THE COMPLETE

ELFQUEST®

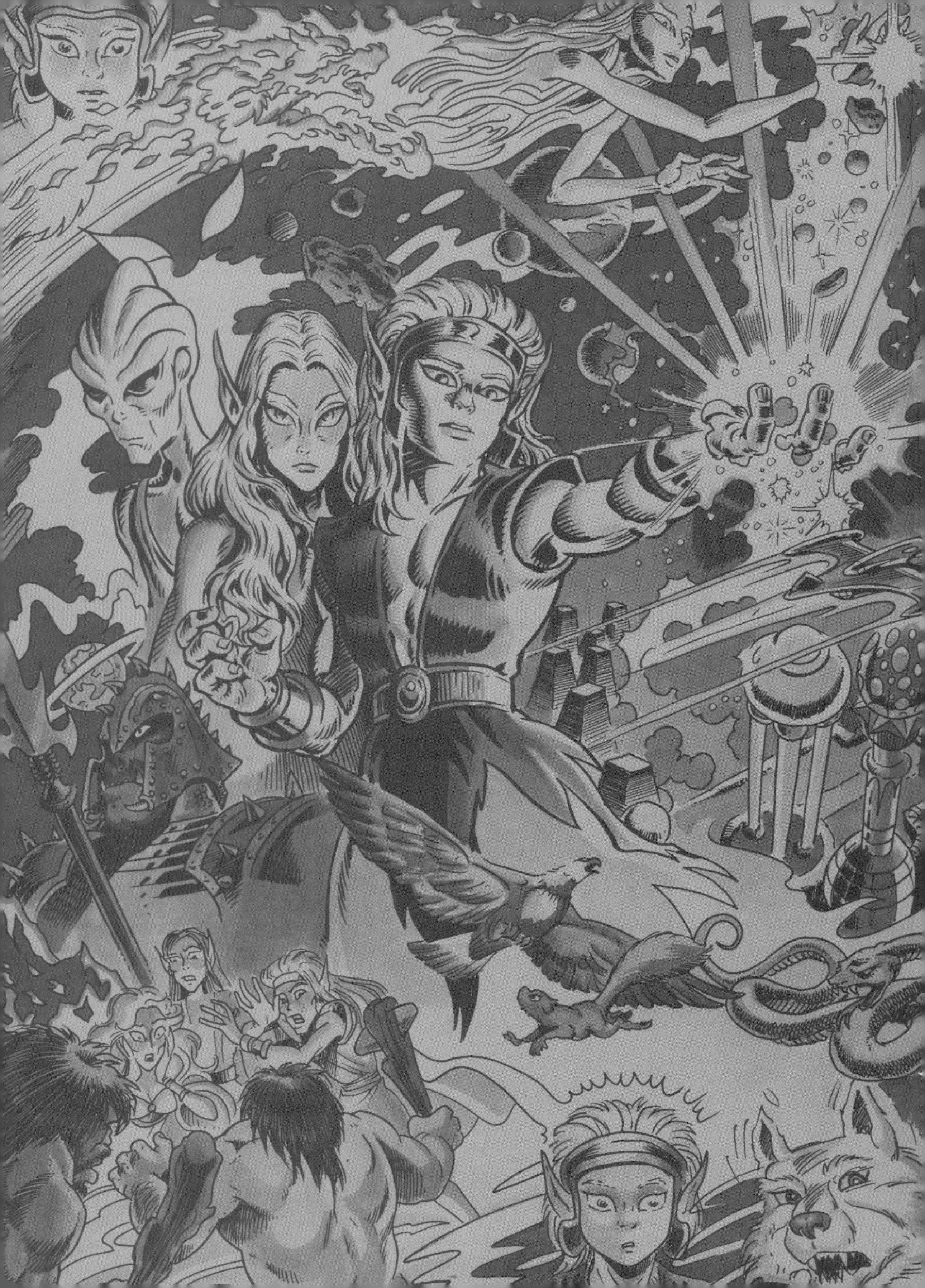

THE COMPLETE ELFQUEST

VOLUME FIVE

BY WENDY AND RICHARD PINI

STORY BY
WENDY AND RICHARD PINI
WENDY LEE
(HIDDEN YEARS #16–#20)
JOELLYN AUKLANDUS
(HIDDEN YEARS #17–#29, WILD HUNT PARTS 1–24)

SCRIPTS BY
WENDI LEE
(HIDDEN YEARS #16–#20)
RICHARD PINI
(HIDDEN YEARS #16–#24)
JOELLYN AUKLANDUS
(HIDDEN YEARS #17–#29, WILD HUNT PARTS 1–24)

PENCILS BY
O.F. ROKO
(HIDDEN YEARS #16, #17)
STEVE BLEVINS
(HIDDEN YEARS #18–#29, THE WILD HUNT PARTS 1–7)
LORRAINE REYES
(THE WILD HUNT, PARTS 8, 10, 12–24)
CRAIG TAILLEFER
(THE WILD HUNT PARTS 9, 11)

INKS BY
JENNIFER MARRUS
(HIDDEN YEARS #16)
O.F. ROKO
(HIDDEN YEARS #17)

STEVE BLEVINS
(HIDDEN YEARS #18)
TERRY BEATTY
(HIDDEN YEARS #19–#24)
CRAIG TAILLEFER
(HIDDEN YEARS #25–#29, THE WILD HUNT PARTS 9, 11)
DANIEL SHELTON
(WILD HUNT PARTS 1–5)
LORRAINE REYES
(THE WILD HUNT, PARTS 8, 10, 12–24)
ANDY ORJUELA
(THE WILD HUNT, PART 8)
DOUGLAS SMITH
(THE WILD HUNT, PART 8)

LETTERS BY
JOHN J HILL AND RYANE HILL
(HIDDEN YEARS #16, #18–#26, THE WILD HUNT, PARTS 5–7)
LORINA MAPA
(HIDDEN YEARS #17, #27–#29, THE WILD HUNT PART 1–9)
LORRAINE REYES
(THE WILD HUNT, PART 10; 12–24)
CHUCK MALY
(THE WILD HUNT, PART 11)

DARK HORSE BOOKS

President & Publisher MIKE RICHARDSON

Collection Editor KEVIN BURKHALTER

Collection Designer SARAH TERRY

Digital Art Technician ALLYSON HALLER

NEIL HANKERSON Executive Vice President - TOM WEDDLE Chief Financial Officer
RANDY STRADLEY Vice President of Publishing - NICK McWHORTER Chief Business Development Officer
MATT PARKINSON Vice President of Marketing - DALE LaFOUNTAIN Vice President of Information Technology
CARA NIECE Vice President of Production and Scheduling - MARK BERNARDI Vice President of Book Trade and
Digital Sales - KEN LIZZI General Counsel - DAVE MARSHALL Editor in Chief - DAVEY ESTRADA Editorial Director
CHRIS WARNER Senior Books Editor - CARY GRAZZINI Director of Specialty Projects - LIA RIBACCHI Art
Director - VANESSA TODD Director of Print Purchasing - MATT DRYER Director of Digital Art and Prepress
MICHAEL GOMBOS Director of International Publishing and Licensing - KARI YADRO Director of Custom Programs

Published by Dark Horse Books
A division of Dark Horse Comics, Inc.
10956 SE Main Street
Milwaukie, OR 97222

First edition: November 2018
ISBN 978-1-50670-606-1
1 3 5 7 9 10 8 6 4 2
Printed in China

To find a comics shop in your area, visit comicshoplocator.com

Library of Congress Cataloging-in-Publication Data

Names: Pini, Wendy, author, illustrator. | Pini, Richard, author,
    illustrator. | Staton, Joe, inker. | Chiang, Janice, letterer. | Robins,
    Clem, 1955- letterer. | Piekos, Nate, letterer. | Byam, Sarah E., writer.
    | Abrams, Paul, penciller. | Barnett, Charles, III, inker. | Cockrum,
    Paty, colourist. | Dechnik, Suzanne, colourist. | Kato, Gary, letterer. |
    Hill, Ryane, letterer. | Lee, W. W. (Wendi W.), author. | Auklandus,
    Joellyn, author.
Title: The Complete ElfQuest / by Wendy and Richard Pini [and others].
Other titles: Elfquest
Description: Milwaukie, Oregon : Dark Horse Books, 2014- | Volume two: inks
    by Joe Staton ; letters by Janice Chiang, Clem Robins and Nate Piekos of
    Blambot. | Volume three: story by Sarah Byam ; pencils by Paul Abrams ;
    inks by Charles Barnett, John Byrne ; colors by Paty Cockrum, Suzanne
    Dechnik ; letters by Gary Kato [and two others]. | Volume four: pencils by
    Paul Abrams [and two others] ; inks by Charles Barnett III [and five
    others] ; letters by Ryane Hill [and five others]. | Volume five: scripts,
    Wendi Lee, Richard Pini, Joellyn Auklandus ; pencils by O.F. Roko, Steve
    Blevins, Lorraine Reyes, Craig Taillefer ; inks by Jennifer Marrus, O.F.
    Roko, Steve Blevins, Terry Beatty [and others] ; letters by John J Hill,
    Ryane Hill, Lorina Mapa [and others]. | Volume five: "This volume collects
    and reprints the comic books ElfQuest: Hidden Years #16–#29,
    Mertamorphosis #1: Wild Hunt, and ElfQuest V2 Wild Hunt #1?#7, #10–#12,
    #14–#16, #18, #20–#30"
Identifiers: LCCN 2014014517| ISBN 9781616554071 (volume 1 : pbk.) | ISBN
    9781616554088 (volume 2 : pbk.) | ISBN 9781506700809 (volume 3 : pbk.) |
    ISBN 9781506701585 (volume 4 : pbk.) | ISBN 9781506706061 (volume 5 : pbk.)
Subjects: LCSH: Comic books, strips, etc. | BISAC: COMICS & GRAPHIC NOVELS /
    Fantasy.
Classification: LCC PN6728.E45 P53 2014 | DDC 741.5/973-dc23
LC record available at https://lccn.loc.gov/2014014517

TO THOSE WHO HAVE SET OUT

UPON THE MOST WONDERFUL QUEST OF ALL -

TO DISCOVER WHO THEY TRULY ARE.

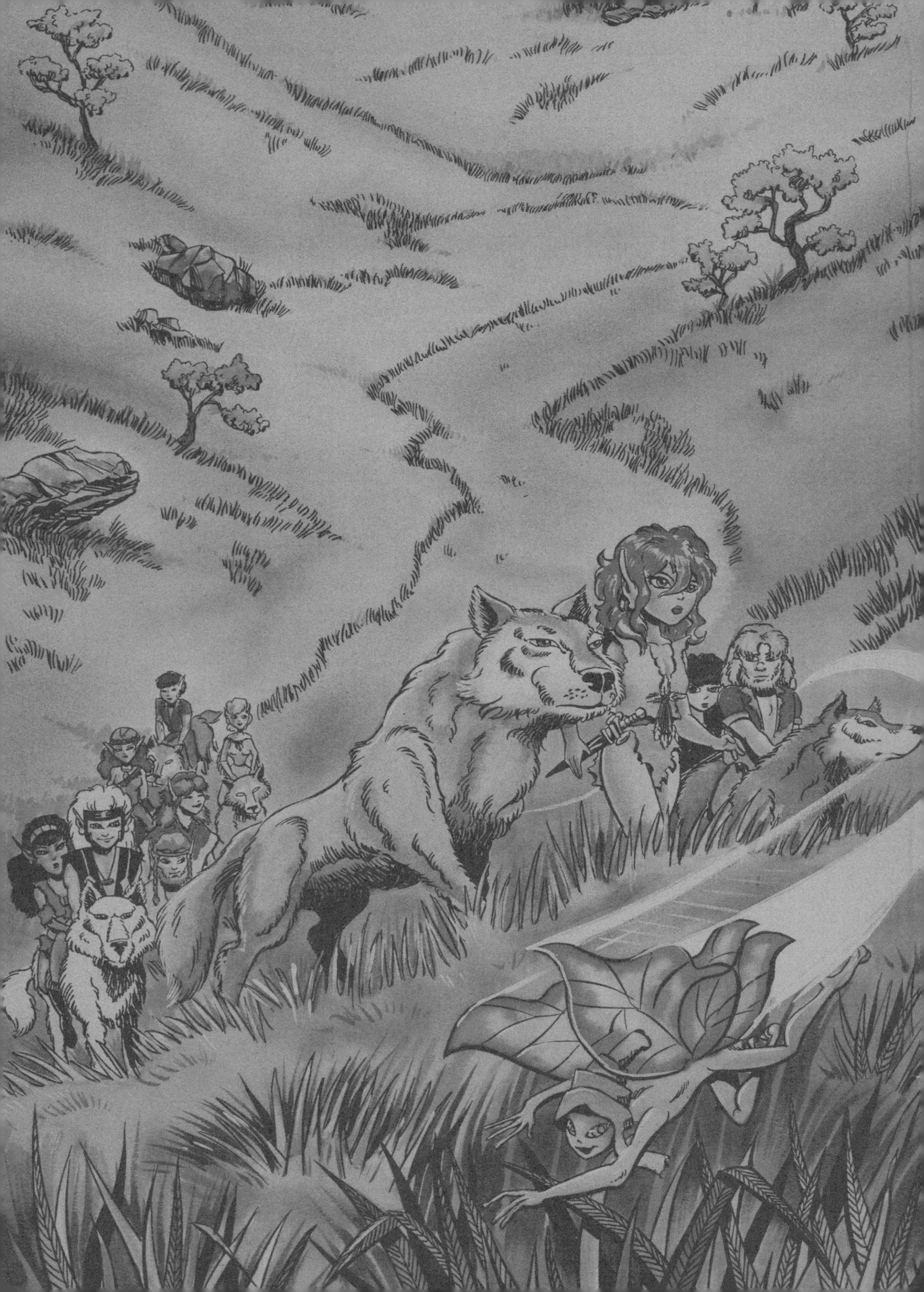

CONTENTS

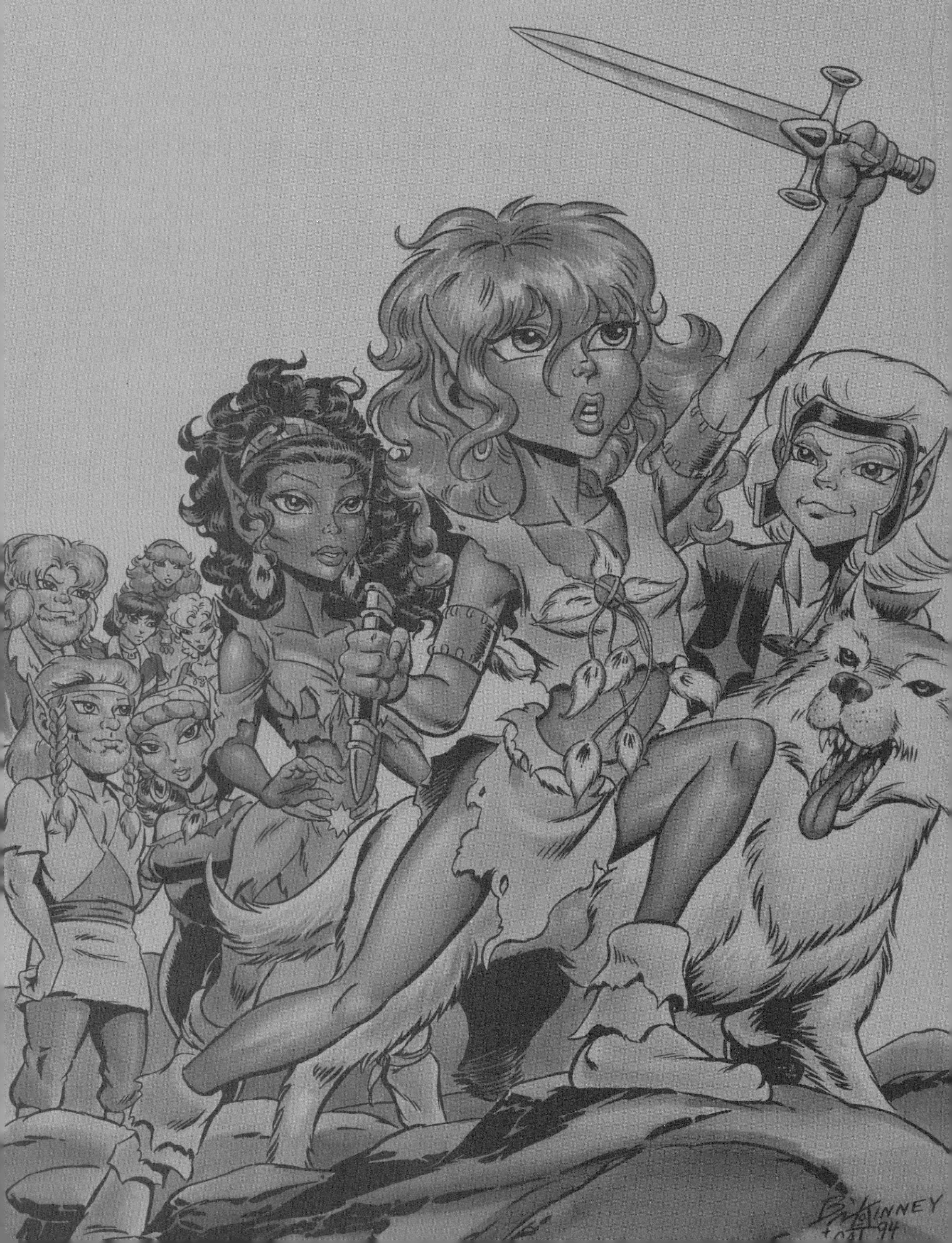

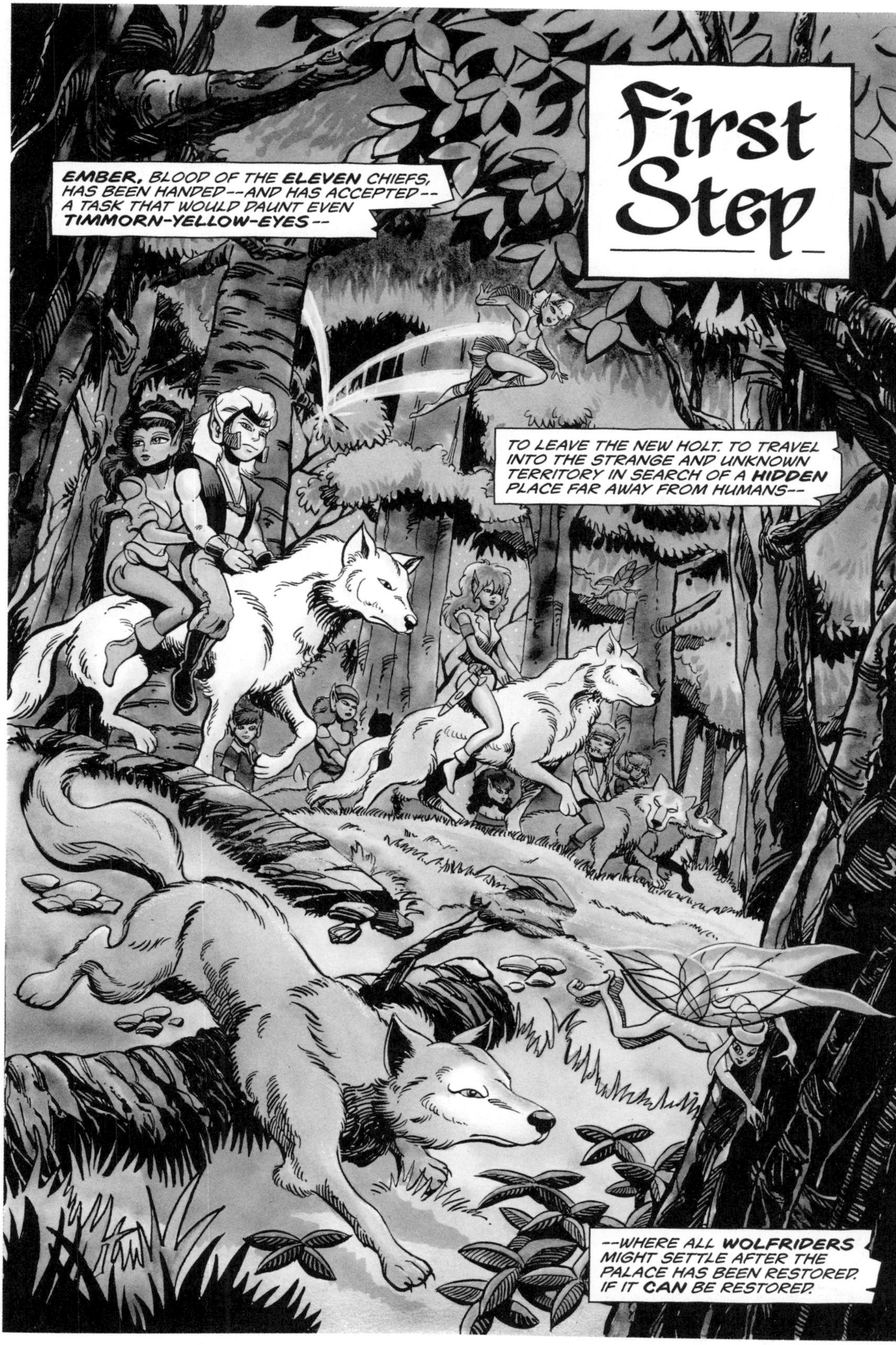
First Step
EMBER, BLOOD OF THE ELEVEN CHIEFS, HAS BEEN HANDED--AND HAS ACCEPTED--A TASK THAT WOULD DAUNT EVEN TIMMORN-YELLOW-EYES--
TO LEAVE THE NEW HOLT. TO TRAVEL INTO THE STRANGE AND UNKNOWN TERRITORY IN SEARCH OF A HIDDEN PLACE FAR AWAY FROM HUMANS--
--WHERE ALL WOLFRIDERS MIGHT SETTLE AFTER THE PALACE HAS BEEN RESTORED. IF IT CAN BE RESTORED.

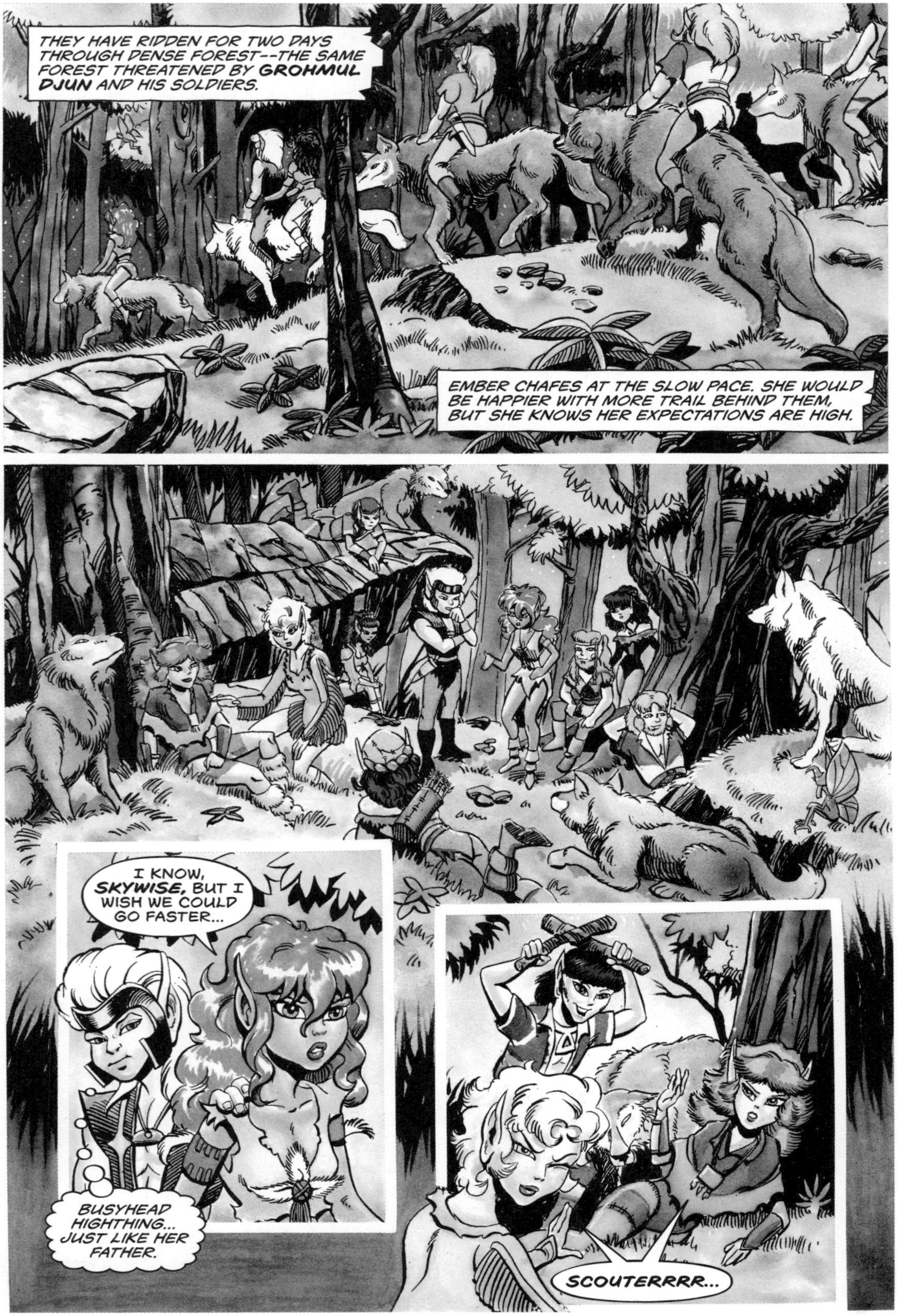

THEY HAVE RIDDEN FOR TWO DAYS THROUGH DENSE FOREST--THE SAME FOREST THREATENED BY GROHMUL DJUN AND HIS SOLDIERS.
EMBER CHAFES AT THE SLOW PACE. SHE WOULD BE HAPPIER WITH MORE TRAIL BEHIND THEM, BUT SHE KNOWS HER EXPECTATIONS ARE HIGH.
I KNOW, SKYWISE, BUT I WISH WE COULD GO FASTER...
BUSYHEAD HIGHTHING... JUST LIKE HER FATHER.
SCOUTERRRR...

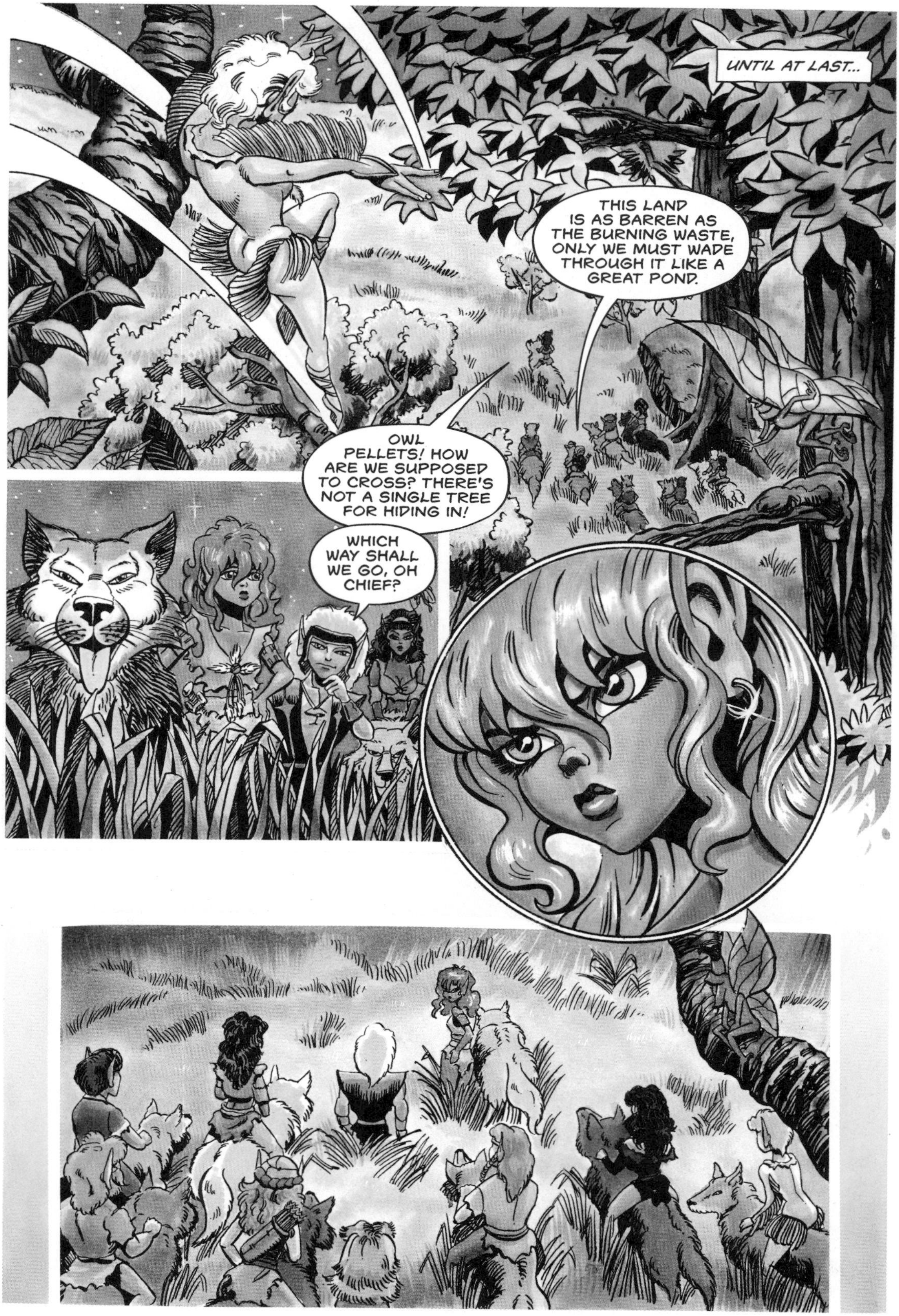
UNTIL AT LAST...
THIS LAND IS AS BARREN AS THE BURNING WASTE, ONLY WE MUST WADE THROUGH IT LIKE A GREAT POND.
OWL PELLETS! HOW ARE WE SUPPOSED TO CROSS? THERE'S NOT A SINGLE TREE FOR HIDING IN!
WHICH WAY SHALL WE GO, OH CHIEF?

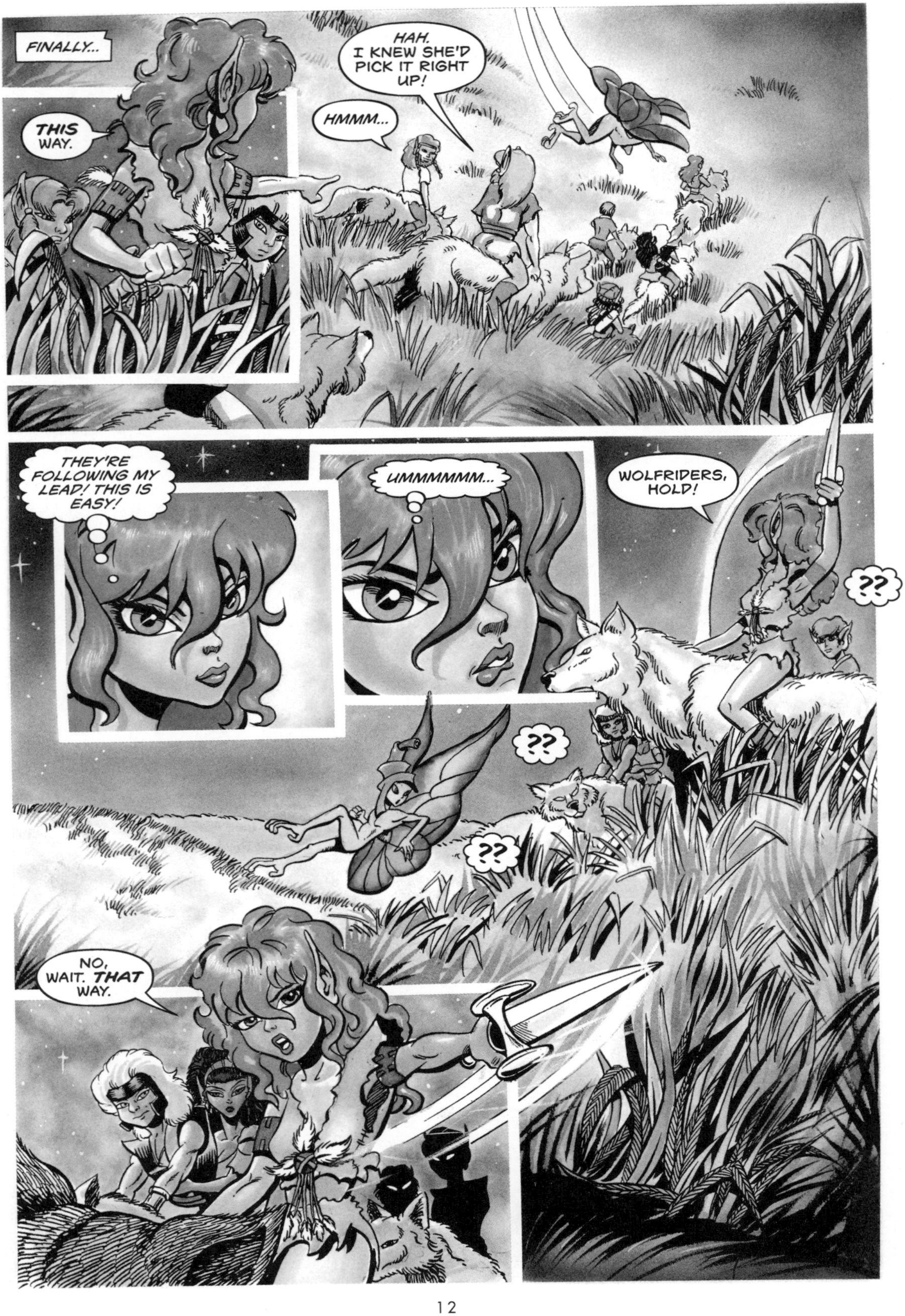

FINALLY...
THIS WAY.
HAH. I KNEW SHE'D PICK IT RIGHT UP!
HMMM...
THEY'RE FOLLOWING MY LEAD! THIS IS EASY!
UMMMMMM...
WOLFRIDERS, HOLD!
??
??
??
NO, WAIT. THAT WAY.

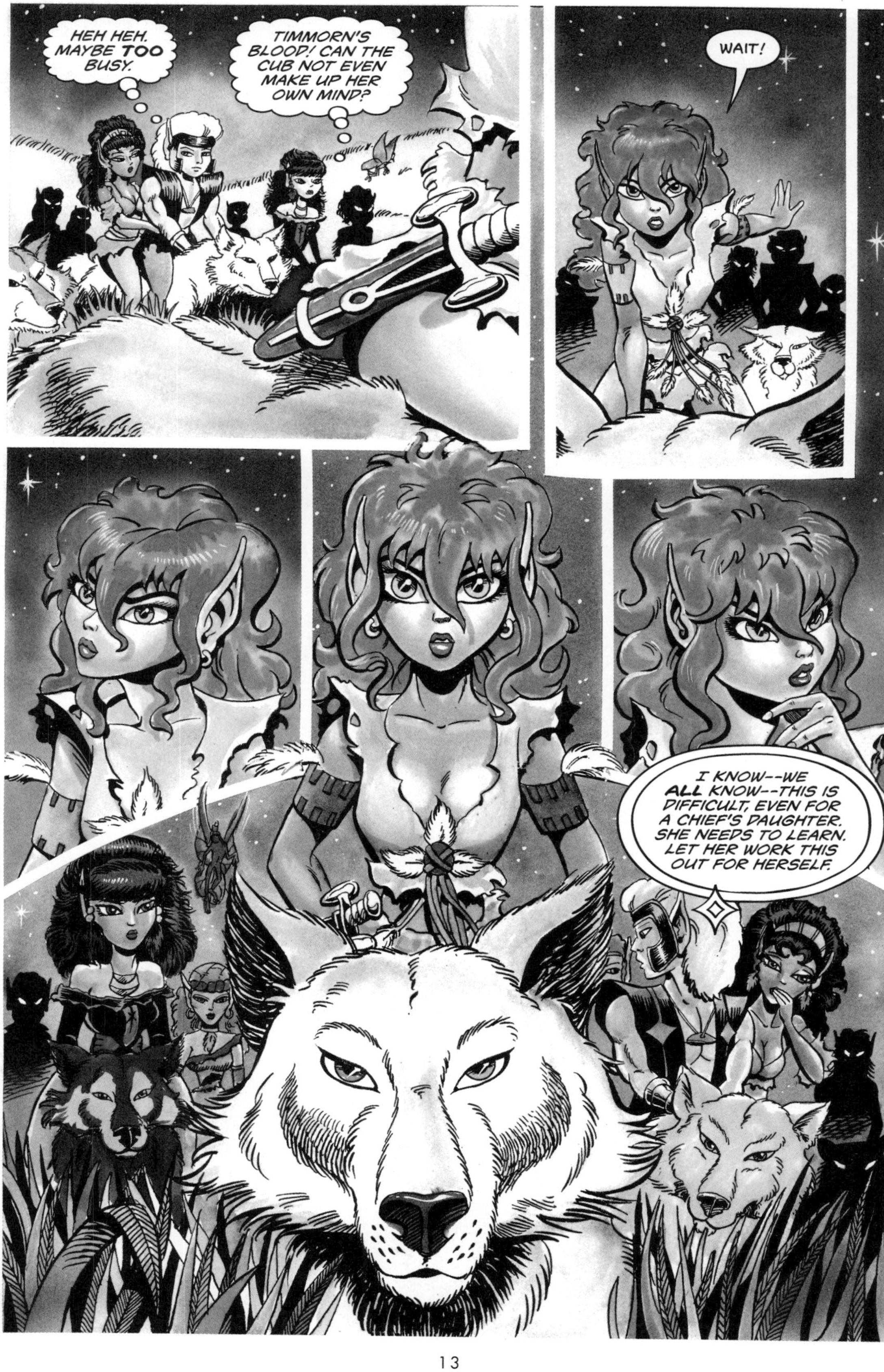
HEH HEH. MAYBE TOO BUSY.
TIMMORN'S BLOOD! CAN THE CUB NOT EVEN MAKE UP HER OWN MIND?
WAIT!
I KNOW--WE ALL KNOW--THIS IS DIFFICULT, EVEN FOR A CHIEF'S DAUGHTER. SHE NEEDS TO LEARN. LET HER WORK THIS OUT FOR HERSELF.

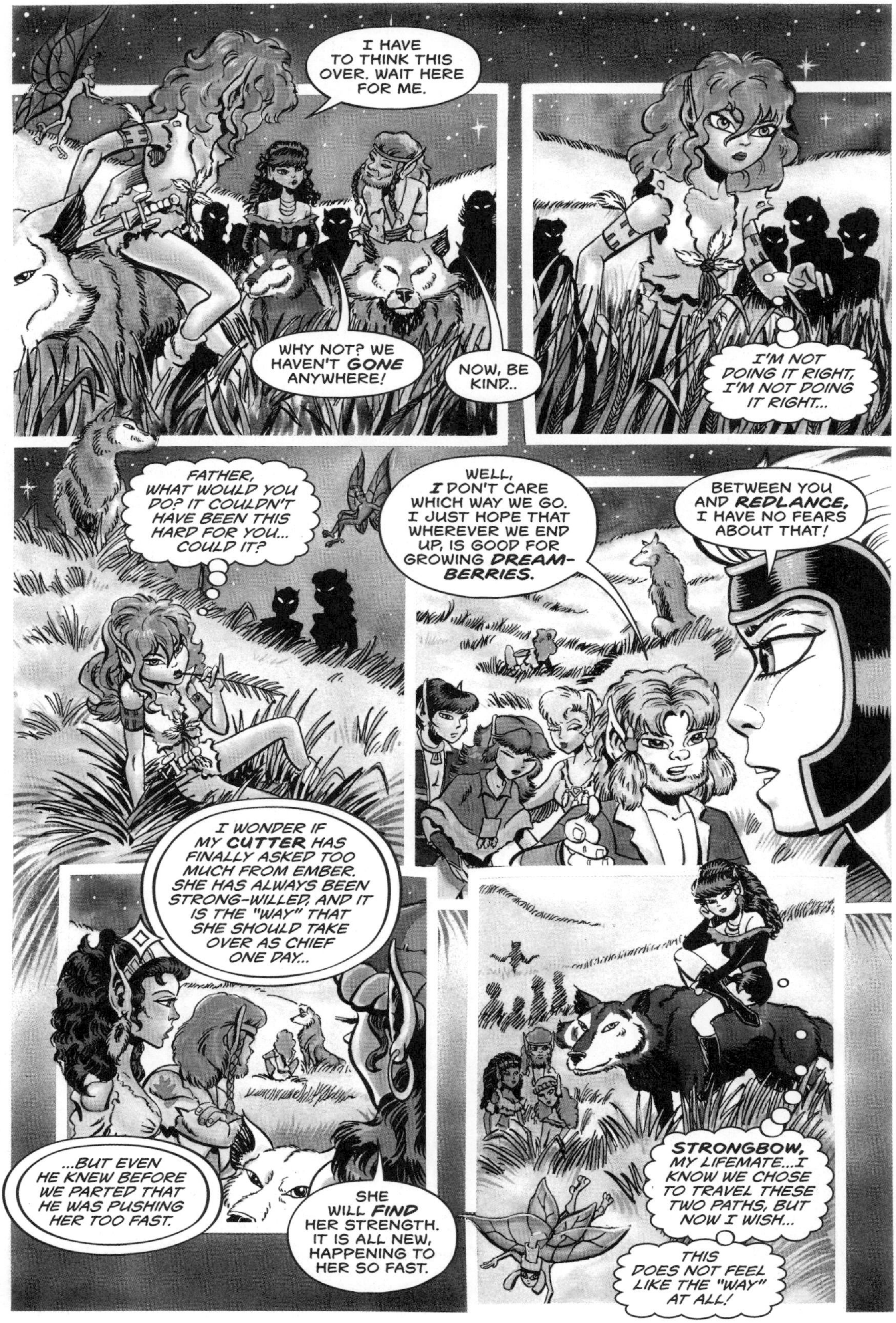
I HAVE TO THINK THIS OVER. WAIT HERE FOR ME.
WHY NOT? WE HAVEN'T GONE ANYWHERE!
NOW, BE KIND...
I'M NOT DOING IT RIGHT, I'M NOT DOING IT RIGHT...
FATHER, WHAT WOULD YOU DO? IT COULDN'T HAVE BEEN THIS HARD FOR YOU... COULD IT?
WELL, I DON'T CARE WHICH WAY WE GO. I JUST HOPE THAT WHEREVER WE END UP, IS GOOD FOR GROWING DREAM-BERRIES.
BETWEEN YOU AND REDLANCE, I HAVE NO FEARS ABOUT THAT!
I WONDER IF MY CUTTER HAS FINALLY ASKED TOO MUCH FROM EMBER. SHE HAS ALWAYS BEEN STRONG-WILLED, AND IT IS THE "WAY" THAT SHE SHOULD TAKE OVER AS CHIEF ONE DAY...
...BUT EVEN HE KNEW BEFORE WE PARTED THAT HE WAS PUSHING HER TOO FAST.
SHE WILL FIND HER STRENGTH. IT IS ALL NEW, HAPPENING TO HER SO FAST.
STRONGBOW, MY LIFEMATE...I KNOW WE CHOSE TO TRAVEL THESE TWO PATHS, BUT NOW I WISH...
THIS DOES NOT FEEL LIKE THE "WAY" AT ALL!

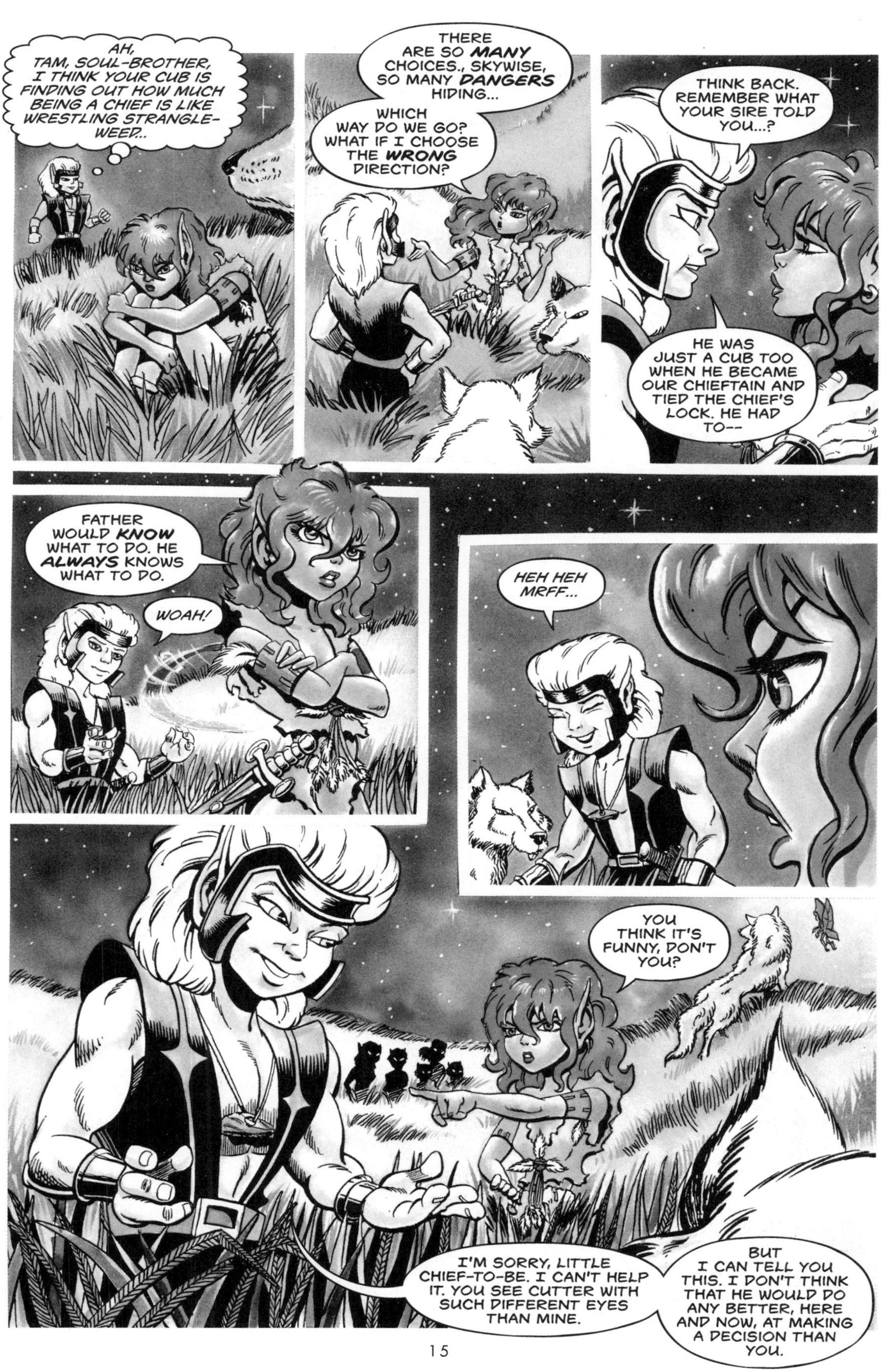
AH, TAM, SOUL-BROTHER, I THINK YOUR CUB IS FINDING OUT HOW MUCH BEING A CHIEF IS LIKE WRESTLING STRANGLE-WEED...
THERE ARE SO MANY CHOICES., SKYWISE, SO MANY DANGERS HIDING...
WHICH WAY DO WE GO? WHAT IF I CHOOSE THE WRONG DIRECTION?
THINK BACK. REMEMBER WHAT YOUR SIRE TOLD YOU...?
HE WAS JUST A CUB TOO WHEN HE BECAME OUR CHIEFTAIN AND TIED THE CHIEF'S LOCK. HE HAD TO--
FATHER WOULD KNOW WHAT TO DO. HE ALWAYS KNOWS WHAT TO DO.
WOAH!
HEH HEH MRFF...
YOU THINK IT'S FUNNY, DON'T YOU?
I'M SORRY, LITTLE CHIEF-TO-BE. I CAN'T HELP IT. YOU SEE CUTTER WITH SUCH DIFFERENT EYES THAN MINE.
BUT I CAN TELL YOU THIS. I DON'T THINK THAT HE WOULD DO ANY BETTER, HERE AND NOW, AT MAKING A DECISION THAN YOU.

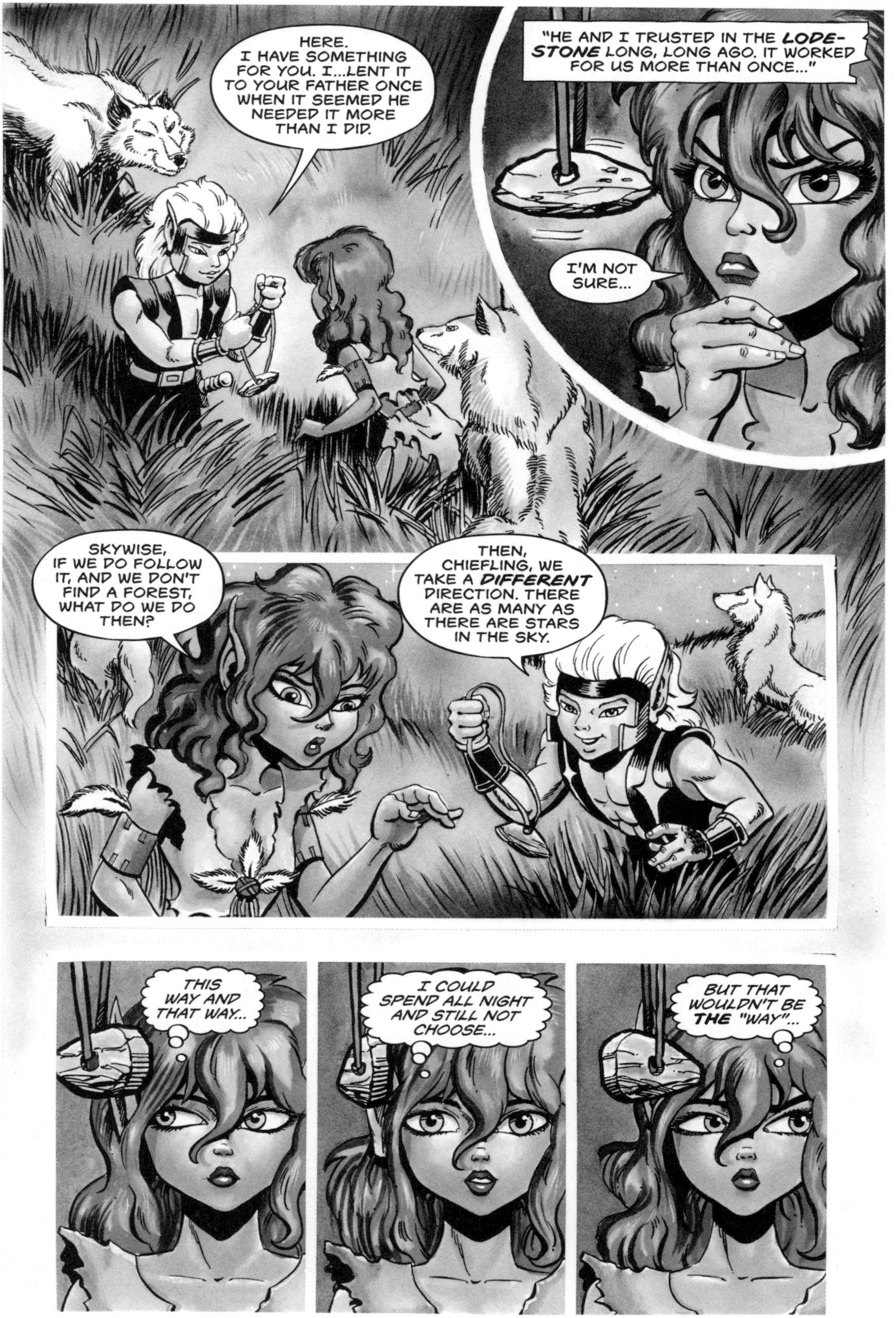
HERE. I HAVE SOMETHING FOR YOU. I...LENT IT TO YOUR FATHER ONCE WHEN IT SEEMED HE NEEDED IT MORE THAN I DID.
"HE AND I TRUSTED IN THE LODE-STONE LONG, LONG AGO. IT WORKED FOR US MORE THAN ONCE..."
I'M NOT SURE...
SKYWISE, IF WE DO FOLLOW IT, AND WE DON'T FIND A FOREST, WHAT DO WE DO THEN?
THEN, CHIEFLING, WE TAKE A DIFFERENT DIRECTION. THERE ARE AS MANY AS THERE ARE STARS IN THE SKY.
THIS WAY AND THAT WAY...
I COULD SPEND ALL NIGHT AND STILL NOT CHOOSE...
BUT THAT WOULDN'T BE THE "WAY"...

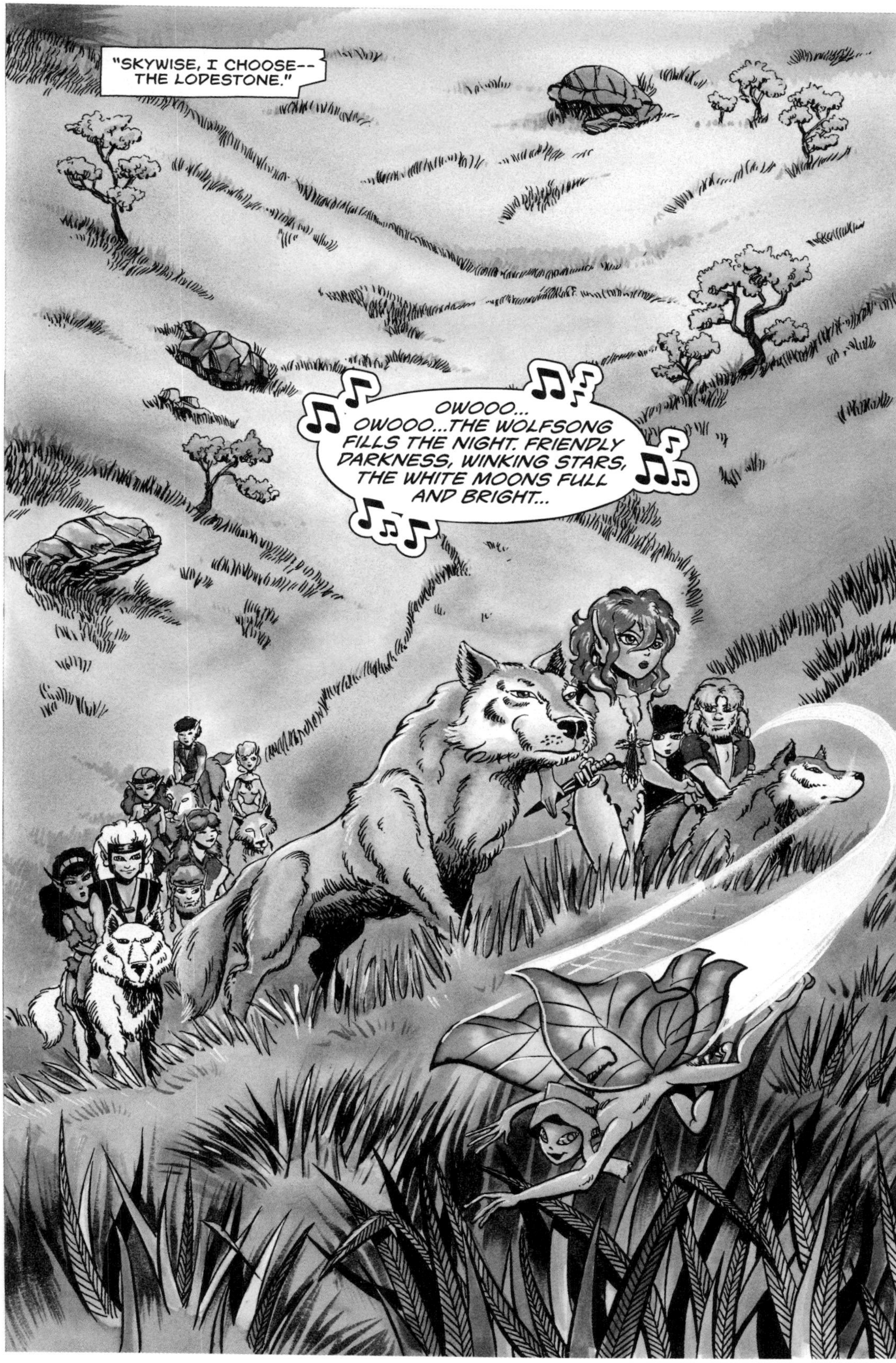
"SKYWISE, I CHOOSE--
THE LODESTONE."
OWOOO...
OWOOO...THE WOLFSONG
FILLS THE NIGHT. FRIENDLY
DARKNESS, WINKING STARS,
THE WHITE MOONS FULL
AND BRIGHT...

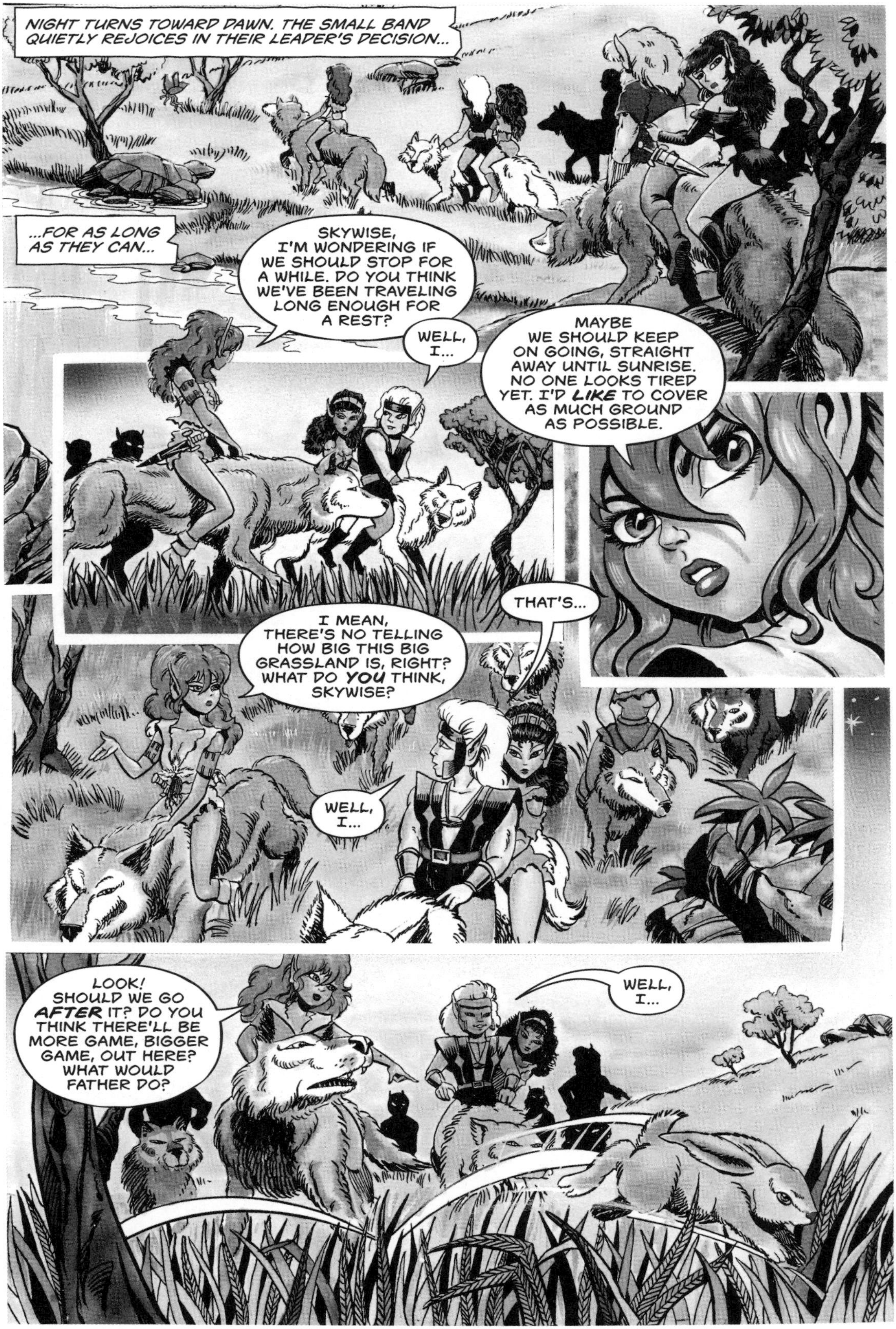
NIGHT TURNS TOWARD DAWN. THE SMALL BAND QUIETLY REJOICES IN THEIR LEADER'S DECISION...
...FOR AS LONG AS THEY CAN...
SKYWISE, I'M WONDERING IF WE SHOULD STOP FOR A WHILE. DO YOU THINK WE'VE BEEN TRAVELING LONG ENOUGH FOR A REST?
WELL, I...
MAYBE WE SHOULD KEEP ON GOING, STRAIGHT AWAY UNTIL SUNRISE. NO ONE LOOKS TIRED YET. I'D LIKE TO COVER AS MUCH GROUND AS POSSIBLE.
THAT'S...
I MEAN, THERE'S NO TELLING HOW BIG THIS BIG GRASSLAND IS, RIGHT? WHAT DO YOU THINK, SKYWISE?
WELL, I...
LOOK! SHOULD WE GO AFTER IT? DO YOU THINK THERE'LL BE MORE GAME, BIGGER GAME, OUT HERE? WHAT WOULD FATHER DO?
WELL, I...

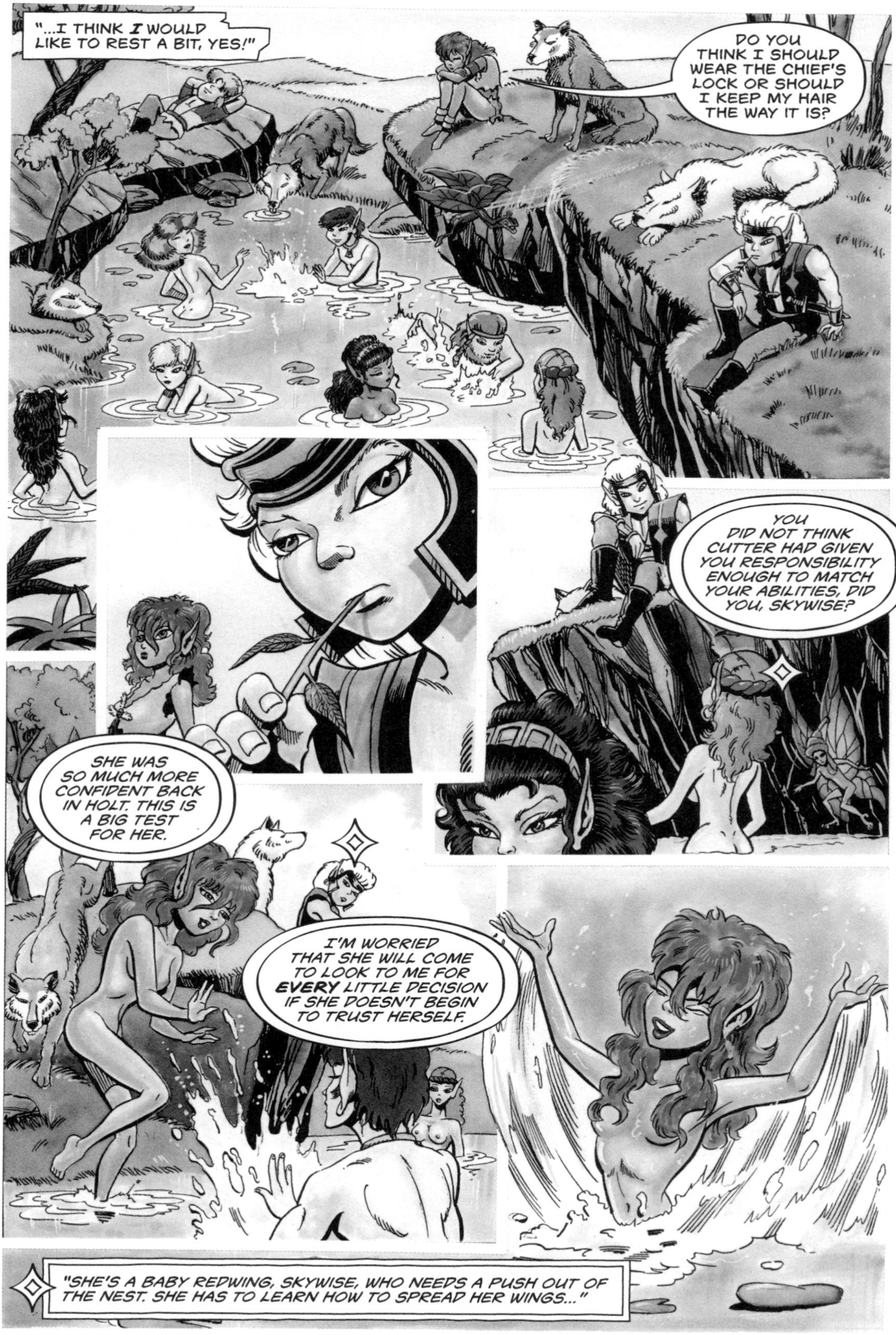
"...I THINK I WOULD LIKE TO REST A BIT, YES!"
DO YOU THINK I SHOULD WEAR THE CHIEF'S LOCK OR SHOULD I KEEP MY HAIR THE WAY IT IS?
YOU DID NOT THINK CUTTER HAD GIVEN YOU RESPONSIBILITY ENOUGH TO MATCH YOUR ABILITIES, DID YOU, SKYWISE?
SHE WAS SO MUCH MORE CONFIDENT BACK IN HOLT. THIS IS A BIG TEST FOR HER.
I'M WORRIED THAT SHE WILL COME TO LOOK TO ME FOR EVERY LITTLE DECISION IF SHE DOESN'T BEGIN TO TRUST HERSELF.
"SHE'S A BABY REDWING, SKYWISE, WHO NEEDS A PUSH OUT OF THE NEST. SHE HAS TO LEARN HOW TO SPREAD HER WINGS..."

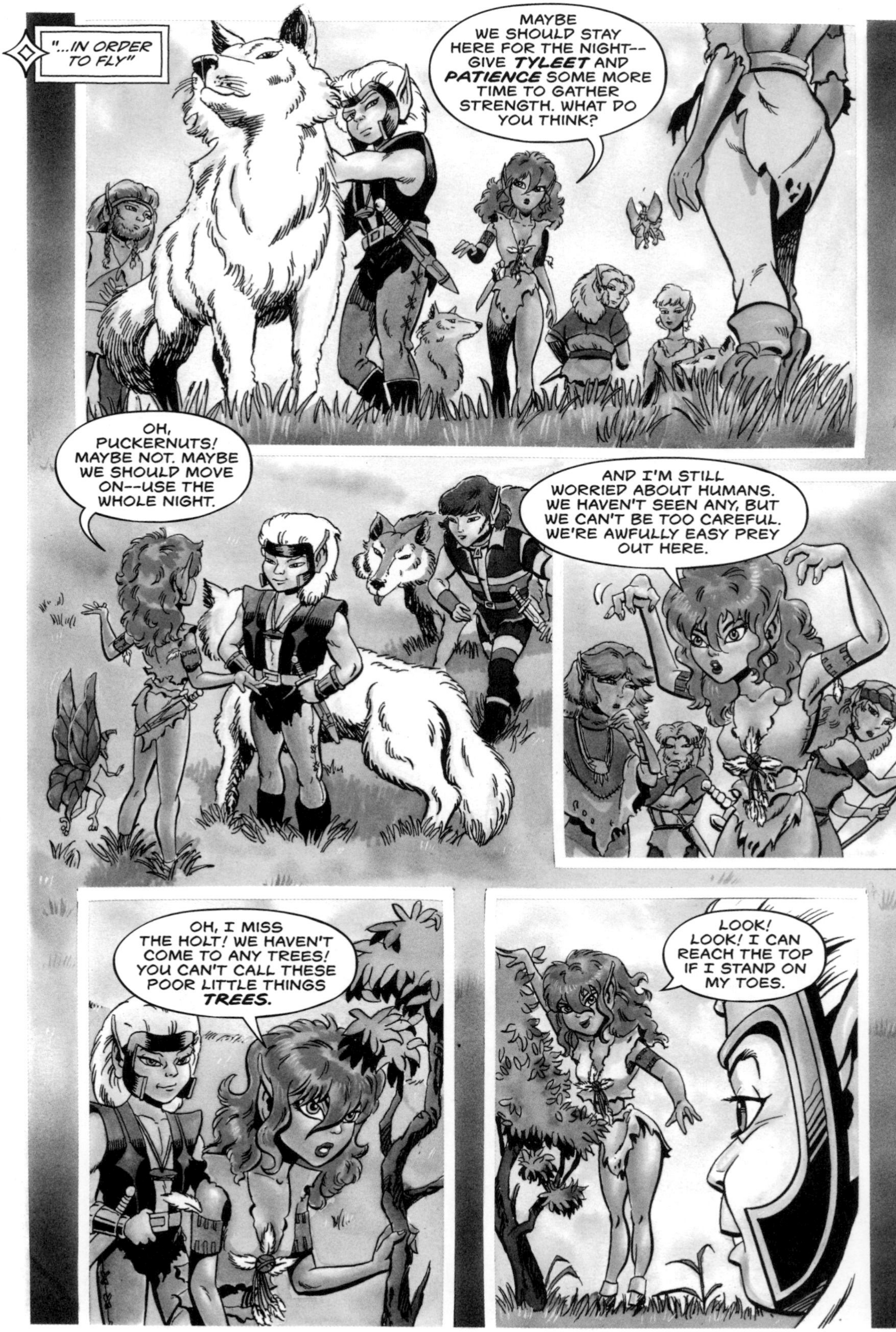
"...IN ORDER TO FLY"
MAYBE WE SHOULD STAY HERE FOR THE NIGHT-- GIVE TYLEET AND PATIENCE SOME MORE TIME TO GATHER STRENGTH. WHAT DO YOU THINK?
OH, PUCKERNUTS! MAYBE NOT. MAYBE WE SHOULD MOVE ON--USE THE WHOLE NIGHT.
AND I'M STILL WORRIED ABOUT HUMANS. WE HAVEN'T SEEN ANY, BUT WE CAN'T BE TOO CAREFUL. WE'RE AWFULLY EASY PREY OUT HERE.
OH, I MISS THE HOLT! WE HAVEN'T COME TO ANY TREES! YOU CAN'T CALL THESE POOR LITTLE THINGS TREES.
LOOK! LOOK! I CAN REACH THE TOP IF I STAND ON MY TOES.

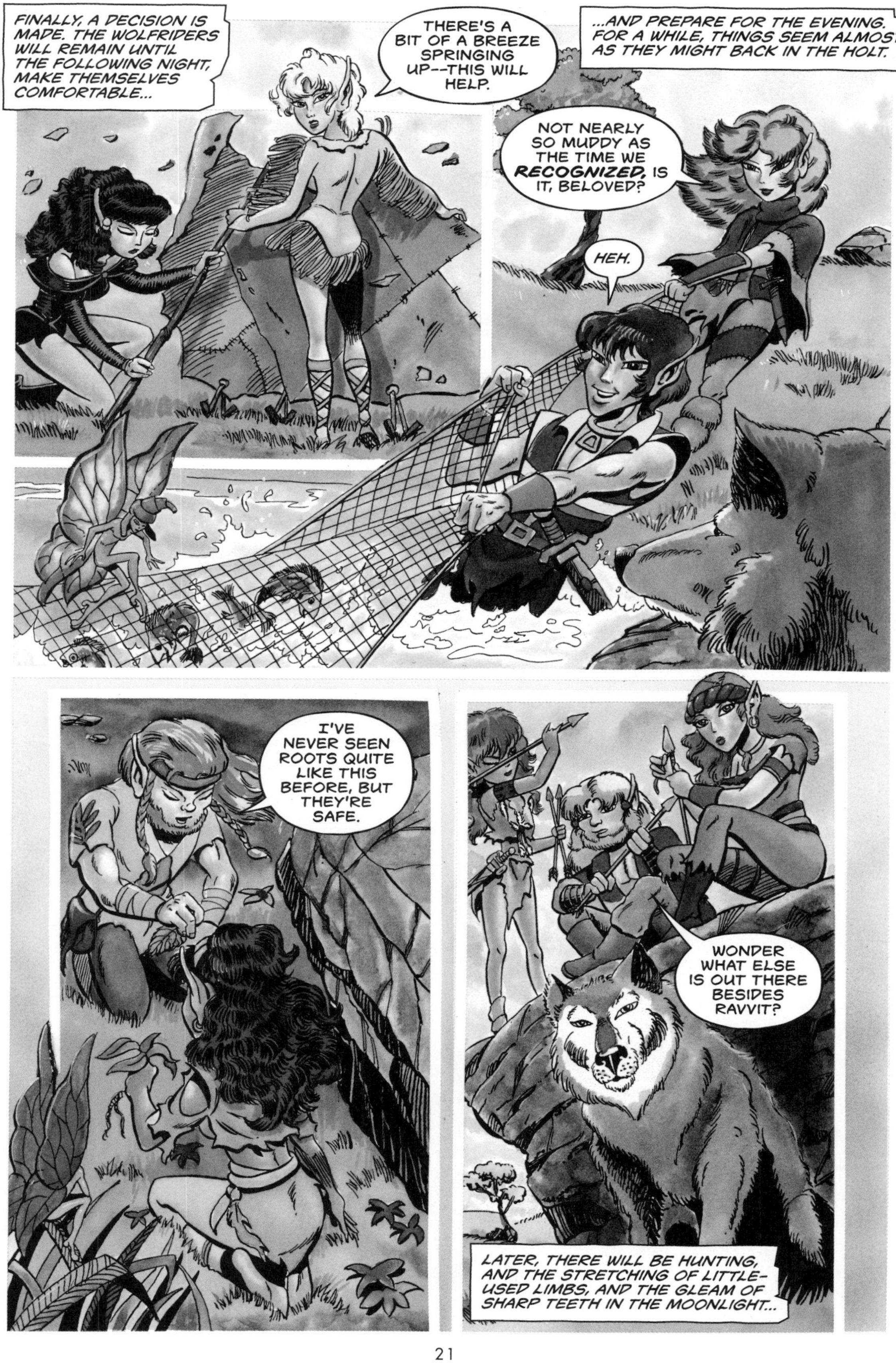
FINALLY, A DECISION IS MADE. THE WOLFRIDERS WILL REMAIN UNTIL THE FOLLOWING NIGHT, MAKE THEMSELVES COMFORTABLE...
THERE'S A BIT OF A BREEZE SPRINGING UP--THIS WILL HELP.
...AND PREPARE FOR THE EVENING. FOR A WHILE, THINGS SEEM ALMOST AS THEY MIGHT BACK IN THE HOLT.
NOT NEARLY SO MUDDY AS THE TIME WE RECOGNIZED, IS IT, BELOVED?
HEH.
I'VE NEVER SEEN ROOTS QUITE LIKE THIS BEFORE, BUT THEY'RE SAFE.
WONDER WHAT ELSE IS OUT THERE BESIDES RAVVIT?
LATER, THERE WILL BE HUNTING, AND THE STRETCHING OF LITTLE-USED LIMBS, AND THE GLEAM OF SHARP TEETH IN THE MOONLIGHT...

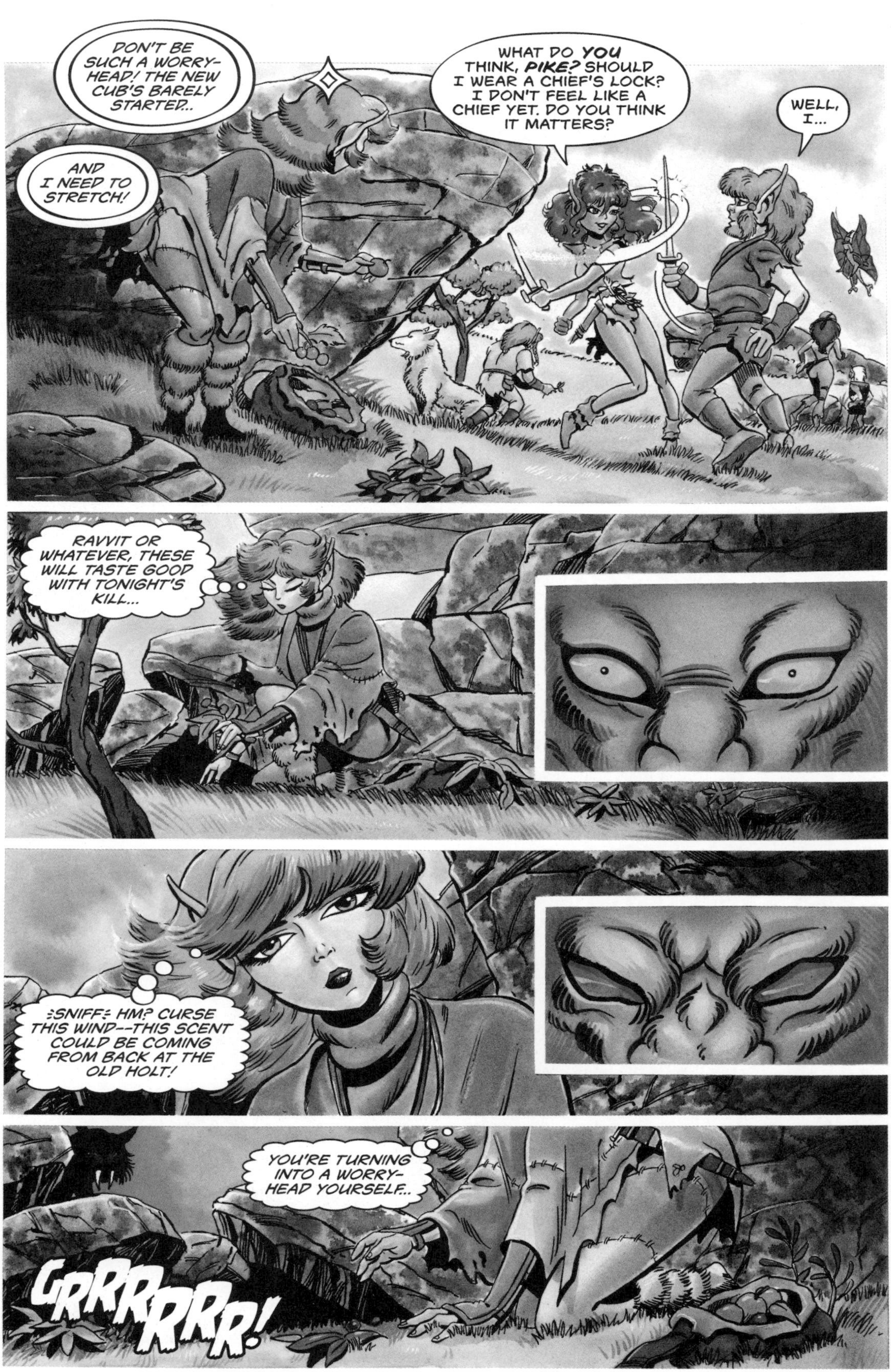
DON'T BE SUCH A WORRY-HEAD! THE NEW CUB'S BARELY STARTED...
AND I NEED TO STRETCH!
WHAT DO YOU THINK, PIKE? SHOULD I WEAR A CHIEF'S LOCK? I DON'T FEEL LIKE A CHIEF YET. DO YOU THINK IT MATTERS?
WELL, I...
RAVVIT OR WHATEVER, THESE WILL TASTE GOOD WITH TONIGHT'S KILL...
:SNIFF: HM? CURSE THIS WIND--THIS SCENT COULD BE COMING FROM BACK AT THE OLD HOLT!
YOU'RE TURNING INTO A WORRY-HEAD YOURSELF...
GRRRRRR!

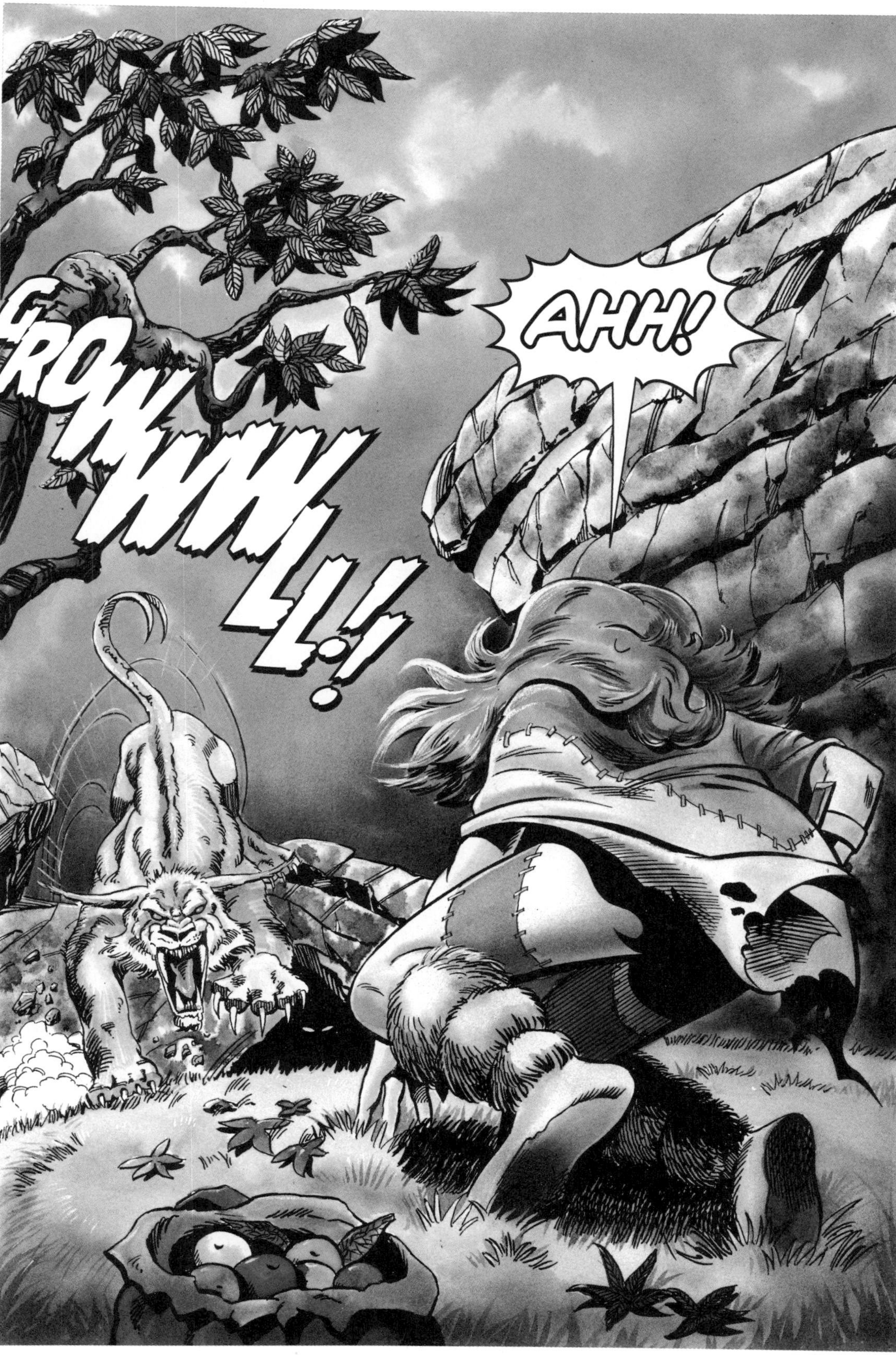
GROWWLL!!
AHH!

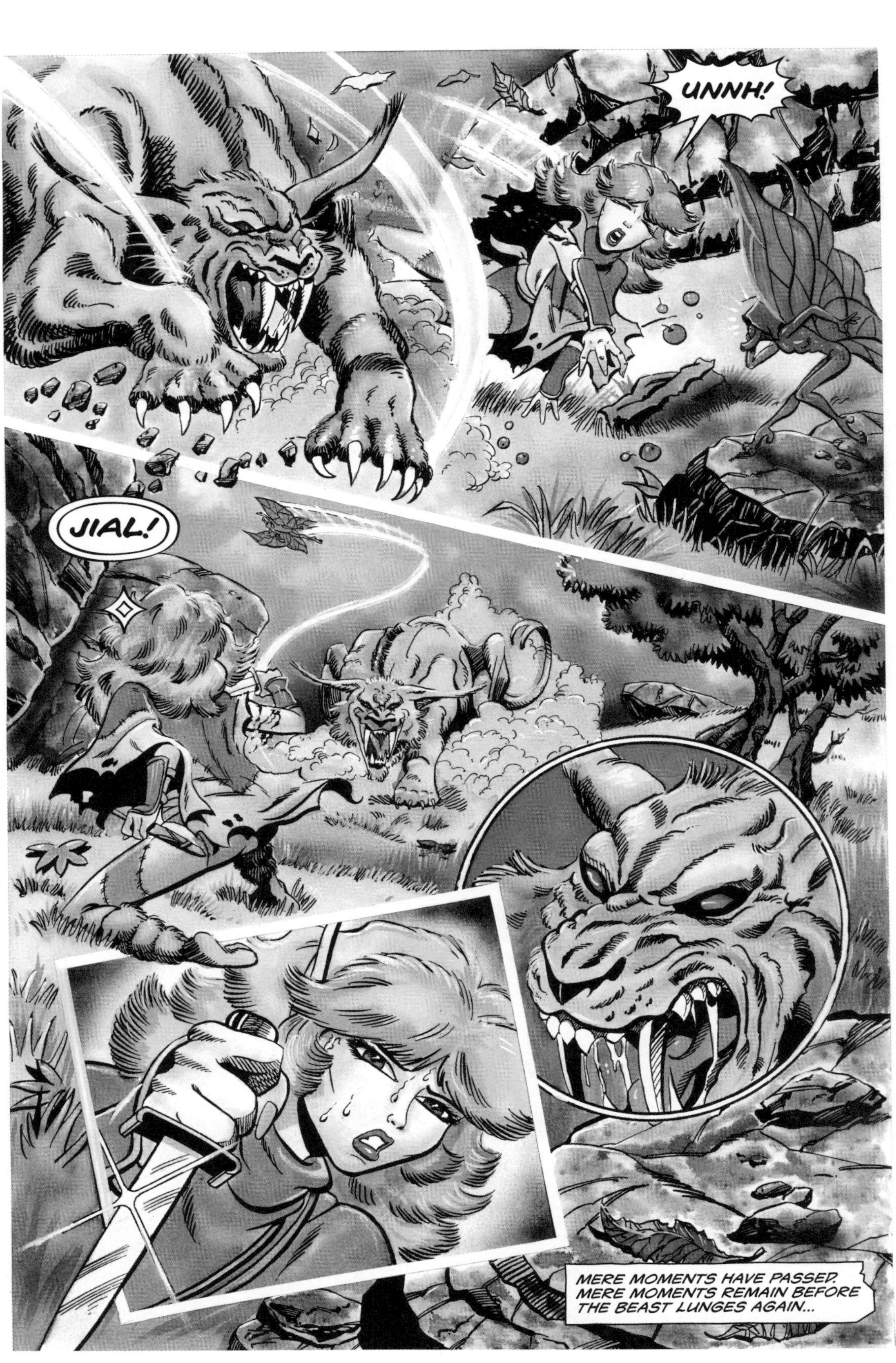
UNNH!
JIAL!
MERE MOMENTS HAVE PASSED. MERE MOMENTS REMAIN BEFORE THE BEAST LUNGES AGAIN...

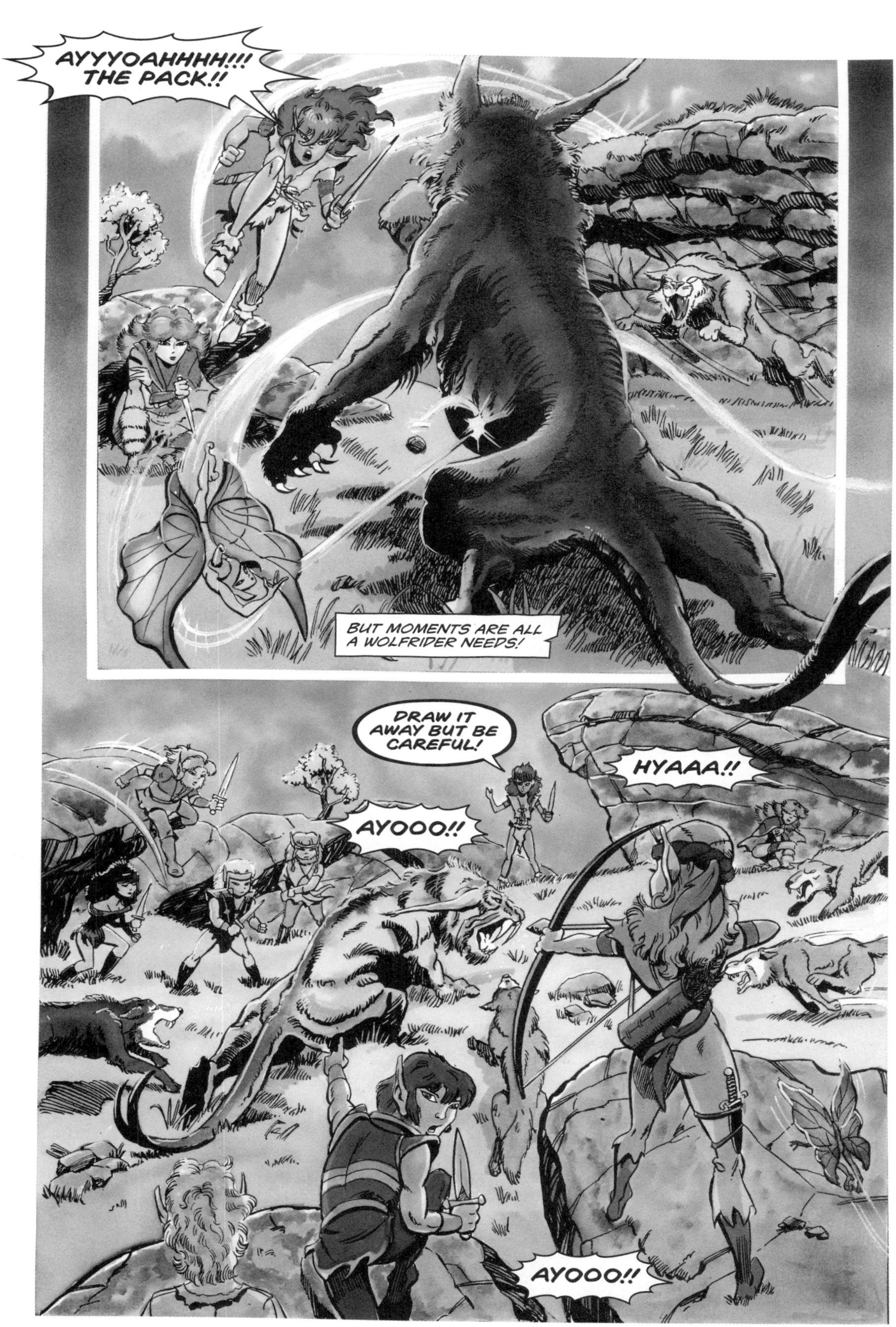
AYYYOAHHHH!!! THE PACK!!
BUT MOMENTS ARE ALL A WOLFRIDER NEEDS!
DRAW IT AWAY BUT BE CAREFUL!
HYAAA!!
AYOOO!!
AYOOO!!

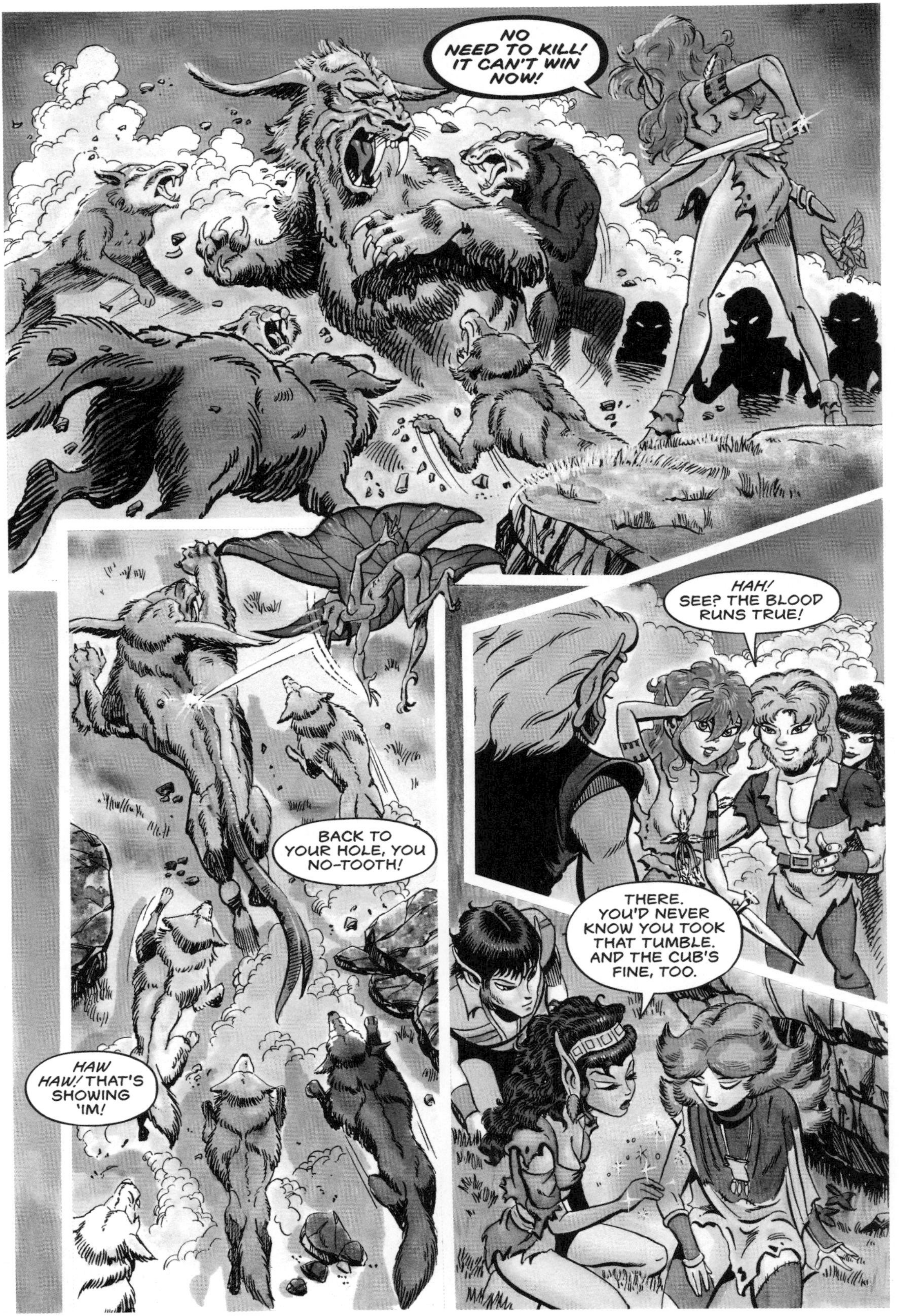
NO NEED TO KILL! IT CAN'T WIN NOW!
BACK TO YOUR HOLE, YOU NO-TOOTH!
HAW HAW! THAT'S SHOWING 'IM!
HAH! SEE? THE BLOOD RUNS TRUE!
THERE. YOU'D NEVER KNOW YOU TOOK THAT TUMBLE. AND THE CUB'S FINE, TOO.

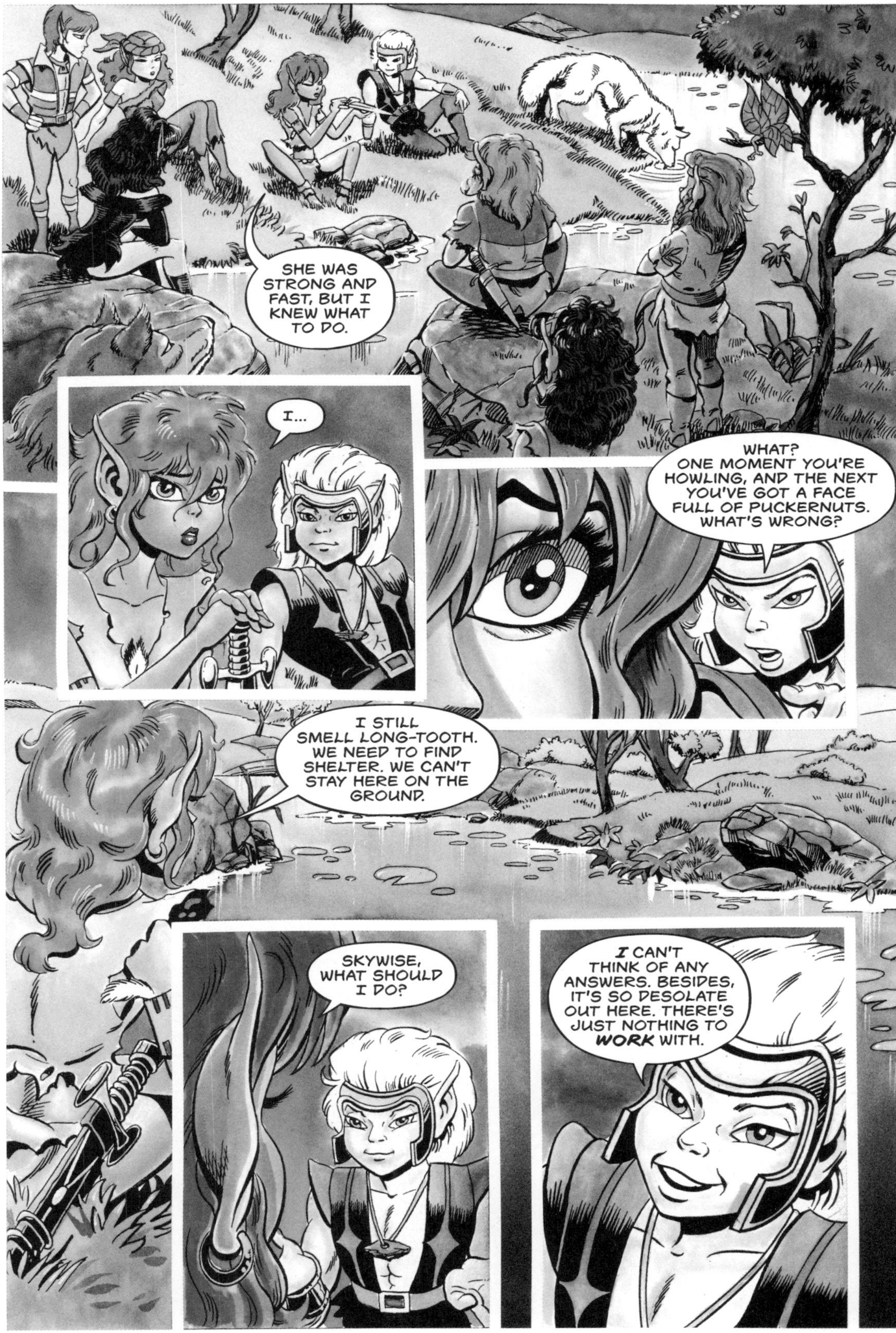
SHE WAS STRONG AND FAST, BUT I KNEW WHAT TO DO.
I...
WHAT? ONE MOMENT YOU'RE HOWLING, AND THE NEXT YOU'VE GOT A FACE FULL OF PUCKERNUTS. WHAT'S WRONG?
I STILL SMELL LONG-TOOTH. WE NEED TO FIND SHELTER. WE CAN'T STAY HERE ON THE GROUND.
SKYWISE, WHAT SHOULD I DO?
I CAN'T THINK OF ANY ANSWERS. BESIDES, IT'S SO DESOLATE OUT HERE. THERE'S JUST NOTHING TO ***WORK*** WITH.

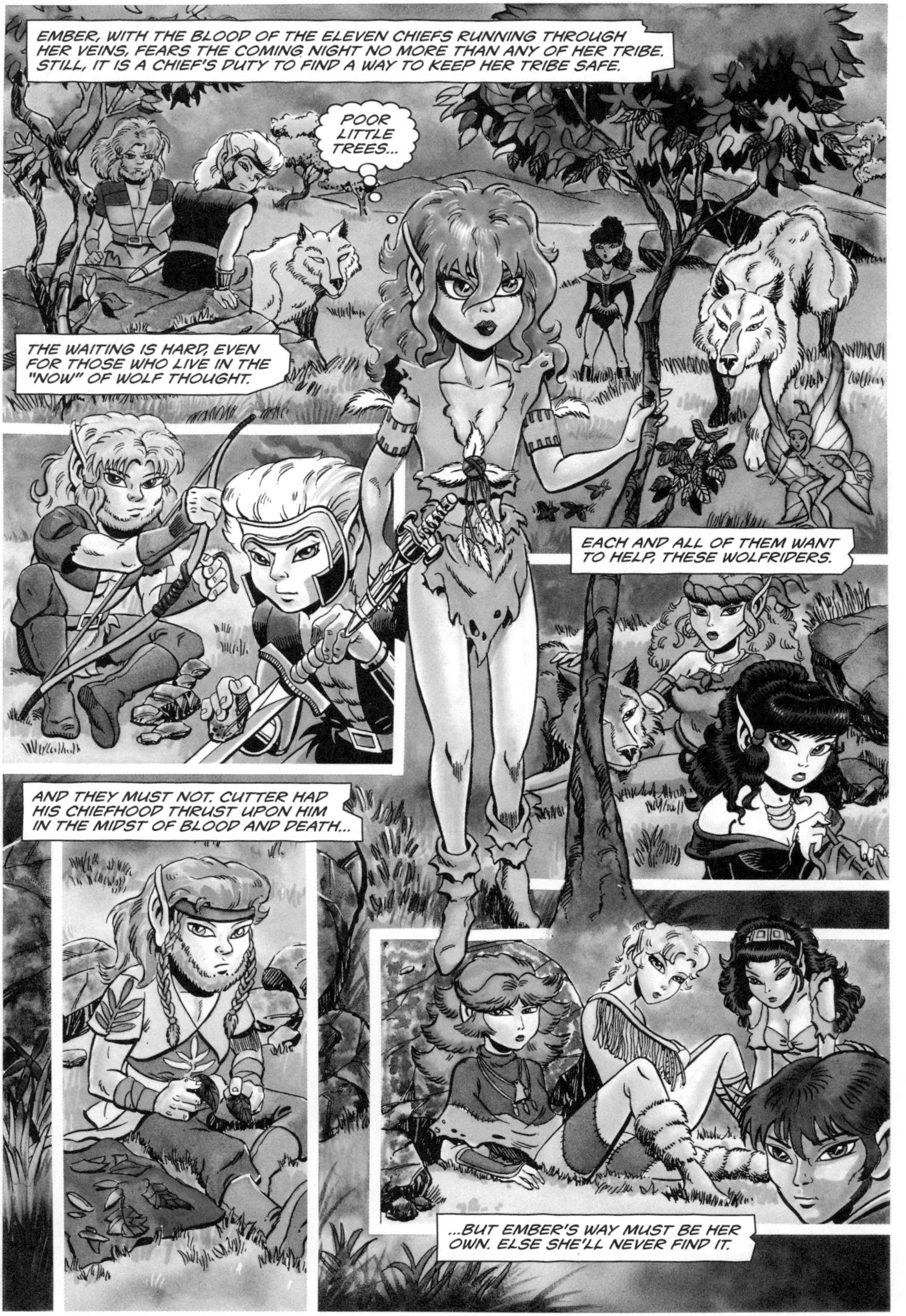
EMBER, WITH THE BLOOD OF THE ELEVEN CHIEFS RUNNING THROUGH HER VEINS, FEARS THE COMING NIGHT NO MORE THAN ANY OF HER TRIBE. STILL, IT IS A CHIEF'S DUTY TO FIND A WAY TO KEEP HER TRIBE SAFE.
POOR LITTLE TREES...
THE WAITING IS HARD, EVEN FOR THOSE WHO LIVE IN THE "NOW" OF WOLF THOUGHT.
EACH AND ALL OF THEM WANT TO HELP, THESE WOLFRIDERS.
AND THEY MUST NOT. CUTTER HAD HIS CHIEFHOOD THRUST UPON HIM IN THE MIDST OF BLOOD AND DEATH...
...BUT EMBER'S WAY MUST BE HER OWN. ELSE SHE'LL NEVER FIND IT.

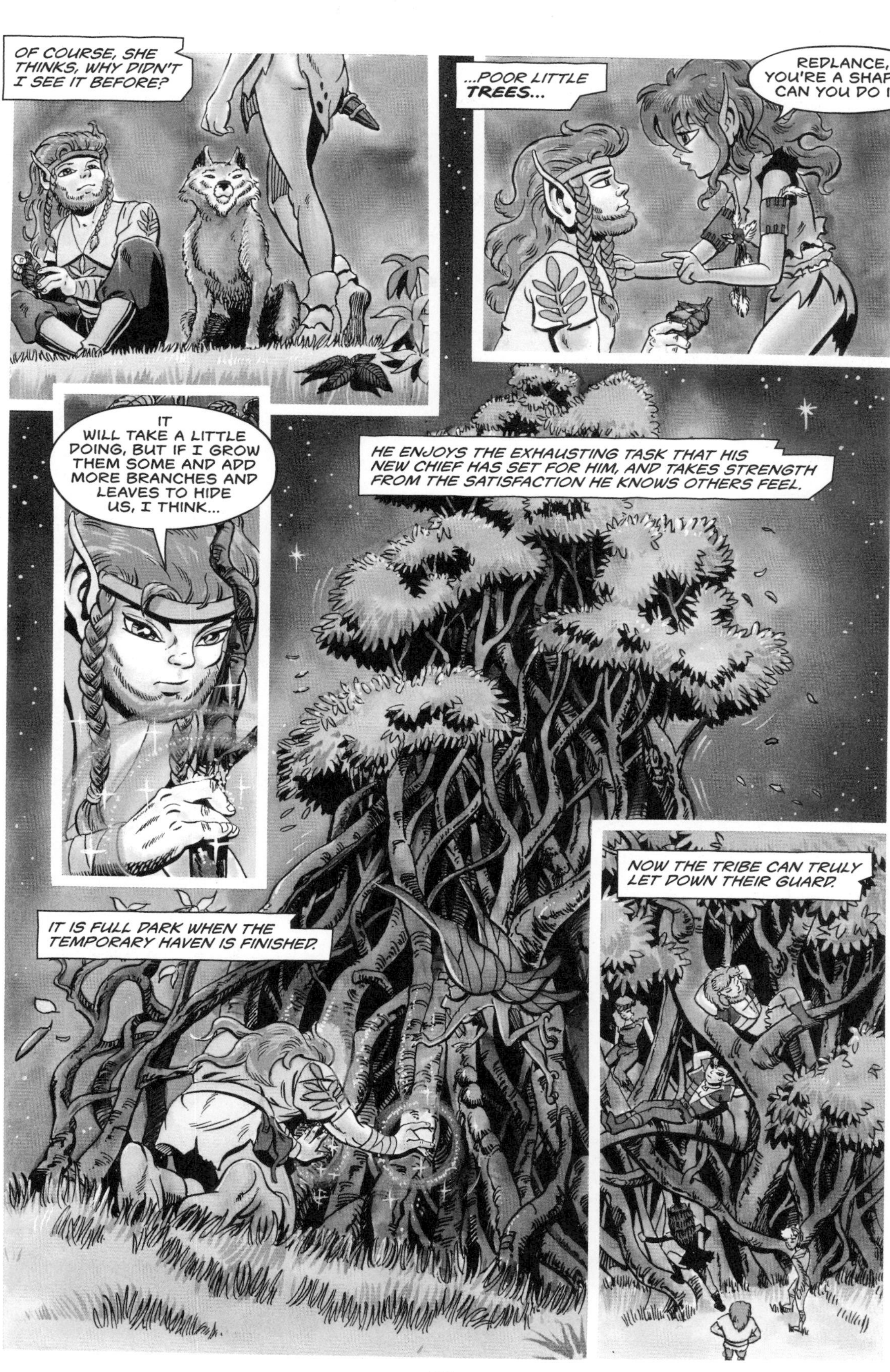

OF COURSE, SHE THINKS, WHY DIDN'T I SEE IT BEFORE?
...POOR LITTLE TREES...
REDLANCE, YOU'RE A SHAPER. CAN YOU DO IT?
IT WILL TAKE A LITTLE DOING, BUT IF I GROW THEM SOME AND ADD MORE BRANCHES AND LEAVES TO HIDE US, I THINK...
HE ENJOYS THE EXHAUSTING TASK THAT HIS NEW CHIEF HAS SET FOR HIM, AND TAKES STRENGTH FROM THE SATISFACTION HE KNOWS OTHERS FEEL.
IT IS FULL DARK WHEN THE TEMPORARY HAVEN IS FINISHED.
NOW THE TRIBE CAN TRULY LET DOWN THEIR GUARD.

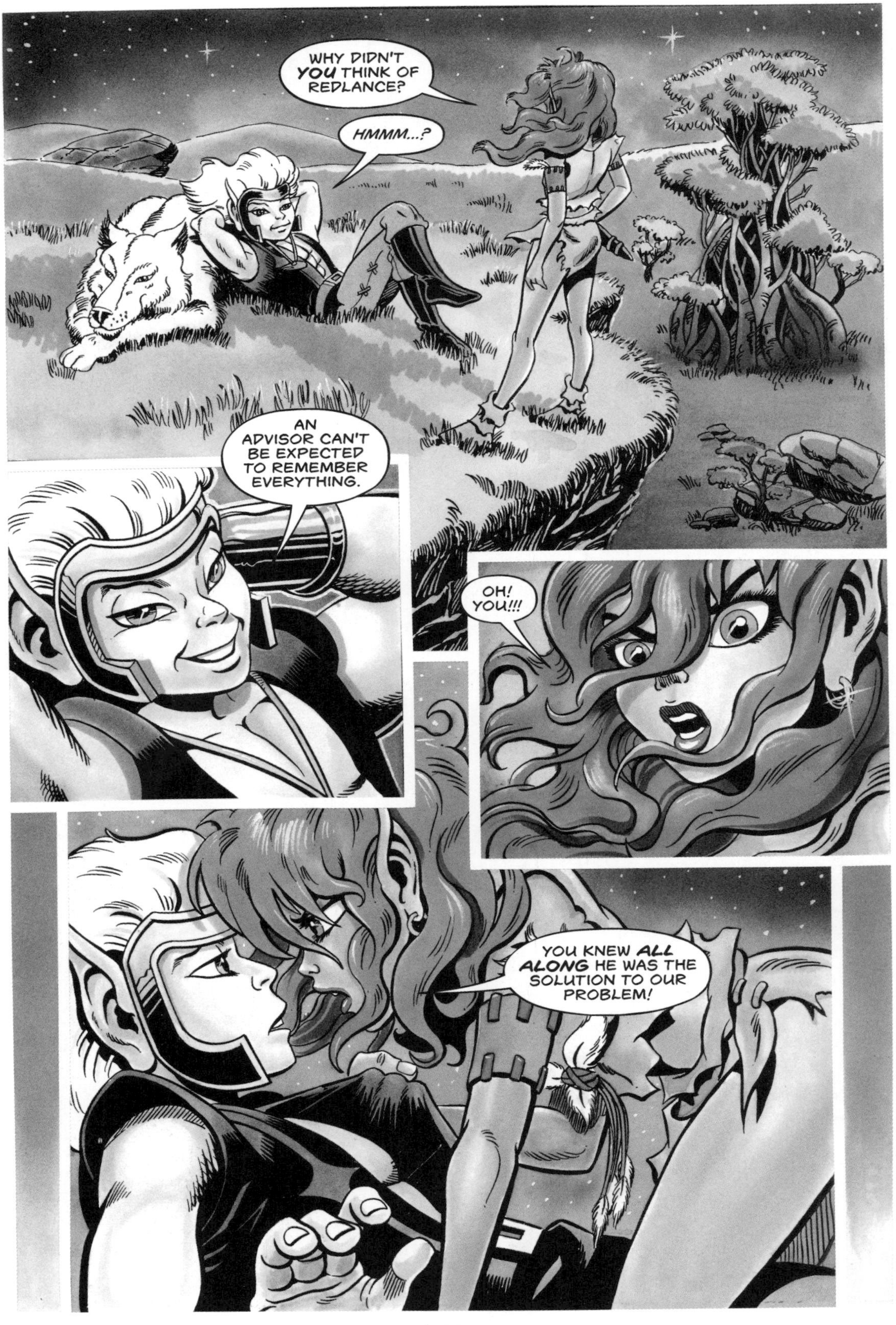
WHY DIDN'T YOU THINK OF REDLANCE?
HMMM...?
AN ADVISOR CAN'T BE EXPECTED TO REMEMBER EVERYTHING.
OH! YOU!!!
YOU KNEW ALL ALONG HE WAS THE SOLUTION TO OUR PROBLEM!

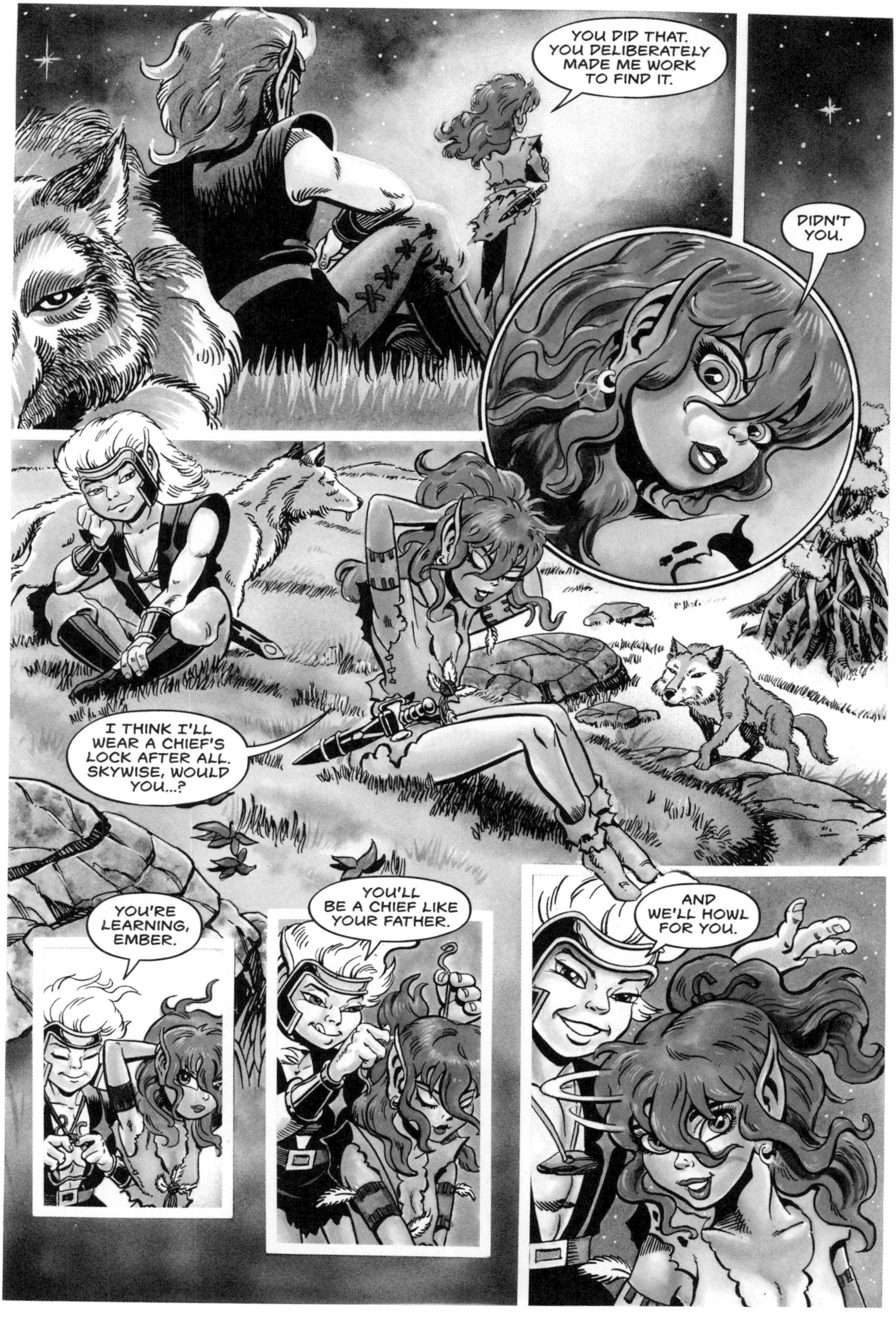
YOU DID THAT. YOU DELIBERATELY MADE ME WORK TO FIND IT.
DIDN'T YOU.
I THINK I'LL WEAR A CHIEF'S LOCK AFTER ALL. SKYWISE, WOULD YOU...?
YOU'RE LEARNING, EMBER.
YOU'LL BE A CHIEF LIKE YOUR FATHER.
AND WE'LL HOWL FOR YOU.

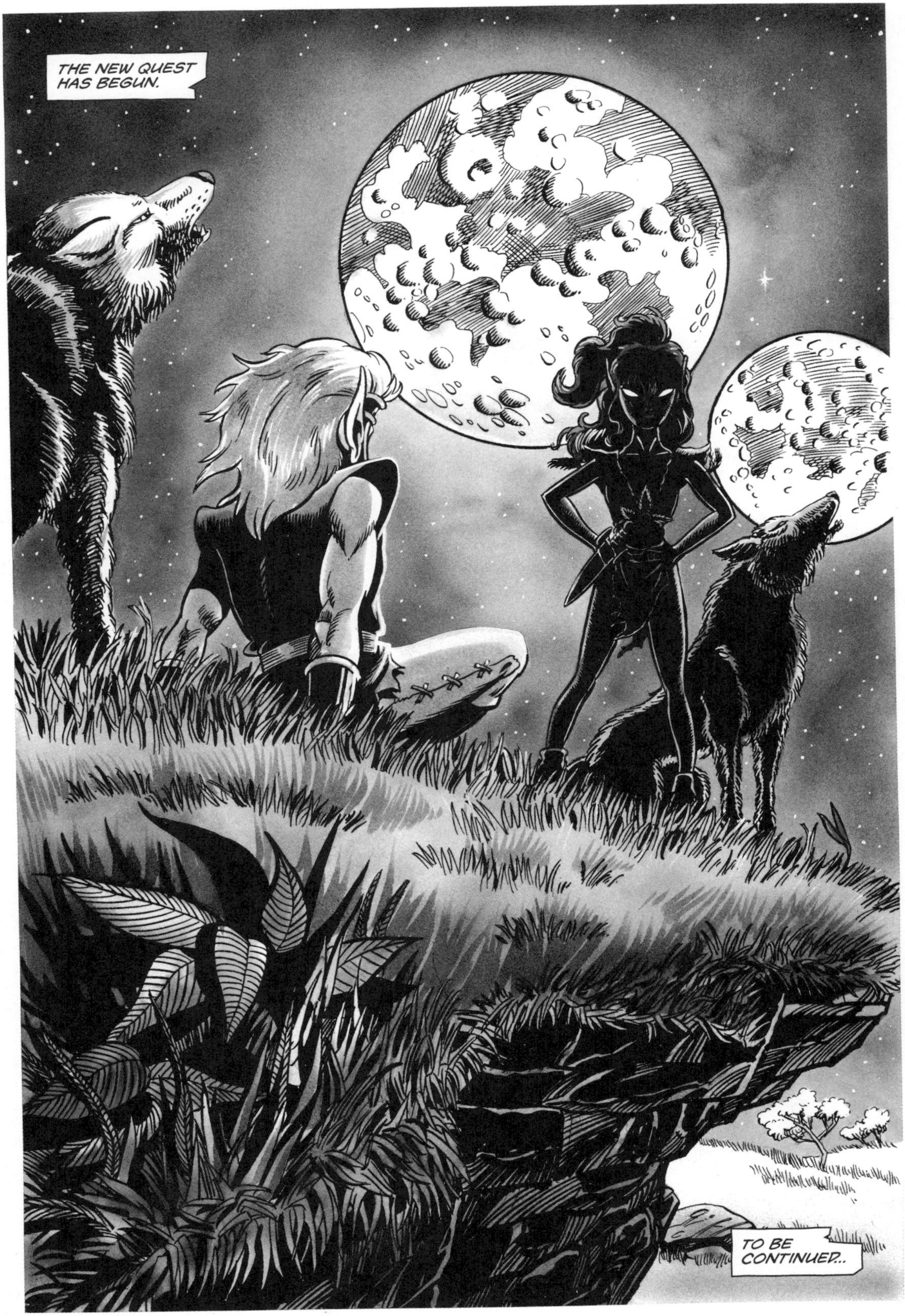
THE NEW QUEST HAS BEGUN.
TO BE CONTINUED...

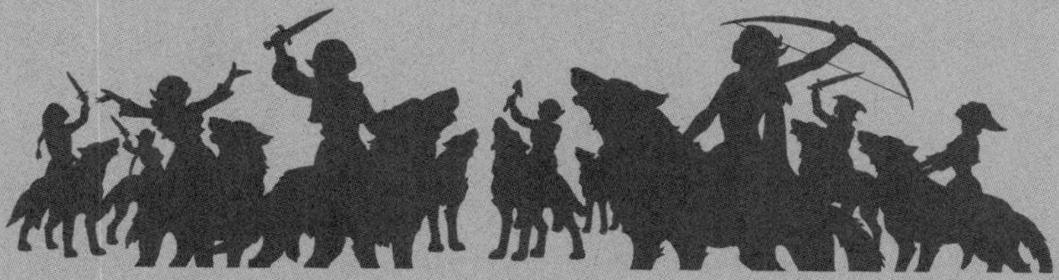

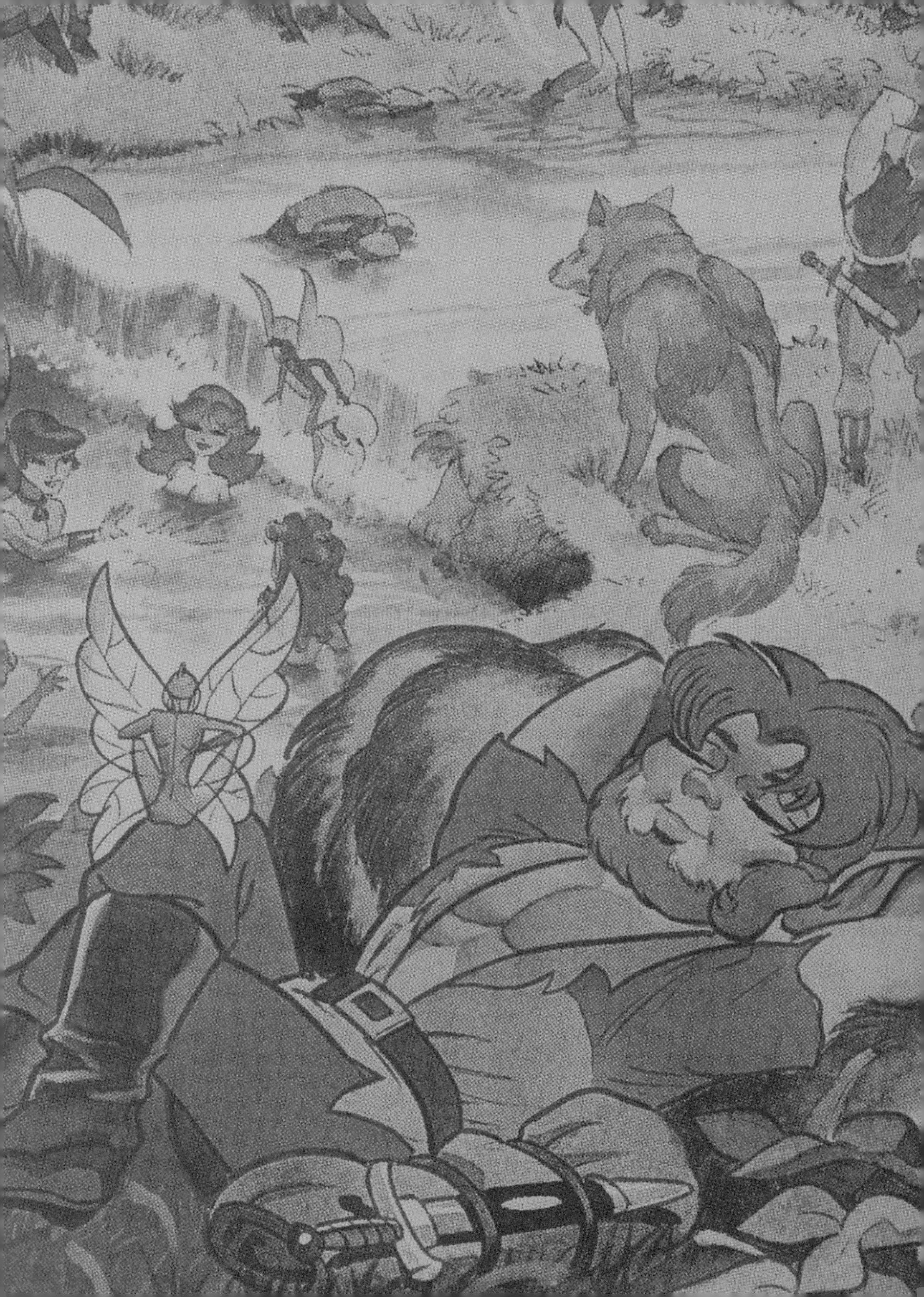

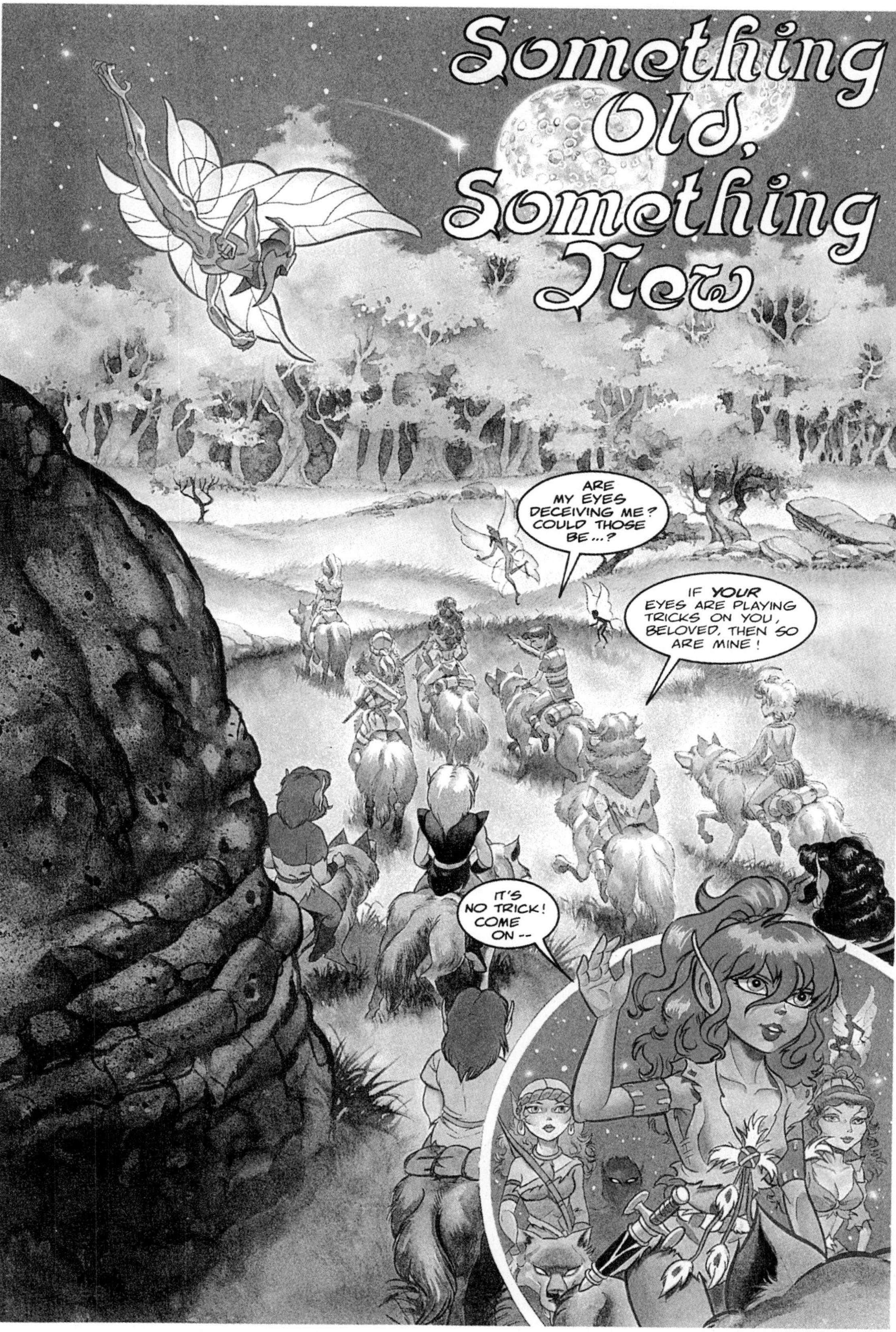

Something Old, Something New
ARE MY EYES DECEIVING ME? COULD THOSE BE...?
IF YOUR EYES ARE PLAYING TRICKS ON YOU, BELOVED, THEN SO ARE MINE!
IT'S NO TRICK! COME ON--

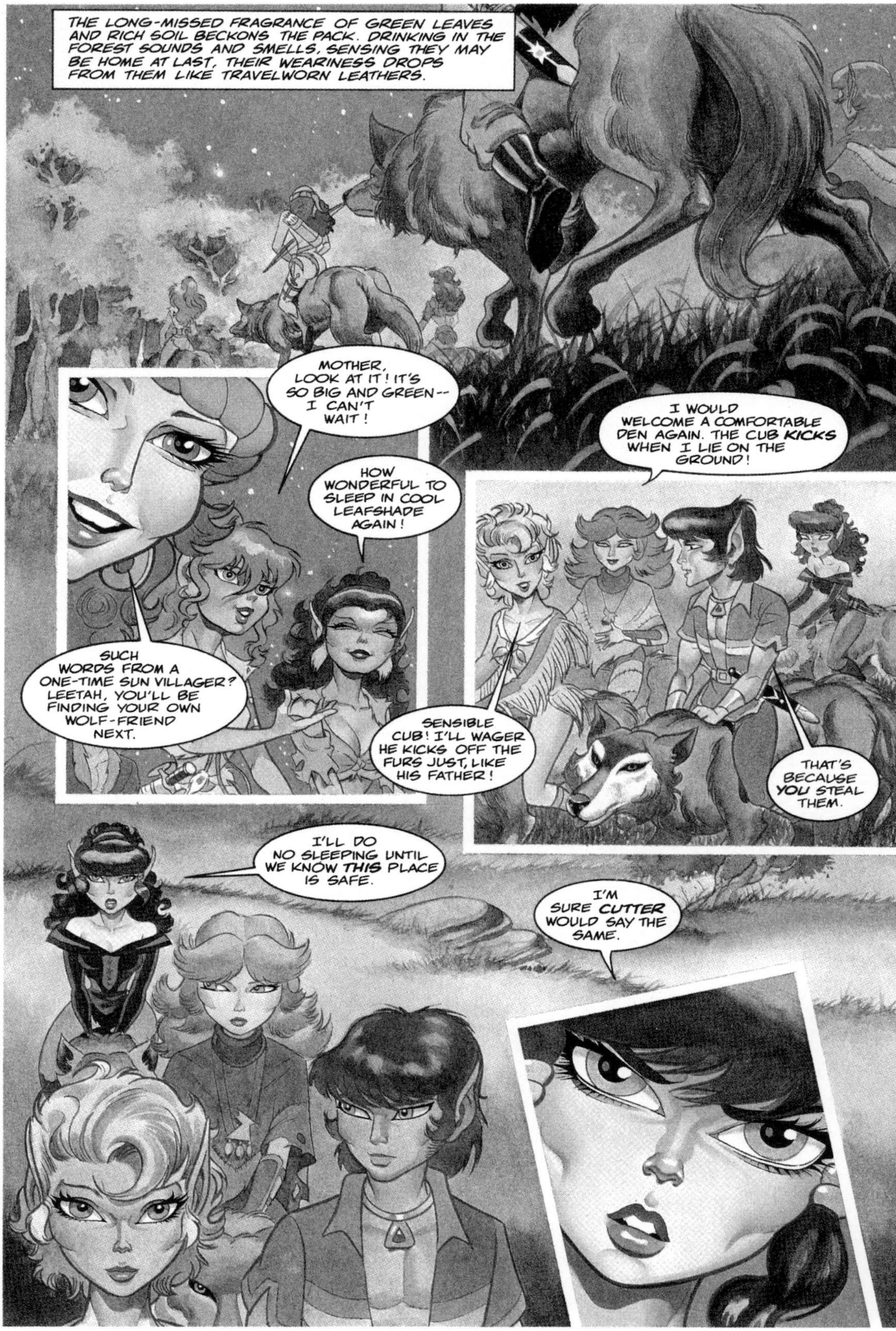

THE LONG-MISSED FRAGRANCE OF GREEN LEAVES AND RICH SOIL BECKONS THE PACK. DRINKING IN THE FOREST SOUNDS AND SMELLS, SENSING THEY MAY BE HOME AT LAST, THEIR WEARINESS DROPS FROM THEM LIKE TRAVELWORN LEATHERS.
MOTHER, LOOK AT IT! IT'S SO BIG AND GREEN-- I CAN'T WAIT!
HOW WONDERFUL TO SLEEP IN COOL LEAFSHADE AGAIN!
SUCH WORDS FROM A ONE-TIME SUN VILLAGER? LEETAH, YOU'LL BE FINDING YOUR OWN WOLF-FRIEND NEXT.
I WOULD WELCOME A COMFORTABLE DEN AGAIN. THE CUB KICKS WHEN I LIE ON THE GROUND!
SENSIBLE CUB! I'LL WAGER HE KICKS OFF THE FURS JUST, LIKE HIS FATHER!
THAT'S BECAUSE YOU STEAL THEM.
I'LL DO NO SLEEPING UNTIL WE KNOW THIS PLACE IS SAFE.
I'M SURE CUTTER WOULD SAY THE SAME.

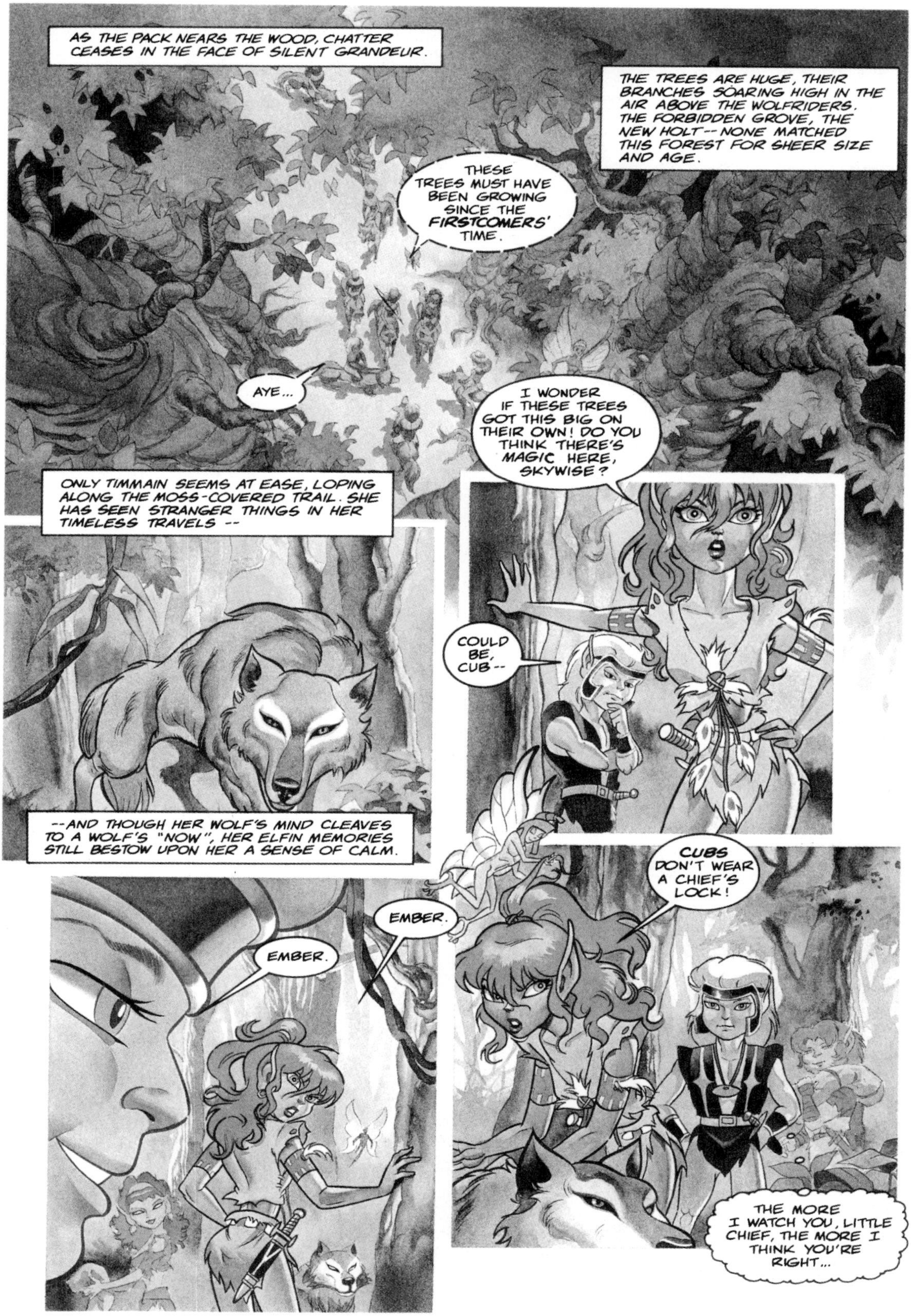
AS THE PACK NEARS THE WOOD, CHATTER CEASES IN THE FACE OF SILENT GRANDEUR.
THE TREES ARE HUGE, THEIR BRANCHES SOARING HIGH IN THE AIR ABOVE THE WOLFRIDERS. THE FORBIDDEN GROVE, THE NEW HOLT--NONE MATCHED THIS FOREST FOR SHEER SIZE AND AGE.
THESE TREES MUST HAVE BEEN GROWING SINCE THE FIRSTCOMERS' TIME.
AYE...
I WONDER IF THESE TREES GOT THIS BIG ON THEIR OWN! DO YOU THINK THERE'S MAGIC HERE, SKYWISE?
ONLY TIMMAIN SEEMS AT EASE, LOPING ALONG THE MOSS-COVERED TRAIL. SHE HAS SEEN STRANGER THINGS IN HER TIMELESS TRAVELS --
--AND THOUGH HER WOLF'S MIND CLEAVES TO A WOLF'S "NOW", HER ELFIN MEMORIES STILL BESTOW UPON HER A SENSE OF CALM.
COULD BE, CUB--
EMBER.
EMBER.
CUBS DON'T WEAR A CHIEF'S LOCK!
THE MORE I WATCH YOU, LITTLE CHIEF, THE MORE I THINK YOU'RE RIGHT...

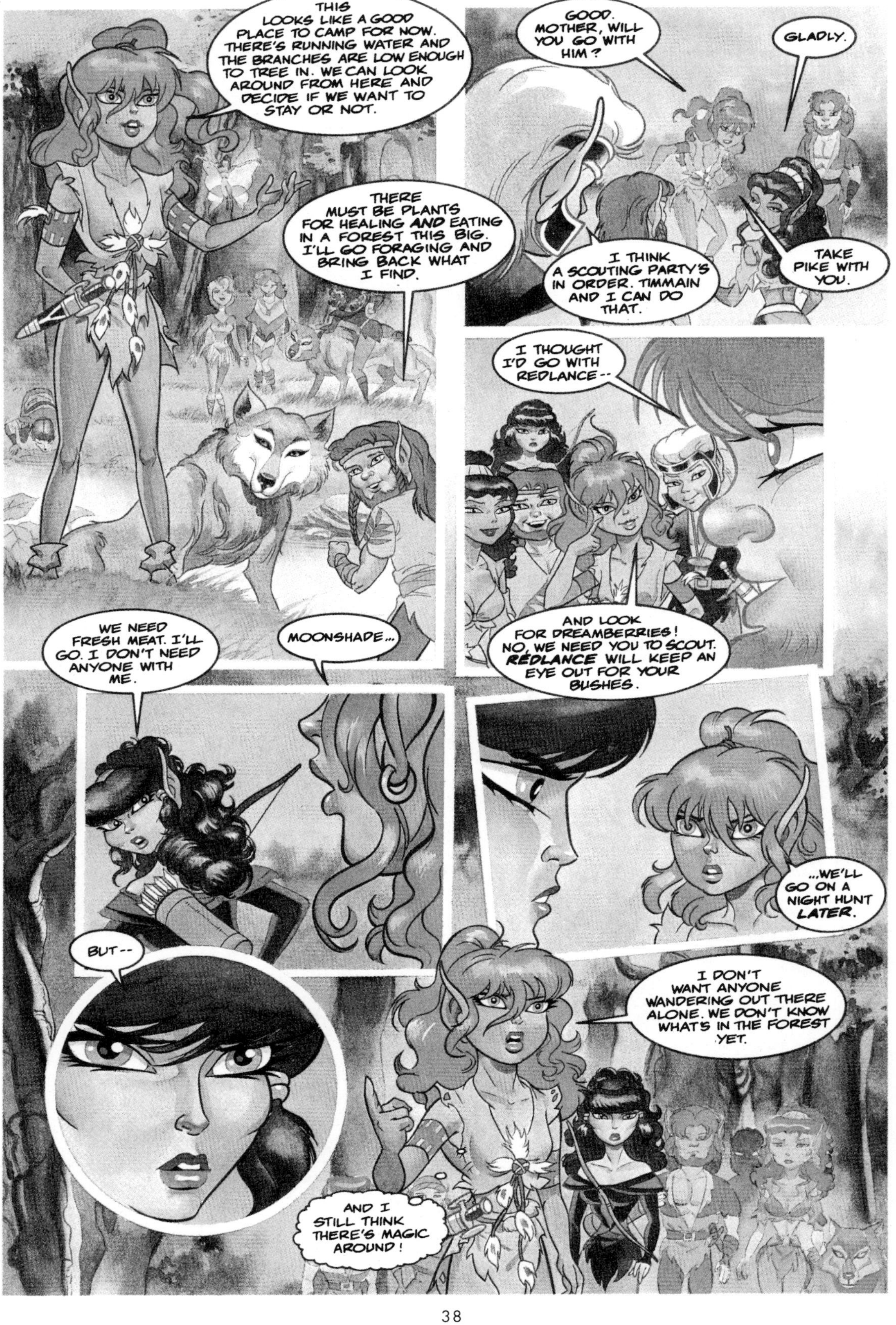
THIS LOOKS LIKE A GOOD PLACE TO CAMP FOR NOW. THERE'S RUNNING WATER AND THE BRANCHES ARE LOW ENOUGH TO TREE IN. WE CAN LOOK AROUND FROM HERE AND DECIDE IF WE WANT TO STAY OR NOT.
THERE MUST BE PLANTS FOR HEALING AND EATING IN A FOREST THIS BIG. I'LL GO FORAGING AND BRING BACK WHAT I FIND.
I THINK A SCOUTING PARTY'S IN ORDER. TIMMAIN AND I CAN DO THAT.
GOOD. MOTHER, WILL YOU GO WITH HIM?
GLADLY.
TAKE PIKE WITH YOU.
I THOUGHT I'D GO WITH REDLANCE--
AND LOOK FOR DREAMBERRIES! NO, WE NEED YOU TO SCOUT. REDLANCE WILL KEEP AN EYE OUT FOR YOUR BUSHES.
WE NEED FRESH MEAT. I'LL GO. I DON'T NEED ANYONE WITH ME.
MOONSHADE...
...WE'LL GO ON A NIGHT HUNT LATER.
BUT--
I DON'T WANT ANYONE WANDERING OUT THERE ALONE. WE DON'T KNOW WHAT'S IN THE FOREST YET.
AND I STILL THINK THERE'S MAGIC AROUND!

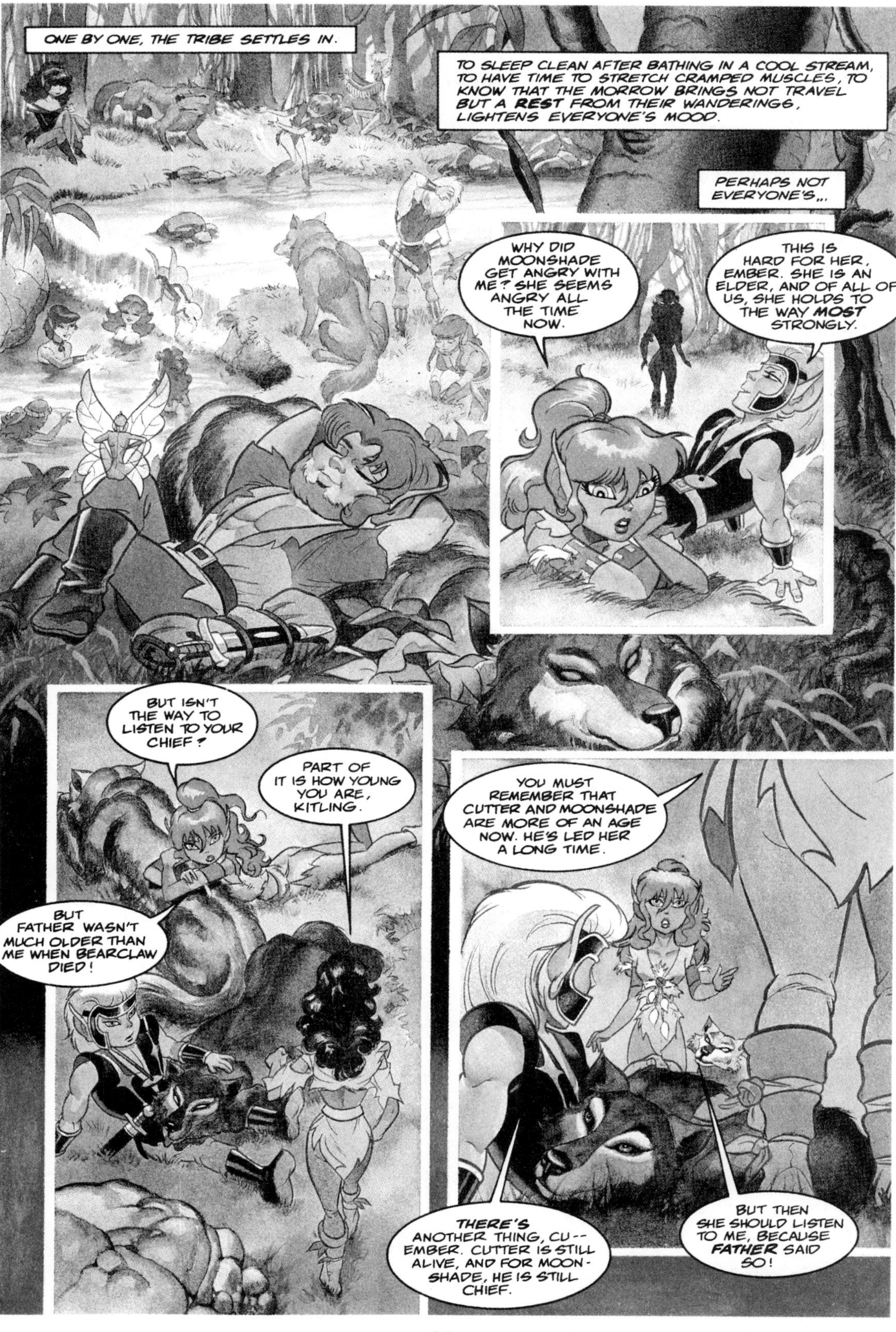
ONE BY ONE, THE TRIBE SETTLES IN.
TO SLEEP CLEAN AFTER BATHING IN A COOL STREAM, TO HAVE TIME TO STRETCH CRAMPED MUSCLES, TO KNOW THAT THE MORROW BRINGS NOT TRAVEL BUT A REST FROM THEIR WANDERINGS, LIGHTENS EVERYONE'S MOOD.
PERHAPS NOT EVERYONE'S...
WHY DID MOONSHADE GET ANGRY WITH ME? SHE SEEMS ANGRY ALL THE TIME NOW.
THIS IS HARD FOR HER, EMBER. SHE IS AN ELDER, AND OF ALL OF US, SHE HOLDS TO THE WAY MOST STRONGLY.
BUT ISN'T THE WAY TO LISTEN TO YOUR CHIEF?
PART OF IT IS HOW YOUNG YOU ARE, KITLING.
BUT FATHER WASN'T MUCH OLDER THAN ME WHEN BEARCLAW DIED!
YOU MUST REMEMBER THAT CUTTER AND MOONSHADE ARE MORE OF AN AGE NOW. HE'S LED HER A LONG TIME.
THERE'S ANOTHER THING, CU-- EMBER. CUTTER IS STILL ALIVE, AND FOR MOON-SHADE, HE IS STILL CHIEF.
BUT THEN SHE SHOULD LISTEN TO ME, BECAUSE FATHER SAID SO!

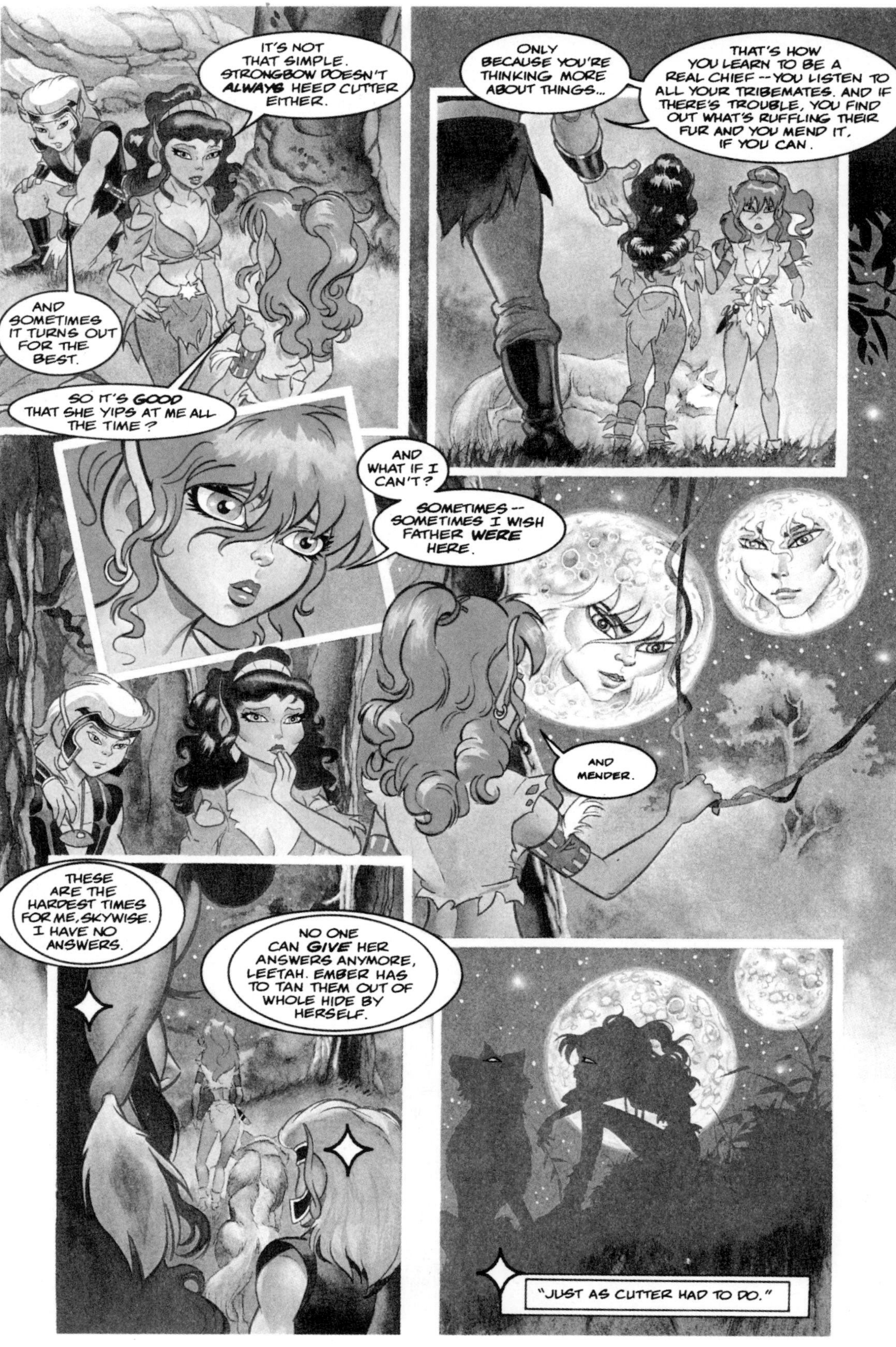
IT'S NOT THAT SIMPLE. STRONGBOW DOESN'T ALWAYS HEED CUTTER EITHER.
AND SOMETIMES IT TURNS OUT FOR THE BEST.
SO IT'S GOOD THAT SHE YIPS AT ME ALL THE TIME?
ONLY BECAUSE YOU'RE THINKING MORE ABOUT THINGS...
THAT'S HOW YOU LEARN TO BE A REAL CHIEF --YOU LISTEN TO ALL YOUR TRIBEMATES. AND IF THERE'S TROUBLE, YOU FIND OUT WHAT'S RUFFLING THEIR FUR AND YOU MEND IT, IF YOU CAN.
AND WHAT IF I CAN'T?
SOMETIMES -- SOMETIMES I WISH FATHER WERE HERE.
AND MENDER.
THESE ARE THE HARDEST TIMES FOR ME, SKYWISE. I HAVE NO ANSWERS.
NO ONE CAN GIVE HER ANSWERS ANYMORE, LEETAH. EMBER HAS TO TAN THEM OUT OF WHOLE HIDE BY HERSELF.
"JUST AS CUTTER HAD TO DO."

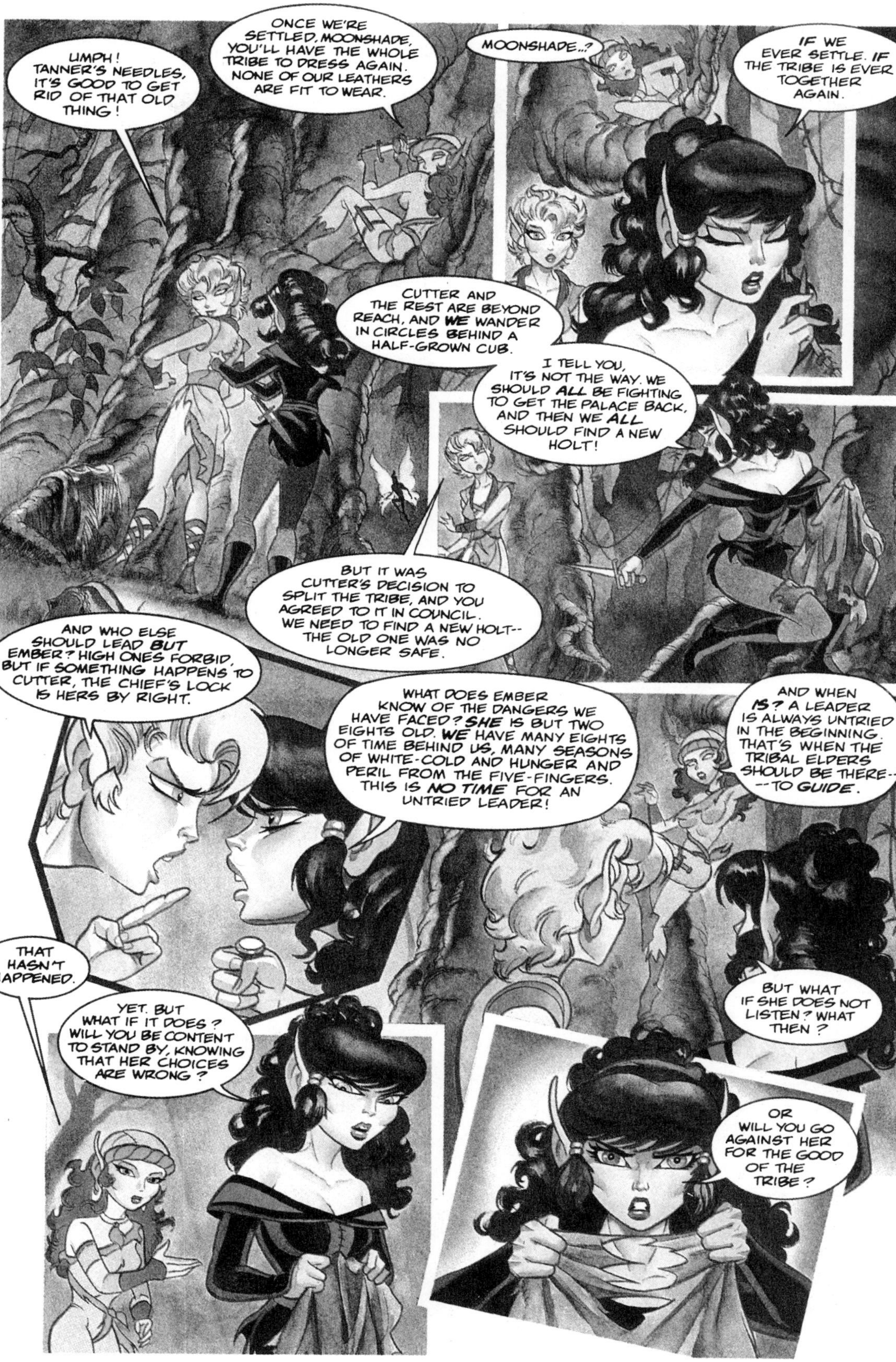
UMPH! TANNER'S NEEDLES, IT'S GOOD TO GET RID OF THAT OLD THING!
ONCE WE'RE SETTLED, MOONSHADE, YOU'LL HAVE THE WHOLE TRIBE TO DRESS AGAIN. NONE OF OUR LEATHERS ARE FIT TO WEAR.
MOONSHADE...?
IF WE EVER SETTLE. IF THE TRIBE IS EVER TOGETHER AGAIN.
CUTTER AND THE REST ARE BEYOND REACH, AND WE WANDER IN CIRCLES BEHIND A HALF-GROWN CUB.
I TELL YOU, IT'S NOT THE WAY. WE SHOULD ALL BE FIGHTING TO GET THE PALACE BACK, AND THEN WE ALL SHOULD FIND A NEW HOLT!
BUT IT WAS CUTTER'S DECISION TO SPLIT THE TRIBE, AND YOU AGREED TO IT IN COUNCIL. WE NEED TO FIND A NEW HOLT-- THE OLD ONE WAS NO LONGER SAFE.
AND WHO ELSE SHOULD LEAD BUT EMBER? HIGH ONES FORBID, BUT IF SOMETHING HAPPENS TO CUTTER, THE CHIEF'S LOCK IS HERS BY RIGHT.
WHAT DOES EMBER KNOW OF THE DANGERS WE HAVE FACED? SHE IS BUT TWO EIGHTS OLD. WE HAVE MANY EIGHTS OF TIME BEHIND US, MANY SEASONS OF WHITE-COLD AND HUNGER AND PERIL FROM THE FIVE-FINGERS. THIS IS NO TIME FOR AN UNTRIED LEADER!
AND WHEN IS? A LEADER IS ALWAYS UNTRIED IN THE BEGINNING. THAT'S WHEN THE TRIBAL ELDERS SHOULD BE THERE-- --TO GUIDE.
THAT HASN'T HAPPENED.
YET. BUT WHAT IF IT DOES? WILL YOU BE CONTENT TO STAND BY, KNOWING THAT HER CHOICES ARE WRONG?
BUT WHAT IF SHE DOES NOT LISTEN? WHAT THEN?
OR WILL YOU GO AGAINST HER FOR THE GOOD OF THE TRIBE?

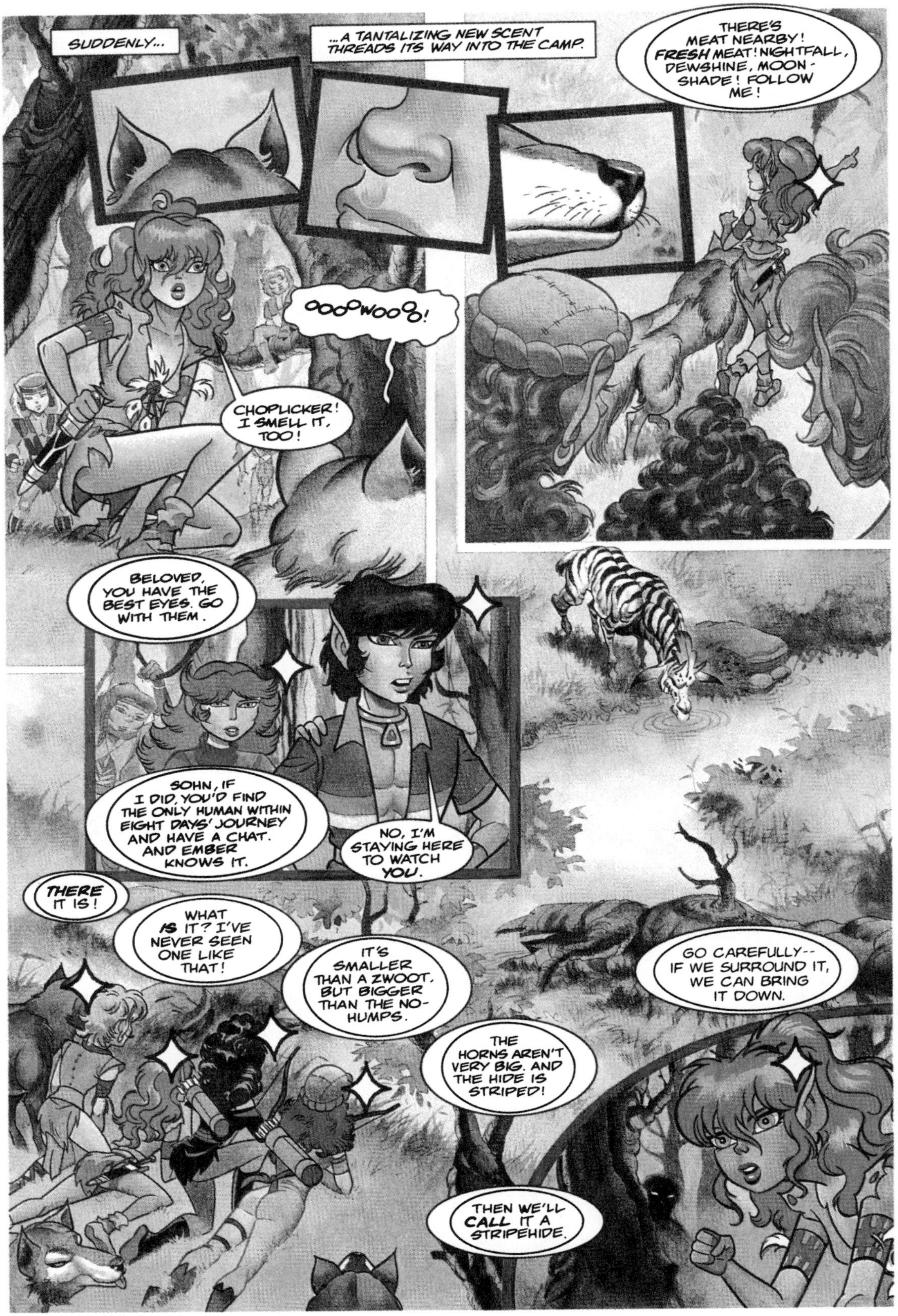
SUDDENLY...
...A TANTALIZING NEW SCENT THREADS ITS WAY INTO THE CAMP.
THERE'S MEAT NEARBY! FRESH MEAT! NIGHTFALL, DEWSHINE, MOON-SHADE! FOLLOW ME!
OOOOWOOOO!
CHOPLICKER! I SMELL IT, TOO!
BELOVED, YOU HAVE THE BEST EYES. GO WITH THEM.
SOHN, IF I DID, YOU'D FIND THE ONLY HUMAN WITHIN EIGHT DAYS' JOURNEY AND HAVE A CHAT. AND EMBER KNOWS IT.
NO, I'M STAYING HERE TO WATCH YOU.
THERE IT IS!
WHAT IS IT? I'VE NEVER SEEN ONE LIKE THAT!
IT'S SMALLER THAN A ZWOOT, BUT BIGGER THAN THE NO-HUMPS.
GO CAREFULLY-- IF WE SURROUND IT, WE CAN BRING IT DOWN.
THE HORNS AREN'T VERY BIG. AND THE HIDE IS STRIPED!
THEN WE'LL CALL IT A STRIPEHIDE.

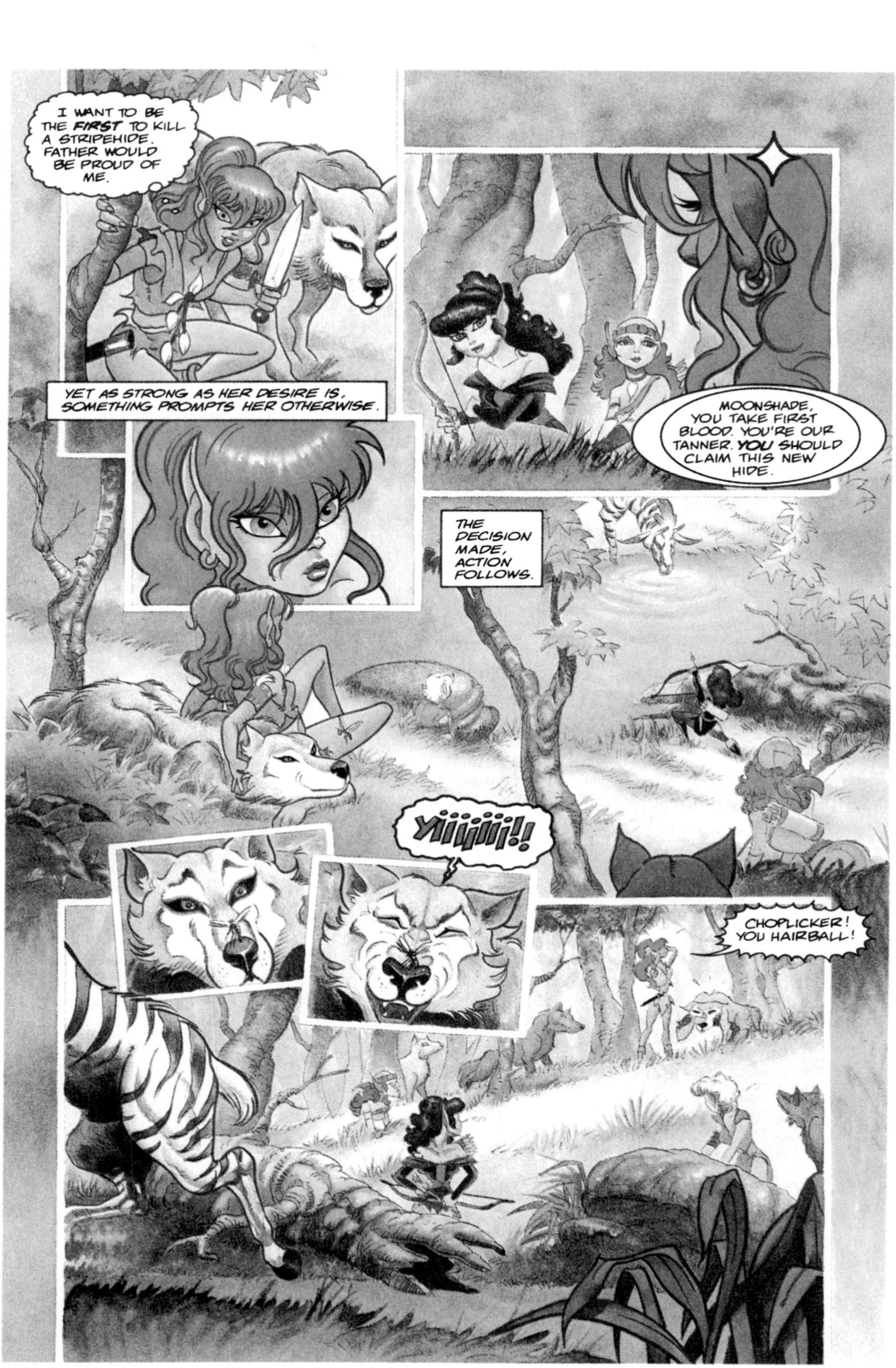
I WANT TO BE THE FIRST TO KILL A STRIPEHIDE. FATHER WOULD BE PROUD OF ME.
YET AS STRONG AS HER DESIRE IS, SOMETHING PROMPTS HER OTHERWISE.
MOONSHADE, YOU TAKE FIRST BLOOD. YOU'RE OUR TANNER. YOU SHOULD CLAIM THIS NEW HIDE.
THE DECISION MADE, ACTION FOLLOWS.
YIIIIII!!
CHOPLICKER! YOU HAIRBALL!

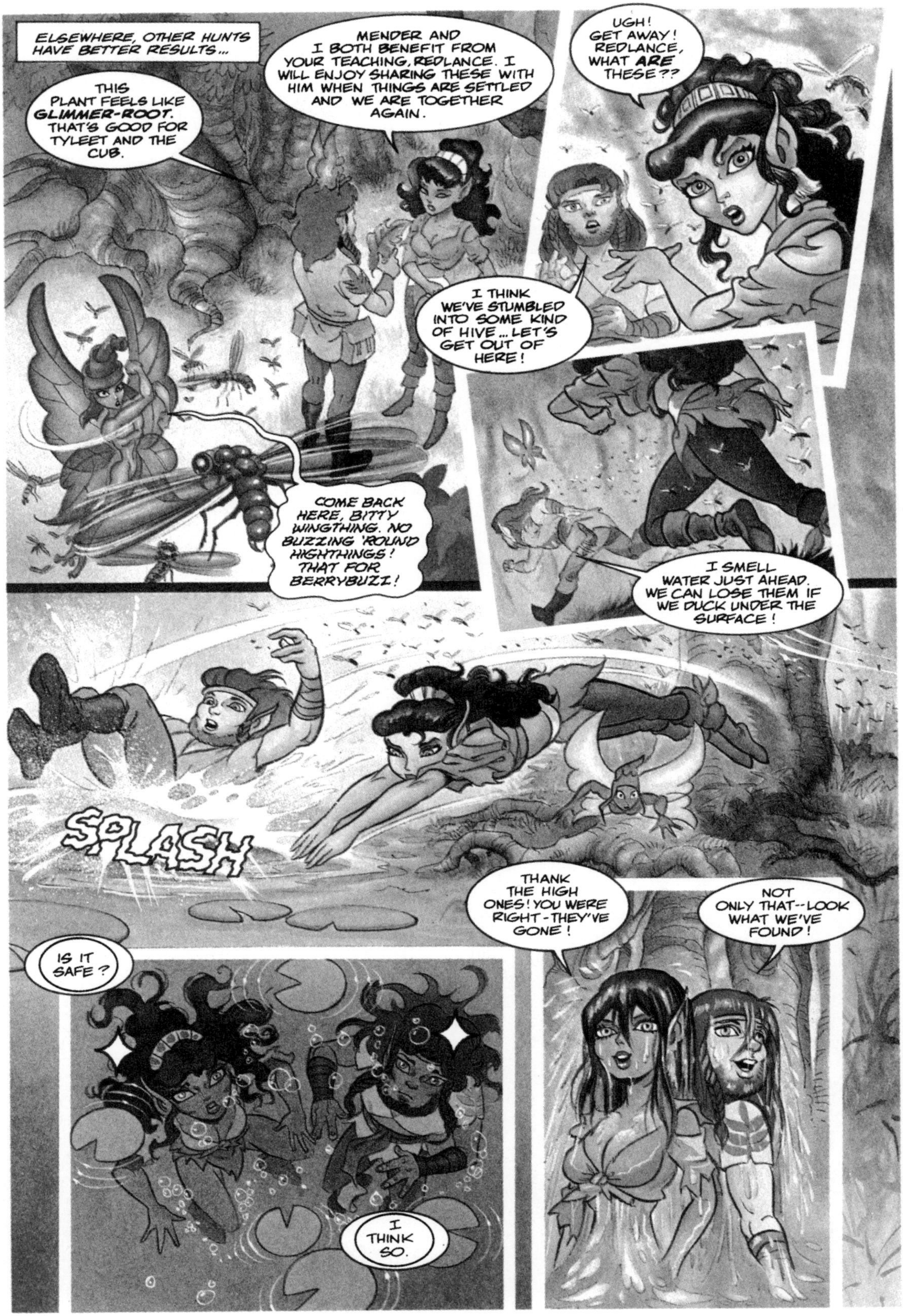
ELSEWHERE, OTHER HUNTS HAVE BETTER RESULTS...
THIS PLANT FEELS LIKE GLIMMER-ROOT. THAT'S GOOD FOR TYLEET AND THE CUB.
MENDER AND I BOTH BENEFIT FROM YOUR TEACHING, REDLANCE. I WILL ENJOY SHARING THESE WITH HIM WHEN THINGS ARE SETTLED AND WE ARE TOGETHER AGAIN.
COME BACK HERE, BITTY WINGTHING. NO BUZZING 'ROUND HIGHTHINGS! THAT FOR BERRYBUZZ!
UGH! GET AWAY! REDLANCE, WHAT ARE THESE??
I THINK WE'VE STUMBLED INTO SOME KIND OF HIVE... LET'S GET OUT OF HERE!
I SMELL WATER JUST AHEAD. WE CAN LOSE THEM IF WE DUCK UNDER THE SURFACE!
SPLASH
IS IT SAFE?
I THINK SO.
THANK THE HIGH ONES! YOU WERE RIGHT - THEY'VE GONE!
NOT ONLY THAT--LOOK WHAT WE'VE FOUND!

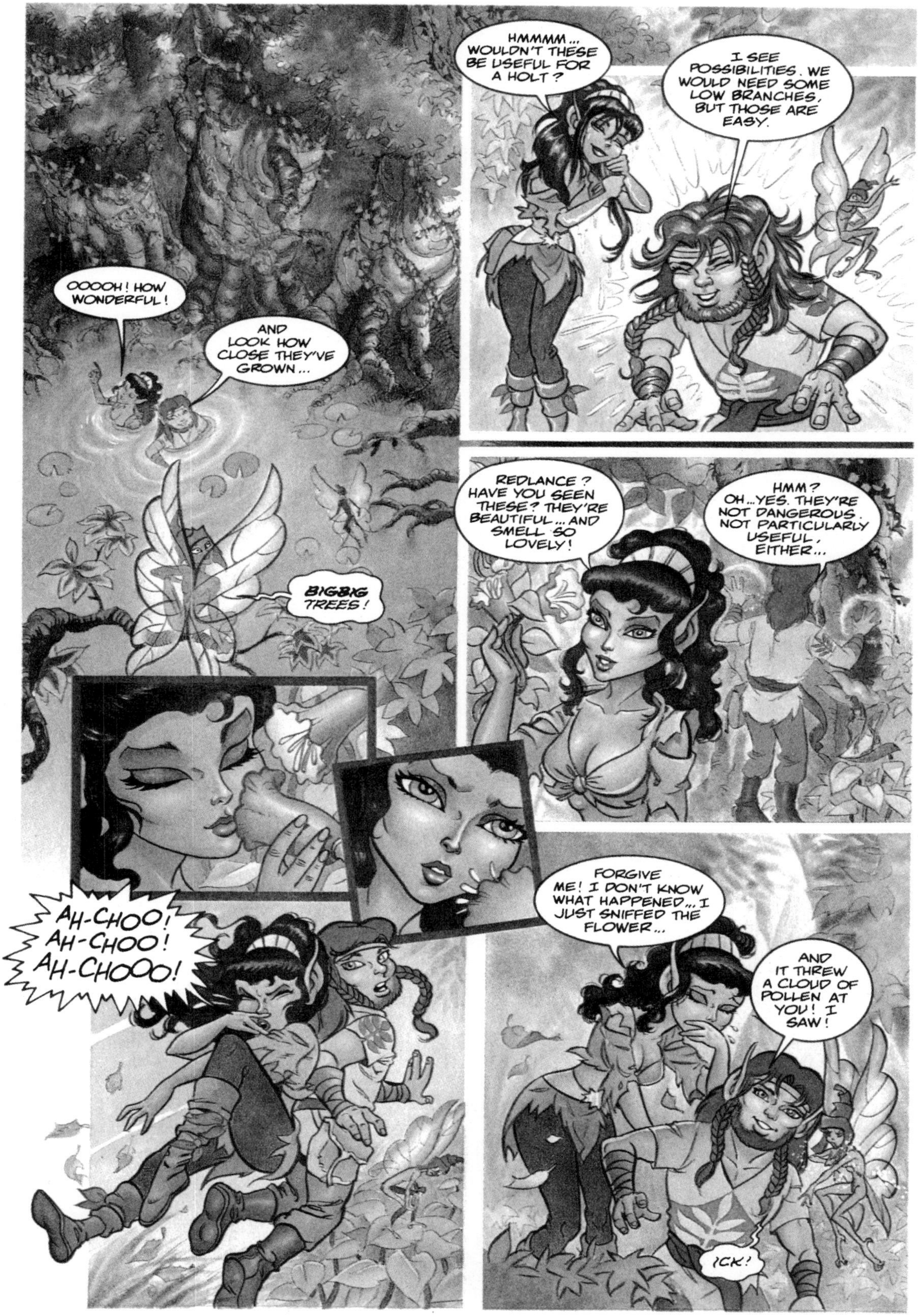
OOOOH! HOW WONDERFUL!
AND LOOK HOW CLOSE THEY'VE GROWN...
BIGBIG TREES!
HMMMM... WOULDN'T THESE BE USEFUL FOR A HOLT?
I SEE POSSIBILITIES. WE WOULD NEED SOME LOW BRANCHES, BUT THOSE ARE EASY.
REDLANCE? HAVE YOU SEEN THESE? THEY'RE BEAUTIFUL... AND SMELL SO LOVELY!
HMM? OH... YES. THEY'RE NOT DANGEROUS. NOT PARTICULARLY USEFUL, EITHER...
AH-CHOO! AH-CHOO! AH-CHOOO!
FORGIVE ME! I DON'T KNOW WHAT HAPPENED... I JUST SNIFFED THE FLOWER...
AND IT THREW A CLOUD OF POLLEN AT YOU! I SAW!
ICK!

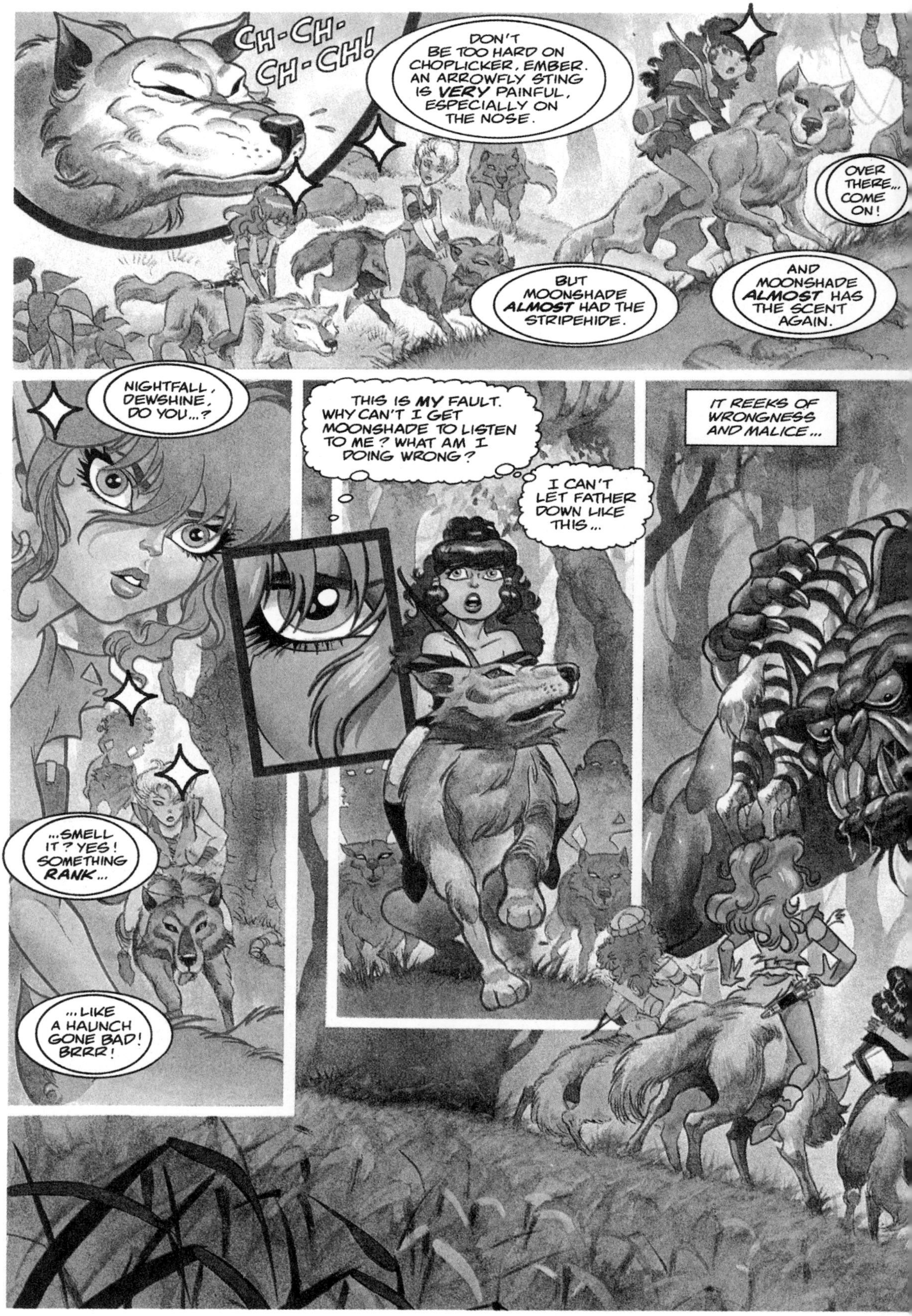
CH-CH-CH-CH!
DON'T BE TOO HARD ON CHOPLICKER, EMBER. AN ARROWFLY STING IS VERY PAINFUL, ESPECIALLY ON THE NOSE.
BUT MOONSHADE ALMOST HAD THE STRIPEHIDE.
OVER THERE... COME ON!
AND MOONSHADE ALMOST HAS THE SCENT AGAIN.
NIGHTFALL, DEWSHINE, DO YOU...?
...SMELL IT? YES! SOMETHING RANK...
...LIKE A HAUNCH GONE BAD! BRRR!
THIS IS MY FAULT. WHY CAN'T I GET MOONSHADE TO LISTEN TO ME? WHAT AM I DOING WRONG?
I CAN'T LET FATHER DOWN LIKE THIS...
IT REEKS OF WRONGNESS AND MALICE...

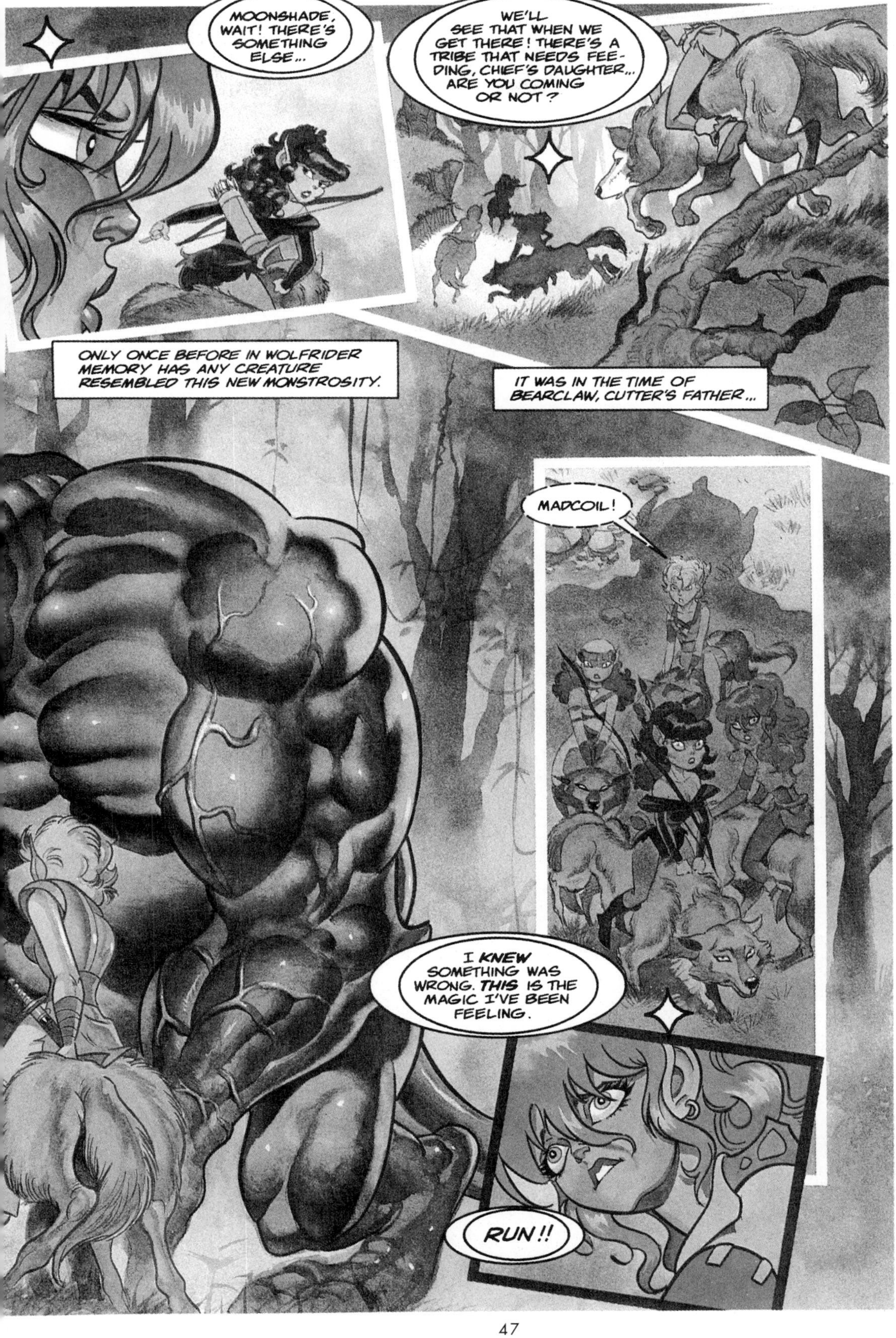
MOONSHADE, WAIT! THERE'S SOMETHING ELSE...
WE'LL SEE THAT WHEN WE GET THERE! THERE'S A TRIBE THAT NEEDS FEE-DING, CHIEF'S DAUGHTER... ARE YOU COMING OR NOT?
ONLY ONCE BEFORE IN WOLFRIDER MEMORY HAS ANY CREATURE RESEMBLED THIS NEW MONSTROSITY.
IT WAS IN THE TIME OF BEARCLAW, CUTTER'S FATHER...
MADCOIL!
I KNEW SOMETHING WAS WRONG. THIS IS THE MAGIC I'VE BEEN FEELING.
RUN!!

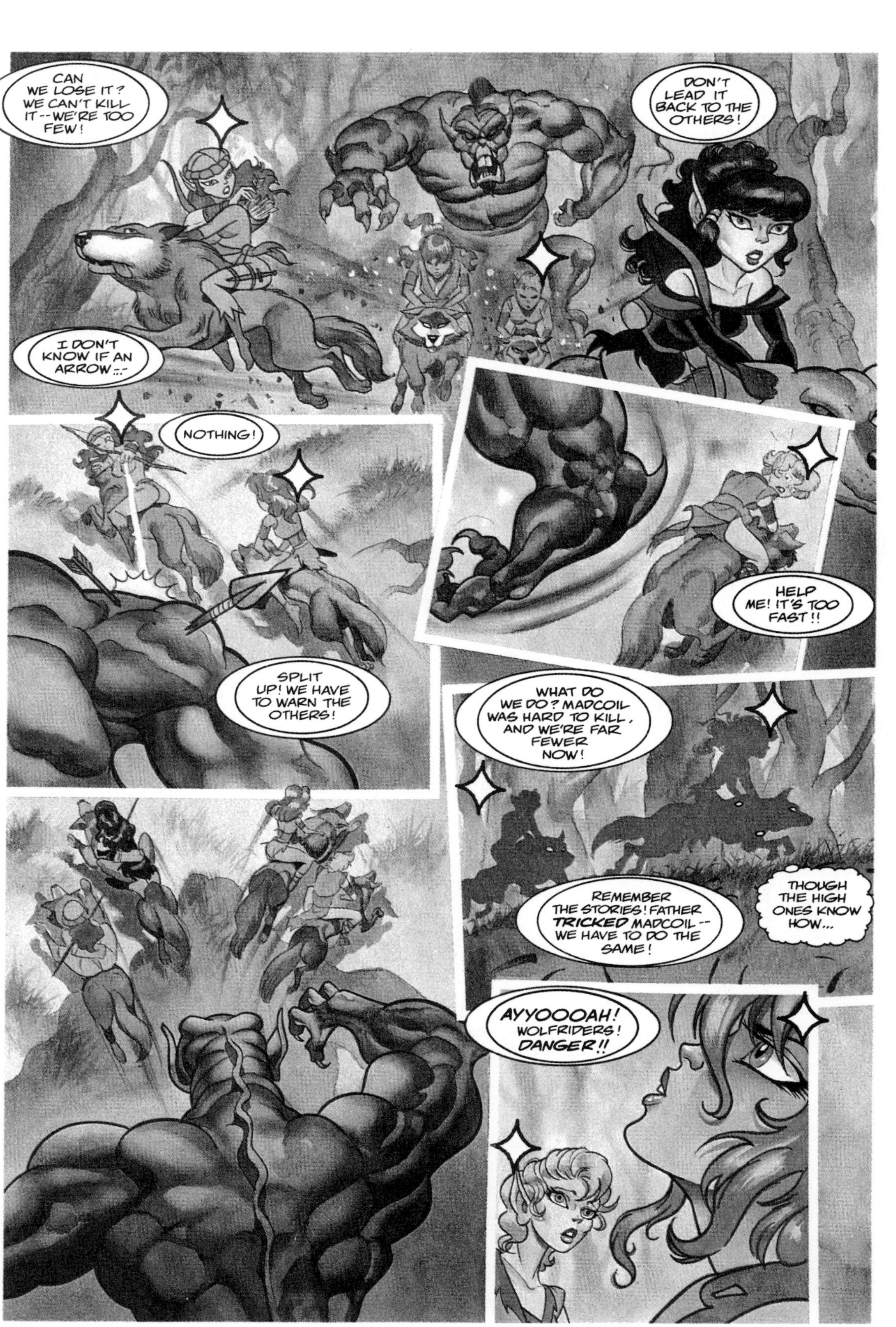
CAN WE LOSE IT? WE CAN'T KILL IT--WE'RE TOO FEW!
DON'T LEAD IT BACK TO THE OTHERS!
I DON'T KNOW IF AN ARROW...
NOTHING!
HELP ME! IT'S TOO FAST!!
SPLIT UP! WE HAVE TO WARN THE OTHERS!
WHAT DO WE DO? MADCOIL WAS HARD TO KILL, AND WE'RE FAR FEWER NOW!
REMEMBER THE STORIES! FATHER TRICKED MADCOIL-- WE HAVE TO DO THE SAME!
THOUGH THE HIGH ONES KNOW HOW...
AYYOOOAH! WOLFRIDERS! DANGER!!

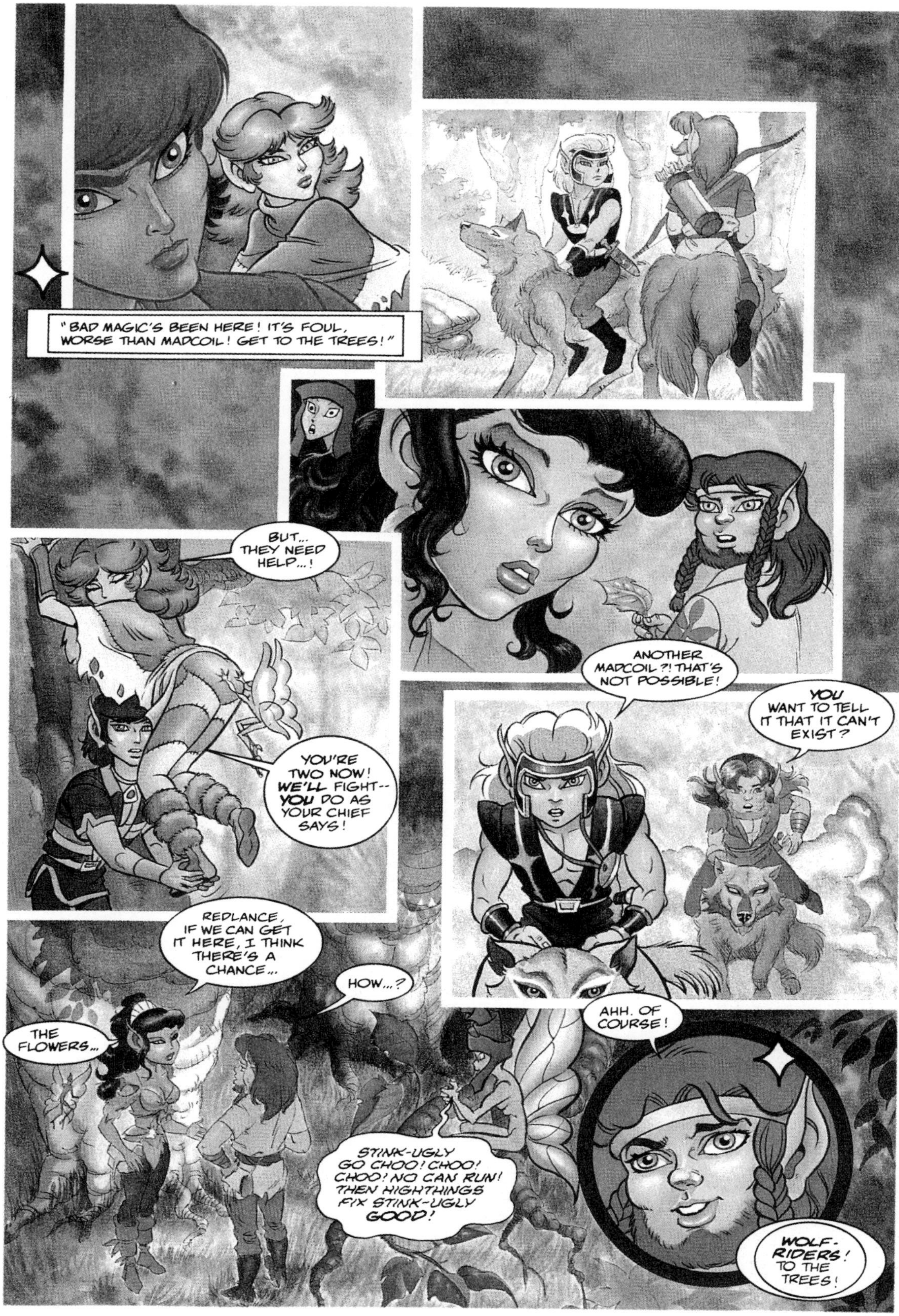
"BAD MAGIC'S BEEN HERE! IT'S FOUL, WORSE THAN MADCOIL! GET TO THE TREES!"
BUT... THEY NEED HELP...!
ANOTHER MADCOIL?! THAT'S NOT POSSIBLE!
YOU WANT TO TELL IT THAT IT CAN'T EXIST?
YOU'RE TWO NOW! WE'LL FIGHT-- YOU DO AS YOUR CHIEF SAYS!
REDLANCE, IF WE CAN GET IT HERE, I THINK THERE'S A CHANCE...
HOW...?
THE FLOWERS...
AHH. OF COURSE!
STINK-UGLY GO CHOO! CHOO! CHOO! NO CAN RUN! THEN HIGHTHINGS FIX STINK-UGLY GOOD!
WOLF-RIDERS! TO THE TREES!

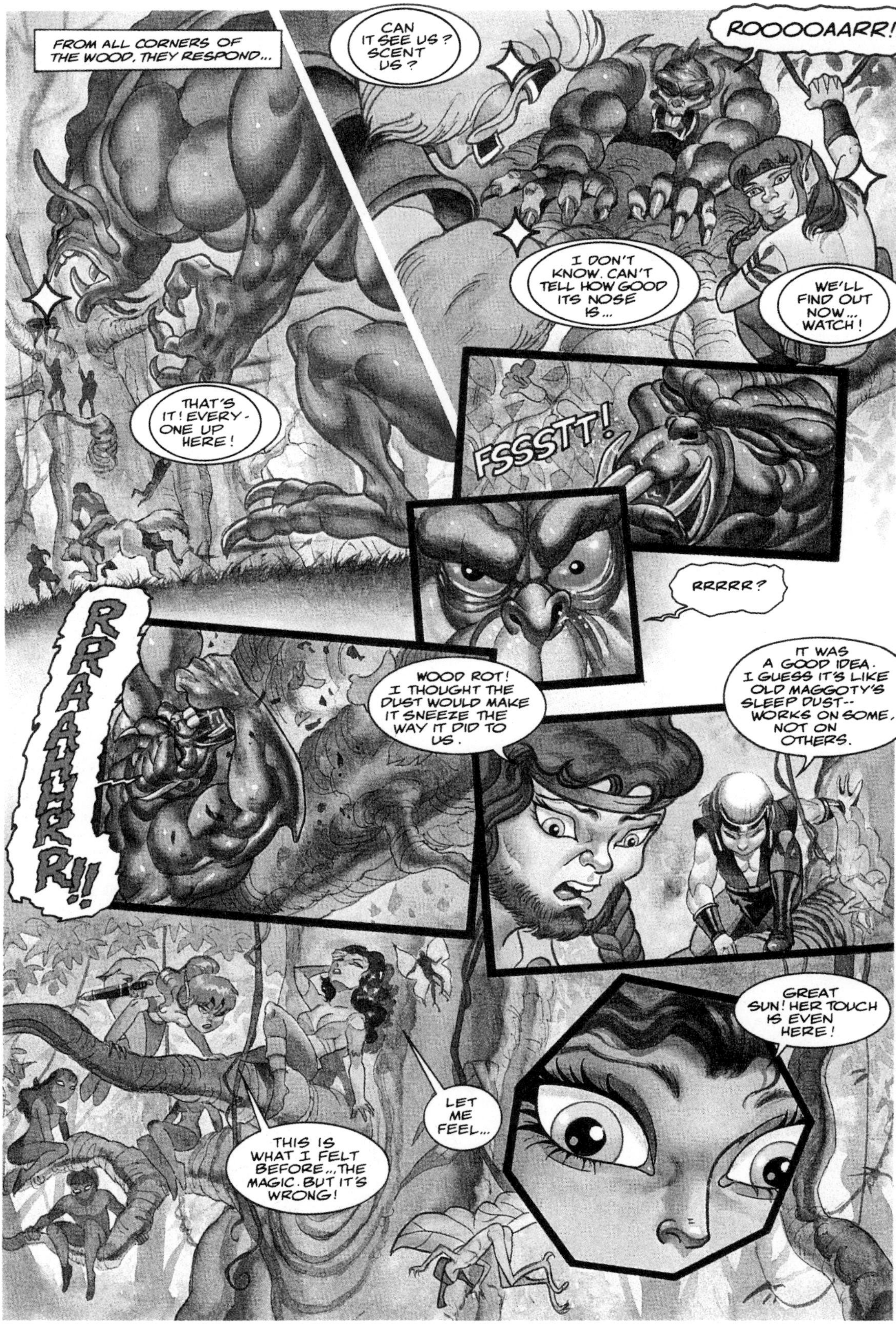
FROM ALL CORNERS OF THE WOOD, THEY RESPOND...
CAN IT SEE US? SCENT US?
ROOOOAARR!!
I DON'T KNOW. CAN'T TELL HOW GOOD ITS NOSE IS...
WE'LL FIND OUT NOW... WATCH!
THAT'S IT! EVERY-ONE UP HERE!
FSSSTT!
RRRRR?
RRAAAHHRR!!
WOOD ROT! I THOUGHT THE DUST WOULD MAKE IT SNEEZE THE WAY IT DID TO US.
IT WAS A GOOD IDEA. I GUESS IT'S LIKE OLD MAGGOTY'S SLEEP DUST-- WORKS ON SOME, NOT ON OTHERS.
GREAT SUN! HER TOUCH IS EVEN HERE!
LET ME FEEL...
THIS IS WHAT I FELT BEFORE... THE MAGIC. BUT IT'S WRONG!

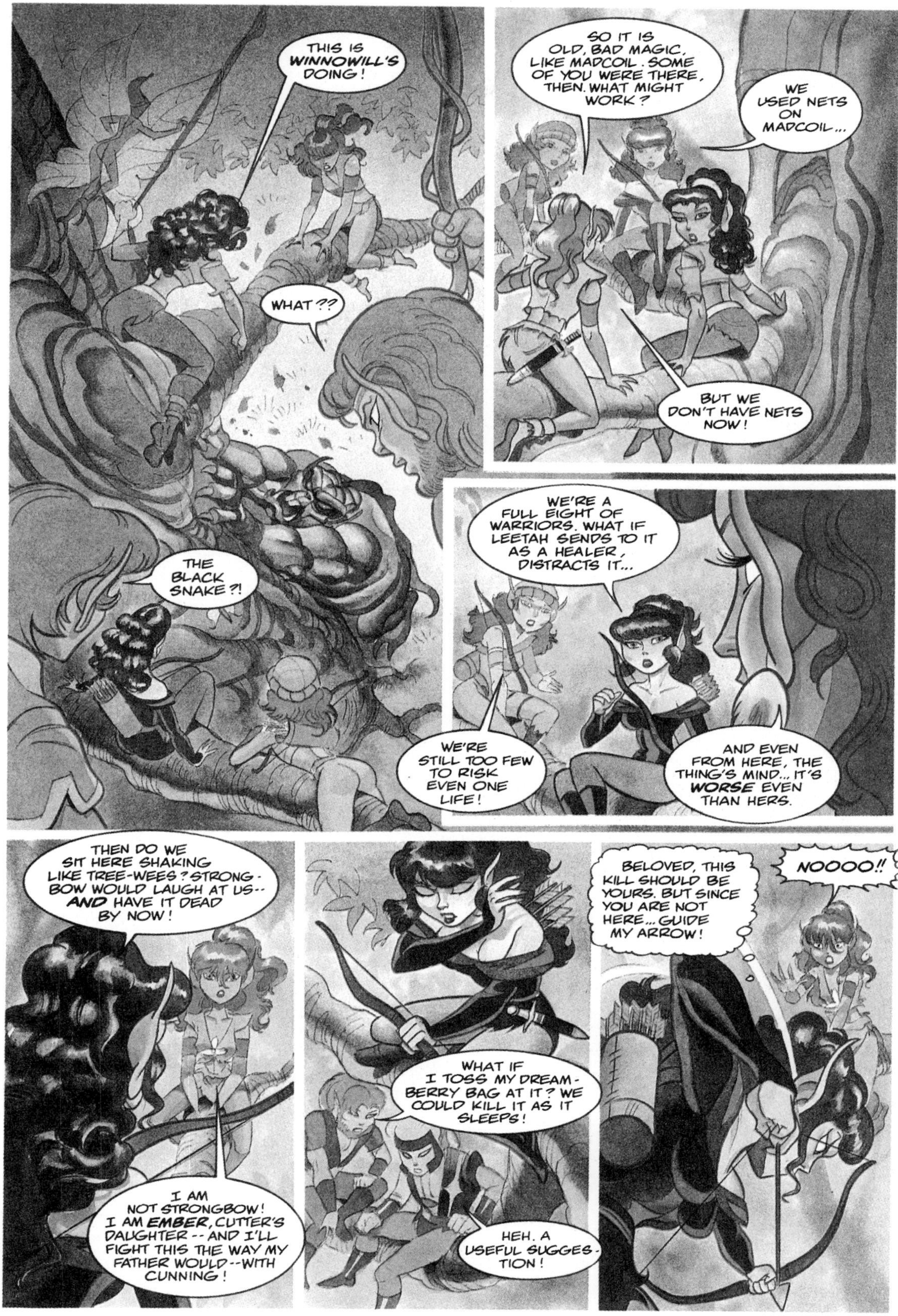
THIS IS WINNOWILL'S DOING!
WHAT??
THE BLACK SNAKE?!
SO IT IS OLD, BAD MAGIC, LIKE MADCOIL. SOME OF YOU WERE THERE, THEN. WHAT MIGHT WORK?
WE USED NETS ON MADCOIL...
BUT WE DON'T HAVE NETS NOW!
WE'RE A FULL EIGHT OF WARRIORS. WHAT IF LEETAH SENDS TO IT AS A HEALER, DISTRACTS IT...
WE'RE STILL TOO FEW TO RISK EVEN ONE LIFE!
AND EVEN FROM HERE, THE THING'S MIND... IT'S WORSE EVEN THAN HERS.
THEN DO WE SIT HERE SHAKING LIKE TREE-WEES? STRONG-BOW WOULD LAUGH AT US-- AND HAVE IT DEAD BY NOW!
I AM NOT STRONGBOW! I AM EMBER, CUTTER'S DAUGHTER -- AND I'LL FIGHT THIS THE WAY MY FATHER WOULD--WITH CUNNING!
WHAT IF I TOSS MY DREAM-BERRY BAG AT IT? WE COULD KILL IT AS IT SLEEPS!
HEH. A USEFUL SUGGES-TION!
BELOVED, THIS KILL SHOULD BE YOURS. BUT SINCE YOU ARE NOT HERE... GUIDE MY ARROW!
NOOOO!!

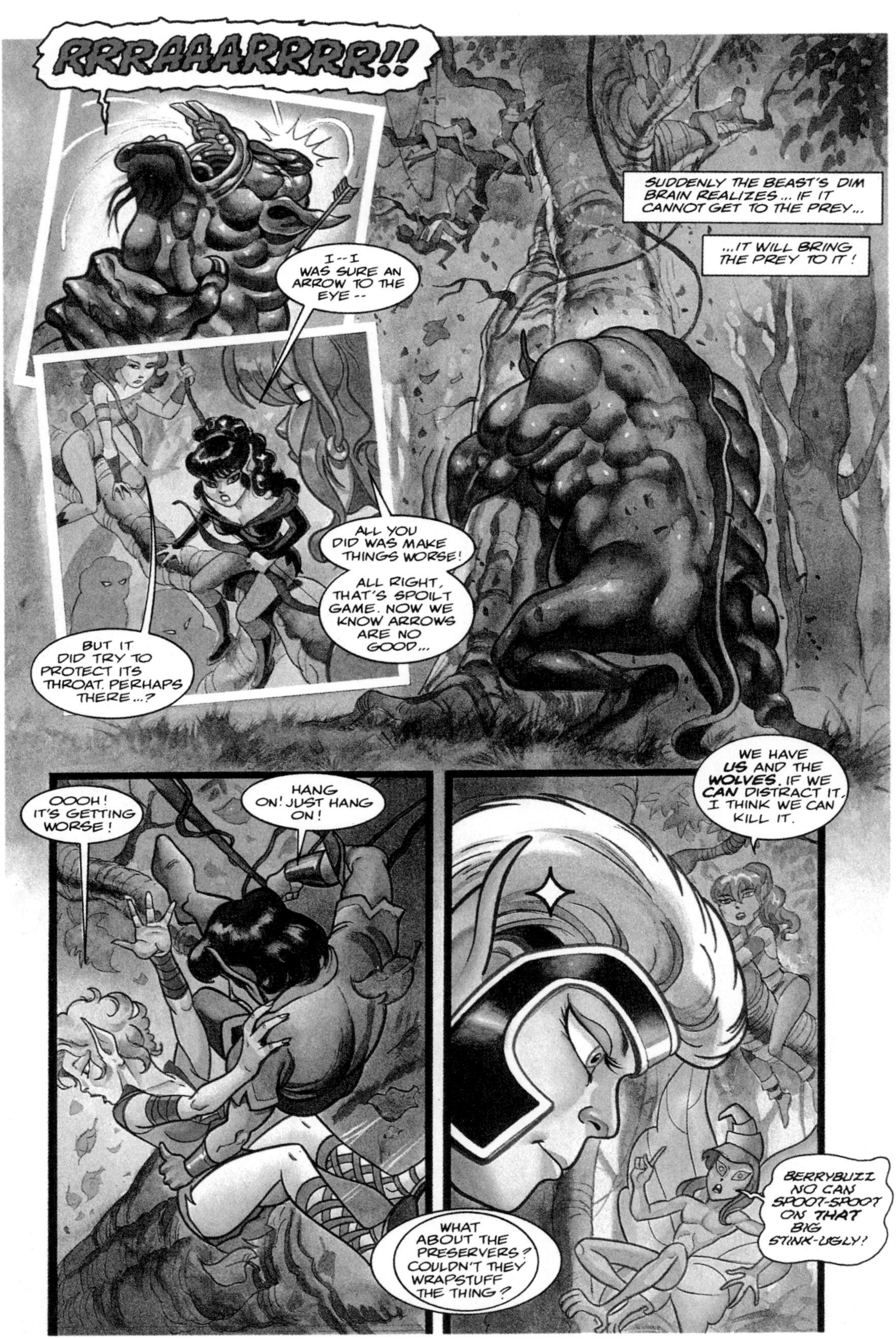
RRRAAARRRR!!
I--I WAS SURE AN ARROW TO THE EYE--
ALL YOU DID WAS MAKE THINGS WORSE!
ALL RIGHT, THAT'S SPOILT GAME. NOW WE KNOW ARROWS ARE NO GOOD...
BUT IT DID TRY TO PROTECT ITS THROAT. PERHAPS THERE...?
SUDDENLY THE BEAST'S DIM BRAIN REALIZES... IF IT CANNOT GET TO THE PREY...
...IT WILL BRING THE PREY TO IT!
OOOH! IT'S GETTING WORSE!
HANG ON! JUST HANG ON!
WE HAVE US AND THE WOLVES. IF WE CAN DISTRACT IT, I THINK WE CAN KILL IT.
WHAT ABOUT THE PRESERVERS? COULDN'T THEY WRAPSTUFF THE THING?
BERRYBUZZ NO CAN SPOOT-SPOOT ON THAT BIG STINK-UGLY!

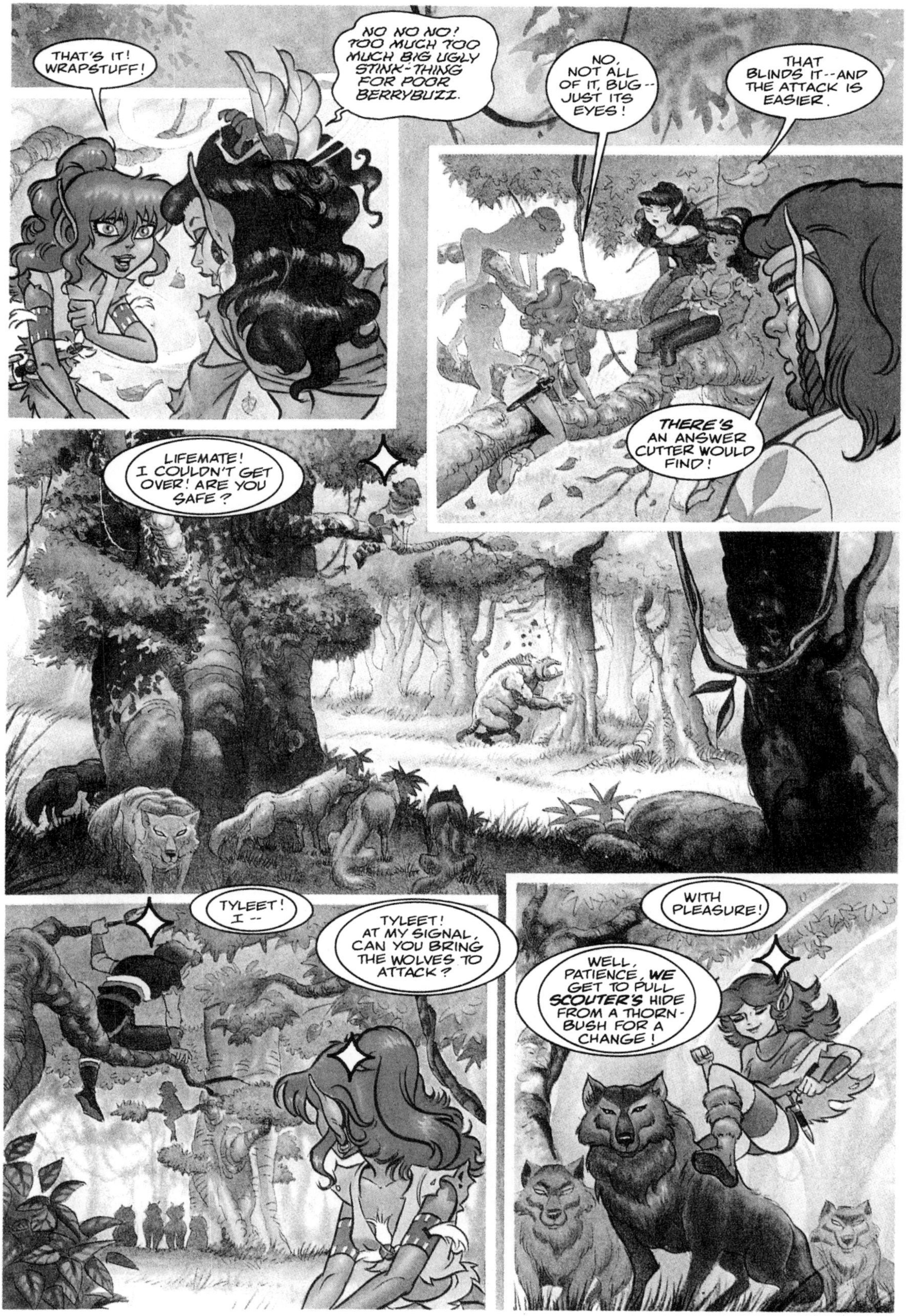
THAT'S IT! WRAPSTUFF!
NO NO NO! TOO MUCH TOO MUCH BIG UGLY STINK-THING FOR POOR BERRYBUZZ.
NO, NOT ALL OF IT, BUG-- JUST ITS EYES!
THAT BLINDS IT--AND THE ATTACK IS EASIER.
THERE'S AN ANSWER CUTTER WOULD FIND!
LIFEMATE! I COULDN'T GET OVER! ARE YOU SAFE?
TYLEET! I --
TYLEET! AT MY SIGNAL, CAN YOU BRING THE WOLVES TO ATTACK?
WITH PLEASURE!
WELL, PATIENCE, WE GET TO PULL SCOUTER'S HIDE FROM A THORN-BUSH FOR A CHANGE!

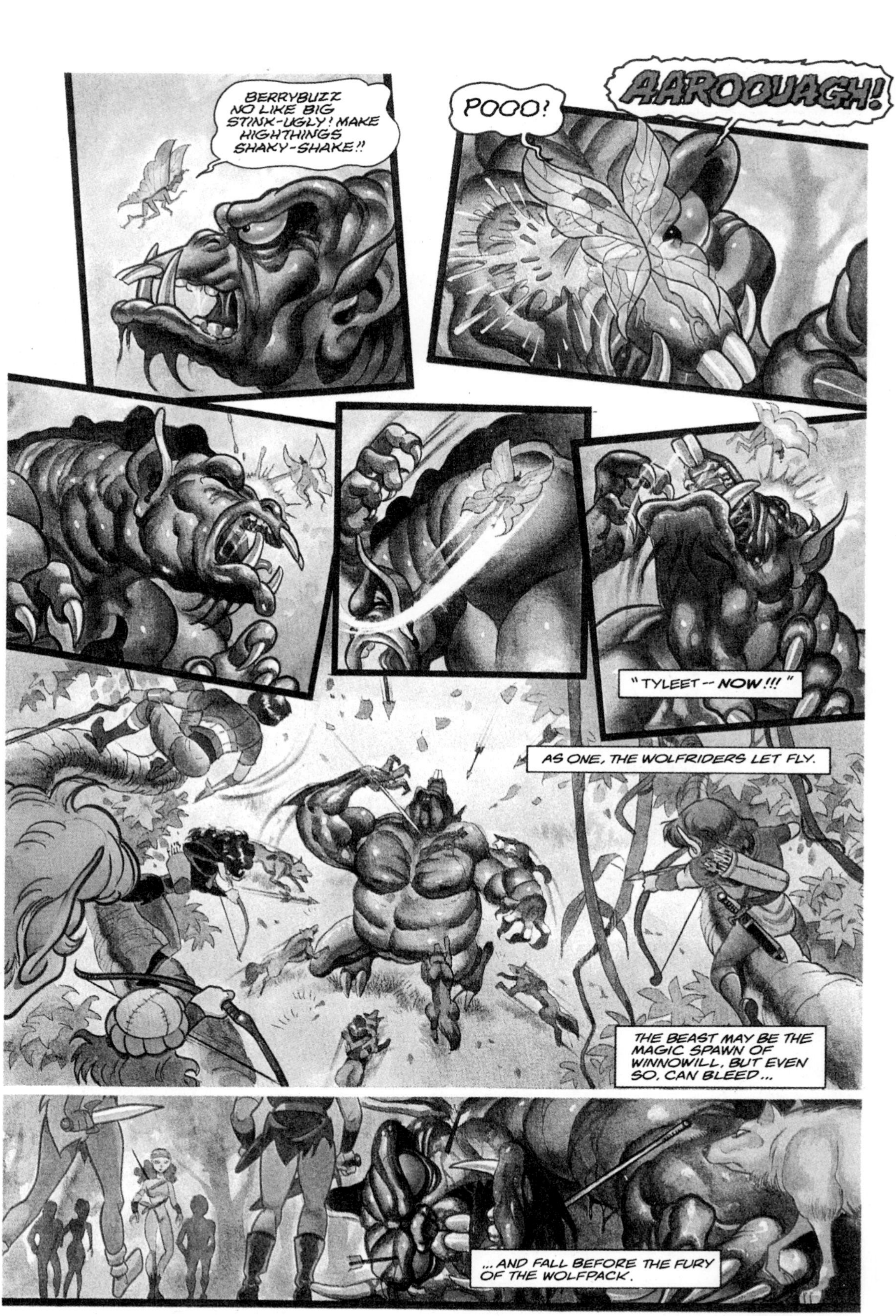
BERRYBUZZ NO LIKE BIG STINK-UGLY! MAKE HIGHTHINGS SHAKY-SHAKE!!
POOO?
AAROOUAGH!
"TYLEET -- NOW!!!"
AS ONE, THE WOLFRIDERS LET FLY.
THE BEAST MAY BE THE MAGIC SPAWN OF WINNOWILL, BUT EVEN SO, CAN BLEED...
...AND FALL BEFORE THE FURY OF THE WOLFPACK.

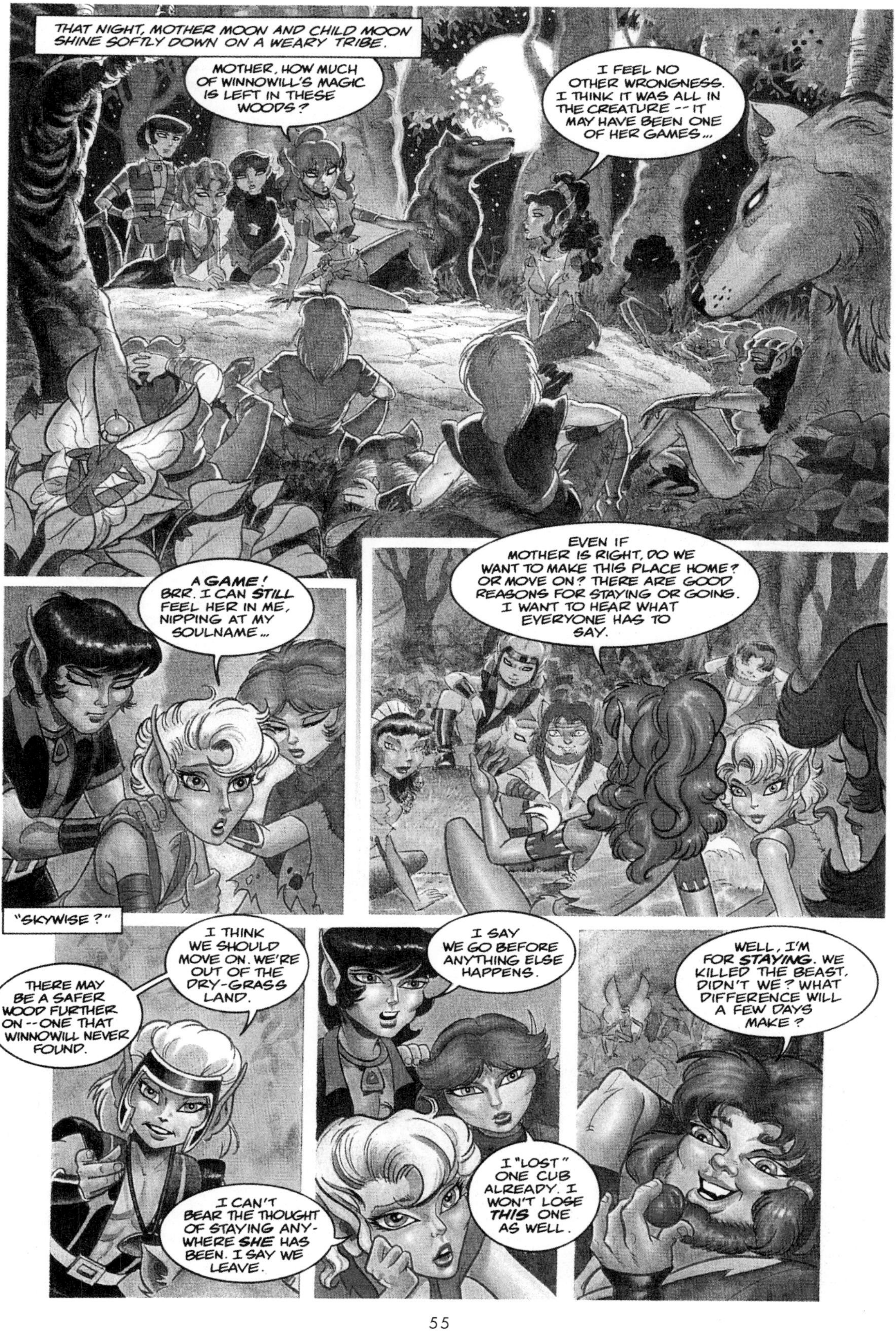
THAT NIGHT, MOTHER MOON AND CHILD MOON SHINE SOFTLY DOWN ON A WEARY TRIBE.
MOTHER, HOW MUCH OF WINNOWILL'S MAGIC IS LEFT IN THESE WOODS?
I FEEL NO OTHER WRONGNESS. I THINK IT WAS ALL IN THE CREATURE -- IT MAY HAVE BEEN ONE OF HER GAMES...
A GAME! BRR. I CAN STILL FEEL HER IN ME, NIPPING AT MY SOULNAME...
EVEN IF MOTHER IS RIGHT, DO WE WANT TO MAKE THIS PLACE HOME? OR MOVE ON? THERE ARE GOOD REASONS FOR STAYING OR GOING. I WANT TO HEAR WHAT EVERYONE HAS TO SAY.
"SKYWISE?"
I THINK WE SHOULD MOVE ON. WE'RE OUT OF THE DRY-GRASS LAND.
THERE MAY BE A SAFER WOOD FURTHER ON -- ONE THAT WINNOWILL NEVER FOUND.
I CAN'T BEAR THE THOUGHT OF STAYING ANY-WHERE SHE HAS BEEN. I SAY WE LEAVE.
I SAY WE GO BEFORE ANYTHING ELSE HAPPENS.
I "LOST" ONE CUB ALREADY. I WON'T LOSE THIS ONE AS WELL.
WELL, I'M FOR STAYING. WE KILLED THE BEAST, DIDN'T WE? WHAT DIFFERENCE WILL A FEW DAYS MAKE?

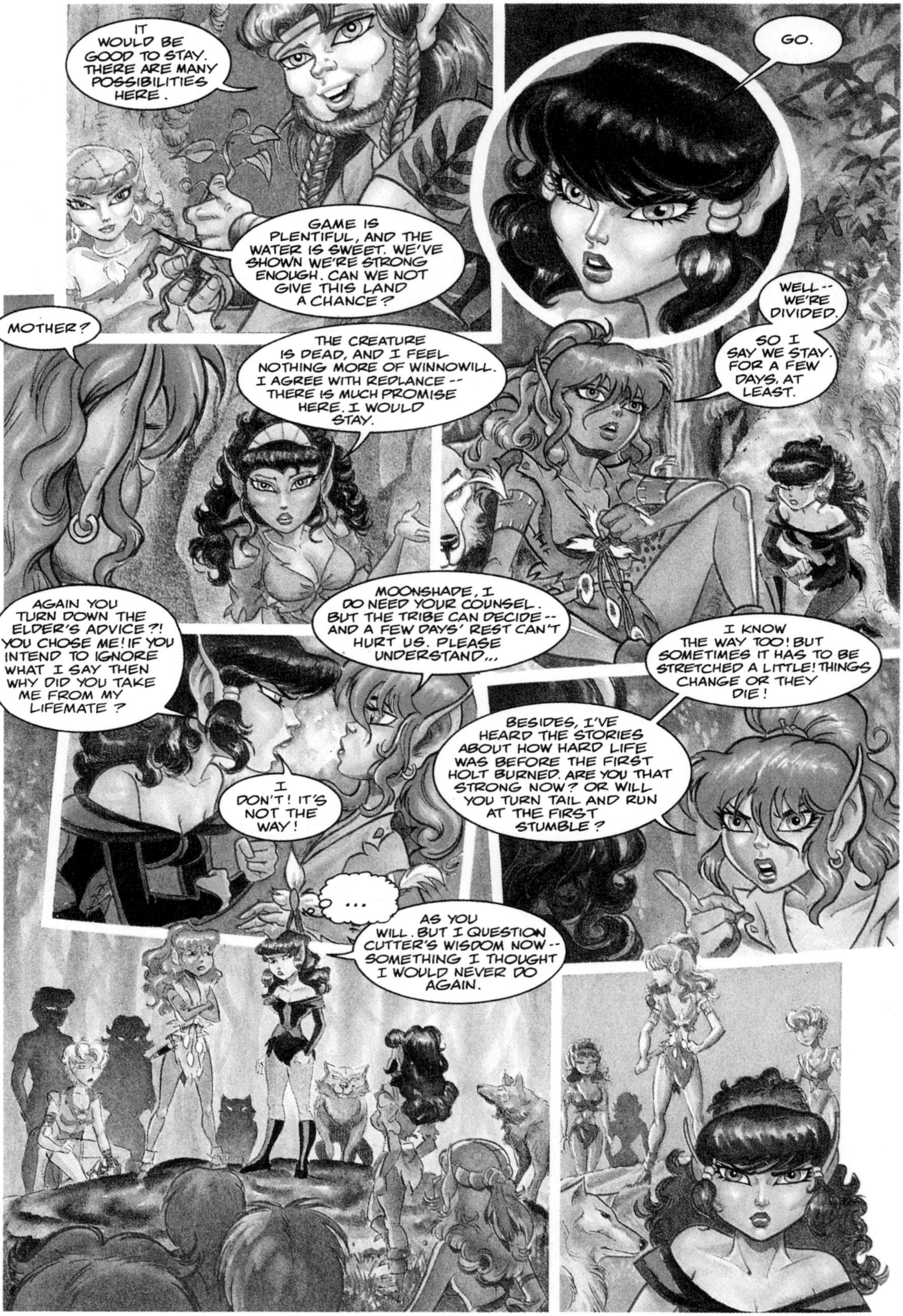
IT WOULD BE GOOD TO STAY. THERE ARE MANY POSSIBILITIES HERE.
GAME IS PLENTIFUL, AND THE WATER IS SWEET. WE'VE SHOWN WE'RE STRONG ENOUGH. CAN WE NOT GIVE THIS LAND A CHANCE?
GO.
MOTHER?
THE CREATURE IS DEAD, AND I FEEL NOTHING MORE OF WINNOWILL. I AGREE WITH REDLANCE -- THERE IS MUCH PROMISE HERE. I WOULD STAY.
WELL -- WE'RE DIVIDED.
SO I SAY WE STAY. FOR A FEW DAYS, AT LEAST.
AGAIN YOU TURN DOWN THE ELDER'S ADVICE?! YOU CHOSE ME! IF YOU INTEND TO IGNORE WHAT I SAY THEN WHY DID YOU TAKE ME FROM MY LIFEMATE?
MOONSHADE, I DO NEED YOUR COUNSEL. BUT THE TRIBE CAN DECIDE -- AND A FEW DAYS' REST CAN'T HURT US. PLEASE UNDERSTAND...
I DON'T! IT'S NOT THE WAY!
I KNOW THE WAY TOO! BUT SOMETIMES IT HAS TO BE STRETCHED A LITTLE! THINGS CHANGE OR THEY DIE!
BESIDES, I'VE HEARD THE STORIES ABOUT HOW HARD LIFE WAS BEFORE THE FIRST HOLT BURNED. ARE YOU THAT STRONG NOW? OR WILL YOU TURN TAIL AND RUN AT THE FIRST STUMBLE?
...
AS YOU WILL. BUT I QUESTION CUTTER'S WISDOM NOW -- SOMETHING I THOUGHT I WOULD NEVER DO AGAIN.

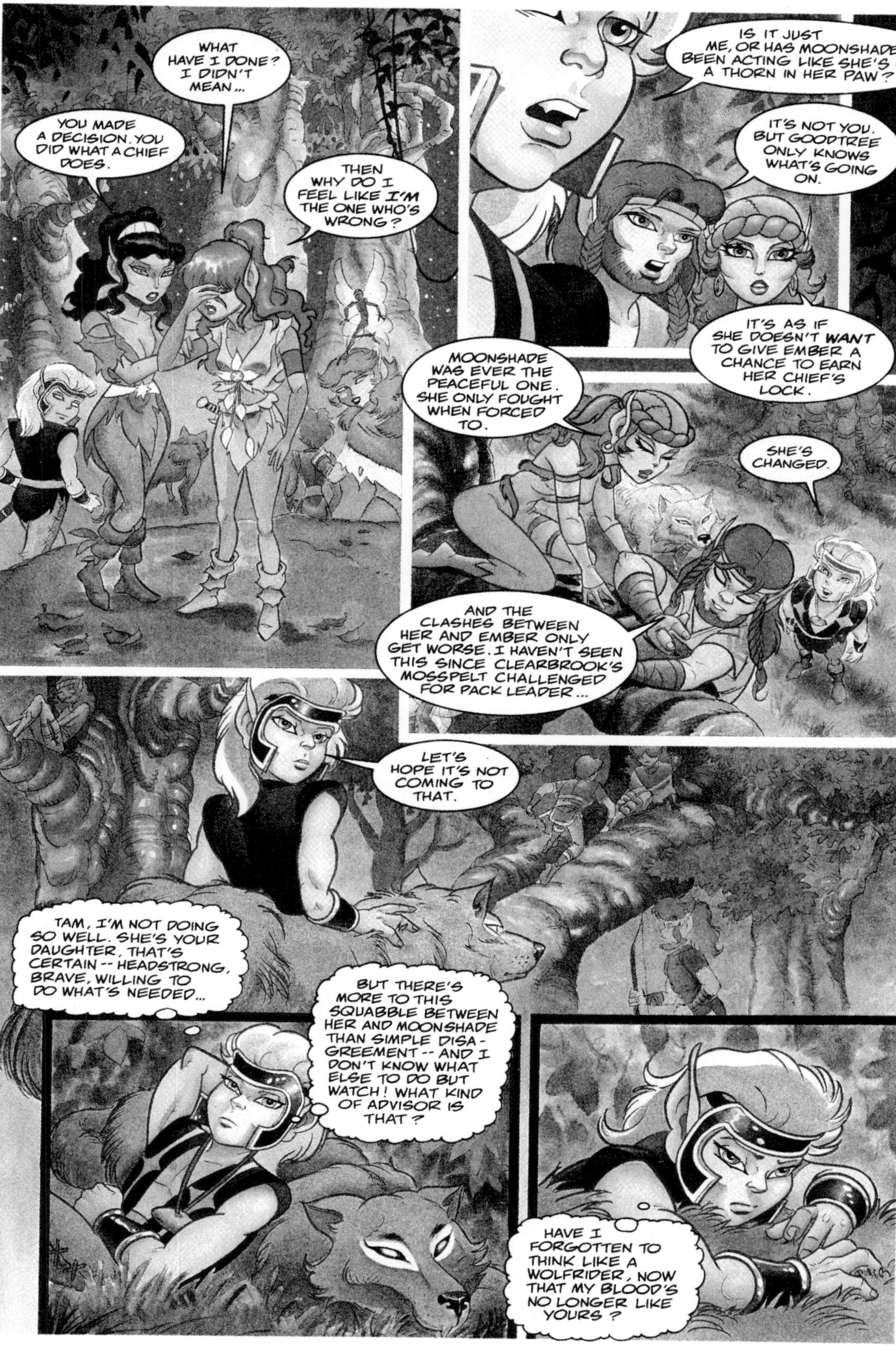
WHAT HAVE I DONE? I DIDN'T MEAN...
YOU MADE A DECISION. YOU DID WHAT A CHIEF DOES.
THEN WHY DO I FEEL LIKE I'M THE ONE WHO'S WRONG?
IS IT JUST ME, OR HAS MOONSHADE BEEN ACTING LIKE SHE'S GOT A THORN IN HER PAW?
IT'S NOT YOU. BUT GOODTREE ONLY KNOWS WHAT'S GOING ON.
IT'S AS IF SHE DOESN'T WANT TO GIVE EMBER A CHANCE TO EARN HER CHIEF'S LOCK.
MOONSHADE WAS EVER THE PEACEFUL ONE. SHE ONLY FOUGHT WHEN FORCED TO.
SHE'S CHANGED.
AND THE CLASHES BETWEEN HER AND EMBER ONLY GET WORSE. I HAVEN'T SEEN THIS SINCE CLEARBROOK'S MOSSPELT CHALLENGED FOR PACK LEADER...
LET'S HOPE IT'S NOT COMING TO THAT.
TAM, I'M NOT DOING SO WELL. SHE'S YOUR DAUGHTER, THAT'S CERTAIN -- HEADSTRONG, BRAVE, WILLING TO DO WHAT'S NEEDED...
BUT THERE'S MORE TO THIS SQUABBLE BETWEEN HER AND MOONSHADE THAN SIMPLE DISA-GREEMENT -- AND I DON'T KNOW WHAT ELSE TO DO BUT WATCH! WHAT KIND OF ADVISOR IS THAT?
HAVE I FORGOTTEN TO THINK LIKE A WOLFRIDER, NOW THAT MY BLOOD'S NO LONGER LIKE YOURS?

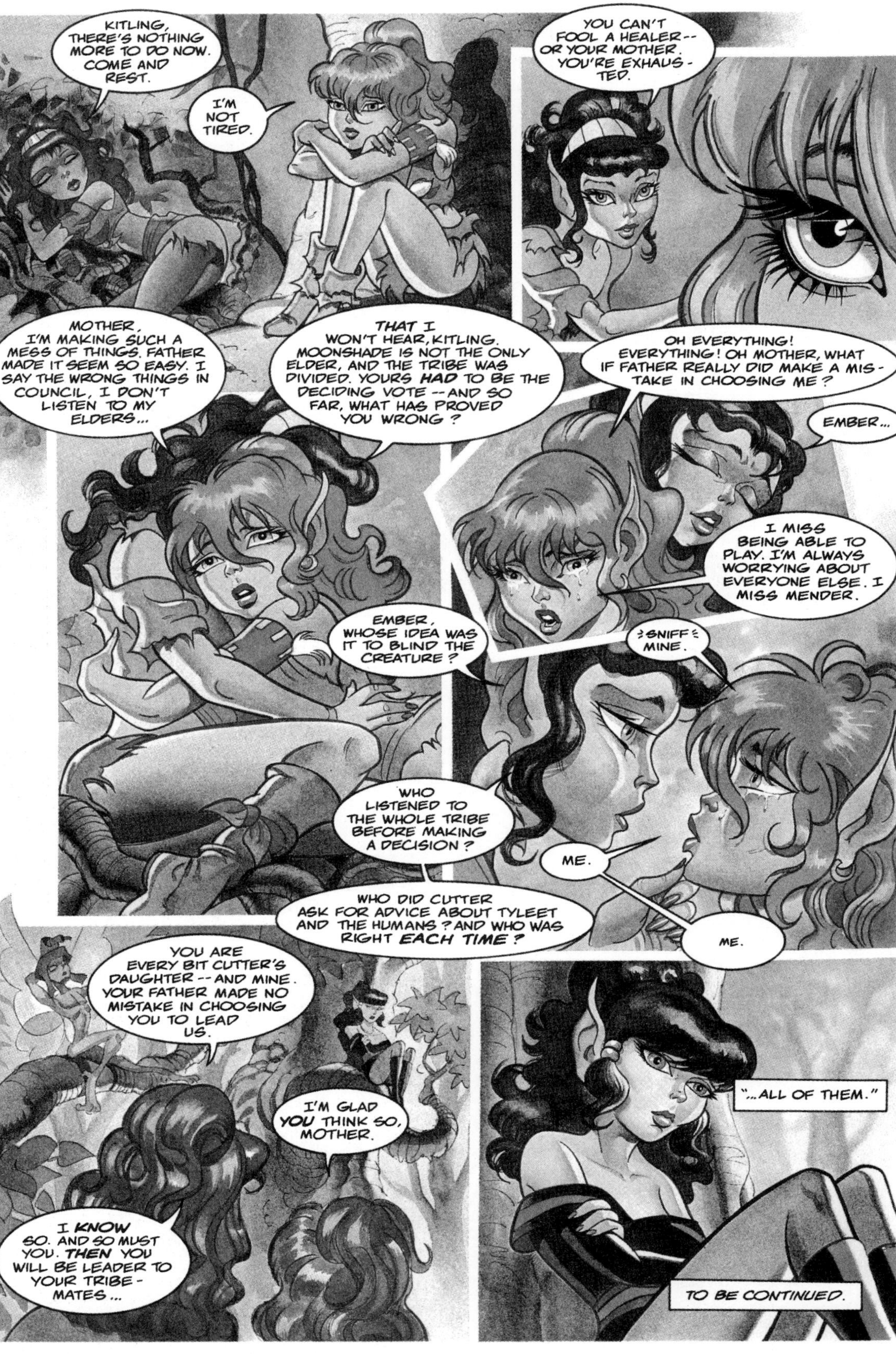
KITLING, THERE'S NOTHING MORE TO DO NOW. COME AND REST.
I'M NOT TIRED.
YOU CAN'T FOOL A HEALER-- OR YOUR MOTHER. YOU'RE EXHAUS-TED.
MOTHER, I'M MAKING SUCH A MESS OF THINGS. FATHER MADE IT SEEM SO EASY. I SAY THE WRONG THINGS IN COUNCIL, I DON'T LISTEN TO MY ELDERS...
THAT I WON'T HEAR, KITLING. MOONSHADE IS NOT THE ONLY ELDER, AND THE TRIBE WAS DIVIDED. YOURS HAD TO BE THE DECIDING VOTE --AND SO FAR, WHAT HAS PROVED YOU WRONG?
OH EVERYTHING! EVERYTHING! OH MOTHER, WHAT IF FATHER REALLY DID MAKE A MIS-TAKE IN CHOOSING ME?
EMBER...
I MISS BEING ABLE TO PLAY. I'M ALWAYS WORRYING ABOUT EVERYONE ELSE. I MISS MENDER.
EMBER, WHOSE IDEA WAS IT TO BLIND THE CREATURE?
SNIFF MINE.
WHO LISTENED TO THE WHOLE TRIBE BEFORE MAKING A DECISION?
ME.
WHO DID CUTTER ASK FOR ADVICE ABOUT TYLEET AND THE HUMANS? AND WHO WAS RIGHT EACH TIME?
ME.
YOU ARE EVERY BIT CUTTER'S DAUGHTER --AND MINE. YOUR FATHER MADE NO MISTAKE IN CHOOSING YOU TO LEAD US.
I'M GLAD YOU THINK SO, MOTHER.
I KNOW SO. AND SO MUST YOU. THEN YOU WILL BE LEADER TO YOUR TRIBE-MATES...
"...ALL OF THEM."
TO BE CONTINUED.

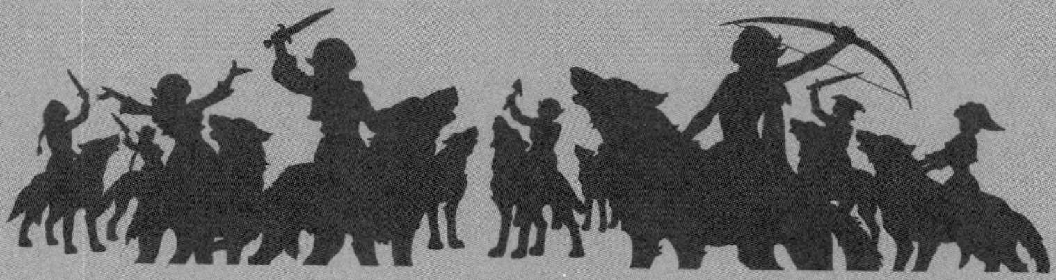

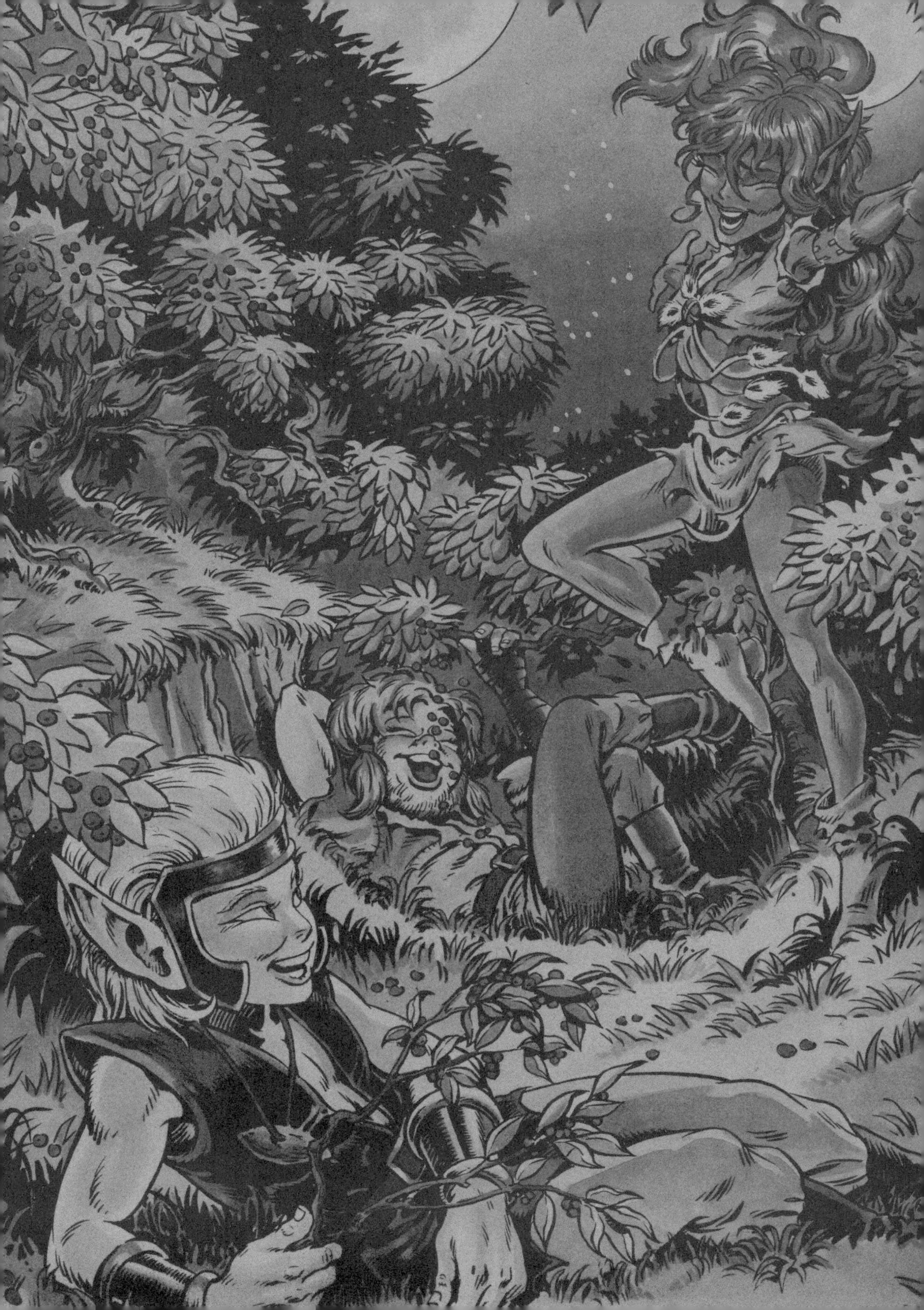

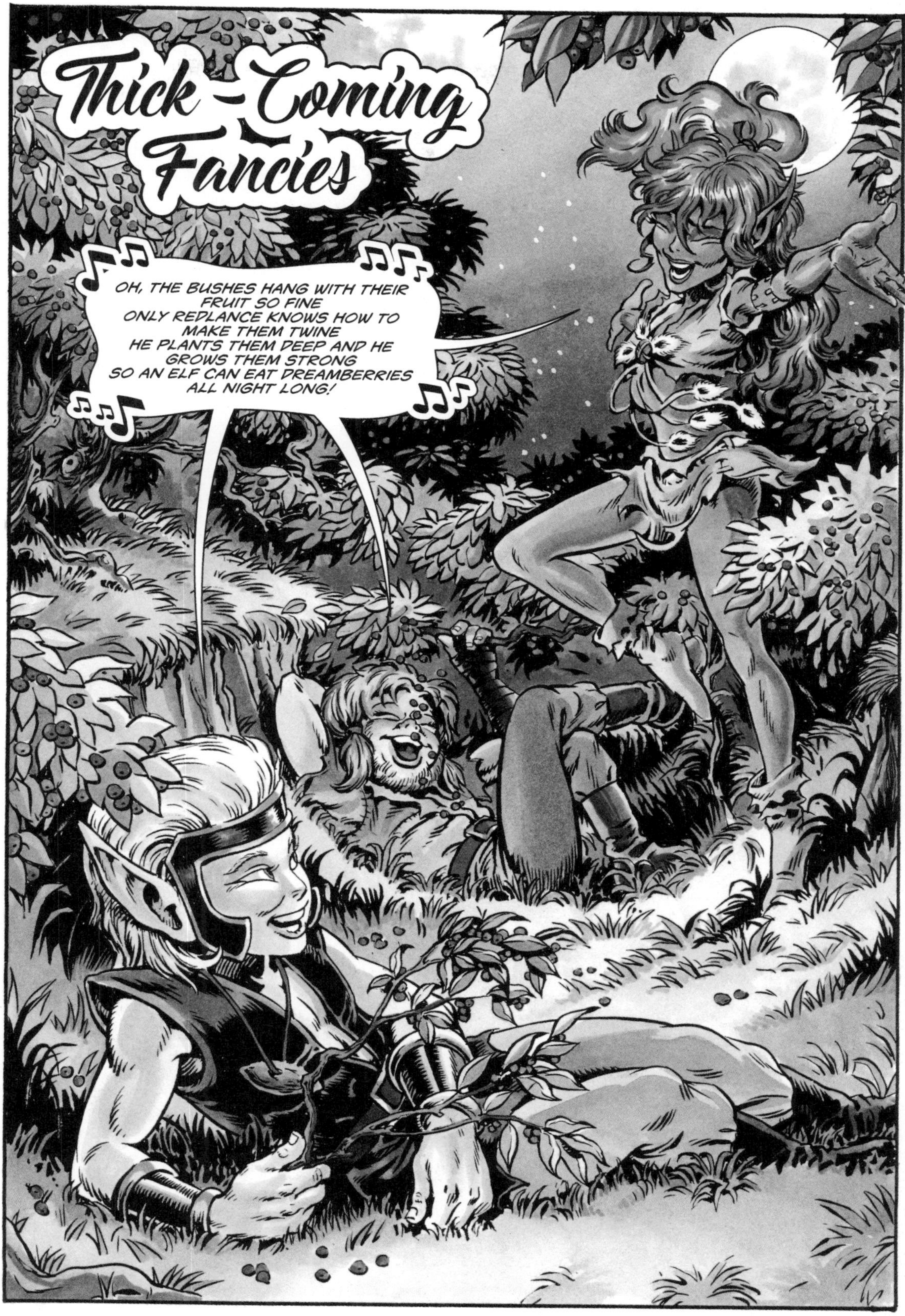
Thick-Coming Fancies
OH, THE BUSHES HANG WITH THEIR FRUIT SO FINE ONLY REDLANCE KNOWS HOW TO MAKE THEM TWINE HE PLANTS THEM DEEP AND HE GROWS THEM STRONG SO AN ELF CAN EAT DREAMBERRIES ALL NIGHT LONG!

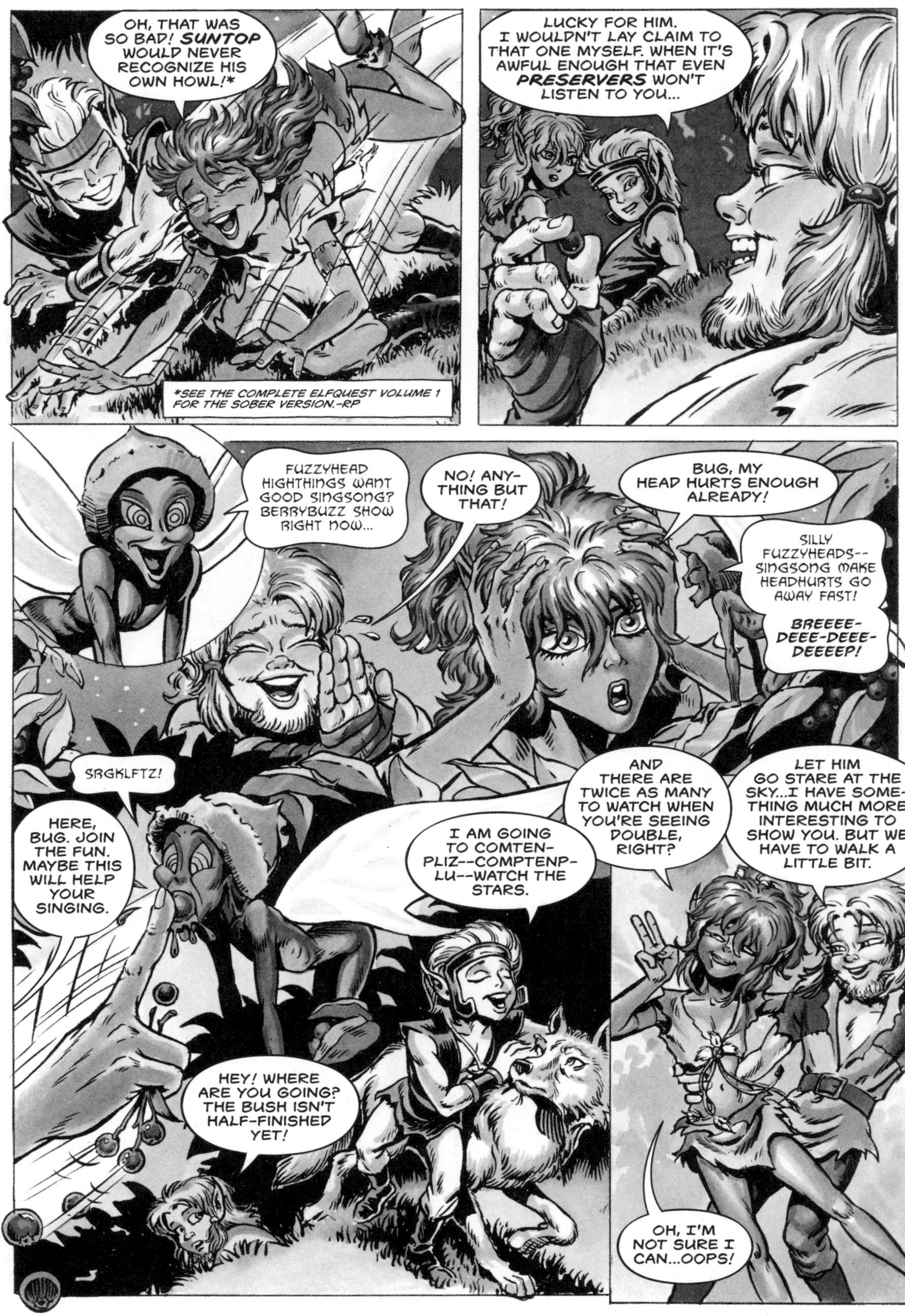
OH, THAT WAS SO BAD! SUNTOP WOULD NEVER RECOGNIZE HIS OWN HOWL!*
*SEE THE COMPLETE ELFQUEST VOLUME 1 FOR THE SOBER VERSION.-RP
LUCKY FOR HIM. I WOULDN'T LAY CLAIM TO THAT ONE MYSELF. WHEN IT'S AWFUL ENOUGH THAT EVEN PRESERVERS WON'T LISTEN TO YOU...
FUZZYHEAD HIGHTHINGS WANT GOOD SINGSONG? BERRYBUZZ SHOW RIGHT NOW...
NO! ANYTHING BUT THAT!
BUG, MY HEAD HURTS ENOUGH ALREADY!
SILLY FUZZYHEADS--SINGSONG MAKE HEADHURTS GO AWAY FAST!
BREEEE-DEEE-DEEE-DEEEEP!
SRGKLFTZ!
HERE, BUG. JOIN THE FUN. MAYBE THIS WILL HELP YOUR SINGING.
I AM GOING TO COMTENPLIZ--COMPTENPLU--WATCH THE STARS.
AND THERE ARE TWICE AS MANY TO WATCH WHEN YOU'RE SEEING DOUBLE, RIGHT?
LET HIM GO STARE AT THE SKY...I HAVE SOMETHING MUCH MORE INTERESTING TO SHOW YOU. BUT WE HAVE TO WALK A LITTLE BIT.
HEY! WHERE ARE YOU GOING? THE BUSH ISN'T HALF-FINISHED YET!
OH, I'M NOT SURE I CAN...OOPS!

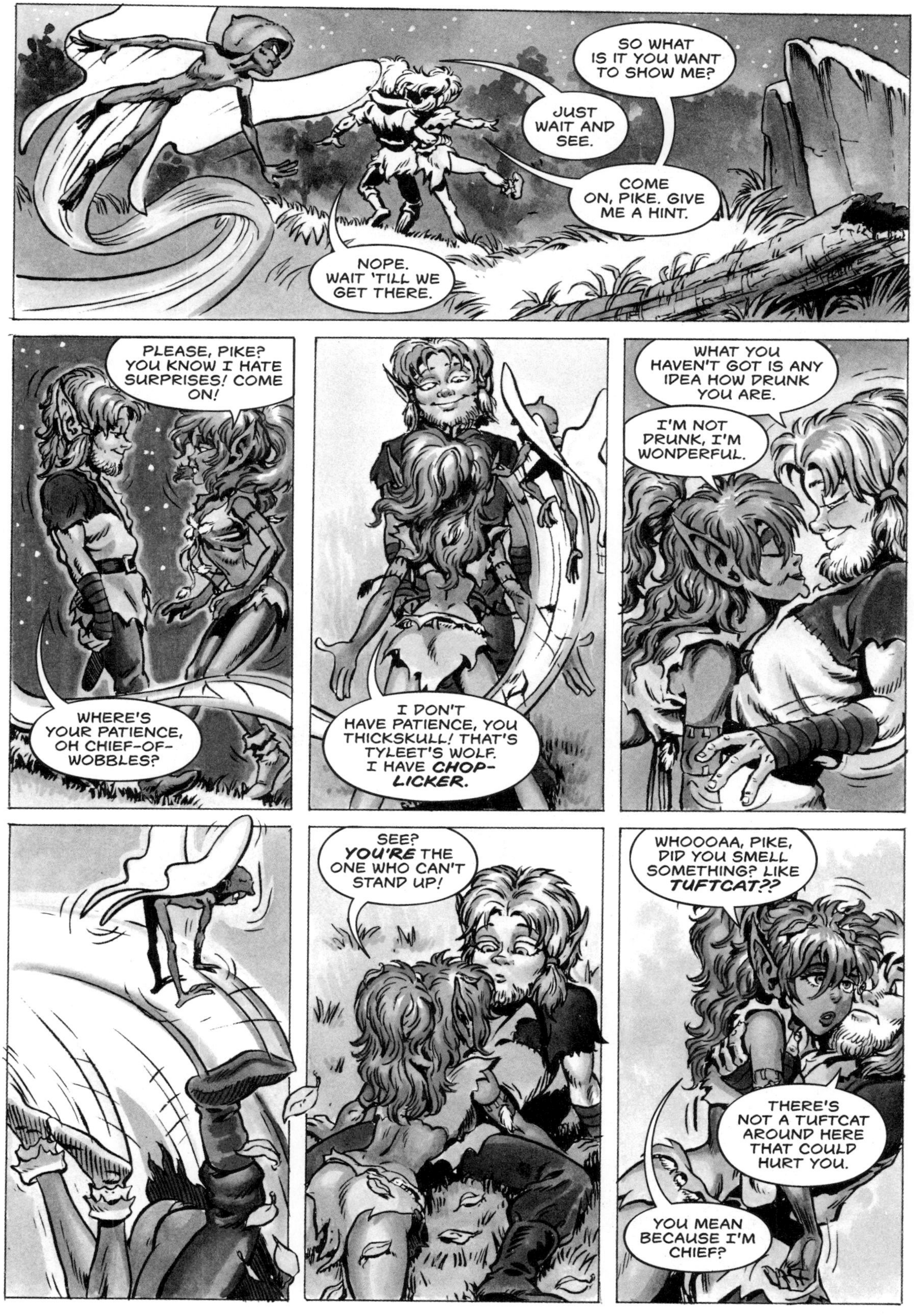
SO WHAT IS IT YOU WANT TO SHOW ME?
JUST WAIT AND SEE.
COME ON, PIKE. GIVE ME A HINT.
NOPE. WAIT 'TILL WE GET THERE.
PLEASE, PIKE? YOU KNOW I HATE SURPRISES! COME ON!
WHERE'S YOUR PATIENCE, OH CHIEF-OF-WOBBLES?
I DON'T HAVE PATIENCE, YOU THICKSKULL! THAT'S TYLEET'S WOLF. I HAVE **CHOP-LICKER.**
WHAT YOU HAVEN'T GOT IS ANY IDEA HOW DRUNK YOU ARE.
I'M NOT DRUNK, I'M WONDERFUL.
SEE? ***YOU'RE*** THE ONE WHO CAN'T STAND UP!
WHOOOAA, PIKE, DID YOU SMELL SOMETHING? LIKE ***TUFTCAT??***
THERE'S NOT A TUFTCAT AROUND HERE THAT COULD HURT YOU.
YOU MEAN BECAUSE I'M CHIEF?

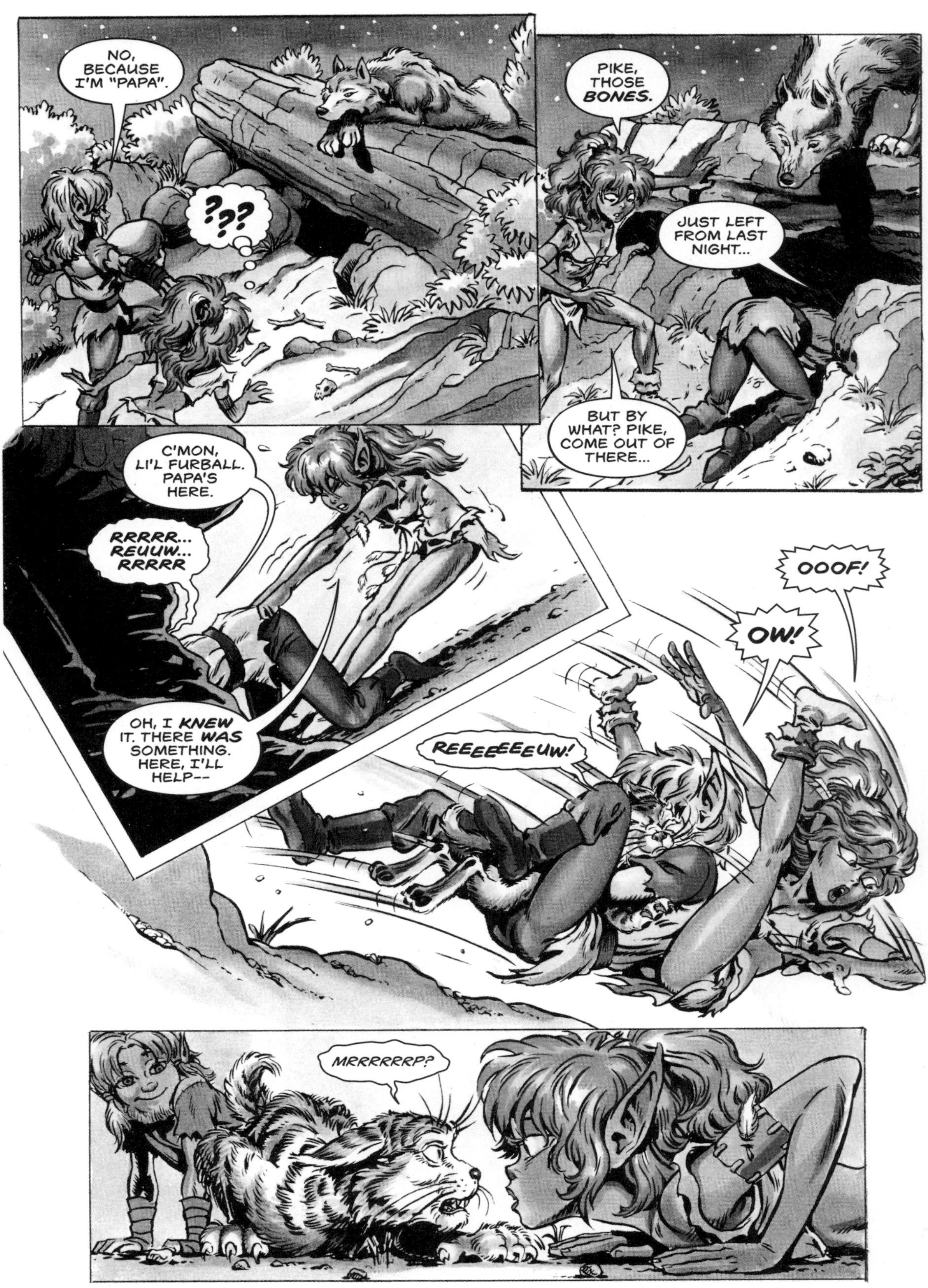
NO, BECAUSE I'M "PAPA".
???
PIKE, THOSE BONES.
JUST LEFT FROM LAST NIGHT...
BUT BY WHAT? PIKE, COME OUT OF THERE...
C'MON, LI'L FURBALL. PAPA'S HERE.
RRRRR... REUUW... RRRRR
OH, I KNEW IT. THERE WAS SOMETHING. HERE, I'LL HELP--
REEEEEEEUW!
OW!
OOOF!
MRRRRRRP?

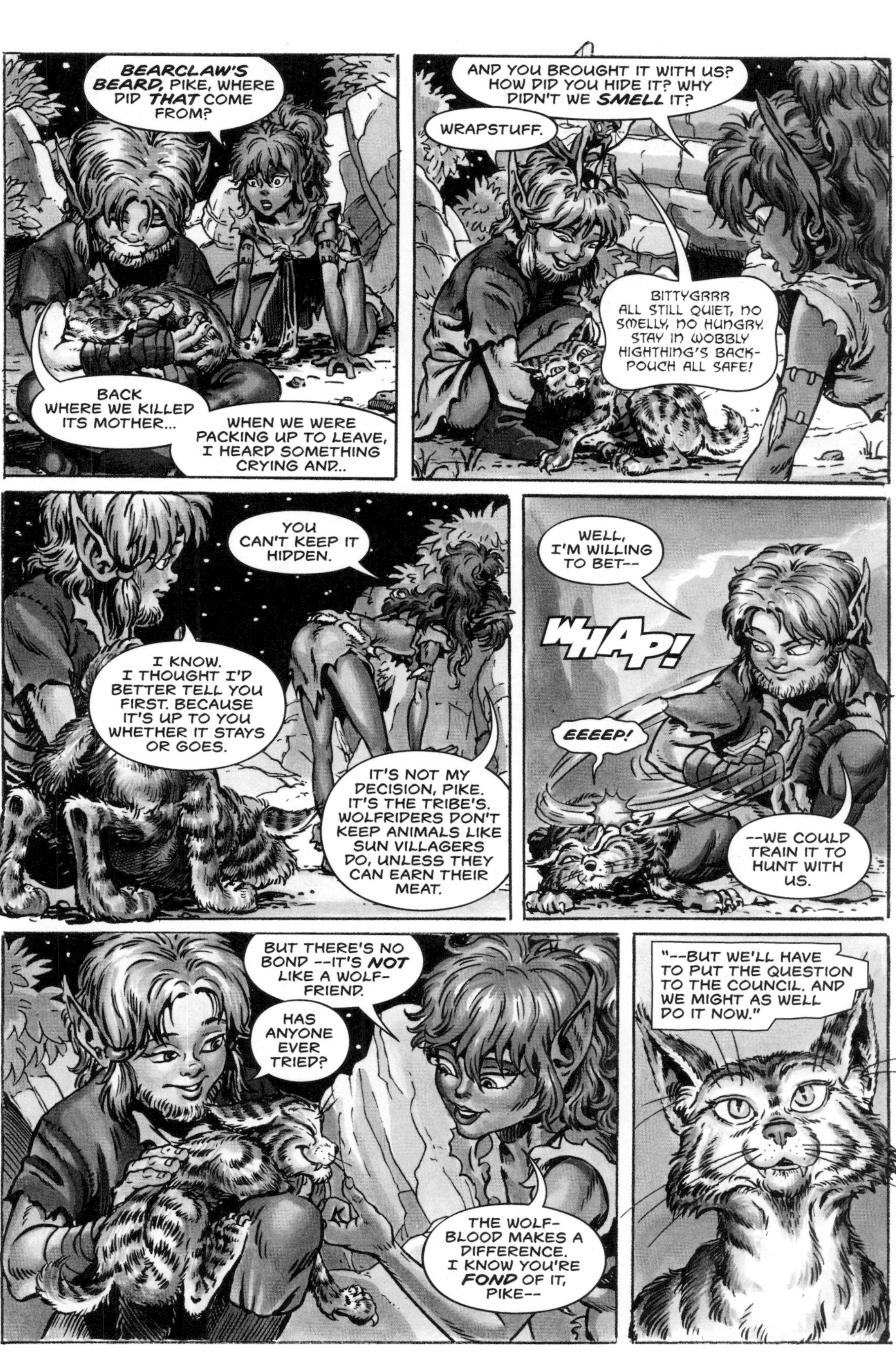
BEARCLAW'S BEARD, PIKE, WHERE DID THAT COME FROM?
BACK WHERE WE KILLED ITS MOTHER...
WHEN WE WERE PACKING UP TO LEAVE, I HEARD SOMETHING CRYING AND...
AND YOU BROUGHT IT WITH US? HOW DID YOU HIDE IT? WHY DIDN'T WE SMELL IT?
WRAPSTUFF.
BITTYGRRR ALL STILL QUIET, NO SMELLY, NO HUNGRY. STAY IN WOBBLY HIGHTHING'S BACK-POUCH ALL SAFE!
YOU CAN'T KEEP IT HIDDEN.
I KNOW. I THOUGHT I'D BETTER TELL YOU FIRST. BECAUSE IT'S UP TO YOU WHETHER IT STAYS OR GOES.
IT'S NOT MY DECISION, PIKE. IT'S THE TRIBE'S. WOLFRIDERS DON'T KEEP ANIMALS LIKE SUN VILLAGERS DO, UNLESS THEY CAN EARN THEIR MEAT.
WELL, I'M WILLING TO BET--
WHAP!
EEEEP!
--WE COULD TRAIN IT TO HUNT WITH US.
BUT THERE'S NO BOND --IT'S NOT LIKE A WOLF-FRIEND.
HAS ANYONE EVER TRIED?
THE WOLF-BLOOD MAKES A DIFFERENCE. I KNOW YOU'RE FOND OF IT, PIKE--
"--BUT WE'LL HAVE TO PUT THE QUESTION TO THE COUNCIL. AND WE MIGHT AS WELL DO IT NOW."

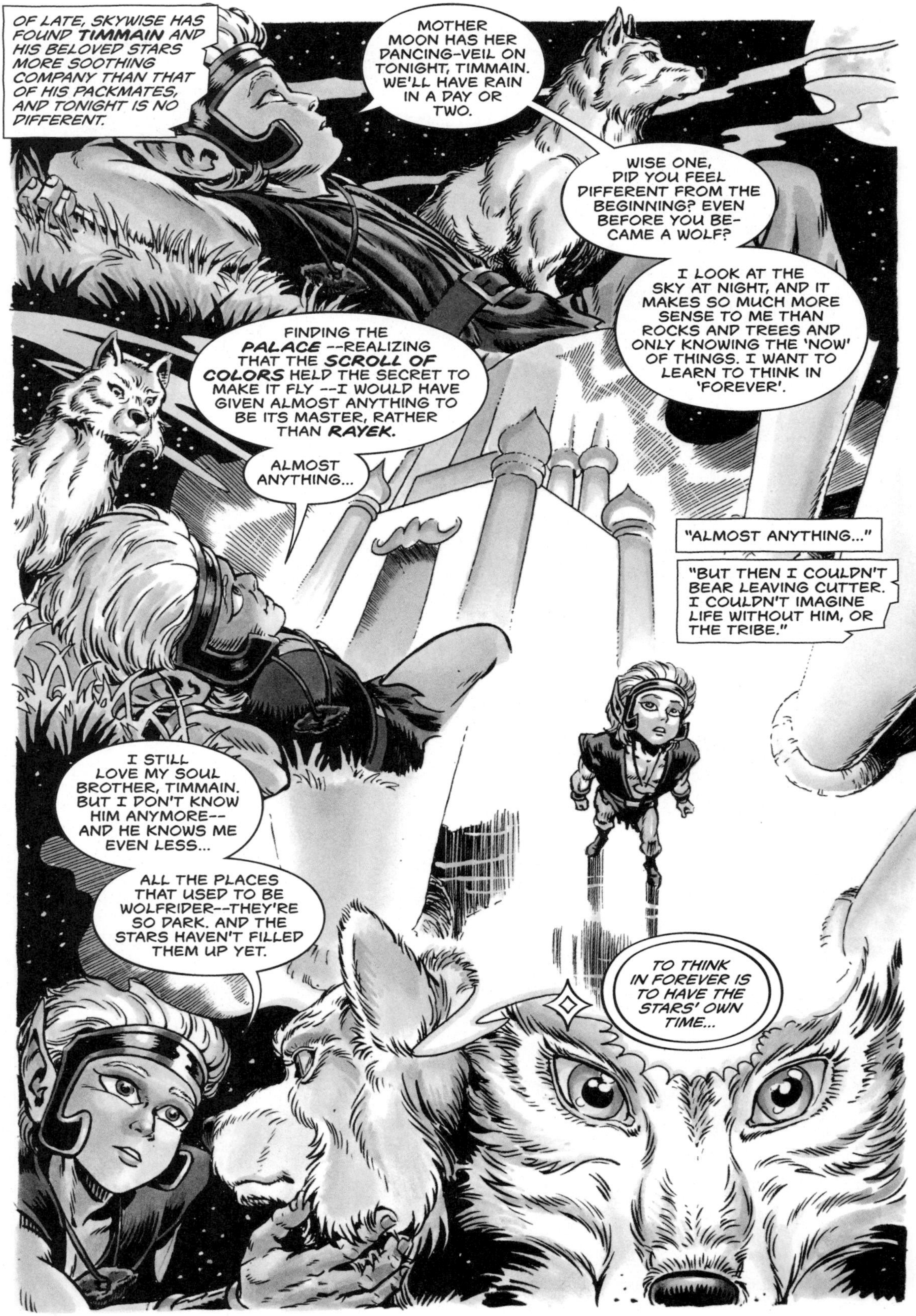

OF LATE, SKYWISE HAS FOUND TIMMAIN AND HIS BELOVED STARS MORE SOOTHING COMPANY THAN THAT OF HIS PACKMATES, AND TONIGHT IS NO DIFFERENT.
MOTHER MOON HAS HER DANCING-VEIL ON TONIGHT, TIMMAIN. WE'LL HAVE RAIN IN A DAY OR TWO.
WISE ONE, DID YOU FEEL DIFFERENT FROM THE BEGINNING? EVEN BEFORE YOU BE-CAME A WOLF?
I LOOK AT THE SKY AT NIGHT, AND IT MAKES SO MUCH MORE SENSE TO ME THAN ROCKS AND TREES AND ONLY KNOWING THE 'NOW' OF THINGS. I WANT TO LEARN TO THINK IN 'FOREVER'.
FINDING THE PALACE --REALIZING THAT THE SCROLL OF COLORS HELD THE SECRET TO MAKE IT FLY --I WOULD HAVE GIVEN ALMOST ANYTHING TO BE ITS MASTER, RATHER THAN RAYEK.
ALMOST ANYTHING...
"ALMOST ANYTHING..."
"BUT THEN I COULDN'T BEAR LEAVING CUTTER. I COULDN'T IMAGINE LIFE WITHOUT HIM, OR THE TRIBE."
I STILL LOVE MY SOUL BROTHER, TIMMAIN. BUT I DON'T KNOW HIM ANYMORE-- AND HE KNOWS ME EVEN LESS...
ALL THE PLACES THAT USED TO BE WOLFRIDER--THEY'RE SO DARK. AND THE STARS HAVEN'T FILLED THEM UP YET.
TO THINK IN FOREVER IS TO HAVE THE STARS' OWN TIME...

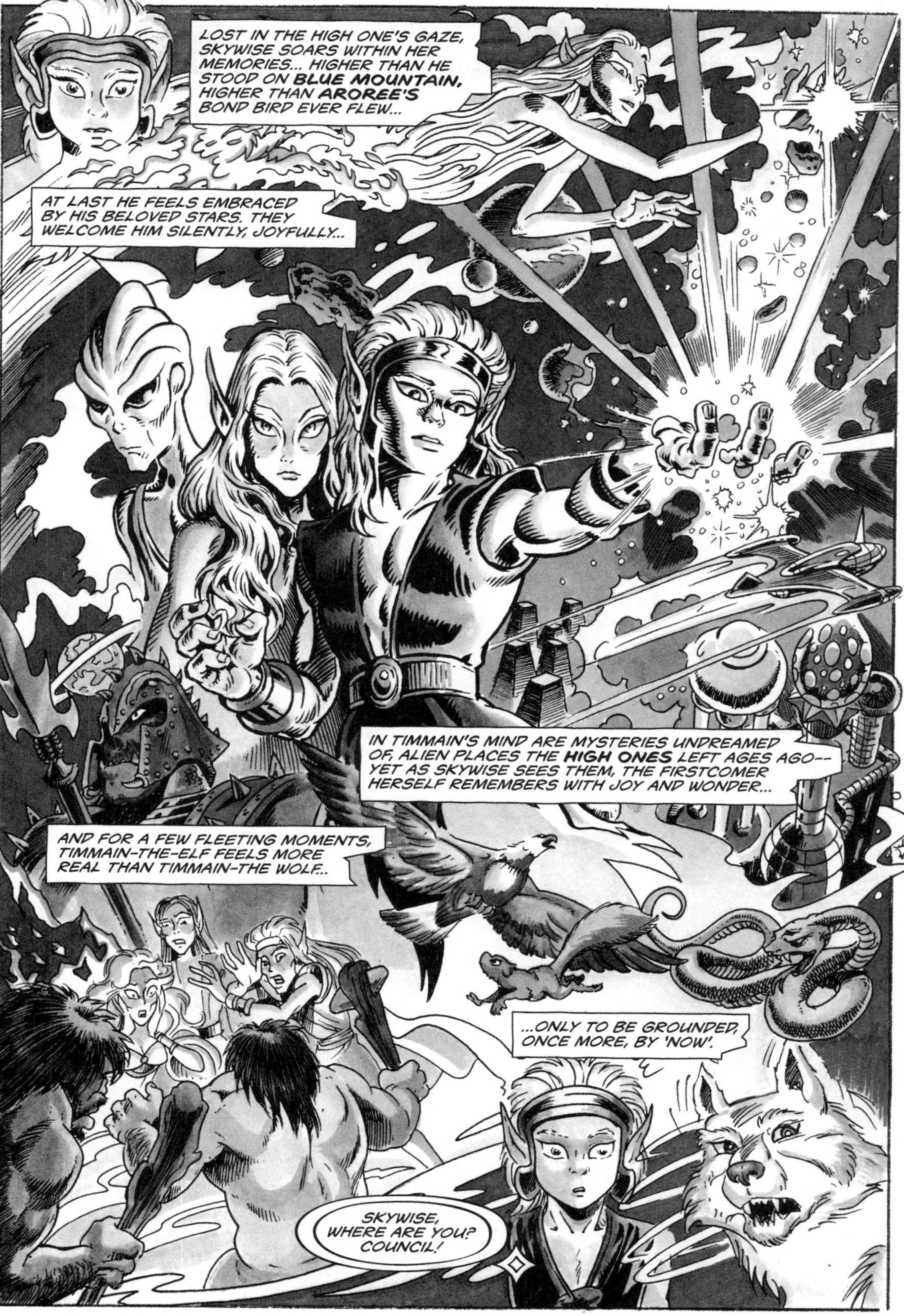
LOST IN THE HIGH ONE'S GAZE, SKYWISE SOARS WITHIN HER MEMORIES... HIGHER THAN HE STOOD ON **BLUE MOUNTAIN,** HIGHER THAN **AROREE'S** BOND BIRD EVER FLEW...
AT LAST HE FEELS EMBRACED BY HIS BELOVED STARS. THEY WELCOME HIM SILENTLY, JOYFULLY...
IN TIMMAIN'S MIND ARE MYSTERIES UNDREAMED OF, ALIEN PLACES THE **HIGH ONES** LEFT AGES AGO-- YET AS SKYWISE SEES THEM, THE FIRSTCOMER HERSELF REMEMBERS WITH JOY AND WONDER...
AND FOR A FEW FLEETING MOMENTS, TIMMAIN-THE-ELF FEELS MORE REAL THAN TIMMAIN-THE WOLF...
...ONLY TO BE GROUNDED, ONCE MORE, BY 'NOW'.
SKYWISE, WHERE ARE YOU? COUNCIL!

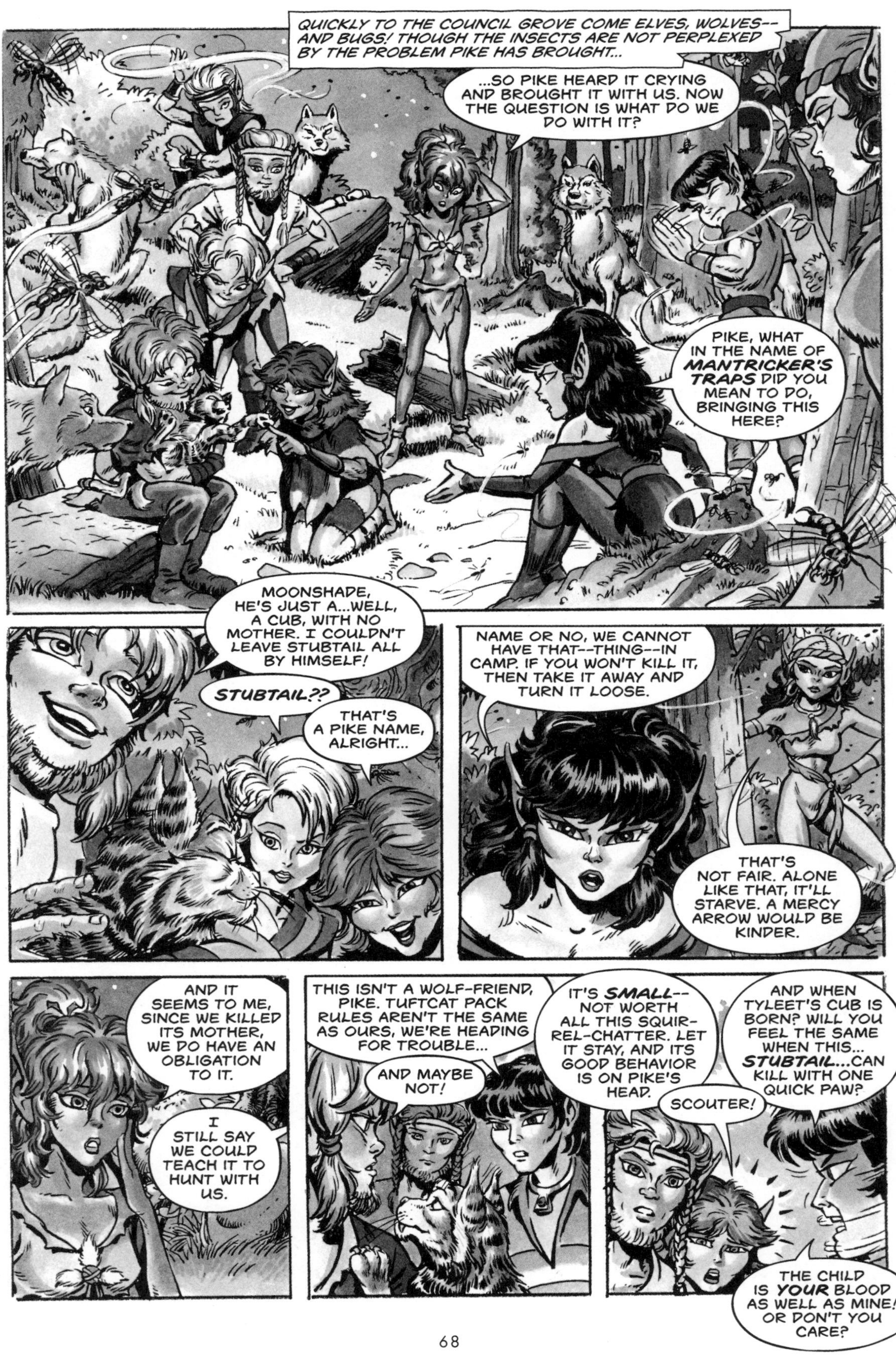
QUICKLY TO THE COUNCIL GROVE COME ELVES, WOLVES-- AND BUGS! THOUGH THE INSECTS ARE NOT PERPLEXED BY THE PROBLEM PIKE HAS BROUGHT...
...SO PIKE HEARD IT CRYING AND BROUGHT IT WITH US. NOW THE QUESTION IS WHAT DO WE DO WITH IT?
PIKE, WHAT IN THE NAME OF MANTRICKER'S TRAPS DID YOU MEAN TO DO, BRINGING THIS HERE?
MOONSHADE, HE'S JUST A...WELL, A CUB, WITH NO MOTHER. I COULDN'T LEAVE STUBTAIL ALL BY HIMSELF!
STUBTAIL??
THAT'S A PIKE NAME, ALRIGHT...
NAME OR NO, WE CANNOT HAVE THAT--THING--IN CAMP. IF YOU WON'T KILL IT, THEN TAKE IT AWAY AND TURN IT LOOSE.
THAT'S NOT FAIR. ALONE LIKE THAT, IT'LL STARVE. A MERCY ARROW WOULD BE KINDER.
AND IT SEEMS TO ME, SINCE WE KILLED ITS MOTHER, WE DO HAVE AN OBLIGATION TO IT.
I STILL SAY WE COULD TEACH IT TO HUNT WITH US.
THIS ISN'T A WOLF-FRIEND, PIKE. TUFTCAT PACK RULES AREN'T THE SAME AS OURS, WE'RE HEADING FOR TROUBLE...
AND MAYBE NOT!
IT'S SMALL-- NOT WORTH ALL THIS SQUIR-REL-CHATTER. LET IT STAY, AND ITS GOOD BEHAVIOR IS ON PIKE'S HEAD.
AND WHEN TYLEET'S CUB IS BORN? WILL YOU FEEL THE SAME WHEN THIS... STUBTAIL...CAN KILL WITH ONE QUICK PAW?
SCOUTER!
THE CHILD IS YOUR BLOOD AS WELL AS MINE! OR DON'T YOU CARE?

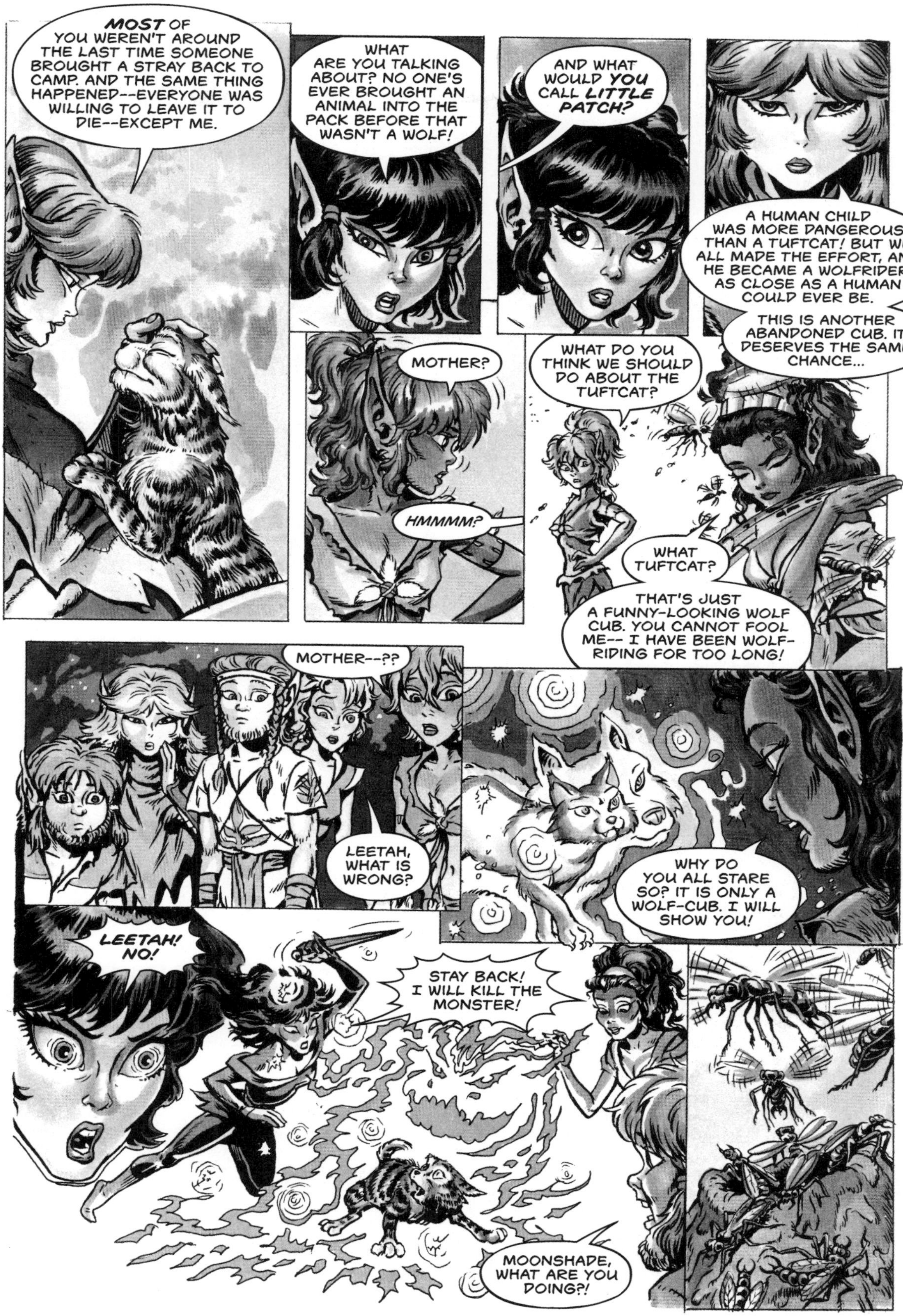
MOST OF YOU WEREN'T AROUND THE LAST TIME SOMEONE BROUGHT A STRAY BACK TO CAMP. AND THE SAME THING HAPPENED--EVERYONE WAS WILLING TO LEAVE IT TO DIE--EXCEPT ME.
WHAT ARE YOU TALKING ABOUT? NO ONE'S EVER BROUGHT AN ANIMAL INTO THE PACK BEFORE THAT WASN'T A WOLF!
AND WHAT WOULD YOU CALL LITTLE PATCH?
A HUMAN CHILD WAS MORE DANGEROUS THAN A TUFTCAT! BUT WE ALL MADE THE EFFORT, AND HE BECAME A WOLFRIDER, AS CLOSE AS A HUMAN COULD EVER BE.
THIS IS ANOTHER ABANDONED CUB. IT DESERVES THE SAME CHANCE...
MOTHER?
HMMMM?
WHAT DO YOU THINK WE SHOULD DO ABOUT THE TUFTCAT?
WHAT TUFTCAT?
THAT'S JUST A FUNNY-LOOKING WOLF CUB. YOU CANNOT FOOL ME-- I HAVE BEEN WOLF-RIDING FOR TOO LONG!
MOTHER--??
LEETAH, WHAT IS WRONG?
WHY DO YOU ALL STARE SO? IT IS ONLY A WOLF-CUB. I WILL SHOW YOU!
LEETAH! NO!
STAY BACK! I WILL KILL THE MONSTER!
MOONSHADE, WHAT ARE YOU DOING?!

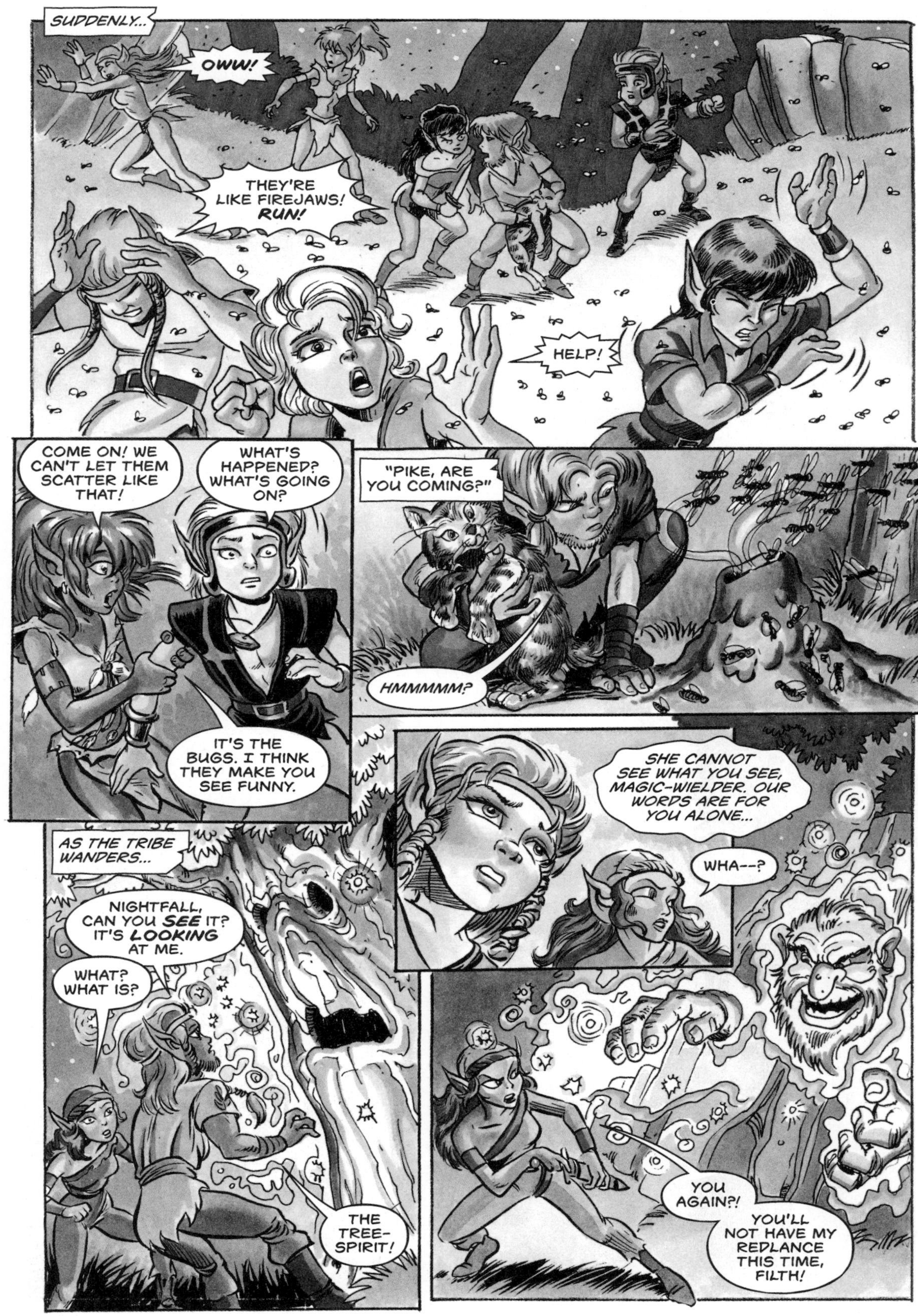
SUDDENLY...
OWW!
THEY'RE LIKE FIREJAWS! RUN!
HELP!
COME ON! WE CAN'T LET THEM SCATTER LIKE THAT!
WHAT'S HAPPENED? WHAT'S GOING ON?
IT'S THE BUGS. I THINK THEY MAKE YOU SEE FUNNY.
"PIKE, ARE YOU COMING?"
HMMMMM?
AS THE TRIBE WANDERS...
NIGHTFALL, CAN YOU SEE IT? IT'S LOOKING AT ME.
WHAT? WHAT IS?
THE TREE-SPIRIT!
SHE CANNOT SEE WHAT YOU SEE, MAGIC-WIELDER. OUR WORDS ARE FOR YOU ALONE...
WHA--?
YOU AGAIN?!
YOU'LL NOT HAVE MY REDLANCE THIS TIME, FILTH!

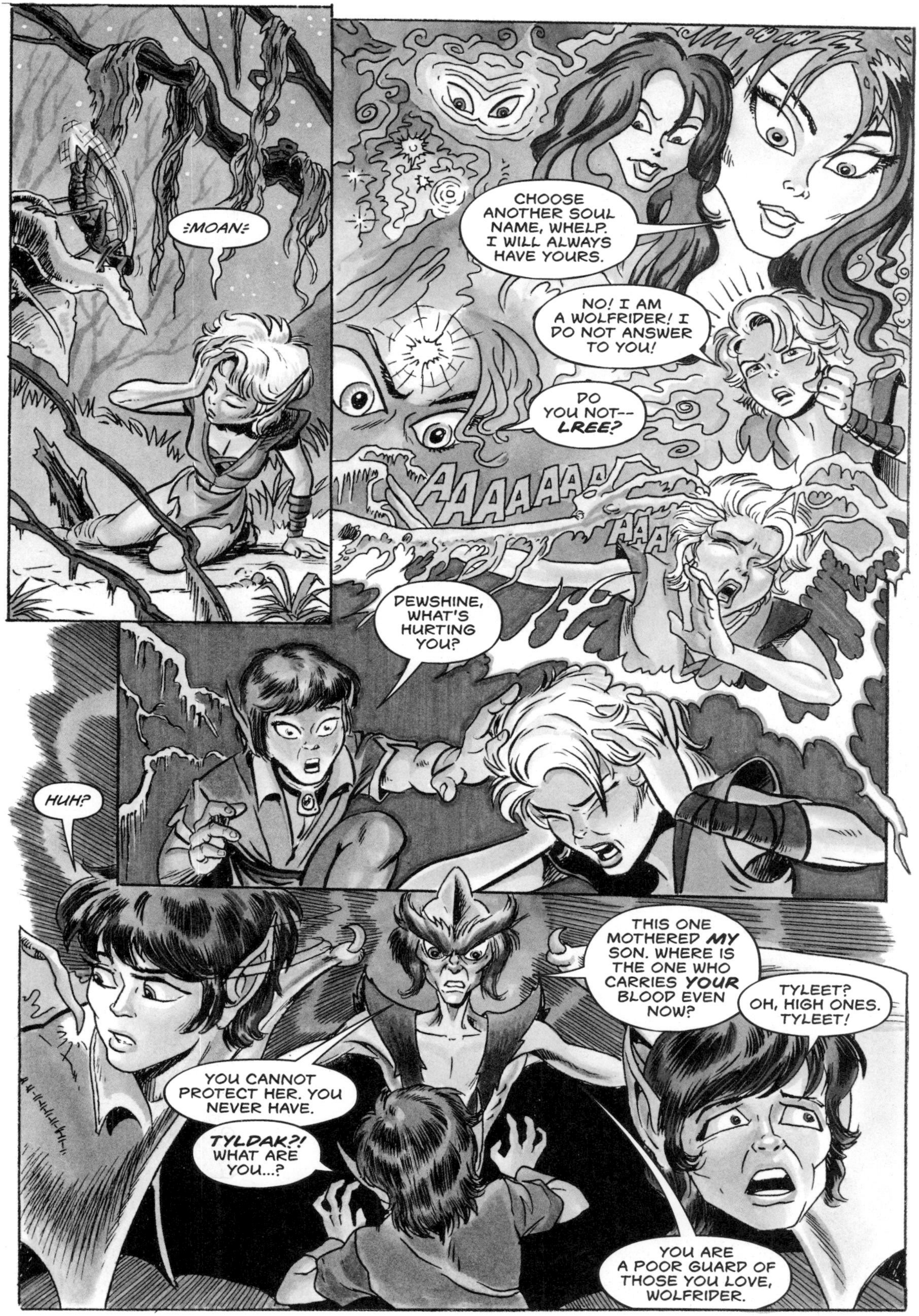

MOAN
CHOOSE ANOTHER SOUL NAME, WHELP. I WILL ALWAYS HAVE YOURS.
NO! I AM A WOLFRIDER! I DO NOT ANSWER TO YOU!
DO YOU NOT-- LREE?
AAAAAAA!
AAA
DEWSHINE, WHAT'S HURTING YOU?
HUH?
THIS ONE MOTHERED MY SON. WHERE IS THE ONE WHO CARRIES YOUR BLOOD EVEN NOW?
TYLEET? OH, HIGH ONES. TYLEET!
YOU CANNOT PROTECT HER. YOU NEVER HAVE.
TYLDAK?! WHAT ARE YOU...?
YOU ARE A POOR GUARD OF THOSE YOU LOVE, WOLFRIDER.

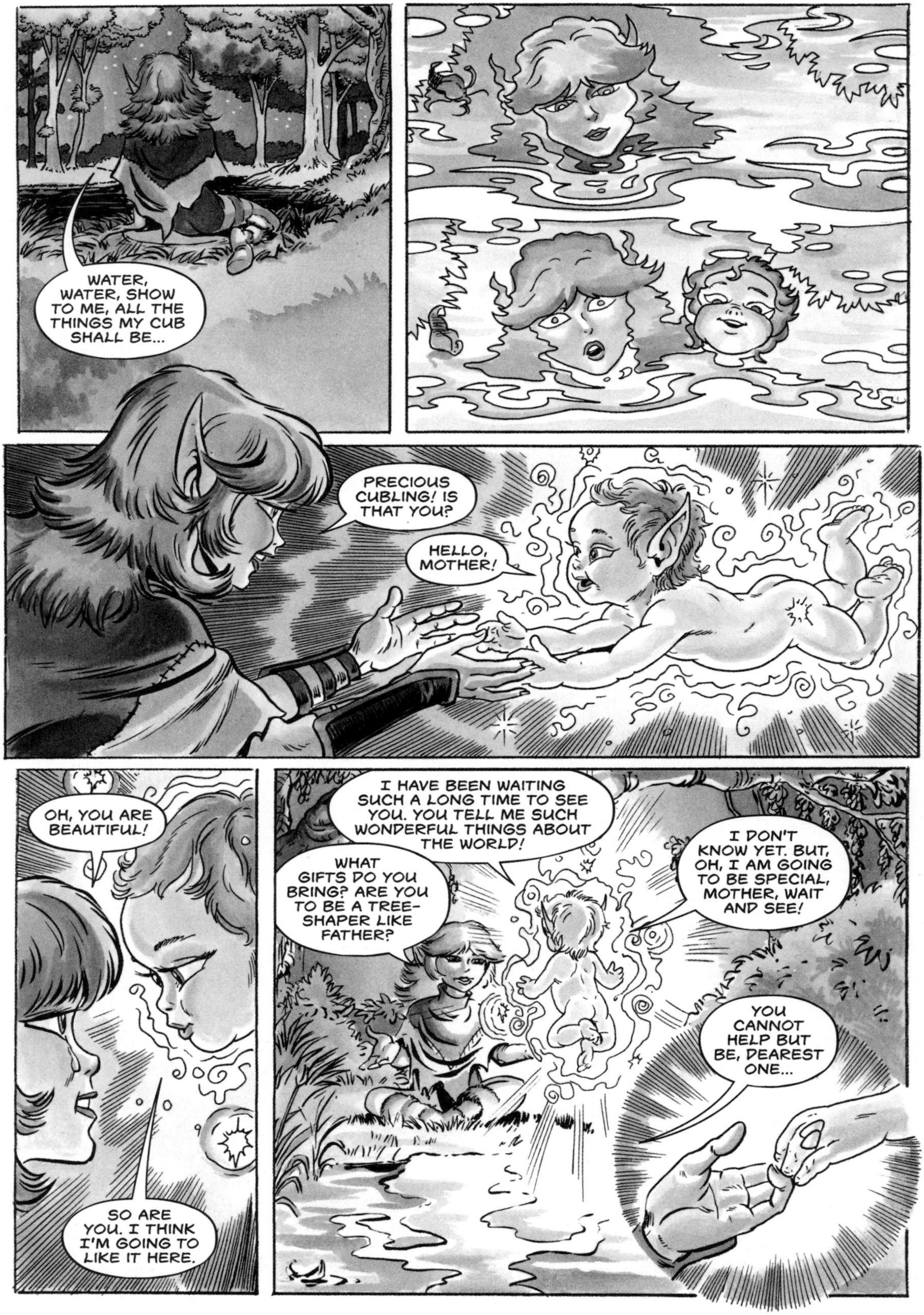
WATER, WATER, SHOW TO ME, ALL THE THINGS MY CUB SHALL BE...
PRECIOUS CUBLING! IS THAT YOU?
HELLO, MOTHER!
OH, YOU ARE BEAUTIFUL!
SO ARE YOU. I THINK I'M GOING TO LIKE IT HERE.
I HAVE BEEN WAITING SUCH A LONG TIME TO SEE YOU. YOU TELL ME SUCH WONDERFUL THINGS ABOUT THE WORLD!
WHAT GIFTS DO YOU BRING? ARE YOU TO BE A TREE-SHAPER LIKE FATHER?
I DON'T KNOW YET. BUT, OH, I AM GOING TO BE SPECIAL, MOTHER, WAIT AND SEE!
YOU CANNOT HELP BUT BE, DEAREST ONE...

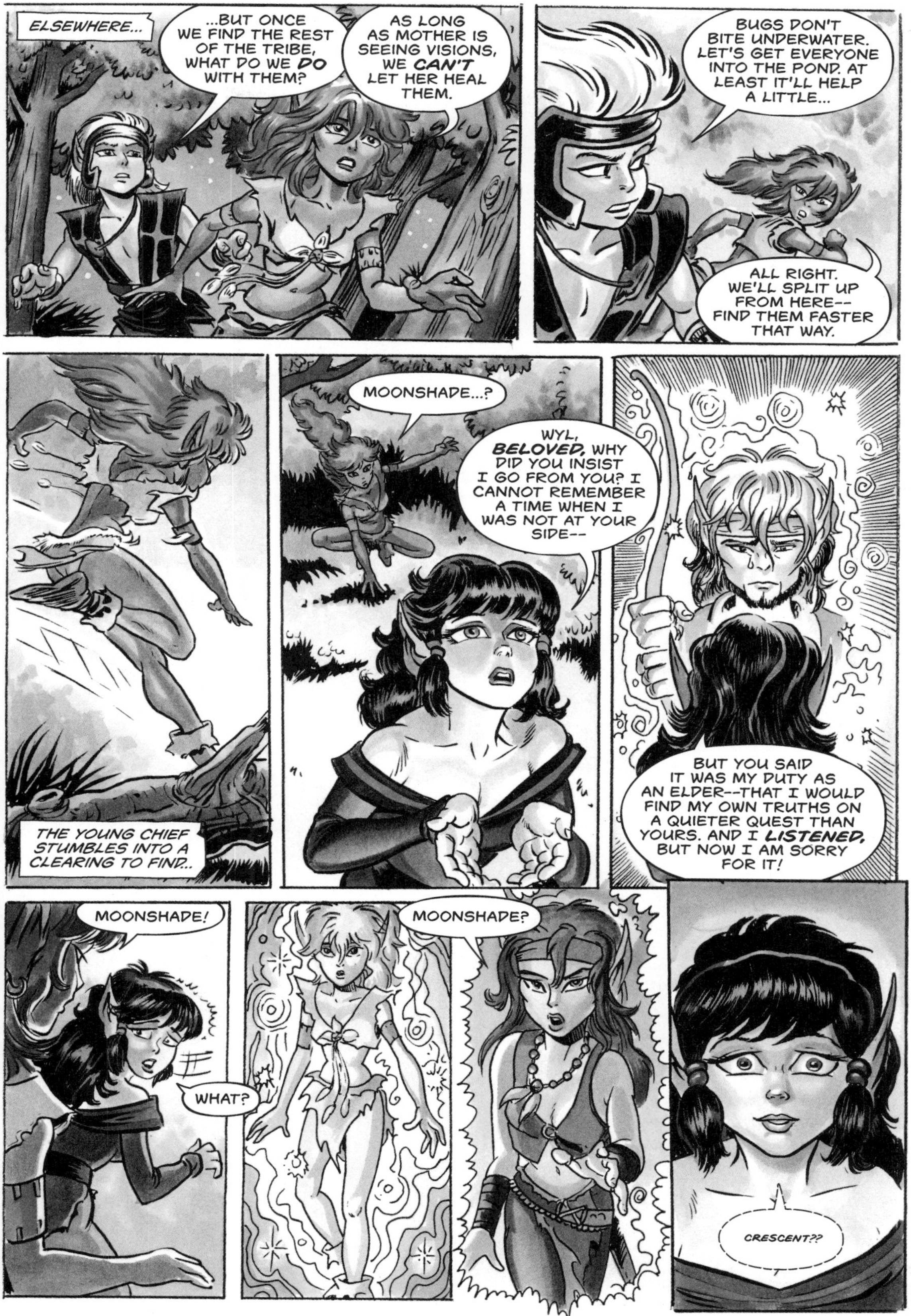
ELSEWHERE...
...BUT ONCE WE FIND THE REST OF THE TRIBE, WHAT DO WE DO WITH THEM?
AS LONG AS MOTHER IS SEEING VISIONS, WE CAN'T LET HER HEAL THEM.
BUGS DON'T BITE UNDERWATER. LET'S GET EVERYONE INTO THE POND. AT LEAST IT'LL HELP A LITTLE...
ALL RIGHT. WE'LL SPLIT UP FROM HERE-- FIND THEM FASTER THAT WAY.
THE YOUNG CHIEF STUMBLES INTO A CLEARING TO FIND...
MOONSHADE...?
WYL, BELOVED, WHY DID YOU INSIST I GO FROM YOU? I CANNOT REMEMBER A TIME WHEN I WAS NOT AT YOUR SIDE--
BUT YOU SAID IT WAS MY DUTY AS AN ELDER--THAT I WOULD FIND MY OWN TRUTHS ON A QUIETER QUEST THAN YOURS. AND I LISTENED, BUT NOW I AM SORRY FOR IT!
MOONSHADE!
WHAT?
MOONSHADE?
CRESCENT??

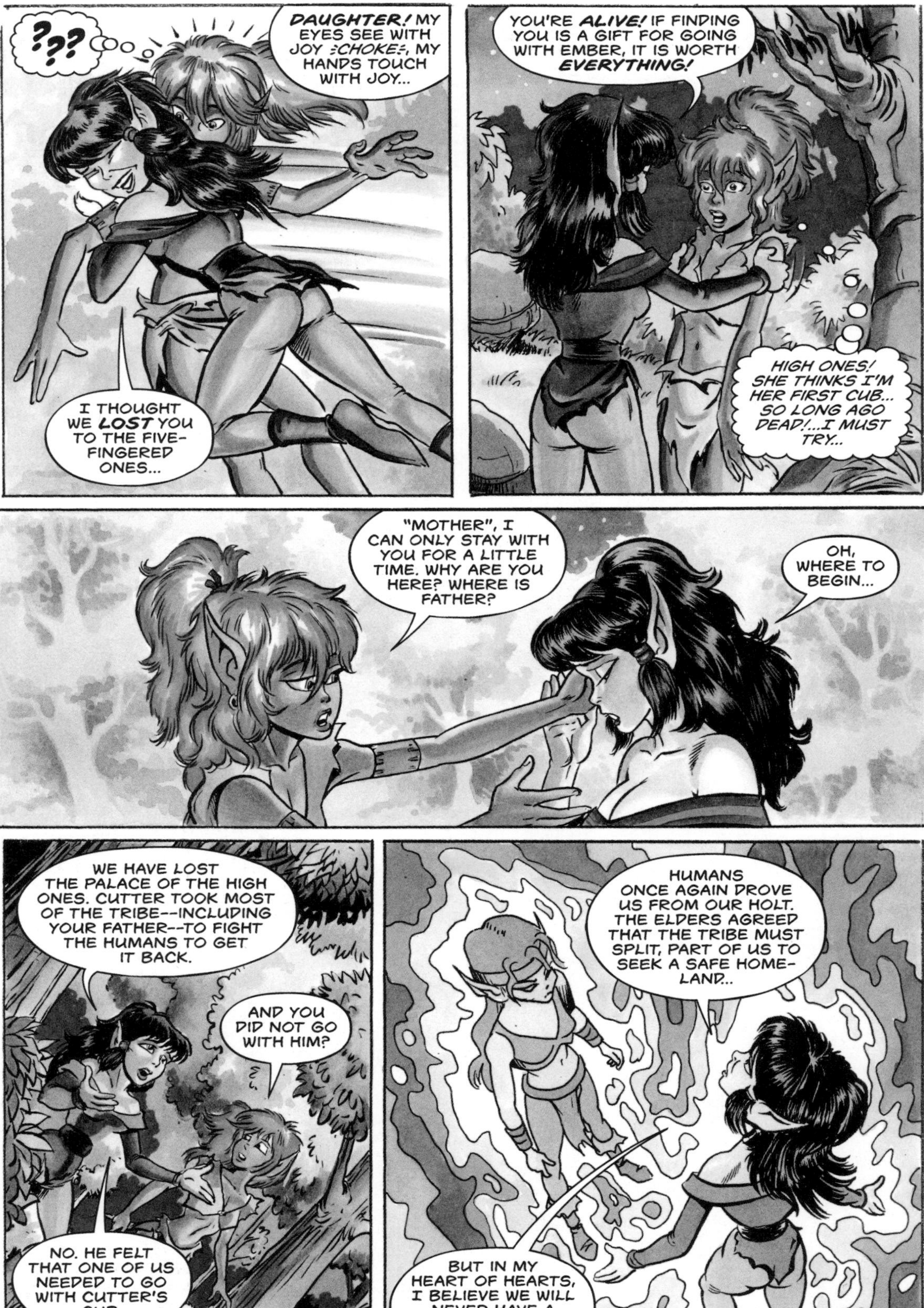
???
DAUGHTER! MY EYES SEE WITH JOY :CHOKE:, MY HANDS TOUCH WITH JOY...
I THOUGHT WE LOST YOU TO THE FIVE-FINGERED ONES...
YOU'RE ALIVE! IF FINDING YOU IS A GIFT FOR GOING WITH EMBER, IT IS WORTH EVERYTHING!
HIGH ONES! SHE THINKS I'M HER FIRST CUB... SO LONG AGO DEAD!...I MUST TRY...
"MOTHER", I CAN ONLY STAY WITH YOU FOR A LITTLE TIME. WHY ARE YOU HERE? WHERE IS FATHER?
OH, WHERE TO BEGIN...
WE HAVE LOST THE PALACE OF THE HIGH ONES. CUTTER TOOK MOST OF THE TRIBE--INCLUDING YOUR FATHER--TO FIGHT THE HUMANS TO GET IT BACK.
AND YOU DID NOT GO WITH HIM?
NO. HE FELT THAT ONE OF US NEEDED TO GO WITH CUTTER'S CUB.
HUMANS ONCE AGAIN DROVE US FROM OUR HOLT. THE ELDERS AGREED THAT THE TRIBE MUST SPLIT, PART OF US TO SEEK A SAFE HOMELAND...
BUT IN MY HEART OF HEARTS, I BELIEVE WE WILL NEVER HAVE A TRUE HOLT AGAIN!

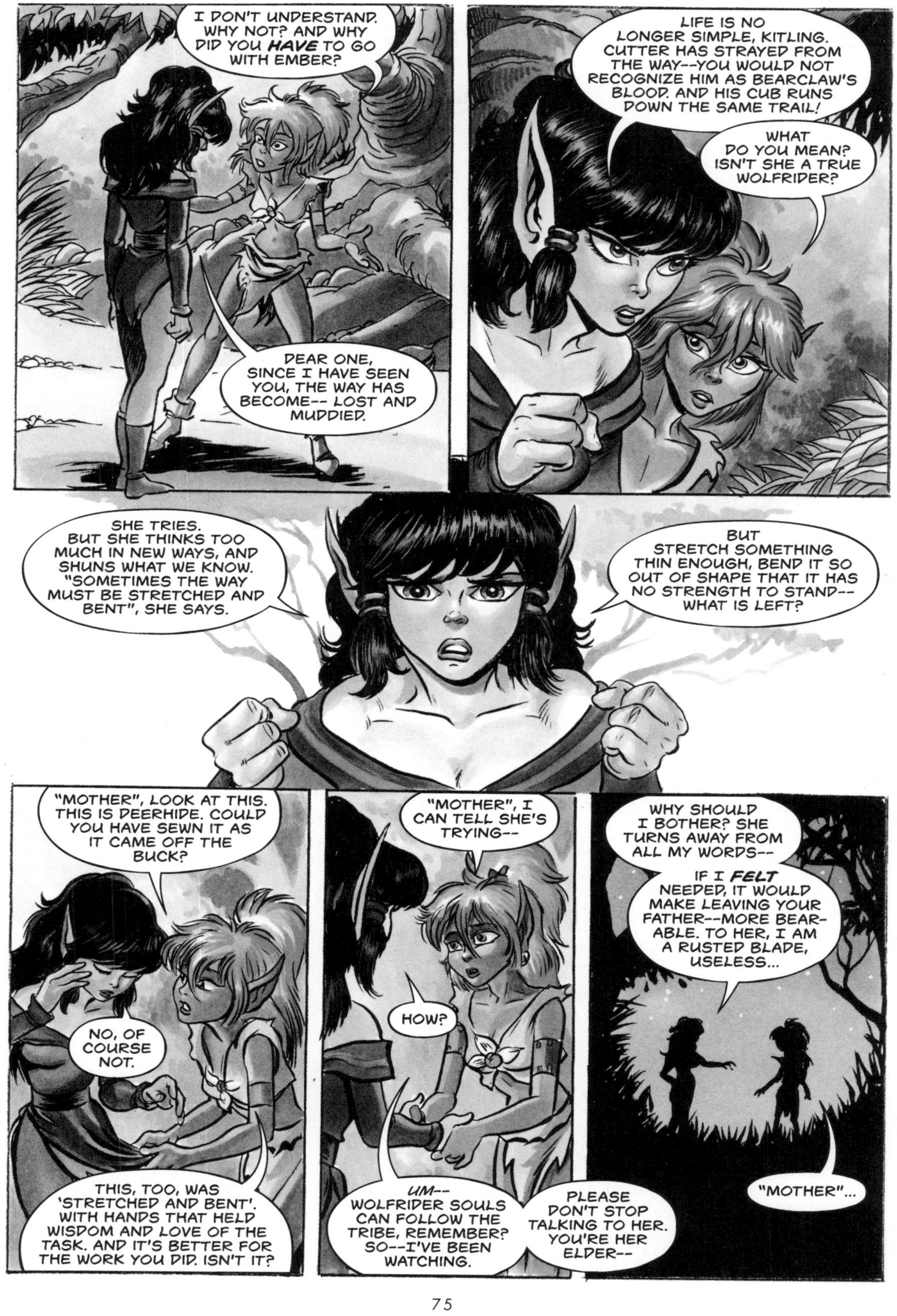
I DON'T UNDERSTAND. WHY NOT? AND WHY DID YOU HAVE TO GO WITH EMBER?
DEAR ONE, SINCE I HAVE SEEN YOU, THE WAY HAS BECOME-- LOST AND MUDDIED.
LIFE IS NO LONGER SIMPLE, KITLING. CUTTER HAS STRAYED FROM THE WAY--YOU WOULD NOT RECOGNIZE HIM AS BEARCLAW'S BLOOD. AND HIS CUB RUNS DOWN THE SAME TRAIL!
WHAT DO YOU MEAN? ISN'T SHE A TRUE WOLFRIDER?
SHE TRIES. BUT SHE THINKS TOO MUCH IN NEW WAYS, AND SHUNS WHAT WE KNOW. "SOMETIMES THE WAY MUST BE STRETCHED AND BENT", SHE SAYS.
BUT STRETCH SOMETHING THIN ENOUGH, BEND IT SO OUT OF SHAPE THAT IT HAS NO STRENGTH TO STAND-- WHAT IS LEFT?
"MOTHER", LOOK AT THIS. THIS IS DEERHIDE. COULD YOU HAVE SEWN IT AS IT CAME OFF THE BUCK?
NO, OF COURSE NOT.
THIS, TOO, WAS 'STRETCHED AND BENT'. WITH HANDS THAT HELD WISDOM AND LOVE OF THE TASK. AND IT'S BETTER FOR THE WORK YOU DID. ISN'T IT?
"MOTHER", I CAN TELL SHE'S TRYING--
HOW?
UM-- WOLFRIDER SOULS CAN FOLLOW THE TRIBE, REMEMBER? SO--I'VE BEEN WATCHING.
PLEASE DON'T STOP TALKING TO HER. YOU'RE HER ELDER--
WHY SHOULD I BOTHER? SHE TURNS AWAY FROM ALL MY WORDS--
IF I FELT NEEDED, IT WOULD MAKE LEAVING YOUR FATHER--MORE BEARABLE. TO HER, I AM A RUSTED BLADE, USELESS...
"MOTHER"...

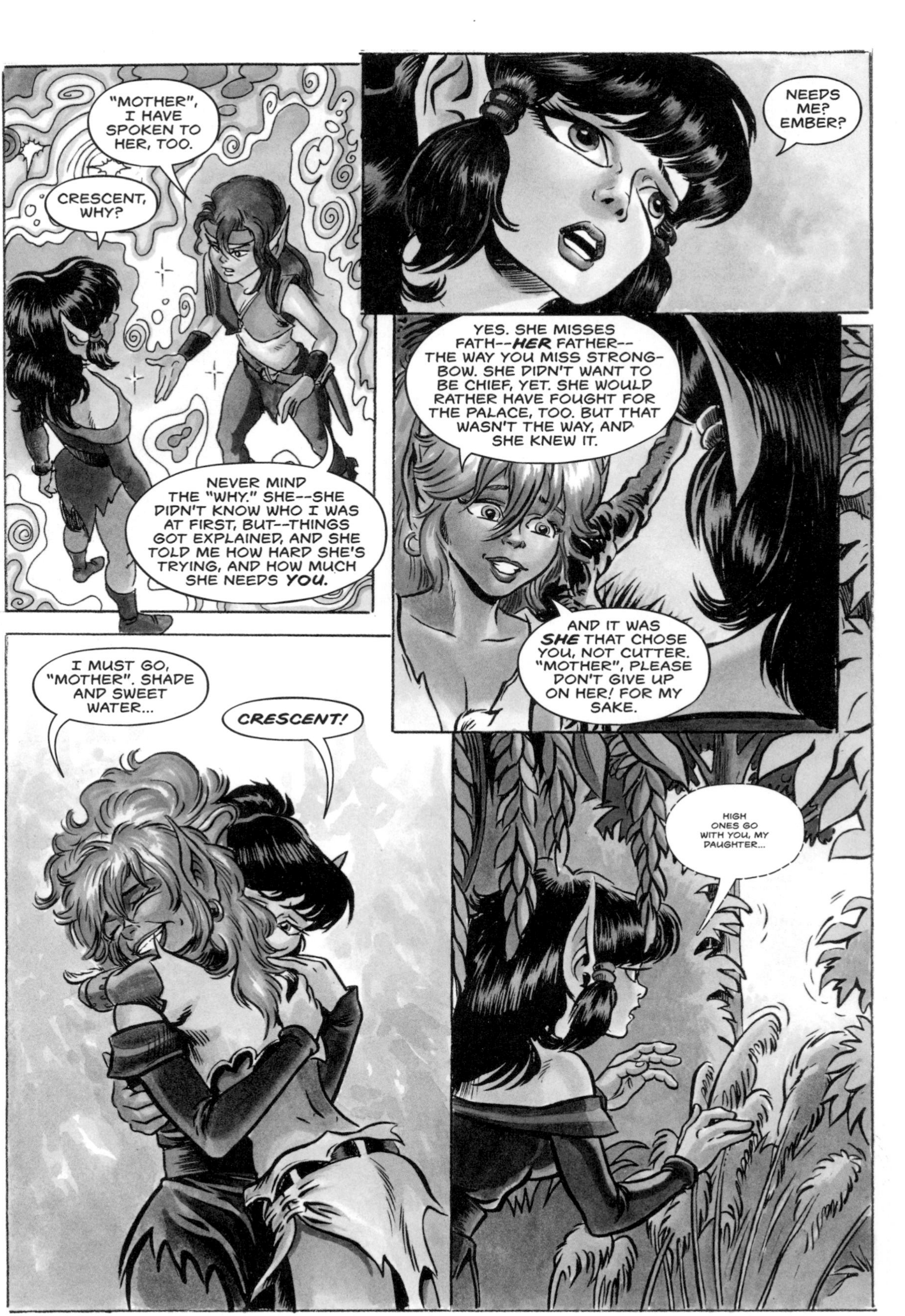

"MOTHER", I HAVE SPOKEN TO HER, TOO.
CRESCENT, WHY?
NEVER MIND THE "WHY." SHE--SHE DIDN'T KNOW WHO I WAS AT FIRST, BUT--THINGS GOT EXPLAINED, AND SHE TOLD ME HOW HARD SHE'S TRYING, AND HOW MUCH SHE NEEDS YOU.
NEEDS ME? EMBER?
YES. SHE MISSES FATH--HER FATHER--THE WAY YOU MISS STRONG-BOW. SHE DIDN'T WANT TO BE CHIEF, YET. SHE WOULD RATHER HAVE FOUGHT FOR THE PALACE, TOO. BUT THAT WASN'T THE WAY, AND SHE KNEW IT.
AND IT WAS SHE THAT CHOSE YOU, NOT CUTTER. "MOTHER", PLEASE DON'T GIVE UP ON HER! FOR MY SAKE.
I MUST GO, "MOTHER". SHADE AND SWEET WATER...
CRESCENT!
HIGH ONES GO WITH YOU, MY DAUGHTER...

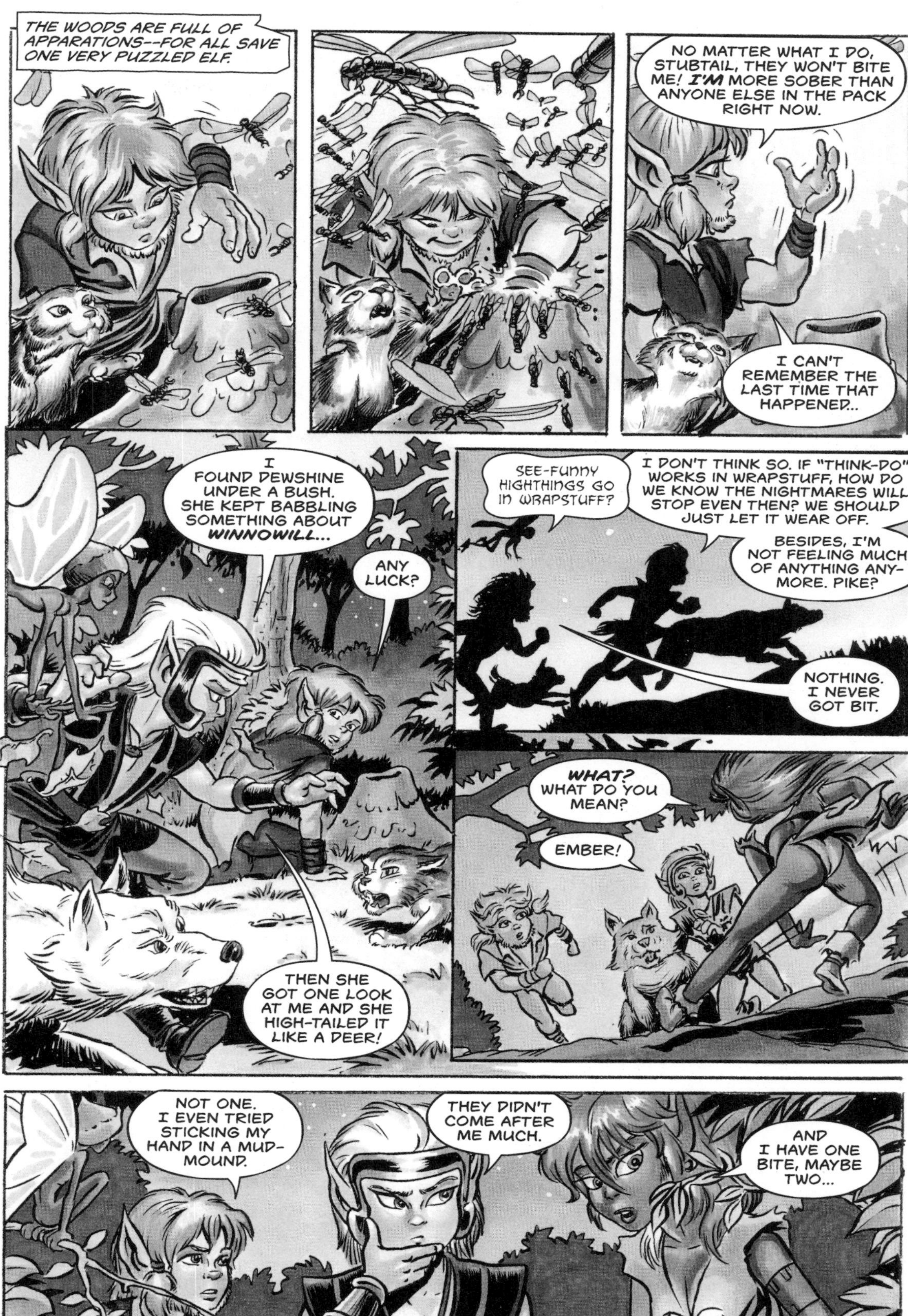
THE WOODS ARE FULL OF APPARATIONS--FOR ALL SAVE ONE VERY PUZZLED ELF.
NO MATTER WHAT I DO, STUBTAIL, THEY WON'T BITE ME! I'M MORE SOBER THAN ANYONE ELSE IN THE PACK RIGHT NOW.
I CAN'T REMEMBER THE LAST TIME THAT HAPPENED...
I FOUND DEWSHINE UNDER A BUSH. SHE KEPT BABBLING SOMETHING ABOUT WINNOWILL...
ANY LUCK?
THEN SHE GOT ONE LOOK AT ME AND SHE HIGH-TAILED IT LIKE A DEER!
SEE-FUNNY HIGHTHINGS GO IN WRAPSTUFF?
I DON'T THINK SO. IF "THINK-DO" WORKS IN WRAPSTUFF, HOW DO WE KNOW THE NIGHTMARES WILL STOP EVEN THEN? WE SHOULD JUST LET IT WEAR OFF.
BESIDES, I'M NOT FEELING MUCH OF ANYTHING ANYMORE. PIKE?
NOTHING. I NEVER GOT BIT.
WHAT? WHAT DO YOU MEAN?
EMBER!
NOT ONE. I EVEN TRIED STICKING MY HAND IN A MUD-MOUND.
THEY DIDN'T COME AFTER ME MUCH.
AND I HAVE ONE BITE, MAYBE TWO...

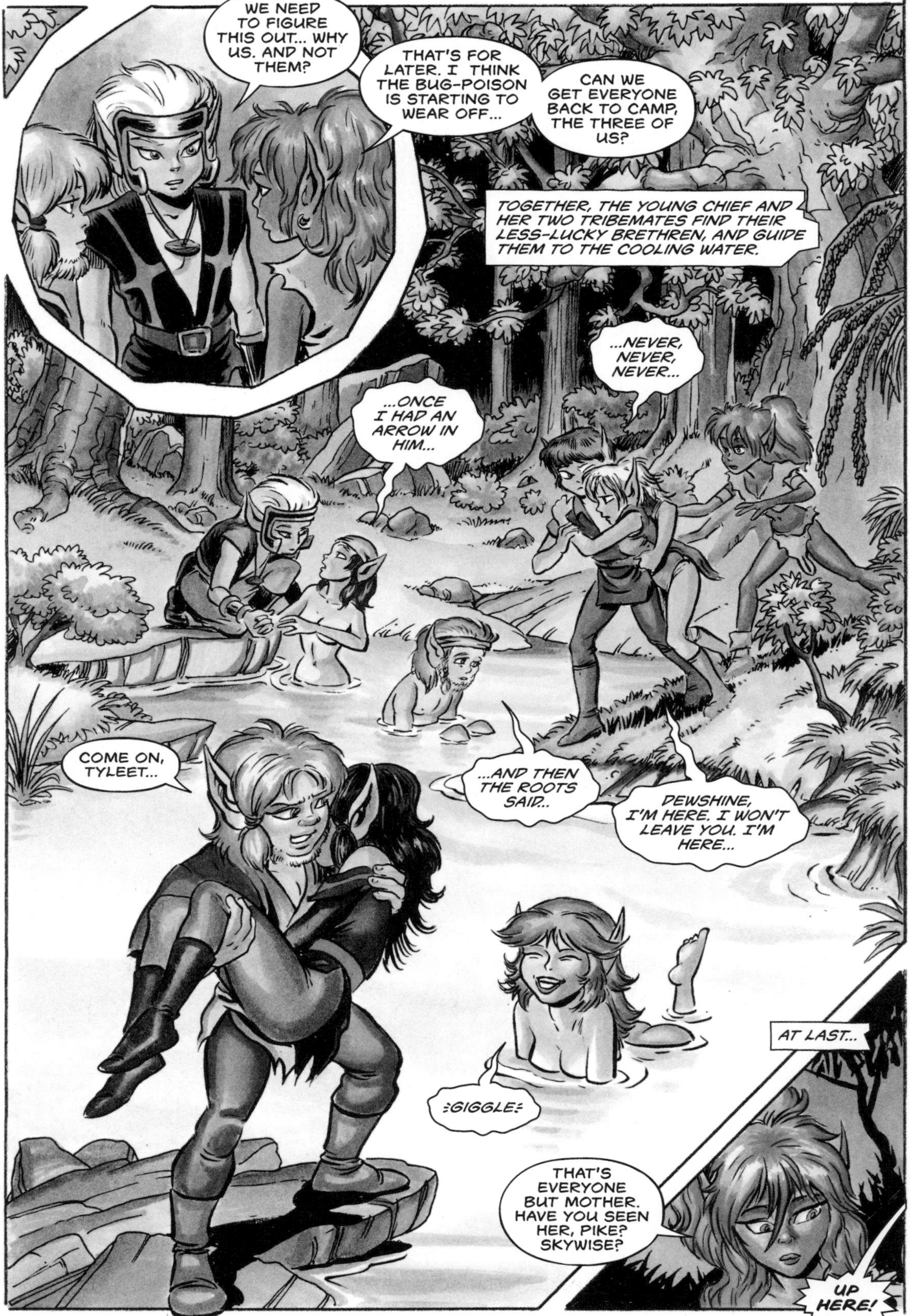
WE NEED TO FIGURE THIS OUT... WHY US. AND NOT THEM?
THAT'S FOR LATER. I THINK THE BUG-POISON IS STARTING TO WEAR OFF...
CAN WE GET EVERYONE BACK TO CAMP, THE THREE OF US?
TOGETHER, THE YOUNG CHIEF AND HER TWO TRIBEMATES FIND THEIR LESS-LUCKY BRETHREN, AND GUIDE THEM TO THE COOLING WATER.
...ONCE I HAD AN ARROW IN HIM...
...NEVER, NEVER, NEVER...
COME ON, TYLEET...
...AND THEN THE ROOTS SAID..
DEWSHINE, I'M HERE. I WON'T LEAVE YOU. I'M HERE...
GIGGLE
AT LAST...
THAT'S EVERYONE BUT MOTHER. HAVE YOU SEEN HER, PIKE? SKYWISE?
UP HERE!

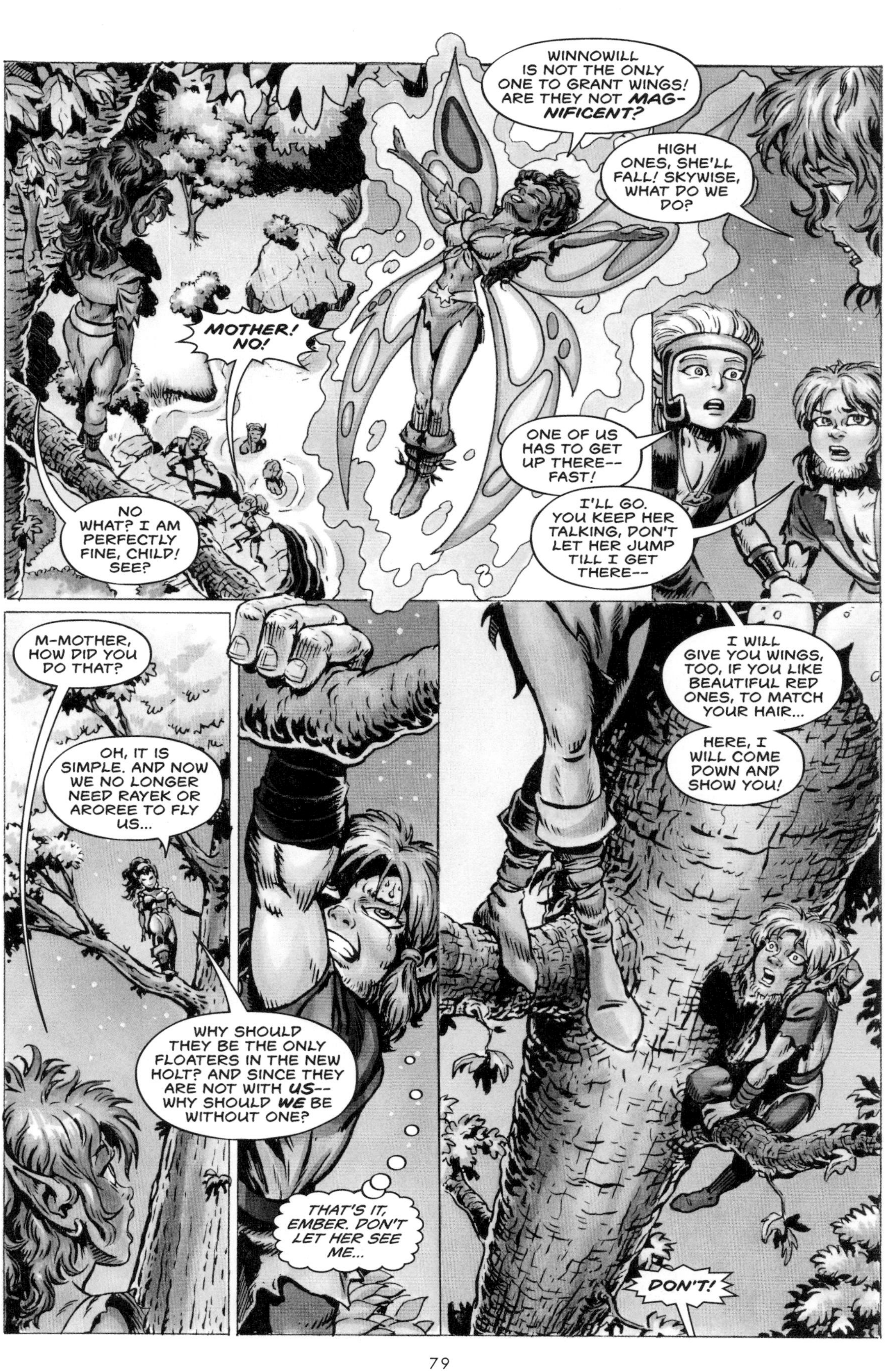

WINNOWILL IS NOT THE ONLY ONE TO GRANT WINGS! ARE THEY NOT MAG-NIFICENT?
MOTHER! NO!
NO WHAT? I AM PERFECTLY FINE, CHILD! SEE?
HIGH ONES, SHE'LL FALL! SKYWISE, WHAT DO WE DO?
ONE OF US HAS TO GET UP THERE-- FAST!
I'LL GO. YOU KEEP HER TALKING, DON'T LET HER JUMP TILL I GET THERE--
M-MOTHER, HOW DID YOU DO THAT?
OH, IT IS SIMPLE. AND NOW WE NO LONGER NEED RAYEK OR AROREE TO FLY US...
WHY SHOULD THEY BE THE ONLY FLOATERS IN THE NEW HOLT? AND SINCE THEY ARE NOT WITH US-- WHY SHOULD WE BE WITHOUT ONE?
THAT'S IT, EMBER. DON'T LET HER SEE ME...
I WILL GIVE YOU WINGS, TOO, IF YOU LIKE BEAUTIFUL RED ONES, TO MATCH YOUR HAIR...
HERE, I WILL COME DOWN AND SHOW YOU!
DON'T!

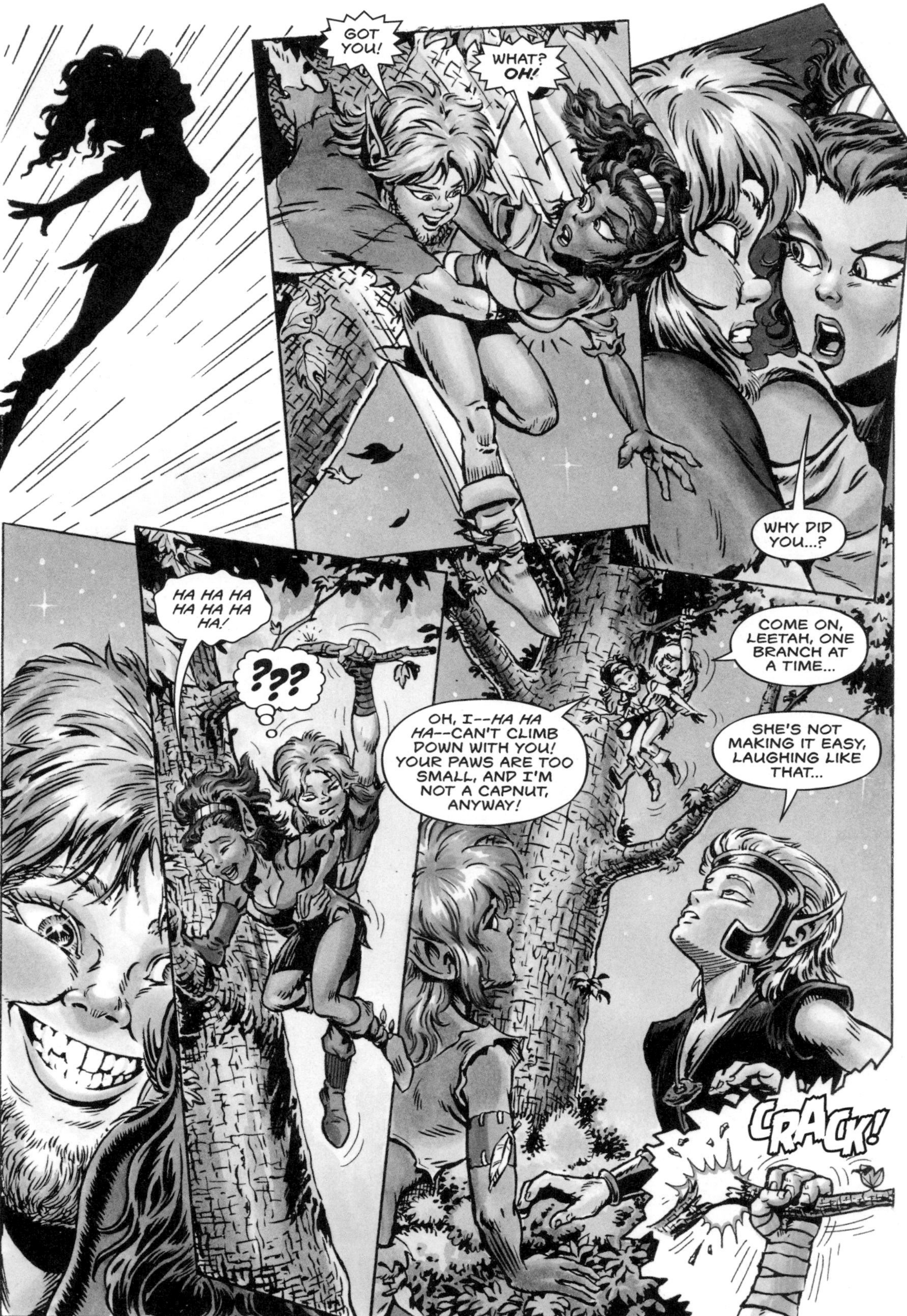
GOT YOU!
WHAT? OH!
WHY DID YOU...?
HA HA HA HA HA HA HA!
???
OH, I--HA HA HA--CAN'T CLIMB DOWN WITH YOU! YOUR PAWS ARE TOO SMALL, AND I'M NOT A CAPNUT, ANYWAY!
COME ON, LEETAH, ONE BRANCH AT A TIME...
SHE'S NOT MAKING IT EASY, LAUGHING LIKE THAT...
CRACK!

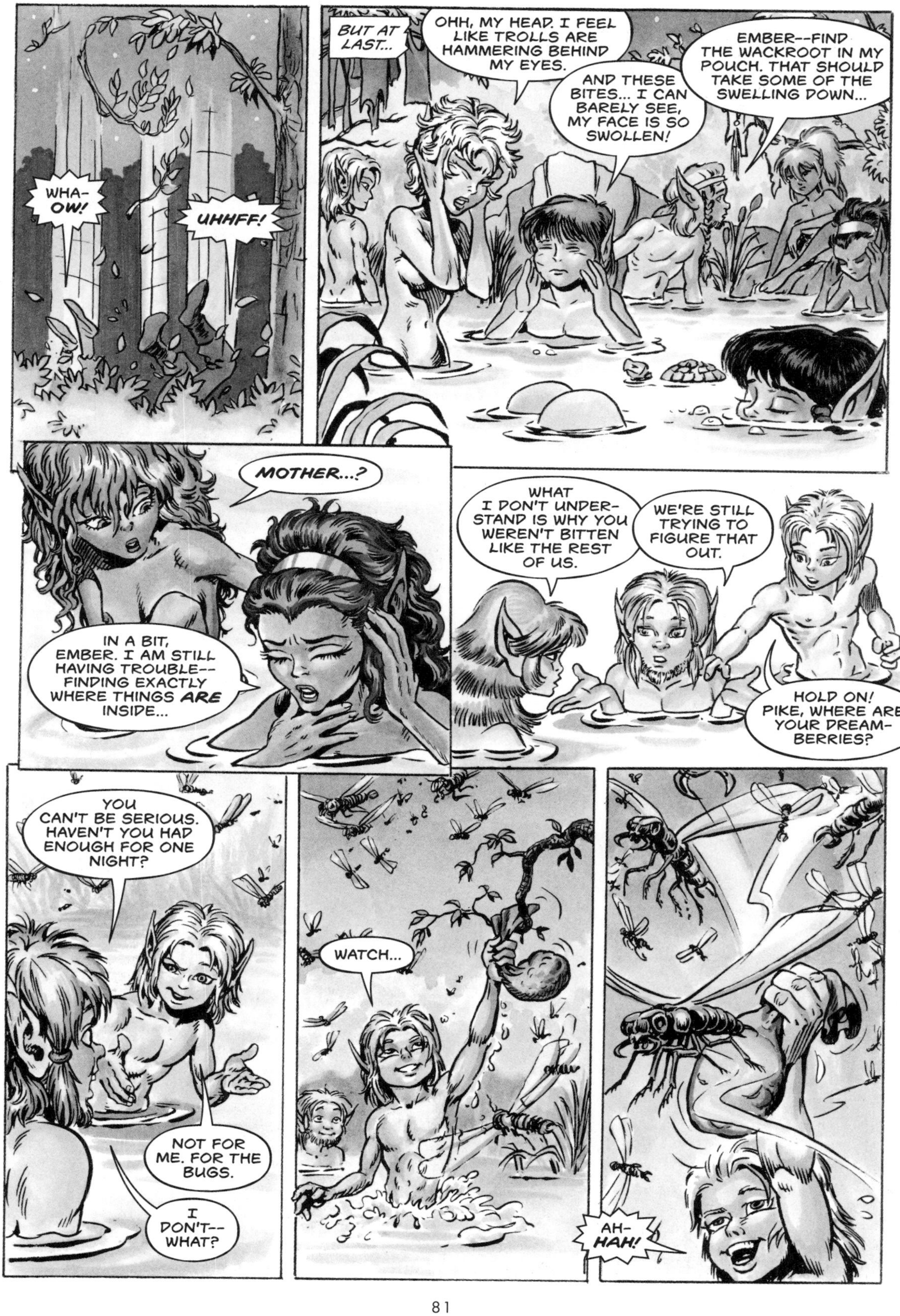
WHA-OW!
UHHFF!
BUT AT LAST...
OHH, MY HEAD. I FEEL LIKE TROLLS ARE HAMMERING BEHIND MY EYES.
AND THESE BITES... I CAN BARELY SEE, MY FACE IS SO SWOLLEN!
EMBER--FIND THE WACKROOT IN MY POUCH. THAT SHOULD TAKE SOME OF THE SWELLING DOWN...
MOTHER...?
IN A BIT, EMBER. I AM STILL HAVING TROUBLE--FINDING EXACTLY WHERE THINGS ARE INSIDE...
WHAT I DON'T UNDERSTAND IS WHY YOU WEREN'T BITTEN LIKE THE REST OF US.
WE'RE STILL TRYING TO FIGURE THAT OUT.
HOLD ON! PIKE, WHERE ARE YOUR DREAM-BERRIES?
YOU CAN'T BE SERIOUS. HAVEN'T YOU HAD ENOUGH FOR ONE NIGHT?
NOT FOR ME. FOR THE BUGS.
I DON'T--WHAT?
WATCH...
AH-HAH!

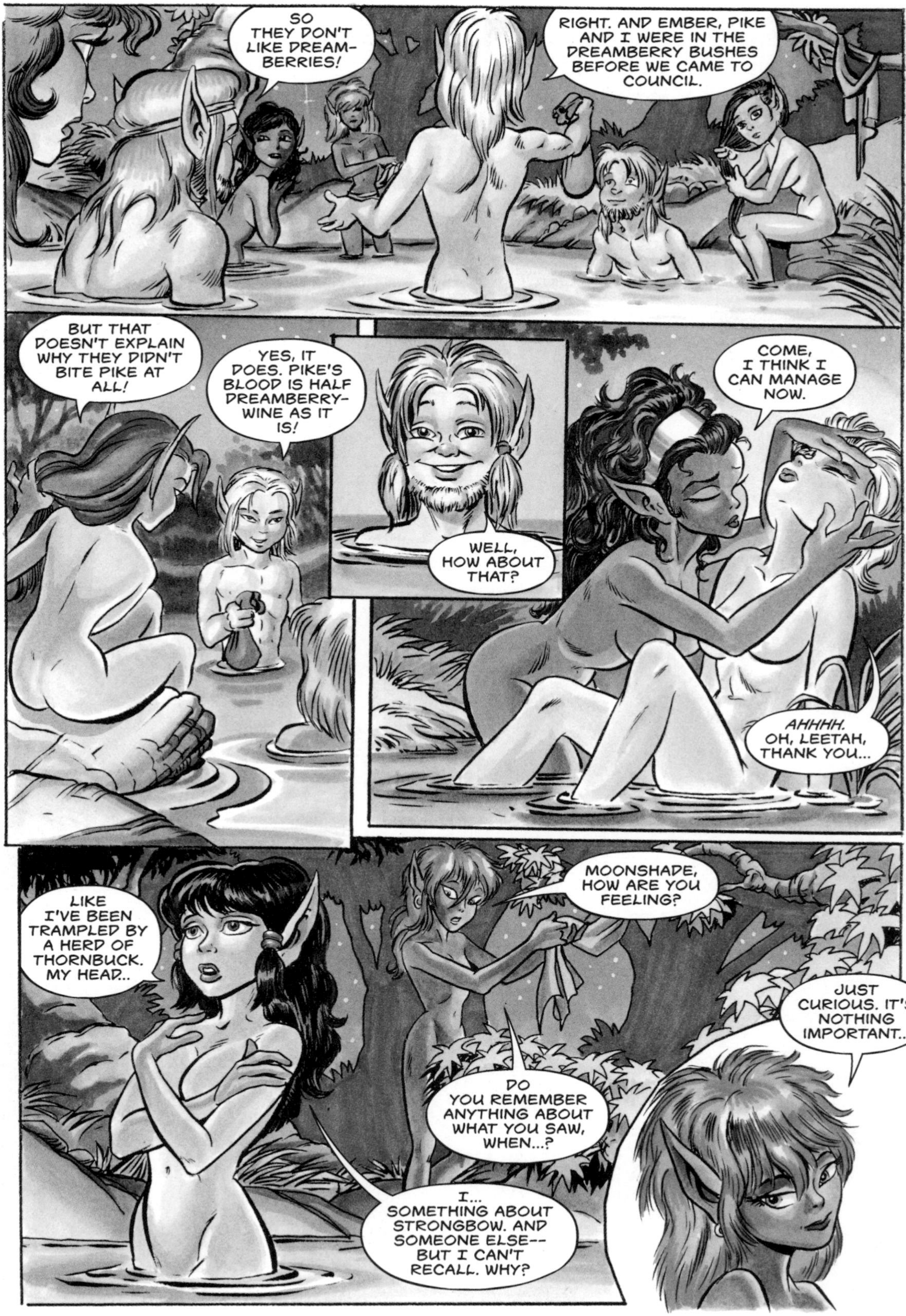
SO THEY DON'T LIKE DREAM-BERRIES!
RIGHT. AND EMBER, PIKE AND I WERE IN THE DREAMBERRY BUSHES BEFORE WE CAME TO COUNCIL.
BUT THAT DOESN'T EXPLAIN WHY THEY DIDN'T BITE PIKE AT ALL!
YES, IT DOES. PIKE'S BLOOD IS HALF DREAMBERRY-WINE AS IT IS!
WELL, HOW ABOUT THAT?
COME, I THINK I CAN MANAGE NOW.
AHHHH. OH, LEETAH, THANK YOU...
MOONSHADE, HOW ARE YOU FEELING?
LIKE I'VE BEEN TRAMPLED BY A HERD OF THORNBUCK. MY HEAD...
DO YOU REMEMBER ANYTHING ABOUT WHAT YOU SAW, WHEN...?
I... SOMETHING ABOUT STRONGBOW. AND SOMEONE ELSE-- BUT I CAN'T RECALL. WHY?
JUST CURIOUS. IT'S NOTHING IMPORTANT...

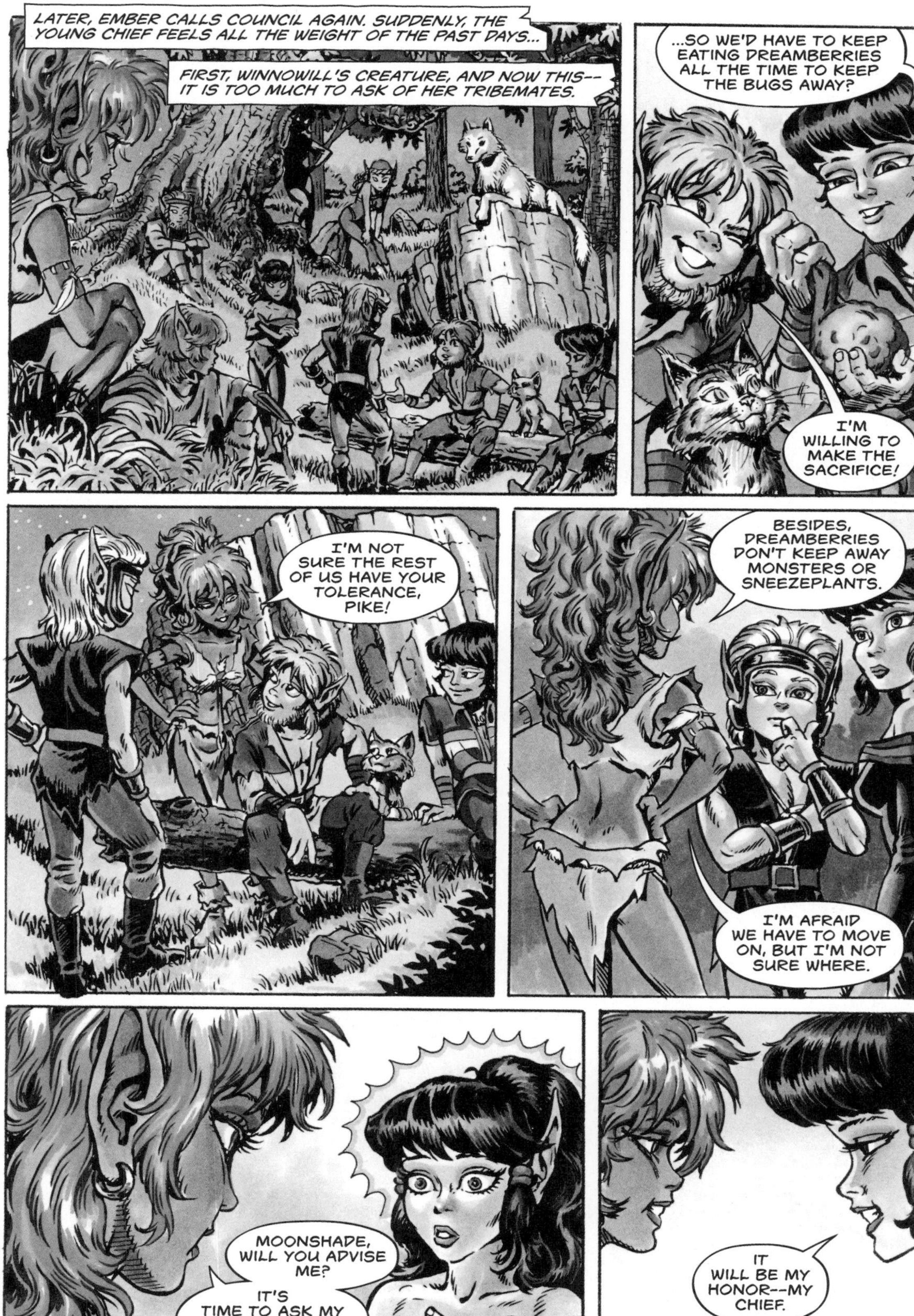
LATER, EMBER CALLS COUNCIL AGAIN. SUDDENLY, THE YOUNG CHIEF FEELS ALL THE WEIGHT OF THE PAST DAYS...
FIRST, WINNOWILL'S CREATURE, AND NOW THIS-- IT IS TOO MUCH TO ASK OF HER TRIBEMATES.
...SO WE'D HAVE TO KEEP EATING DREAMBERRIES ALL THE TIME TO KEEP THE BUGS AWAY?
I'M WILLING TO MAKE THE SACRIFICE!
I'M NOT SURE THE REST OF US HAVE YOUR TOLERANCE, PIKE!
BESIDES, DREAMBERRIES DON'T KEEP AWAY MONSTERS OR SNEEZEPLANTS.
I'M AFRAID WE HAVE TO MOVE ON, BUT I'M NOT SURE WHERE.
MOONSHADE, WILL YOU ADVISE ME?
IT'S TIME TO ASK MY ELDER'S GUIDANCE, I THINK.
IT WILL BE MY HONOR--MY CHIEF.

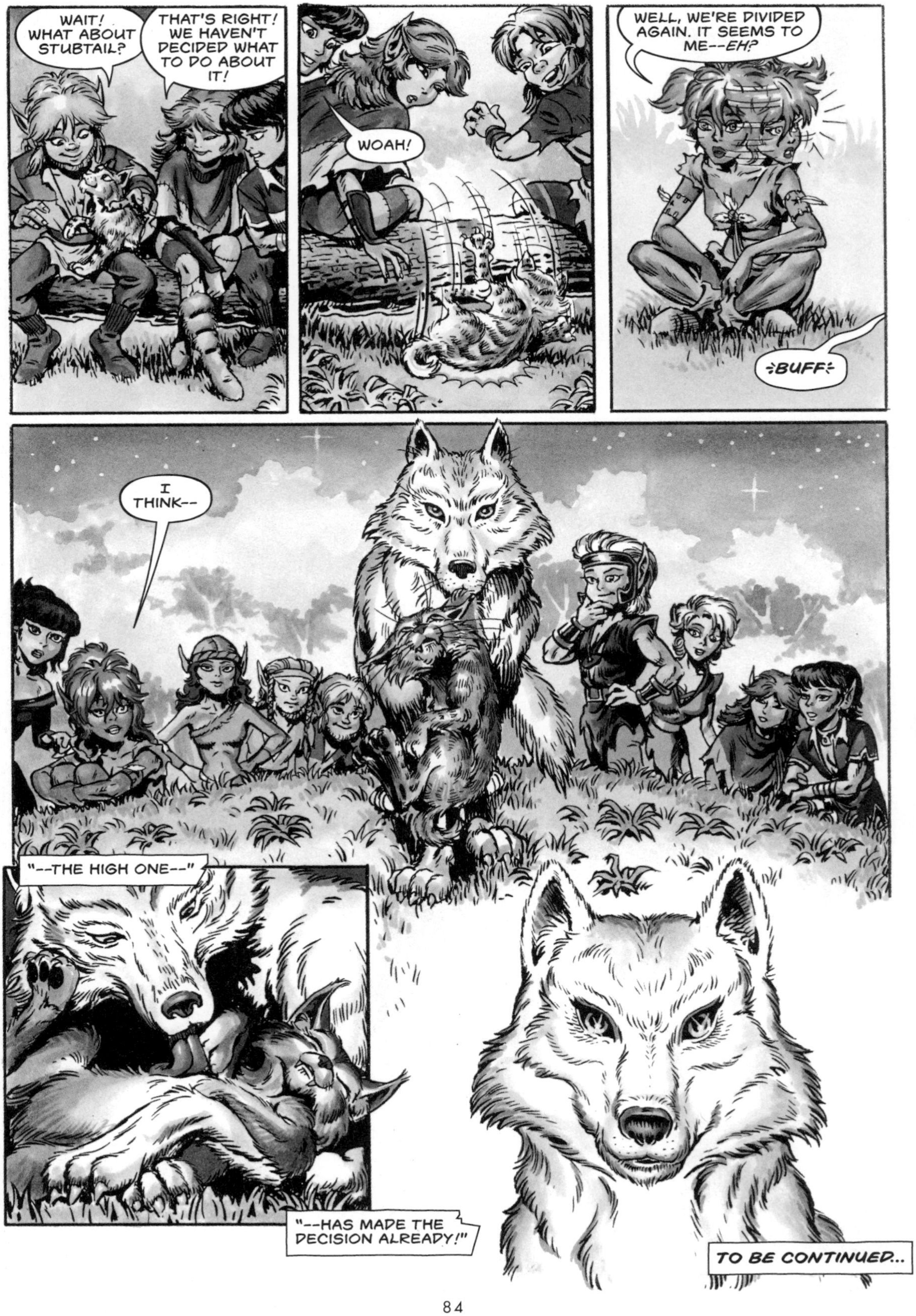
WAIT! WHAT ABOUT STUBTAIL?
THAT'S RIGHT! WE HAVEN'T DECIDED WHAT TO DO ABOUT IT!
WOAH!
WELL, WE'RE DIVIDED AGAIN. IT SEEMS TO ME--EH?
BUFF
I THINK--
"--THE HIGH ONE--"
"--HAS MADE THE DECISION ALREADY!"
TO BE CONTINUED...

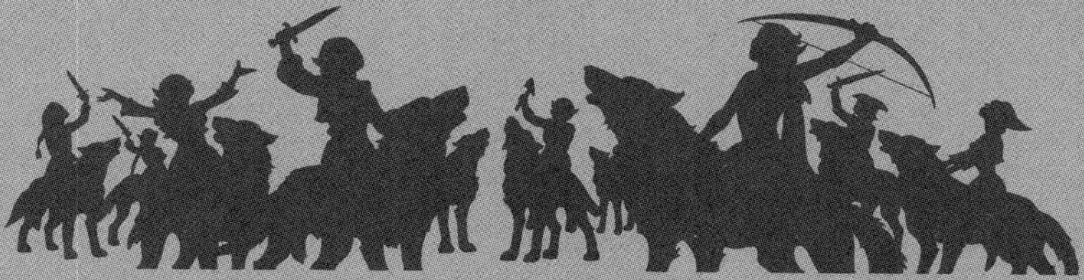

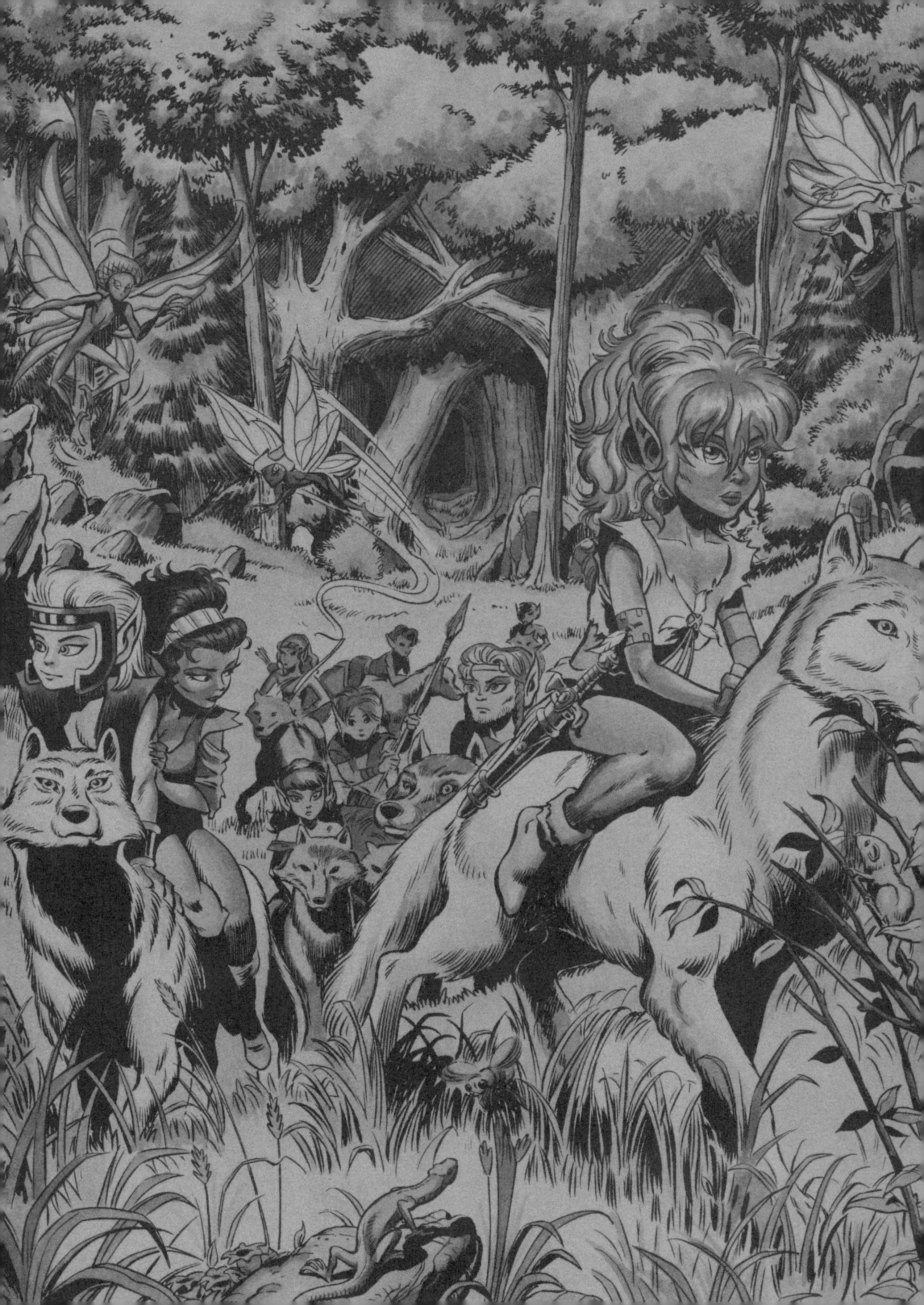

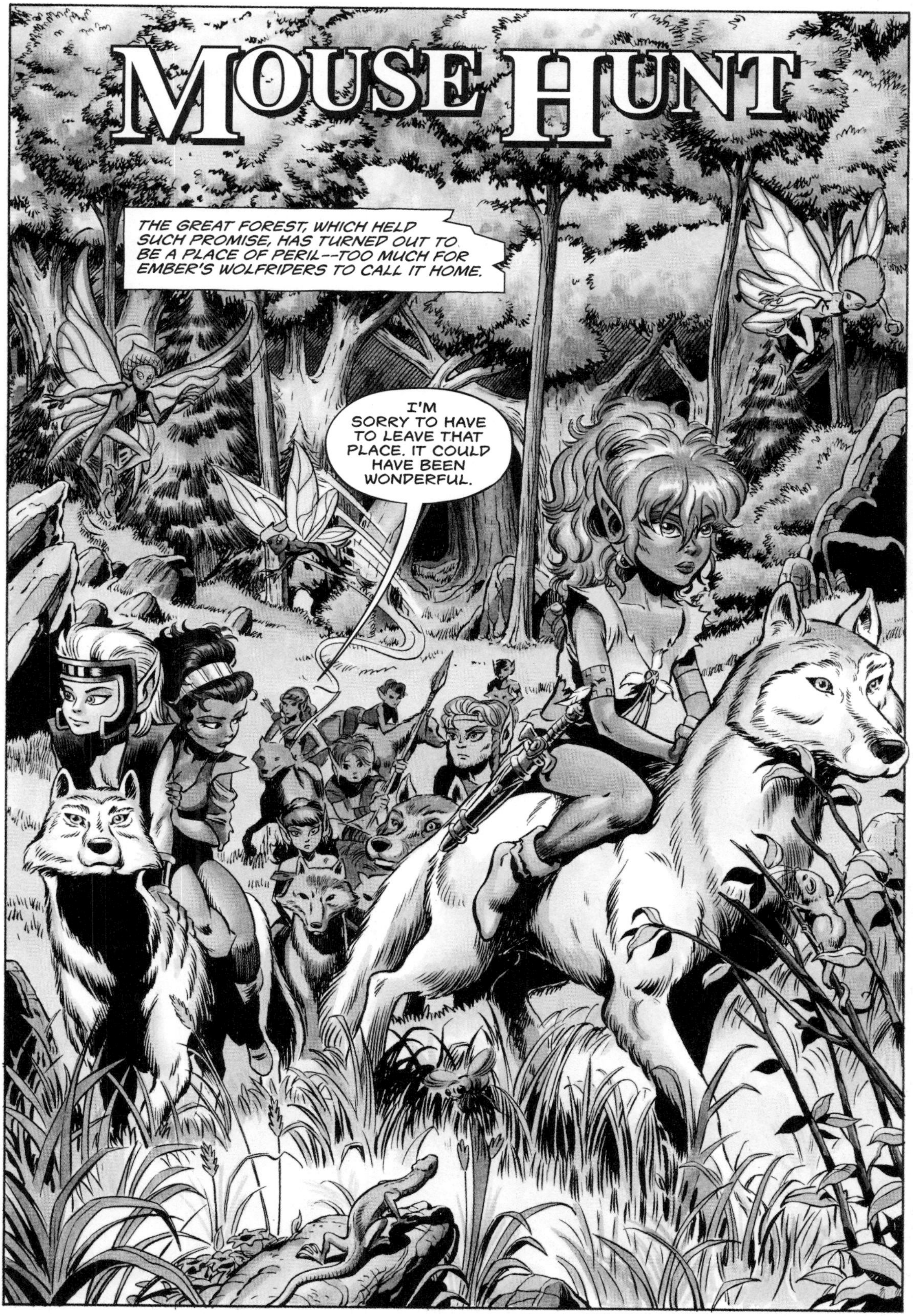
MOUSE HUNT
THE GREAT FOREST, WHICH HELD SUCH PROMISE, HAS TURNED OUT TO BE A PLACE OF PERIL--TOO MUCH FOR EMBER'S WOLFRIDERS TO CALL IT HOME.
I'M SORRY TO HAVE TO LEAVE THAT PLACE. IT COULD HAVE BEEN WONDERFUL.

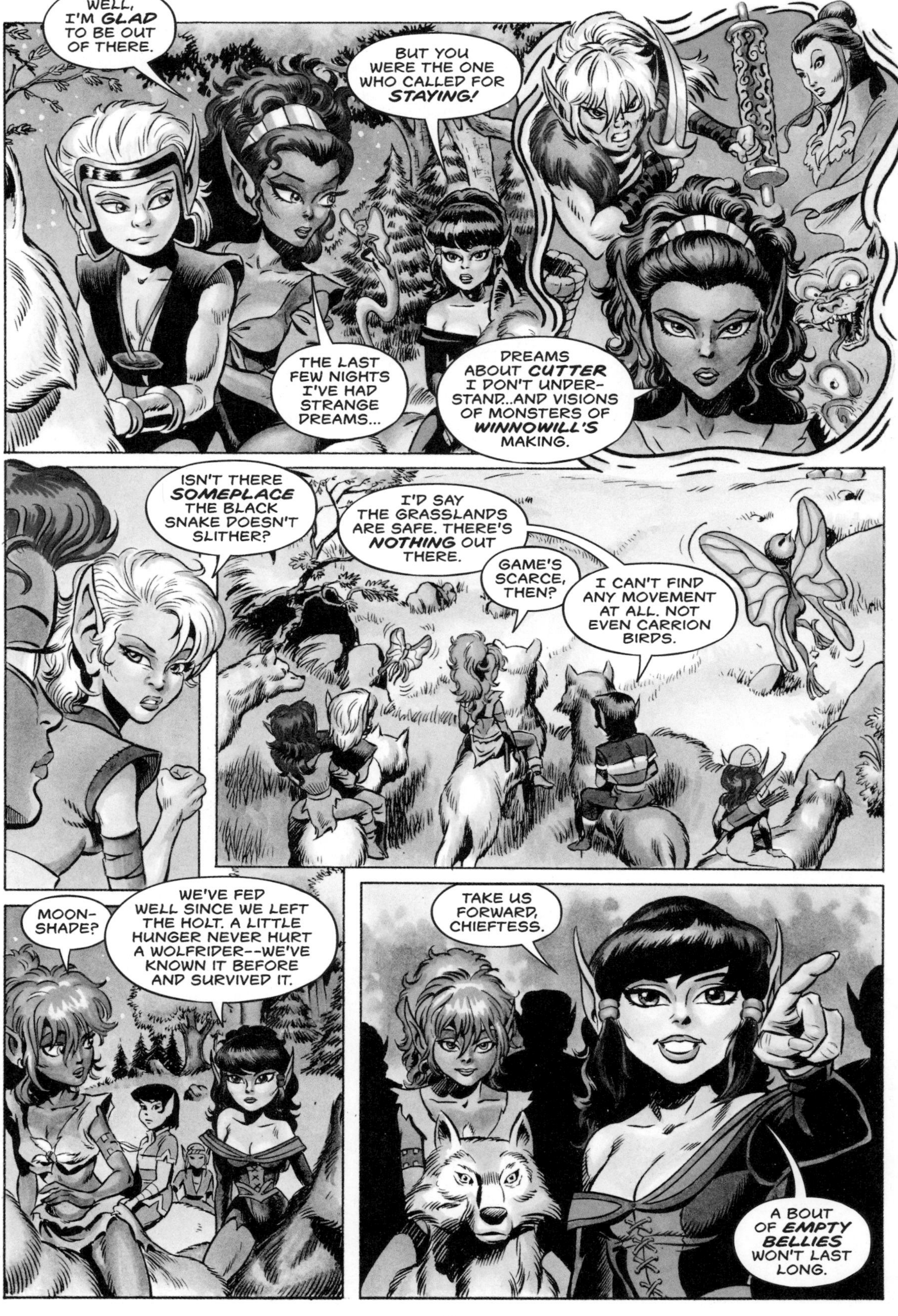

WELL, I'M GLAD TO BE OUT OF THERE.
BUT YOU WERE THE ONE WHO CALLED FOR STAYING!
THE LAST FEW NIGHTS I'VE HAD STRANGE DREAMS...
DREAMS ABOUT CUTTER I DON'T UNDER-STAND...AND VISIONS OF MONSTERS OF WINNOWILL'S MAKING.
ISN'T THERE SOMEPLACE THE BLACK SNAKE DOESN'T SLITHER?
I'D SAY THE GRASSLANDS ARE SAFE. THERE'S NOTHING OUT THERE.
GAME'S SCARCE, THEN?
I CAN'T FIND ANY MOVEMENT AT ALL. NOT EVEN CARRION BIRDS.
MOON-SHADE?
WE'VE FED WELL SINCE WE LEFT THE HOLT. A LITTLE HUNGER NEVER HURT A WOLFRIDER--WE'VE KNOWN IT BEFORE AND SURVIVED IT.
TAKE US FORWARD, CHIEFTESS.
A BOUT OF EMPTY BELLIES WON'T LAST LONG.

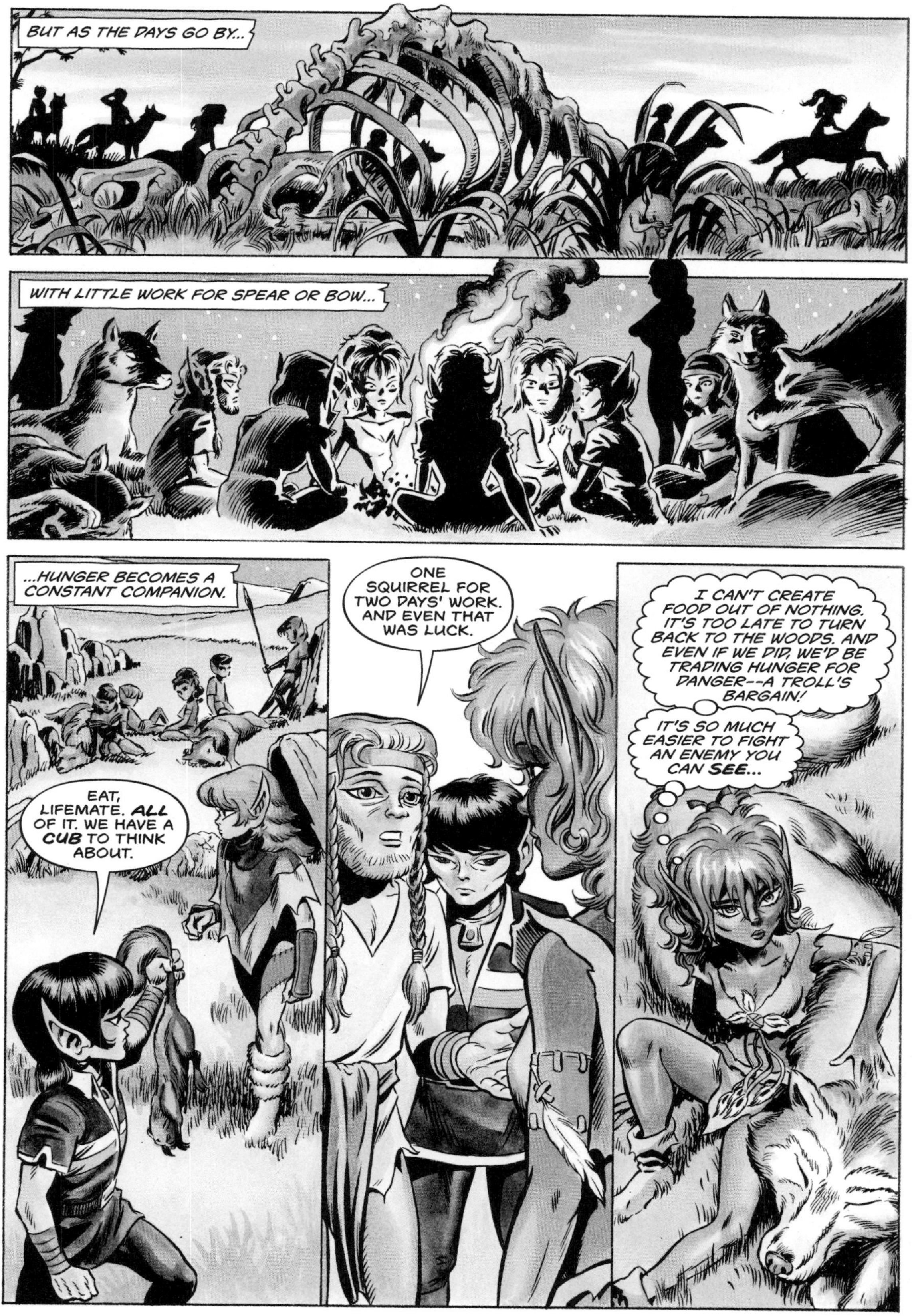

BUT AS THE DAYS GO BY...
WITH LITTLE WORK FOR SPEAR OR BOW...
...HUNGER BECOMES A CONSTANT COMPANION.
EAT, LIFEMATE. ALL OF IT. WE HAVE A CUB TO THINK ABOUT.
ONE SQUIRREL FOR TWO DAYS' WORK. AND EVEN THAT WAS LUCK.
I CAN'T CREATE FOOD OUT OF NOTHING. IT'S TOO LATE TO TURN BACK TO THE WOODS. AND EVEN IF WE DID, WE'D BE TRADING HUNGER FOR DANGER--A TROLL'S BARGAIN!
IT'S SO MUCH EASIER TO FIGHT AN ENEMY YOU CAN SEE...

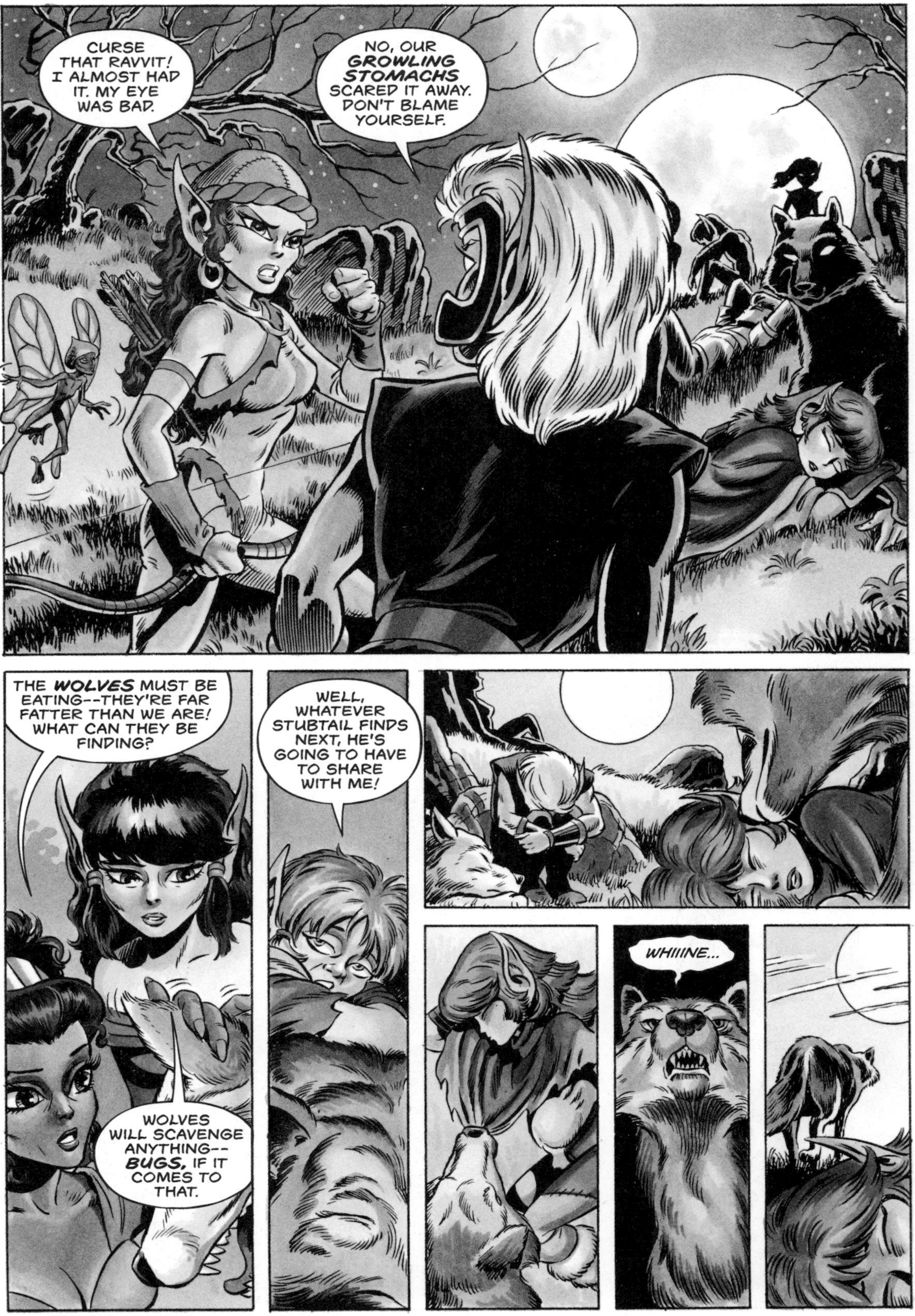
CURSE THAT RAVVIT! I ALMOST HAD IT. MY EYE WAS BAD.
NO, OUR **GROWLING STOMACHS** SCARED IT AWAY. DON'T BLAME YOURSELF.
THE **WOLVES** MUST BE EATING--THEY'RE FAR FATTER THAN WE ARE! WHAT CAN THEY BE FINDING?
WOLVES WILL SCAVENGE ANYTHING-- **BUGS,** IF IT COMES TO THAT.
WELL, WHATEVER STUBTAIL FINDS NEXT, HE'S GOING TO HAVE TO SHARE WITH ME!
WHIIINE...

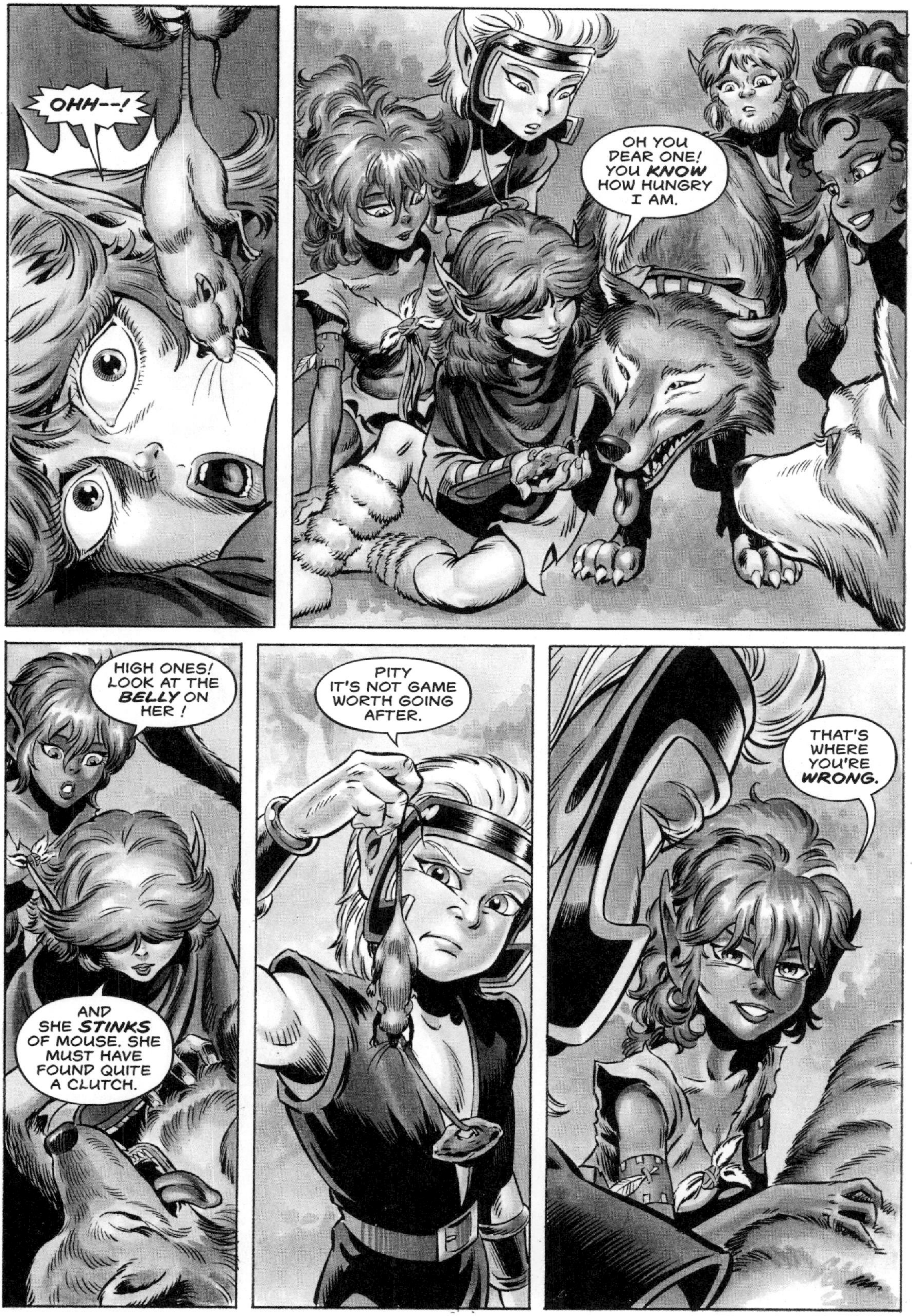
OHH--!
OH YOU DEAR ONE! YOU KNOW HOW HUNGRY I AM.
HIGH ONES! LOOK AT THE BELLY ON HER !
AND SHE STINKS OF MOUSE. SHE MUST HAVE FOUND QUITE A CLUTCH.
PITY IT'S NOT GAME WORTH GOING AFTER.
THAT'S WHERE YOU'RE WRONG.

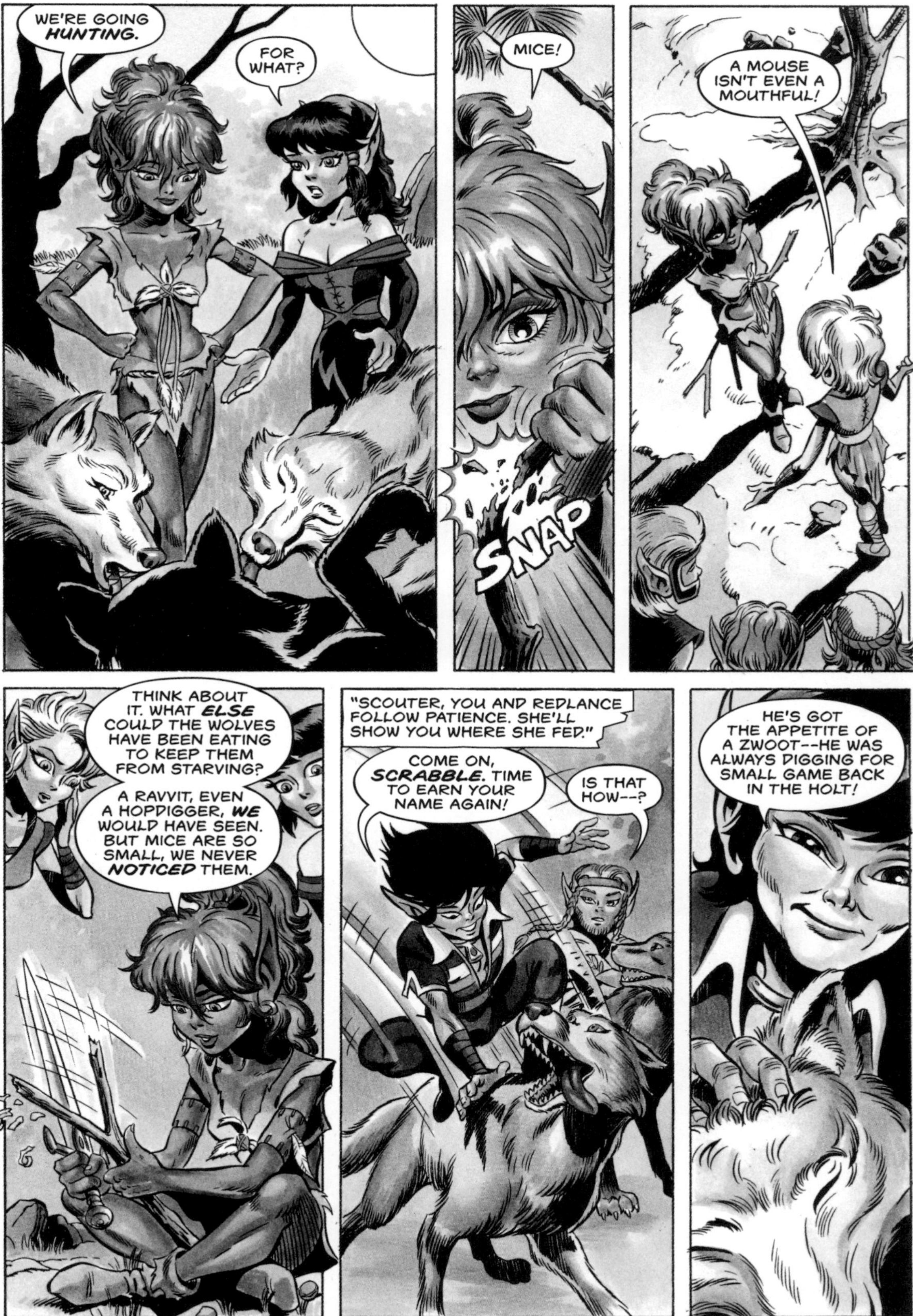
WE'RE GOING HUNTING.
FOR WHAT?
MICE!
SNAP
A MOUSE ISN'T EVEN A MOUTHFUL!
THINK ABOUT IT. WHAT ELSE COULD THE WOLVES HAVE BEEN EATING TO KEEP THEM FROM STARVING?
A RAVVIT, EVEN A HOPDIGGER, WE WOULD HAVE SEEN. BUT MICE ARE SO SMALL, WE NEVER NOTICED THEM.
"SCOUTER, YOU AND REDLANCE FOLLOW PATIENCE. SHE'LL SHOW YOU WHERE SHE FED."
COME ON, SCRABBLE. TIME TO EARN YOUR NAME AGAIN!
IS THAT HOW--?
HE'S GOT THE APPETITE OF A ZWOOT--HE WAS ALWAYS DIGGING FOR SMALL GAME BACK IN THE HOLT!

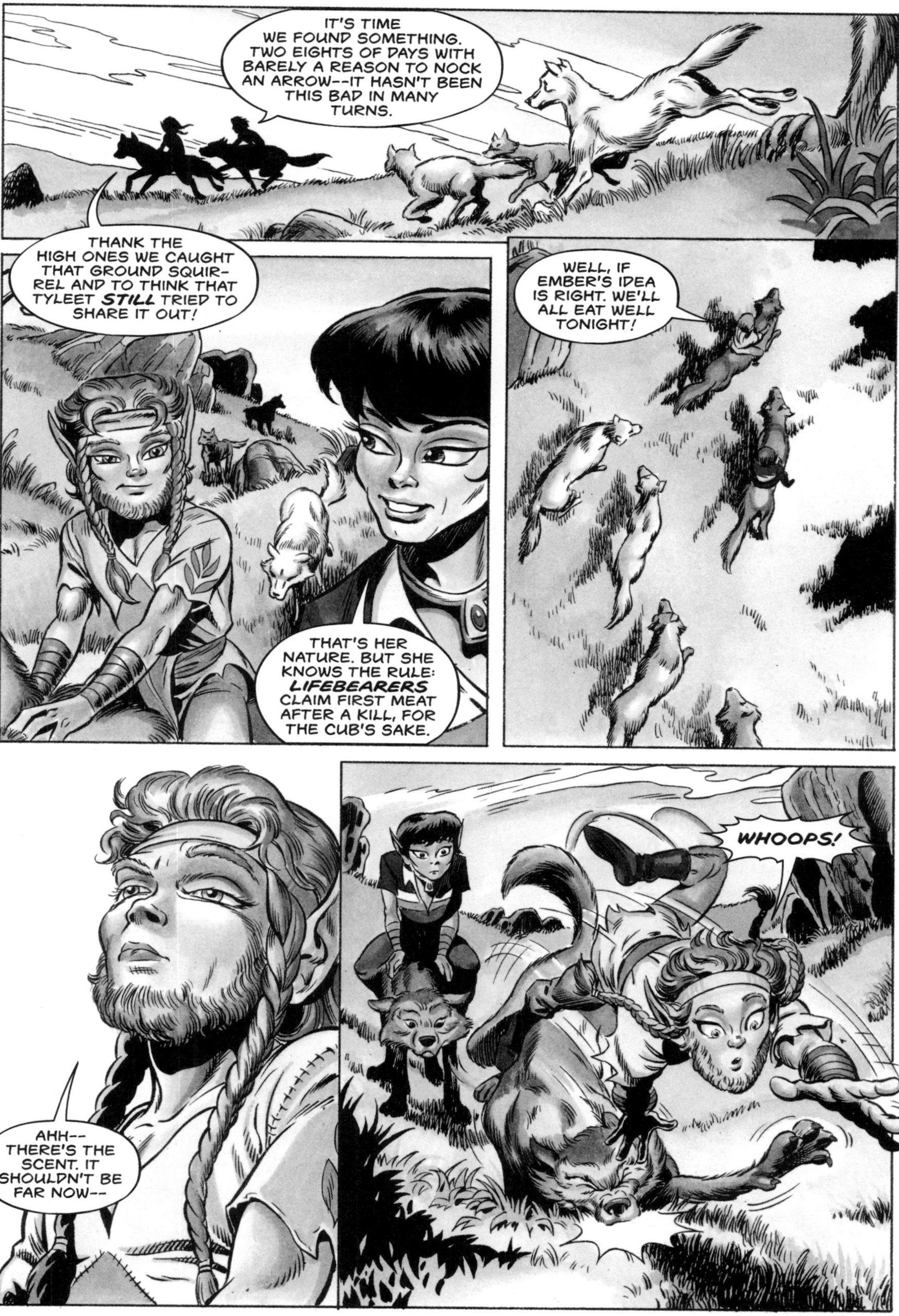
IT'S TIME WE FOUND SOMETHING. TWO EIGHTS OF DAYS WITH BARELY A REASON TO NOCK AN ARROW--IT HASN'T BEEN THIS BAD IN MANY TURNS.
THANK THE HIGH ONES WE CAUGHT THAT GROUND SQUIR-REL AND TO THINK THAT TYLEET STILL TRIED TO SHARE IT OUT!
THAT'S HER NATURE. BUT SHE KNOWS THE RULE: LIFEBEARERS CLAIM FIRST MEAT AFTER A KILL, FOR THE CUB'S SAKE.
WELL, IF EMBER'S IDEA IS RIGHT. WE'LL ALL EAT WELL TONIGHT!
AHH-- THERE'S THE SCENT. IT SHOULDN'T BE FAR NOW--
WHOOPS!

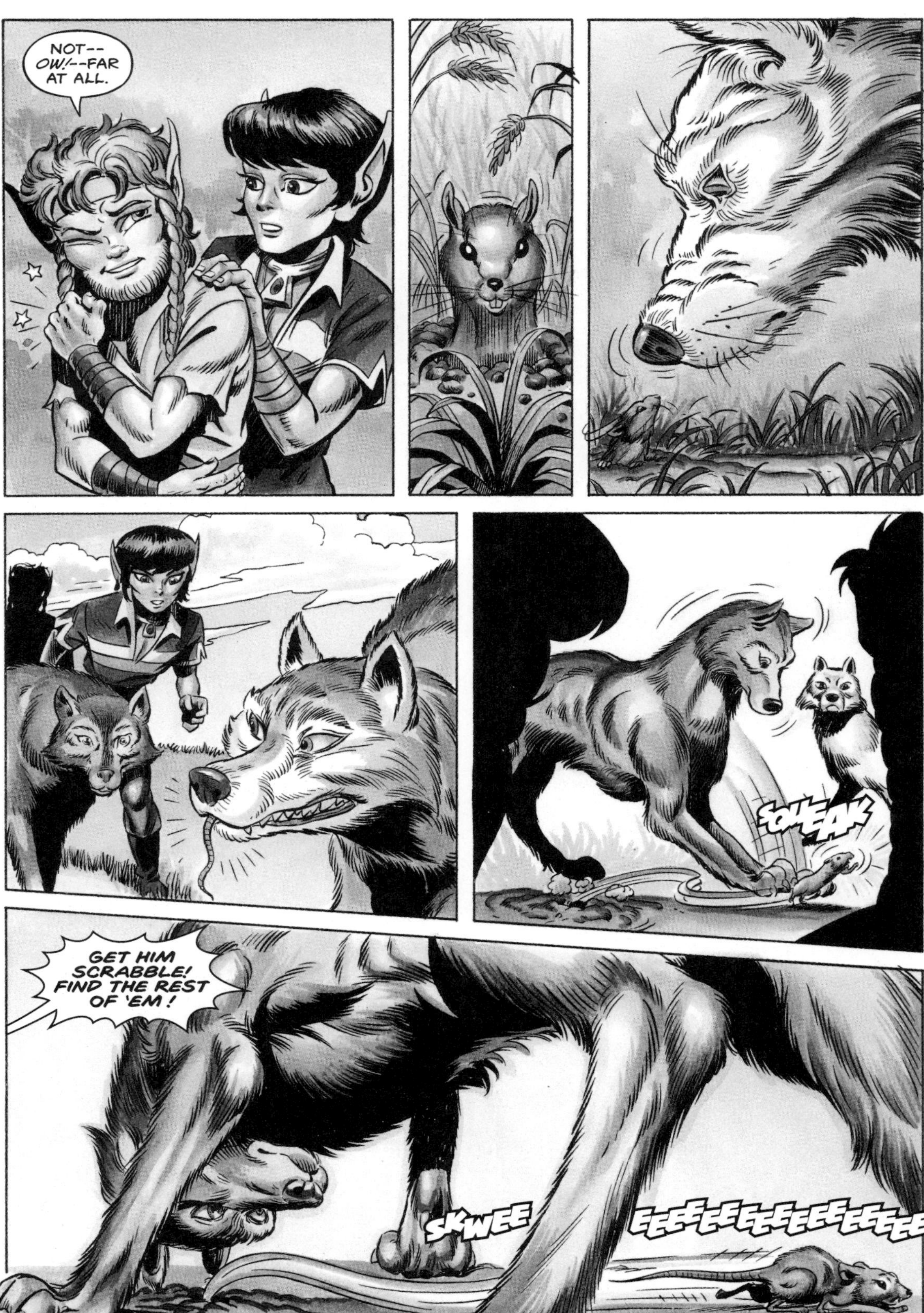
NOT-- OW!--FAR AT ALL.
SQUEAK
GET HIM SCRABBLE! FIND THE REST OF 'EM!
SKWEEEEEEEEEEEEEEEEEEEE

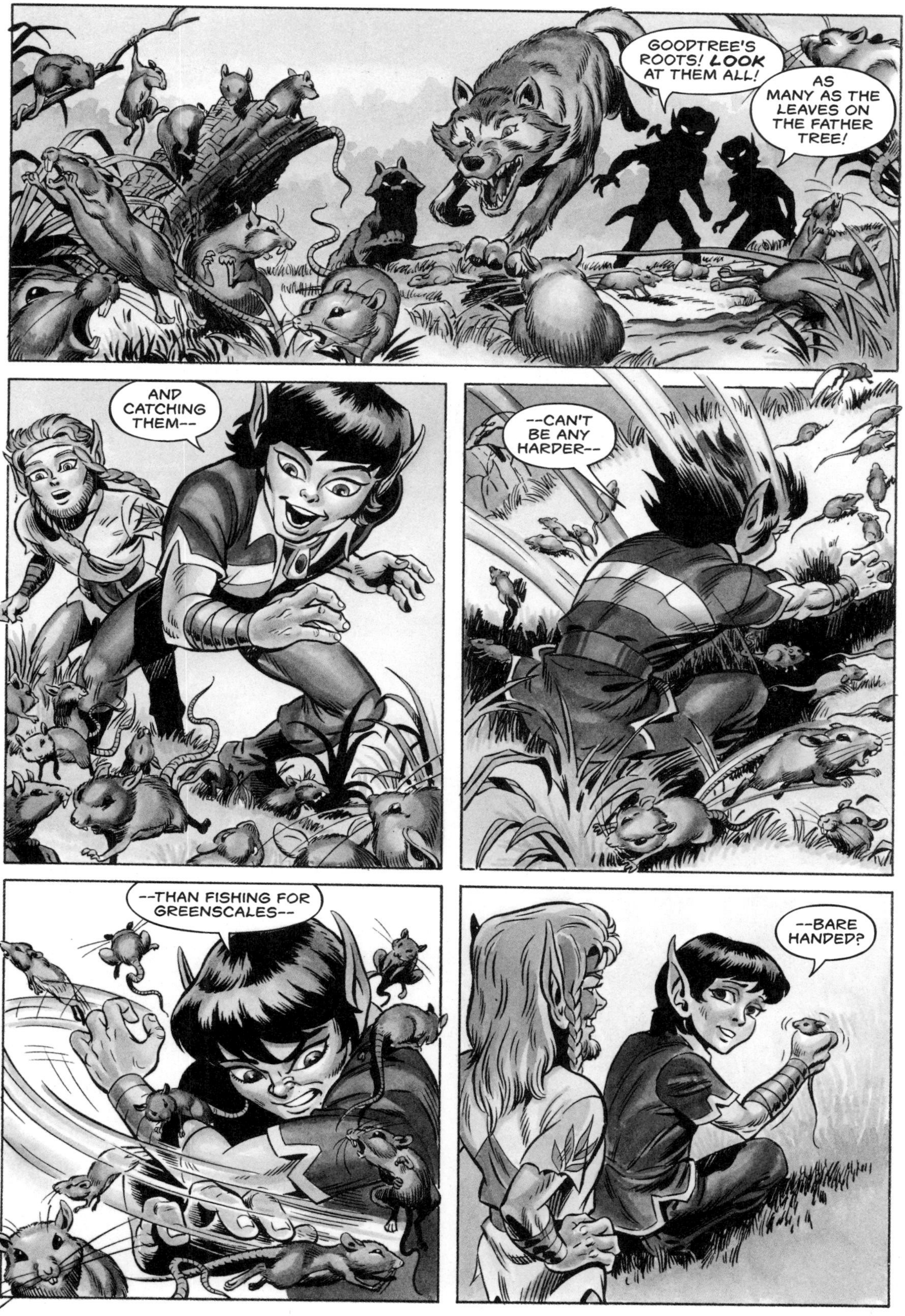
GOODTREE'S ROOTS! **LOOK** AT THEM ALL!
AS MANY AS THE LEAVES ON THE FATHER TREE!
AND CATCHING THEM--
--CAN'T BE ANY HARDER--
--THAN FISHING FOR GREENSCALES--
--BARE HANDED?

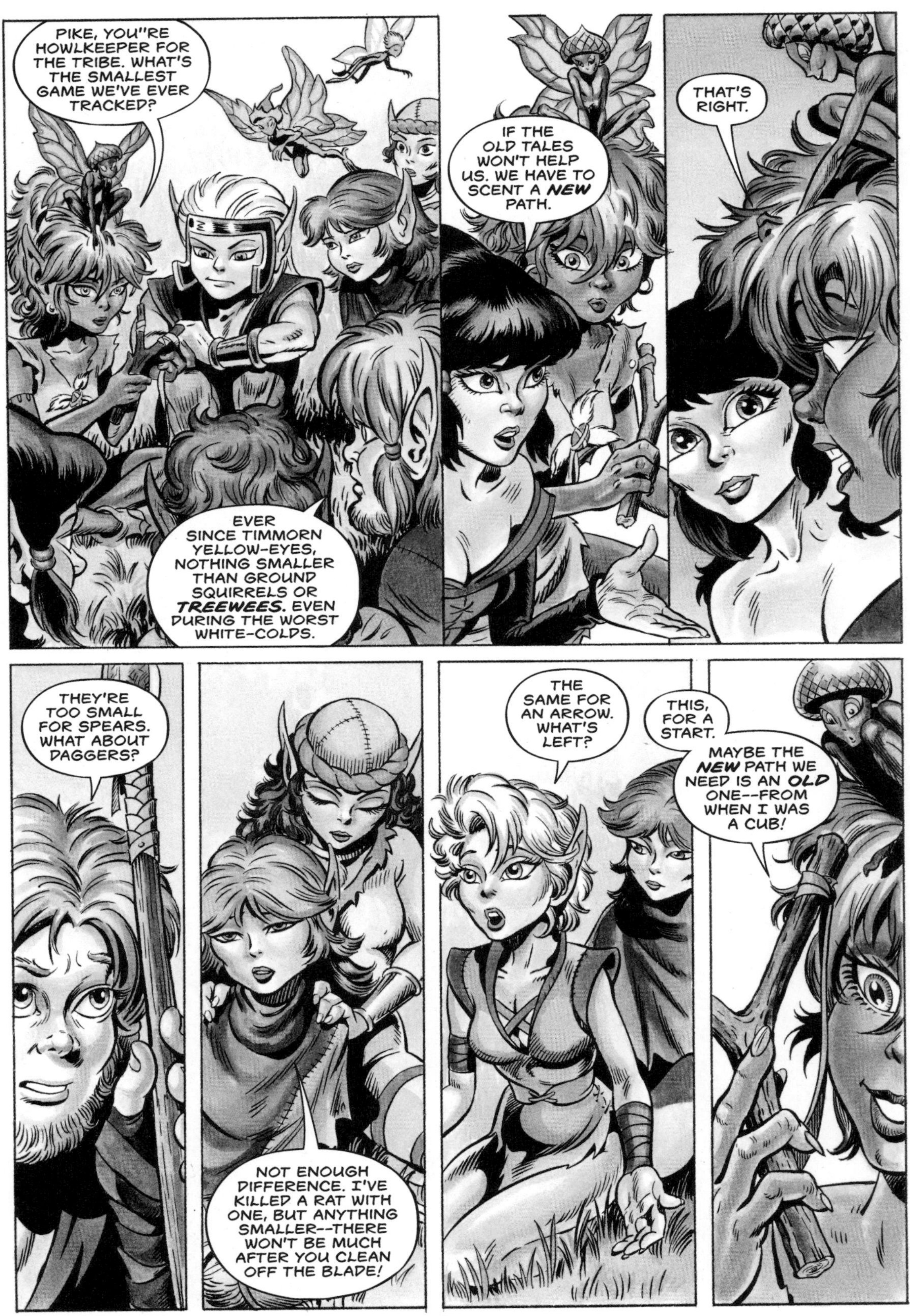
PIKE, YOU''RE HOWLKEEPER FOR THE TRIBE. WHAT'S THE SMALLEST GAME WE'VE EVER TRACKED?
EVER SINCE TIMMORN YELLOW-EYES, NOTHING SMALLER THAN GROUND SQUIRRELS OR TREEWEES. EVEN DURING THE WORST WHITE-COLDS.
IF THE OLD TALES WON'T HELP US. WE HAVE TO SCENT A NEW PATH.
THAT'S RIGHT.
THEY'RE TOO SMALL FOR SPEARS. WHAT ABOUT DAGGERS?
NOT ENOUGH DIFFERENCE. I'VE KILLED A RAT WITH ONE, BUT ANYTHING SMALLER--THERE WON'T BE MUCH AFTER YOU CLEAN OFF THE BLADE!
THE SAME FOR AN ARROW. WHAT'S LEFT?
THIS, FOR A START.
MAYBE THE NEW PATH WE NEED IS AN OLD ONE--FROM WHEN I WAS A CUB!

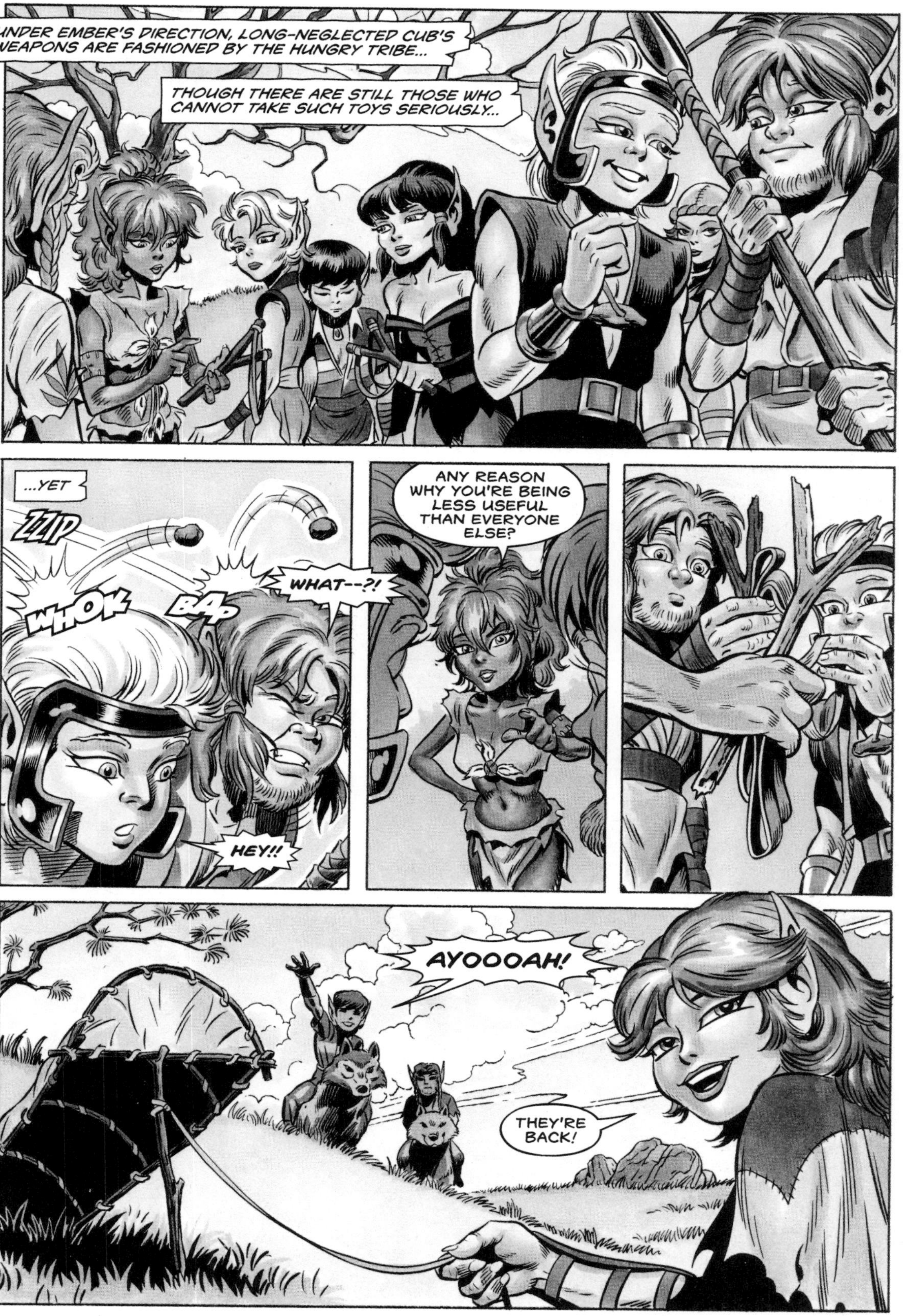
UNDER EMBER'S DIRECTION, LONG-NEGLECTED CUB'S WEAPONS ARE FASHIONED BY THE HUNGRY TRIBE...
THOUGH THERE ARE STILL THOSE WHO CANNOT TAKE SUCH TOYS SERIOUSLY...
...YET
ZZIP
WHOK
BAP
WHAT--?!
HEY!!
ANY REASON WHY YOU'RE BEING LESS USEFUL THAN EVERYONE ELSE?
AYOOOAH!
THEY'RE BACK!

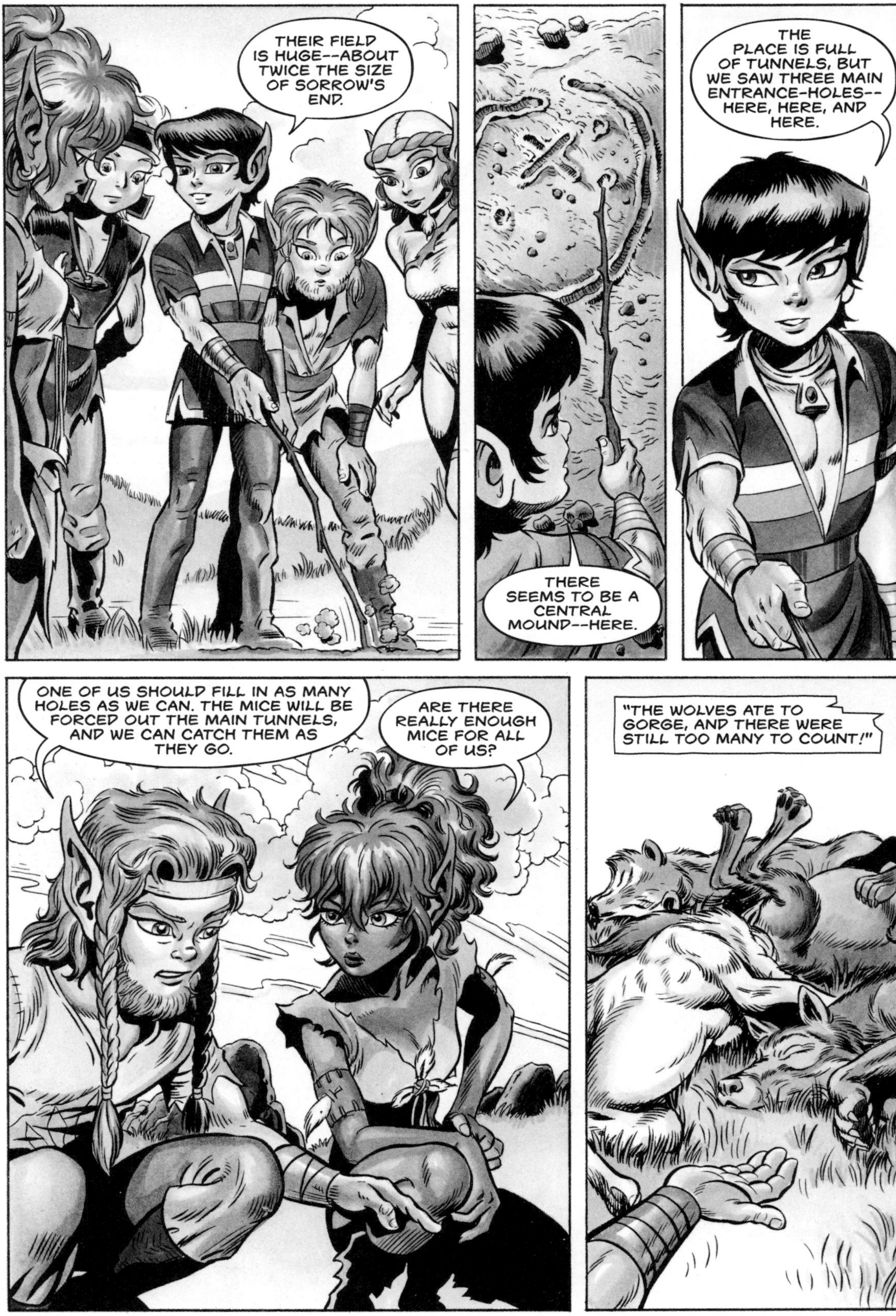
THEIR FIELD IS HUGE--ABOUT TWICE THE SIZE OF SORROW'S END.
THERE SEEMS TO BE A CENTRAL MOUND--HERE.
THE PLACE IS FULL OF TUNNELS, BUT WE SAW THREE MAIN ENTRANCE-HOLES--HERE, HERE, AND HERE.
ONE OF US SHOULD FILL IN AS MANY HOLES AS WE CAN. THE MICE WILL BE FORCED OUT THE MAIN TUNNELS, AND WE CAN CATCH THEM AS THEY GO.
ARE THERE REALLY ENOUGH MICE FOR ALL OF US?
"THE WOLVES ATE TO GORGE, AND THERE WERE STILL TOO MANY TO COUNT!"

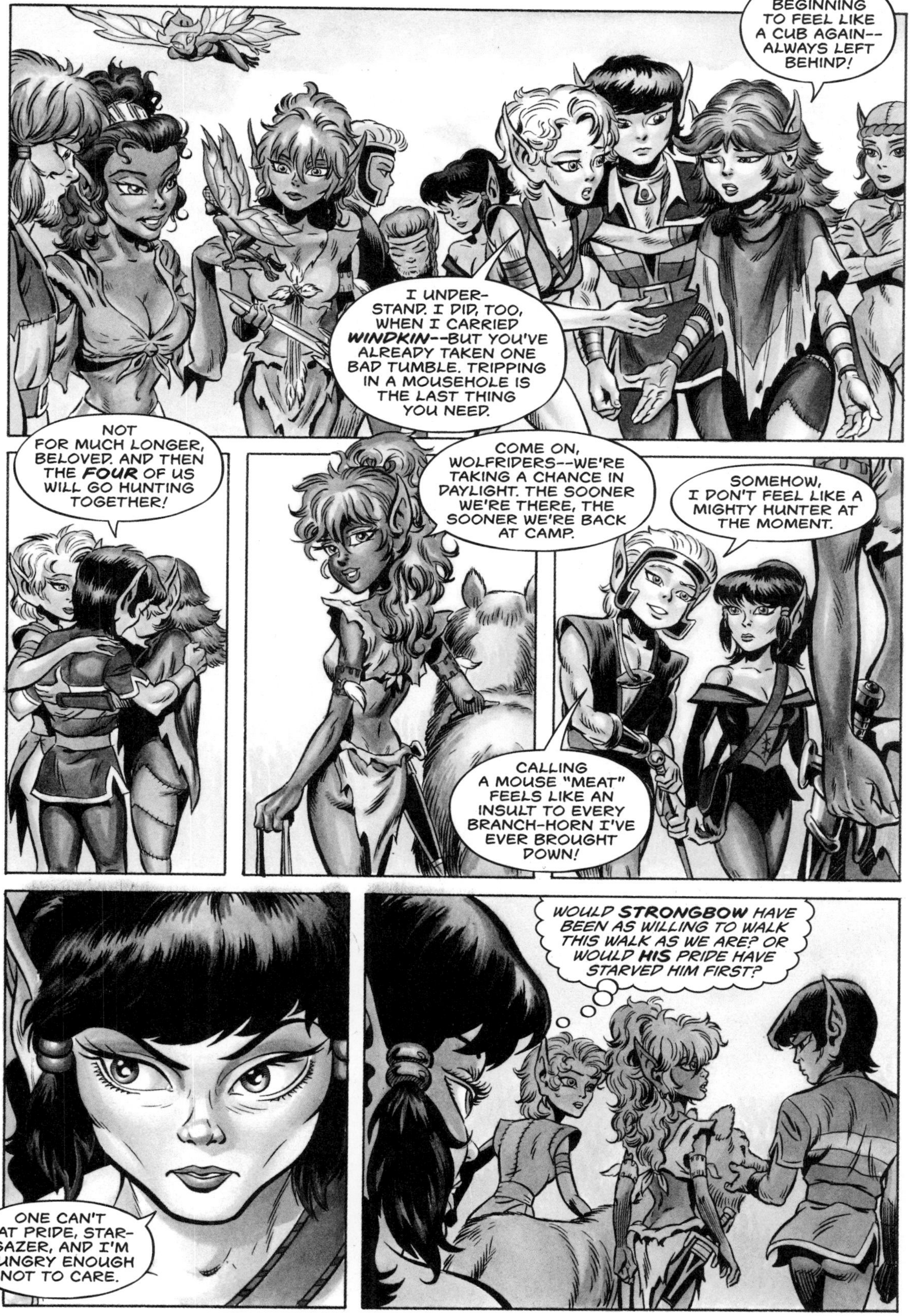

I'M BEGINNING TO FEEL LIKE A CUB AGAIN-- ALWAYS LEFT BEHIND!
I UNDER-STAND. I DID, TOO, WHEN I CARRIED WINDKIN--BUT YOU'VE ALREADY TAKEN ONE BAD TUMBLE. TRIPPING IN A MOUSEHOLE IS THE LAST THING YOU NEED.
NOT FOR MUCH LONGER, BELOVED. AND THEN THE FOUR OF US WILL GO HUNTING TOGETHER!
COME ON, WOLFRIDERS--WE'RE TAKING A CHANCE IN DAYLIGHT. THE SOONER WE'RE THERE, THE SOONER WE'RE BACK AT CAMP.
SOMEHOW, I DON'T FEEL LIKE A MIGHTY HUNTER AT THE MOMENT.
CALLING A MOUSE "MEAT" FEELS LIKE AN INSULT TO EVERY BRANCH-HORN I'VE EVER BROUGHT DOWN!
ONE CAN'T EAT PRIDE, STAR-GAZER, AND I'M HUNGRY ENOUGH NOT TO CARE.
WOULD STRONGBOW HAVE BEEN AS WILLING TO WALK THIS WALK AS WE ARE? OR WOULD HIS PRIDE HAVE STARVED HIM FIRST?

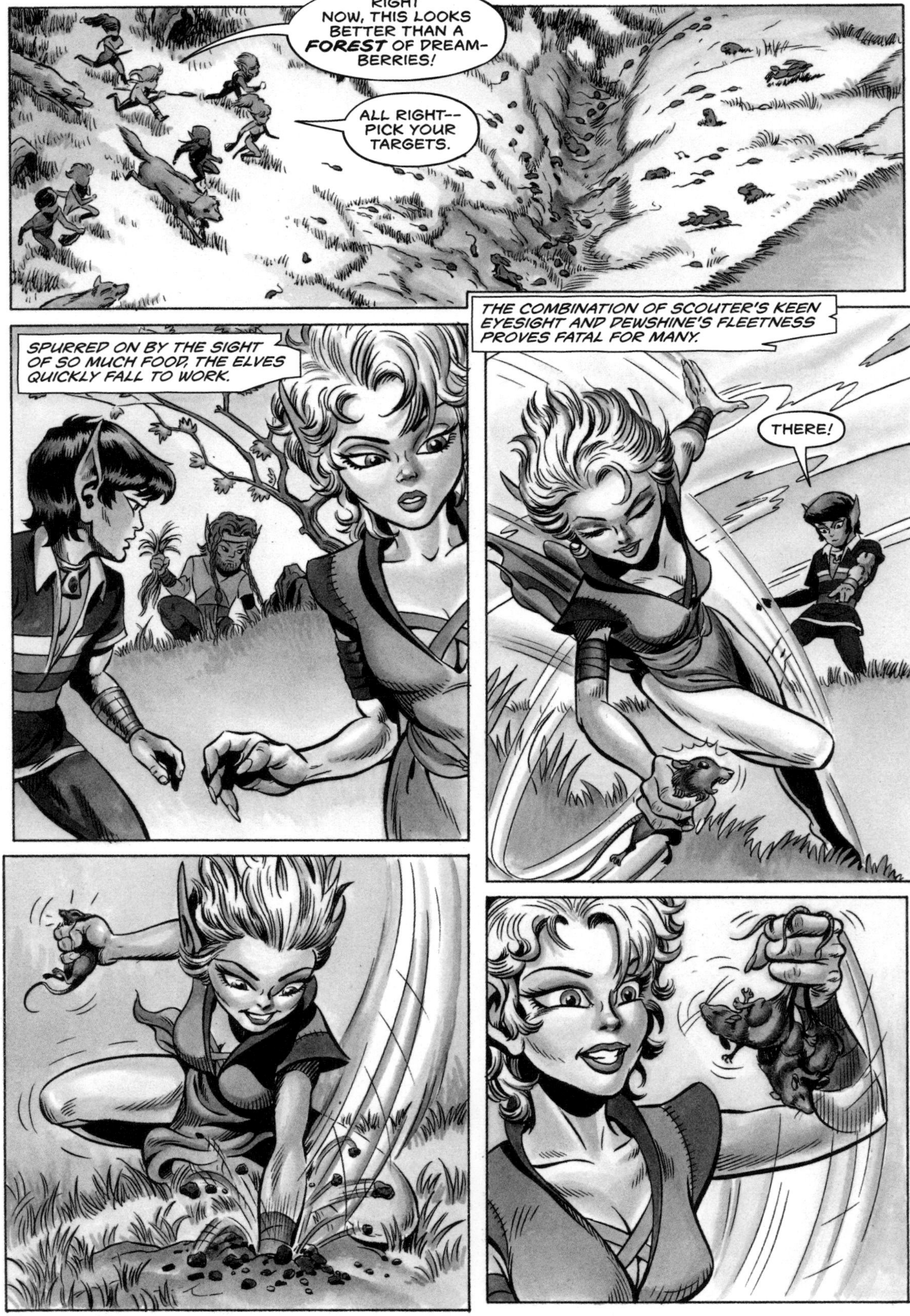
RIGHT NOW, THIS LOOKS BETTER THAN A FOREST OF DREAM-BERRIES!
ALL RIGHT-- PICK YOUR TARGETS.
SPURRED ON BY THE SIGHT OF SO MUCH FOOD, THE ELVES QUICKLY FALL TO WORK.
THE COMBINATION OF SCOUTER'S KEEN EYESIGHT AND DEWSHINE'S FLEETNESS PROVES FATAL FOR MANY.
THERE!

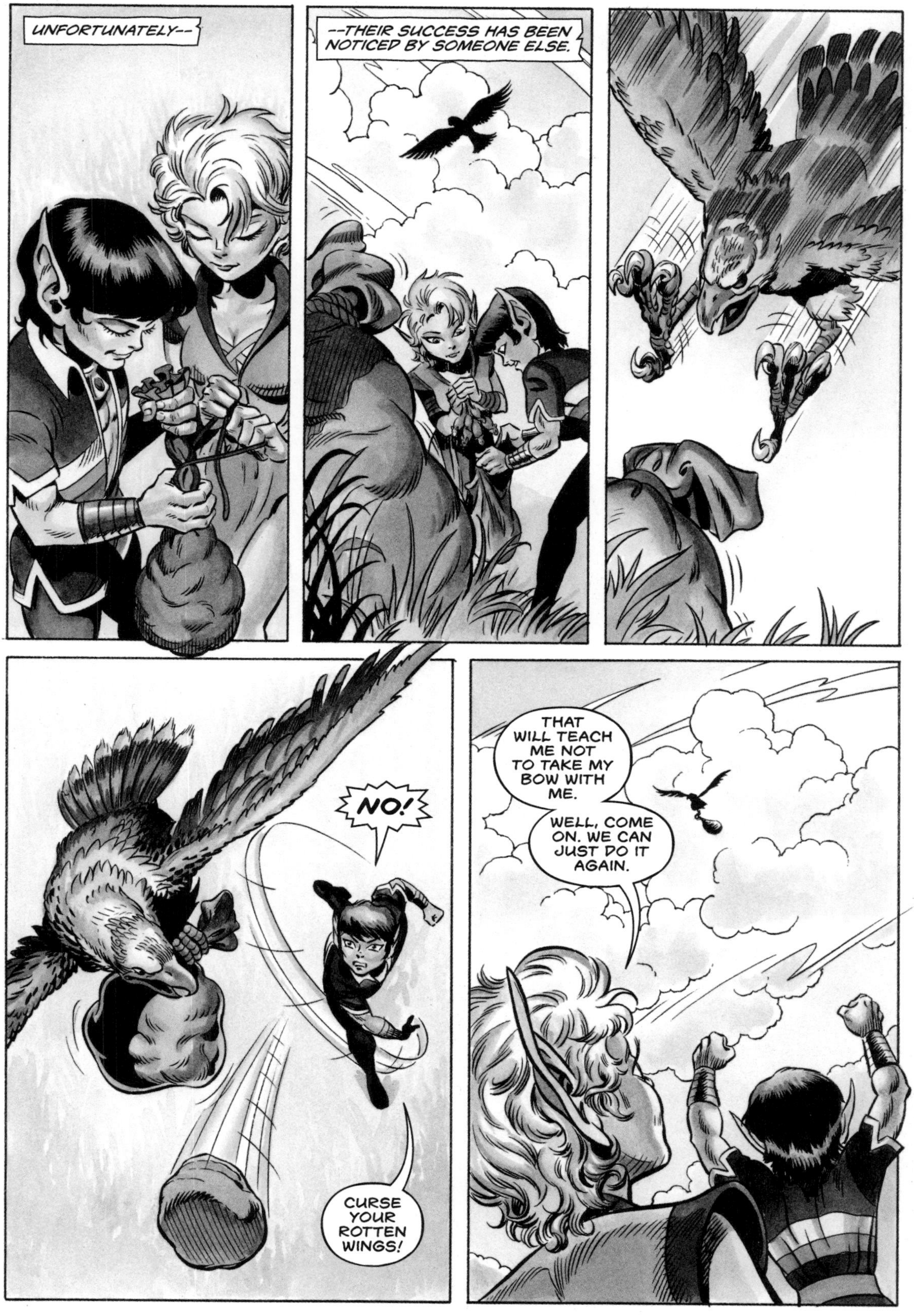
UNFORTUNATELY--
--THEIR SUCCESS HAS BEEN NOTICED BY SOMEONE ELSE.
NO!
CURSE YOUR ROTTEN WINGS!
THAT WILL TEACH ME NOT TO TAKE MY BOW WITH ME.
WELL, COME ON. WE CAN JUST DO IT AGAIN.

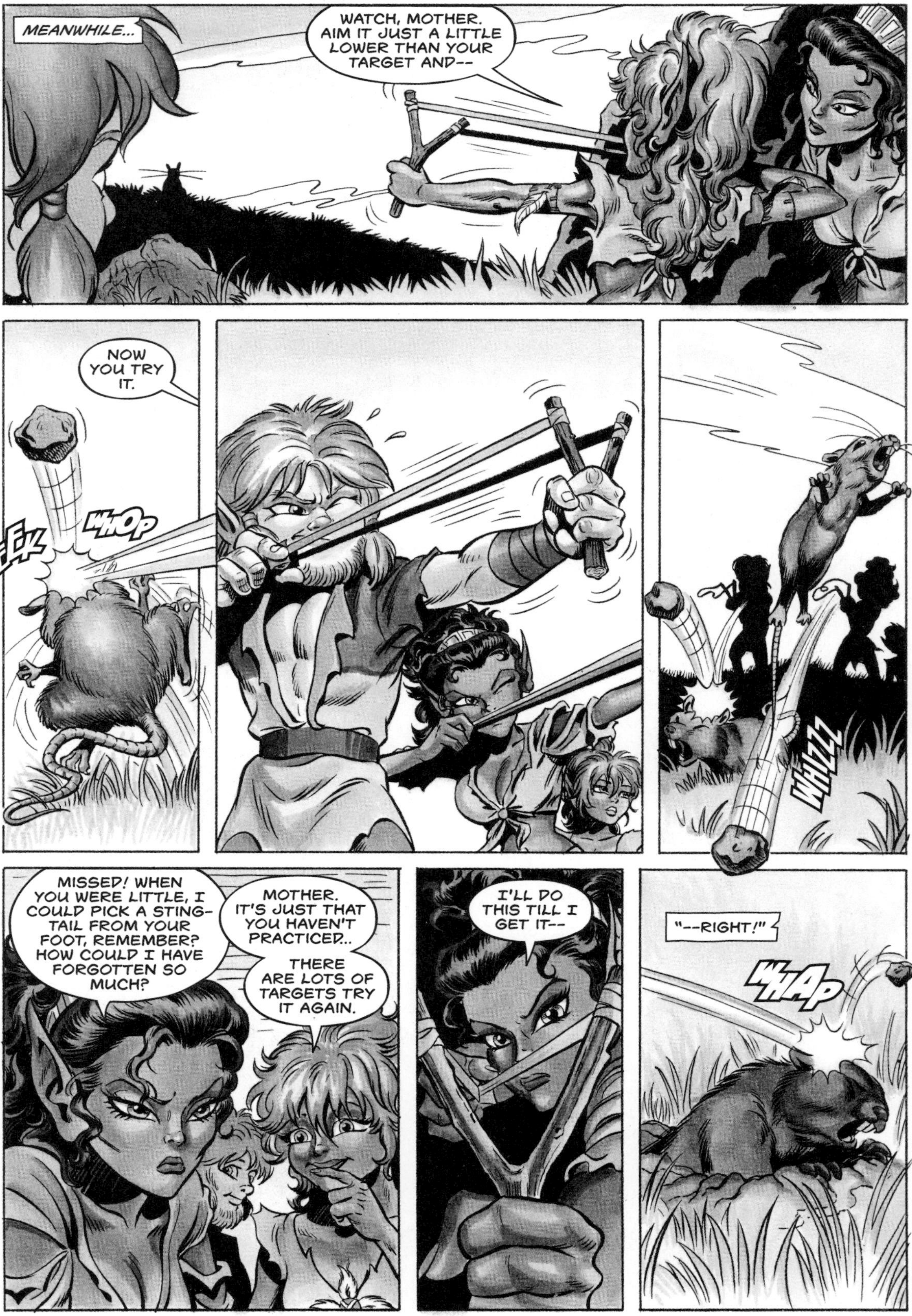
MEANWHILE...
WATCH, MOTHER. AIM IT JUST A LITTLE LOWER THAN YOUR TARGET AND--
NOW YOU TRY IT.
EEK
WHOP
WHIZZZ
MISSED! WHEN YOU WERE LITTLE, I COULD PICK A STING-TAIL FROM YOUR FOOT, REMEMBER? HOW COULD I HAVE FORGOTTEN SO MUCH?
MOTHER. IT'S JUST THAT YOU HAVEN'T PRACTICED...
THERE ARE LOTS OF TARGETS TRY IT AGAIN.
I'LL DO THIS TILL I GET IT--
"--RIGHT!"
WHAP

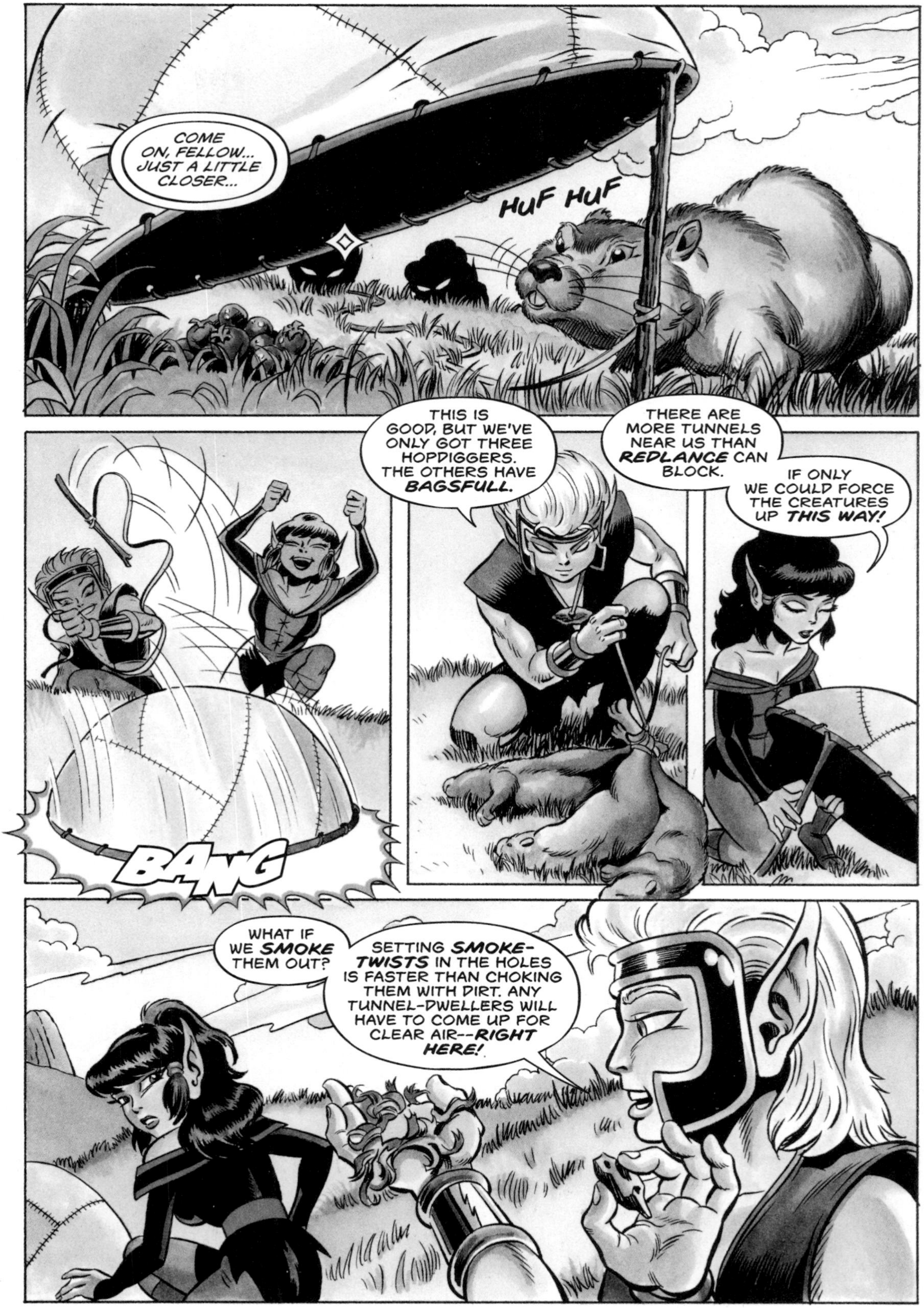
COME ON, FELLOW... JUST A LITTLE CLOSER...
HUF HUF
BANG
THIS IS GOOD, BUT WE'VE ONLY GOT THREE HOPDIGGERS. THE OTHERS HAVE **BAGSFULL.**
THERE ARE MORE TUNNELS NEAR US THAN **REDLANCE** CAN BLOCK.
IF ONLY WE COULD FORCE THE CREATURES UP **THIS WAY!**
WHAT IF WE **SMOKE** THEM OUT?
SETTING **SMOKE-TWISTS** IN THE HOLES IS FASTER THAN CHOKING THEM WITH DIRT. ANY TUNNEL-DWELLERS WILL HAVE TO COME UP FOR CLEAR AIR--**RIGHT HERE!**

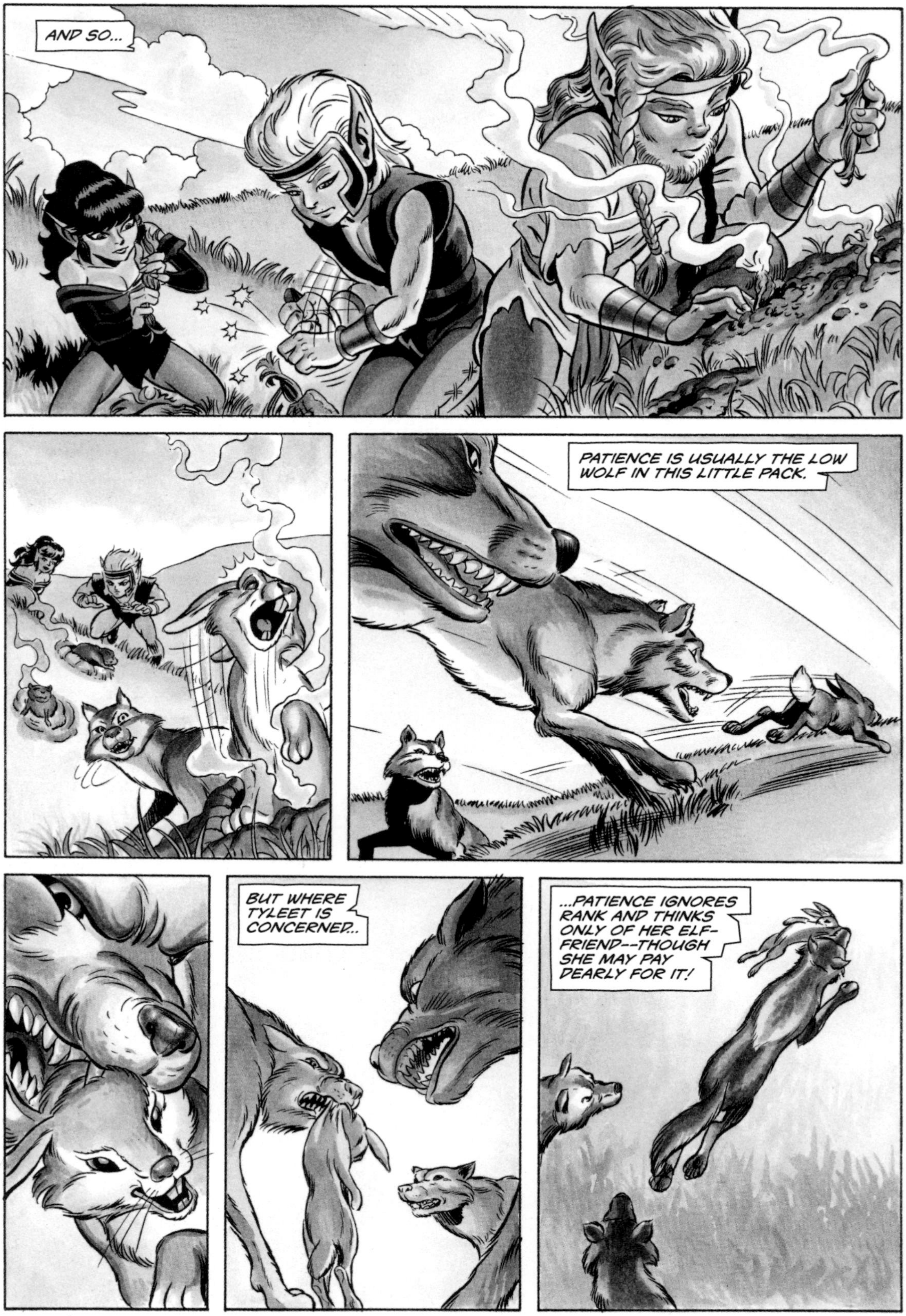
AND SO...
PATIENCE IS USUALLY THE LOW WOLF IN THIS LITTLE PACK.
BUT WHERE TYLEET IS CONCERNED...
...PATIENCE IGNORES RANK AND THINKS ONLY OF HER ELF-FRIEND--THOUGH SHE MAY PAY DEARLY FOR IT!

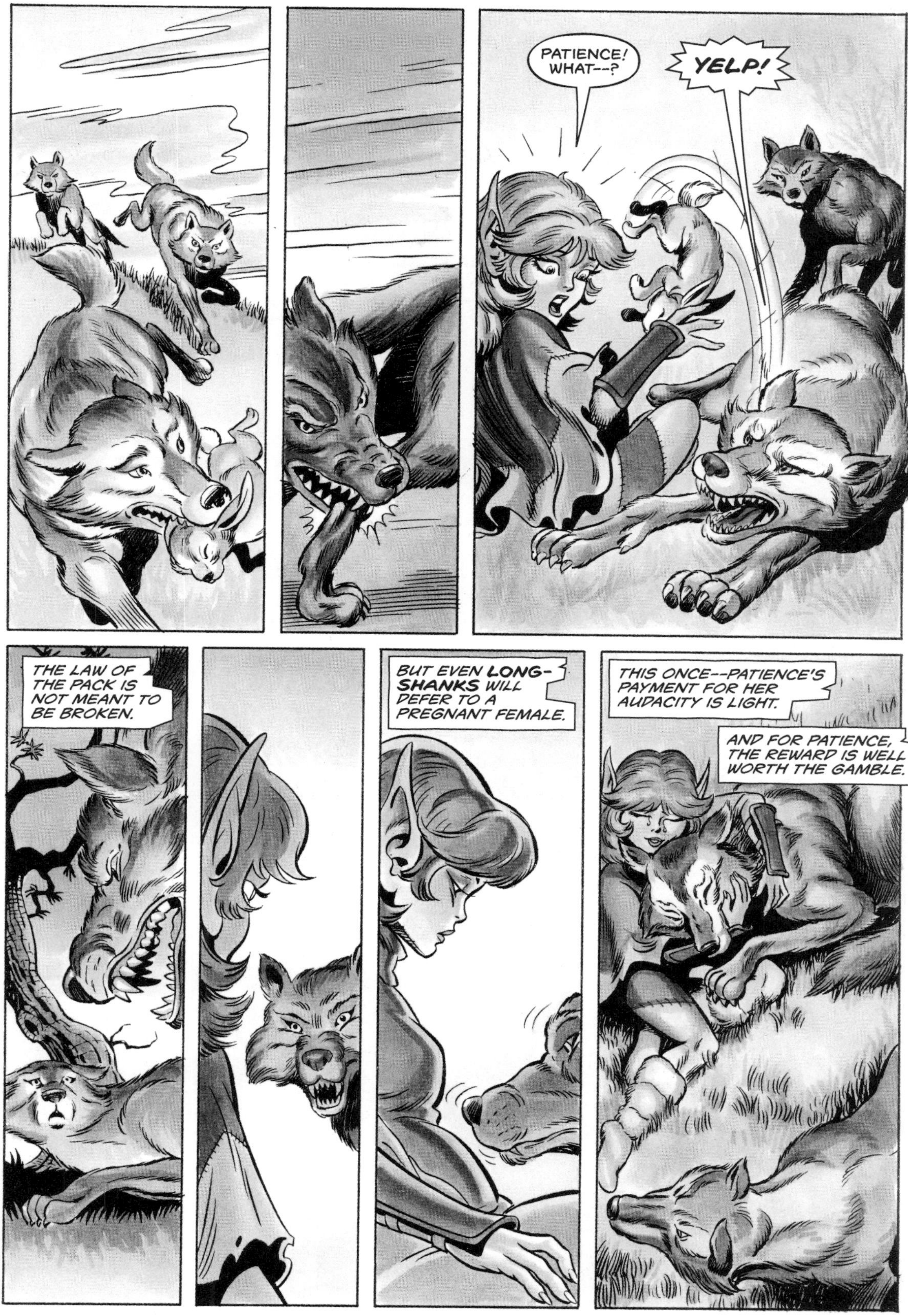
PATIENCE! WHAT--?
YELP!
THE LAW OF THE PACK IS NOT MEANT TO BE BROKEN.
BUT EVEN LONG-SHANKS WILL DEFER TO A PREGNANT FEMALE.
THIS ONCE--PATIENCE'S PAYMENT FOR HER AUDACITY IS LIGHT.
AND FOR PATIENCE, THE REWARD IS WELL WORTH THE GAMBLE.

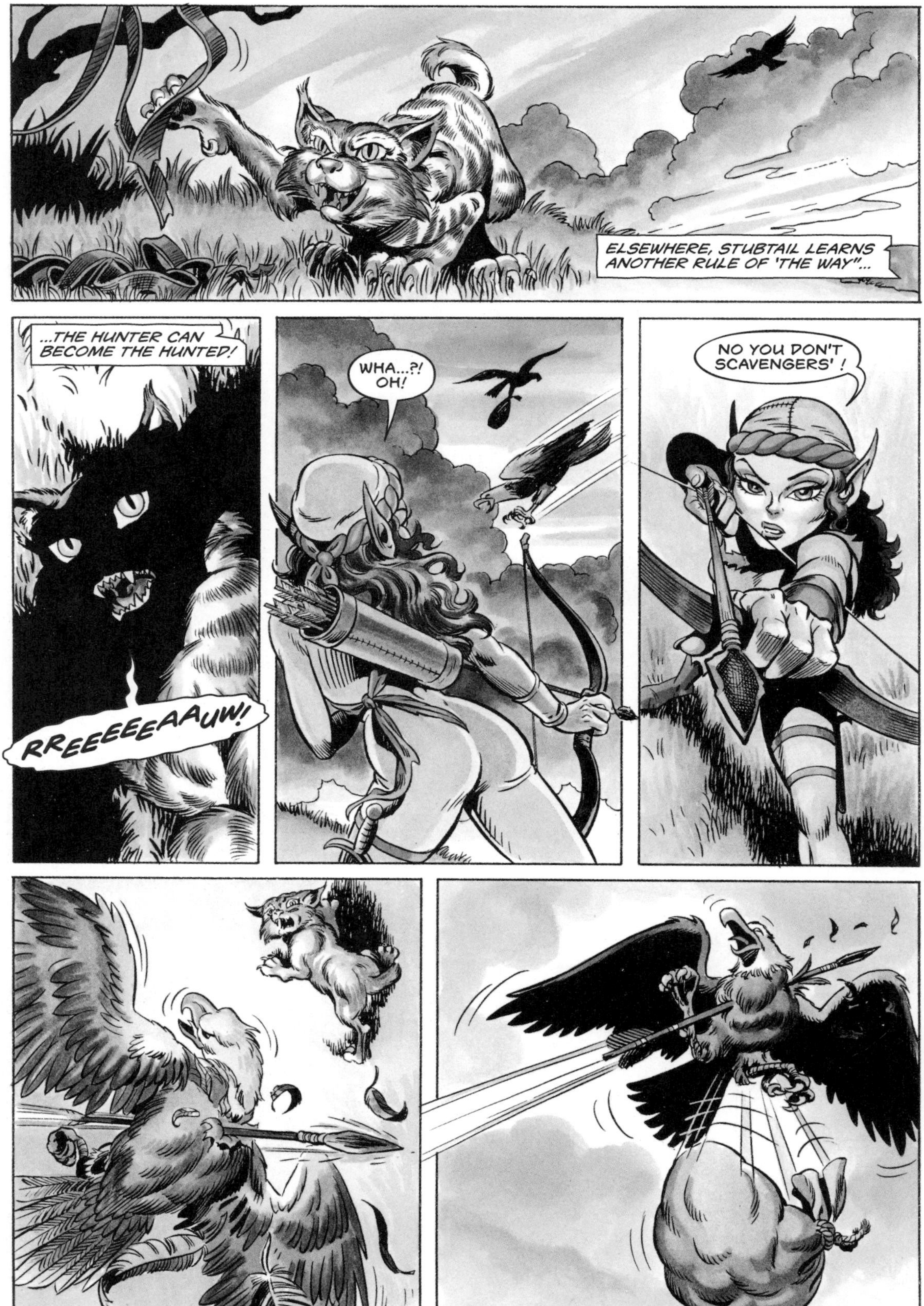
ELSEWHERE, STUBTAIL LEARNS ANOTHER RULE OF 'THE WAY"...
...THE HUNTER CAN BECOME THE HUNTED!
RREEEEEEAAUW!
WHA...?! OH!
NO YOU DON'T SCAVENGERS' !

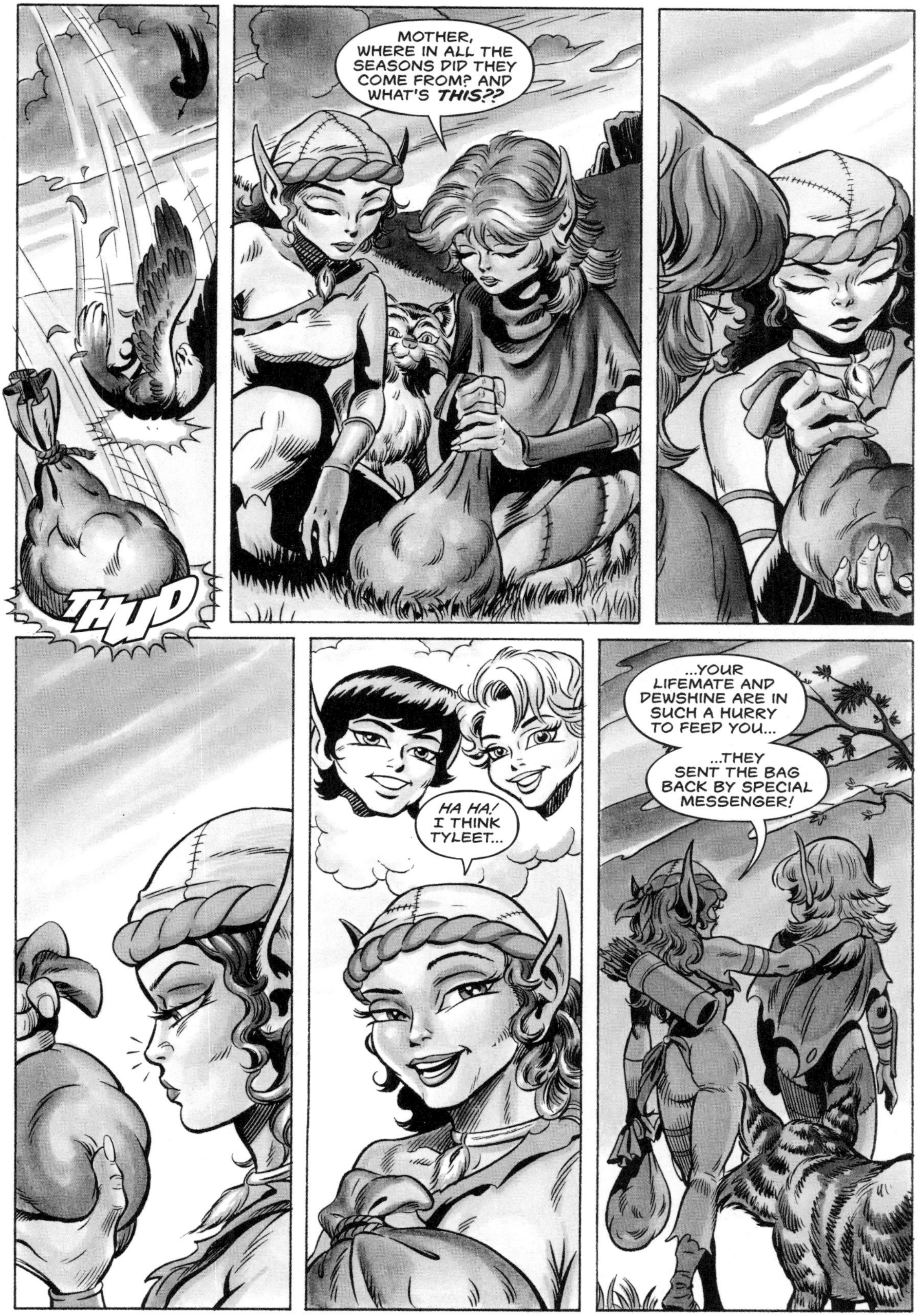

MOTHER, WHERE IN ALL THE SEASONS DID THEY COME FROM? AND WHAT'S *THIS??*
THUD
HA HA! I THINK TYLEET...
...YOUR LIFEMATE AND DEWSHINE ARE IN SUCH A HURRY TO FEED YOU...
...THEY SENT THE BAG BACK BY SPECIAL MESSENGER!

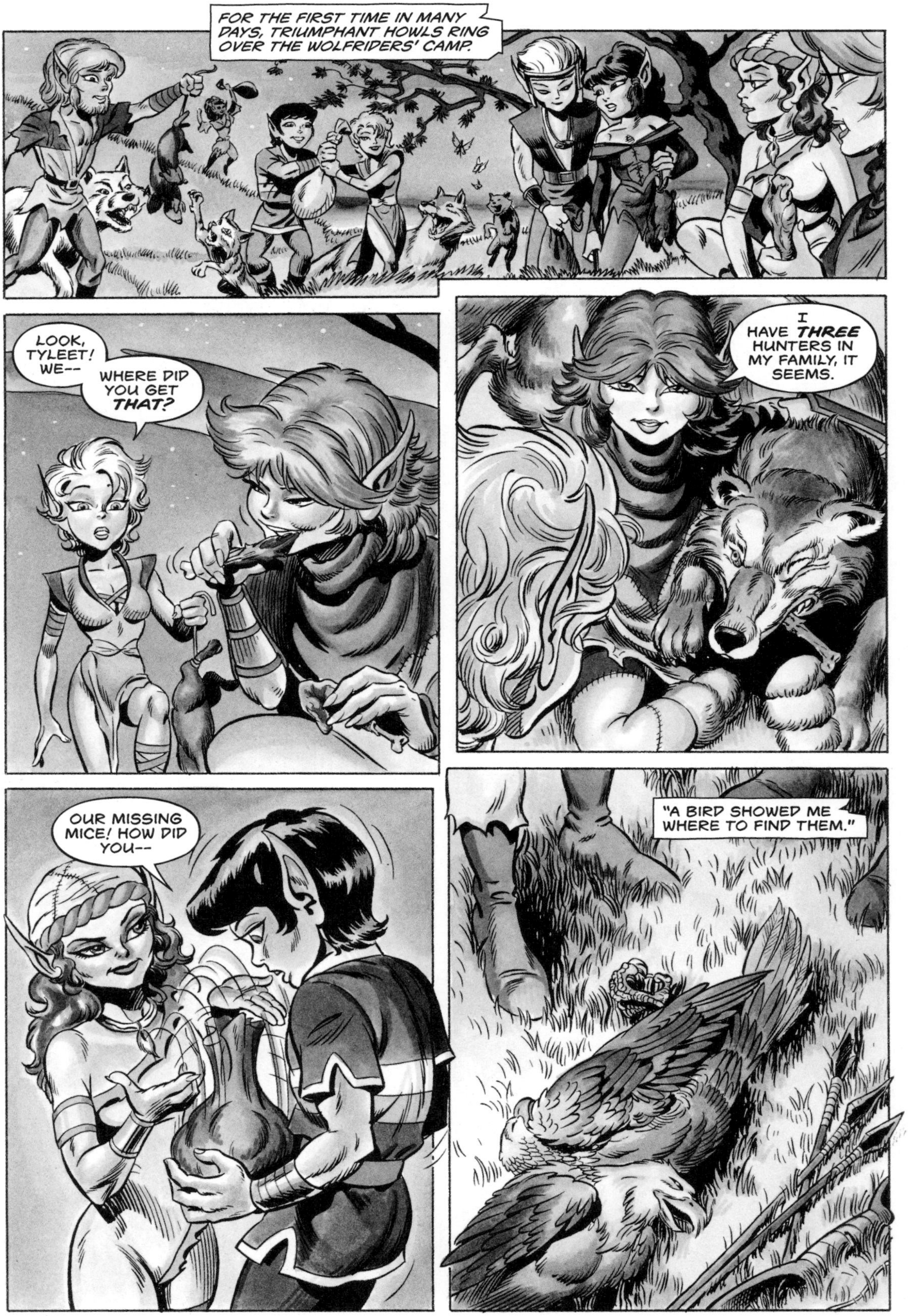
FOR THE FIRST TIME IN MANY DAYS, TRIUMPHANT HOWLS RING OVER THE WOLFRIDERS' CAMP.
LOOK, TYLEET! WE--
WHERE DID YOU GET THAT?
I HAVE THREE HUNTERS IN MY FAMILY, IT SEEMS.
OUR MISSING MICE! HOW DID YOU--
"A BIRD SHOWED ME WHERE TO FIND THEM."

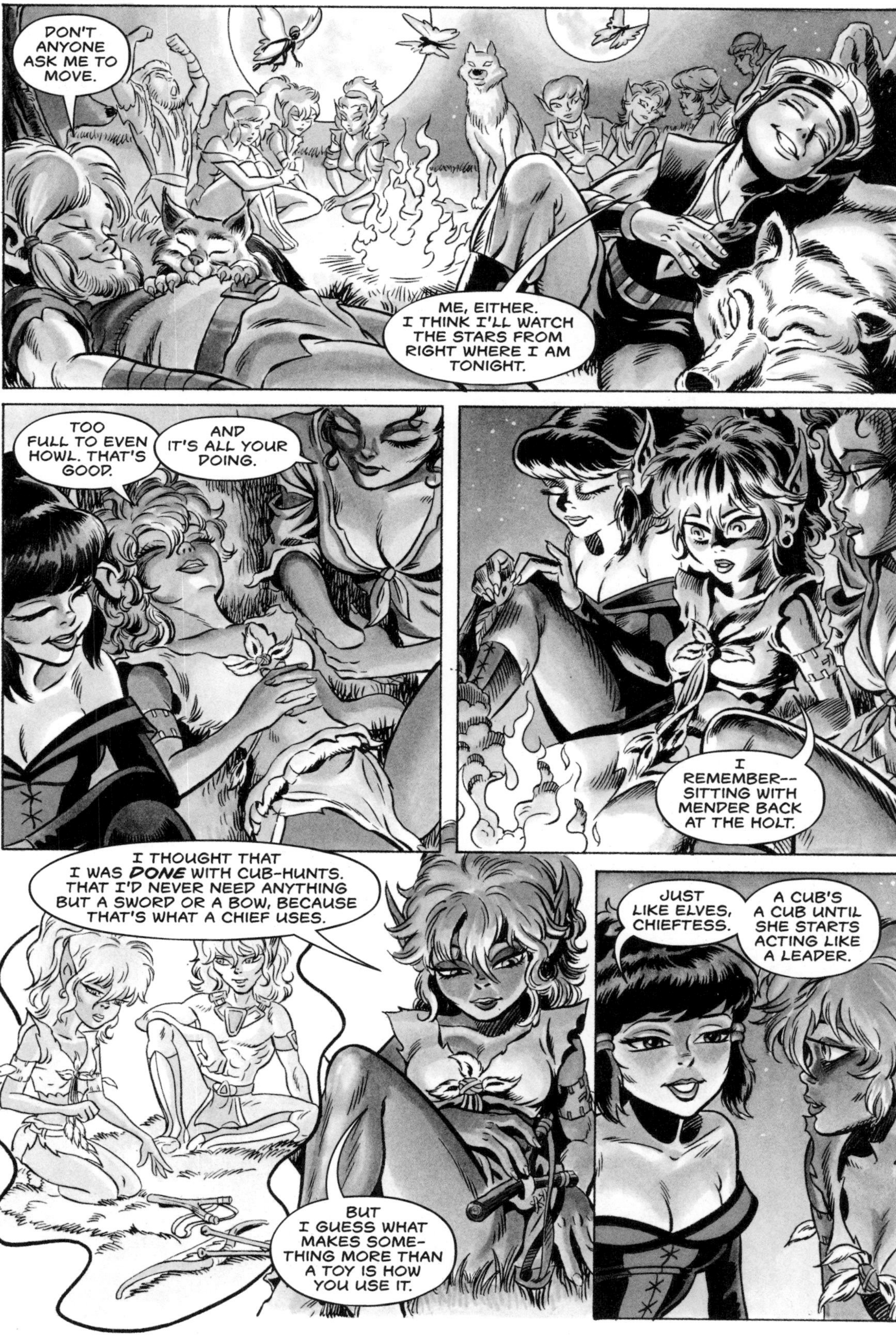
DON'T ANYONE ASK ME TO MOVE.
ME, EITHER. I THINK I'LL WATCH THE STARS FROM RIGHT WHERE I AM TONIGHT.
TOO FULL TO EVEN HOWL. THAT'S GOOD.
AND IT'S ALL YOUR DOING.
I REMEMBER-- SITTING WITH MENDER BACK AT THE HOLT.
I THOUGHT THAT I WAS **DONE** WITH CUB-HUNTS. THAT I'D NEVER NEED ANYTHING BUT A SWORD OR A BOW, BECAUSE THAT'S WHAT A CHIEF USES.
BUT I GUESS WHAT MAKES SOME-THING MORE THAN A TOY IS HOW YOU USE IT.
JUST LIKE ELVES, CHIEFTESS.
A CUB'S A CUB UNTIL SHE STARTS ACTING LIKE A LEADER.

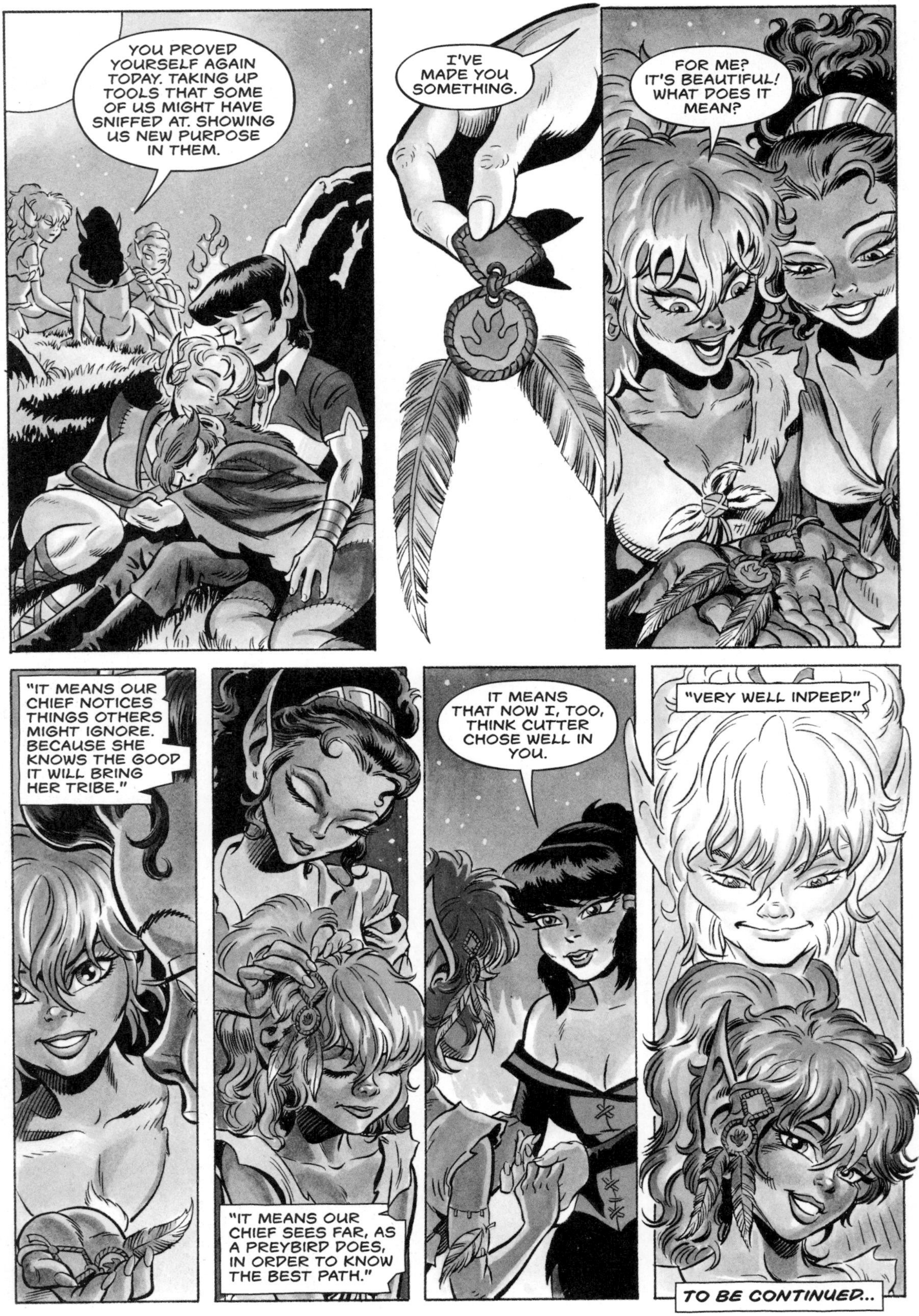
YOU PROVED YOURSELF AGAIN TODAY. TAKING UP TOOLS THAT SOME OF US MIGHT HAVE SNIFFED AT. SHOWING US NEW PURPOSE IN THEM.
I'VE MADE YOU SOMETHING.
FOR ME? IT'S BEAUTIFUL! WHAT DOES IT MEAN?
"IT MEANS OUR CHIEF NOTICES THINGS OTHERS MIGHT IGNORE. BECAUSE SHE KNOWS THE GOOD IT WILL BRING HER TRIBE."
"IT MEANS OUR CHIEF SEES FAR, AS A PREYBIRD DOES, IN ORDER TO KNOW THE BEST PATH."
IT MEANS THAT NOW I, TOO, THINK CUTTER CHOSE WELL IN YOU.
"VERY WELL INDEED."
TO BE CONTINUED...

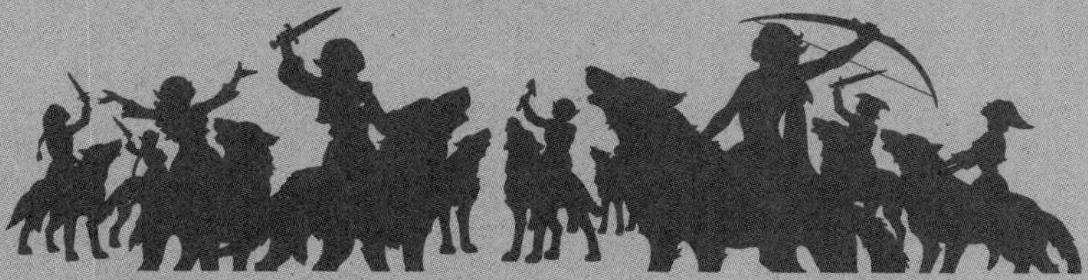

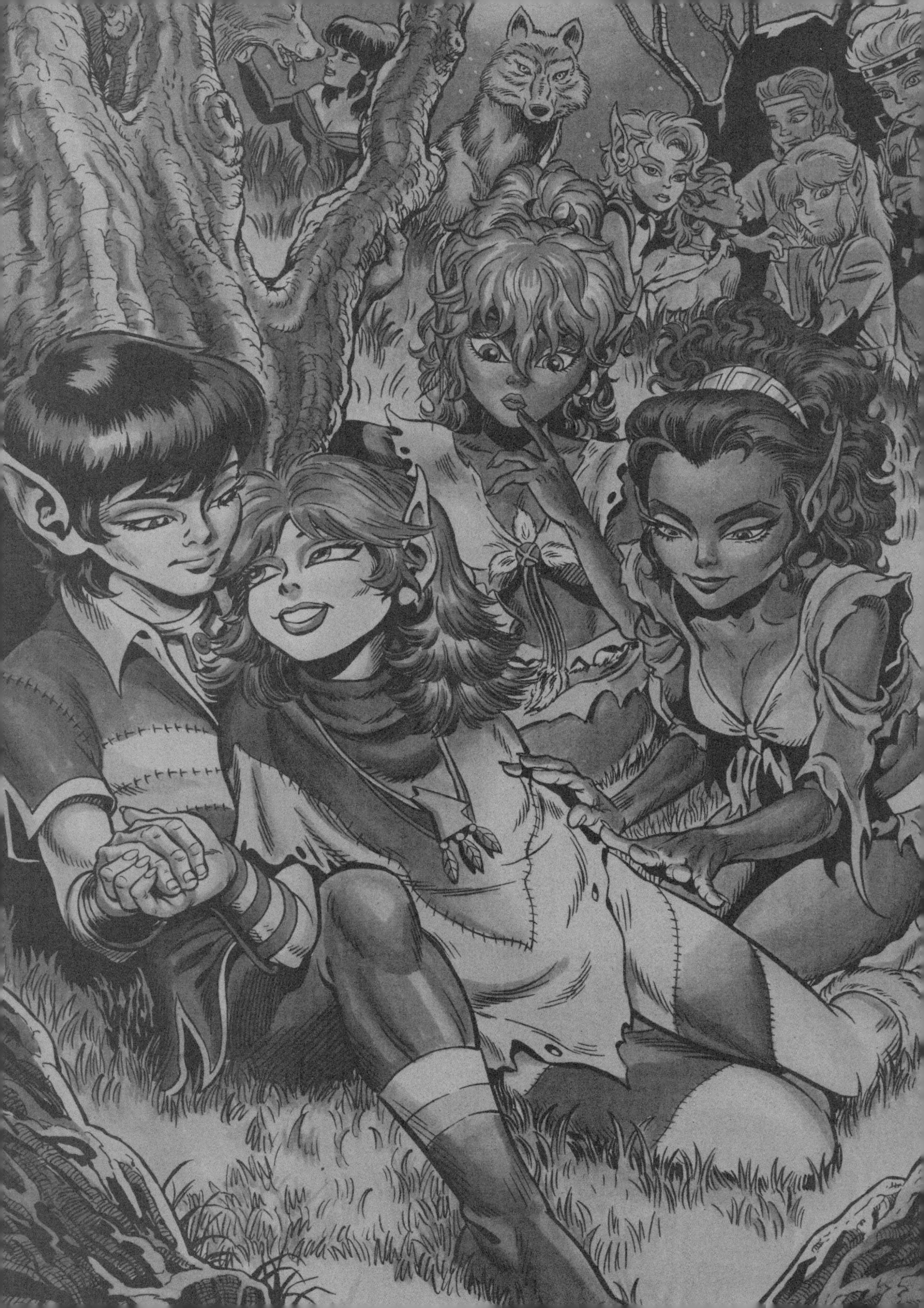

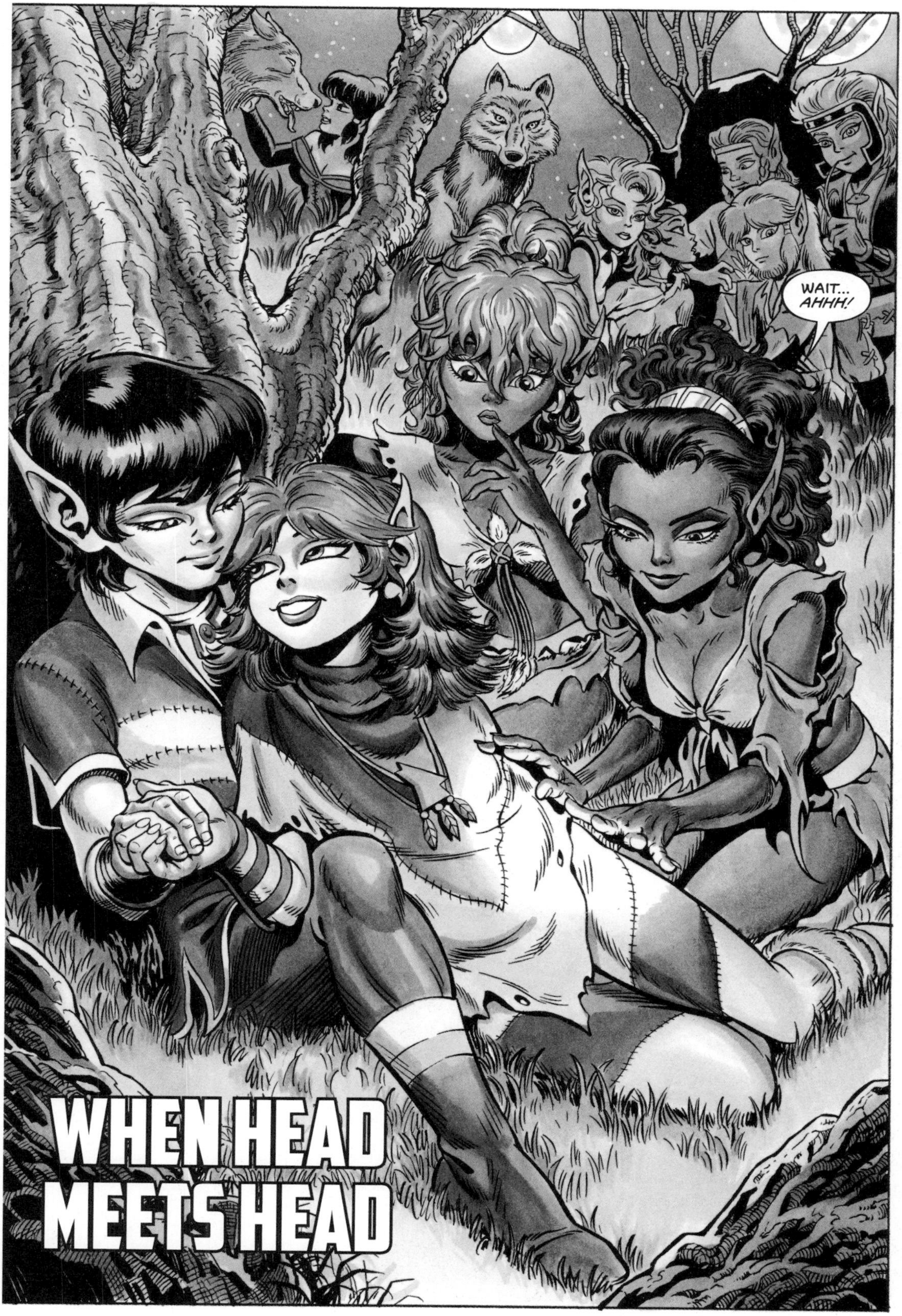
WAIT... AHHH!
WHEN HEAD MEETS HEAD

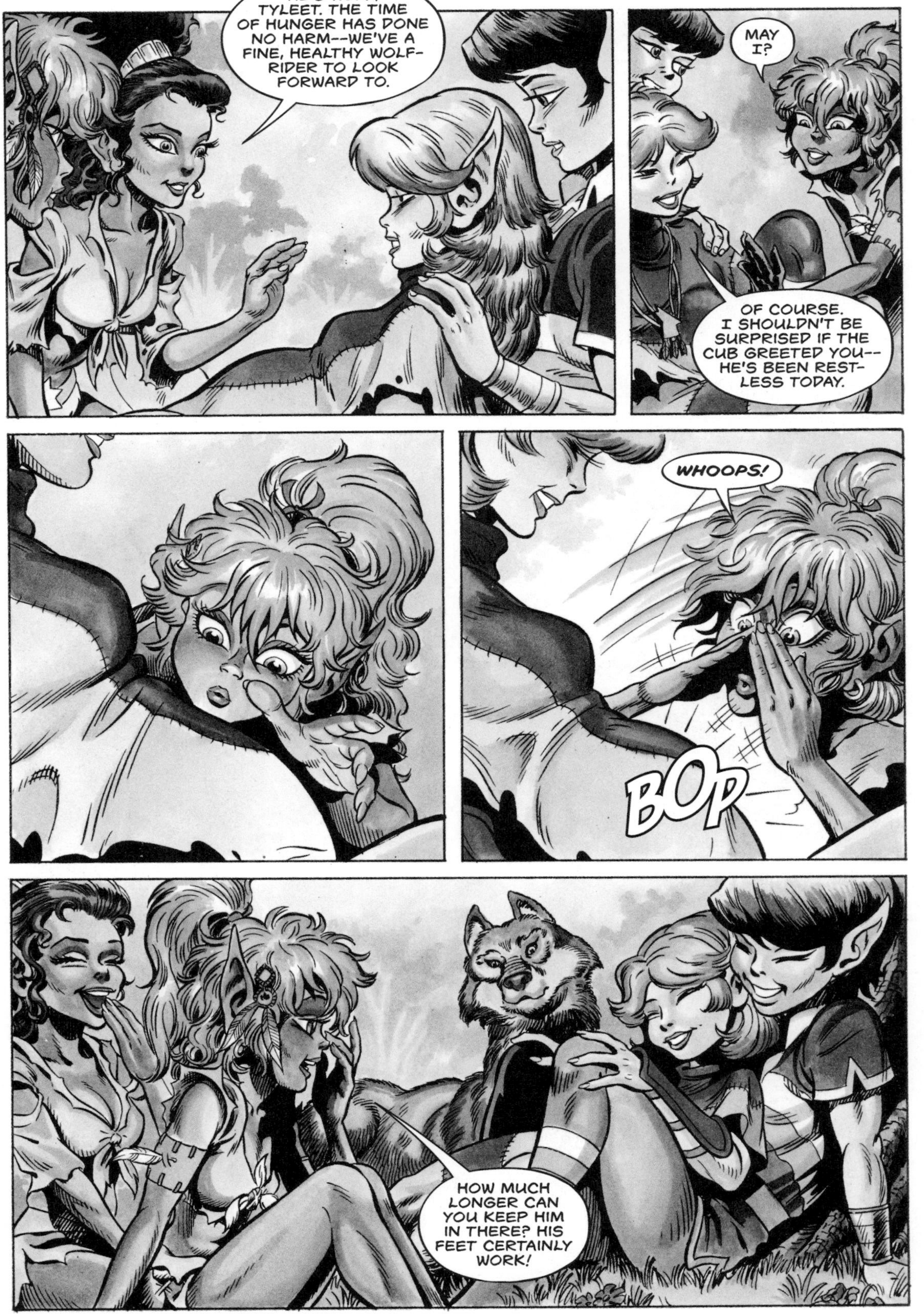
HE'S WELL, TYLEET. THE TIME OF HUNGER HAS DONE NO HARM--WE'VE A FINE, HEALTHY WOLF-RIDER TO LOOK FORWARD TO.
MAY I?
OF COURSE. I SHOULDN'T BE SURPRISED IF THE CUB GREETED YOU--HE'S BEEN REST-LESS TODAY.
WHOOPS!
BOP
HOW MUCH LONGER CAN YOU KEEP HIM IN THERE? HIS FEET CERTAINLY WORK!

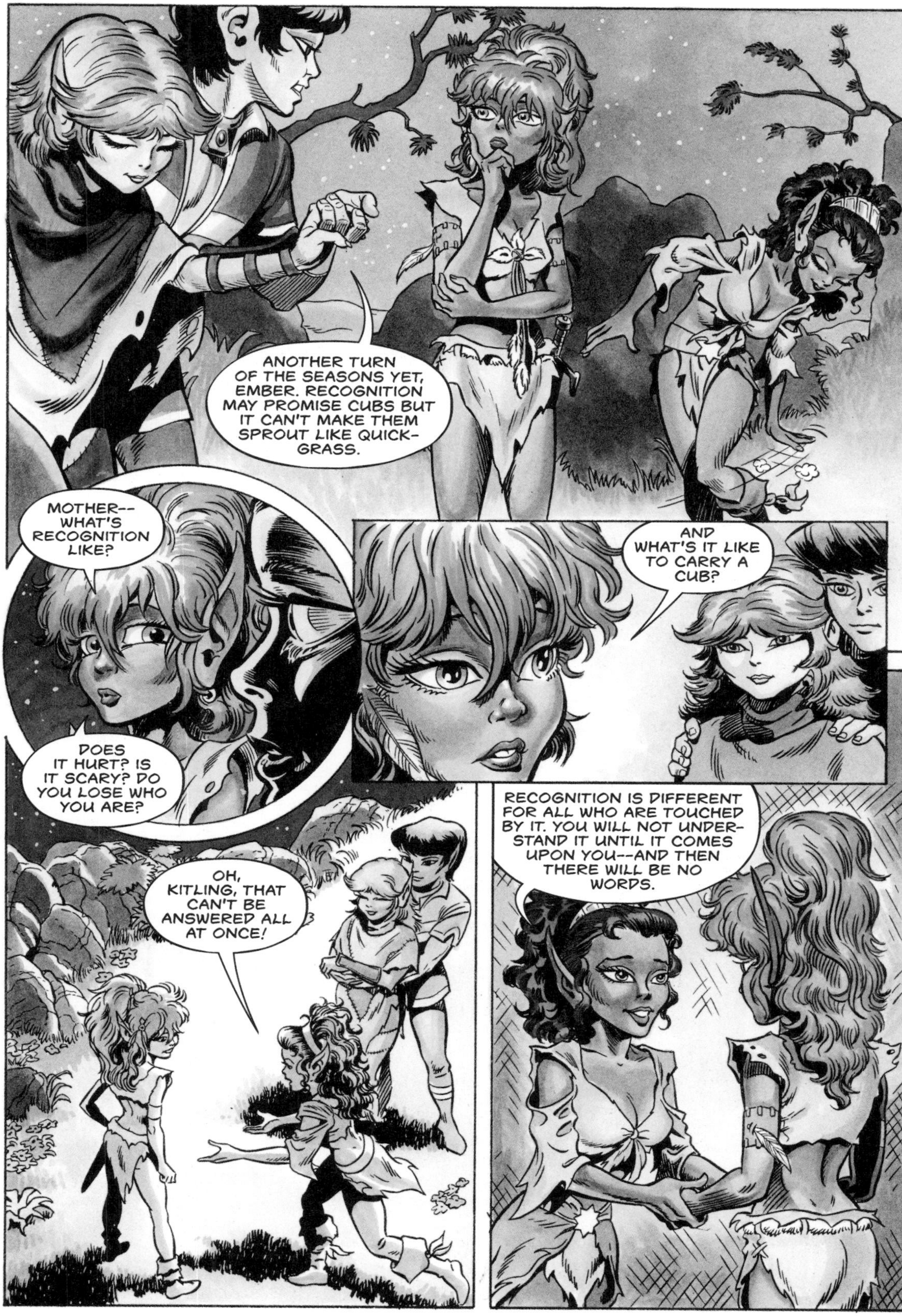
ANOTHER TURN OF THE SEASONS YET, EMBER. RECOGNITION MAY PROMISE CUBS BUT IT CAN'T MAKE THEM SPROUT LIKE QUICK-GRASS.
MOTHER--WHAT'S RECOGNITION LIKE?
AND WHAT'S IT LIKE TO CARRY A CUB?
DOES IT HURT? IS IT SCARY? DO YOU LOSE WHO YOU ARE?
OH, KITLING, THAT CAN'T BE ANSWERED ALL AT ONCE!
RECOGNITION IS DIFFERENT FOR ALL WHO ARE TOUCHED BY IT. YOU WILL NOT UNDER-STAND IT UNTIL IT COMES UPON YOU--AND THEN THERE WILL BE NO WORDS.

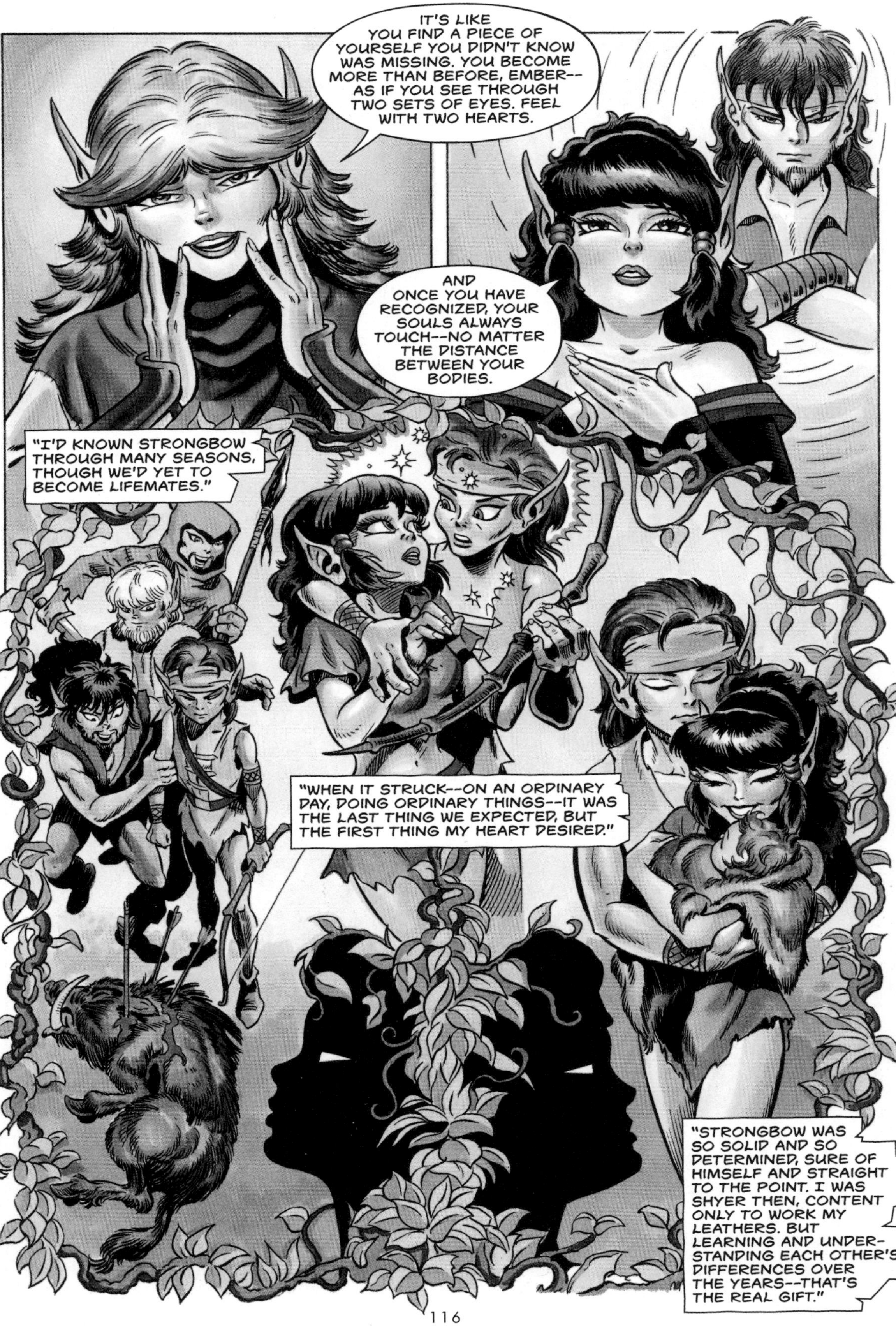
IT'S LIKE YOU FIND A PIECE OF YOURSELF YOU DIDN'T KNOW WAS MISSING. YOU BECOME MORE THAN BEFORE, EMBER-- AS IF YOU SEE THROUGH TWO SETS OF EYES. FEEL WITH TWO HEARTS.
AND ONCE YOU HAVE RECOGNIZED, YOUR SOULS ALWAYS TOUCH--NO MATTER THE DISTANCE BETWEEN YOUR BODIES.
"I'D KNOWN STRONGBOW THROUGH MANY SEASONS, THOUGH WE'D YET TO BECOME LIFEMATES."
"WHEN IT STRUCK--ON AN ORDINARY DAY, DOING ORDINARY THINGS--IT WAS THE LAST THING WE EXPECTED, BUT THE FIRST THING MY HEART DESIRED."
"STRONGBOW WAS SO SOLID AND SO DETERMINED, SURE OF HIMSELF AND STRAIGHT TO THE POINT. I WAS SHYER THEN, CONTENT ONLY TO WORK MY LEATHERS. BUT LEARNING AND UNDER-STANDING EACH OTHER'S DIFFERENCES OVER THE YEARS--THAT'S THE REAL GIFT."

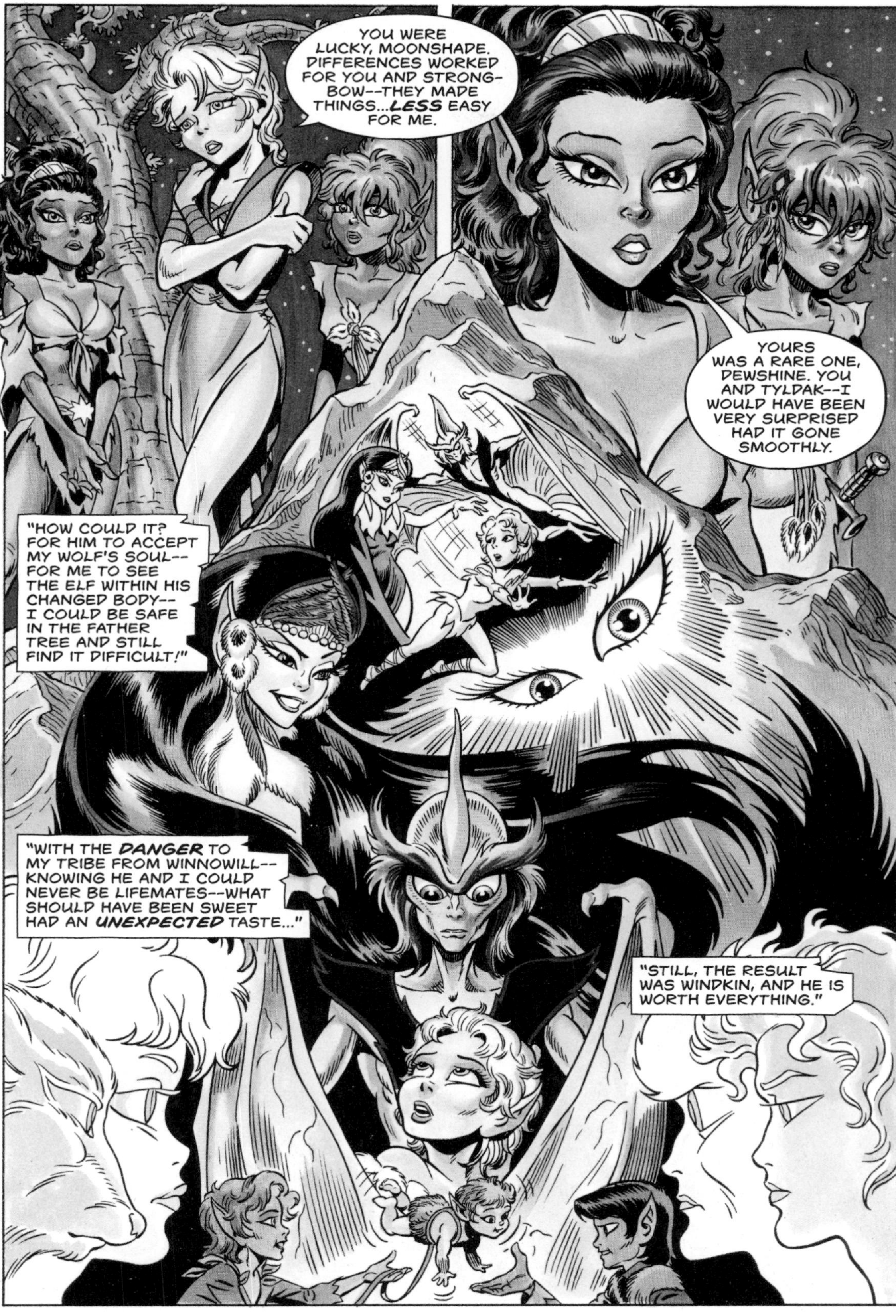
YOU WERE LUCKY, MOONSHADE. DIFFERENCES WORKED FOR YOU AND STRONG-BOW--THEY MADE THINGS...LESS EASY FOR ME.
YOURS WAS A RARE ONE, DEWSHINE. YOU AND TYLDAK--I WOULD HAVE BEEN VERY SURPRISED HAD IT GONE SMOOTHLY.
"HOW COULD IT? FOR HIM TO ACCEPT MY WOLF'S SOUL--FOR ME TO SEE THE ELF WITHIN HIS CHANGED BODY--I COULD BE SAFE IN THE FATHER TREE AND STILL FIND IT DIFFICULT!"
"WITH THE DANGER TO MY TRIBE FROM WINNOWILL--KNOWING HE AND I COULD NEVER BE LIFEMATES--WHAT SHOULD HAVE BEEN SWEET HAD AN UNEXPECTED TASTE..."
"STILL, THE RESULT WAS WINDKIN, AND HE IS WORTH EVERYTHING."

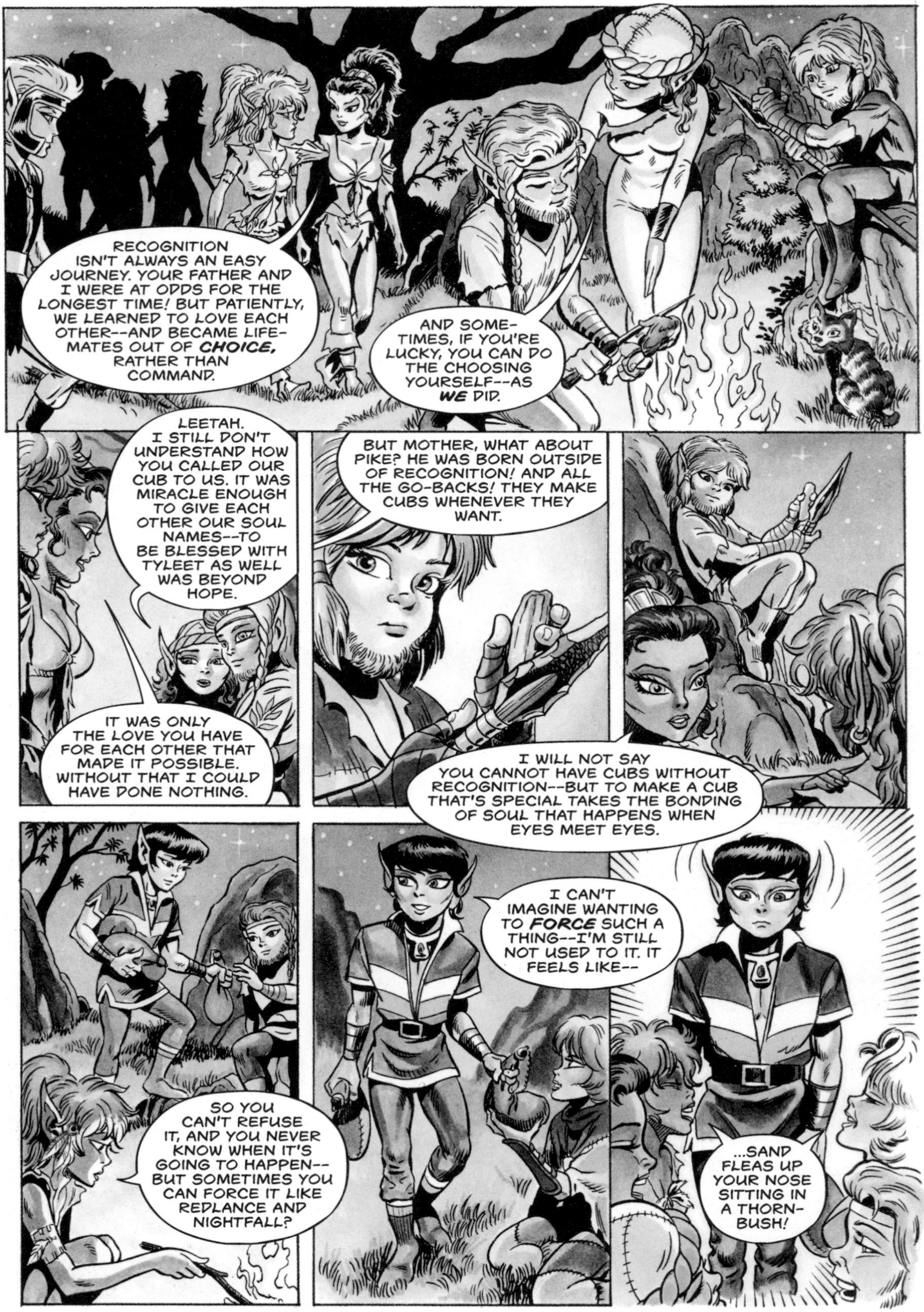
RECOGNITION ISN'T ALWAYS AN EASY JOURNEY. YOUR FATHER AND I WERE AT ODDS FOR THE LONGEST TIME! BUT PATIENTLY, WE LEARNED TO LOVE EACH OTHER--AND BECAME LIFE-MATES OUT OF CHOICE, RATHER THAN COMMAND.
AND SOME-TIMES, IF YOU'RE LUCKY, YOU CAN DO THE CHOOSING YOURSELF--AS WE DID.
LEETAH. I STILL DON'T UNDERSTAND HOW YOU CALLED OUR CUB TO US. IT WAS MIRACLE ENOUGH TO GIVE EACH OTHER OUR SOUL NAMES--TO BE BLESSED WITH TYLEET AS WELL WAS BEYOND HOPE.
IT WAS ONLY THE LOVE YOU HAVE FOR EACH OTHER THAT MADE IT POSSIBLE. WITHOUT THAT I COULD HAVE DONE NOTHING.
BUT MOTHER, WHAT ABOUT PIKE? HE WAS BORN OUTSIDE OF RECOGNITION! AND ALL THE GO-BACKS! THEY MAKE CUBS WHENEVER THEY WANT.
I WILL NOT SAY YOU CANNOT HAVE CUBS WITHOUT RECOGNITION--BUT TO MAKE A CUB THAT'S SPECIAL TAKES THE BONDING OF SOUL THAT HAPPENS WHEN EYES MEET EYES.
SO YOU CAN'T REFUSE IT, AND YOU NEVER KNOW WHEN IT'S GOING TO HAPPEN--BUT SOMETIMES YOU CAN FORCE IT LIKE REDLANCE AND NIGHTFALL?
I CAN'T IMAGINE WANTING TO FORCE SUCH A THING--I'M STILL NOT USED TO IT. IT FEELS LIKE--
...SAND FLEAS UP YOUR NOSE SITTING IN A THORN-BUSH!

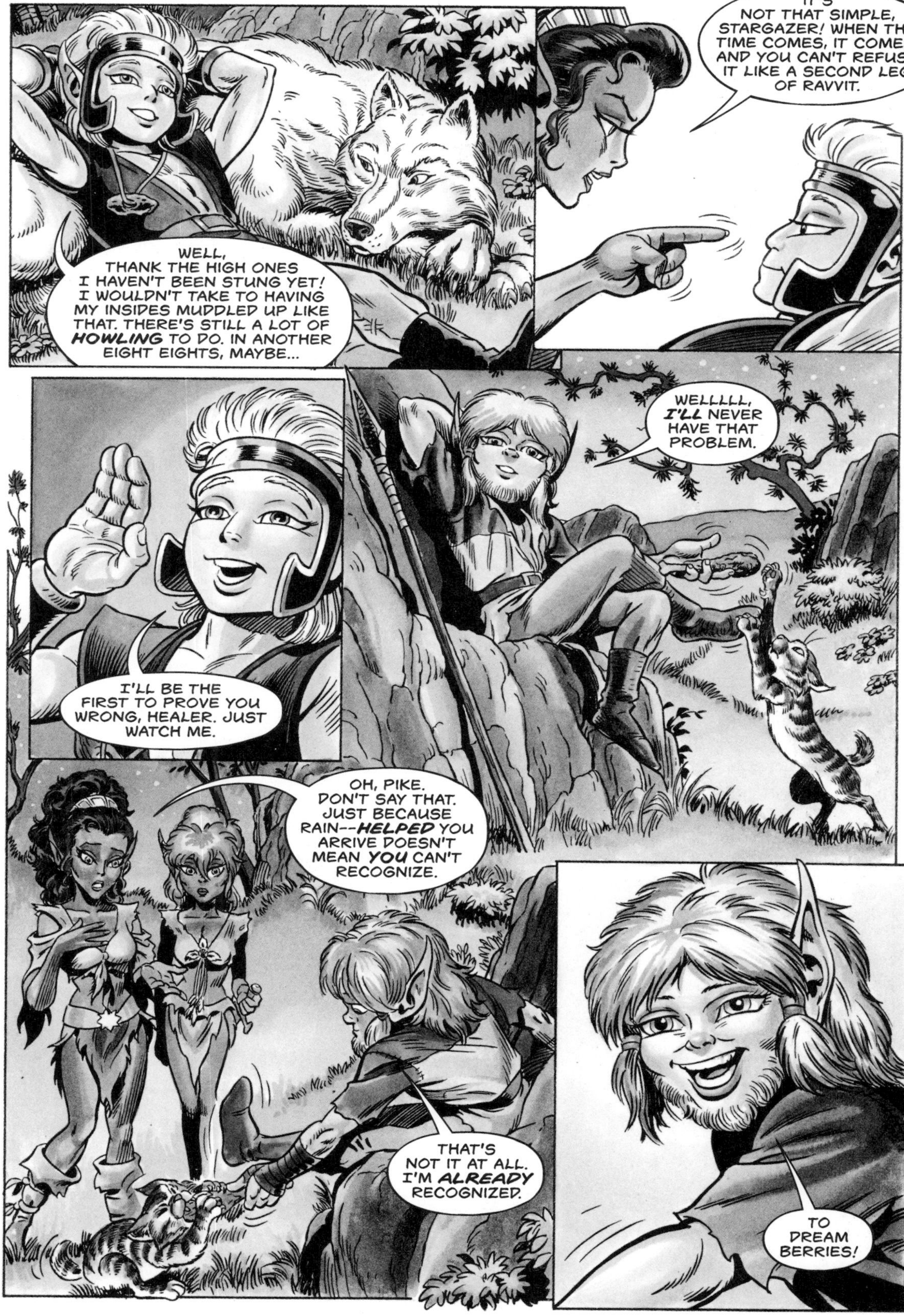
WELL, THANK THE HIGH ONES I HAVEN'T BEEN STUNG YET! I WOULDN'T TAKE TO HAVING MY INSIDES MUDDLED UP LIKE THAT. THERE'S STILL A LOT OF HOWLING TO DO. IN ANOTHER EIGHT EIGHTS, MAYBE...
IT'S NOT THAT SIMPLE, STARGAZER! WHEN THE TIME COMES, IT COMES, AND YOU CAN'T REFUSE IT LIKE A SECOND LEG OF RAVVIT.
I'LL BE THE FIRST TO PROVE YOU WRONG, HEALER. JUST WATCH ME.
WELLLLLL, I'LL NEVER HAVE THAT PROBLEM.
OH, PIKE. DON'T SAY THAT. JUST BECAUSE RAIN--HELPED YOU ARRIVE DOESN'T MEAN YOU CAN'T RECOGNIZE.
THAT'S NOT IT AT ALL. I'M ALREADY RECOGNIZED.
TO DREAM BERRIES!

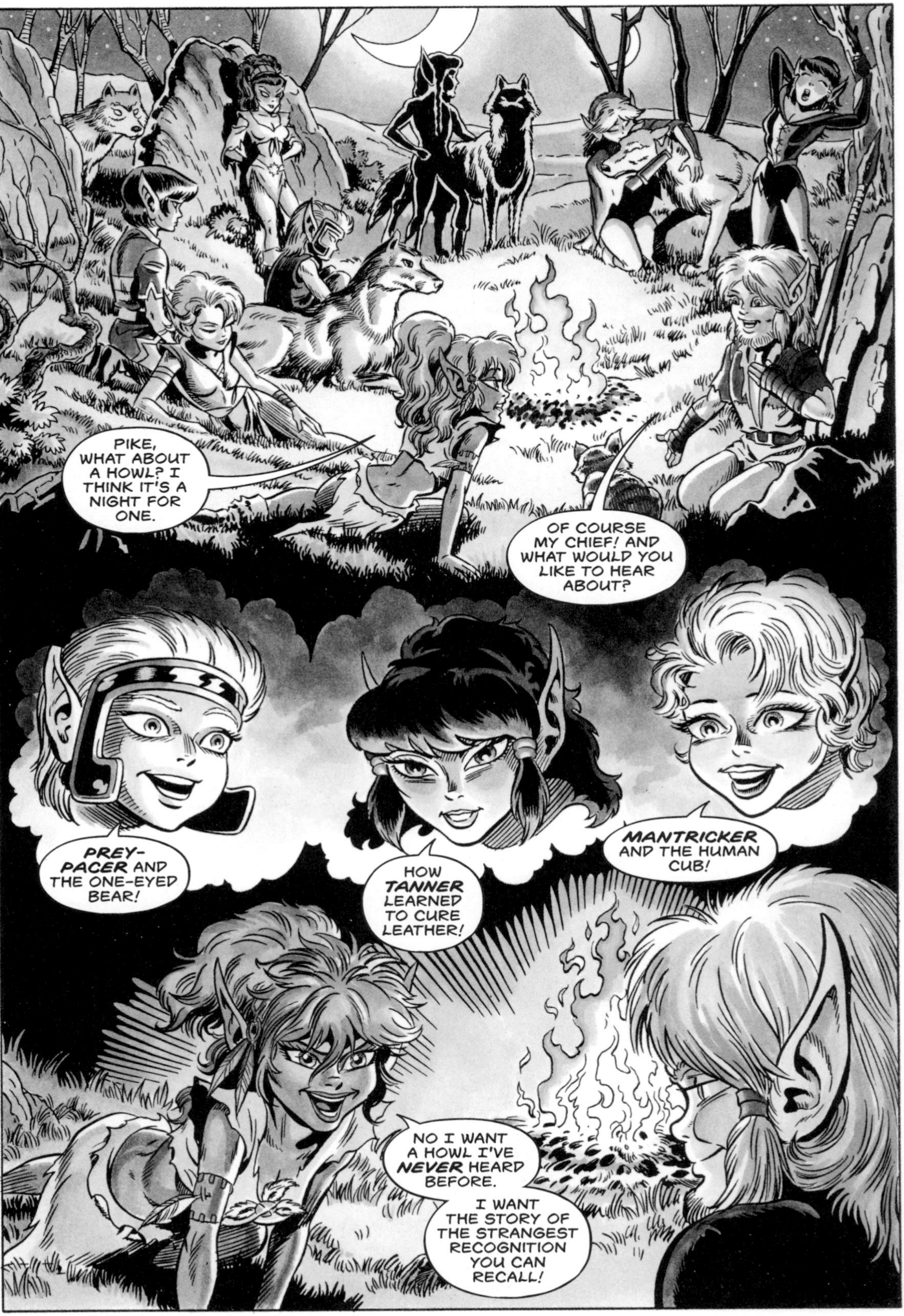
PIKE, WHAT ABOUT A HOWL? I THINK IT'S A NIGHT FOR ONE.
OF COURSE MY CHIEF! AND WHAT WOULD YOU LIKE TO HEAR ABOUT?
PREY-PACER AND THE ONE-EYED BEAR!
HOW TANNER LEARNED TO CURE LEATHER!
MANTRICKER AND THE HUMAN CUB!
NO I WANT A HOWL I'VE NEVER HEARD BEFORE.
I WANT THE STORY OF THE STRANGEST RECOGNITION YOU CAN RECALL!

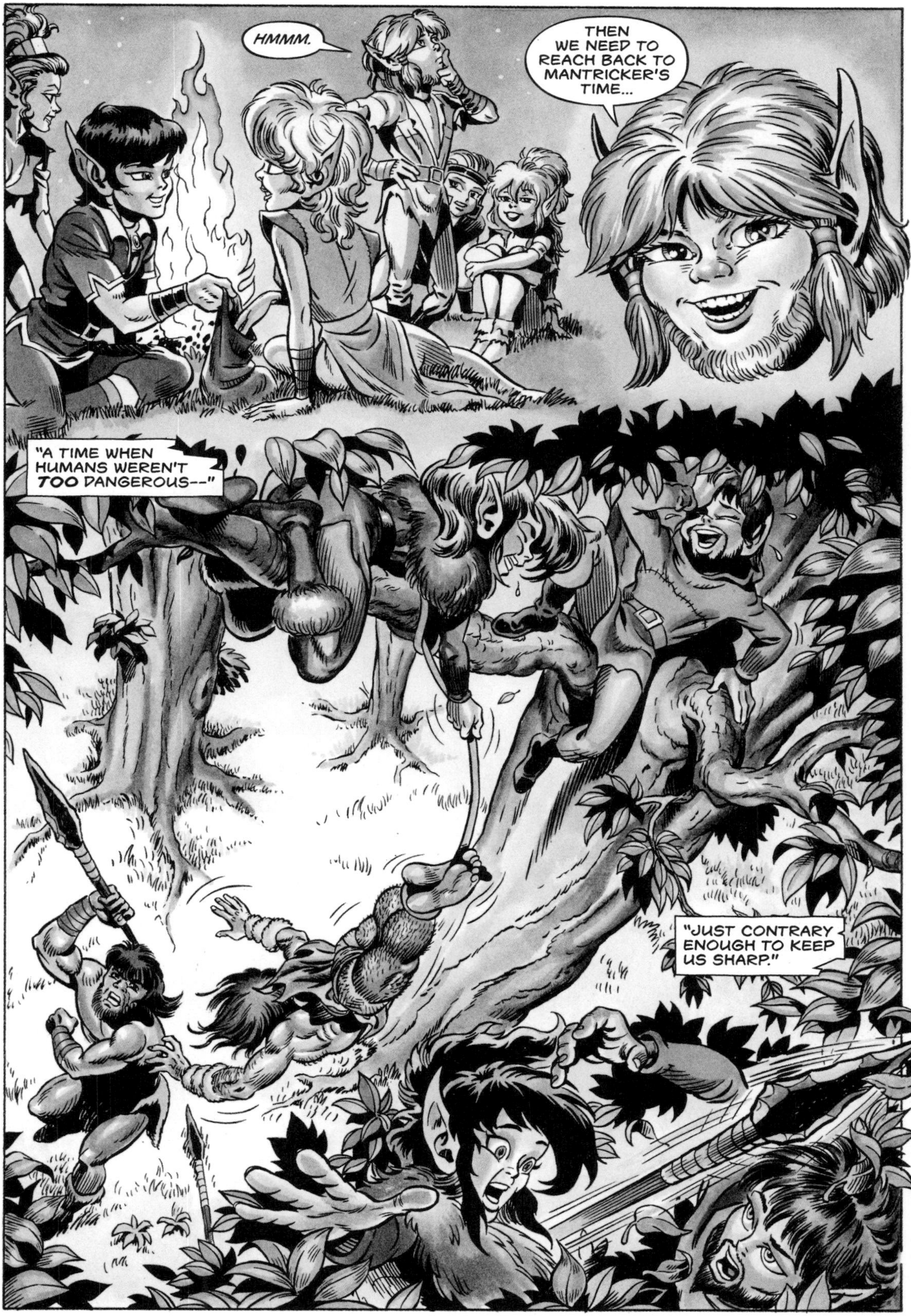
HMMM.
THEN WE NEED TO REACH BACK TO MANTRICKER'S TIME...
"A TIME WHEN HUMANS WEREN'T TOO DANGEROUS--"
"JUST CONTRARY ENOUGH TO KEEP US SHARP."

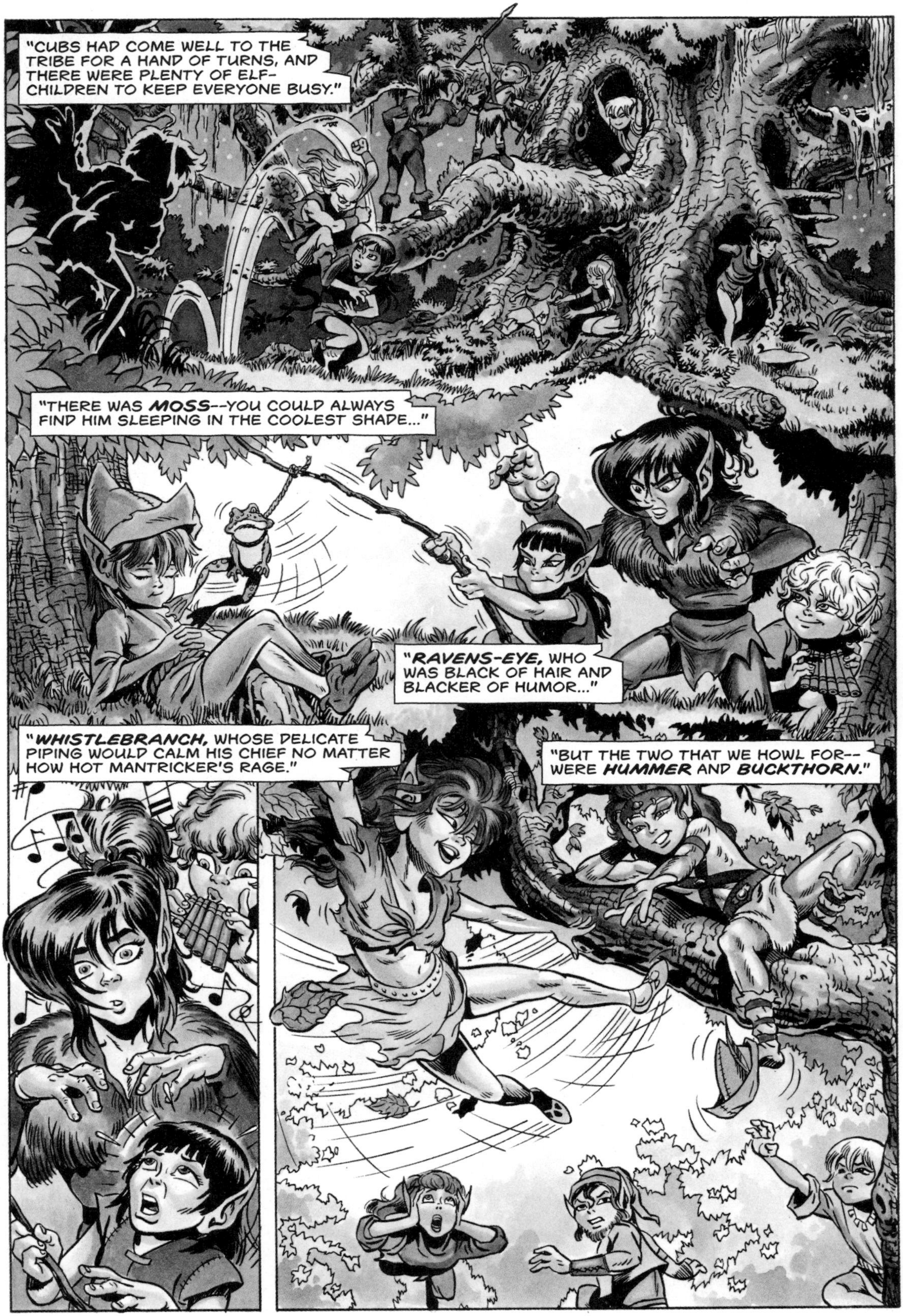
"CUBS HAD COME WELL TO THE TRIBE FOR A HAND OF TURNS, AND THERE WERE PLENTY OF ELF-CHILDREN TO KEEP EVERYONE BUSY."
"THERE WAS MOSS--YOU COULD ALWAYS FIND HIM SLEEPING IN THE COOLEST SHADE..."
"RAVENS-EYE, WHO WAS BLACK OF HAIR AND BLACKER OF HUMOR..."
"WHISTLEBRANCH, WHOSE DELICATE PIPING WOULD CALM HIS CHIEF NO MATTER HOW HOT MANTRICKER'S RAGE."
"BUT THE TWO THAT WE HOWL FOR--WERE HUMMER AND BUCKTHORN."

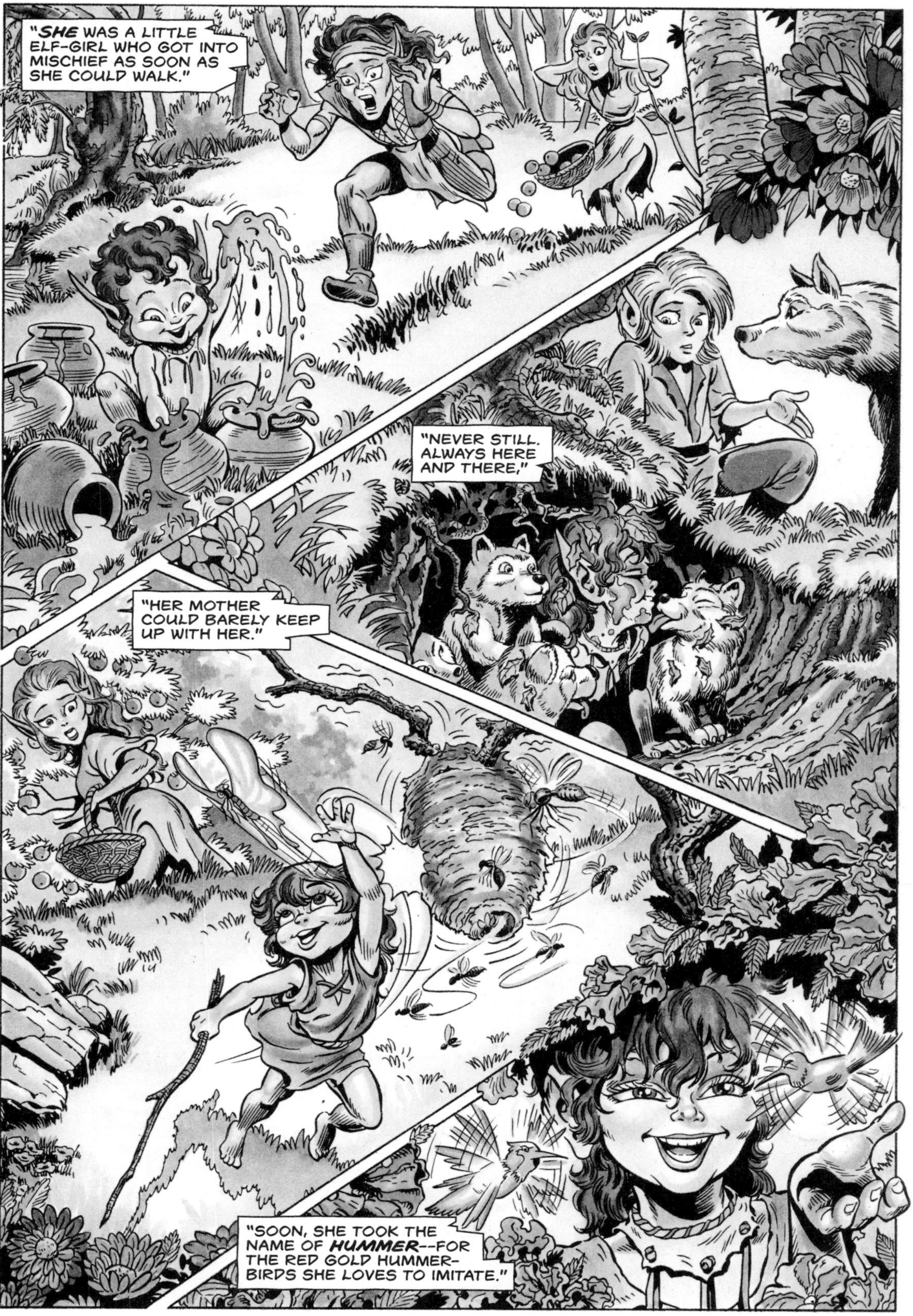
"SHE WAS A LITTLE ELF-GIRL WHO GOT INTO MISCHIEF AS SOON AS SHE COULD WALK."
"NEVER STILL. ALWAYS HERE AND THERE,"
"HER MOTHER COULD BARELY KEEP UP WITH HER."
"SOON, SHE TOOK THE NAME OF HUMMER--FOR THE RED GOLD HUMMER-BIRDS SHE LOVES TO IMITATE."

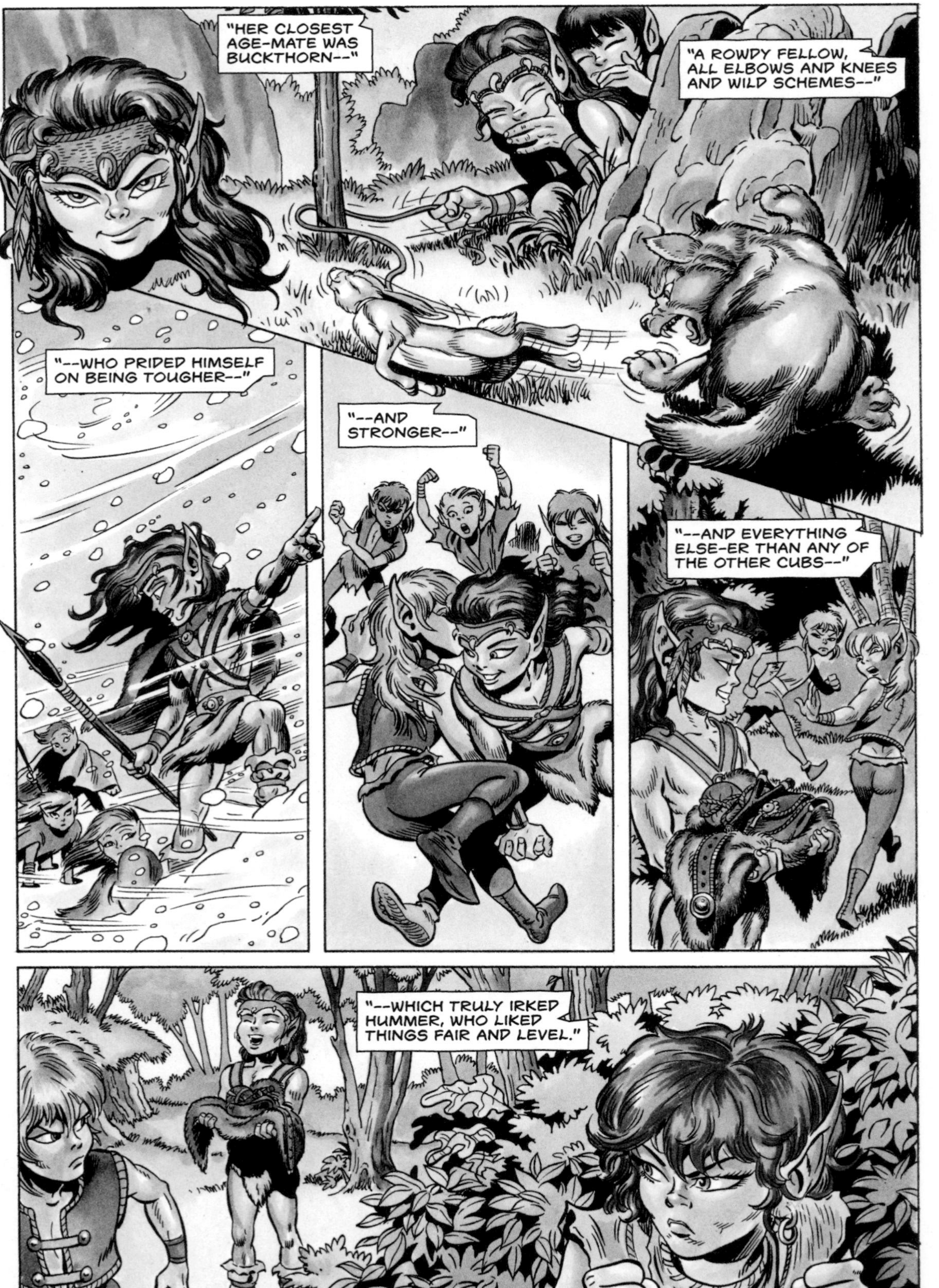
"HER CLOSEST AGE-MATE WAS BUCKTHORN--"
"A ROWDY FELLOW, ALL ELBOWS AND KNEES AND WILD SCHEMES--"
"--WHO PRIDED HIMSELF ON BEING TOUGHER--"
"--AND STRONGER--"
"--AND EVERYTHING ELSE-ER THAN ANY OF THE OTHER CUBS--"
"--WHICH TRULY IRKED HUMMER, WHO LIKED THINGS FAIR AND LEVEL."

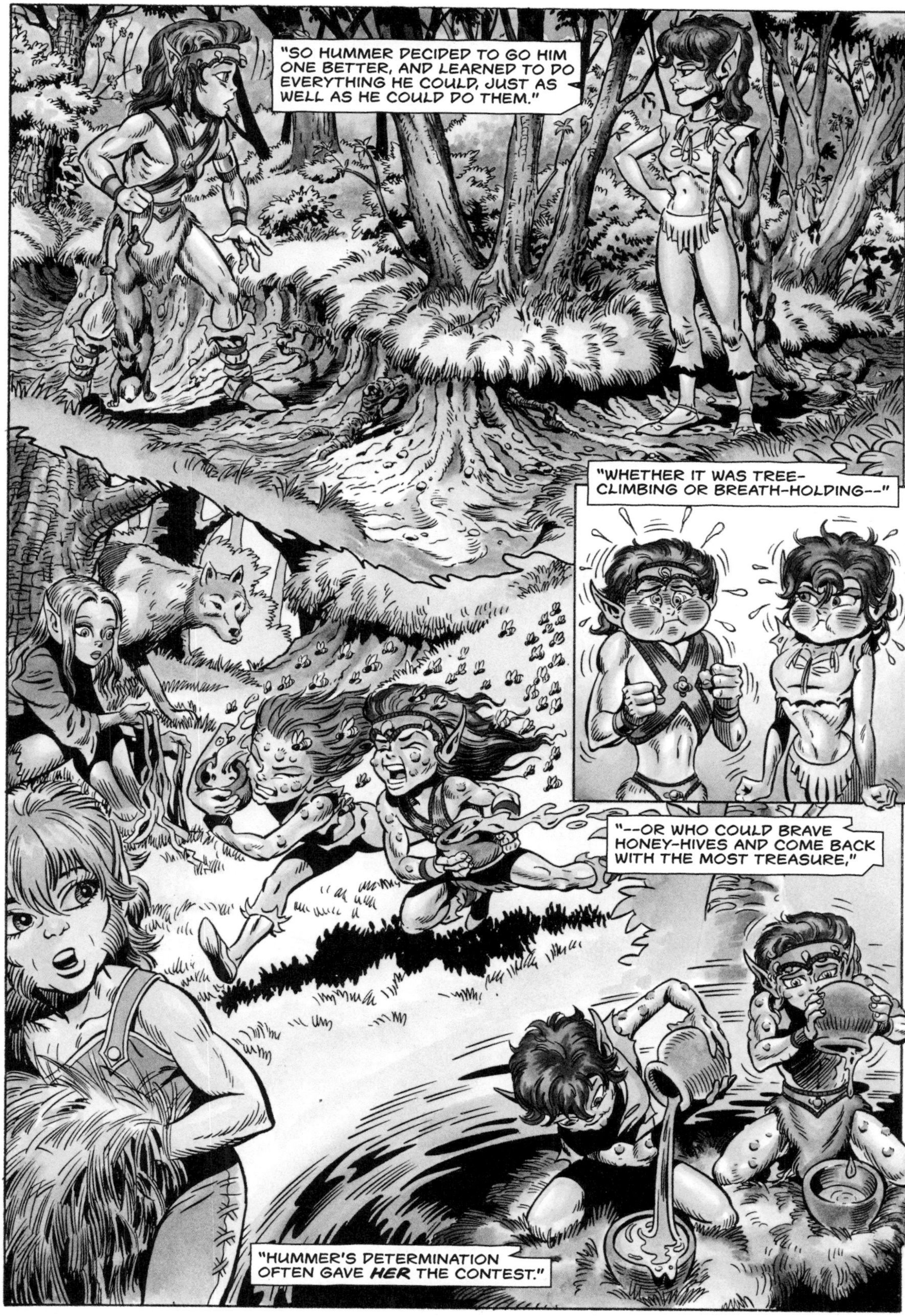
"SO HUMMER DECIDED TO GO HIM ONE BETTER, AND LEARNED TO DO EVERYTHING HE COULD, JUST AS WELL AS HE COULD DO THEM."
"WHETHER IT WAS TREE-CLIMBING OR BREATH-HOLDING--"
"--OR WHO COULD BRAVE HONEY-HIVES AND COME BACK WITH THE MOST TREASURE,"
"HUMMER'S DETERMINATION OFTEN GAVE ***HER*** THE CONTEST."

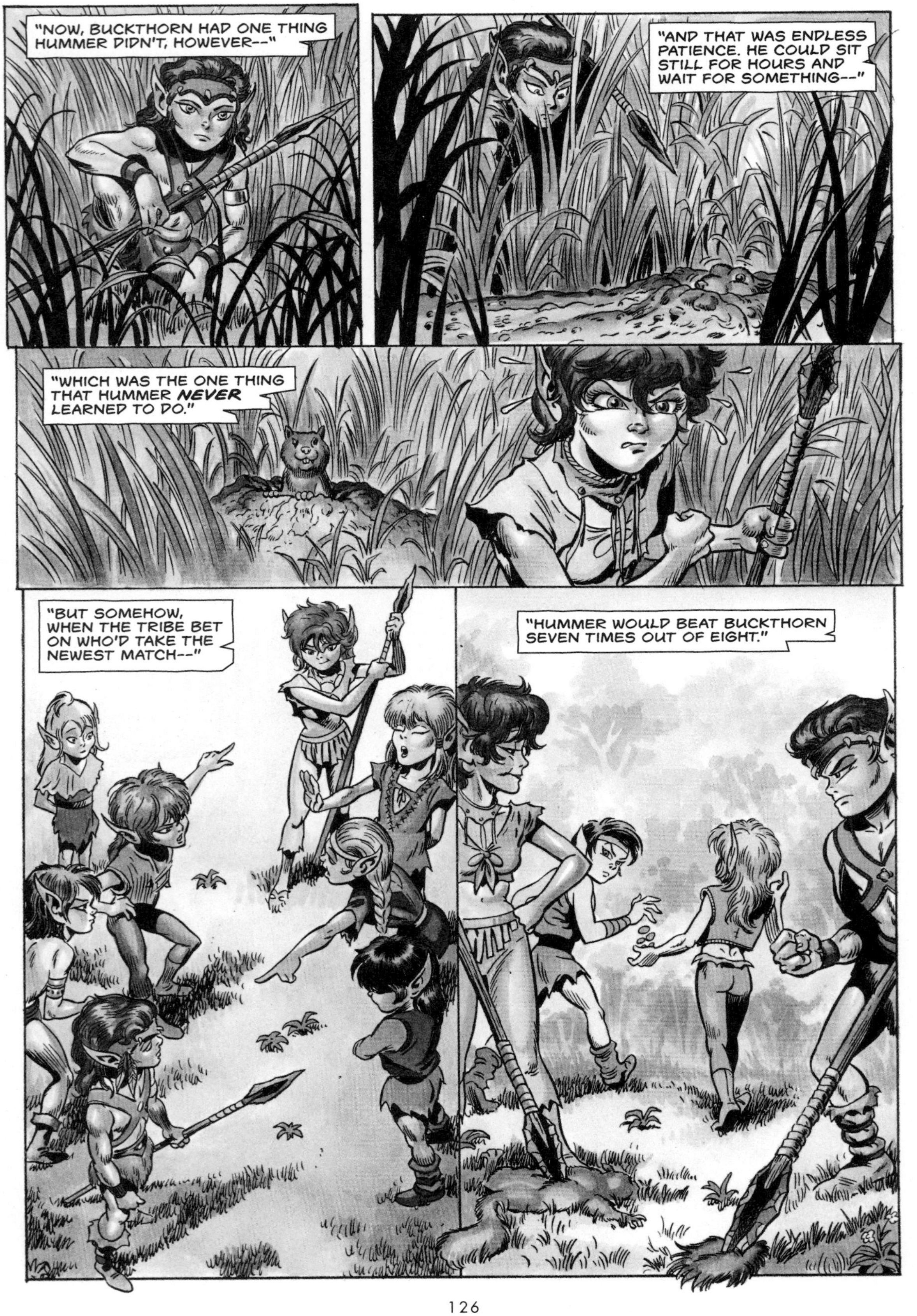
"NOW, BUCKTHORN HAD ONE THING HUMMER DIDN'T, HOWEVER--"
"AND THAT WAS ENDLESS PATIENCE. HE COULD SIT STILL FOR HOURS AND WAIT FOR SOMETHING--"
"WHICH WAS THE ONE THING THAT HUMMER *NEVER* LEARNED TO DO."
"BUT SOMEHOW, WHEN THE TRIBE BET ON WHO'D TAKE THE NEWEST MATCH--"
"HUMMER WOULD BEAT BUCKTHORN SEVEN TIMES OUT OF EIGHT."

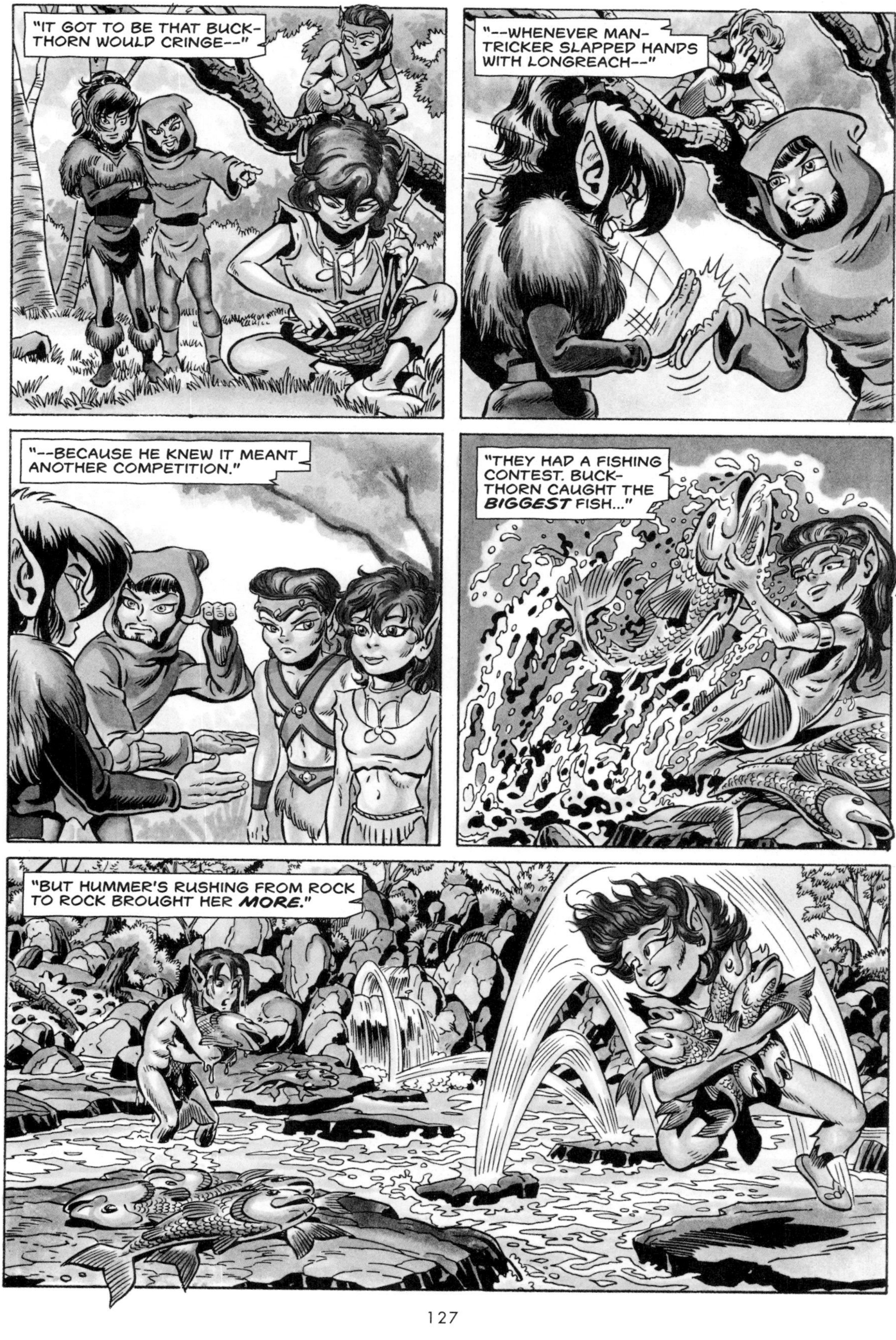
"IT GOT TO BE THAT BUCK-THORN WOULD CRINGE--"
"--WHENEVER MAN-TRICKER SLAPPED HANDS WITH LONGREACH--"
"--BECAUSE HE KNEW IT MEANT ANOTHER COMPETITION."
"THEY HAD A FISHING CONTEST. BUCK-THORN CAUGHT THE BIGGEST FISH..."
"BUT HUMMER'S RUSHING FROM ROCK TO ROCK BROUGHT HER MORE."

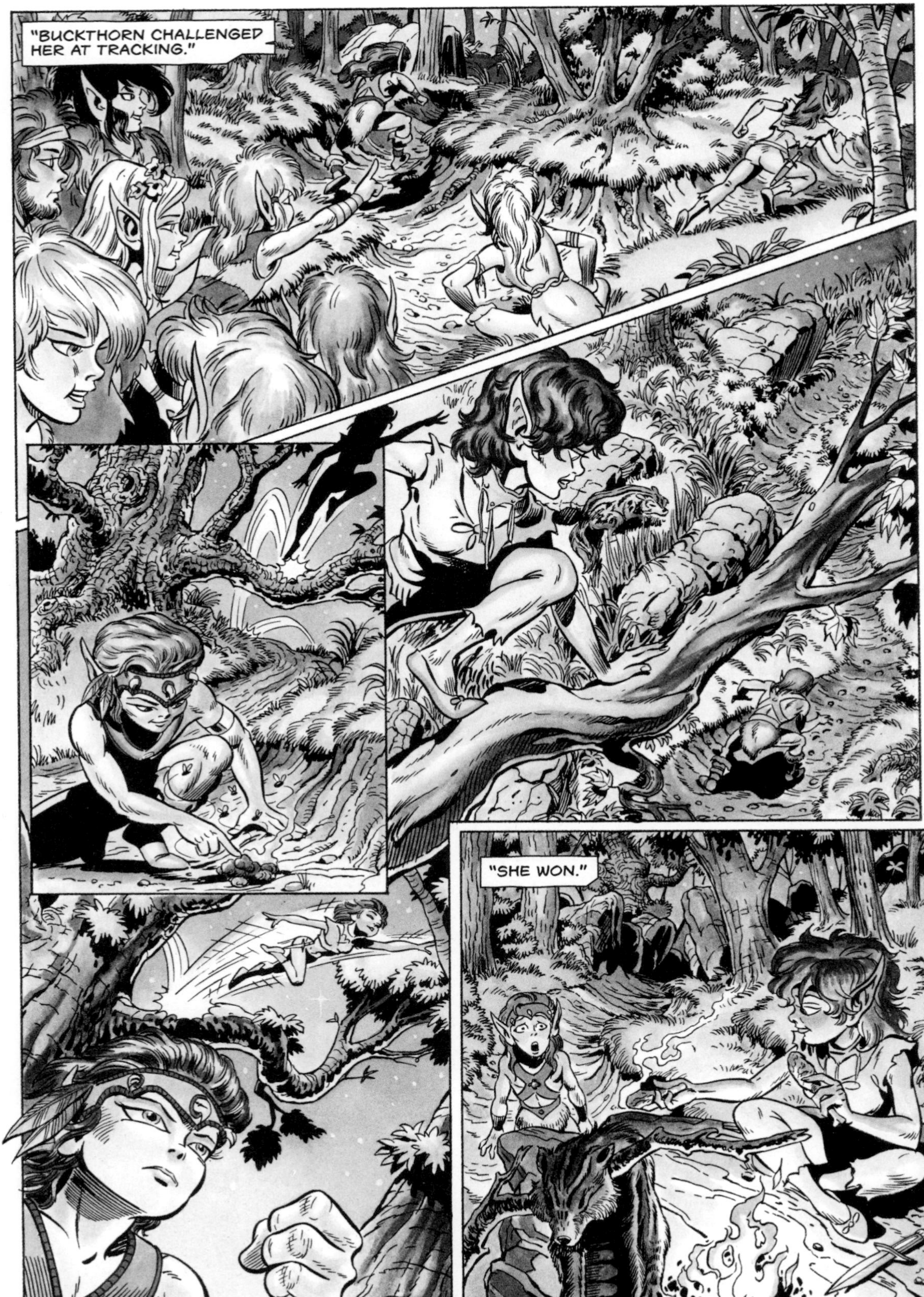
"BUCKTHORN CHALLENGED HER AT TRACKING."
"SHE WON."

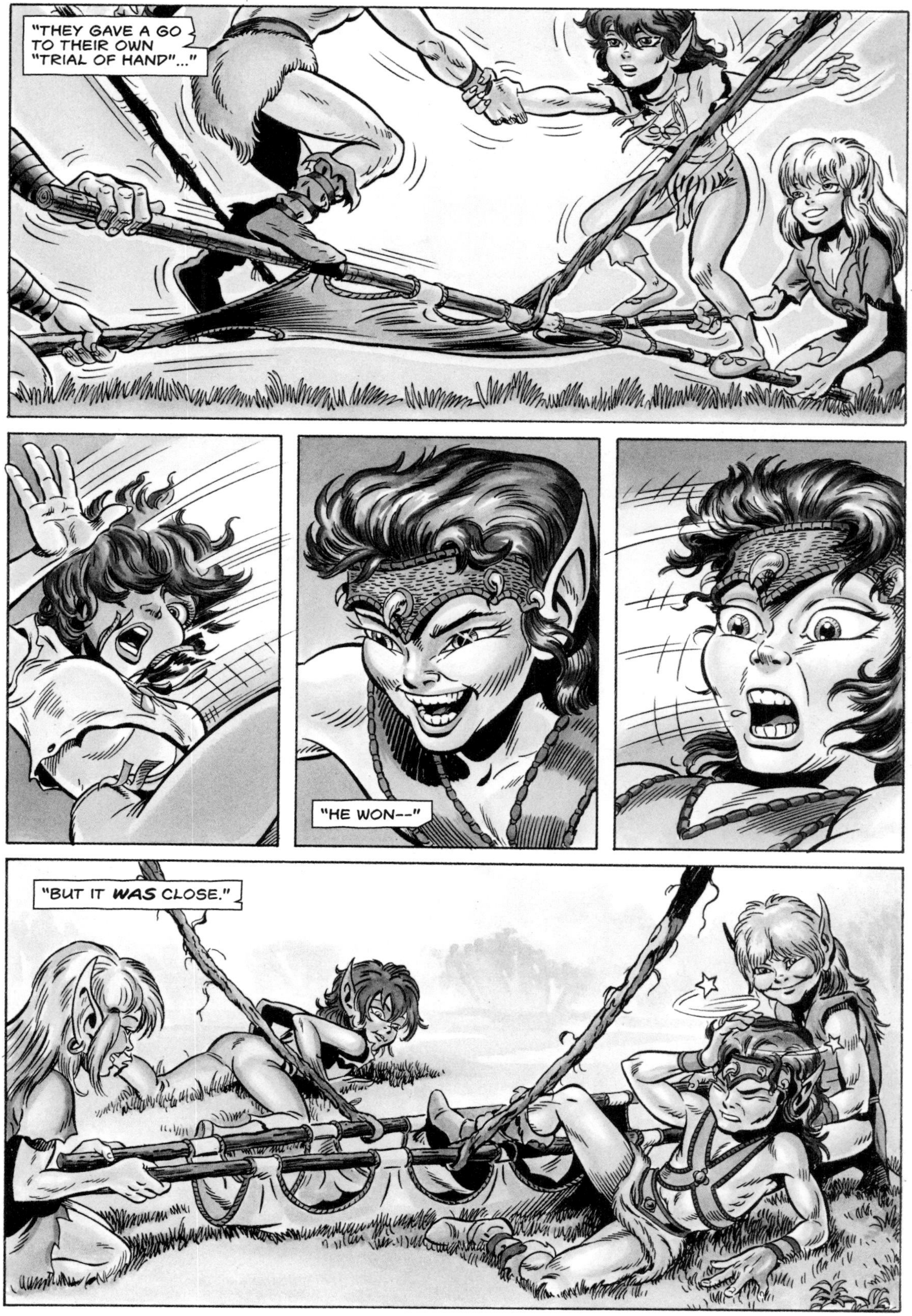
"THEY GAVE A GO
TO THEIR OWN
"TRIAL OF HAND"..."
"HE WON--"
"BUT IT *WAS* CLOSE."

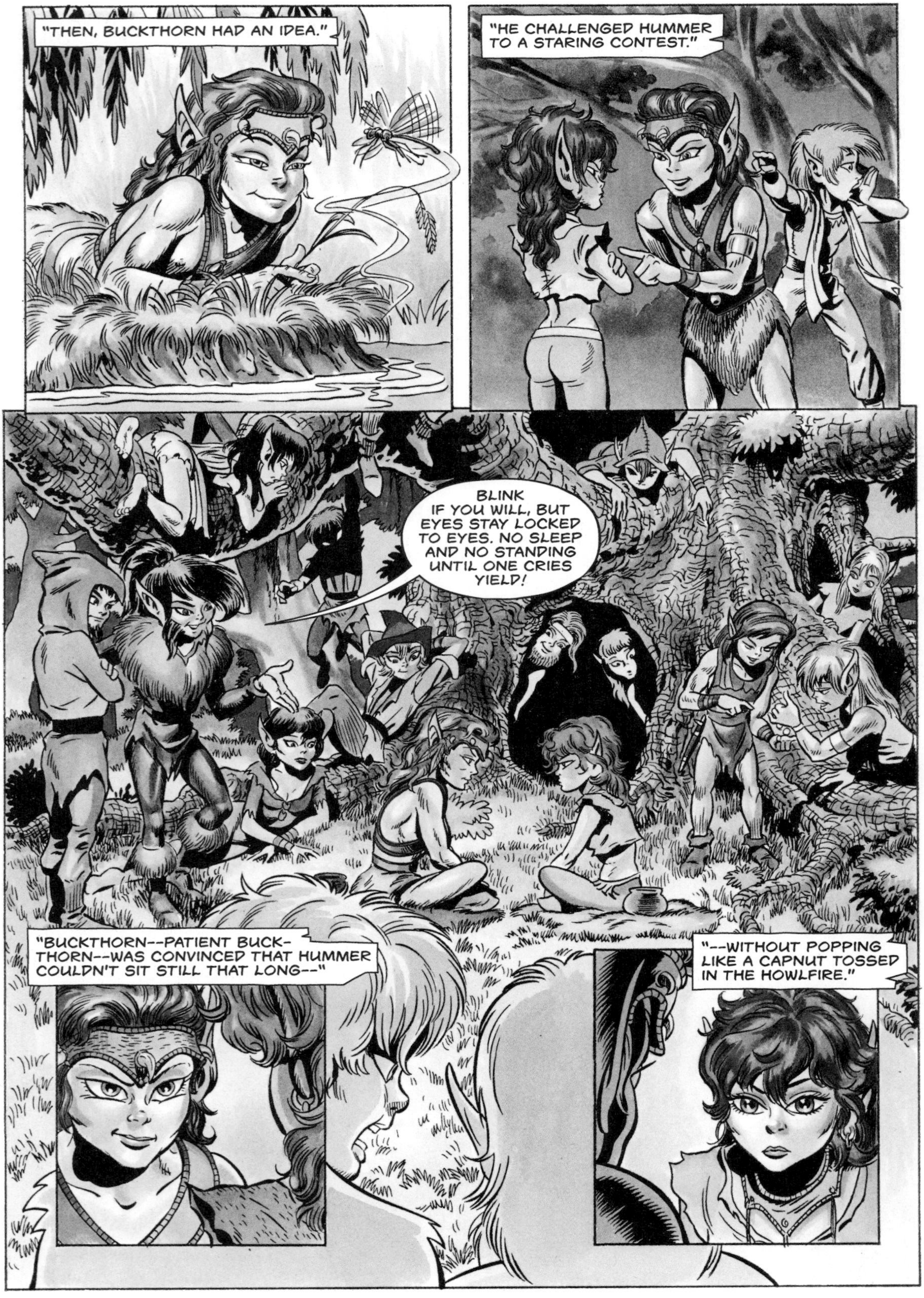
"THEN, BUCKTHORN HAD AN IDEA."
"HE CHALLENGED HUMMER TO A STARING CONTEST."
BLINK IF YOU WILL, BUT EYES STAY LOCKED TO EYES. NO SLEEP AND NO STANDING UNTIL ONE CRIES YIELD!
"BUCKTHORN--PATIENT BUCK-THORN--WAS CONVINCED THAT HUMMER COULDN'T SIT STILL THAT LONG--"
"--WITHOUT POPPING LIKE A CAPNUT TOSSED IN THE HOWLFIRE."

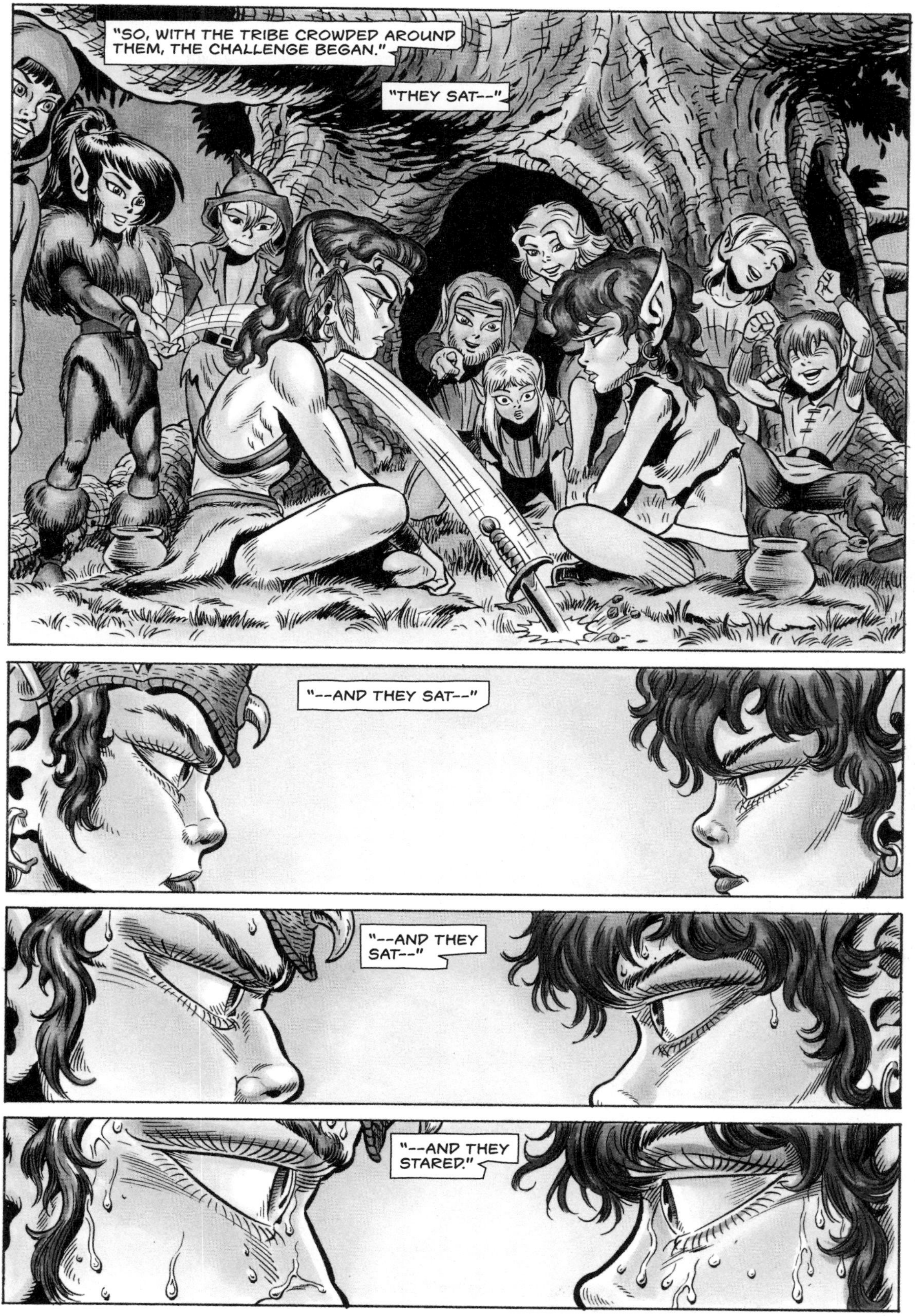
"SO, WITH THE TRIBE CROWDED AROUND THEM, THE CHALLENGE BEGAN."
"THEY SAT--"
"--AND THEY SAT--"
"--AND THEY SAT--"
"--AND THEY STARED."

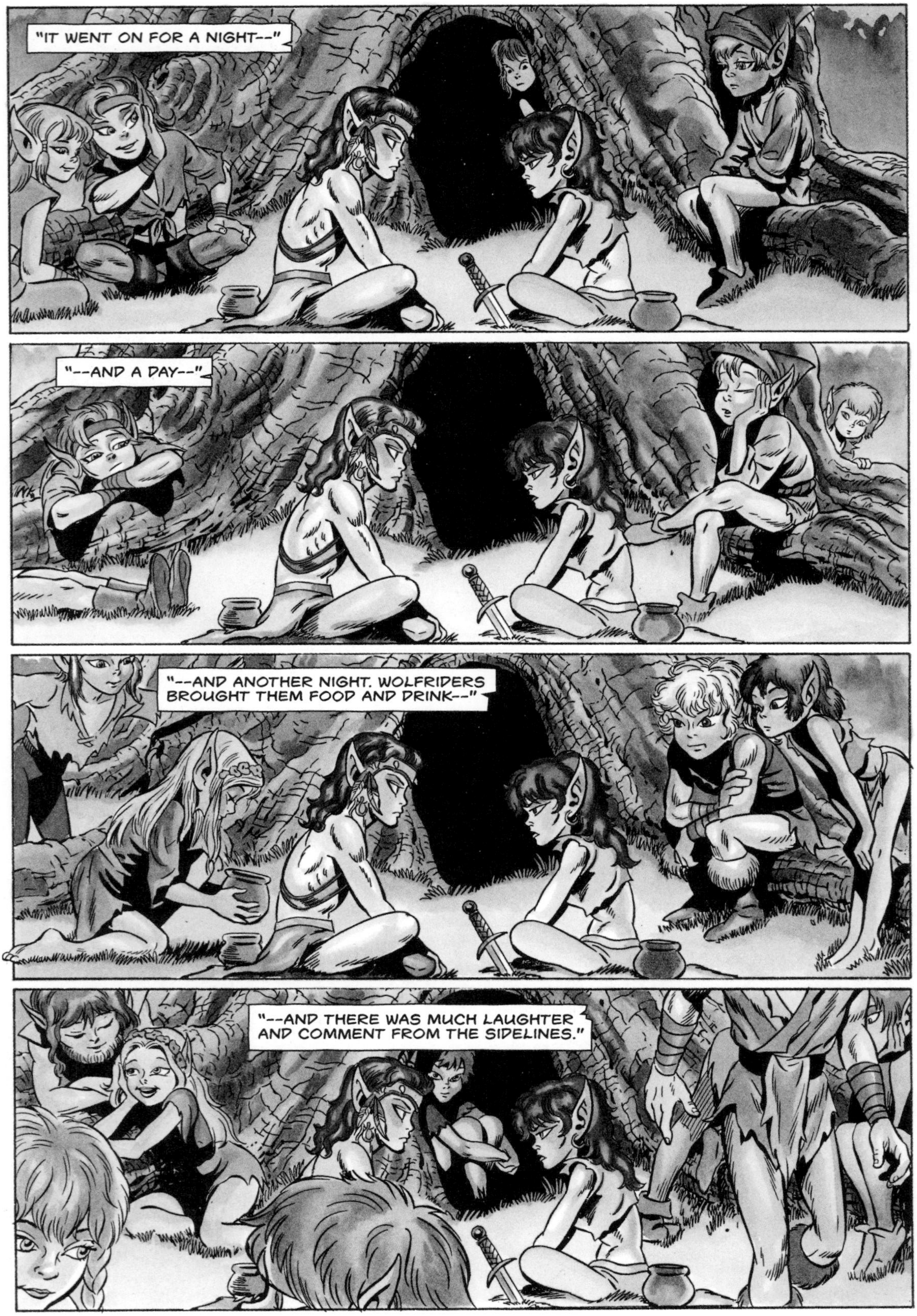
"IT WENT ON FOR A NIGHT--"
"--AND A DAY--"
"--AND ANOTHER NIGHT. WOLFRIDERS BROUGHT THEM FOOD AND DRINK--"
"--AND THERE WAS MUCH LAUGHTER AND COMMENT FROM THE SIDELINES."

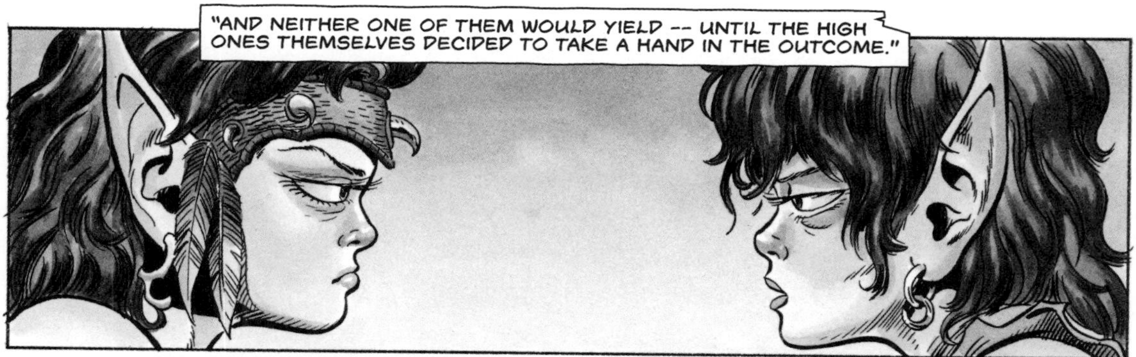
"AND NEITHER ONE OF THEM WOULD YIELD -- UNTIL THE HIGH ONES THEMSELVES DECIDED TO TAKE A HAND IN THE OUTCOME."

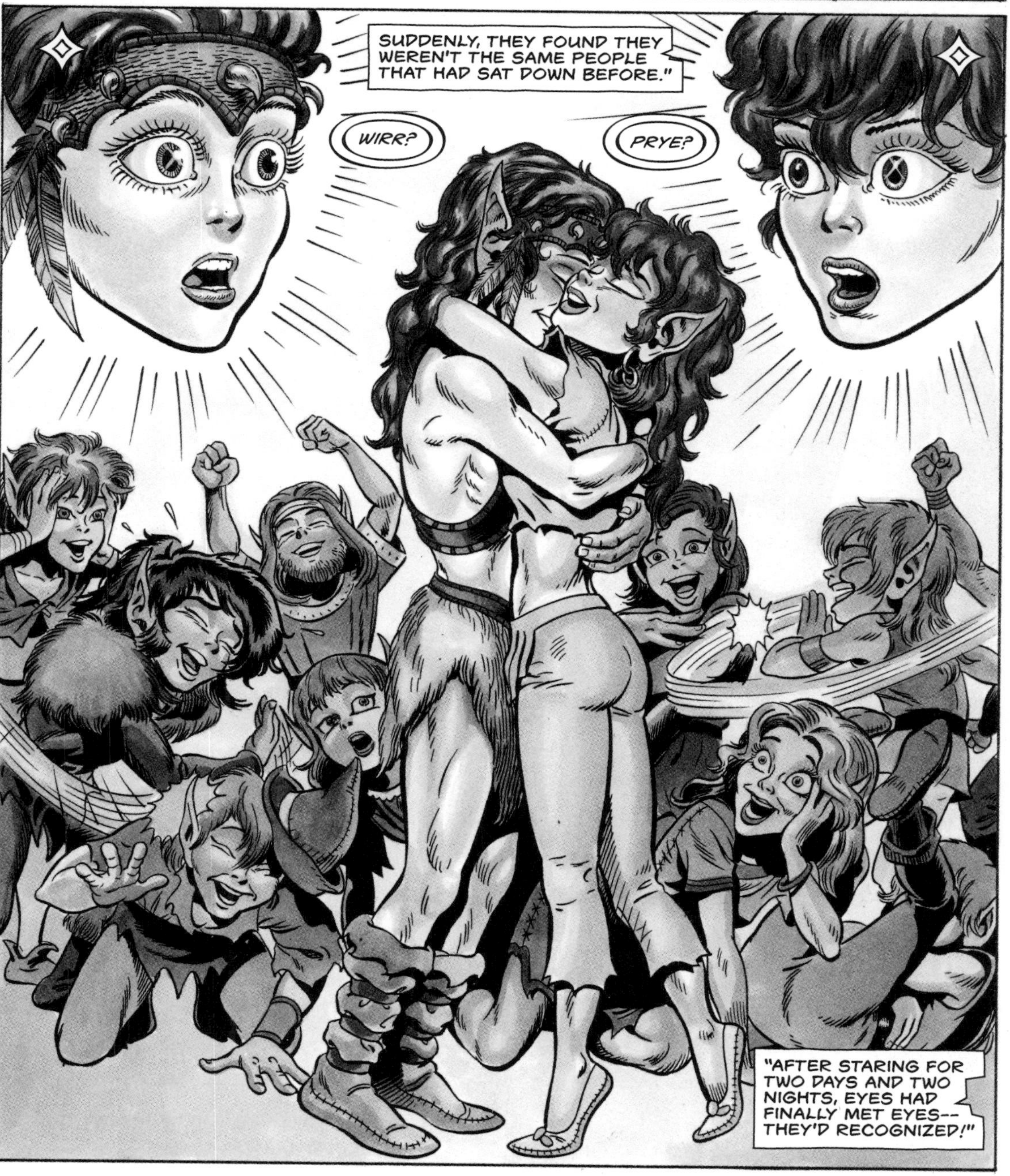
SUDDENLY, THEY FOUND THEY WEREN'T THE SAME PEOPLE THAT HAD SAT DOWN BEFORE."
WIRR?
PRYE?
"AFTER STARING FOR TWO DAYS AND TWO NIGHTS, EYES HAD FINALLY MET EYES-- THEY'D RECOGNIZED!"

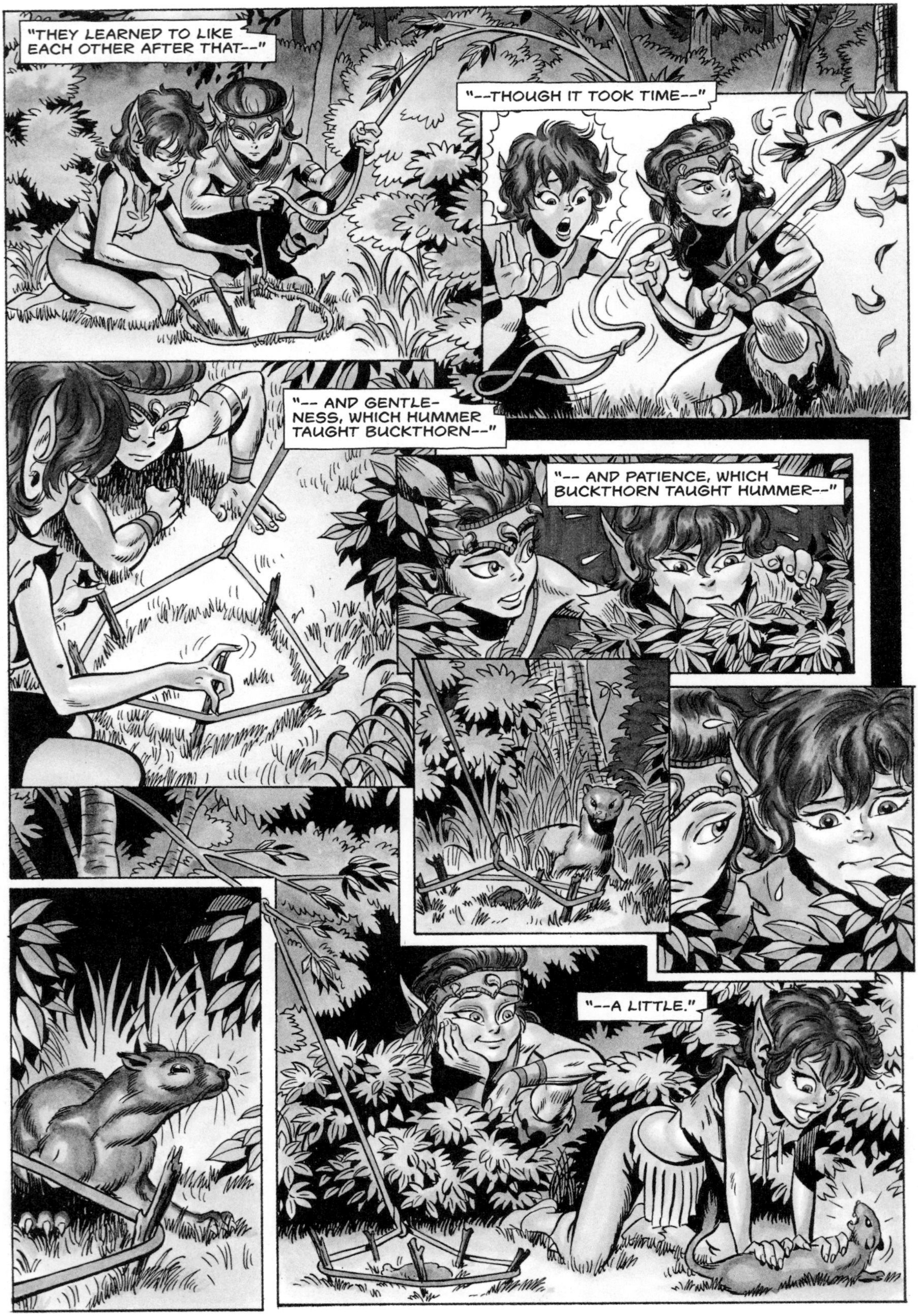
"THEY LEARNED TO LIKE EACH OTHER AFTER THAT--"
"--THOUGH IT TOOK TIME--"
"-- AND GENTLE-NESS, WHICH HUMMER TAUGHT BUCKTHORN--"
"-- AND PATIENCE, WHICH BUCKTHORN TAUGHT HUMMER--"
"--A LITTLE."

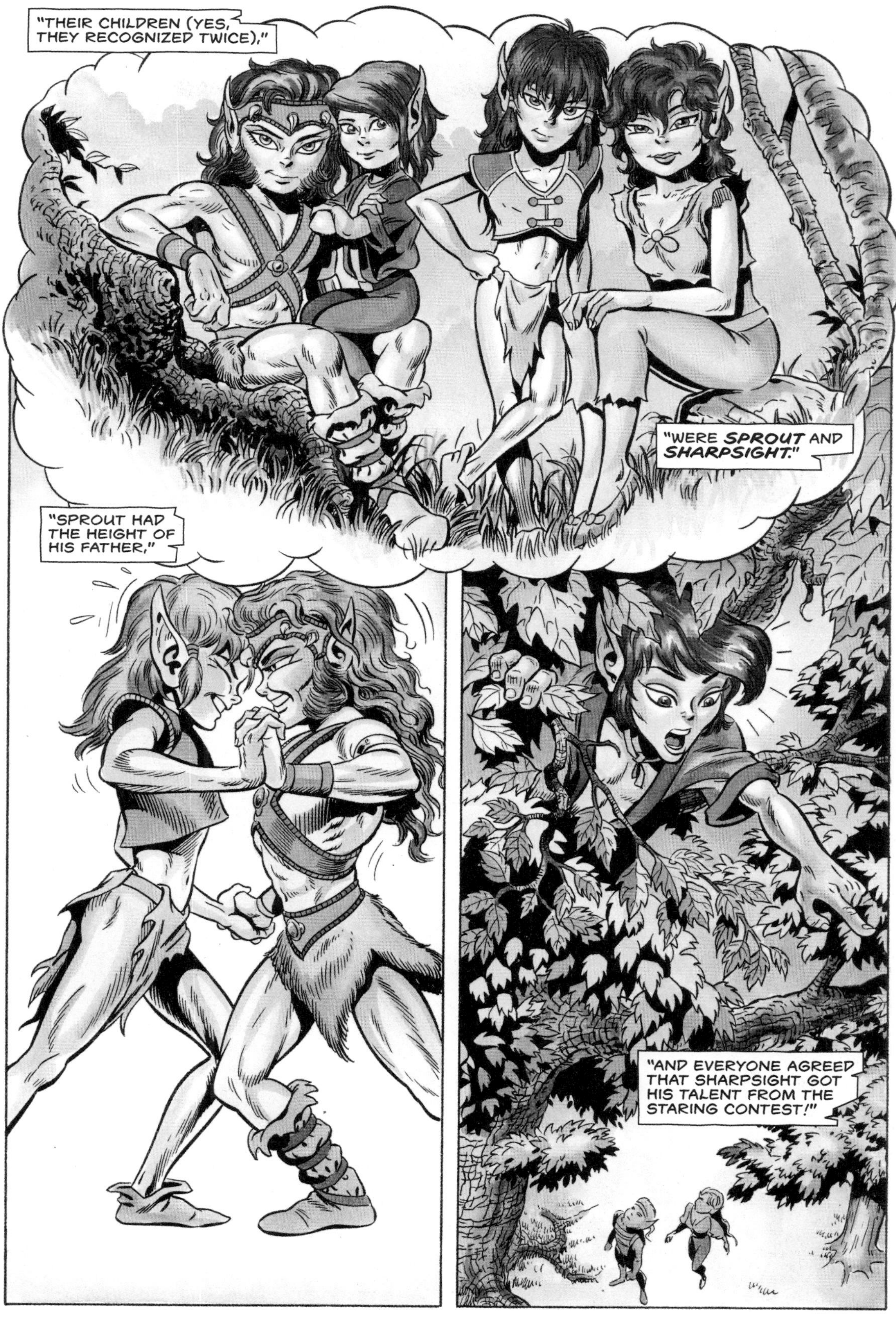
"THEIR CHILDREN (YES, THEY RECOGNIZED TWICE),"
"WERE SPROUT AND SHARPSIGHT."
"SPROUT HAD THE HEIGHT OF HIS FATHER,"
"AND EVERYONE AGREED THAT SHARPSIGHT GOT HIS TALENT FROM THE STARING CONTEST!"

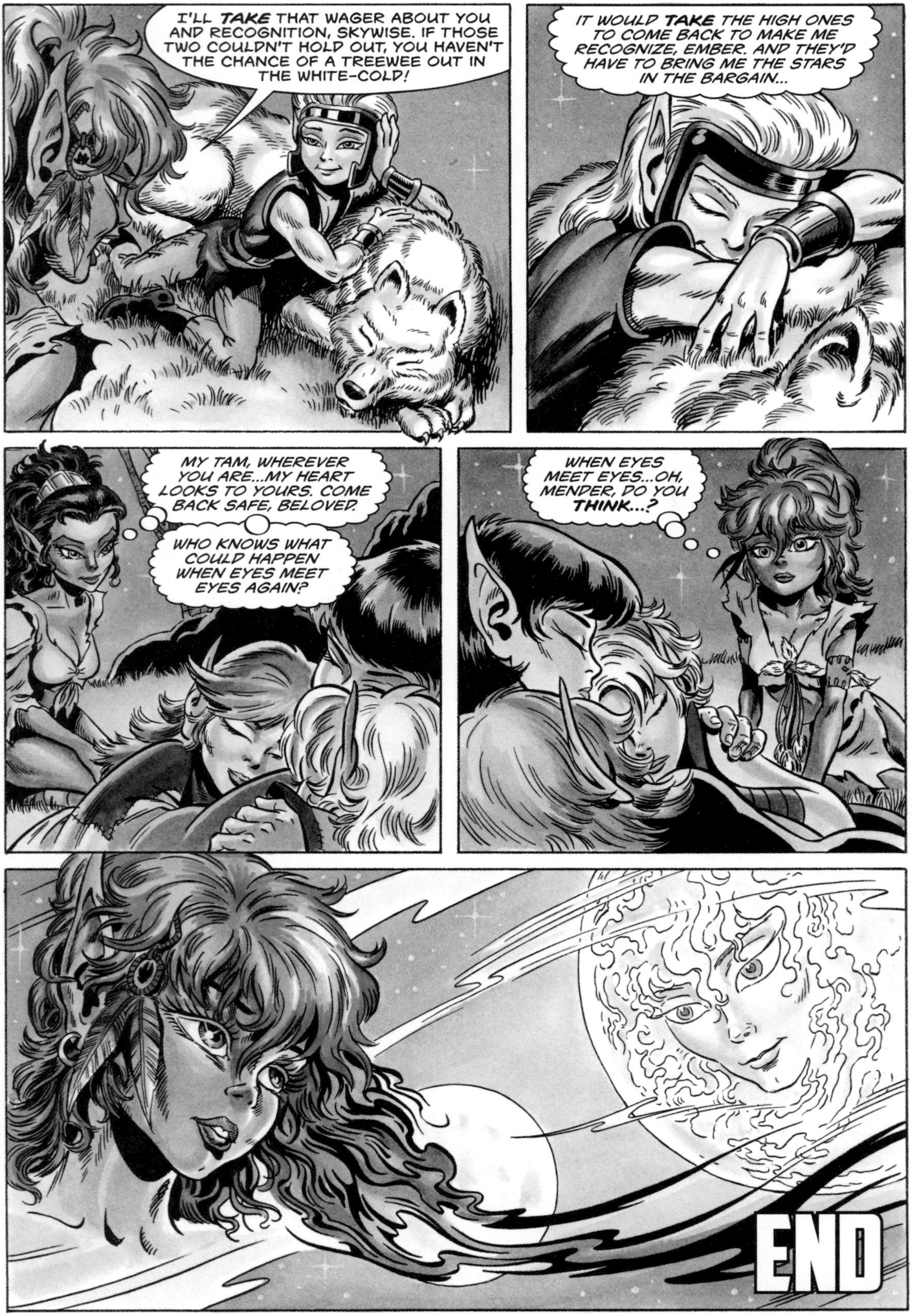
I'LL TAKE THAT WAGER ABOUT YOU AND RECOGNITION, SKYWISE. IF THOSE TWO COULDN'T HOLD OUT, YOU HAVEN'T THE CHANCE OF A TREEWEE OUT IN THE WHITE-COLD!
IT WOULD TAKE THE HIGH ONES TO COME BACK TO MAKE ME RECOGNIZE, EMBER. AND THEY'D HAVE TO BRING ME THE STARS IN THE BARGAIN...
MY TAM, WHEREVER YOU ARE...MY HEART LOOKS TO YOURS. COME BACK SAFE, BELOVED.
WHO KNOWS WHAT COULD HAPPEN WHEN EYES MEET EYES AGAIN?
WHEN EYES MEET EYES...OH, MENDER, DO YOU THINK...?
END

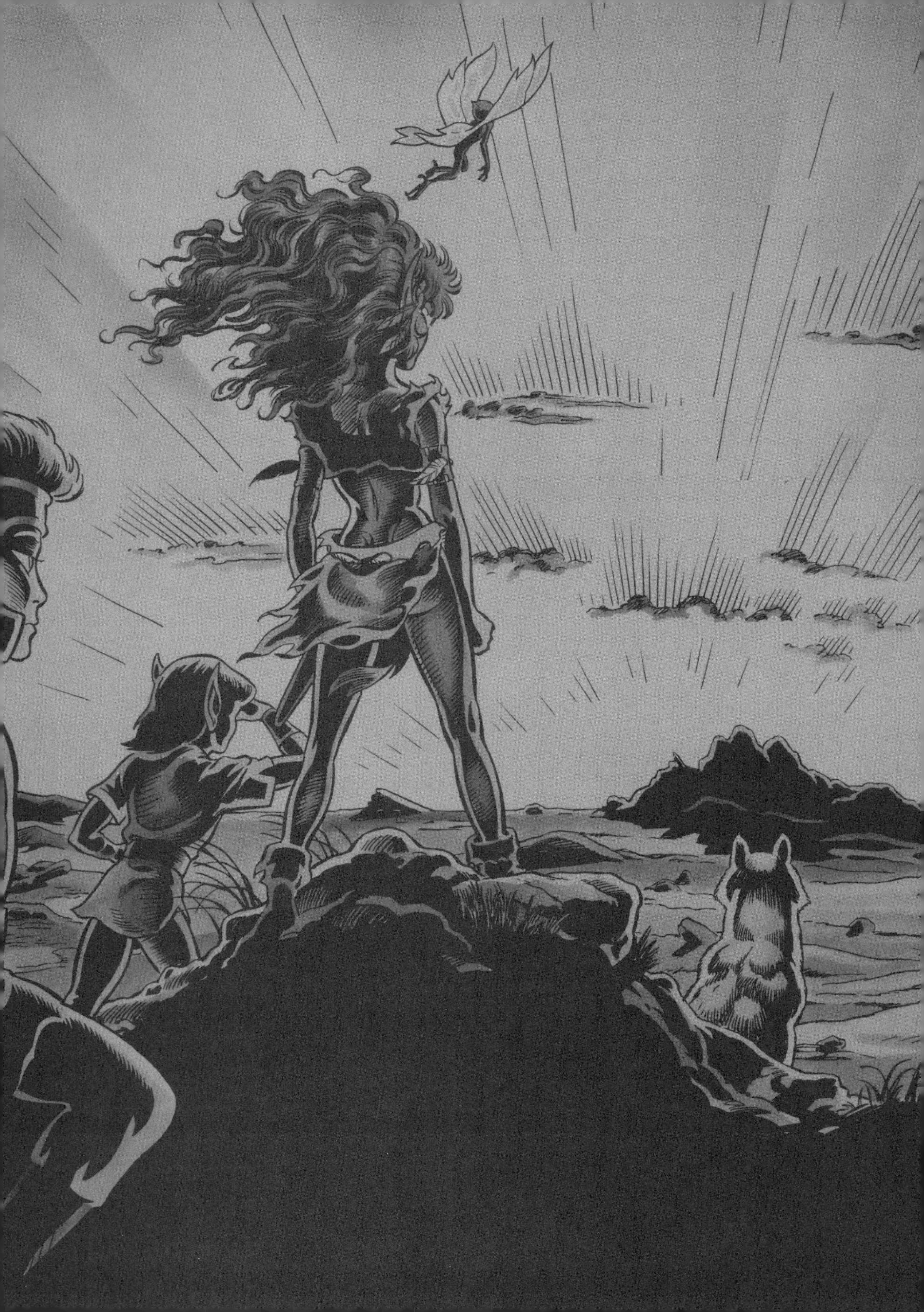

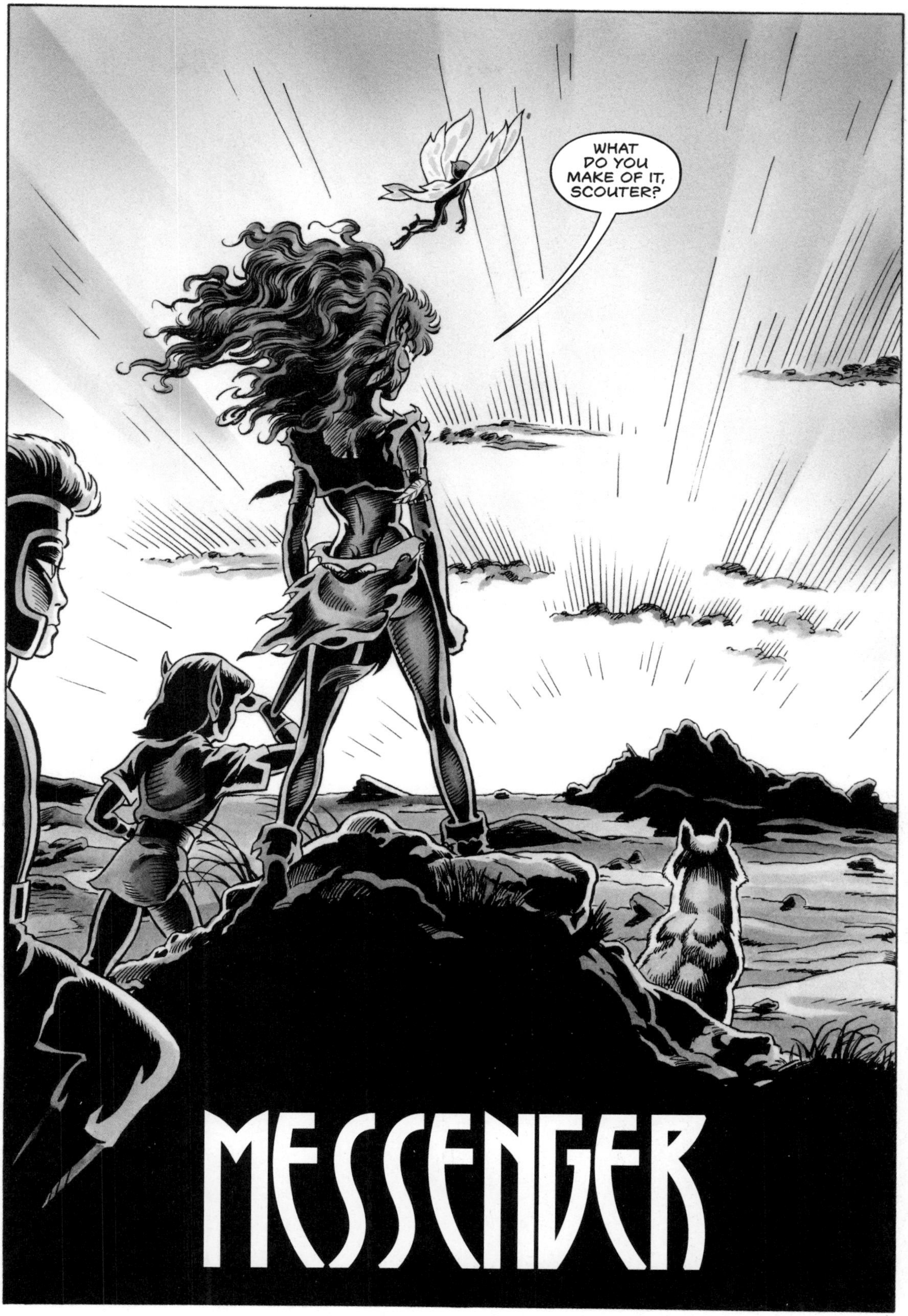
WHAT DO YOU MAKE OF IT, SCOUTER?
MESSENGER

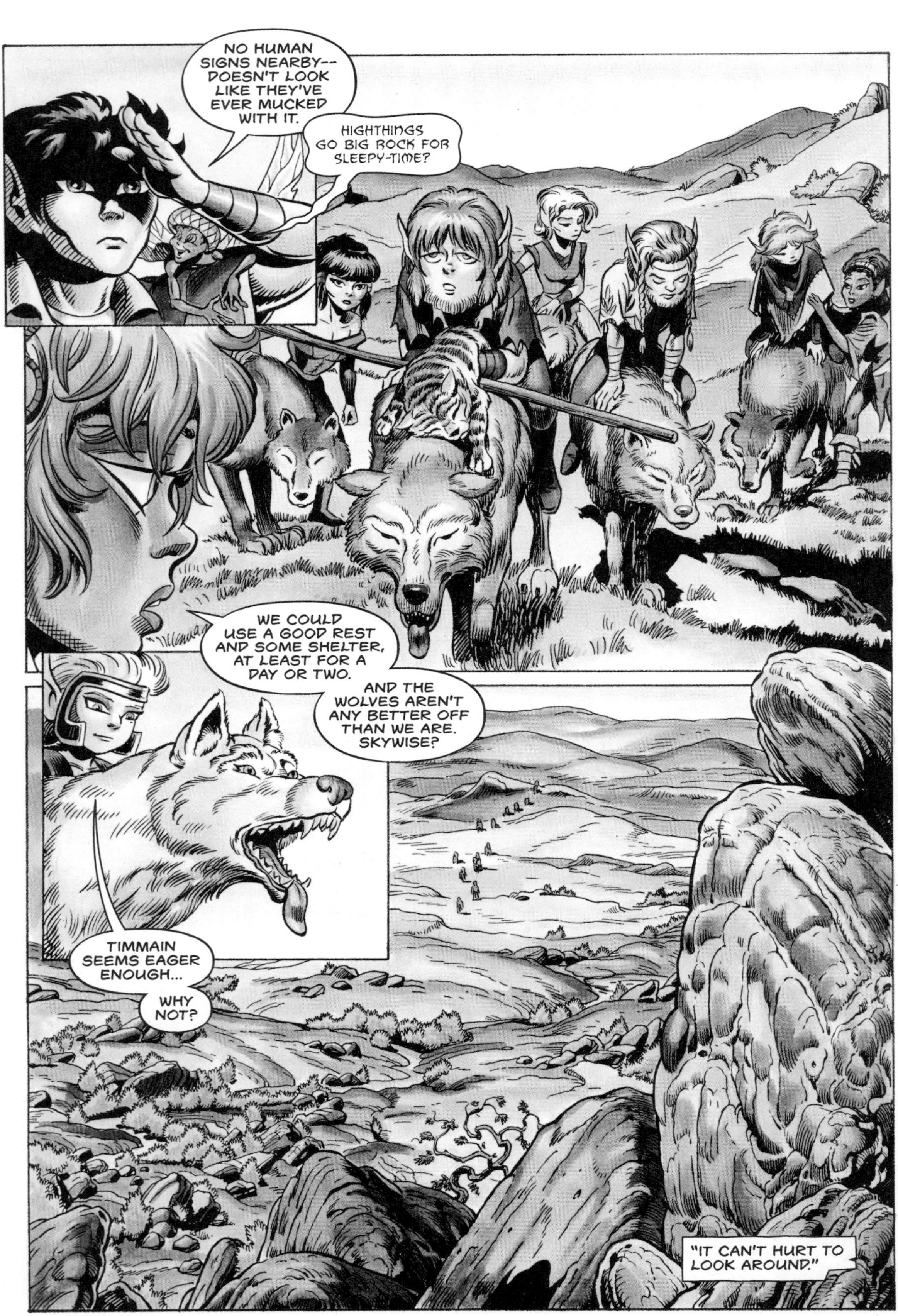
NO HUMAN SIGNS NEARBY-- DOESN'T LOOK LIKE THEY'VE EVER MUCKED WITH IT.
HIGHTHINGS GO BIG ROCK FOR SLEEPY-TIME?
WE COULD USE A GOOD REST AND SOME SHELTER, AT LEAST FOR A DAY OR TWO.
AND THE WOLVES AREN'T ANY BETTER OFF THAN WE ARE. SKYWISE?
TIMMAIN SEEMS EAGER ENOUGH...
WHY NOT?
"IT CAN'T HURT TO LOOK AROUND."

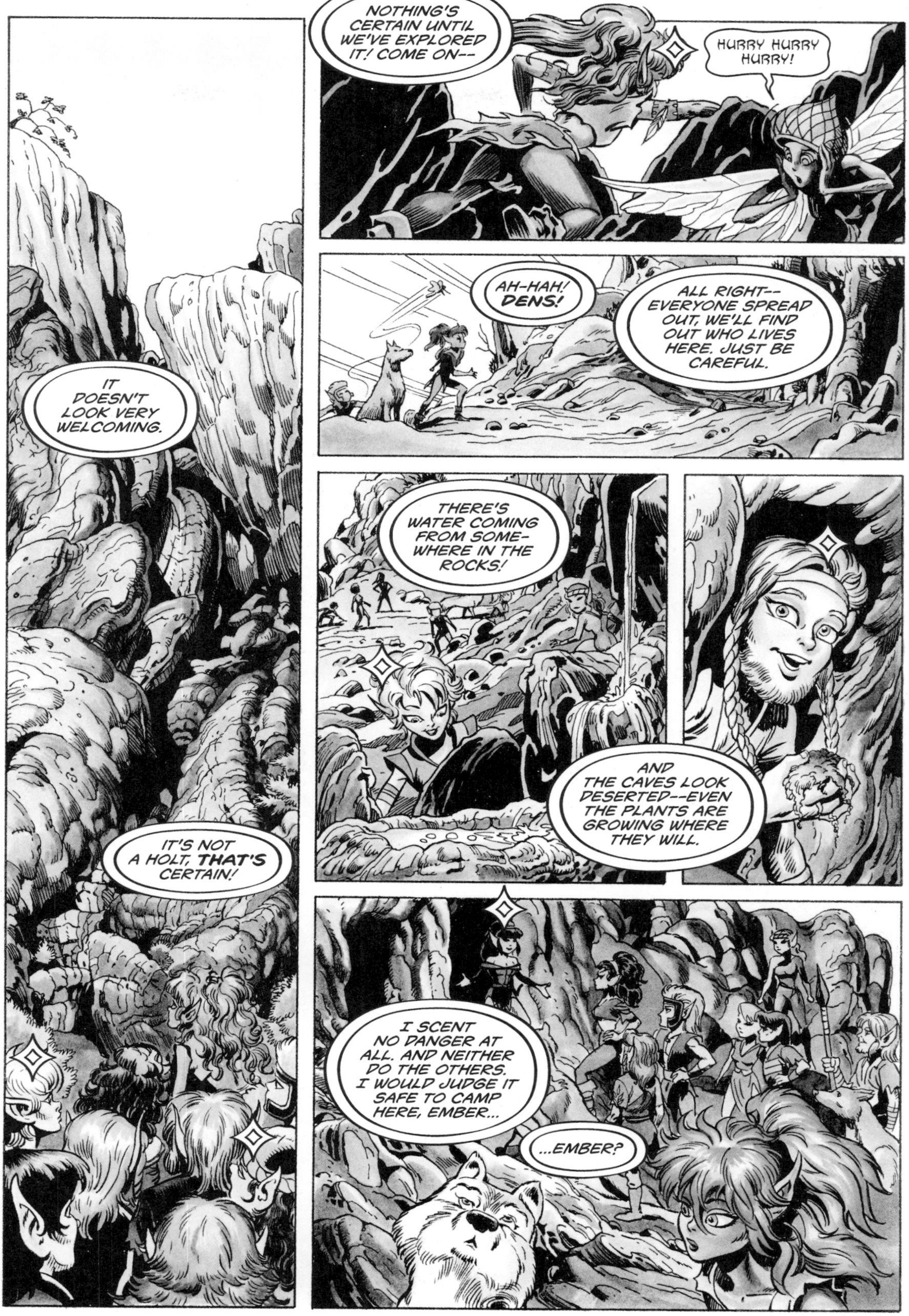
IT DOESN'T LOOK VERY WELCOMING.
IT'S NOT A HOLT, THAT'S CERTAIN!
NOTHING'S CERTAIN UNTIL WE'VE EXPLORED IT! COME ON--
HURRY HURRY HURRY!
AH-HAH! DENS!
ALL RIGHT-- EVERYONE SPREAD OUT, WE'LL FIND OUT WHO LIVES HERE. JUST BE CAREFUL.
THERE'S WATER COMING FROM SOME-WHERE IN THE ROCKS!
AND THE CAVES LOOK DESERTED--EVEN THE PLANTS ARE GROWING WHERE THEY WILL.
I SCENT NO DANGER AT ALL. AND NEITHER DO THE OTHERS. I WOULD JUDGE IT SAFE TO CAMP HERE, EMBER...
...EMBER?

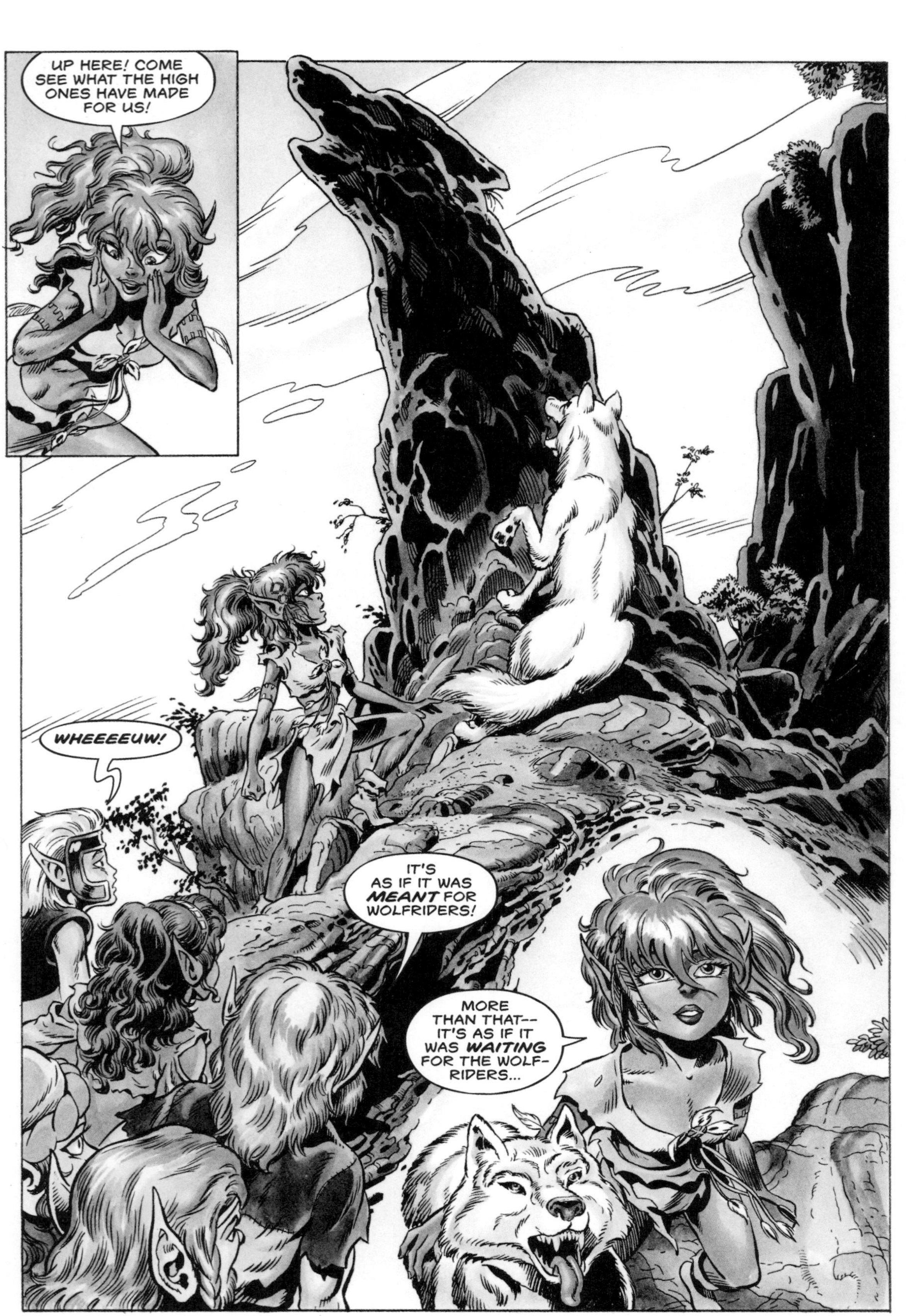
UP HERE! COME SEE WHAT THE HIGH ONES HAVE MADE FOR US!
WHEEEEEUW!
IT'S AS IF IT WAS MEANT FOR WOLFRIDERS!
MORE THAN THAT-- IT'S AS IF IT WAS WAITING FOR THE WOLF-RIDERS...

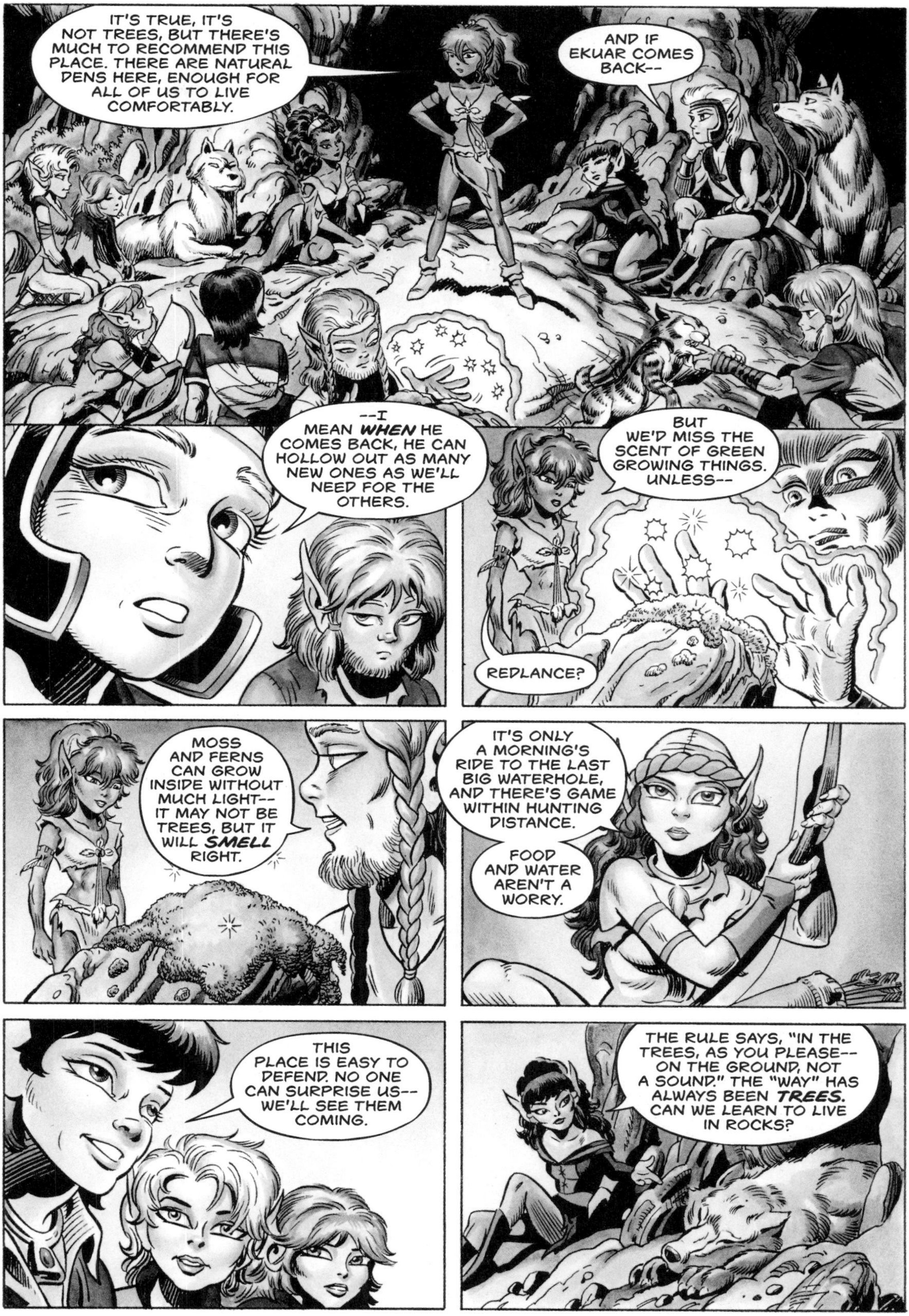
IT'S TRUE, IT'S NOT TREES, BUT THERE'S MUCH TO RECOMMEND THIS PLACE. THERE ARE NATURAL DENS HERE, ENOUGH FOR ALL OF US TO LIVE COMFORTABLY.
AND IF EKUAR COMES BACK--
--I MEAN ***WHEN*** HE COMES BACK, HE CAN HOLLOW OUT AS MANY NEW ONES AS WE'LL NEED FOR THE OTHERS.
BUT WE'D MISS THE SCENT OF GREEN GROWING THINGS. UNLESS--
REDLANCE?
MOSS AND FERNS CAN GROW INSIDE WITHOUT MUCH LIGHT-- IT MAY NOT BE TREES, BUT IT WILL ***SMELL*** RIGHT.
IT'S ONLY A MORNING'S RIDE TO THE LAST BIG WATERHOLE, AND THERE'S GAME WITHIN HUNTING DISTANCE.
FOOD AND WATER AREN'T A WORRY.
THIS PLACE IS EASY TO DEFEND. NO ONE CAN SURPRISE US-- WE'LL SEE THEM COMING.
THE RULE SAYS, "IN THE TREES, AS YOU PLEASE-- ON THE GROUND, NOT A SOUND." THE "WAY" HAS ALWAYS BEEN ***TREES.*** CAN WE LEARN TO LIVE IN ROCKS?

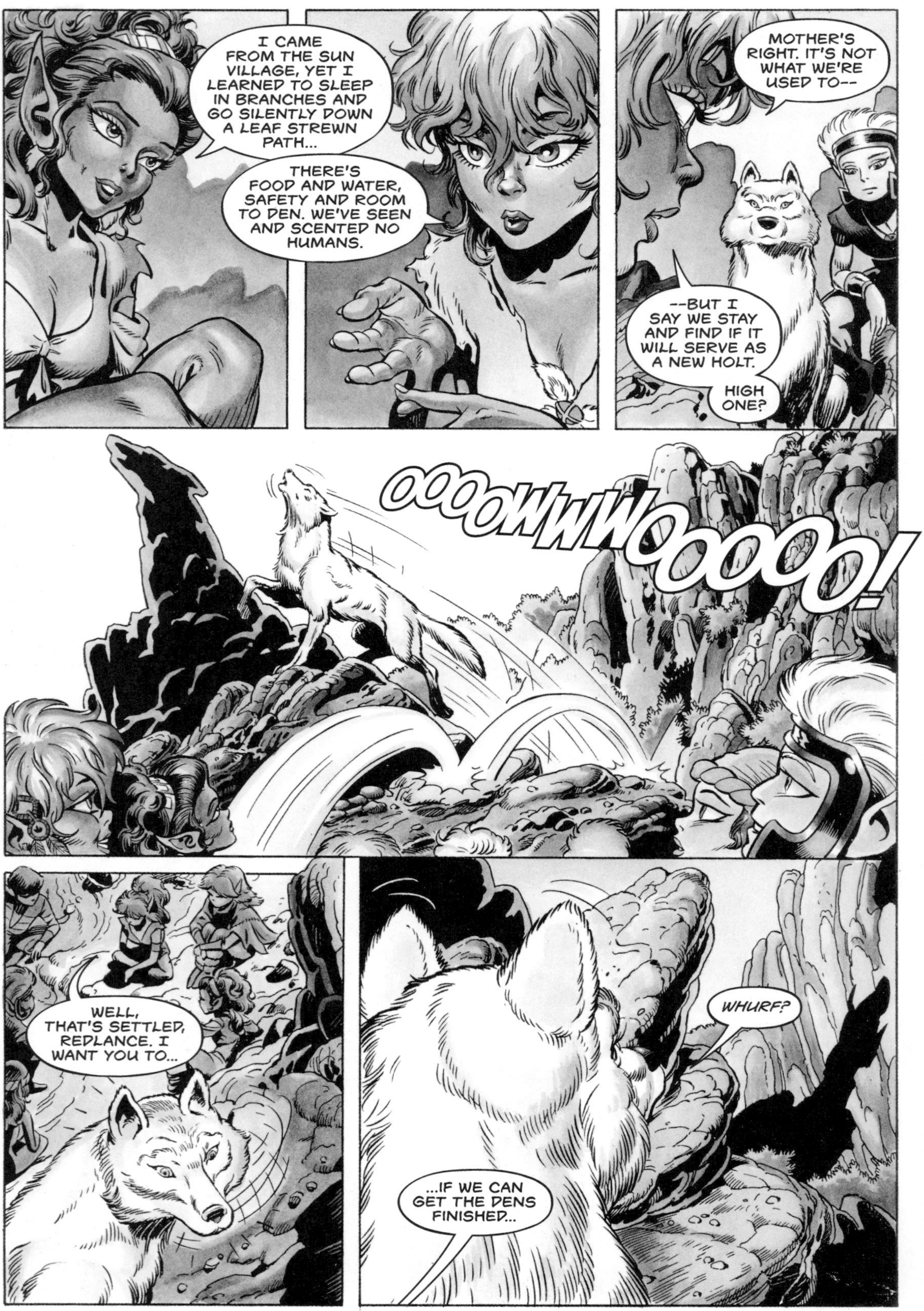

I CAME FROM THE SUN VILLAGE, YET I LEARNED TO SLEEP IN BRANCHES AND GO SILENTLY DOWN A LEAF STREWN PATH...
THERE'S FOOD AND WATER, SAFETY AND ROOM TO DEN. WE'VE SEEN AND SCENTED NO HUMANS.
MOTHER'S RIGHT. IT'S NOT WHAT WE'RE USED TO--
--BUT I SAY WE STAY AND FIND IF IT WILL SERVE AS A NEW HOLT.
HIGH ONE?
OOOOOWWWOOOOOO!
WELL, THAT'S SETTLED, REDLANCE. I WANT YOU TO...
WHURF?
...IF WE CAN GET THE DENS FINISHED...

...SHOULD BE ABLE TO STORE THINGS IN...

RRRRR...

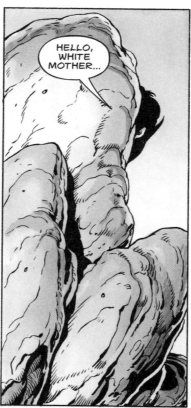

HELLO, WHITE MOTHER...

WHINNNNE...?

SSSHHHH...

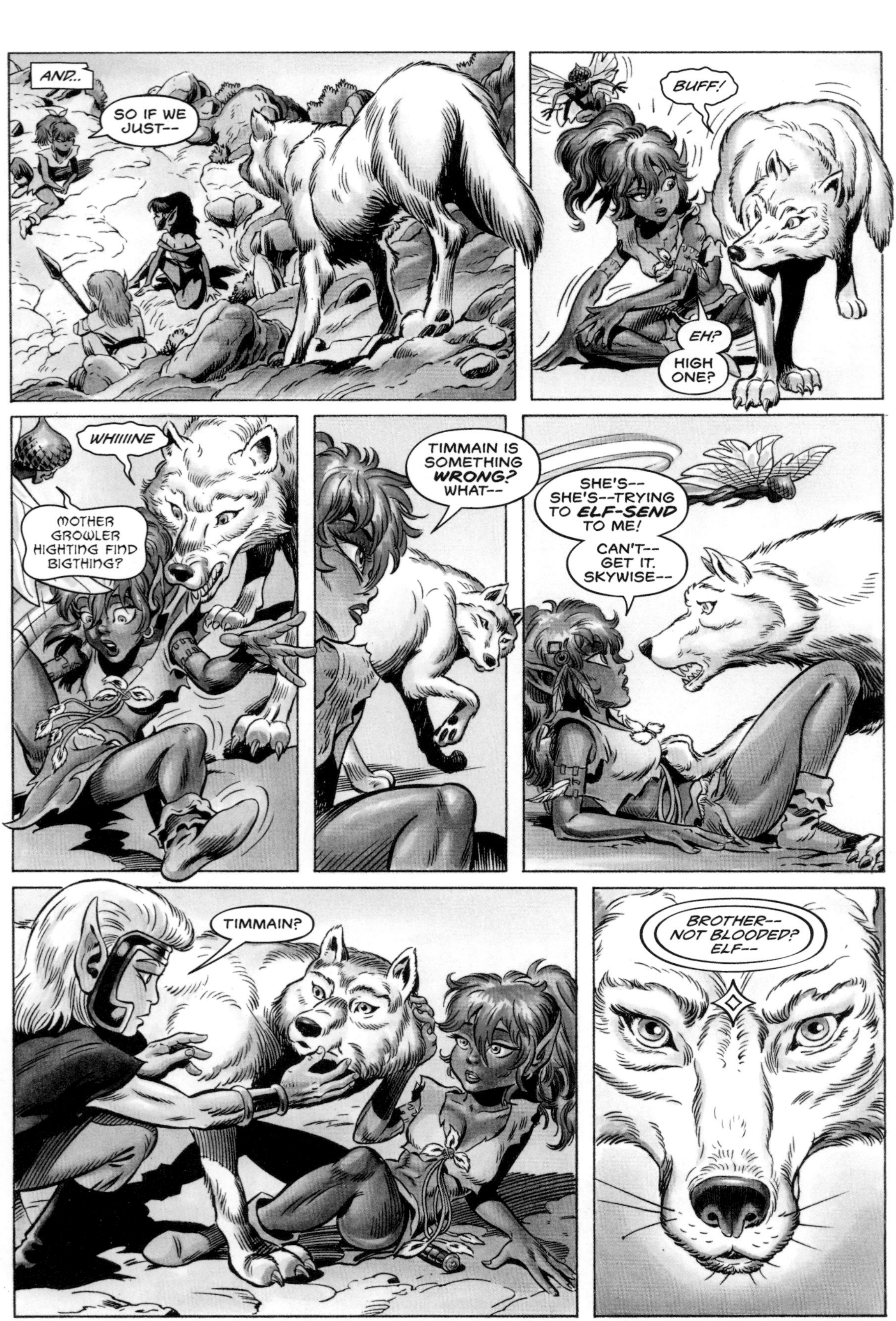
AND..
SO IF WE JUST--
BUFF!
EH? HIGH ONE?
WHIIIINE
MOTHER GROWLER HIGHTING FIND BIGTHING?
TIMMAIN IS SOMETHING WRONG? WHAT--
SHE'S-- SHE'S--TRYING TO ELF-SEND TO ME!
CAN'T-- GET IT. SKYWISE--
TIMMAIN?
BROTHER-- NOT BLOODED? ELF--

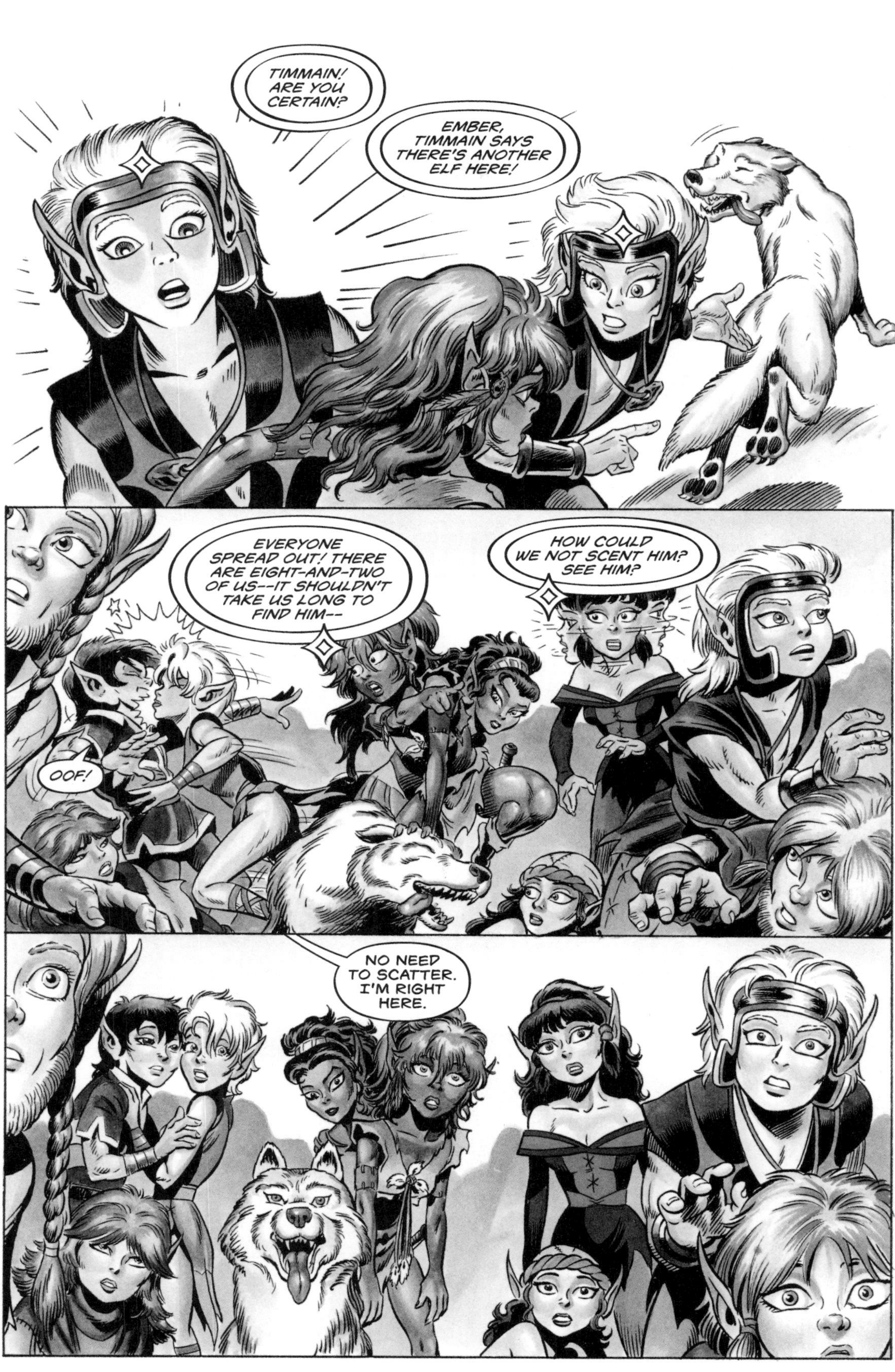
TIMMAIN! ARE YOU CERTAIN?
EMBER, TIMMAIN SAYS THERE'S ANOTHER ELF HERE!
EVERYONE SPREAD OUT! THERE ARE EIGHT-AND-TWO OF US--IT SHOULDN'T TAKE US LONG TO FIND HIM--
HOW COULD WE NOT SCENT HIM? SEE HIM?
OOF!
NO NEED TO SCATTER. I'M RIGHT HERE.

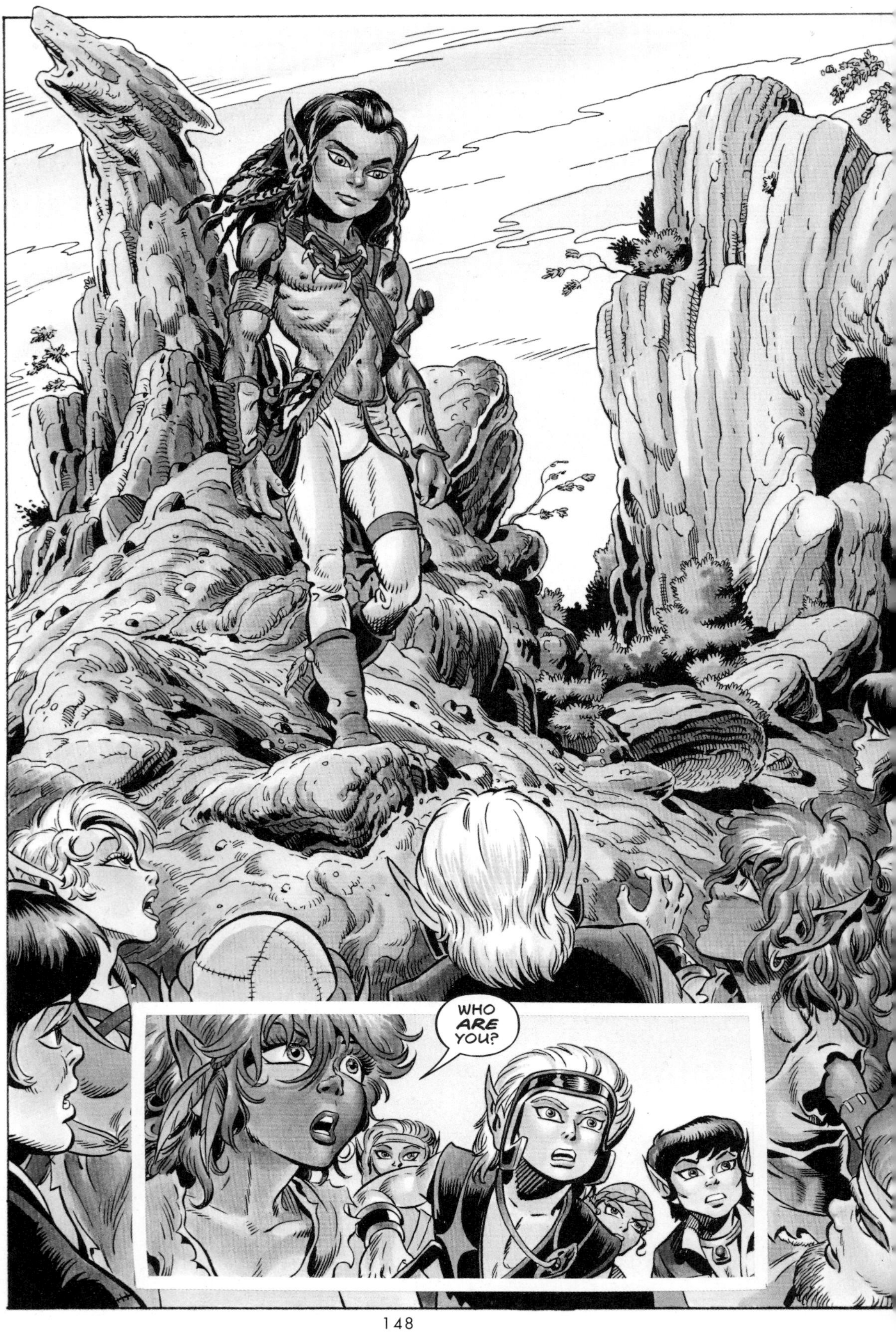
WHO ARE YOU?

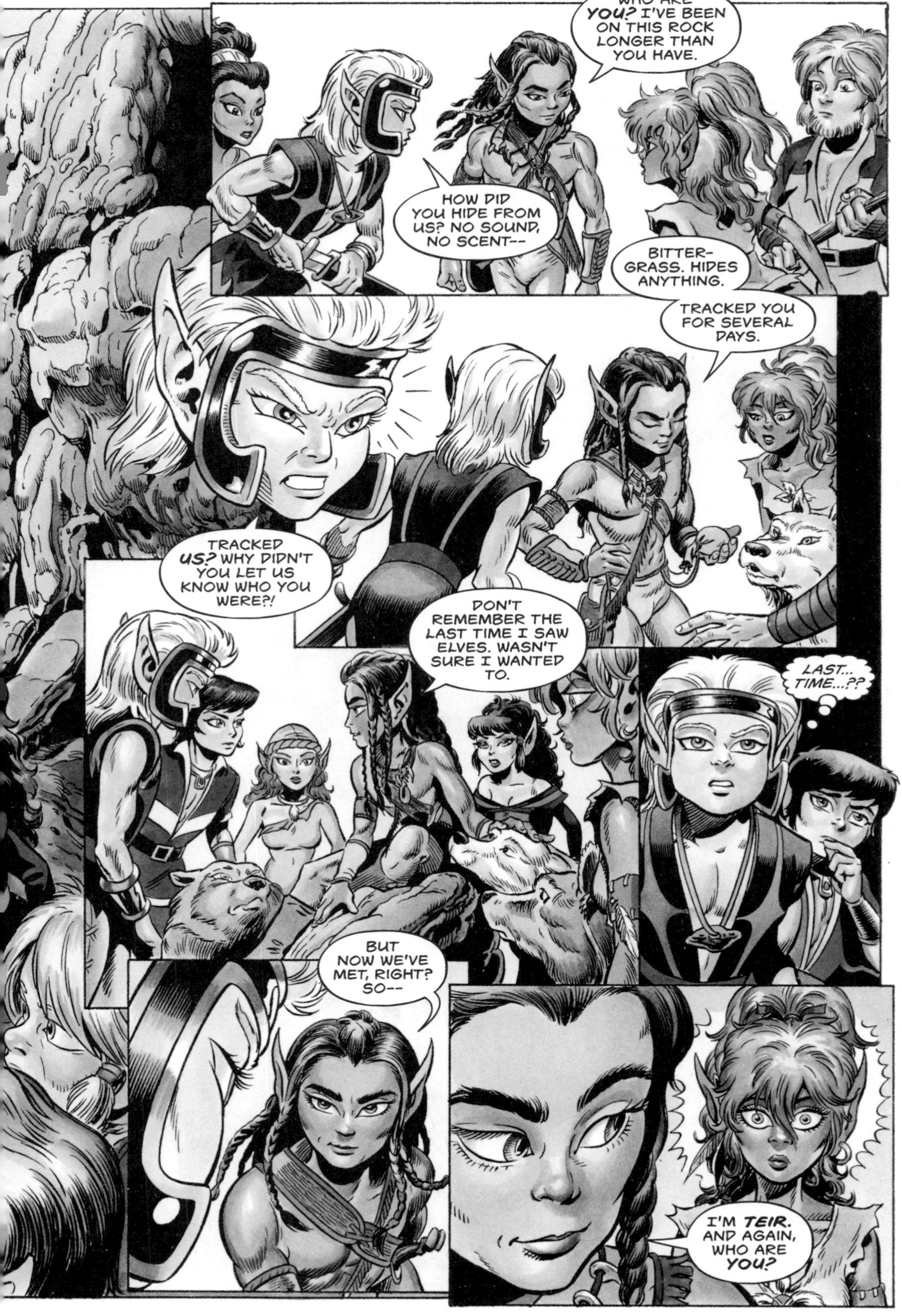
WHO ARE YOU? I'VE BEEN ON THIS ROCK LONGER THAN YOU HAVE.
HOW DID YOU HIDE FROM US? NO SOUND, NO SCENT--
BITTER-GRASS. HIDES ANYTHING.
TRACKED YOU FOR SEVERAL DAYS.
TRACKED US? WHY DIDN'T YOU LET US KNOW WHO YOU WERE?!
DON'T REMEMBER THE LAST TIME I SAW ELVES. WASN'T SURE I WANTED TO.
LAST... TIME...??
BUT NOW WE'VE MET, RIGHT? SO--
I'M TEIR. AND AGAIN, WHO ARE YOU?

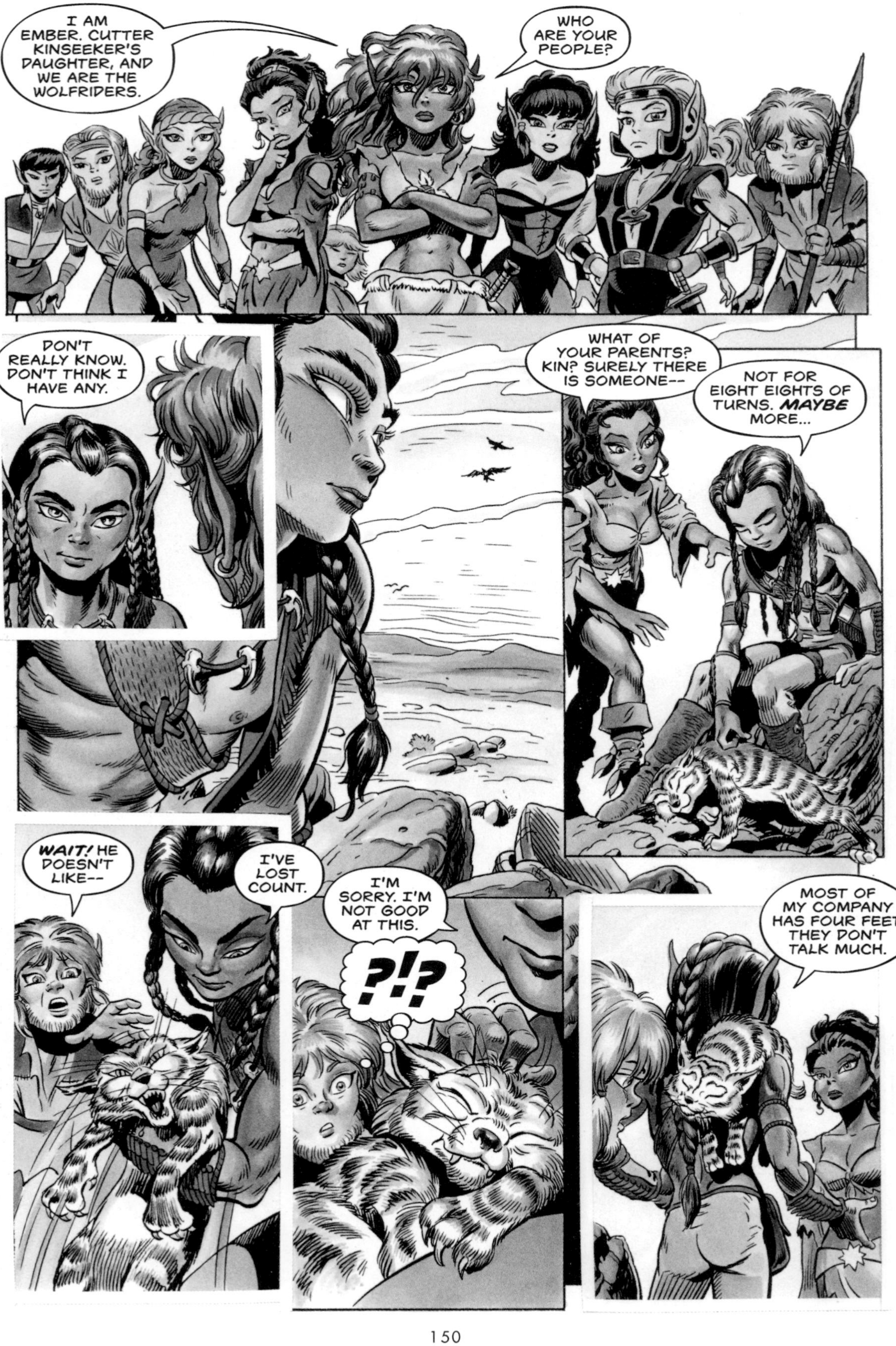
I AM EMBER. CUTTER KINSEEKER'S DAUGHTER, AND WE ARE THE WOLFRIDERS.
WHO ARE YOUR PEOPLE?
DON'T REALLY KNOW. DON'T THINK I HAVE ANY.
WHAT OF YOUR PARENTS? KIN? SURELY THERE IS SOMEONE--
NOT FOR EIGHT EIGHTS OF TURNS. MAYBE MORE...
WAIT! HE DOESN'T LIKE--
I'VE LOST COUNT.
I'M SORRY. I'M NOT GOOD AT THIS.
?!?
MOST OF MY COMPANY HAS FOUR FEET. THEY DON'T TALK MUCH.

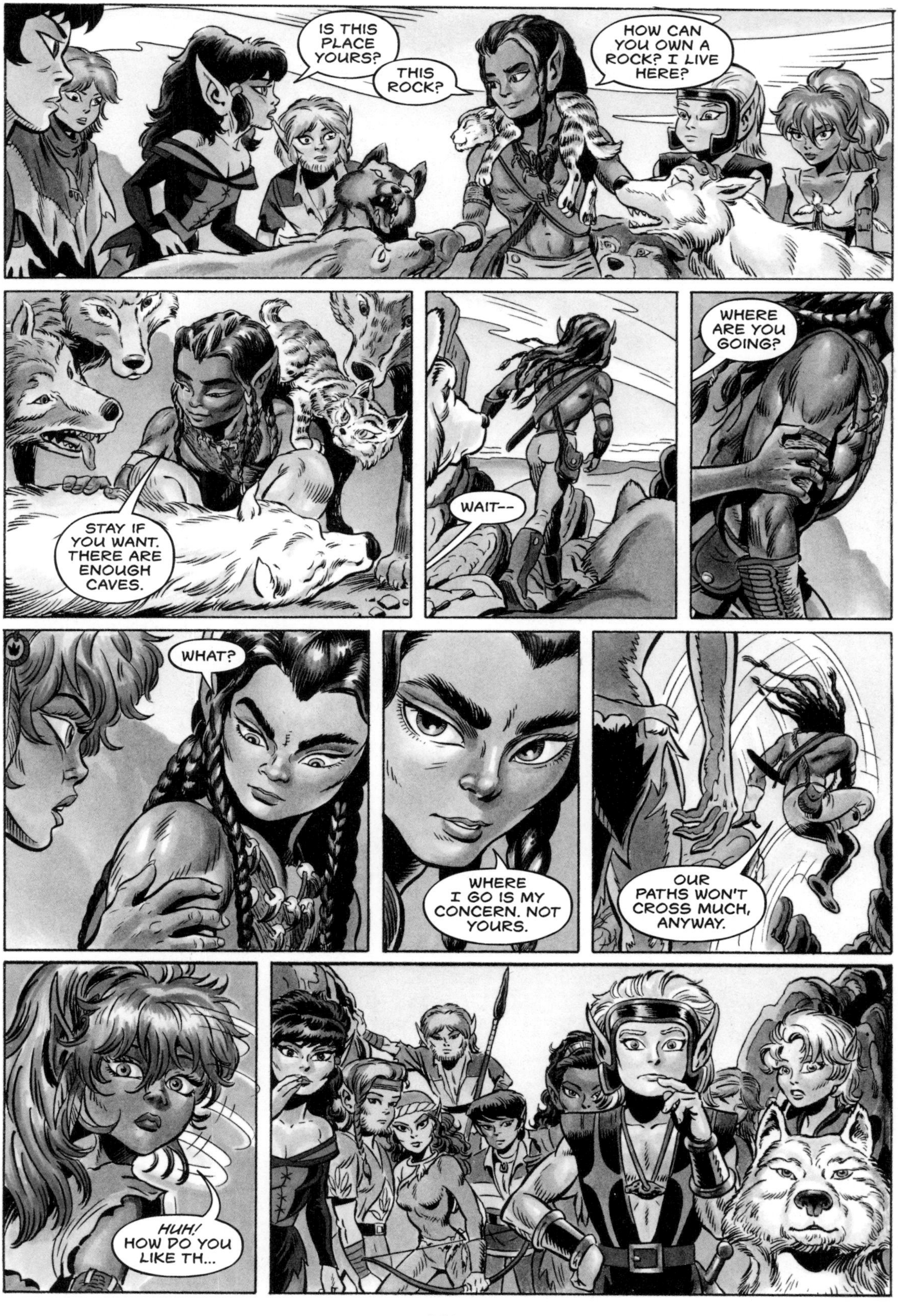

IS THIS PLACE YOURS?
THIS ROCK?
HOW CAN YOU OWN A ROCK? I LIVE HERE?
STAY IF YOU WANT. THERE ARE ENOUGH CAVES.
WAIT--
WHERE ARE YOU GOING?
WHAT?
WHERE I GO IS MY CONCERN. NOT YOURS.
OUR PATHS WON'T CROSS MUCH, ANYWAY.
HUH! HOW DO YOU LIKE TH...

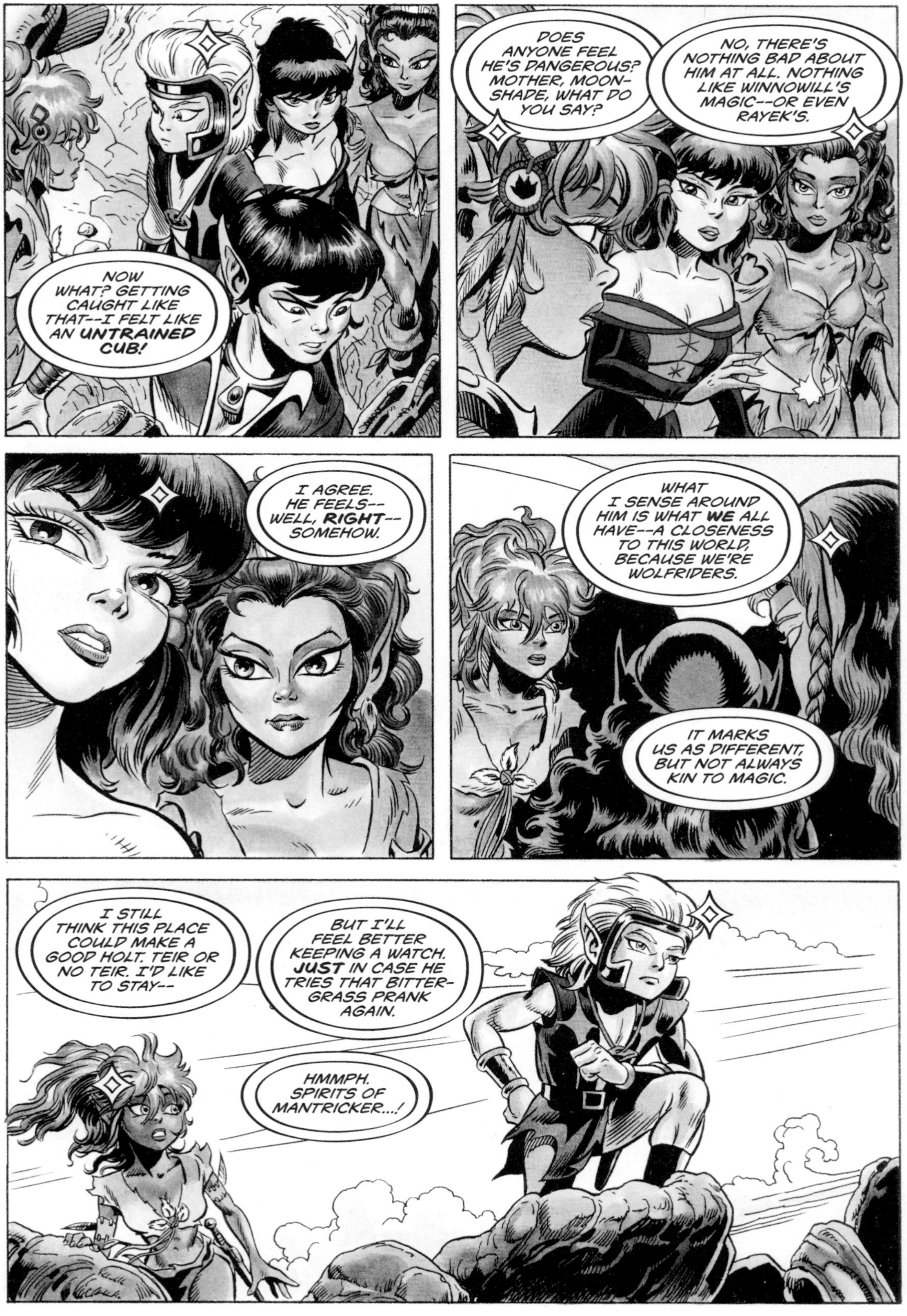
NOW WHAT? GETTING CAUGHT LIKE THAT--I FELT LIKE AN **UNTRAINED CUB!**
DOES ANYONE FEEL HE'S DANGEROUS? MOTHER, MOON-SHADE, WHAT DO YOU SAY?
NO, THERE'S NOTHING BAD ABOUT HIM AT ALL. NOTHING LIKE WINNOWILL'S MAGIC--OR EVEN RAYEK'S.
I AGREE. HE FEELS--WELL, **RIGHT**--SOMEHOW.
WHAT I SENSE AROUND HIM IS WHAT **WE** ALL HAVE--A CLOSENESS TO THIS WORLD, BECAUSE WE'RE WOLFRIDERS.
IT MARKS US AS DIFFERENT, BUT NOT ALWAYS KIN TO MAGIC.
I STILL THINK THIS PLACE COULD MAKE A GOOD HOLT. TEIR OR NO TEIR. I'D LIKE TO STAY--
BUT I'LL FEEL BETTER KEEPING A WATCH. **JUST** IN CASE HE TRIES THAT BITTER-GRASS PRANK AGAIN.
HMMPH. SPIRITS OF MANTRICKER...!

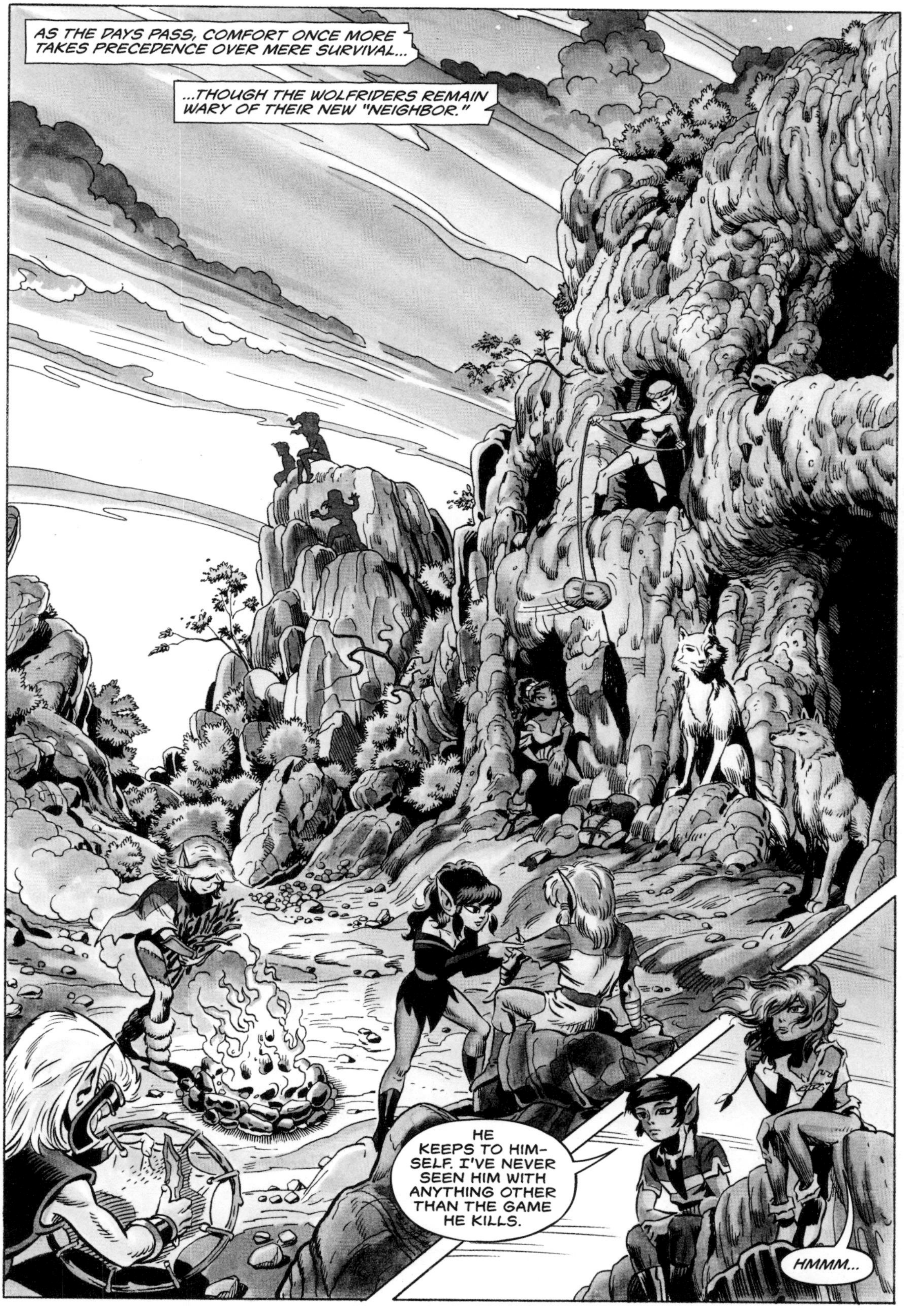
AS THE DAYS PASS, COMFORT ONCE MORE TAKES PRECEDENCE OVER MERE SURVIVAL...
...THOUGH THE WOLFRIDERS REMAIN WARY OF THEIR NEW "NEIGHBOR."
HE KEEPS TO HIMSELF. I'VE NEVER SEEN HIM WITH ANYTHING OTHER THAN THE GAME HE KILLS.
HMMM...

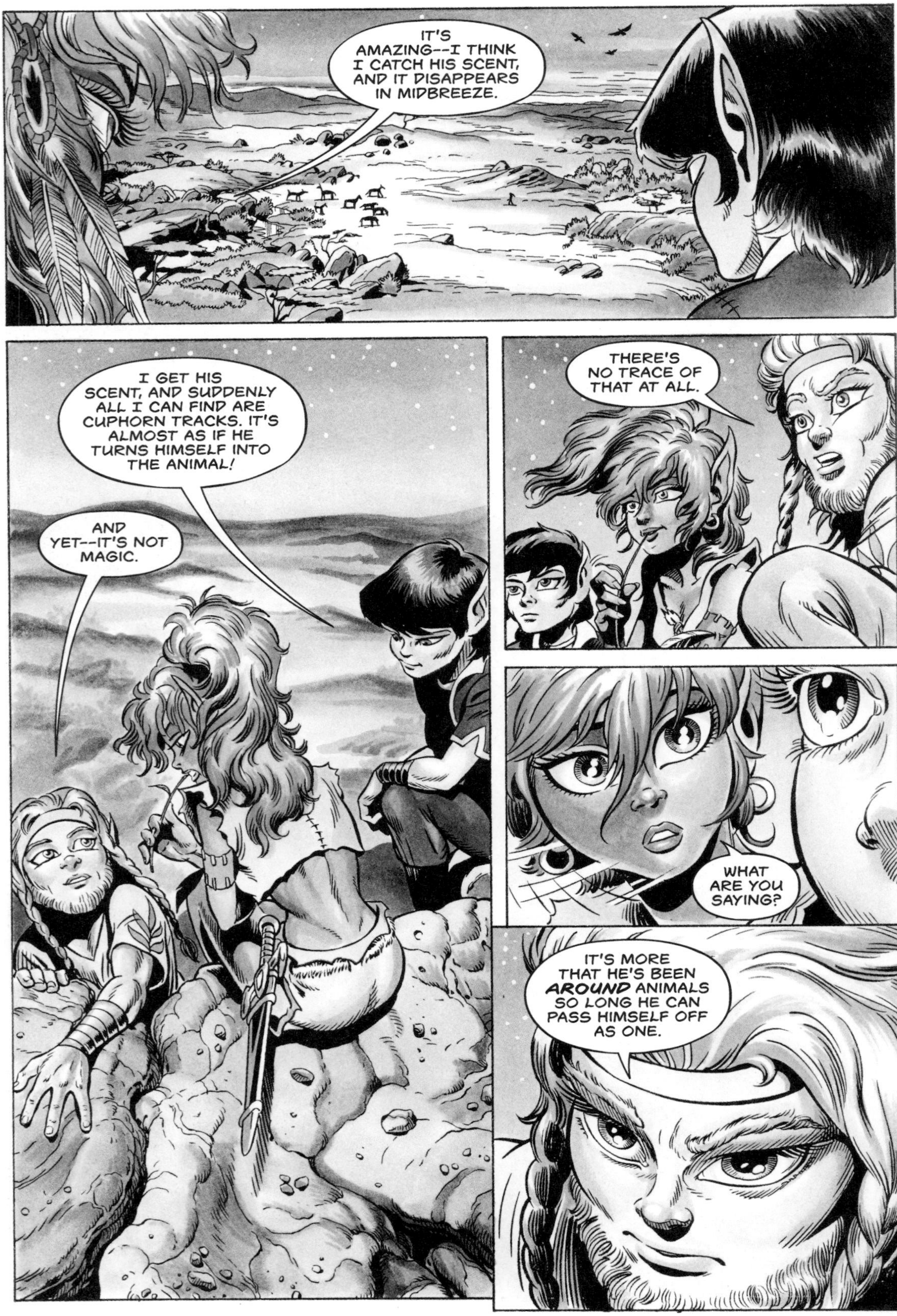
IT'S AMAZING--I THINK I CATCH HIS SCENT, AND IT DISAPPEARS IN MIDBREEZE.
I GET HIS SCENT, AND SUDDENLY ALL I CAN FIND ARE CUPHORN TRACKS. IT'S ALMOST AS IF HE TURNS HIMSELF INTO THE ANIMAL!
AND YET--IT'S NOT MAGIC.
THERE'S NO TRACE OF THAT AT ALL.
WHAT ARE YOU SAYING?
IT'S MORE THAT HE'S BEEN AROUND ANIMALS SO LONG HE CAN PASS HIMSELF OFF AS ONE.

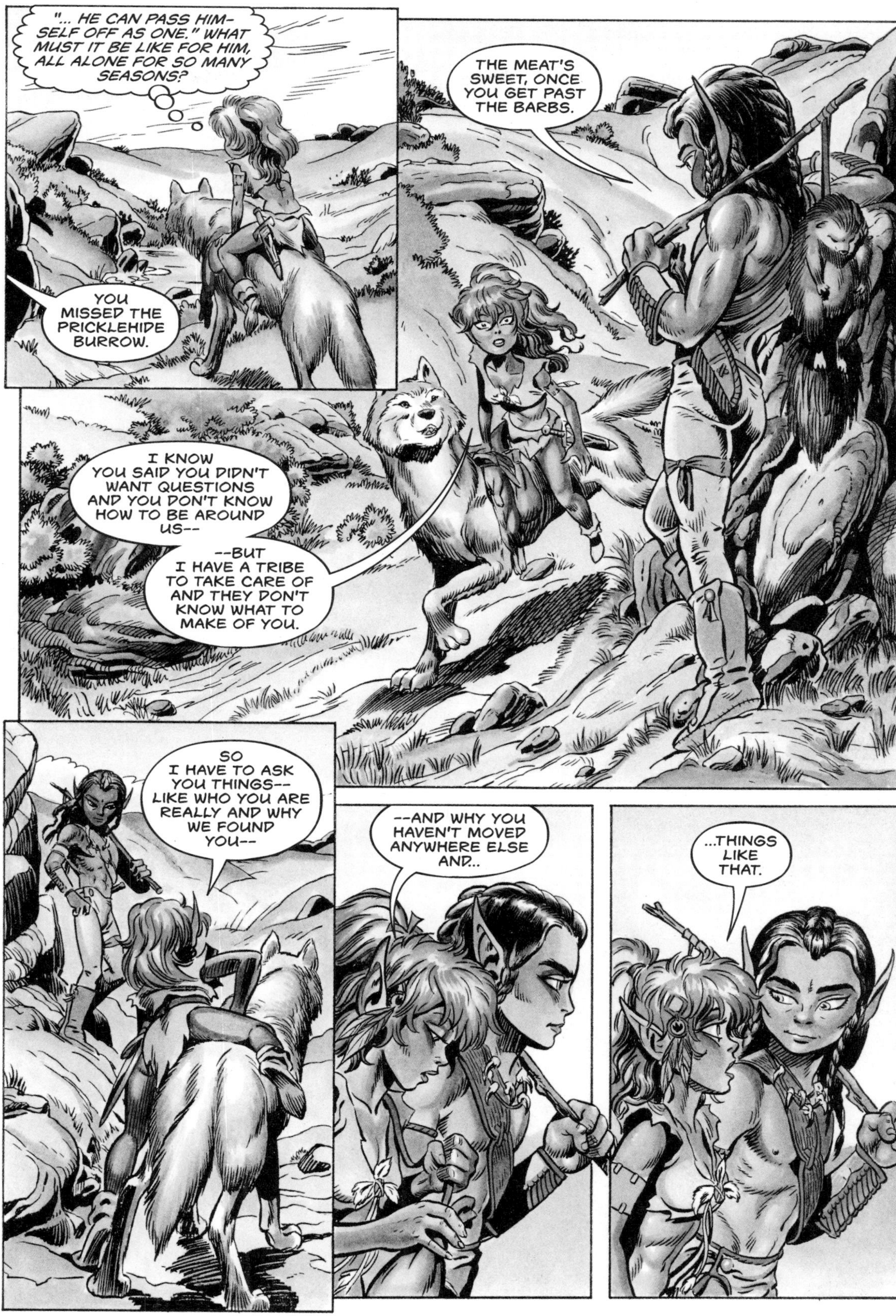
"... HE CAN PASS HIMSELF OFF AS ONE." WHAT MUST IT BE LIKE FOR HIM, ALL ALONE FOR SO MANY SEASONS?
YOU MISSED THE PRICKLEHIDE BURROW.
THE MEAT'S SWEET, ONCE YOU GET PAST THE BARBS.
I KNOW YOU SAID YOU DIDN'T WANT QUESTIONS AND YOU DON'T KNOW HOW TO BE AROUND US--
--BUT I HAVE A TRIBE TO TAKE CARE OF AND THEY DON'T KNOW WHAT TO MAKE OF YOU.
SO I HAVE TO ASK YOU THINGS-- LIKE WHO YOU ARE REALLY AND WHY WE FOUND YOU--
--AND WHY YOU HAVEN'T MOVED ANYWHERE ELSE AND...
...THINGS LIKE THAT.

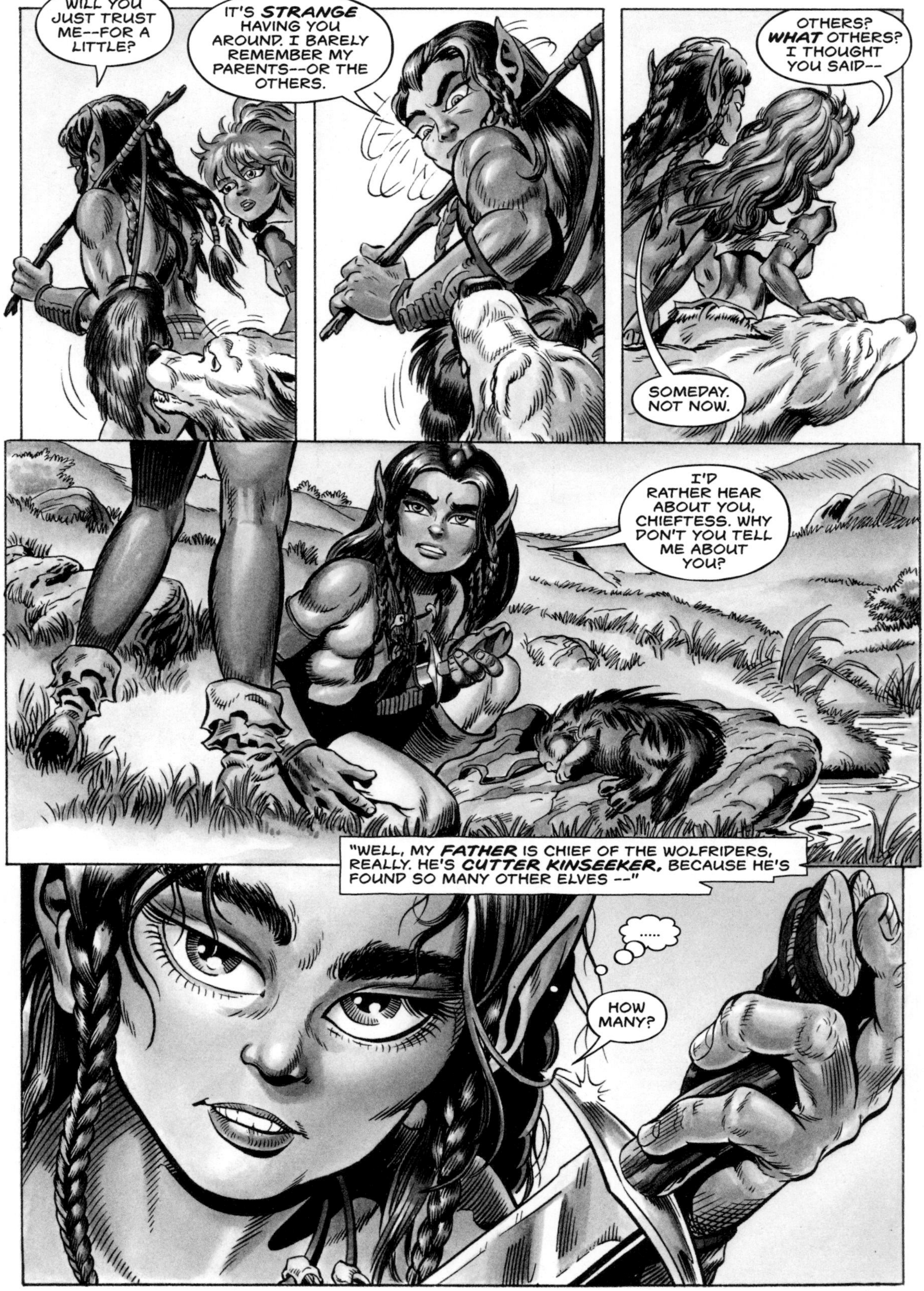
WILL YOU JUST TRUST ME--FOR A LITTLE?
IT'S STRANGE HAVING YOU AROUND. I BARELY REMEMBER MY PARENTS--OR THE OTHERS.
OTHERS? WHAT OTHERS? I THOUGHT YOU SAID--
SOMEDAY. NOT NOW.
I'D RATHER HEAR ABOUT YOU, CHIEFTESS. WHY DON'T YOU TELL ME ABOUT YOU?
"WELL, MY FATHER IS CHIEF OF THE WOLFRIDERS, REALLY. HE'S CUTTER KINSEEKER, BECAUSE HE'S FOUND SO MANY OTHER ELVES --"
.....
HOW MANY?

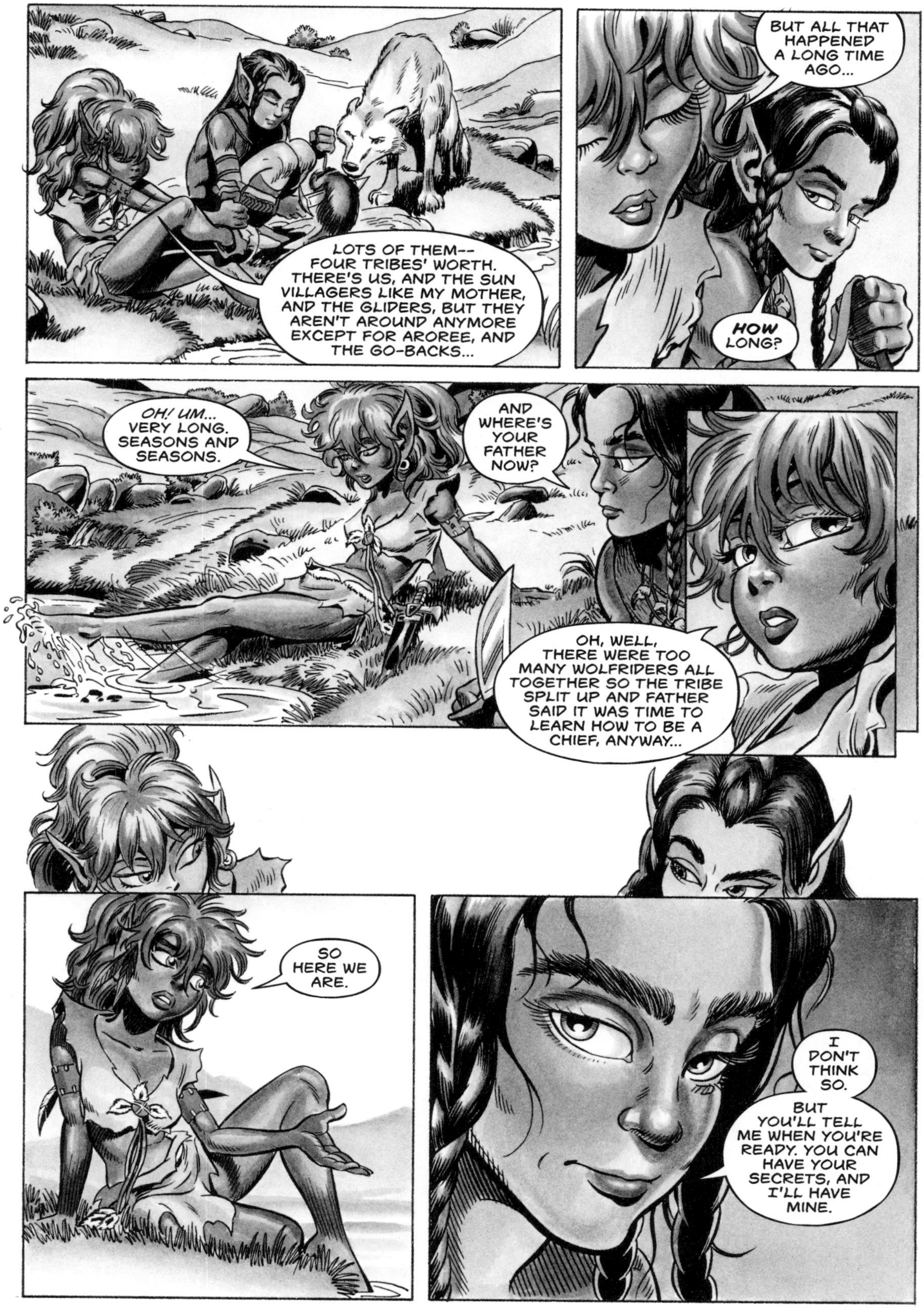
LOTS OF THEM--
FOUR TRIBES' WORTH.
THERE'S US, AND THE SUN
VILLAGERS LIKE MY MOTHER,
AND THE GLIDERS, BUT THEY
AREN'T AROUND ANYMORE
EXCEPT FOR AROREE, AND
THE GO-BACKS...
BUT ALL THAT HAPPENED A LONG TIME AGO...
HOW LONG?
OH! UM... VERY LONG. SEASONS AND SEASONS.
AND WHERE'S YOUR FATHER NOW?
OH, WELL, THERE WERE TOO MANY WOLFRIDERS ALL TOGETHER SO THE TRIBE SPLIT UP AND FATHER SAID IT WAS TIME TO LEARN HOW TO BE A CHIEF, ANYWAY...
SO HERE WE ARE.
I DON'T THINK SO.
BUT YOU'LL TELL ME WHEN YOU'RE READY. YOU CAN HAVE YOUR SECRETS, AND I'LL HAVE MINE.

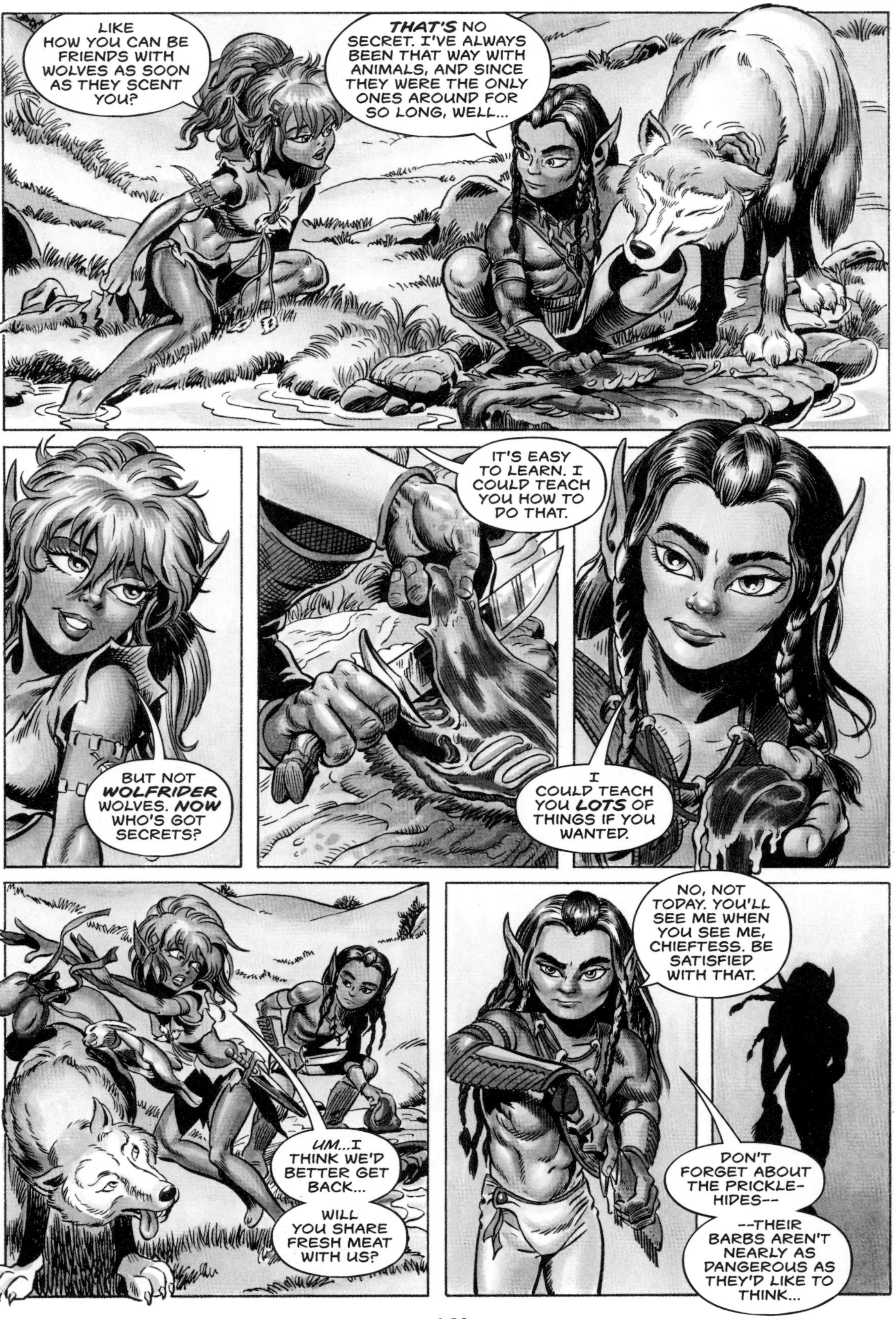

LIKE HOW YOU CAN BE FRIENDS WITH WOLVES AS SOON AS THEY SCENT YOU?
THAT'S NO SECRET. I'VE ALWAYS BEEN THAT WAY WITH ANIMALS, AND SINCE THEY WERE THE ONLY ONES AROUND FOR SO LONG, WELL...
BUT NOT WOLFRIDER WOLVES. NOW WHO'S GOT SECRETS?
IT'S EASY TO LEARN. I COULD TEACH YOU HOW TO DO THAT.
I COULD TEACH YOU LOTS OF THINGS IF YOU WANTED.
UM...I THINK WE'D BETTER GET BACK...
WILL YOU SHARE FRESH MEAT WITH US?
NO, NOT TODAY. YOU'LL SEE ME WHEN YOU SEE ME, CHIEFTESS. BE SATISFIED WITH THAT.
DON'T FORGET ABOUT THE PRICKLE-HIDES--
--THEIR BARBS AREN'T NEARLY AS DANGEROUS AS THEY'D LIKE TO THINK...

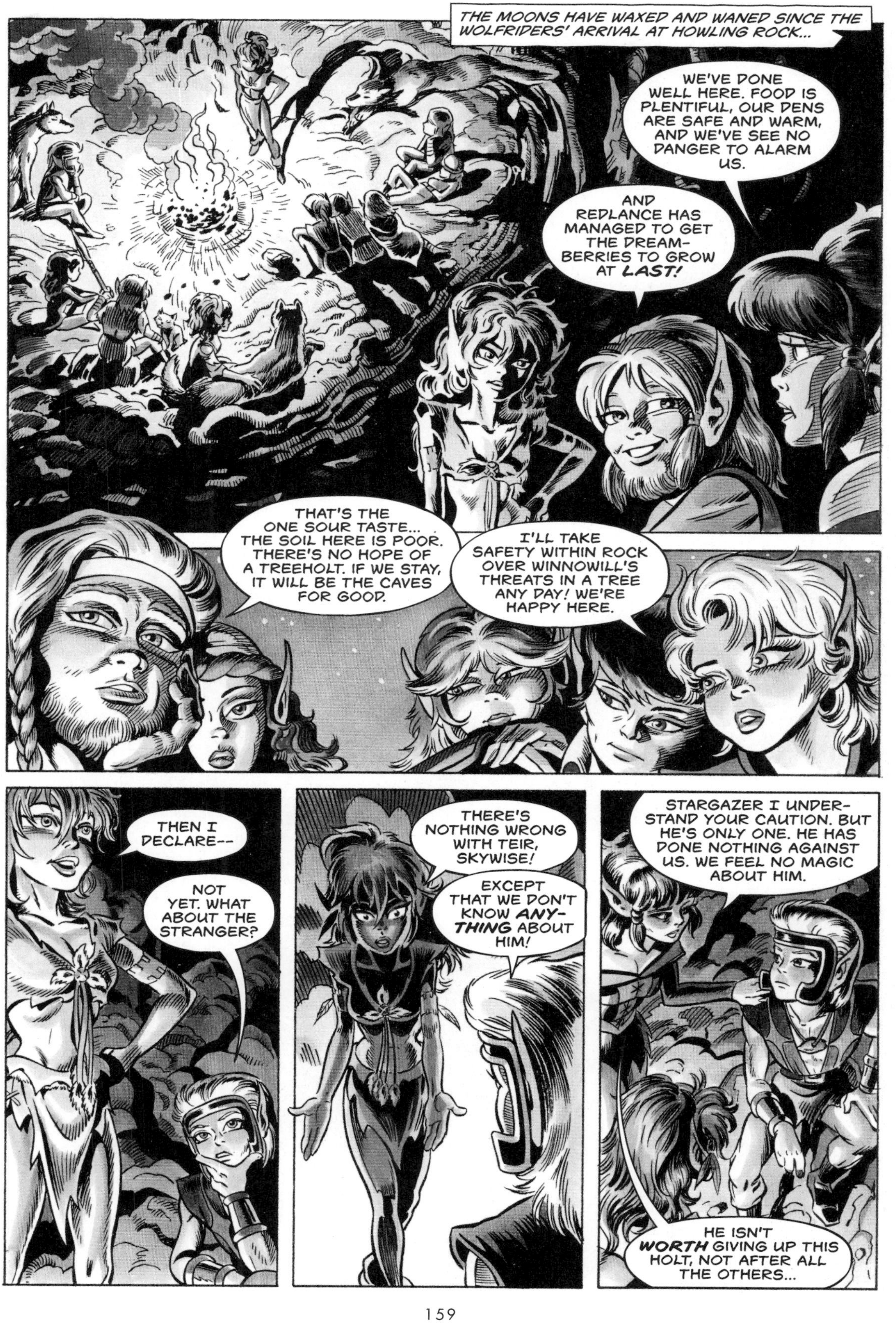

THE MOONS HAVE WAXED AND WANED SINCE THE WOLFRIDERS' ARRIVAL AT HOWLING ROCK...
WE'VE DONE WELL HERE. FOOD IS PLENTIFUL, OUR DENS ARE SAFE AND WARM, AND WE'VE SEE NO DANGER TO ALARM US.
AND REDLANCE HAS MANAGED TO GET THE DREAM-BERRIES TO GROW AT LAST!
THAT'S THE ONE SOUR TASTE... THE SOIL HERE IS POOR. THERE'S NO HOPE OF A TREEHOLT. IF WE STAY, IT WILL BE THE CAVES FOR GOOD.
I'LL TAKE SAFETY WITHIN ROCK OVER WINNOWILL'S THREATS IN A TREE ANY DAY! WE'RE HAPPY HERE.
THEN I DECLARE--
NOT YET. WHAT ABOUT THE STRANGER?
THERE'S NOTHING WRONG WITH TEIR, SKYWISE!
EXCEPT THAT WE DON'T KNOW ANYTHING ABOUT HIM!
STARGAZER I UNDERSTAND YOUR CAUTION. BUT HE'S ONLY ONE. HE HAS DONE NOTHING AGAINST US. WE FEEL NO MAGIC ABOUT HIM.
HE ISN'T WORTH GIVING UP THIS HOLT, NOT AFTER ALL THE OTHERS...

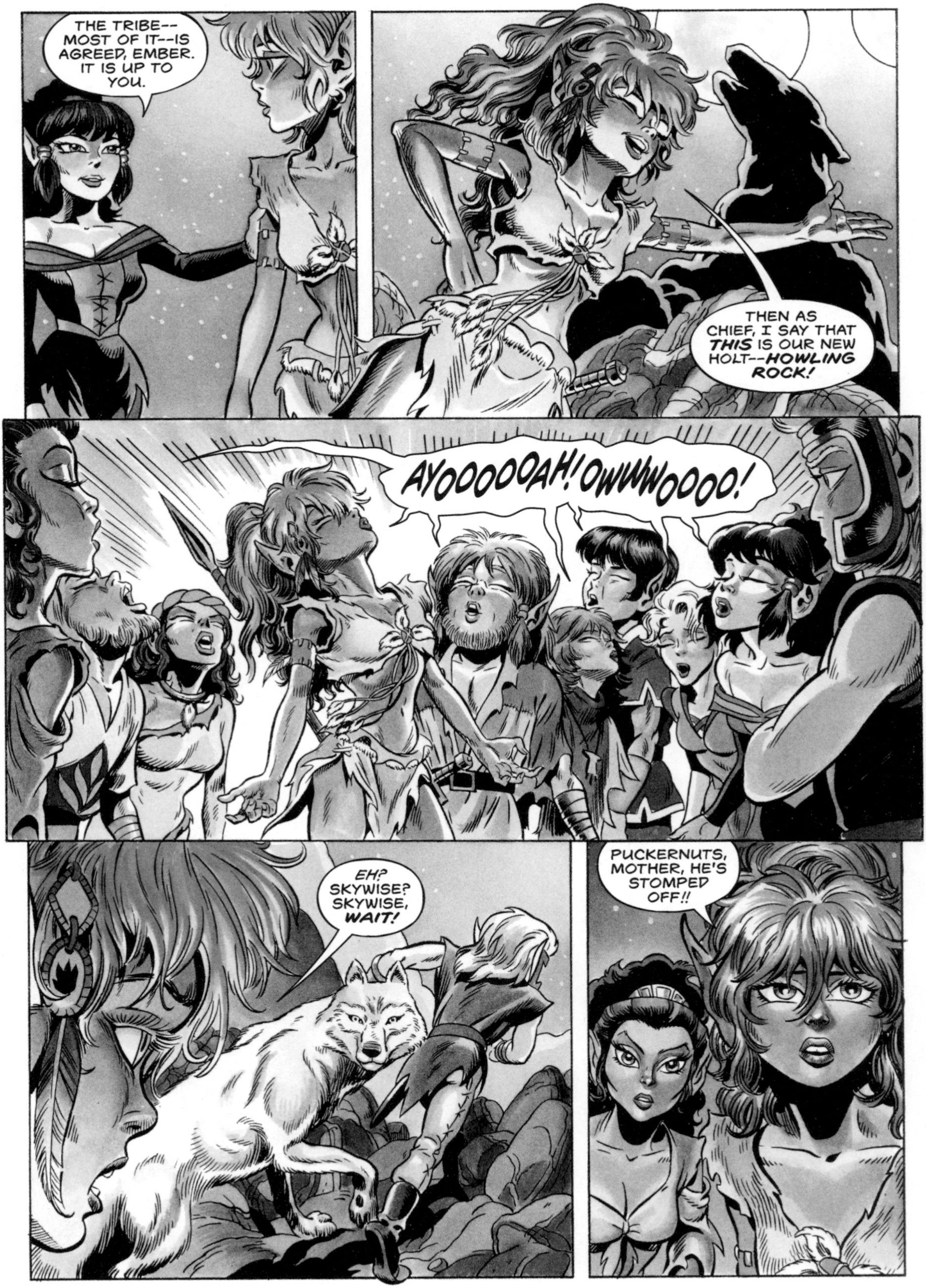
THE TRIBE-- MOST OF IT--IS AGREED, EMBER. IT IS UP TO YOU.
THEN AS CHIEF, I SAY THAT *THIS* IS OUR NEW HOLT--*HOWLING ROCK!*
AYOOOOOAH! OWWWOOOO!
EH? SKYWISE? SKYWISE, *WAIT!*
PUCKERNUTS, MOTHER, HE'S STOMPED OFF!!

WILL YOU STOP ACTING LIKE A TROLL ABOUT THIS??

OH! I'D SWEAR I'M DEALING WITH *TRINKET!*

GENTLY, KITLING--

"YOU'RE NOT THE ONLY ONE SEEKING ANSWERS..."

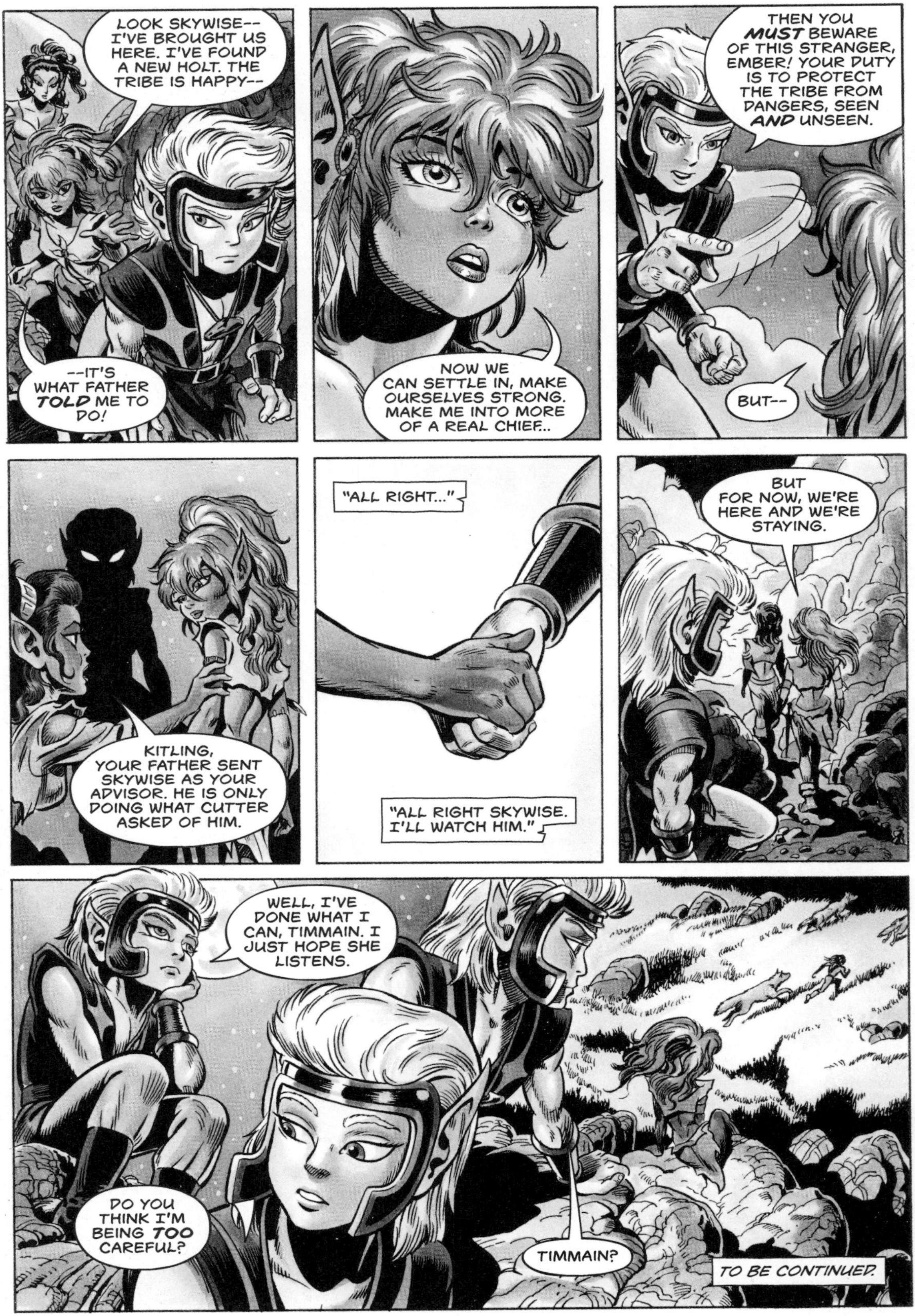
LOOK SKYWISE-- I'VE BROUGHT US HERE. I'VE FOUND A NEW HOLT. THE TRIBE IS HAPPY--
--IT'S WHAT FATHER TOLD ME TO DO!
NOW WE CAN SETTLE IN, MAKE OURSELVES STRONG. MAKE ME INTO MORE OF A REAL CHIEF...
THEN YOU MUST BEWARE OF THIS STRANGER, EMBER! YOUR DUTY IS TO PROTECT THE TRIBE FROM DANGERS, SEEN AND UNSEEN.
BUT--
KITLING, YOUR FATHER SENT SKYWISE AS YOUR ADVISOR. HE IS ONLY DOING WHAT CUTTER ASKED OF HIM.
"ALL RIGHT..."
"ALL RIGHT SKYWISE. I'LL WATCH HIM."
BUT FOR NOW, WE'RE HERE AND WE'RE STAYING.
WELL, I'VE DONE WHAT I CAN, TIMMAIN. I JUST HOPE SHE LISTENS.
DO YOU THINK I'M BEING TOO CAREFUL?
TIMMAIN?
TO BE CONTINUED.

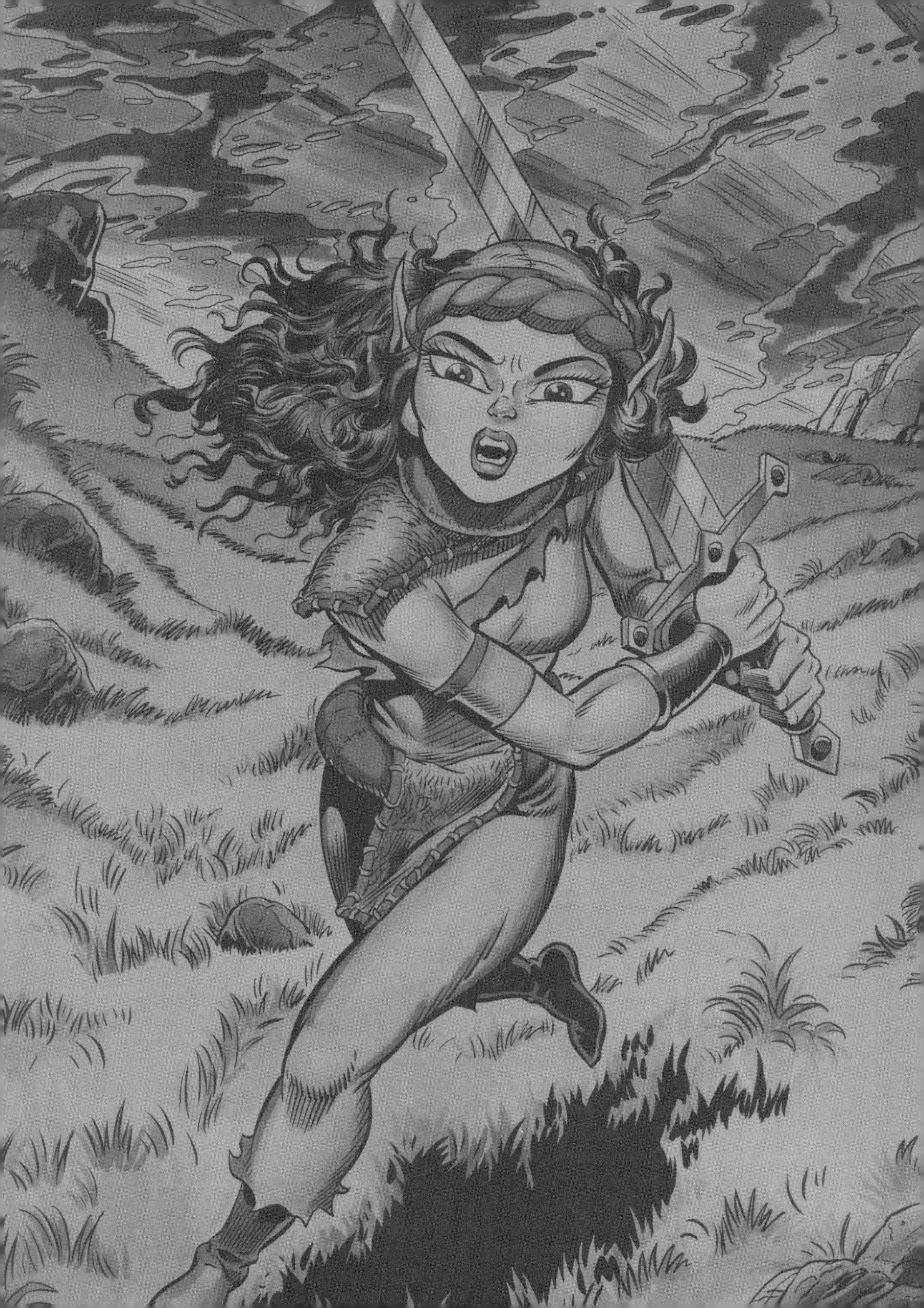

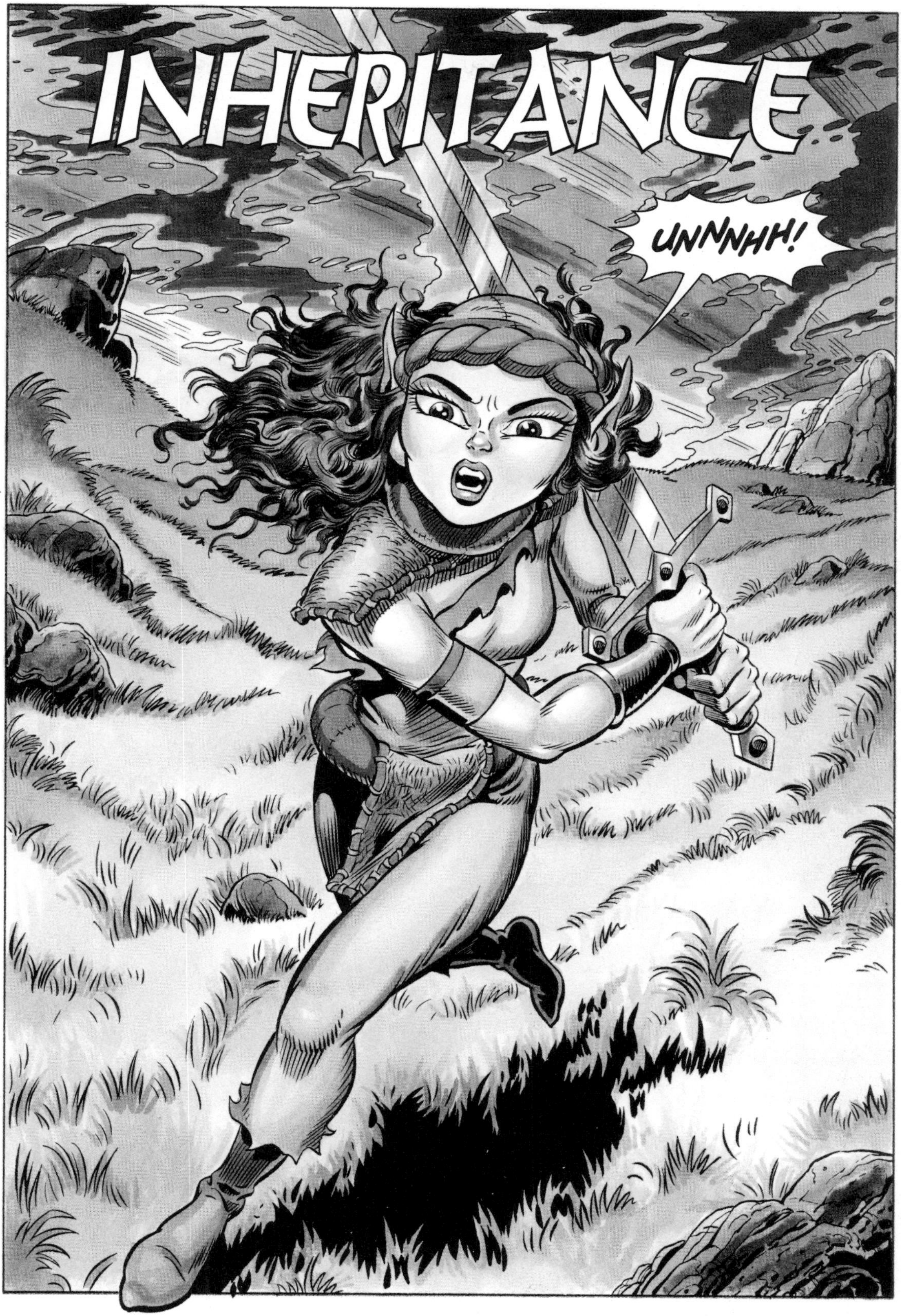
INHERITANCE
UNNNHH!

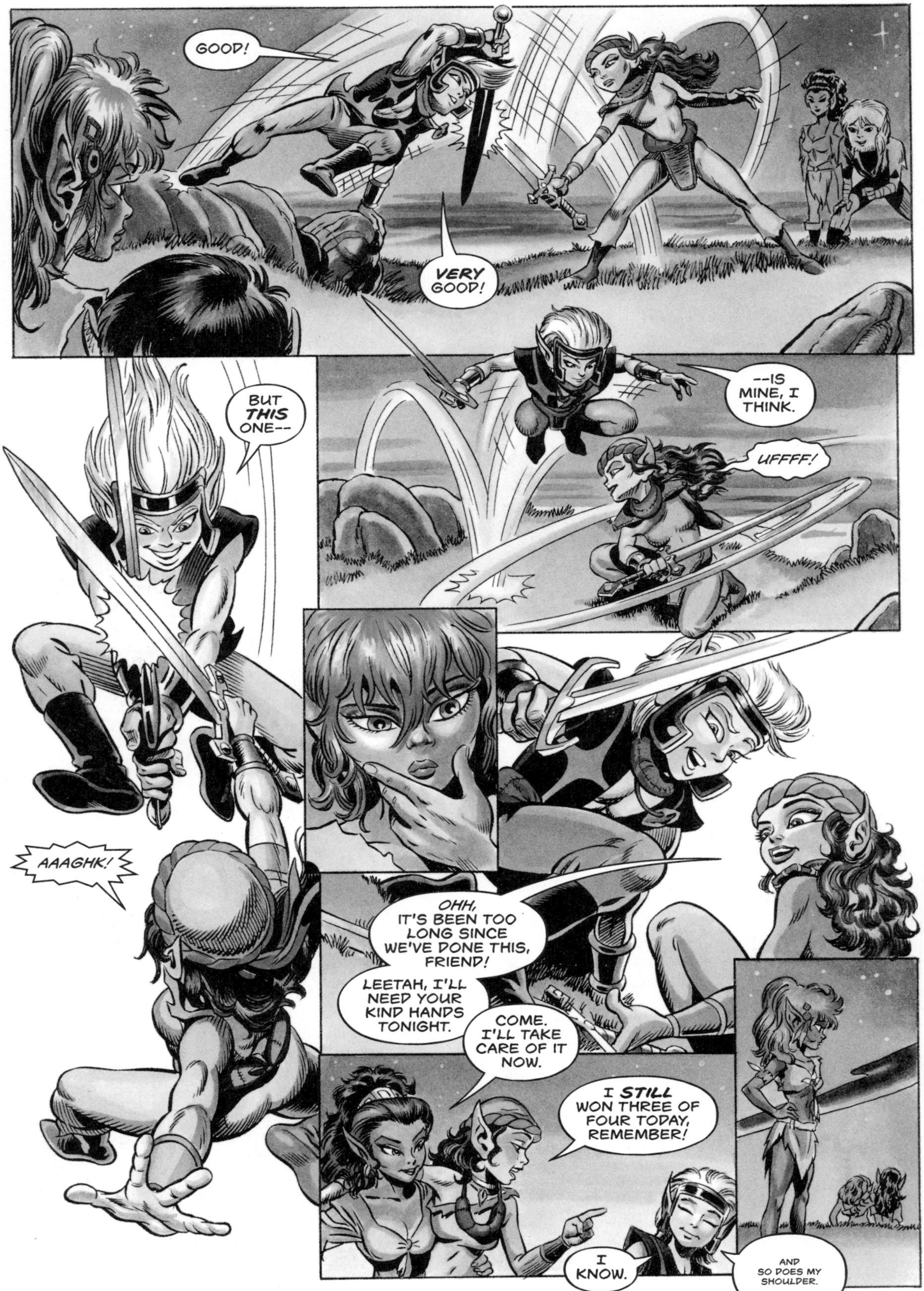
GOOD!
VERY GOOD!
BUT THIS ONE--
--IS MINE, I THINK.
UFFFF!
AAAGHK!
OHH, IT'S BEEN TOO LONG SINCE WE'VE DONE THIS, FRIEND!
LEETAH, I'LL NEED YOUR KIND HANDS TONIGHT.
COME. I'LL TAKE CARE OF IT NOW.
I STILL WON THREE OF FOUR TODAY, REMEMBER!
I KNOW.
AND SO DOES MY SHOULDER.

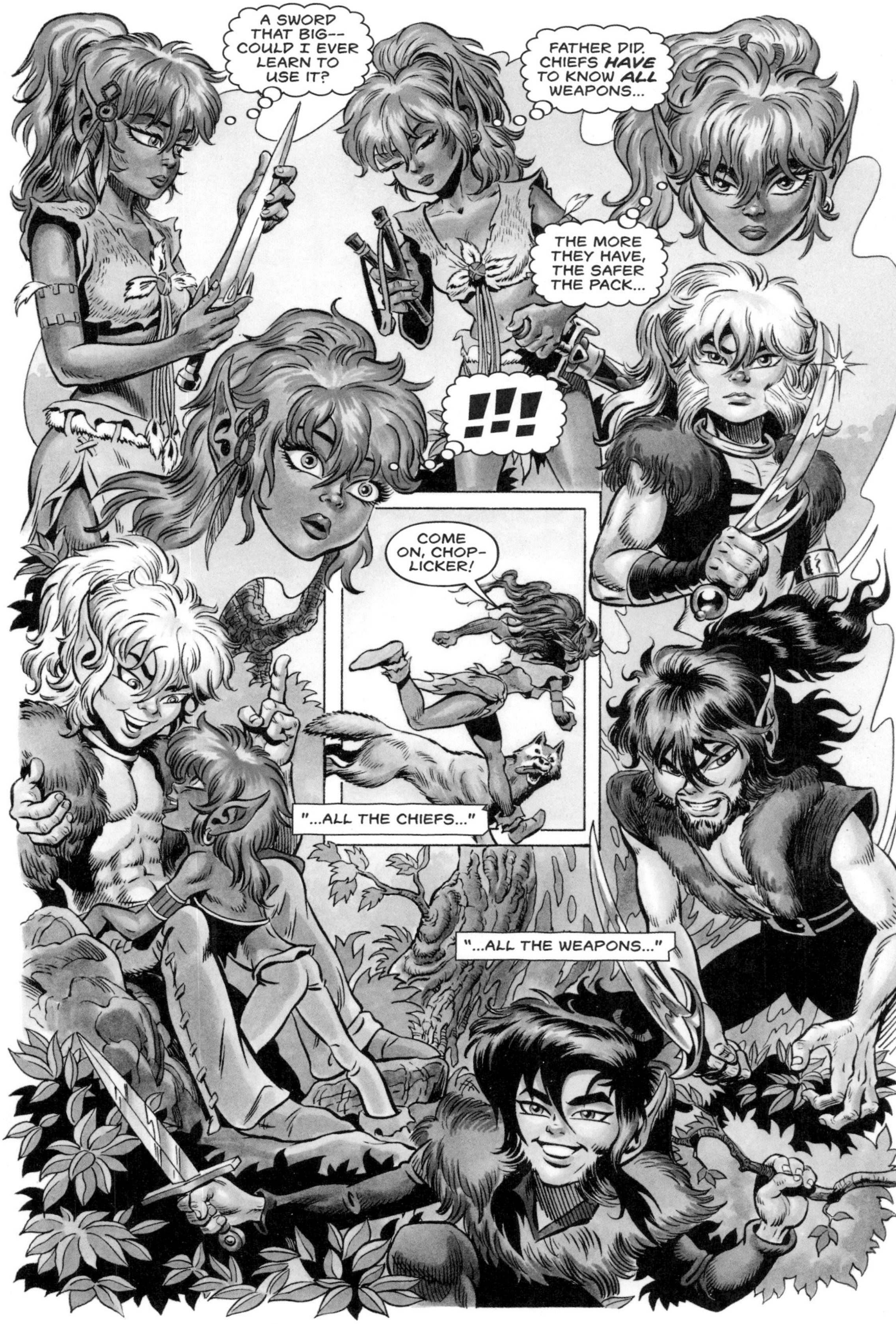
A SWORD THAT BIG-- COULD I EVER LEARN TO USE IT?
FATHER DID. CHIEFS HAVE TO KNOW ALL WEAPONS...
THE MORE THEY HAVE, THE SAFER THE PACK...
!!!
COME ON, CHOP-LICKER!
"...ALL THE CHIEFS..."
"...ALL THE WEAPONS..."

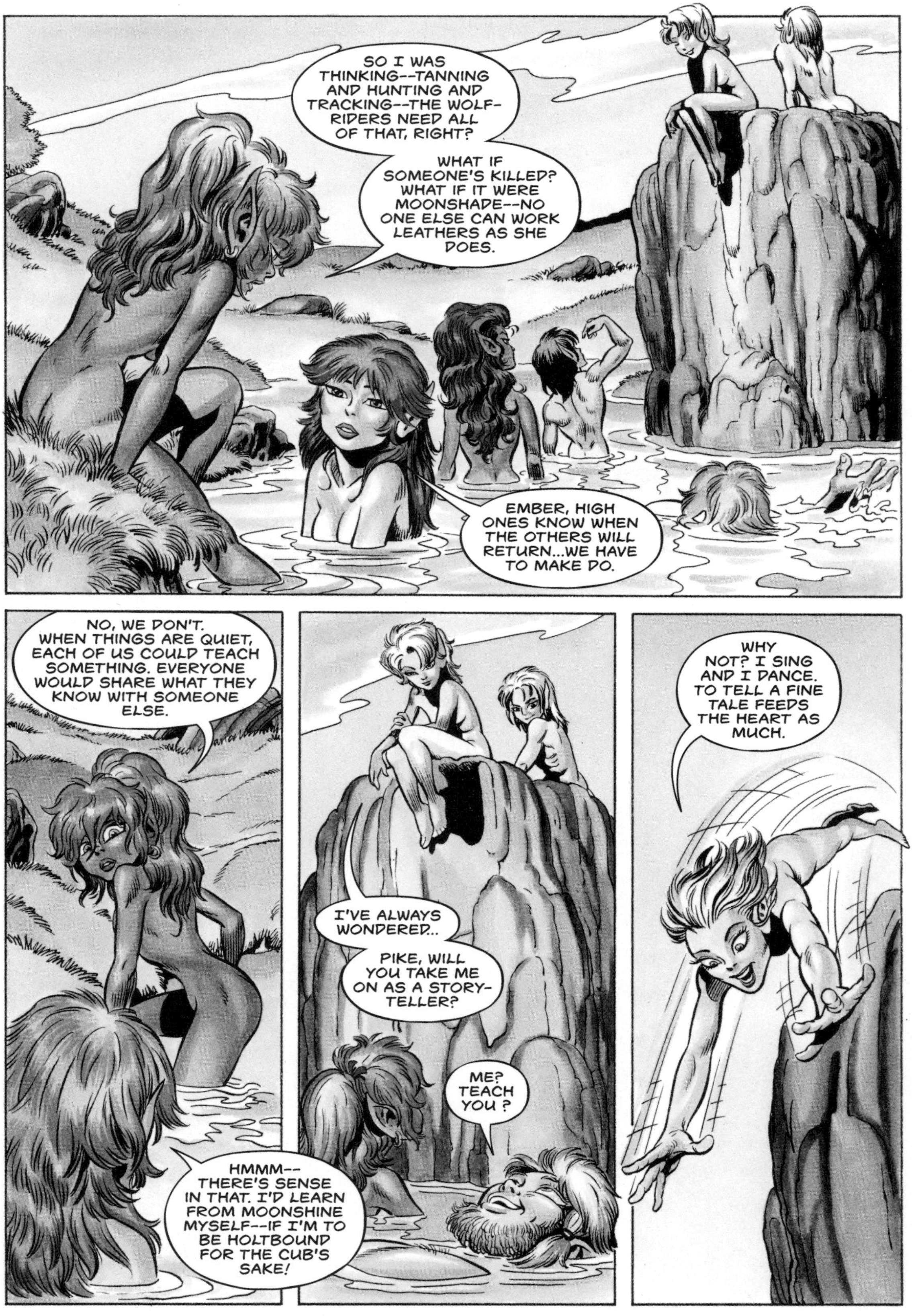
SO I WAS THINKING--TANNING AND HUNTING AND TRACKING--THE WOLF-RIDERS NEED ALL OF THAT, RIGHT?
WHAT IF SOMEONE'S KILLED? WHAT IF IT WERE MOONSHADE--NO ONE ELSE CAN WORK LEATHERS AS SHE DOES.
EMBER, HIGH ONES KNOW WHEN THE OTHERS WILL RETURN...WE HAVE TO MAKE DO.
NO, WE DON'T. WHEN THINGS ARE QUIET, EACH OF US COULD TEACH SOMETHING. EVERYONE WOULD SHARE WHAT THEY KNOW WITH SOMEONE ELSE.
HMMM--THERE'S SENSE IN THAT. I'D LEARN FROM MOONSHINE MYSELF--IF I'M TO BE HOLTBOUND FOR THE CUB'S SAKE!
I'VE ALWAYS WONDERED...
PIKE, WILL YOU TAKE ME ON AS A STORY-TELLER?
ME? TEACH YOU ?
WHY NOT? I SING AND I DANCE. TO TELL A FINE TALE FEEDS THE HEART AS MUCH.

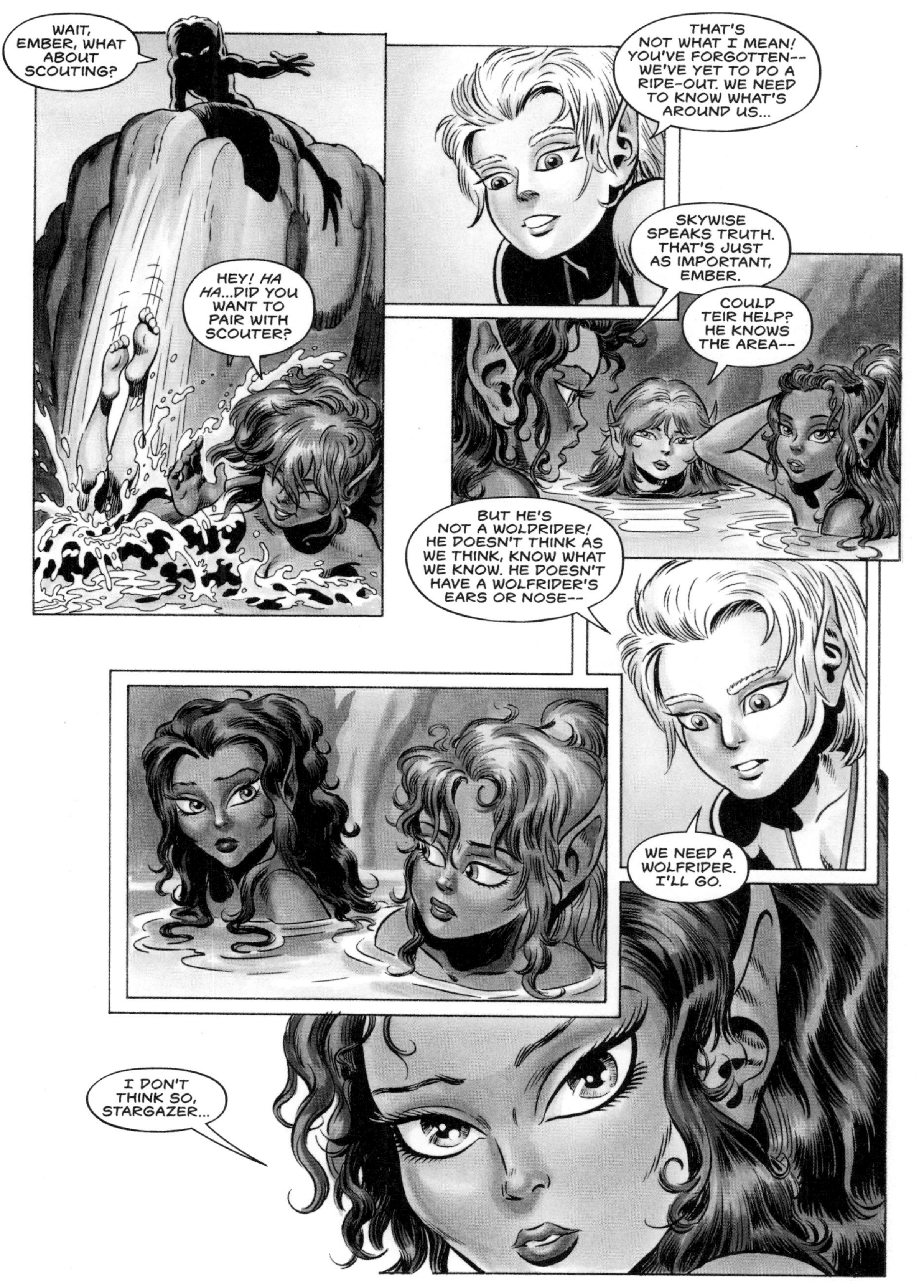
WAIT, EMBER, WHAT ABOUT SCOUTING?
HEY! *HA HA*...DID YOU WANT TO PAIR WITH SCOUTER?
THAT'S NOT WHAT I MEAN! YOU'VE FORGOTTEN-- WE'VE YET TO DO A RIDE-OUT. WE NEED TO KNOW WHAT'S AROUND US...
SKYWISE SPEAKS TRUTH. THAT'S JUST AS IMPORTANT, EMBER.
COULD TEIR HELP? HE KNOWS THE AREA--
BUT HE'S NOT A WOLFRIDER! HE DOESN'T THINK AS WE THINK, KNOW WHAT WE KNOW. HE DOESN'T HAVE A WOLFRIDER'S EARS OR NOSE--
WE NEED A WOLFRIDER. I'LL GO.
I DON'T THINK SO, STARGAZER...

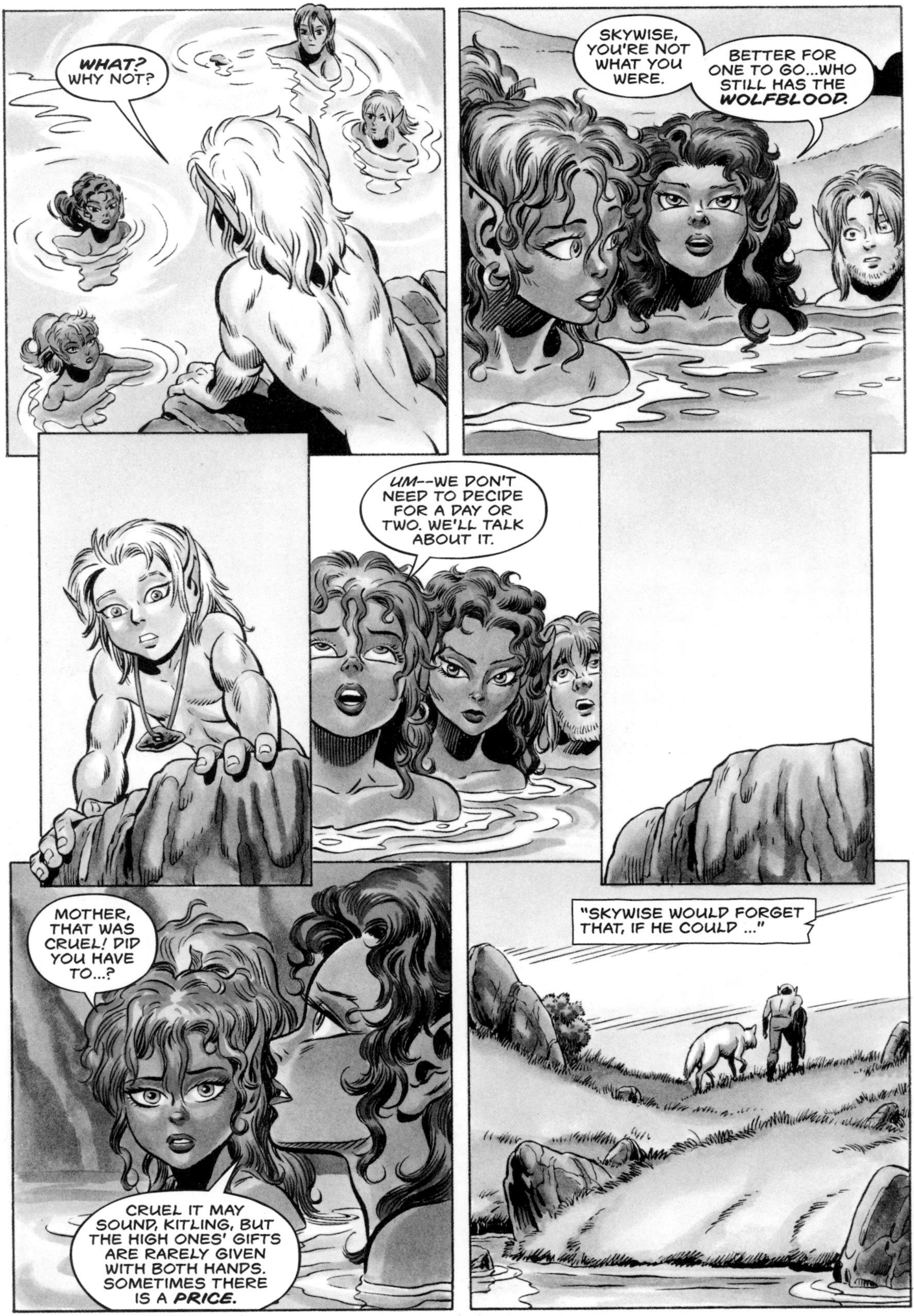

WHAT? WHY NOT?
SKYWISE, YOU'RE NOT WHAT YOU WERE.
BETTER FOR ONE TO GO...WHO STILL HAS THE WOLFBLOOD.
UM--WE DON'T NEED TO DECIDE FOR A DAY OR TWO. WE'LL TALK ABOUT IT.
MOTHER, THAT WAS CRUEL! DID YOU HAVE TO...?
CRUEL IT MAY SOUND, KITLING, BUT THE HIGH ONES' GIFTS ARE RARELY GIVEN WITH BOTH HANDS. SOMETIMES THERE IS A PRICE.
"SKYWISE WOULD FORGET THAT, IF HE COULD ..."

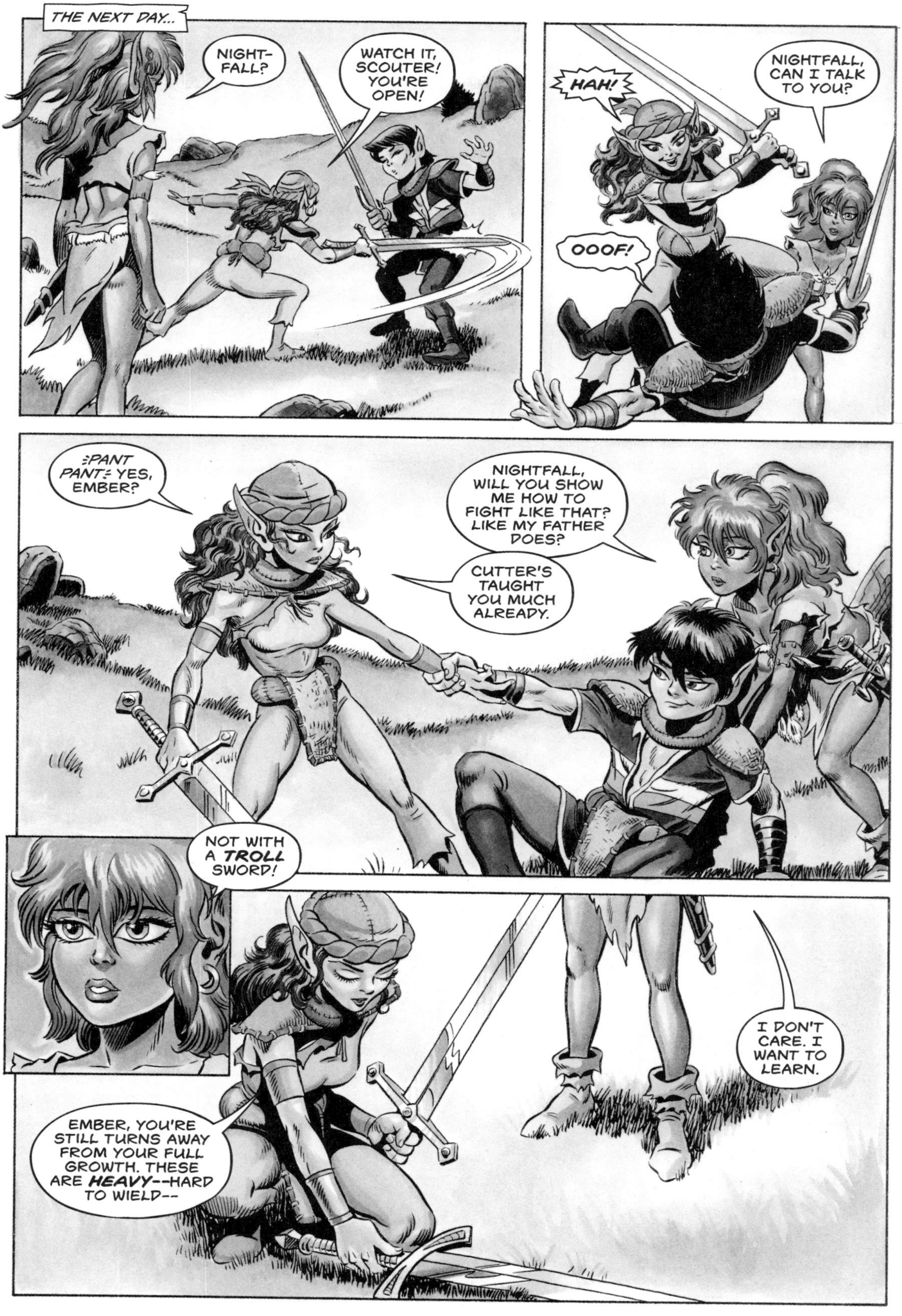
THE NEXT DAY...
NIGHT-FALL?
WATCH IT, SCOUTER! YOU'RE OPEN!
HAH!
NIGHTFALL, CAN I TALK TO YOU?
OOOF!
:PANT PANT: YES, EMBER?
NIGHTFALL, WILL YOU SHOW ME HOW TO FIGHT LIKE THAT? LIKE MY FATHER DOES?
CUTTER'S TAUGHT YOU MUCH ALREADY.
NOT WITH A *TROLL* SWORD!
EMBER, YOU'RE STILL TURNS AWAY FROM YOUR FULL GROWTH. THESE ARE *HEAVY*--HARD TO WIELD--
I DON'T CARE. I WANT TO LEARN.

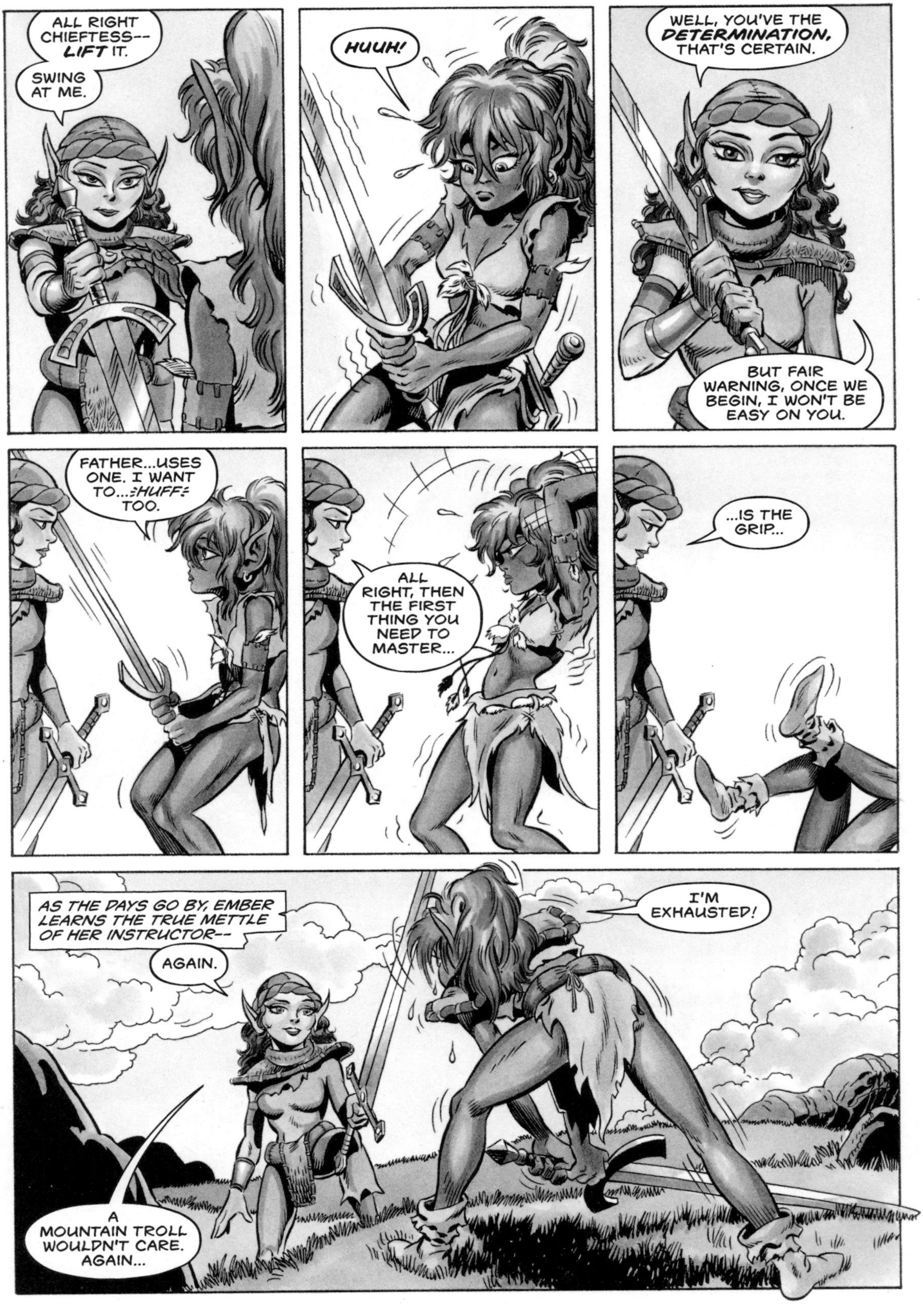
ALL RIGHT CHIEFTESS-- LIFT IT.
SWING AT ME.
HUUH!
WELL, YOU'VE THE DETERMINATION, THAT'S CERTAIN.
BUT FAIR WARNING, ONCE WE BEGIN, I WON'T BE EASY ON YOU.
FATHER...USES ONE. I WANT TO... HUFF TOO.
ALL RIGHT, THEN THE FIRST THING YOU NEED TO MASTER...
...IS THE GRIP...
AS THE DAYS GO BY, EMBER LEARNS THE TRUE METTLE OF HER INSTRUCTOR--
I'M EXHAUSTED!
AGAIN.
A MOUNTAIN TROLL WOULDN'T CARE. AGAIN...

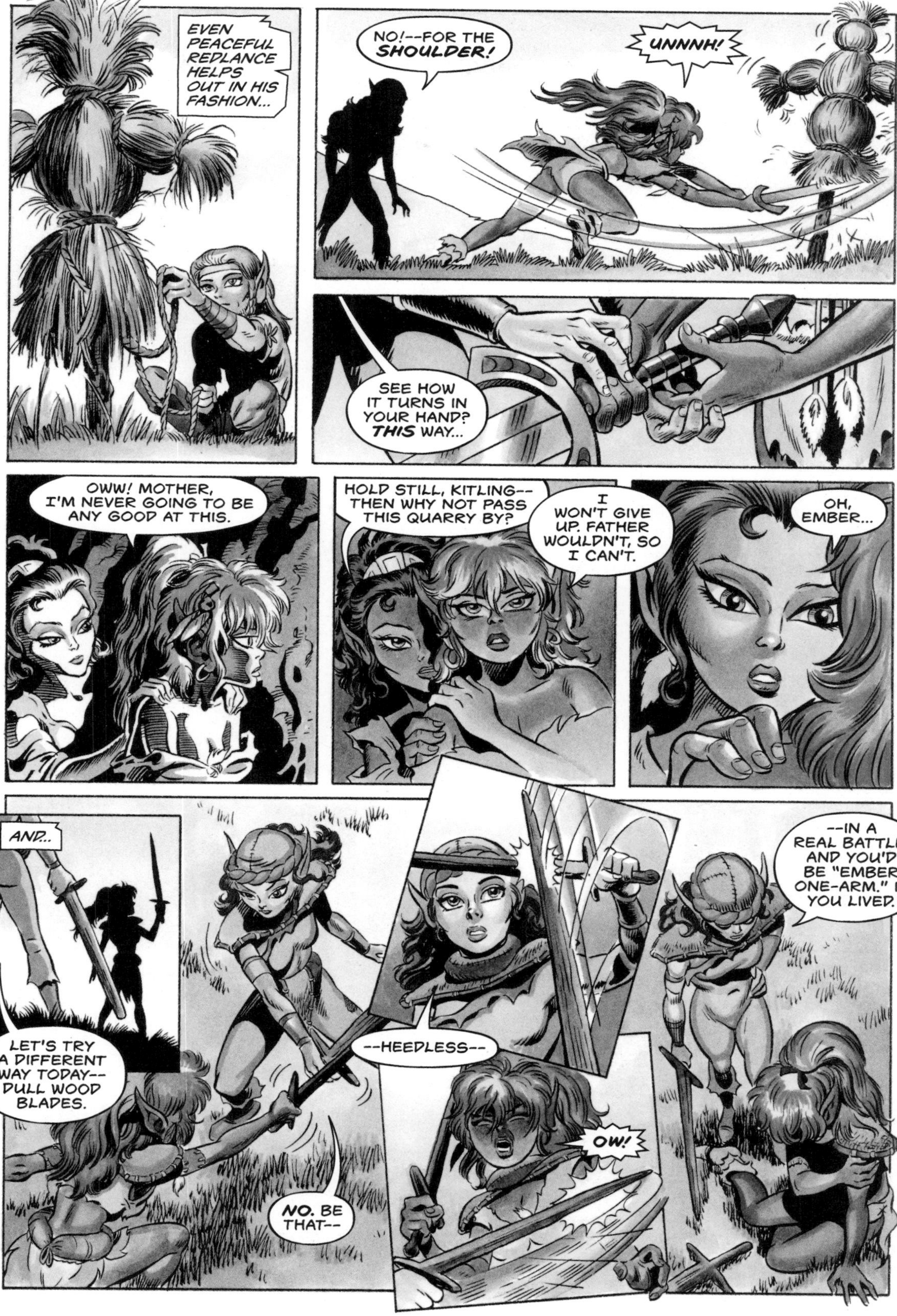
EVEN PEACEFUL REDLANCE HELPS OUT IN HIS FASHION...
NO!--FOR THE SHOULDER!
UNNNH!
SEE HOW IT TURNS IN YOUR HAND? THIS WAY...
OWW! MOTHER, I'M NEVER GOING TO BE ANY GOOD AT THIS.
HOLD STILL, KITLING-- THEN WHY NOT PASS THIS QUARRY BY?
I WON'T GIVE UP. FATHER WOULDN'T, SO I CAN'T.
OH, EMBER...
AND...
LET'S TRY A DIFFERENT WAY TODAY-- DULL WOOD BLADES.
NO. BE THAT--
--HEEDLESS--
OW!
--IN A REAL BATTLE, AND YOU'D BE "EMBER ONE-ARM." IF YOU LIVED.

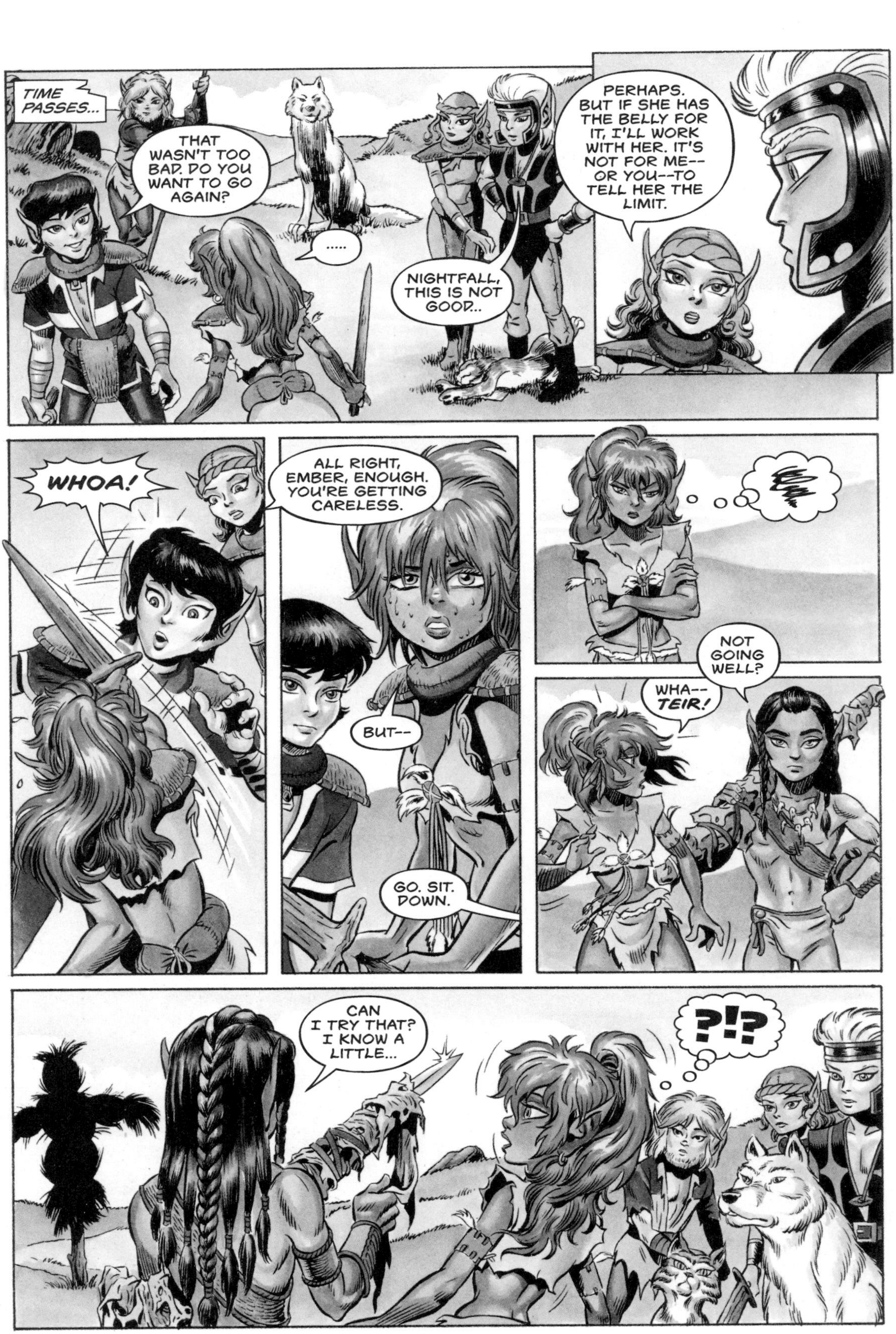

TIME PASSES...
THAT WASN'T TOO BAD. DO YOU WANT TO GO AGAIN?
.....
NIGHTFALL, THIS IS NOT GOOD...
PERHAPS. BUT IF SHE HAS THE BELLY FOR IT, I'LL WORK WITH HER. IT'S NOT FOR ME-- OR YOU--TO TELL HER THE LIMIT.
WHOA!
ALL RIGHT, EMBER, ENOUGH. YOU'RE GETTING CARELESS.
BUT--
GO. SIT. DOWN.
NOT GOING WELL?
WHA-- TEIR!
CAN I TRY THAT? I KNOW A LITTLE...
?!?

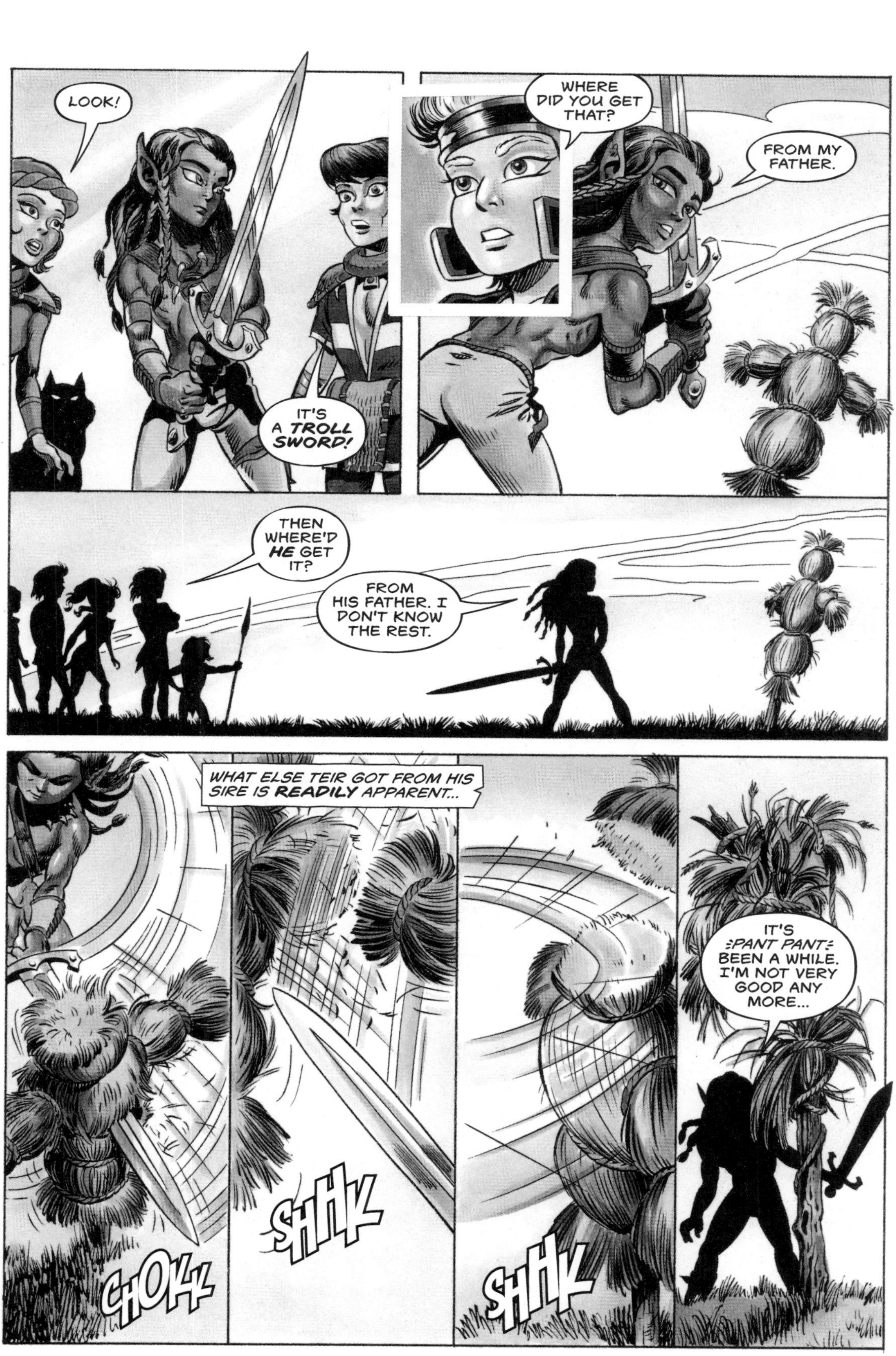
LOOK!
IT'S A TROLL SWORD!
WHERE DID YOU GET THAT?
FROM MY FATHER.
THEN WHERE'D HE GET IT?
FROM HIS FATHER. I DON'T KNOW THE REST.
WHAT ELSE TEIR GOT FROM HIS SIRE IS READILY APPARENT...
CHOKK
SHHK
SHHK
IT'S =PANT PANT= BEEN A WHILE. I'M NOT VERY GOOD ANY MORE...

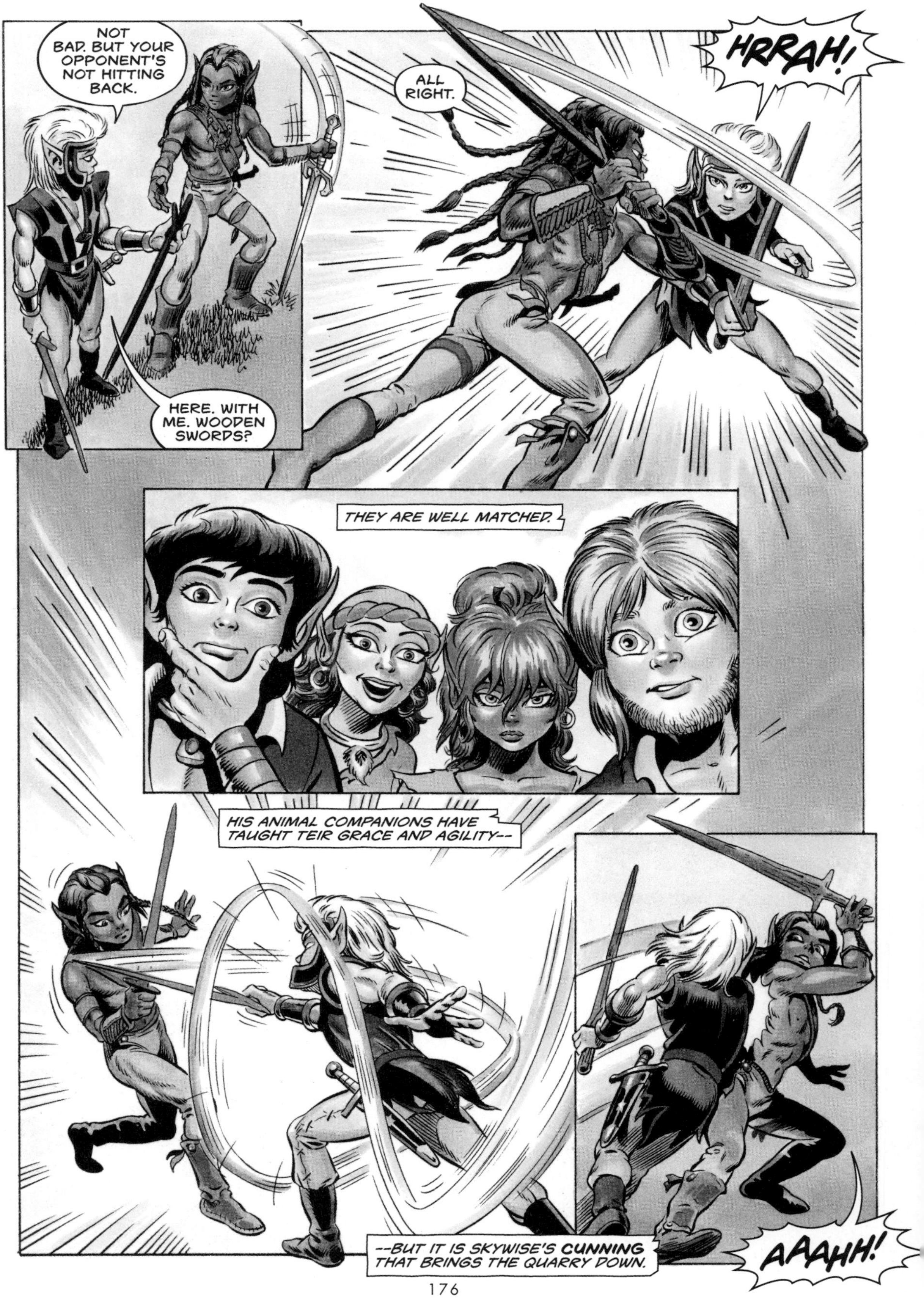
NOT BAD. BUT YOUR OPPONENT'S NOT HITTING BACK.
HERE. WITH ME. WOODEN SWORDS?
ALL RIGHT.
HRRAH!
THEY ARE WELL MATCHED.
HIS ANIMAL COMPANIONS HAVE TAUGHT TEIR GRACE AND AGILITY--
--BUT IT IS SKYWISE'S CUNNING THAT BRINGS THE QUARRY DOWN.
AAAHH!

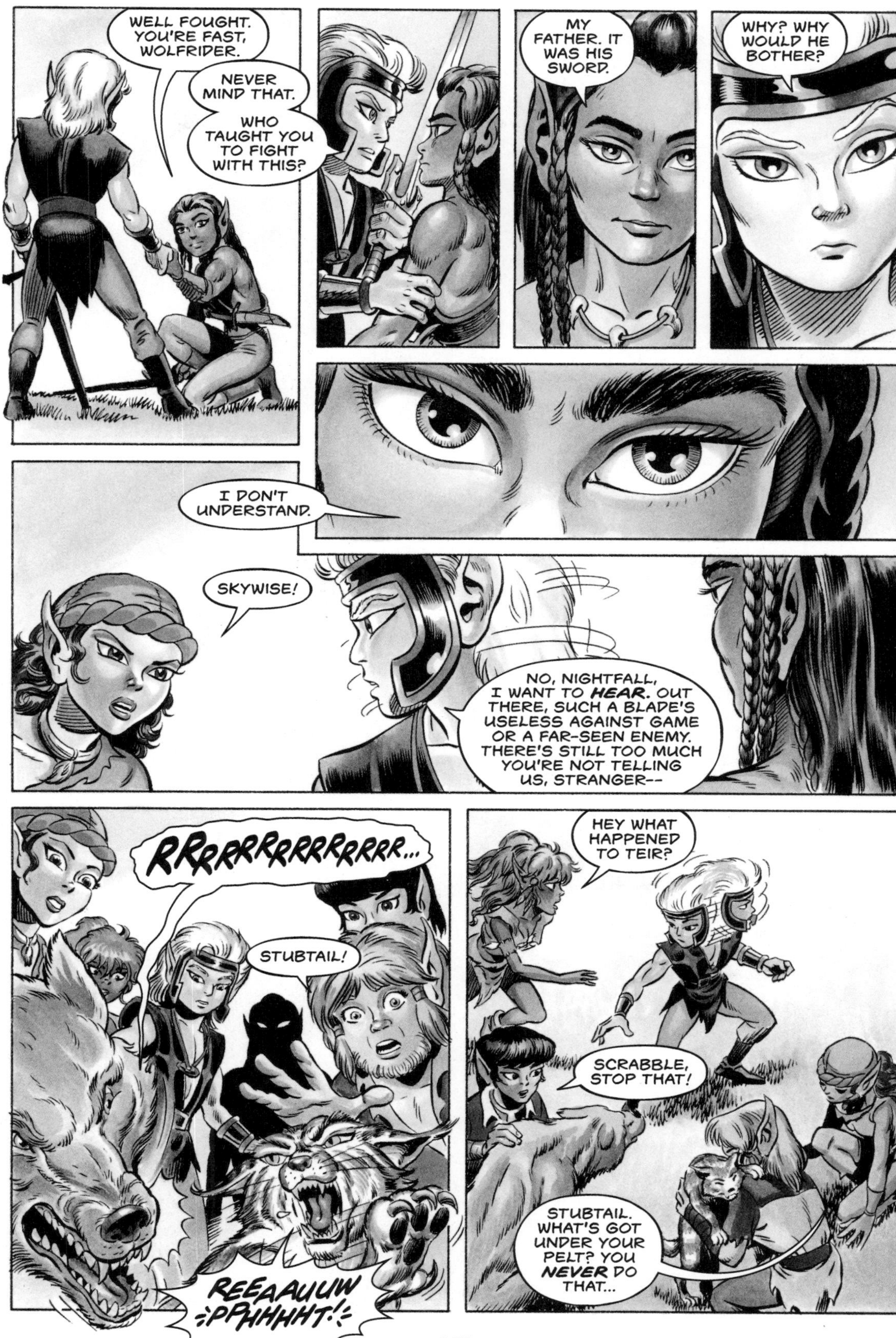

WELL FOUGHT. YOU'RE FAST, WOLFRIDER.
NEVER MIND THAT.
WHO TAUGHT YOU TO FIGHT WITH THIS?
MY FATHER. IT WAS HIS SWORD.
WHY? WHY WOULD HE BOTHER?
I DON'T UNDERSTAND.
SKYWISE!
NO, NIGHTFALL, I WANT TO HEAR. OUT THERE, SUCH A BLADE'S USELESS AGAINST GAME OR A FAR-SEEN ENEMY. THERE'S STILL TOO MUCH YOU'RE NOT TELLING US, STRANGER--
RRRRRRRRRRRRR...
STUBTAIL!
REEAAUUW PPHHHHT!
HEY WHAT HAPPENED TO TEIR?
SCRABBLE, STOP THAT!
STUBTAIL. WHAT'S GOT UNDER YOUR PELT? YOU NEVER DO THAT...

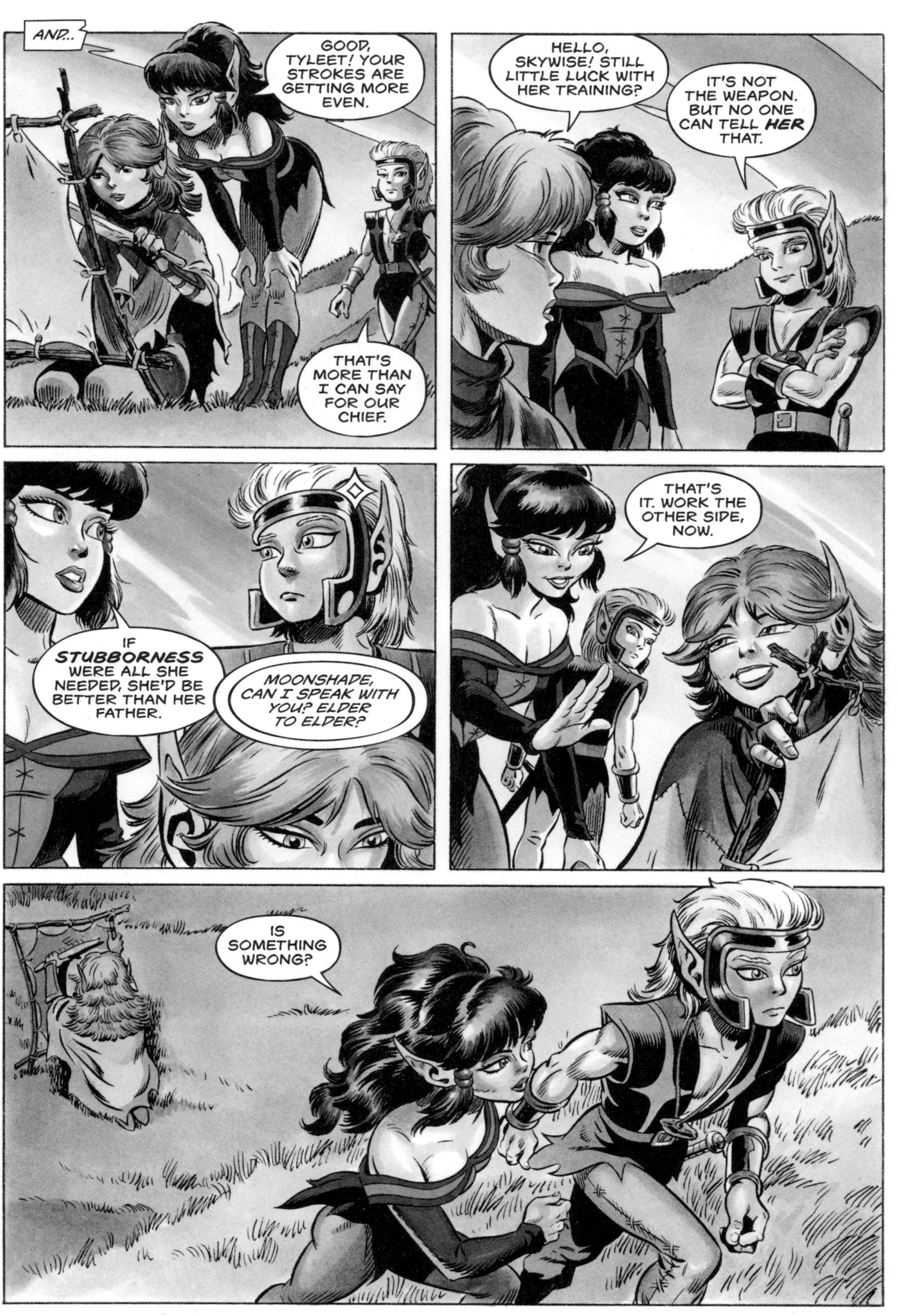
AND...
GOOD, TYLEET! YOUR STROKES ARE GETTING MORE EVEN.
THAT'S MORE THAN I CAN SAY FOR OUR CHIEF.
HELLO, SKYWISE! STILL LITTLE LUCK WITH HER TRAINING?
IT'S NOT THE WEAPON. BUT NO ONE CAN TELL HER THAT.
IF STUBBORNESS WERE ALL SHE NEEDED, SHE'D BE BETTER THAN HER FATHER.
MOONSHADE, CAN I SPEAK WITH YOU? ELDER TO ELDER?
THAT'S IT. WORK THE OTHER SIDE, NOW.
IS SOMETHING WRONG?

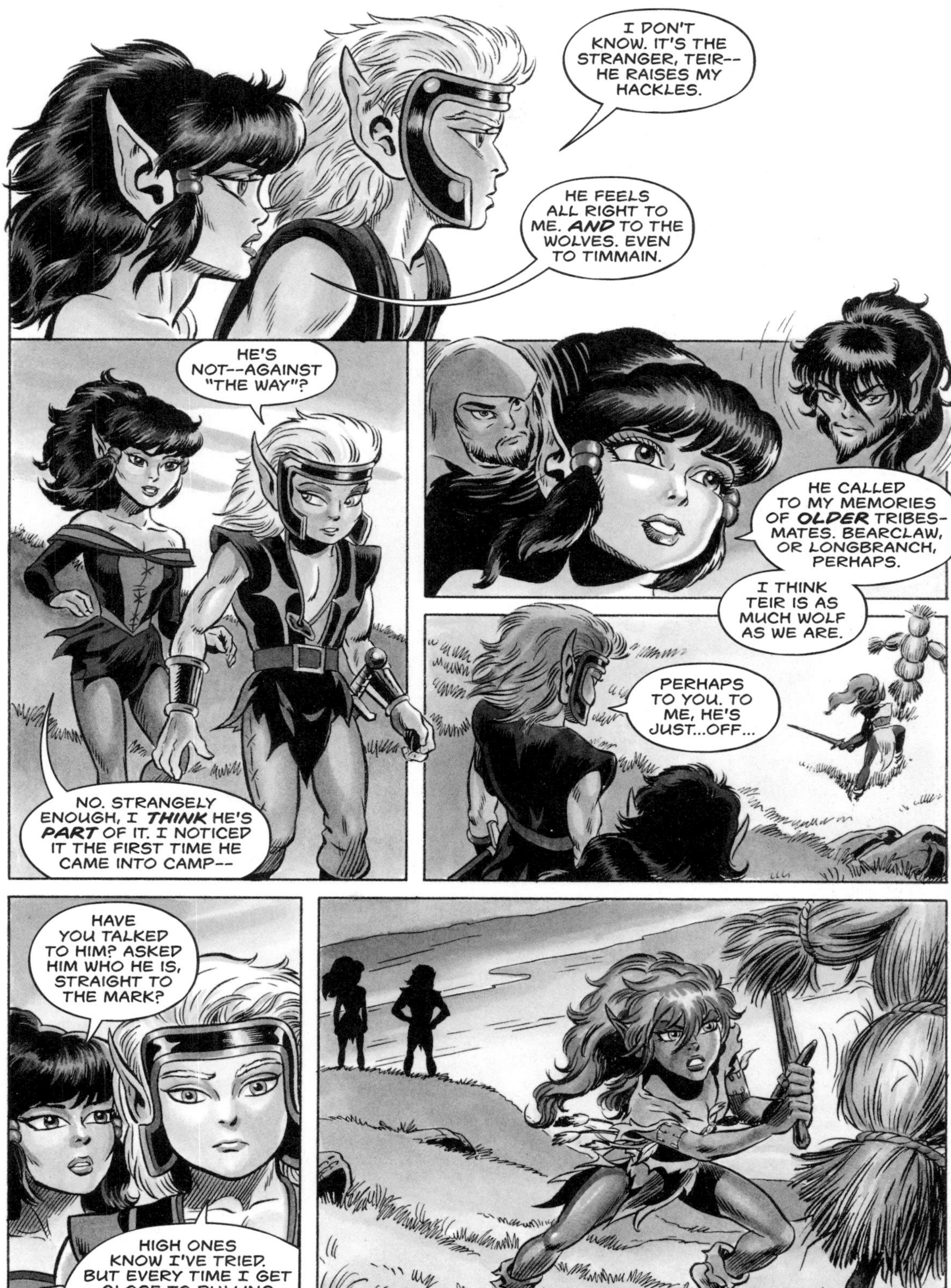
I DON'T KNOW. IT'S THE STRANGER, TEIR-- HE RAISES MY HACKLES.
HE FEELS ALL RIGHT TO ME. AND TO THE WOLVES. EVEN TO TIMMAIN.
HE'S NOT--AGAINST "THE WAY"?
NO. STRANGELY ENOUGH, I THINK HE'S PART OF IT. I NOTICED IT THE FIRST TIME HE CAME INTO CAMP--
HE CALLED TO MY MEMORIES OF OLDER TRIBES-MATES. BEARCLAW, OR LONGBRANCH, PERHAPS.
I THINK TEIR IS AS MUCH WOLF AS WE ARE.
PERHAPS TO YOU. TO ME, HE'S JUST...OFF...
HAVE YOU TALKED TO HIM? ASKED HIM WHO HE IS, STRAIGHT TO THE MARK?
HIGH ONES KNOW I'VE TRIED. BUT EVERY TIME I GET CLOSE TO PULLING AN ANSWER FROM HIM, SOMETHING HAPPENS. I GET DISTRACTED-- OR HE DISAPPEARS.
"I'D GIVE HALF THE LODESTONE TO KNOW WHO HIS KIN REALLY WERE..."

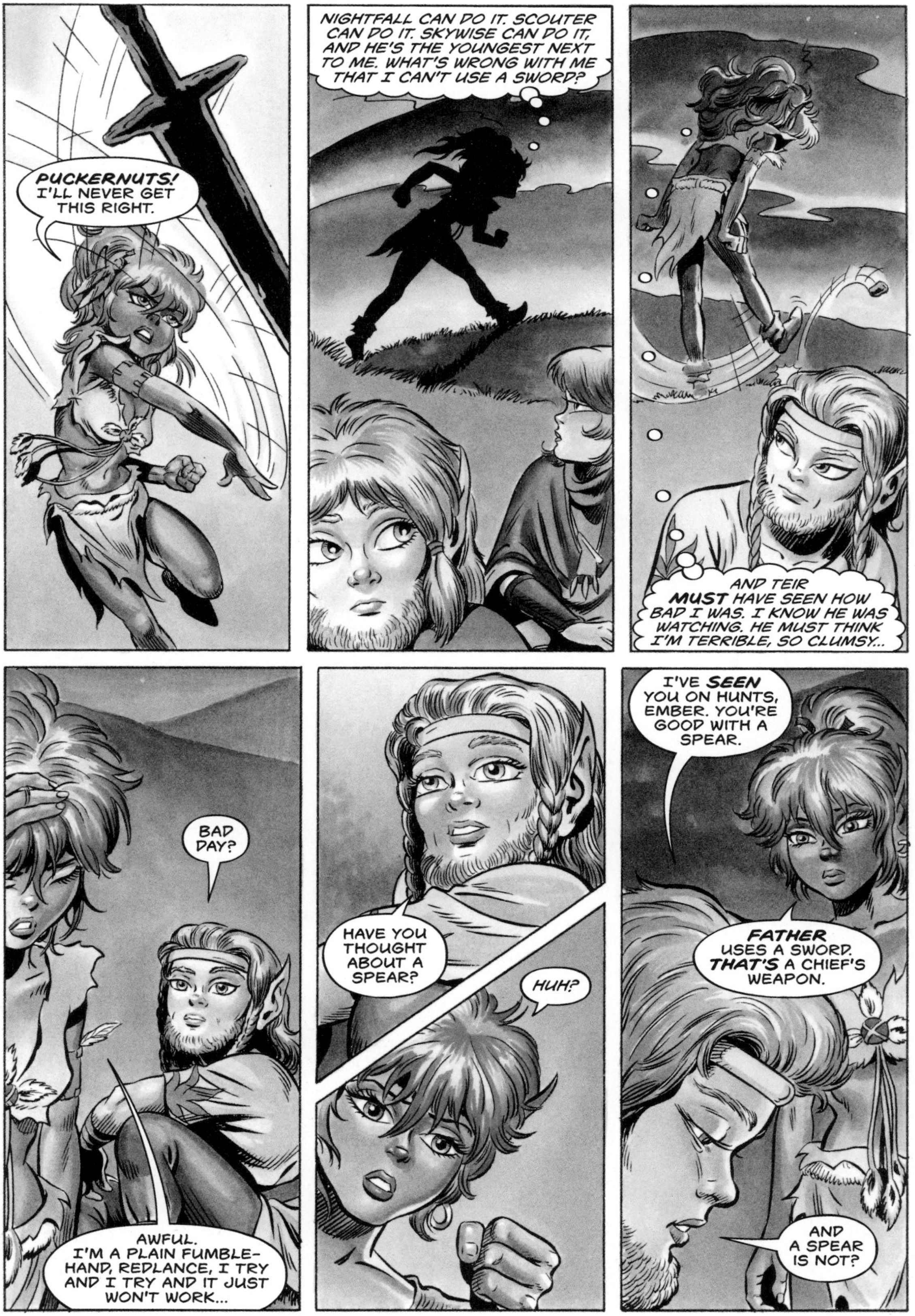
PUCKERNUTS! I'LL NEVER GET THIS RIGHT.
NIGHTFALL CAN DO IT. SCOUTER CAN DO IT. SKYWISE CAN DO IT, AND HE'S THE YOUNGEST NEXT TO ME. WHAT'S WRONG WITH ME THAT I CAN'T USE A SWORD?
AND TEIR MUST HAVE SEEN HOW BAD I WAS. I KNOW HE WAS WATCHING. HE MUST THINK I'M TERRIBLE, SO CLUMSY...
BAD DAY?
AWFUL. I'M A PLAIN FUMBLE-HAND, REDLANCE, I TRY AND I TRY AND IT JUST WON'T WORK...
HAVE YOU THOUGHT ABOUT A SPEAR?
HUH?
I'VE SEEN YOU ON HUNTS, EMBER. YOU'RE GOOD WITH A SPEAR.
FATHER USES A SWORD. THAT'S A CHIEF'S WEAPON.
AND A SPEAR IS NOT?

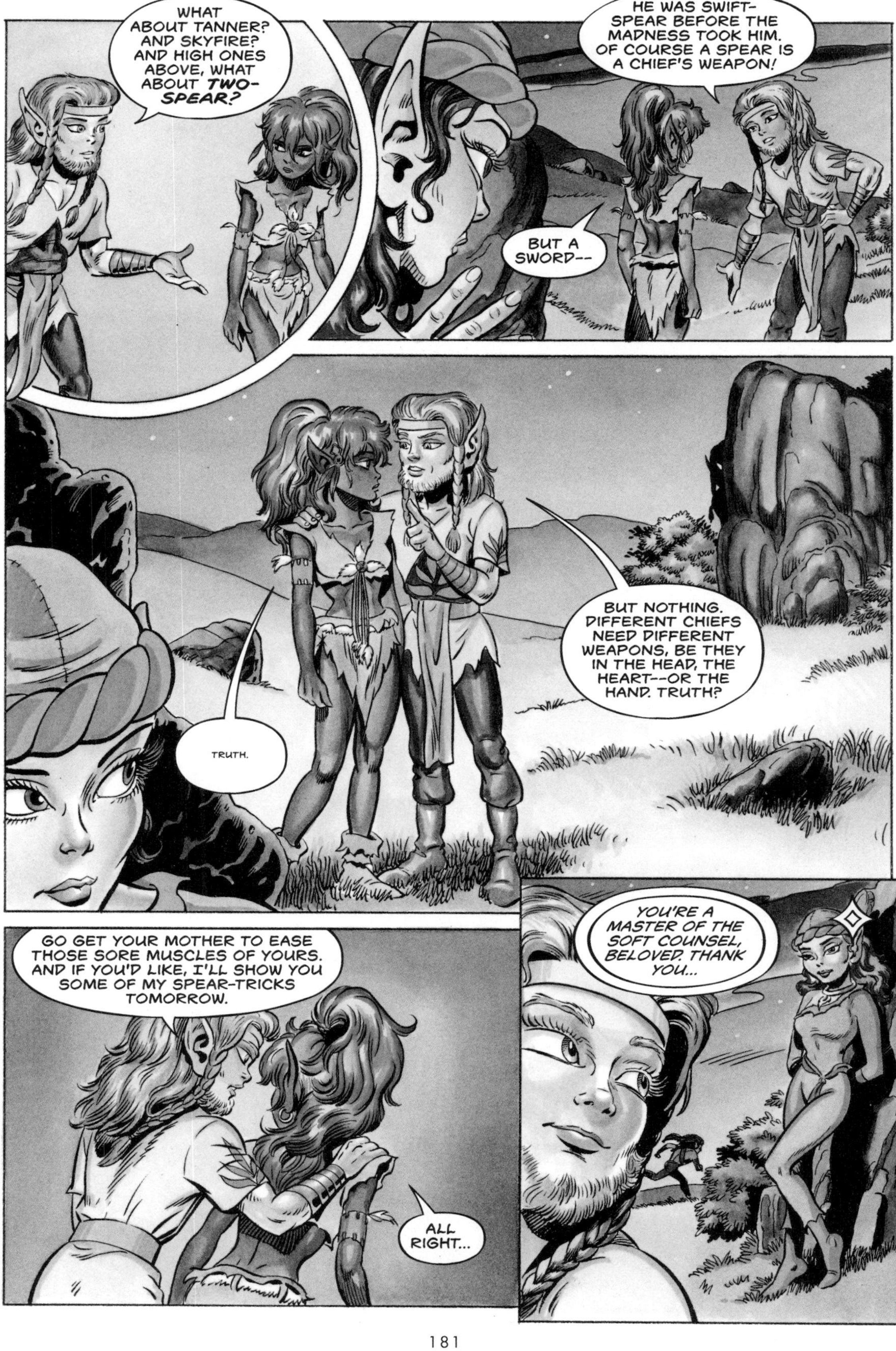
WHAT ABOUT TANNER? AND SKYFIRE? AND HIGH ONES ABOVE, WHAT ABOUT *TWO-SPEAR?*
HE WAS SWIFT-SPEAR BEFORE THE MADNESS TOOK HIM. OF COURSE A SPEAR IS A CHIEF'S WEAPON!
BUT A SWORD--
BUT NOTHING. DIFFERENT CHIEFS NEED DIFFERENT WEAPONS, BE THEY IN THE HEAD, THE HEART--OR THE HAND. TRUTH?
TRUTH.
GO GET YOUR MOTHER TO EASE THOSE SORE MUSCLES OF YOURS. AND IF YOU'D LIKE, I'LL SHOW YOU SOME OF MY SPEAR-TRICKS TOMORROW.
ALL RIGHT...
YOU'RE A MASTER OF THE SOFT COUNSEL, BELOVED. THANK YOU...

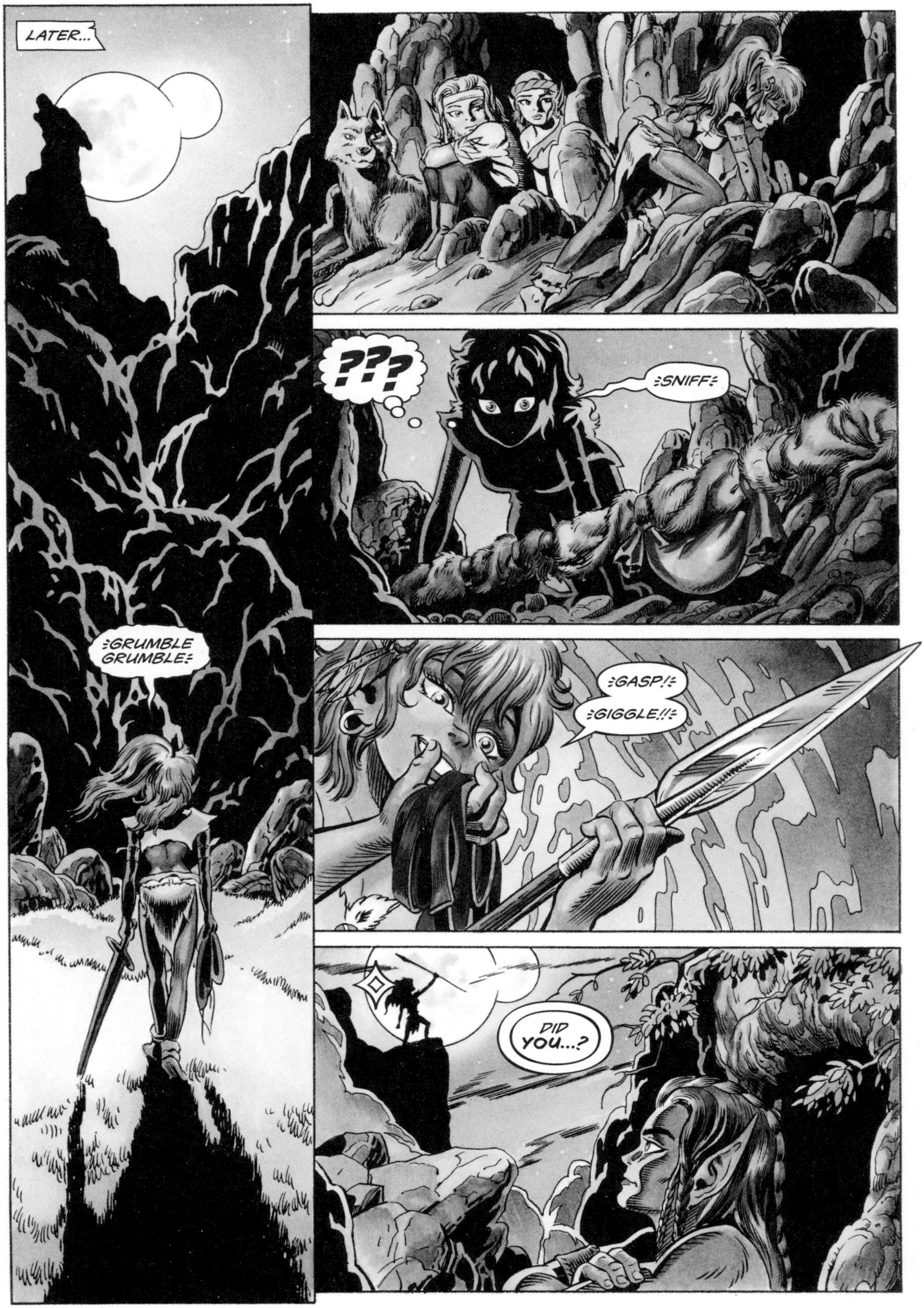
LATER...
GRUMBLE GRUMBLE
???
SNIFF
GASP!
GIGGLE!!
DID YOU...?

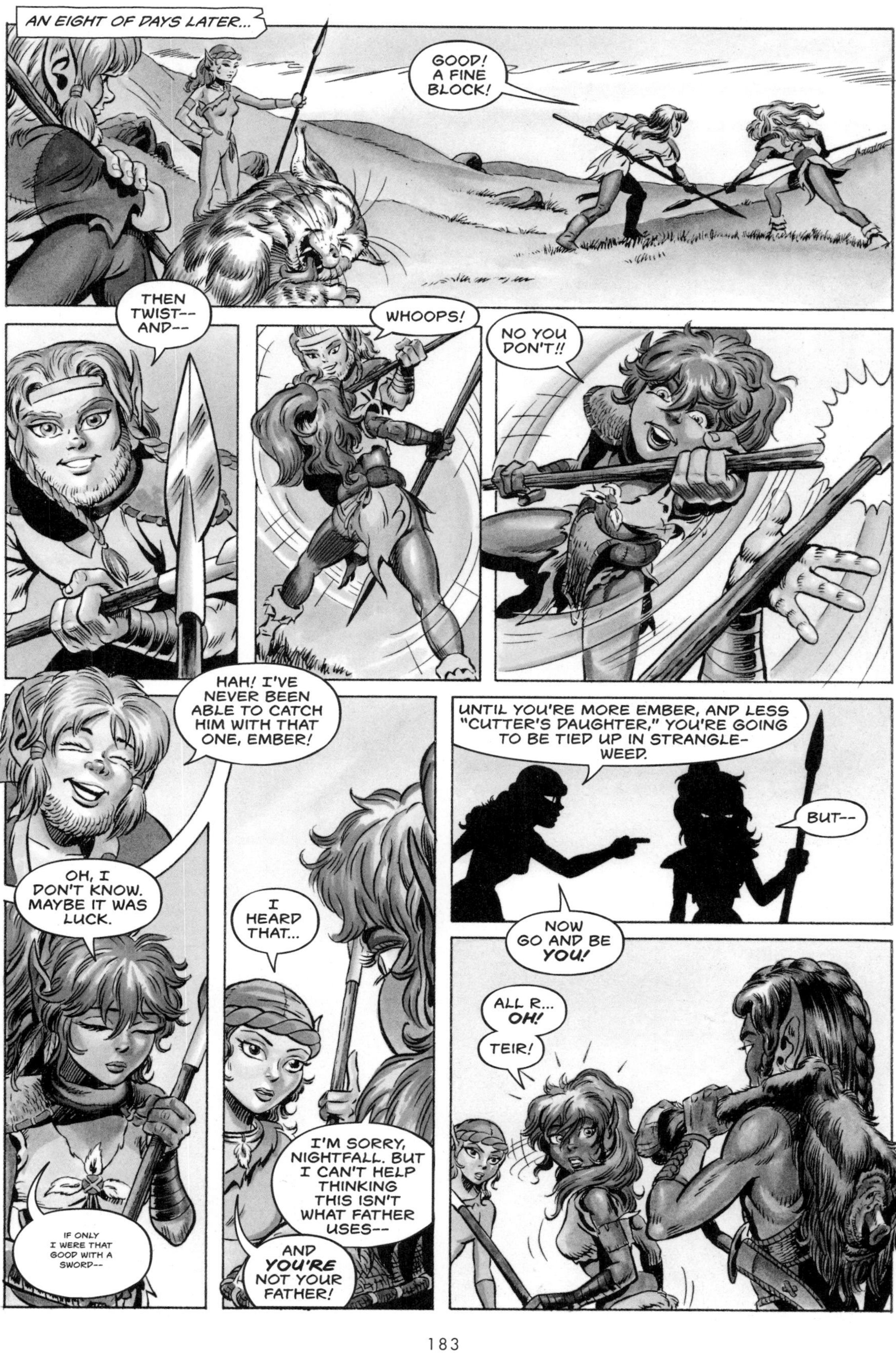

AN EIGHT OF DAYS LATER...
GOOD! A FINE BLOCK!
THEN TWIST-- AND--
WHOOPS!
NO YOU DON'T!!
HAH! I'VE NEVER BEEN ABLE TO CATCH HIM WITH THAT ONE, EMBER!
OH, I DON'T KNOW. MAYBE IT WAS LUCK.
IF ONLY I WERE THAT GOOD WITH A SWORD--
I HEARD THAT...
I'M SORRY, NIGHTFALL. BUT I CAN'T HELP THINKING THIS ISN'T WHAT FATHER USES--
AND YOU'RE NOT YOUR FATHER!
UNTIL YOU'RE MORE EMBER, AND LESS "CUTTER'S DAUGHTER," YOU'RE GOING TO BE TIED UP IN STRANGLE-WEED.
BUT--
NOW GO AND BE YOU!
ALL R... OH!
TEIR!

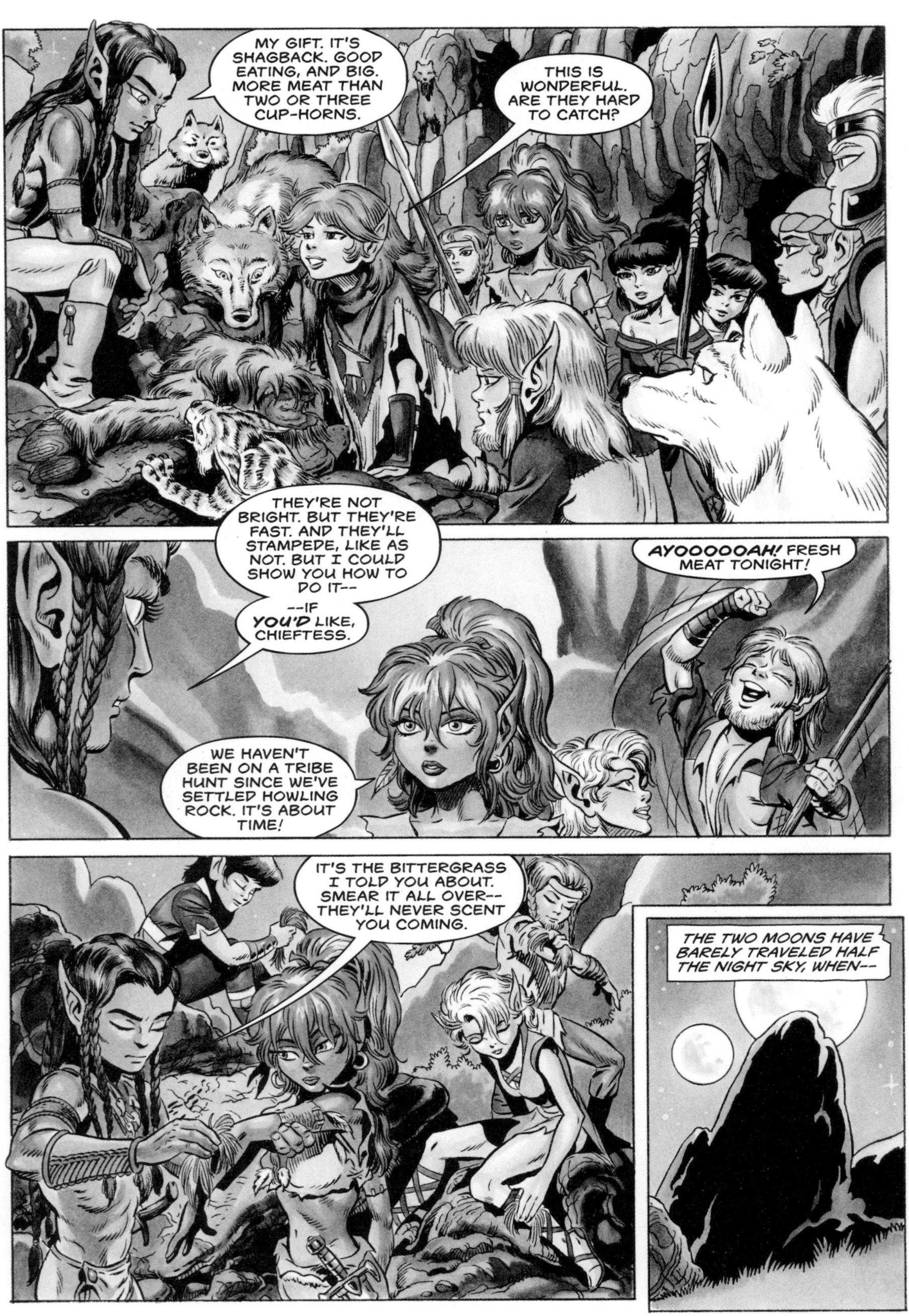
MY GIFT. IT'S SHAGBACK. GOOD EATING, AND BIG. MORE MEAT THAN TWO OR THREE CUP-HORNS.
THIS IS WONDERFUL. ARE THEY HARD TO CATCH?
THEY'RE NOT BRIGHT. BUT THEY'RE FAST. AND THEY'LL STAMPEDE, LIKE AS NOT. BUT I COULD SHOW YOU HOW TO DO IT--
--IF YOU'D LIKE, CHIEFTESS.
AYOOOOOAH! FRESH MEAT TONIGHT!
WE HAVEN'T BEEN ON A TRIBE HUNT SINCE WE'VE SETTLED HOWLING ROCK. IT'S ABOUT TIME!
IT'S THE BITTERGRASS I TOLD YOU ABOUT. SMEAR IT ALL OVER-- THEY'LL NEVER SCENT YOU COMING.
THE TWO MOONS HAVE BARELY TRAVELED HALF THE NIGHT SKY, WHEN--

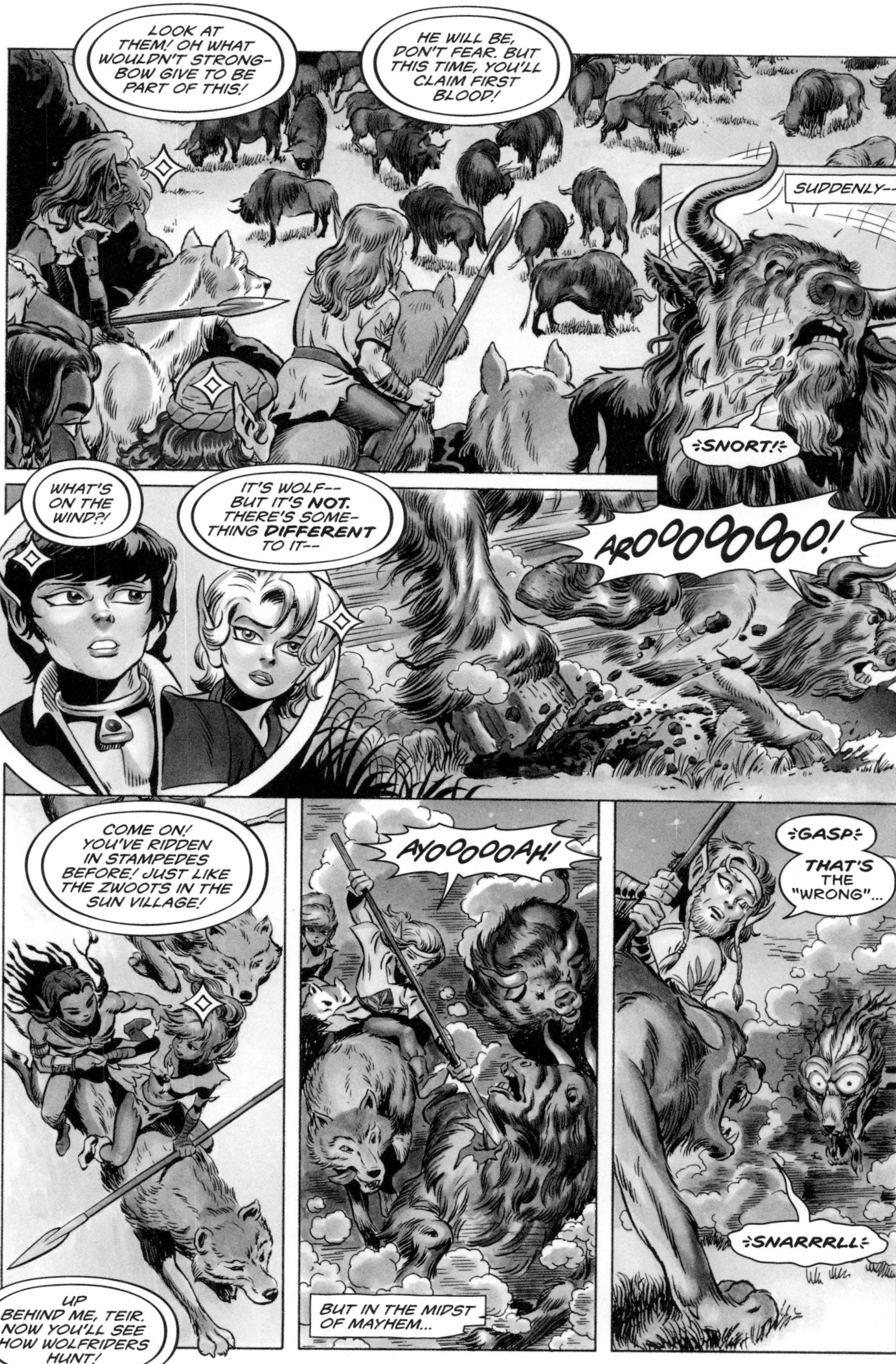
LOOK AT THEM! OH WHAT WOULDN'T STRONG-BOW GIVE TO BE PART OF THIS!
HE WILL BE, DON'T FEAR. BUT THIS TIME, YOU'LL CLAIM FIRST BLOOD!
SUDDENLY--
SNORT!
WHAT'S ON THE WIND?!
IT'S WOLF-- BUT IT'S NOT. THERE'S SOME-THING DIFFERENT TO IT--
AROOOOOOOOO!
COME ON! YOU'VE RIDDEN IN STAMPEDES BEFORE! JUST LIKE THE ZWOOTS IN THE SUN VILLAGE!
UP BEHIND ME, TEIR. NOW YOU'LL SEE HOW WOLFRIDERS HUNT!
AYOOOOOAH!
BUT IN THE MIDST OF MAYHEM...
GASP
THAT'S THE "WRONG"...
SNARRRLL

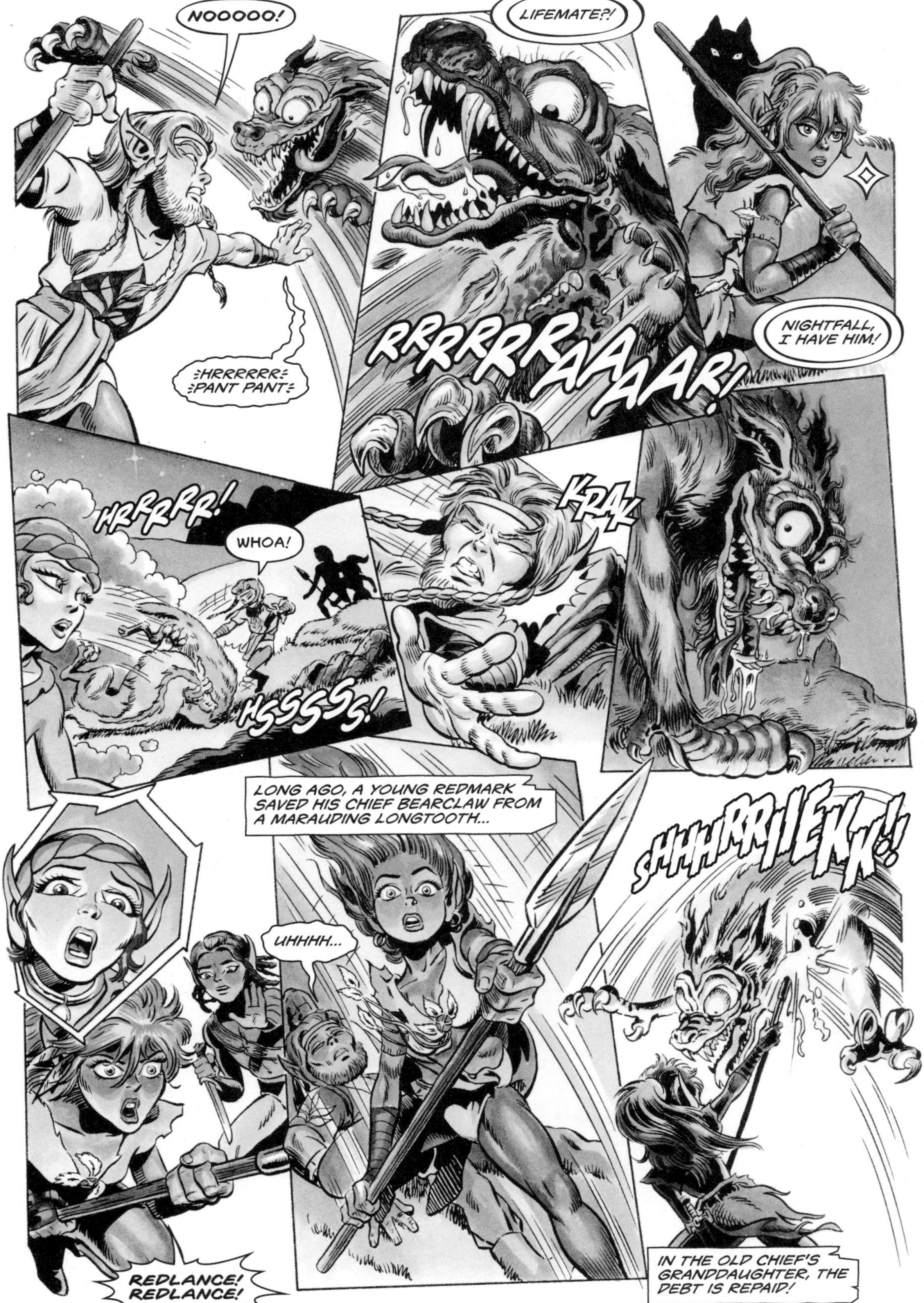
NOOOOO!
HRRRRRR PANT PANT
LIFEMATE?!
RRRRRRAAAAAR!
NIGHTFALL, I HAVE HIM!
HRRRRR!
WHOA!
HSSSSS!
KRAK
LONG AGO, A YOUNG REDMARK SAVED HIS CHIEF BEARCLAW FROM A MARAUDING LONGTOOTH...
UHHHH...
SHHHRRIIEKK!!
REDLANCE! REDLANCE!
IN THE OLD CHIEF'S GRANDDAUGHTER, THE DEBT IS REPAID!

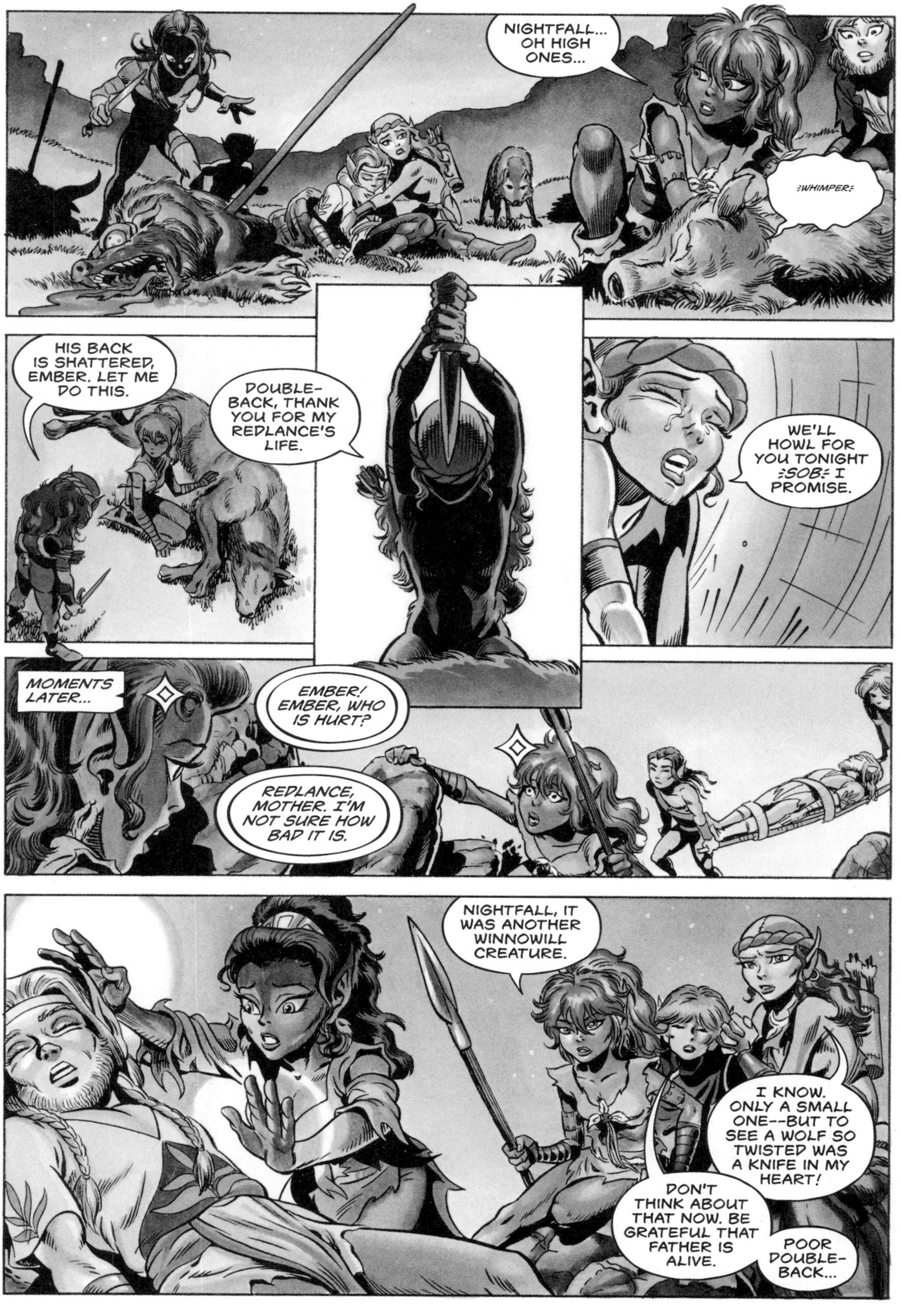
NIGHTFALL... OH HIGH ONES...
WHIMPER
HIS BACK IS SHATTERED, EMBER. LET ME DO THIS.
DOUBLE-BACK, THANK YOU FOR MY REDLANCE'S LIFE.
WE'LL HOWL FOR YOU TONIGHT SOB I PROMISE.
MOMENTS LATER...
EMBER! EMBER, WHO IS HURT?
REDLANCE, MOTHER. I'M NOT SURE HOW BAD IT IS.
NIGHTFALL, IT WAS ANOTHER WINNOWILL CREATURE.
I KNOW. ONLY A SMALL ONE--BUT TO SEE A WOLF SO TWISTED WAS A KNIFE IN MY HEART!
DON'T THINK ABOUT THAT NOW. BE GRATEFUL THAT FATHER IS ALIVE.
POOR DOUBLE-BACK...

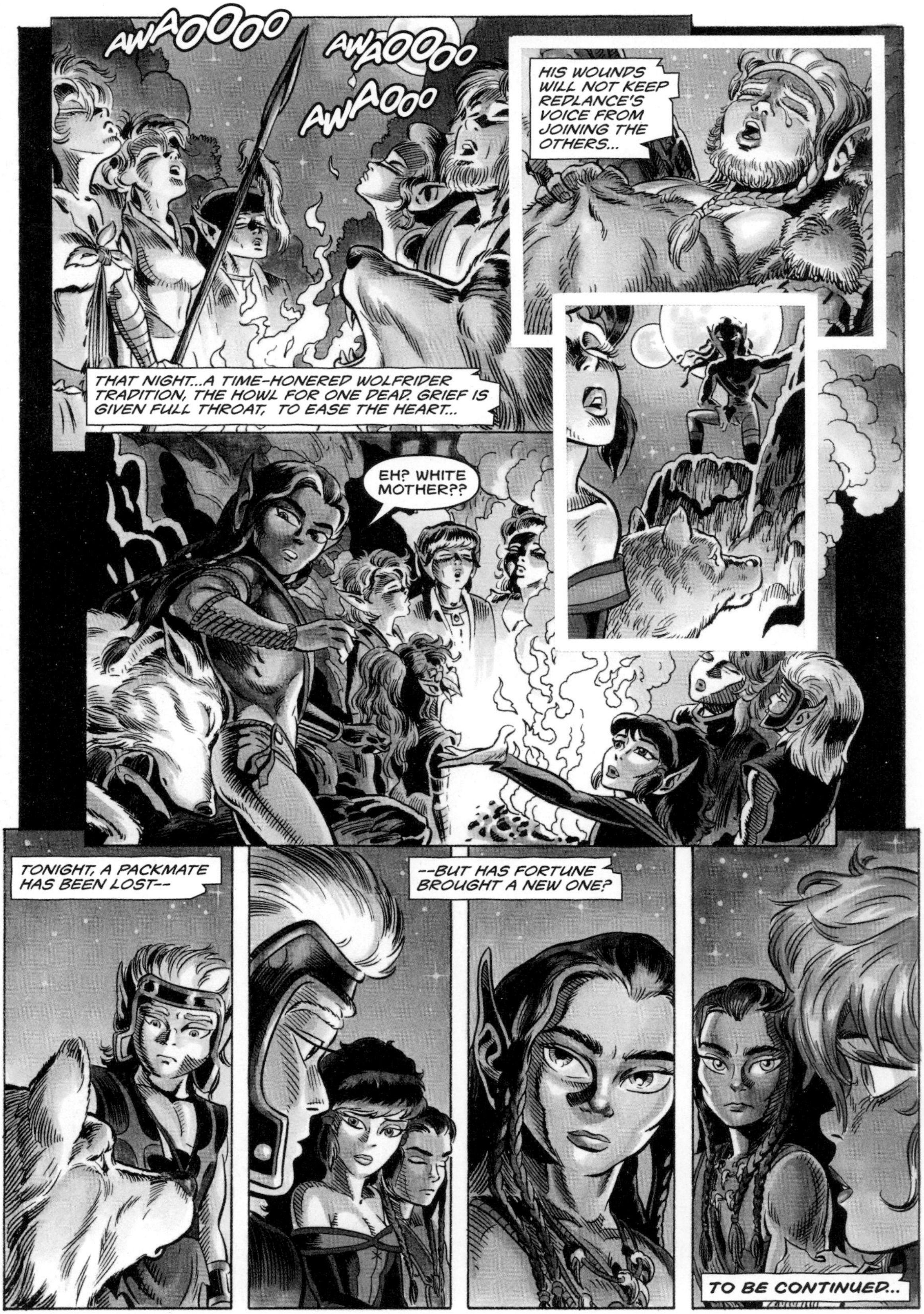
AWAOOOOO
AWAOOOOO
AWAOOO
HIS WOUNDS WILL NOT KEEP REDLANCE'S VOICE FROM JOINING THE OTHERS...
THAT NIGHT...A TIME-HONERED WOLFRIDER TRADITION, THE HOWL FOR ONE DEAD. GRIEF IS GIVEN FULL THROAT, TO EASE THE HEART...
EH? WHITE MOTHER??
TONIGHT, A PACKMATE HAS BEEN LOST--
--BUT HAS FORTUNE BROUGHT A NEW ONE?
TO BE CONTINUED...

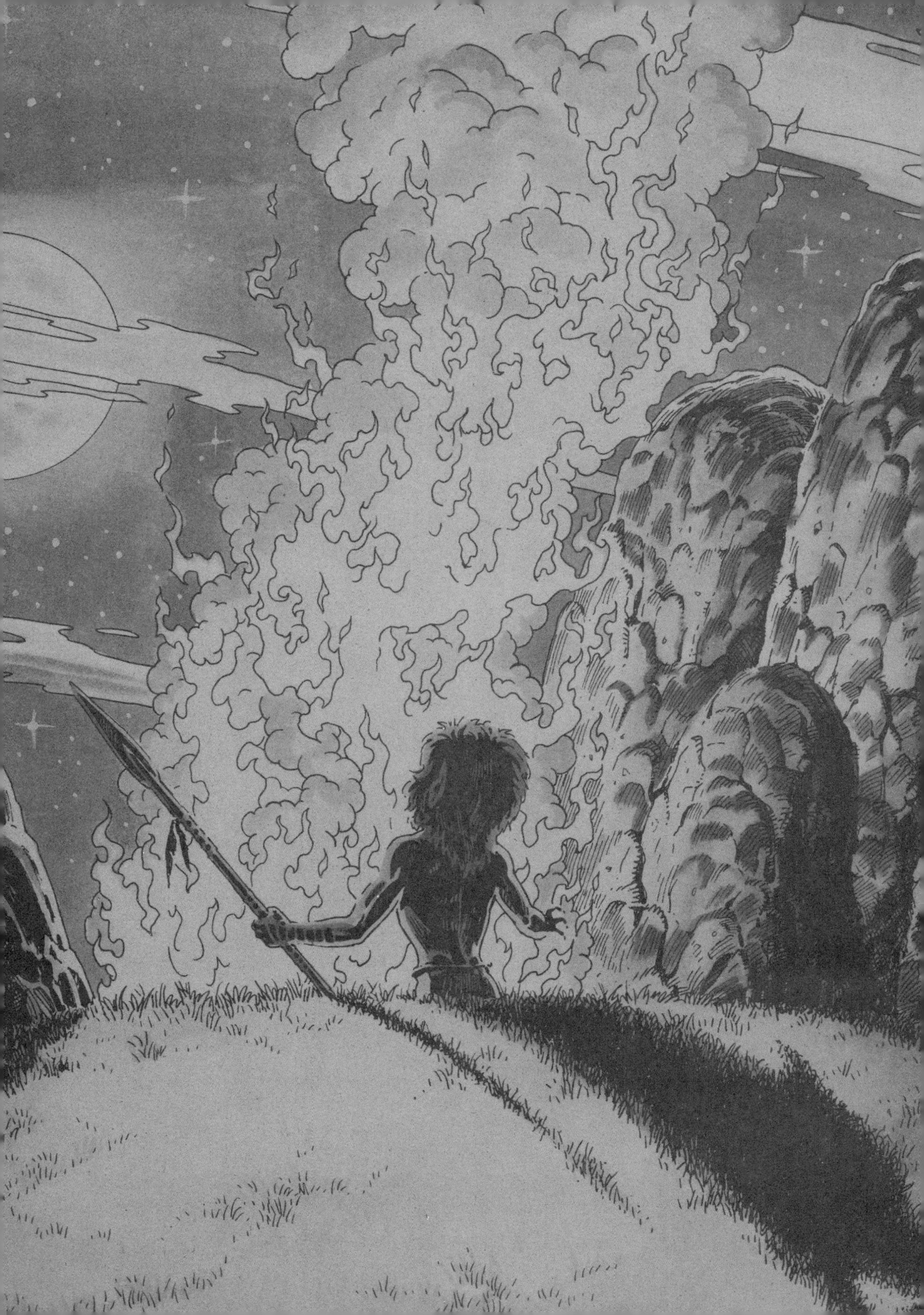

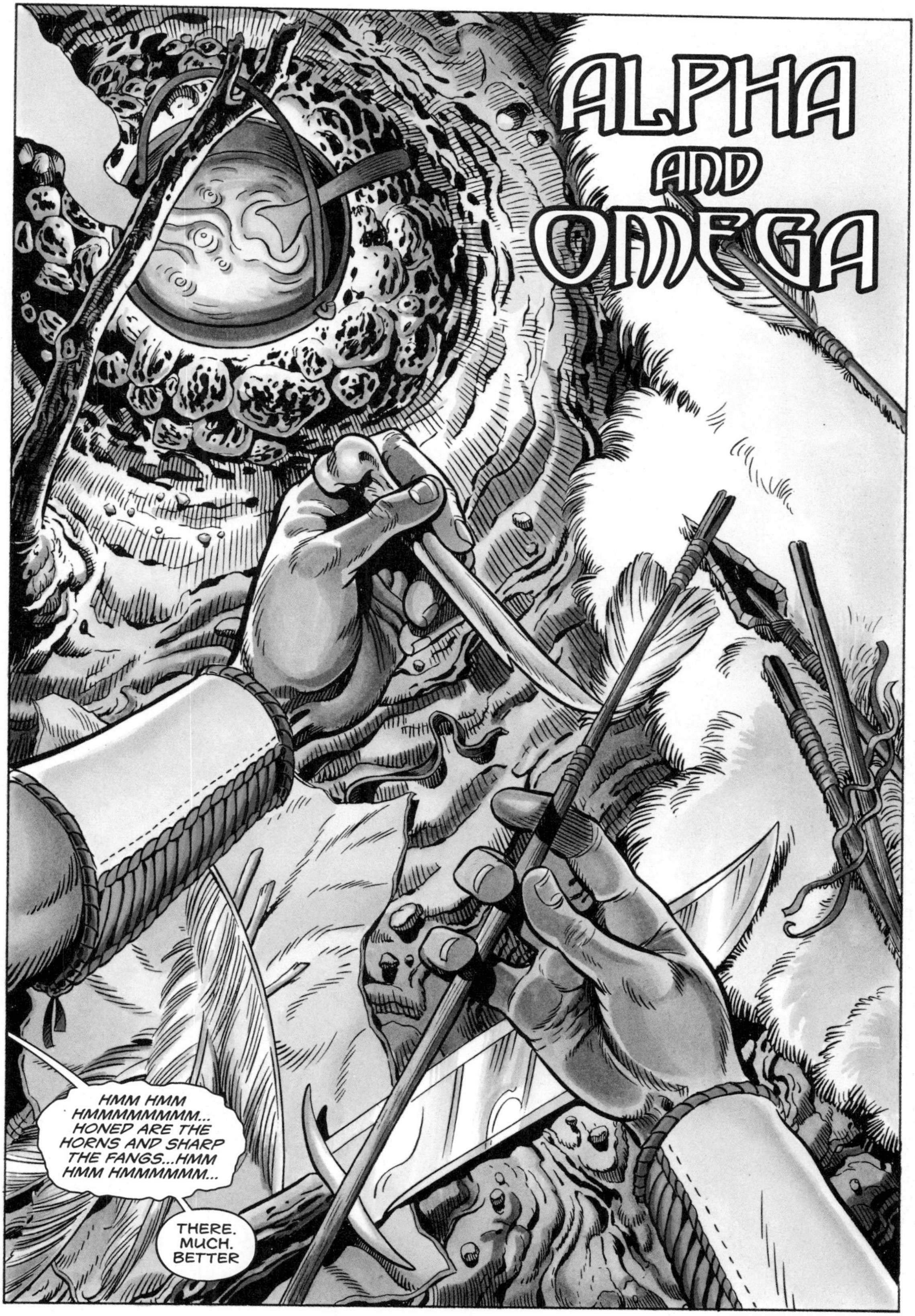
ALPHA AND OMEGA
HMM HMM HMMMMMMMMM... HONED ARE THE HORNS AND SHARP THE FANGS...HMM HMM HMMMMMMM...
THERE. MUCH. BETTER

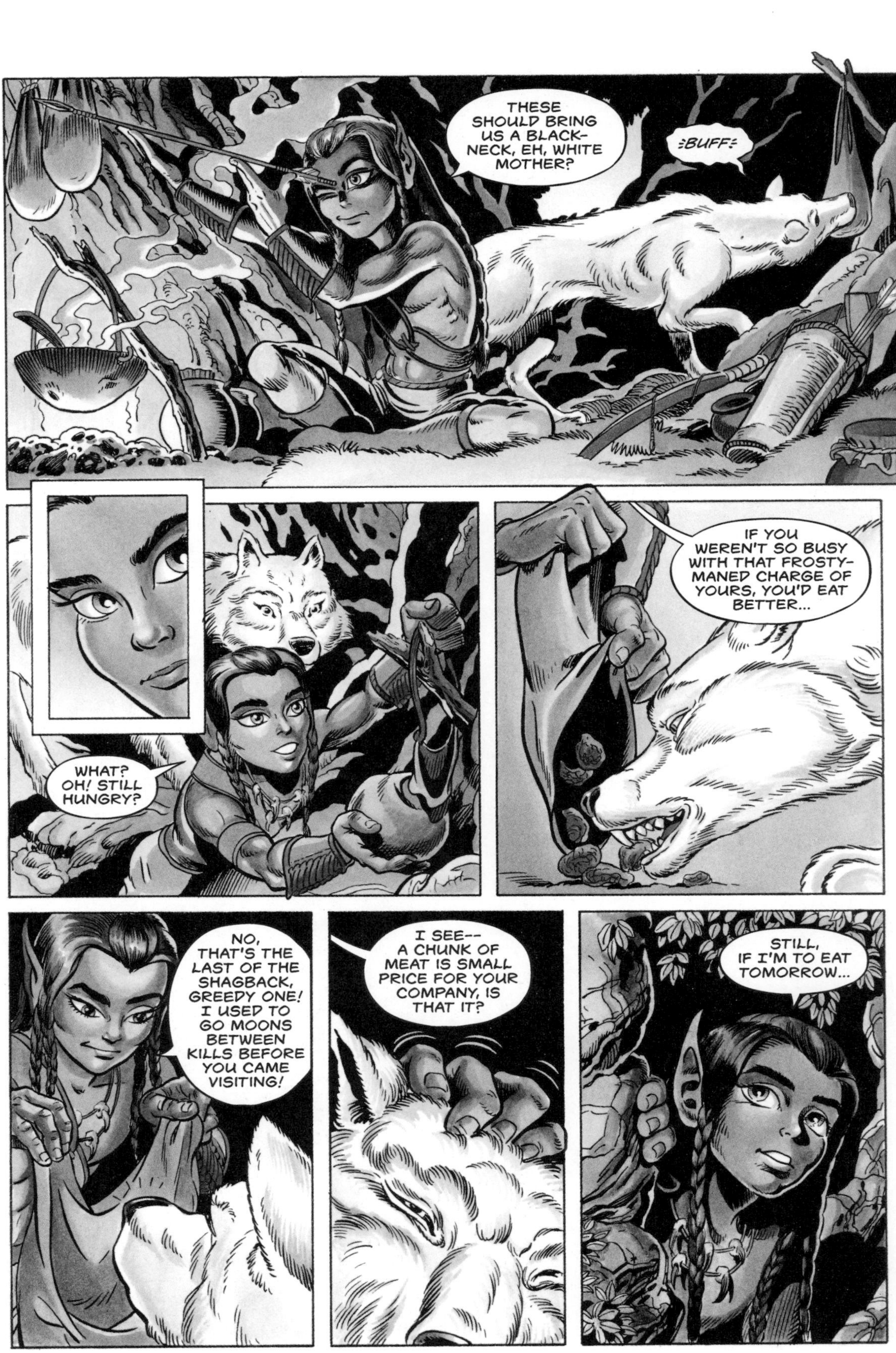
THESE SHOULD BRING US A BLACK-NECK, EH, WHITE MOTHER?
BUFF
WHAT? OH! STILL HUNGRY?
IF YOU WEREN'T SO BUSY WITH THAT FROSTY-MANED CHARGE OF YOURS, YOU'D EAT BETTER...
NO, THAT'S THE LAST OF THE SHAGBACK, GREEDY ONE! I USED TO GO MOONS BETWEEN KILLS BEFORE YOU CAME VISITING!
I SEE-- A CHUNK OF MEAT IS SMALL PRICE FOR YOUR COMPANY, IS THAT IT?
STILL, IF I'M TO EAT TOMORROW...

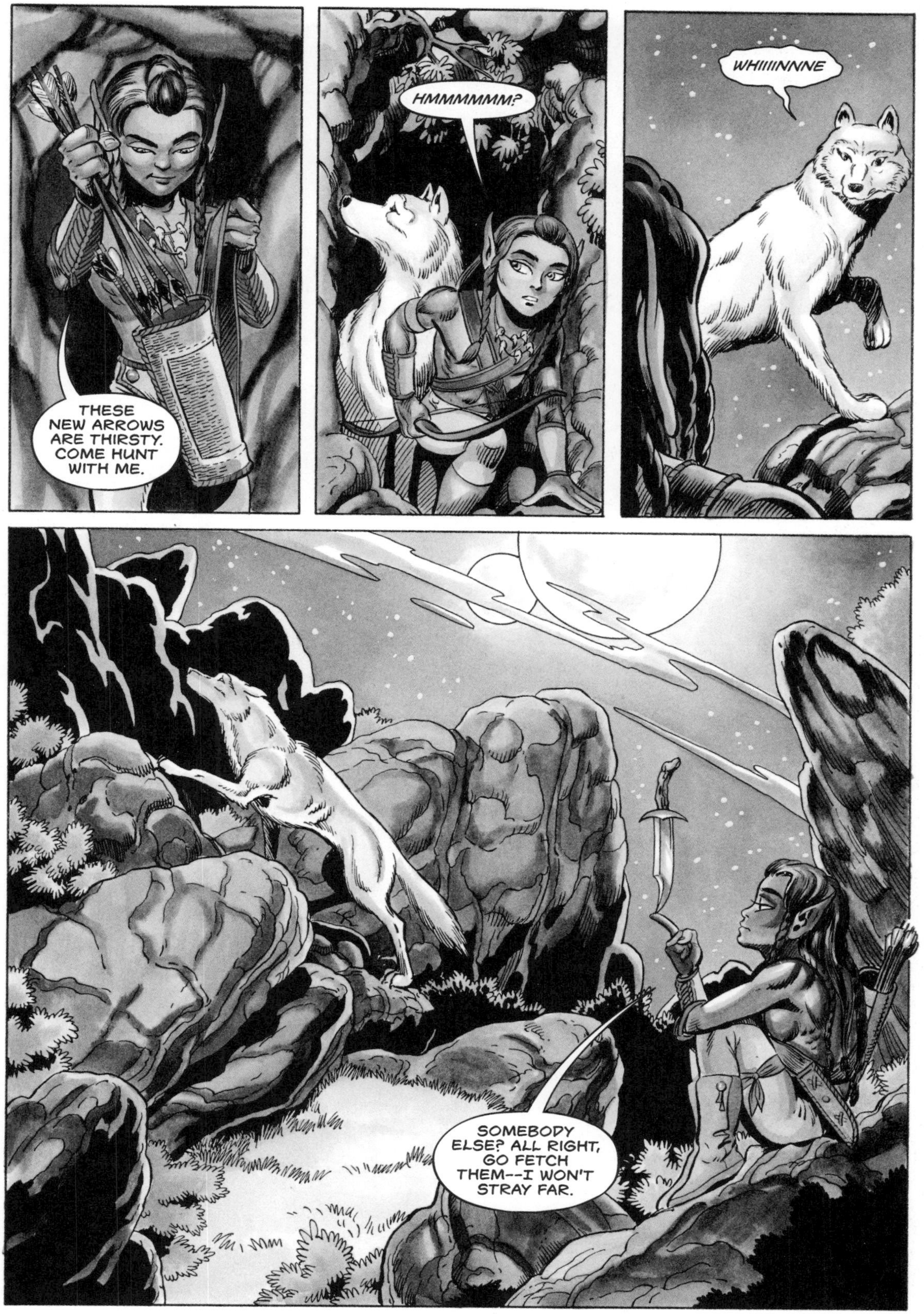
THESE NEW ARROWS ARE THIRSTY. COME HUNT WITH ME.
HMMMMMM?
WHIIIINNNE
SOMEBODY ELSE? ALL RIGHT, GO FETCH THEM--I WON'T STRAY FAR.

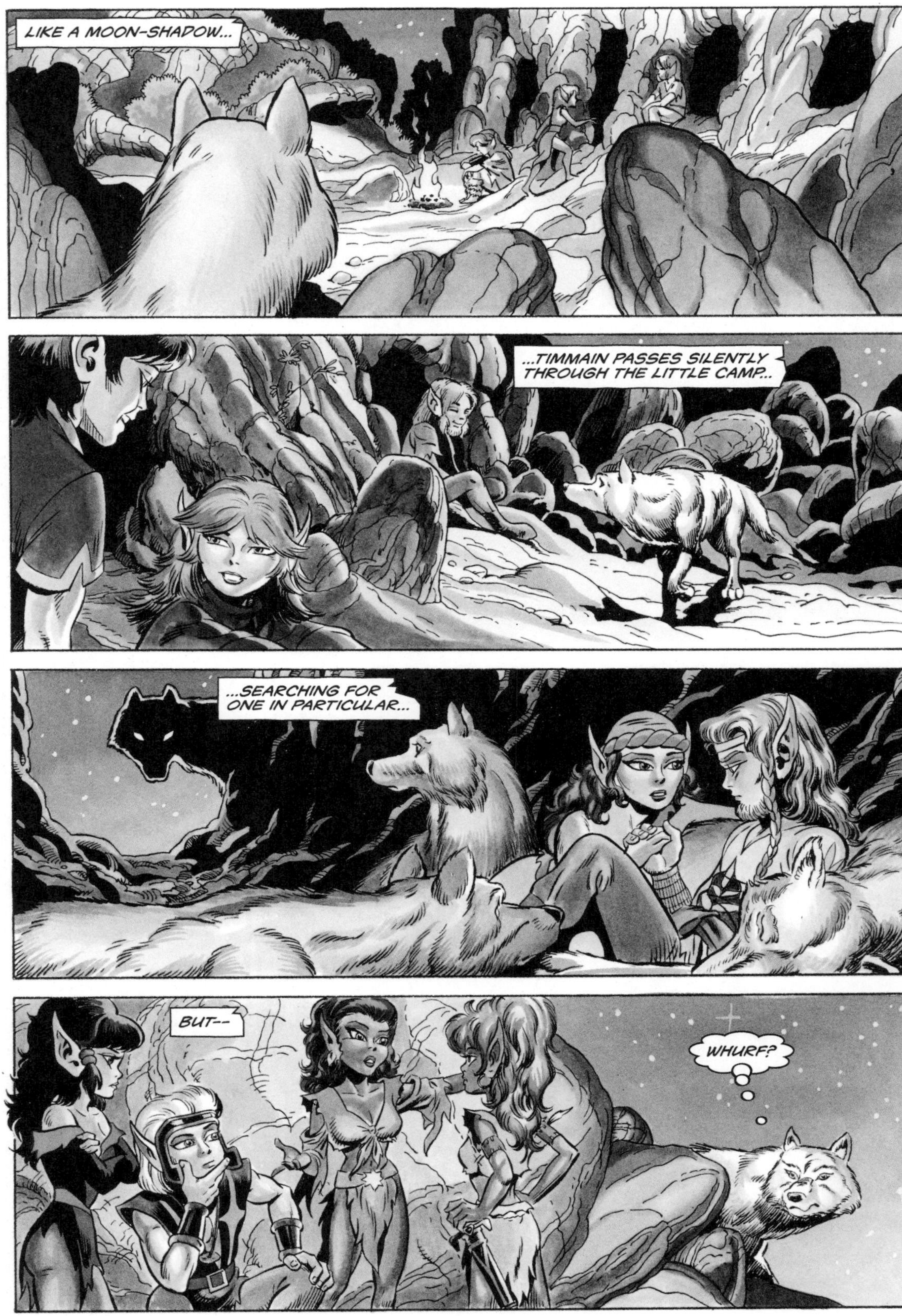
LIKE A MOON-SHADOW...
...TIMMAIN PASSES SILENTLY THROUGH THE LITTLE CAMP...
...SEARCHING FOR ONE IN PARTICULAR...
BUT--
WHURF?

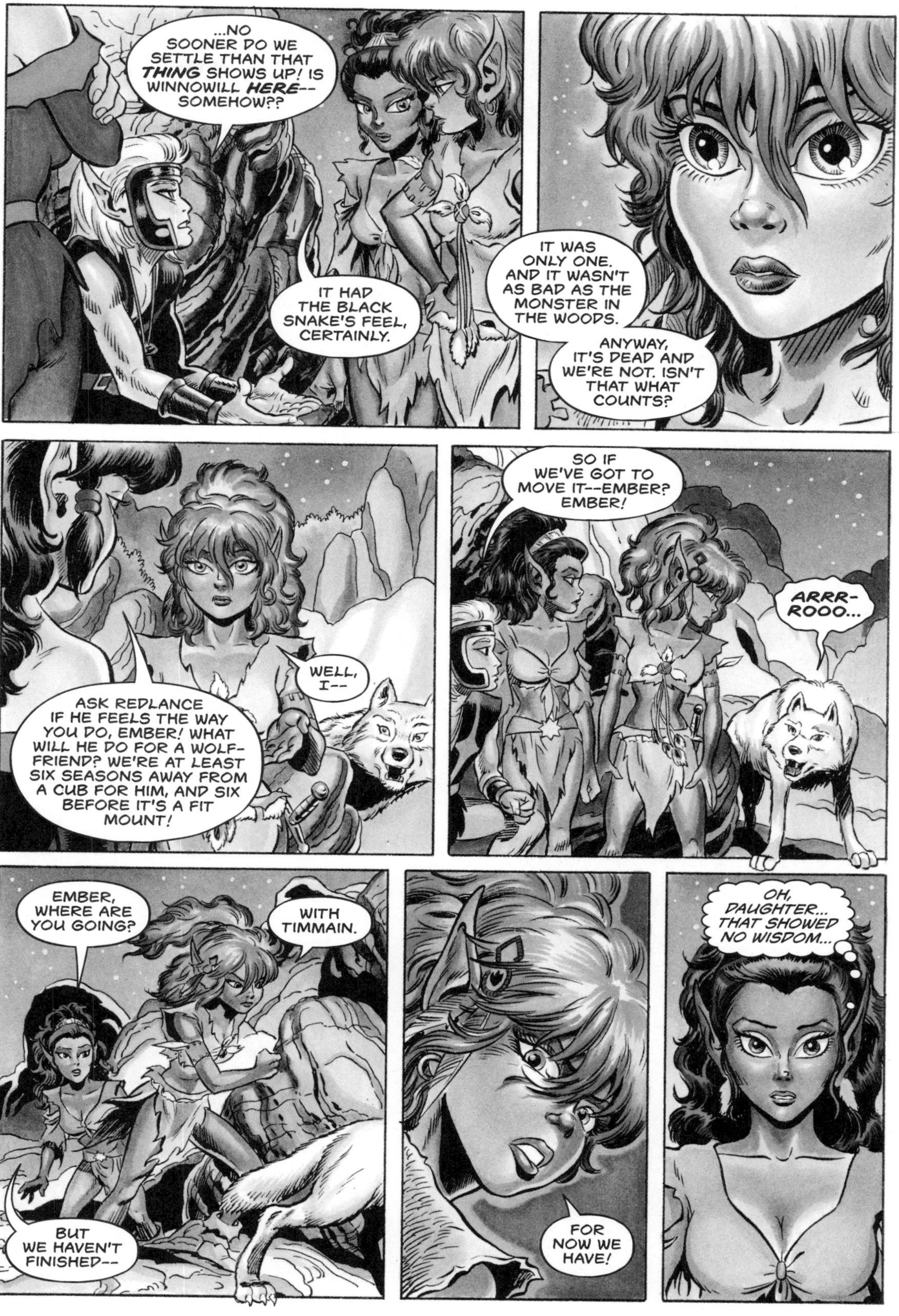
...NO SOONER DO WE SETTLE THAN THAT THING SHOWS UP! IS WINNOWILL HERE-- SOMEHOW??
IT HAD THE BLACK SNAKE'S FEEL, CERTAINLY.
IT WAS ONLY ONE. AND IT WASN'T AS BAD AS THE MONSTER IN THE WOODS.
ANYWAY, IT'S DEAD AND WE'RE NOT. ISN'T THAT WHAT COUNTS?
ASK REDLANCE IF HE FEELS THE WAY YOU DO, EMBER! WHAT WILL HE DO FOR A WOLF-FRIEND? WE'RE AT LEAST SIX SEASONS AWAY FROM A CUB FOR HIM, AND SIX BEFORE IT'S A FIT MOUNT!
WELL, I--
SO IF WE'VE GOT TO MOVE IT--EMBER? EMBER!
ARRR-ROOO...
EMBER, WHERE ARE YOU GOING?
WITH TIMMAIN.
BUT WE HAVEN'T FINISHED--
FOR NOW WE HAVE!
OH, DAUGHTER... THAT SHOWED NO WISDOM...

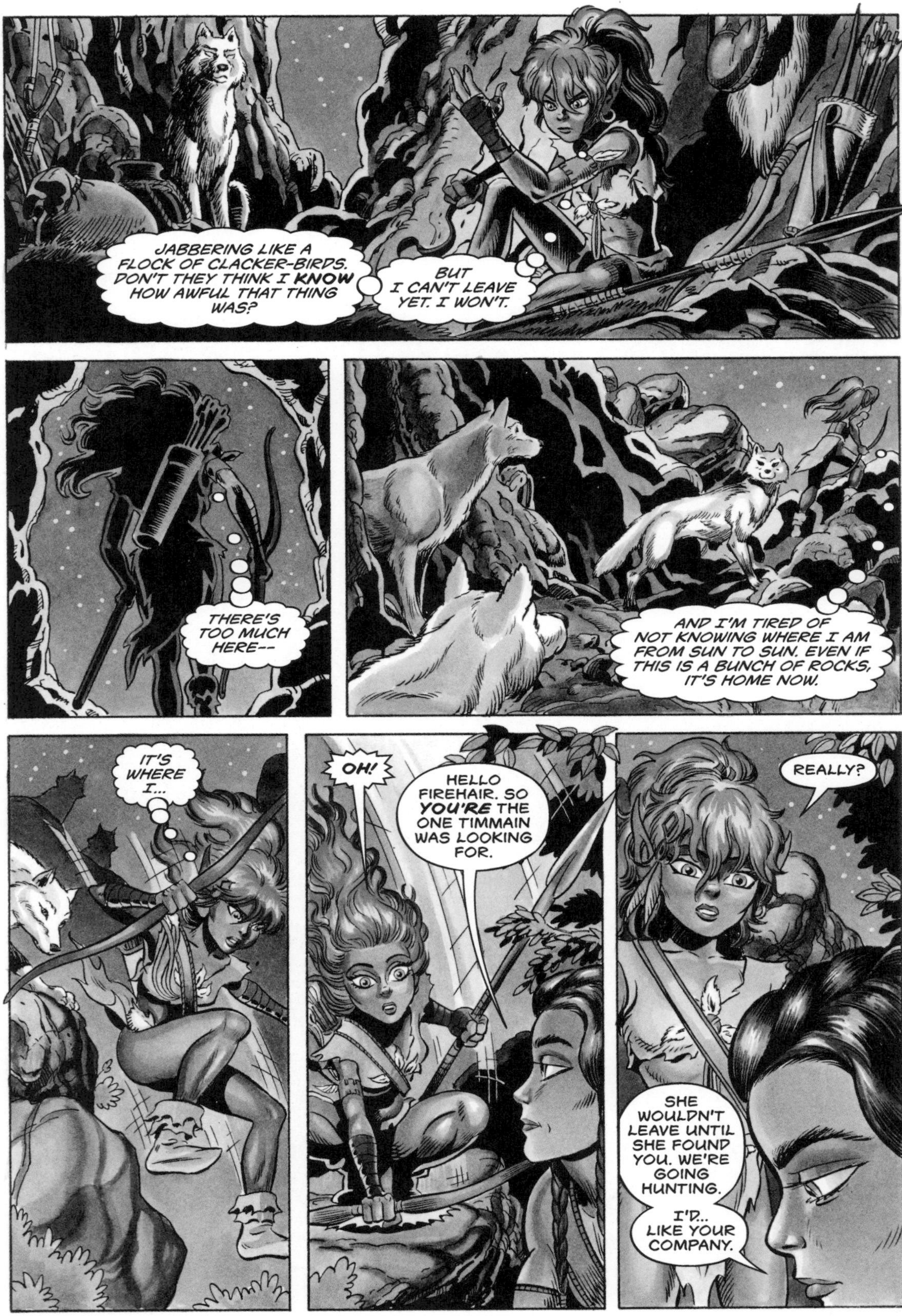
JABBERING LIKE A FLOCK OF CLACKER-BIRDS. DON'T THEY THINK I KNOW HOW AWFUL THAT THING WAS?
BUT I CAN'T LEAVE YET. I WON'T.
THERE'S TOO MUCH HERE--
AND I'M TIRED OF NOT KNOWING WHERE I AM FROM SUN TO SUN. EVEN IF THIS IS A BUNCH OF ROCKS, IT'S HOME NOW.
IT'S WHERE I...
OH!
HELLO FIREHAIR. SO YOU'RE THE ONE TIMMAIN WAS LOOKING FOR.
REALLY?
SHE WOULDN'T LEAVE UNTIL SHE FOUND YOU. WE'RE GOING HUNTING.
I'D.. LIKE YOUR COMPANY.

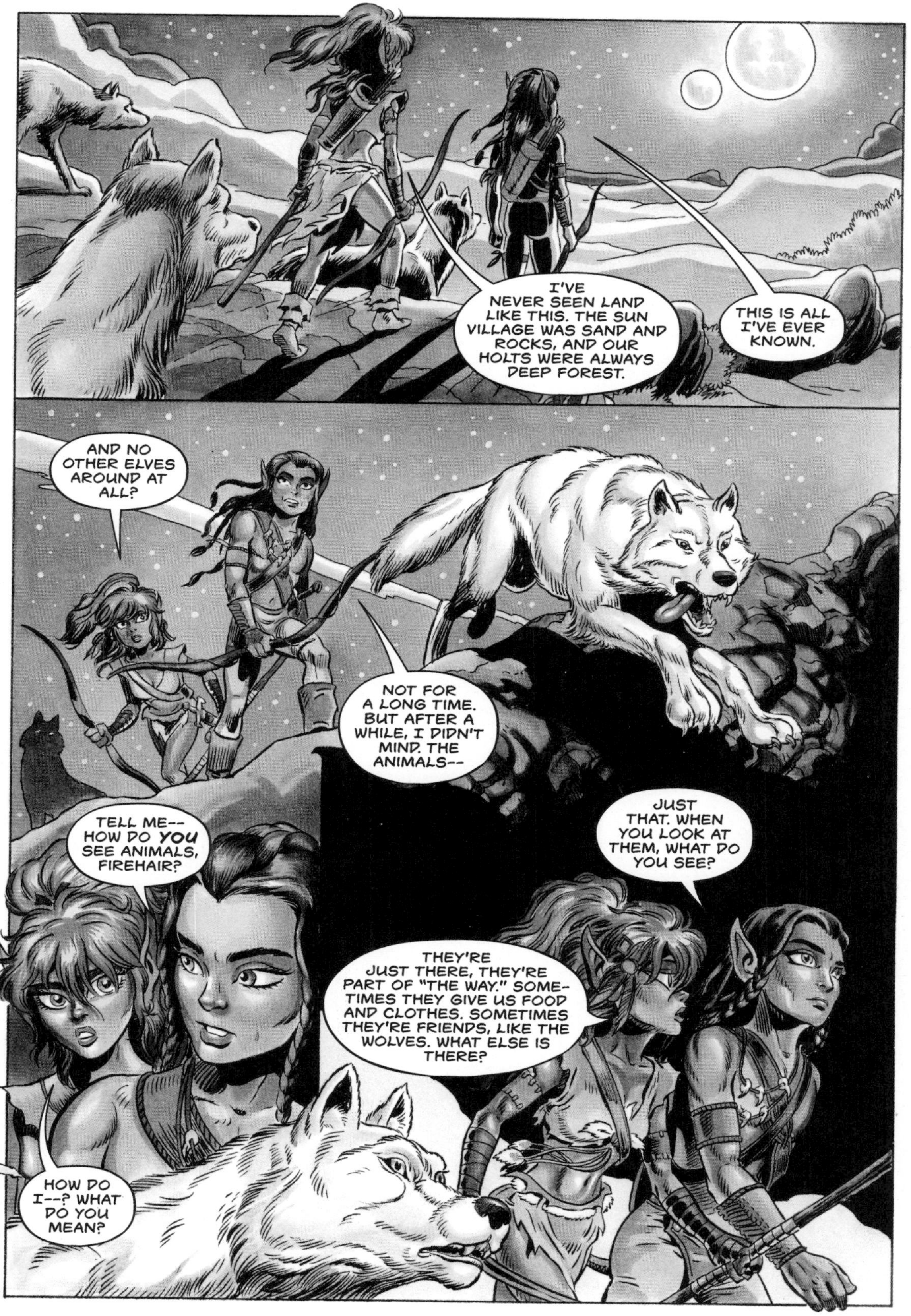
I'VE NEVER SEEN LAND LIKE THIS. THE SUN VILLAGE WAS SAND AND ROCKS, AND OUR HOLTS WERE ALWAYS DEEP FOREST.
THIS IS ALL I'VE EVER KNOWN.
AND NO OTHER ELVES AROUND AT ALL?
NOT FOR A LONG TIME. BUT AFTER A WHILE, I DIDN'T MIND. THE ANIMALS--
TELL ME-- HOW DO *YOU* SEE ANIMALS, FIREHAIR?
HOW DO I--? WHAT DO YOU MEAN?
JUST THAT. WHEN YOU LOOK AT THEM, WHAT DO YOU SEE?
THEY'RE JUST THERE, THEY'RE PART OF "THE WAY." SOMETIMES THEY GIVE US FOOD AND CLOTHES. SOMETIMES THEY'RE FRIENDS, LIKE THE WOLVES. WHAT ELSE IS THERE?

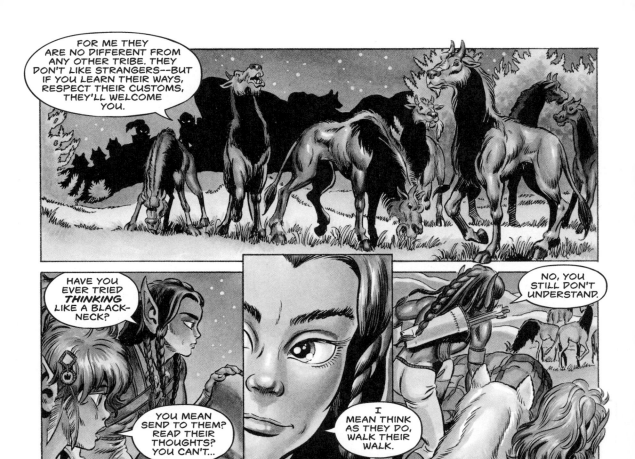

FOR ME THEY ARE NO DIFFERENT FROM ANY OTHER TRIBE. THEY DON'T LIKE STRANGERS--BUT IF YOU LEARN THEIR WAYS, RESPECT THEIR CUSTOMS, THEY'LL WELCOME YOU.

HAVE YOU EVER TRIED *THINKING* LIKE A BLACK-NECK?

YOU MEAN SEND TO THEM? READ THEIR THOUGHTS? YOU CAN'T...

I MEAN THINK AS THEY DO, WALK THEIR WALK.

NO, YOU STILL DON'T UNDERSTAND.

WATCH.

FOR AN INSTANT, THE SHY CREATURES SENSE AN INTRUDER.

BUT IN A SPACE OF A SINGLE BREATH...

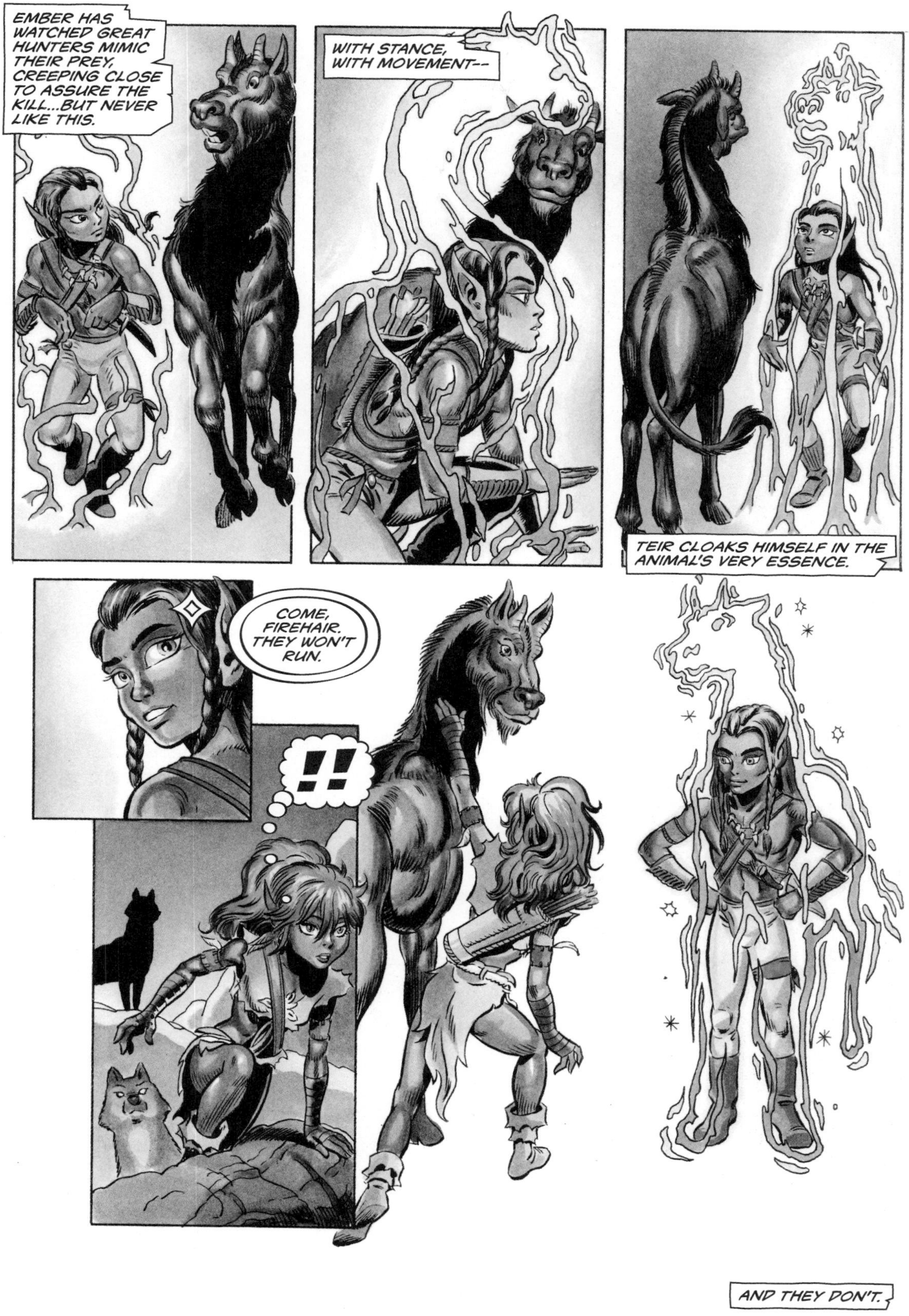
EMBER HAS WATCHED GREAT HUNTERS MIMIC THEIR PREY, CREEPING CLOSE TO ASSURE THE KILL...BUT NEVER LIKE THIS.
WITH STANCE, WITH MOVEMENT--
TEIR CLOAKS HIMSELF IN THE ANIMAL'S VERY ESSENCE.
COME, FIREHAIR. THEY WON'T RUN.
!!
AND THEY DON'T.

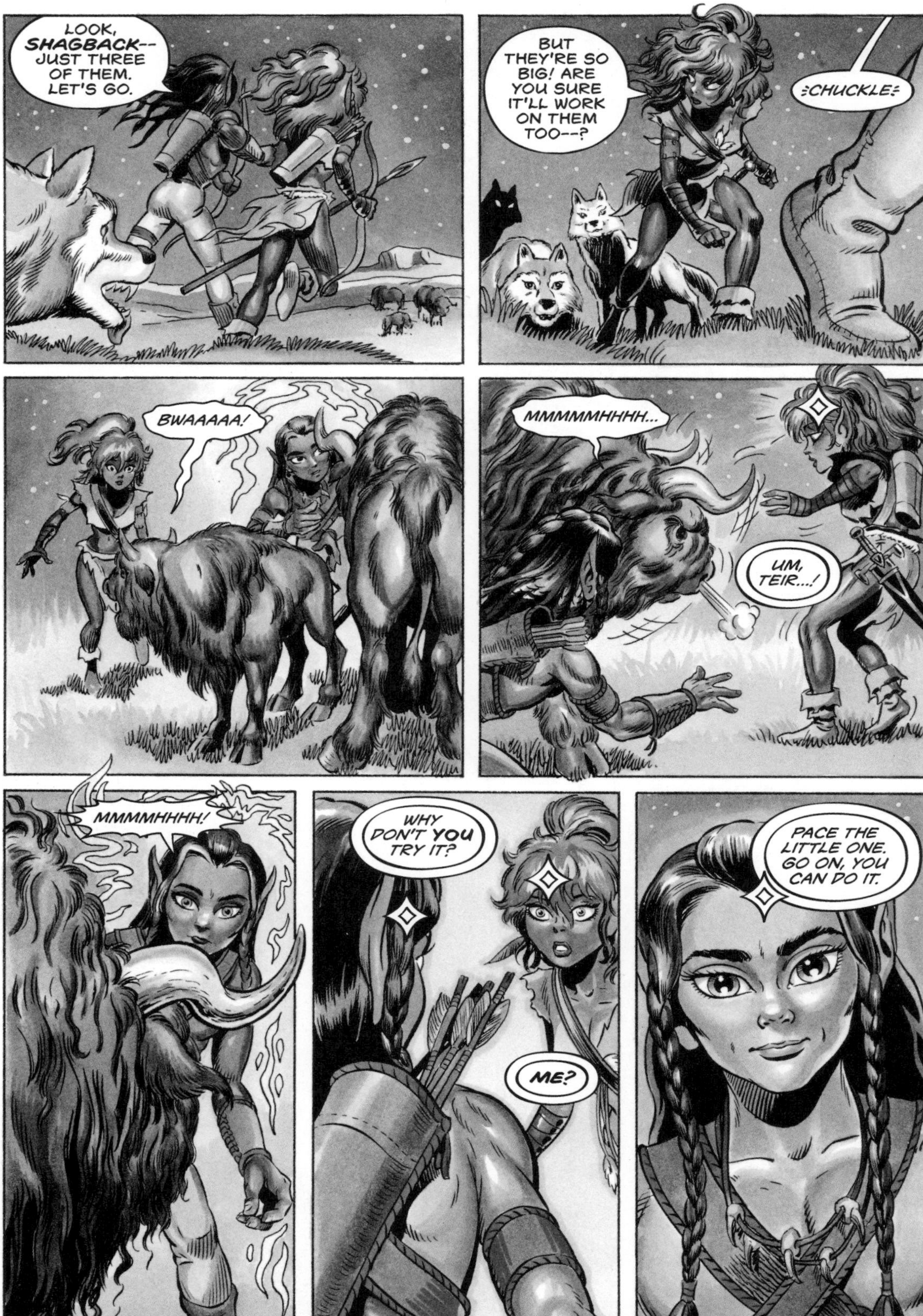
LOOK, SHAGBACK-- JUST THREE OF THEM. LET'S GO.
BUT THEY'RE SO BIG! ARE YOU SURE IT'LL WORK ON THEM TOO--?
:CHUCKLE:
BWAAAAA!
MMMMMHHHH...
UM, TEIR...!
MMMMHHHH!
WHY DON'T YOU TRY IT?
ME?
PACE THE LITTLE ONE. GO ON, YOU CAN DO IT.

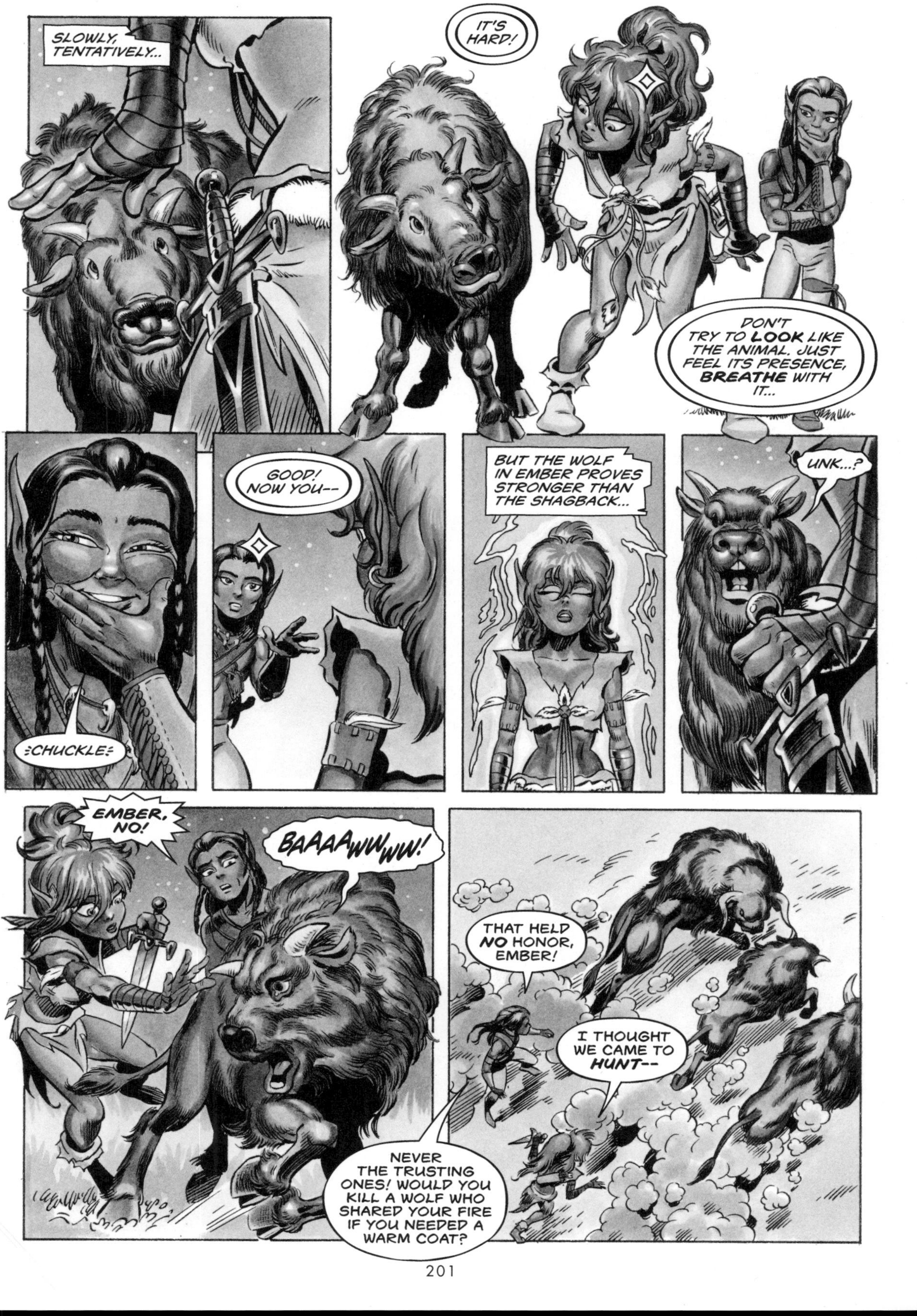
SLOWLY, TENTATIVELY...
IT'S HARD!
DON'T TRY TO LOOK LIKE THE ANIMAL. JUST FEEL ITS PRESENCE, BREATHE WITH IT...
:CHUCKLE:
GOOD! NOW YOU--
BUT THE WOLF IN EMBER PROVES STRONGER THAN THE SHAGBACK...
UNK...?
EMBER, NO!
BAAAAWWWWW!
THAT HELD NO HONOR, EMBER!
I THOUGHT WE CAME TO HUNT--
NEVER THE TRUSTING ONES! WOULD YOU KILL A WOLF WHO SHARED YOUR FIRE IF YOU NEEDED A WARM COAT?

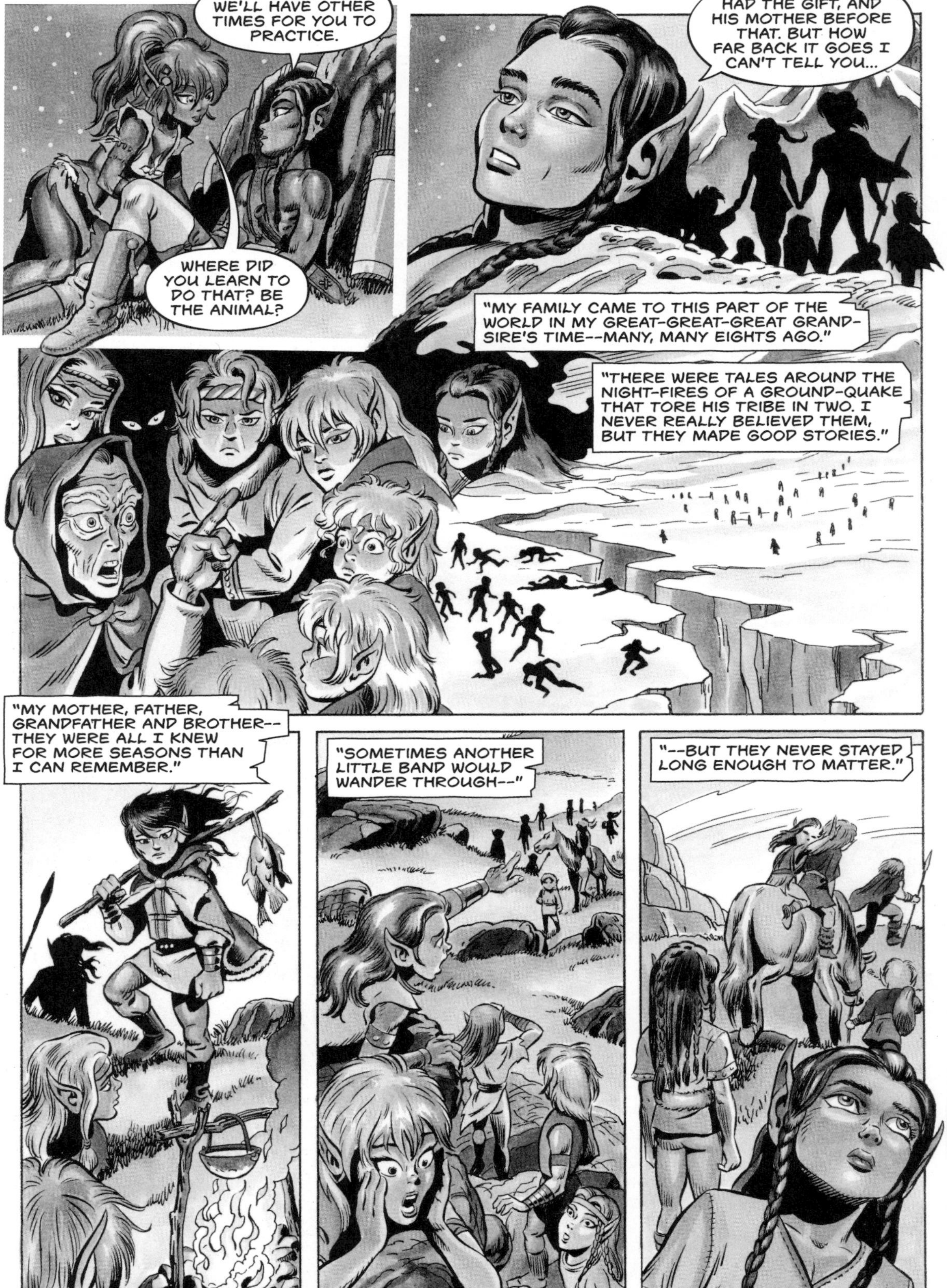
NO MATTER. WE'LL HAVE OTHER TIMES FOR YOU TO PRACTICE.
WHERE DID YOU LEARN TO DO THAT? BE THE ANIMAL?
MY FATHER HAD THE GIFT, AND HIS MOTHER BEFORE THAT. BUT HOW FAR BACK IT GOES I CAN'T TELL YOU...
"MY FAMILY CAME TO THIS PART OF THE WORLD IN MY GREAT-GREAT-GREAT GRANDSIRE'S TIME--MANY, MANY EIGHTS AGO."
"THERE WERE TALES AROUND THE NIGHT-FIRES OF A GROUND-QUAKE THAT TORE HIS TRIBE IN TWO. I NEVER REALLY BELIEVED THEM, BUT THEY MADE GOOD STORIES."
"MY MOTHER, FATHER, GRANDFATHER AND BROTHER--THEY WERE ALL I KNEW FOR MORE SEASONS THAN I CAN REMEMBER."
"SOMETIMES ANOTHER LITTLE BAND WOULD WANDER THROUGH--"
"--BUT THEY NEVER STAYED LONG ENOUGH TO MATTER."

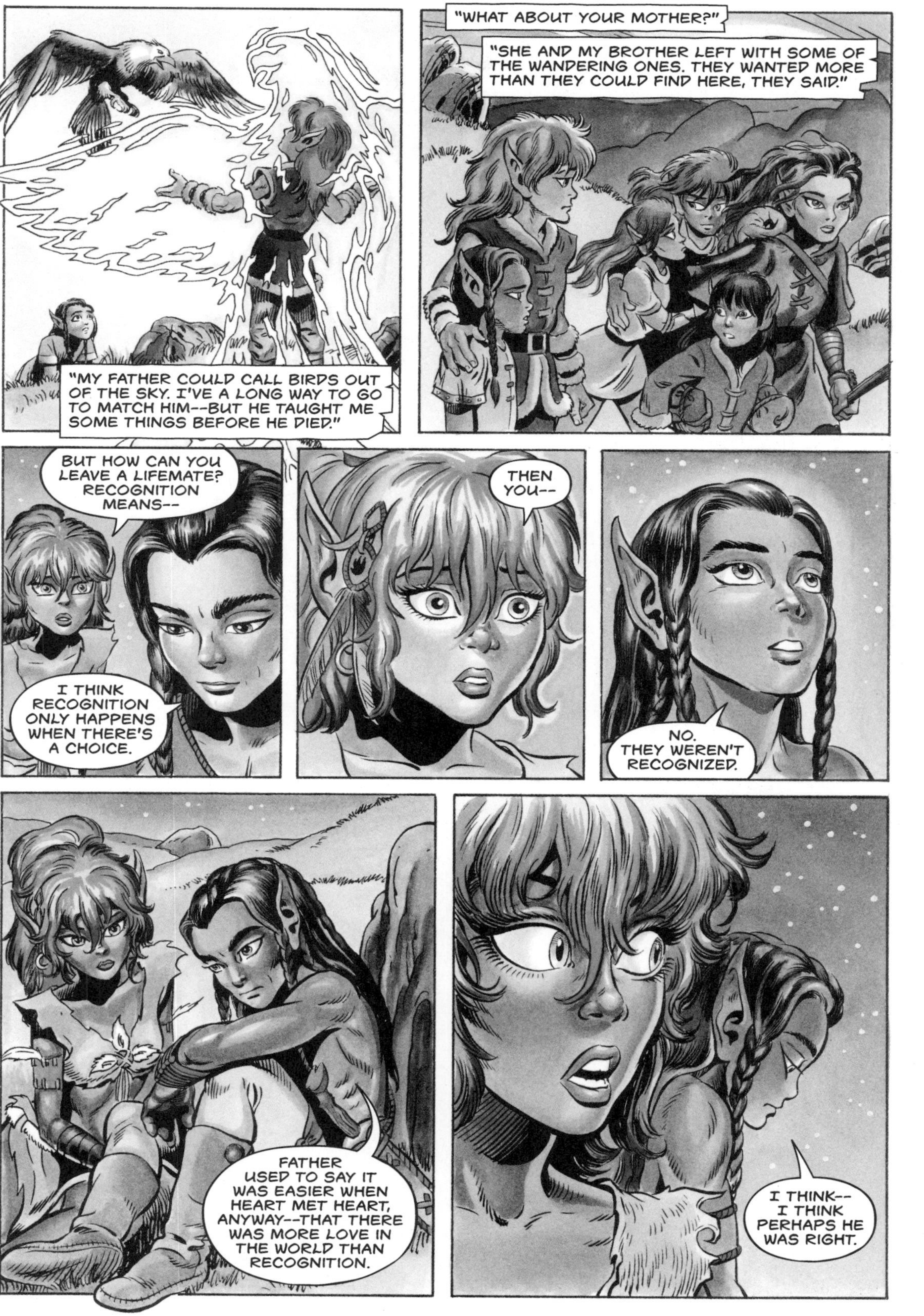
"MY FATHER COULD CALL BIRDS OUT OF THE SKY. I'VE A LONG WAY TO GO TO MATCH HIM--BUT HE TAUGHT ME SOME THINGS BEFORE HE DIED."
"WHAT ABOUT YOUR MOTHER?"
"SHE AND MY BROTHER LEFT WITH SOME OF THE WANDERING ONES. THEY WANTED MORE THAN THEY COULD FIND HERE, THEY SAID."
BUT HOW CAN YOU LEAVE A LIFEMATE? RECOGNITION MEANS--
I THINK RECOGNITION ONLY HAPPENS WHEN THERE'S A CHOICE.
THEN YOU--
NO. THEY WEREN'T RECOGNIZED.
FATHER USED TO SAY IT WAS EASIER WHEN HEART MET HEART, ANYWAY--THAT THERE WAS MORE LOVE IN THE WORLD THAN RECOGNITION.
I THINK-- I THINK PERHAPS HE WAS RIGHT.

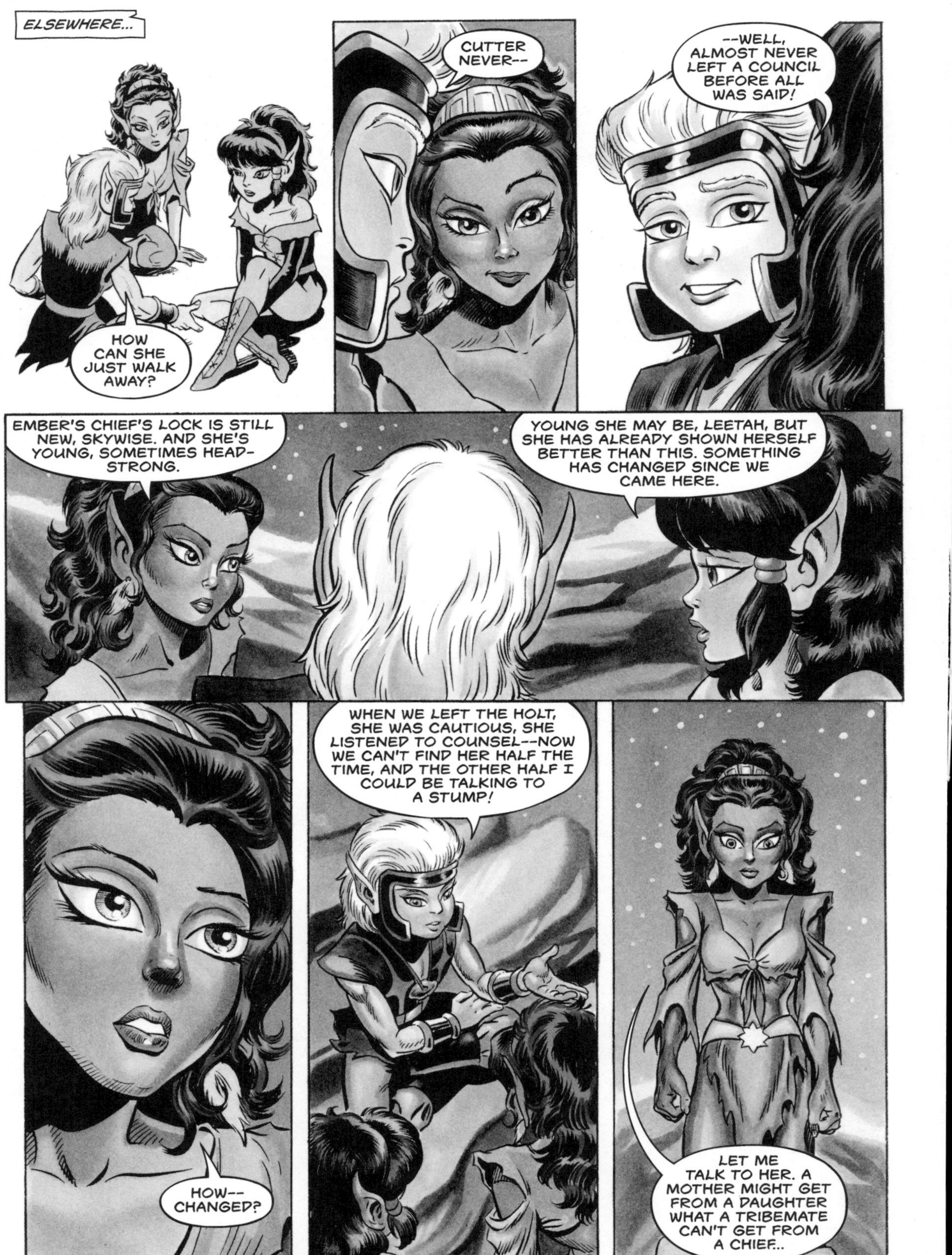
ELSEWHERE...
HOW CAN SHE JUST WALK AWAY?
CUTTER NEVER--
--WELL, ALMOST NEVER LEFT A COUNCIL BEFORE ALL WAS SAID!
EMBER'S CHIEF'S LOCK IS STILL NEW, SKYWISE. AND SHE'S YOUNG, SOMETIMES HEAD-STRONG.
YOUNG SHE MAY BE, LEETAH, BUT SHE HAS ALREADY SHOWN HERSELF BETTER THAN THIS. SOMETHING HAS CHANGED SINCE WE CAME HERE.
HOW--CHANGED?
WHEN WE LEFT THE HOLT, SHE WAS CAUTIOUS, SHE LISTENED TO COUNSEL--NOW WE CAN'T FIND HER HALF THE TIME, AND THE OTHER HALF I COULD BE TALKING TO A STUMP!
LET ME TALK TO HER. A MOTHER MIGHT GET FROM A DAUGHTER WHAT A TRIBEMATE CAN'T GET FROM A CHIEF...

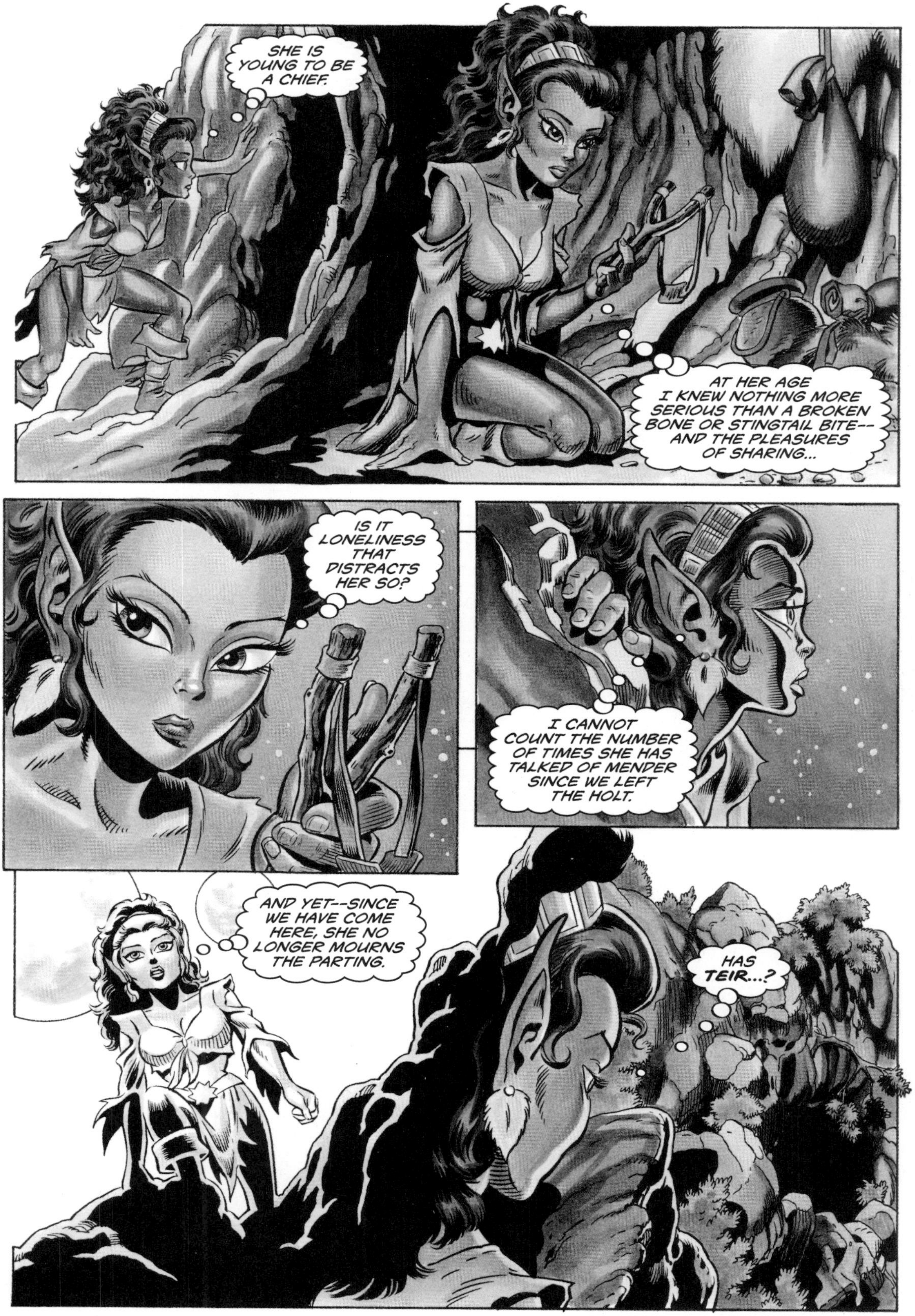
SHE IS YOUNG TO BE A CHIEF.
AT HER AGE I KNEW NOTHING MORE SERIOUS THAN A BROKEN BONE OR STINGTAIL BITE-- AND THE PLEASURES OF SHARING...
IS IT LONELINESS THAT DISTRACTS HER SO?
I CANNOT COUNT THE NUMBER OF TIMES SHE HAS TALKED OF MENDER SINCE WE LEFT THE HOLT.
AND YET--SINCE WE HAVE COME HERE, SHE NO LONGER MOURNS THE PARTING.
HAS **TEIR**...?

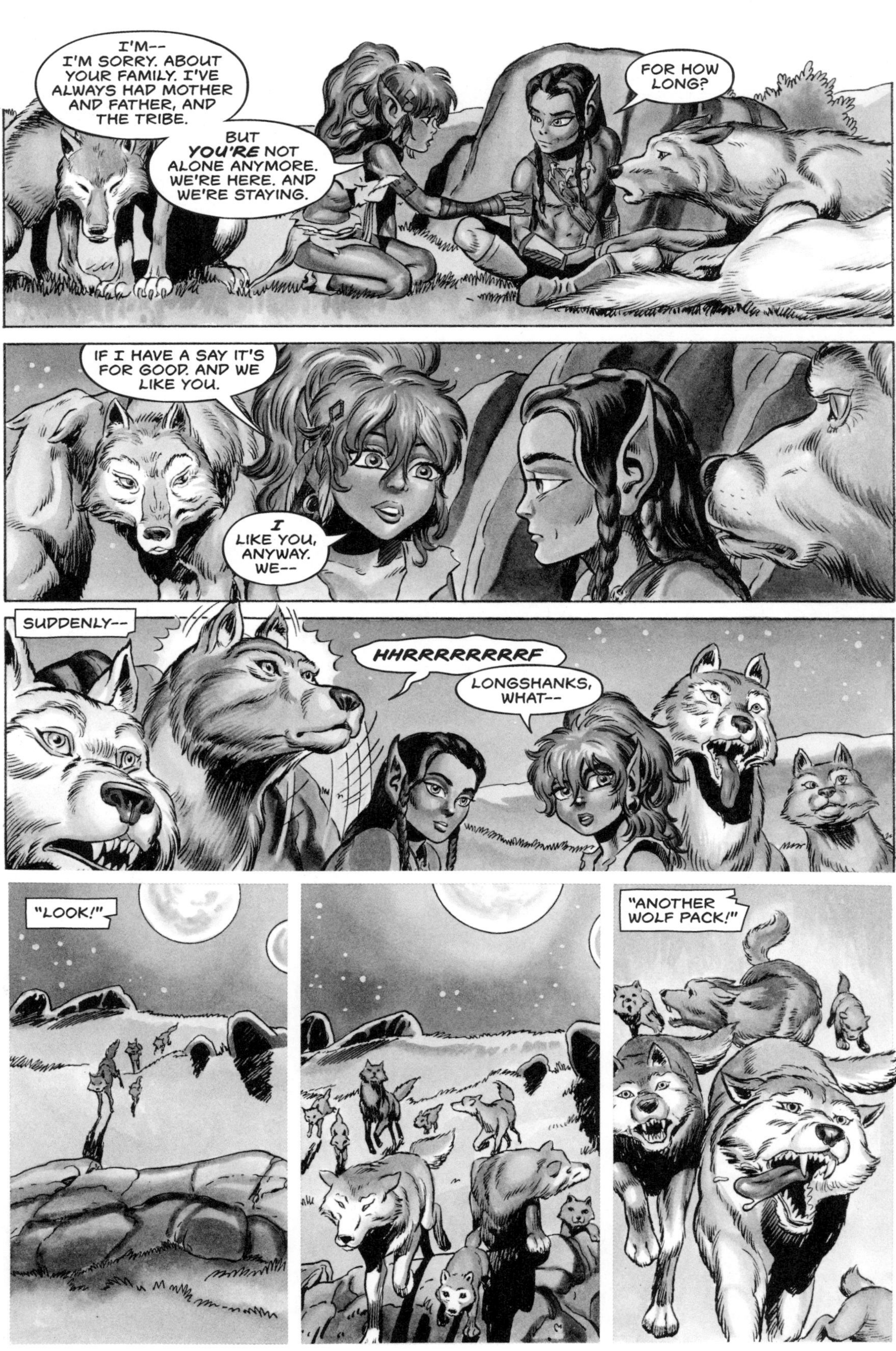
I'M-- I'M SORRY. ABOUT YOUR FAMILY. I'VE ALWAYS HAD MOTHER AND FATHER, AND THE TRIBE.
BUT *YOU'RE* NOT ALONE ANYMORE. WE'RE HERE. AND WE'RE STAYING.
FOR HOW LONG?
IF I HAVE A SAY IT'S FOR GOOD. AND WE LIKE YOU.
I LIKE YOU, ANYWAY. WE--
SUDDENLY--
HHRRRRRRRRF
LONGSHANKS, WHAT--
"LOOK!"
"ANOTHER WOLF PACK!"

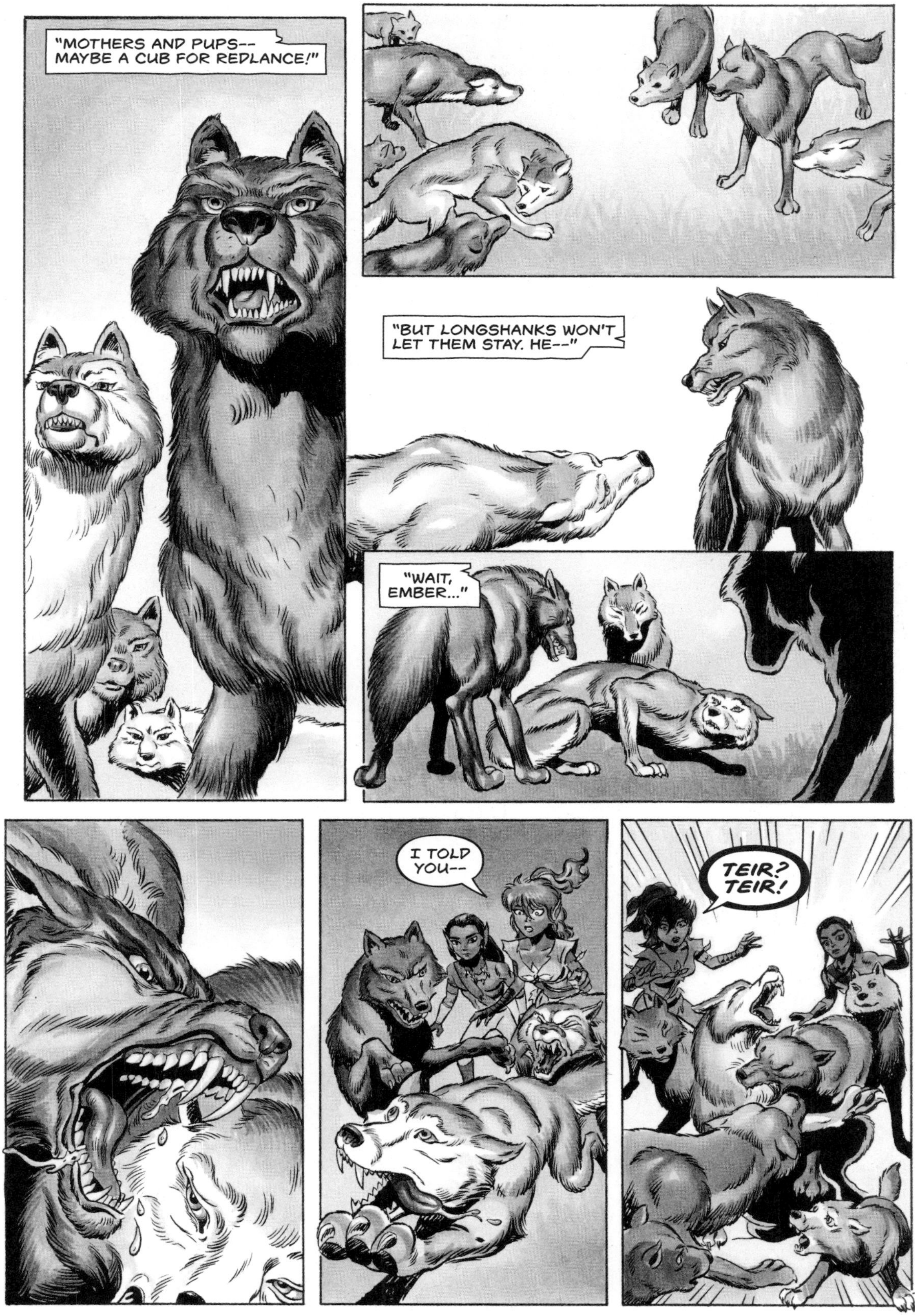
"MOTHERS AND PUPS-- MAYBE A CUB FOR REDLANCE!"
"BUT LONGSHANKS WON'T LET THEM STAY. HE--"
"WAIT, EMBER..."
I TOLD YOU--
TEIR? TEIR!

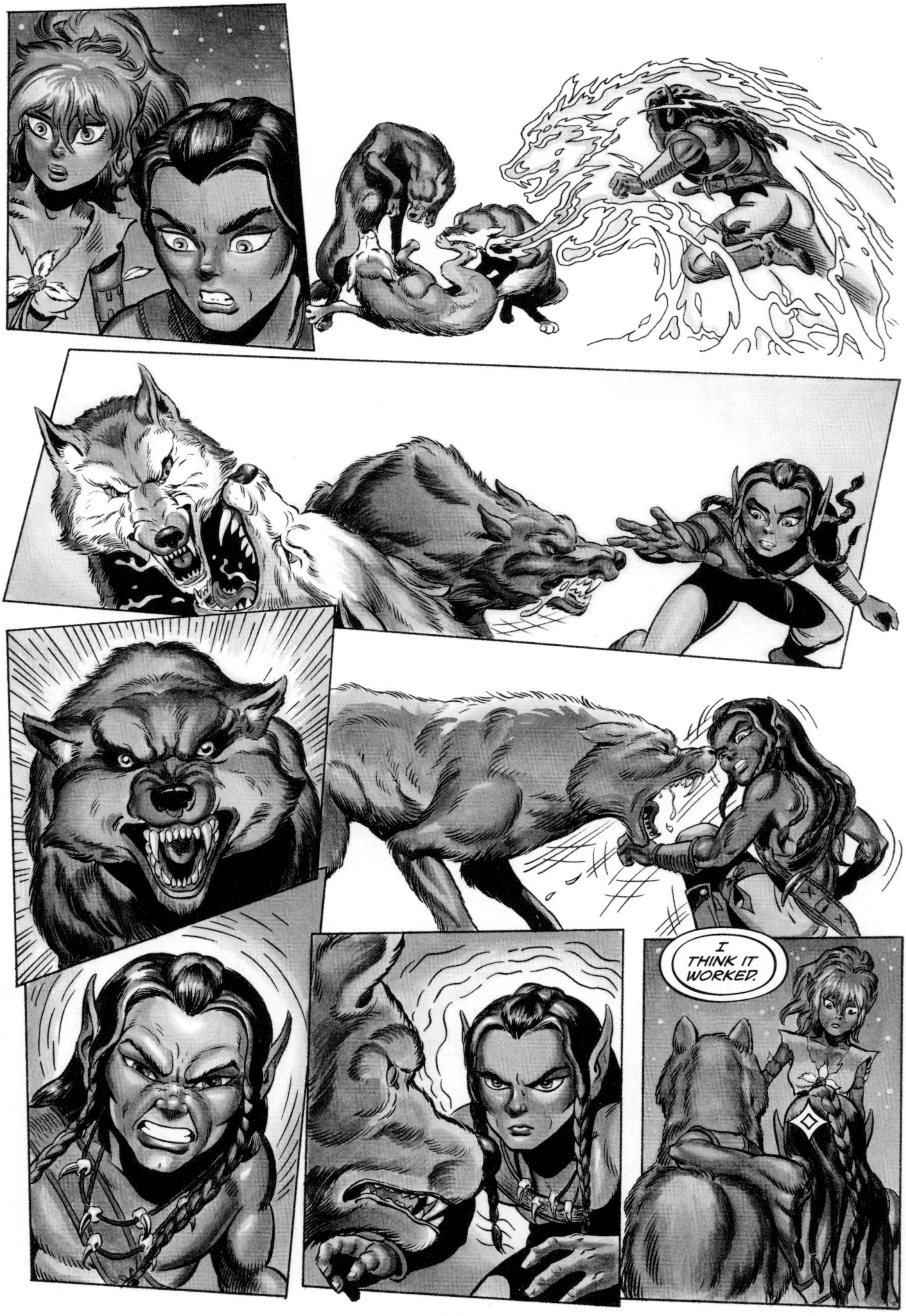
I THINK IT WORKED.

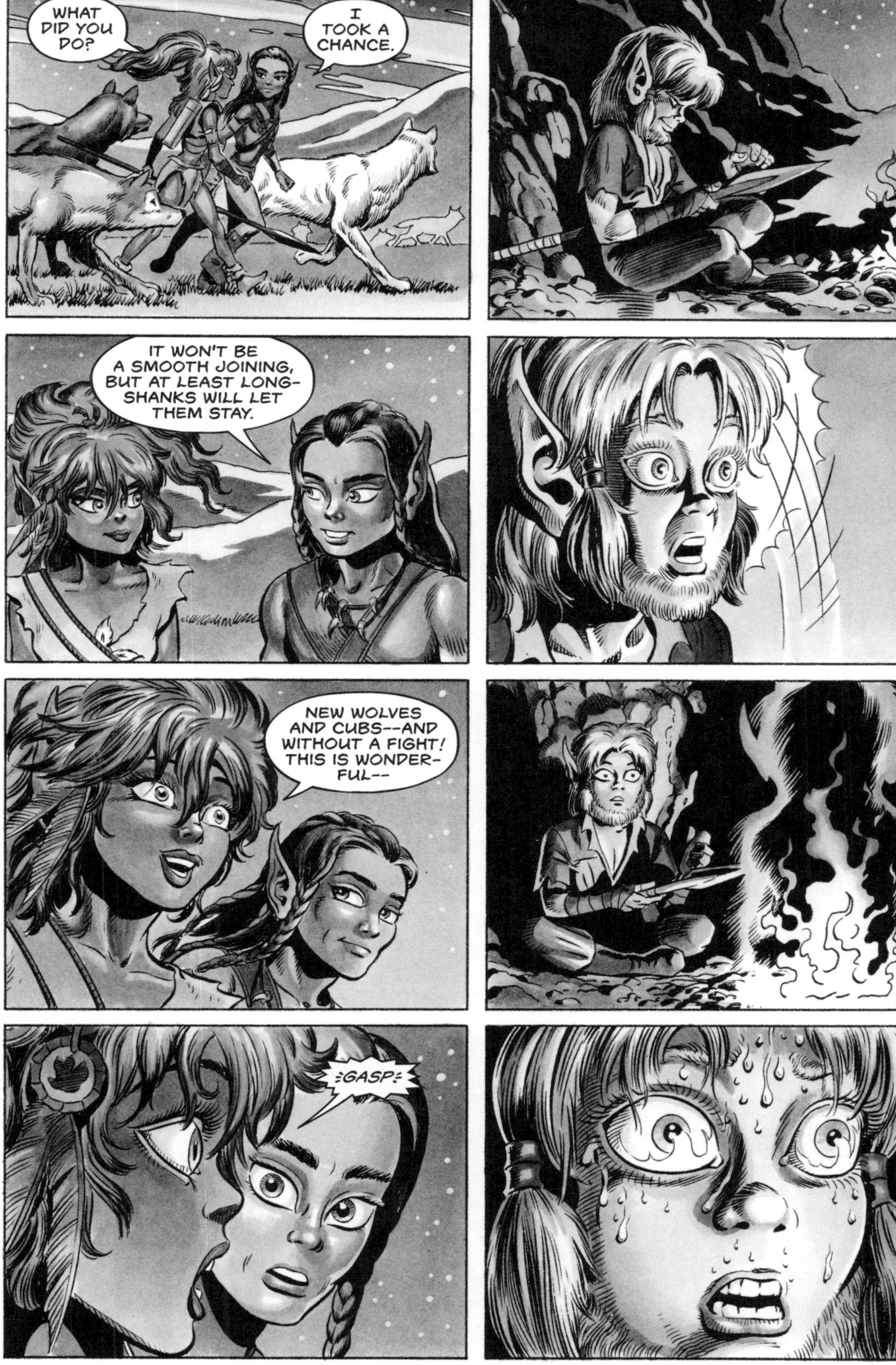
WHAT DID YOU DO?
I TOOK A CHANCE.
IT WON'T BE A SMOOTH JOINING, BUT AT LEAST LONG-SHANKS WILL LET THEM STAY.
NEW WOLVES AND CUBS--AND WITHOUT A FIGHT! THIS IS WONDER-FUL--
GASP

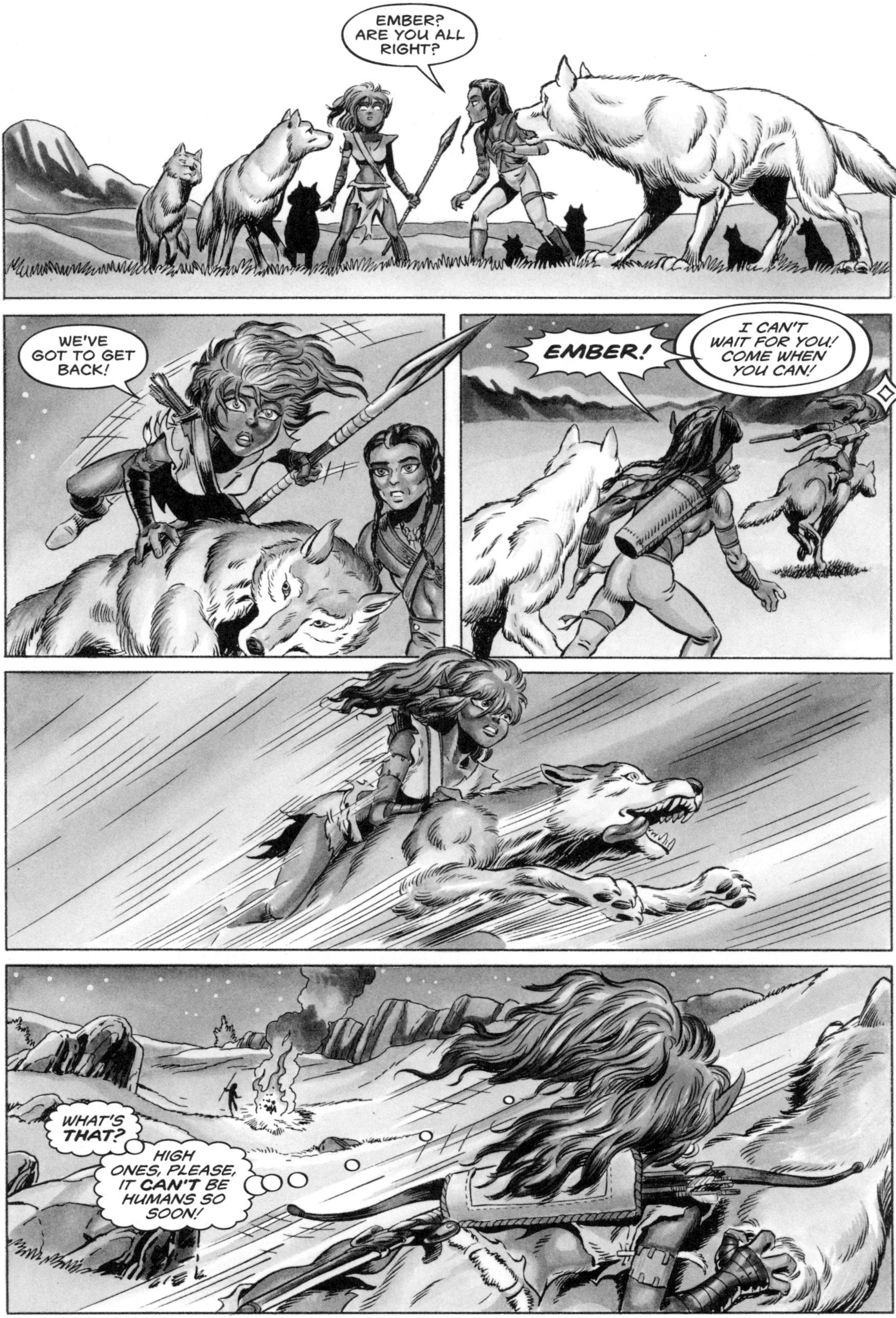

EMBER? ARE YOU ALL RIGHT?
WE'VE GOT TO GET BACK!
EMBER!
I CAN'T WAIT FOR YOU! COME WHEN YOU CAN!
WHAT'S THAT?
HIGH ONES, PLEASE, IT CAN'T BE HUMANS SO SOON!

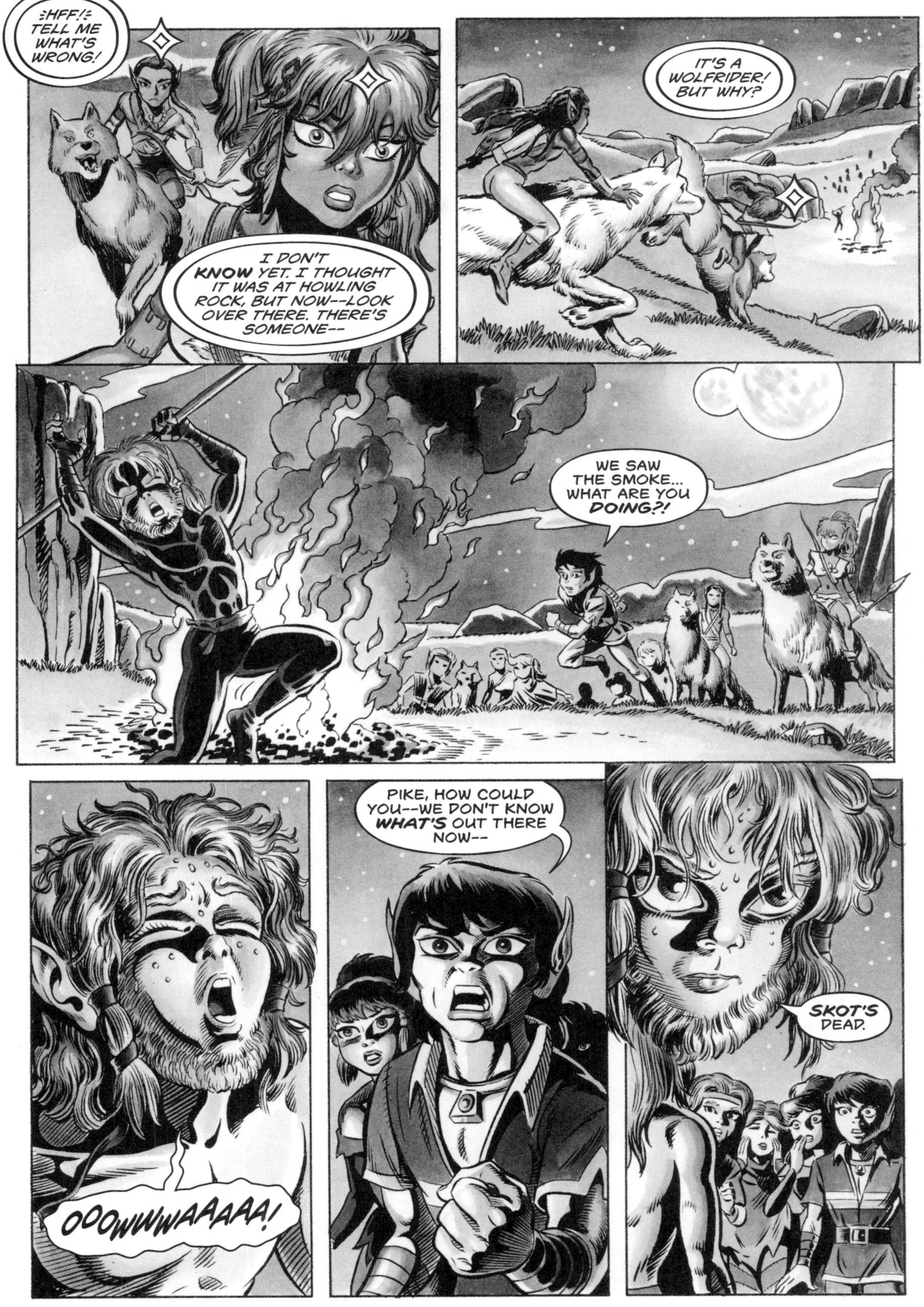
HFF! TELL ME WHAT'S WRONG!
I DON'T KNOW YET. I THOUGHT IT WAS AT HOWLING ROCK, BUT NOW--LOOK OVER THERE. THERE'S SOMEONE--
IT'S A WOLFRIDER! BUT WHY?
WE SAW THE SMOKE... WHAT ARE YOU DOING?!
OOOWWWAAAAA!
PIKE, HOW COULD YOU--WE DON'T KNOW WHAT'S OUT THERE NOW--
SKOT'S DEAD.

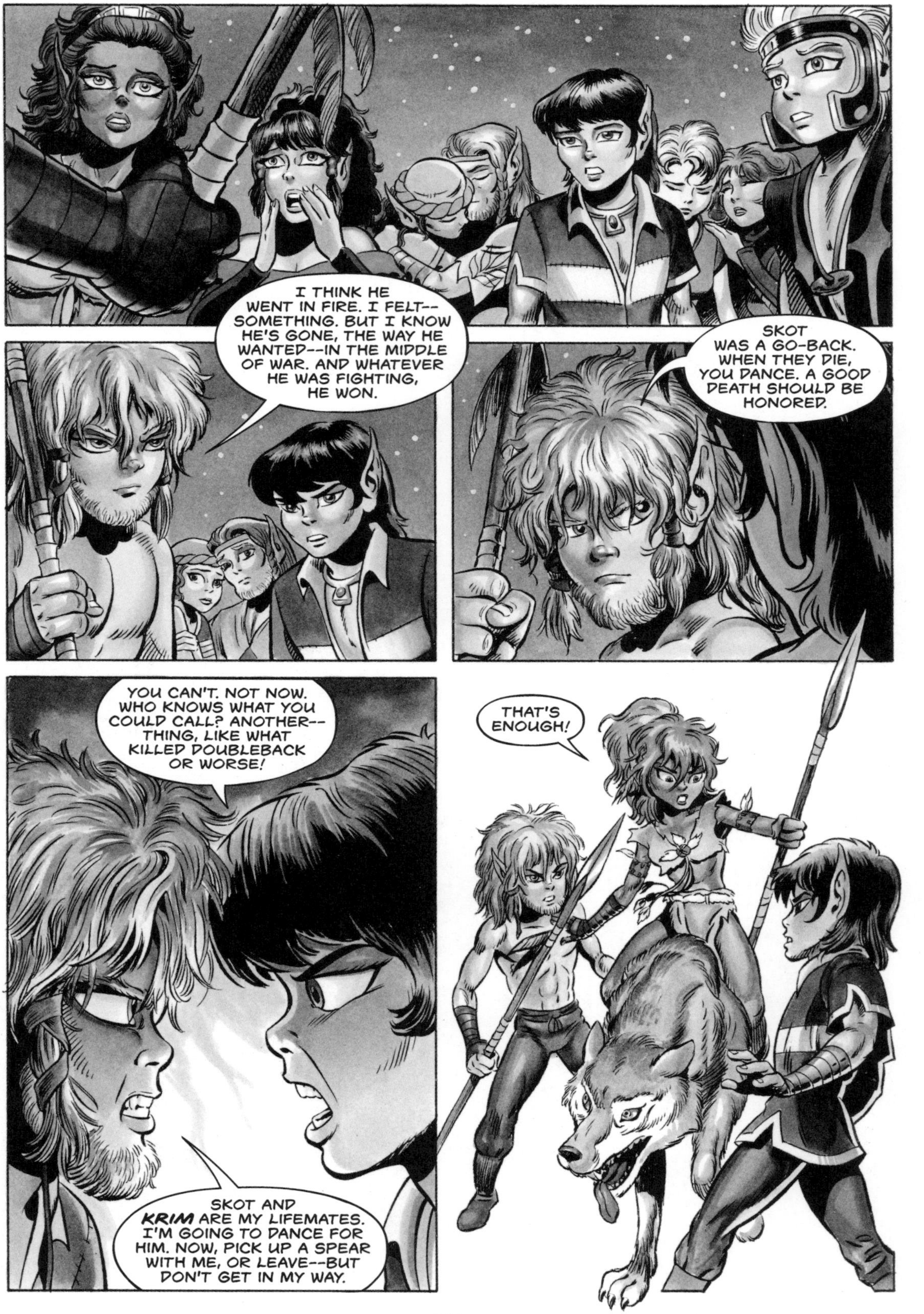
I THINK HE WENT IN FIRE. I FELT--SOMETHING. BUT I KNOW HE'S GONE, THE WAY HE WANTED--IN THE MIDDLE OF WAR. AND WHATEVER HE WAS FIGHTING, HE WON.
SKOT WAS A GO-BACK. WHEN THEY DIE, YOU DANCE. A GOOD DEATH SHOULD BE HONORED.
YOU CAN'T. NOT NOW. WHO KNOWS WHAT YOU COULD CALL? ANOTHER--THING, LIKE WHAT KILLED DOUBLEBACK OR WORSE!
SKOT AND KRIM ARE MY LIFEMATES. I'M GOING TO DANCE FOR HIM. NOW, PICK UP A SPEAR WITH ME, OR LEAVE--BUT DON'T GET IN MY WAY.
THAT'S ENOUGH!

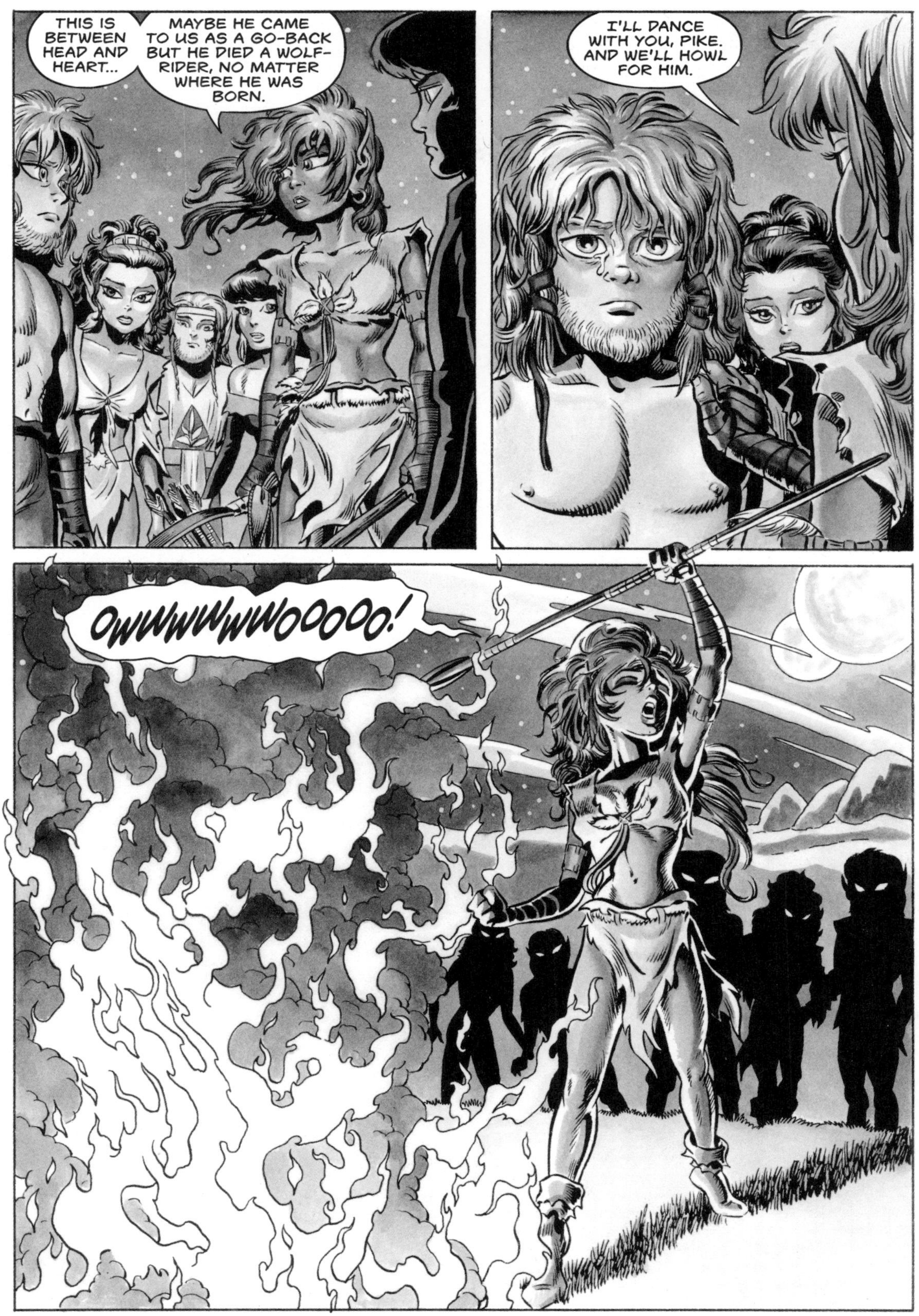
THIS IS BETWEEN HEAD AND HEART...
MAYBE HE CAME TO US AS A GO-BACK BUT HE DIED A WOLF-RIDER, NO MATTER WHERE HE WAS BORN.
I'LL DANCE WITH YOU, PIKE. AND WE'LL HOWL FOR HIM.
OWWWWWWOOOOO!

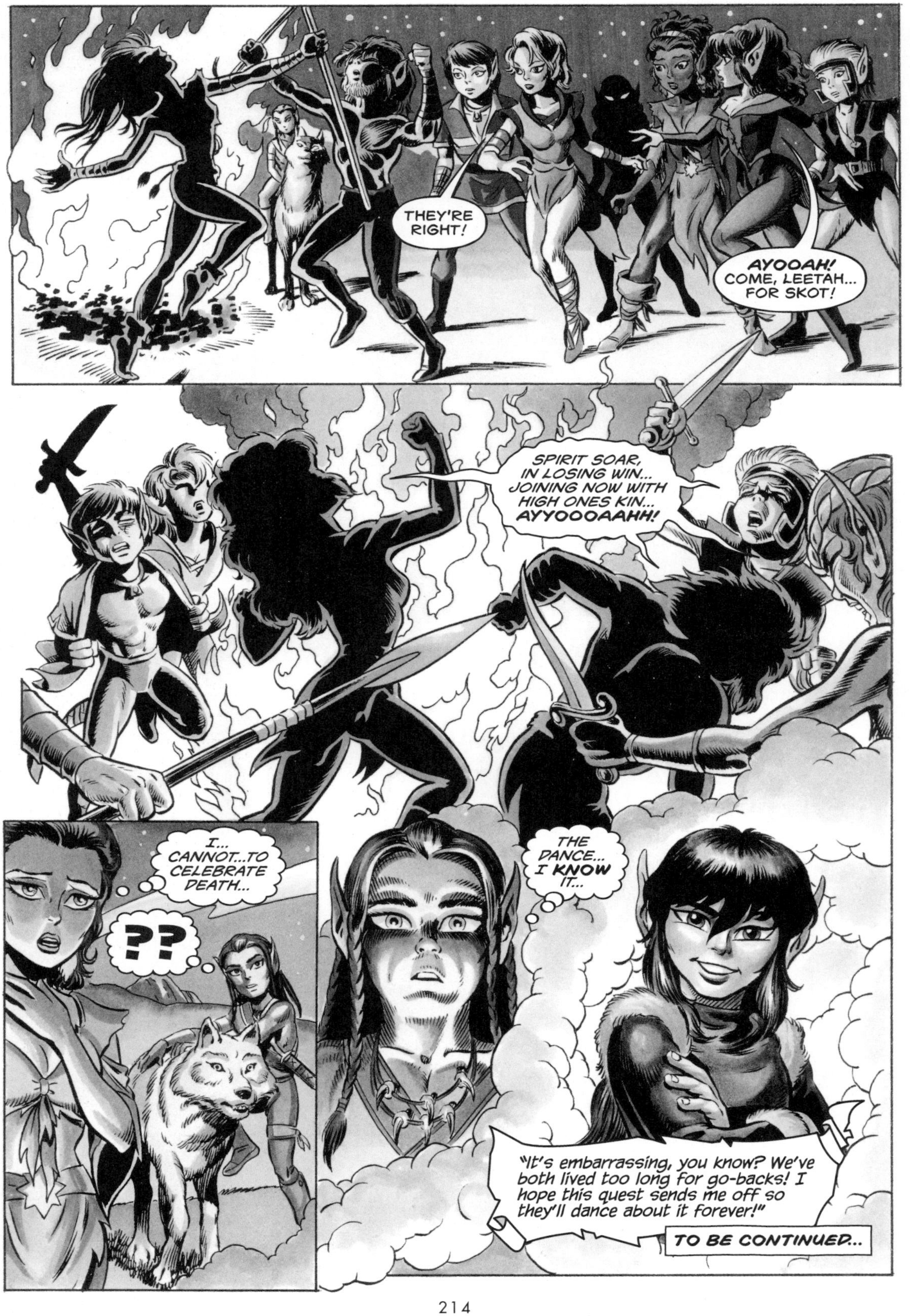
THEY'RE RIGHT!
AYOOAH! COME, LEETAH... FOR SKOT!
SPIRIT SOAR, IN LOSING WIN... JOINING NOW WITH HIGH ONES KIN... AYYOOOAAHH!
I... CANNOT...TO CELEBRATE DEATH...
??
THE DANCE... I KNOW IT...
"It's embarrassing, you know? We've both lived too long for go-backs! I hope this quest sends me off so they'll dance about it forever!"
TO BE CONTINUED...

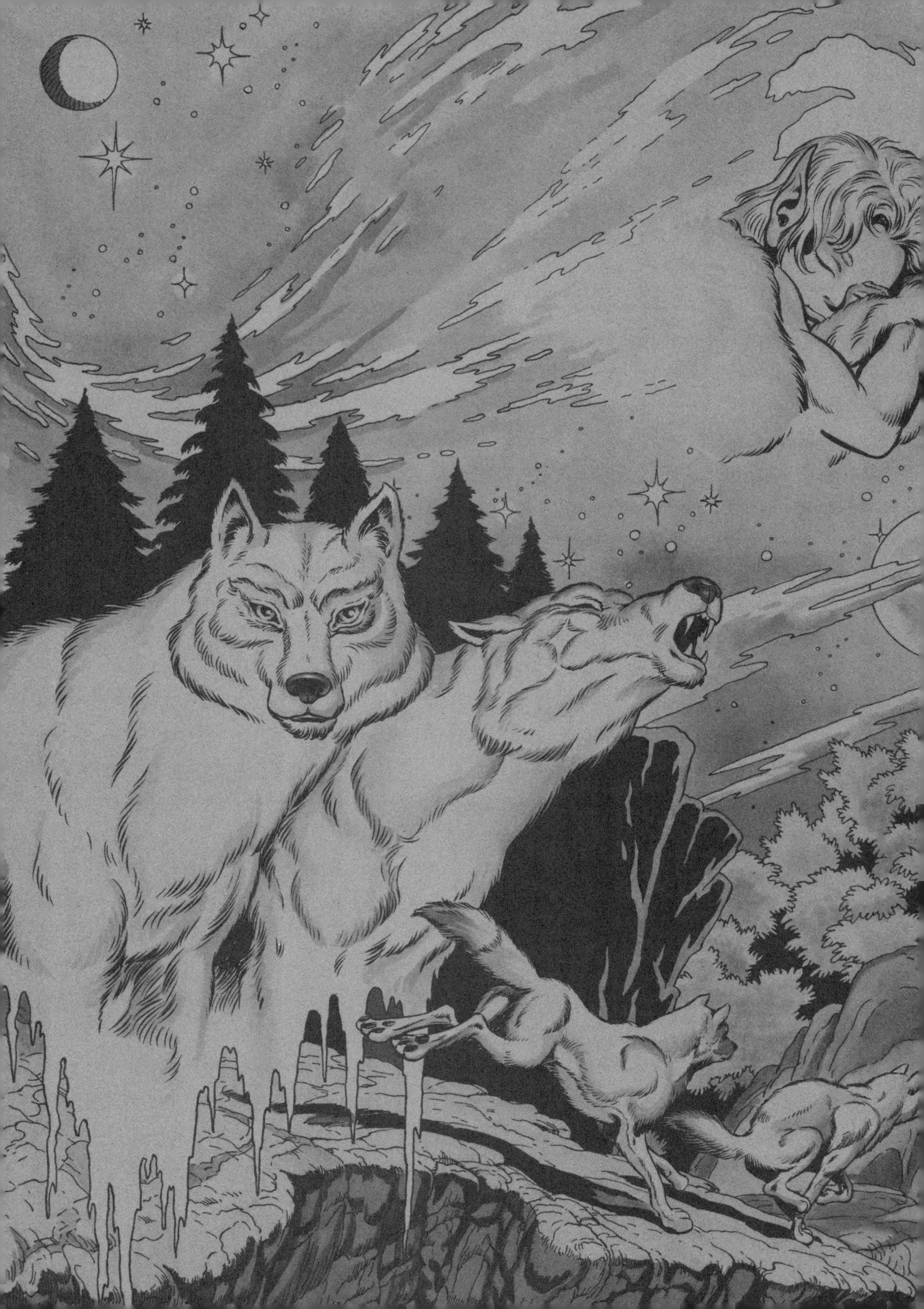

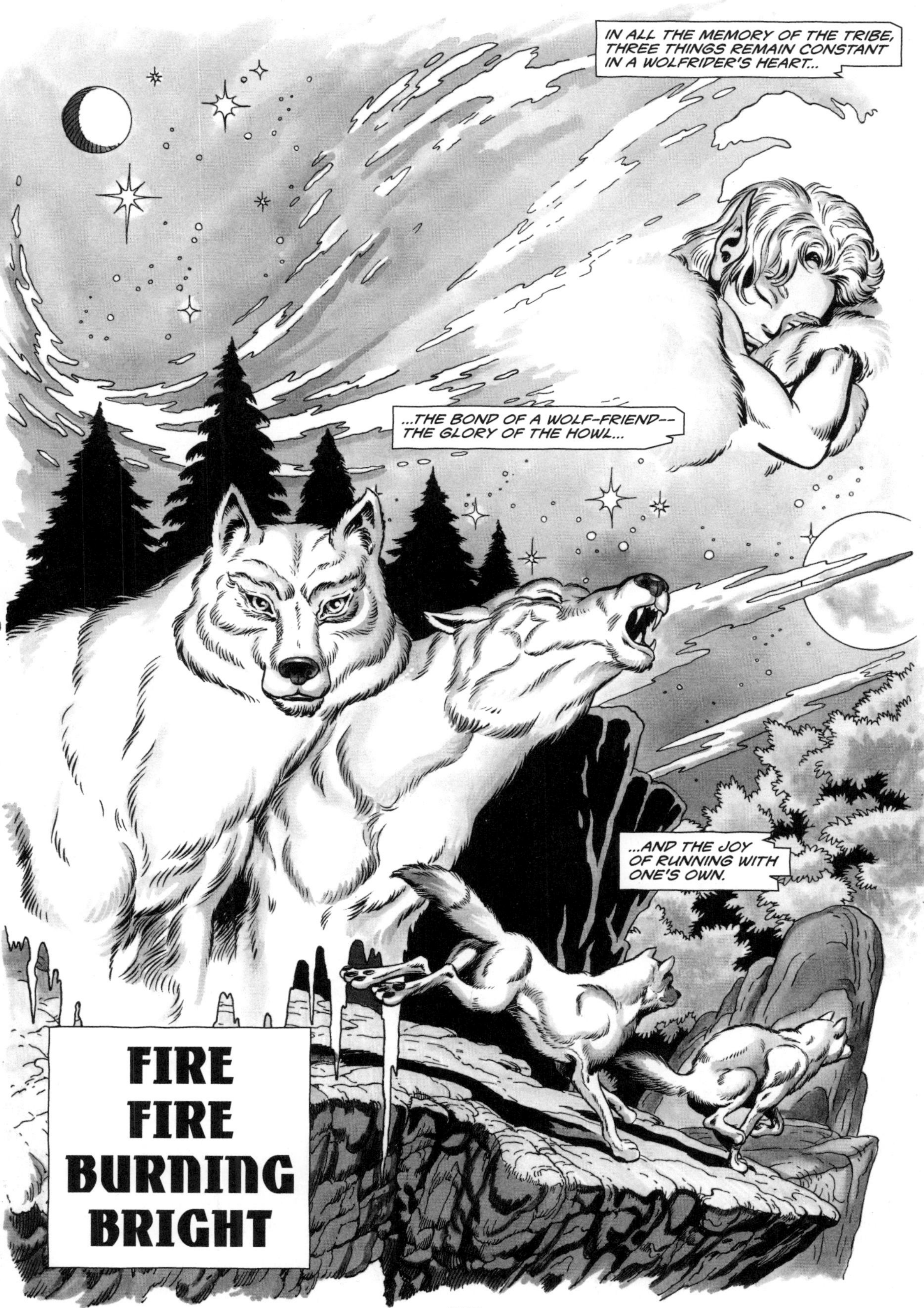
IN ALL THE MEMORY OF THE TRIBE, THREE THINGS REMAIN CONSTANT IN A WOLFRIDER'S HEART...
...THE BOND OF A WOLF-FRIEND-- THE GLORY OF THE HOWL...
...AND THE JOY OF RUNNING WITH ONE'S OWN.
FIRE FIRE BURNING BRIGHT

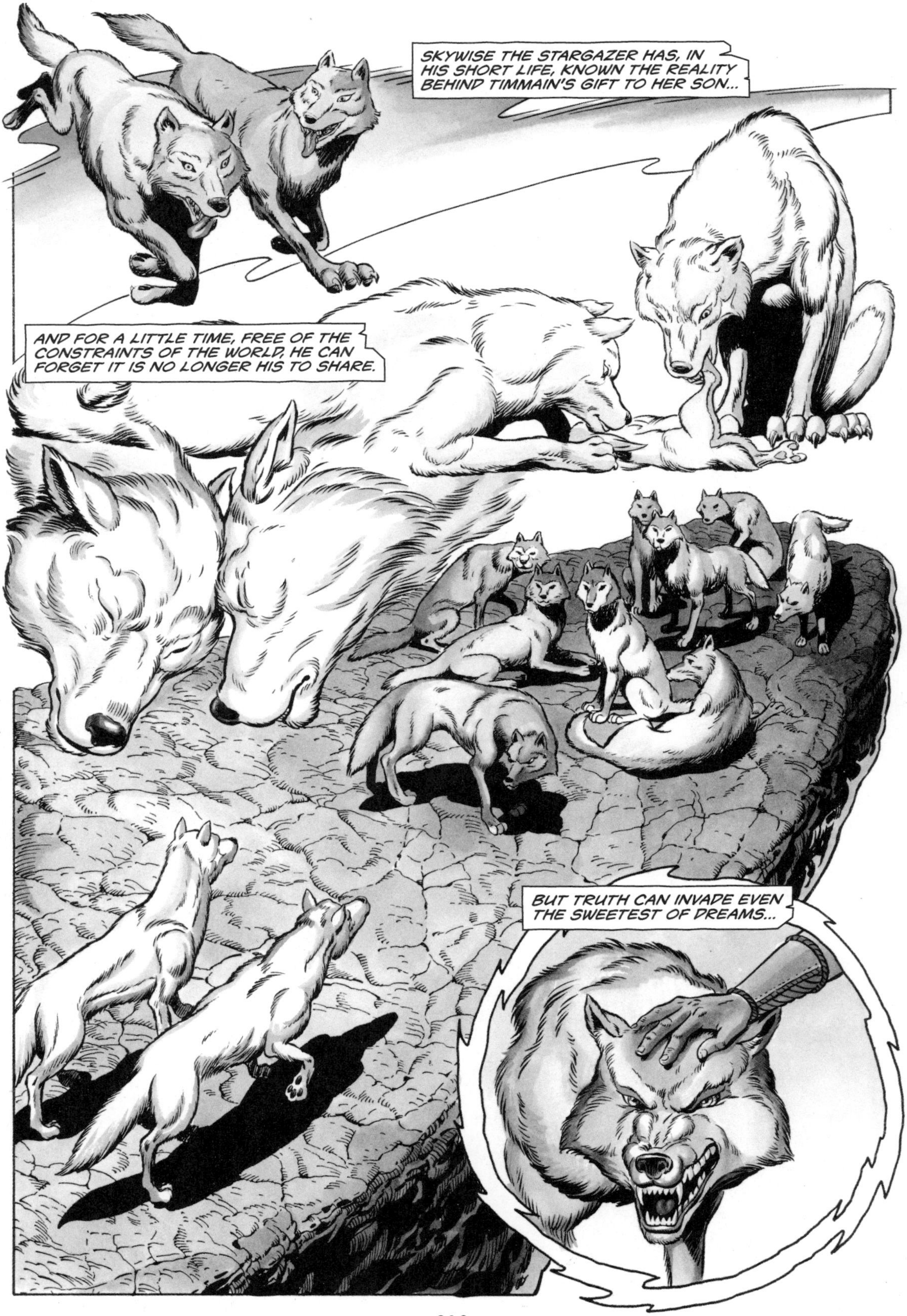
SKYWISE THE STARGAZER HAS, IN HIS SHORT LIFE, KNOWN THE REALITY BEHIND TIMMAIN'S GIFT TO HER SON...
AND FOR A LITTLE TIME, FREE OF THE CONSTRAINTS OF THE WORLD, HE CAN FORGET IT IS NO LONGER HIS TO SHARE.
BUT TRUTH CAN INVADE EVEN THE SWEETEST OF DREAMS...

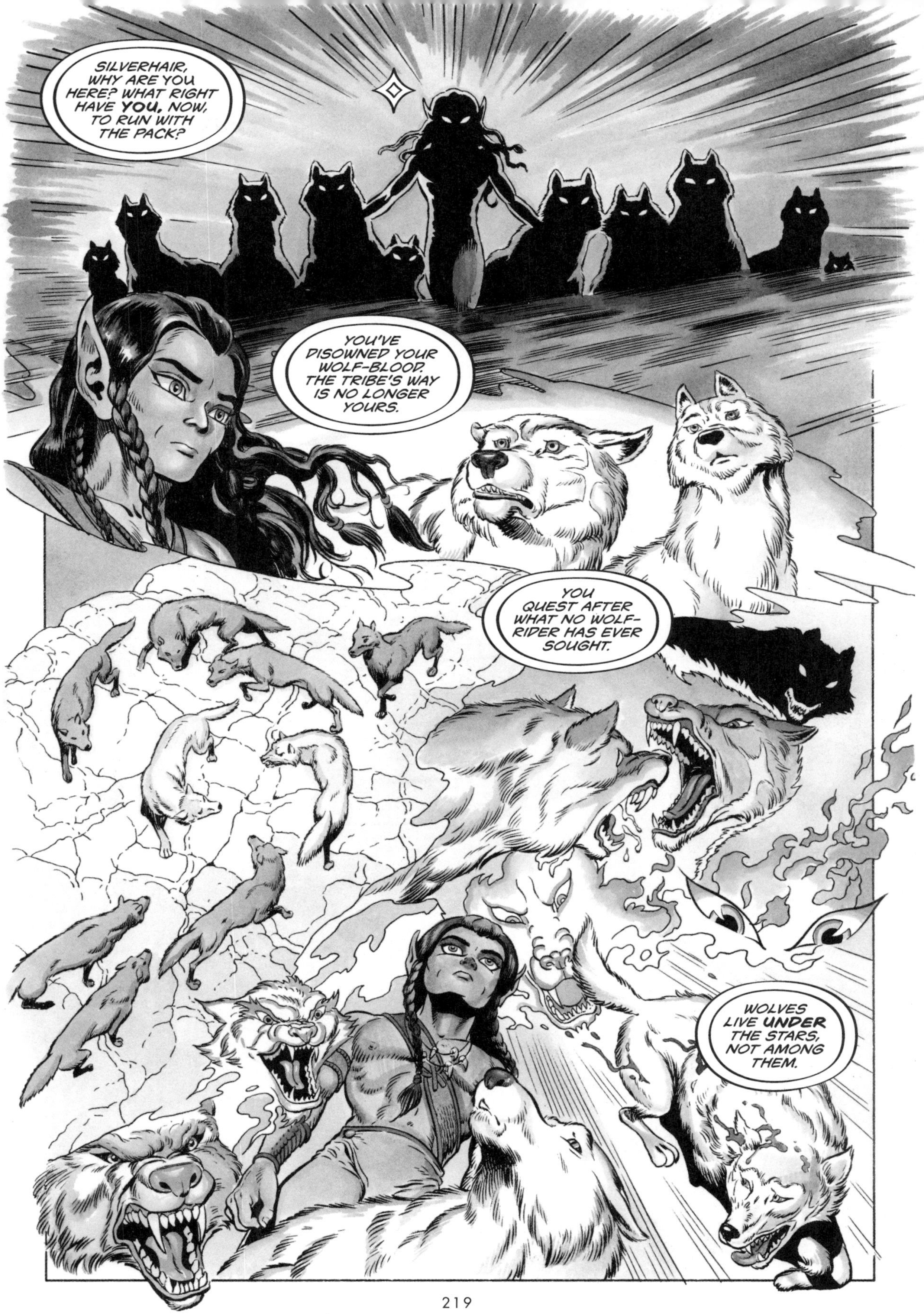
SILVERHAIR, WHY ARE YOU HERE? WHAT RIGHT HAVE YOU, NOW, TO RUN WITH THE PACK?
YOU'VE DISOWNED YOUR WOLF-BLOOD. THE TRIBE'S WAY IS NO LONGER YOURS.
YOU QUEST AFTER WHAT NO WOLF-RIDER HAS EVER SOUGHT.
WOLVES LIVE UNDER THE STARS, NOT AMONG THEM.

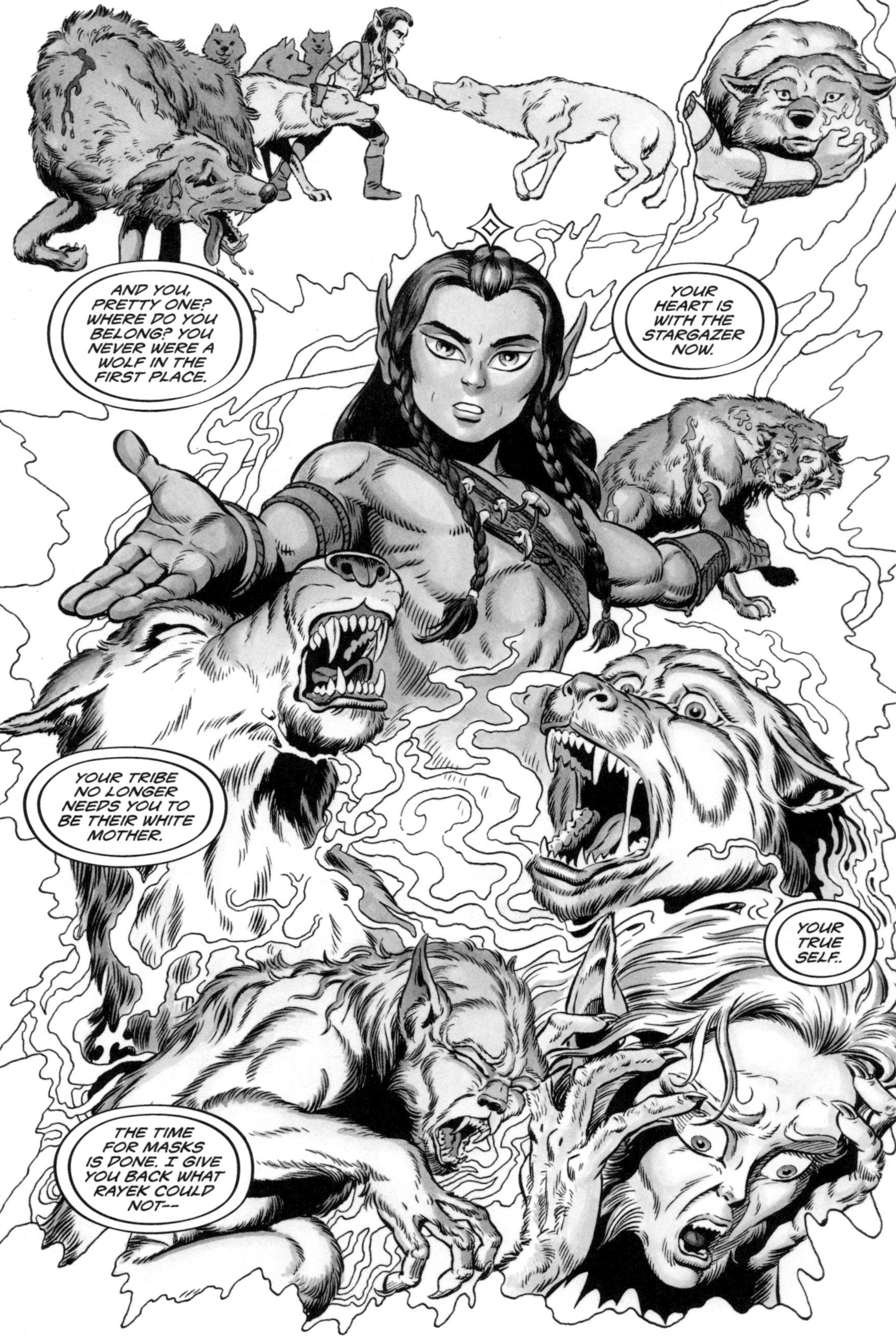
AND YOU, PRETTY ONE? WHERE DO YOU BELONG? YOU NEVER WERE A WOLF IN THE FIRST PLACE.
YOUR HEART IS WITH THE STARGAZER NOW.
YOUR TRIBE NO LONGER NEEDS YOU TO BE THEIR WHITE MOTHER.
YOUR TRUE SELF..
THE TIME FOR MASKS IS DONE. I GIVE YOU BACK WHAT RAYEK COULD NOT--

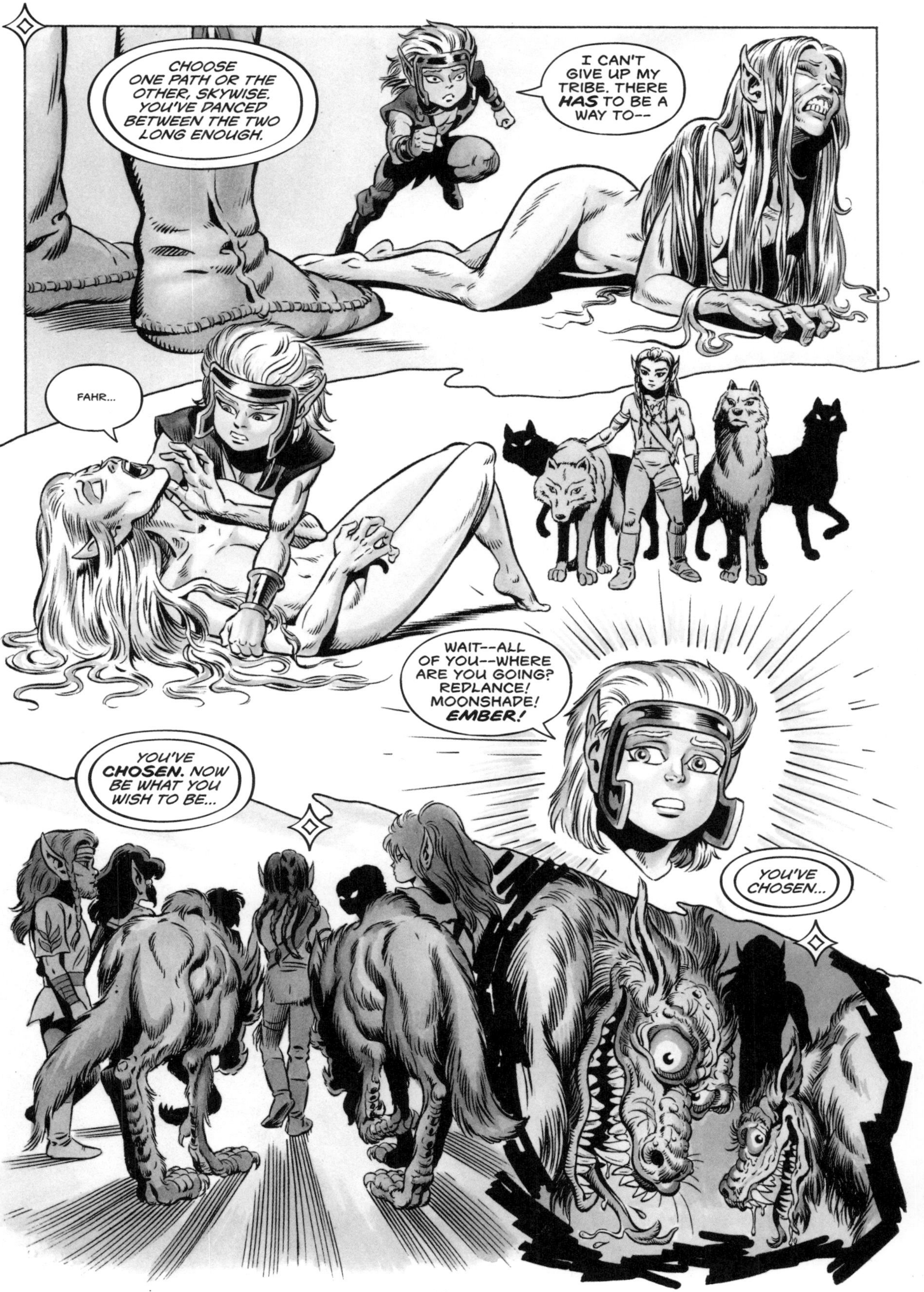
CHOOSE ONE PATH OR THE OTHER, SKYWISE. YOU'VE DANCED BETWEEN THE TWO LONG ENOUGH.
I CAN'T GIVE UP MY TRIBE. THERE HAS TO BE A WAY TO--
FAHR...
WAIT--ALL OF YOU--WHERE ARE YOU GOING? REDLANCE! MOONSHADE! EMBER!
YOU'VE CHOSEN. NOW BE WHAT YOU WISH TO BE...
YOU'VE CHOSEN...

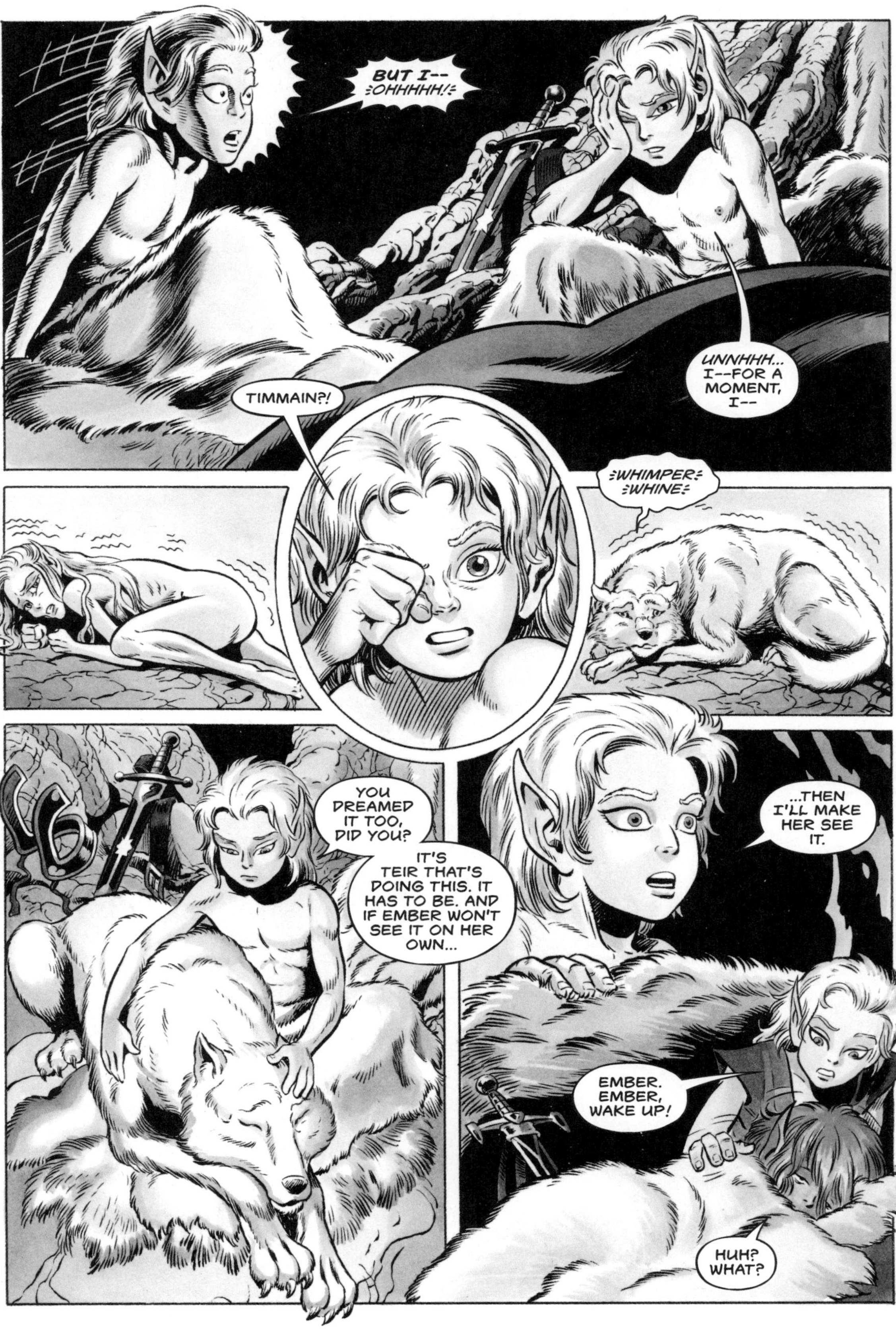
BUT I--
OHHHHH!
UNNHHH... I--FOR A MOMENT, I--
TIMMAIN?!
WHIMPER WHINE
YOU DREAMED IT TOO, DID YOU?
IT'S TEIR THAT'S DOING THIS. IT HAS TO BE. AND IF EMBER WON'T SEE IT ON HER OWN...
...THEN I'LL MAKE HER SEE IT.
EMBER. EMBER, WAKE UP!
HUH? WHAT?

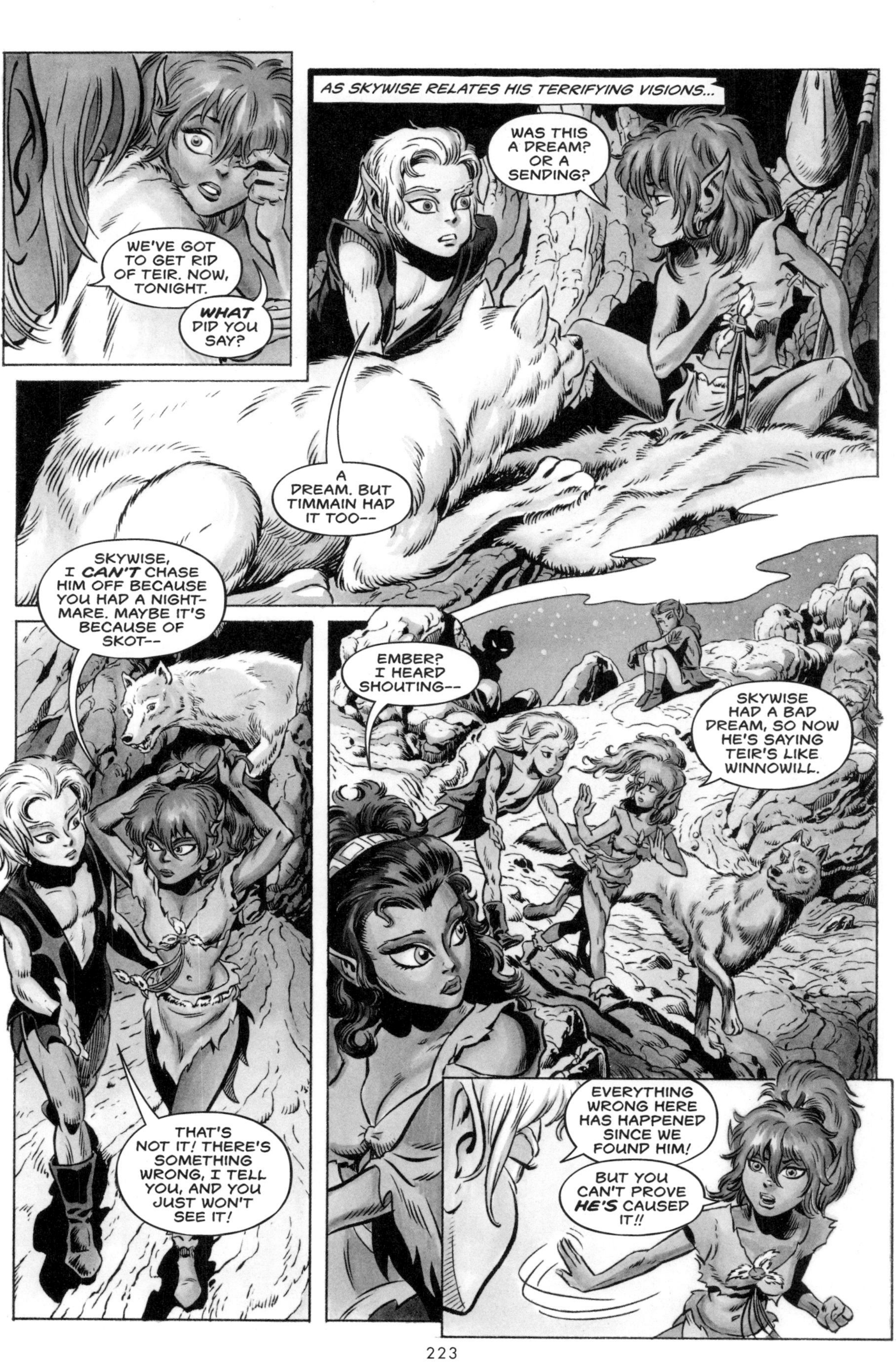
WE'VE GOT TO GET RID OF TEIR. NOW, TONIGHT.
WHAT DID YOU SAY?
AS SKYWISE RELATES HIS TERRIFYING VISIONS...
WAS THIS A DREAM? OR A SENDING?
A DREAM. BUT TIMMAIN HAD IT TOO--
SKYWISE, I CAN'T CHASE HIM OFF BECAUSE YOU HAD A NIGHT-MARE. MAYBE IT'S BECAUSE OF SKOT--
THAT'S NOT IT! THERE'S SOMETHING WRONG, I TELL YOU, AND YOU JUST WON'T SEE IT!
EMBER? I HEARD SHOUTING--
SKYWISE HAD A BAD DREAM, SO NOW HE'S SAYING TEIR'S LIKE WINNOWILL.
EVERYTHING WRONG HERE HAS HAPPENED SINCE WE FOUND HIM!
BUT YOU CAN'T PROVE HE'S CAUSED IT!!

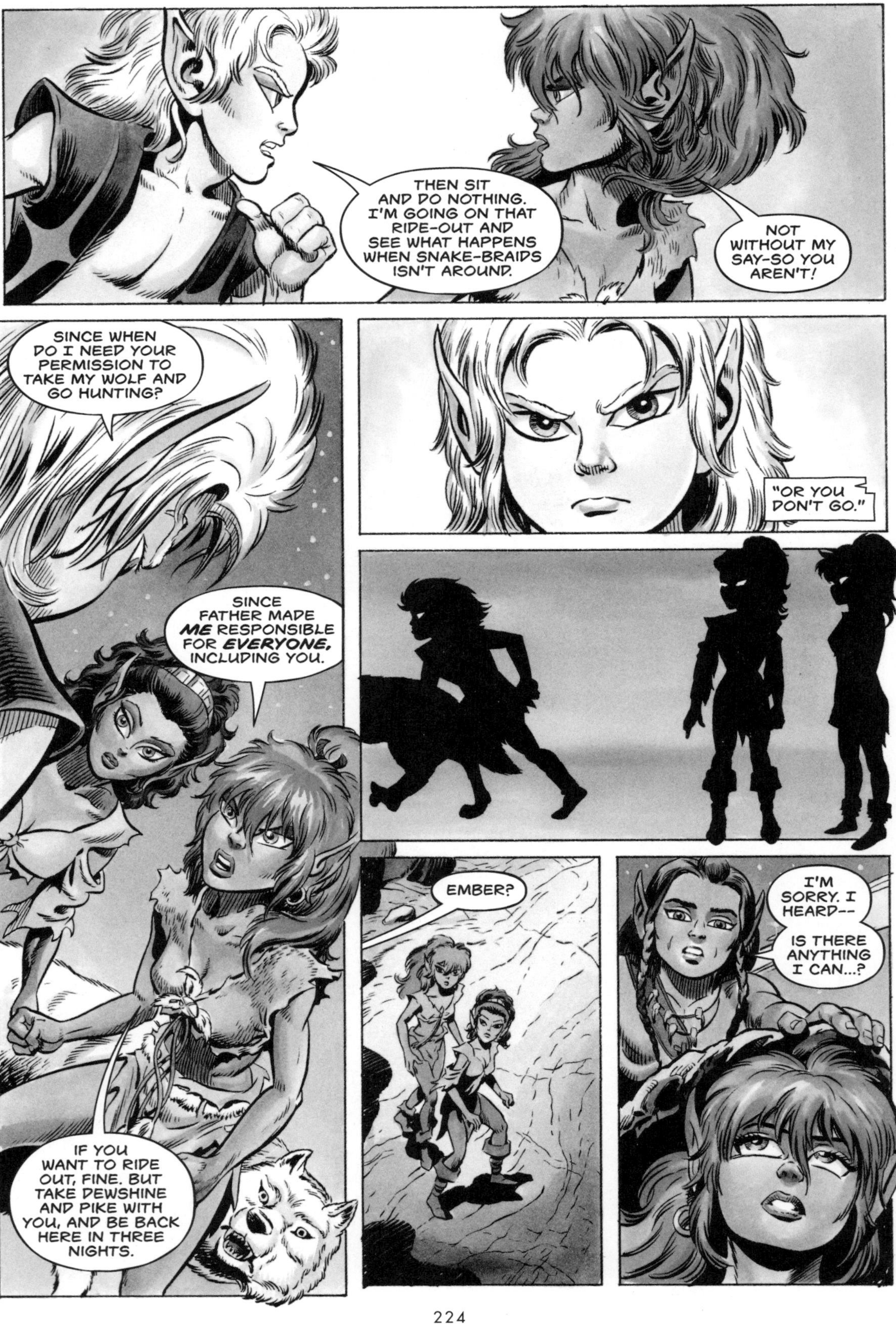
THEN SIT AND DO NOTHING. I'M GOING ON THAT RIDE-OUT AND SEE WHAT HAPPENS WHEN SNAKE-BRAIDS ISN'T AROUND.
NOT WITHOUT MY SAY-SO YOU AREN'T!
SINCE WHEN DO I NEED YOUR PERMISSION TO TAKE MY WOLF AND GO HUNTING?
SINCE FATHER MADE ***ME*** RESPONSIBLE FOR ***EVERYONE,*** INCLUDING YOU.
IF YOU WANT TO RIDE OUT, FINE. BUT TAKE DEWSHINE AND PIKE WITH YOU, AND BE BACK HERE IN THREE NIGHTS.
"OR YOU DON'T GO."
EMBER?
I'M SORRY. I HEARD--
IS THERE ANYTHING I CAN...?

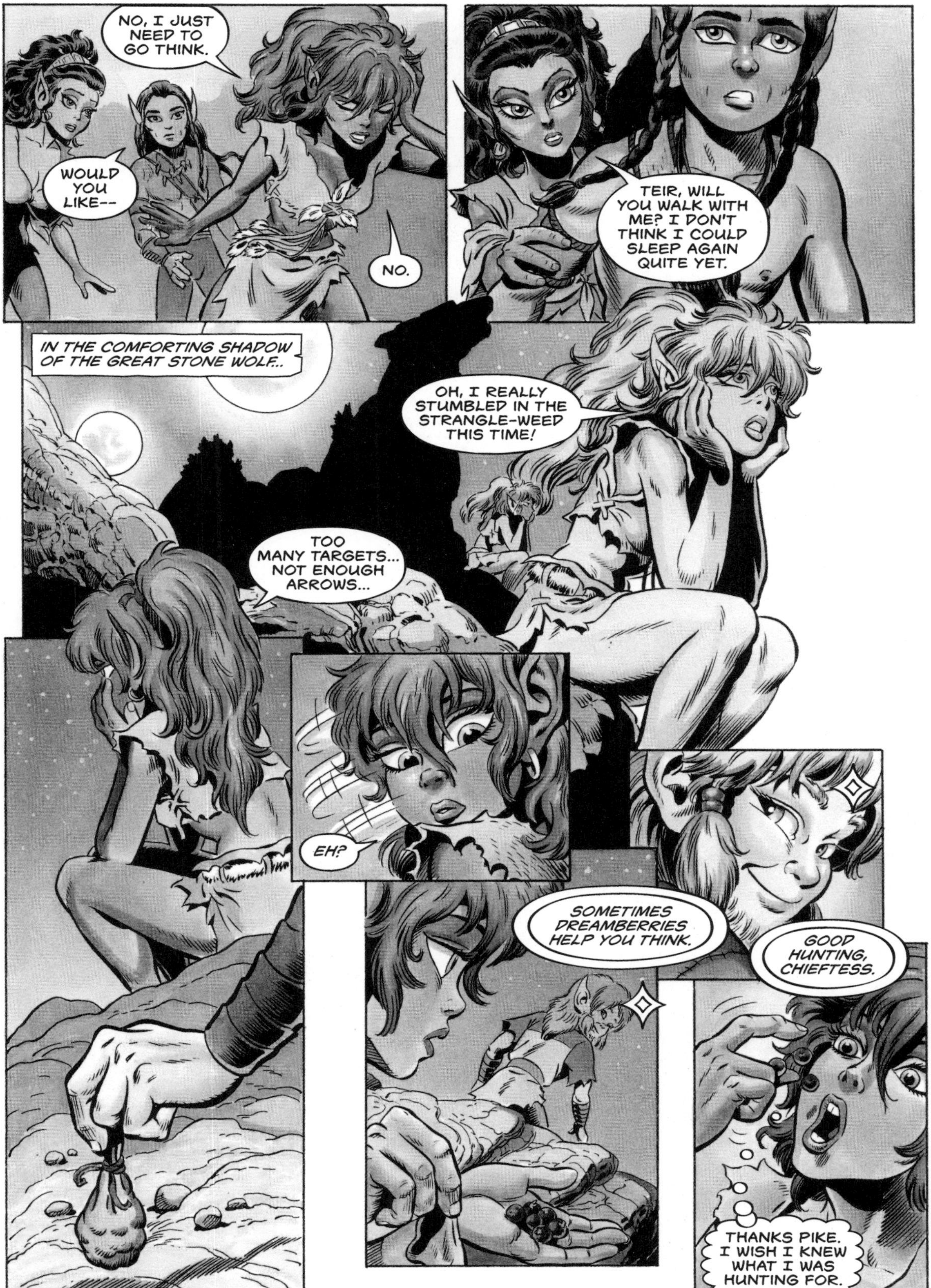
NO, I JUST NEED TO GO THINK.
WOULD YOU LIKE--
NO.
TEIR, WILL YOU WALK WITH ME? I DON'T THINK I COULD SLEEP AGAIN QUITE YET.
IN THE COMFORTING SHADOW OF THE GREAT STONE WOLF...
OH, I REALLY STUMBLED IN THE STRANGLE-WEED THIS TIME!
TOO MANY TARGETS... NOT ENOUGH ARROWS...
EH?
SOMETIMES DREAMBERRIES HELP YOU THINK.
GOOD HUNTING, CHIEFTESS.
THANKS PIKE. I WISH I KNEW WHAT I WAS HUNTING FOR.

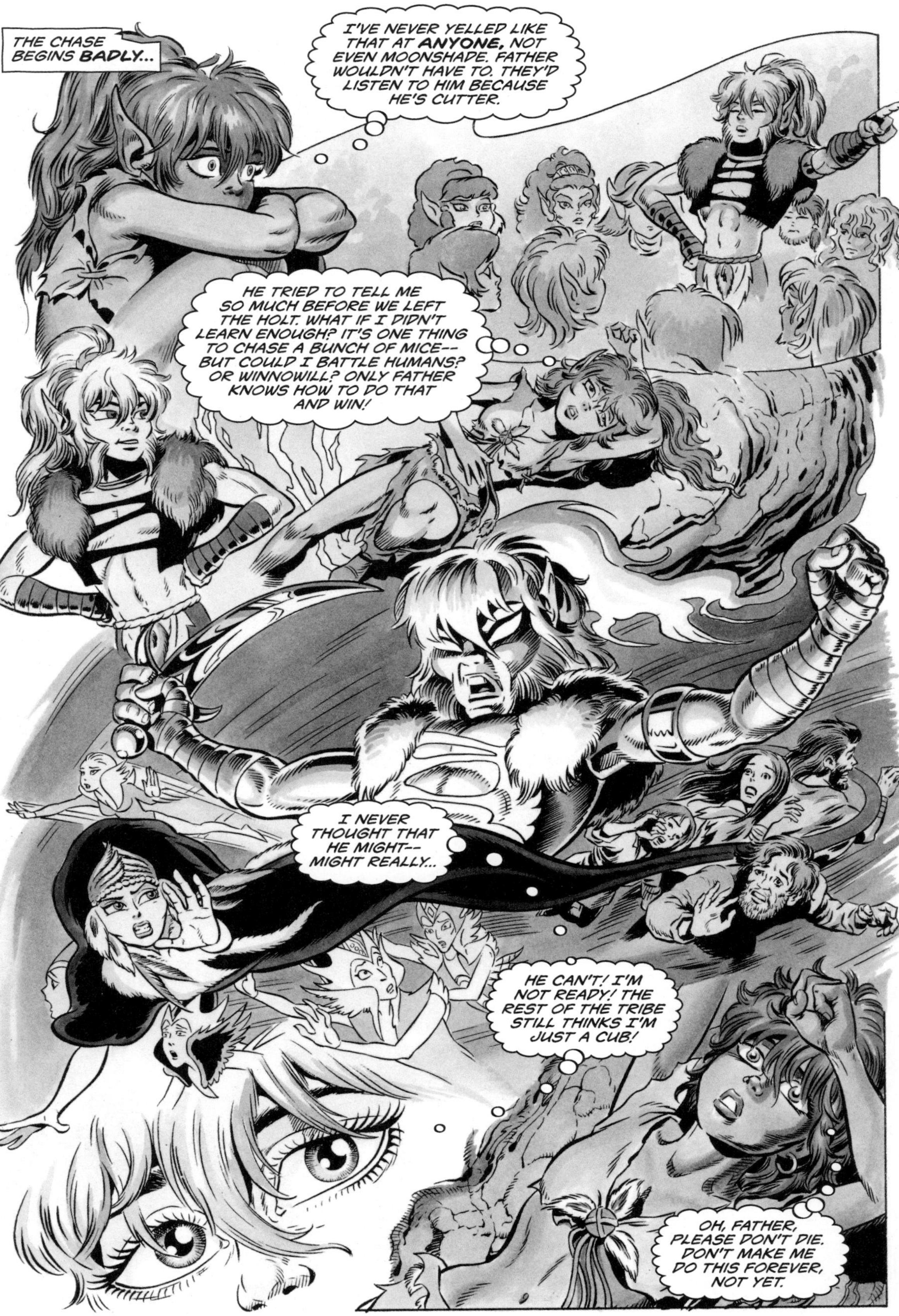
THE CHASE BEGINS BADLY...
I'VE NEVER YELLED LIKE THAT AT ANYONE, NOT EVEN MOONSHADE. FATHER WOULDN'T HAVE TO. THEY'D LISTEN TO HIM BECAUSE HE'S CUTTER.
HE TRIED TO TELL ME SO MUCH BEFORE WE LEFT THE HOLT. WHAT IF I DIDN'T LEARN ENOUGH? IT'S ONE THING TO CHASE A BUNCH OF MICE-- BUT COULD I BATTLE HUMANS? OR WINNOWILL? ONLY FATHER KNOWS HOW TO DO THAT AND WIN!
I NEVER THOUGHT THAT HE MIGHT-- MIGHT REALLY...
HE CAN'T! I'M NOT READY! THE REST OF THE TRIBE STILL THINKS I'M JUST A CUB!
OH, FATHER, PLEASE DON'T DIE. DON'T MAKE ME DO THIS FOREVER, NOT YET.

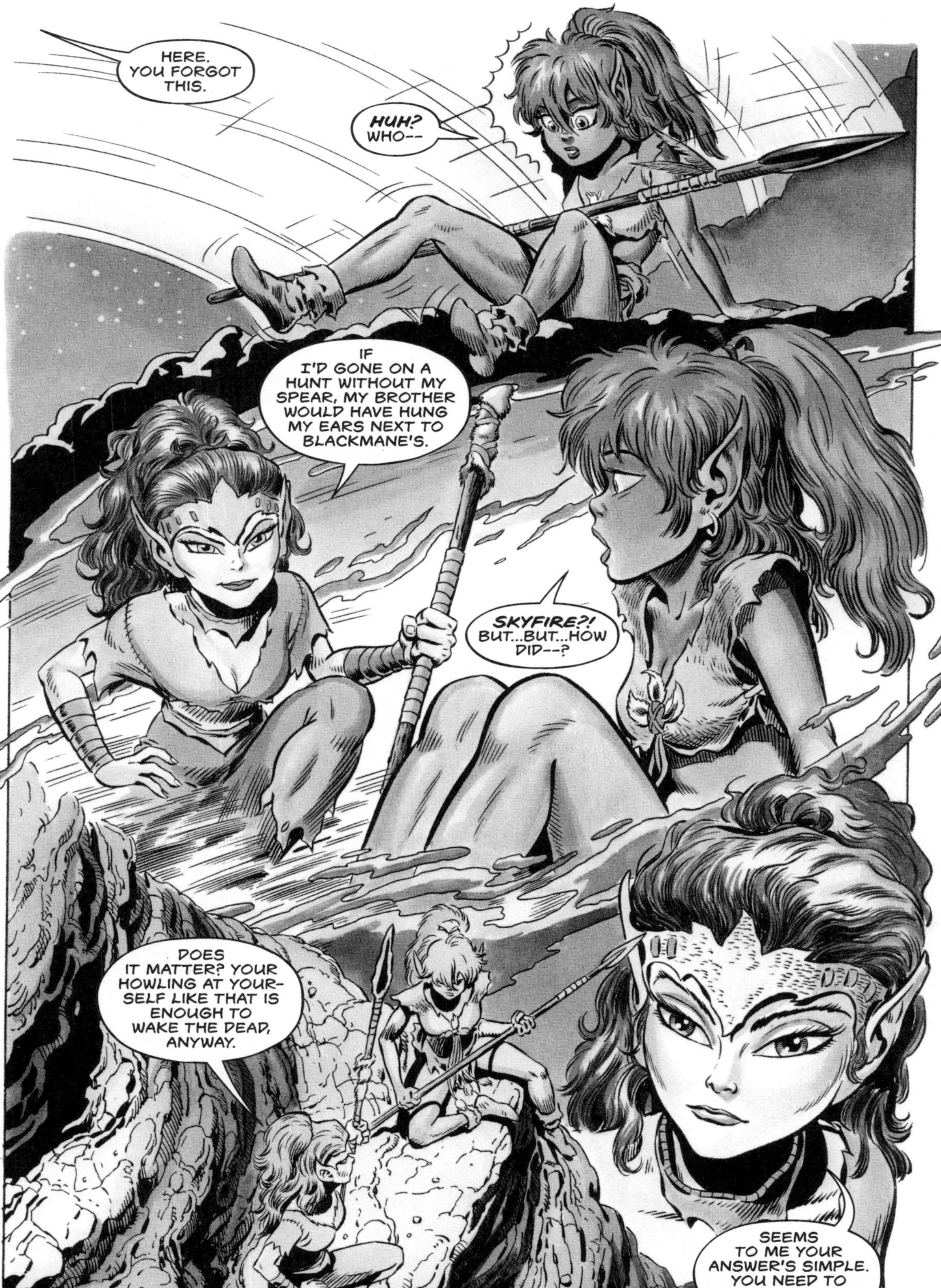
HERE. YOU FORGOT THIS.
HUH? WHO--
IF I'D GONE ON A HUNT WITHOUT MY SPEAR, MY BROTHER WOULD HAVE HUNG MY EARS NEXT TO BLACKMANE'S.
SKYFIRE?! BUT...BUT...HOW DID--?
DOES IT MATTER? YOUR HOWLING AT YOUR-SELF LIKE THAT IS ENOUGH TO WAKE THE DEAD, ANYWAY.
SEEMS TO ME YOUR ANSWER'S SIMPLE. YOU NEED TO FIND "THE WAY" AGAIN.

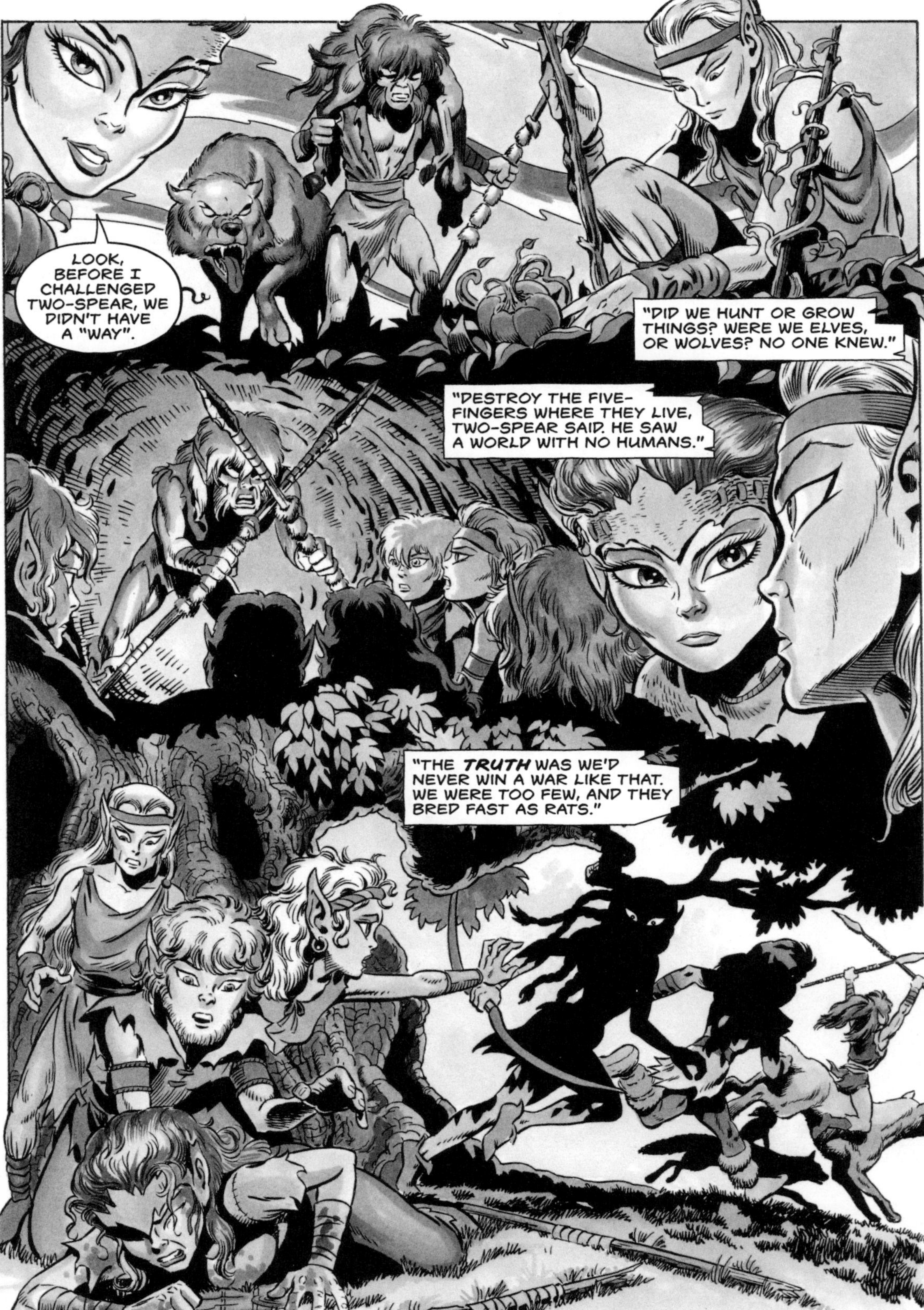
LOOK, BEFORE I CHALLENGED TWO-SPEAR, WE DIDN'T HAVE A "WAY".
"DID WE HUNT OR GROW THINGS? WERE WE ELVES, OR WOLVES? NO ONE KNEW."
"DESTROY THE FIVE-FINGERS WHERE THEY LIVE, TWO-SPEAR SAID. HE SAW A WORLD WITH NO HUMANS."
"THE *TRUTH* WAS WE'D NEVER WIN A WAR LIKE THAT. WE WERE TOO FEW, AND THEY BRED FAST AS RATS."
"TO SAVE THE TRIBE, I CHALLENGED HIM. HE WON--BUT HE LEFT ANYWAY. AND I HAD TO PICK UP THE PIECES."

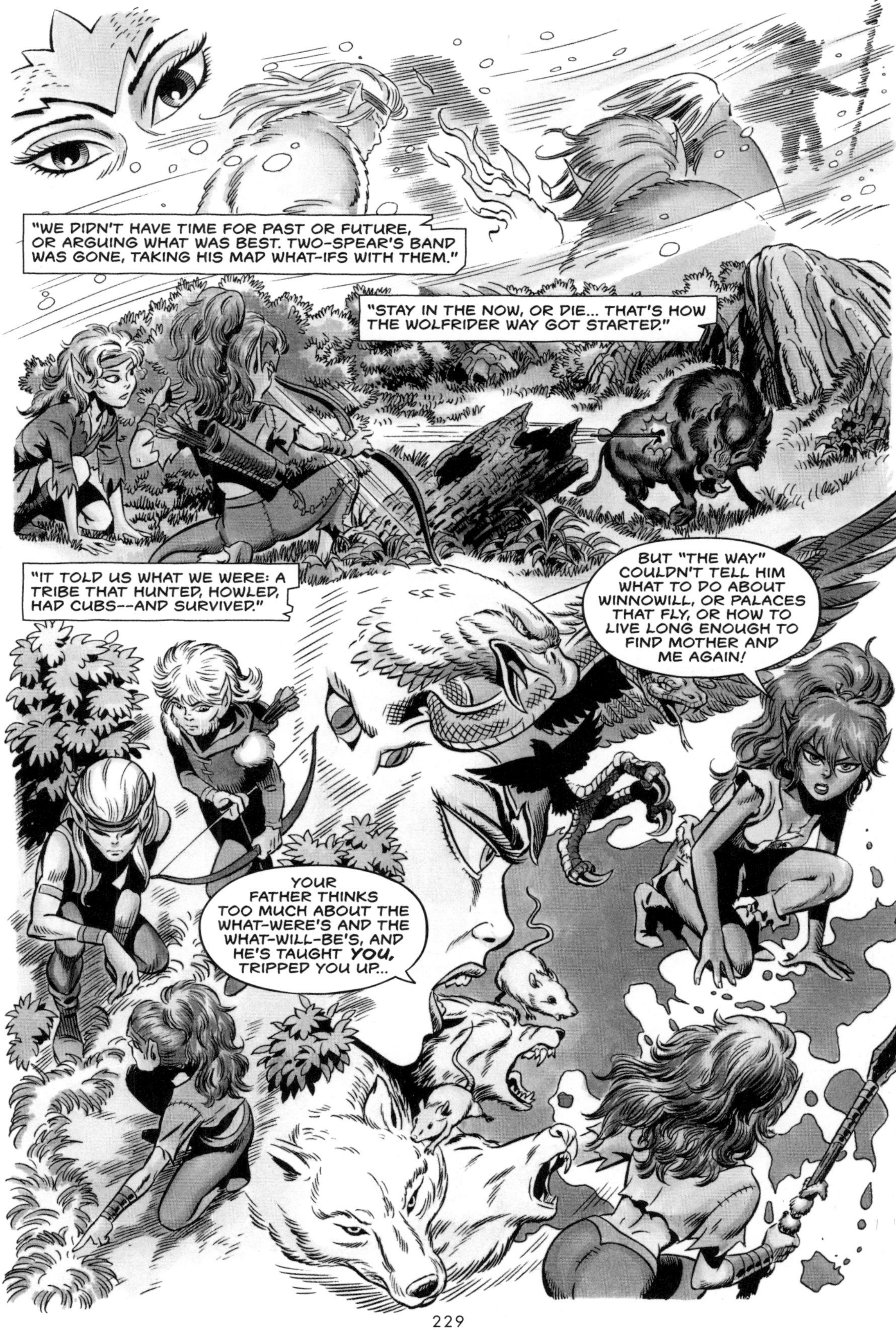
"WE DIDN'T HAVE TIME FOR PAST OR FUTURE, OR ARGUING WHAT WAS BEST. TWO-SPEAR'S BAND WAS GONE, TAKING HIS MAD WHAT-IFS WITH THEM."
"STAY IN THE NOW, OR DIE... THAT'S HOW THE WOLFRIDER WAY GOT STARTED."
"IT TOLD US WHAT WE WERE: A TRIBE THAT HUNTED, HOWLED, HAD CUBS--AND SURVIVED."
BUT "THE WAY" COULDN'T TELL HIM WHAT TO DO ABOUT WINNOWILL, OR PALACES THAT FLY, OR HOW TO LIVE LONG ENOUGH TO FIND MOTHER AND ME AGAIN!
YOUR FATHER THINKS TOO MUCH ABOUT THE WHAT-WERE'S AND THE WHAT-WILL-BE'S, AND HE'S TAUGHT *YOU*, TRIPPED YOU UP...

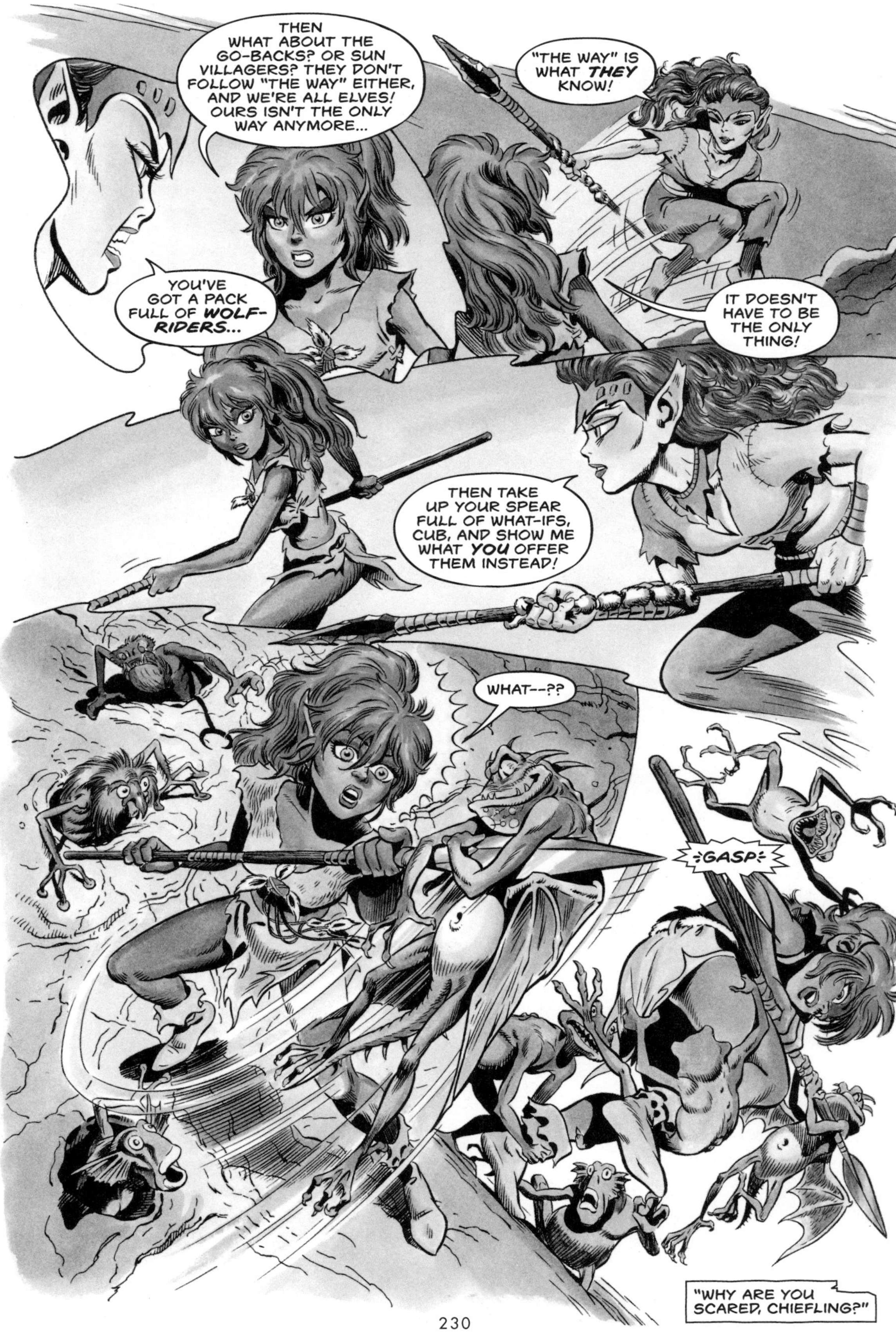

THEN WHAT ABOUT THE GO-BACKS? OR SUN VILLAGERS? THEY DON'T FOLLOW "THE WAY" EITHER, AND WE'RE ALL ELVES! OURS ISN'T THE ONLY WAY ANYMORE...
"THE WAY" IS WHAT *THEY* KNOW!
YOU'VE GOT A PACK FULL OF ***WOLF-RIDERS***...
IT DOESN'T HAVE TO BE THE ONLY THING!
THEN TAKE UP YOUR SPEAR FULL OF WHAT-IFS, CUB, AND SHOW ME WHAT ***YOU*** OFFER THEM INSTEAD!
WHAT--??
GASP
"WHY ARE YOU SCARED, CHIEFLING?"

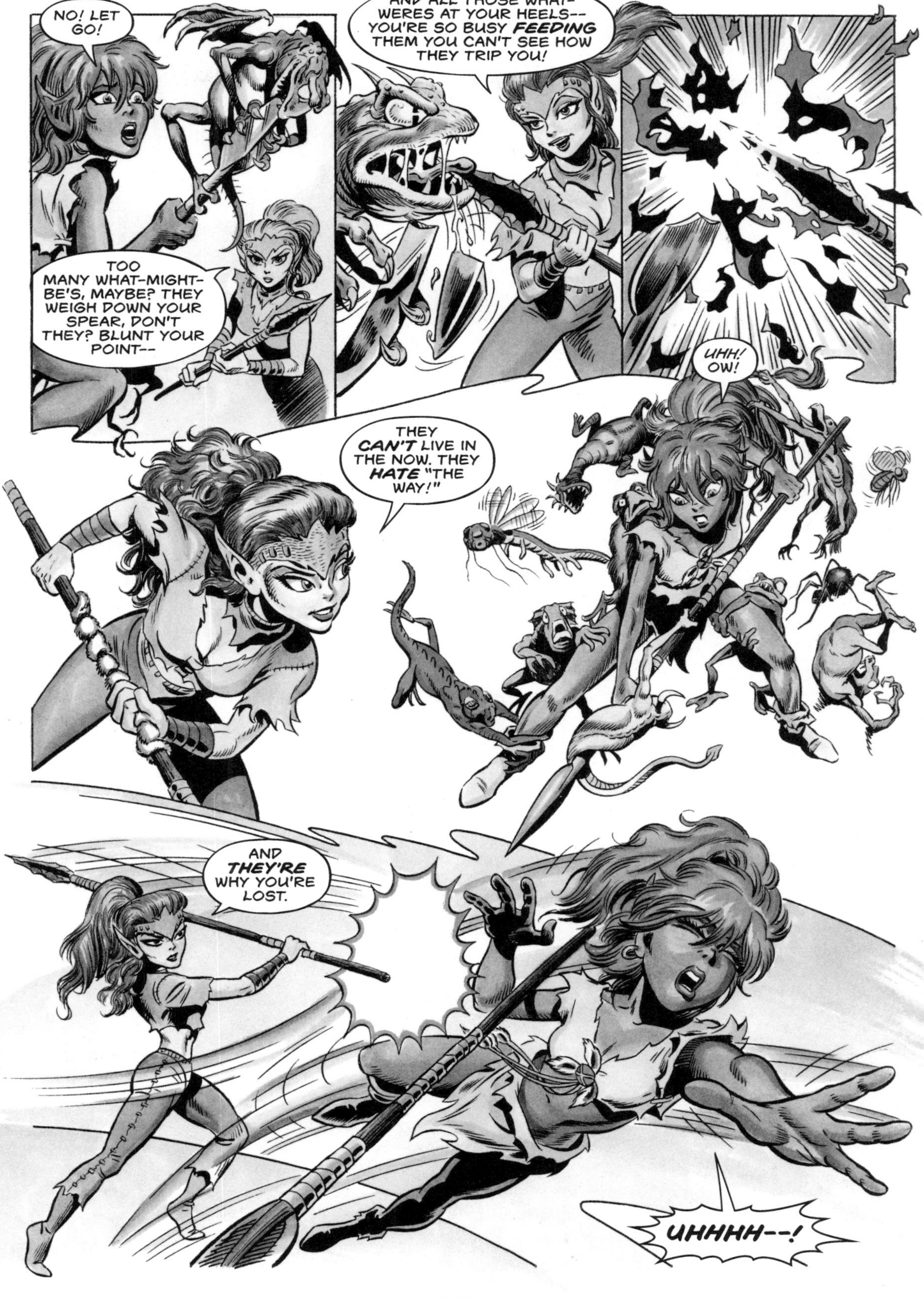
NO! LET GO!
TOO MANY WHAT-MIGHT-BE'S, MAYBE? THEY WEIGH DOWN YOUR SPEAR, DON'T THEY? BLUNT YOUR POINT--
AND ALL THOSE WHAT-WERES AT YOUR HEELS-- YOU'RE SO BUSY FEEDING THEM YOU CAN'T SEE HOW THEY TRIP YOU!
UHH! OW!
THEY CAN'T LIVE IN THE NOW. THEY HATE "THE WAY!"
AND THEY'RE WHY YOU'RE LOST.
UHHHH--!

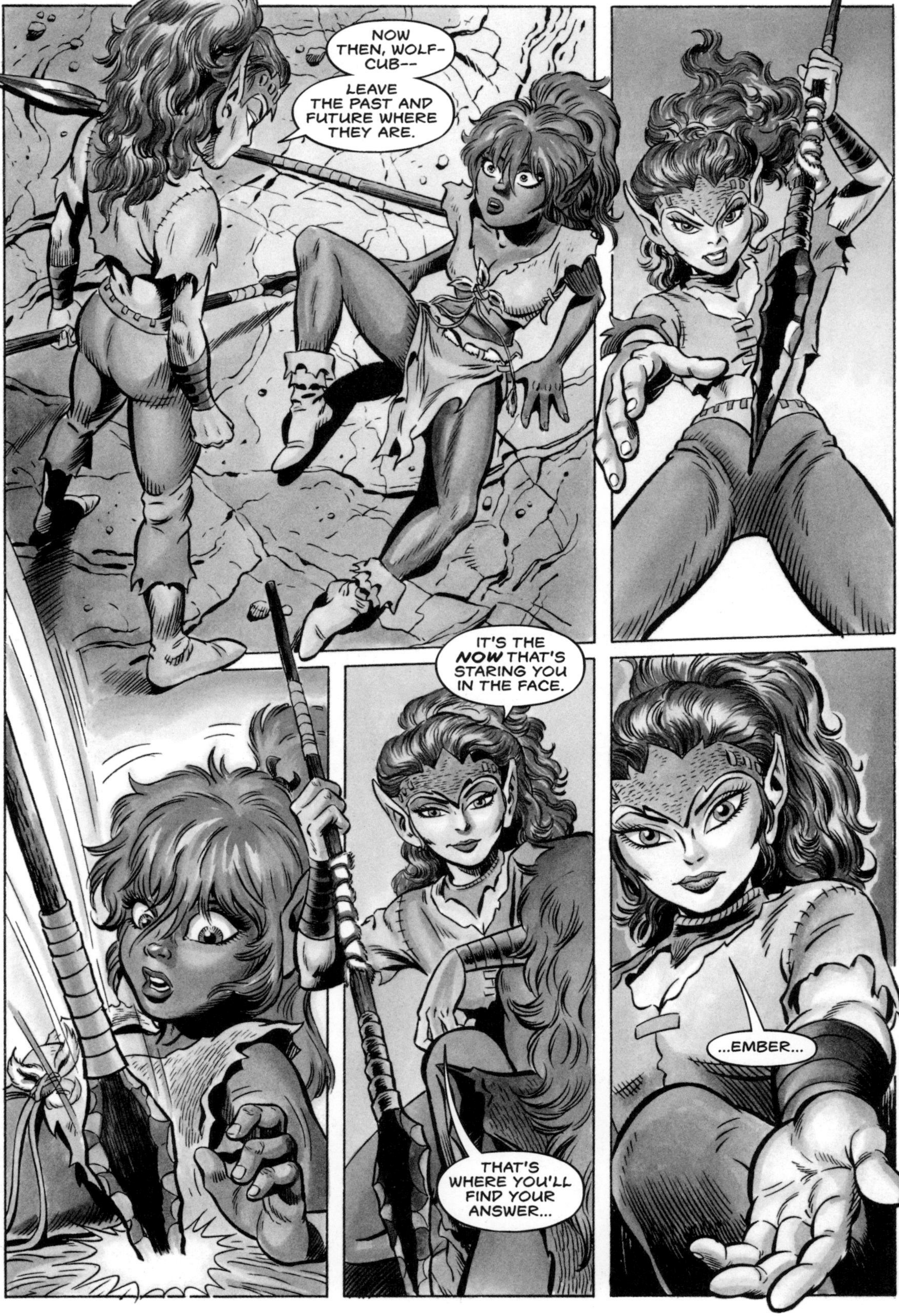
NOW THEN, WOLF-CUB--
LEAVE THE PAST AND FUTURE WHERE THEY ARE.
IT'S THE NOW THAT'S STARING YOU IN THE FACE.
THAT'S WHERE YOU'LL FIND YOUR ANSWER...
...EMBER...

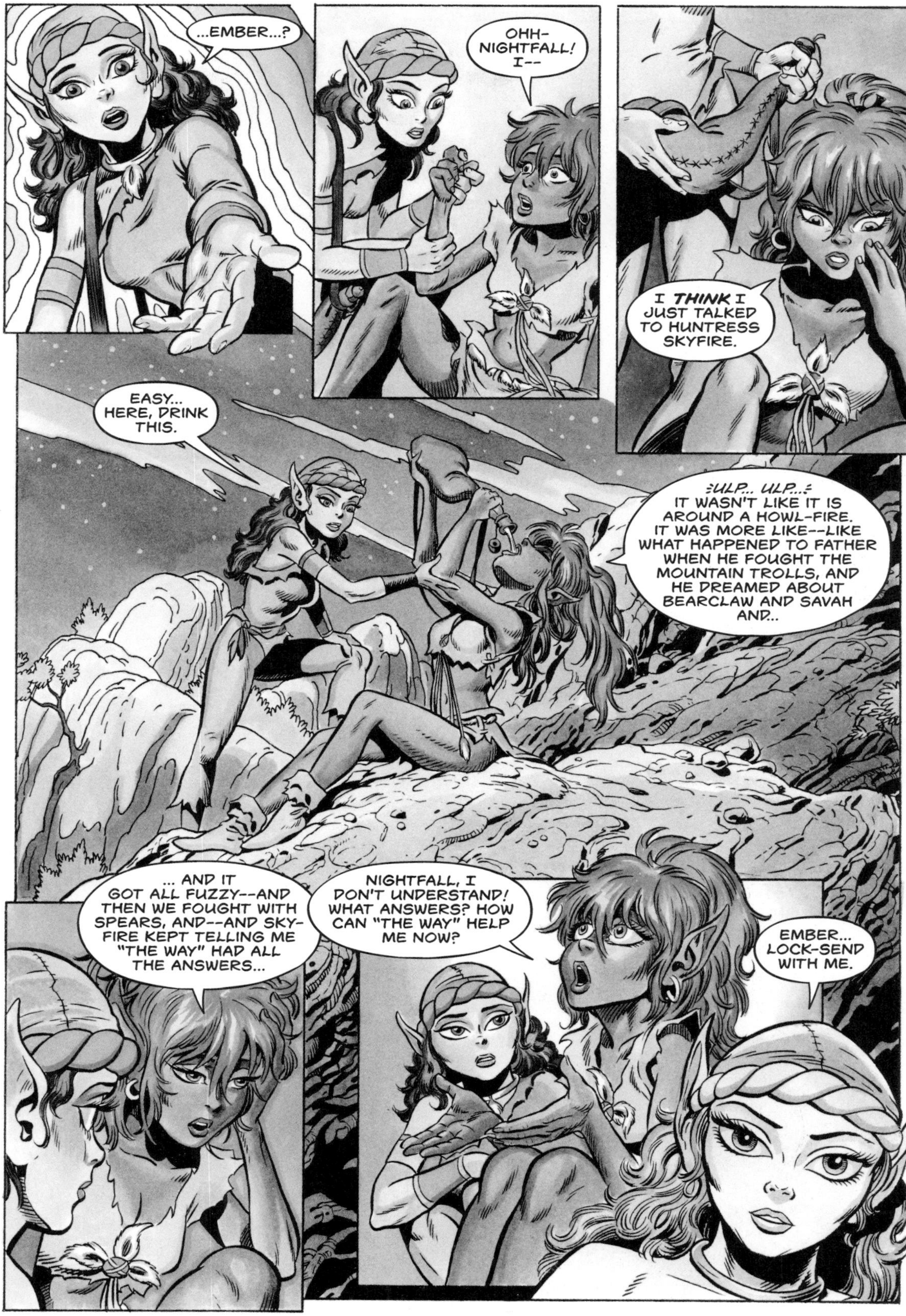
...EMBER...?
OHH-NIGHTFALL! I--
I THINK I JUST TALKED TO HUNTRESS SKYFIRE.
EASY... HERE, DRINK THIS.
ULP... ULP...
IT WASN'T LIKE IT IS AROUND A HOWL-FIRE. IT WAS MORE LIKE--LIKE WHAT HAPPENED TO FATHER WHEN HE FOUGHT THE MOUNTAIN TROLLS, AND HE DREAMED ABOUT BEARCLAW AND SAVAH AND...
... AND IT GOT ALL FUZZY--AND THEN WE FOUGHT WITH SPEARS, AND--AND SKY-FIRE KEPT TELLING ME "THE WAY" HAD ALL THE ANSWERS...
NIGHTFALL, I DON'T UNDERSTAND! WHAT ANSWERS? HOW CAN "THE WAY" HELP ME NOW?
EMBER... LOCK-SEND WITH ME.

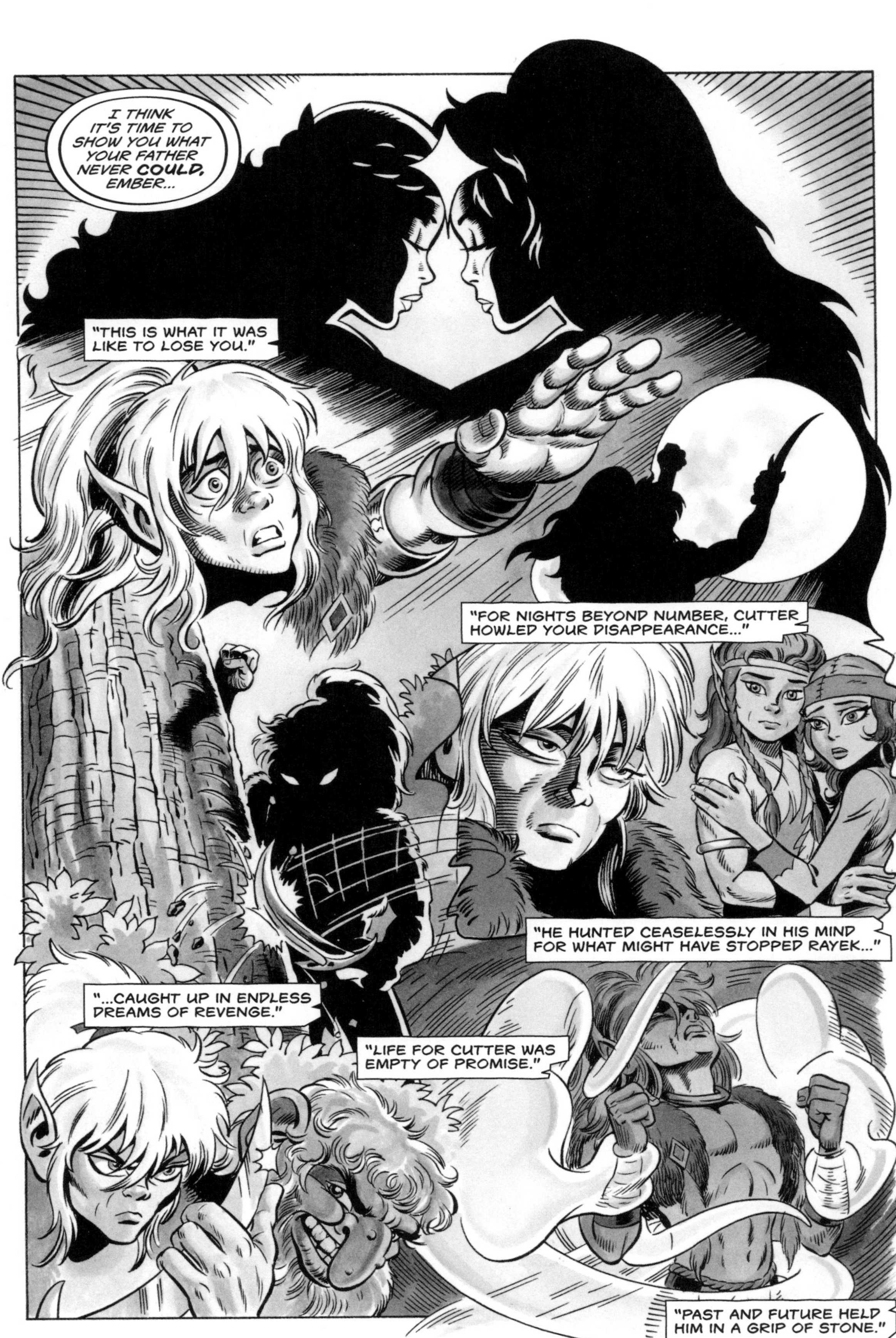
I THINK IT'S TIME TO SHOW YOU WHAT YOUR FATHER NEVER COULD, EMBER...
"THIS IS WHAT IT WAS LIKE TO LOSE YOU."
"FOR NIGHTS BEYOND NUMBER, CUTTER HOWLED YOUR DISAPPEARANCE..."
"HE HUNTED CEASELESSLY IN HIS MIND FOR WHAT MIGHT HAVE STOPPED RAYEK..."
"...CAUGHT UP IN ENDLESS DREAMS OF REVENGE."
"LIFE FOR CUTTER WAS EMPTY OF PROMISE."
"PAST AND FUTURE HELD HIM IN A GRIP OF STONE."

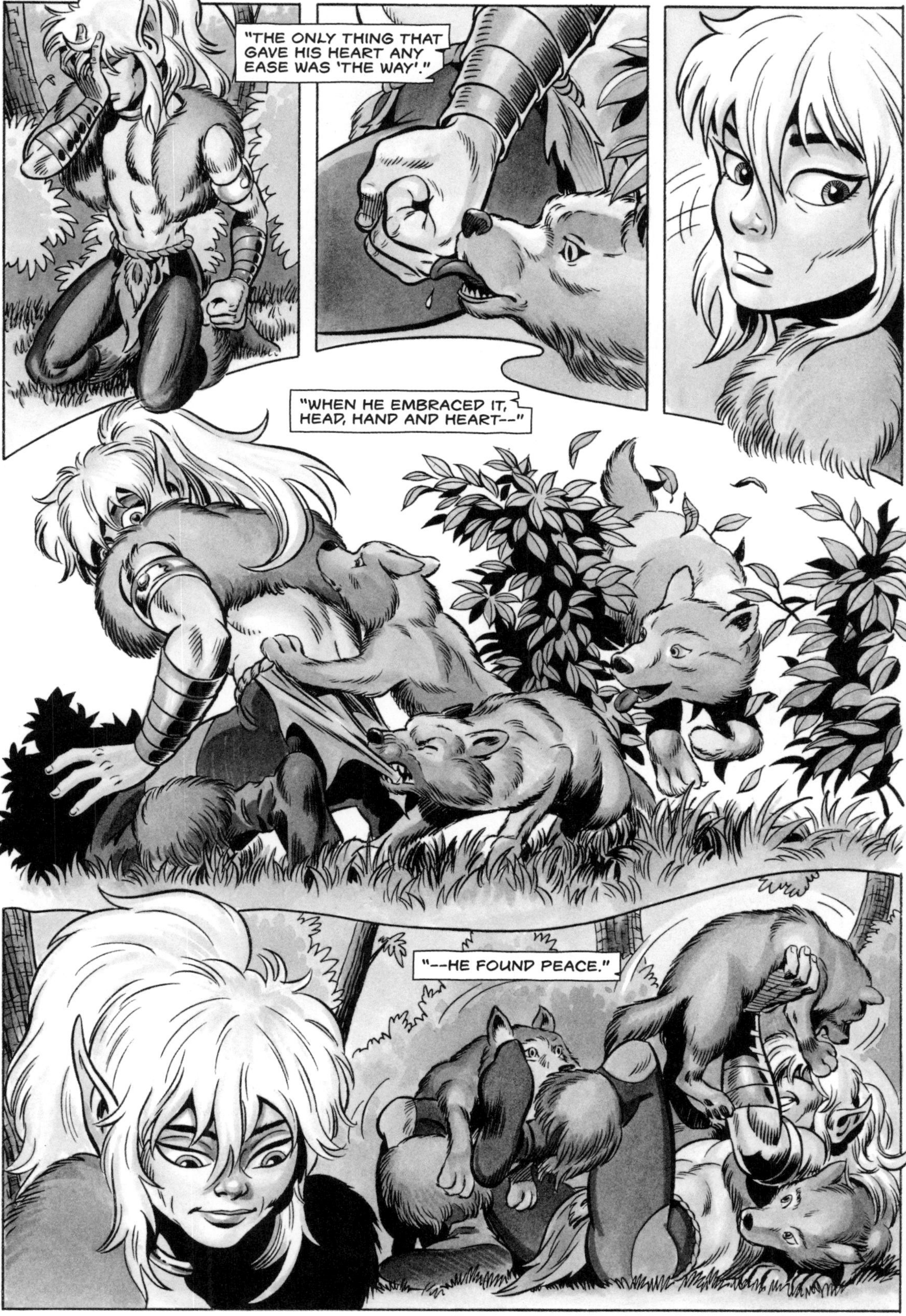
"THE ONLY THING THAT GAVE HIS HEART ANY EASE WAS 'THE WAY'."
"WHEN HE EMBRACED IT, HEAD, HAND AND HEART--"
"--HE FOUND PEACE."

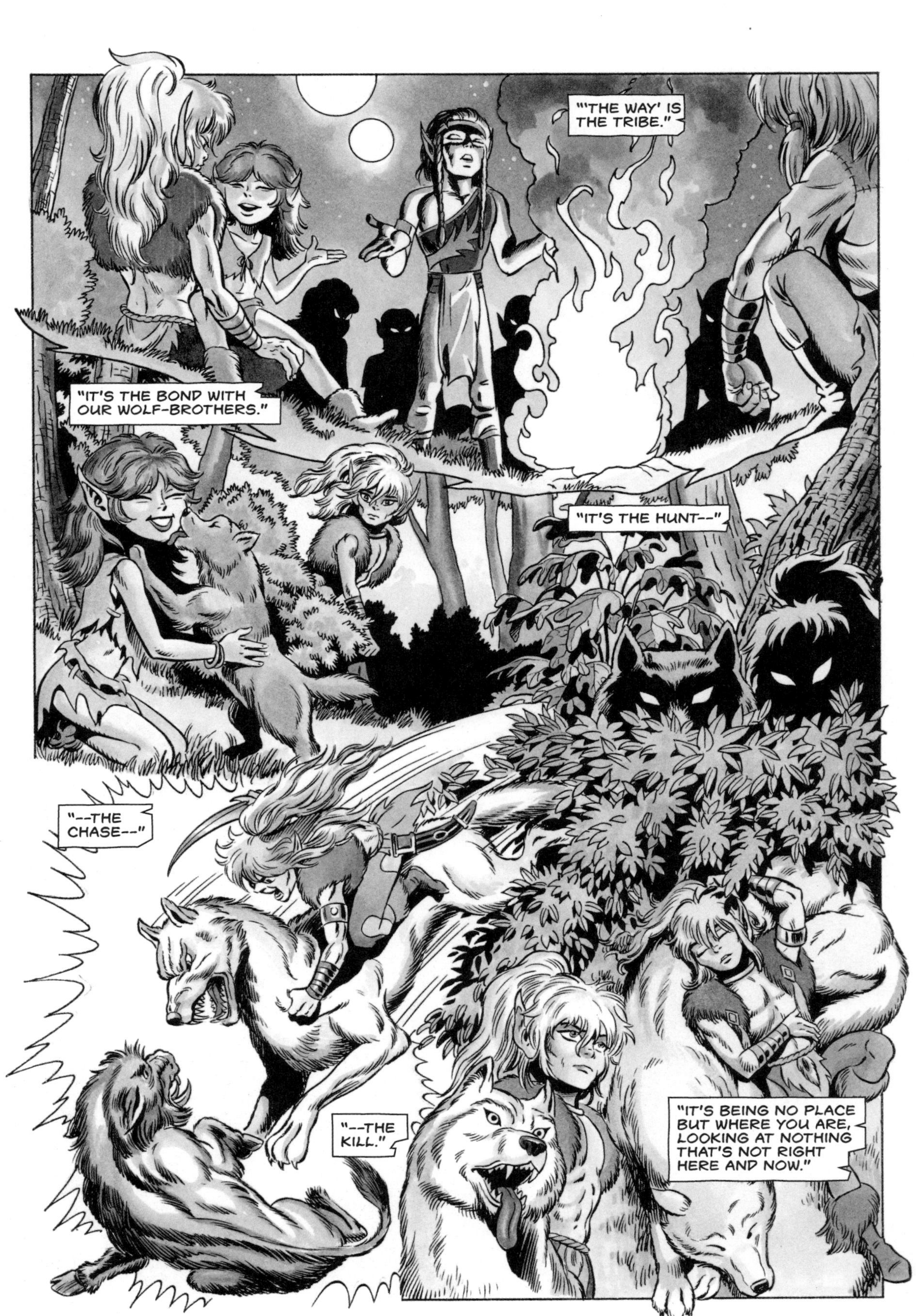
"'THE WAY' IS THE TRIBE."
"IT'S THE BOND WITH OUR WOLF-BROTHERS."
"IT'S THE HUNT--"
"--THE CHASE--"
"--THE KILL."
"IT'S BEING NO PLACE BUT WHERE YOU ARE, LOOKING AT NOTHING THAT'S NOT RIGHT HERE AND NOW."

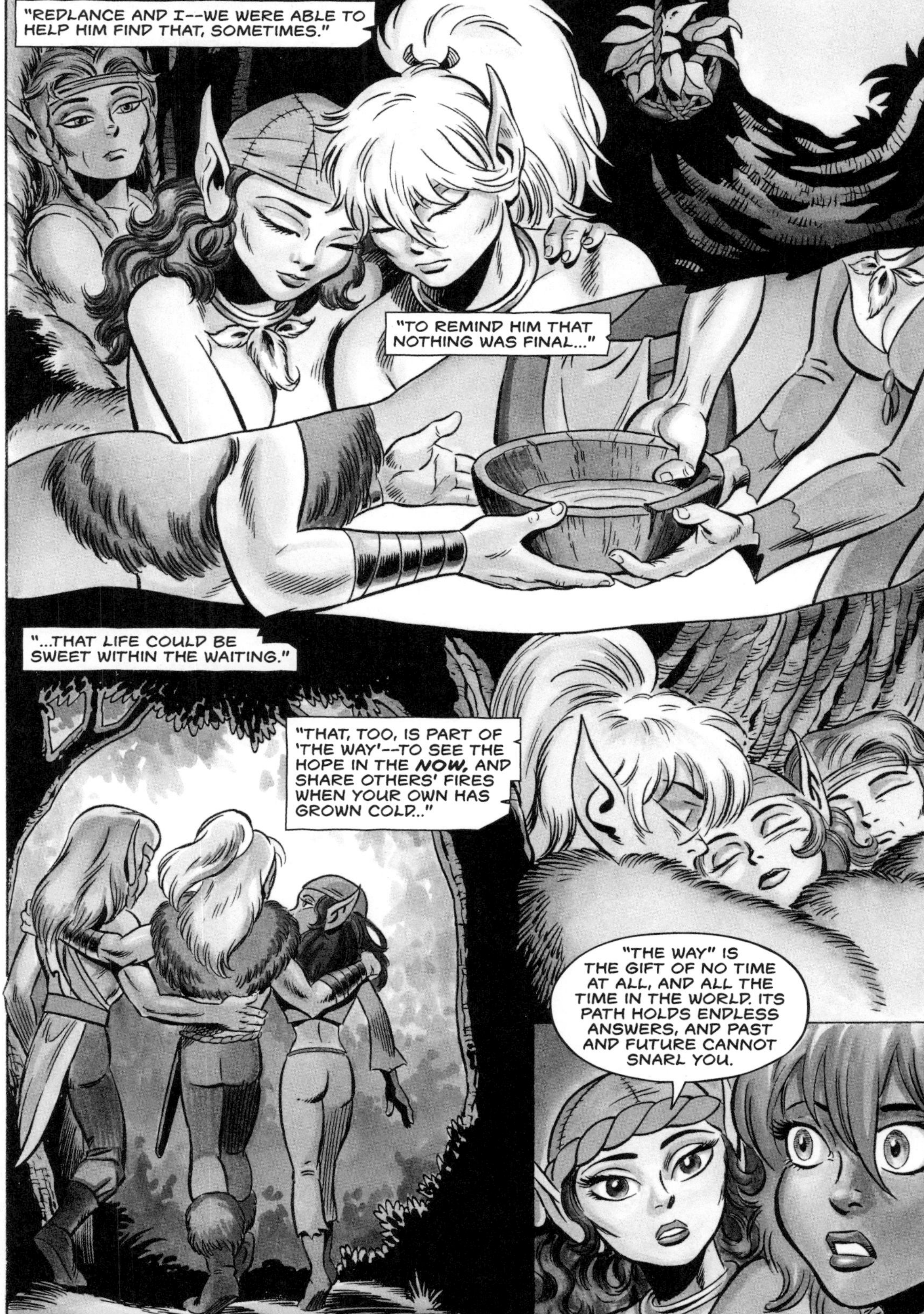
"REDLANCE AND I--WE WERE ABLE TO HELP HIM FIND THAT, SOMETIMES."
"TO REMIND HIM THAT NOTHING WAS FINAL..."
"...THAT LIFE COULD BE SWEET WITHIN THE WAITING."
"THAT, TOO, IS PART OF 'THE WAY'--TO SEE THE HOPE IN THE NOW, AND SHARE OTHERS' FIRES WHEN YOUR OWN HAS GROWN COLD..."
"THE WAY" IS THE GIFT OF NO TIME AT ALL, AND ALL THE TIME IN THE WORLD. ITS PATH HOLDS ENDLESS ANSWERS, AND PAST AND FUTURE CANNOT SNARL YOU.

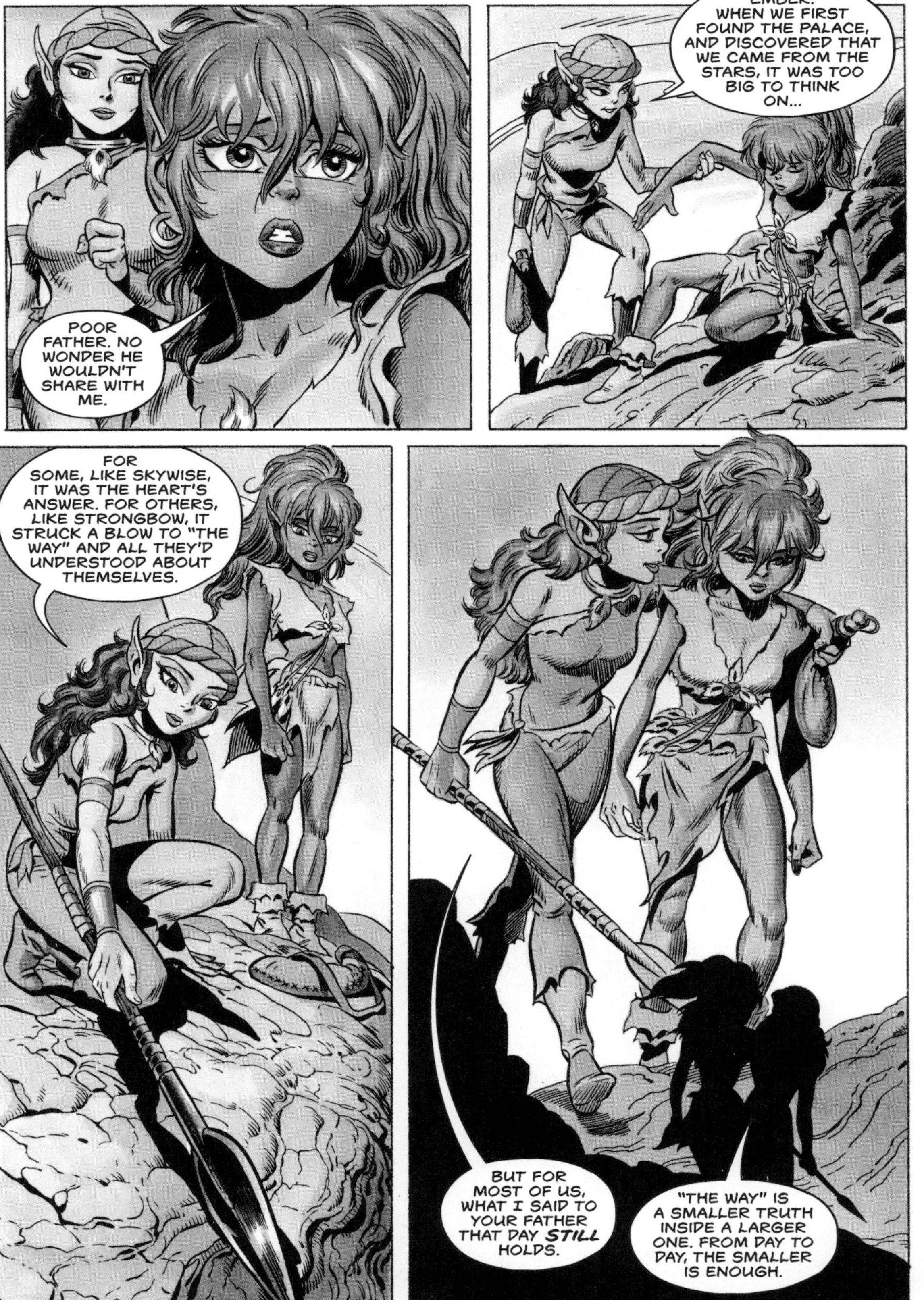
POOR FATHER. NO WONDER HE WOULDN'T SHARE WITH ME.
EMBER. WHEN WE FIRST FOUND THE PALACE, AND DISCOVERED THAT WE CAME FROM THE STARS, IT WAS TOO BIG TO THINK ON...
FOR SOME, LIKE SKYWISE, IT WAS THE HEART'S ANSWER. FOR OTHERS, LIKE STRONGBOW, IT STRUCK A BLOW TO "THE WAY" AND ALL THEY'D UNDERSTOOD ABOUT THEMSELVES.
BUT FOR MOST OF US, WHAT I SAID TO YOUR FATHER THAT DAY STILL HOLDS.
"THE WAY" IS A SMALLER TRUTH INSIDE A LARGER ONE. FROM DAY TO DAY, THE SMALLER IS ENOUGH.

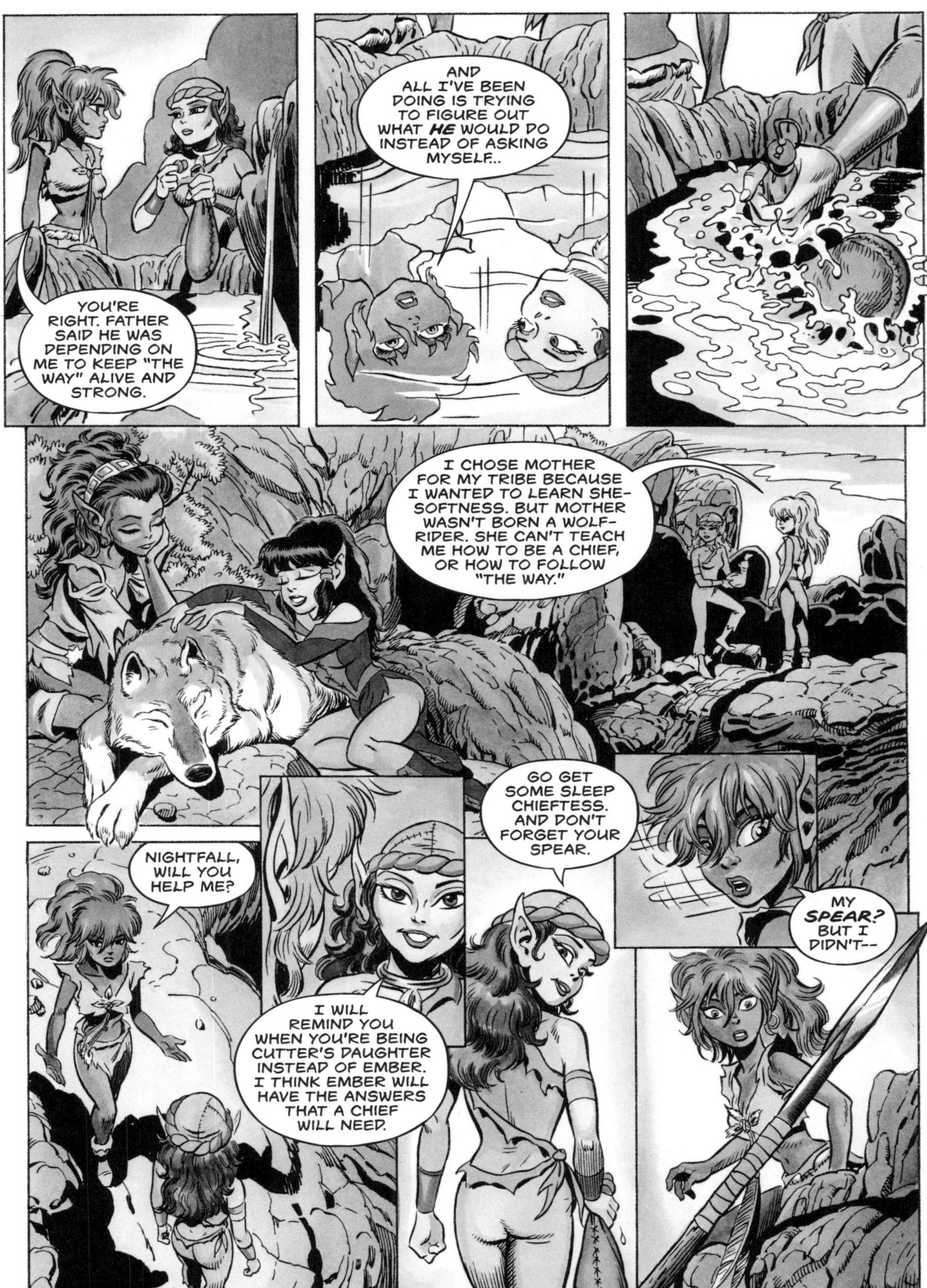
YOU'RE RIGHT. FATHER SAID HE WAS DEPENDING ON ME TO KEEP "THE WAY" ALIVE AND STRONG.
AND ALL I'VE BEEN DOING IS TRYING TO FIGURE OUT WHAT HE WOULD DO INSTEAD OF ASKING MYSELF...
I CHOSE MOTHER FOR MY TRIBE BECAUSE I WANTED TO LEARN SHE-SOFTNESS. BUT MOTHER WASN'T BORN A WOLF-RIDER. SHE CAN'T TEACH ME HOW TO BE A CHIEF, OR HOW TO FOLLOW "THE WAY."
NIGHTFALL, WILL YOU HELP ME?
I WILL REMIND YOU WHEN YOU'RE BEING CUTTER'S DAUGHTER INSTEAD OF EMBER. I THINK EMBER WILL HAVE THE ANSWERS THAT A CHIEF WILL NEED.
GO GET SOME SLEEP CHIEFTESS. AND DON'T FORGET YOUR SPEAR.
MY SPEAR? BUT I DIDN'T--

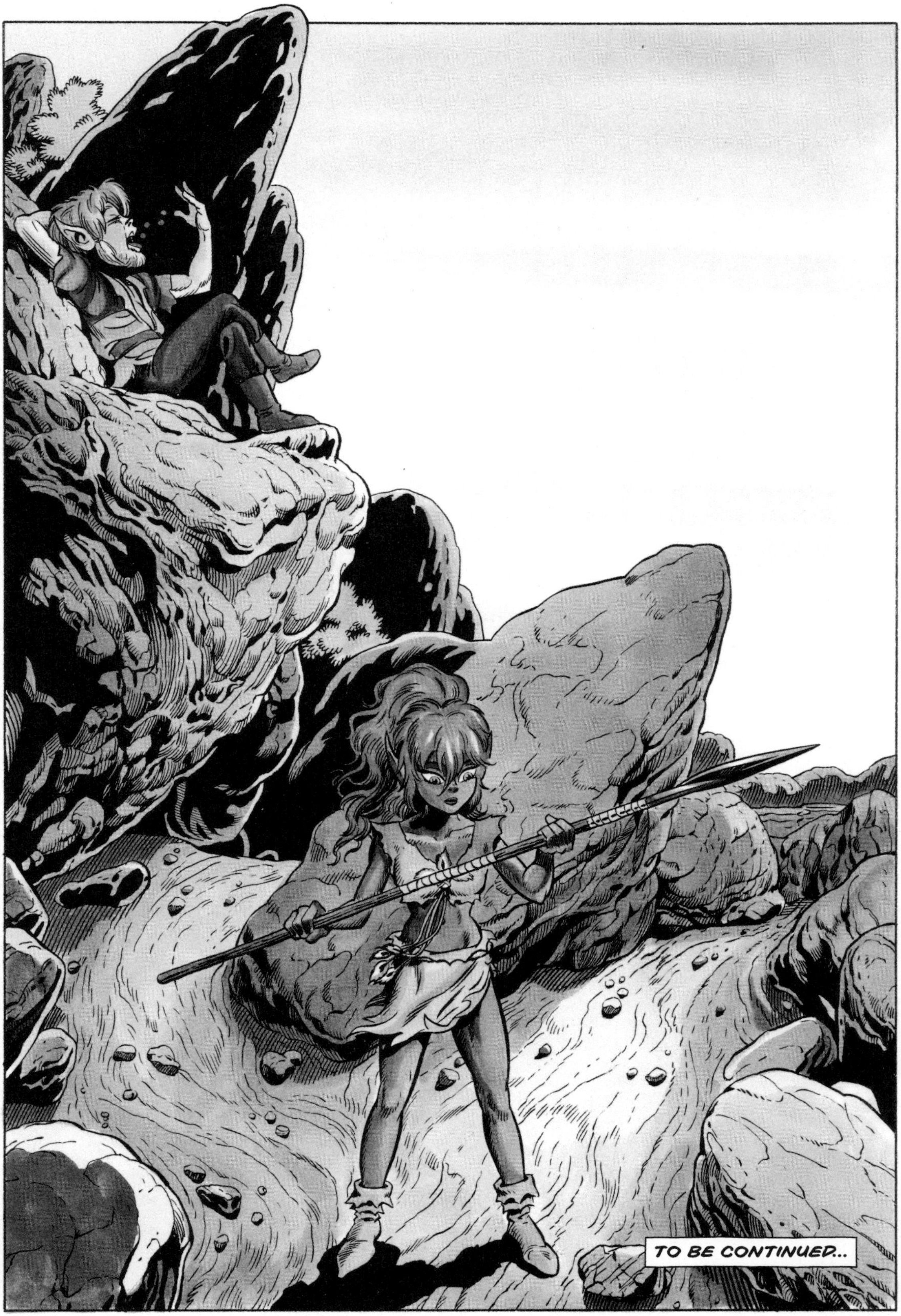
TO BE CONTINUED...

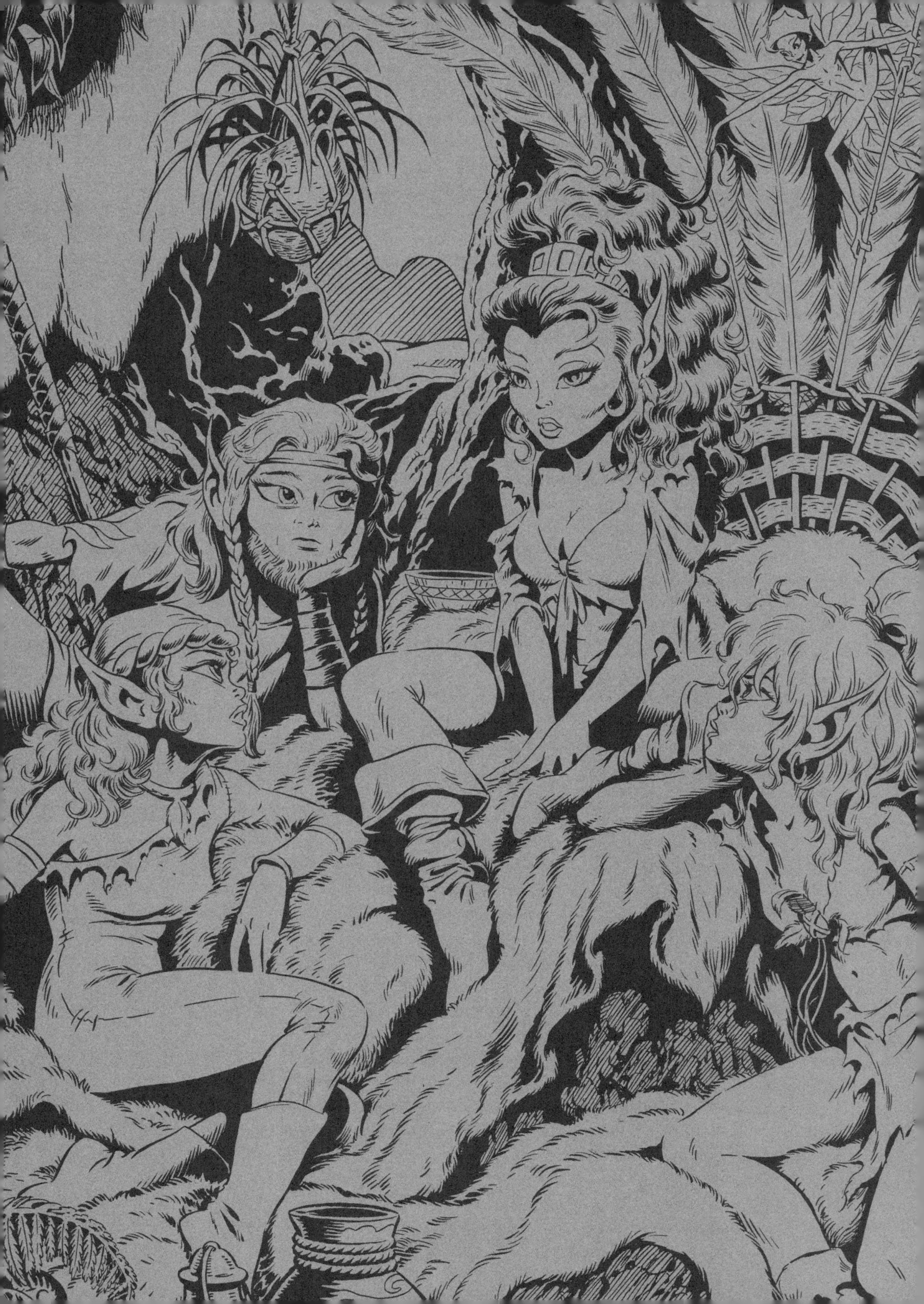

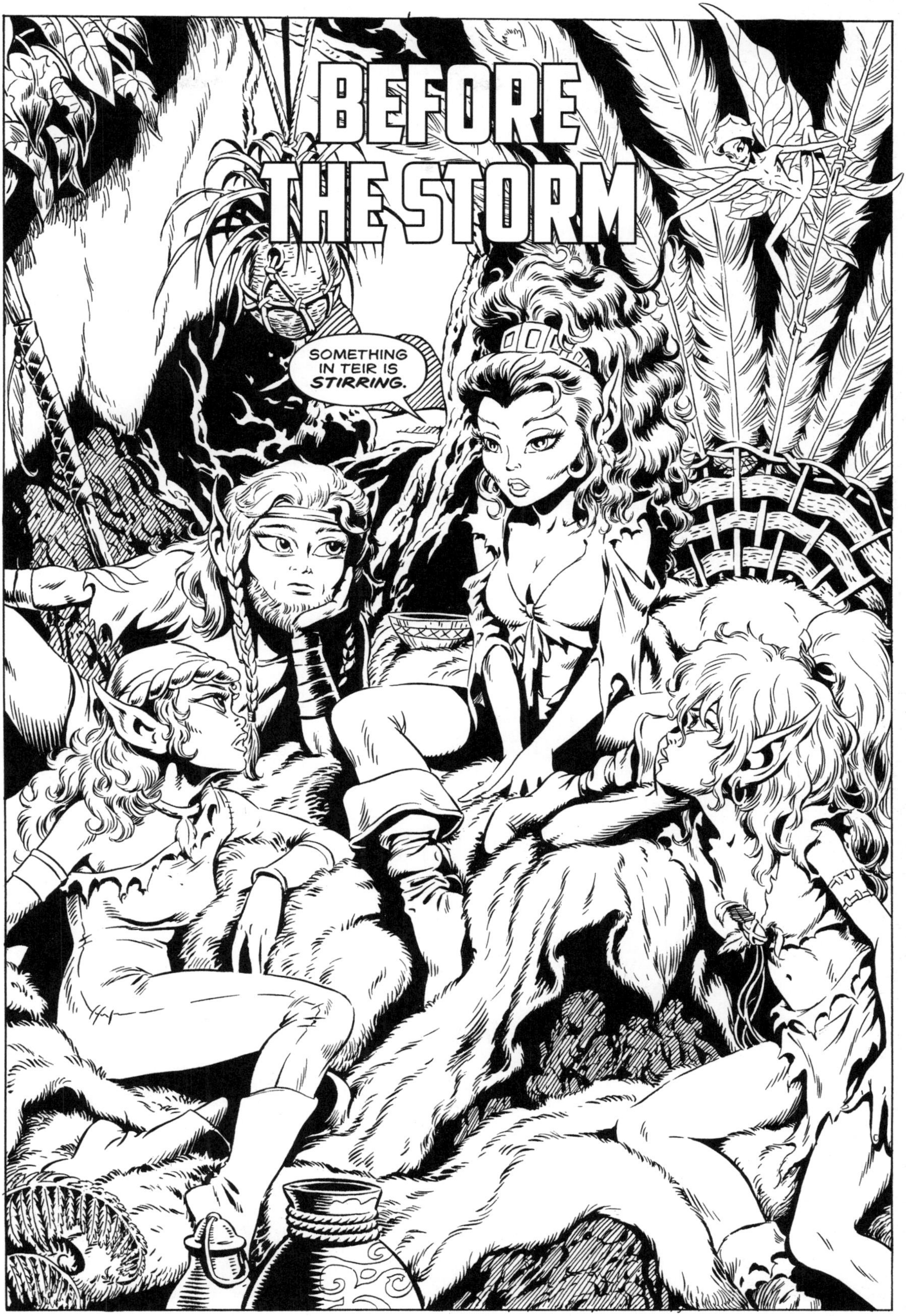
BEFORE THE STORM
SOMETHING IN TEIR IS STIRRING.

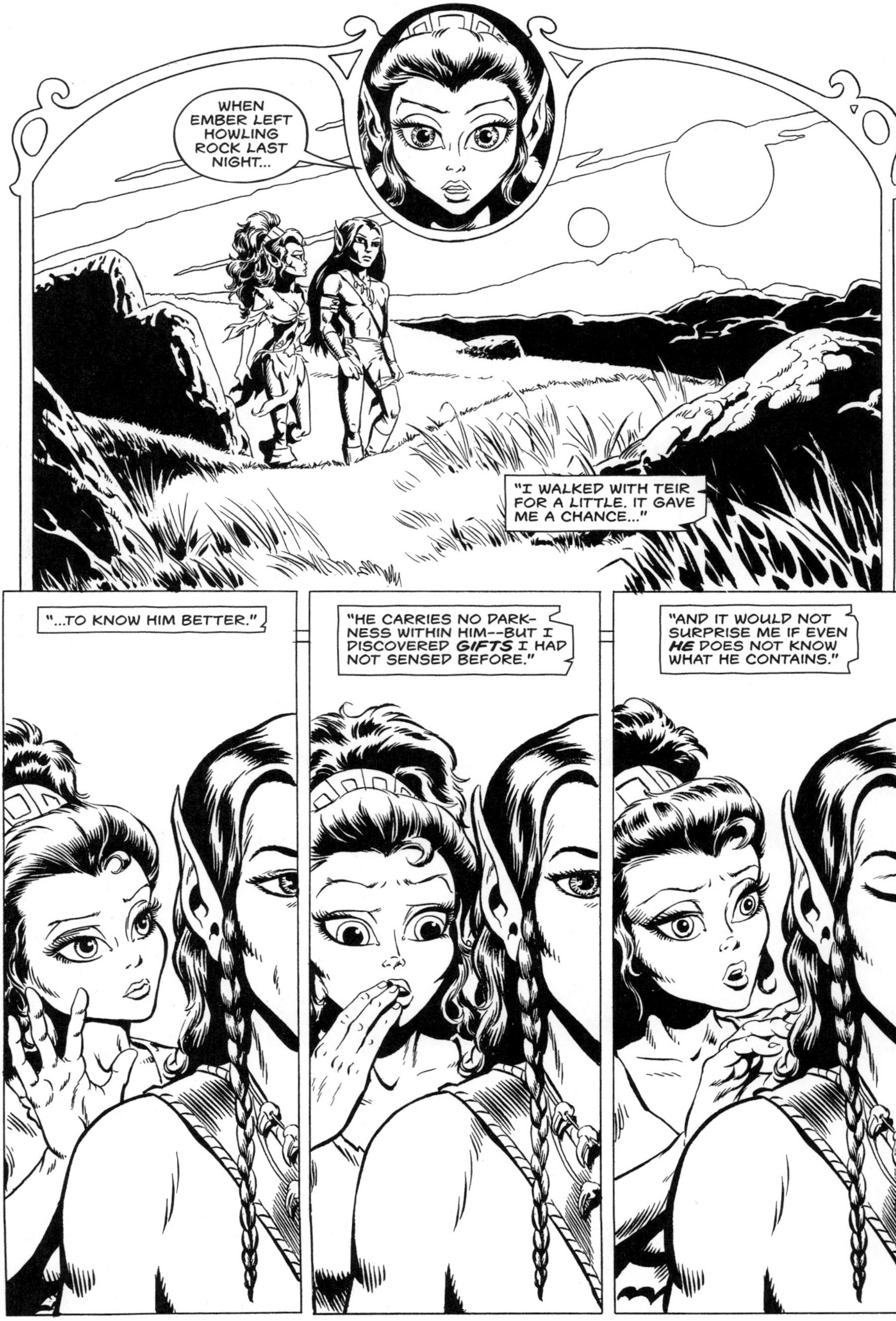
WHEN EMBER LEFT HOWLING ROCK LAST NIGHT...
"I WALKED WITH TEIR FOR A LITTLE. IT GAVE ME A CHANCE..."
"...TO KNOW HIM BETTER."
"HE CARRIES NO DARKNESS WITHIN HIM--BUT I DISCOVERED GIFTS I HAD NOT SENSED BEFORE."
"AND IT WOULD NOT SURPRISE ME IF EVEN HE DOES NOT KNOW WHAT HE CONTAINS."

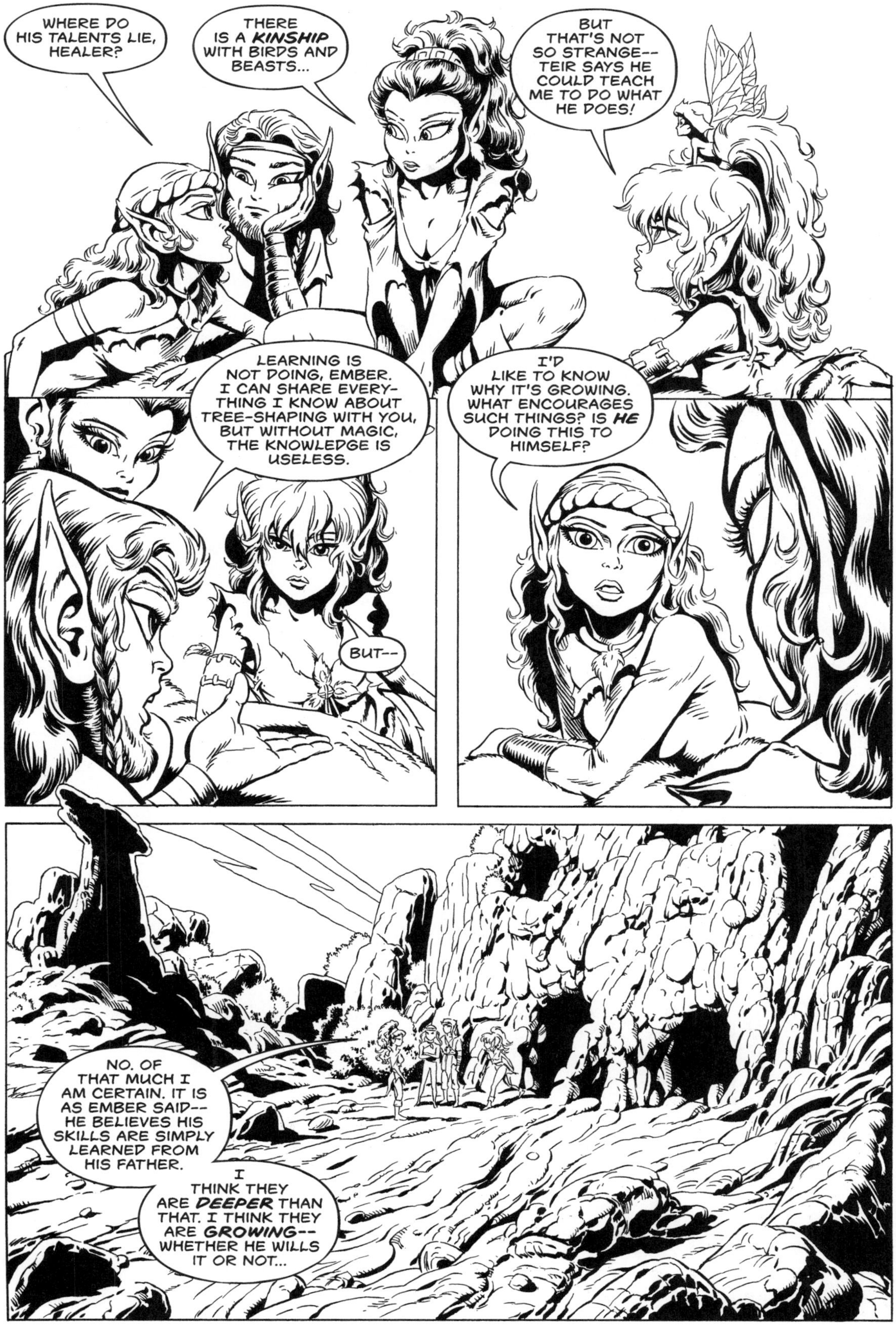
WHERE DO HIS TALENTS LIE, HEALER?
THERE IS A KINSHIP WITH BIRDS AND BEASTS...
BUT THAT'S NOT SO STRANGE-- TEIR SAYS HE COULD TEACH ME TO DO WHAT HE DOES!
LEARNING IS NOT DOING, EMBER. I CAN SHARE EVERYTHING I KNOW ABOUT TREE-SHAPING WITH YOU, BUT WITHOUT MAGIC, THE KNOWLEDGE IS USELESS.
BUT--
I'D LIKE TO KNOW WHY IT'S GROWING. WHAT ENCOURAGES SUCH THINGS? IS HE DOING THIS TO HIMSELF?
NO. OF THAT MUCH I AM CERTAIN. IT IS AS EMBER SAID-- HE BELIEVES HIS SKILLS ARE SIMPLY LEARNED FROM HIS FATHER.
I THINK THEY ARE DEEPER THAN THAT. I THINK THEY ARE GROWING-- WHETHER HE WILLS IT OR NOT...

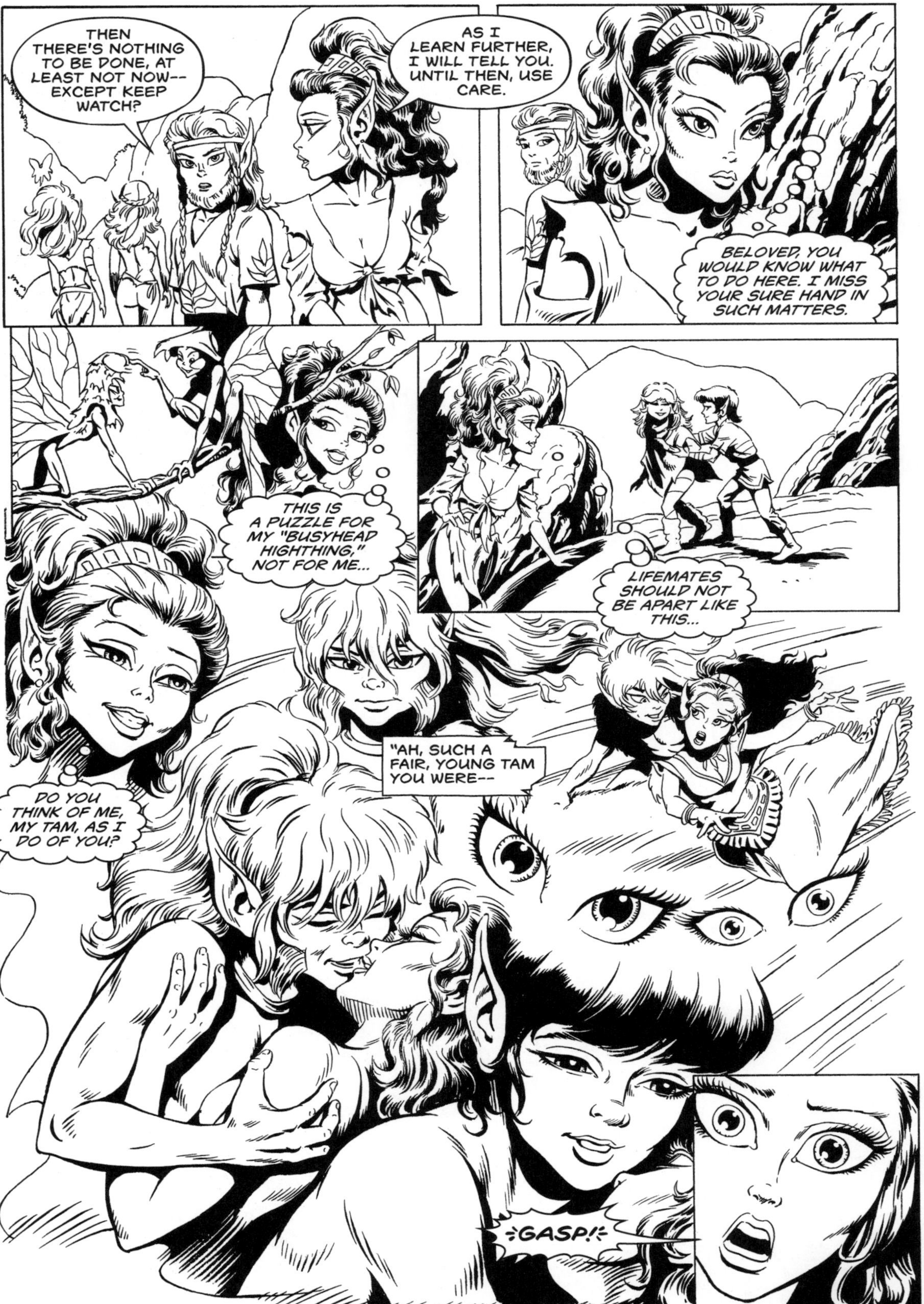
THEN THERE'S NOTHING TO BE DONE, AT LEAST NOT NOW-- EXCEPT KEEP WATCH?
AS I LEARN FURTHER, I WILL TELL YOU. UNTIL THEN, USE CARE.
BELOVED, YOU WOULD KNOW WHAT TO DO HERE. I MISS YOUR SURE HAND IN SUCH MATTERS.
THIS IS A PUZZLE FOR MY "BUSYHEAD HIGHTHING," NOT FOR ME...
LIFEMATES SHOULD NOT BE APART LIKE THIS...
"AH, SUCH A FAIR, YOUNG TAM YOU WERE--
DO YOU THINK OF ME, MY TAM, AS I DO OF YOU?
GASP!

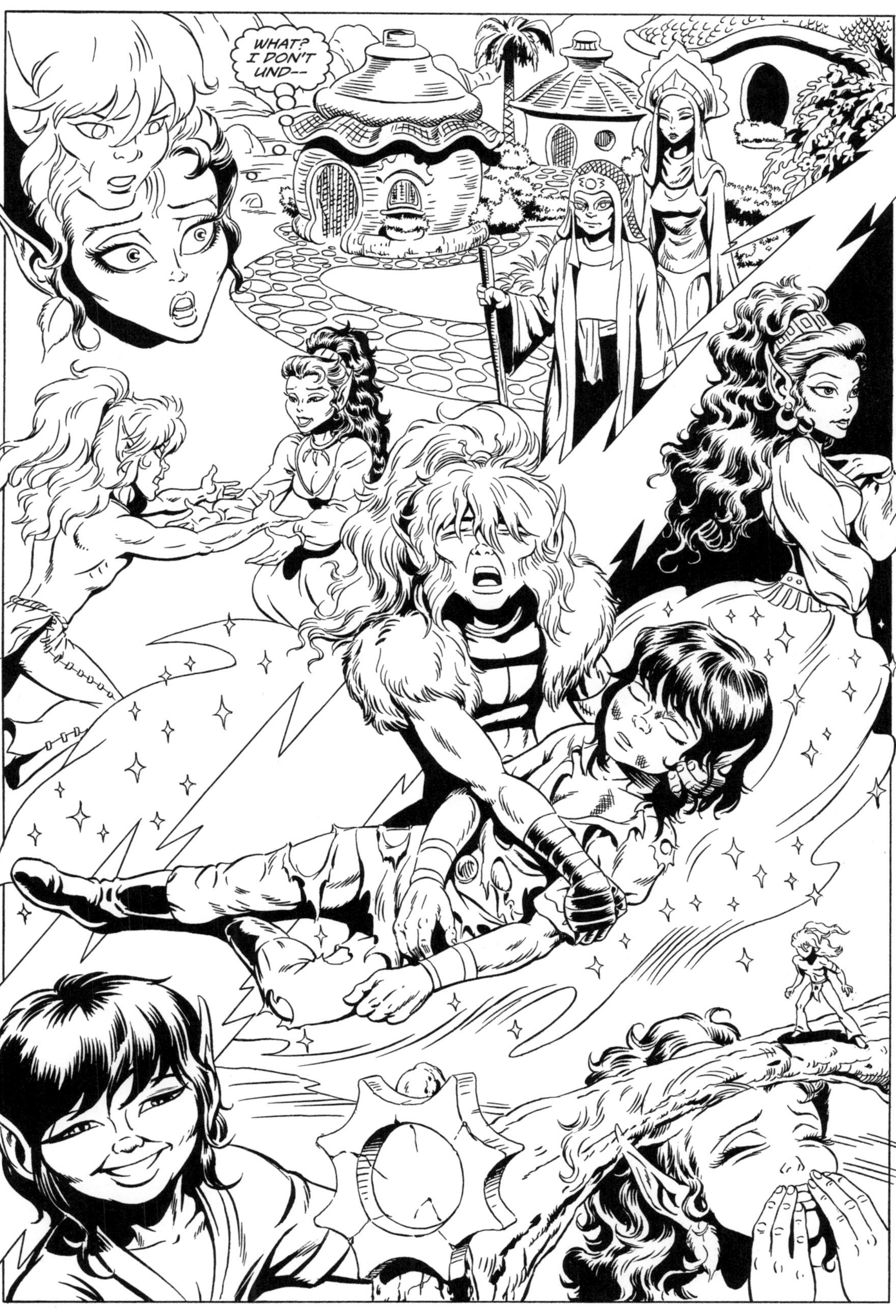
WHAT? I DON'T UND--

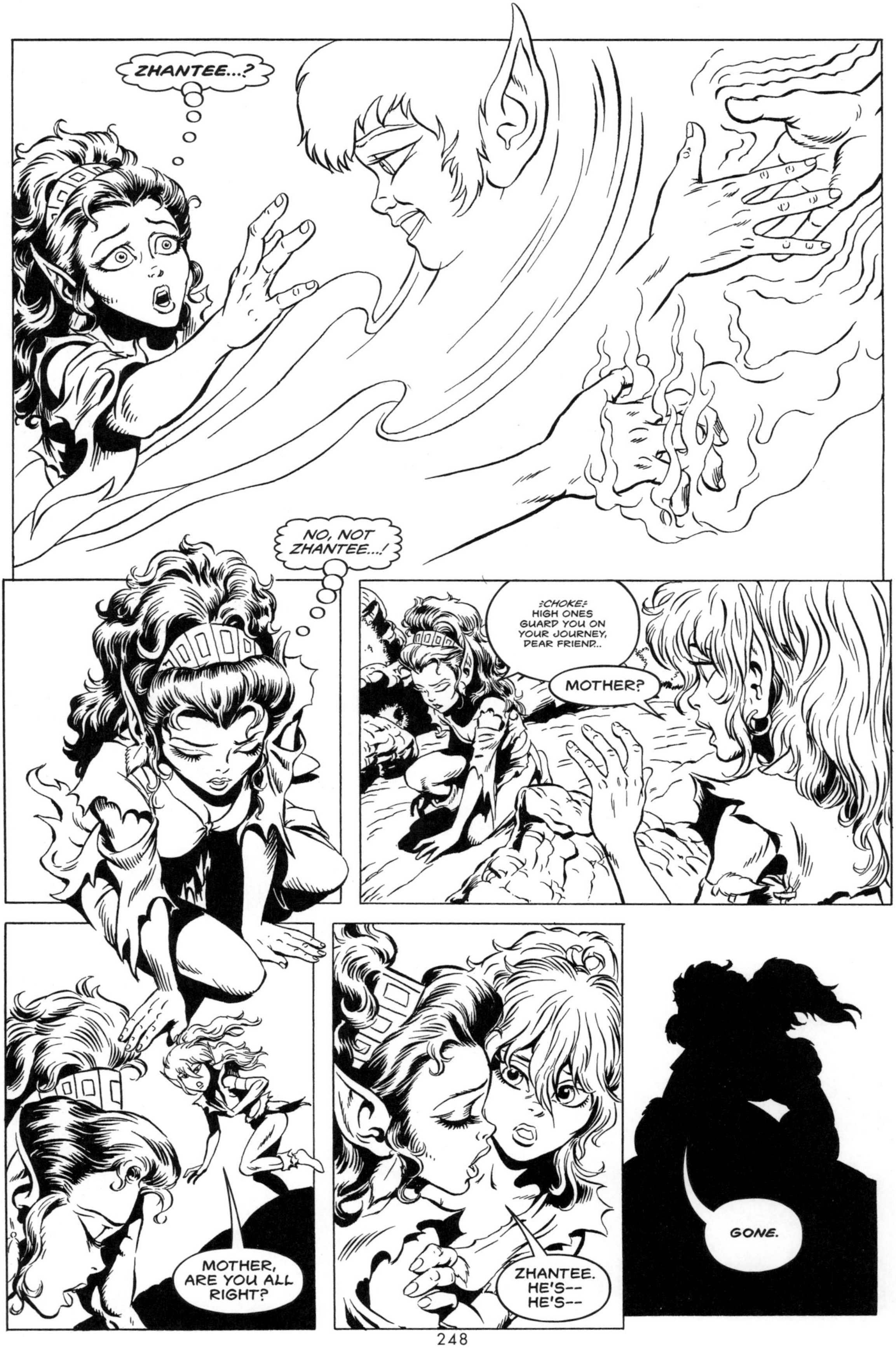
ZHANTEE...?
NO, NOT ZHANTEE...!
CHOKE HIGH ONES GUARD YOU ON YOUR JOURNEY, DEAR FRIEND...
MOTHER?
MOTHER, ARE YOU ALL RIGHT?
ZHANTEE. HE'S-- HE'S--
GONE.

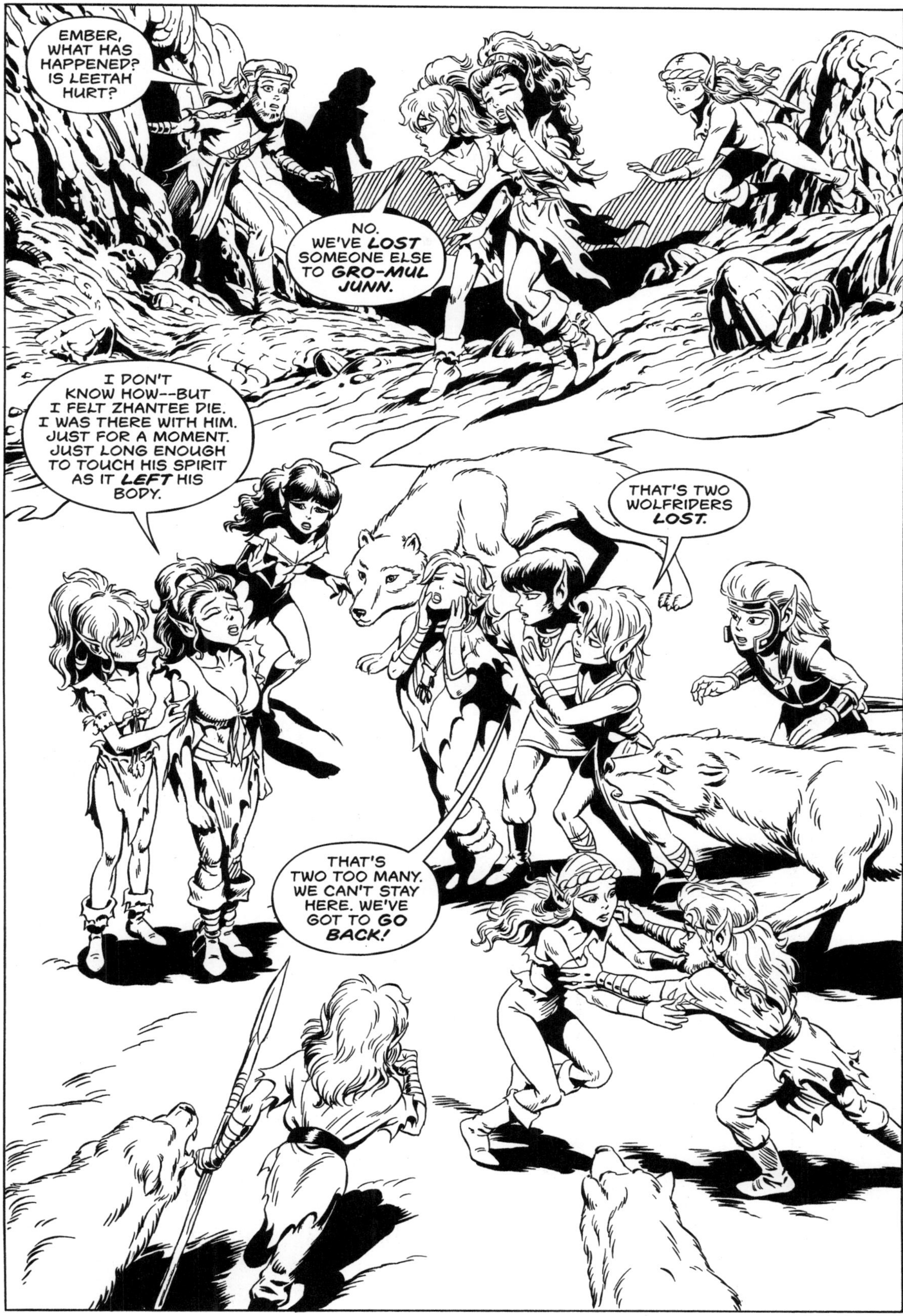
EMBER, WHAT HAS HAPPENED? IS LEETAH HURT?
NO. WE'VE LOST SOMEONE ELSE TO GRO-MUL JUNN.
I DON'T KNOW HOW--BUT I FELT ZHANTEE DIE. I WAS THERE WITH HIM. JUST FOR A MOMENT. JUST LONG ENOUGH TO TOUCH HIS SPIRIT AS IT LEFT HIS BODY.
THAT'S TWO WOLFRIDERS LOST.
THAT'S TWO TOO MANY. WE CAN'T STAY HERE. WE'VE GOT TO GO BACK!

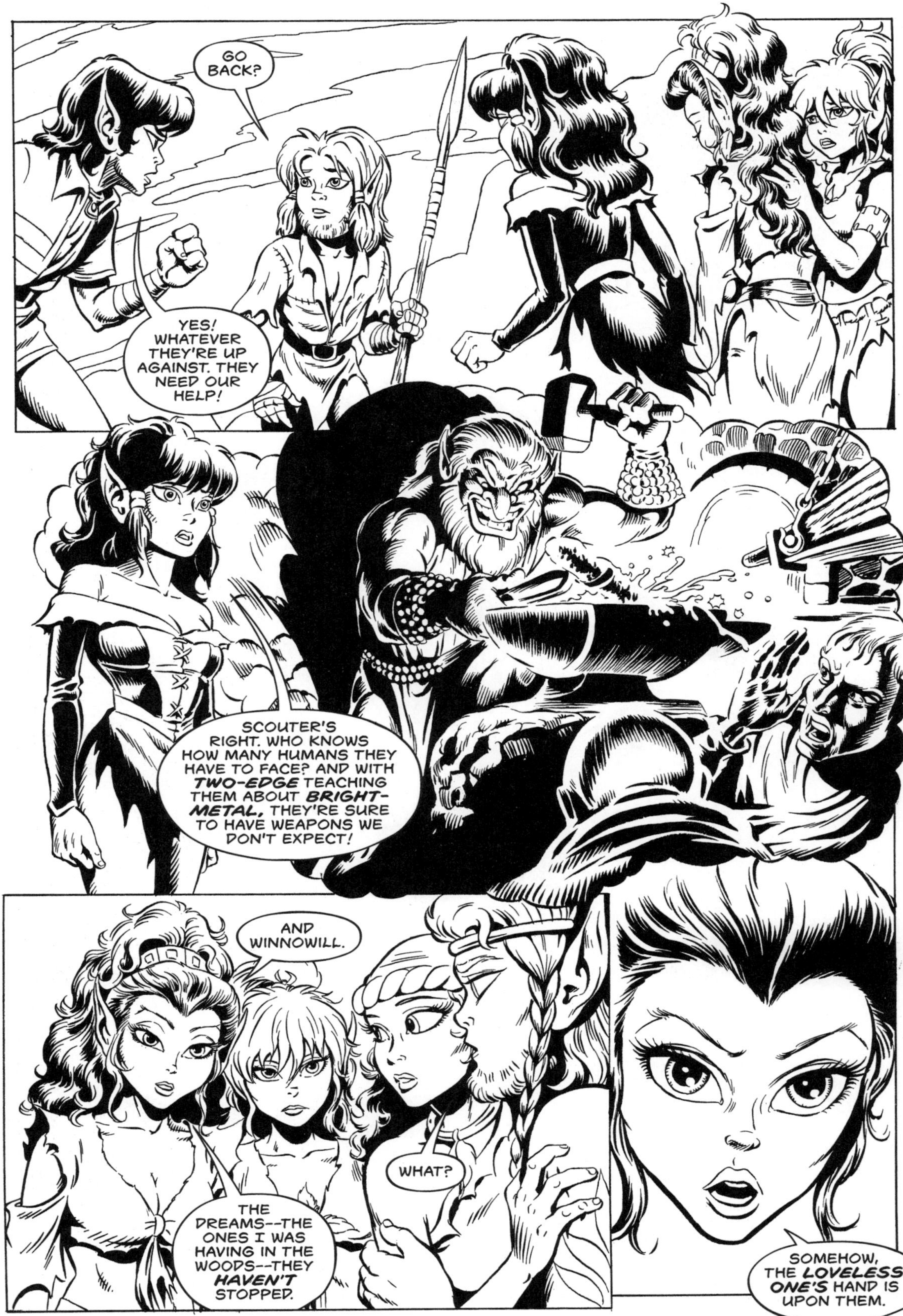
GO BACK?
YES! WHATEVER THEY'RE UP AGAINST. THEY NEED OUR HELP!
SCOUTER'S RIGHT. WHO KNOWS HOW MANY HUMANS THEY HAVE TO FACE? AND WITH TWO-EDGE TEACHING THEM ABOUT BRIGHT-METAL, THEY'RE SURE TO HAVE WEAPONS WE DON'T EXPECT!
AND WINNOWILL.
WHAT?
THE DREAMS--THE ONES I WAS HAVING IN THE WOODS--THEY HAVEN'T STOPPED.
SOMEHOW, THE LOVELESS ONE'S HAND IS UPON THEM.

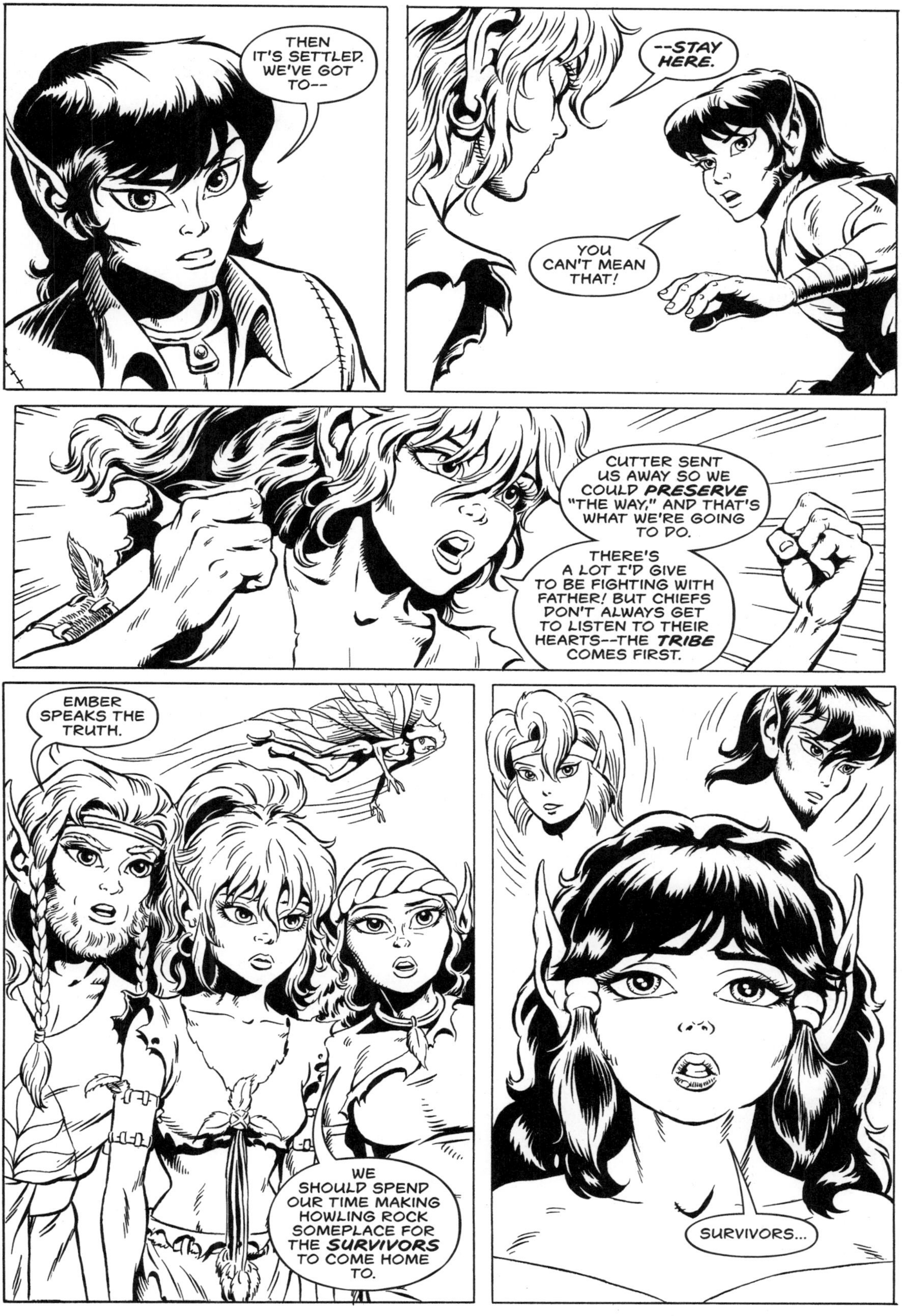
THEN IT'S SETTLED. WE'VE GOT TO--
--STAY HERE.
YOU CAN'T MEAN THAT!
CUTTER SENT US AWAY SO WE COULD PRESERVE "THE WAY," AND THAT'S WHAT WE'RE GOING TO DO.
THERE'S A LOT I'D GIVE TO BE FIGHTING WITH FATHER! BUT CHIEFS DON'T ALWAYS GET TO LISTEN TO THEIR HEARTS--THE TRIBE COMES FIRST.
EMBER SPEAKS THE TRUTH.
WE SHOULD SPEND OUR TIME MAKING HOWLING ROCK SOMEPLACE FOR THE SURVIVORS TO COME HOME TO.
SURVIVORS...

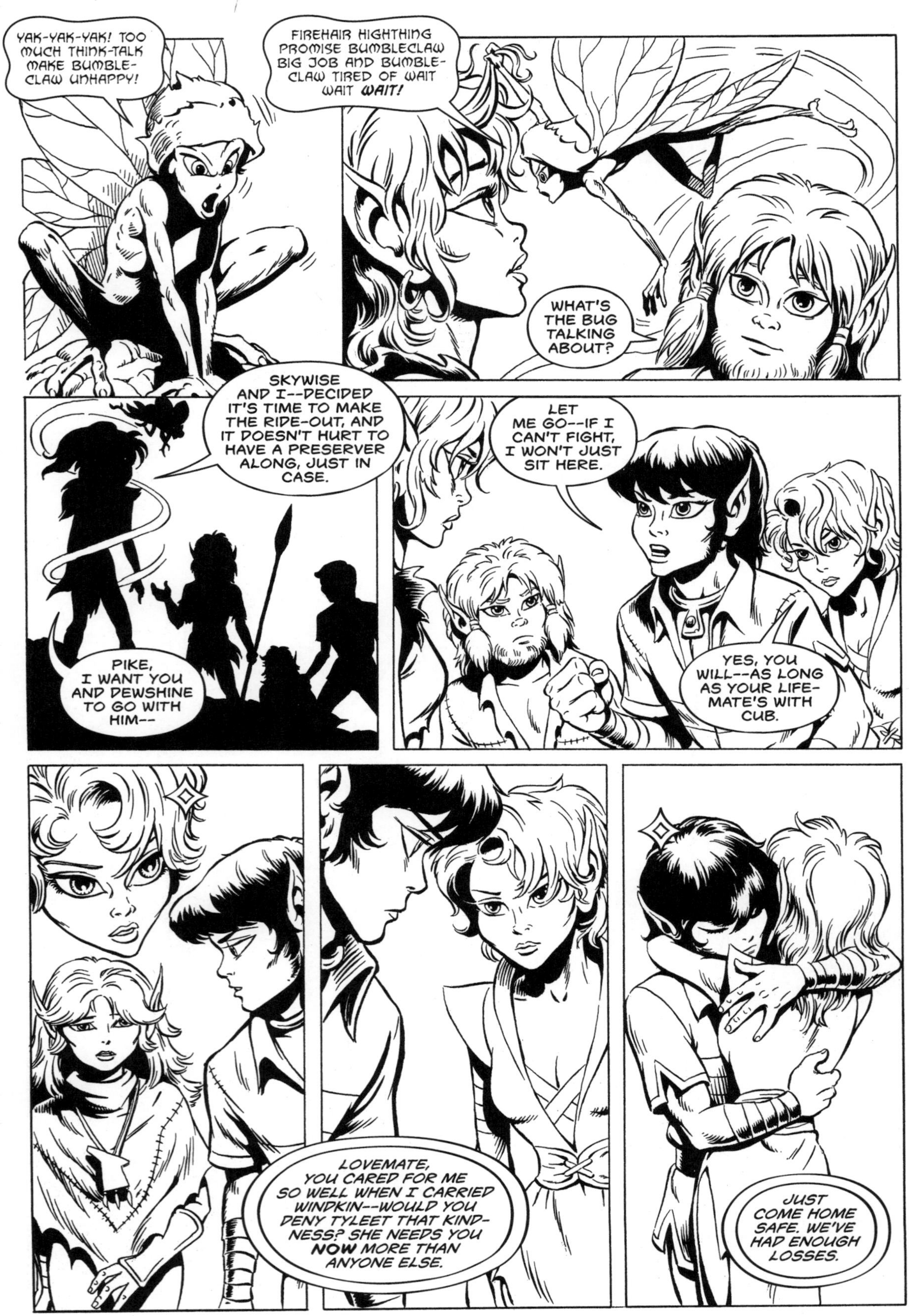
YAK-YAK-YAK! TOO MUCH THINK-TALK MAKE BUMBLE-CLAW UNHAPPY!
FIREHAIR HIGHTHING PROMISE BUMBLECLAW BIG JOB AND BUMBLE-CLAW TIRED OF WAIT WAIT **WAIT!**
WHAT'S THE BUG TALKING ABOUT?
SKYWISE AND I--DECIDED IT'S TIME TO MAKE THE RIDE-OUT, AND IT DOESN'T HURT TO HAVE A PRESERVER ALONG, JUST IN CASE.
PIKE, I WANT YOU AND DEWSHINE TO GO WITH HIM--
LET ME GO--IF I CAN'T FIGHT, I WON'T JUST SIT HERE.
YES, YOU WILL--AS LONG AS YOUR LIFE-MATE'S WITH CUB.
LOVEMATE, YOU CARED FOR ME SO WELL WHEN I CARRIED WINDKIN--WOULD YOU DENY TYLEET THAT KIND-NESS? SHE NEEDS YOU ***NOW*** *MORE THAN ANYONE ELSE.*
JUST COME HOME SAFE. WE'VE HAD ENOUGH LOSSES.

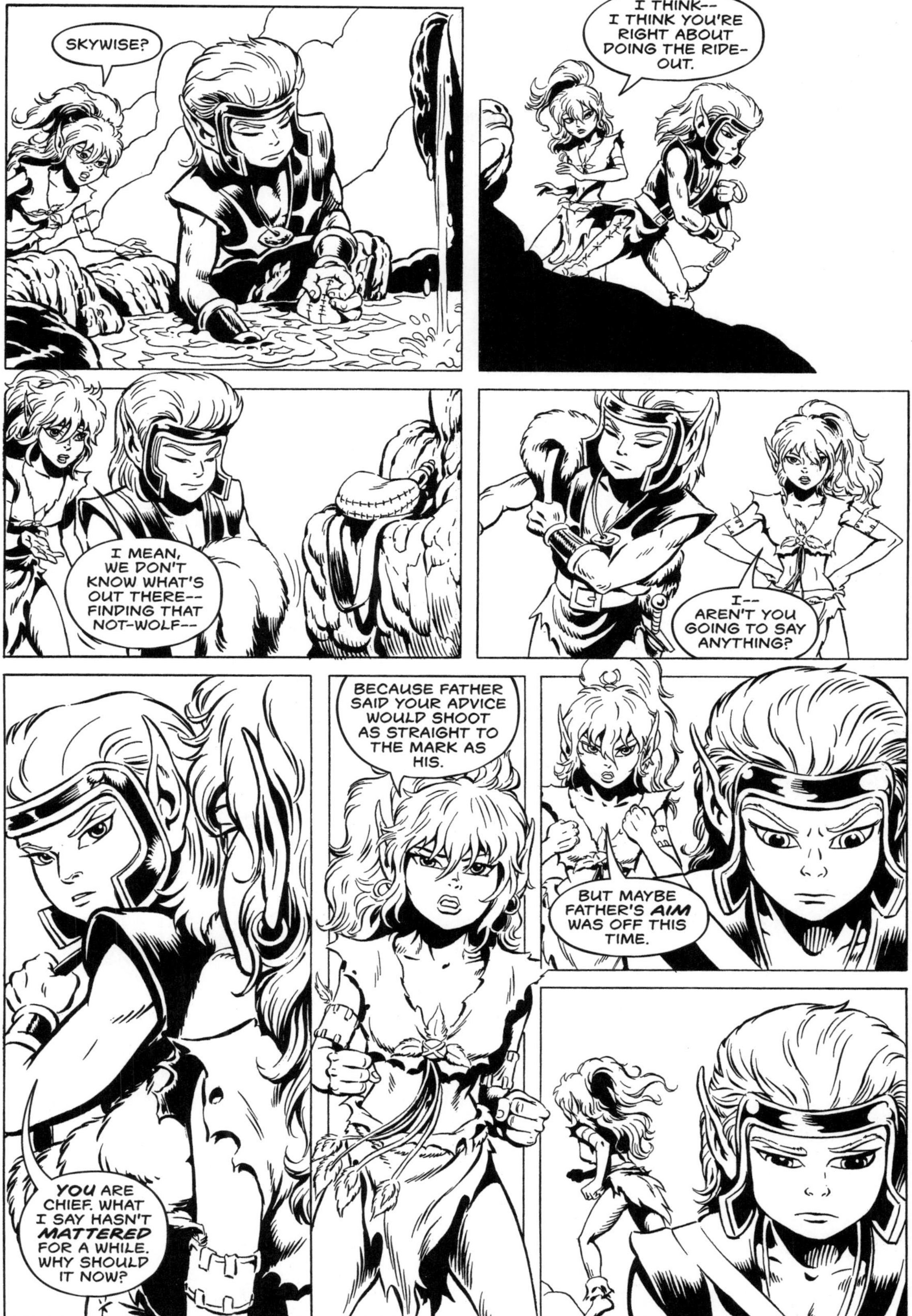
SKYWISE?
I THINK-- I THINK YOU'RE RIGHT ABOUT DOING THE RIDE-OUT.
I MEAN, WE DON'T KNOW WHAT'S OUT THERE-- FINDING THAT NOT-WOLF--
I-- AREN'T YOU GOING TO SAY ANYTHING?
YOU ARE CHIEF. WHAT I SAY HASN'T MATTERED FOR A WHILE. WHY SHOULD IT NOW?
BECAUSE FATHER SAID YOUR ADVICE WOULD SHOOT AS STRAIGHT TO THE MARK AS HIS.
BUT MAYBE FATHER'S AIM WAS OFF THIS TIME.

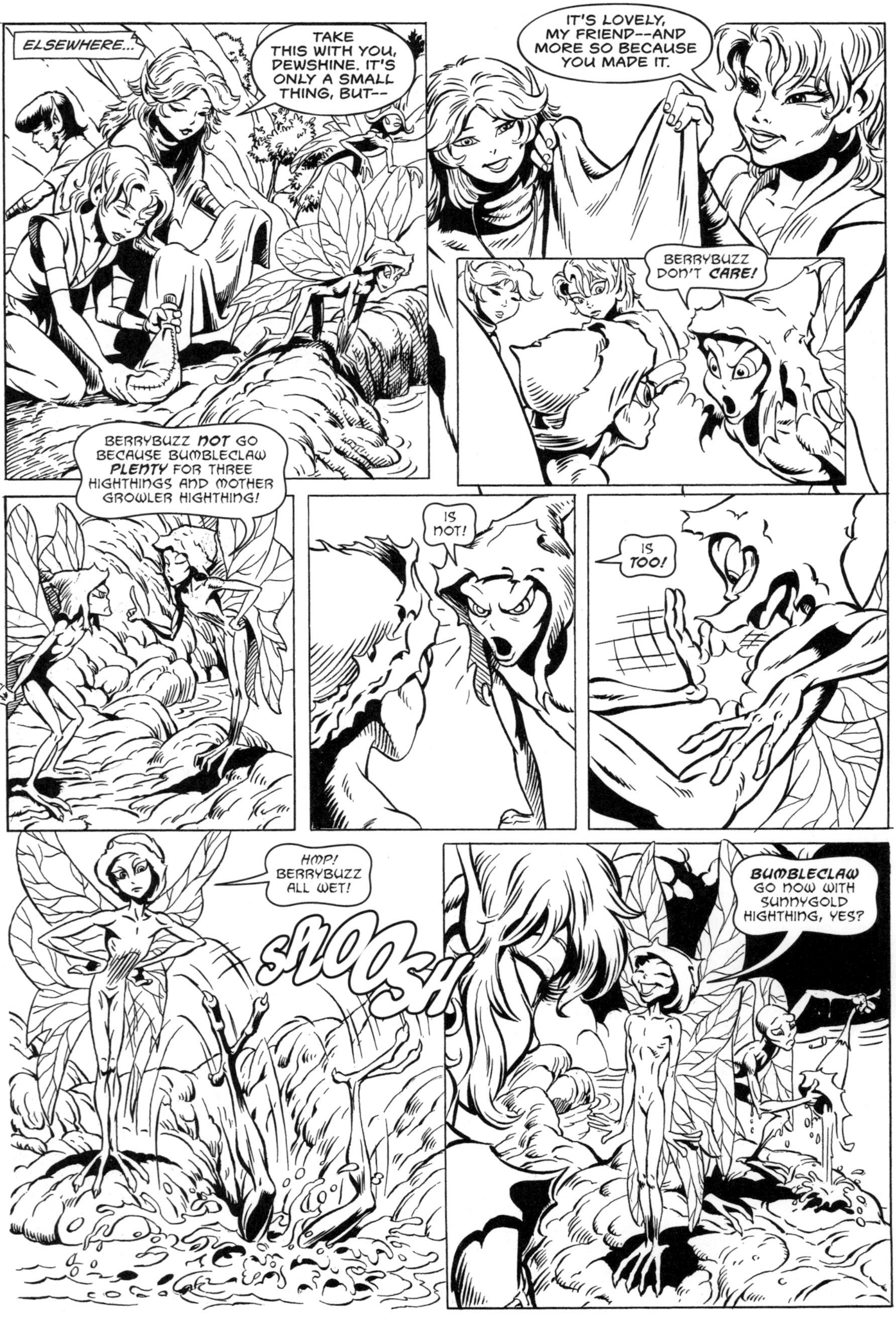
ELSEWHERE...
TAKE THIS WITH YOU, DEWSHINE. IT'S ONLY A SMALL THING, BUT--
IT'S LOVELY, MY FRIEND--AND MORE SO BECAUSE YOU MADE IT.
BERRYBUZZ DON'T CARE!
BERRYBUZZ NOT GO BECAUSE BUMBLECLAW PLENTY FOR THREE HIGHTHINGS AND MOTHER GROWLER HIGHTHING!
IS NOT!
IS TOO!
HMP! BERRYBUZZ ALL WET!
SHOOSH
BUMBLECLAW GO NOW WITH SUNNYGOLD HIGHTHING, YES?

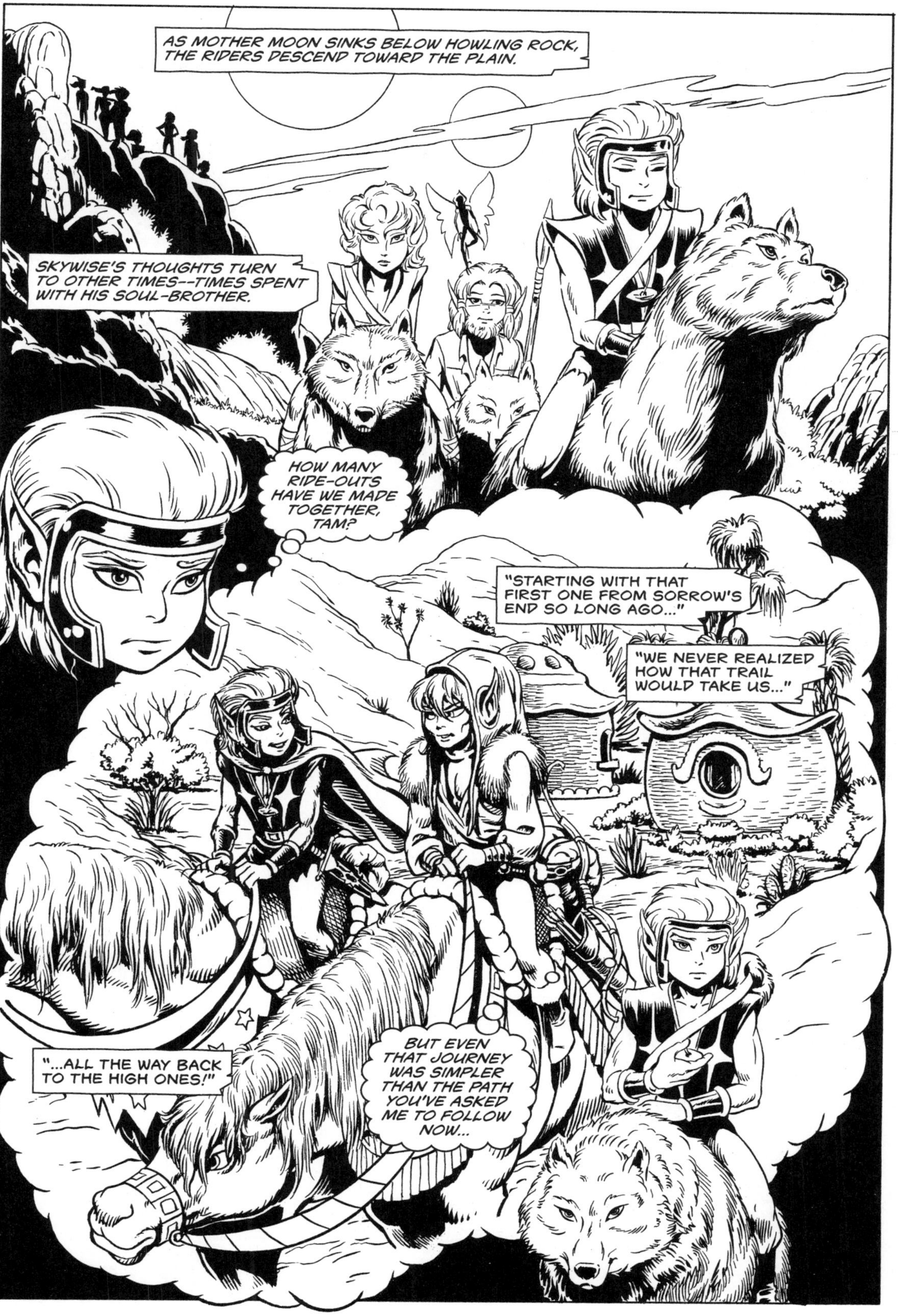
AS MOTHER MOON SINKS BELOW HOWLING ROCK, THE RIDERS DESCEND TOWARD THE PLAIN.
SKYWISE'S THOUGHTS TURN TO OTHER TIMES--TIMES SPENT WITH HIS SOUL-BROTHER.
HOW MANY RIDE-OUTS HAVE WE MADE TOGETHER, TAM?
"STARTING WITH THAT FIRST ONE FROM SORROW'S END SO LONG AGO..."
"WE NEVER REALIZED HOW THAT TRAIL WOULD TAKE US..."
"...ALL THE WAY BACK TO THE HIGH ONES!"
BUT EVEN THAT JOURNEY WAS SIMPLER THAN THE PATH YOU'VE ASKED ME TO FOLLOW NOW...

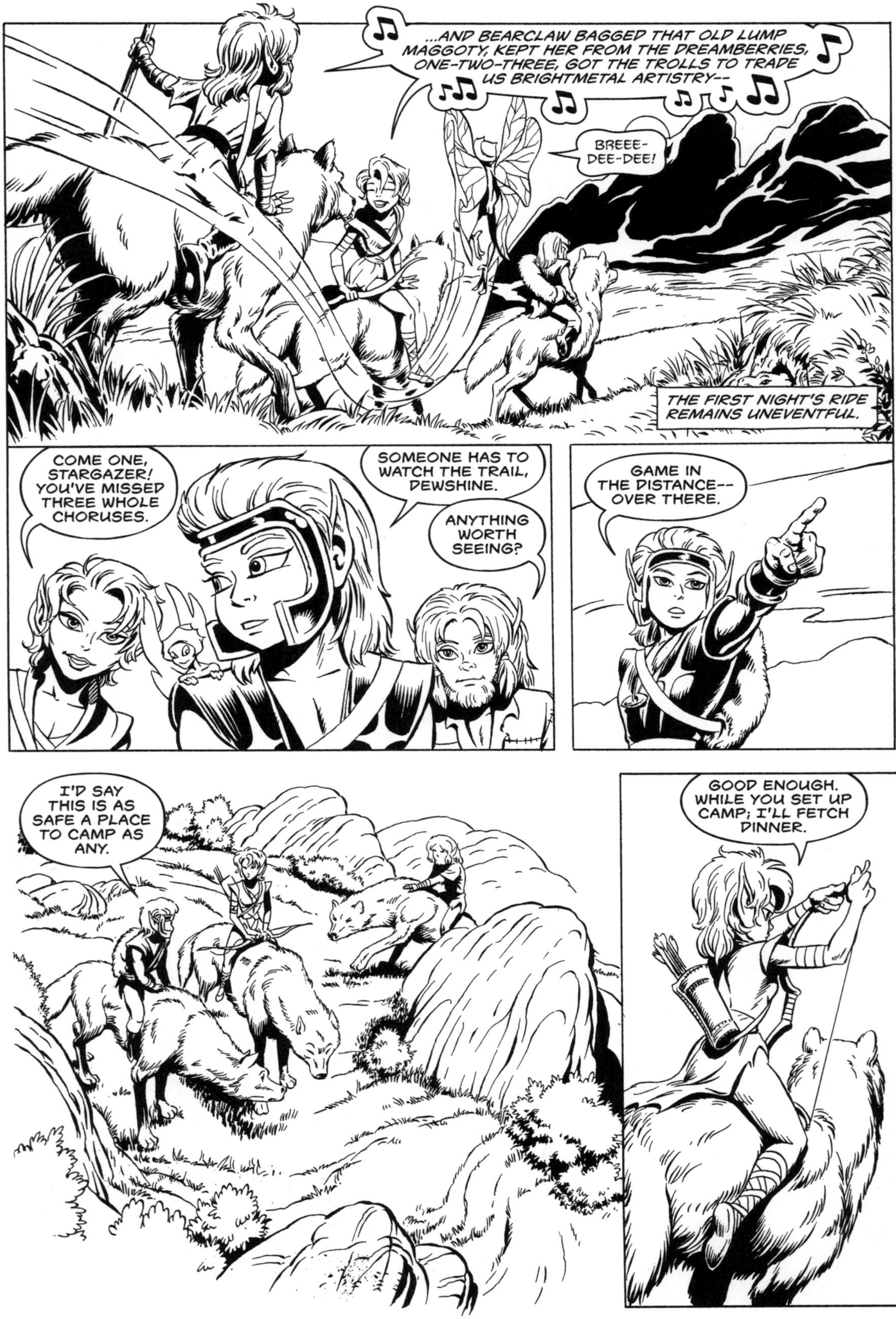
...AND BEARCLAW BAGGED THAT OLD LUMP MAGGOTY, KEPT HER FROM THE DREAMBERRIES, ONE-TWO-THREE, GOT THE TROLLS TO TRADE US BRIGHTMETAL ARTISTRY--
BREEE-DEE-DEE!
THE FIRST NIGHT'S RIDE REMAINS UNEVENTFUL.
COME ONE, STARGAZER! YOU'VE MISSED THREE WHOLE CHORUSES.
SOMEONE HAS TO WATCH THE TRAIL, DEWSHINE.
ANYTHING WORTH SEEING?
GAME IN THE DISTANCE-- OVER THERE.
I'D SAY THIS IS AS SAFE A PLACE TO CAMP AS ANY.
GOOD ENOUGH. WHILE YOU SET UP CAMP; I'LL FETCH DINNER.

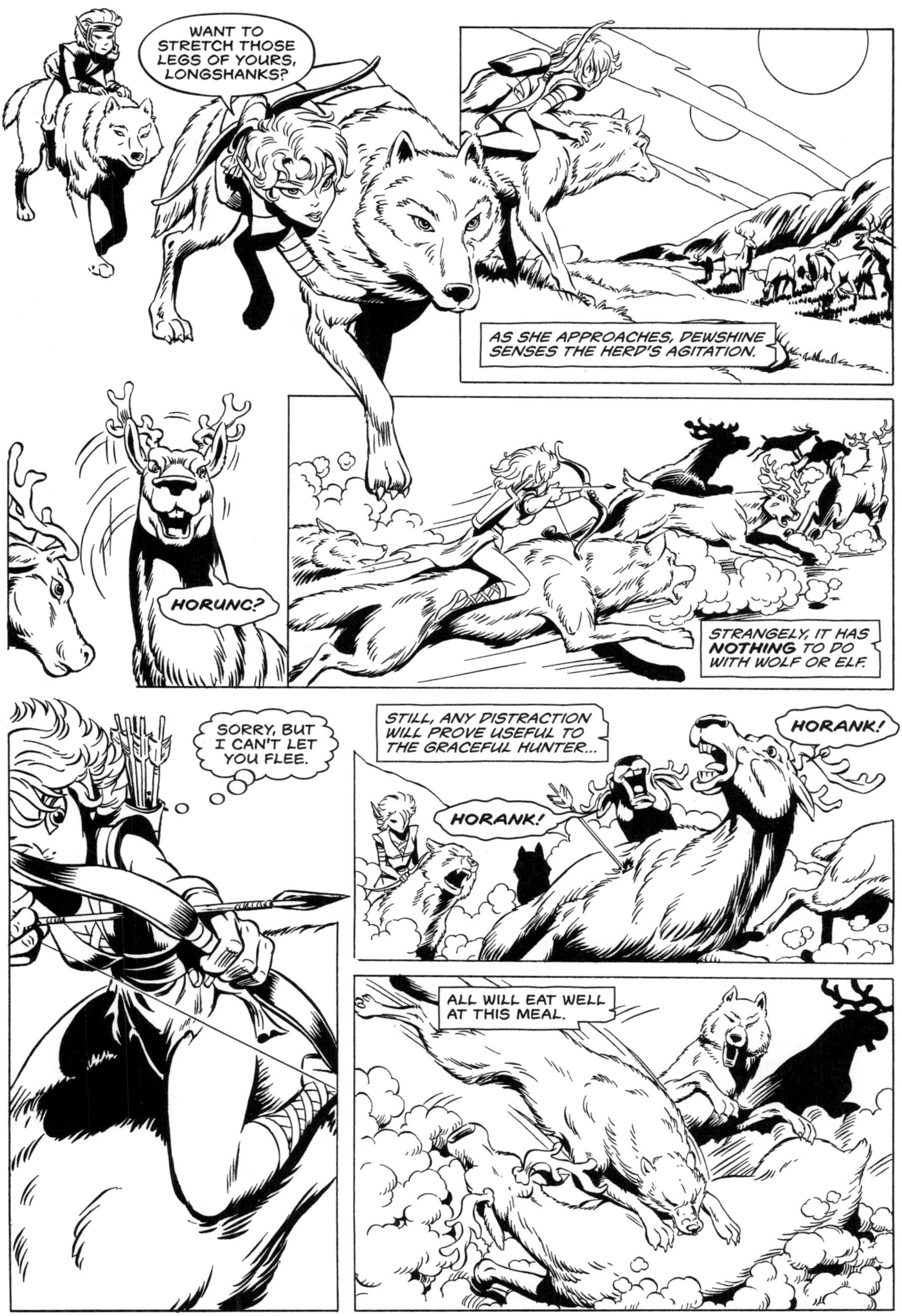

WANT TO STRETCH THOSE LEGS OF YOURS, LONGSHANKS?
AS SHE APPROACHES, DEWSHINE SENSES THE HERD'S AGITATION.
HORUNC?
STRANGELY, IT HAS NOTHING TO DO WITH WOLF OR ELF.
SORRY, BUT I CAN'T LET YOU FLEE.
STILL, ANY DISTRACTION WILL PROVE USEFUL TO THE GRACEFUL HUNTER...
HORANK!
HORANK!
ALL WILL EAT WELL AT THIS MEAL.

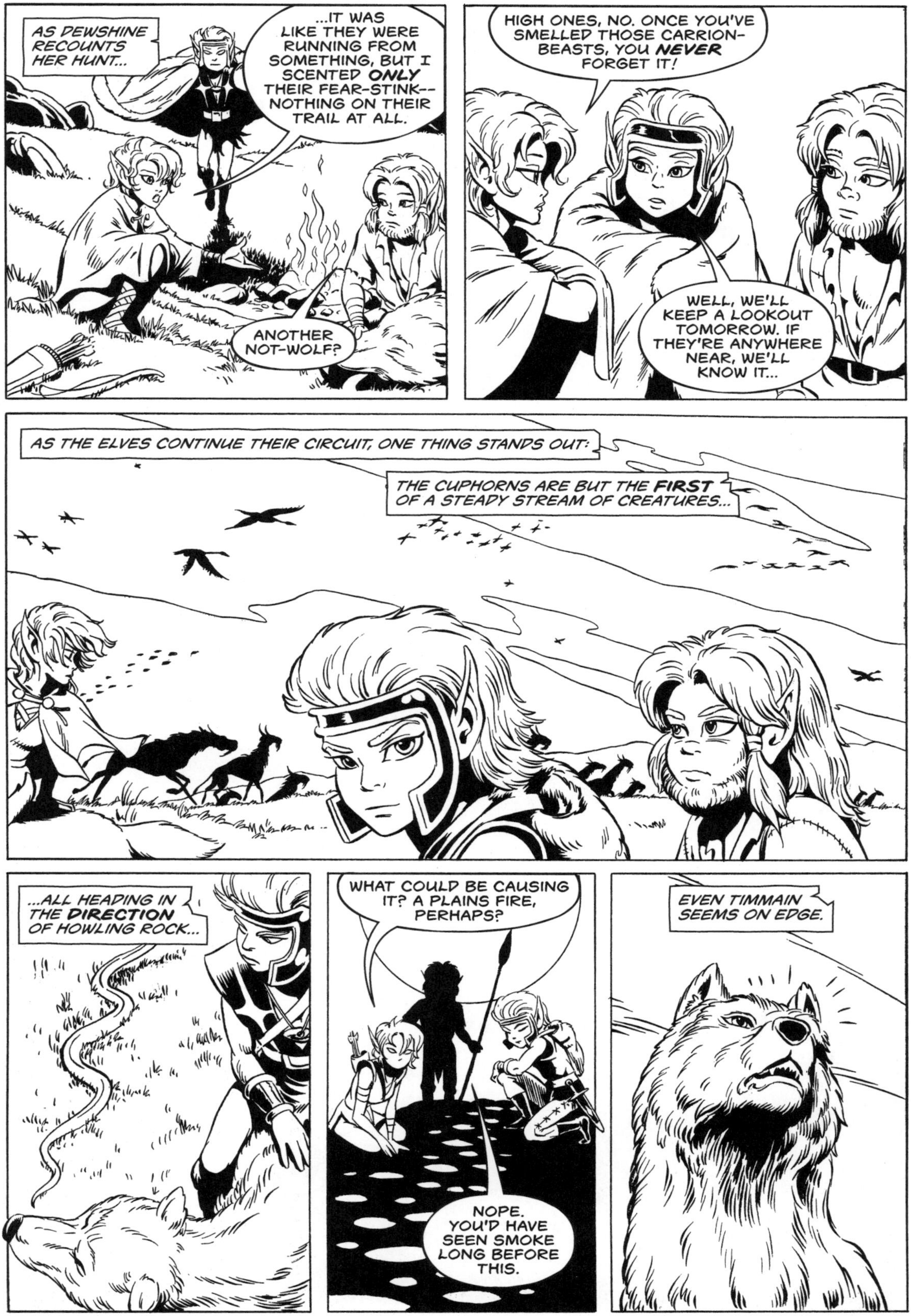

AS DEWSHINE RECOUNTS HER HUNT...
...IT WAS LIKE THEY WERE RUNNING FROM SOMETHING, BUT I SCENTED **ONLY** THEIR FEAR-STINK-- NOTHING ON THEIR TRAIL AT ALL.
ANOTHER NOT-WOLF?
HIGH ONES, NO. ONCE YOU'VE SMELLED THOSE CARRION-BEASTS, YOU **NEVER** FORGET IT!
WELL, WE'LL KEEP A LOOKOUT TOMORROW. IF THEY'RE ANYWHERE NEAR, WE'LL KNOW IT...
AS THE ELVES CONTINUE THEIR CIRCUIT, ONE THING STANDS OUT:
THE CUPHORNS ARE BUT THE **FIRST** OF A STEADY STREAM OF CREATURES...
...ALL HEADING IN THE **DIRECTION** OF HOWLING ROCK...
WHAT COULD BE CAUSING IT? A PLAINS FIRE, PERHAPS?
NOPE. YOU'D HAVE SEEN SMOKE LONG BEFORE THIS.
EVEN TIMMAIN SEEMS ON EDGE.

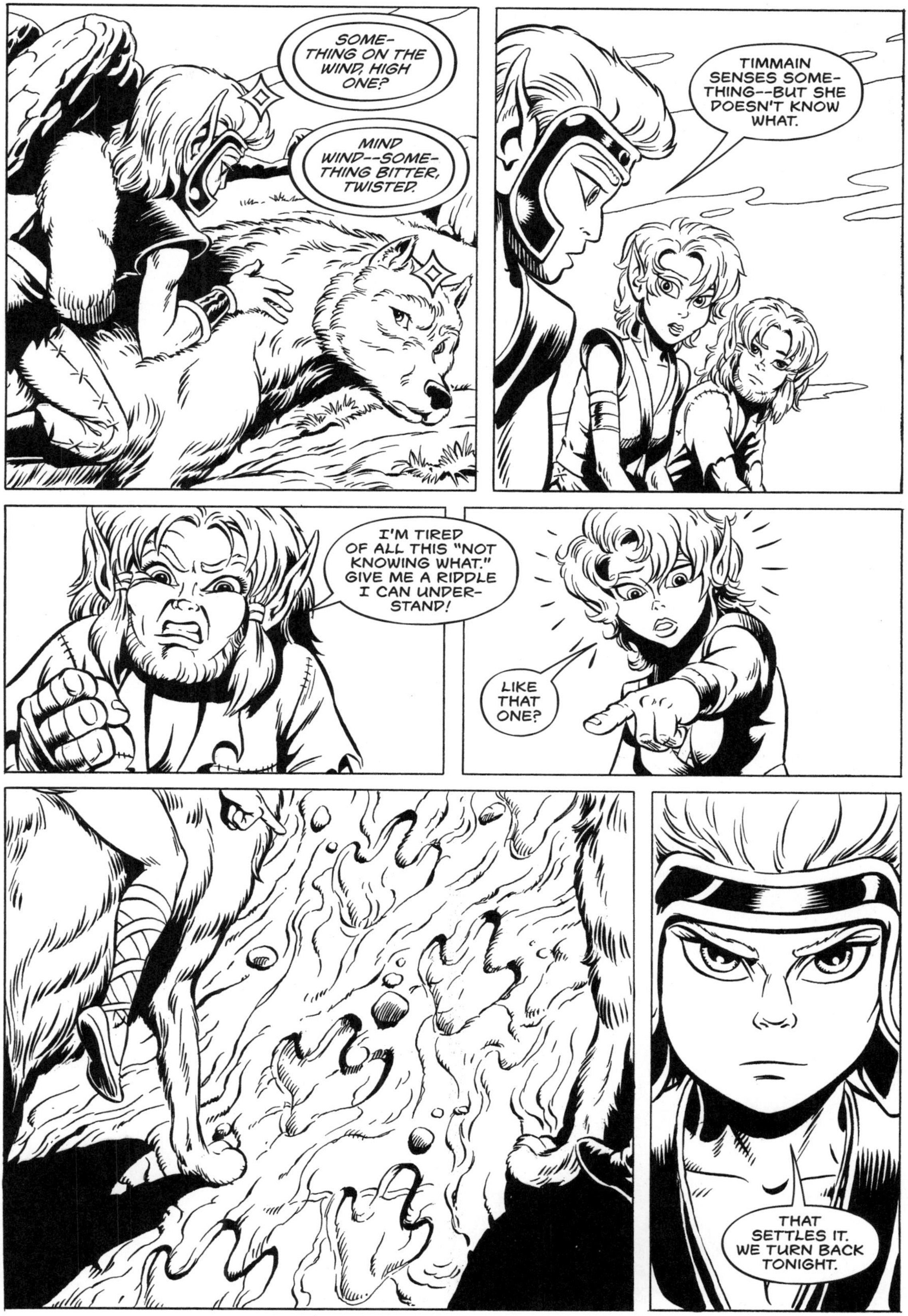
SOME-THING ON THE WIND, HIGH ONE?
MIND WIND--SOME-THING BITTER, TWISTED.
TIMMAIN SENSES SOME-THING--BUT SHE DOESN'T KNOW WHAT.
I'M TIRED OF ALL THIS "NOT KNOWING WHAT." GIVE ME A RIDDLE I CAN UNDER-STAND!
LIKE THAT ONE?
THAT SETTLES IT. WE TURN BACK TONIGHT.

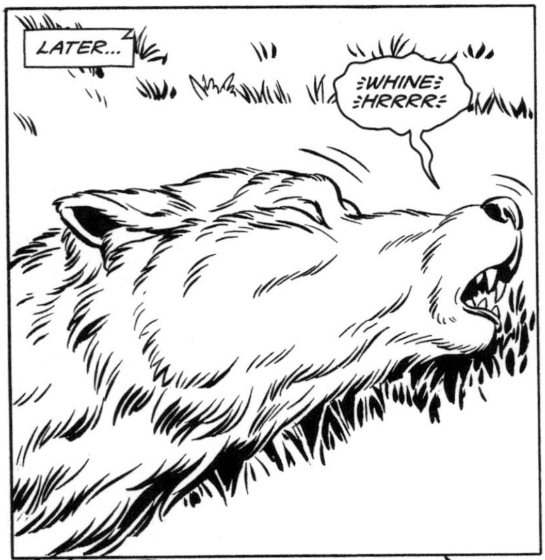
LATER...
:WHINE: HRRRR:

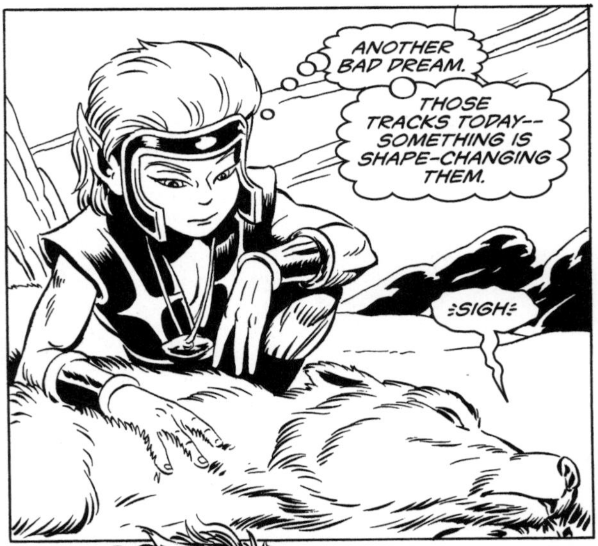
ANOTHER BAD DREAM.
THOSE TRACKS TODAY-- SOMETHING IS SHAPE-CHANGING THEM.
:SIGH:

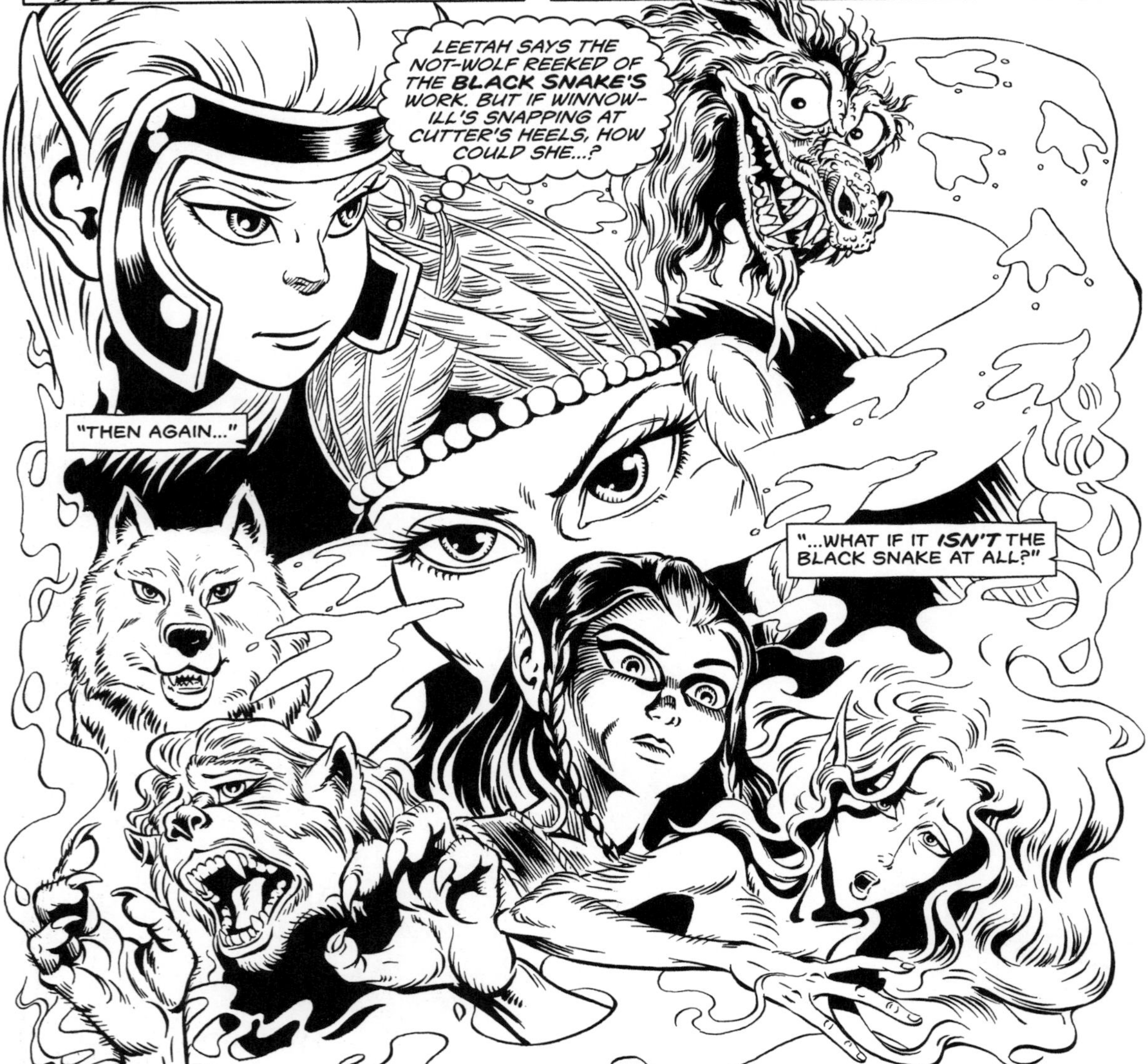
LEETAH SAYS THE NOT-WOLF REEKED OF THE BLACK SNAKE'S WORK. BUT IF WINNOW-ILL'S SNAPPING AT CUTTER'S HEELS, HOW COULD SHE...?
"THEN AGAIN..."
"...WHAT IF IT ISN'T THE BLACK SNAKE AT ALL?"

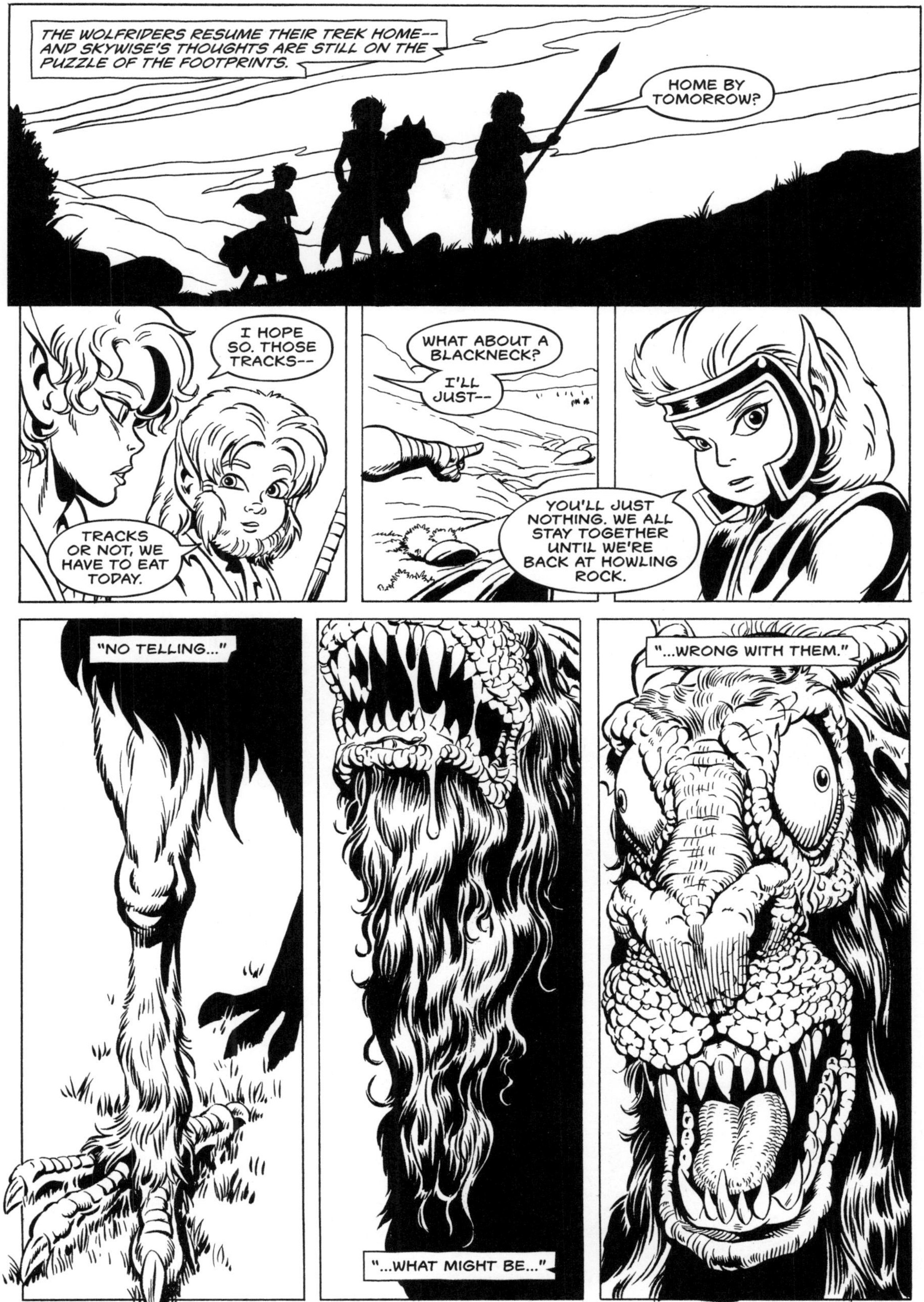

THE WOLFRIDERS RESUME THEIR TREK HOME-- AND SKYWISE'S THOUGHTS ARE STILL ON THE PUZZLE OF THE FOOTPRINTS.
HOME BY TOMORROW?
I HOPE SO. THOSE TRACKS--
TRACKS OR NOT, WE HAVE TO EAT TODAY.
WHAT ABOUT A BLACKNECK?
I'LL JUST--
YOU'LL JUST NOTHING. WE ALL STAY TOGETHER UNTIL WE'RE BACK AT HOWLING ROCK.
"NO TELLING..."
"...WHAT MIGHT BE..."
"...WRONG WITH THEM."

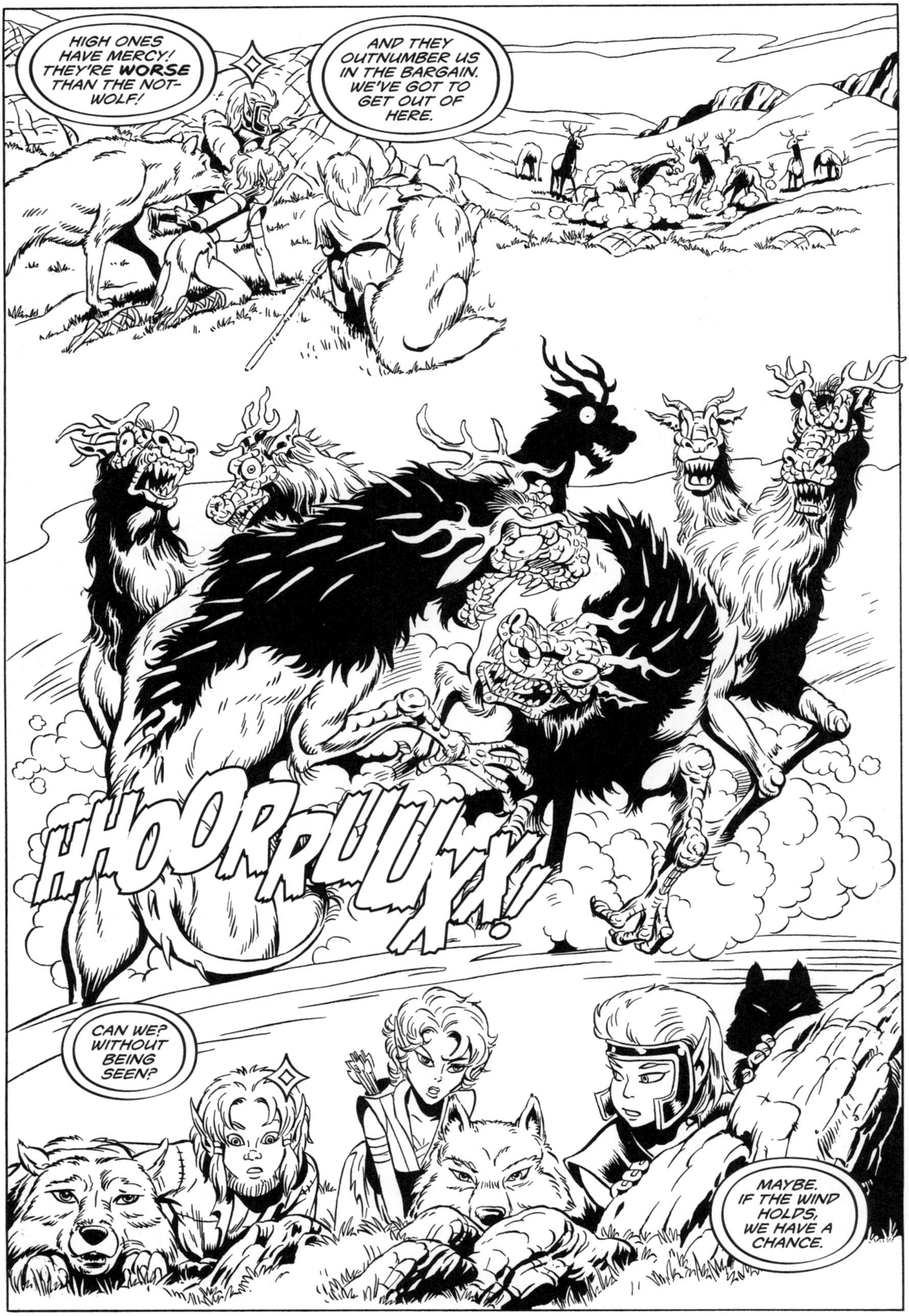
HIGH ONES HAVE MERCY! THEY'RE **WORSE** THAN THE NOT-WOLF!
AND THEY OUTNUMBER US IN THE BARGAIN. WE'VE GOT TO GET OUT OF HERE.
HHOORRRUUUXX!
CAN WE? WITHOUT BEING SEEN?
MAYBE. IF THE WIND HOLDS, WE HAVE A CHANCE.

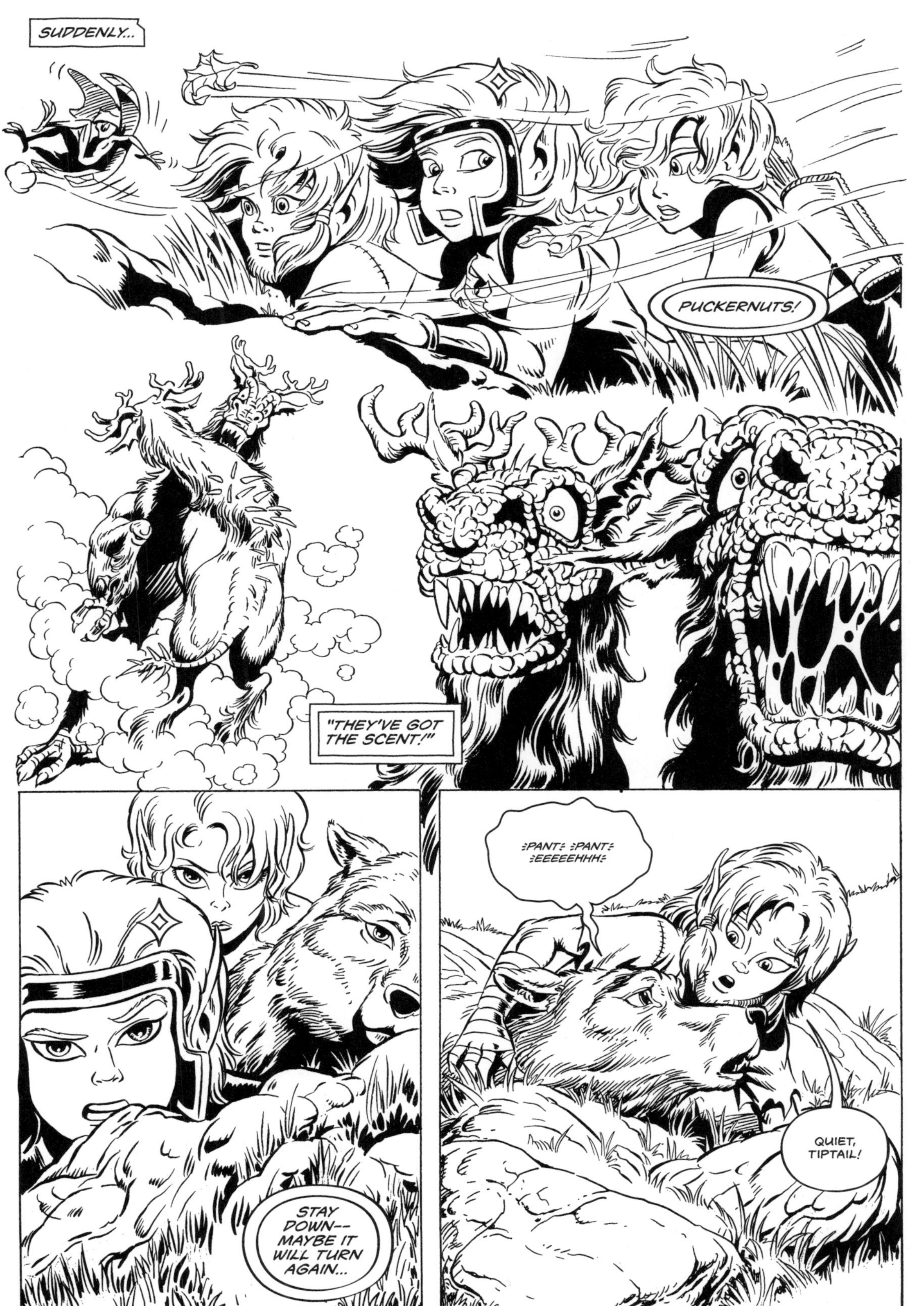
SUDDENLY...
PUCKERNUTS!
"THEY'VE GOT THE SCENT!"
STAY DOWN-- MAYBE IT WILL TURN AGAIN...
PANT PANT EEEEEHHH
QUIET, TIPTAIL!

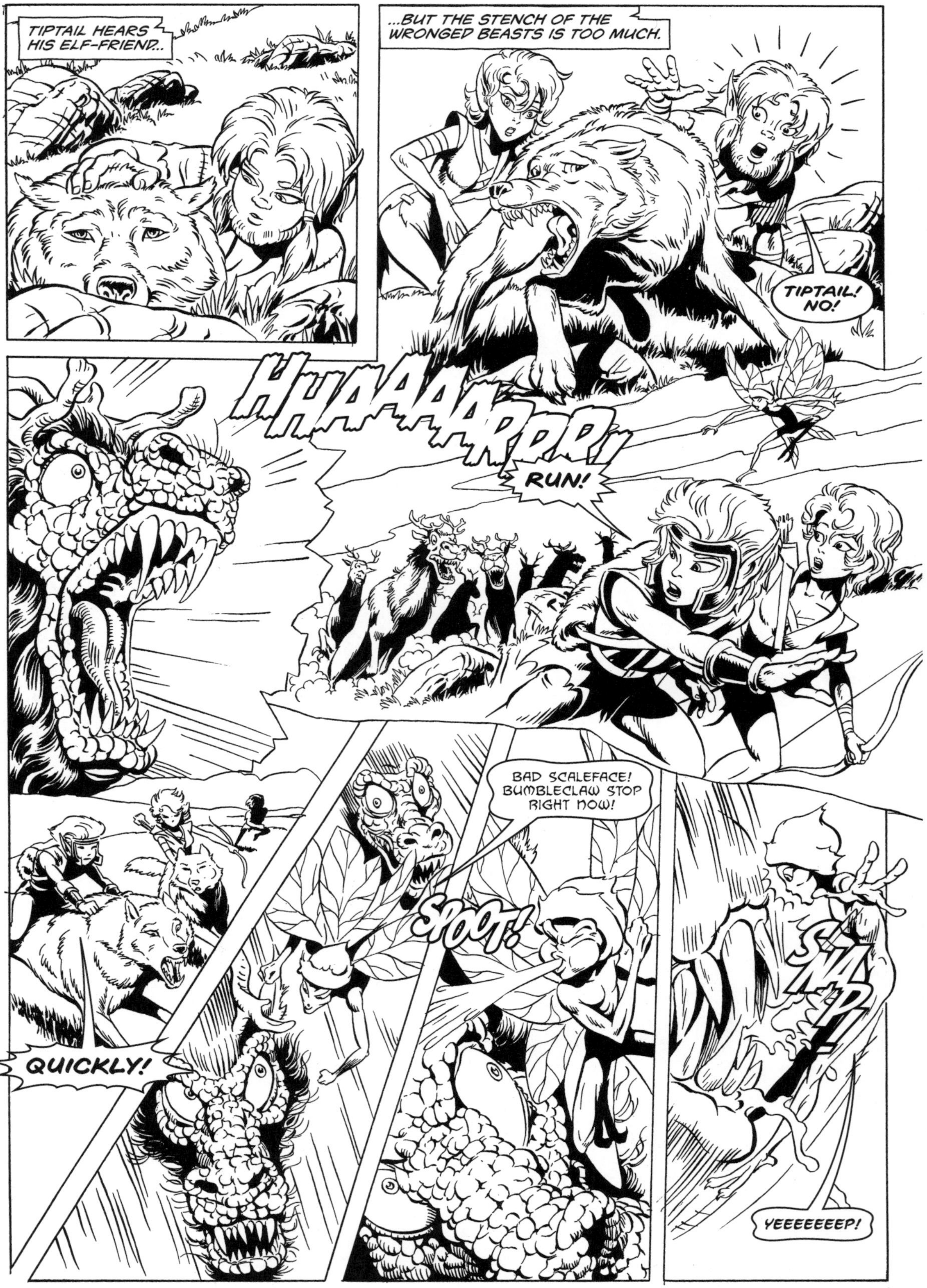

TIPTAIL HEARS HIS ELF-FRIEND...
...BUT THE STENCH OF THE WRONGED BEASTS IS TOO MUCH.
TIPTAIL! NO!
HHAAAARRR!
RUN!
QUICKLY!
BAD SCALEFACE! BUMBLECLAW STOP RIGHT NOW!
SPOOT!
SNAP!
YEEEEEEEP!

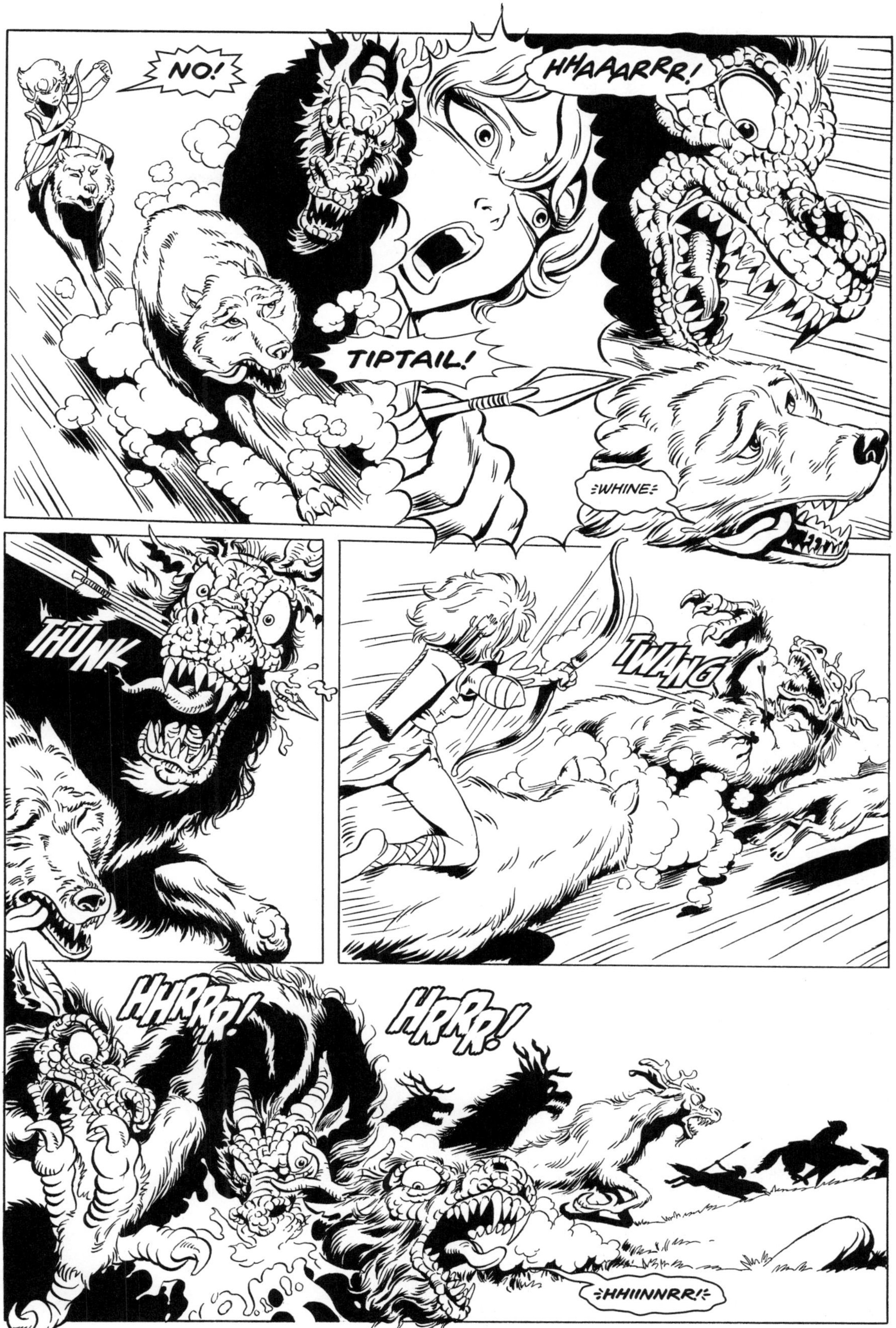
NO!
HHAAARRR!
TIPTAIL!
WHINE
THUNK
TWANG
HHRRR!
HRRR!
HHIINNRR!

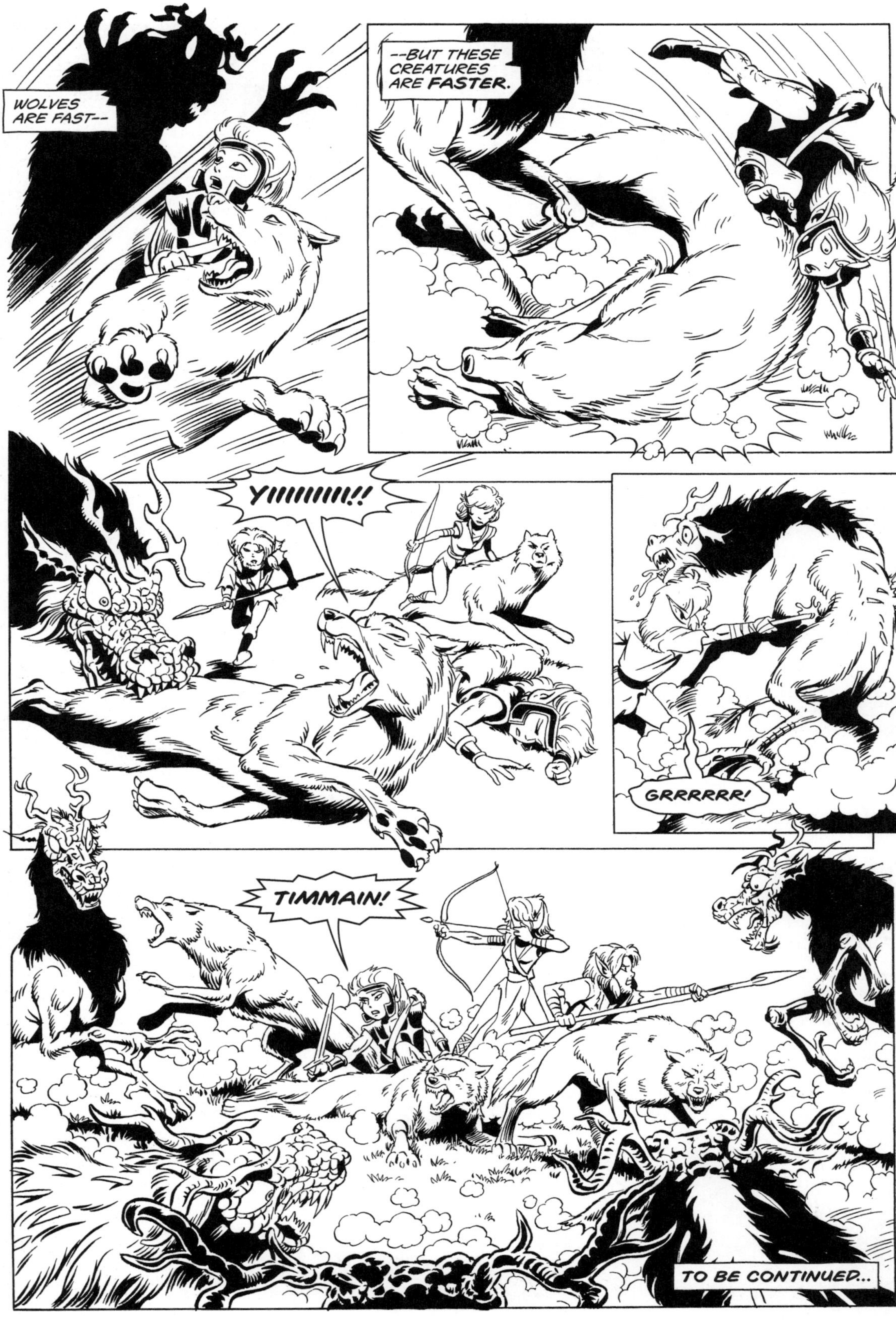
WOLVES ARE FAST--
--BUT THESE CREATURES ARE FASTER.
YIIIIIIIII!!
GRRRRRR!
TIMMAIN!
TO BE CONTINUED...

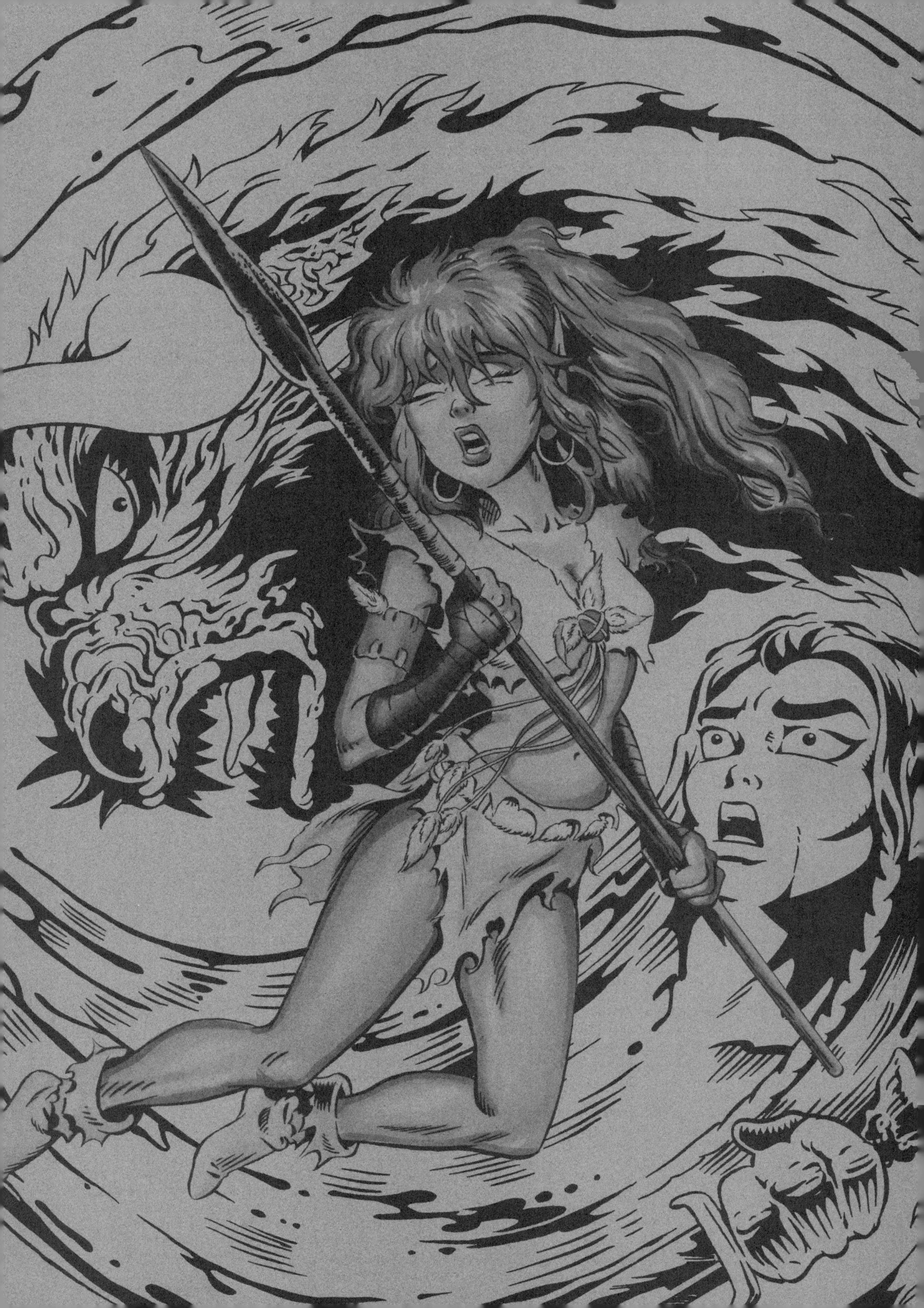

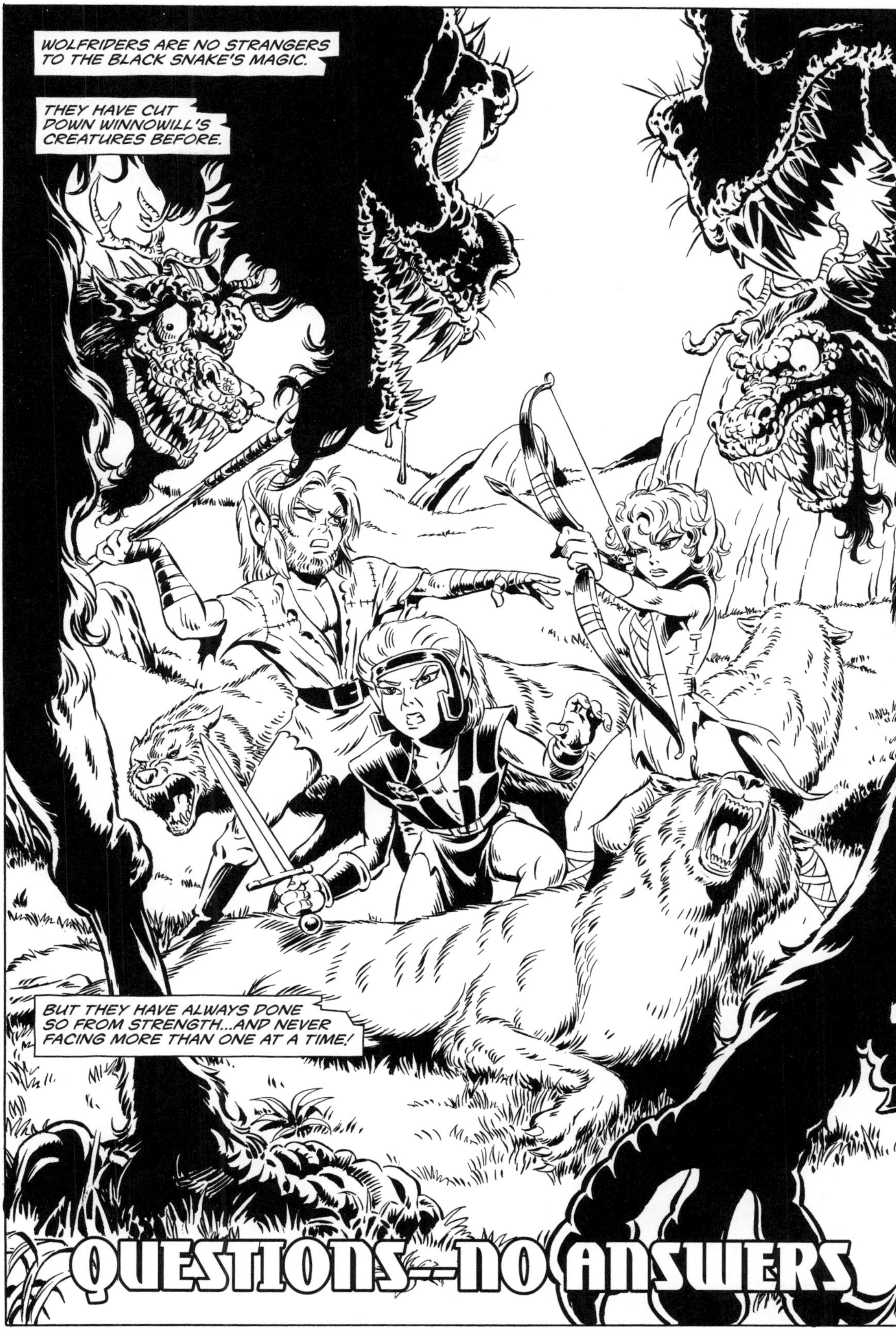
WOLFRIDERS ARE NO STRANGERS TO THE BLACK SNAKE'S MAGIC.
THEY HAVE CUT DOWN WINNOWILL'S CREATURES BEFORE.
BUT THEY HAVE ALWAYS DONE SO FROM STRENGTH...AND NEVER FACING MORE THAN ONE AT A TIME!
QUESTIONS--NO ANSWERS

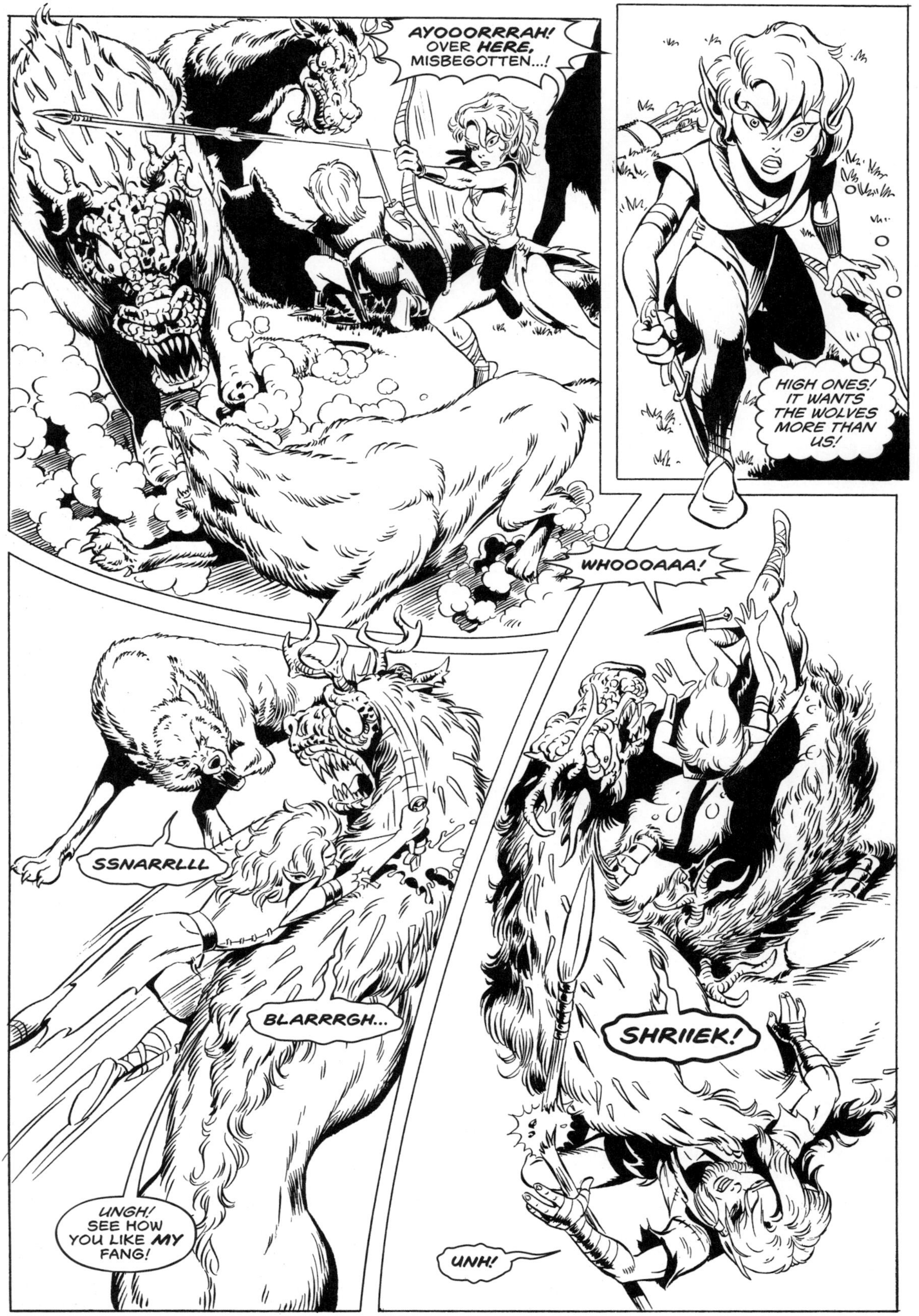
AYOOORRRAH! OVER HERE, MISBEGOTTEN...!
HIGH ONES! IT WANTS THE WOLVES MORE THAN US!
WHOOOAAA!
SSNARRLLL
BLARRRGH...
UNGH! SEE HOW YOU LIKE MY FANG!
SHRIIEK!
UNH!

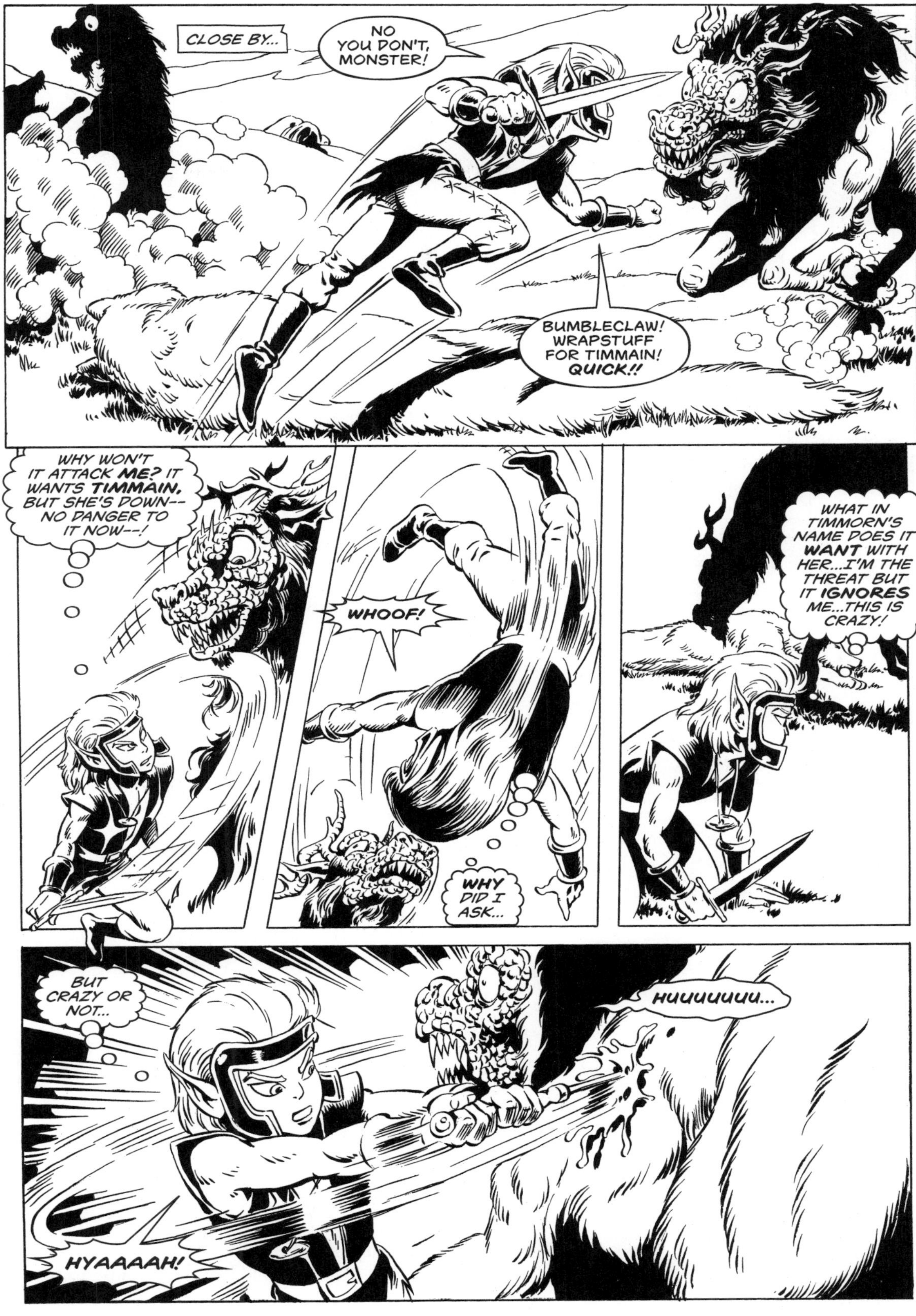
CLOSE BY...
NO YOU DON'T, MONSTER!
BUMBLECLAW! WRAPSTUFF FOR TIMMAIN! QUICK!!
WHY WON'T IT ATTACK ME? IT WANTS TIMMAIN. BUT SHE'S DOWN-- NO DANGER TO IT NOW--!
WHOOF!
WHY DID I ASK...
WHAT IN TIMMORN'S NAME DOES IT WANT WITH HER...I'M THE THREAT BUT IT IGNORES ME...THIS IS CRAZY!
BUT CRAZY OR NOT...
HUUUUUUU...
HYAAAAH!

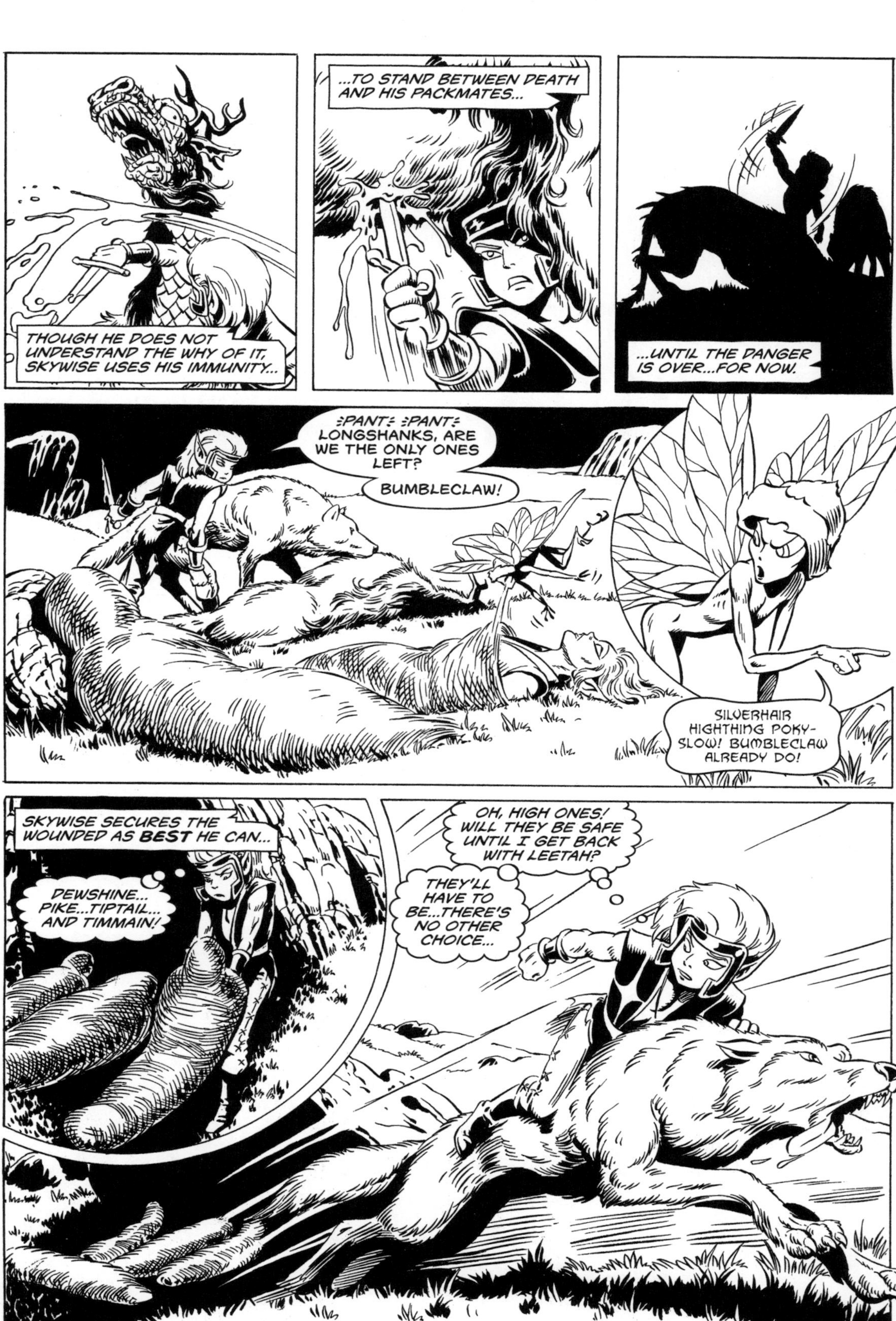

THOUGH HE DOES NOT UNDERSTAND THE WHY OF IT, SKYWISE USES HIS IMMUNITY...
...TO STAND BETWEEN DEATH AND HIS PACKMATES...
...UNTIL THE DANGER IS OVER...FOR NOW.
PANT PANT LONGSHANKS, ARE WE THE ONLY ONES LEFT?
BUMBLECLAW!
SILVERHAIR HIGHTHING POKY-SLOW! BUMBLECLAW ALREADY DO!
SKYWISE SECURES THE WOUNDED AS BEST HE CAN...
DEWSHINE... PIKE...TIPTAIL... AND TIMMAIN!
OH, HIGH ONES! WILL THEY BE SAFE UNTIL I GET BACK WITH LEETAH?
THEY'LL HAVE TO BE...THERE'S NO OTHER CHOICE...

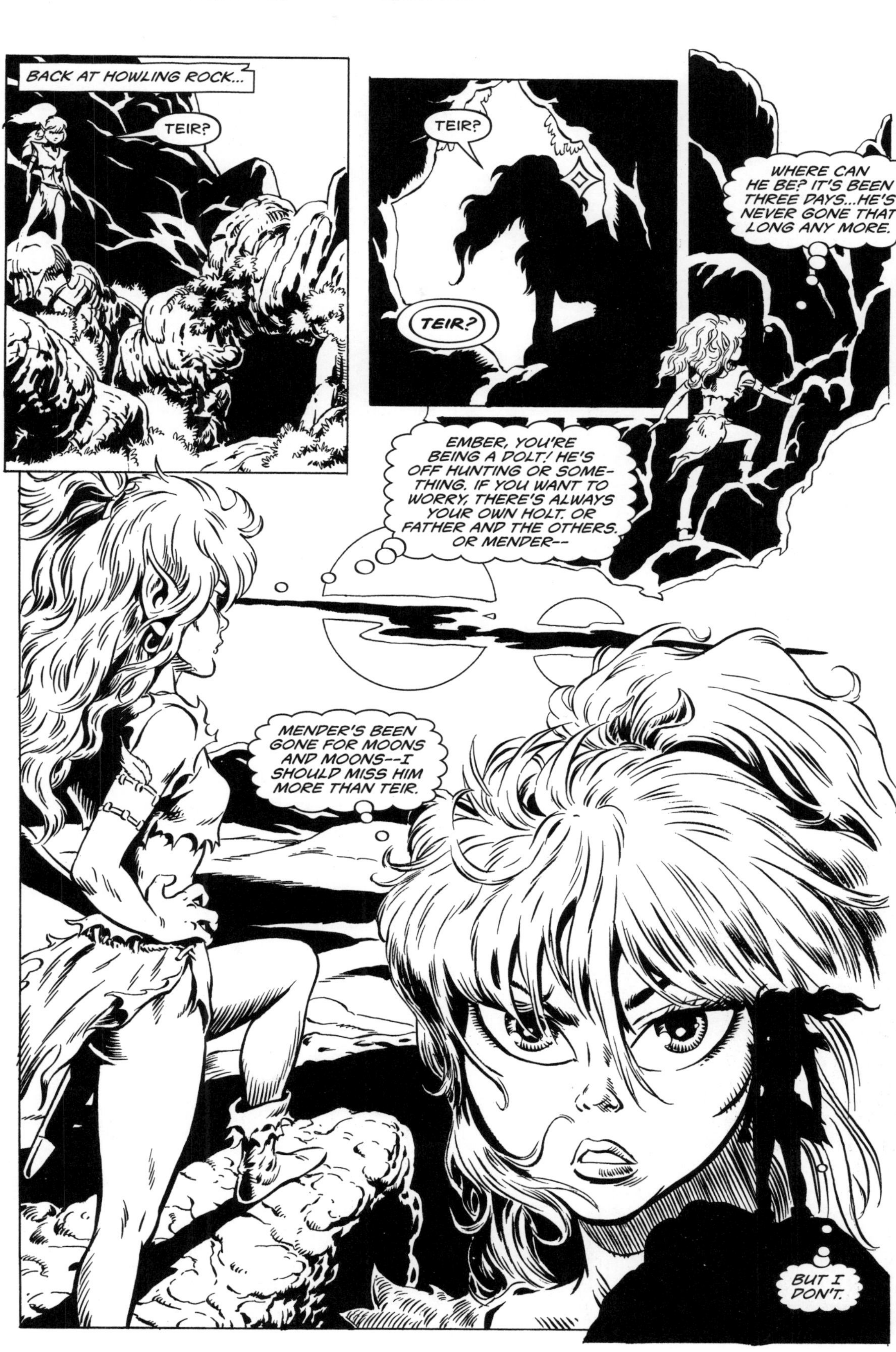
BACK AT HOWLING ROCK...
TEIR?
TEIR?
TEIR?
WHERE CAN HE BE? IT'S BEEN THREE DAYS...HE'S NEVER GONE THAT LONG ANY MORE.
EMBER, YOU'RE BEING A DOLT! HE'S OFF HUNTING OR SOME-THING. IF YOU WANT TO WORRY, THERE'S ALWAYS YOUR OWN HOLT. OR FATHER AND THE OTHERS. OR MENDER--
MENDER'S BEEN GONE FOR MOONS AND MOONS--I SHOULD MISS HIM MORE THAN TEIR.
BUT I DON'T.

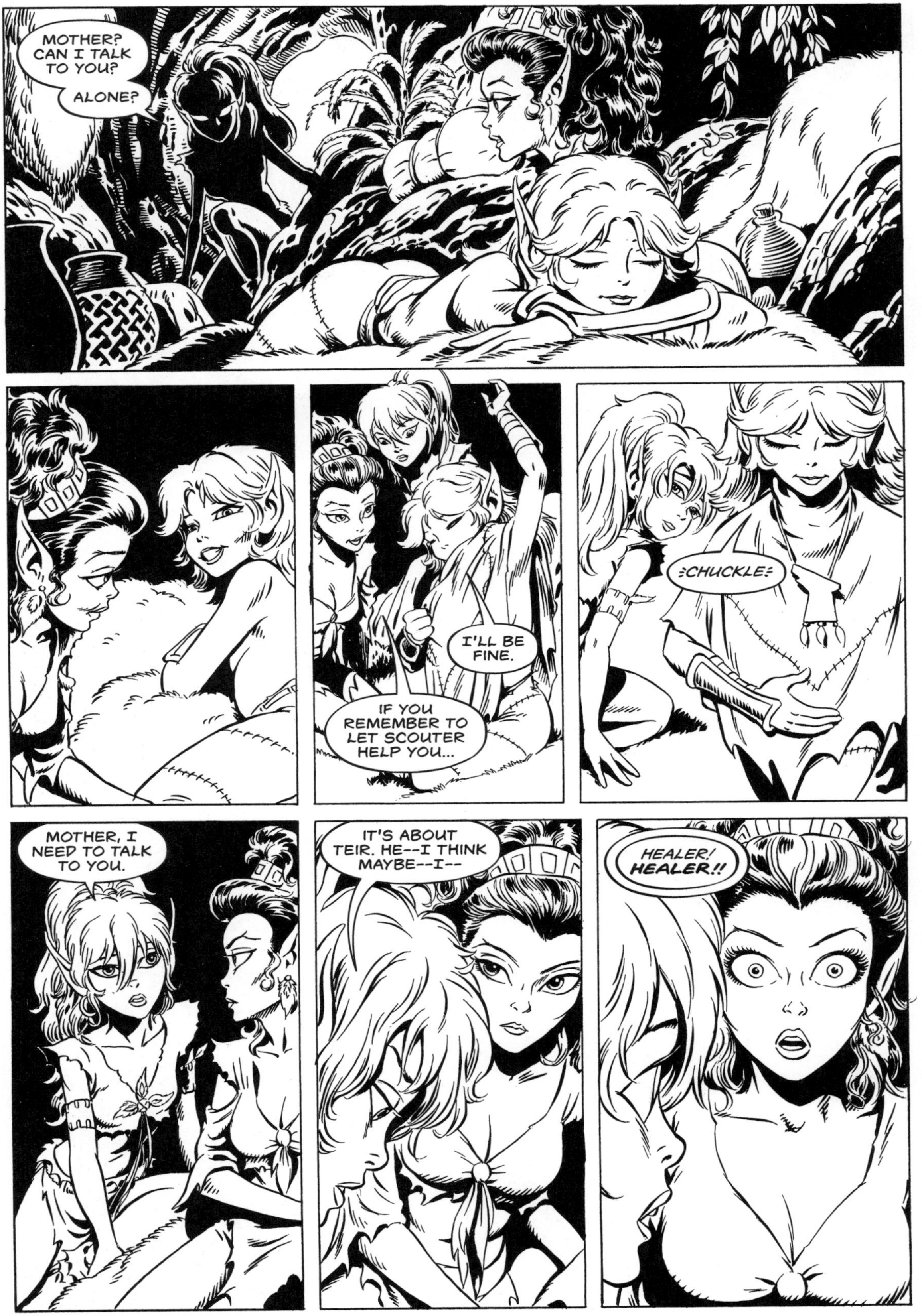
MOTHER? CAN I TALK TO YOU?
ALONE?
I'LL BE FINE.
IF YOU REMEMBER TO LET SCOUTER HELP YOU...
CHUCKLE
MOTHER, I NEED TO TALK TO YOU.
IT'S ABOUT TEIR. HE--I THINK MAYBE--I--
HEALER!
HEALER!!

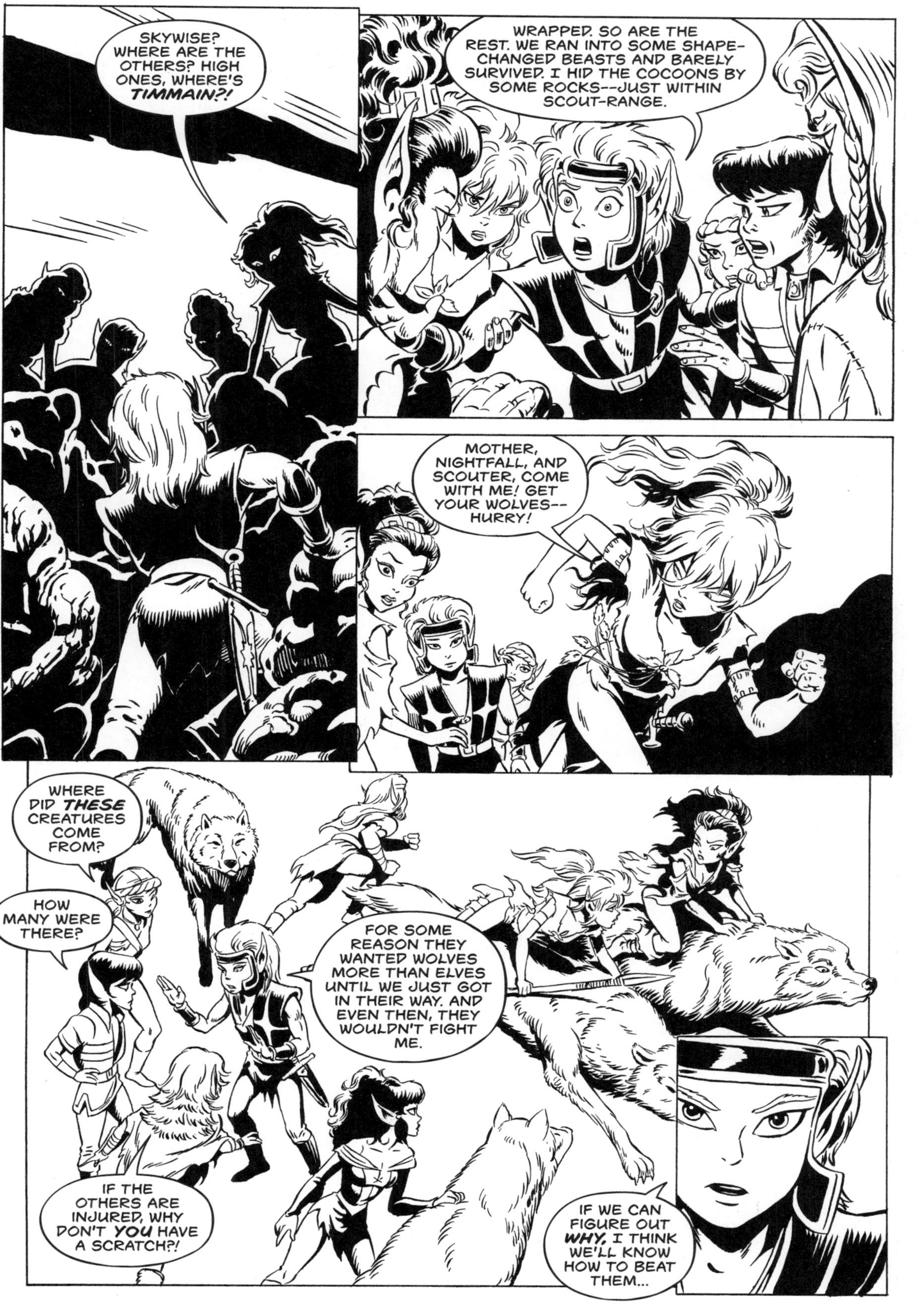

SKYWISE? WHERE ARE THE OTHERS? HIGH ONES, WHERE'S TIMMAIN?!
WRAPPED. SO ARE THE REST. WE RAN INTO SOME SHAPE-CHANGED BEASTS AND BARELY SURVIVED. I HID THE COCOONS BY SOME ROCKS--JUST WITHIN SCOUT-RANGE.
MOTHER, NIGHTFALL, AND SCOUTER, COME WITH ME! GET YOUR WOLVES--HURRY!
WHERE DID THESE CREATURES COME FROM?
HOW MANY WERE THERE?
FOR SOME REASON THEY WANTED WOLVES MORE THAN ELVES UNTIL WE JUST GOT IN THEIR WAY. AND EVEN THEN, THEY WOULDN'T FIGHT ME.
IF THE OTHERS ARE INJURED, WHY DON'T YOU HAVE A SCRATCH?!
IF WE CAN FIGURE OUT WHY, I THINK WE'LL KNOW HOW TO BEAT THEM...

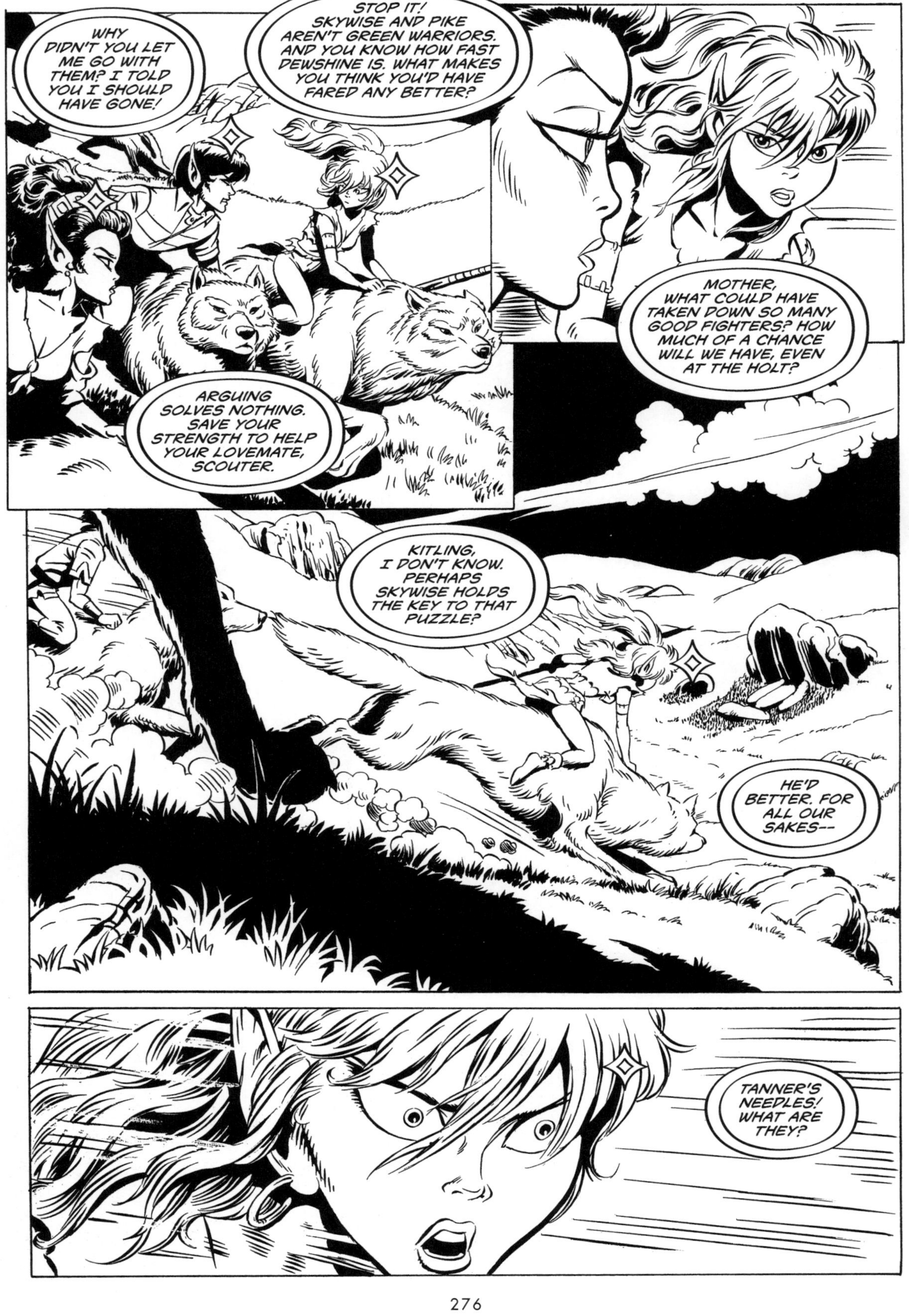
WHY DIDN'T YOU LET ME GO WITH THEM? I TOLD YOU I SHOULD HAVE GONE!
STOP IT! SKYWISE AND PIKE AREN'T GREEN WARRIORS. AND YOU KNOW HOW FAST DEWSHINE IS. WHAT MAKES YOU THINK YOU'D HAVE FARED ANY BETTER?
ARGUING SOLVES NOTHING. SAVE YOUR STRENGTH TO HELP YOUR LOVEMATE, SCOUTER.
MOTHER, WHAT COULD HAVE TAKEN DOWN SO MANY GOOD FIGHTERS? HOW MUCH OF A CHANCE WILL WE HAVE, EVEN AT THE HOLT?
KITLING, I DON'T KNOW. PERHAPS SKYWISE HOLDS THE KEY TO THAT PUZZLE?
HE'D BETTER. FOR ALL OUR SAKES--
TANNER'S NEEDLES! WHAT ARE THEY?

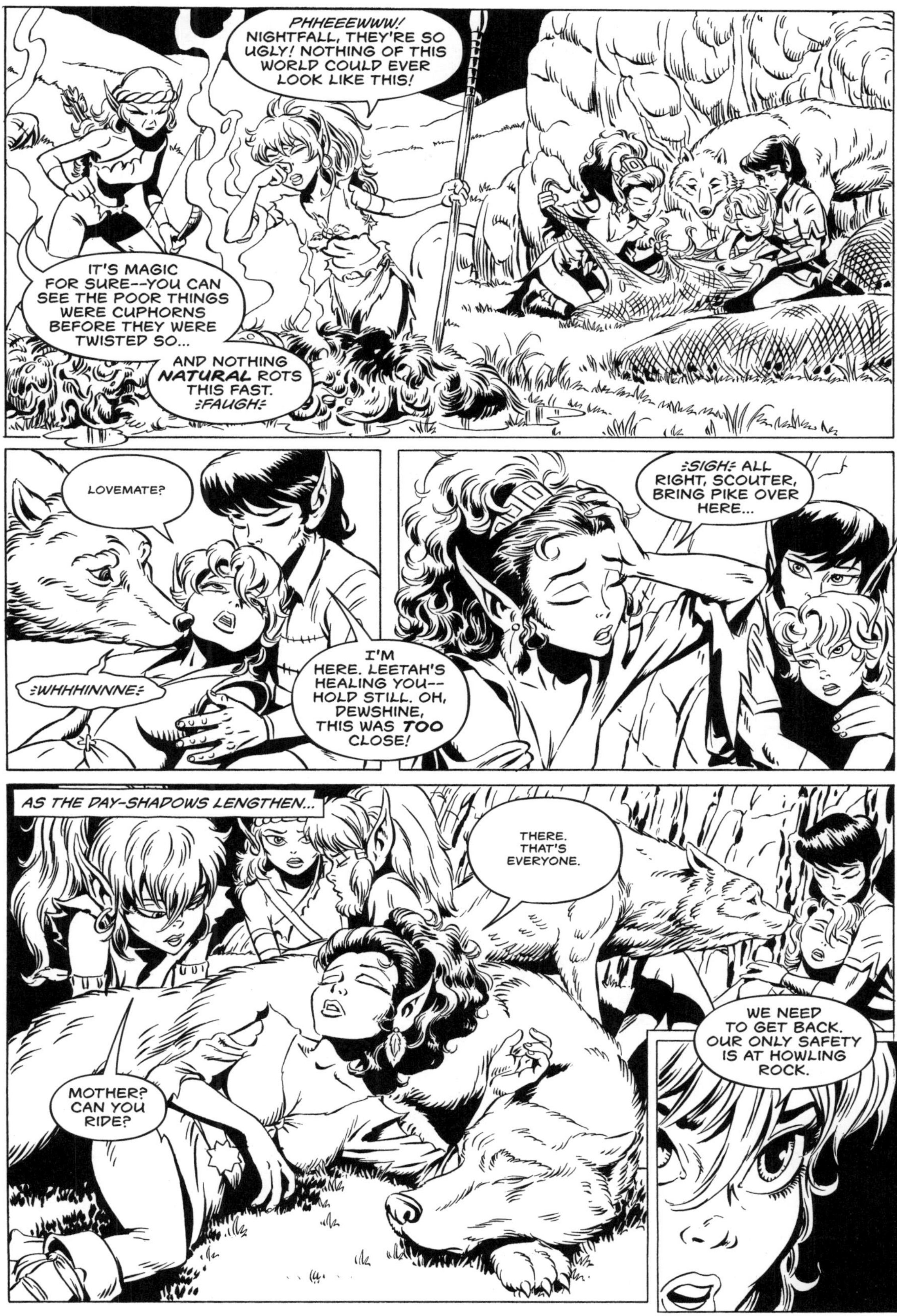

PHHEEEWWW! NIGHTFALL, THEY'RE SO UGLY! NOTHING OF THIS WORLD COULD EVER LOOK LIKE THIS!
IT'S MAGIC FOR SURE--YOU CAN SEE THE POOR THINGS WERE CUPHORNS BEFORE THEY WERE TWISTED SO...
AND NOTHING NATURAL ROTS THIS FAST. FAUGH
LOVEMATE?
WHHHINNNE
I'M HERE. LEETAH'S HEALING YOU--HOLD STILL. OH, DEWSHINE, THIS WAS TOO CLOSE!
SIGH ALL RIGHT, SCOUTER, BRING PIKE OVER HERE...
AS THE DAY-SHADOWS LENGTHEN...
THERE. THAT'S EVERYONE.
MOTHER? CAN YOU RIDE?
WE NEED TO GET BACK. OUR ONLY SAFETY IS AT HOWLING ROCK.

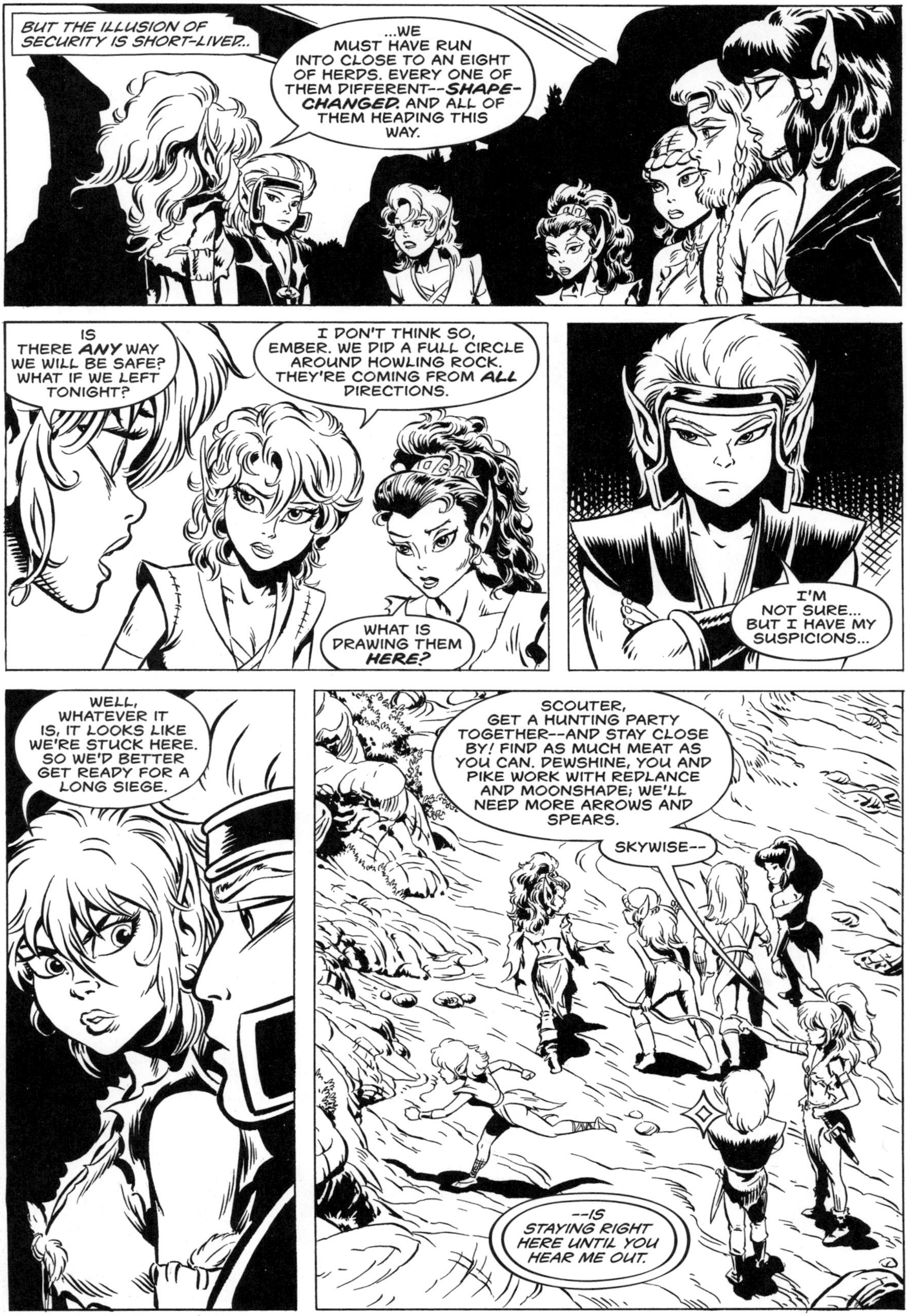
BUT THE ILLUSION OF SECURITY IS SHORT-LIVED...
...WE MUST HAVE RUN INTO CLOSE TO AN EIGHT OF HERDS. EVERY ONE OF THEM DIFFERENT--SHAPE-CHANGED. AND ALL OF THEM HEADING THIS WAY.
IS THERE ANY WAY WE WILL BE SAFE? WHAT IF WE LEFT TONIGHT?
I DON'T THINK SO, EMBER. WE DID A FULL CIRCLE AROUND HOWLING ROCK. THEY'RE COMING FROM ALL DIRECTIONS.
WHAT IS DRAWING THEM HERE?
I'M NOT SURE... BUT I HAVE MY SUSPICIONS...
WELL, WHATEVER IT IS, IT LOOKS LIKE WE'RE STUCK HERE. SO WE'D BETTER GET READY FOR A LONG SIEGE.
SCOUTER, GET A HUNTING PARTY TOGETHER--AND STAY CLOSE BY! FIND AS MUCH MEAT AS YOU CAN. DEWSHINE, YOU AND PIKE WORK WITH REDLANCE AND MOONSHADE; WE'LL NEED MORE ARROWS AND SPEARS.
SKYWISE--
--IS STAYING RIGHT HERE UNTIL YOU HEAR ME OUT.

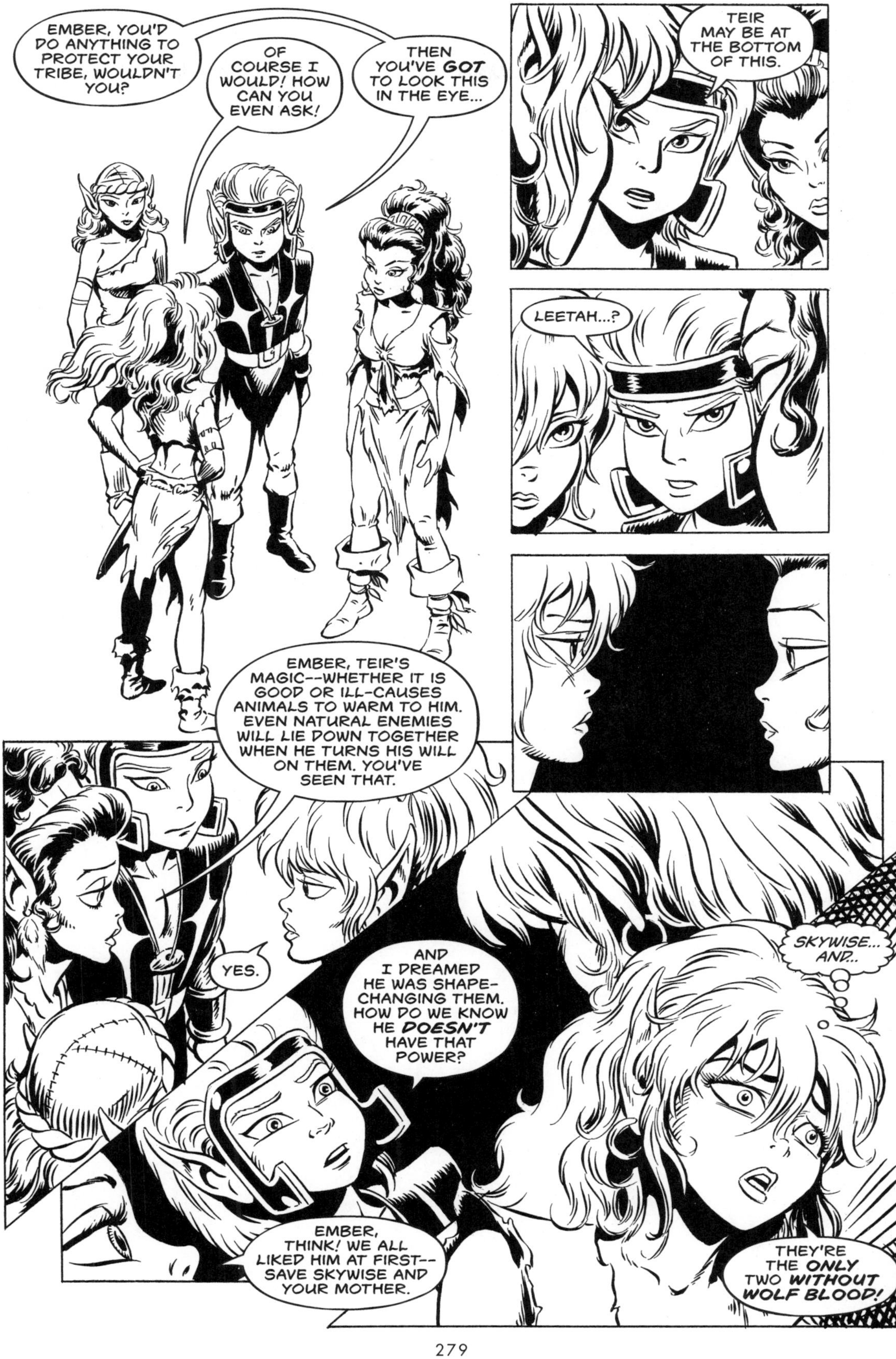

EMBER, YOU'D DO ANYTHING TO PROTECT YOUR TRIBE, WOULDN'T YOU?
OF COURSE I WOULD! HOW CAN YOU EVEN ASK!
THEN YOU'VE **GOT** TO LOOK THIS IN THE EYE...
TEIR MAY BE AT THE BOTTOM OF THIS.
LEETAH...?
EMBER, TEIR'S MAGIC--WHETHER IT IS GOOD OR ILL-CAUSES ANIMALS TO WARM TO HIM. EVEN NATURAL ENEMIES WILL LIE DOWN TOGETHER WHEN HE TURNS HIS WILL ON THEM. YOU'VE SEEN THAT.
YES.
AND I DREAMED HE WAS SHAPE-CHANGING THEM. HOW DO WE KNOW HE ***DOESN'T*** HAVE THAT POWER?
SKYWISE... AND...
EMBER, THINK! WE ALL LIKED HIM AT FIRST--SAVE SKYWISE AND YOUR MOTHER.
THEY'RE THE ***ONLY*** TWO ***WITHOUT WOLF BLOOD!***

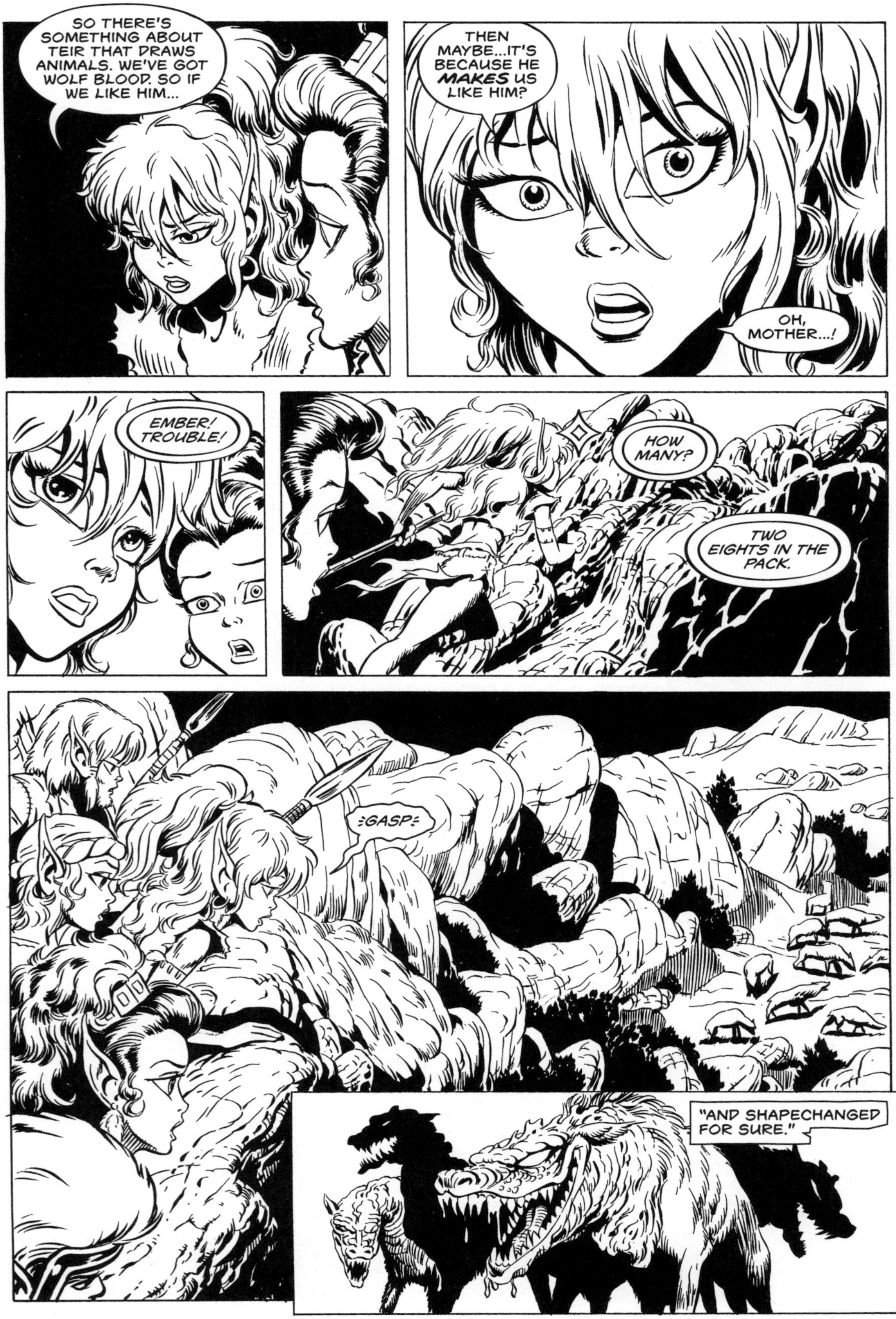
SO THERE'S SOMETHING ABOUT TEIR THAT DRAWS ANIMALS. WE'VE GOT WOLF BLOOD. SO IF WE LIKE HIM...
THEN MAYBE...IT'S BECAUSE HE **MAKES** US LIKE HIM?
OH, MOTHER...!
EMBER! TROUBLE!
HOW MANY?
TWO EIGHTS IN THE PACK.
GASP
"AND SHAPECHANGED FOR SURE."

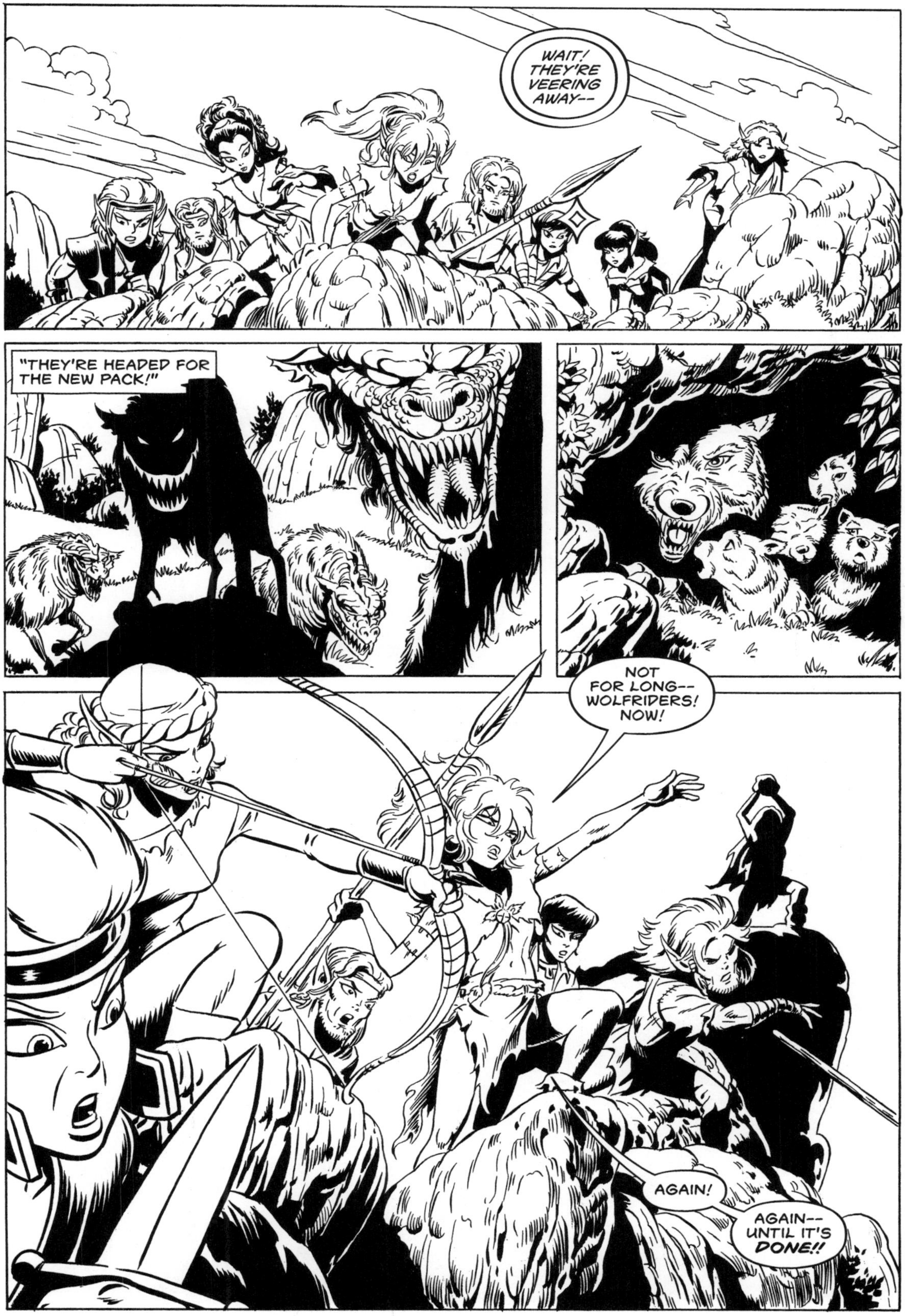
WAIT! THEY'RE VEERING AWAY--
"THEY'RE HEADED FOR THE NEW PACK!"
NOT FOR LONG-- WOLFRIDERS! NOW!
AGAIN!
AGAIN-- UNTIL IT'S DONE!!

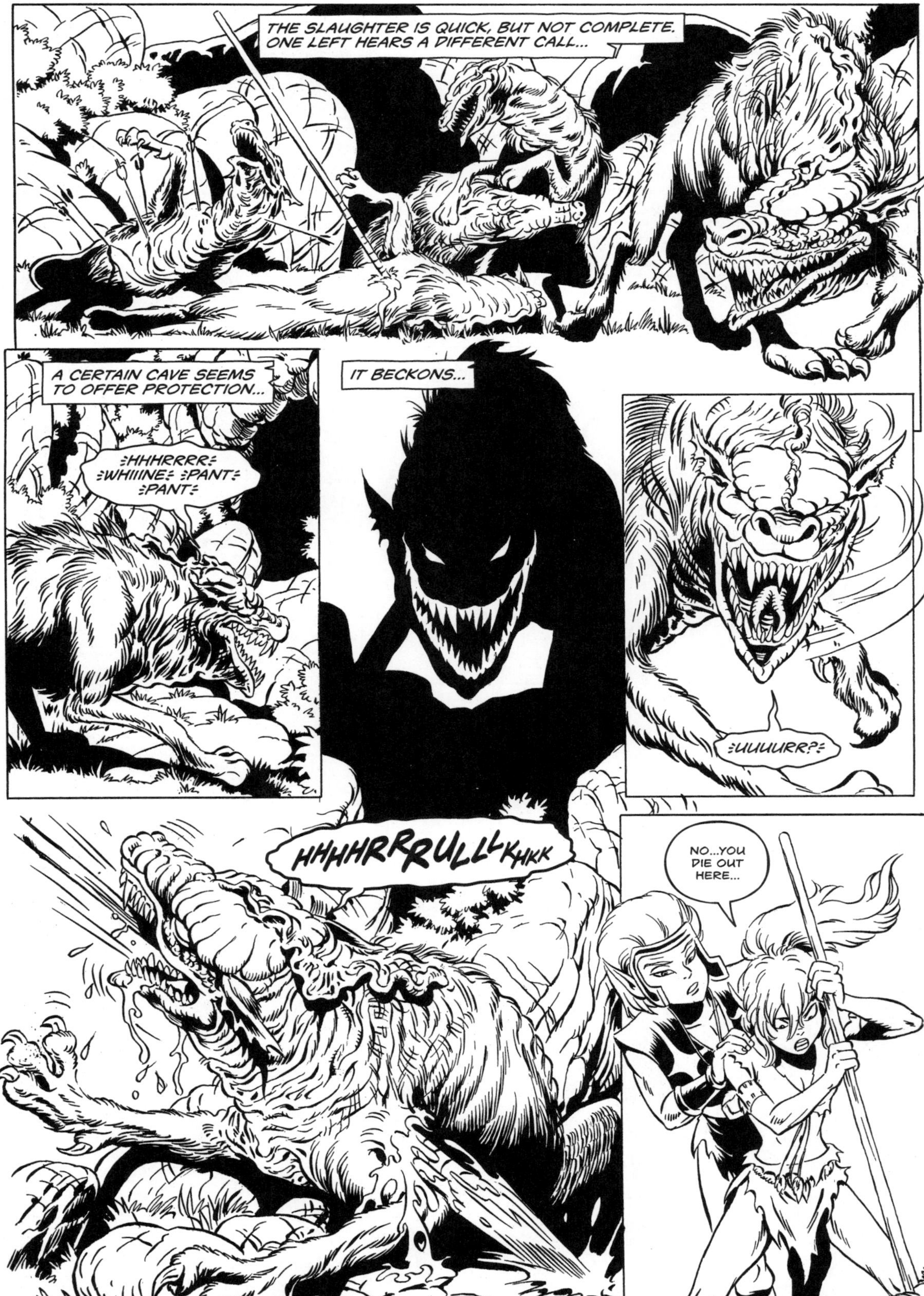
THE SLAUGHTER IS QUICK, BUT NOT COMPLETE. ONE LEFT HEARS A DIFFERENT CALL...
A CERTAIN CAVE SEEMS TO OFFER PROTECTION...
HHHRRRR WHIIINE PANT PANT
IT BECKONS...
UUUURR?
HHHHRRRRULLLKHKK
NO...YOU DIE OUT HERE...

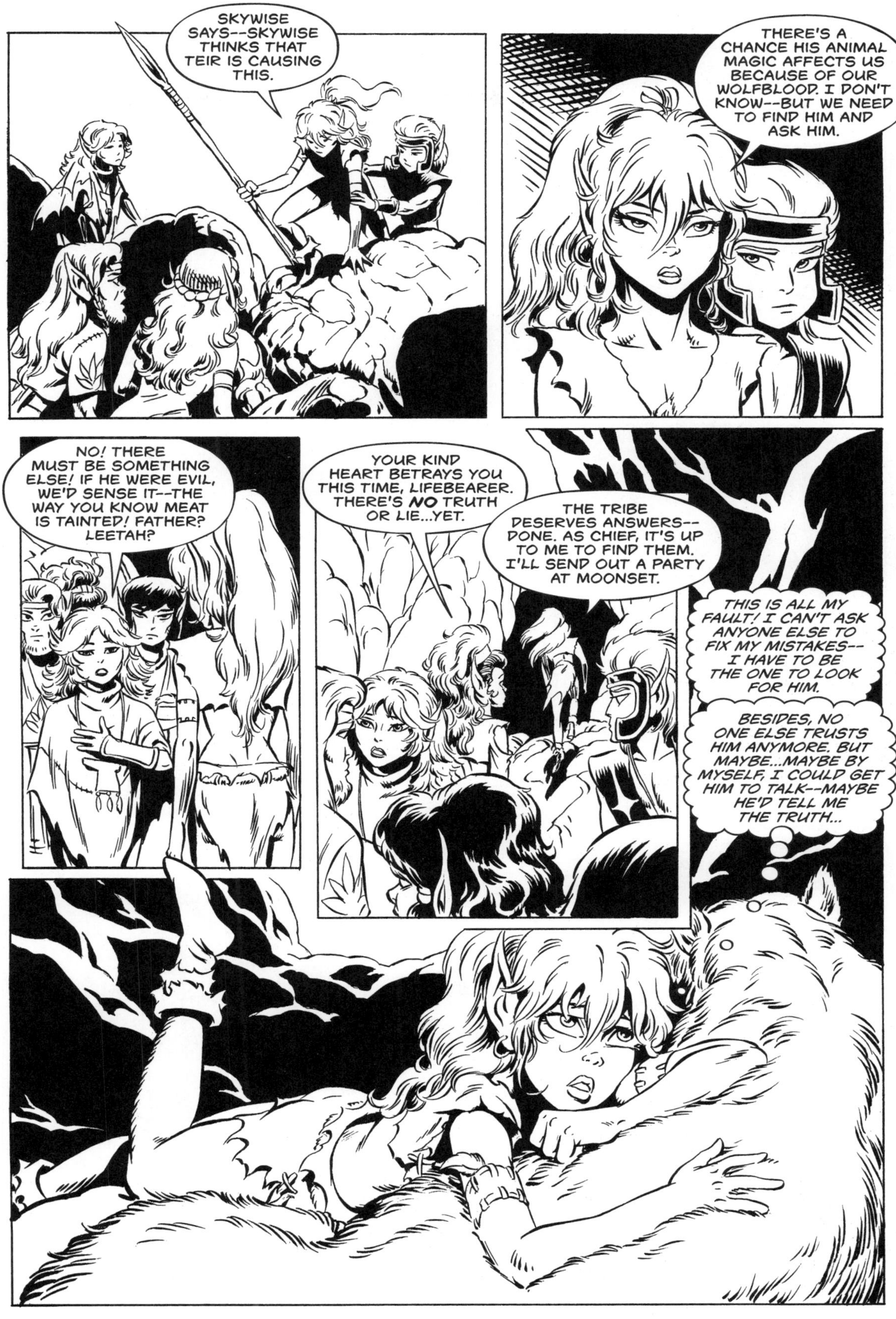
SKYWISE SAYS--SKYWISE THINKS THAT TEIR IS CAUSING THIS.
THERE'S A CHANCE HIS ANIMAL MAGIC AFFECTS US BECAUSE OF OUR WOLFBLOOD. I DON'T KNOW--BUT WE NEED TO FIND HIM AND ASK HIM.
NO! THERE MUST BE SOMETHING ELSE! IF HE WERE EVIL, WE'D SENSE IT--THE WAY YOU KNOW MEAT IS TAINTED! FATHER? LEETAH?
YOUR KIND HEART BETRAYS YOU THIS TIME, LIFEBEARER. THERE'S NO TRUTH OR LIE...YET.
THE TRIBE DESERVES ANSWERS--DONE. AS CHIEF, IT'S UP TO ME TO FIND THEM. I'LL SEND OUT A PARTY AT MOONSET.
THIS IS ALL MY FAULT! I CAN'T ASK ANYONE ELSE TO FIX MY MISTAKES--I HAVE TO BE THE ONE TO LOOK FOR HIM.
BESIDES, NO ONE ELSE TRUSTS HIM ANYMORE. BUT MAYBE...MAYBE BY MYSELF, I COULD GET HIM TO TALK--MAYBE HE'D TELL ME THE TRUTH...

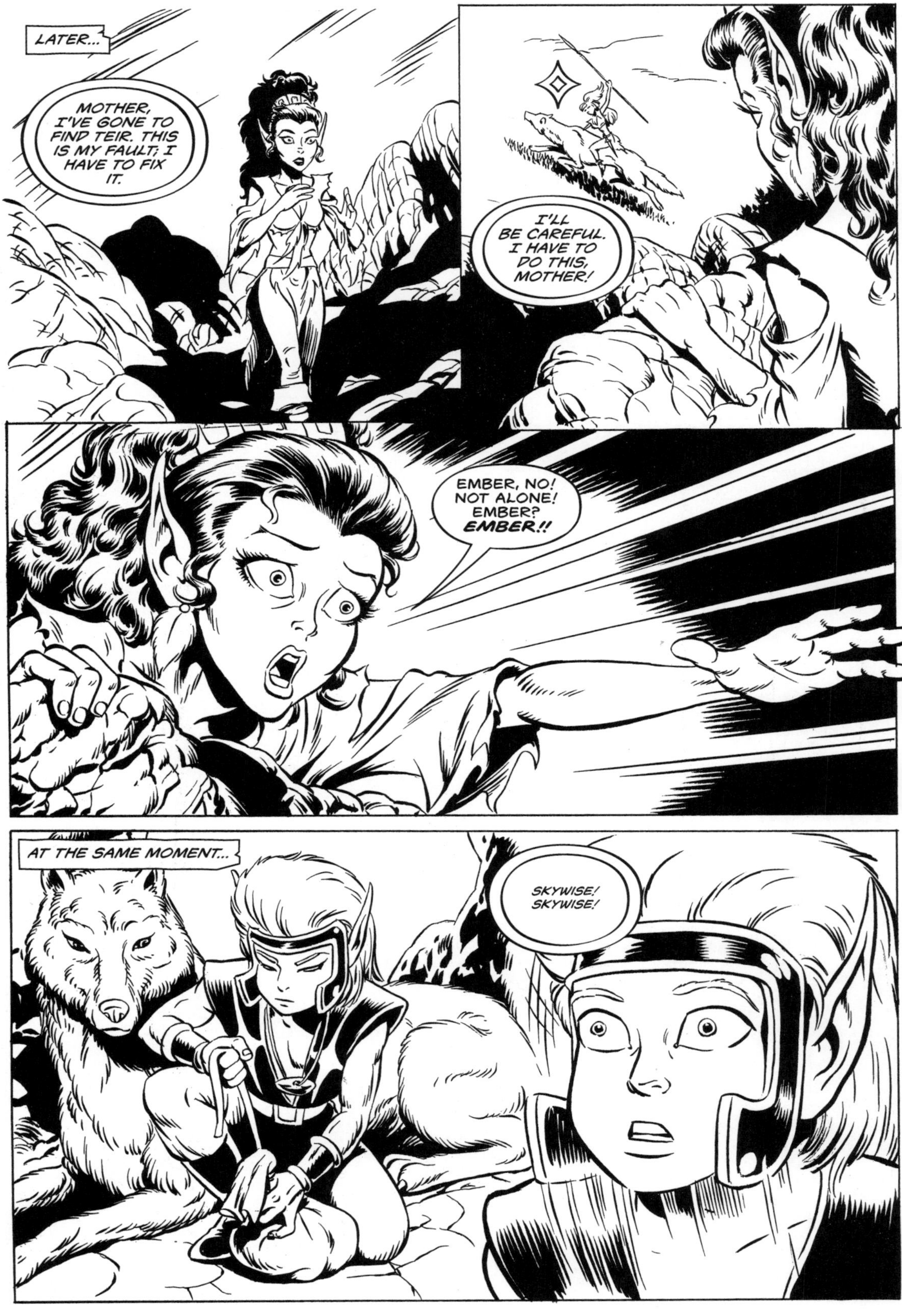
LATER...
MOTHER, I'VE GONE TO FIND TEIR. THIS IS MY FAULT; I HAVE TO FIX IT.
I'LL BE CAREFUL. I HAVE TO DO THIS, MOTHER!
EMBER, NO! NOT ALONE! EMBER? EMBER!!
AT THE SAME MOMENT...
SKYWISE! SKYWISE!

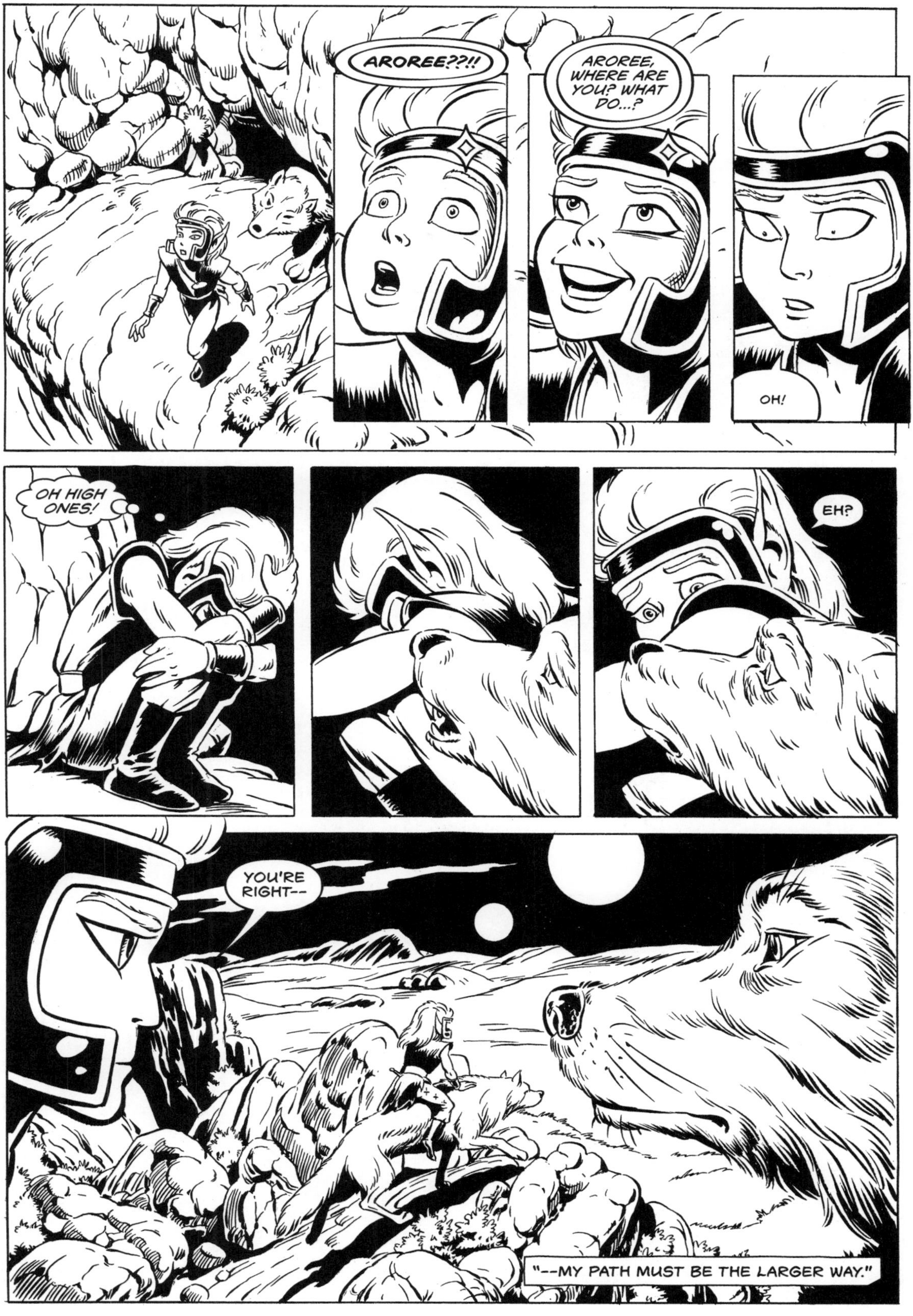

AROREE??!!
AROREE, WHERE ARE YOU? WHAT DO...?
OH!
OH HIGH ONES!
EH?
YOU'RE RIGHT--
"--MY PATH MUST BE THE LARGER WAY."

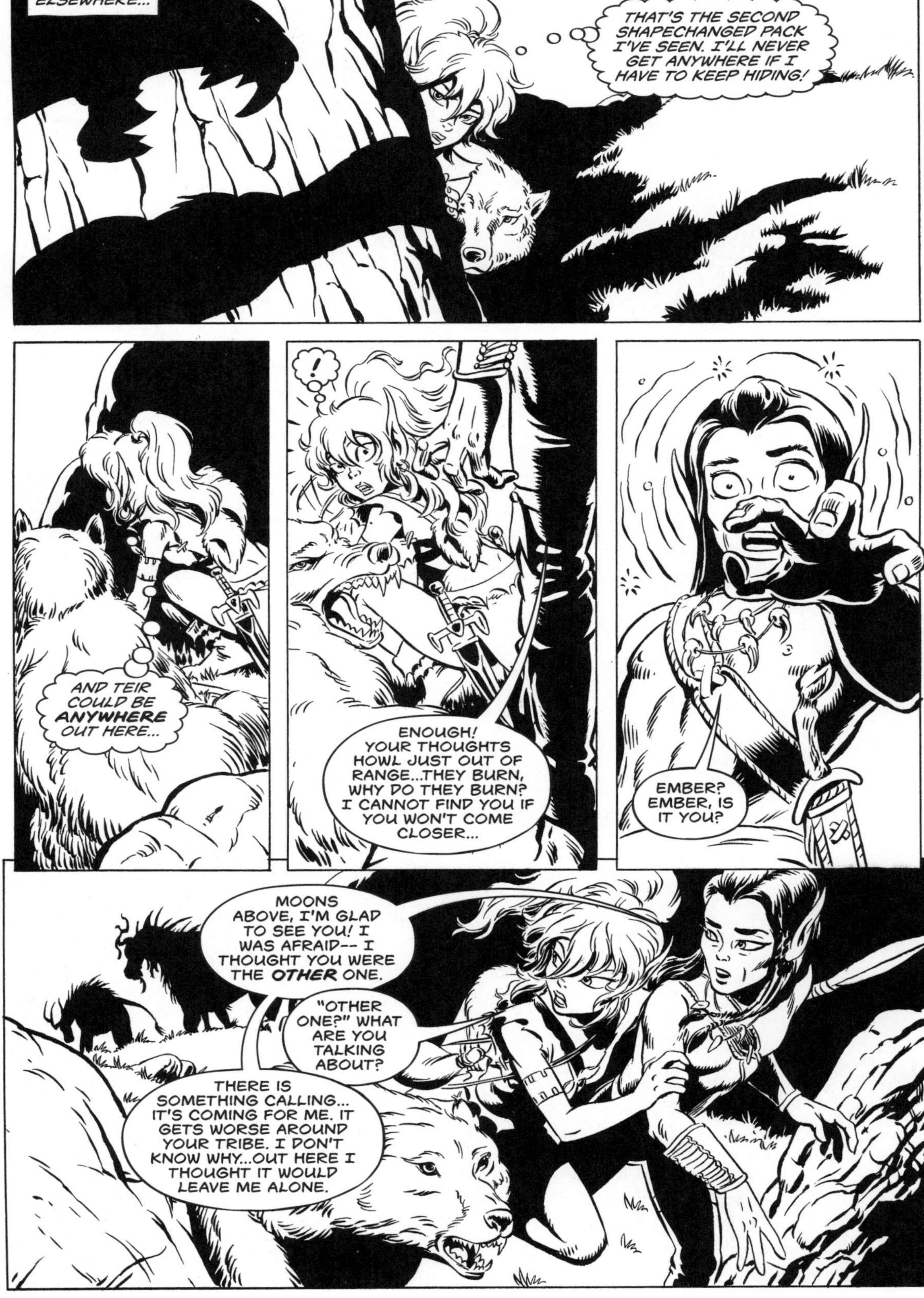
ELSEWHERE...
THAT'S THE SECOND SHAPECHANGED PACK I'VE SEEN. I'LL NEVER GET ANYWHERE IF I HAVE TO KEEP HIDING!
AND TEIR COULD BE ANYWHERE OUT HERE...
!
ENOUGH! YOUR THOUGHTS HOWL JUST OUT OF RANGE...THEY BURN, WHY DO THEY BURN? I CANNOT FIND YOU IF YOU WON'T COME CLOSER...
EMBER? EMBER, IS IT YOU?
MOONS ABOVE, I'M GLAD TO SEE YOU! I WAS AFRAID-- I THOUGHT YOU WERE THE OTHER ONE.
"OTHER ONE?" WHAT ARE YOU TALKING ABOUT?
THERE IS SOMETHING CALLING... IT'S COMING FOR ME. IT GETS WORSE AROUND YOUR TRIBE. I DON'T KNOW WHY...OUT HERE I THOUGHT IT WOULD LEAVE ME ALONE.

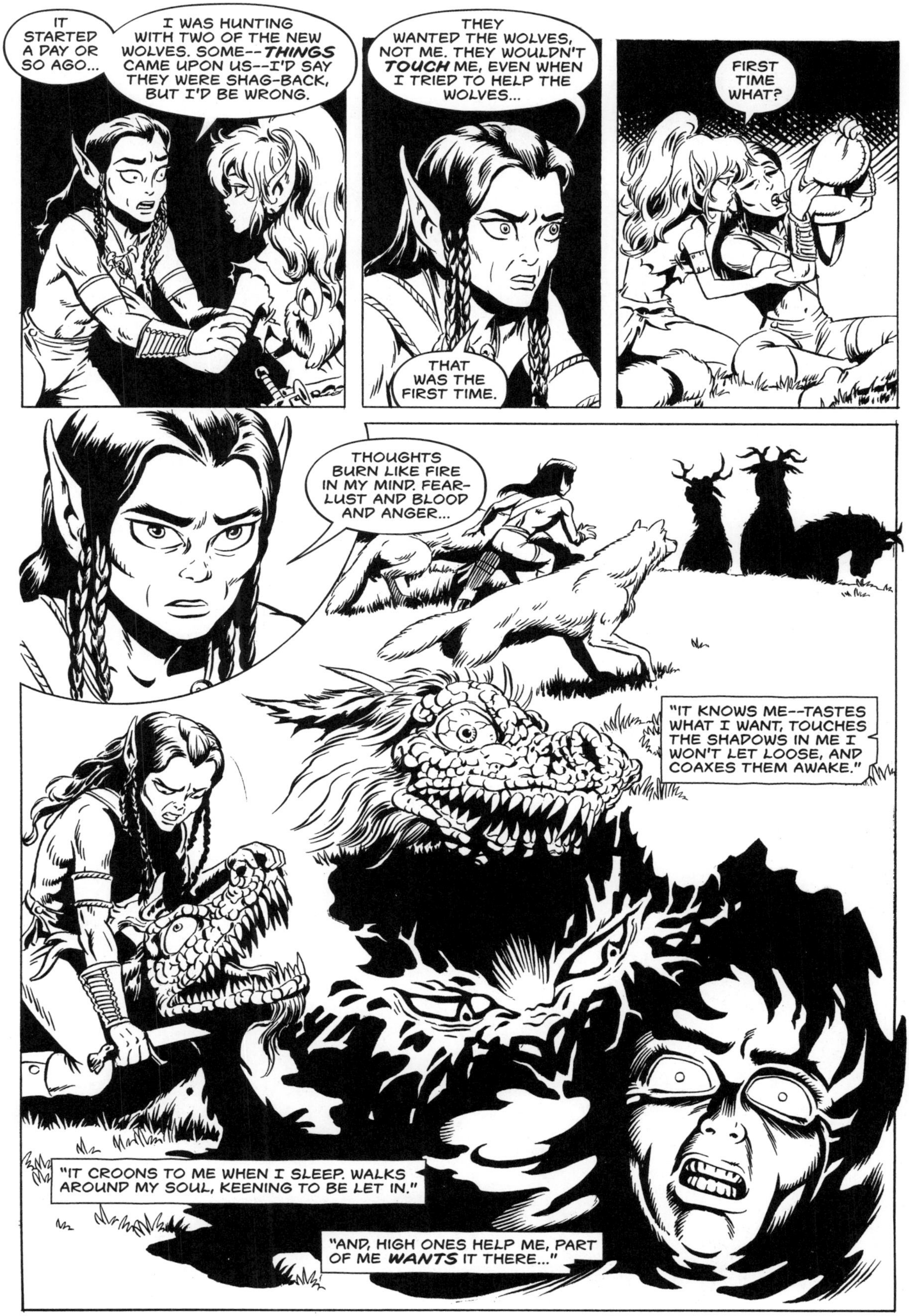
IT STARTED A DAY OR SO AGO...
I WAS HUNTING WITH TWO OF THE NEW WOLVES. SOME--THINGS CAME UPON US--I'D SAY THEY WERE SHAG-BACK, BUT I'D BE WRONG.
THEY WANTED THE WOLVES, NOT ME. THEY WOULDN'T TOUCH ME, EVEN WHEN I TRIED TO HELP THE WOLVES...
THAT WAS THE FIRST TIME.
FIRST TIME WHAT?
THOUGHTS BURN LIKE FIRE IN MY MIND. FEAR-LUST AND BLOOD AND ANGER...
"IT KNOWS ME--TASTES WHAT I WANT, TOUCHES THE SHADOWS IN ME I WON'T LET LOOSE, AND COAXES THEM AWAKE."
"IT CROONS TO ME WHEN I SLEEP. WALKS AROUND MY SOUL, KEENING TO BE LET IN."
"AND, HIGH ONES HELP ME, PART OF ME WANTS IT THERE..."

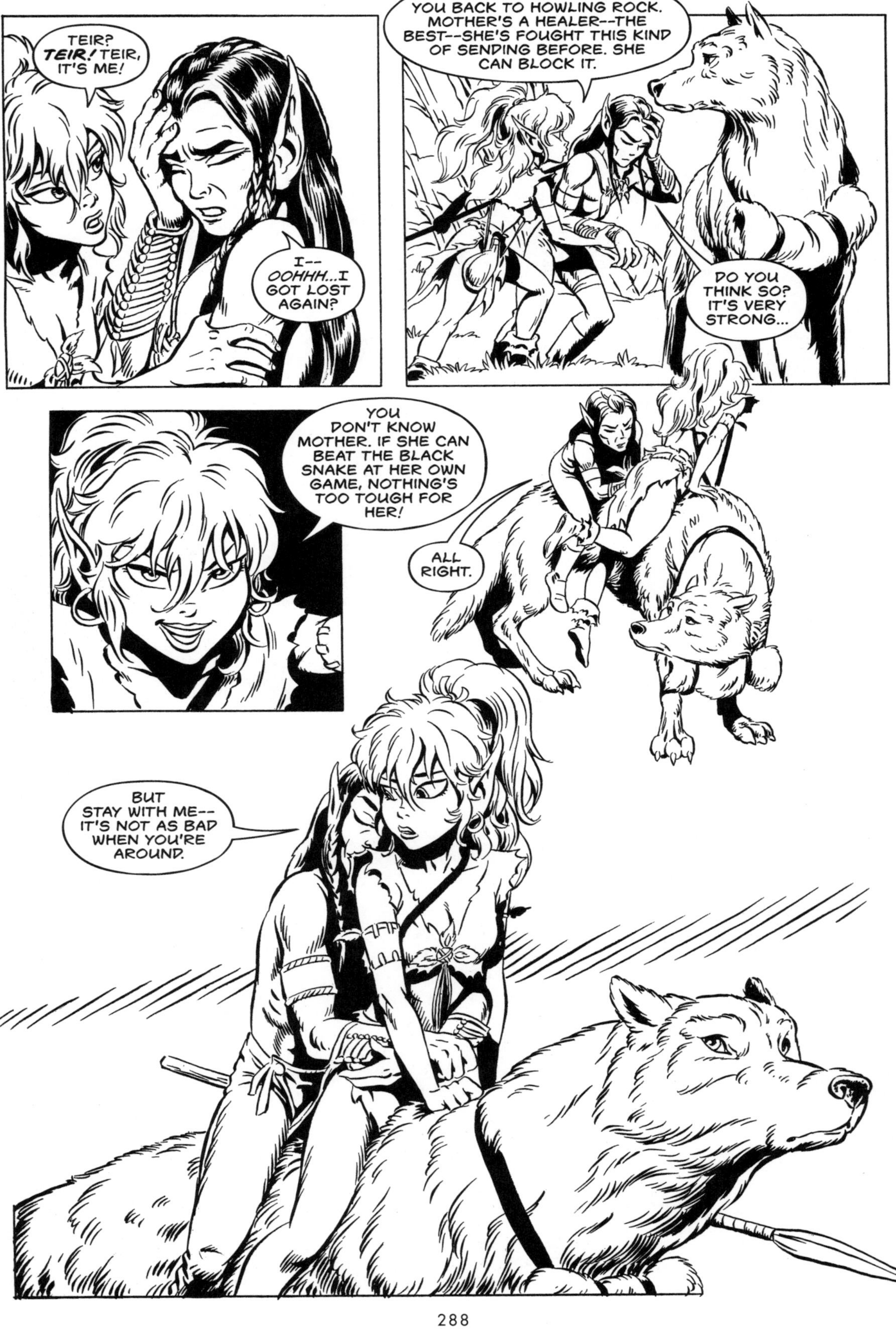
TEIR? *TEIR!* TEIR, IT'S ME!
I-- *OOHHH*...I GOT LOST AGAIN?
YES...LET ME TAKE YOU BACK TO HOWLING ROCK. MOTHER'S A HEALER--THE BEST--SHE'S FOUGHT THIS KIND OF SENDING BEFORE. SHE CAN BLOCK IT.
DO YOU THINK SO? IT'S VERY STRONG...
YOU DON'T KNOW MOTHER. IF SHE CAN BEAT THE BLACK SNAKE AT HER OWN GAME, NOTHING'S TOO TOUGH FOR HER!
ALL RIGHT.
BUT STAY WITH ME-- IT'S NOT AS BAD WHEN YOU'RE AROUND.

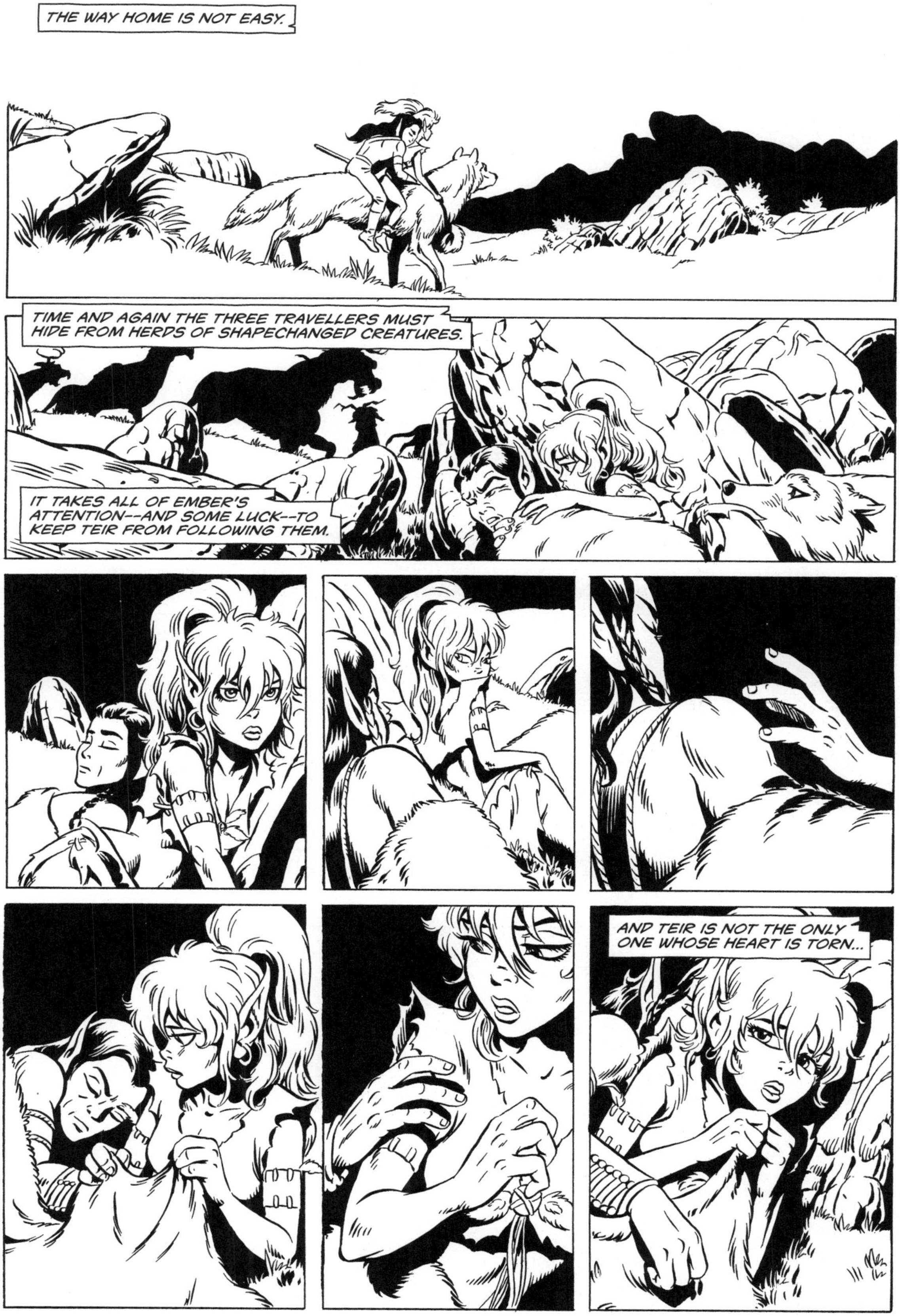
THE WAY HOME IS NOT EASY.
TIME AND AGAIN THE THREE TRAVELLERS MUST HIDE FROM HERDS OF SHAPECHANGED CREATURES.
IT TAKES ALL OF EMBER'S ATTENTION--AND SOME LUCK--TO KEEP TEIR FROM FOLLOWING THEM.
AND TEIR IS NOT THE ONLY ONE WHOSE HEART IS TORN...

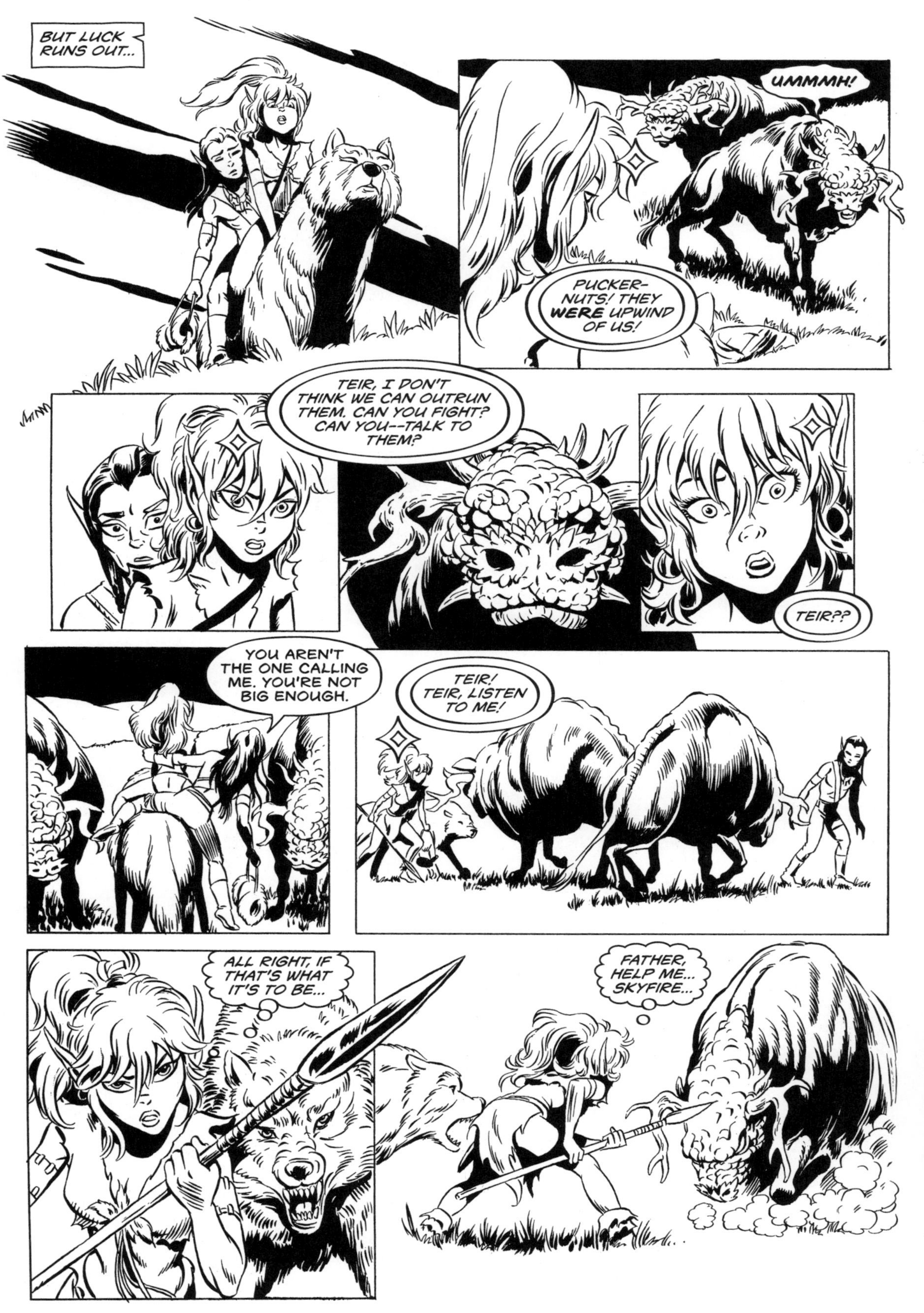

BUT LUCK RUNS OUT...
UMMMH!
PUCKER-NUTS! THEY **WERE** UPWIND OF US!
TEIR, I DON'T THINK WE CAN OUTRUN THEM. CAN YOU FIGHT? CAN YOU--TALK TO THEM?
TEIR??
YOU AREN'T THE ONE CALLING ME. YOU'RE NOT BIG ENOUGH.
TEIR! TEIR, LISTEN TO ME!
ALL RIGHT, IF THAT'S WHAT IT'S TO BE...
FATHER, HELP ME... SKYFIRE...

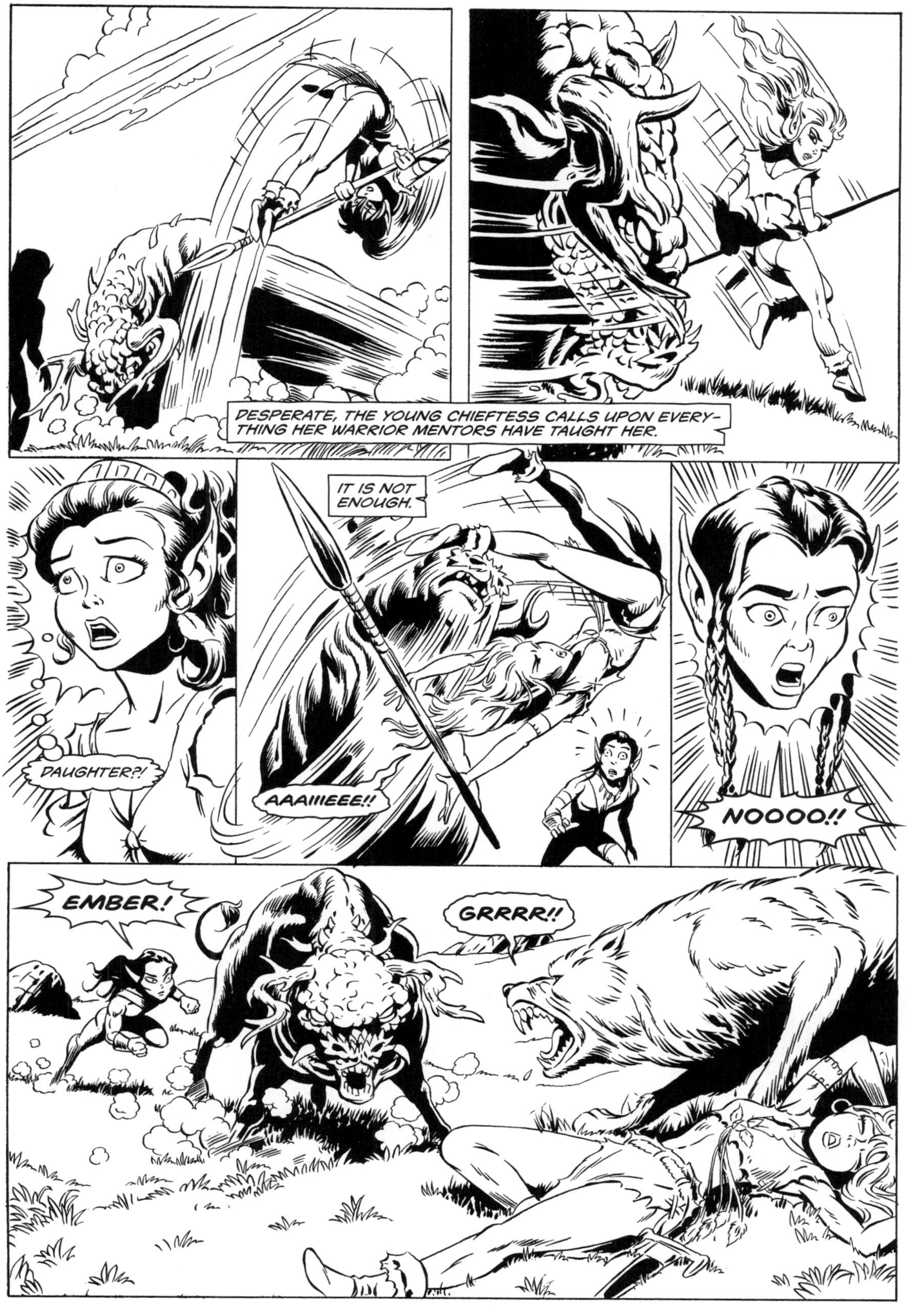
DESPERATE, THE YOUNG CHIEFTESS CALLS UPON EVERYTHING HER WARRIOR MENTORS HAVE TAUGHT HER.
DAUGHTER?!
IT IS NOT ENOUGH.
AAAIIIEEE!!
NOOOO!!
EMBER!
GRRRR!!

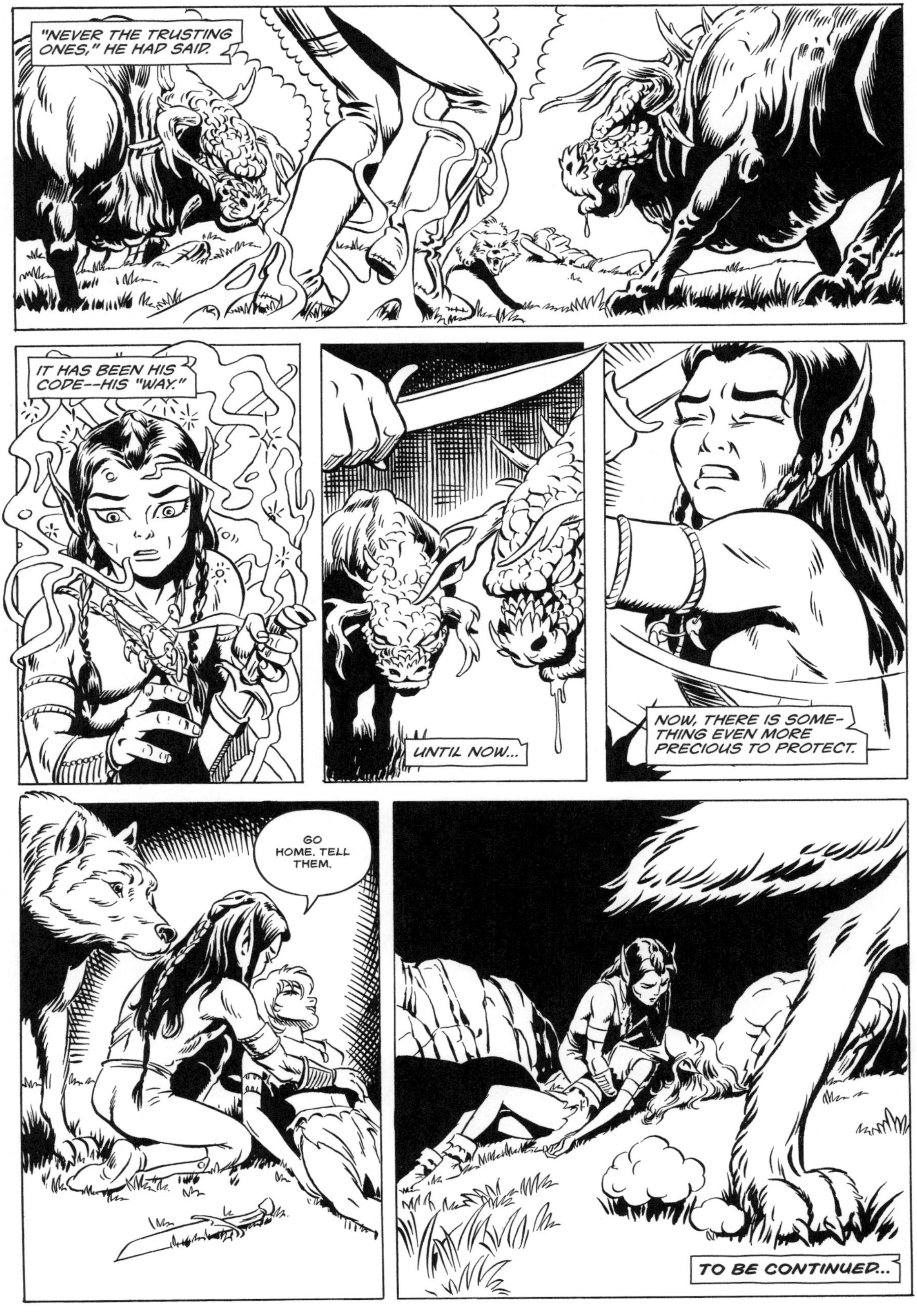
"NEVER THE TRUSTING ONES," HE HAD SAID.
IT HAS BEEN HIS CODE--HIS "WAY."
UNTIL NOW...
NOW, THERE IS SOMETHING EVEN MORE PRECIOUS TO PROTECT.
GO HOME. TELL THEM.
TO BE CONTINUED...

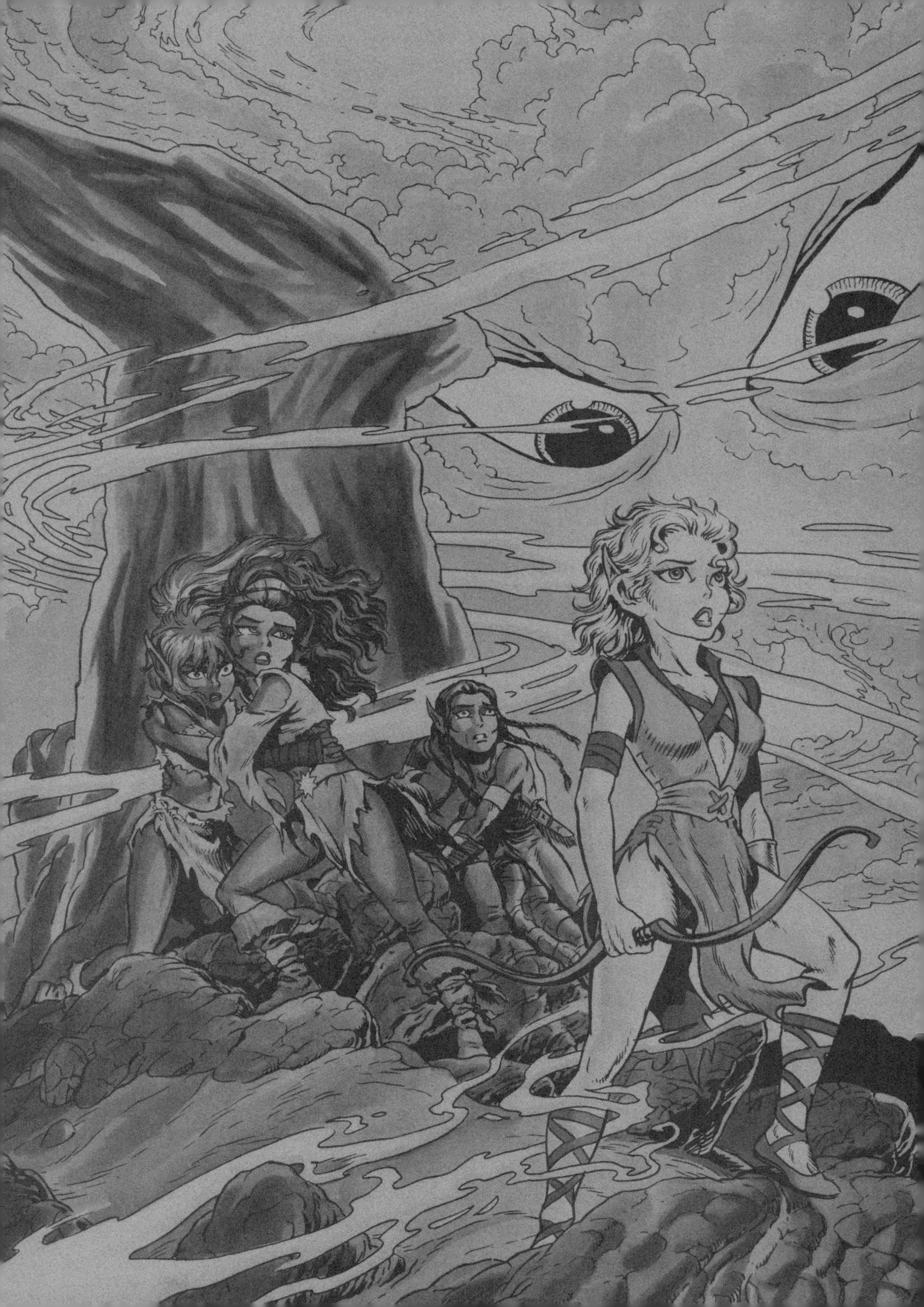

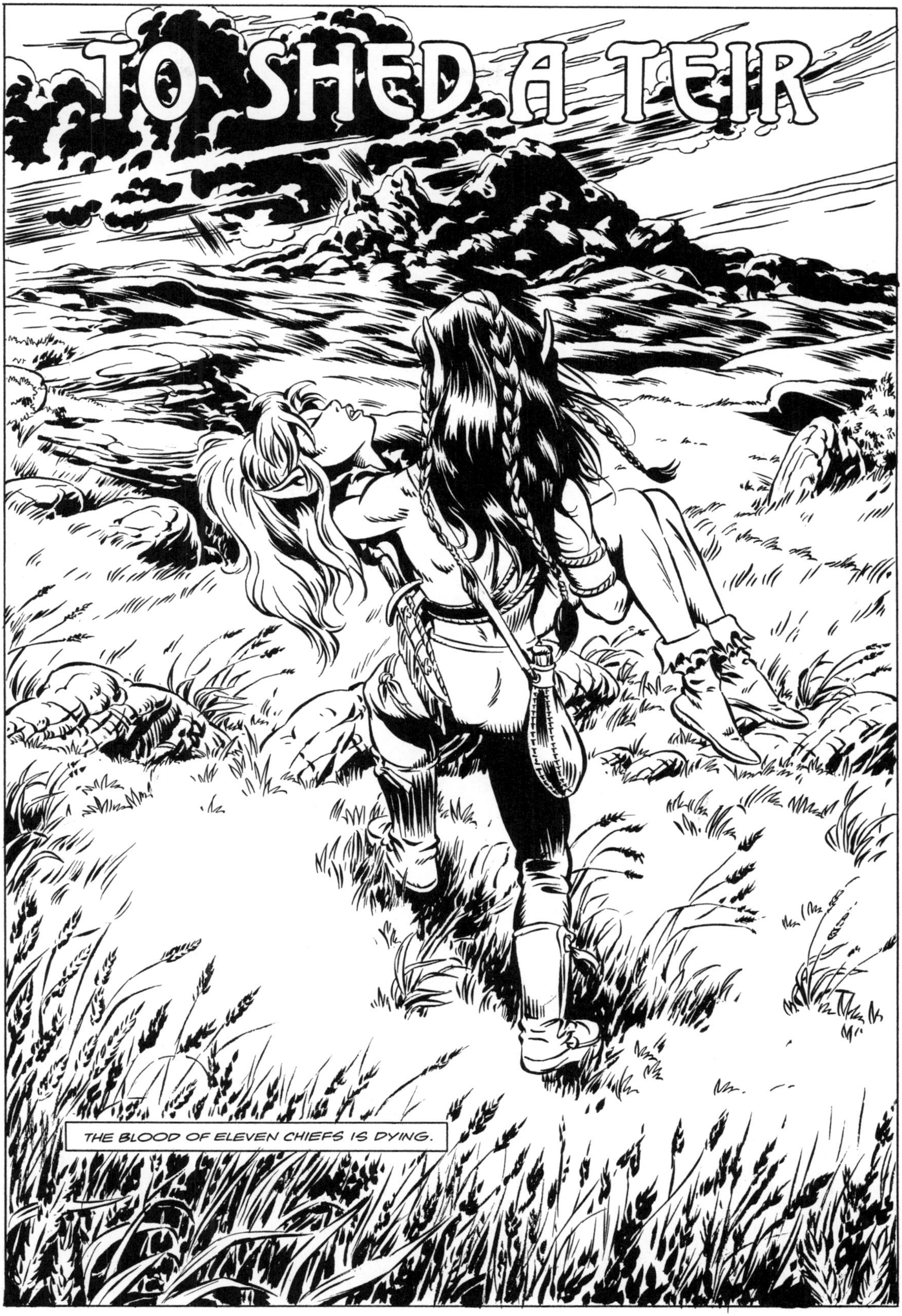
TO SHED A TEIR
THE BLOOD OF ELEVEN CHIEFS IS DYING.

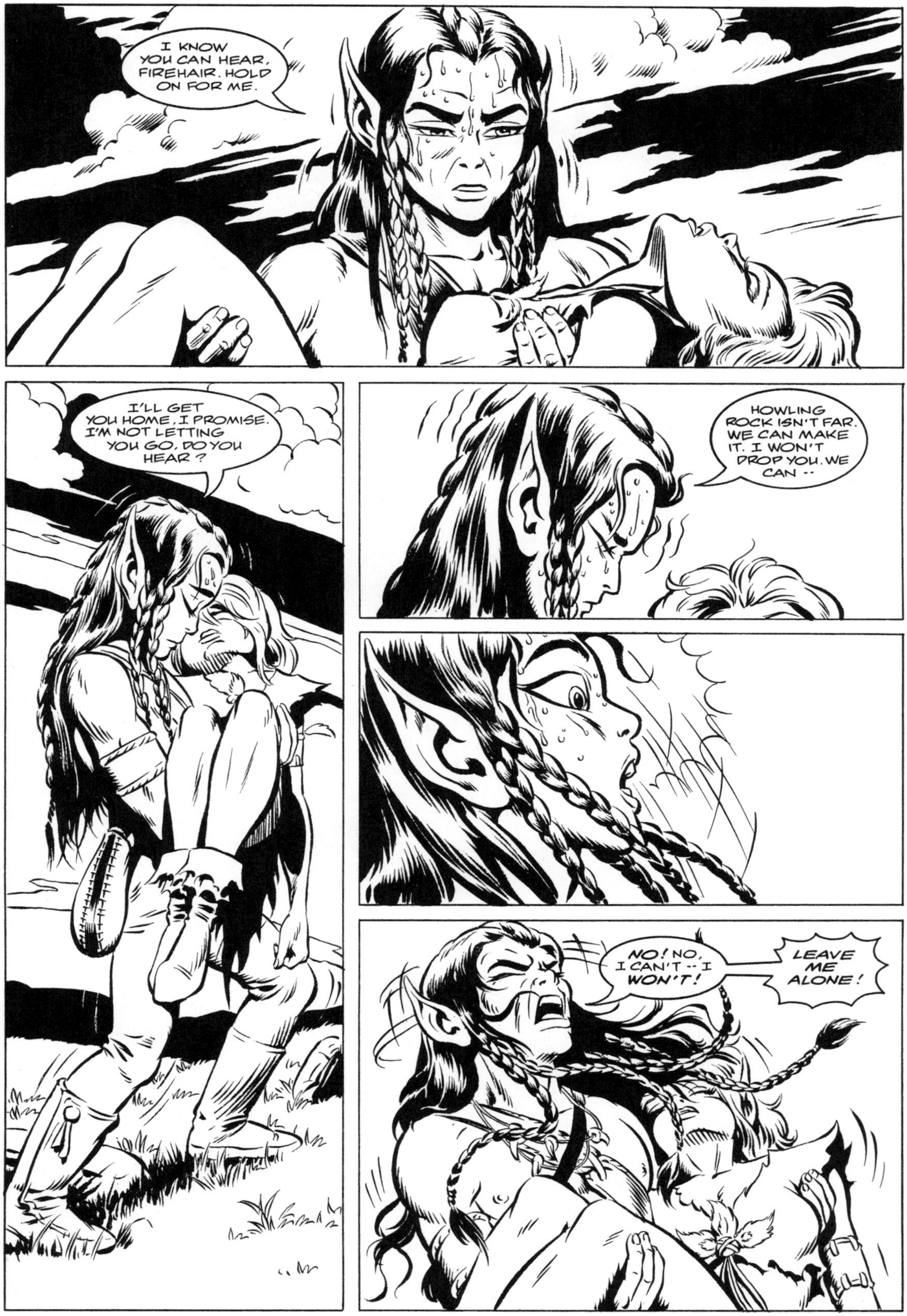
I KNOW YOU CAN HEAR, FIREHAIR. HOLD ON FOR ME.
I'LL GET YOU HOME, I PROMISE. I'M NOT LETTING YOU GO, DO YOU HEAR?
HOWLING ROCK ISN'T FAR. WE CAN MAKE IT. I WON'T DROP YOU. WE CAN --
NO! NO, I CAN'T -- I WON'T!
LEAVE ME ALONE!

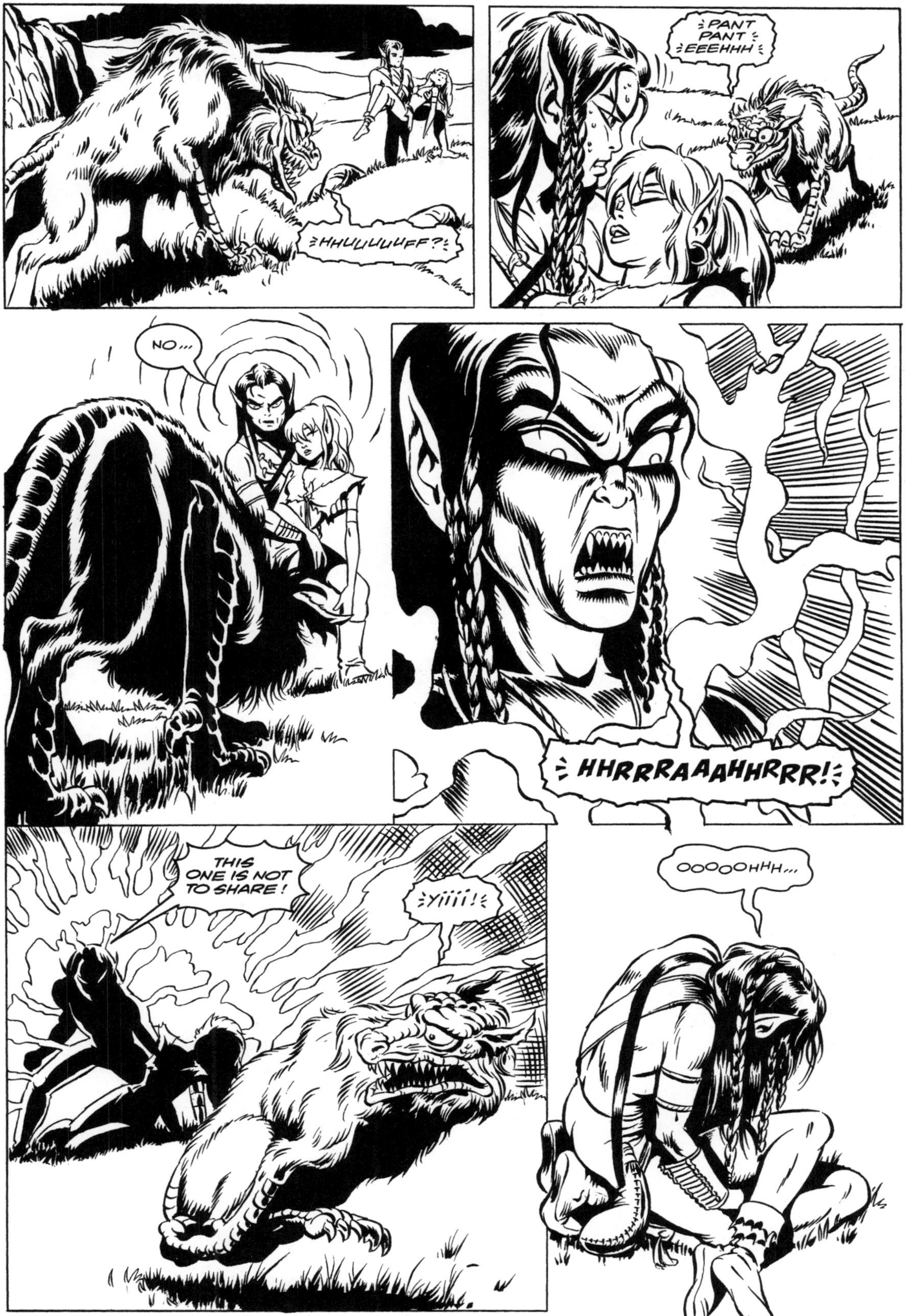
HHUUUUUFF?!
PANT PANT EEEHHH
NO...
HHRRRAAAHHRRR!
THIS ONE IS NOT TO SHARE!
YIIII!
OOOOOHHH...

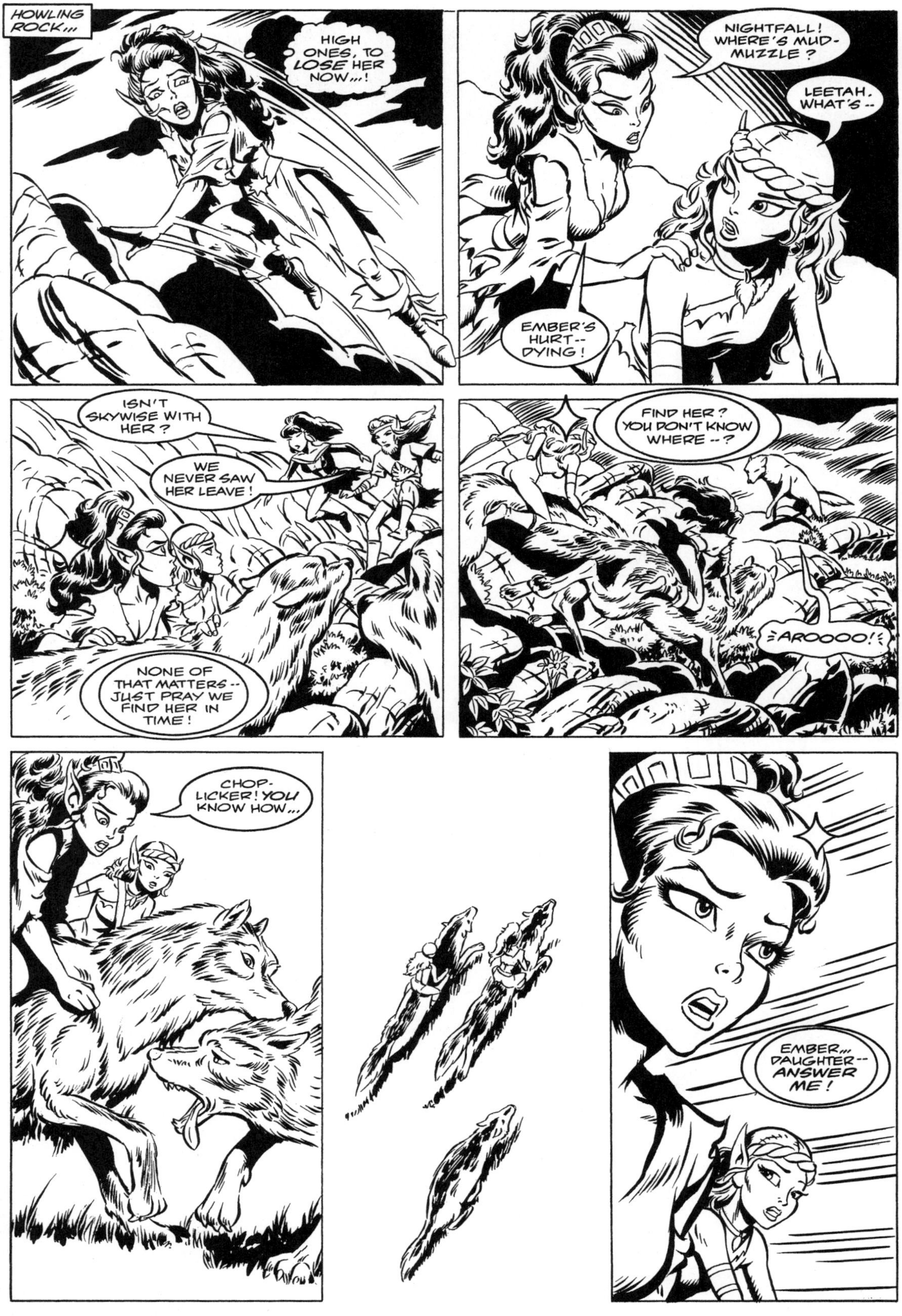
HOWLING ROCK...
HIGH ONES, TO LOSE HER NOW...!
NIGHTFALL! WHERE'S MUD-MUZZLE?
LEETAH, WHAT'S --
EMBER'S HURT-- DYING!
ISN'T SKYWISE WITH HER?
WE NEVER SAW HER LEAVE!
NONE OF THAT MATTERS -- JUST PRAY WE FIND HER IN TIME!
FIND HER? YOU DON'T KNOW WHERE --?
AROOOO!
CHOP-LICKER! YOU KNOW HOW...
EMBER... DAUGHTER-- ANSWER ME!

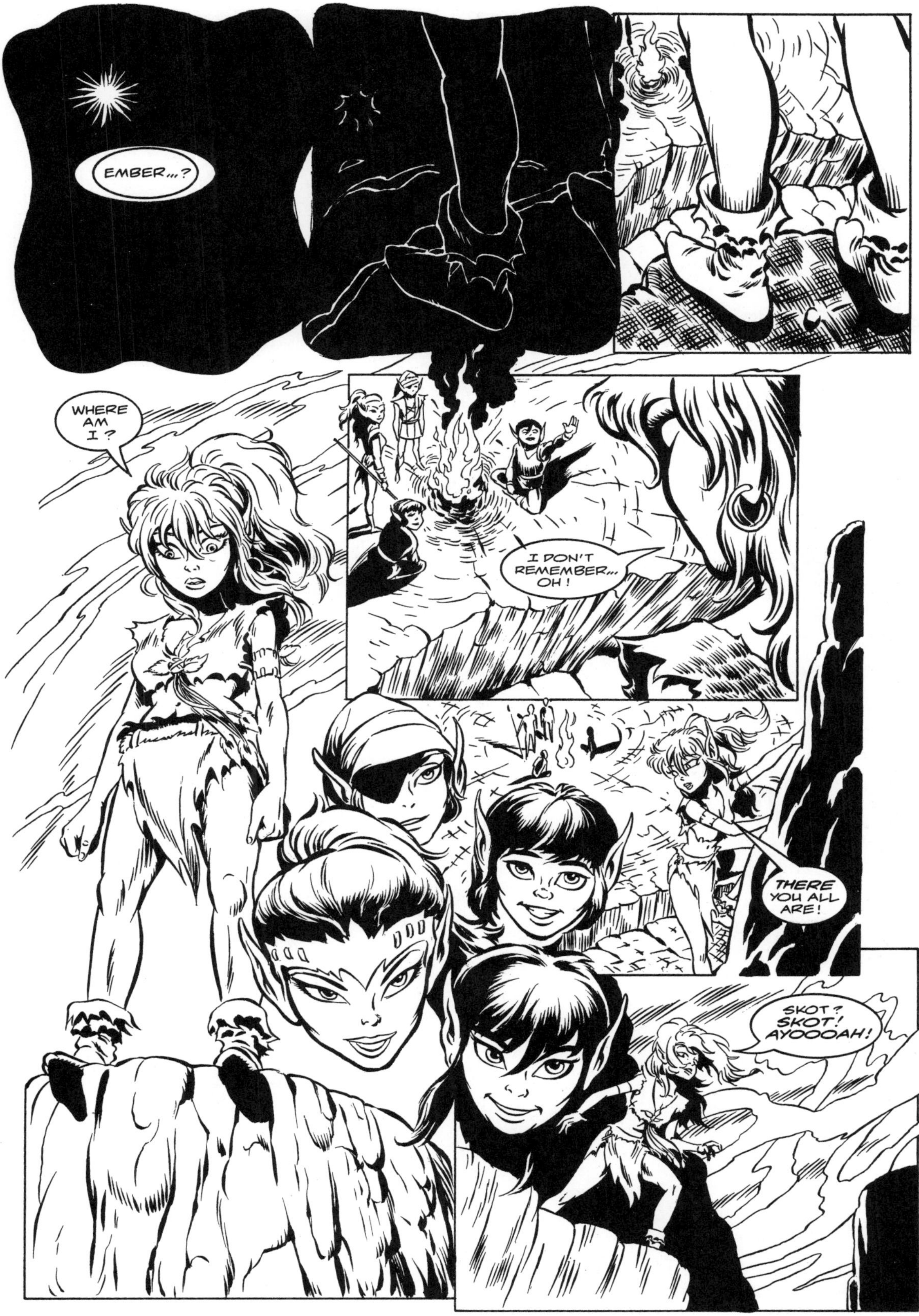
EMBER...?
WHERE AM I?
I DON'T REMEMBER... OH!
THERE YOU ALL ARE!
SKOT? SKOT! AYOOOAH!

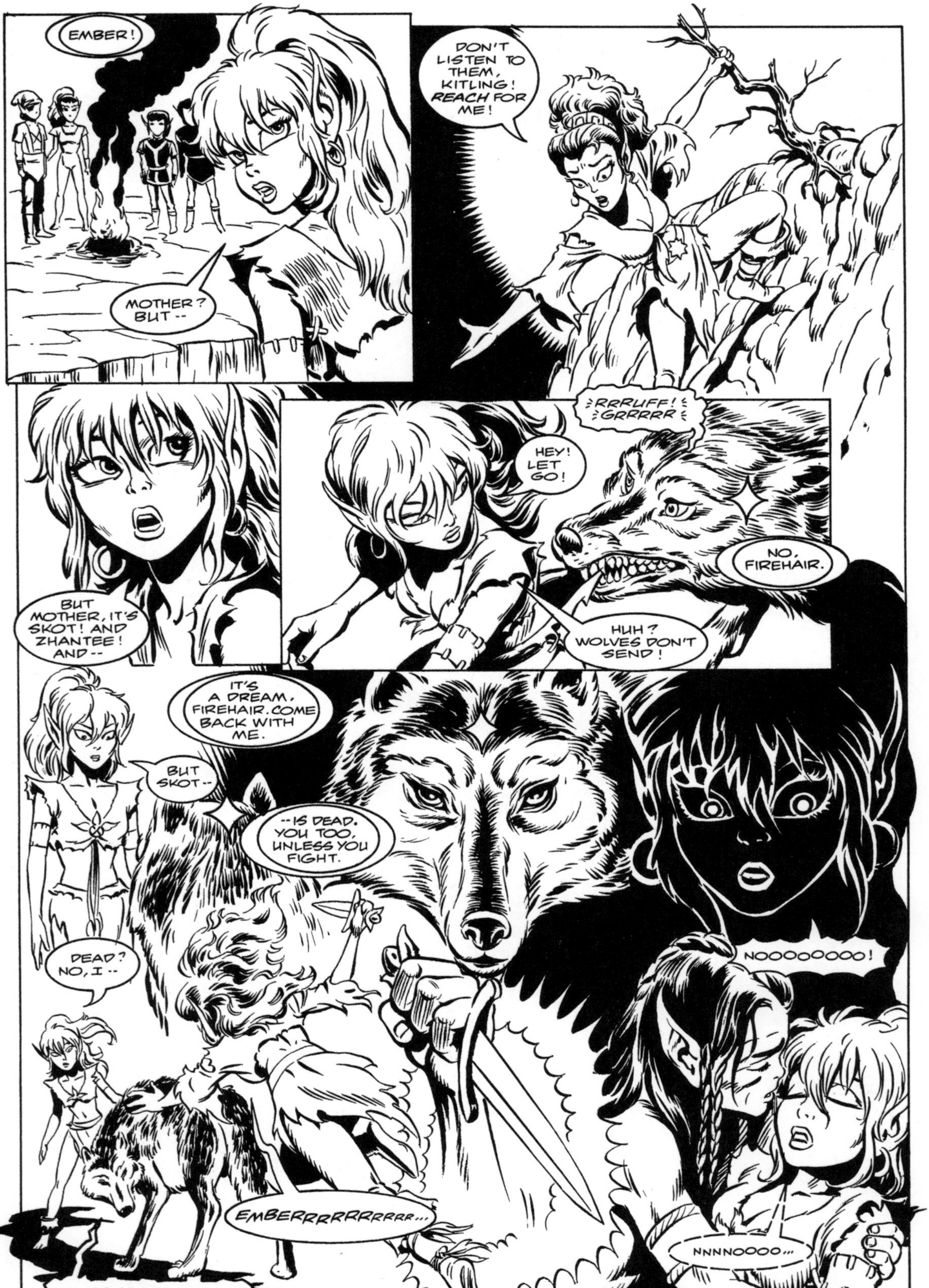
EMBER!
MOTHER? BUT --
DON'T LISTEN TO THEM, KITLING! *REACH* FOR ME!
BUT MOTHER, IT'S SKOT! AND ZHANTEE! AND --
RRRUFF! GRRRRR
HEY! LET GO!
NO, FIREHAIR.
HUH? WOLVES DON'T SEND!
IT'S A DREAM, FIREHAIR. COME BACK WITH ME.
BUT SKOT--
--IS DEAD. YOU TOO, UNLESS YOU FIGHT.
DEAD? NO, I --
NOOOOOOOO!
EMBERRRRRRRRR...
NNNNOOOO...
RRRAHARRHHHRRR!

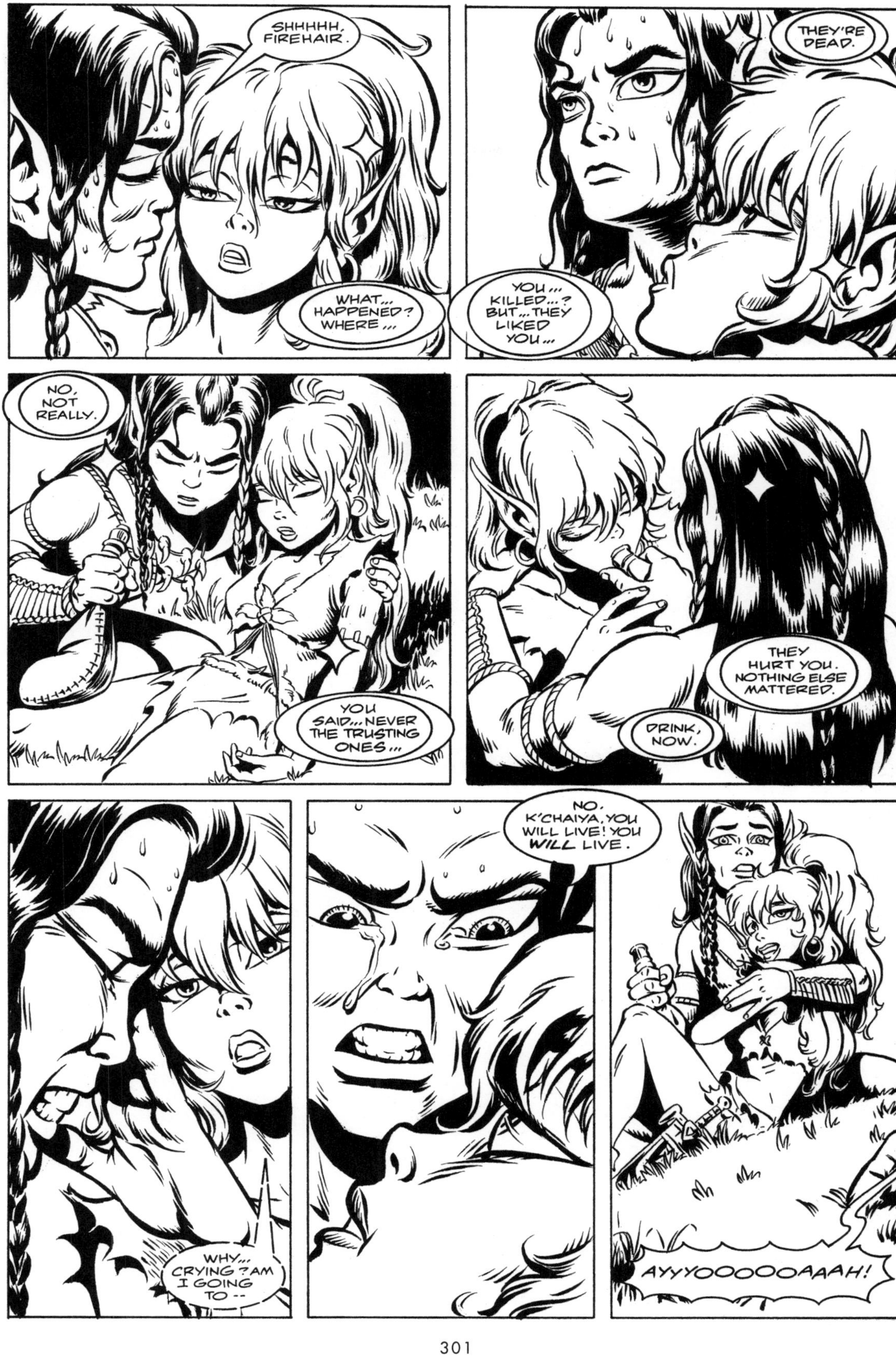
SHHHHH, FIREHAIR.
WHAT... HAPPENED? WHERE...
THEY'RE DEAD.
YOU... KILLED...? BUT... THEY LIKED YOU...
NO, NOT REALLY.
YOU SAID... NEVER THE TRUSTING ONES...
THEY HURT YOU. NOTHING ELSE MATTERED.
DRINK, NOW.
WHY... CRYING? AM I GOING TO --
NO. K'CHAIYA, YOU WILL LIVE! YOU **WILL** LIVE.
AYYYOOOOOOAAAH!

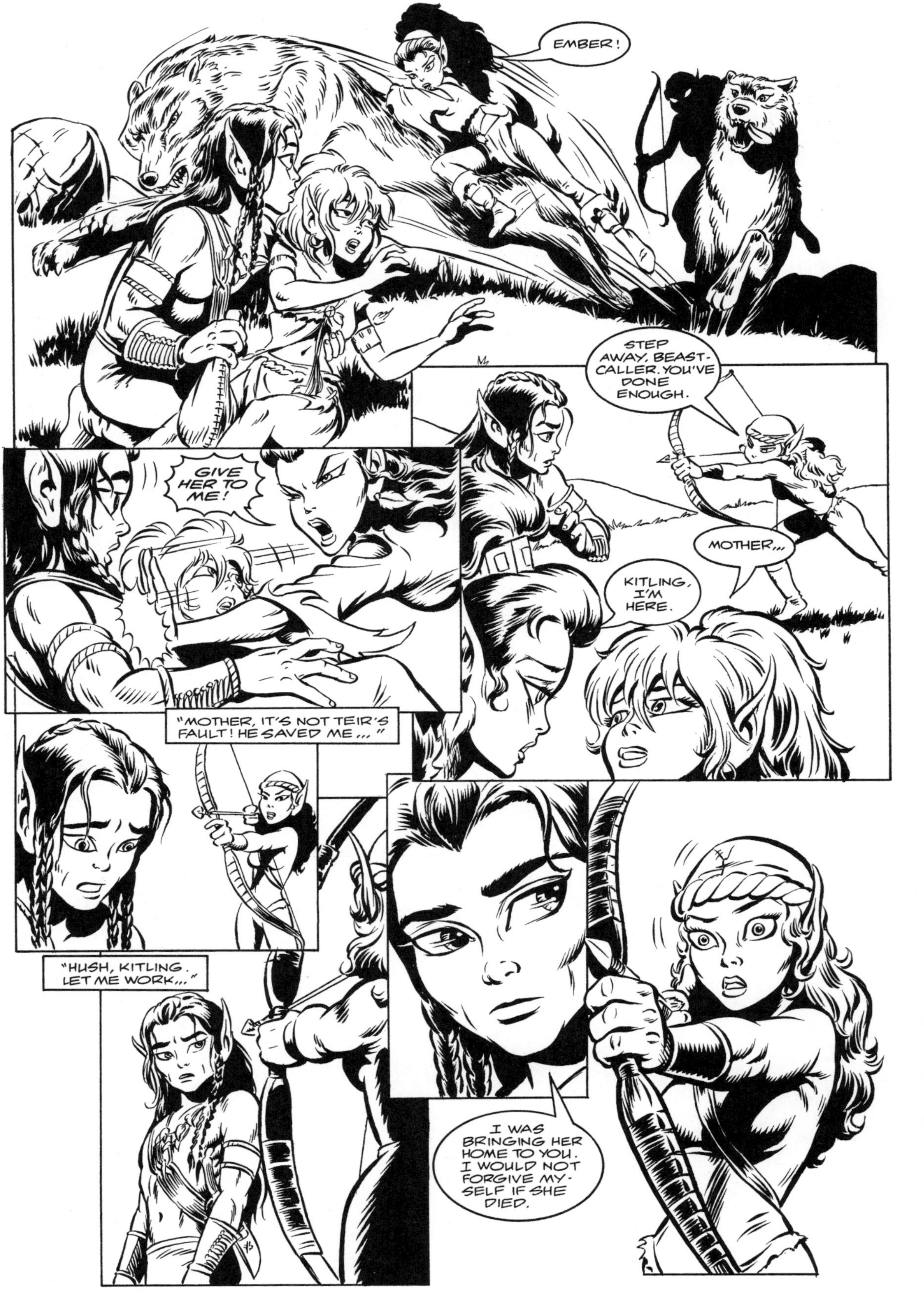
EMBER!
STEP AWAY, BEAST-CALLER. YOU'VE DONE ENOUGH.
GIVE HER TO ME!
MOTHER...
KITLING, I'M HERE.
"MOTHER, IT'S NOT TEIR'S FAULT! HE SAVED ME..."
"HUSH, KITLING. LET ME WORK..."
I WAS BRINGING HER HOME TO YOU. I WOULD NOT FORGIVE MY-SELF IF SHE DIED.

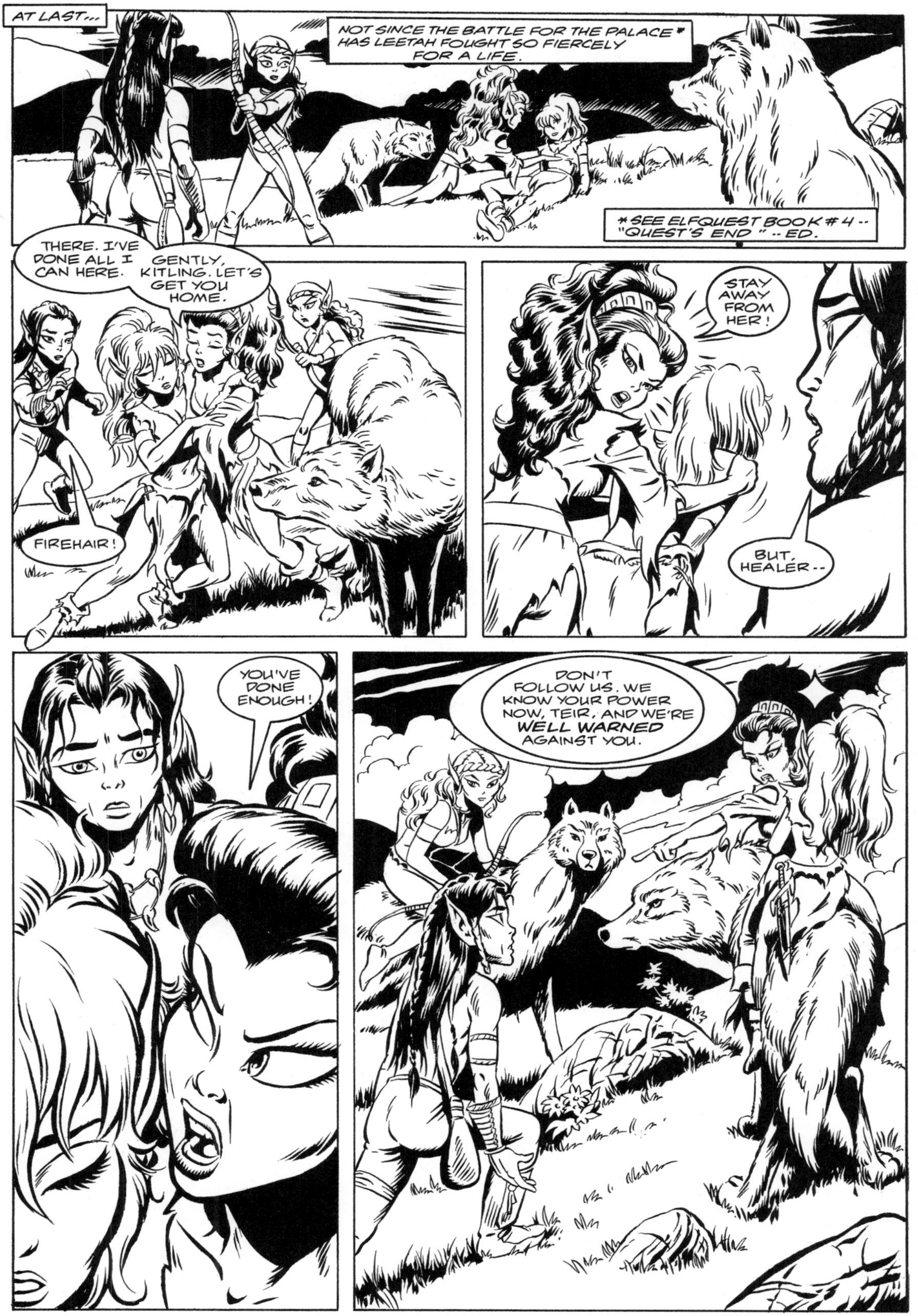

AT LAST...
NOT SINCE THE BATTLE FOR THE PALACE* HAS LEETAH FOUGHT SO FIERCELY FOR A LIFE.
*SEE ELFQUEST BOOK #4 -- "QUEST'S END" -- ED.
THERE. I'VE DONE ALL I CAN HERE.
GENTLY, KITLING. LET'S GET YOU HOME.
FIREHAIR!
STAY AWAY FROM HER!
BUT, HEALER--
YOU'VE DONE ENOUGH!
DON'T FOLLOW US. WE KNOW YOUR POWER NOW, TEIR, AND WE'RE WELL WARNED AGAINST YOU.

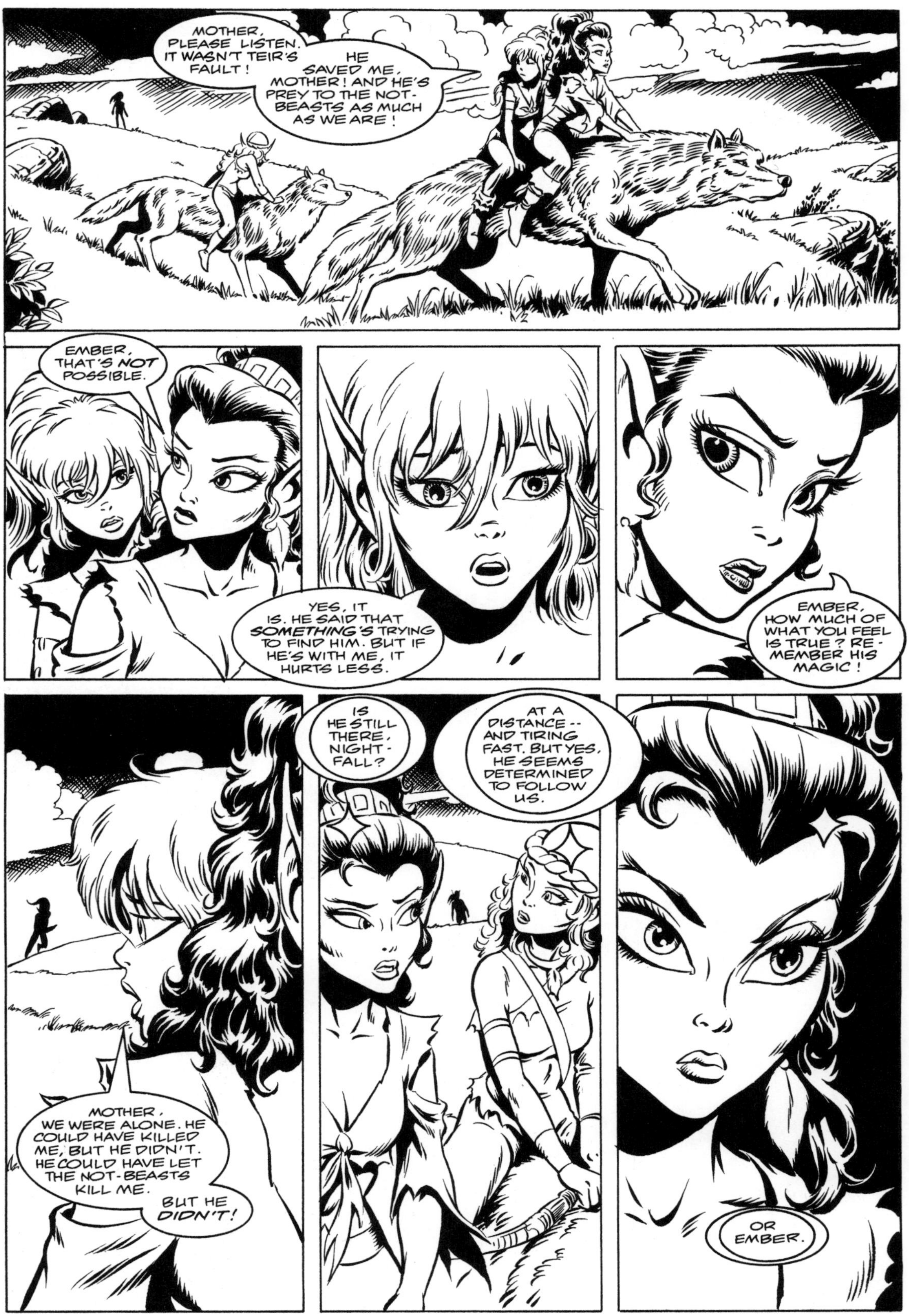
MOTHER, PLEASE LISTEN. IT WASN'T TEIR'S FAULT!
HE SAVED ME, MOTHER! AND HE'S PREY TO THE NOT-BEASTS AS MUCH AS WE ARE!
EMBER, THAT'S NOT POSSIBLE.
YES, IT IS. HE SAID THAT SOMETHING'S TRYING TO FIND HIM. BUT IF HE'S WITH ME, IT HURTS LESS.
EMBER, HOW MUCH OF WHAT YOU FEEL IS TRUE? RE-MEMBER HIS MAGIC!
MOTHER, WE WERE ALONE. HE COULD HAVE KILLED ME, BUT HE DIDN'T. HE COULD HAVE LET THE NOT-BEASTS KILL ME.
BUT HE DIDN'T!
IS HE STILL THERE, NIGHT-FALL?
AT A DISTANCE -- AND TIRING FAST. BUT YES, HE SEEMS DETERMINED TO FOLLOW US.
OR EMBER.

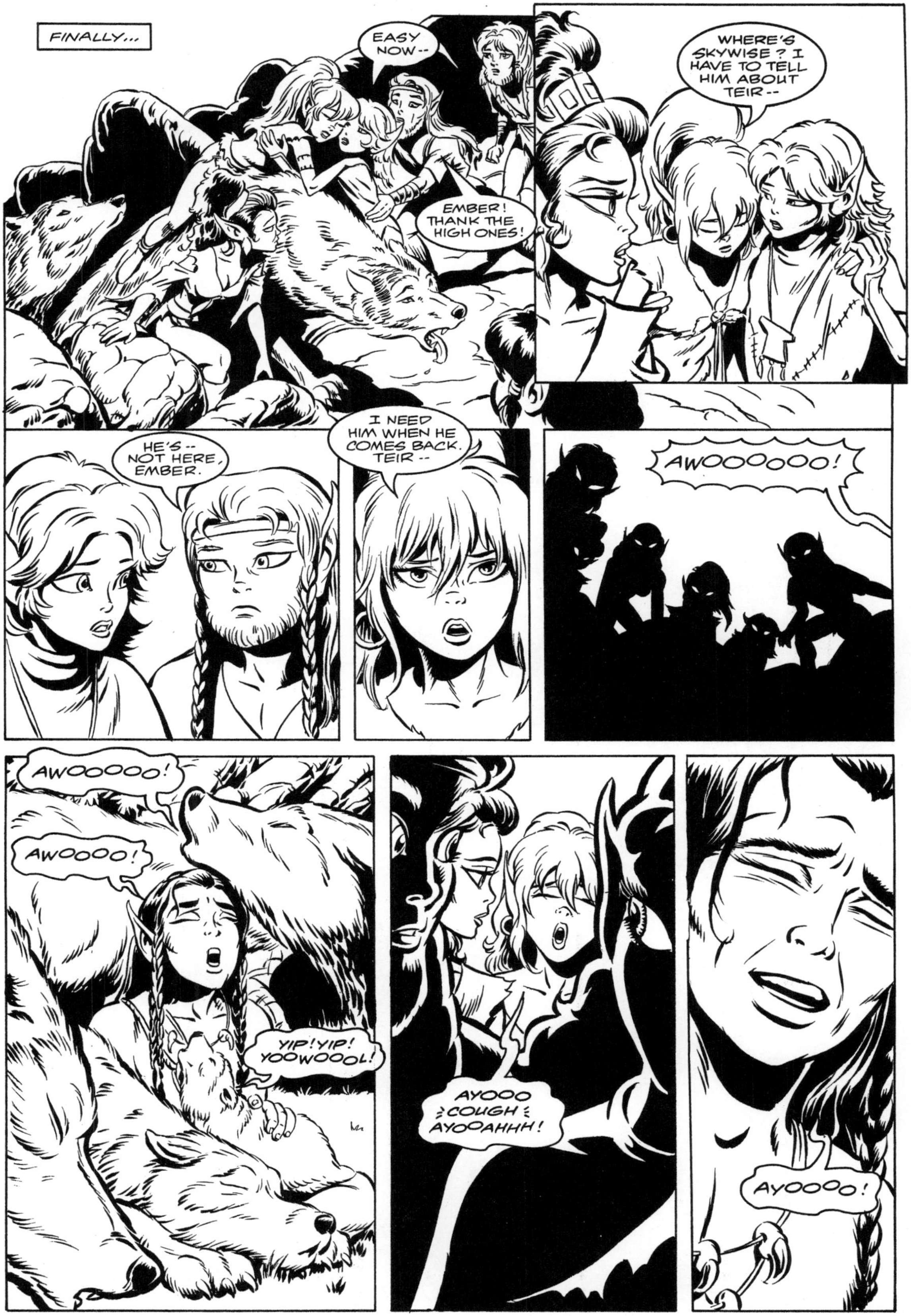

FINALLY...
EASY NOW --
EMBER! THANK THE HIGH ONES!
WHERE'S SKYWISE? I HAVE TO TELL HIM ABOUT TEIR --
HE'S -- NOT HERE, EMBER.
I NEED HIM WHEN HE COMES BACK. TEIR --
AWOOOOOOO!
AWOOOOOO!
AWOOOO!
YIP! YIP! YOOWOOOL!
AYOOO COUGH AYOOAHHH!
AYOOOO!

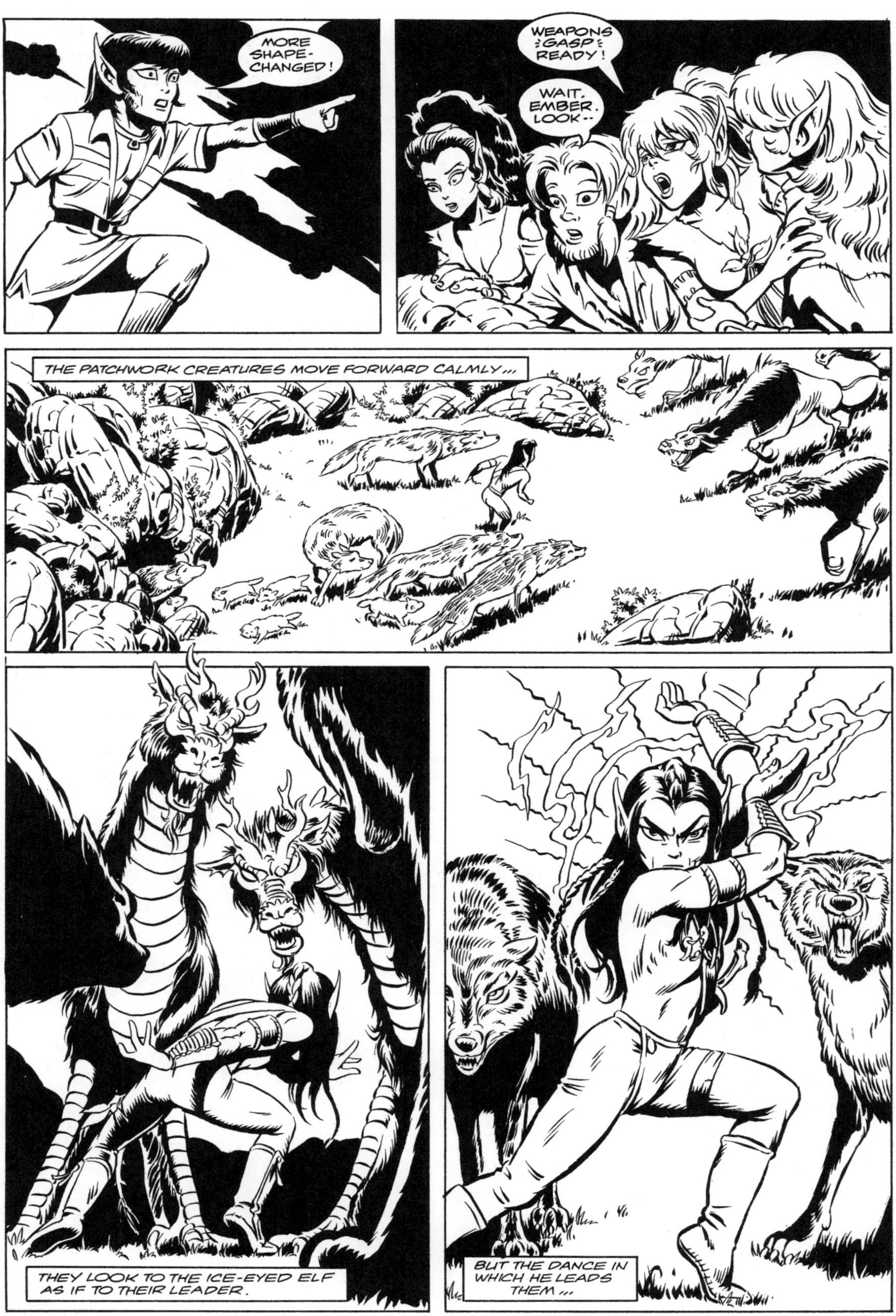
MORE SHAPE-CHANGED!
WEAPONS :GASP: READY!
WAIT, EMBER. LOOK--
THE PATCHWORK CREATURES MOVE FORWARD CALMLY...
THEY LOOK TO THE ICE-EYED ELF AS IF TO THEIR LEADER.
BUT THE DANCE IN WHICH HE LEADS THEM...

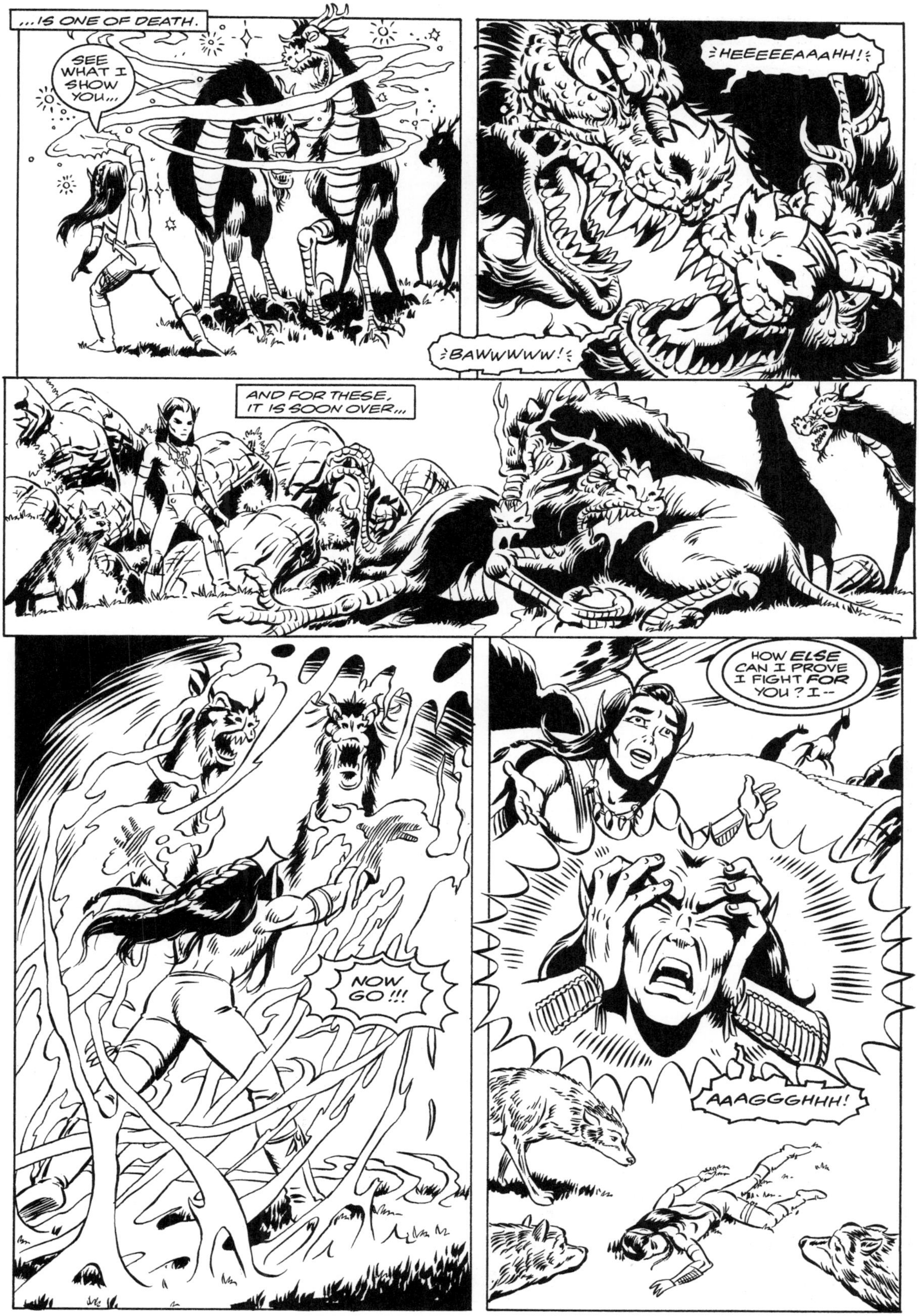
...IS ONE OF DEATH.
SEE WHAT I SHOW YOU...
HEEEEEAAAHH!
BAWWWWW!
AND FOR THESE, IT IS SOON OVER...
NOW GO!!!
HOW ELSE CAN I PROVE I FIGHT FOR YOU? I--
AAAGGGHHH!

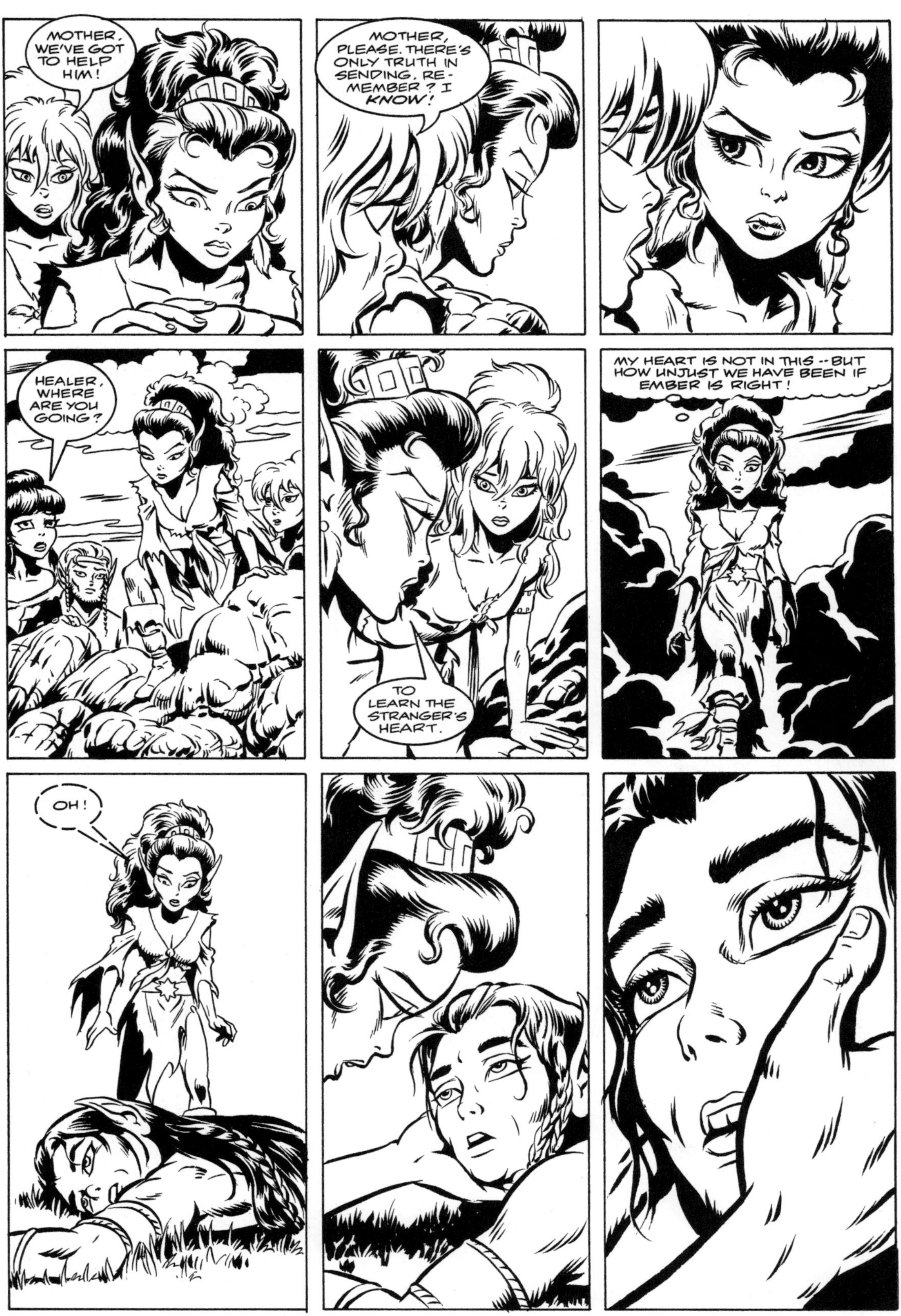
MOTHER, WE'VE GOT TO HELP HIM!
MOTHER, PLEASE. THERE'S ONLY TRUTH IN SENDING, RE- MEMBER? I KNOW!
HEALER, WHERE ARE YOU GOING?
TO LEARN THE STRANGER'S HEART.
MY HEART IS NOT IN THIS -- BUT HOW UNJUST WE HAVE BEEN IF EMBER IS RIGHT!
OH!

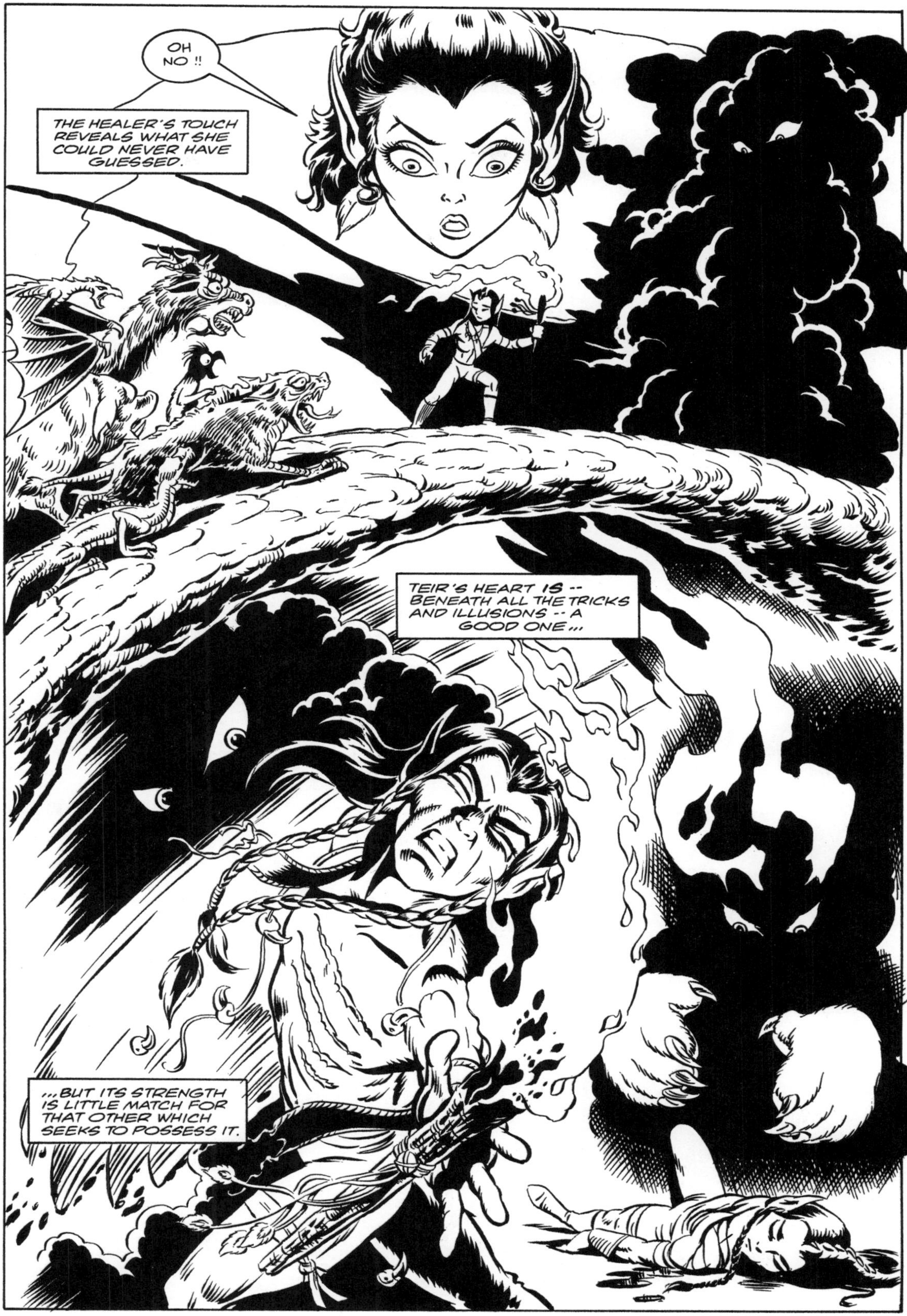

OH NO !!
THE HEALER'S TOUCH REVEALS WHAT SHE COULD NEVER HAVE GUESSED.
TEIR'S HEART IS -- BENEATH ALL THE TRICKS AND ILLUSIONS -- A GOOD ONE...
...BUT ITS STRENGTH IS LITTLE MATCH FOR THAT OTHER WHICH SEEKS TO POSSESS IT.

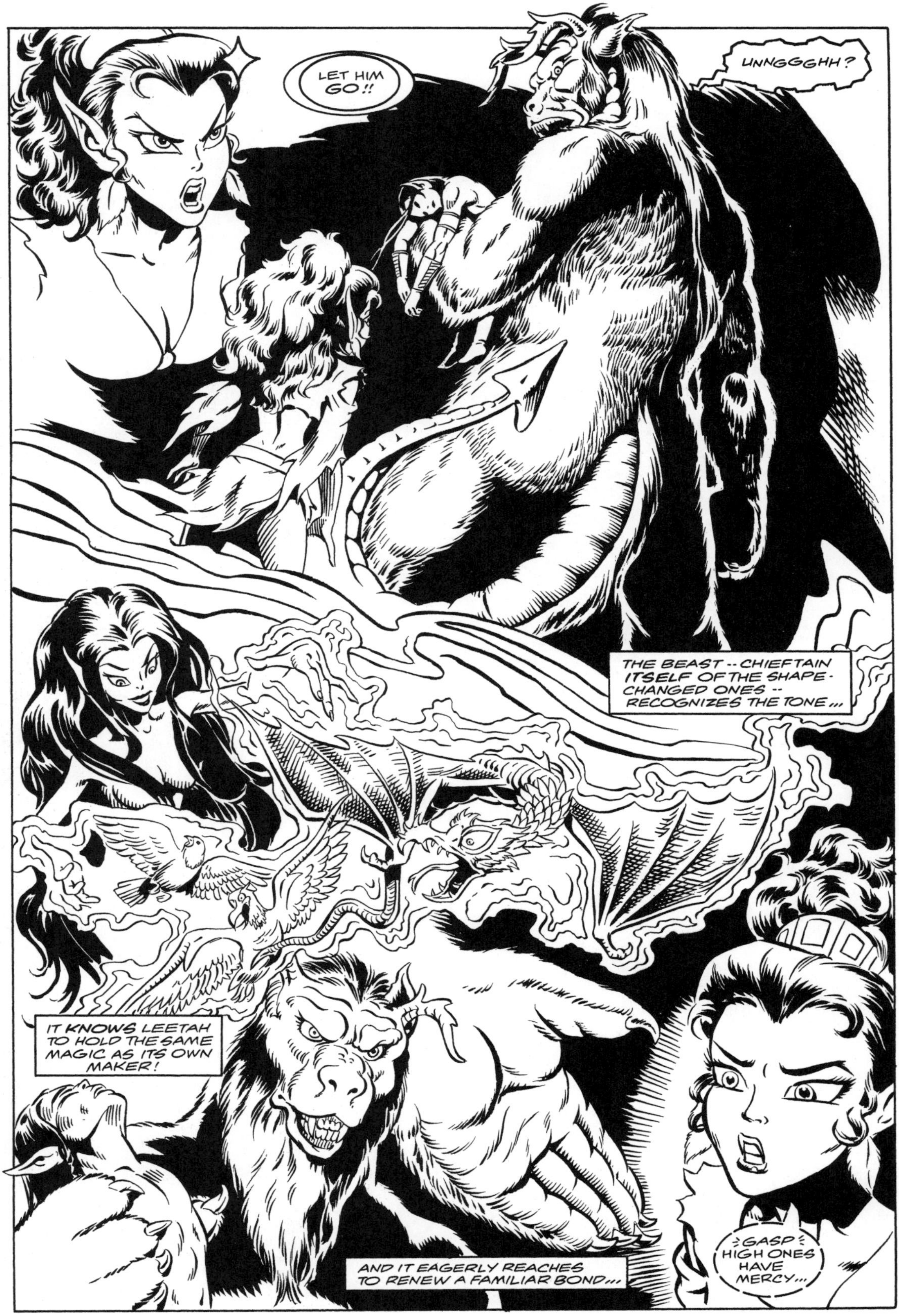
LET HIM GO!!
UNNGGGHH?
THE BEAST -- CHIEFTAIN ITSELF OF THE SHAPE-CHANGED ONES -- RECOGNIZES THE TONE...
IT KNOWS LEETAH TO HOLD THE SAME MAGIC AS ITS OWN MAKER!
AND IT EAGERLY REACHES TO RENEW A FAMILIAR BOND...
GASP HIGH ONES HAVE MERCY...

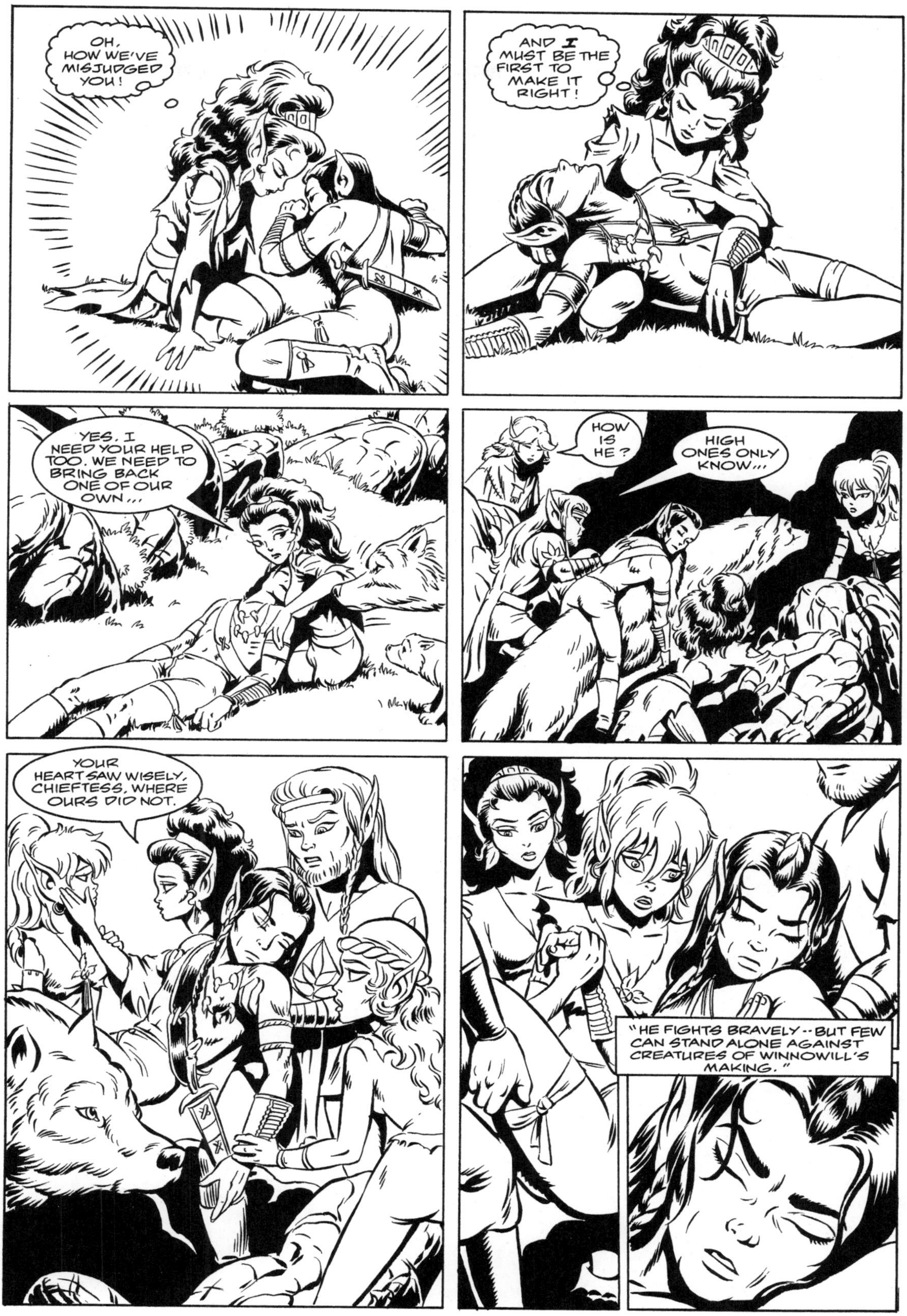

OH, HOW WE'VE MISJUDGED YOU!
AND I MUST BE THE FIRST TO MAKE IT RIGHT!
YES, I NEED YOUR HELP TOO. WE NEED TO BRING BACK ONE OF OUR OWN...
HOW IS HE?
HIGH ONES ONLY KNOW...
YOUR HEART SAW WISELY, CHIEFTESS, WHERE OURS DID NOT.
"HE FIGHTS BRAVELY -- BUT FEW CAN STAND ALONE AGAINST CREATURES OF WINNOWILL'S MAKING."

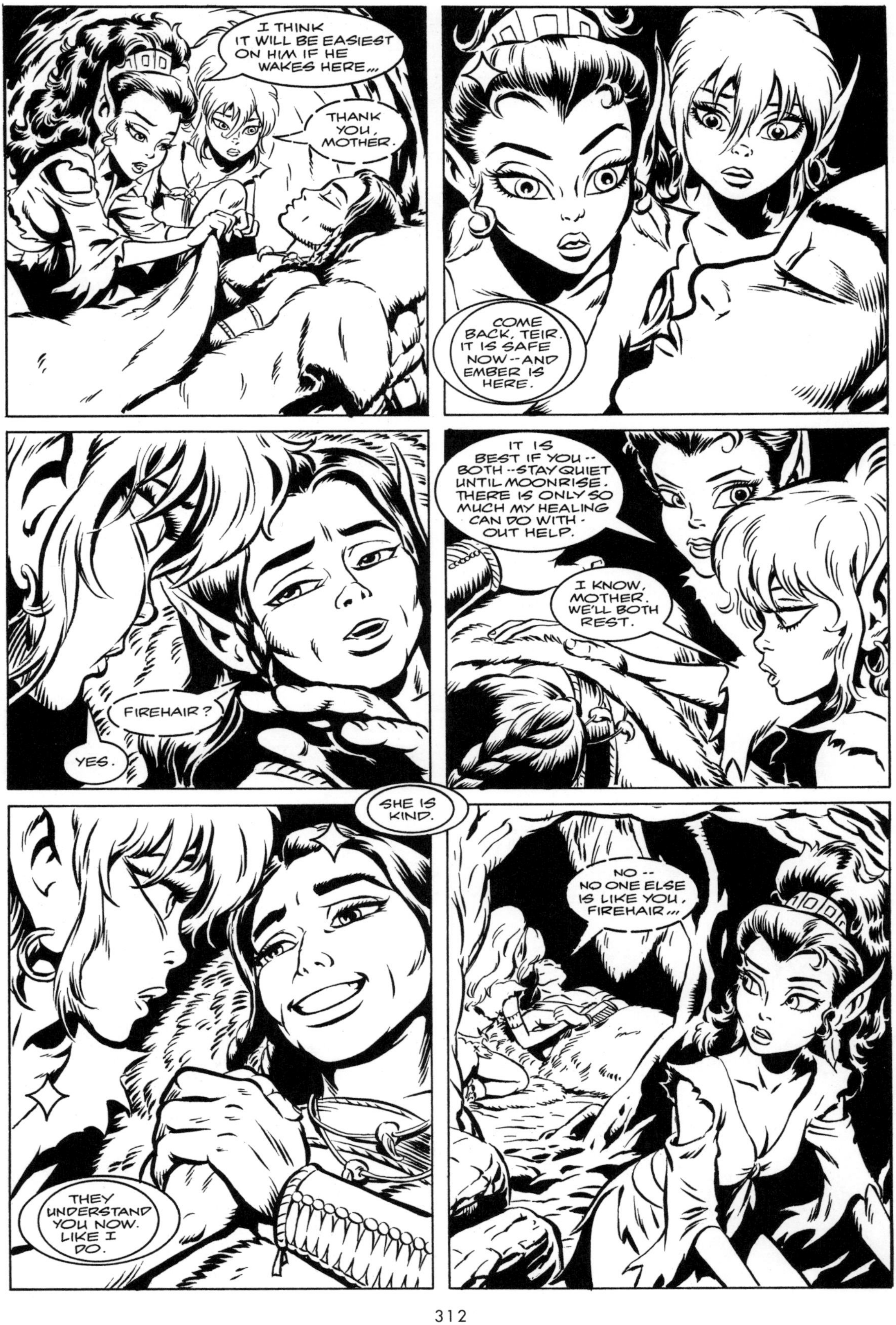
I THINK IT WILL BE EASIEST ON HIM IF HE WAKES HERE...
THANK YOU, MOTHER.
COME BACK, TEIR. IT IS SAFE NOW--AND EMBER IS HERE.
FIREHAIR?
YES.
IT IS BEST IF YOU-- BOTH--STAY QUIET UNTIL MOONRISE. THERE IS ONLY SO MUCH MY HEALING CAN DO WITH-OUT HELP.
I KNOW, MOTHER. WE'LL BOTH REST.
SHE IS KIND.
THEY UNDERSTAND YOU NOW. LIKE I DO.
NO-- NO ONE ELSE IS LIKE YOU, FIREHAIR...

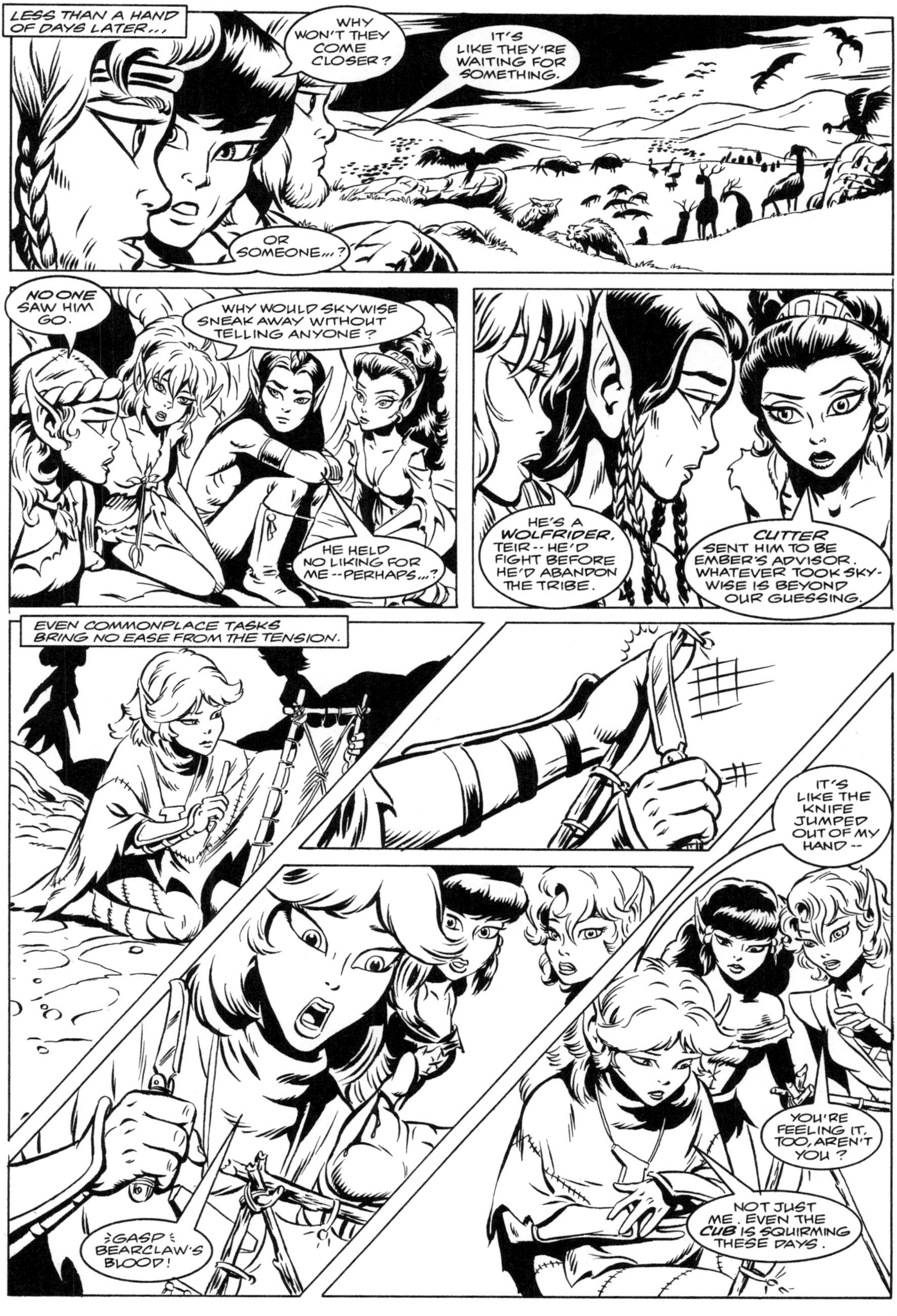
LESS THAN A HAND OF DAYS LATER...
WHY WON'T THEY COME CLOSER?
IT'S LIKE THEY'RE WAITING FOR SOMETHING.
OR SOMEONE...?
NO ONE SAW HIM GO.
WHY WOULD SKYWISE SNEAK AWAY WITHOUT TELLING ANYONE?
HE HELD NO LIKING FOR ME--PERHAPS...?
HE'S A WOLFRIDER, TEIR--HE'D FIGHT BEFORE HE'D ABANDON THE TRIBE.
CUTTER SENT HIM TO BE EMBER'S ADVISOR. WHATEVER TOOK SKYWISE IS BEYOND OUR GUESSING.
EVEN COMMONPLACE TASKS BRING NO EASE FROM THE TENSION.
IT'S LIKE THE KNIFE JUMPED OUT OF MY HAND--
GASP BEARCLAW'S BLOOD!
YOU'RE FEELING IT, TOO, AREN'T YOU?
NOT JUST ME. EVEN THE CUB IS SQUIRMING THESE DAYS.

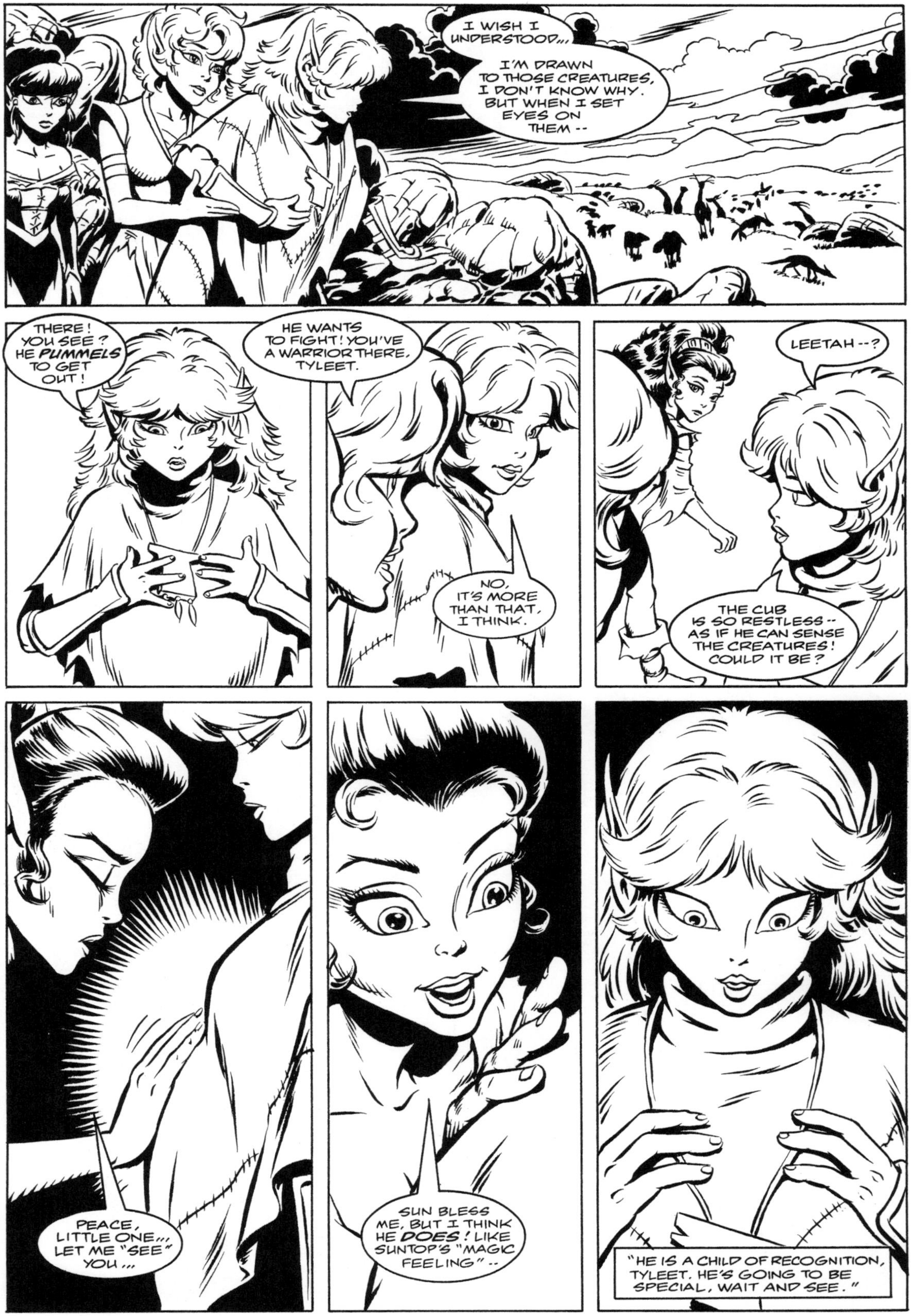
I WISH I UNDERSTOOD...
I'M DRAWN TO THOSE CREATURES, I DON'T KNOW WHY. BUT WHEN I SET EYES ON THEM --
THERE! YOU SEE? HE *PUMMELS* TO GET OUT!
HE WANTS TO FIGHT! YOU'VE A WARRIOR THERE, TYLEET.
NO, IT'S MORE THAN THAT, I THINK.
LEETAH --?
THE CUB IS SO RESTLESS -- AS IF HE CAN SENSE THE CREATURES! COULD IT BE?
PEACE, LITTLE ONE... LET ME "SEE" YOU...
SUN BLESS ME, BUT I THINK HE *DOES*! LIKE SUNTOP'S "MAGIC FEELING" ..
"HE IS A CHILD OF RECOGNITION, TYLEET. HE'S GOING TO BE SPECIAL, WAIT AND SEE."

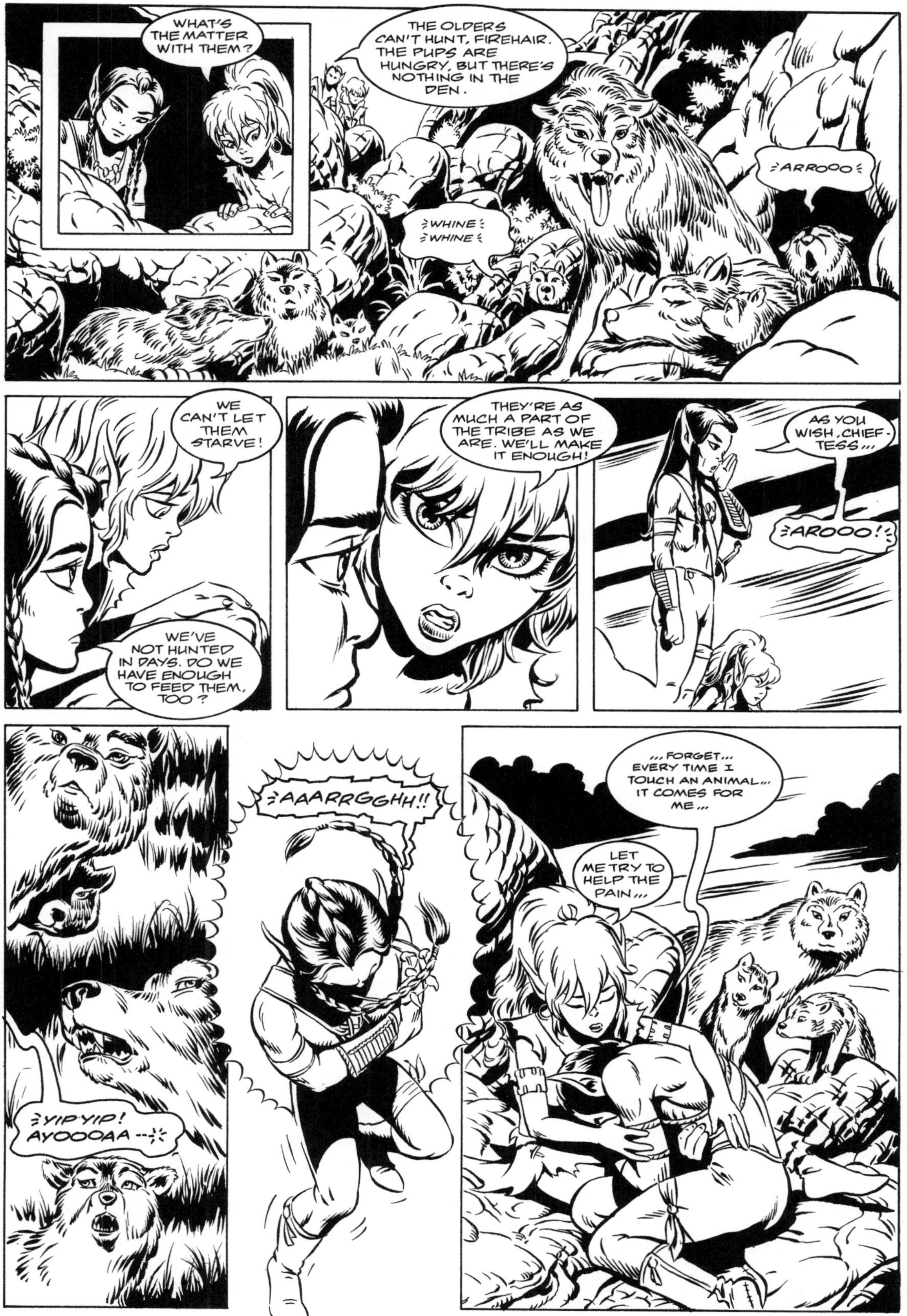

WHAT'S THE MATTER WITH THEM?
THE OLDERS CAN'T HUNT, FIREHAIR. THE PUPS ARE HUNGRY, BUT THERE'S NOTHING IN THE DEN.
ARROOO
WHINE WHINE
WE CAN'T LET THEM STARVE!
WE'VE NOT HUNTED IN DAYS. DO WE HAVE ENOUGH TO FEED THEM, TOO?
THEY'RE AS MUCH A PART OF THE TRIBE AS WE ARE. WE'LL MAKE IT ENOUGH!
AS YOU WISH, CHIEFTESS...
AROOO!
YIP YIP! AYOOOAA --
AAAARRGGHH!!
...FORGET... EVERY TIME I TOUCH AN ANIMAL... IT COMES FOR ME...
LET ME TRY TO HELP THE PAIN...

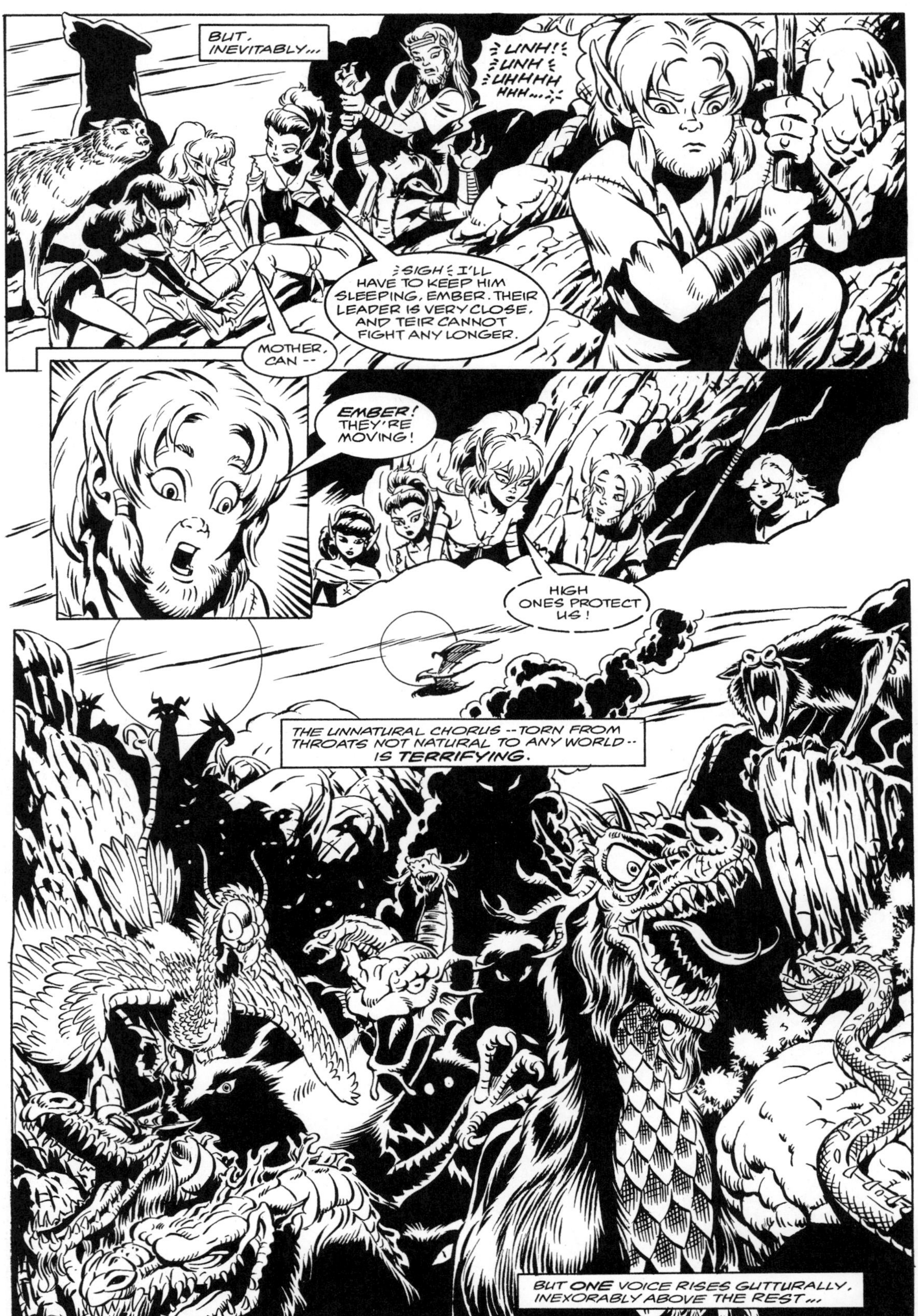

BUT, INEVITABLY...
UNH!! UNH UHHHHH HHH...
SIGH I'LL HAVE TO KEEP HIM SLEEPING, EMBER. THEIR LEADER IS VERY CLOSE, AND TEIR CANNOT FIGHT ANY LONGER.
MOTHER, CAN --
EMBER! THEY'RE MOVING!
HIGH ONES PROTECT US!
THE UNNATURAL CHORUS -- TORN FROM THROATS NOT NATURAL TO ANY WORLD -- IS TERRIFYING.
BUT ONE VOICE RISES GUTTURALLY, INEXORABLY ABOVE THE REST...

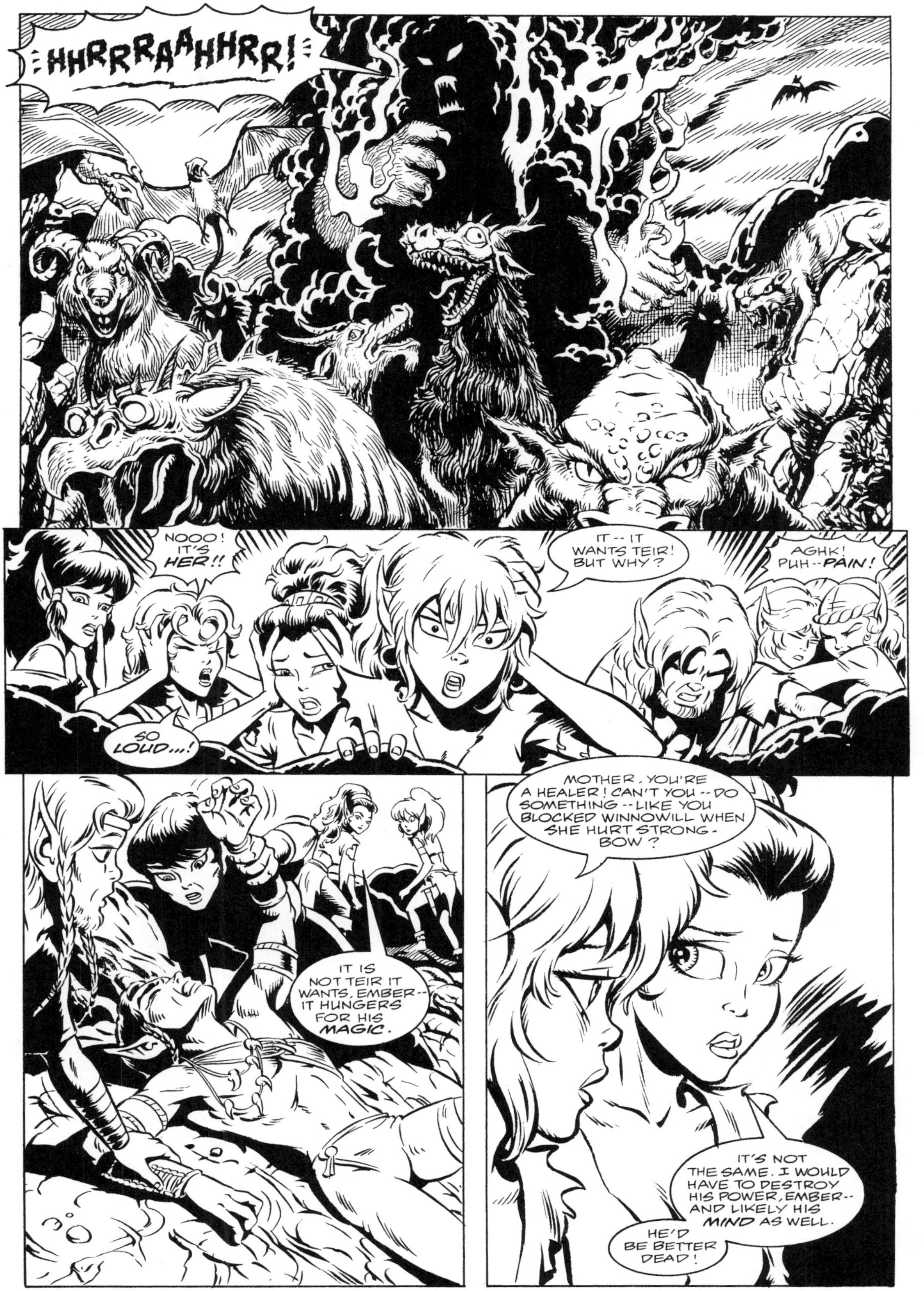
HHRRRAAHHRR!
NOOO! IT'S HER!!
SO LOUD...!
IT -- IT WANTS TEIR! BUT WHY?
AGHK! PUH--PAIN!
IT IS NOT TEIR IT WANTS, EMBER-- IT HUNGERS FOR HIS MAGIC.
MOTHER, YOU'RE A HEALER! CAN'T YOU--DO SOMETHING--LIKE YOU BLOCKED WINNOWILL WHEN SHE HURT STRONG-BOW?
IT'S NOT THE SAME. I WOULD HAVE TO DESTROY HIS POWER, EMBER-- AND LIKELY HIS MIND AS WELL.
HE'D BE BETTER DEAD!

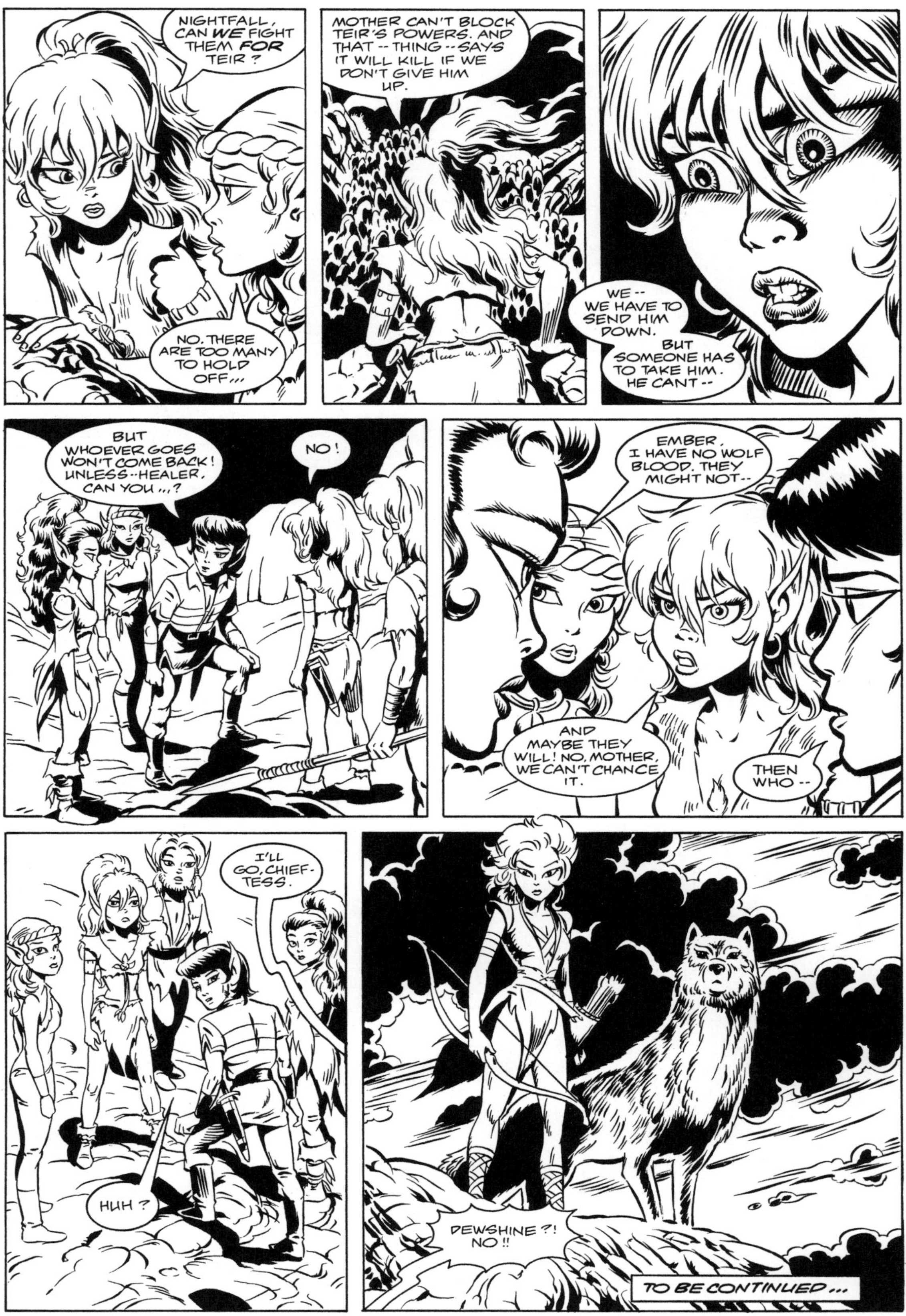

NIGHTFALL, CAN *WE* FIGHT THEM *FOR* TEIR?
NO. THERE ARE TOO MANY TO HOLD OFF...
MOTHER CAN'T BLOCK TEIR'S POWERS. AND THAT -- THING -- SAYS IT WILL KILL IF WE DON'T GIVE HIM UP.
WE -- WE HAVE TO SEND HIM DOWN.
BUT SOMEONE HAS TO TAKE HIM. HE CANT --
BUT WHOEVER GOES WON'T COME BACK! UNLESS -- HEALER, CAN YOU...?
NO!
EMBER, I HAVE NO WOLF BLOOD. THEY MIGHT NOT --
AND MAYBE THEY WILL! NO, MOTHER, WE CAN'T CHANCE IT.
THEN WHO --
I'LL GO, CHIEF-TESS.
HUH?
DEWSHINE?! NO!!
TO BE CONTINUED...

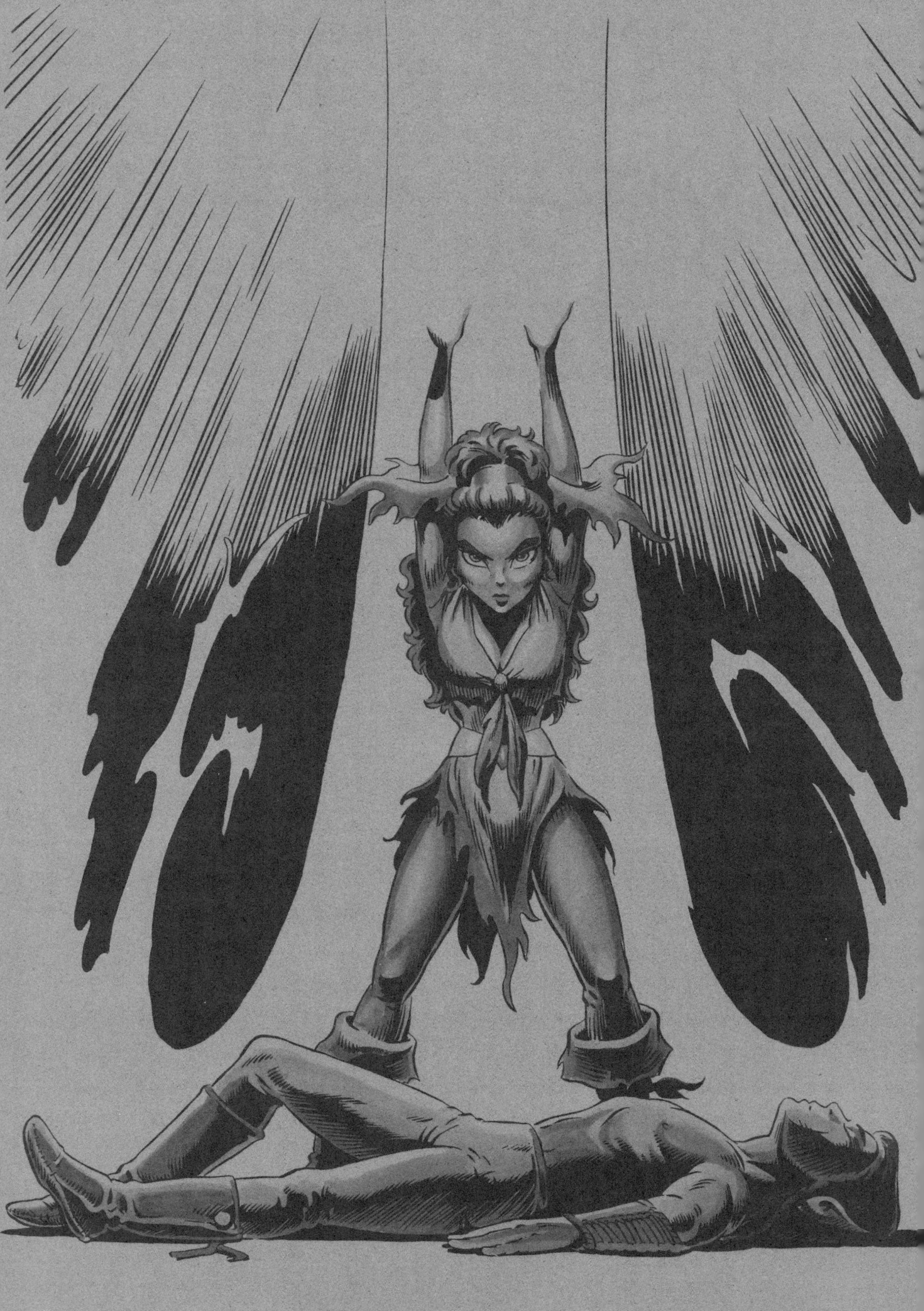

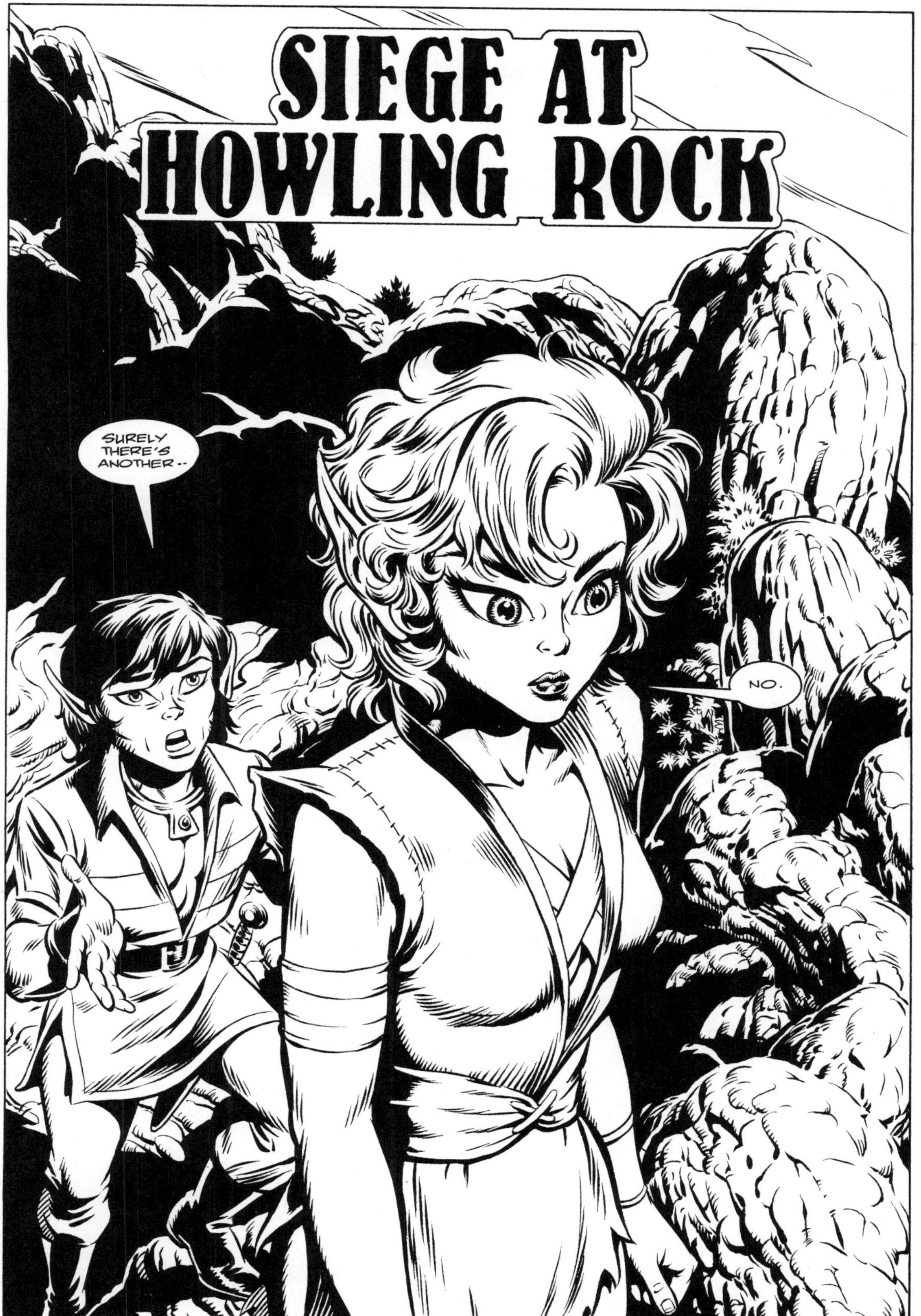
SIEGE AT HOWLING ROCK
SURELY THERE'S ANOTHER--
NO.

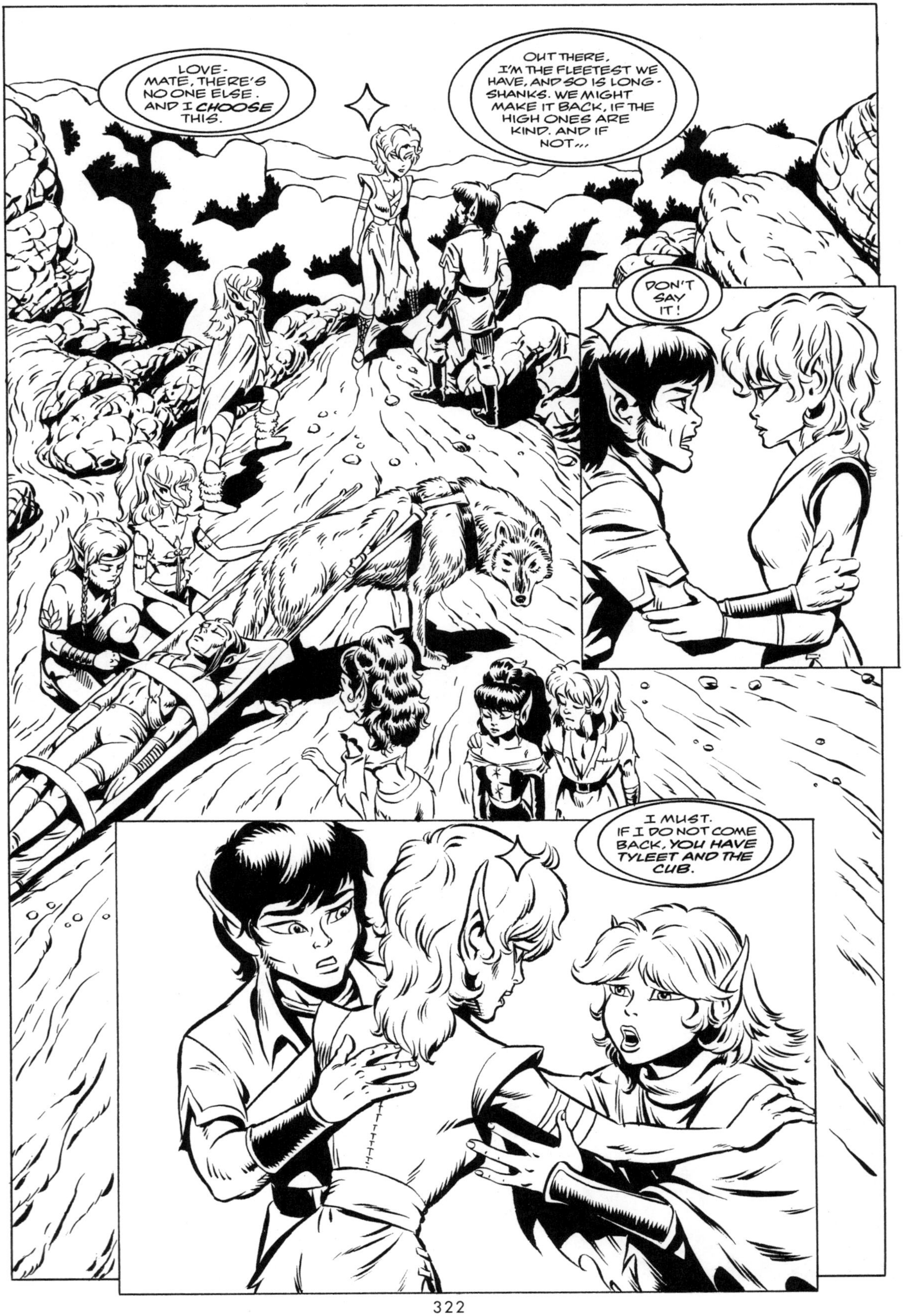
LOVE-MATE, THERE'S NO ONE ELSE. AND I CHOOSE THIS.
OUT THERE, I'M THE FLEETEST WE HAVE, AND SO IS LONG-SHANKS. WE MIGHT MAKE IT BACK, IF THE HIGH ONES ARE KIND. AND IF NOT...
DON'T SAY IT!
I MUST. IF I DO NOT COME BACK, YOU HAVE TYLEET AND THE CUB.

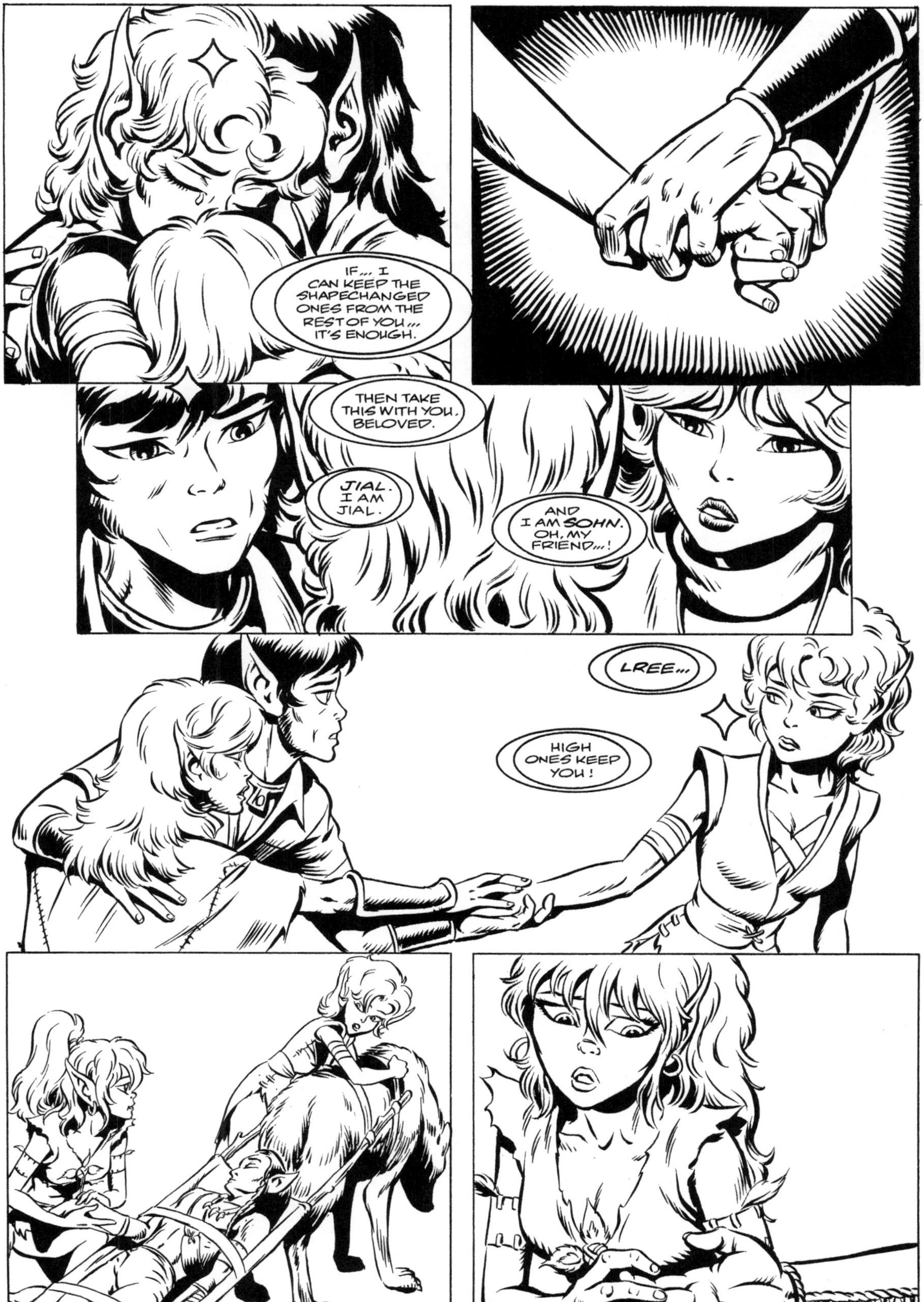
IF... I CAN KEEP THE SHAPECHANGED ONES FROM THE REST OF YOU... IT'S ENOUGH.
THEN TAKE THIS WITH YOU, BELOVED.
JIAL. I AM JIAL.
AND I AM SOHN. OH, MY FRIEND...!
LREE...
HIGH ONES KEEP YOU!

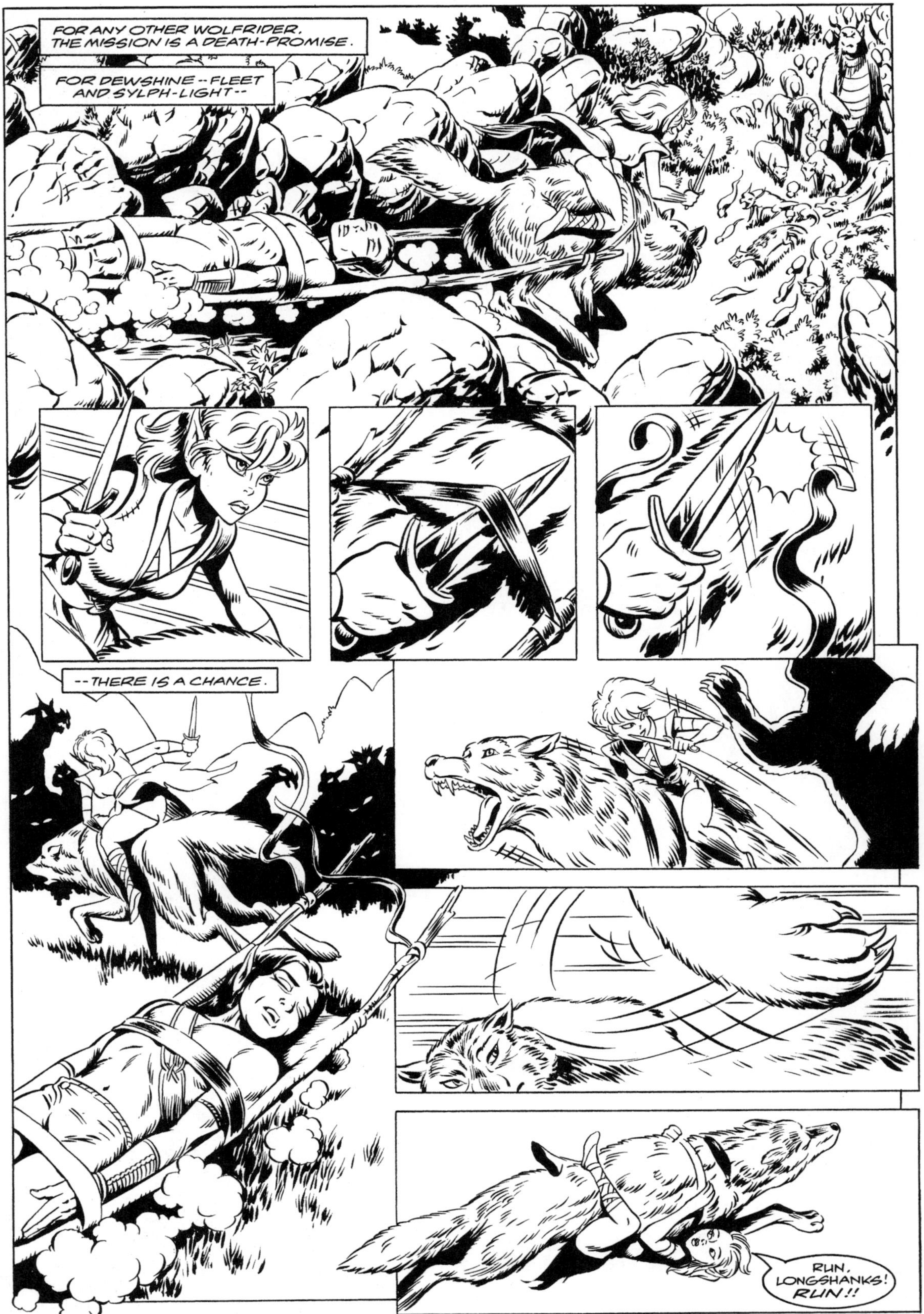
FOR ANY OTHER WOLFRIDER, THE MISSION IS A DEATH-PROMISE.
FOR DEWSHINE -- FLEET AND SYLPH-LIGHT --
-- THERE IS A CHANCE.
RUN, LONGSHANKS! RUN!!

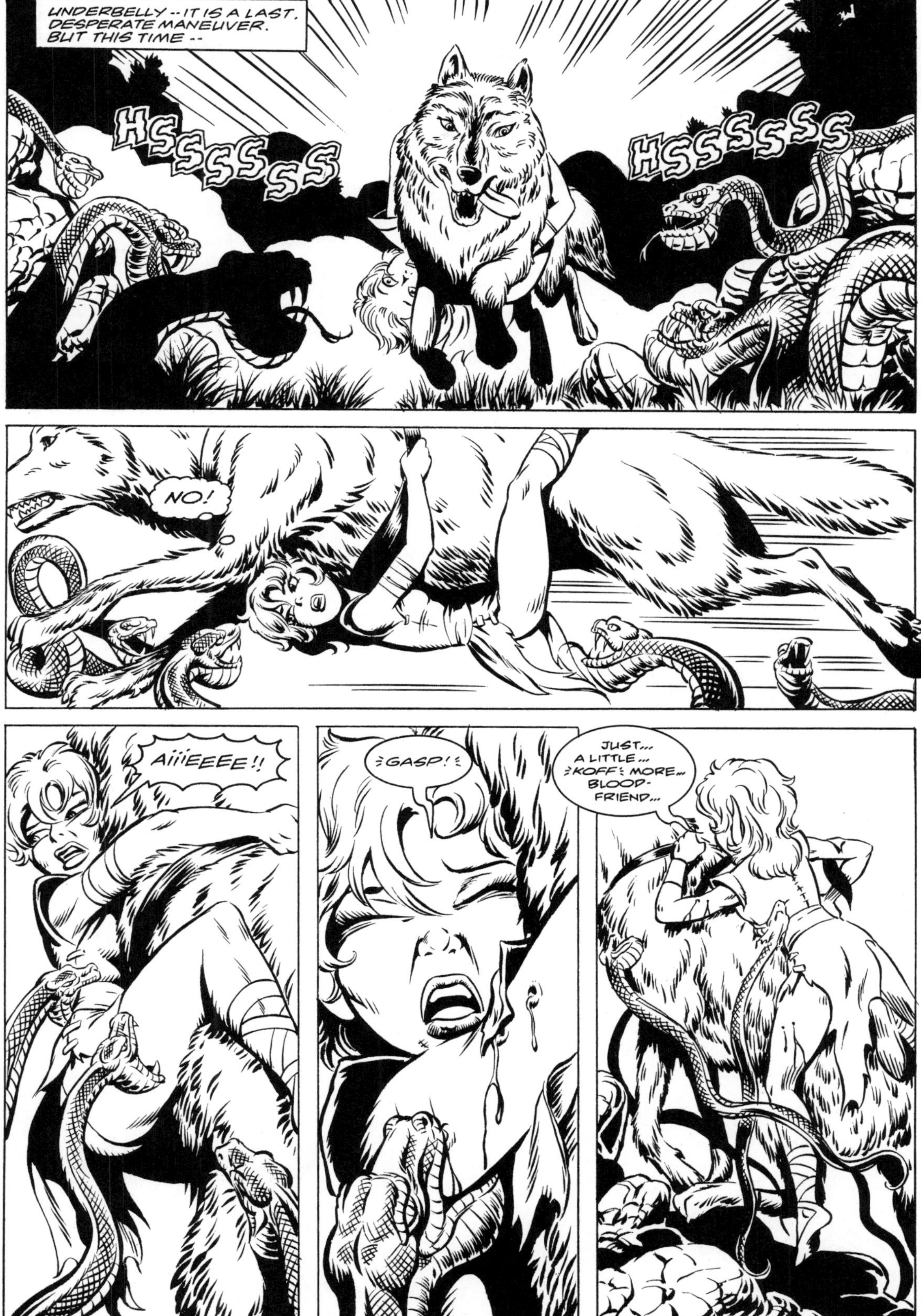
UNDERBELLY -- IT IS A LAST, DESPERATE MANEUVER. BUT THIS TIME --
HSSSSSSS
HSSSSSSS
NO!
AiiiEEEE!!
GASP!
JUST... A LITTLE... KOFF MORE... BLOOD-FRIEND...

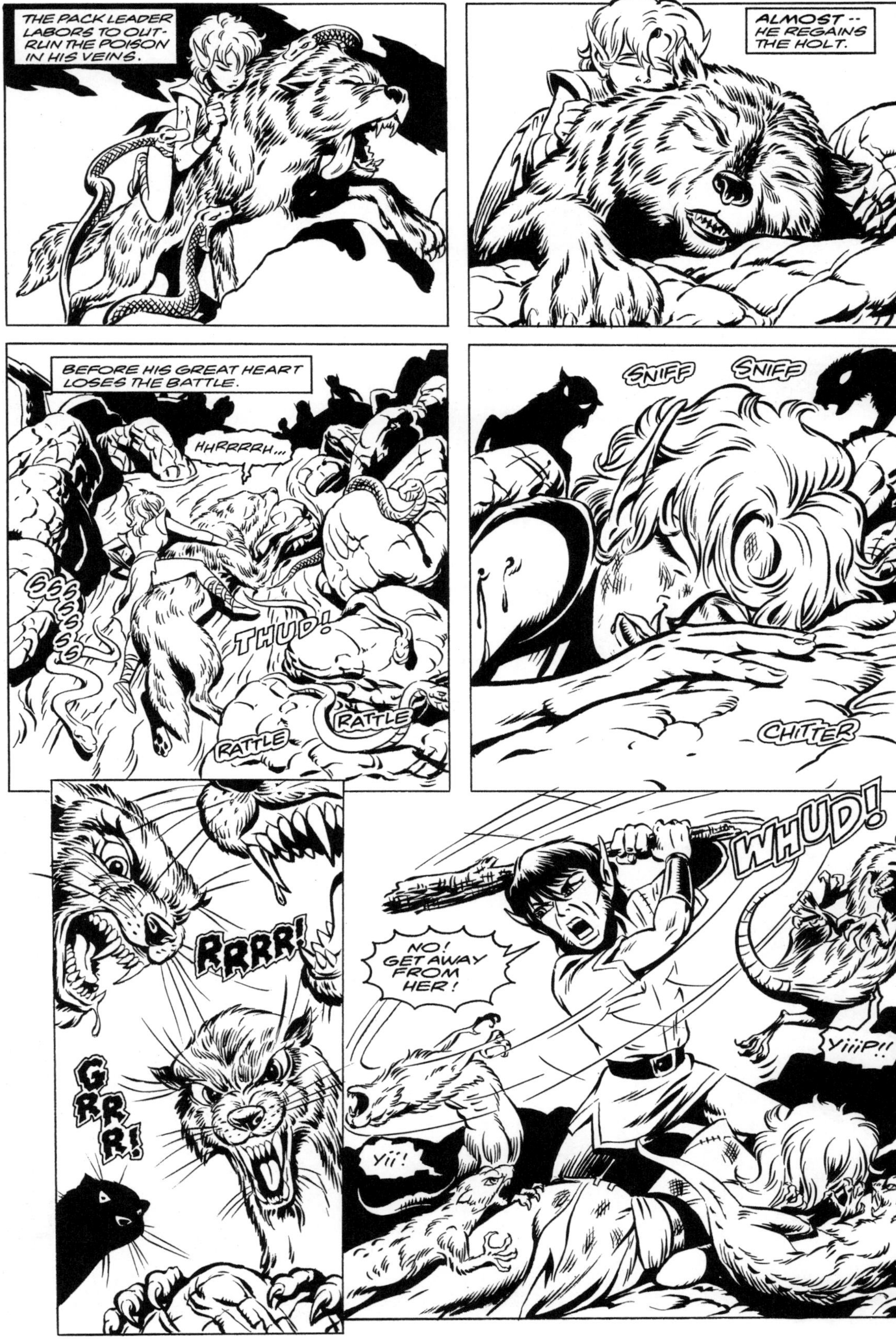
THE PACK LEADER LABORS TO OUT-RUN THE POISON IN HIS VEINS.
ALMOST -- HE REGAINS THE HOLT.
BEFORE HIS GREAT HEART LOSES THE BATTLE.
HHRRRRH...
SSSSSSSS
THUD!
RATTLE
RATTLE
SNIFF
SNIFF
CHITTER
RRRR!
GRRR!
WHUD!
NO! GET AWAY FROM HER!
YiiiP!!
Yii!

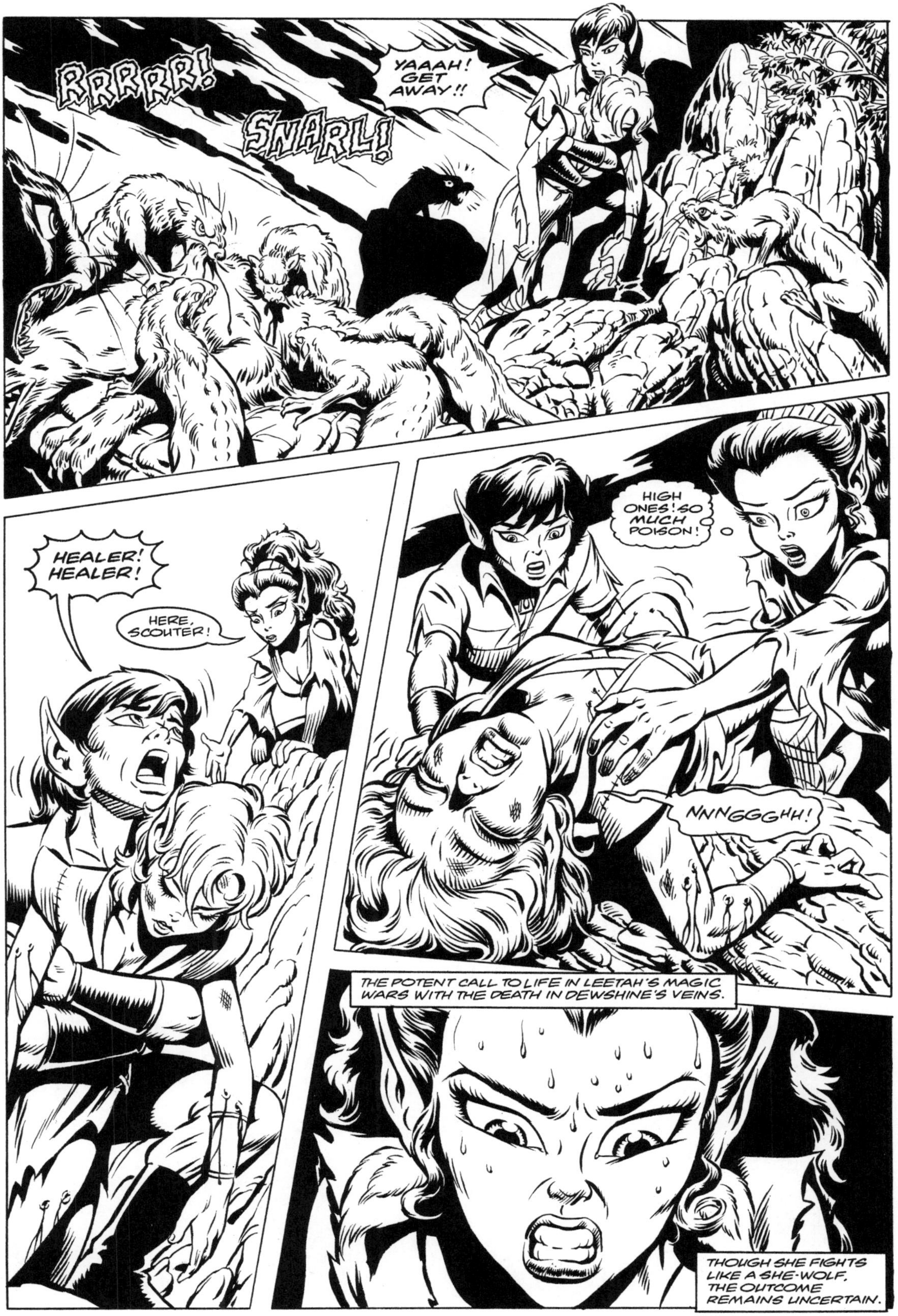

RRRRR!
SNARL!
YAAAH! GET AWAY!!
HEALER! HEALER!
HERE, SCOUTER!
HIGH ONES! SO MUCH POISON!
NNNGGGHH!
THE POTENT CALL TO LIFE IN LEETAH'S MAGIC WARS WITH THE DEATH IN DEWSHINE'S VEINS.
THOUGH SHE FIGHTS LIKE A SHE-WOLF, THE OUTCOME REMAINS UNCERTAIN.

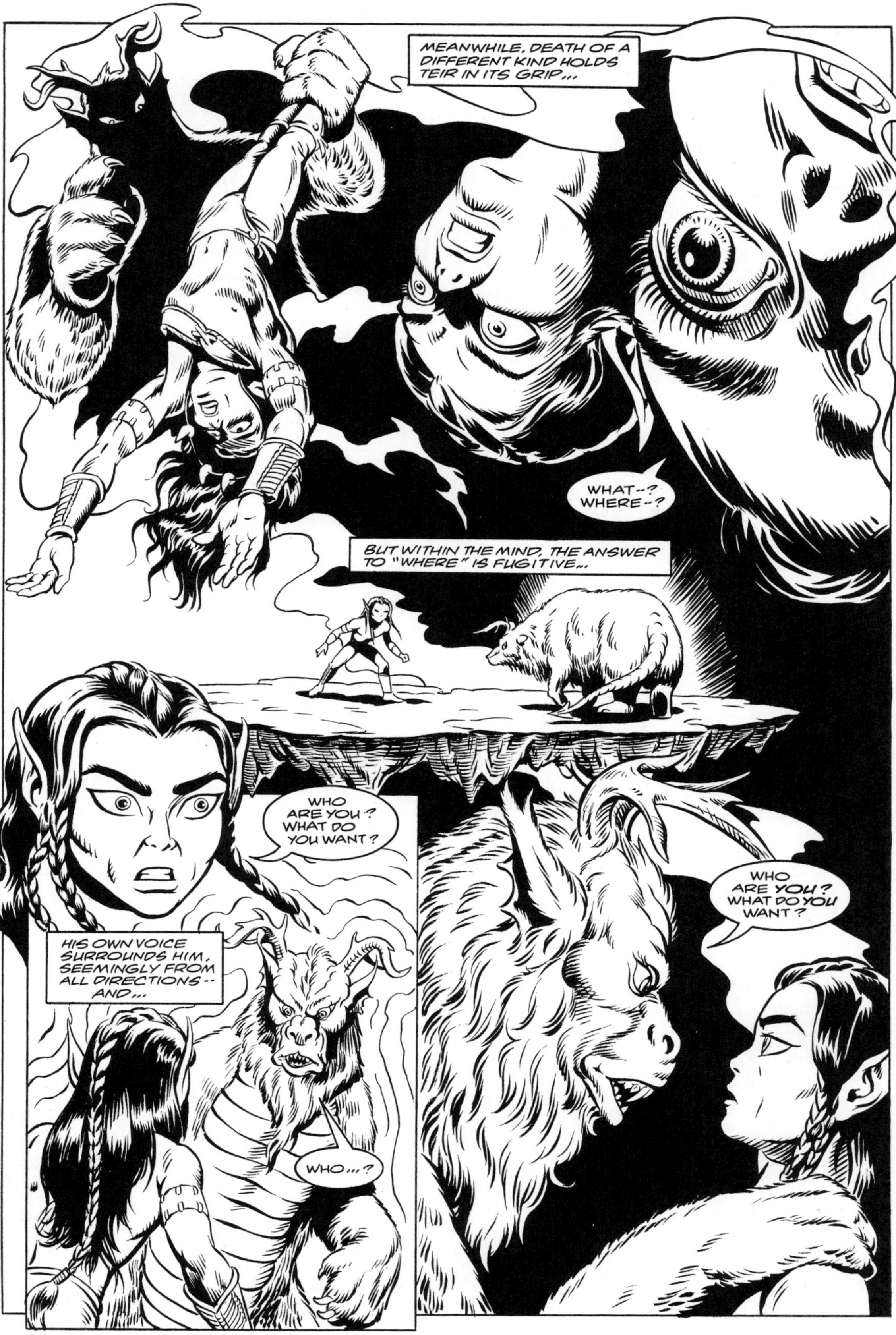

MEANWHILE, DEATH OF A DIFFERENT KIND HOLDS TEIR IN ITS GRIP...
WHAT--? WHERE--?
BUT WITHIN THE MIND, THE ANSWER TO "WHERE" IS FUGITIVE...
WHO ARE YOU? WHAT DO YOU WANT?
WHO ARE YOU? WHAT DO YOU WANT?
HIS OWN VOICE SURROUNDS HIM, SEEMINGLY FROM ALL DIRECTIONS -- AND...
WHO...?

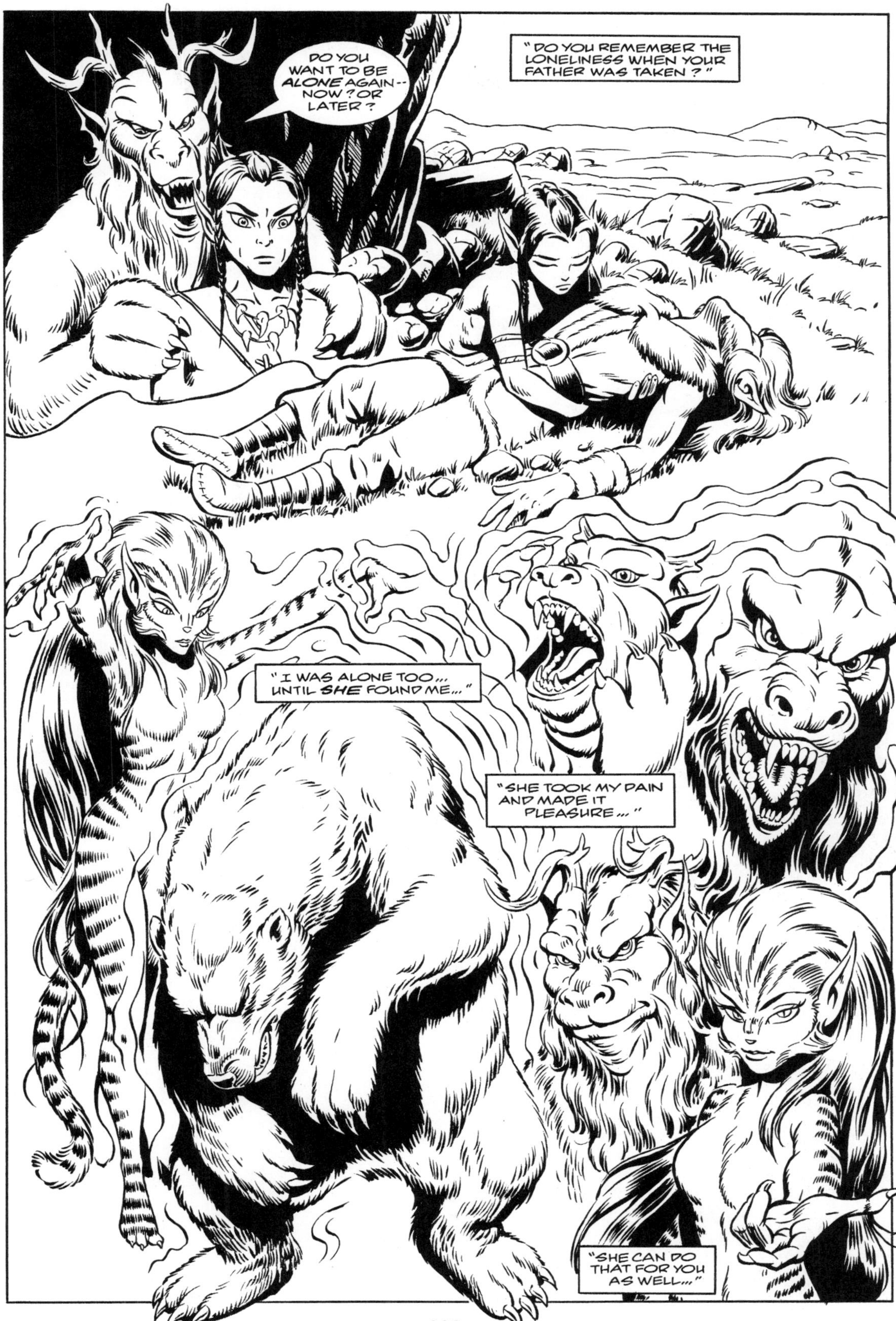
"DO YOU REMEMBER THE LONELINESS WHEN YOUR FATHER WAS TAKEN?"
DO YOU WANT TO BE ALONE AGAIN-- NOW? OR LATER?
"I WAS ALONE TOO... UNTIL SHE FOUND ME..."
"SHE TOOK MY PAIN AND MADE IT PLEASURE..."
"SHE CAN DO THAT FOR YOU AS WELL..."

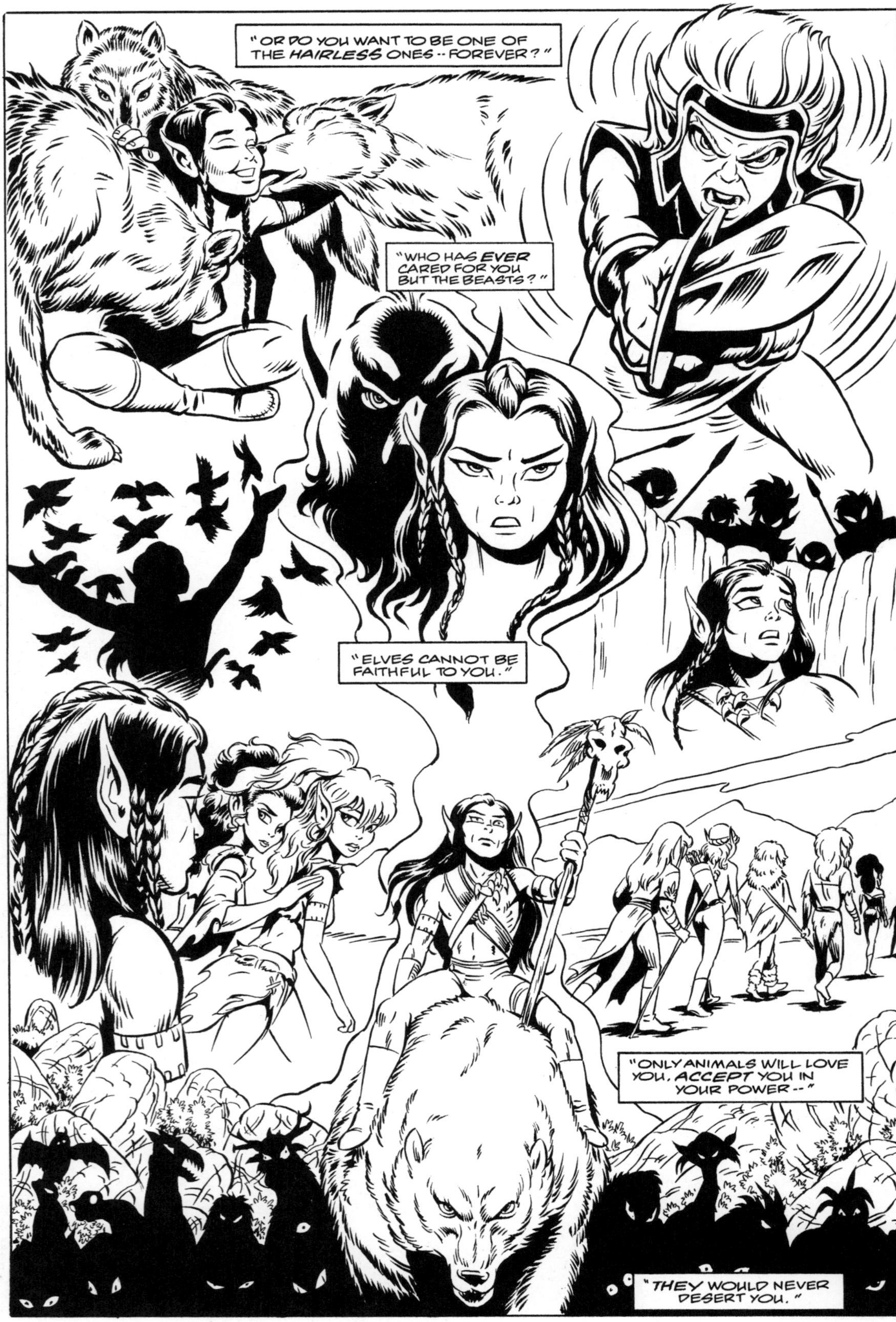
"OR DO YOU WANT TO BE ONE OF THE HAIRLESS ONES -- FOREVER?"
"WHO HAS EVER CARED FOR YOU BUT THE BEASTS?"
"ELVES CANNOT BE FAITHFUL TO YOU."
"ONLY ANIMALS WILL LOVE YOU, ACCEPT YOU IN YOUR POWER --"
"THEY WOULD NEVER DESERT YOU."

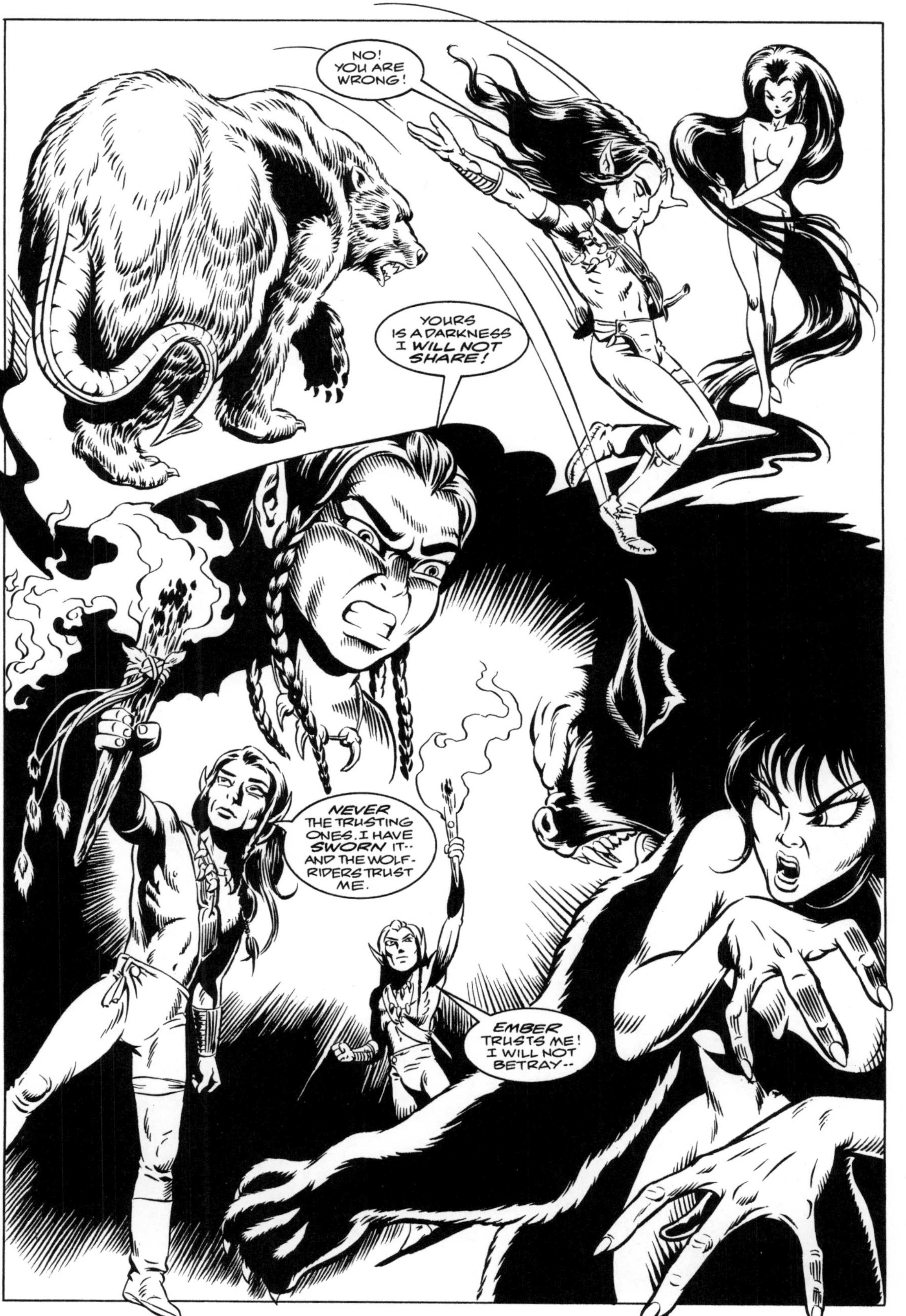
NO! YOU ARE WRONG!
YOURS IS A DARKNESS I WILL NOT SHARE!
NEVER THE TRUSTING ONES. I HAVE SWORN IT-- AND THE WOLFRIDERS TRUST ME.
EMBER TRUSTS ME! I WILL NOT BETRAY--

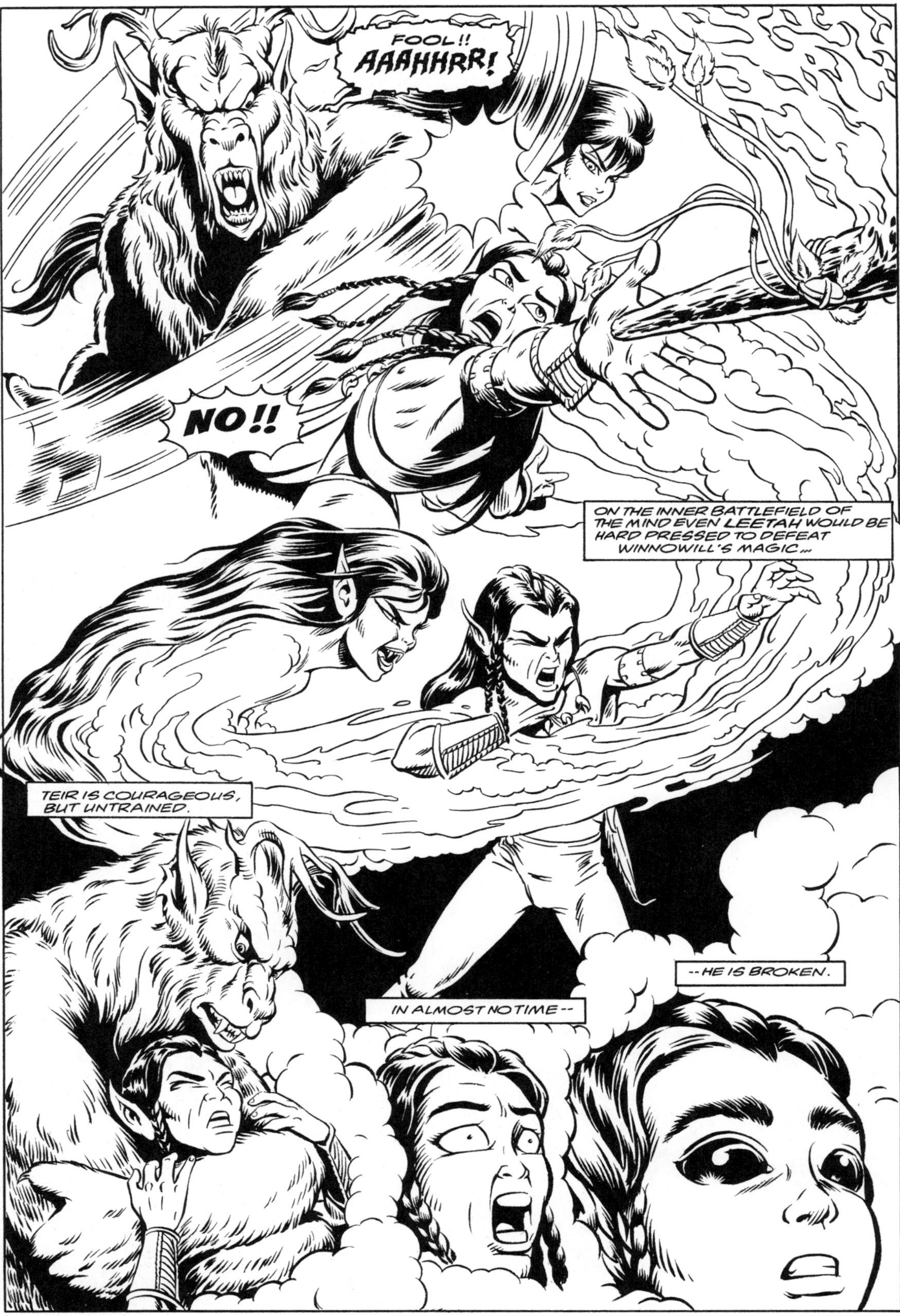
FOOL!! AAAHHRR!
NO!!
ON THE INNER BATTLEFIELD OF THE MIND EVEN LEETAH WOULD BE HARD PRESSED TO DEFEAT WINNOWILL'S MAGIC...
TEIR IS COURAGEOUS, BUT UNTRAINED.
IN ALMOST NO TIME--
--HE IS BROKEN.

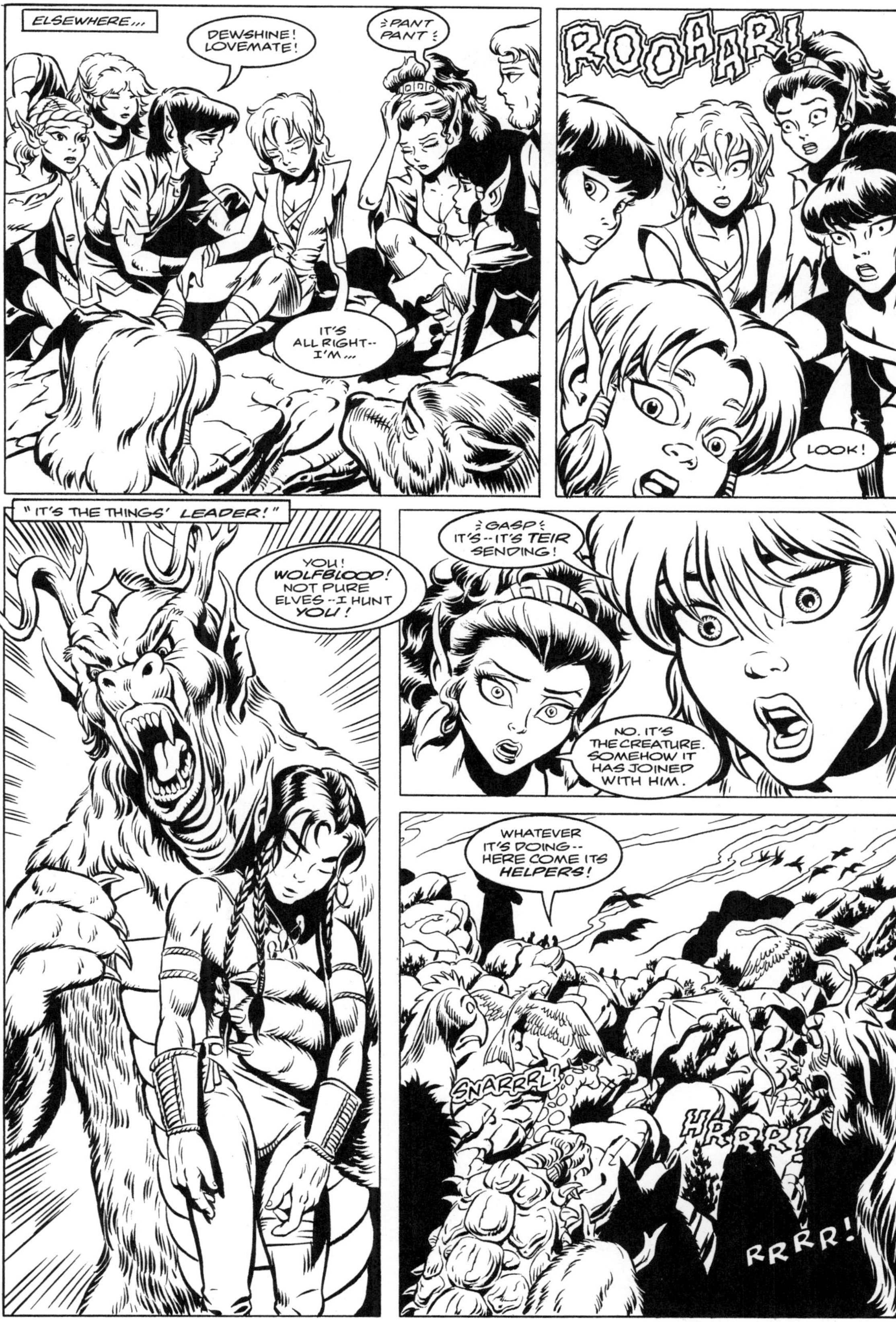
ELSEWHERE...
DEWSHINE! LOVEMATE!
PANT PANT
IT'S ALL RIGHT-- I'M...
ROOAAR!
LOOK!
"IT'S THE THINGS' LEADER!"
YOU! WOLFBLOOD! NOT PURE ELVES--I HUNT YOU!
GASP IT'S--IT'S TEIR SENDING!
NO. IT'S THE CREATURE. SOMEHOW IT HAS JOINED WITH HIM.
WHATEVER IT'S DOING-- HERE COME ITS HELPERS!
SNARRRL!
HRRR!
RRRR!

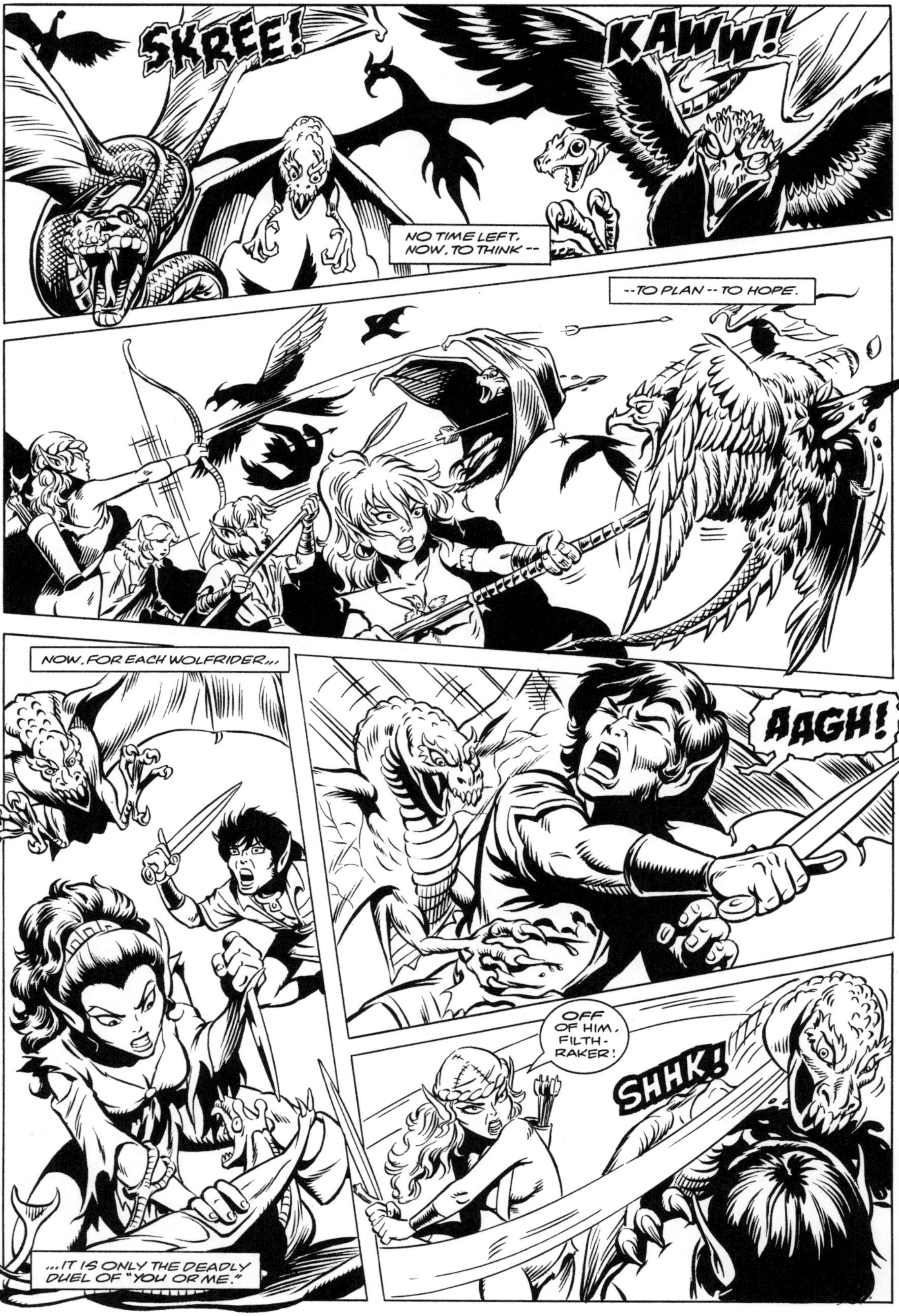
SKREE!
KAWW!
NO TIME LEFT, NOW, TO THINK --
--TO PLAN -- TO HOPE.
NOW, FOR EACH WOLFRIDER...
AAGH!
OFF OF HIM, FILTH-RAKER!
SHHK!
...IT IS ONLY THE DEADLY DUEL OF "YOU OR ME."

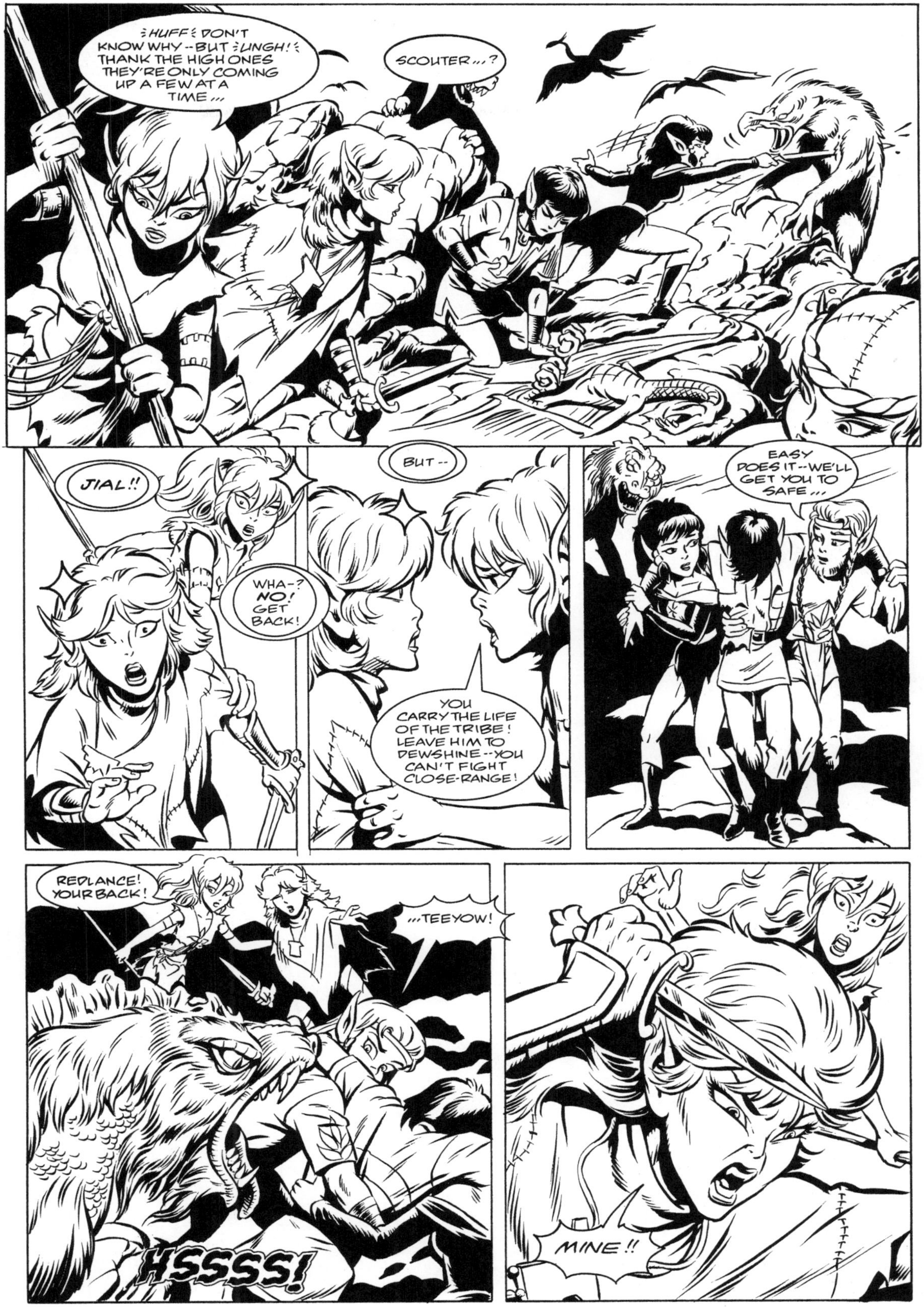

;HUFF; DON'T KNOW WHY--BUT ;UNGH!; THANK THE HIGH ONES THEY'RE ONLY COMING UP A FEW AT A TIME...
SCOUTER...?
JIAL!!
WHA-? NO! GET BACK!
BUT--
YOU CARRY THE LIFE OF THE TRIBE! LEAVE HIM TO DEWSHINE--YOU CAN'T FIGHT CLOSE-RANGE!
EASY DOES IT--WE'LL GET YOU TO SAFE...
REDLANCE! YOUR BACK!
...TEEYOW!
HSSSS!
MINE!!

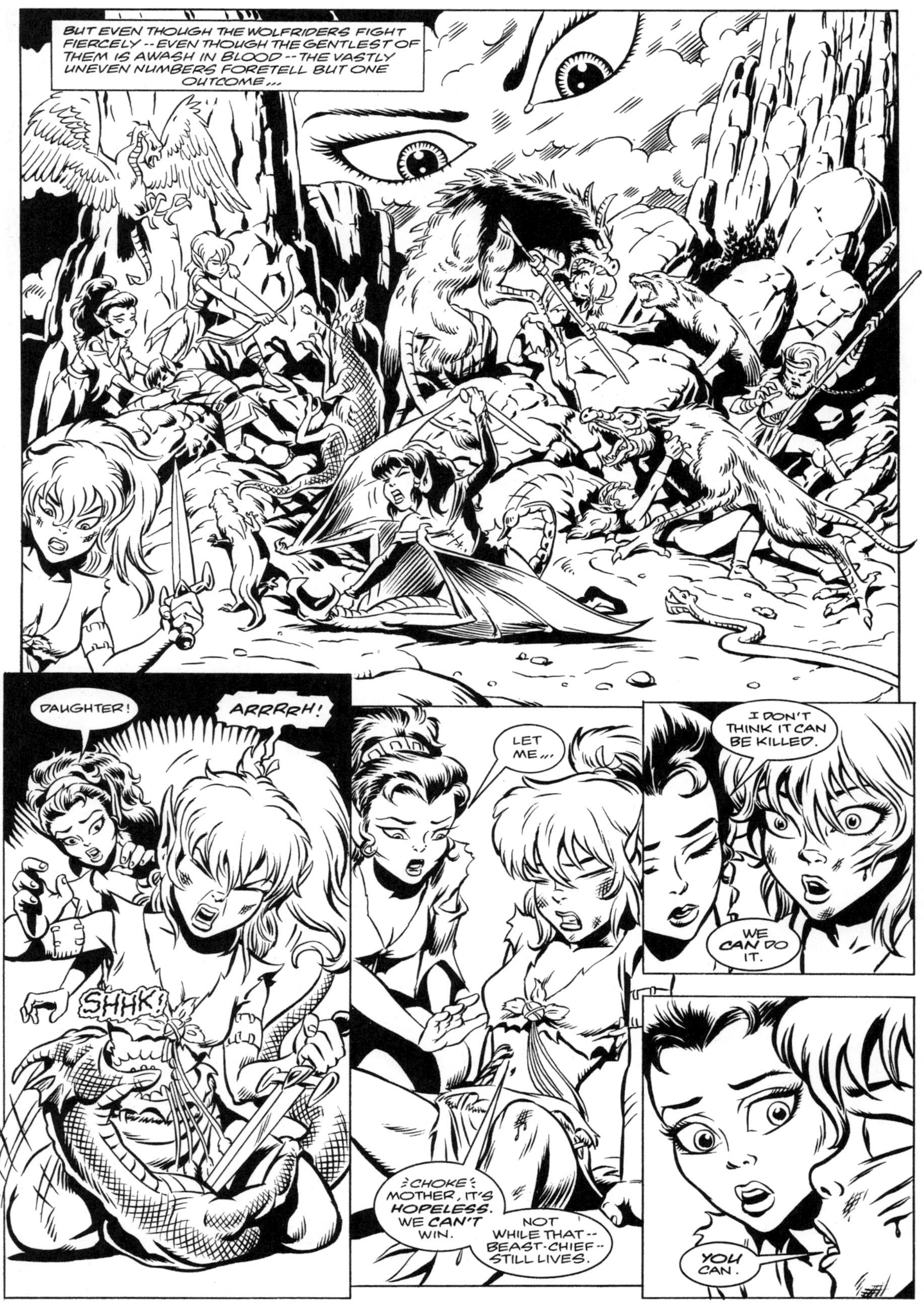
BUT EVEN THOUGH THE WOLFRIDERS FIGHT FIERCELY -- EVEN THOUGH THE GENTLEST OF THEM IS AWASH IN BLOOD -- THE VASTLY UNEVEN NUMBERS FORETELL BUT ONE OUTCOME...
DAUGHTER!
ARRRRH!
SHHK!
LET ME...
CHOKE MOTHER, IT'S HOPELESS. WE CAN'T WIN.
NOT WHILE THAT -- BEAST-CHIEF -- STILL LIVES.
I DON'T THINK IT CAN BE KILLED.
WE CAN DO IT.
YOU CAN.

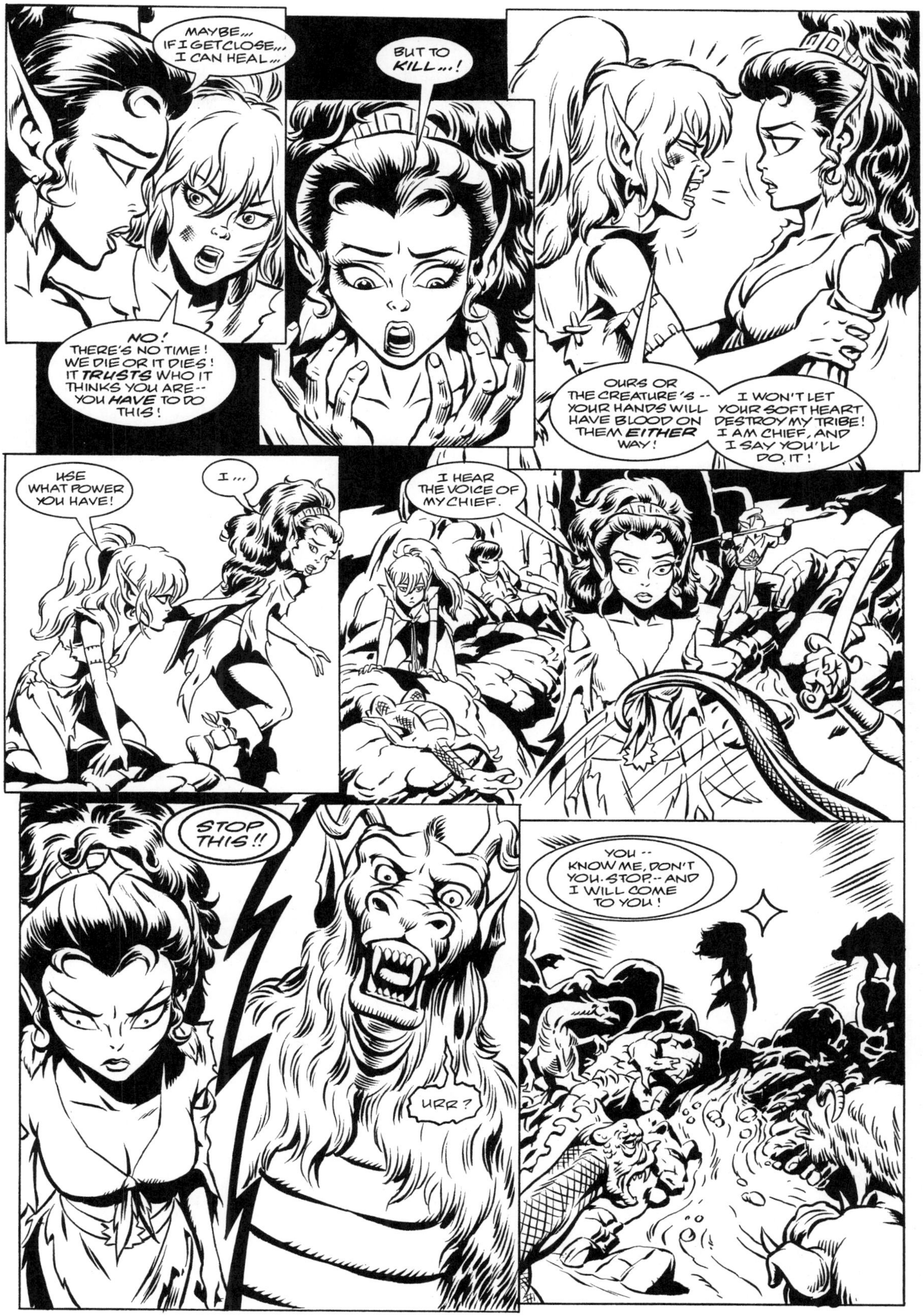
MAYBE... IF I GET CLOSE... I CAN HEAL...
NO! THERE'S NO TIME! WE DIE OR IT DIES! IT TRUSTS WHO IT THINKS YOU ARE-- YOU HAVE TO DO THIS!
BUT TO KILL...!
OURS OR THE CREATURE'S -- YOUR HANDS WILL HAVE BLOOD ON THEM EITHER WAY!
I WON'T LET YOUR SOFT HEART DESTROY MY TRIBE! I AM CHIEF, AND I SAY YOU'LL DO IT!
USE WHAT POWER YOU HAVE!
I...
I HEAR THE VOICE OF MY CHIEF.
STOP THIS!!
URR?
YOU -- KNOW ME, DON'T YOU. STOP.-- AND I WILL COME TO YOU!

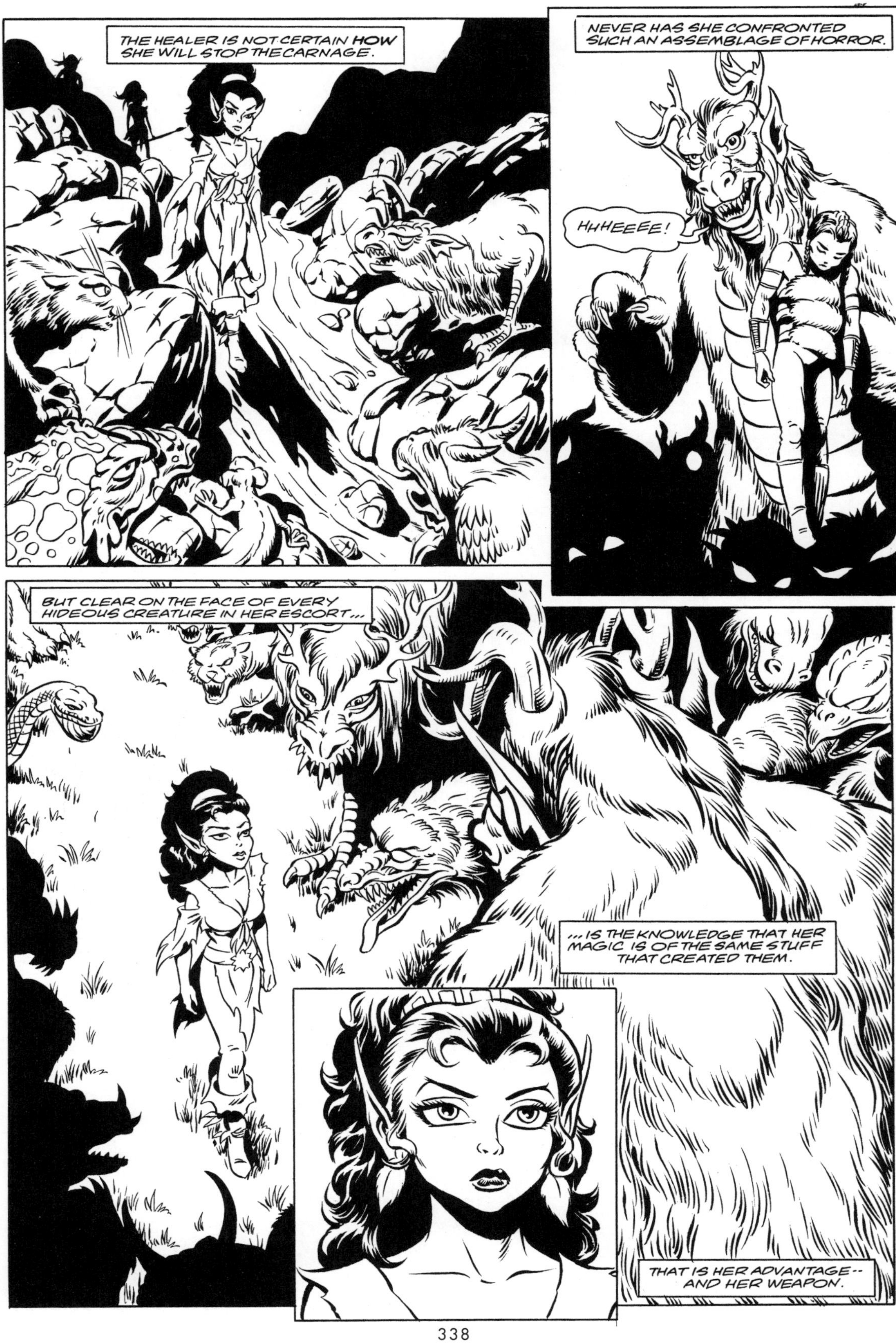
THE HEALER IS NOT CERTAIN HOW SHE WILL STOP THE CARNAGE.
NEVER HAS SHE CONFRONTED SUCH AN ASSEMBLAGE OF HORROR.
HHHEEEEE!
BUT CLEAR ON THE FACE OF EVERY HIDEOUS CREATURE IN HER ESCORT...
...IS THE KNOWLEDGE THAT HER MAGIC IS OF THE SAME STUFF THAT CREATED THEM.
THAT IS HER ADVANTAGE-- AND HER WEAPON.

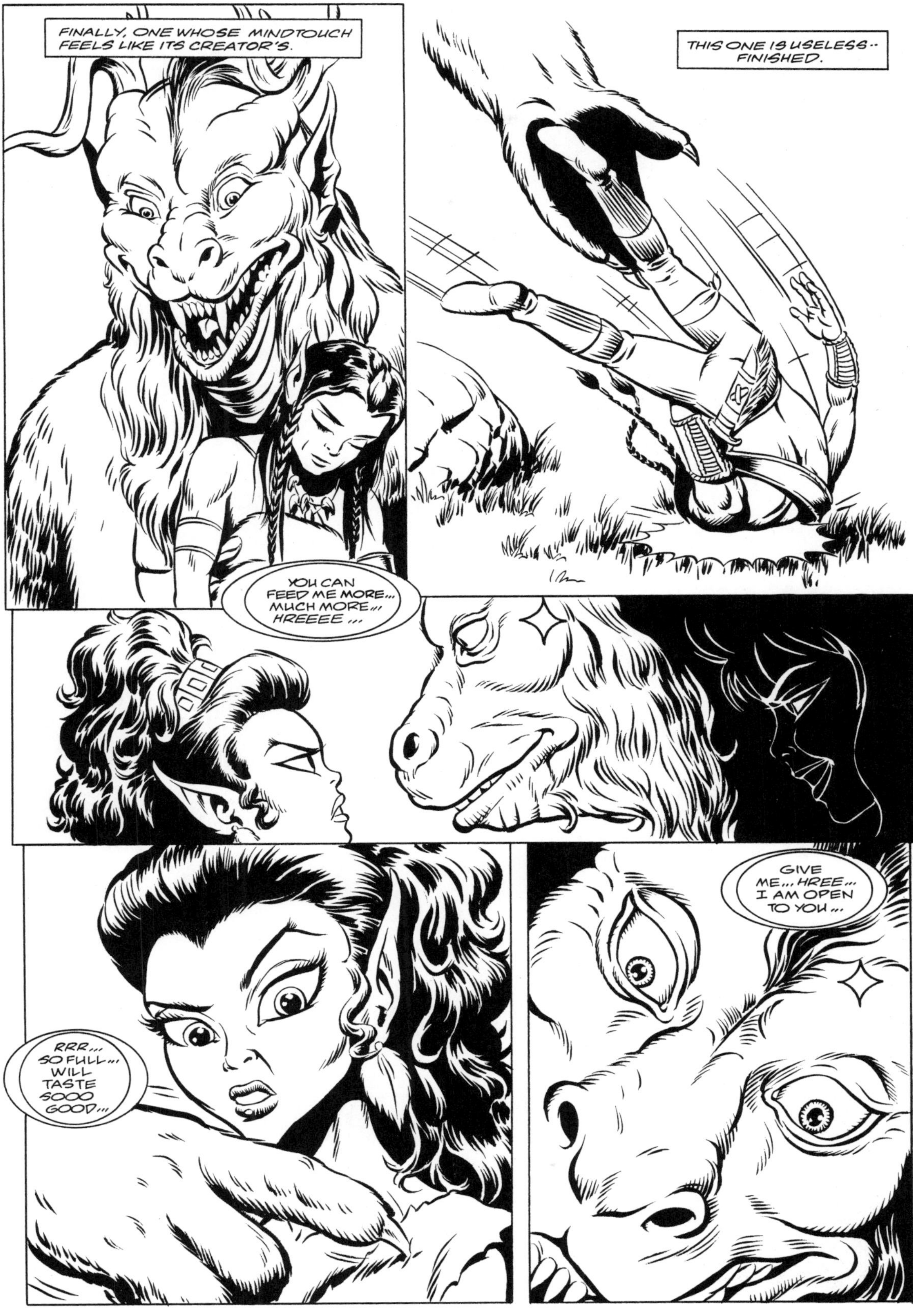
FINALLY, ONE WHOSE MINDTOUCH FEELS LIKE ITS CREATOR'S.
THIS ONE IS USELESS.. FINISHED.
YOU CAN FEED ME MORE... MUCH MORE... HREEEE...
RRR... SO FULL... WILL TASTE SOOO GOOD...
GIVE ME... HREE... I AM OPEN TO YOU...

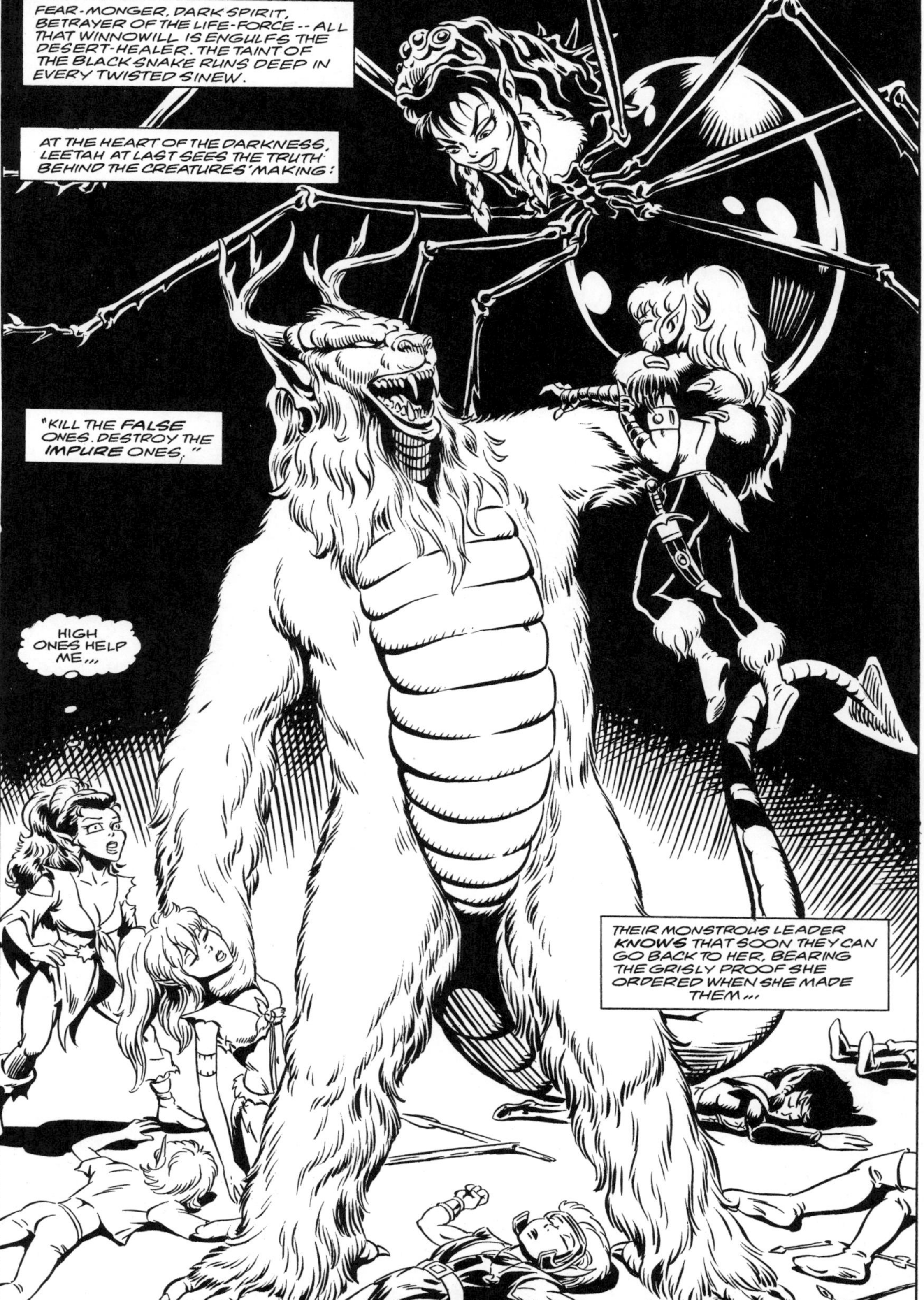

FEAR-MONGER, DARK SPIRIT, BETRAYER OF THE LIFE-FORCE -- ALL THAT WINNOWILL IS ENGULFS THE DESERT-HEALER. THE TAINT OF THE BLACK SNAKE RUNS DEEP IN EVERY TWISTED SINEW.
AT THE HEART OF THE DARKNESS, LEETAH AT LAST SEES THE TRUTH BEHIND THE CREATURES' MAKING:
"KILL THE FALSE ONES. DESTROY THE IMPURE ONES."
HIGH ONES HELP ME...
THEIR MONSTROUS LEADER KNOWS THAT SOON THEY CAN GO BACK TO HER, BEARING THE GRISLY PROOF SHE ORDERED WHEN SHE MADE THEM...

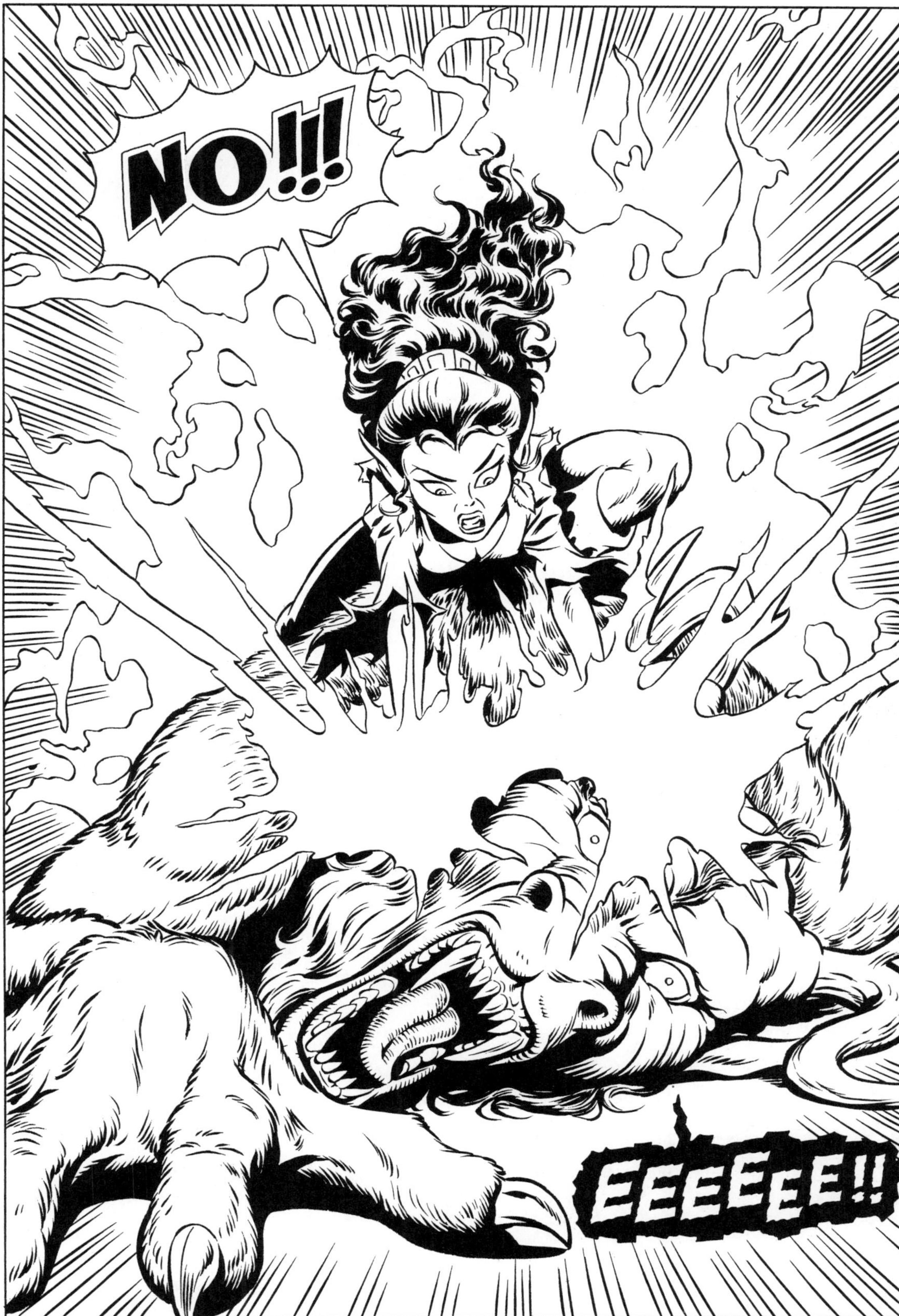
NO!!!
EEEEEEE!!

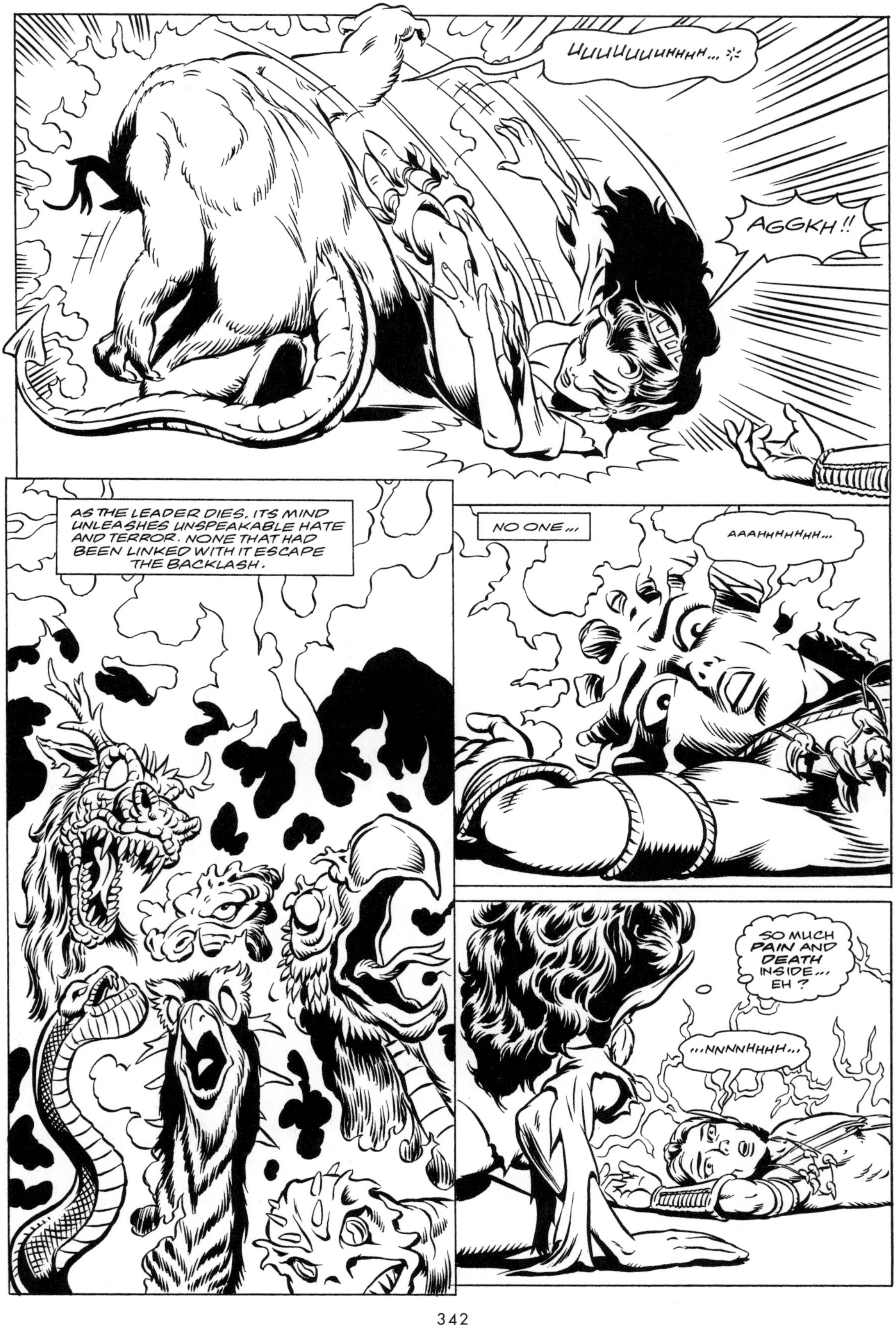
UUUUUUUHHHH...
AGGKH!!
AS THE LEADER DIES, ITS MIND UNLEASHES UNSPEAKABLE HATE AND TERROR. NONE THAT HAD BEEN LINKED WITH IT ESCAPE THE BACKLASH.
NO ONE...
AAAHHHHHHH...
SO MUCH PAIN AND DEATH INSIDE... EH?
...NNNNHHHH...

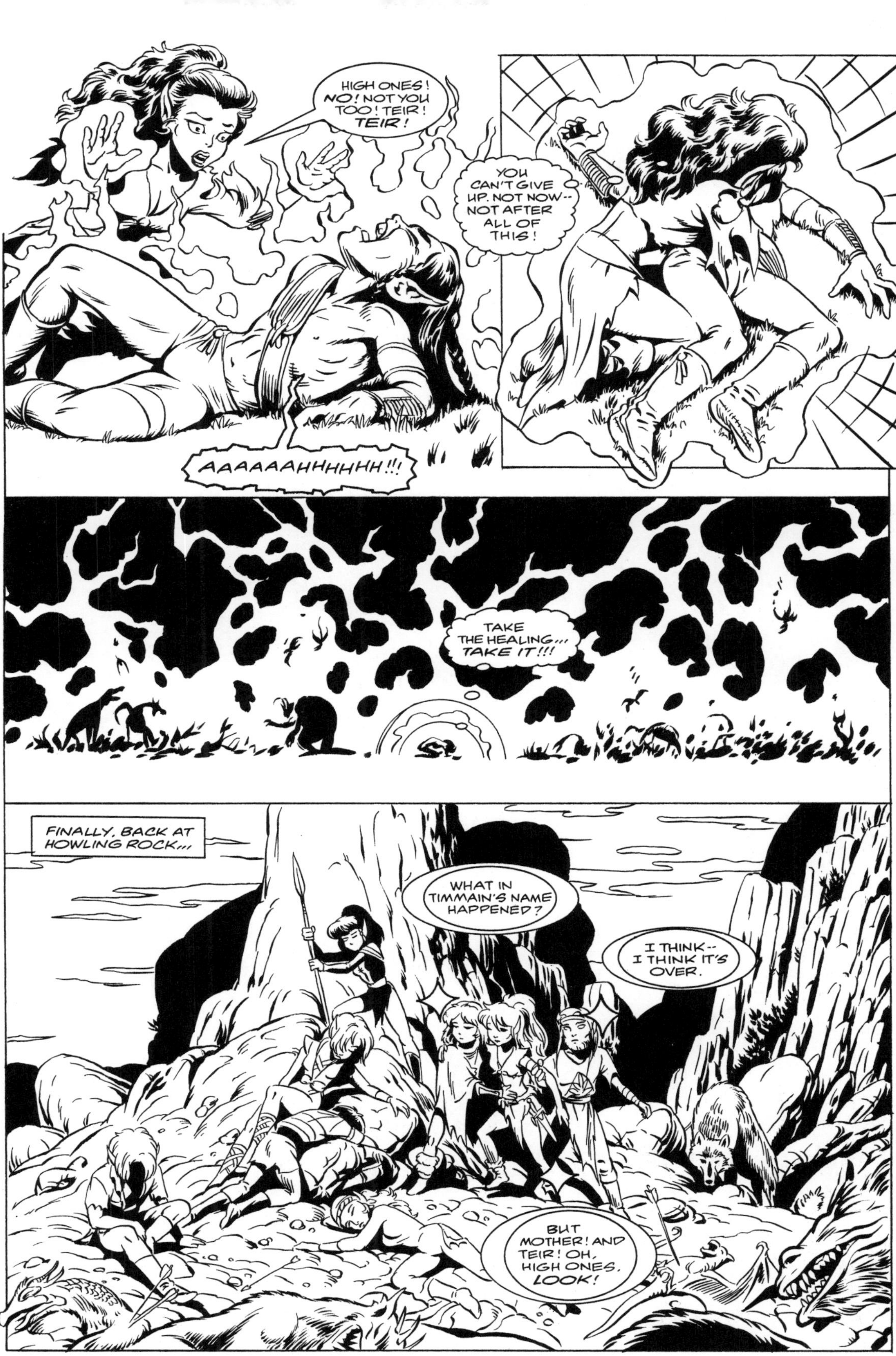
HIGH ONES! NO! NOT YOU TOO! TEIR! TEIR!
YOU CAN'T GIVE UP. NOT NOW-- NOT AFTER ALL OF THIS!
AAAAAAHHHHHH!!!
TAKE THE HEALING... TAKE IT!!!
FINALLY, BACK AT HOWLING ROCK...
WHAT IN TIMMAIN'S NAME HAPPENED?
I THINK-- I THINK IT'S OVER.
BUT MOTHER! AND TEIR! OH, HIGH ONES, LOOK!

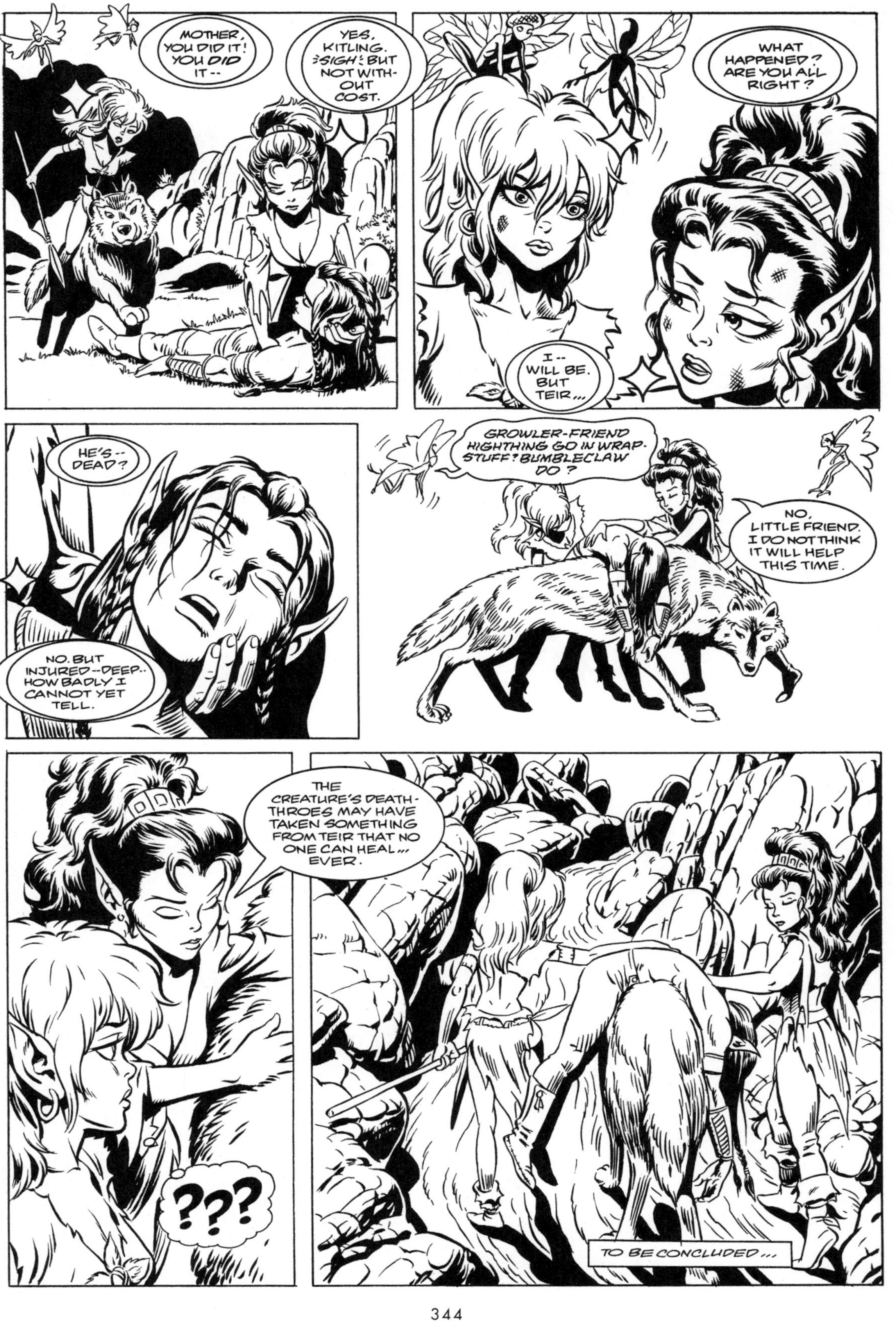
MOTHER, YOU DID IT! YOU DID IT--
YES, KITLING. *SIGH* BUT NOT WITHOUT COST.
WHAT HAPPENED? ARE YOU ALL RIGHT?
I-- WILL BE. BUT TEIR...
HE'S-- DEAD?
NO. BUT INJURED--DEEP.. HOW BADLY I CANNOT YET TELL.
GROWLER-FRIEND HIGHTHING GO IN WRAP-STUFF? BUMBLECLAW DO?
NO, LITTLE FRIEND. I DO NOT THINK IT WILL HELP THIS TIME.
THE CREATURE'S DEATH-THROES MAY HAVE TAKEN SOMETHING FROM TEIR THAT NO ONE CAN HEAL... EVER.
???
TO BE CONCLUDED...

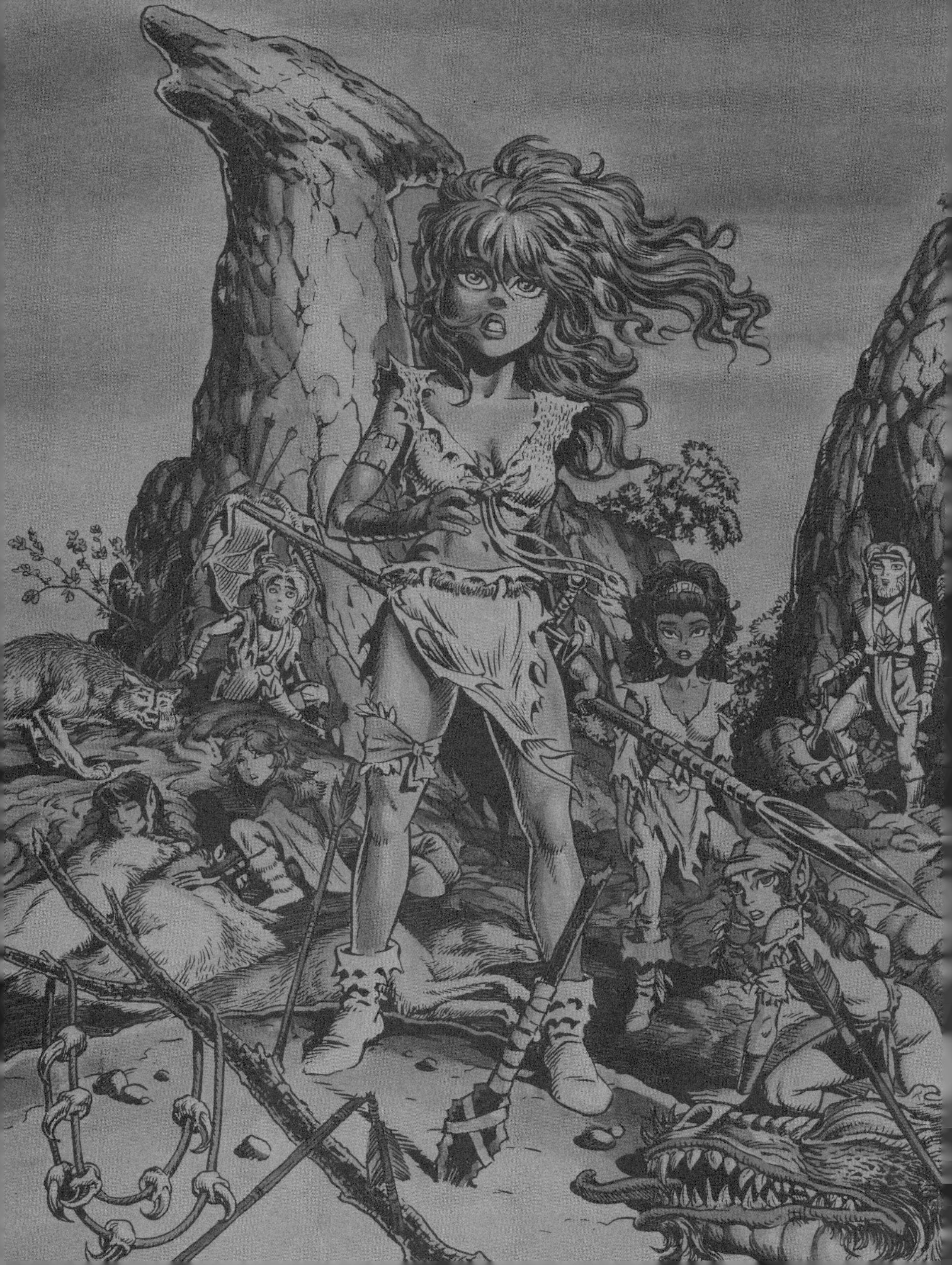

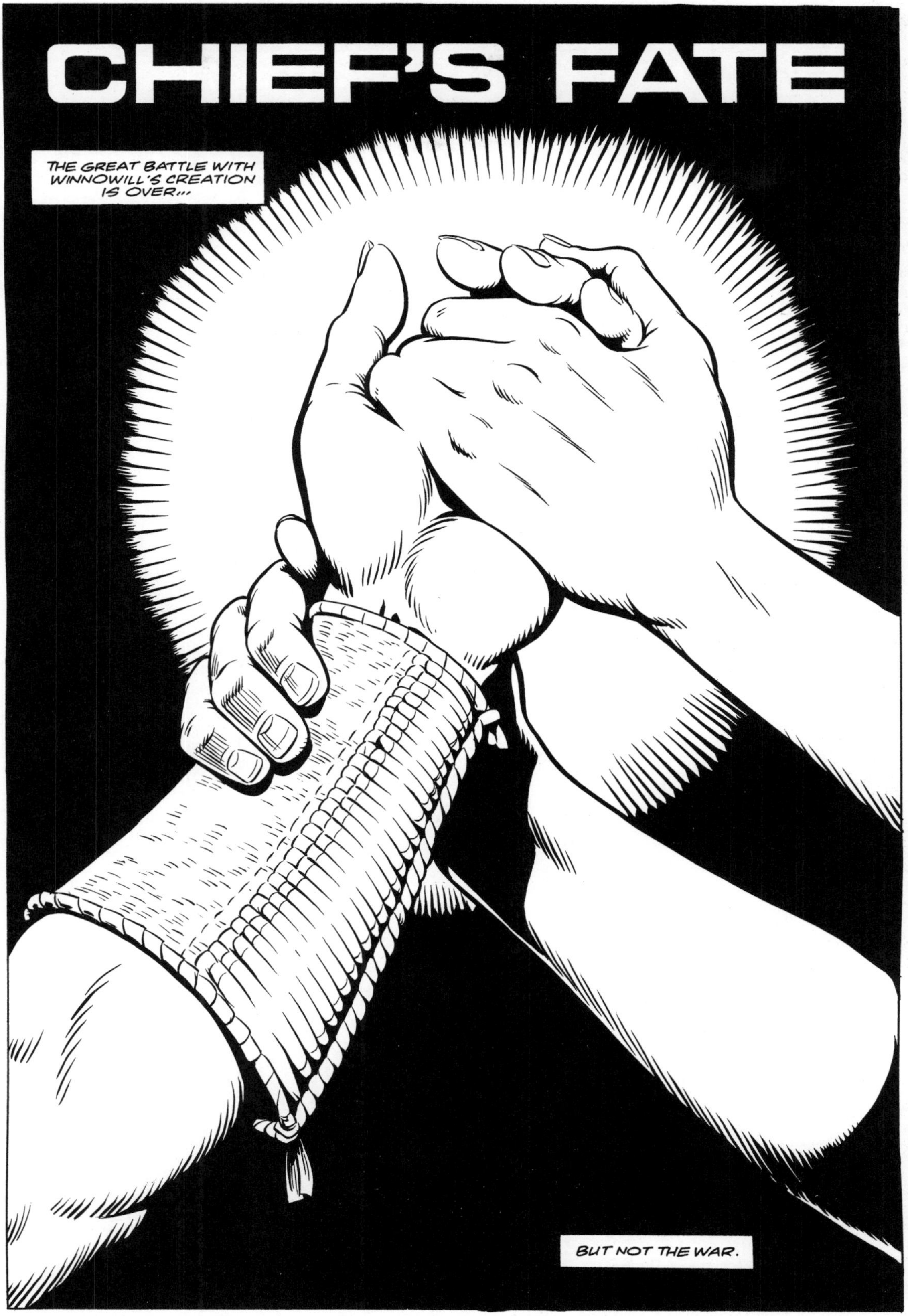
CHIEF'S FATE
THE GREAT BATTLE WITH WINNOWILL'S CREATION IS OVER...
BUT NOT THE WAR.

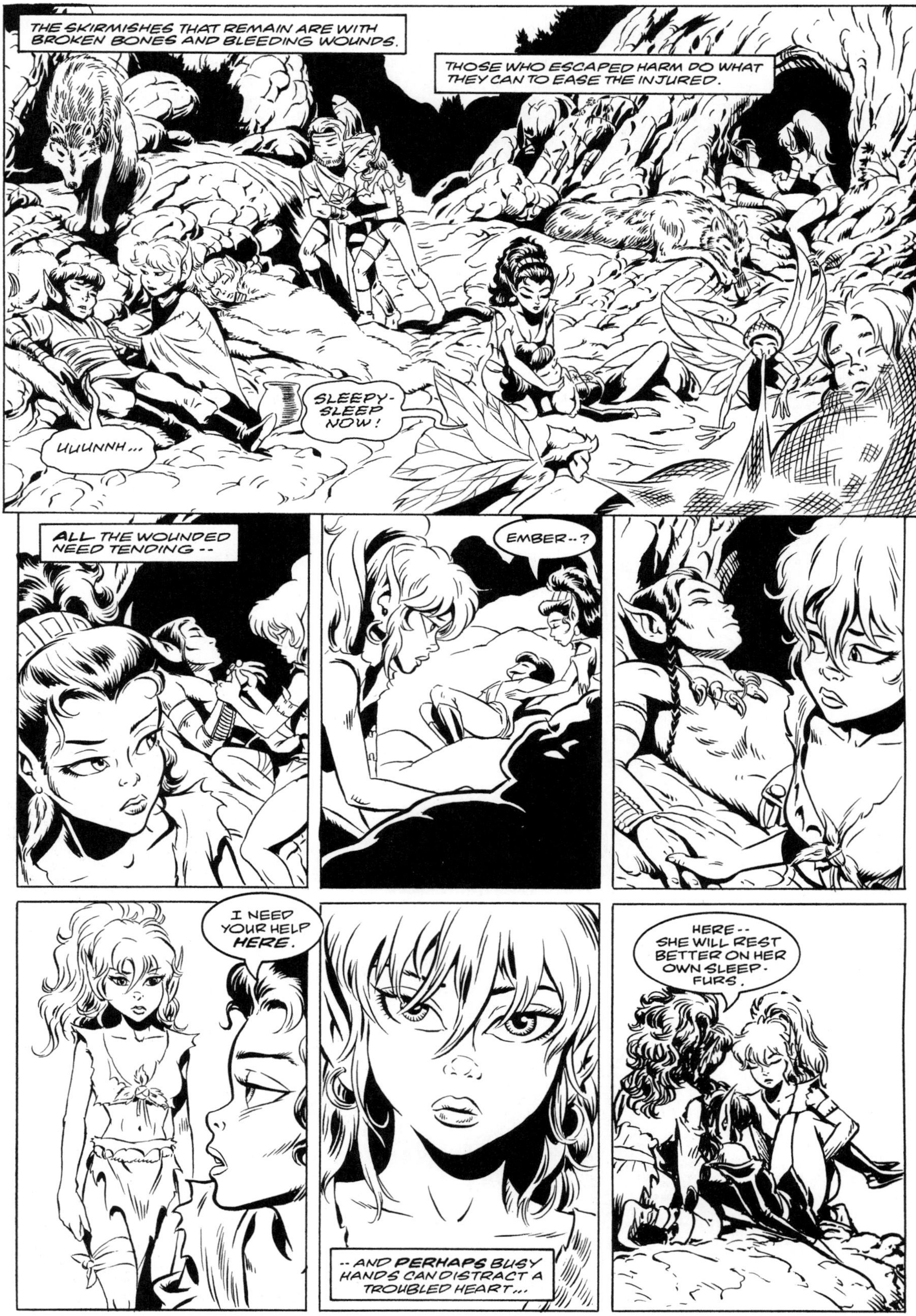
THE SKIRMISHES THAT REMAIN ARE WITH BROKEN BONES AND BLEEDING WOUNDS.
THOSE WHO ESCAPED HARM DO WHAT THEY CAN TO EASE THE INJURED.
SLEEPY-SLEEP NOW!
UUUNNH...
ALL THE WOUNDED NEED TENDING--
EMBER--?
I NEED YOUR HELP HERE.
--AND PERHAPS BUSY HANDS CAN DISTRACT A TROUBLED HEART...
HERE-- SHE WILL REST BETTER ON HER OWN SLEEP-FURS.

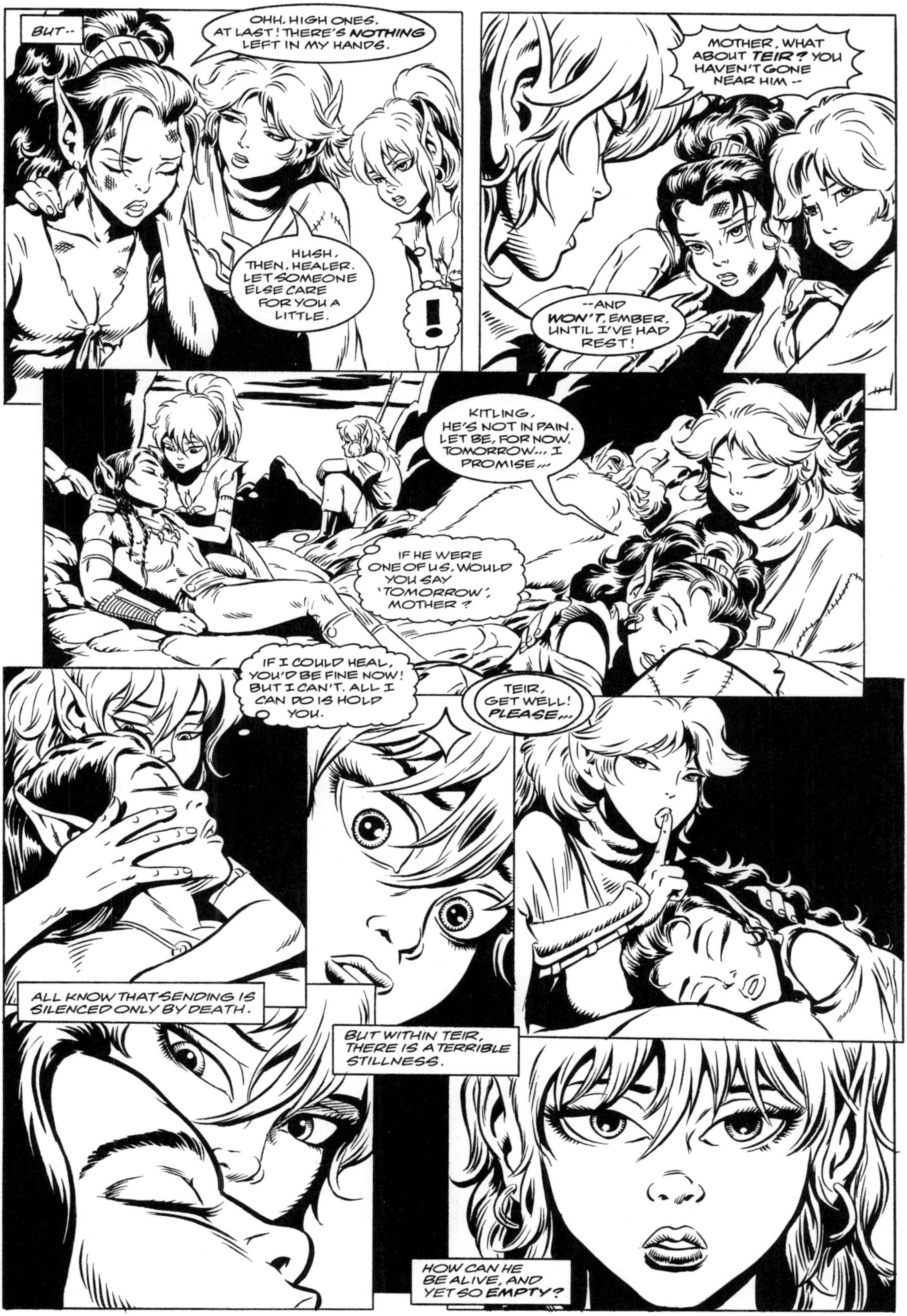

BUT--
OHH, HIGH ONES. AT LAST! THERE'S NOTHING LEFT IN MY HANDS.
HUSH, THEN, HEALER. LET SOMEONE ELSE CARE FOR YOU A LITTLE.
!
MOTHER, WHAT ABOUT TEIR? YOU HAVEN'T GONE NEAR HIM --
--AND WON'T, EMBER, UNTIL I'VE HAD REST!
KITLING, HE'S NOT IN PAIN. LET BE, FOR NOW. TOMORROW... I PROMISE...
IF HE WERE ONE OF US, WOULD YOU SAY 'TOMORROW', MOTHER?
IF I COULD HEAL, YOU'D BE FINE NOW! BUT I CAN'T. ALL I CAN DO IS HOLD YOU.
TEIR, GET WELL! PLEASE...
ALL KNOW THAT SENDING IS SILENCED ONLY BY DEATH.
BUT WITHIN TEIR, THERE IS A TERRIBLE STILLNESS.
HOW CAN HE BE ALIVE, AND YET SO EMPTY?

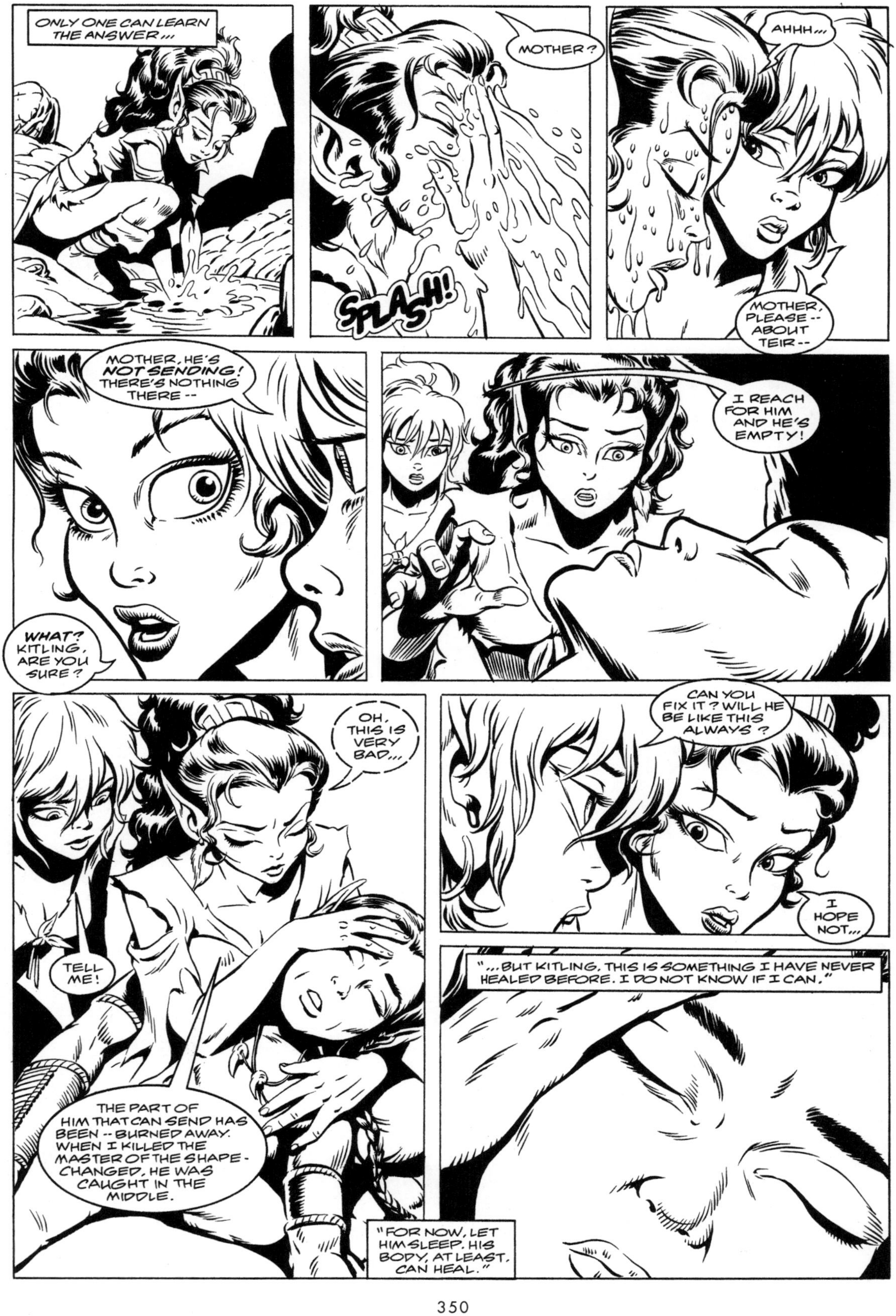
ONLY ONE CAN LEARN THE ANSWER...
MOTHER?
SPLASH!
AHHH...
MOTHER, PLEASE -- ABOUT TEIR--
MOTHER, HE'S **NOT SENDING!** THERE'S NOTHING THERE --
WHAT? KITLING, ARE YOU SURE?
I REACH FOR HIM AND HE'S EMPTY!
OH, THIS IS VERY BAD...
TELL ME!
THE PART OF HIM THAT CAN SEND HAS BEEN -- BURNED AWAY. WHEN I KILLED THE MASTER OF THE SHAPE-CHANGED, HE WAS CAUGHT IN THE MIDDLE.
CAN YOU FIX IT? WILL HE BE LIKE THIS ALWAYS?
I HOPE NOT...
"...BUT KITLING, THIS IS SOMETHING I HAVE NEVER HEALED BEFORE. I DO NOT KNOW IF I CAN."
"FOR NOW, LET HIM SLEEP. HIS BODY, AT LEAST, CAN HEAL."

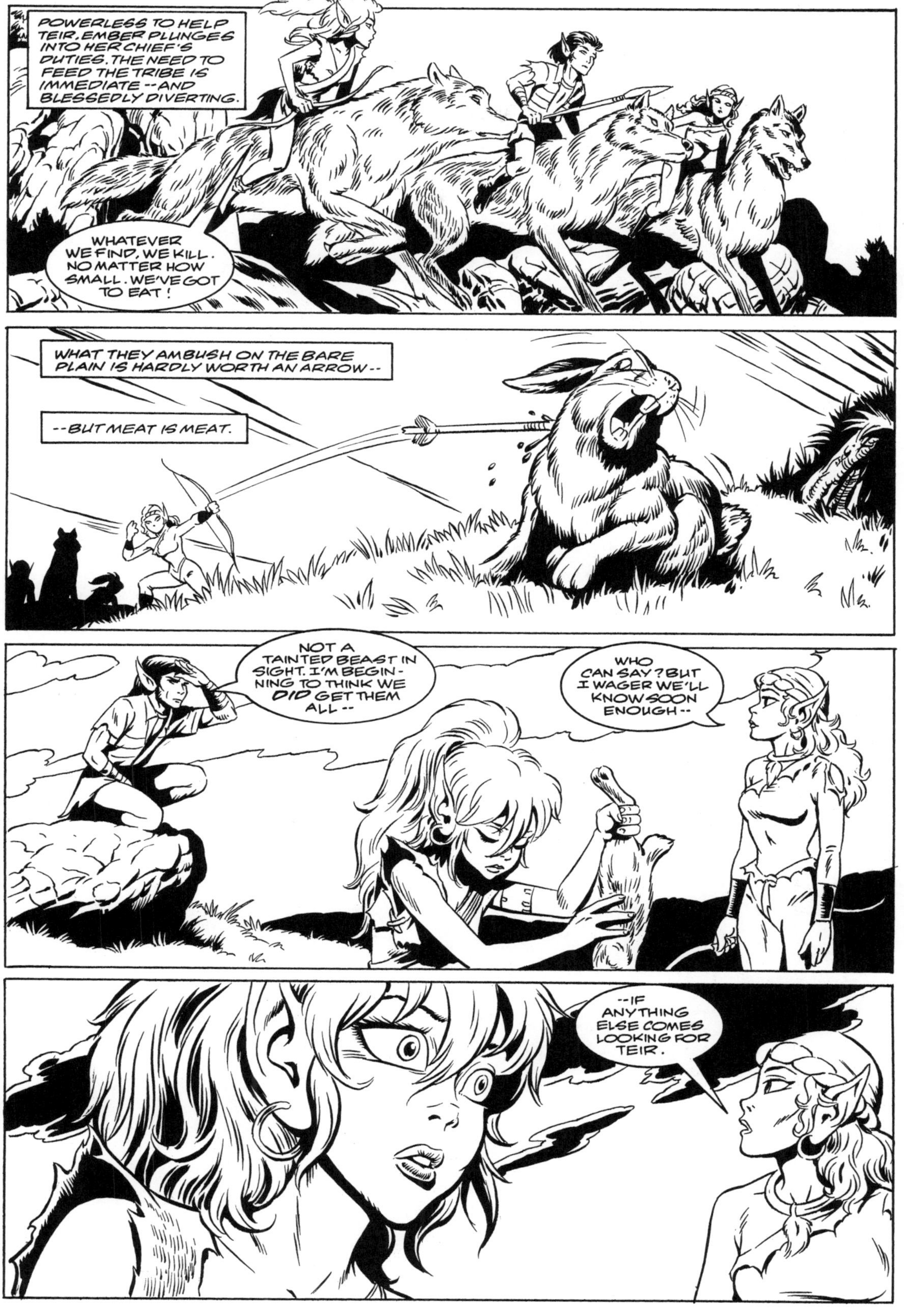
POWERLESS TO HELP TEIR, EMBER PLUNGES INTO HER CHIEF'S DUTIES. THE NEED TO FEED THE TRIBE IS IMMEDIATE -- AND BLESSEDLY DIVERTING.
WHATEVER WE FIND, WE KILL. NO MATTER HOW SMALL. WE'VE GOT TO EAT!
WHAT THEY AMBUSH ON THE BARE PLAIN IS HARDLY WORTH AN ARROW --
-- BUT MEAT IS MEAT.
NOT A TAINTED BEAST IN SIGHT. I'M BEGINNING TO THINK WE DID GET THEM ALL --
WHO CAN SAY? BUT I WAGER WE'LL KNOW SOON ENOUGH --
-- IF ANYTHING ELSE COMES LOOKING FOR TEIR.

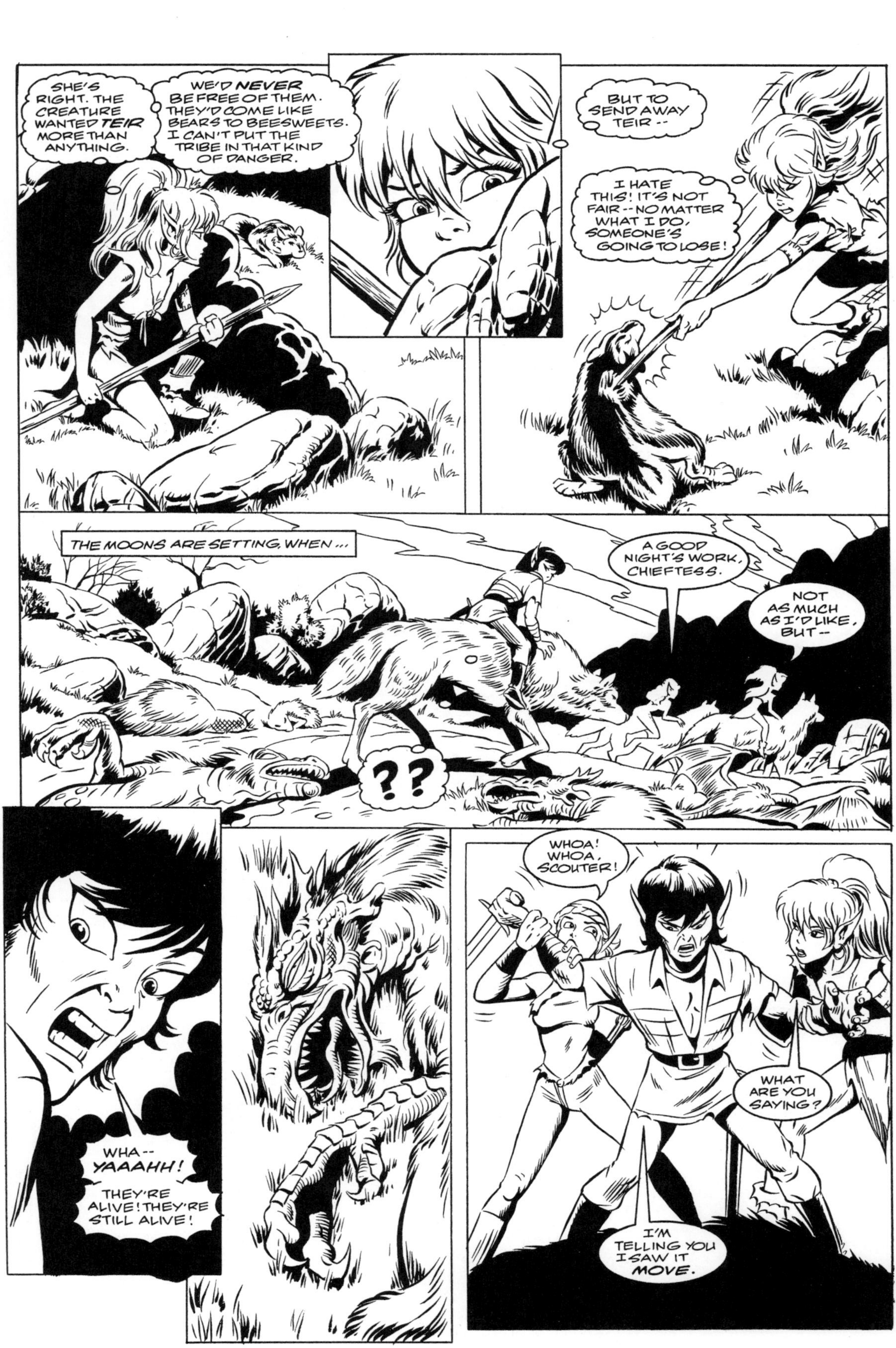
SHE'S RIGHT. THE CREATURE WANTED TEIR MORE THAN ANYTHING.
WE'D NEVER BE FREE OF THEM. THEY'D COME LIKE BEARS TO BEESWEETS. I CAN'T PUT THE TRIBE IN THAT KIND OF DANGER.
BUT TO SEND AWAY TEIR --
I HATE THIS! IT'S NOT FAIR -- NO MATTER WHAT I DO, SOMEONE'S GOING TO LOSE!
THE MOONS ARE SETTING, WHEN ...
A GOOD NIGHT'S WORK, CHIEFTESS.
NOT AS MUCH AS I'D LIKE, BUT --
??
WHA -- YAAAHH!
THEY'RE ALIVE! THEY'RE STILL ALIVE!
WHOA! WHOA, SCOUTER!
WHAT ARE YOU SAYING?
I'M TELLING YOU I SAW IT MOVE.

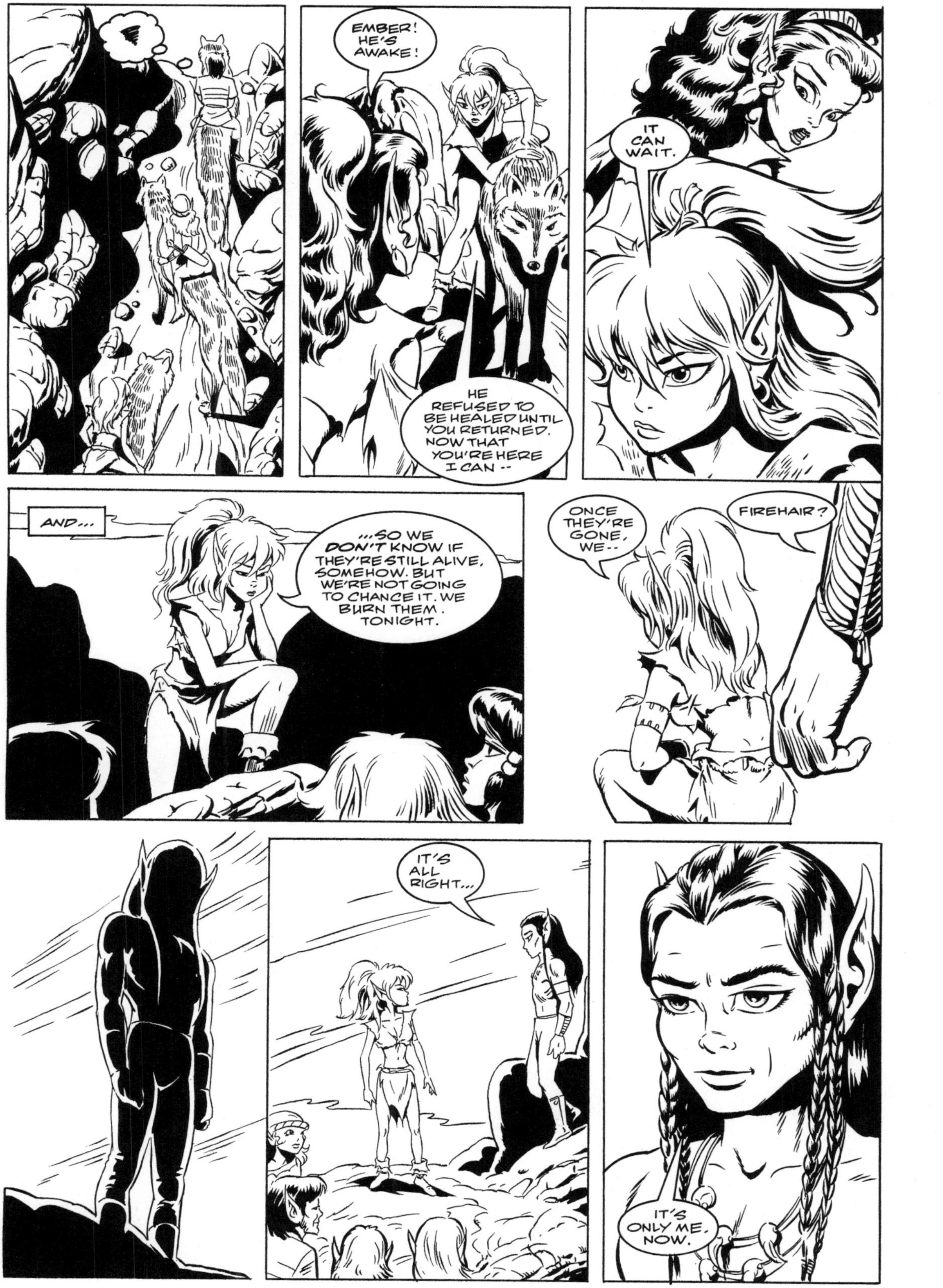
EMBER! HE'S AWAKE!
HE REFUSED TO BE HEALED UNTIL YOU RETURNED. NOW THAT YOU'RE HERE I CAN --
IT CAN WAIT.
AND...
...SO WE DON'T KNOW IF THEY'RE STILL ALIVE, SOMEHOW. BUT WE'RE NOT GOING TO CHANCE IT. WE BURN THEM. TONIGHT.
ONCE THEY'RE GONE, WE--
FIREHAIR?
IT'S ALL RIGHT...
IT'S ONLY ME. NOW.

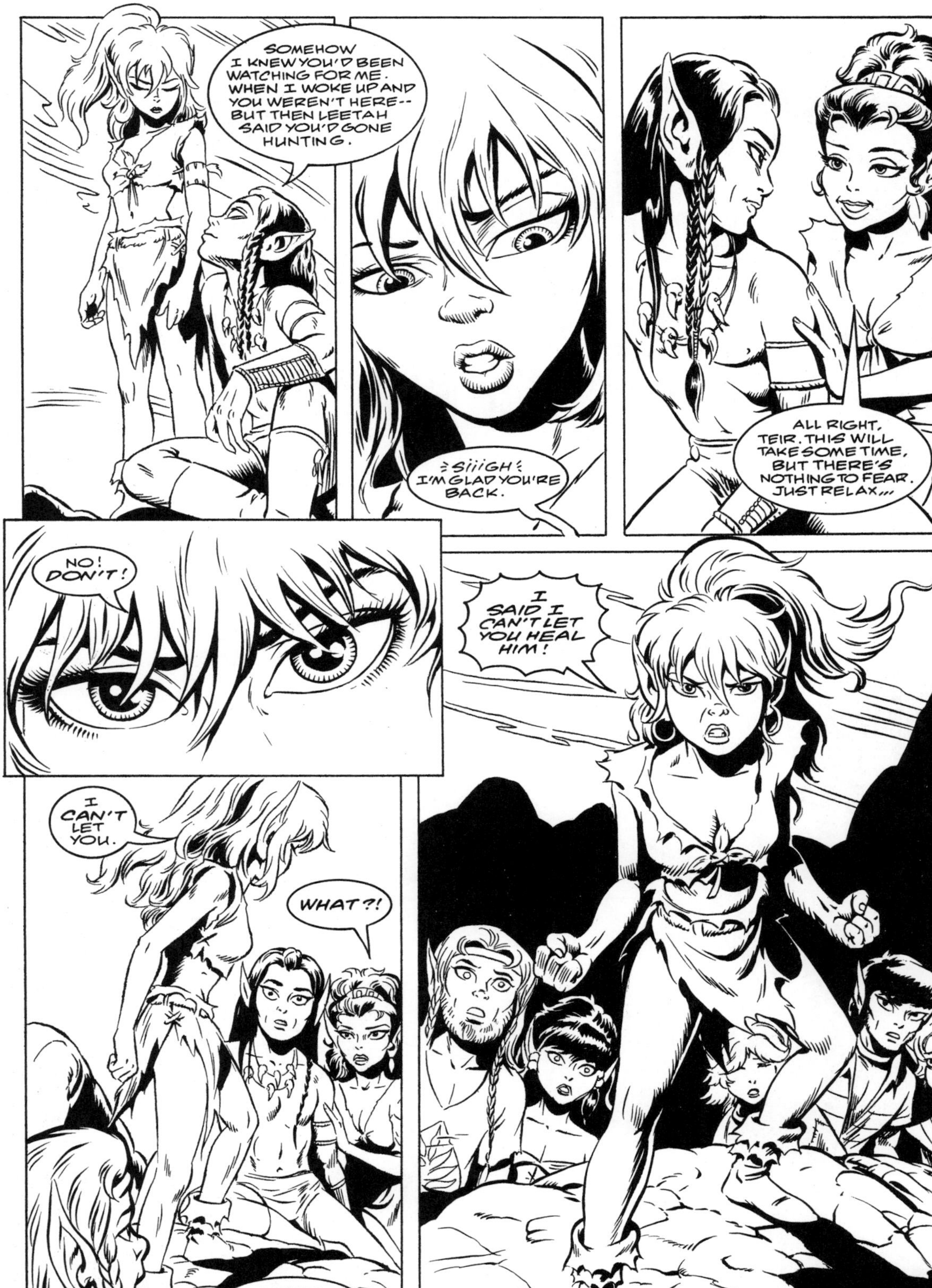

SOMEHOW I KNEW YOU'D BEEN WATCHING FOR ME. WHEN I WOKE UP AND YOU WEREN'T HERE-- BUT THEN LEETAH SAID YOU'D GONE HUNTING.
SIIIGH
I'M GLAD YOU'RE BACK.
ALL RIGHT, TEIR. THIS WILL TAKE SOME TIME, BUT THERE'S NOTHING TO FEAR. JUST RELAX...
NO! DON'T!
I SAID I CAN'T LET YOU HEAL HIM!
I CAN'T LET YOU.
WHAT?!
EMBER. WHAT ARE YOU SAYING?

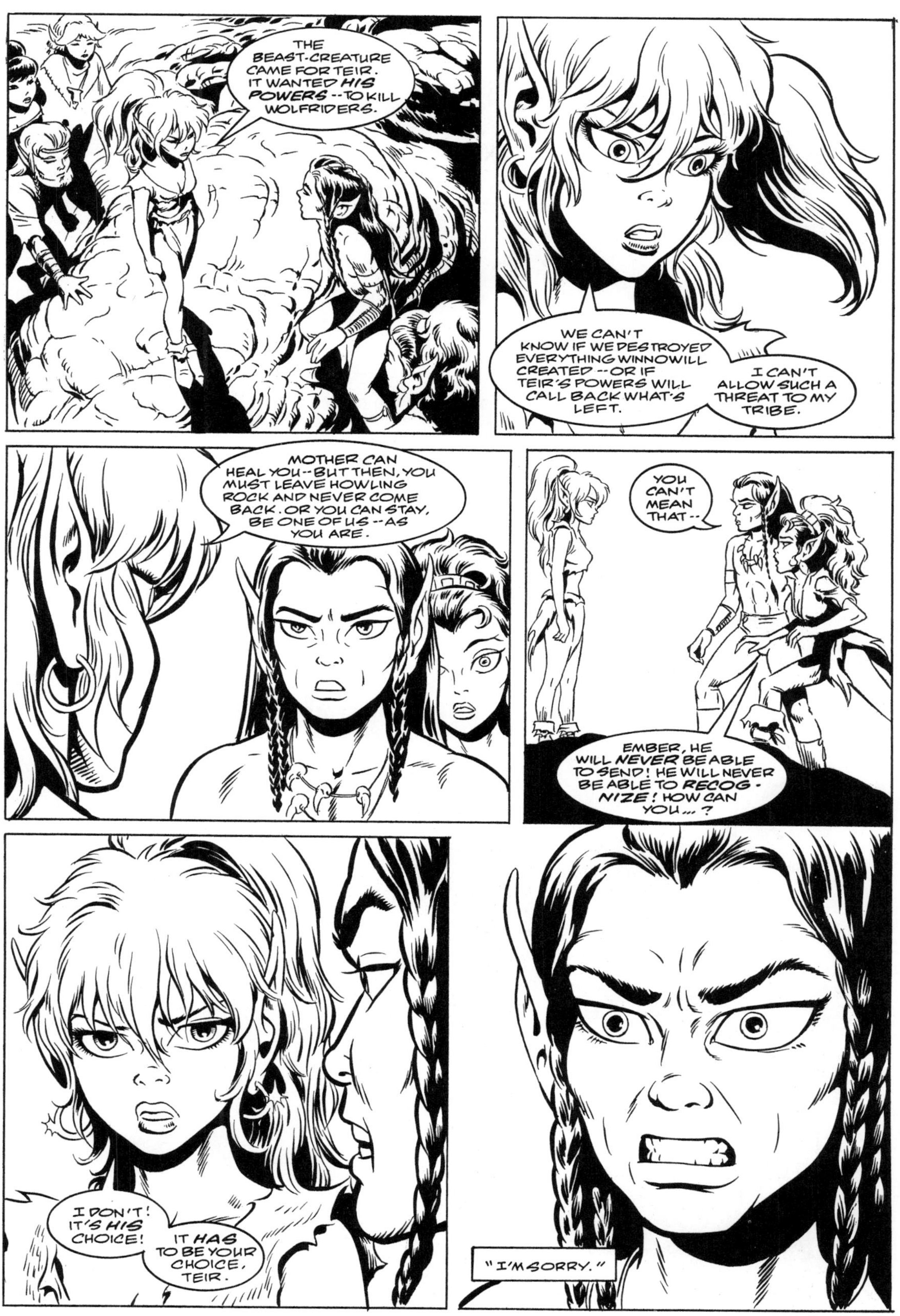
THE BEAST-CREATURE CAME FOR TEIR. IT WANTED HIS POWERS --TO KILL WOLFRIDERS.
WE CAN'T KNOW IF WE DESTROYED EVERYTHING WINNOWILL CREATED --OR IF TEIR'S POWERS WILL CALL BACK WHAT'S LEFT.
I CAN'T ALLOW SUCH A THREAT TO MY TRIBE.
MOTHER CAN HEAL YOU--BUT THEN, YOU MUST LEAVE HOWLING ROCK AND NEVER COME BACK. OR YOU CAN STAY, BE ONE OF US --AS YOU ARE.
YOU CAN'T MEAN THAT--
EMBER, HE WILL NEVER BE ABLE TO SEND! HE WILL NEVER BE ABLE TO RECOG-NIZE! HOW CAN YOU...?
I DON'T! IT'S HIS CHOICE!
IT HAS TO BE YOUR CHOICE, TEIR.
"I'M SORRY."

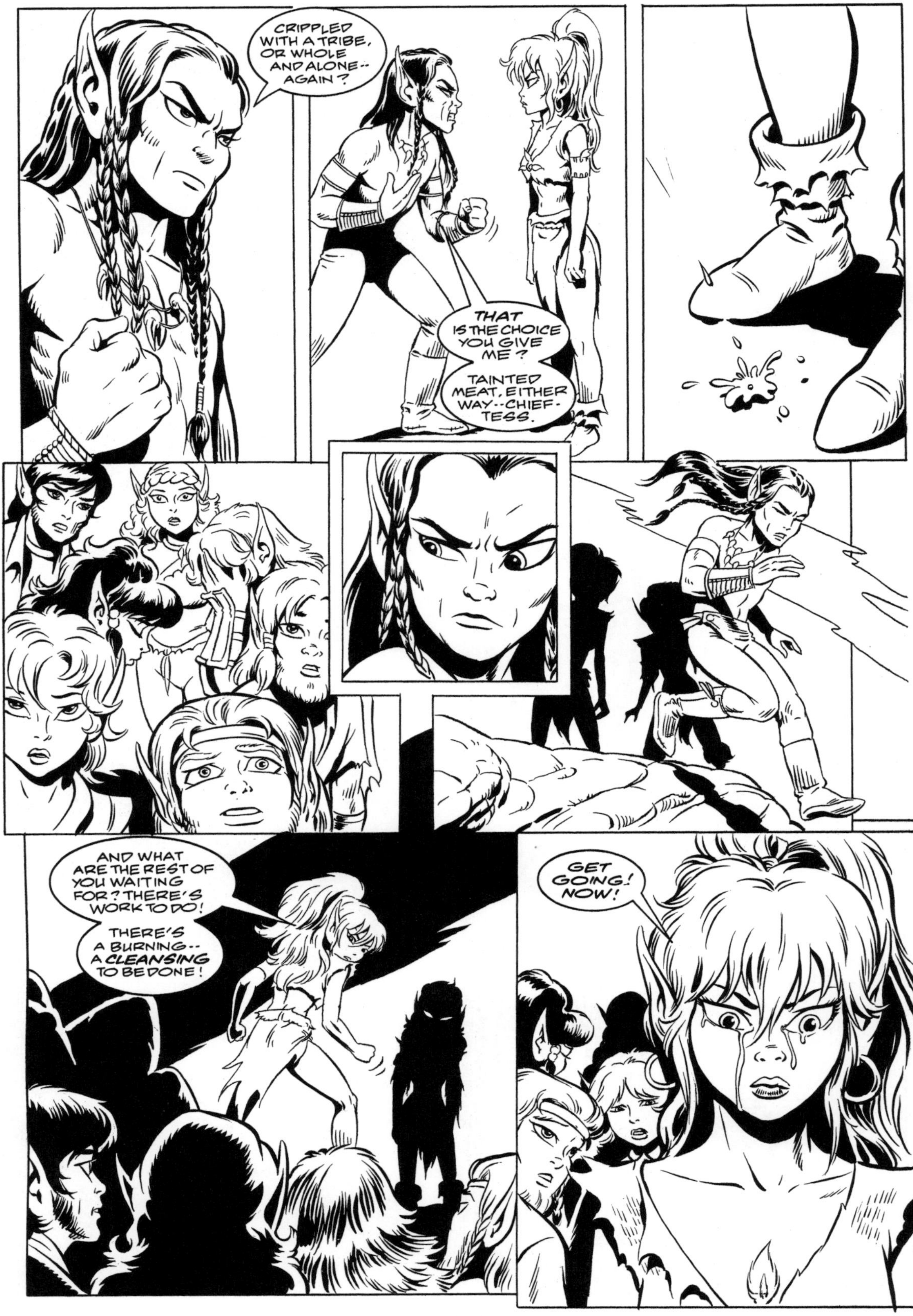
CRIPPLED WITH A TRIBE, OR WHOLE AND ALONE-- AGAIN?
THAT IS THE CHOICE YOU GIVE ME?
TAINTED MEAT, EITHER WAY--CHIEF-TESS.
AND WHAT ARE THE REST OF YOU WAITING FOR? THERE'S WORK TO DO!
THERE'S A BURNING-- A CLEANSING TO BE DONE!
GET GOING! NOW!

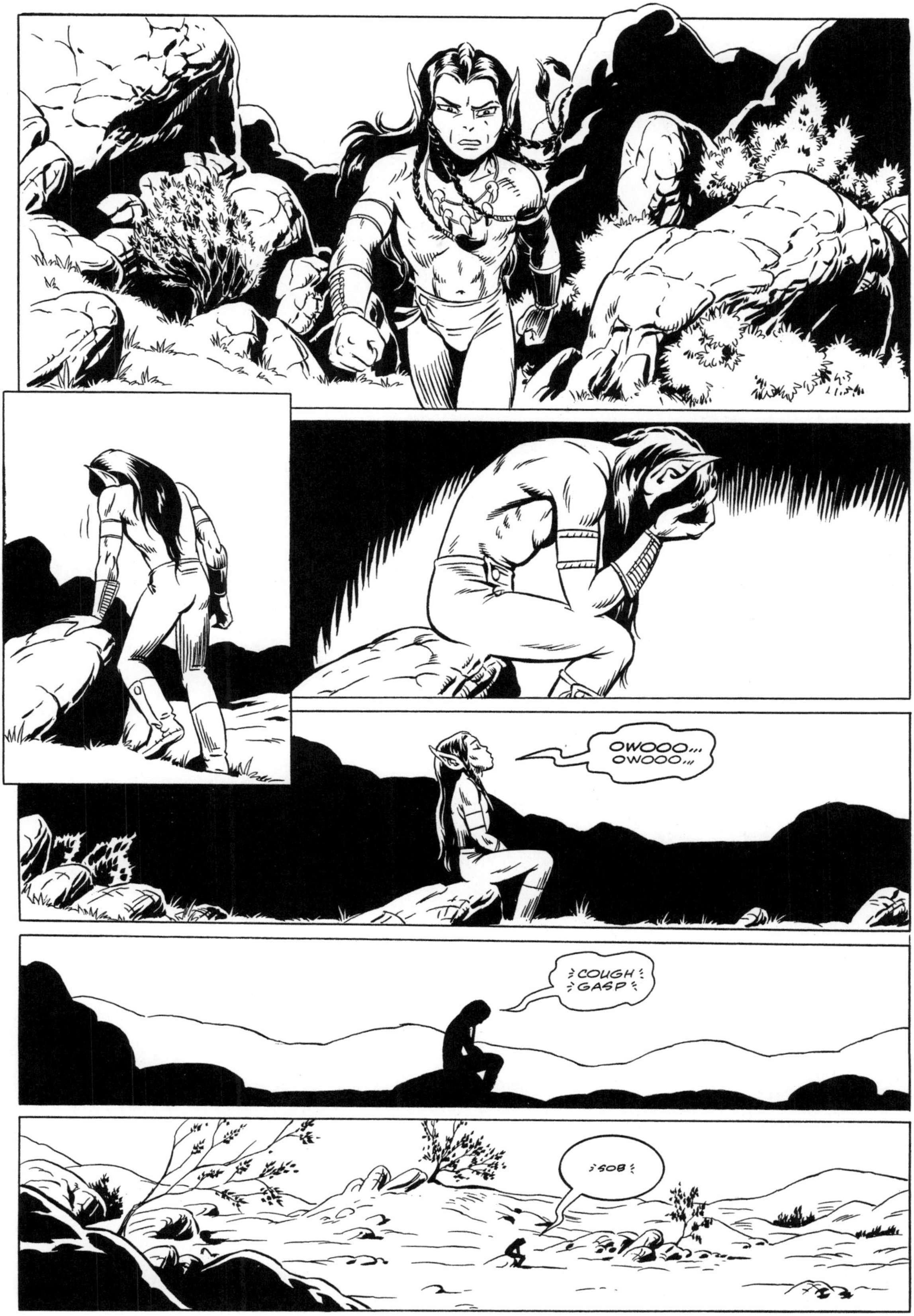
OWOOO...
OWOOO...
COUGH
GASP
SOB

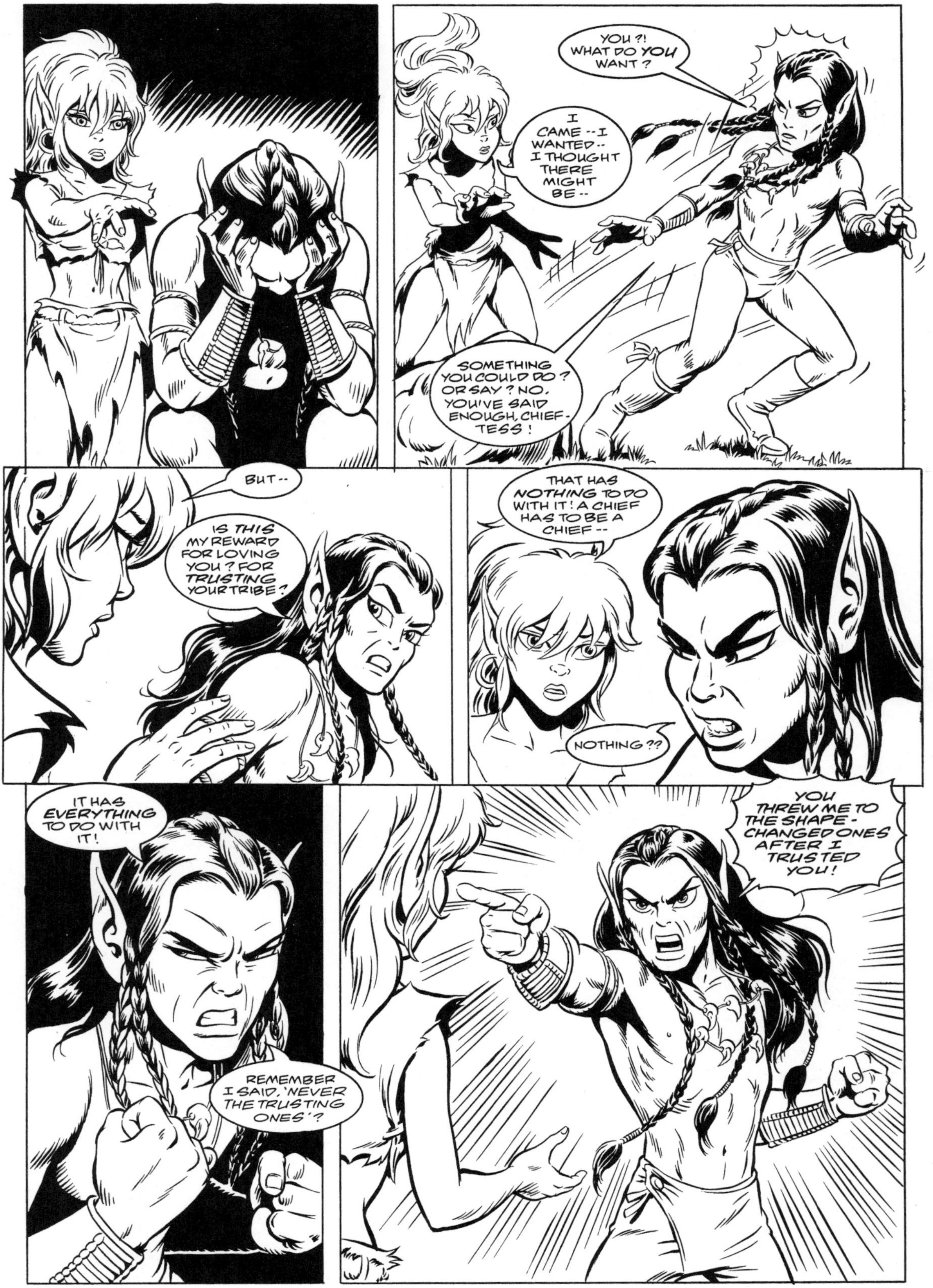

YOU?! WHAT DO YOU WANT?
I CAME -- I WANTED -- I THOUGHT THERE MIGHT BE --
SOMETHING YOU COULD DO? OR SAY? NO. YOU'VE SAID ENOUGH, CHIEF-TESS!
BUT --
IS THIS MY REWARD FOR LOVING YOU? FOR TRUSTING YOUR TRIBE?
THAT HAS NOTHING TO DO WITH IT! A CHIEF HAS TO BE A CHIEF --
NOTHING??
IT HAS EVERYTHING TO DO WITH IT!
REMEMBER I SAID, 'NEVER THE TRUSTING ONES'?
YOU THREW ME TO THE SHAPE-CHANGED ONES AFTER I TRUSTED YOU!

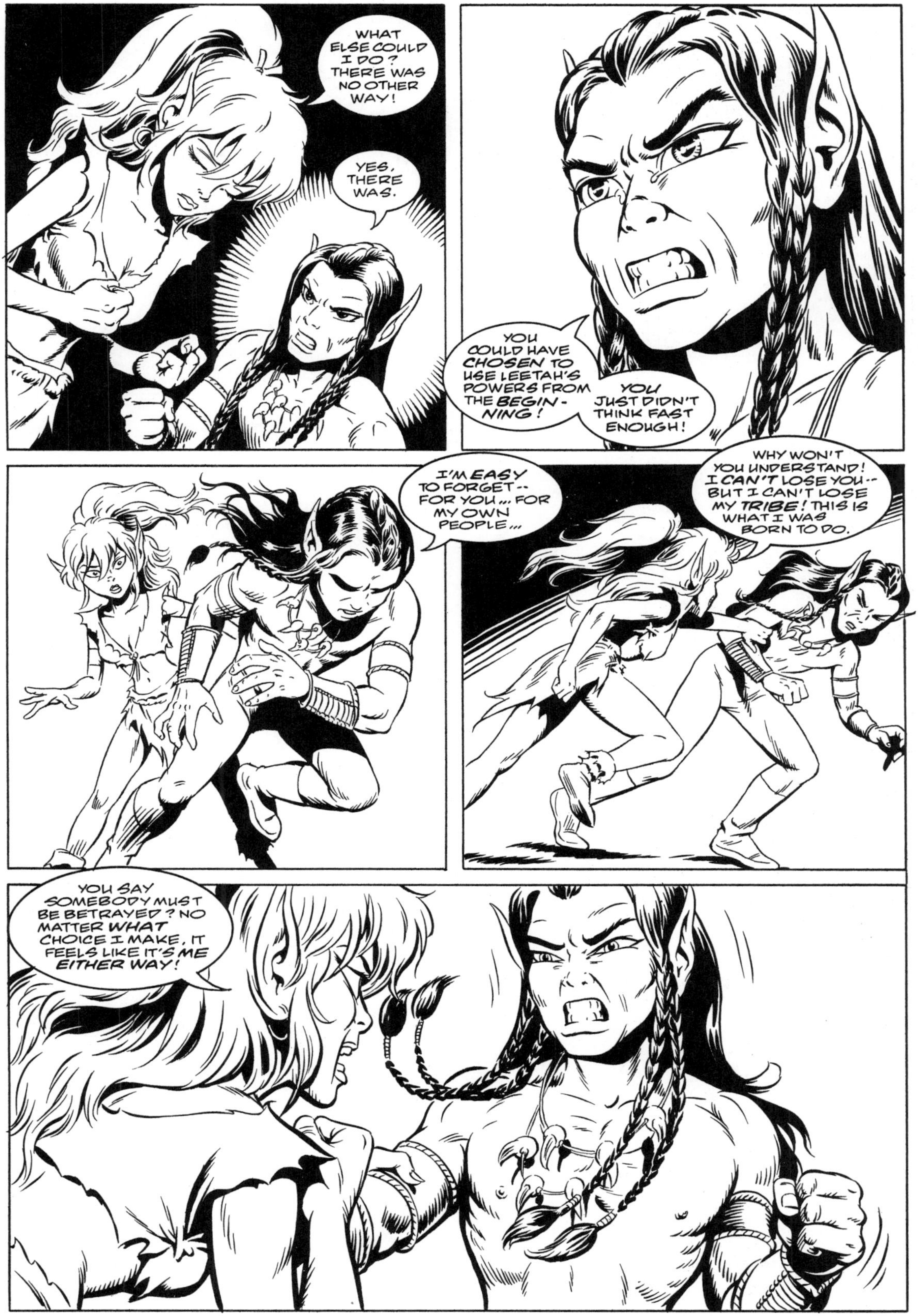
WHAT ELSE COULD I DO? THERE WAS NO OTHER WAY!
YES, THERE WAS.
YOU COULD HAVE CHOSEN TO USE LEETAH'S POWERS FROM THE BEGIN-NING!
YOU JUST DIDN'T THINK FAST ENOUGH!
I'M EASY TO FORGET-- FOR YOU... FOR MY OWN PEOPLE...
WHY WON'T YOU UNDERSTAND! I CAN'T LOSE YOU-- BUT I CAN'T LOSE MY TRIBE! THIS IS WHAT I WAS BORN TO DO.
YOU SAY SOMEBODY MUST BE BETRAYED? NO MATTER WHAT CHOICE I MAKE, IT FEELS LIKE IT'S ME EITHER WAY!

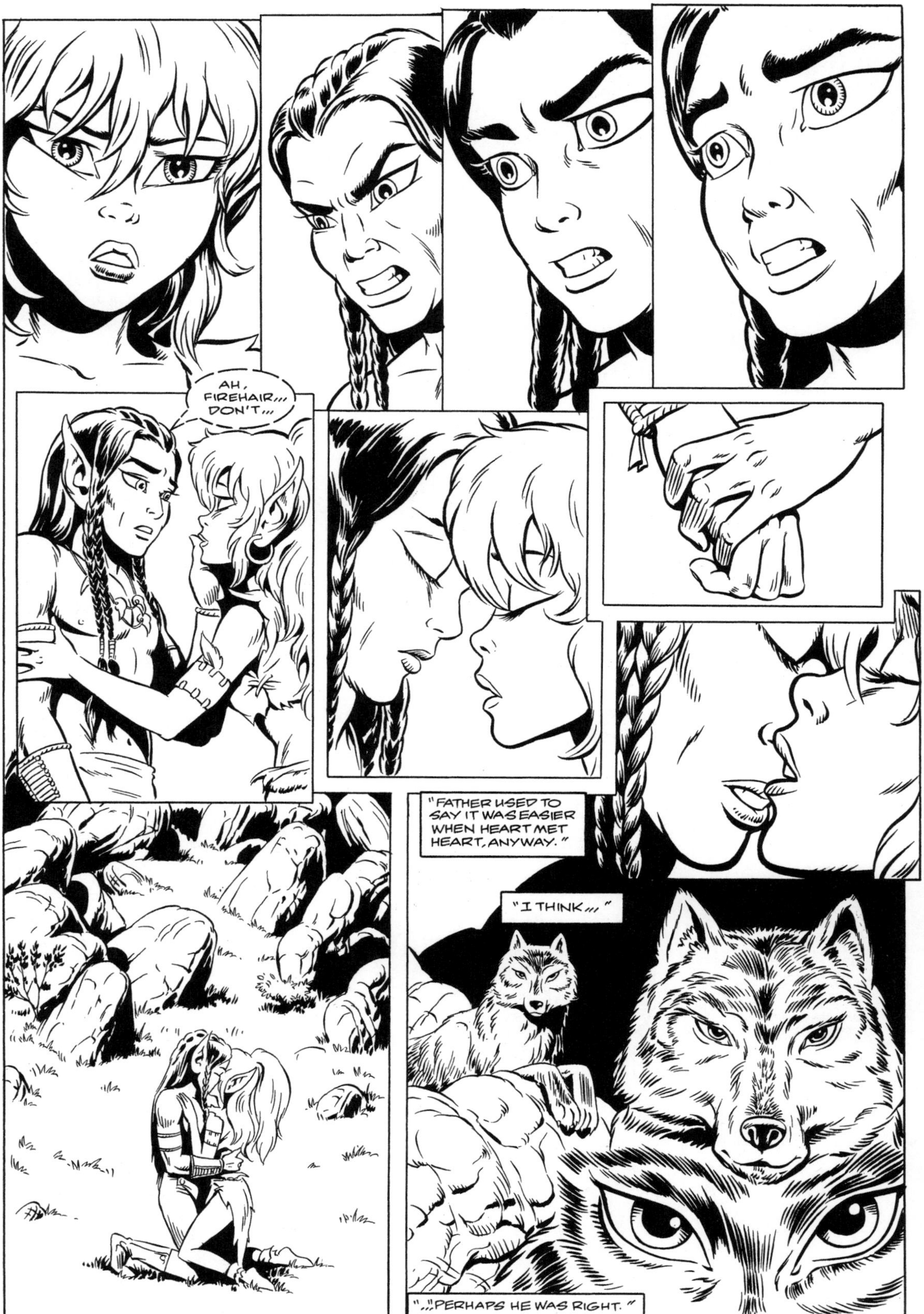

AH, FIREHAIR... DON'T...
"FATHER USED TO SAY IT WAS EASIER WHEN HEART MET HEART, ANYWAY."
"I THINK..."
"...PERHAPS HE WAS RIGHT."

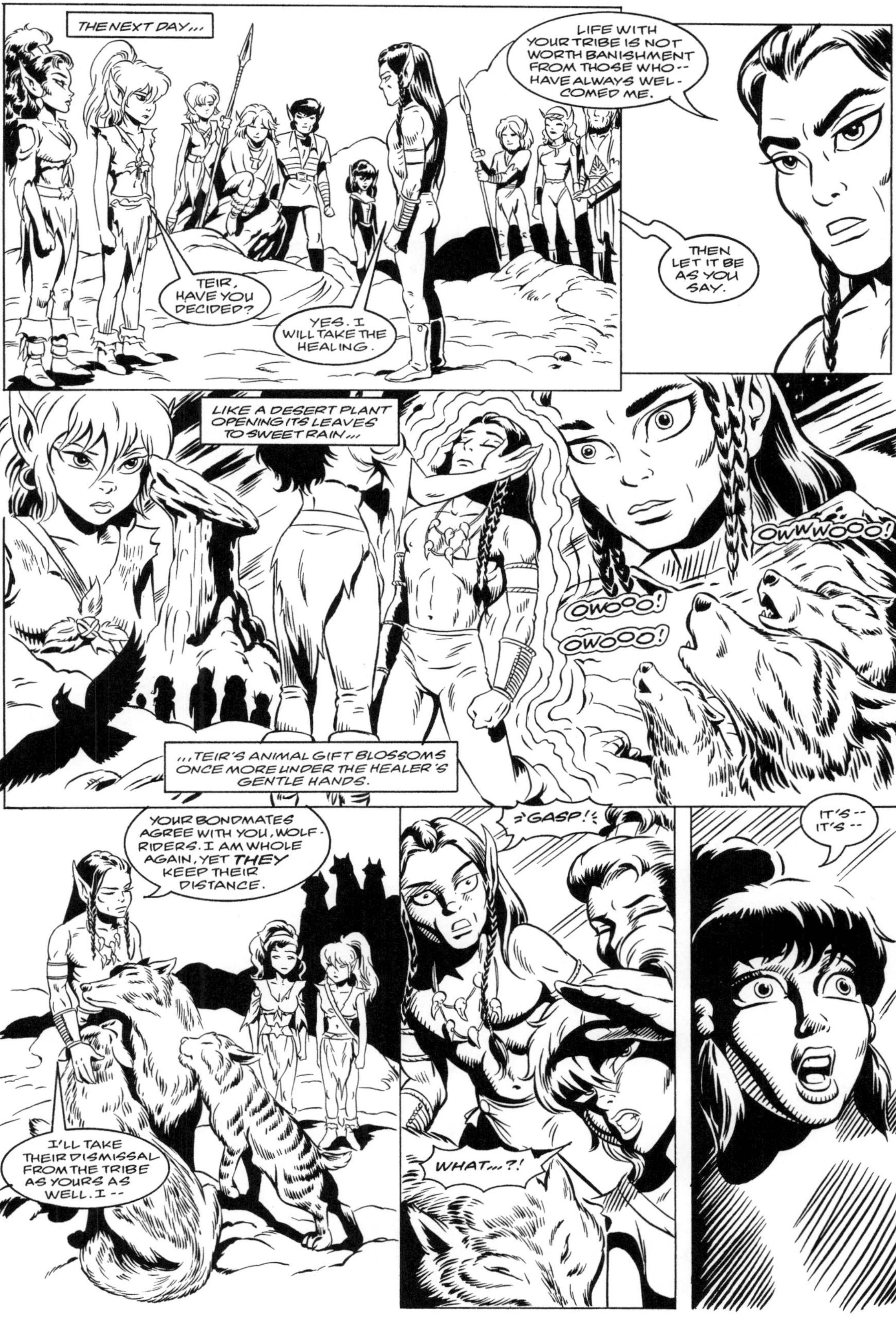
THE NEXT DAY...
TEIR, HAVE YOU DECIDED?
YES. I WILL TAKE THE HEALING.
LIFE WITH YOUR TRIBE IS NOT WORTH BANISHMENT FROM THOSE WHO-- HAVE ALWAYS WEL-COMED ME.
THEN LET IT BE AS YOU SAY.
LIKE A DESERT PLANT OPENING ITS LEAVES TO SWEET RAIN...
...TEIR'S ANIMAL GIFT BLOSSOMS ONCE MORE UNDER THE HEALER'S GENTLE HANDS.
OWWWOOO!
OWOOO!
OWOOO!
YOUR BONDMATES AGREE WITH YOU, WOLF-RIDERS. I AM WHOLE AGAIN, YET THEY KEEP THEIR DISTANCE.
I'LL TAKE THEIR DISMISSAL FROM THE TRIBE AS YOURS AS WELL. I --
GASP!
WHAT...?!
IT'S -- IT'S --

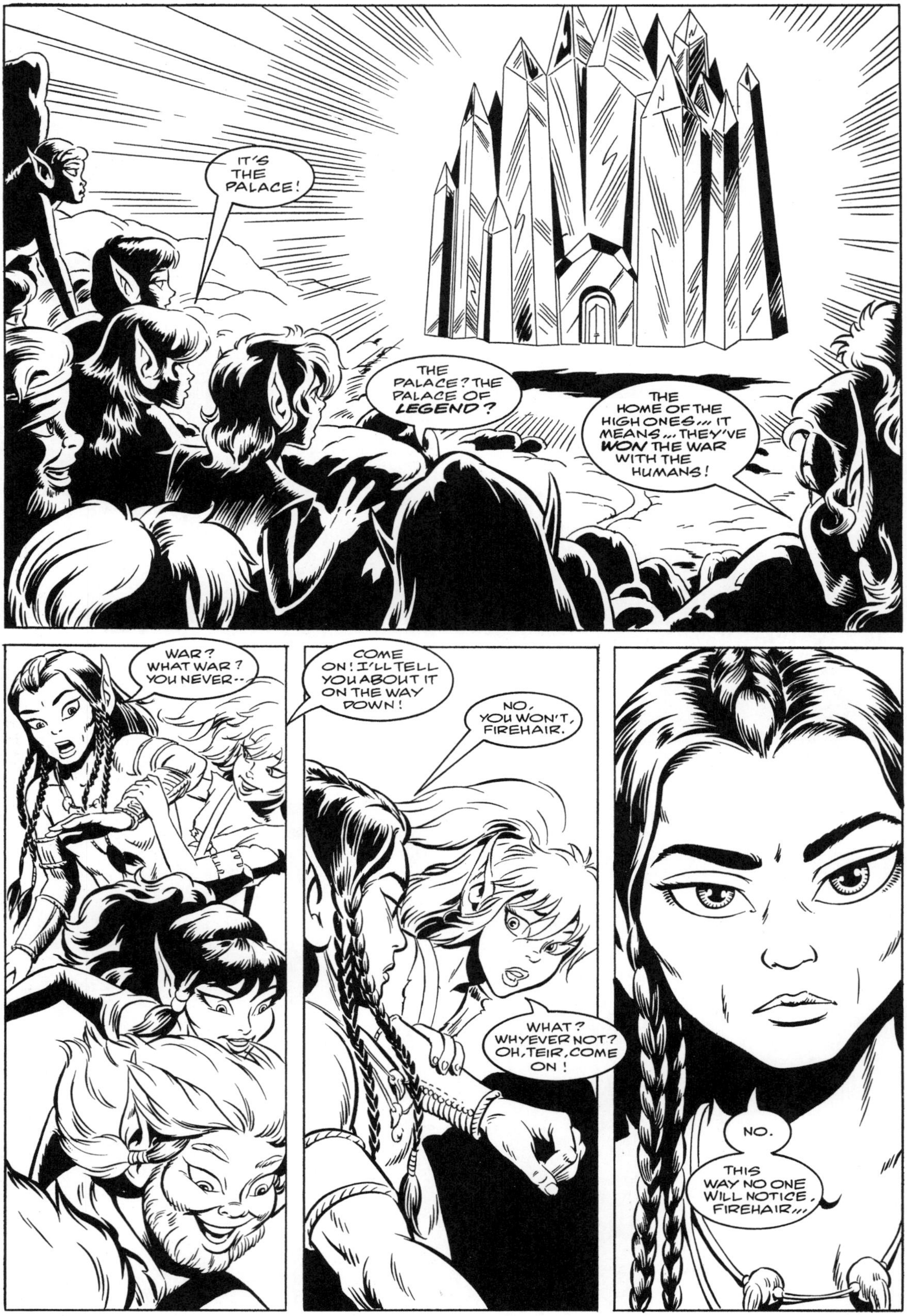
IT'S THE PALACE!
THE PALACE? THE PALACE OF LEGEND?
THE HOME OF THE HIGH ONES... IT MEANS... THEY'VE WON THE WAR WITH THE HUMANS!
WAR? WHAT WAR? YOU NEVER--
COME ON! I'LL TELL YOU ABOUT IT ON THE WAY DOWN!
NO, YOU WON'T, FIREHAIR.
WHAT? WHYEVER NOT? OH, TEIR, COME ON!
NO.
THIS WAY NO ONE WILL NOTICE, FIREHAIR...

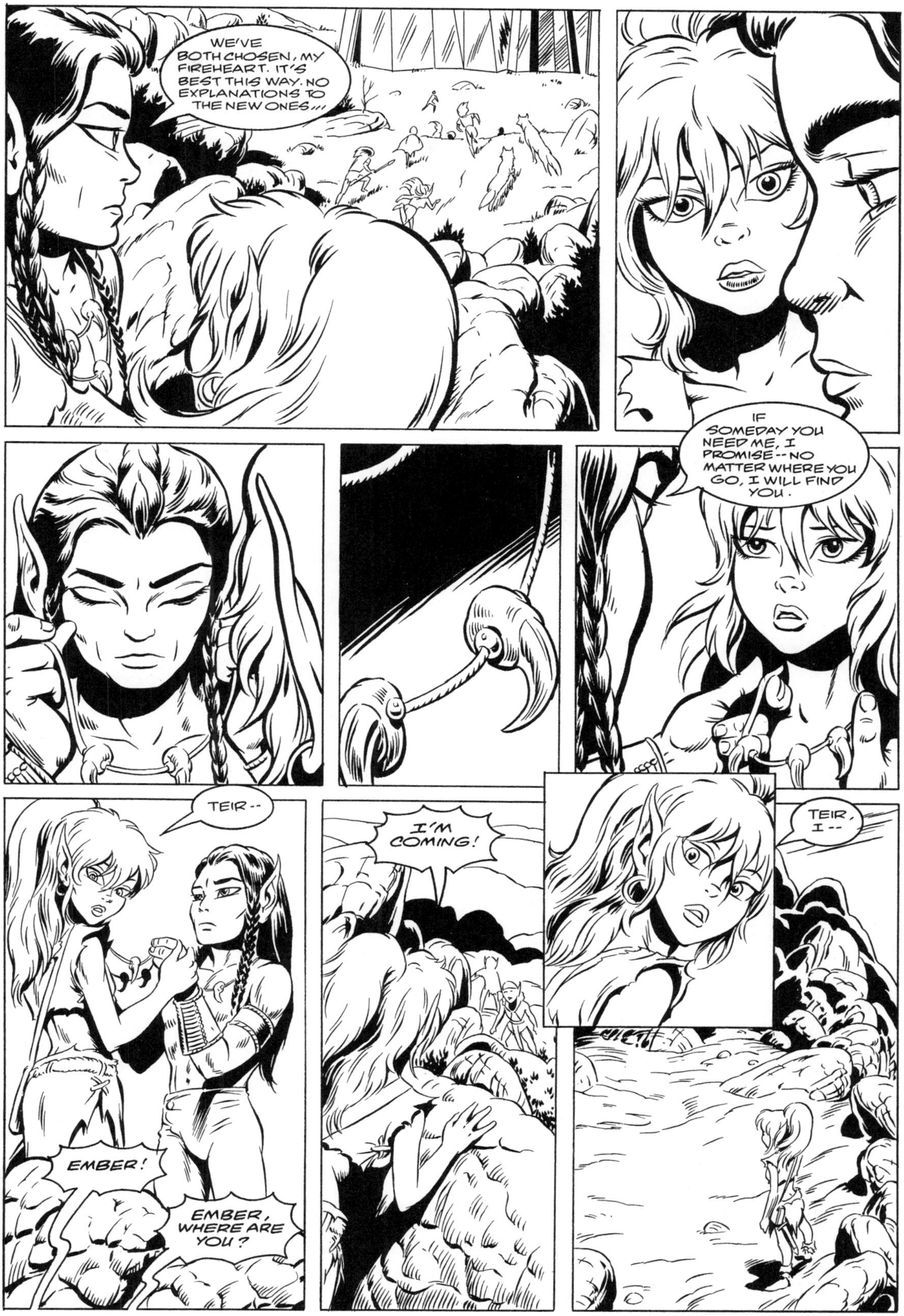
WE'VE BOTH CHOSEN, MY FIREHEART. IT'S BEST THIS WAY. NO EXPLANATIONS TO THE NEW ONES...
IF SOMEDAY YOU NEED ME, I PROMISE--NO MATTER WHERE YOU GO, I WILL FIND YOU.
TEIR--
EMBER!
EMBER, WHERE ARE YOU?
I'M COMING!
TEIR, I--

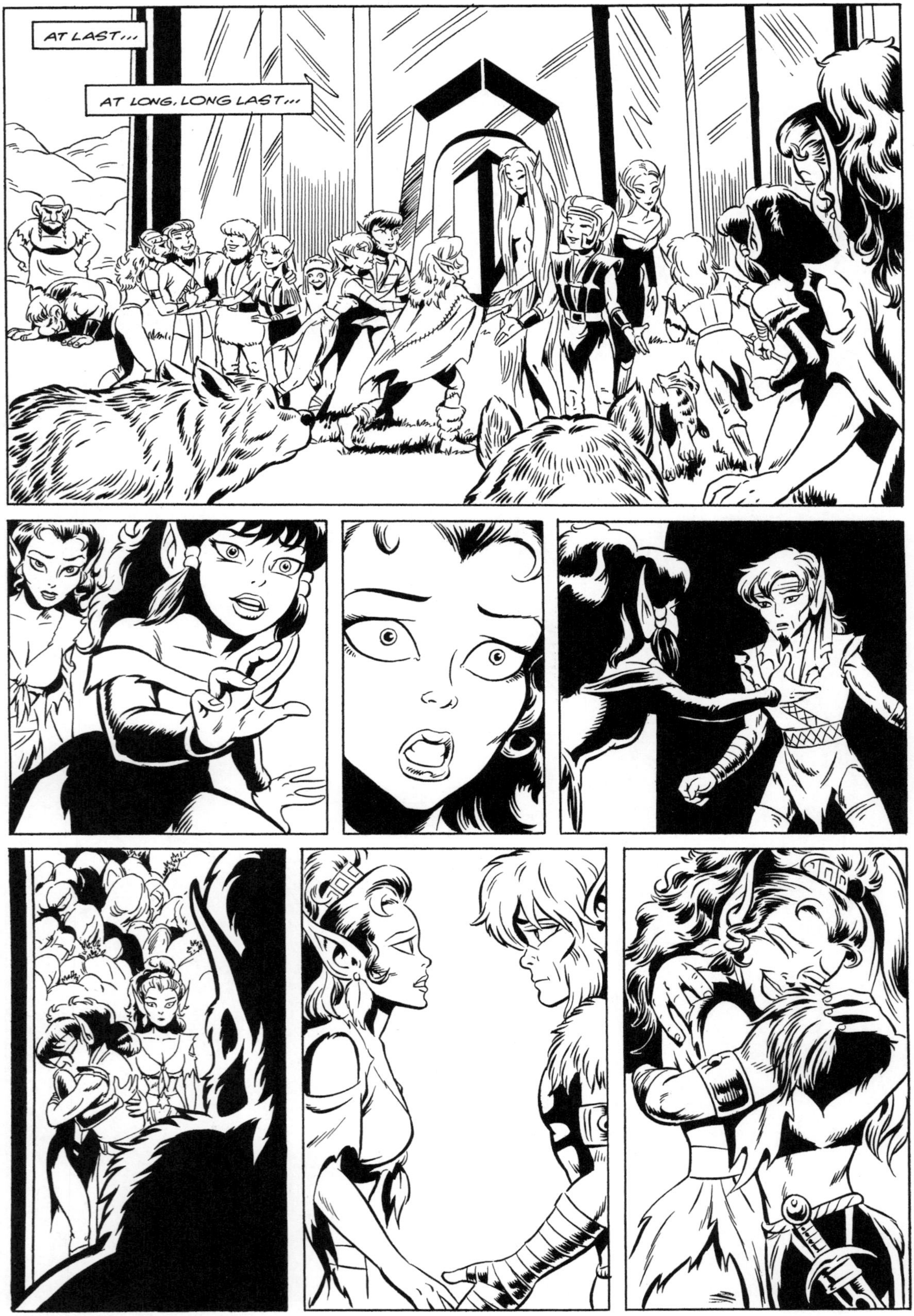
AT LAST...
AT LONG, LONG LAST...

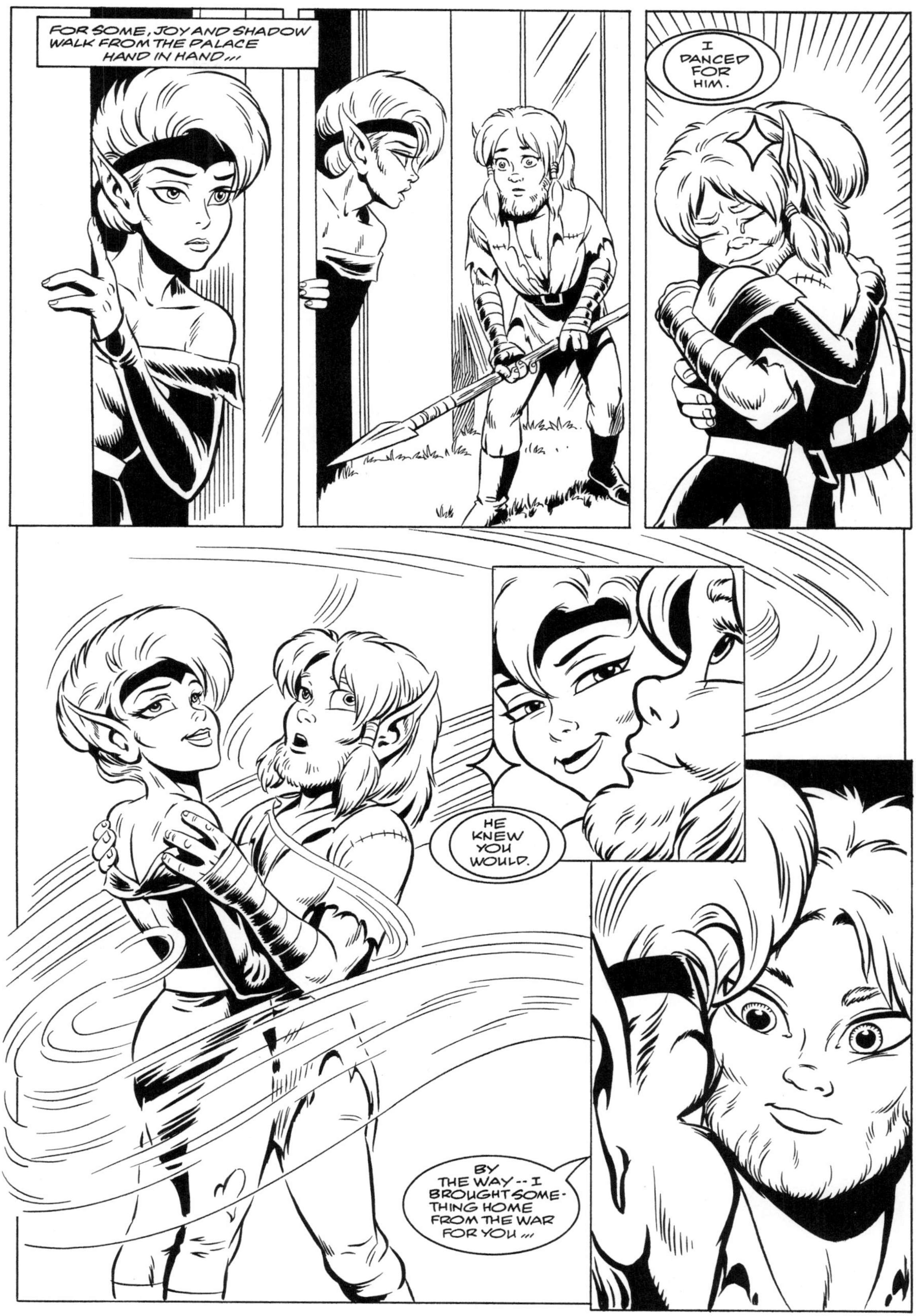
FOR SOME, JOY AND SHADOW WALK FROM THE PALACE HAND IN HAND...
I DANCED FOR HIM.
HE KNEW YOU WOULD.
BY THE WAY -- I BROUGHT SOMETHING HOME FROM THE WAR FOR YOU...

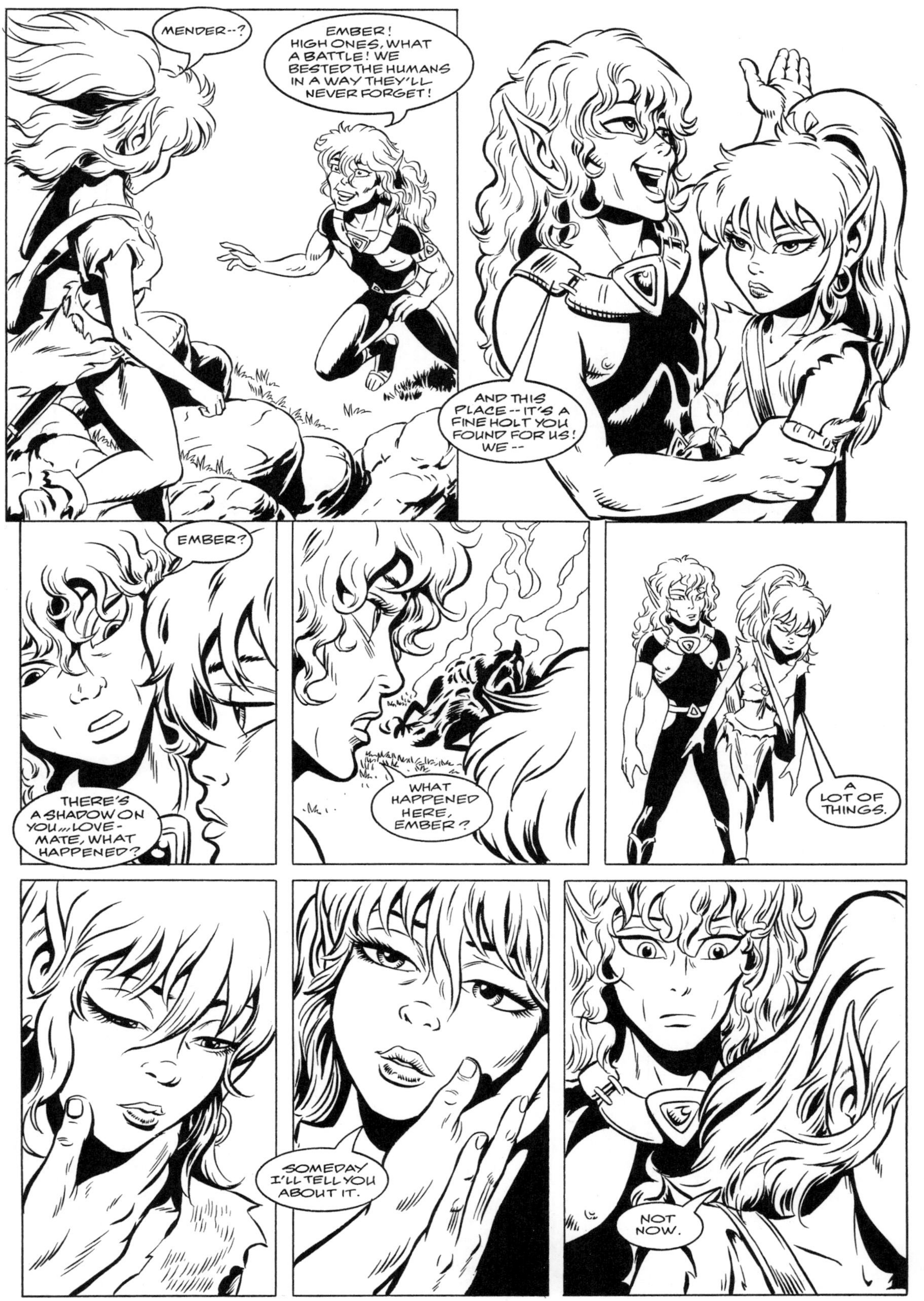
MENDER--?
EMBER! HIGH ONES, WHAT A BATTLE! WE BESTED THE HUMANS IN A WAY THEY'LL NEVER FORGET!
AND THIS PLACE--IT'S A FINE HOLT YOU FOUND FOR US! WE--
EMBER?
THERE'S A SHADOW ON YOU... LOVE-MATE, WHAT HAPPENED?
WHAT HAPPENED HERE, EMBER?
A LOT OF THINGS.
SOMEDAY I'LL TELL YOU ABOUT IT.
NOT NOW.

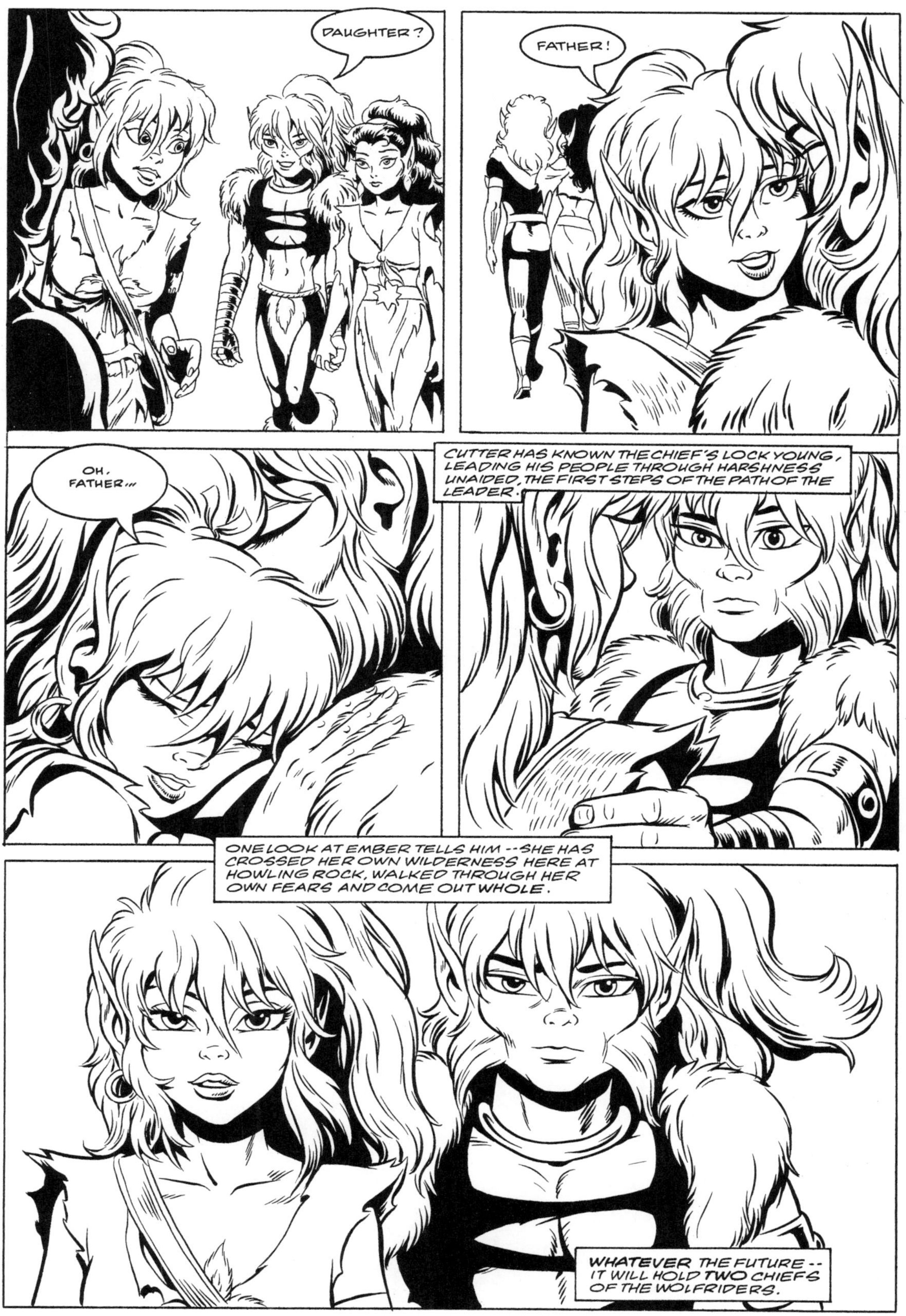
DAUGHTER?
FATHER!
OH, FATHER...
CUTTER HAS KNOWN THE CHIEF'S LOCK YOUNG, LEADING HIS PEOPLE THROUGH HARSHNESS UNAIDED, THE FIRST STEPS OF THE PATH OF THE LEADER.
ONE LOOK AT EMBER TELLS HIM -- SHE HAS CROSSED HER OWN WILDERNESS HERE AT HOWLING ROCK, WALKED THROUGH HER OWN FEARS AND COME OUT WHOLE.
WHATEVER THE FUTURE -- IT WILL HOLD TWO CHIEFS OF THE WOLFRIDERS.

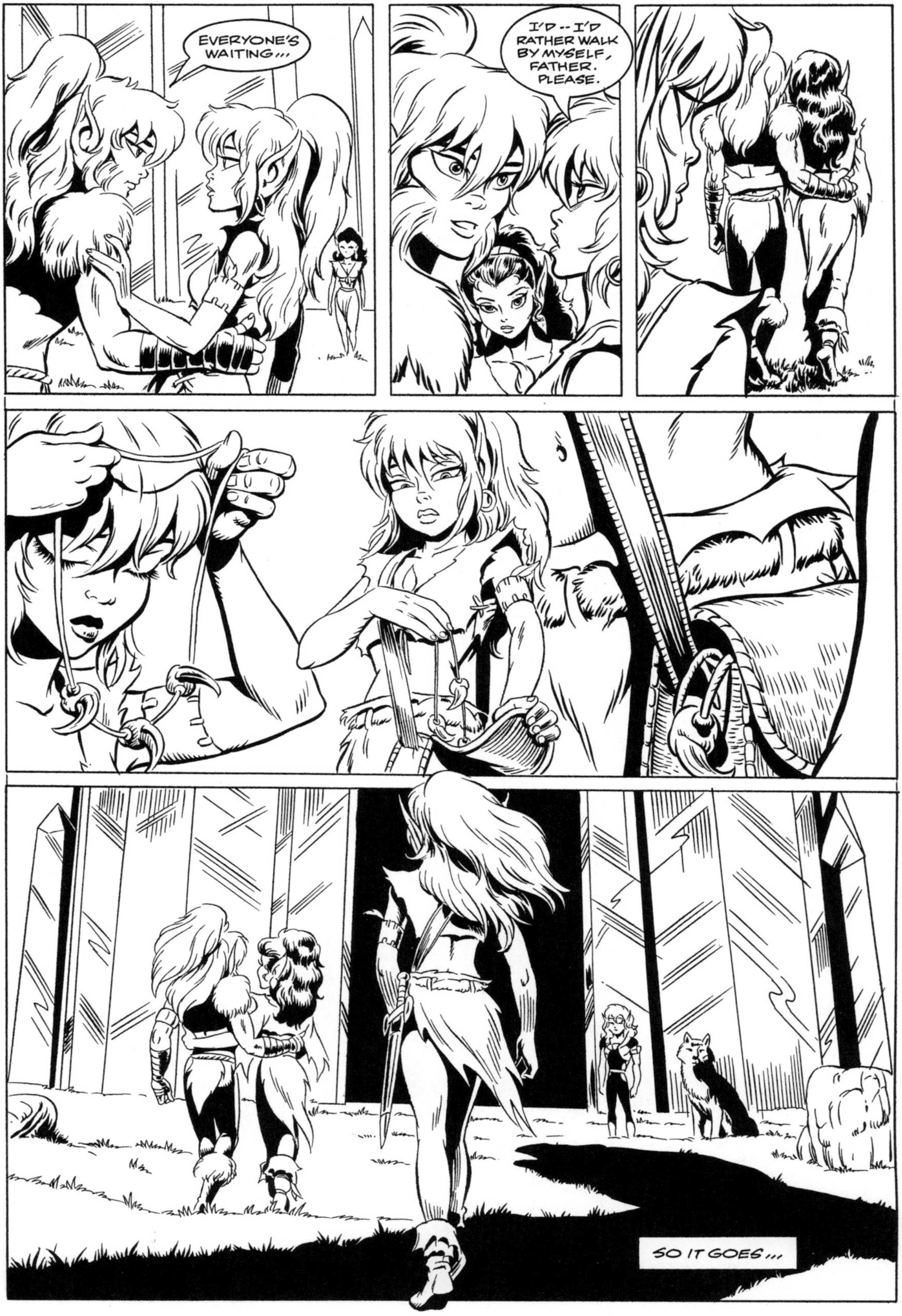
EVERYONE'S WAITING...
I'D -- I'D RATHER WALK BY MYSELF, FATHER. PLEASE.
SO IT GOES...

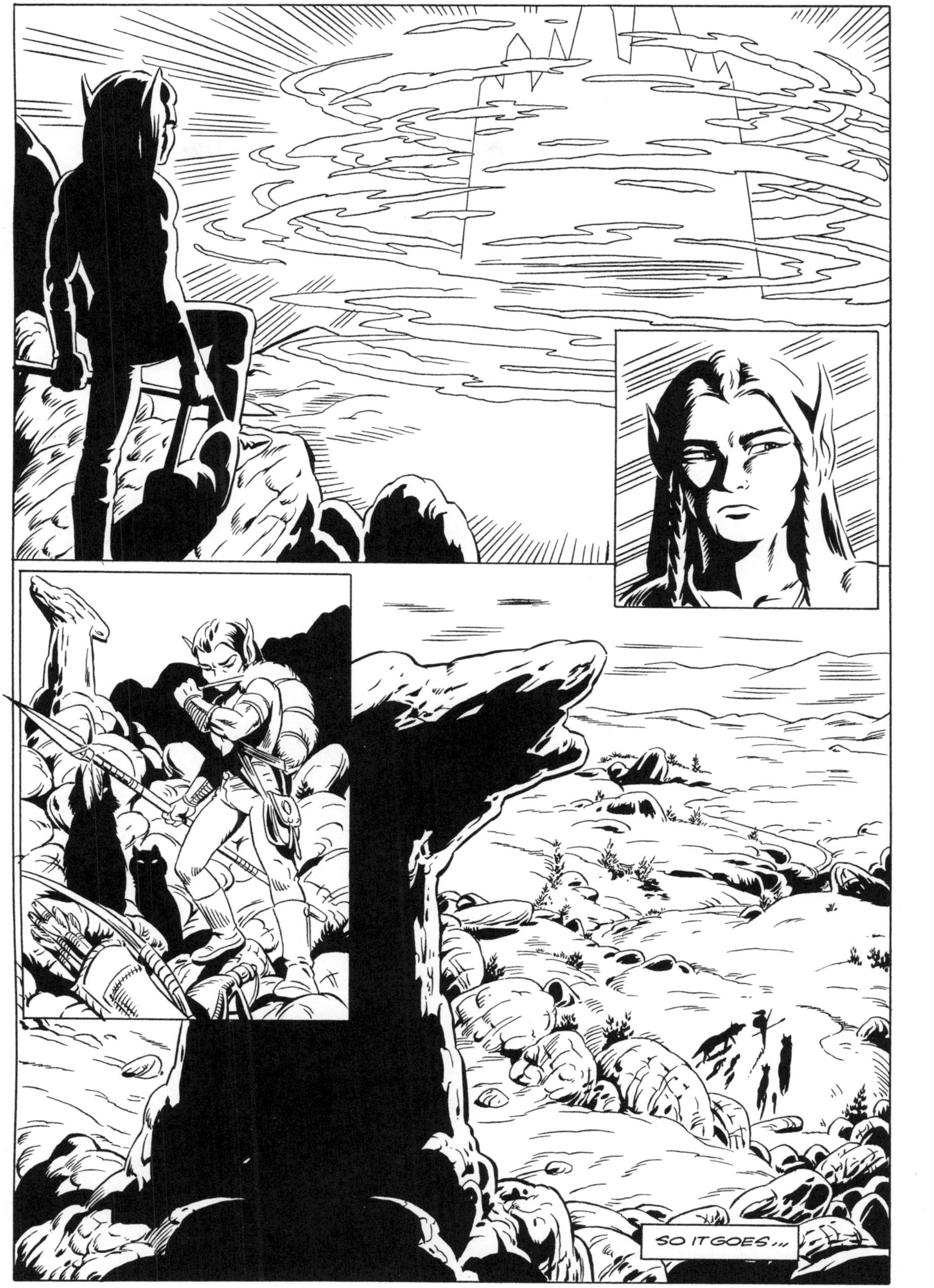
SO IT GOES...

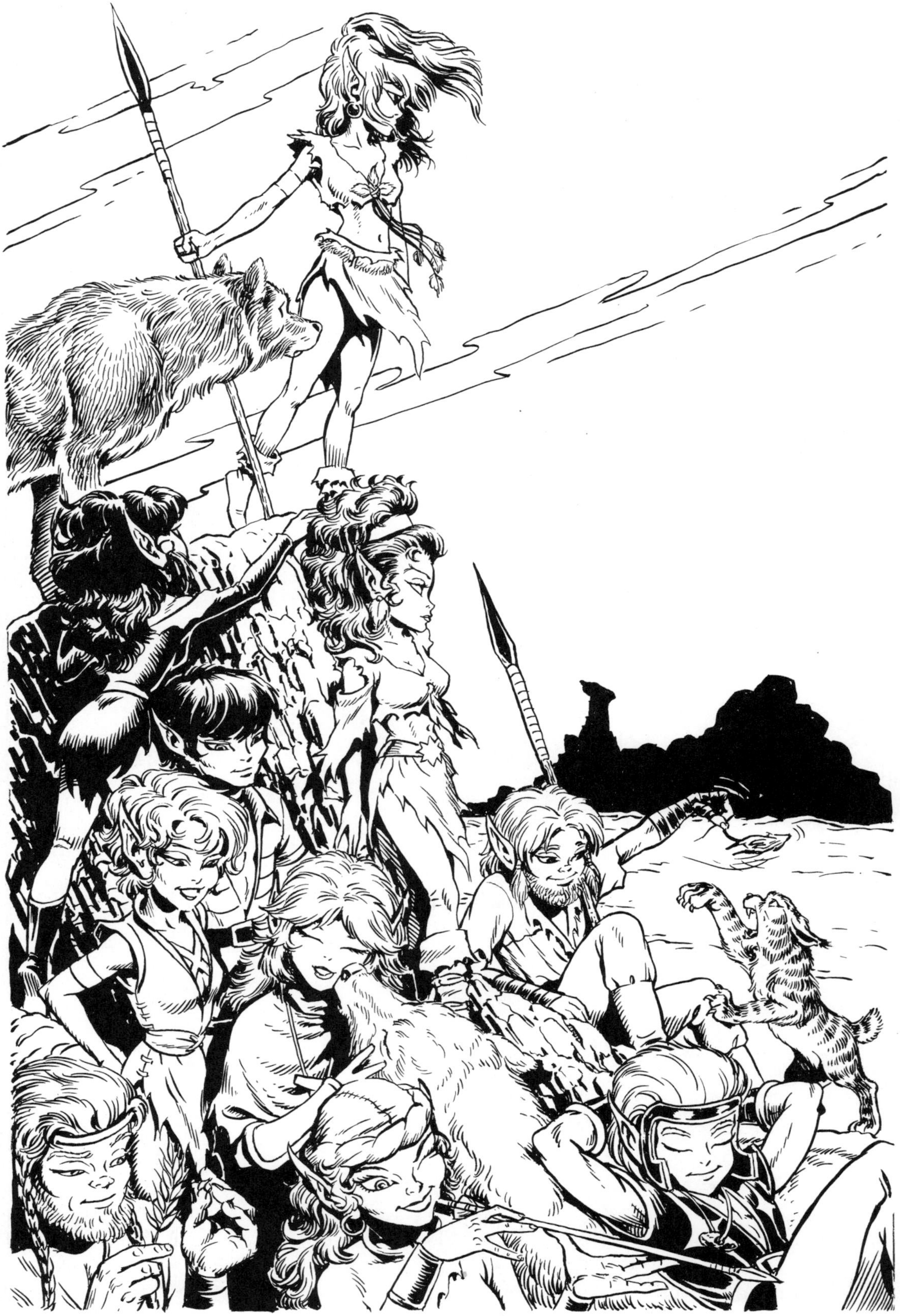

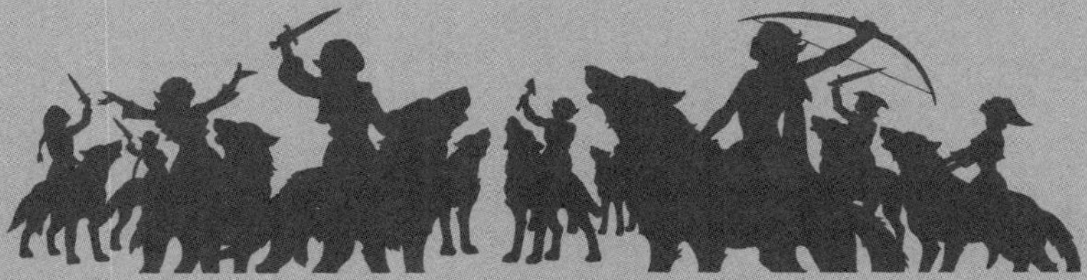

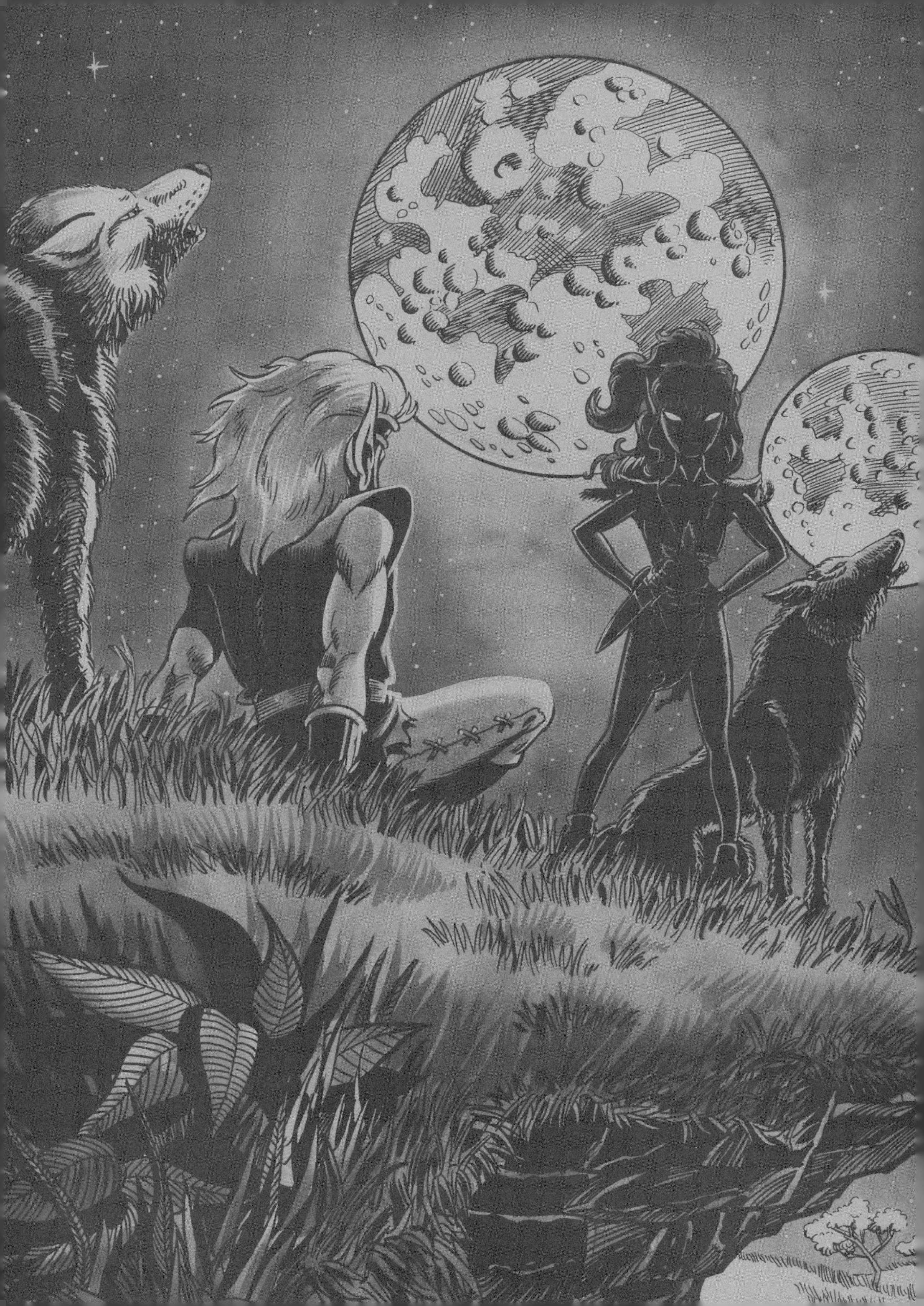

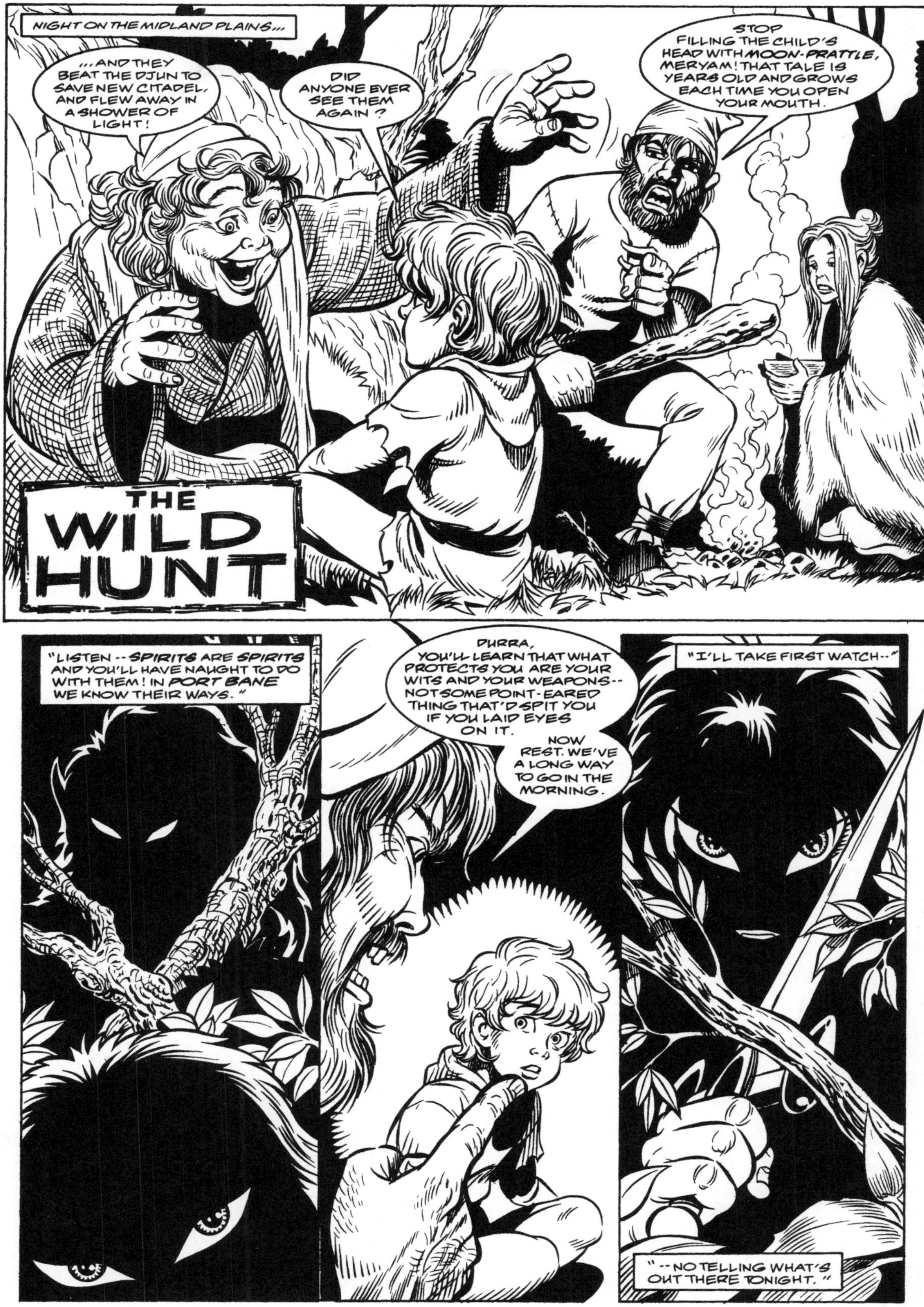
NIGHT ON THE MIDLAND PLAINS...
...AND THEY BEAT THE DJUN TO SAVE NEW CITADEL, AND FLEW AWAY IN A SHOWER OF LIGHT!
DID ANYONE EVER SEE THEM AGAIN?
STOP FILLING THE CHILD'S HEAD WITH MOON-PRATTLE, MERYAM! THAT TALE IS YEARS OLD AND GROWS EACH TIME YOU OPEN YOUR MOUTH.
THE WILD HUNT
"LISTEN -- SPIRITS ARE SPIRITS AND YOU'LL HAVE NAUGHT TO DO WITH THEM! IN PORT BANE WE KNOW THEIR WAYS."
DURRA, YOU'LL LEARN THAT WHAT PROTECTS YOU ARE YOUR WITS AND YOUR WEAPONS-- NOT SOME POINT-EARED THING THAT'D SPIT YOU IF YOU LAID EYES ON IT.
NOW REST. WE'VE A LONG WAY TO GO IN THE MORNING.
"I'LL TAKE FIRST WATCH--"
"--NO TELLING WHAT'S OUT THERE TONIGHT."

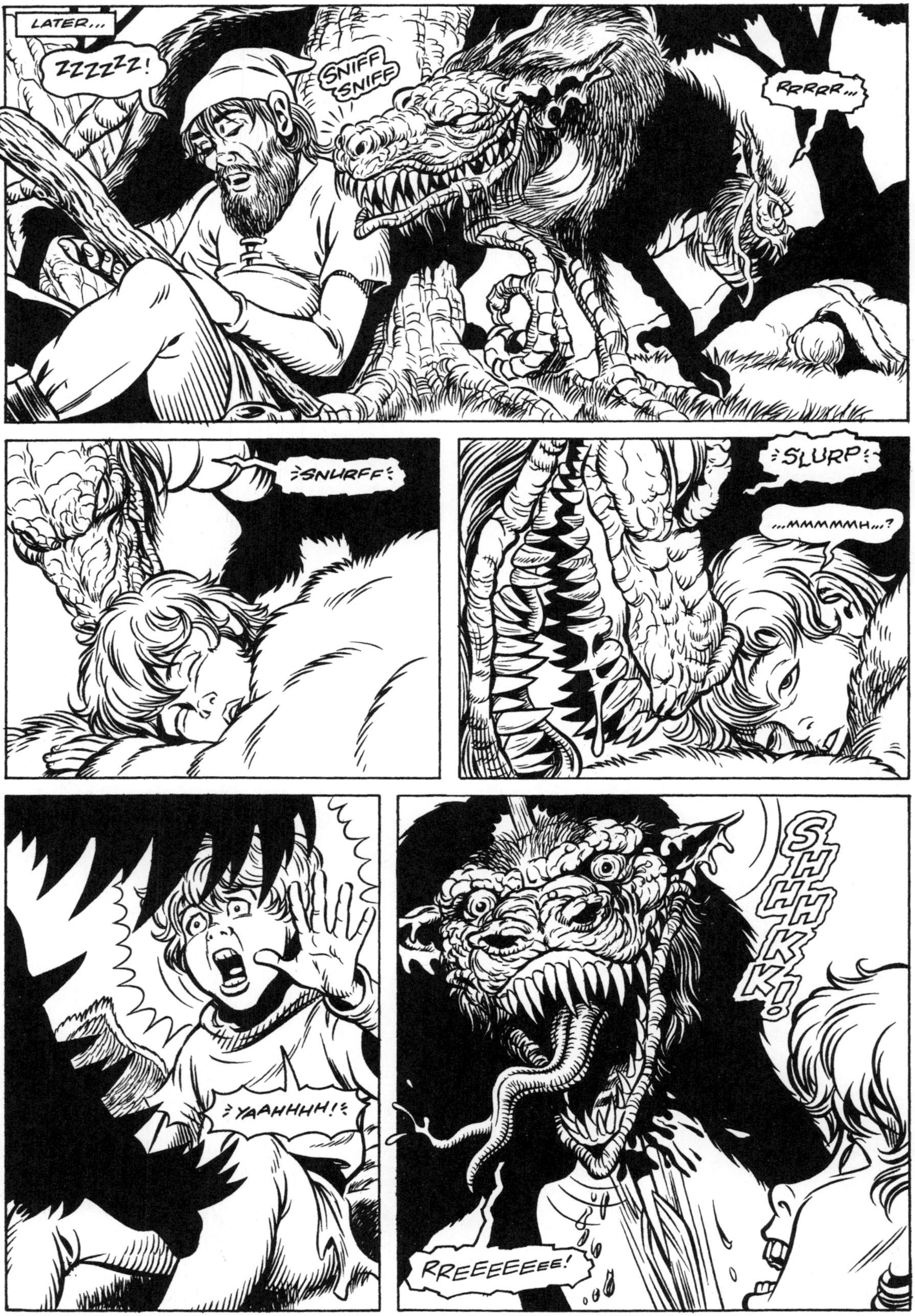
LATER...
ZZZZZZ!
SNIFF SNIFF
RRRRR...
SNURFF
SLURP
...MMMMMH...?
YAAHHHH!
SHHHKK!
RREEEEEEE!

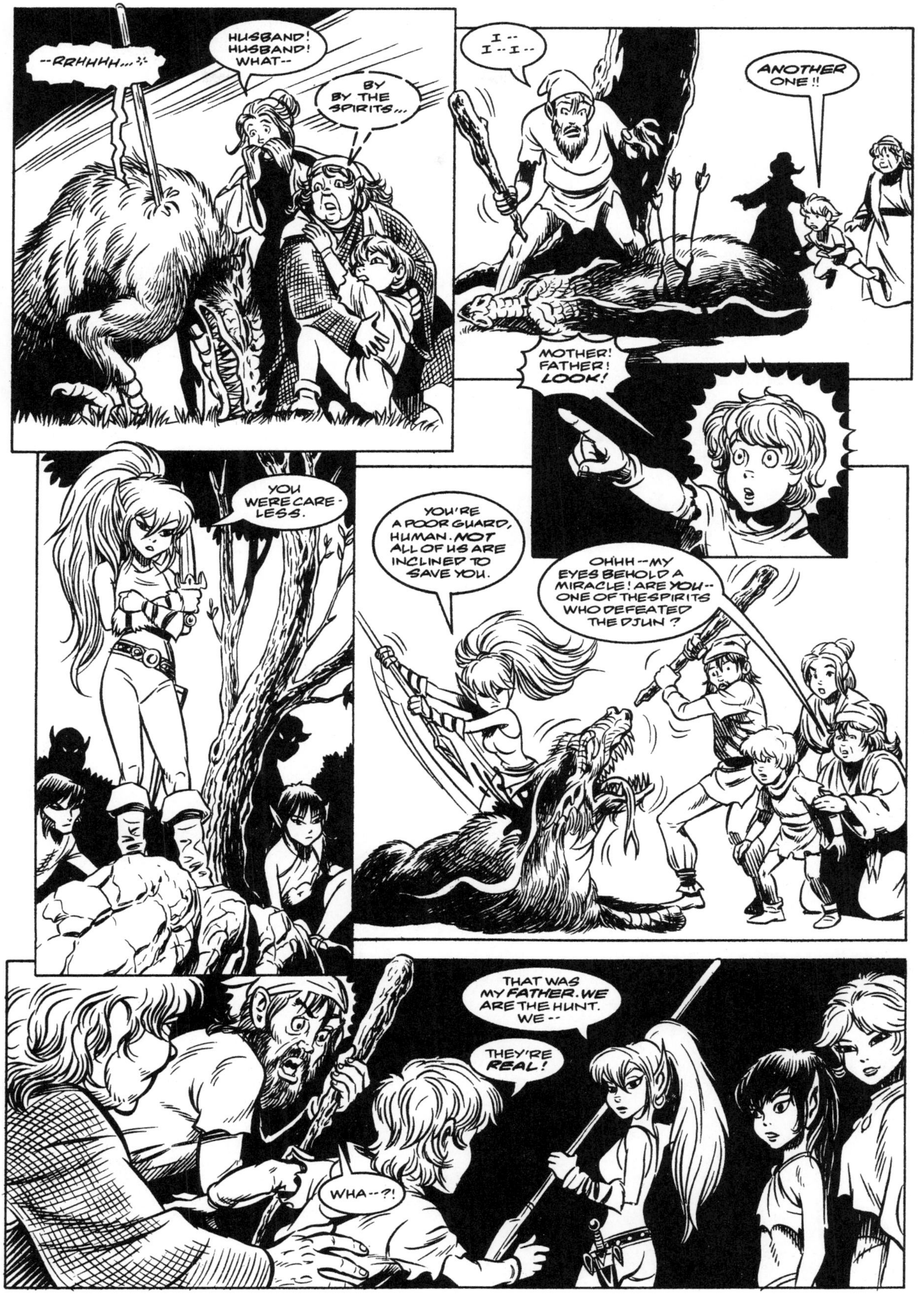

--RRHHHH...
HUSBAND! HUSBAND! WHAT--
BY BY THE SPIRITS...
I -- I -- I --
ANOTHER ONE!!
MOTHER! FATHER! LOOK!
YOU WERE CARE-LESS.
YOU'RE A POOR GUARD, HUMAN. NOT ALL OF US ARE INCLINED TO SAVE YOU.
OHHH--MY EYES BEHOLD A MIRACLE! ARE YOU-- ONE OF THE SPIRITS WHO DEFEATED THE DJUN?
THAT WAS MY FATHER. WE ARE THE HUNT. WE--
THEY'RE REAL!
WHA--?!

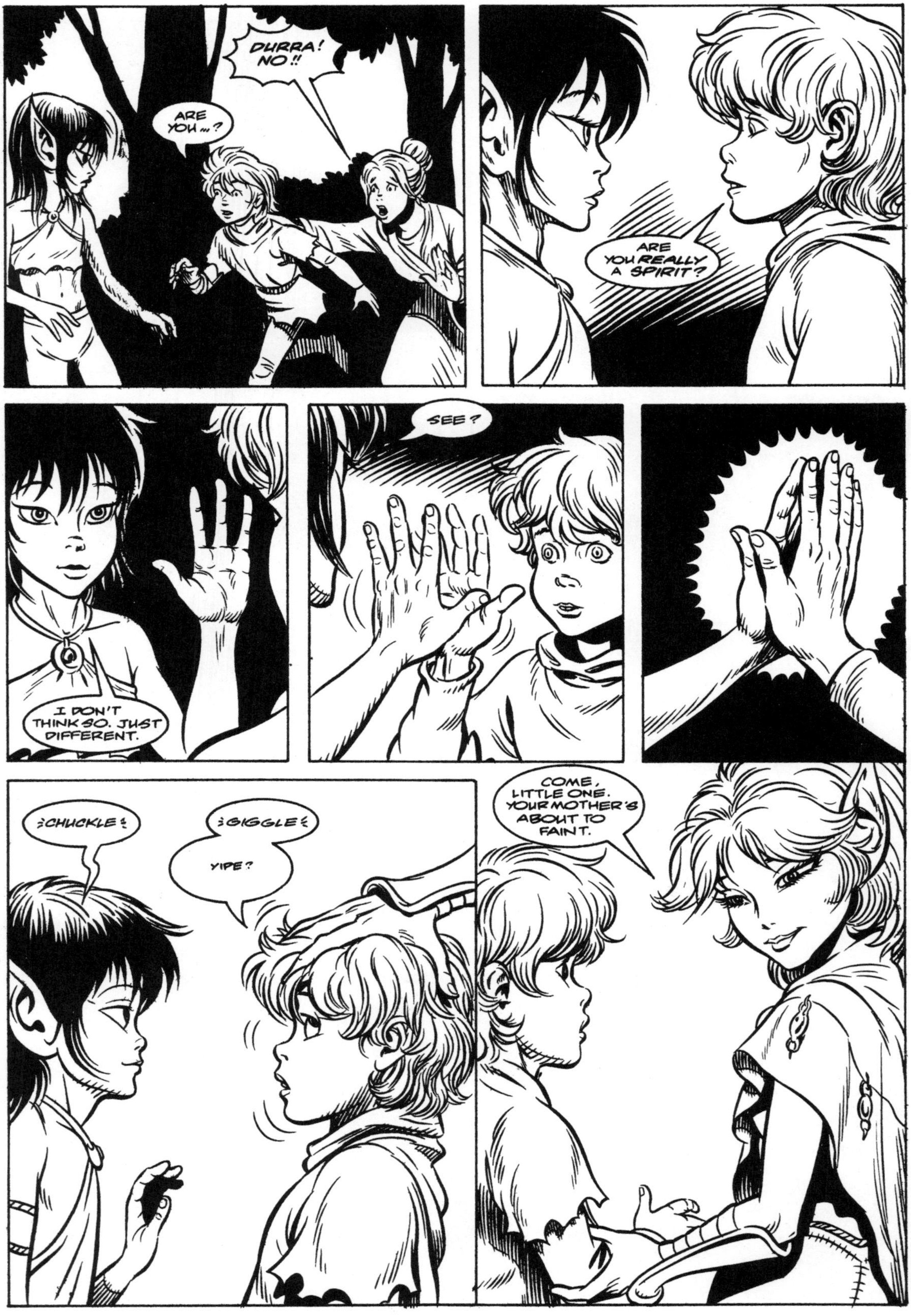
DURRA! NO!!
ARE YOU...?
ARE YOU REALLY A SPIRIT?
I DON'T THINK SO. JUST DIFFERENT.
SEE?
:CHUCKLE:
:GIGGLE:
YIPE?
COME, LITTLE ONE. YOUR MOTHER'S ABOUT TO FAINT.

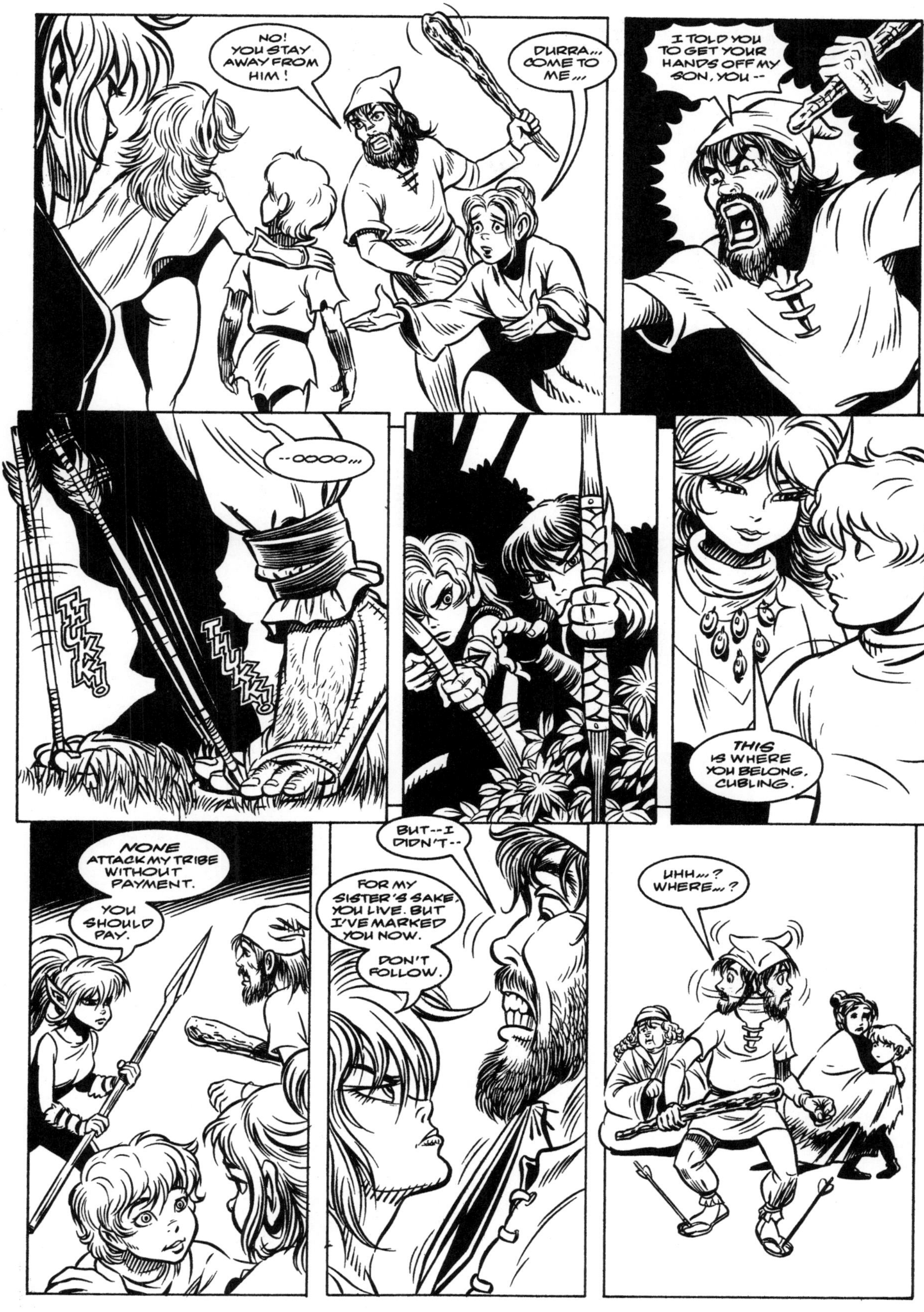
NO! YOU STAY AWAY FROM HIM!
DURRA... COME TO ME...
I TOLD YOU TO GET YOUR HANDS OFF MY SON, YOU --
--OOOO...
THUKK!
THUKK!
THIS IS WHERE YOU BELONG, CUBLING.
NONE ATTACK MY TRIBE WITHOUT PAYMENT.
YOU SHOULD PAY.
BUT--I DIDN'T--
FOR MY SISTER'S SAKE, YOU LIVE. BUT I'VE MARKED YOU NOW.
DON'T FOLLOW.
UHH...? WHERE...?

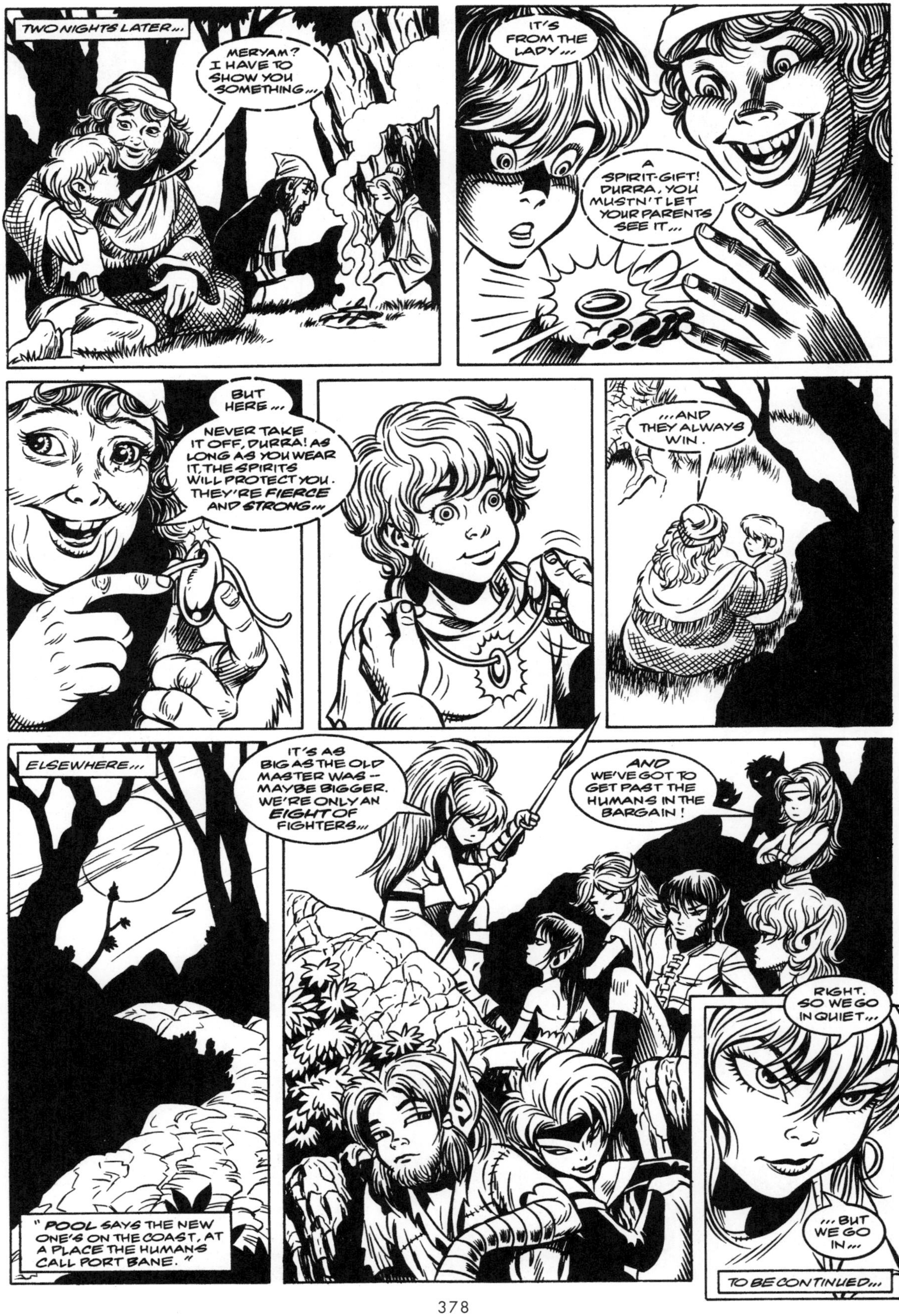
TWO NIGHTS LATER...
MERYAM? I HAVE TO SHOW YOU SOMETHING...
IT'S FROM THE LADY...
A SPIRIT-GIFT! DURRA, YOU MUSTN'T LET YOUR PARENTS SEE IT...
BUT HERE...
NEVER TAKE IT OFF, DURRA! AS LONG AS YOU WEAR IT, THE SPIRITS WILL PROTECT YOU. THEY'RE FIERCE AND STRONG...
...AND THEY ALWAYS WIN.
ELSEWHERE...
IT'S AS BIG AS THE OLD MASTER WAS -- MAYBE BIGGER. WE'RE ONLY AN EIGHT OF FIGHTERS...
AND WE'VE GOT TO GET PAST THE HUMANS IN THE BARGAIN!
"POOL SAYS THE NEW ONE'S ON THE COAST, AT A PLACE THE HUMANS CALL PORT BANE."
RIGHT. SO WE GO IN QUIET...
...BUT WE GO IN...
TO BE CONTINUED...

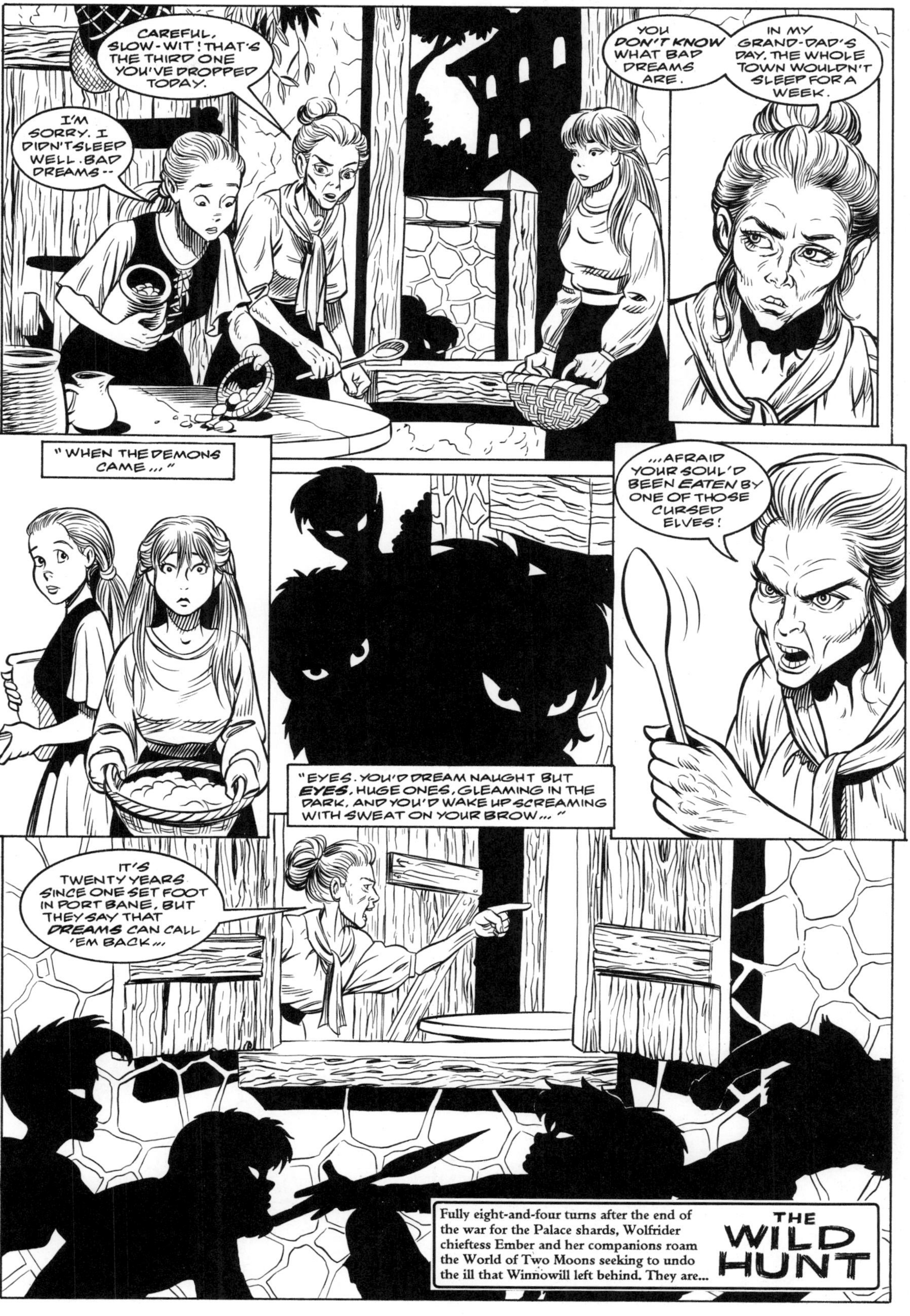
CAREFUL, SLOW-WIT! THAT'S THE THIRD ONE YOU'VE DROPPED TODAY.
I'M SORRY. I DIDN'T SLEEP WELL. BAD DREAMS--
YOU DON'T KNOW WHAT BAD DREAMS ARE.
IN MY GRAND-DAD'S DAY, THE WHOLE TOWN WOULDN'T SLEEP FOR A WEEK.
"WHEN THE DEMONS CAME..."
"EYES. YOU'D DREAM NAUGHT BUT EYES, HUGE ONES, GLEAMING IN THE DARK, AND YOU'D WAKE UP SCREAMING WITH SWEAT ON YOUR BROW..."
...AFRAID YOUR SOUL'D BEEN EATEN BY ONE OF THOSE CURSED ELVES!
IT'S TWENTY YEARS SINCE ONE SET FOOT IN PORT BANE, BUT THEY SAY THAT DREAMS CAN CALL 'EM BACK...
Fully eight-and-four turns after the end of the war for the Palace shards, Wolfrider chieftess Ember and her companions roam the World of Two Moons seeking to undo the ill that Winnowill left behind. They are...
THE WILD HUNT

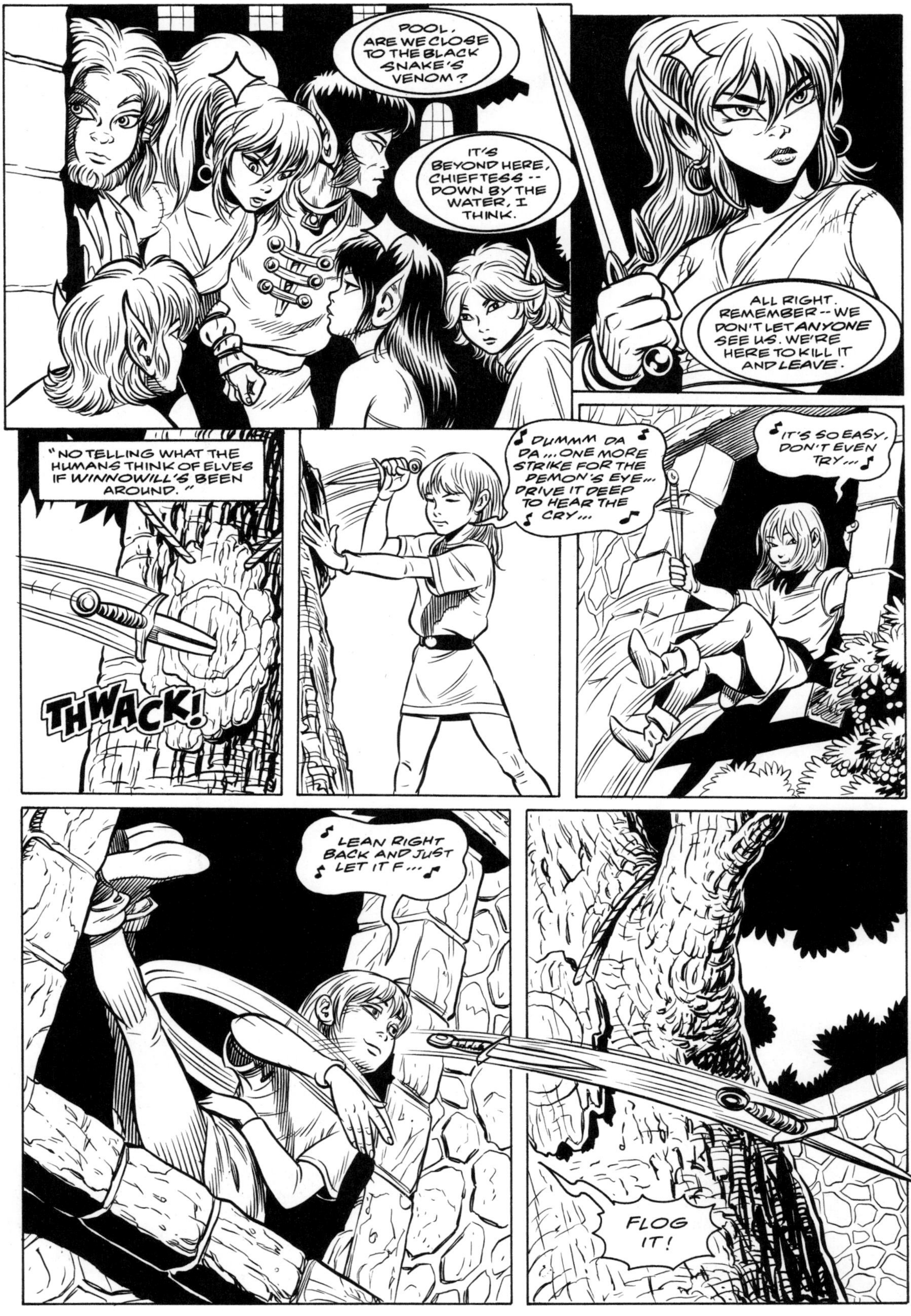

POOL, ARE WE CLOSE TO THE BLACK SNAKE'S VENOM?
IT'S BEYOND HERE, CHIEFTESS -- DOWN BY THE WATER, I THINK.
ALL RIGHT. REMEMBER -- WE DON'T LET ANYONE SEE US. WE'RE HERE TO KILL IT AND LEAVE.
"NO TELLING WHAT THE HUMANS THINK OF ELVES IF WINNOWILL'S BEEN AROUND."
THWACK!
DUMMM DA DA... ONE MORE STRIKE FOR THE DEMON'S EYE... DRIVE IT DEEP TO HEAR THE CRY...
IT'S SO EASY, DON'T EVEN TRY...
LEAN RIGHT BACK AND JUST LET IT F...
FLOG IT!

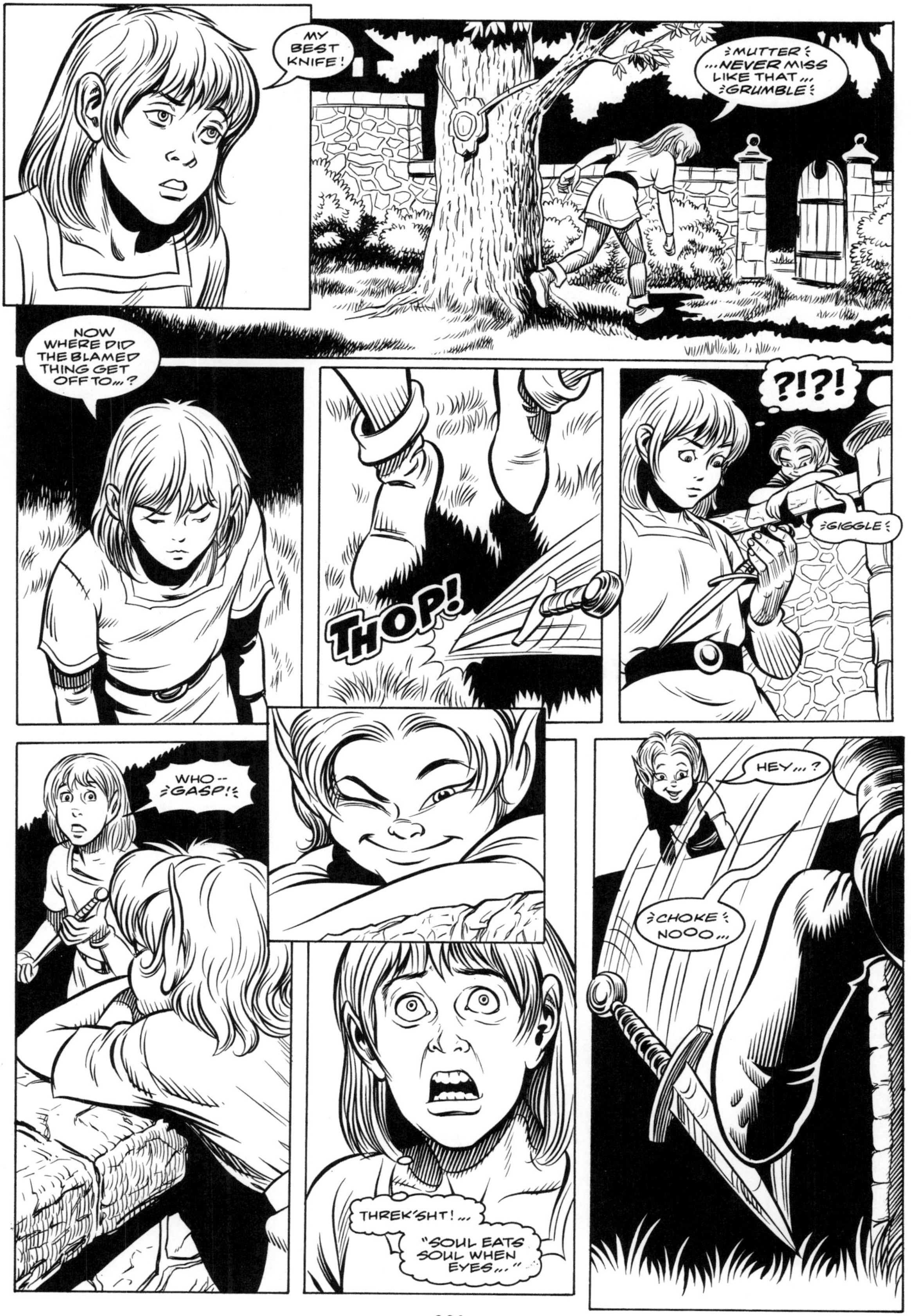
MY BEST KNIFE!
MUTTER ...NEVER MISS LIKE THAT... GRUMBLE
NOW WHERE DID THE BLAMED THING GET OFF TO...?
THOP!
?!?!
GIGGLE
WHO-- GASP!
HEY...?
CHOKE NOOO...
THREK'SHT!...
"SOUL EATS SOUL WHEN EYES..."

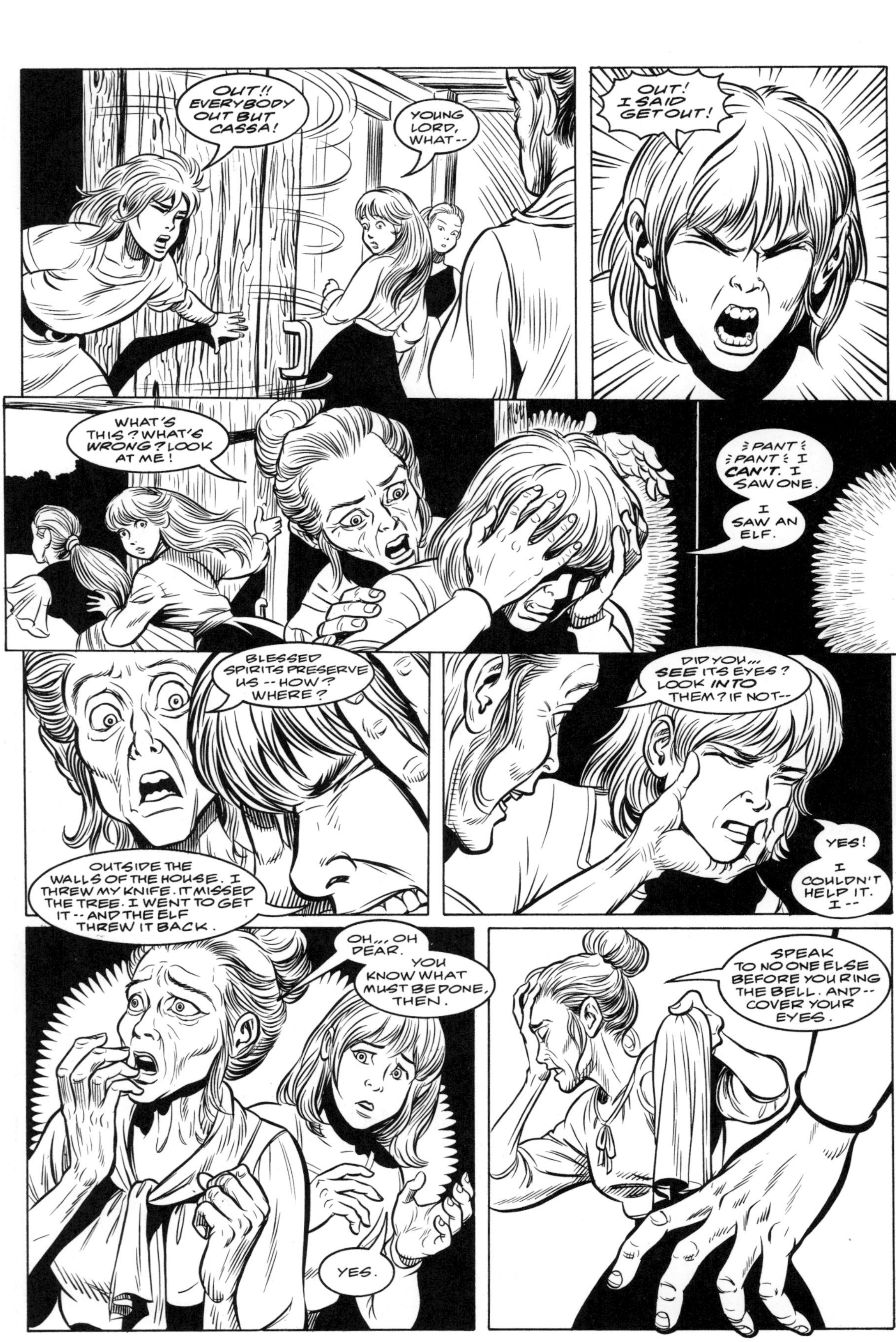
OUT!! EVERYBODY OUT BUT CASSA!
YOUNG LORD, WHAT--
OUT! I SAID GET OUT!
WHAT'S THIS? WHAT'S WRONG? LOOK AT ME!
PANT PANT I CAN'T. I SAW ONE.
I SAW AN ELF.
BLESSED SPIRITS PRESERVE US--HOW? WHERE?
OUTSIDE THE WALLS OF THE HOUSE. I THREW MY KNIFE. IT MISSED THE TREE. I WENT TO GET IT--AND THE ELF THREW IT BACK.
DID YOU... SEE ITS EYES? LOOK INTO THEM? IF NOT--
YES!
I COULDN'T HELP IT. I--
OH... OH DEAR.
YOU KNOW WHAT MUST BE DONE, THEN.
YES.
SPEAK TO NO ONE ELSE BEFORE YOU RING THE BELL. AND--COVER YOUR EYES.

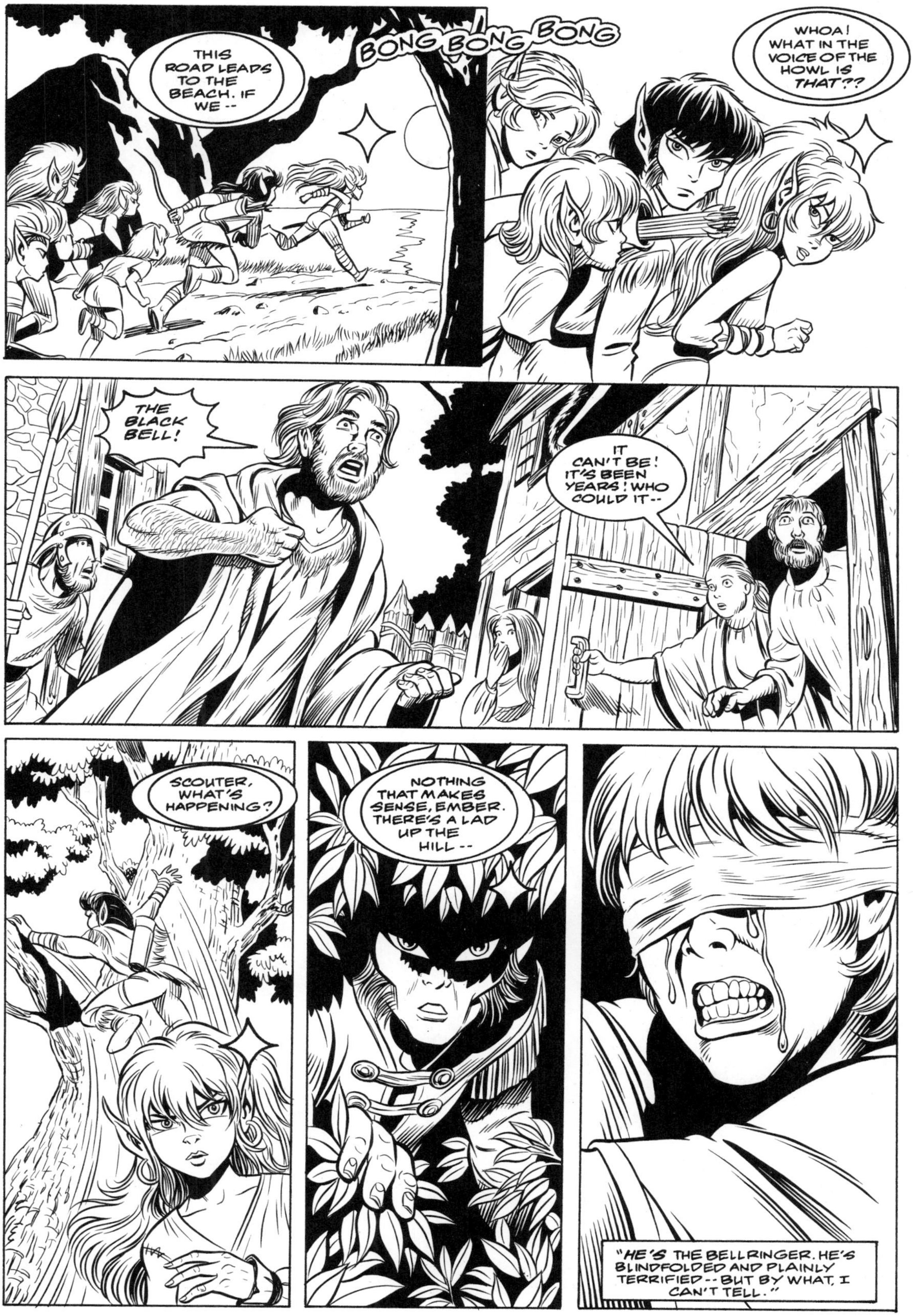
THIS ROAD LEADS TO THE BEACH. IF WE --
BONG BONG BONG
WHOA! WHAT IN THE VOICE OF THE HOWL IS THAT??
THE BLACK BELL!
IT CAN'T BE! IT'S BEEN YEARS! WHO COULD IT --
SCOUTER, WHAT'S HAPPENING?
NOTHING THAT MAKES SENSE, EMBER. THERE'S A LAD UP THE HILL --
"HE'S THE BELLRINGER. HE'S BLINDFOLDED AND PLAINLY TERRIFIED -- BUT BY WHAT, I CAN'T TELL."

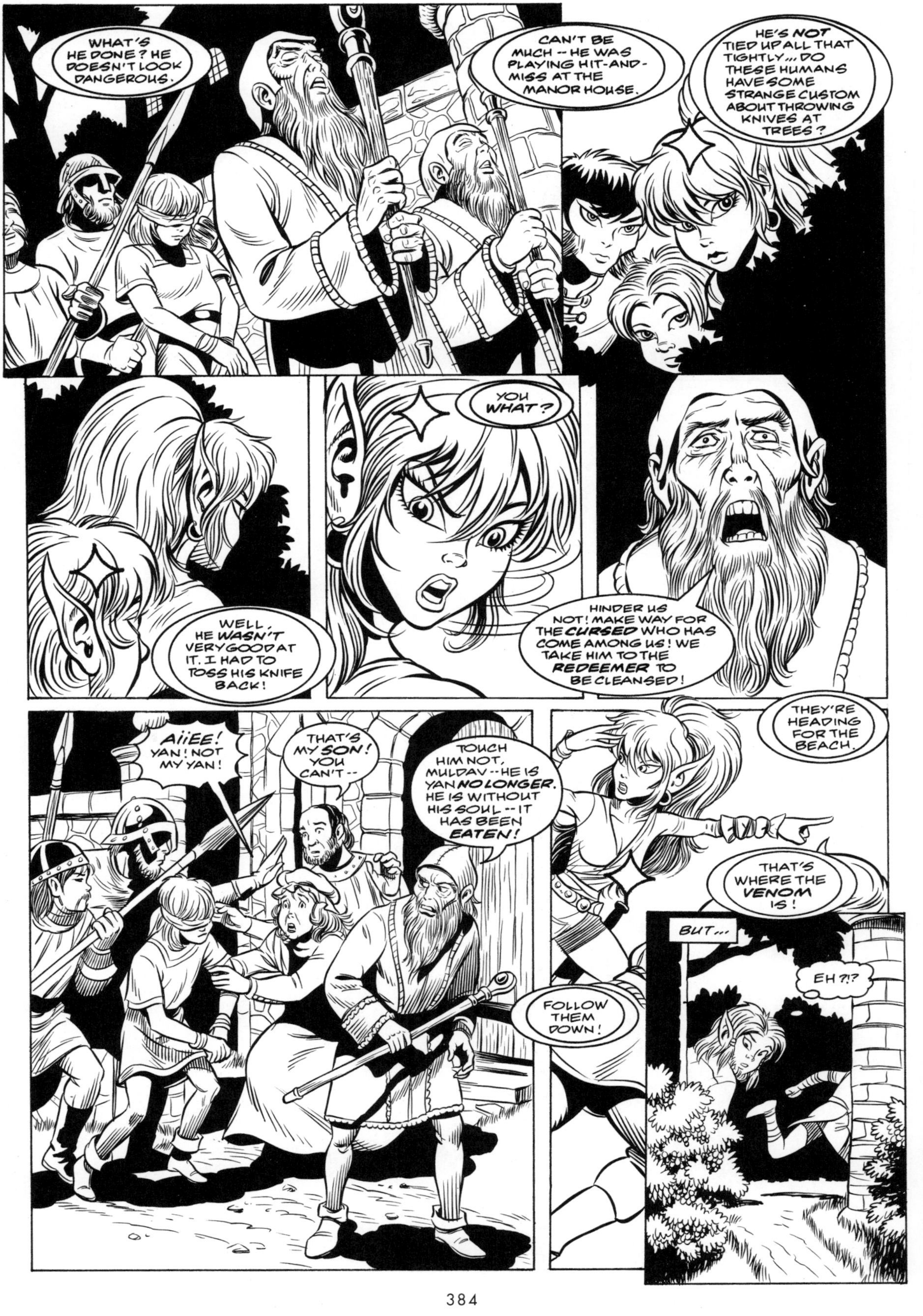
WHAT'S HE DONE? HE DOESN'T LOOK DANGEROUS.
CAN'T BE MUCH -- HE WAS PLAYING HIT-AND-MISS AT THE MANOR HOUSE.
HE'S NOT TIED UP ALL THAT TIGHTLY... DO THESE HUMANS HAVE SOME STRANGE CUSTOM ABOUT THROWING KNIVES AT TREES?
WELL, HE WASN'T VERY GOOD AT IT. I HAD TO TOSS HIS KNIFE BACK!
YOU WHAT?
HINDER US NOT! MAKE WAY FOR THE CURSED WHO HAS COME AMONG US! WE TAKE HIM TO THE REDEEMER TO BE CLEANSED!
AiiEE! YAN! NOT MY YAN!
THAT'S MY SON! YOU CAN'T --
TOUCH HIM NOT, MULDAV -- HE IS YAN NO LONGER. HE IS WITHOUT HIS SOUL -- IT HAS BEEN EATEN!
THEY'RE HEADING FOR THE BEACH.
THAT'S WHERE THE VENOM IS!
FOLLOW THEM DOWN!
BUT...
EH ?!?

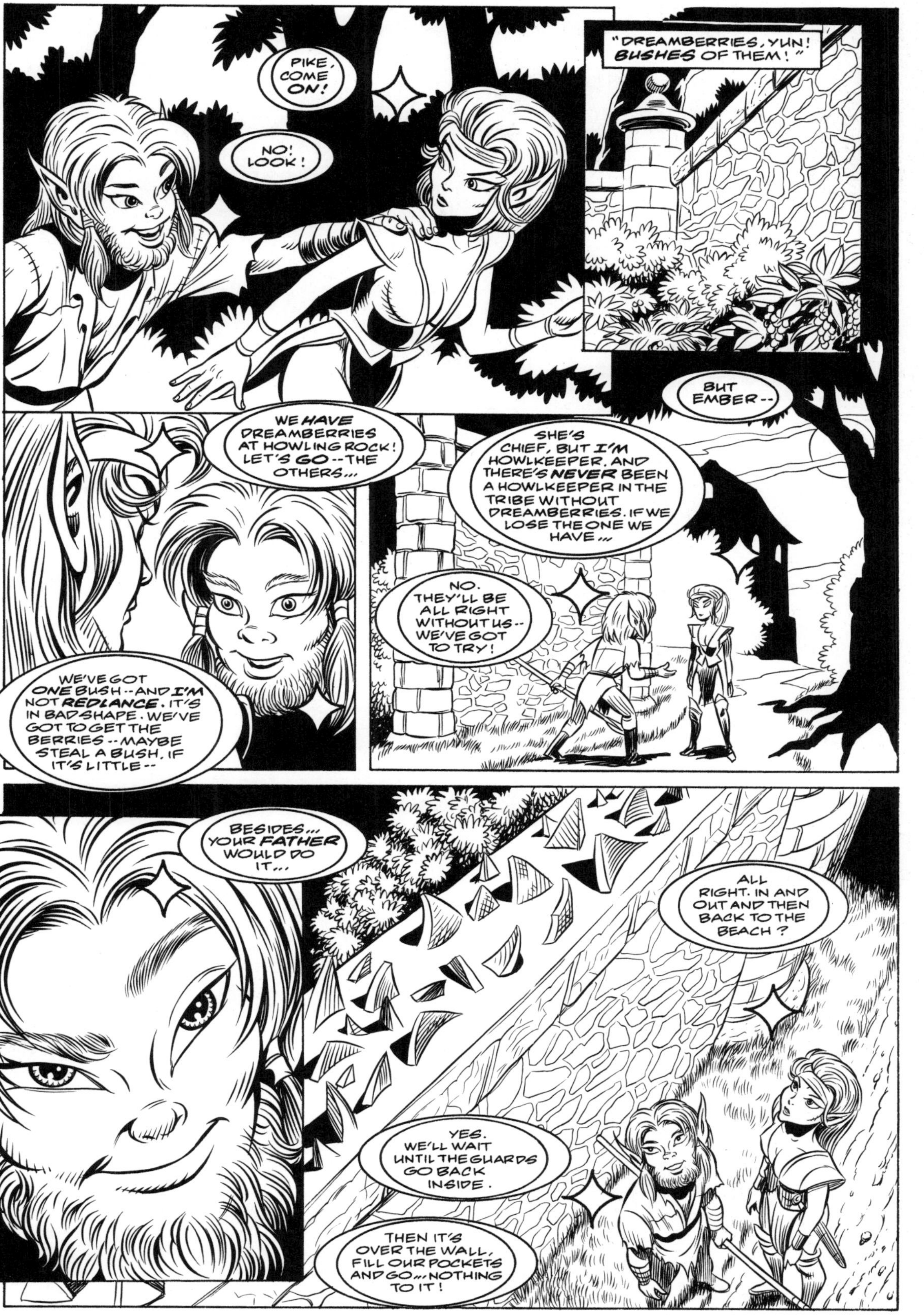

PIKE, COME ON!
NO! LOOK!
"DREAMBERRIES, YUN! BUSHES OF THEM!"
BUT EMBER--
WE HAVE DREAMBERRIES AT HOWLING ROCK! LET'S GO--THE OTHERS...
SHE'S CHIEF, BUT I'M HOWLKEEPER. AND THERE'S NEVER BEEN A HOWLKEEPER IN THE TRIBE WITHOUT DREAMBERRIES. IF WE LOSE THE ONE WE HAVE...
NO. THEY'LL BE ALL RIGHT WITHOUT US--WE'VE GOT TO TRY!
WE'VE GOT ONE BUSH--AND I'M NOT REDLANCE. IT'S IN BAD SHAPE. WE'VE GOT TO GET THE BERRIES--MAYBE STEAL A BUSH, IF IT'S LITTLE--
BESIDES... YOUR FATHER WOULD DO IT...
ALL RIGHT. IN AND OUT AND THEN BACK TO THE BEACH?
YES. WE'LL WAIT UNTIL THE GUARDS GO BACK INSIDE.
THEN IT'S OVER THE WALL, FILL OUR POCKETS AND GO... NOTHING TO IT!

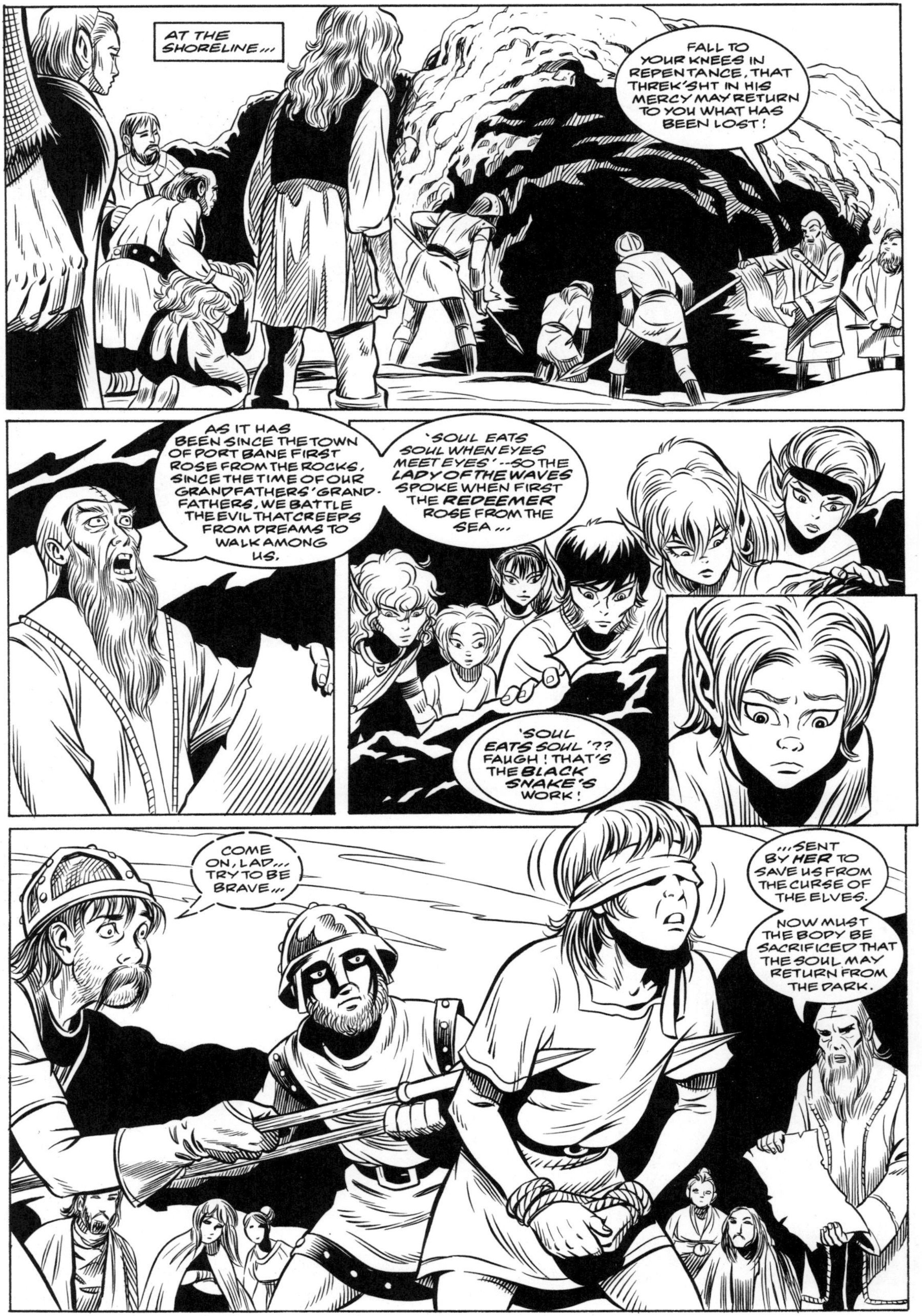
AT THE SHORELINE...
FALL TO YOUR KNEES IN REPENTANCE, THAT THREK'SHT IN HIS MERCY MAY RETURN TO YOU WHAT HAS BEEN LOST!
AS IT HAS BEEN SINCE THE TOWN OF PORT BANE FIRST ROSE FROM THE ROCKS, SINCE THE TIME OF OUR GRANDFATHERS' GRANDFATHERS, WE BATTLE THE EVIL THAT CREEPS FROM DREAMS TO WALK AMONG US.
'SOUL EATS SOUL WHEN EYES MEET EYES'--SO THE LADY OF THE WAVES SPOKE WHEN FIRST THE REDEEMER ROSE FROM THE SEA...
'SOUL EATS SOUL'?? FAUGH! THAT'S THE BLACK SNAKE'S WORK!
COME ON, LAD... TRY TO BE BRAVE...
...SENT BY HER TO SAVE US FROM THE CURSE OF THE ELVES.
NOW MUST THE BODY BE SACRIFICED THAT THE SOUL MAY RETURN FROM THE DARK.

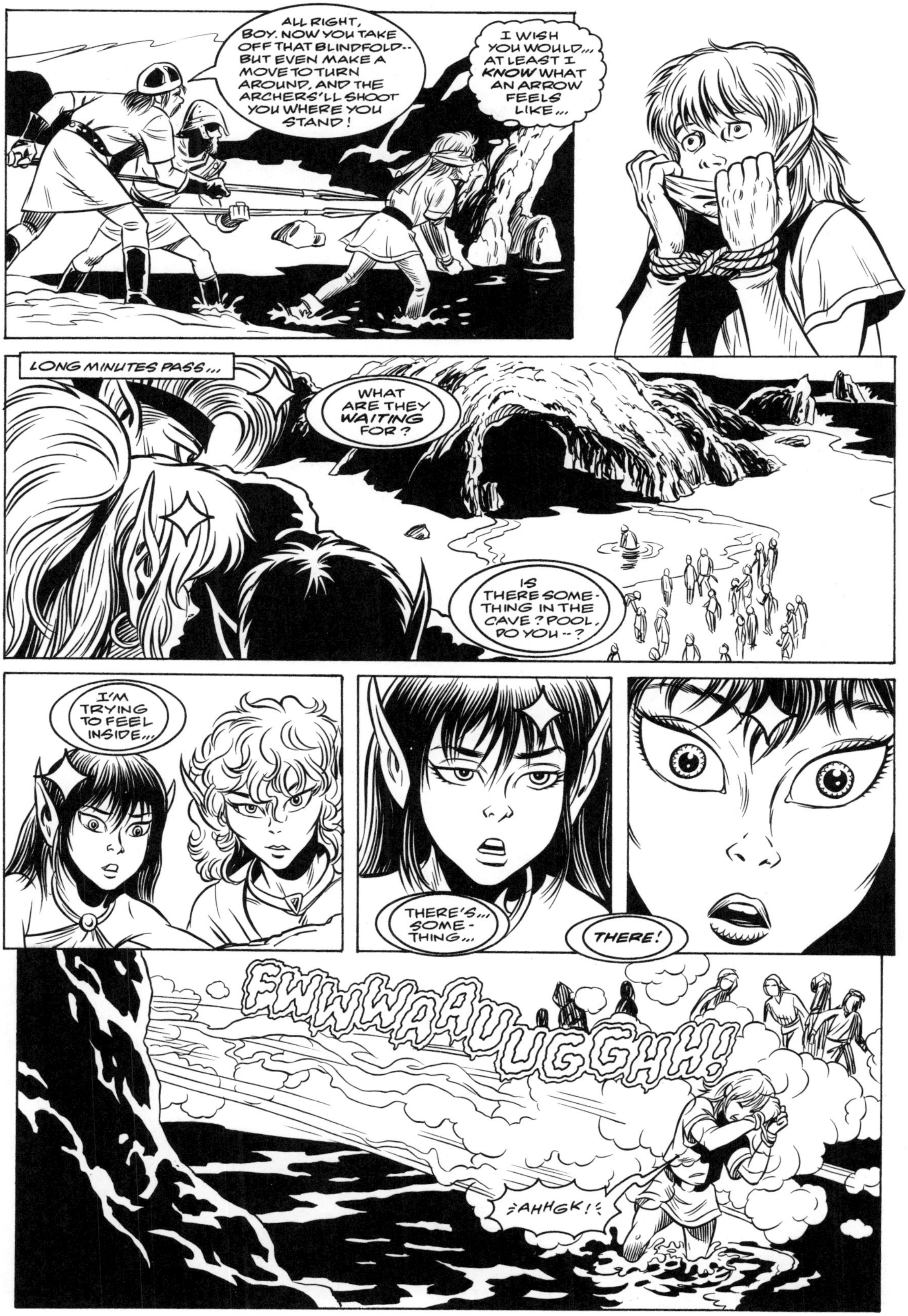
ALL RIGHT, BOY. NOW YOU TAKE OFF THAT BLINDFOLD-- BUT EVEN MAKE A MOVE TO TURN AROUND, AND THE ARCHER'S'LL SHOOT YOU WHERE YOU STAND!
I WISH YOU WOULD... AT LEAST I KNOW WHAT AN ARROW FEELS LIKE...
LONG MINUTES PASS...
WHAT ARE THEY WAITING FOR?
IS THERE SOMETHING IN THE CAVE? POOL, DO YOU--?
I'M TRYING TO FEEL INSIDE...
THERE'S... SOMETHING...
THERE!
FWWWAAUUGGHH!
AHHGK!

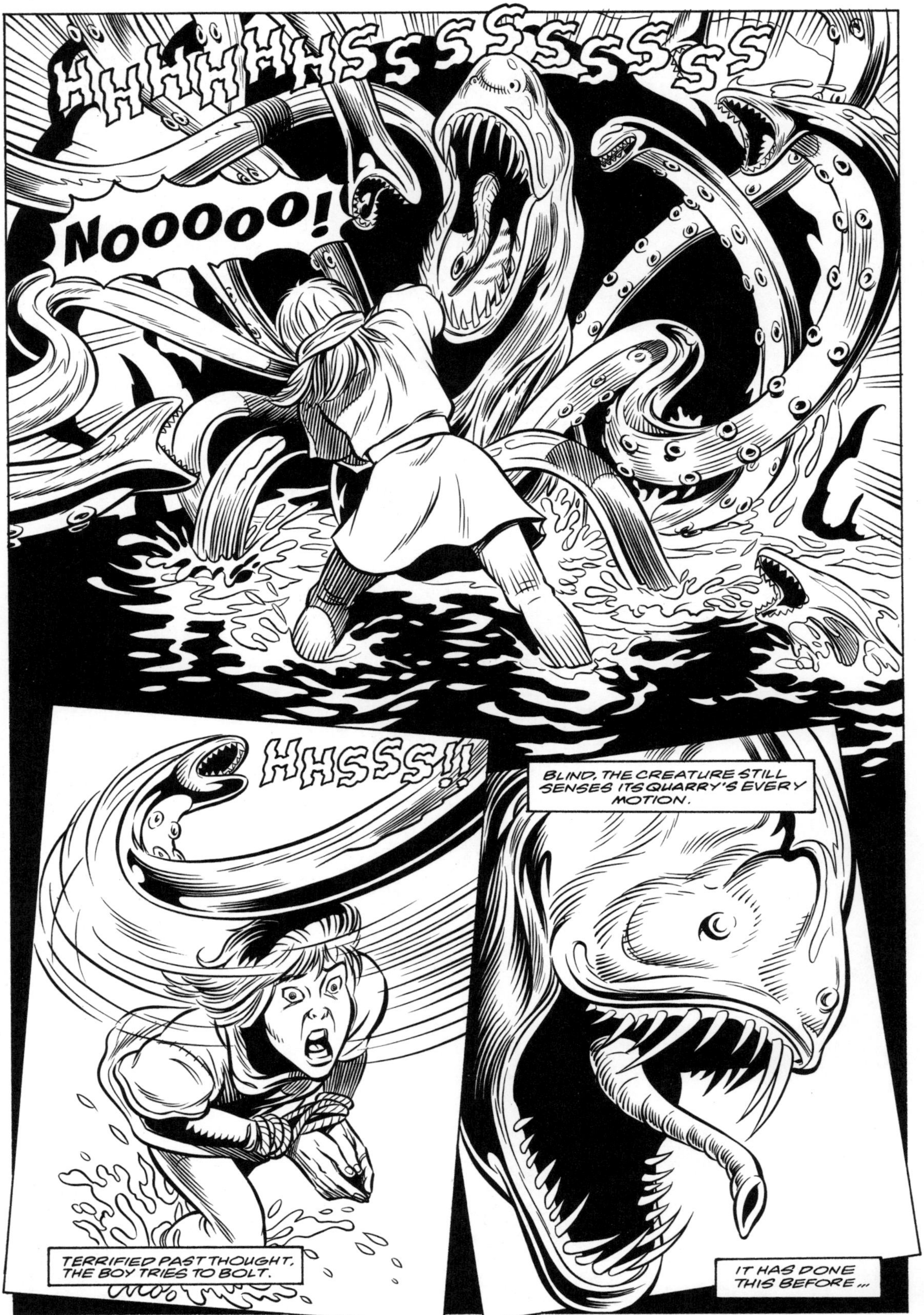
HHHHHHHSsssSSSsssSS
NOOOOO!
HHSSSS!!
BLIND, THE CREATURE STILL SENSES ITS QUARRY'S EVERY MOTION.
TERRIFIED PAST THOUGHT, THE BOY TRIES TO BOLT.
IT HAS DONE THIS BEFORE...

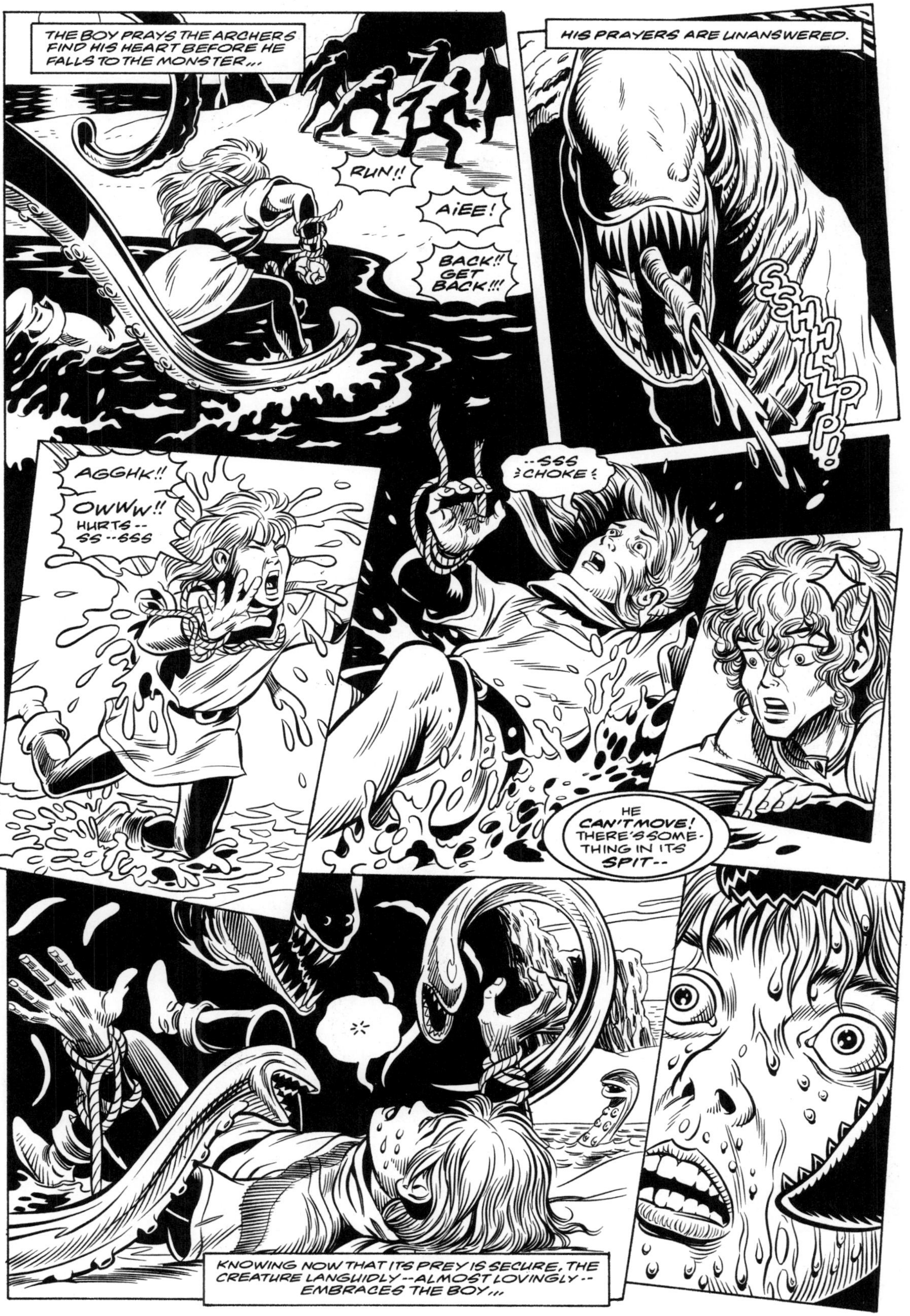
THE BOY PRAYS THE ARCHERS FIND HIS HEART BEFORE HE FALLS TO THE MONSTER...
RUN!!
AiEE!
BACK!! GET BACK!!!
HIS PRAYERS ARE UNANSWERED.
SSHHLLP!
AGGHK!!
OWWW!! HURTS-- SS--SSS
--SSS CHOKE!
HE CAN'T MOVE! THERE'S SOME-THING IN ITS SPIT--
KNOWING NOW THAT ITS PREY IS SECURE, THE CREATURE LANGUIDLY--ALMOST LOVINGLY--EMBRACES THE BOY...

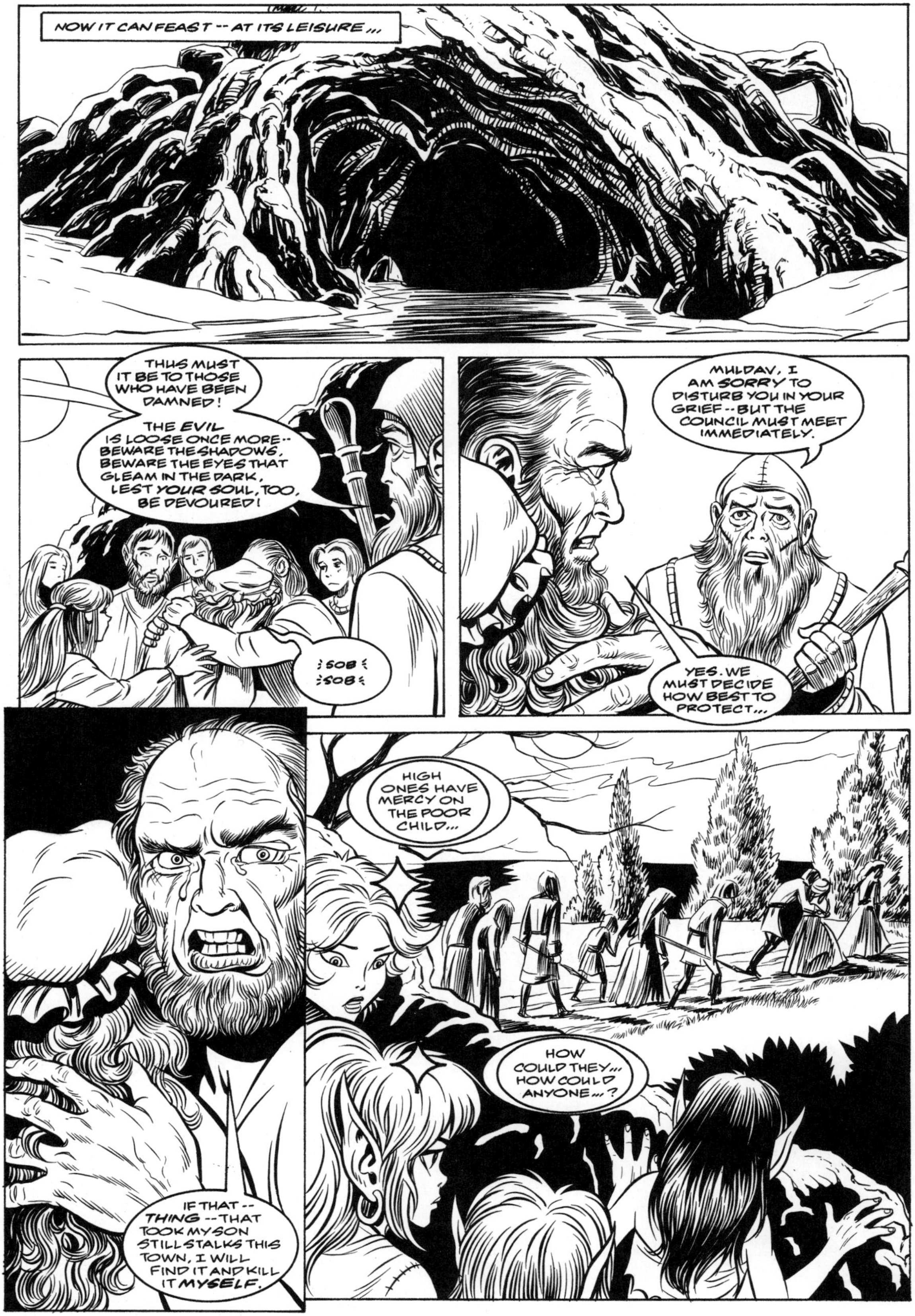
NOW IT CAN FEAST -- AT ITS LEISURE ...
THUS MUST IT BE TO THOSE WHO HAVE BEEN DAMNED!
THE EVIL IS LOOSE ONCE MORE -- BEWARE THE SHADOWS, BEWARE THE EYES THAT GLEAM IN THE DARK, LEST YOUR SOUL, TOO, BE DEVOURED!
SOB SOB
MULDAV, I AM SORRY TO DISTURB YOU IN YOUR GRIEF -- BUT THE COUNCIL MUST MEET IMMEDIATELY.
YES. WE MUST DECIDE HOW BEST TO PROTECT...
IF THAT -- THING -- THAT TOOK MY SON STILL STALKS THIS TOWN, I WILL FIND IT AND KILL IT MYSELF.
HIGH ONES HAVE MERCY ON THE POOR CHILD...
HOW COULD THEY... HOW COULD ANYONE...?

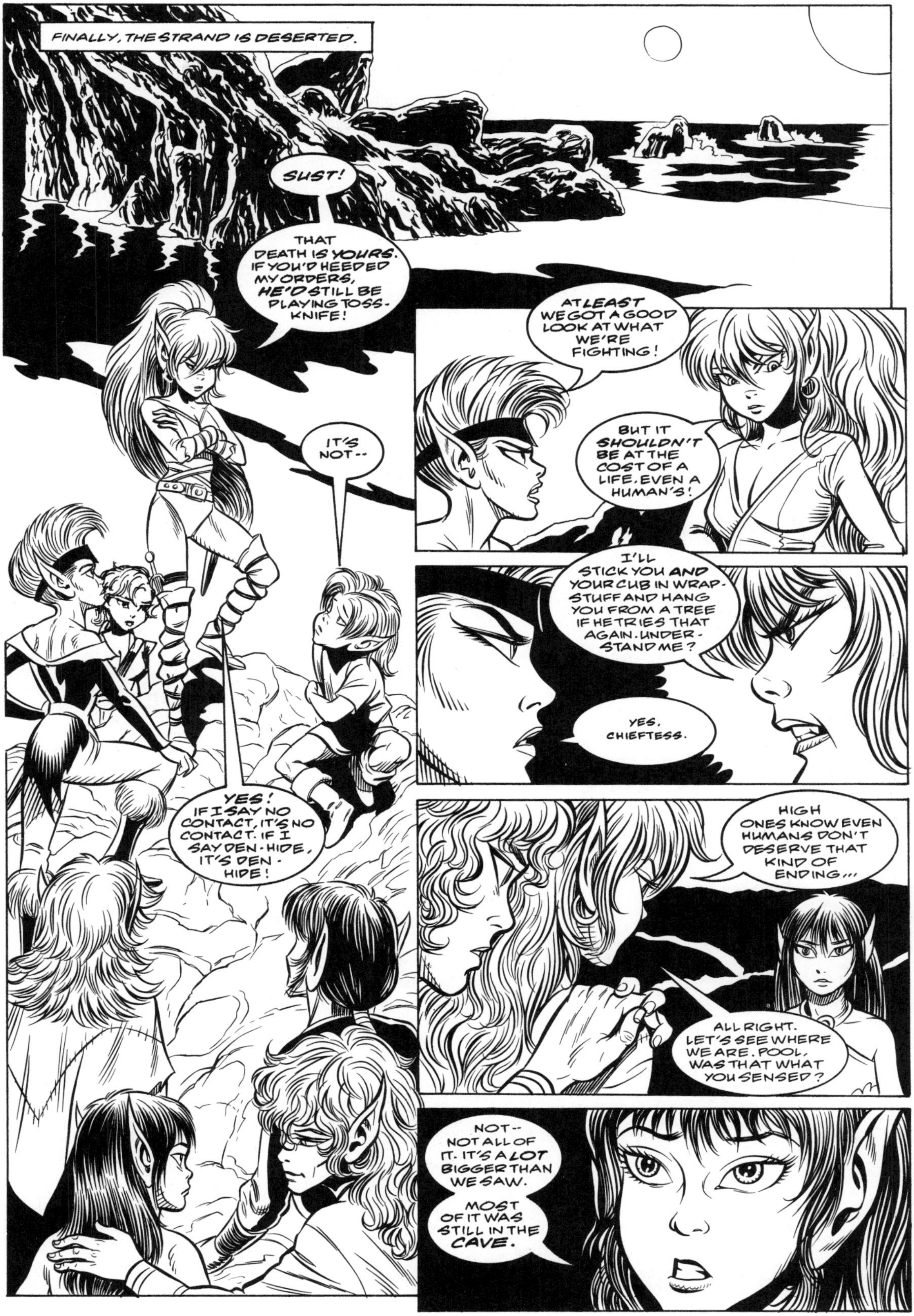
FINALLY, THE STRAND IS DESERTED.
SUST!
THAT DEATH IS YOURS. IF YOU'D HEEDED MY ORDERS, HE'D STILL BE PLAYING TOSS-KNIFE!
IT'S NOT--
YES! IF I SAY NO CONTACT, IT'S NO CONTACT. IF I SAY DEN-HIDE, IT'S DEN-HIDE!
AT LEAST WE GOT A GOOD LOOK AT WHAT WE'RE FIGHTING!
BUT IT SHOULDN'T BE AT THE COST OF A LIFE. EVEN A HUMAN'S!
I'LL STICK YOU AND YOUR CUB IN WRAP-STUFF AND HANG YOU FROM A TREE IF HE TRIES THAT AGAIN. UNDER-STAND ME?
YES, CHIEFTESS.
HIGH ONES KNOW EVEN HUMANS DON'T DESERVE THAT KIND OF ENDING...
ALL RIGHT. LET'S SEE WHERE WE ARE. POOL, WAS THAT WHAT YOU SENSED?
NOT-- NOT ALL OF IT. IT'S A LOT BIGGER THAN WE SAW.
MOST OF IT WAS STILL IN THE CAVE.

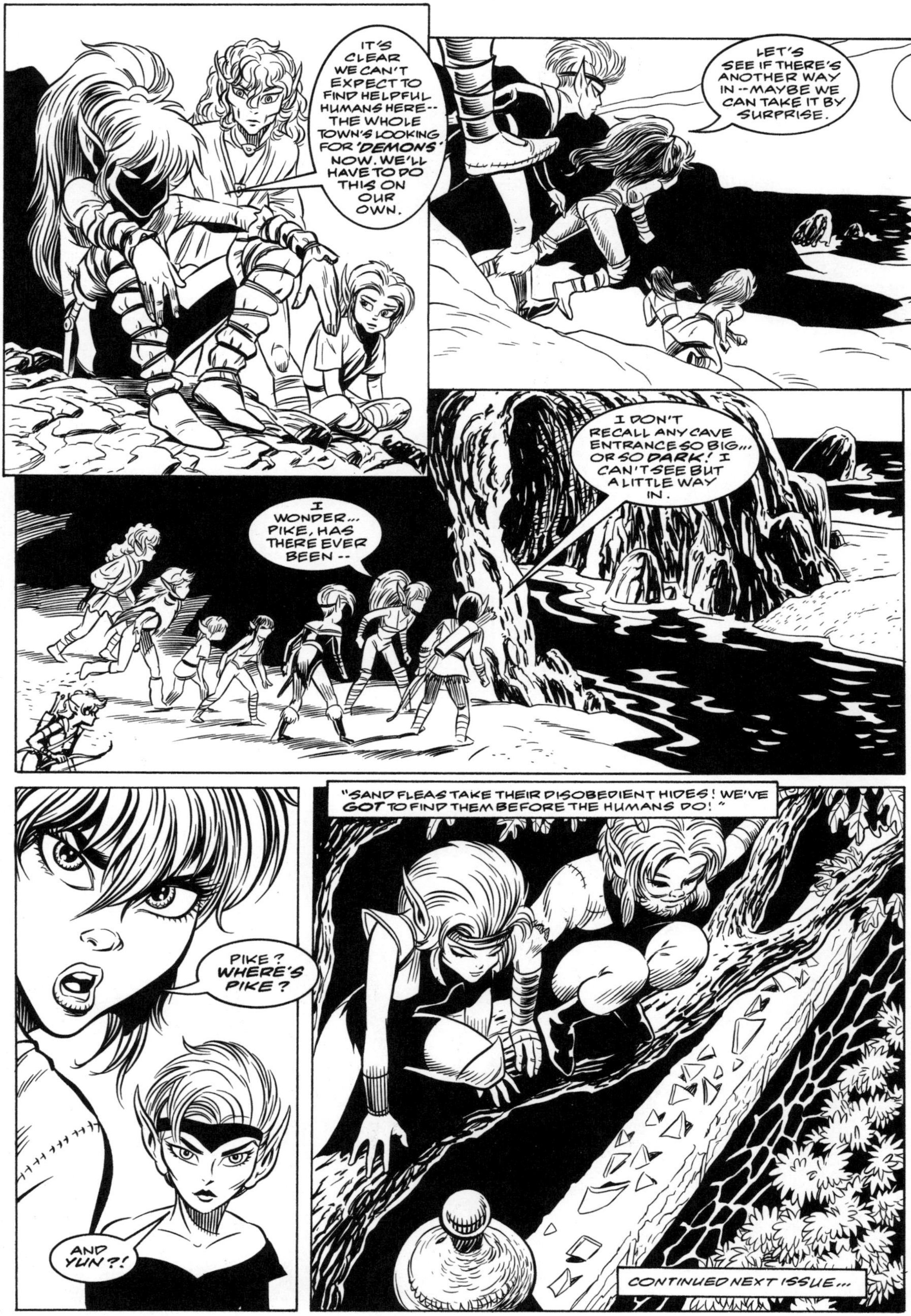
IT'S CLEAR WE CAN'T EXPECT TO FIND HELPFUL HUMANS HERE-- THE WHOLE TOWN'S LOOKING FOR 'DEMONS' NOW. WE'LL HAVE TO DO THIS ON OUR OWN.
LET'S SEE IF THERE'S ANOTHER WAY IN --MAYBE WE CAN TAKE IT BY SURPRISE.
I WONDER... PIKE, HAS THERE EVER BEEN --
I DON'T RECALL ANY CAVE ENTRANCE SO BIG... OR SO DARK! I CAN'T SEE BUT A LITTLE WAY IN.
PIKE? WHERE'S PIKE?
AND YUN?!
"SAND FLEAS TAKE THEIR DISOBEDIENT HIDES! WE'VE GOT TO FIND THEM BEFORE THE HUMANS DO!"
CONTINUED NEXT ISSUE...

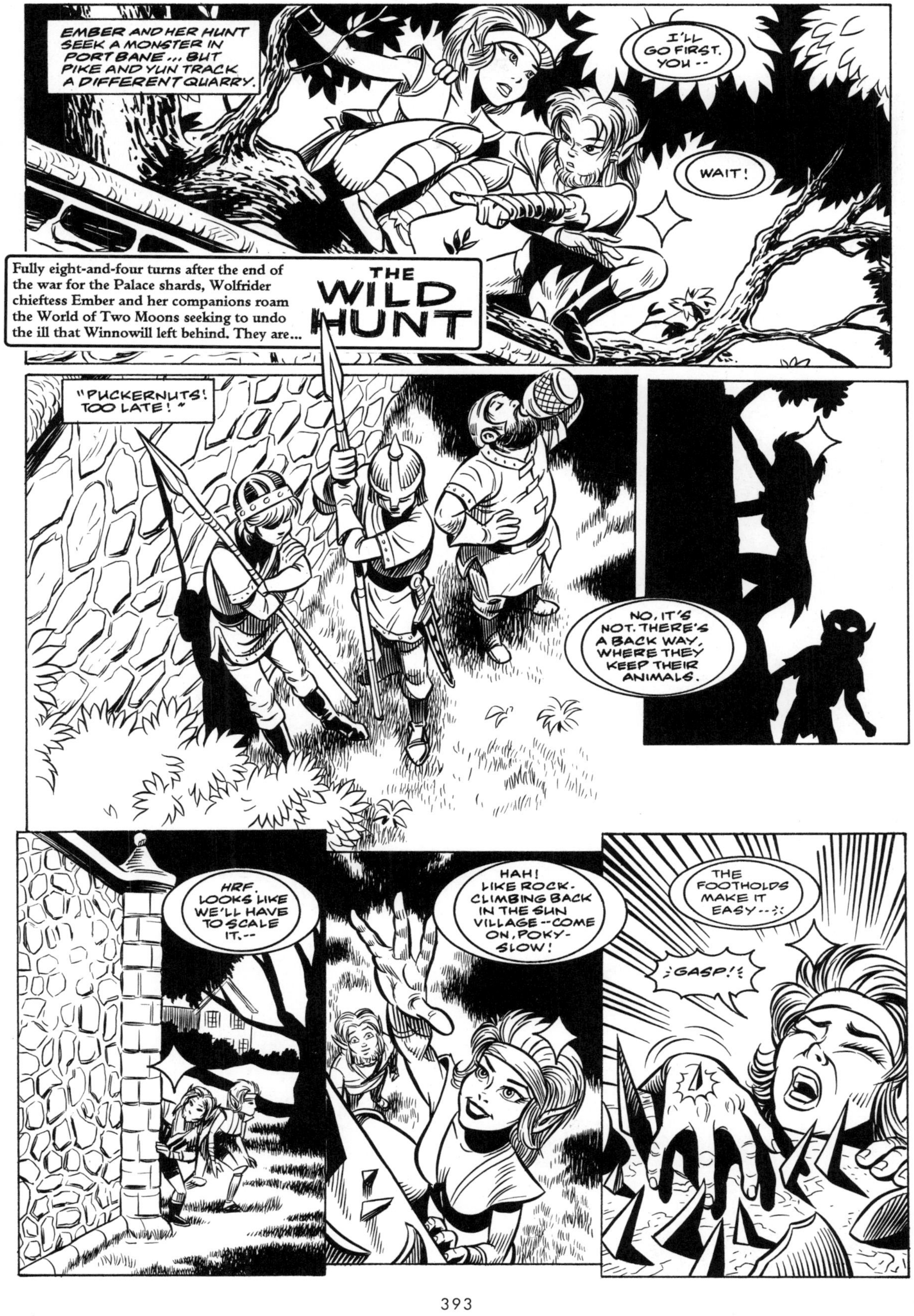

EMBER AND HER HUNT SEEK A MONSTER IN PORT BANE ... BUT PIKE AND YUN TRACK A DIFFERENT QUARRY.
I'LL GO FIRST. YOU --
WAIT!
Fully eight-and-four turns after the end of the war for the Palace shards, Wolfrider chieftess Ember and her companions roam the World of Two Moons seeking to undo the ill that Winnowill left behind. They are...
THE WILD HUNT
"PUCKERNUTS! TOO LATE!"
NO, IT'S NOT. THERE'S A BACK WAY, WHERE THEY KEEP THEIR ANIMALS.
HRF. LOOKS LIKE WE'LL HAVE TO SCALE IT.--
HAH! LIKE ROCK-CLIMBING BACK IN THE SUN VILLAGE --COME ON, POKY-SLOW!
THE FOOTHOLDS MAKE IT EASY --
GASP!

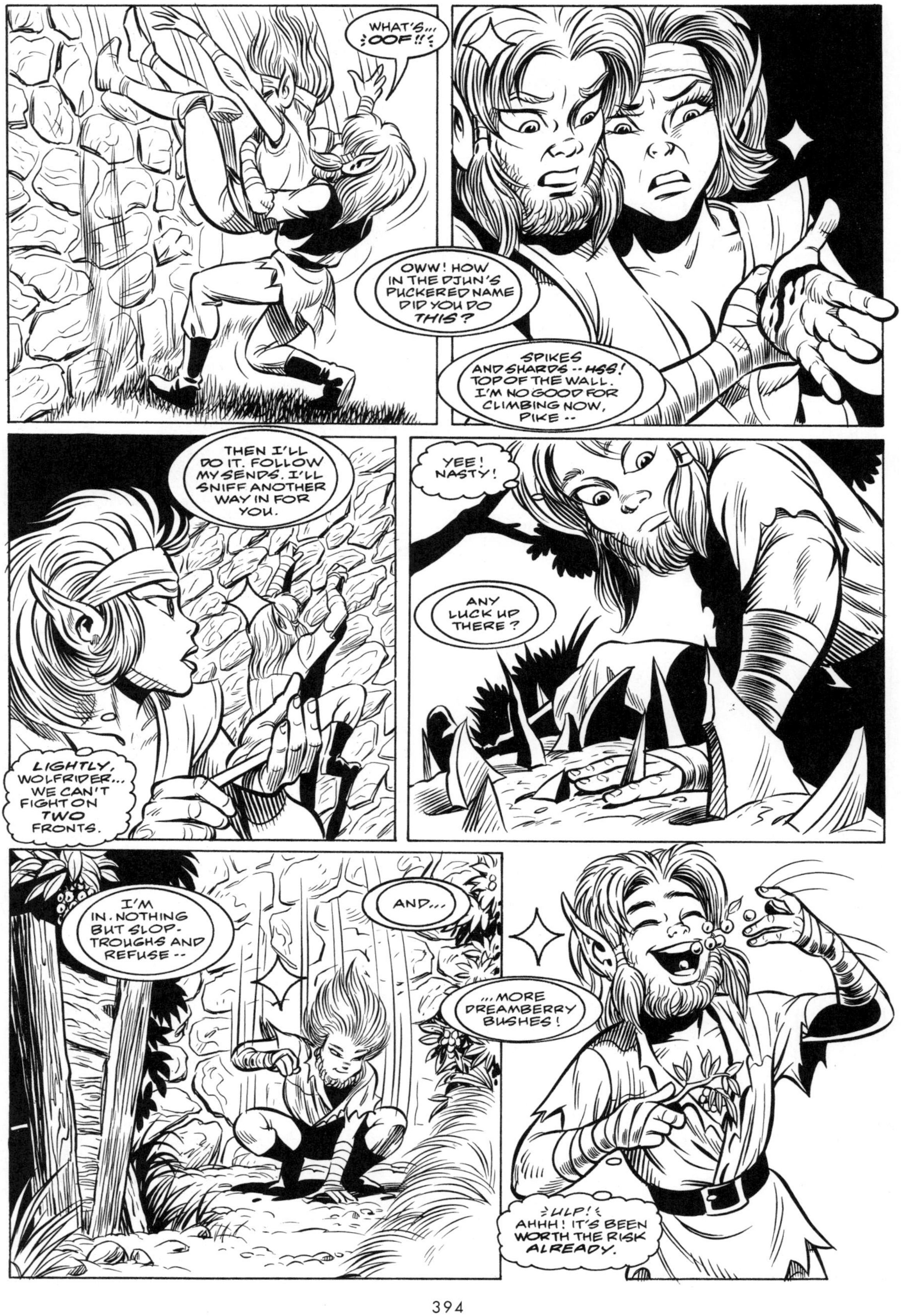
WHAT'S... OOF!!
OWW! HOW IN THE DJUN'S PUCKERED NAME DID YOU DO THIS?
SPIKES AND SHARDS -- HSS! TOP OF THE WALL. I'M NO GOOD FOR CLIMBING NOW, PIKE --
THEN I'LL DO IT. FOLLOW MY SENDS. I'LL SNIFF ANOTHER WAY IN FOR YOU.
LIGHTLY, WOLFRIDER... WE CAN'T FIGHT ON TWO FRONTS.
YEE! NASTY!
ANY LUCK UP THERE?
I'M IN. NOTHING BUT SLOP-TROUGHS AND REFUSE --
AND...
...MORE DREAMBERRY BUSHES!
ULP! AHHH! IT'S BEEN WORTH THE RISK ALREADY.

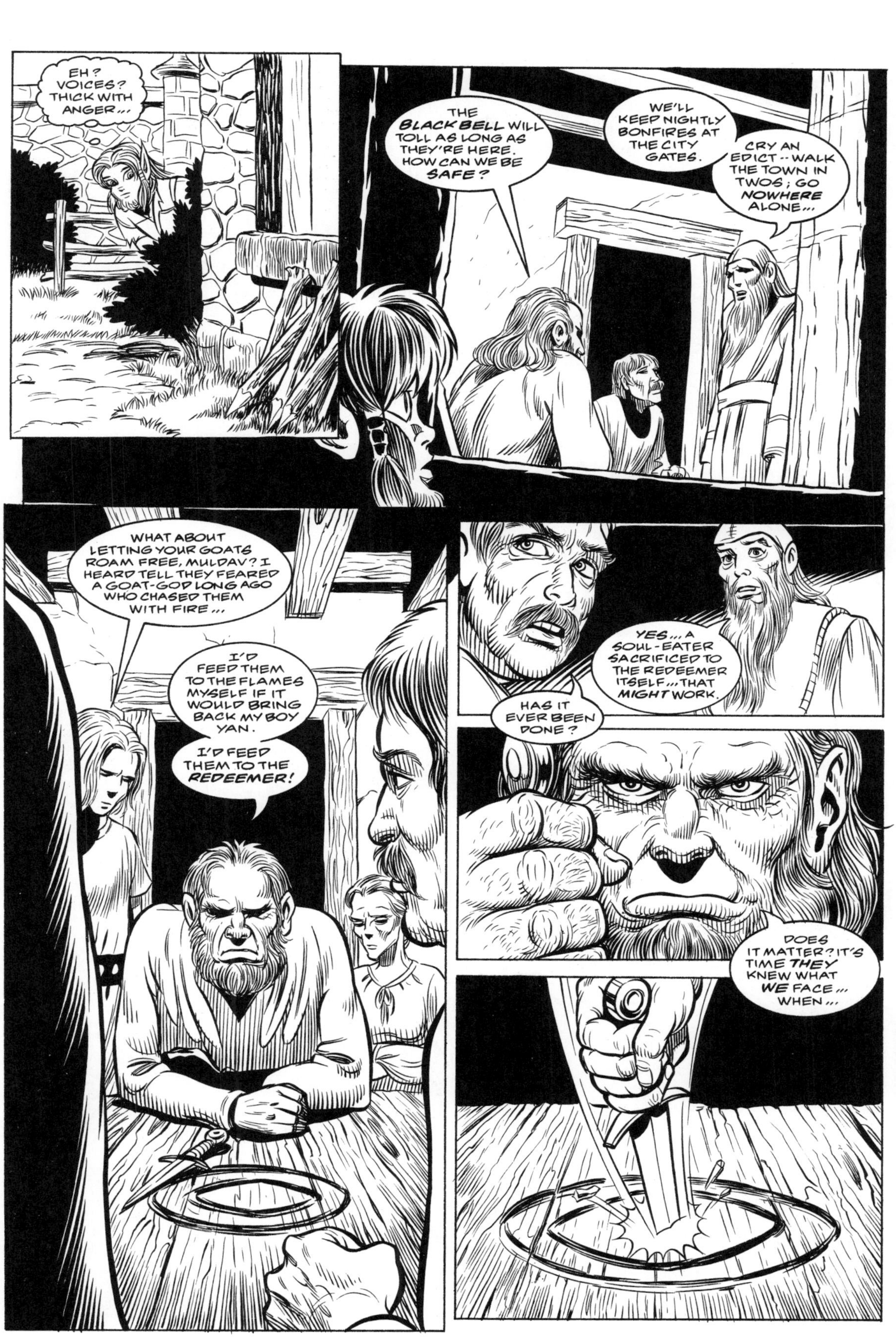
EH? VOICES? THICK WITH ANGER...
THE BLACK BELL WILL TOLL AS LONG AS THEY'RE HERE. HOW CAN WE BE SAFE?
WE'LL KEEP NIGHTLY BONFIRES AT THE CITY GATES.
CRY AN EDICT -- WALK THE TOWN IN TWOS; GO NOWHERE ALONE...
WHAT ABOUT LETTING YOUR GOATS ROAM FREE, MULDAV? I HEARD TELL THEY FEARED A GOAT-GOD LONG AGO WHO CHASED THEM WITH FIRE...
I'D FEED THEM TO THE FLAMES MYSELF IF IT WOULD BRING BACK MY BOY YAN.
I'D FEED THEM TO THE REDEEMER!
YES... A SOUL-EATER SACRIFICED TO THE REDEEMER ITSELF... THAT MIGHT WORK.
HAS IT EVER BEEN DONE?
DOES IT MATTER? IT'S TIME THEY KNEW WHAT WE FACE... WHEN...

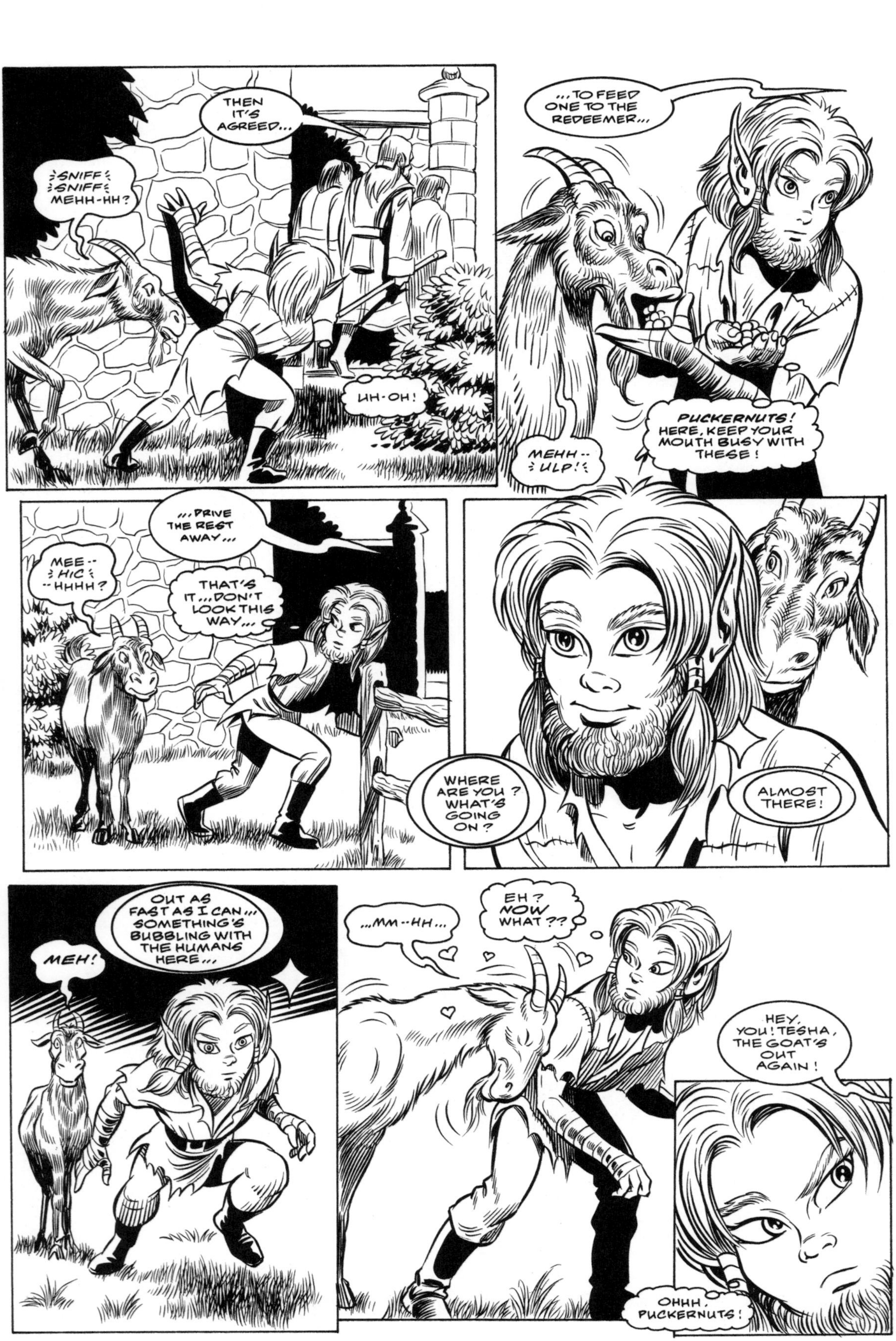
THEN IT'S AGREED...
SNIFF SNIFF MEHH-HH?
UH-OH!
...TO FEED ONE TO THE REDEEMER...
PUCKERNUTS! HERE, KEEP YOUR MOUTH BUSY WITH THESE!
MEHH-- ULP!
...DRIVE THE REST AWAY...
MEE-- HIC --HHHH?
THAT'S IT... DON'T LOOK THIS WAY...
WHERE ARE YOU? WHAT'S GOING ON?
ALMOST THERE!
OUT AS FAST AS I CAN... SOMETHING'S BUBBLING WITH THE HUMANS HERE...
MEH!
...MM--HH...
EH? NOW WHAT??
HEY, YOU! TESHA, THE GOAT'S OUT AGAIN!
OHHH, PUCKERNUTS!

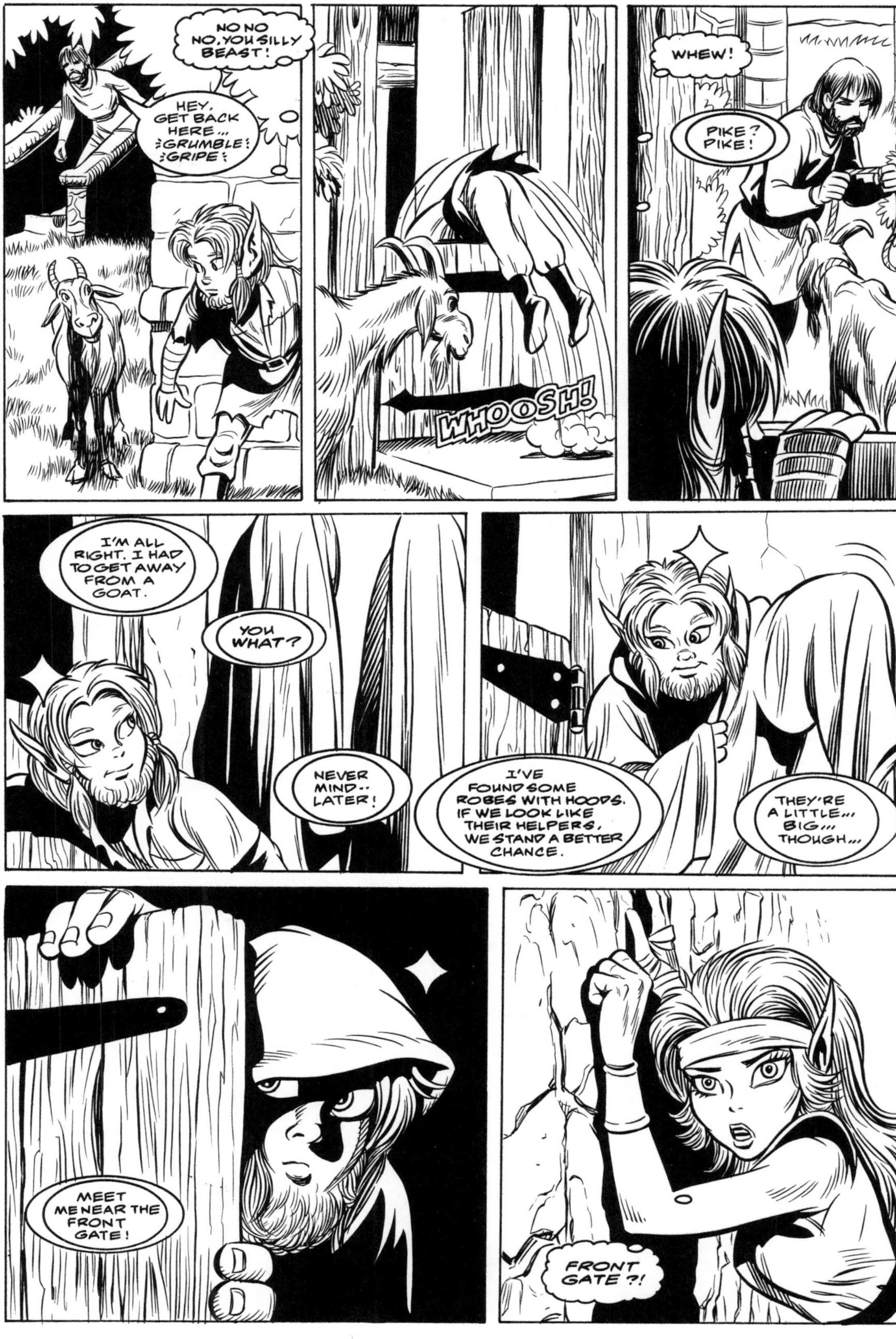
NO NO NO, YOU SILLY BEAST!
HEY, GET BACK HERE... GRUMBLE GRIPE
WHOOSH!
WHEW!
PIKE? PIKE!
I'M ALL RIGHT. I HAD TO GET AWAY FROM A GOAT.
YOU WHAT?
NEVER MIND.. LATER!
I'VE FOUND SOME ROBES WITH HOODS. IF WE LOOK LIKE THEIR HELPERS, WE STAND A BETTER CHANCE.
THEY'RE A LITTLE... BIG... THOUGH...
MEET ME NEAR THE FRONT GATE!
FRONT GATE?!

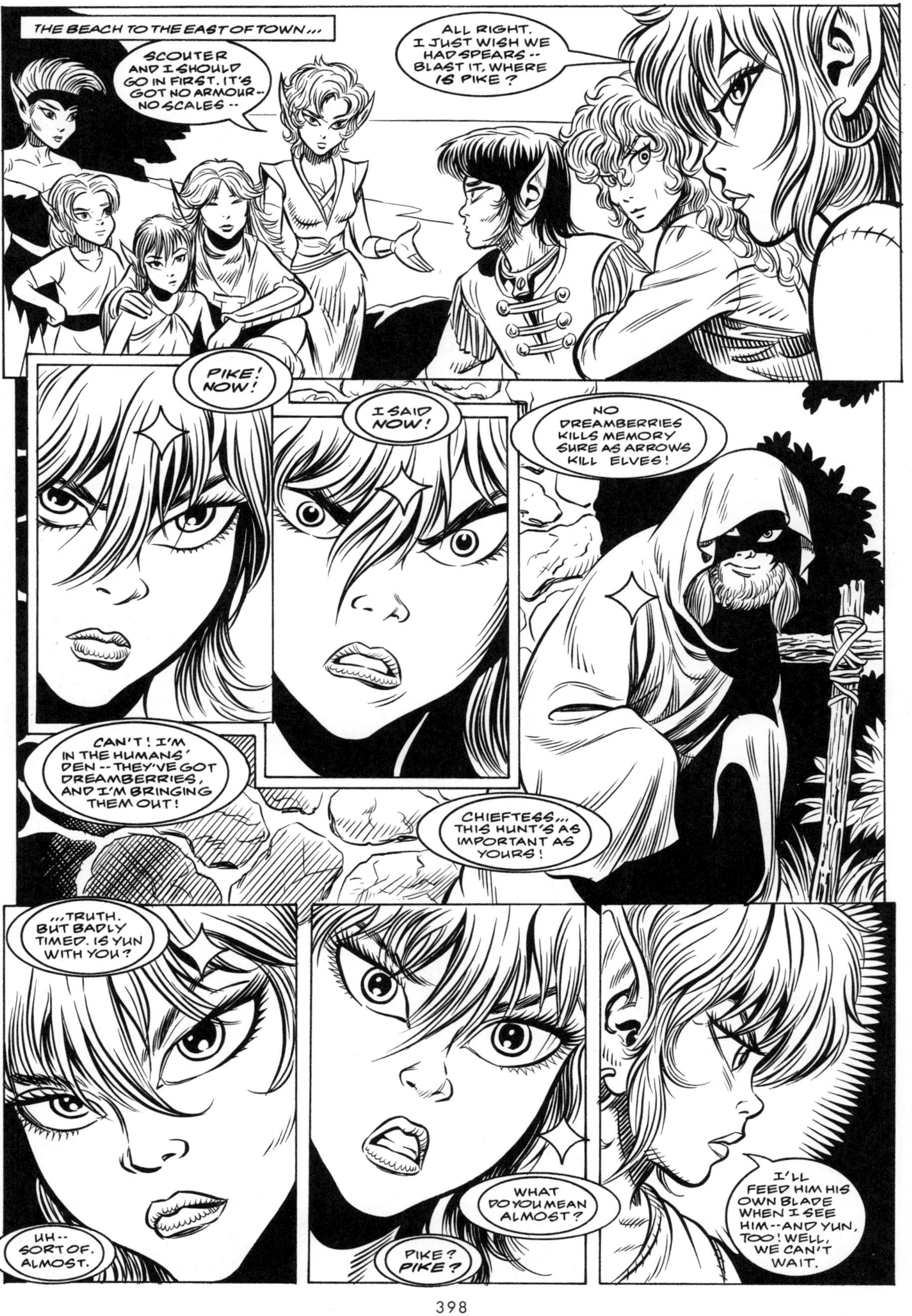

THE BEACH TO THE EAST OF TOWN...
SCOUTER AND I SHOULD GO IN FIRST. IT'S GOT NO ARMOUR -- NO SCALES --
ALL RIGHT. I JUST WISH WE HAD SPEARS -- BLAST IT, WHERE IS PIKE?
PIKE! NOW!
I SAID NOW!
NO DREAMBERRIES KILLS MEMORY SURE AS ARROWS KILL ELVES!
CAN'T! I'M IN THE HUMANS' DEN -- THEY'VE GOT DREAMBERRIES, AND I'M BRINGING THEM OUT!
CHIEFTESS... THIS HUNT'S AS IMPORTANT AS YOURS!
...TRUTH. BUT BADLY TIMED. IS YUN WITH YOU?
UH -- SORT OF. ALMOST.
WHAT DO YOU MEAN ALMOST?
PIKE? PIKE?
I'LL FEED HIM HIS OWN BLADE WHEN I SEE HIM -- AND YUN, TOO! WELL, WE CAN'T WAIT.

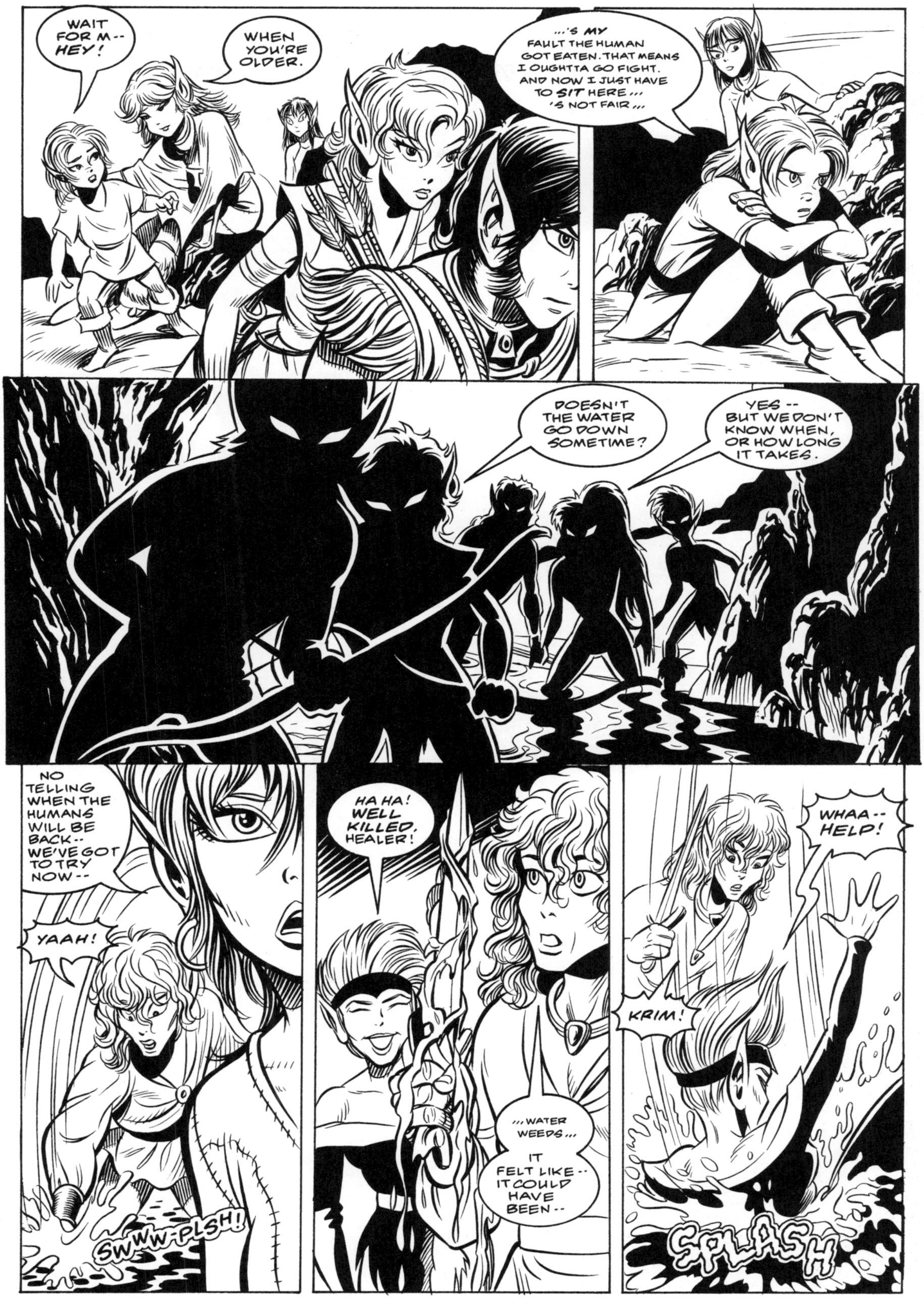
WAIT FOR M-- HEY!
WHEN YOU'RE OLDER.
...'S MY FAULT THE HUMAN GOT EATEN. THAT MEANS I OUGHTTA GO FIGHT. AND NOW I JUST HAVE TO SIT HERE... 'S NOT FAIR...
DOESN'T THE WATER GO DOWN SOMETIME?
YES -- BUT WE DON'T KNOW WHEN, OR HOW LONG IT TAKES.
NO TELLING WHEN THE HUMANS WILL BE BACK-- WE'VE GOT TO TRY NOW--
YAAH!
SWWW-PLSH!
HA HA! WELL KILLED, HEALER!
...WATER WEEDS...
IT FELT LIKE-- IT COULD HAVE BEEN--
WHAA-- HELP!
KRIM!
SPLASH

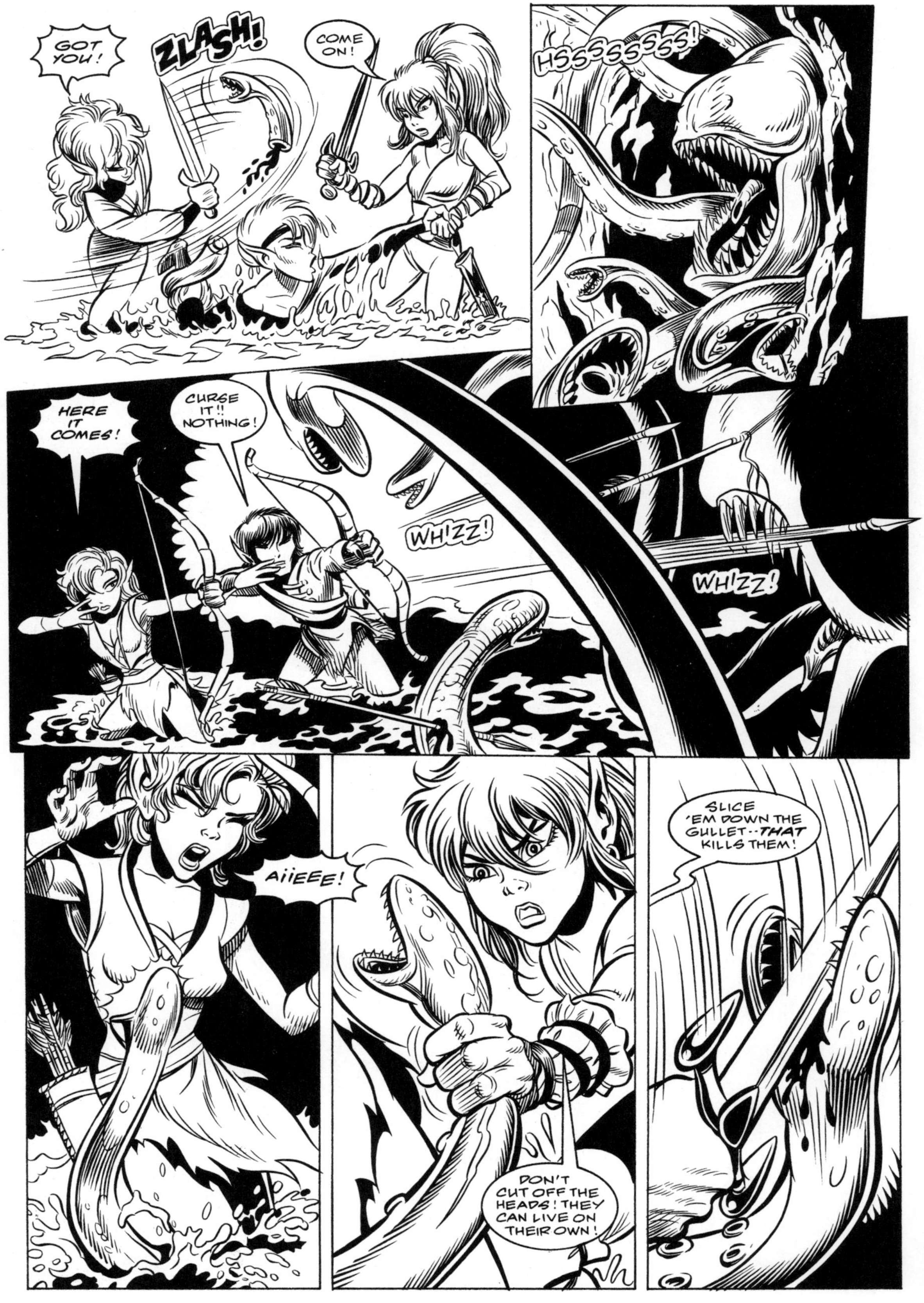
GOT YOU!
ZLASH!
COME ON!
HSSSSSSSS!
HERE IT COMES!
CURSE IT!! NOTHING!
WHIZZ!
WHIZZ!
AIIEEE!
DON'T CUT OFF THE HEADS! THEY CAN LIVE ON THEIR OWN!
SLICE 'EM DOWN THE GULLET--THAT KILLS THEM!

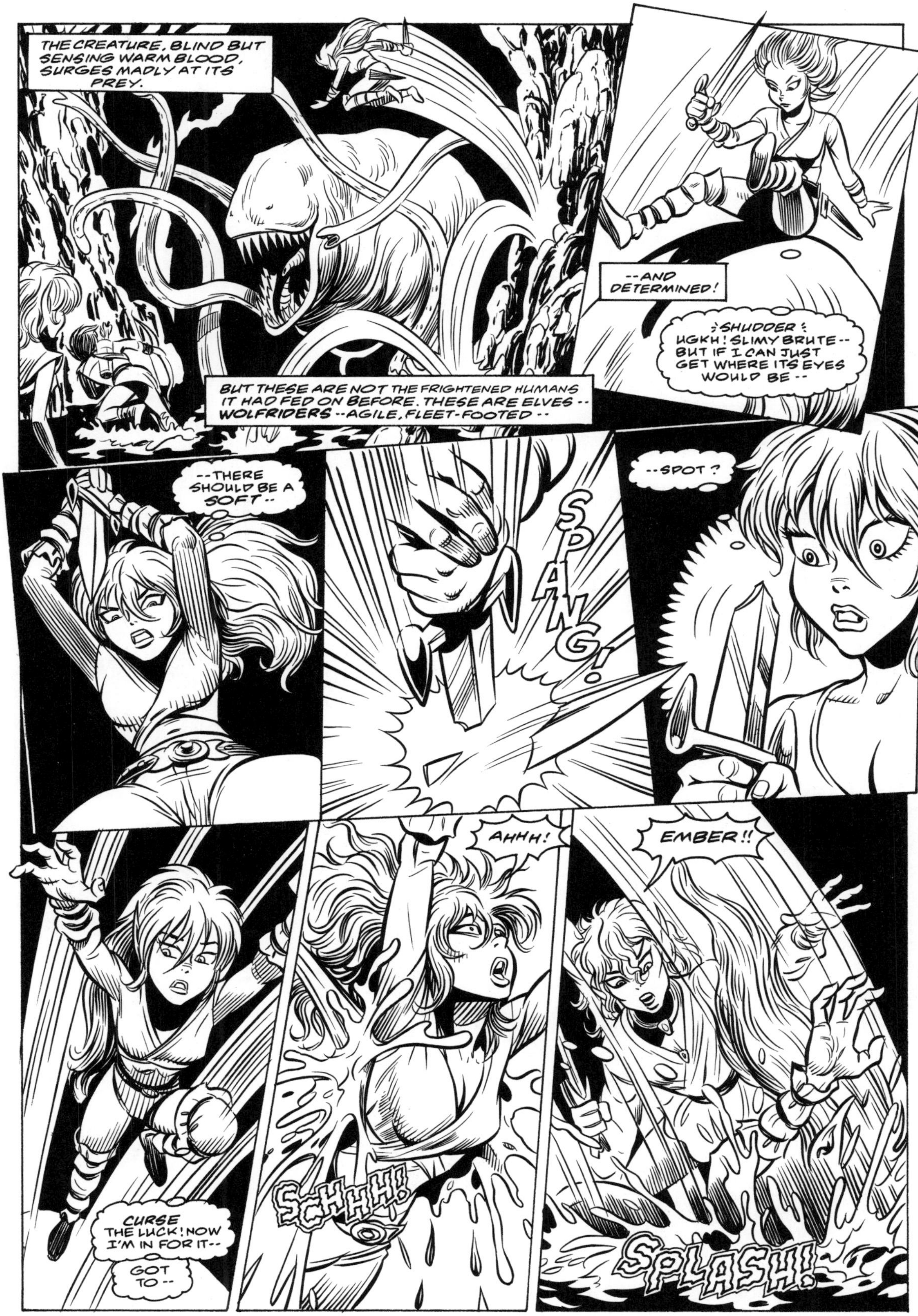
THE CREATURE, BLIND BUT SENSING WARM BLOOD, SURGES MADLY AT ITS PREY.
BUT THESE ARE NOT THE FRIGHTENED HUMANS IT HAD FED ON BEFORE. THESE ARE ELVES -- WOLFRIDERS --AGILE, FLEET-FOOTED --
--AND DETERMINED!
SHUDDER
UGKH! SLIMY BRUTE -- BUT IF I CAN JUST GET WHERE ITS EYES WOULD BE --
--THERE SHOULD BE A SOFT --
SPANG!
--SPOT?
CURSE THE LUCK! NOW I'M IN FOR IT--
GOT TO --
AHHH!
SCHHH!
EMBER!!
SPLASH!

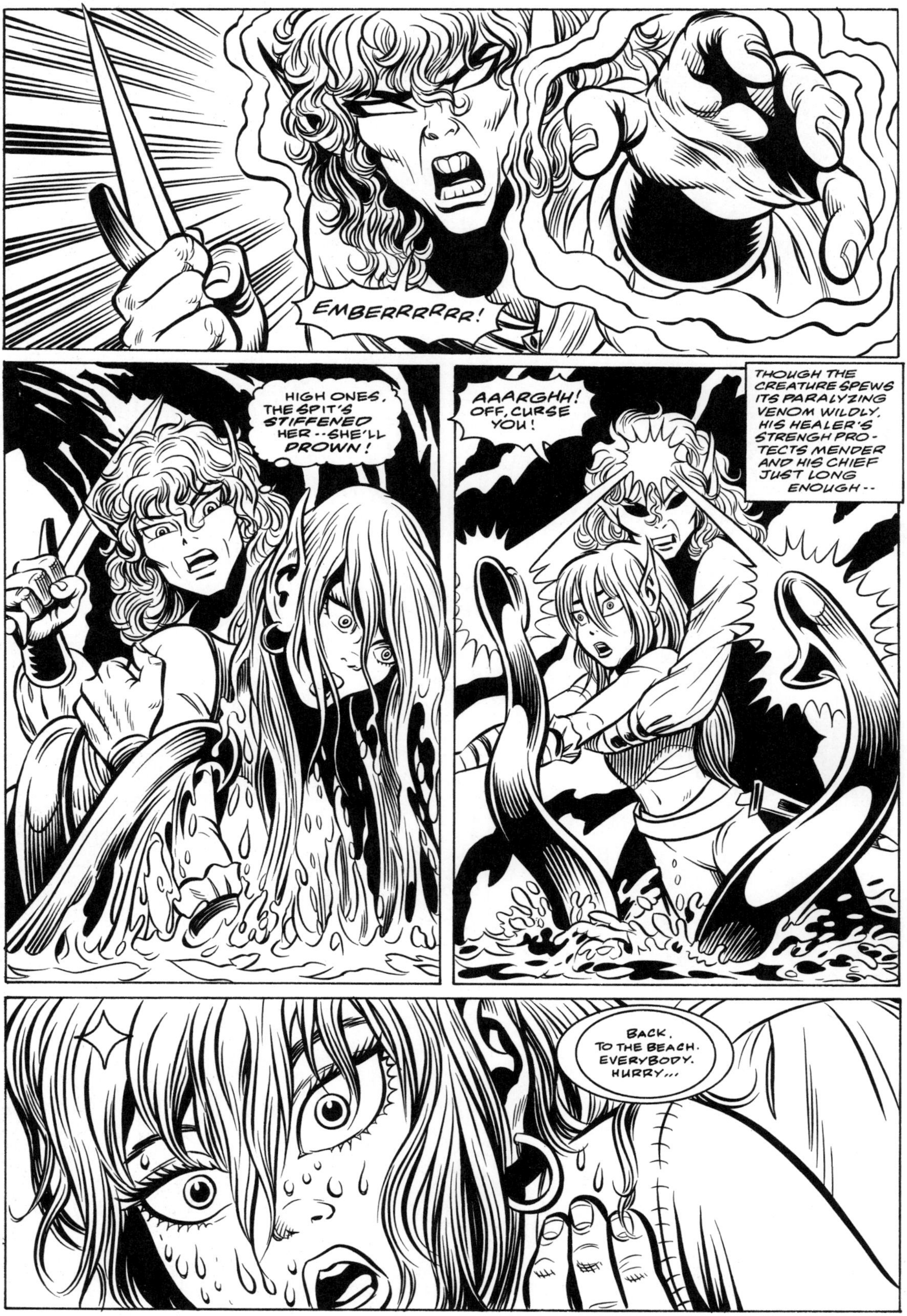
EMBERRRRRR!
HIGH ONES, THE SPIT'S STIFFENED HER--SHE'LL DROWN!
AAARGHH! OFF, CURSE YOU!
THOUGH THE CREATURE SPEWS ITS PARALYZING VENOM WILDLY, HIS HEALER'S STRENGH PROTECTS MENDER AND HIS CHIEF JUST LONG ENOUGH--
BACK. TO THE BEACH. EVERYBODY. HURRY...

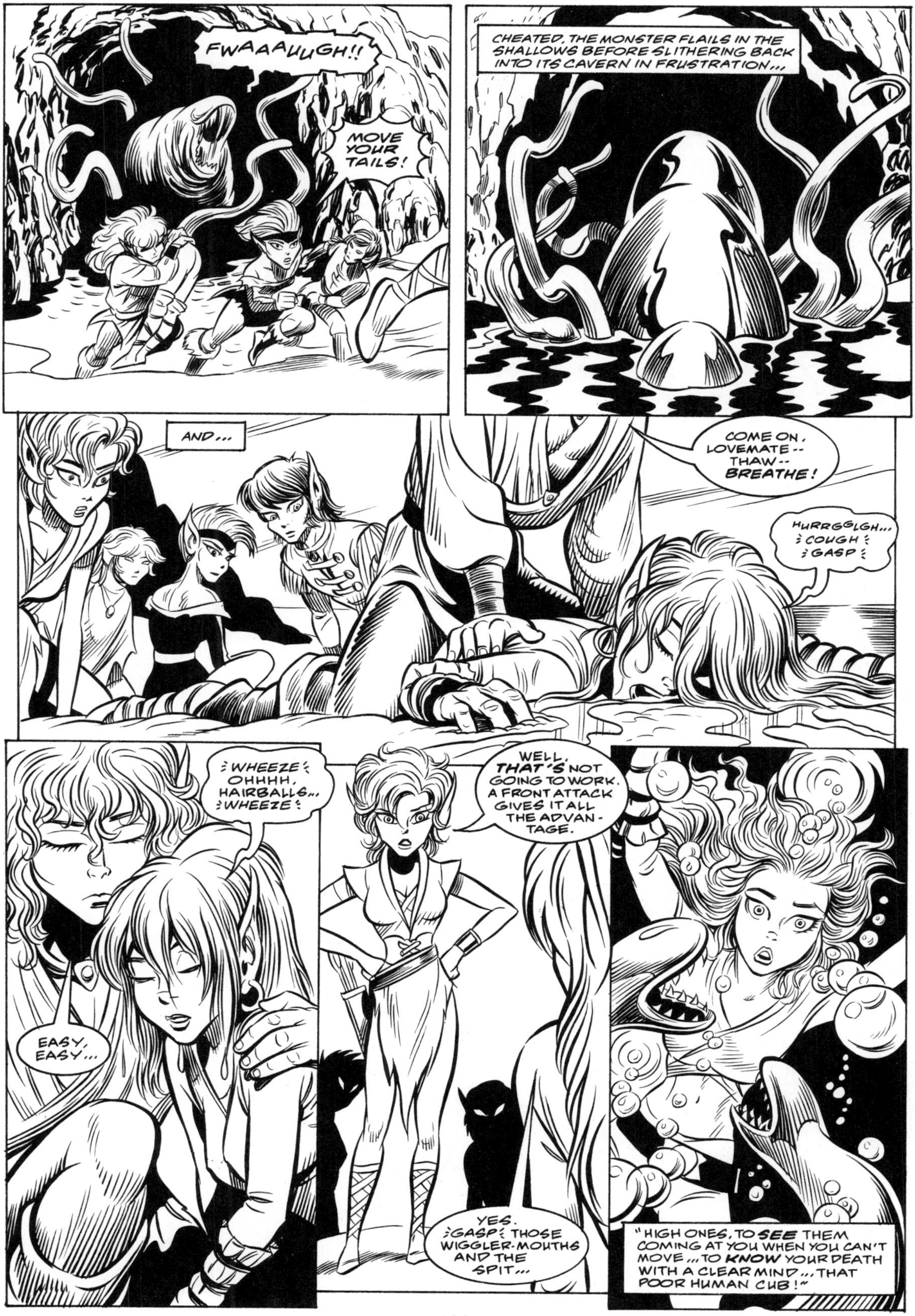
FWAAAUUGH!!
MOVE YOUR TAILS!
CHEATED, THE MONSTER FLAILS IN THE SHALLOWS BEFORE SLITHERING BACK INTO ITS CAVERN IN FRUSTRATION...
AND...
COME ON, LOVEMATE -- THAW -- BREATHE!
HURRGGLGH... COUGH GASP
WHEEZE OHHHH, HAIRBALLS... WHEEZE
EASY, EASY...
WELL, THAT'S NOT GOING TO WORK. A FRONT ATTACK GIVES IT ALL THE ADVAN-TAGE.
YES. GASP THOSE WIGGLER-MOUTHS AND THE SPIT...
"HIGH ONES, TO SEE THEM COMING AT YOU WHEN YOU CAN'T MOVE... TO KNOW YOUR DEATH WITH A CLEAR MIND... THAT POOR HUMAN CUB!"

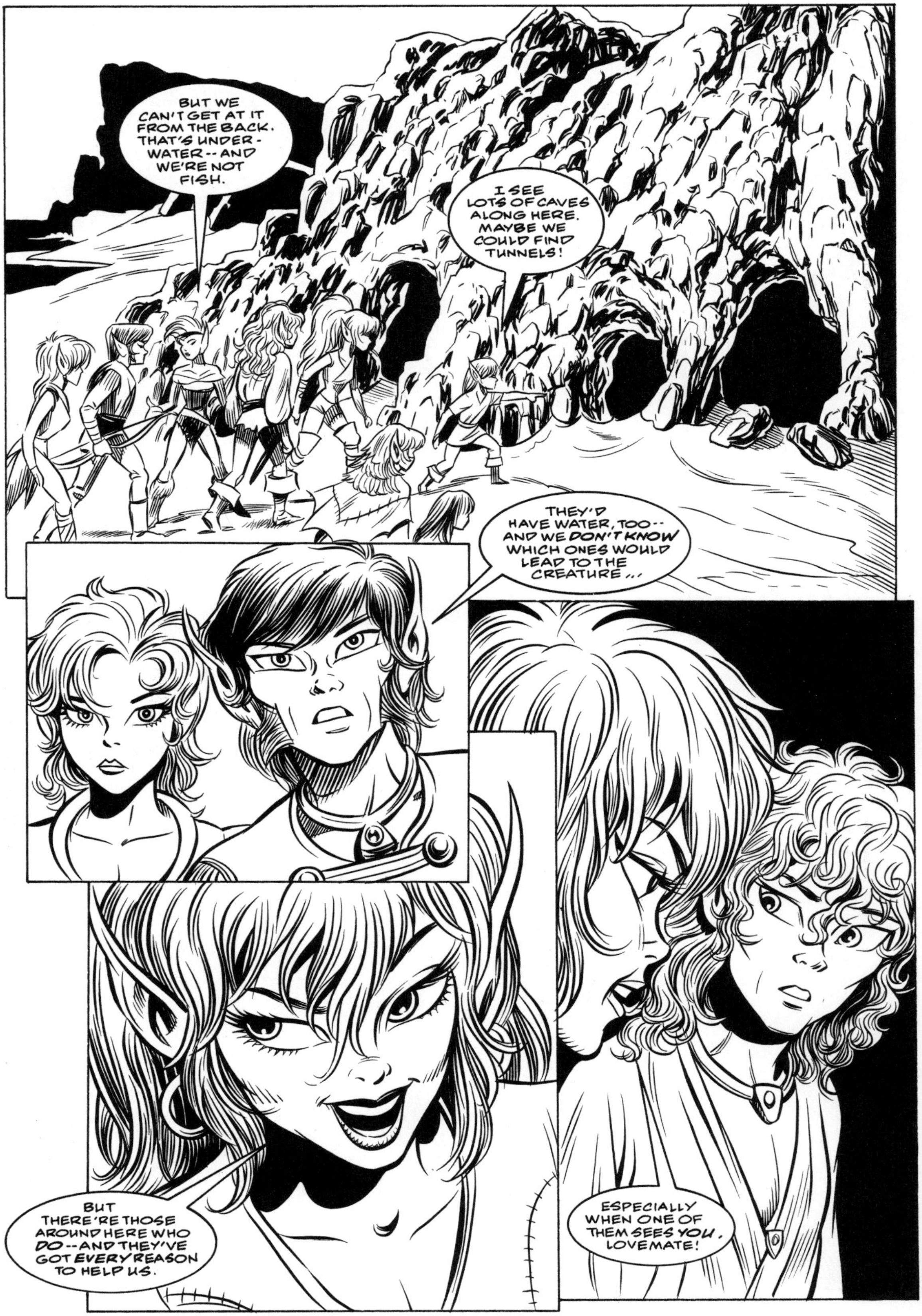
BUT WE CAN'T GET AT IT FROM THE BACK. THAT'S UNDER-WATER -- AND WE'RE NOT FISH.
I SEE LOTS OF CAVES ALONG HERE. MAYBE WE COULD FIND TUNNELS!
THEY'D HAVE WATER, TOO -- AND WE DON'T KNOW WHICH ONES WOULD LEAD TO THE CREATURE ...
BUT THERE'RE THOSE AROUND HERE WHO DO -- AND THEY'VE GOT EVERY REASON TO HELP US.
ESPECIALLY WHEN ONE OF THEM SEES YOU, LOVEMATE!

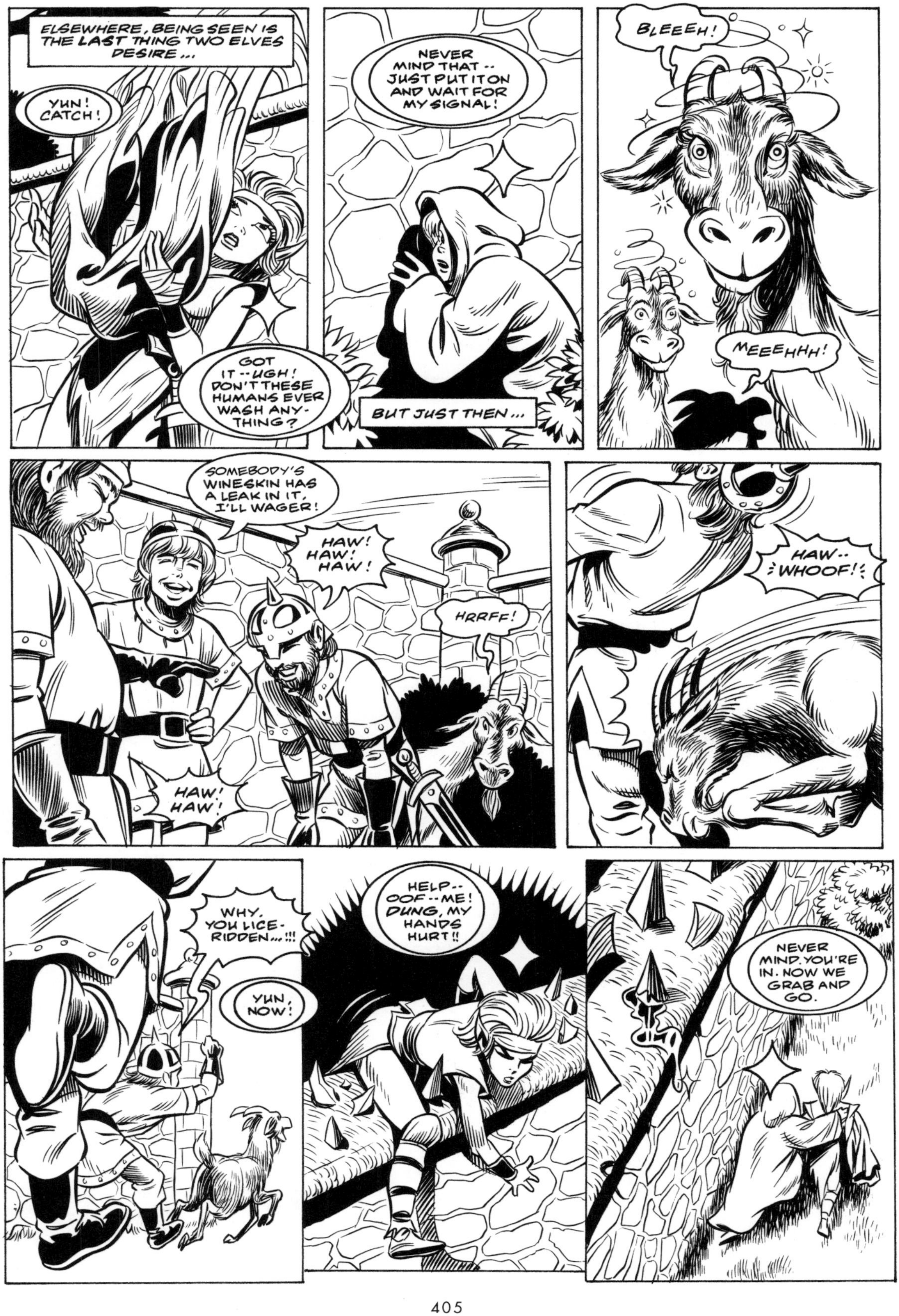
ELSEWHERE, BEING SEEN IS THE LAST THING TWO ELVES DESIRE...
YUN! CATCH!
GOT IT--UGH! DON'T THESE HUMANS EVER WASH ANY-THING?
NEVER MIND THAT-- JUST PUT IT ON AND WAIT FOR MY SIGNAL!
BUT JUST THEN...
BLEEEH!
MEEEHHH!
SOMEBODY'S WINESKIN HAS A LEAK IN IT, I'LL WAGER!
HAW! HAW! HAW!
HRRFF!
HAW! HAW!
HAW-- WHOOF!
WHY, YOU LICE-RIDDEN...!!!
YUN, NOW!
HELP-- OOF--ME! DUNG, MY HANDS HURT!!
NEVER MIND. YOU'RE IN. NOW WE GRAB AND GO.

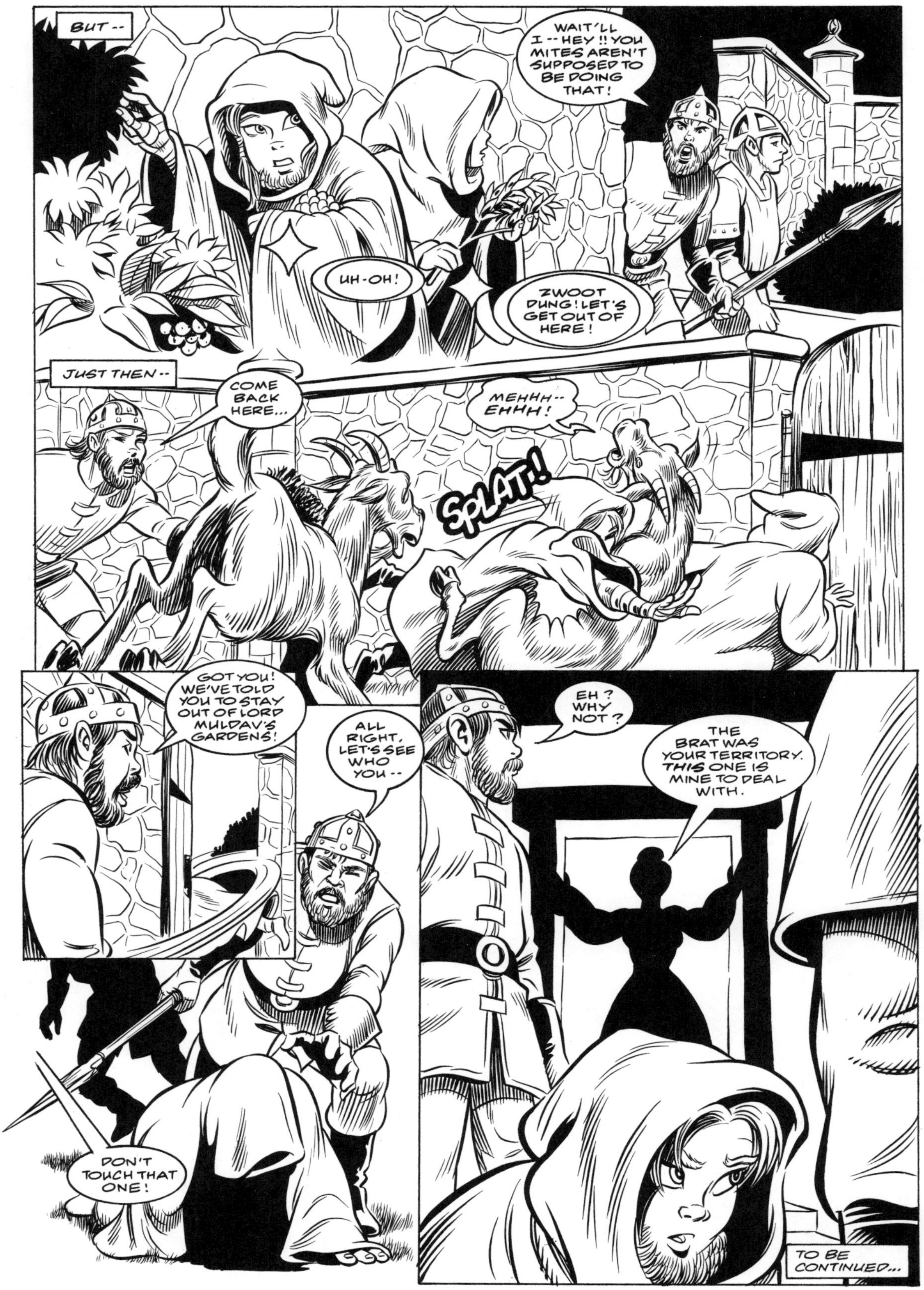
BUT --
WAIT'LL I -- HEY !! YOU MITES AREN'T SUPPOSED TO BE DOING THAT!
UH-OH!
ZWOOT DUNG! LET'S GET OUT OF HERE!
JUST THEN --
COME BACK HERE...
MEHHH-- EHHH!
SPLAT!
GOT YOU! WE'VE TOLD YOU TO STAY OUT OF LORD MULDAV'S GARDENS!
ALL RIGHT, LET'S SEE WHO YOU --
DON'T TOUCH THAT ONE!
EH? WHY NOT?
THE BRAT WAS YOUR TERRITORY. THIS ONE IS MINE TO DEAL WITH.
TO BE CONTINUED...

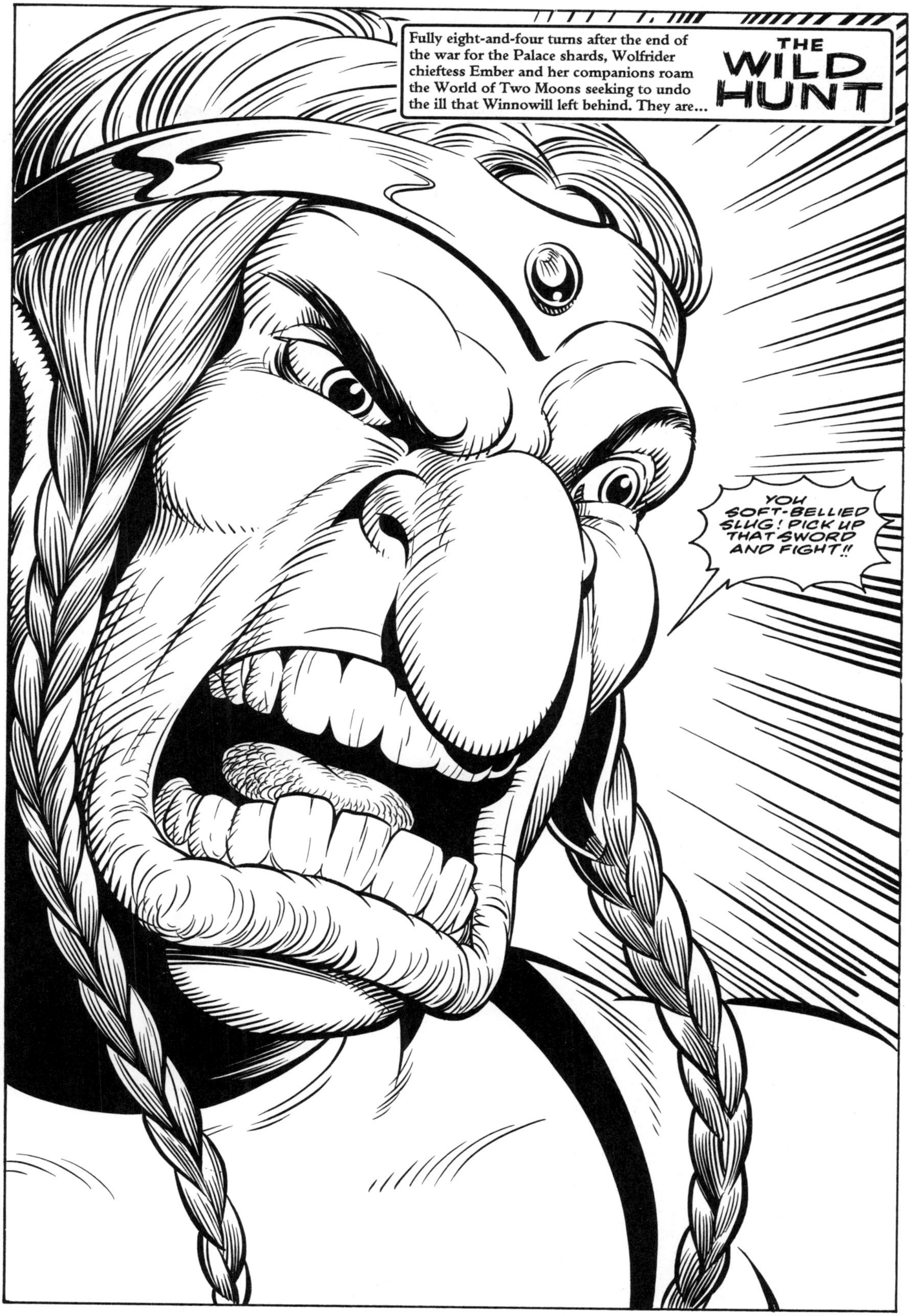

Fully eight-and-four turns after the end of the war for the Palace shards, Wolfrider chieftess Ember and her companions roam the World of Two Moons seeking to undo the ill that Winnowill left behind. They are...
THE WILD HUNT
YOU SOFT-BELLIED SLUG! PICK UP THAT SWORD AND FIGHT!!

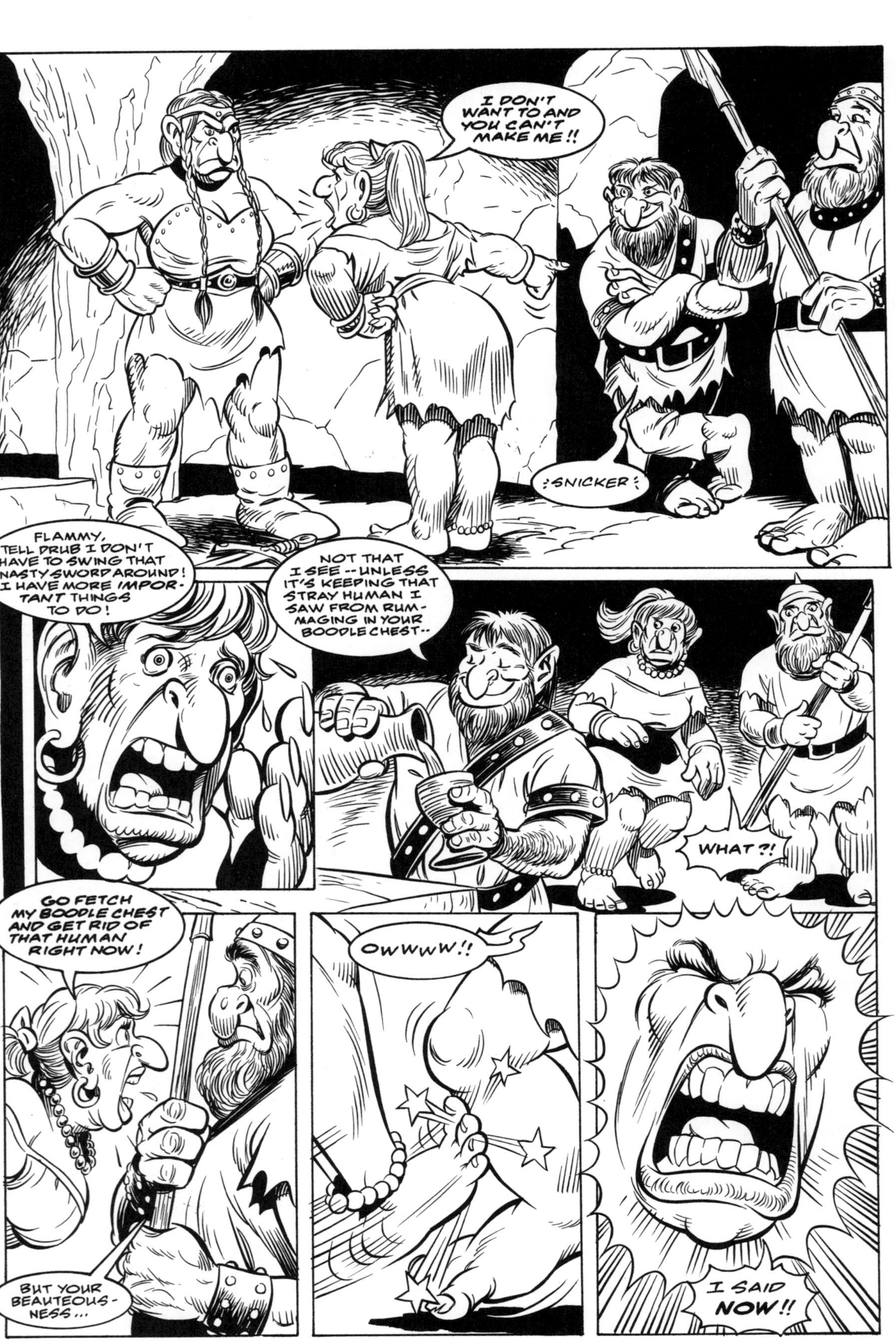

I DON'T WANT TO AND YOU CAN'T MAKE ME!!
SNICKER
FLAMMY, TELL DRUB I DON'T HAVE TO SWING THAT NASTY SWORD AROUND! I HAVE MORE IMPORTANT THINGS TO DO!
NOT THAT I SEE -- UNLESS IT'S KEEPING THAT STRAY HUMAN I SAW FROM RUMMAGING IN YOUR BOODLE CHEST..
WHAT?!
GO FETCH MY BOODLE CHEST AND GET RID OF THAT HUMAN RIGHT NOW!
BUT YOUR BEAUTEOUSNESS...
OWWWW!!
I SAID NOW!!

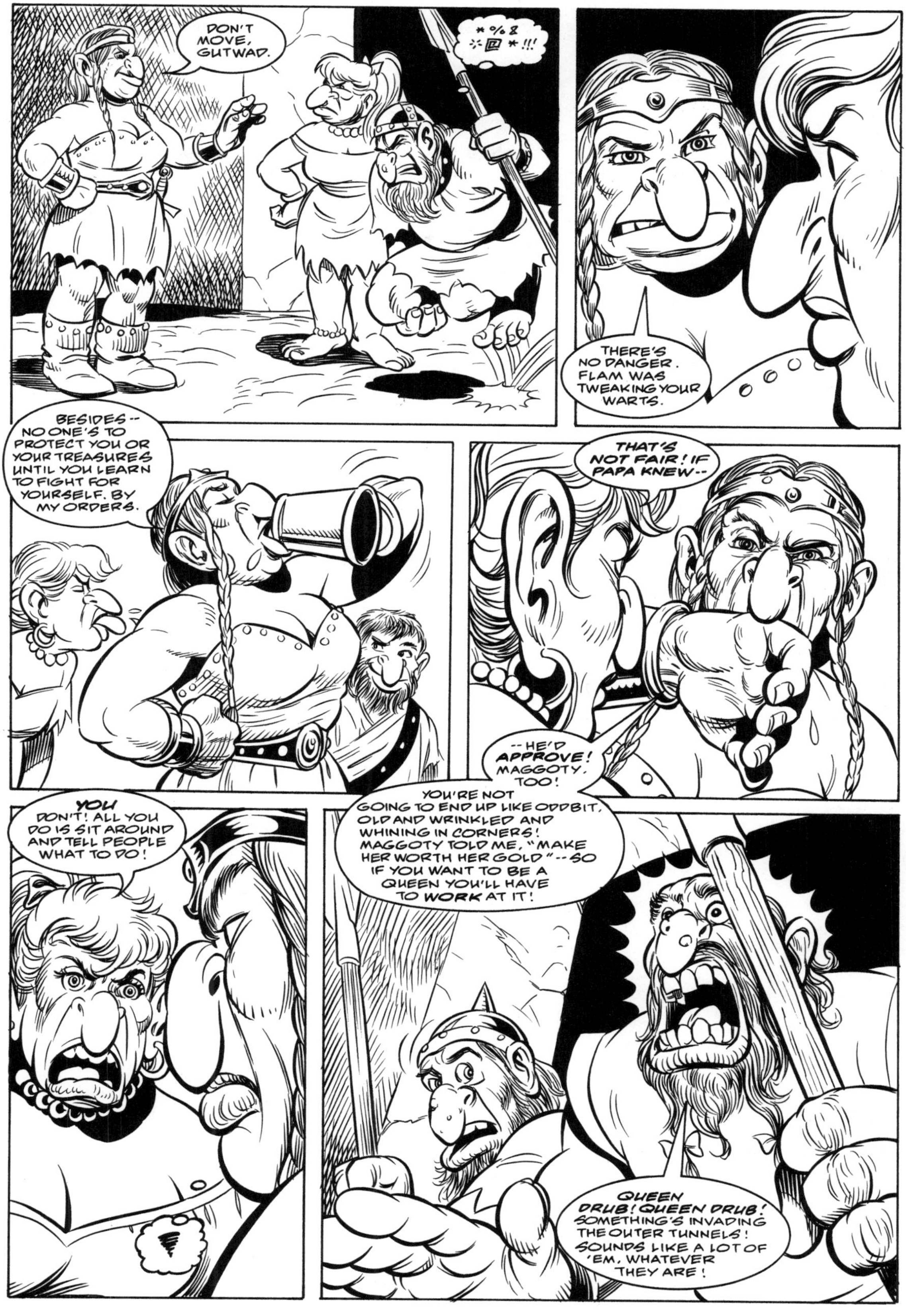
DON'T MOVE, GUTWAD.
*%&
:*:@*!!!
THERE'S NO DANGER. FLAM WAS TWEAKING YOUR WARTS.
BESIDES-- NO ONE'S TO PROTECT YOU OR YOUR TREASURES UNTIL YOU LEARN TO FIGHT FOR YOURSELF. BY MY ORDERS.
THAT'S NOT FAIR! IF PAPA KNEW--
--HE'D APPROVE! MAGGOTY, TOO!
YOU DON'T! ALL YOU DO IS SIT AROUND AND TELL PEOPLE WHAT TO DO!
YOU'RE NOT GOING TO END UP LIKE ODDBIT, OLD AND WRINKLED AND WHINING IN CORNERS! MAGGOTY TOLD ME, "MAKE HER WORTH HER GOLD"-- SO IF YOU WANT TO BE A QUEEN YOU'LL HAVE TO WORK AT IT!
QUEEN DRUB! QUEEN DRUB! SOMETHING'S INVADING THE OUTER TUNNELS! SOUNDS LIKE A LOT OF 'EM, WHATEVER THEY ARE!

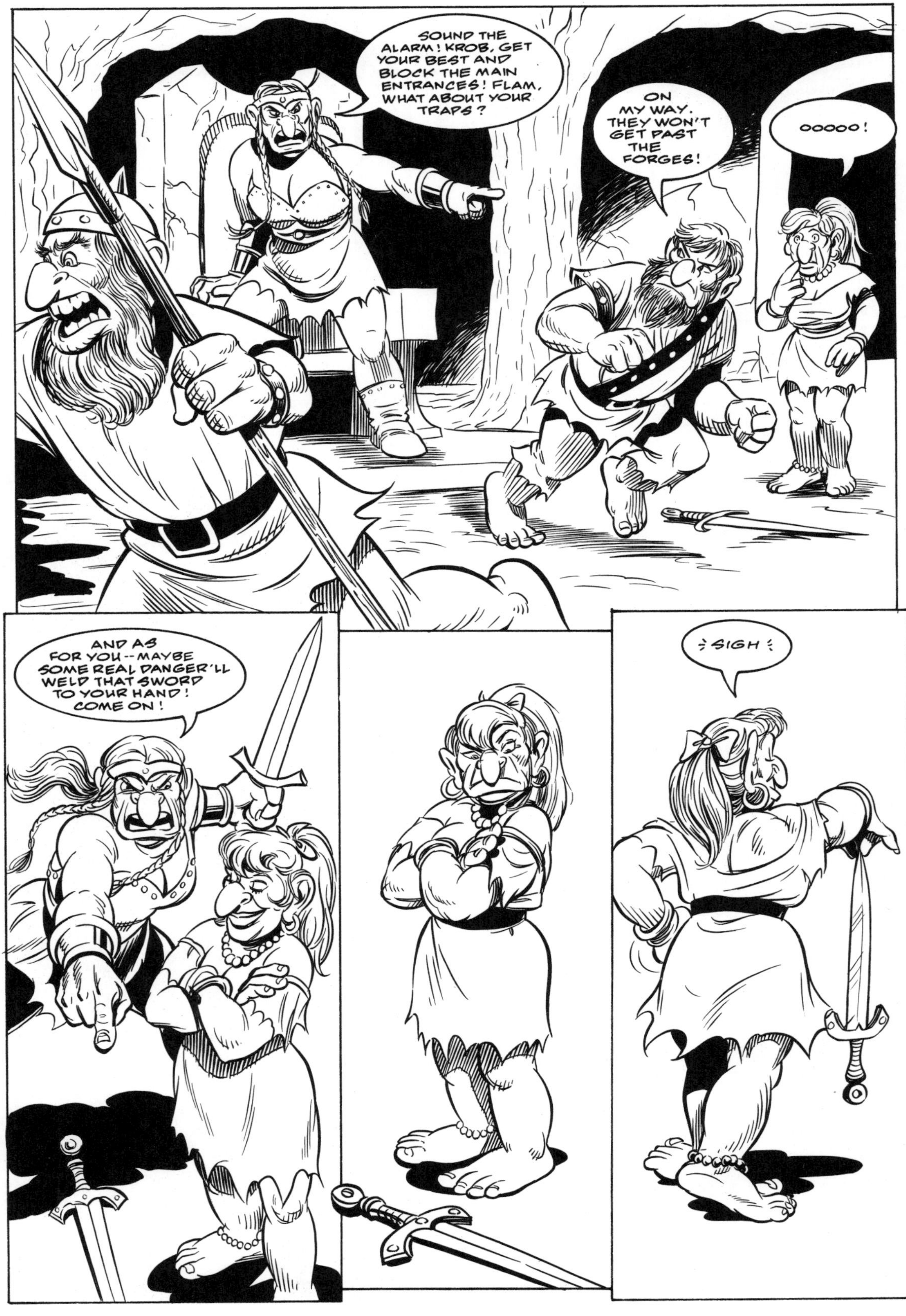

SOUND THE ALARM! KROB, GET YOUR BEST AND BLOCK THE MAIN ENTRANCES! FLAM, WHAT ABOUT YOUR TRAPS?
ON MY WAY. THEY WON'T GET PAST THE FORGES!
OOOOO!
AND AS FOR YOU -- MAYBE SOME REAL DANGER'LL WELD THAT SWORD TO YOUR HAND! COME ON!
SIGH

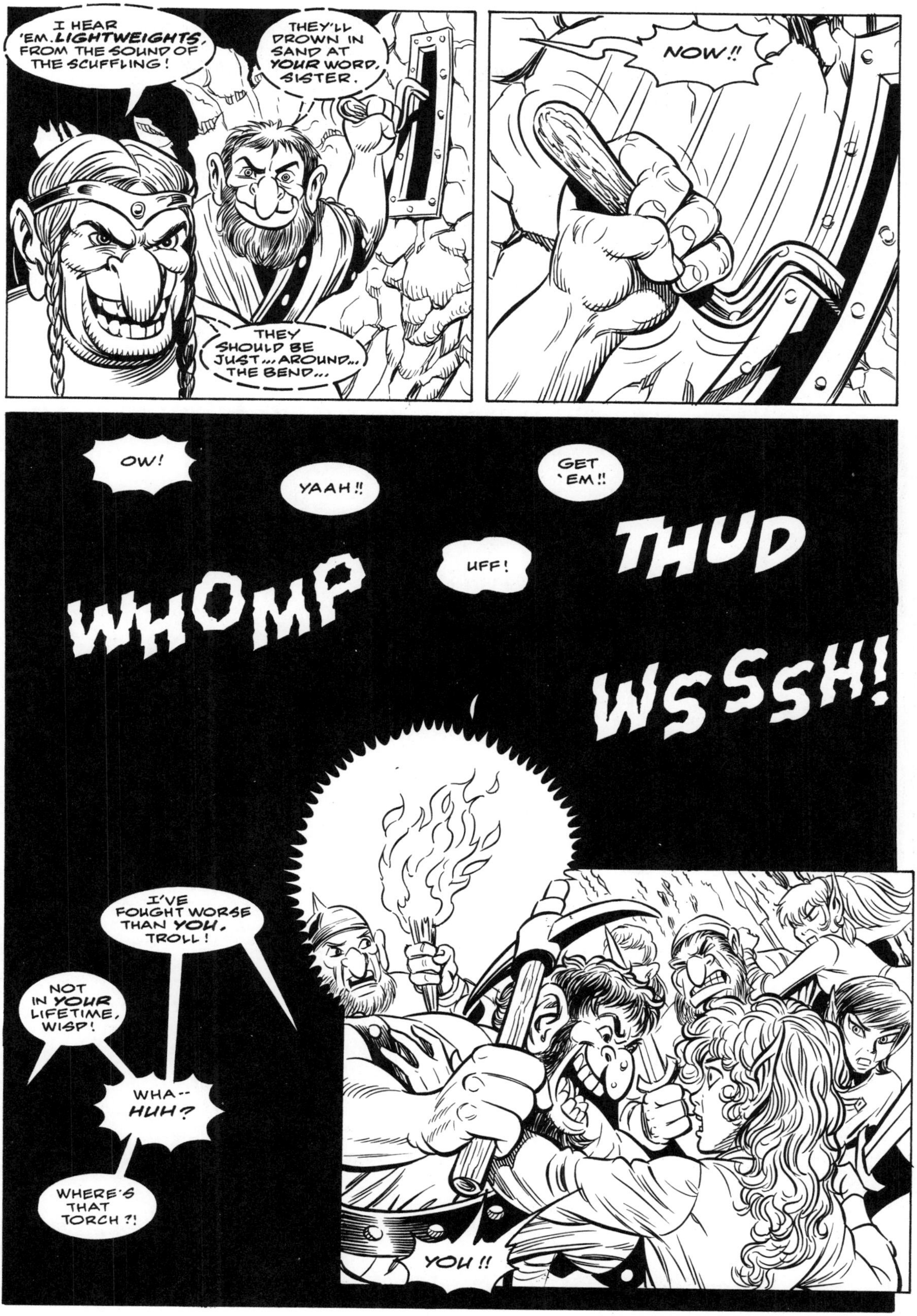
I HEAR 'EM. LIGHTWEIGHTS, FROM THE SOUND OF THE SCUFFLING!
THEY'LL DROWN IN SAND AT YOUR WORD, SISTER.
THEY SHOULD BE JUST... AROUND... THE BEND...
NOW!!
OW!
YAAH!!
GET 'EM!!
WHOMP
UFF!
THUD
WSSSH!
I'VE FOUGHT WORSE THAN YOU, TROLL!
NOT IN YOUR LIFETIME, WISP!
WHA-- HUH?
WHERE'S THAT TORCH?!
YOU!!

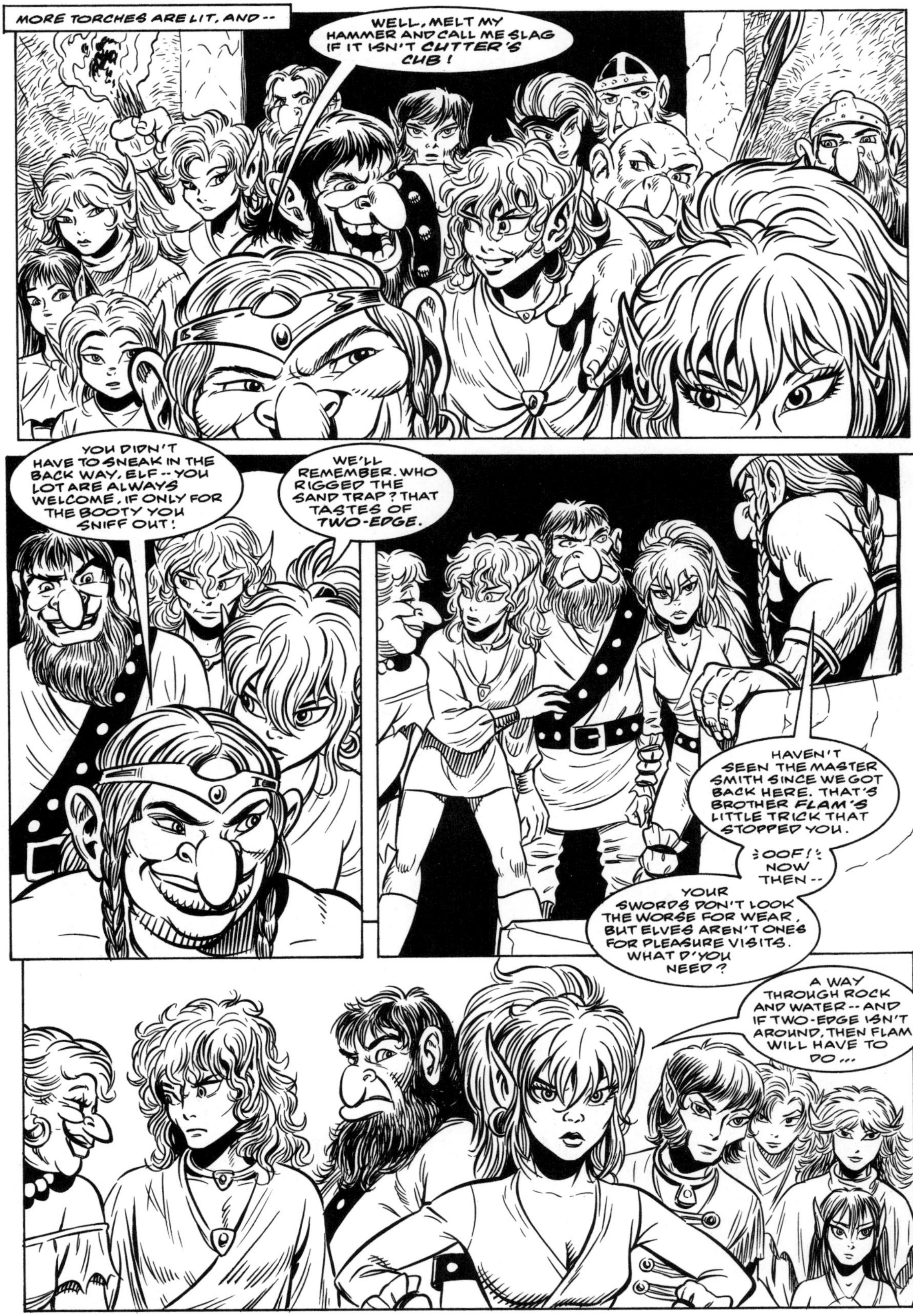
MORE TORCHES ARE LIT, AND --
WELL, MELT MY HAMMER AND CALL ME SLAG IF IT ISN'T CUTTER'S CUB!
YOU DIDN'T HAVE TO SNEAK IN THE BACK WAY, ELF -- YOU LOT ARE ALWAYS WELCOME, IF ONLY FOR THE BOOTY YOU SNIFF OUT!
WE'LL REMEMBER. WHO RIGGED THE SAND TRAP? THAT TASTES OF TWO-EDGE.
HAVEN'T SEEN THE MASTER SMITH SINCE WE GOT BACK HERE. THAT'S BROTHER FLAM'S LITTLE TRICK THAT STOPPED YOU.
OOF! NOW THEN --
YOUR SWORDS DON'T LOOK THE WORSE FOR WEAR, BUT ELVES AREN'T ONES FOR PLEASURE VISITS. WHAT D'YOU NEED?
A WAY THROUGH ROCK AND WATER -- AND IF TWO-EDGE ISN'T AROUND, THEN FLAM WILL HAVE TO DO...

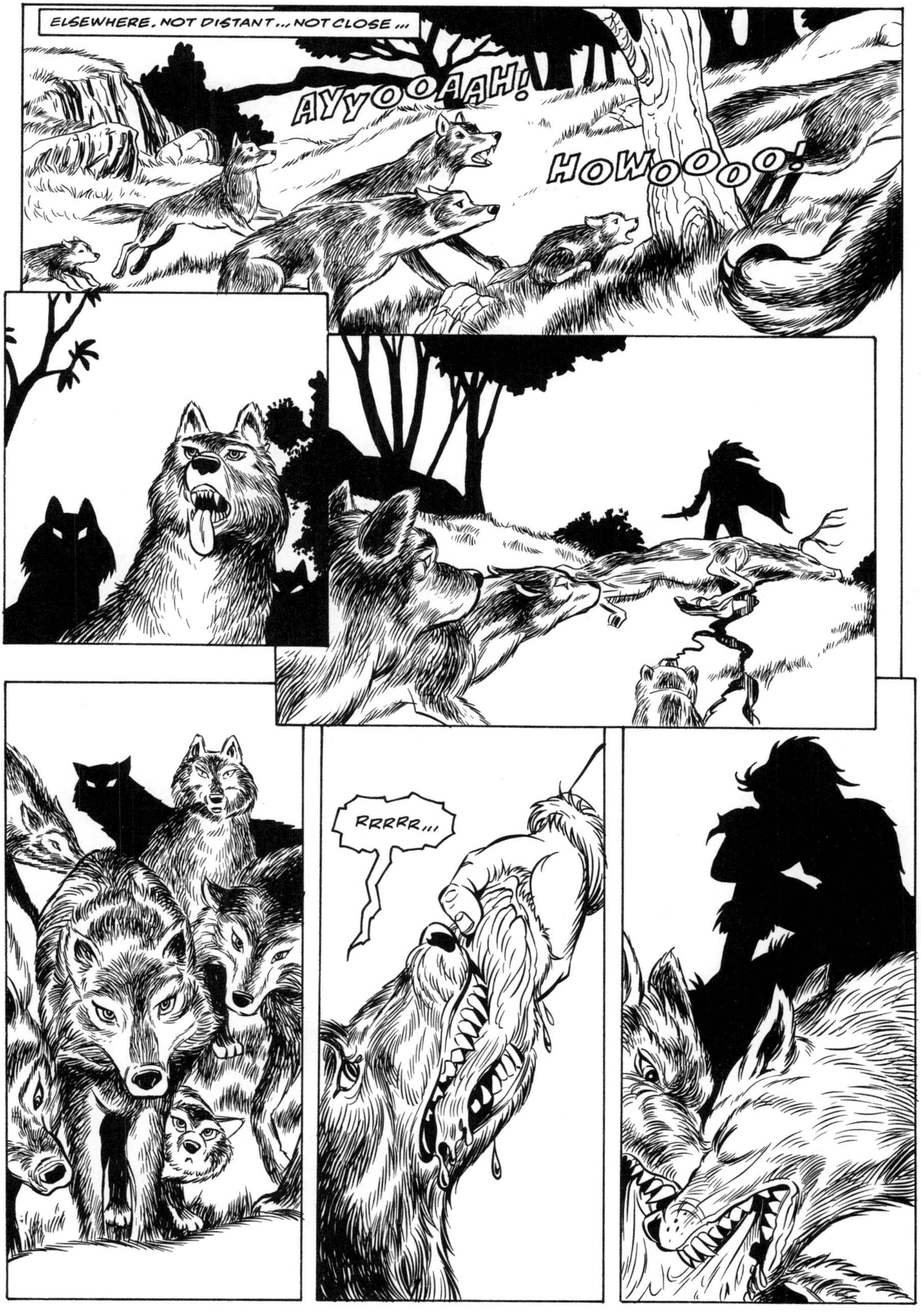
ELSEWHERE. NOT DISTANT... NOT CLOSE...
AYYOOAAAH!
HOWOOOOO!
RRRRR...

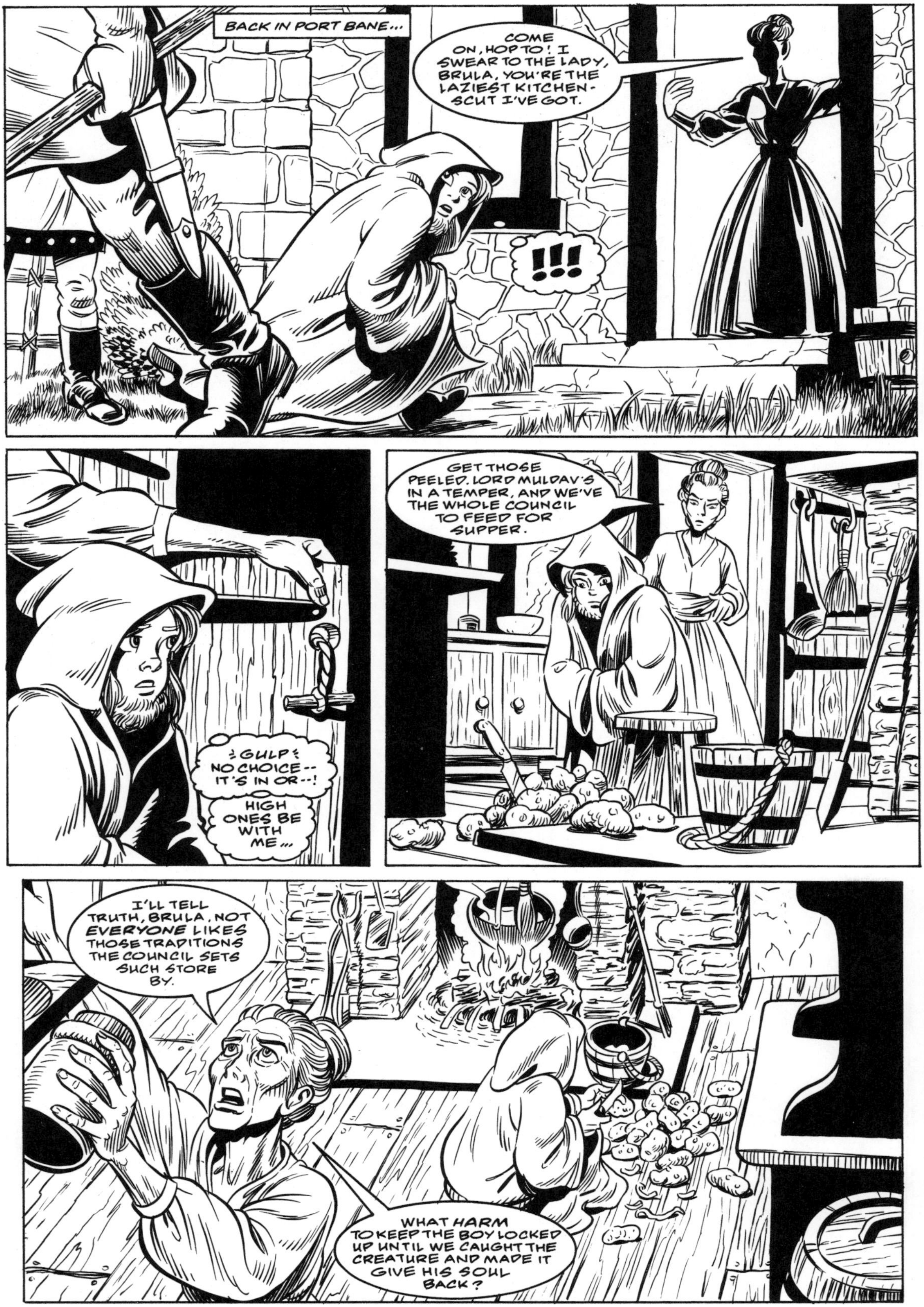
BACK IN PORT BANE...
COME ON, HOP TO! I SWEAR TO THE LADY, BRULA, YOU'RE THE LAZIEST KITCHEN-SCUT I'VE GOT.
!!!
GULP NO CHOICE-- IT'S IN OR--!
HIGH ONES BE WITH ME...
GET THOSE PEELED. LORD MULDAV'S IN A TEMPER, AND WE'VE THE WHOLE COUNCIL TO FEED FOR SUPPER.
I'LL TELL TRUTH, BRULA, NOT EVERYONE LIKES THOSE TRADITIONS THE COUNCIL SETS SUCH STORE BY.
WHAT HARM TO KEEP THE BOY LOCKED UP UNTIL WE CAUGHT THE CREATURE AND MADE IT GIVE HIS SOUL BACK?

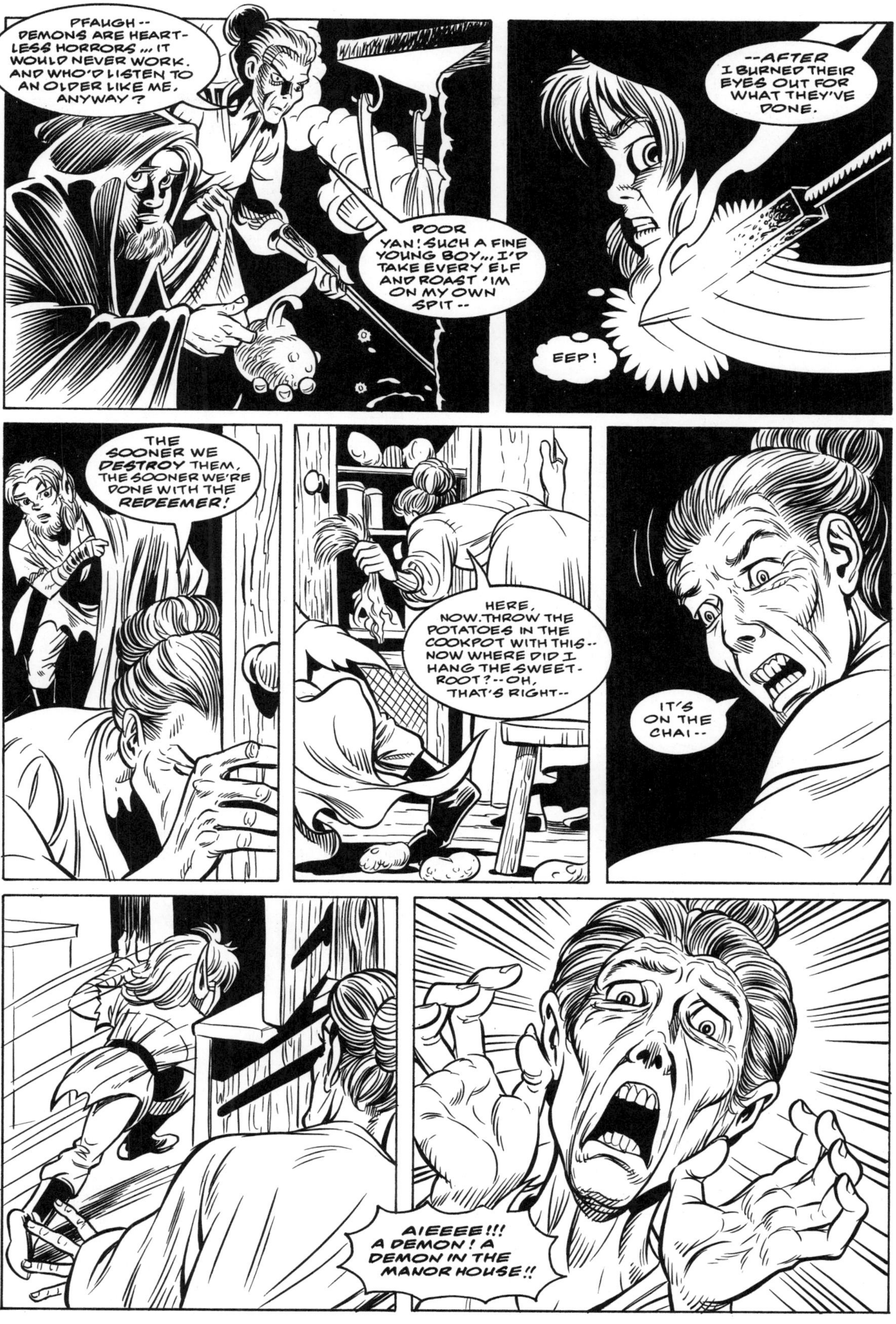
PFAUGH -- DEMONS ARE HEARTLESS HORRORS... IT WOULD NEVER WORK. AND WHO'D LISTEN TO AN OLDER LIKE ME, ANYWAY?
POOR YAN! SUCH A FINE YOUNG BOY... I'D TAKE EVERY ELF AND ROAST 'IM ON MY OWN SPIT --
--AFTER I BURNED THEIR EYES OUT FOR WHAT THEY'VE DONE.
EEP!
THE SOONER WE DESTROY THEM, THE SOONER WE'RE DONE WITH THE REDEEMER!
HERE, NOW. THROW THE POTATOES IN THE COOKPOT WITH THIS -- NOW WHERE DID I HANG THE SWEET-ROOT? -- OH, THAT'S RIGHT--
IT'S ON THE CHAI--
AIEEEE!!! A DEMON! A DEMON IN THE MANOR HOUSE!!

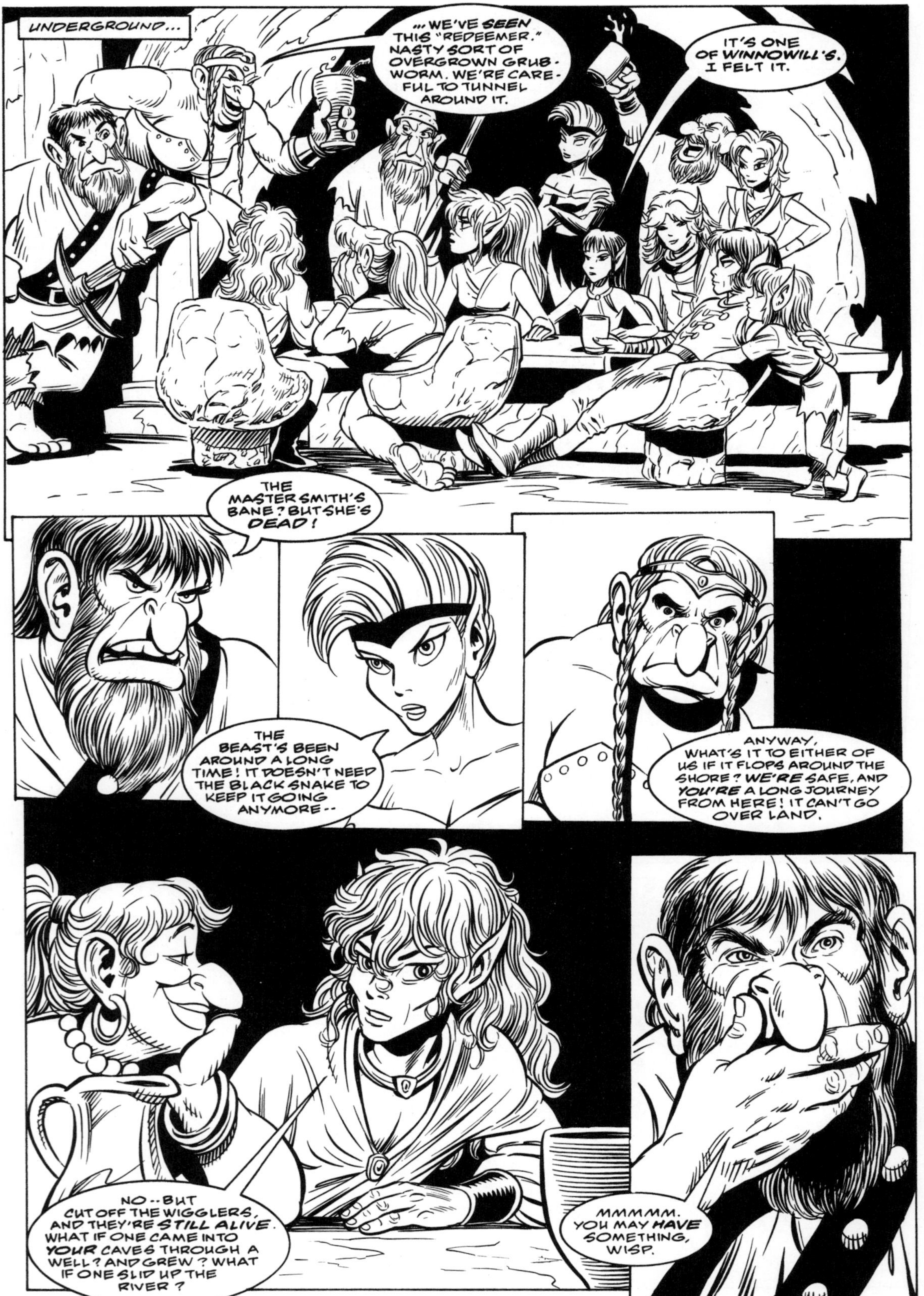
UNDERGROUND...
...WE'VE SEEN THIS "REDEEMER." NASTY SORT OF OVERGROWN GRUB-WORM. WE'RE CARE-FUL TO TUNNEL AROUND IT.
IT'S ONE OF WINNOWILL'S. I FELT IT.
THE MASTER SMITH'S BANE? BUT SHE'S DEAD!
THE BEAST'S BEEN AROUND A LONG TIME! IT DOESN'T NEED THE BLACK SNAKE TO KEEP IT GOING ANYMORE--
ANYWAY, WHAT'S IT TO EITHER OF US IF IT FLOPS AROUND THE SHORE? WE'RE SAFE, AND YOU'RE A LONG JOURNEY FROM HERE! IT CAN'T GO OVER LAND.
NO--BUT CUT OFF THE WIGGLERS, AND THEY'RE STILL ALIVE. WHAT IF ONE CAME INTO YOUR CAVES THROUGH A WELL? AND GREW? WHAT IF ONE SLID UP THE RIVER?
MMMMM. YOU MAY HAVE SOMETHING, WISP.

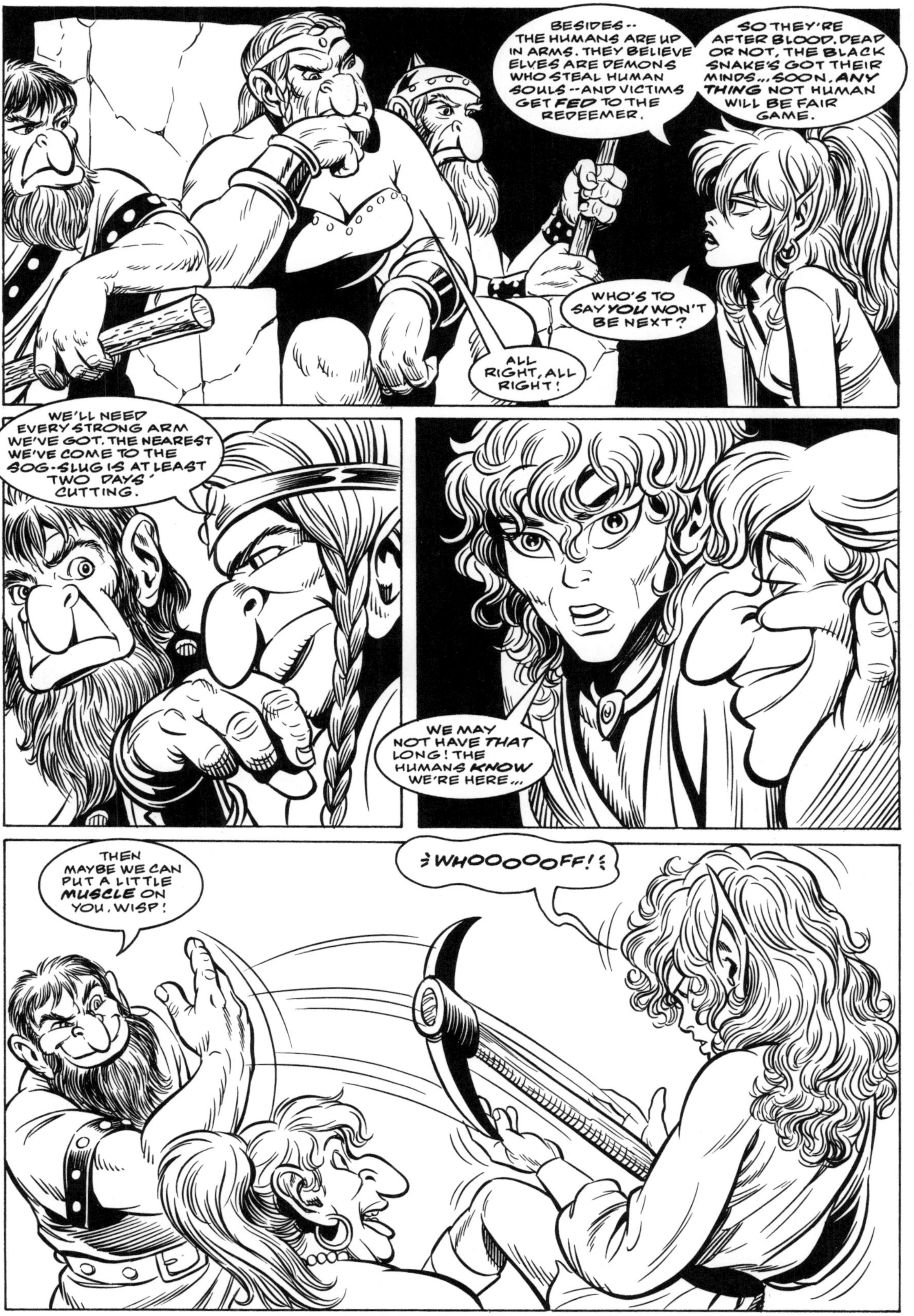
BESIDES -- THE HUMANS ARE UP IN ARMS. THEY BELIEVE ELVES ARE DEMONS WHO STEAL HUMAN SOULS -- AND VICTIMS GET FED TO THE REDEEMER.
SO THEY'RE AFTER BLOOD. DEAD OR NOT, THE BLACK SNAKE'S GOT THEIR MINDS... SOON, ANY THING NOT HUMAN WILL BE FAIR GAME.
WHO'S TO SAY YOU WON'T BE NEXT?
ALL RIGHT, ALL RIGHT!
WE'LL NEED EVERY STRONG ARM WE'VE GOT. THE NEAREST WE'VE COME TO THE SOG-SLUG IS AT LEAST TWO DAYS' CUTTING.
WE MAY NOT HAVE THAT LONG! THE HUMANS KNOW WE'RE HERE...
THEN MAYBE WE CAN PUT A LITTLE MUSCLE ON YOU, WISP!
WHOOOOOOFF!

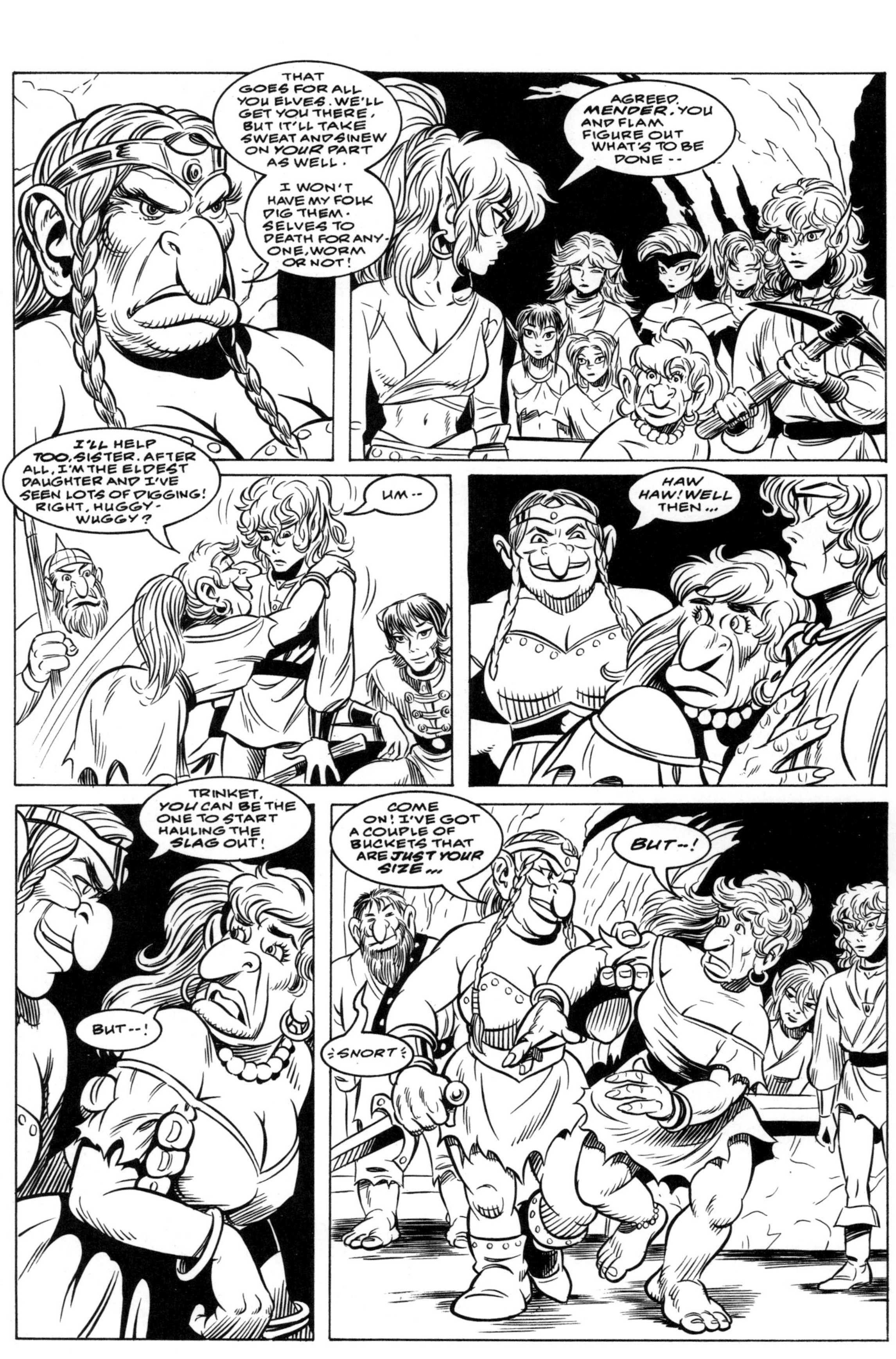
THAT GOES FOR ALL YOU ELVES. WE'LL GET YOU THERE, BUT IT'LL TAKE SWEAT AND SINEW ON YOUR PART AS WELL.
I WON'T HAVE MY FOLK DIG THEMSELVES TO DEATH FOR ANYONE, WORM OR NOT!
AGREED, MENDER. YOU AND FLAM FIGURE OUT WHAT'S TO BE DONE --
I'LL HELP TOO, SISTER. AFTER ALL, I'M THE ELDEST DAUGHTER AND I'VE SEEN LOTS OF DIGGING! RIGHT, HUGGY-WUGGY?
UM --
HAW HAW! WELL THEN...
TRINKET, YOU CAN BE THE ONE TO START HAULING THE SLAG OUT!
BUT --!
COME ON! I'VE GOT A COUPLE OF BUCKETS THAT ARE JUST YOUR SIZE...
BUT --!
SNORT

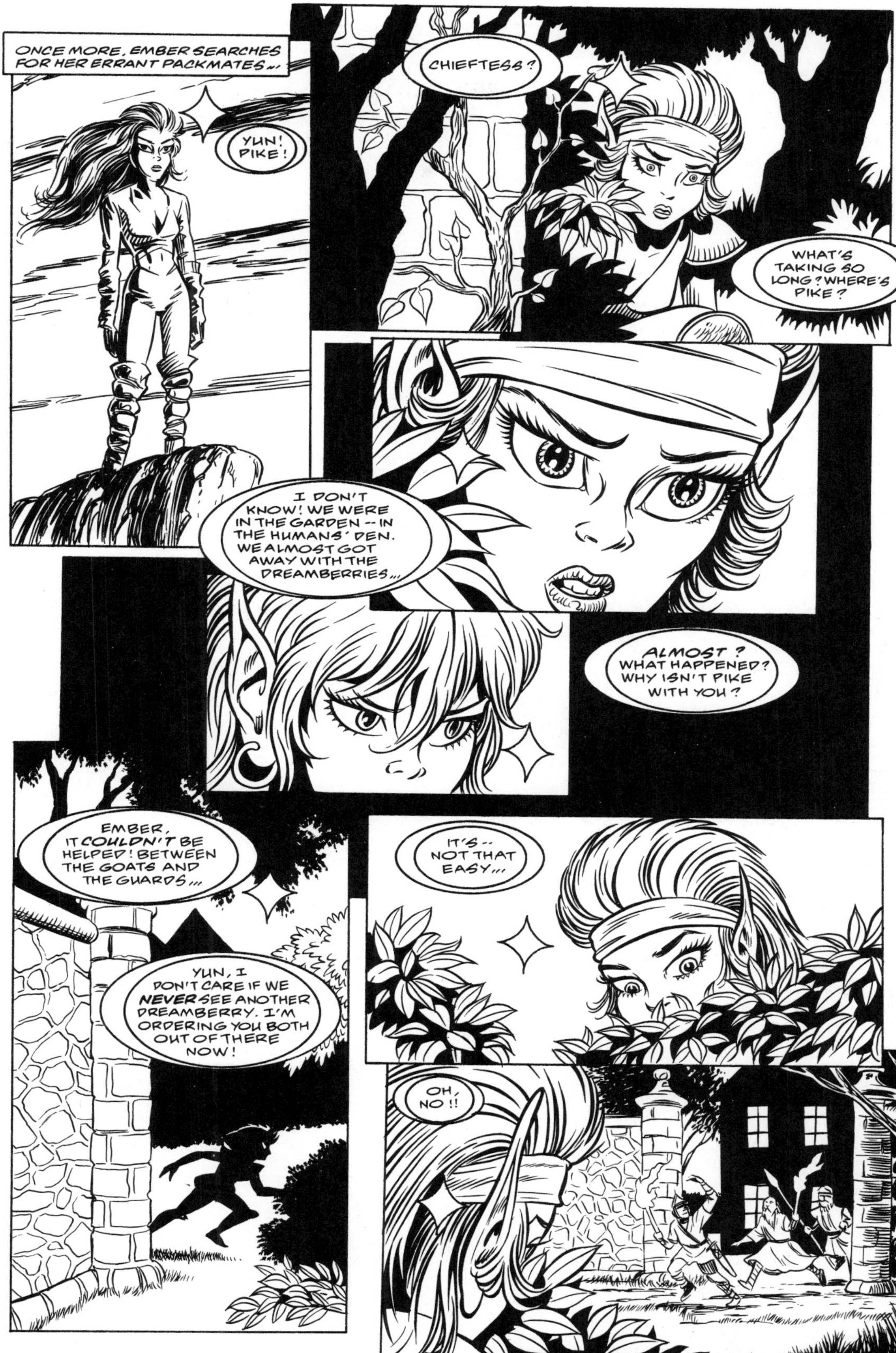
ONCE MORE, EMBER SEARCHES FOR HER ERRANT PACKMATES...
YUN! PIKE!
CHIEFTESS?
WHAT'S TAKING SO LONG? WHERE'S PIKE?
I DON'T KNOW! WE WERE IN THE GARDEN -- IN THE HUMANS' DEN. WE ALMOST GOT AWAY WITH THE DREAMBERRIES...
ALMOST? WHAT HAPPENED? WHY ISN'T PIKE WITH YOU?
EMBER, IT COULDN'T BE HELPED! BETWEEN THE GOATS AND THE GUARDS...
YUN, I DON'T CARE IF WE NEVER SEE ANOTHER DREAMBERRY. I'M ORDERING YOU BOTH OUT OF THERE NOW!
IT'S -- NOT THAT EASY...
OH, NO!!

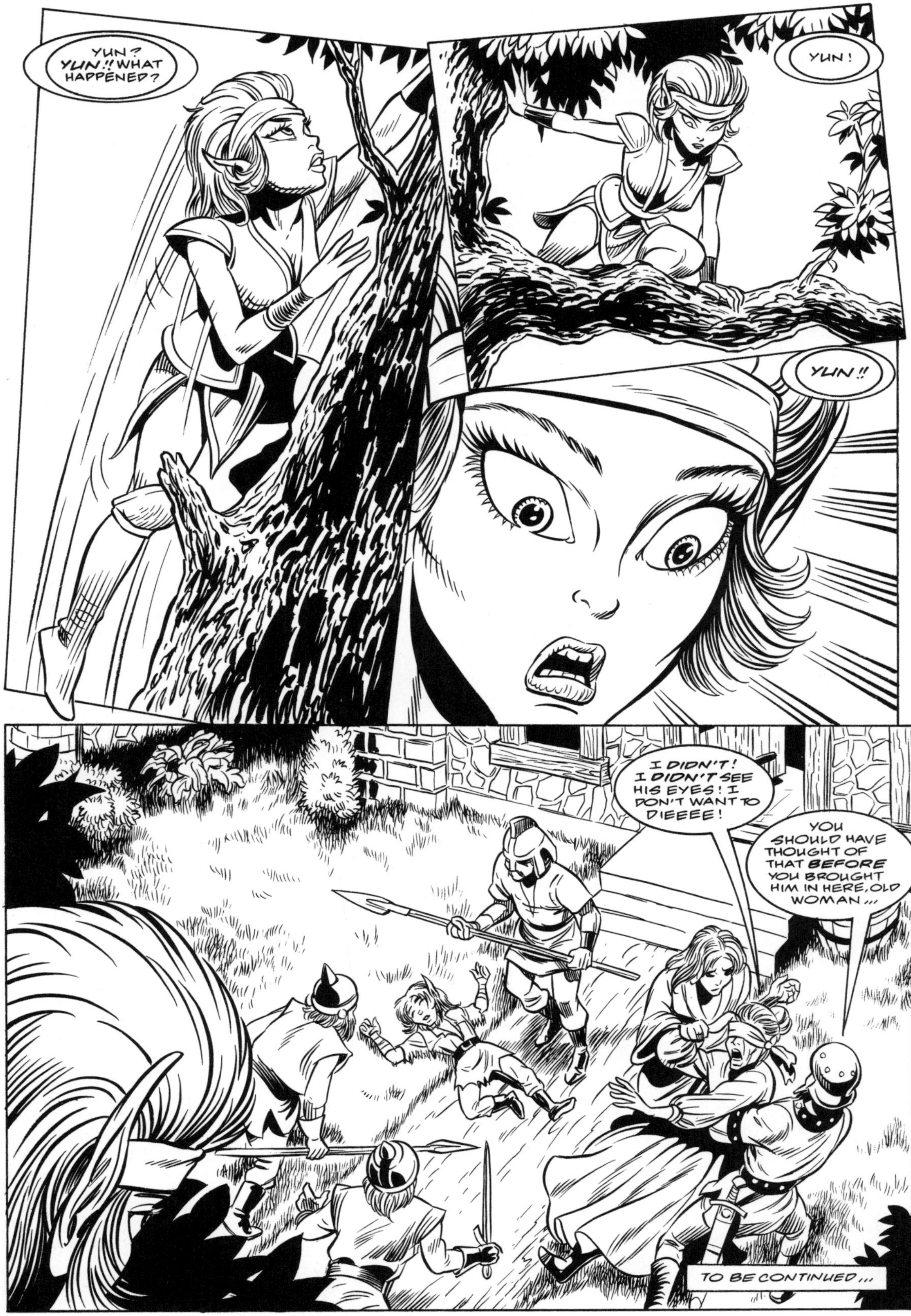
YUN? YUN!! WHAT HAPPENED?
YUN!
YUN!!
I DIDN'T! I DIDN'T SEE HIS EYES! I DON'T WANT TO DIEEEE!
YOU SHOULD HAVE THOUGHT OF THAT BEFORE YOU BROUGHT HIM IN HERE, OLD WOMAN...
TO BE CONTINUED...

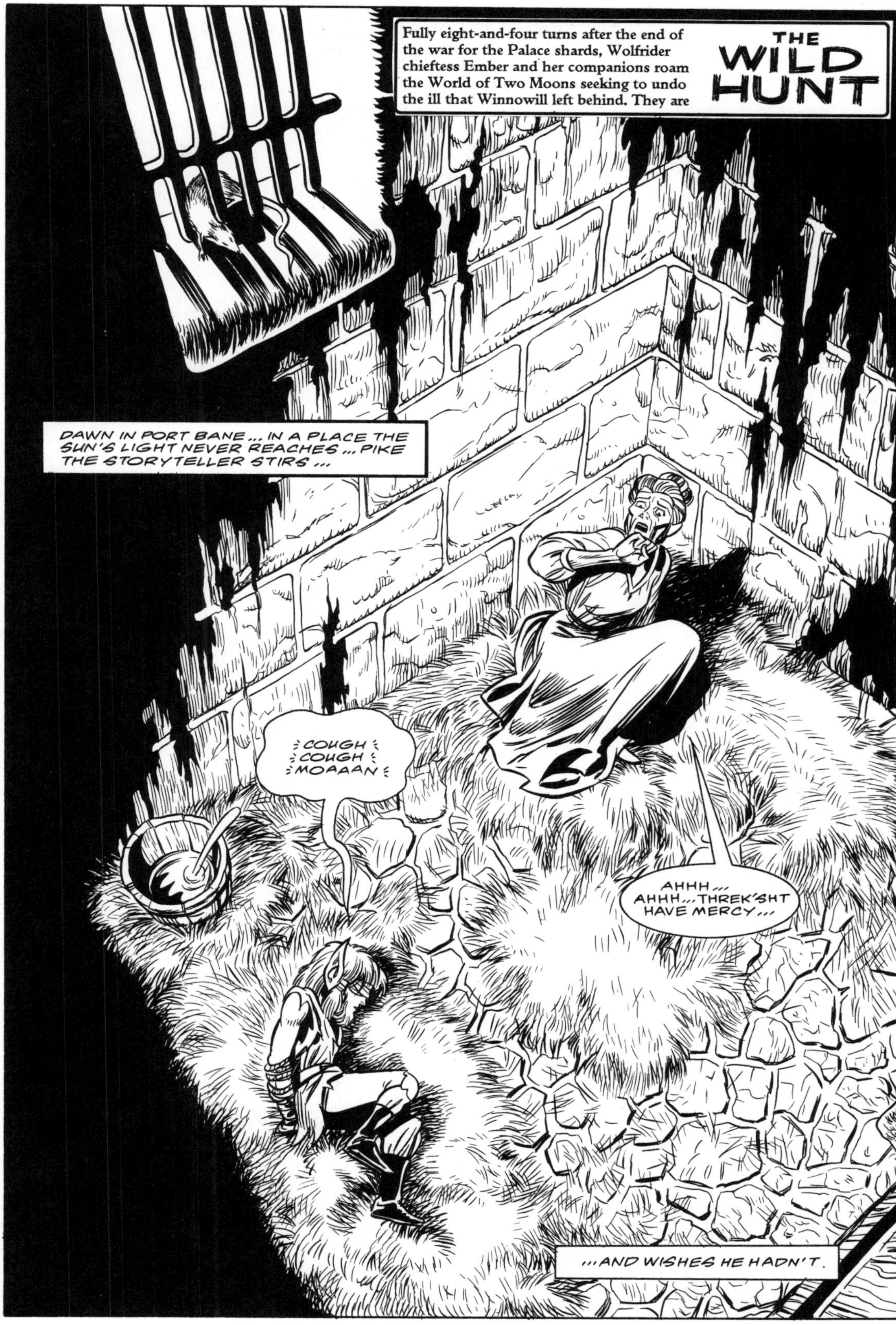
Fully eight-and-four turns after the end of the war for the Palace shards, Wolfrider chieftess Ember and her companions roam the World of Two Moons seeking to undo the ill that Winnowill left behind. They are
THE WILD HUNT
DAWN IN PORT BANE ... IN A PLACE THE SUN'S LIGHT NEVER REACHES ... PIKE THE STORYTELLER STIRS ...
COUGH COUGH MOAAAN
AHHH ... AHHH ... THREK'SHT HAVE MERCY ...
... AND WISHES HE HADN'T.

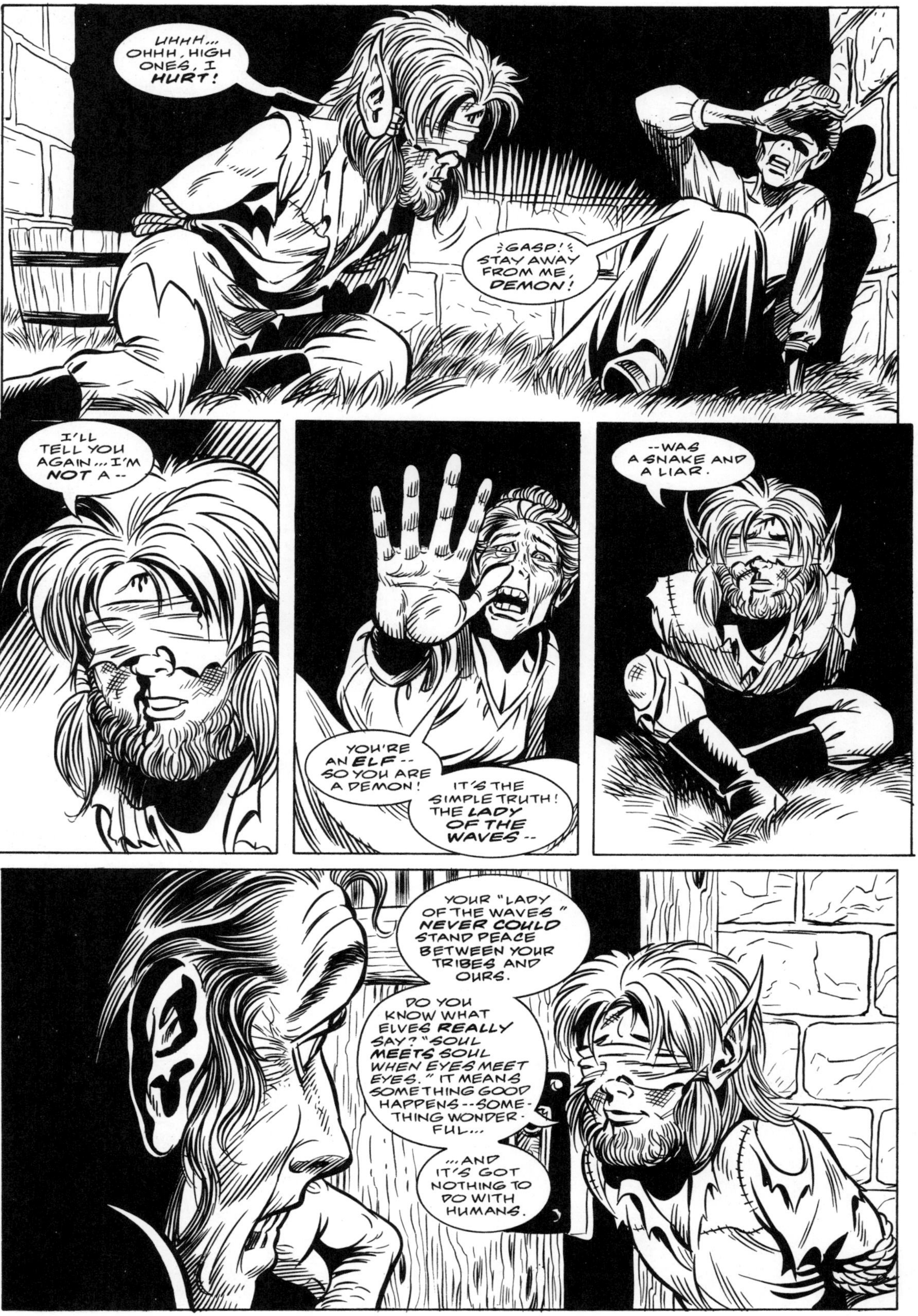
UHHH... OHHH, HIGH ONES, I HURT!
¡GASP!¡ STAY AWAY FROM ME, DEMON!
I'LL TELL YOU AGAIN... I'M NOT A --
YOU'RE AN ELF -- SO YOU ARE A DEMON!
IT'S THE SIMPLE TRUTH! THE LADY OF THE WAVES --
--WAS A SNAKE AND A LIAR.
YOUR "LADY OF THE WAVES" NEVER COULD STAND PEACE BETWEEN YOUR TRIBES AND OURS.
DO YOU KNOW WHAT ELVES REALLY SAY? "SOUL MEETS SOUL WHEN EYES MEET EYES." IT MEANS SOMETHING GOOD HAPPENS -- SOMETHING WONDERFUL...
...AND IT'S GOT NOTHING TO DO WITH HUMANS.

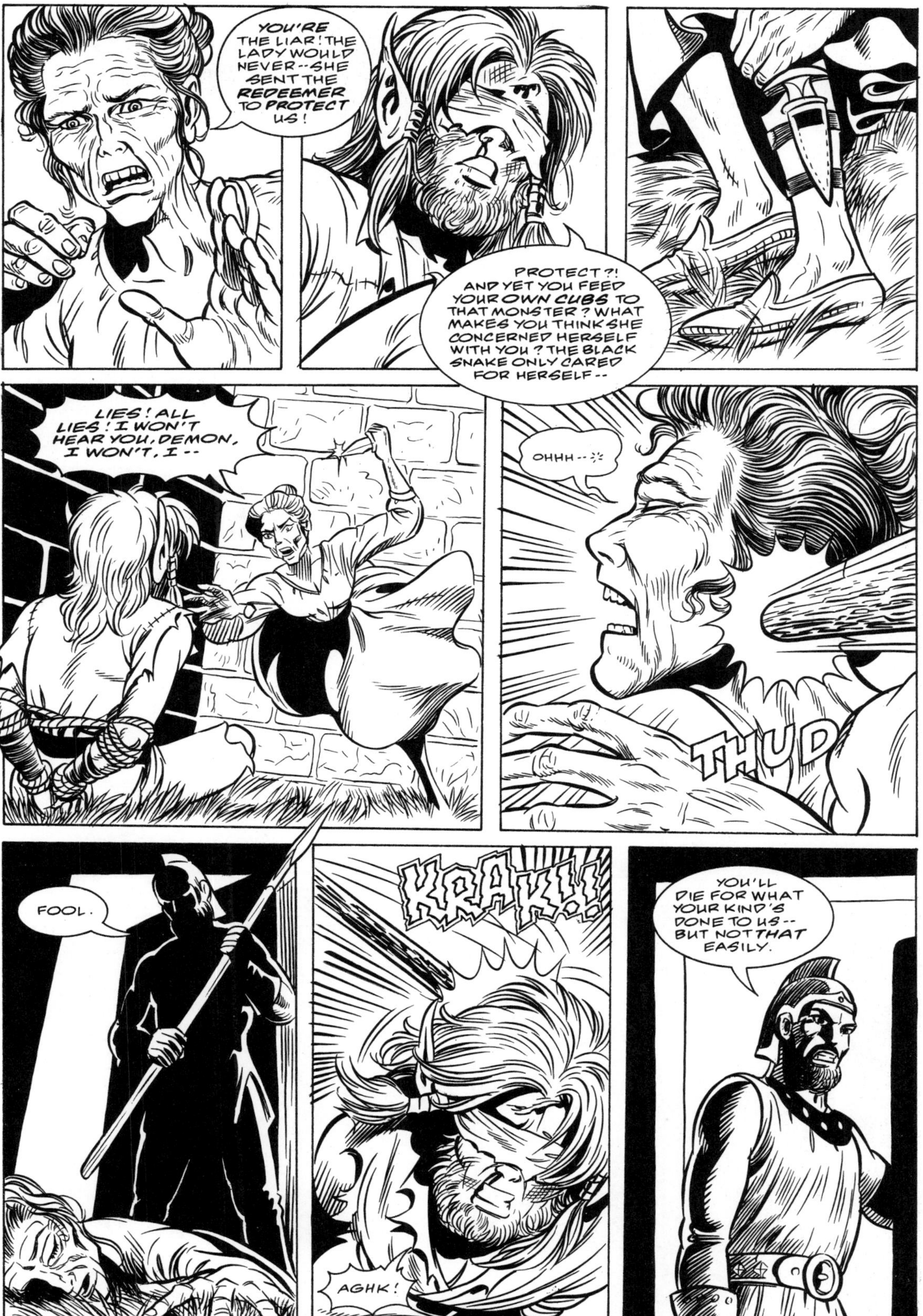
YOU'RE THE LIAR! THE LADY WOULD NEVER--SHE SENT THE REDEEMER TO PROTECT US!
PROTECT?! AND YET YOU FEED YOUR OWN CUBS TO THAT MONSTER? WHAT MAKES YOU THINK SHE CONCERNED HERSELF WITH YOU? THE BLACK SNAKE ONLY CARED FOR HERSELF--
LIES! ALL LIES! I WON'T HEAR YOU, DEMON, I WON'T, I--
OHHH--
THUD
FOOL.
KRAK!!
AGHK!
YOU'LL DIE FOR WHAT YOUR KIND'S DONE TO US--BUT NOT THAT EASILY.

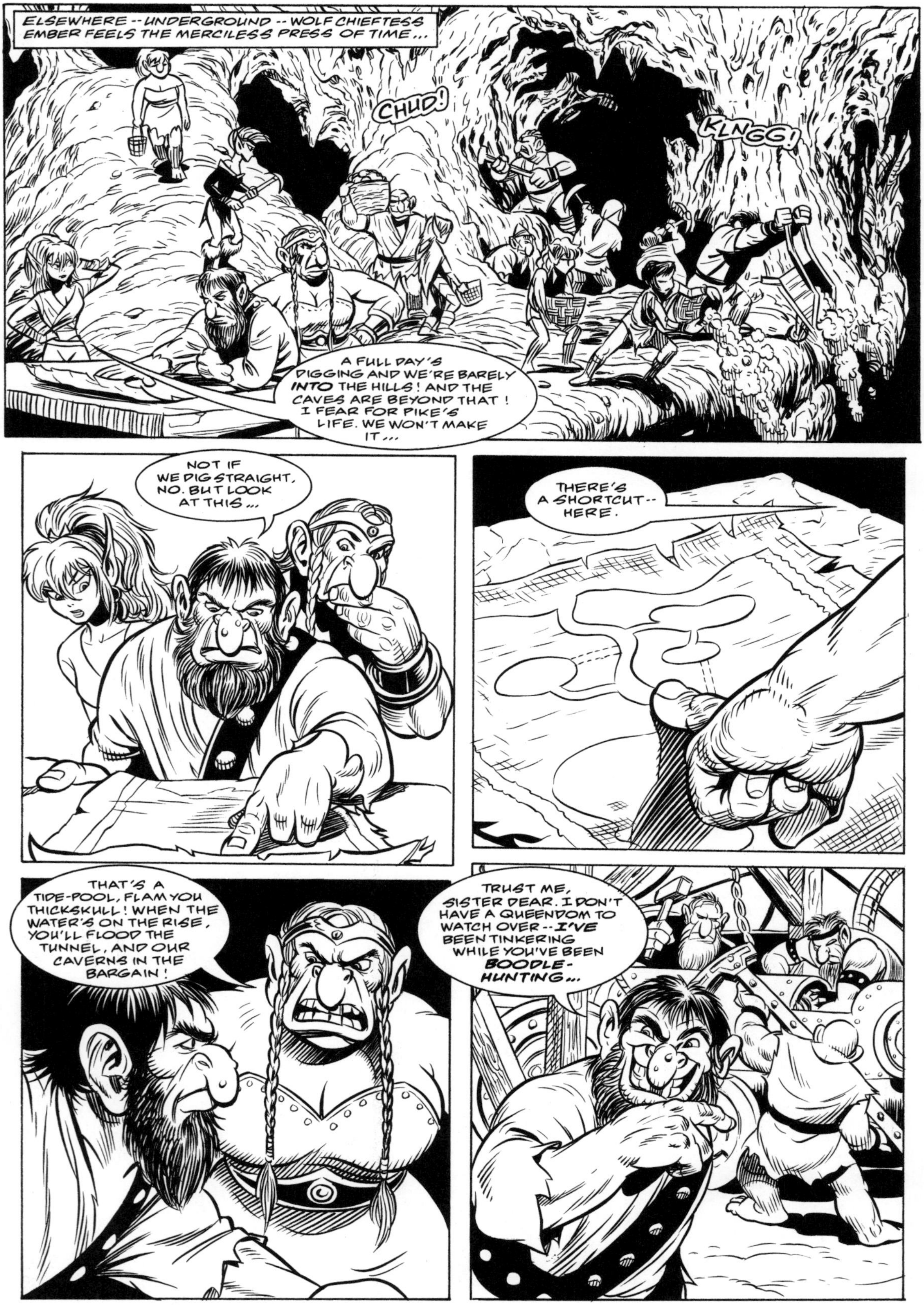
ELSEWHERE -- UNDERGROUND -- WOLF CHIEFTESS EMBER FEELS THE MERCILESS PRESS OF TIME...
CHUD!
KLNGG!
A FULL DAY'S DIGGING AND WE'RE BARELY INTO THE HILLS! AND THE CAVES ARE BEYOND THAT! I FEAR FOR PIKE'S LIFE. WE WON'T MAKE IT...
NOT IF WE DIG STRAIGHT, NO. BUT LOOK AT THIS...
THERE'S A SHORTCUT-- HERE.
THAT'S A TIDE-POOL, FLAM YOU THICKSKULL! WHEN THE WATER'S ON THE RISE, YOU'LL FLOOD THE TUNNEL, AND OUR CAVERNS IN THE BARGAIN!
TRUST ME, SISTER DEAR. I DON'T HAVE A QUEENDOM TO WATCH OVER -- I'VE BEEN TINKERING WHILE YOU'VE BEEN BOODLE-HUNTING...

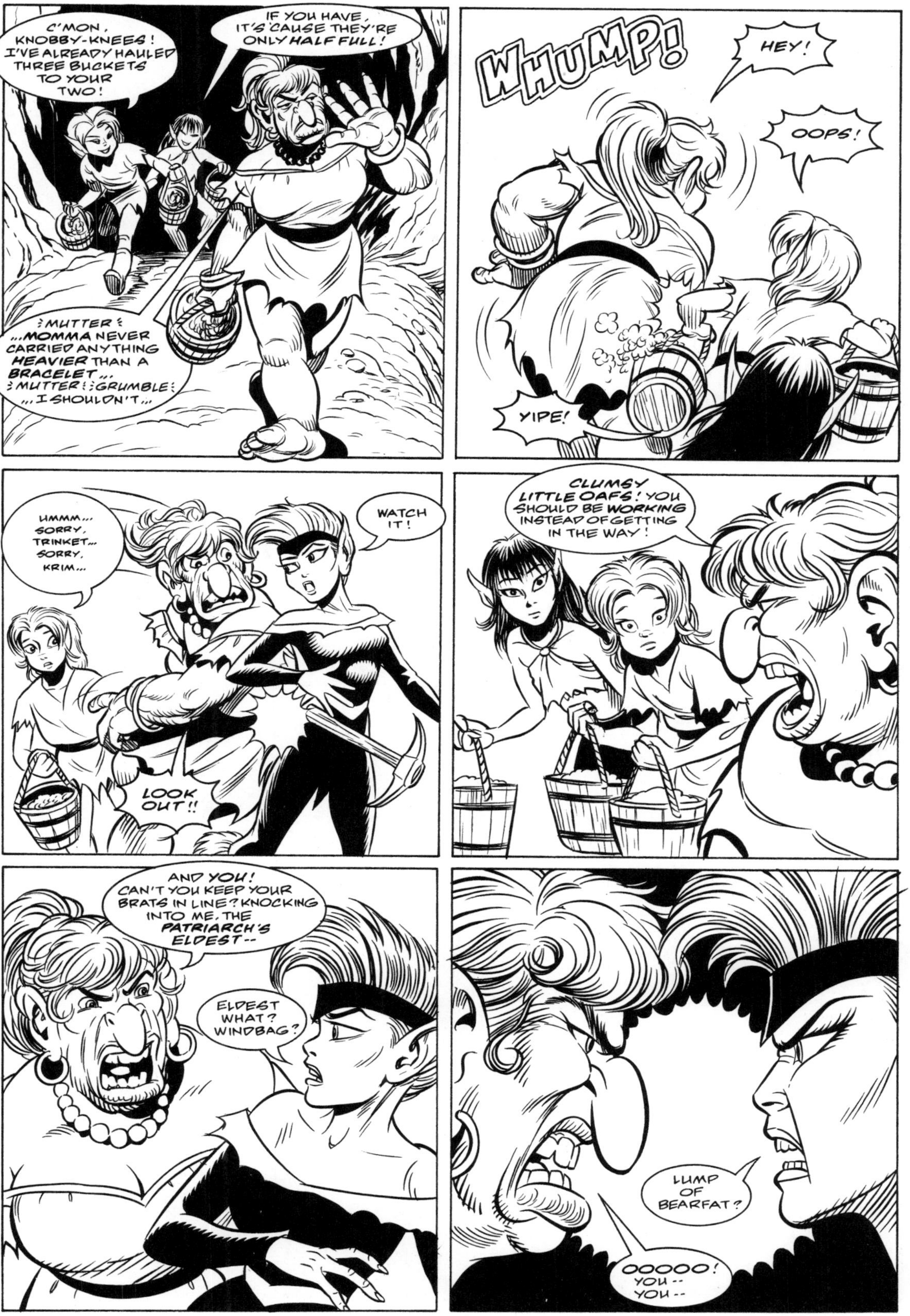
C'MON, KNOBBY-KNEES! I'VE ALREADY HAULED THREE BUCKETS TO YOUR TWO!
IF YOU HAVE, IT'S 'CAUSE THEY'RE ONLY HALF FULL!
MUTTER ...MOMMA NEVER CARRIED ANYTHING HEAVIER THAN A BRACELET... MUTTER GRUMBLE ...I SHOULDN'T...
WHUMP!
HEY!
OOPS!
YIPE!
UMMM... SORRY, TRINKET... SORRY, KRIM...
WATCH IT!
LOOK OUT!!
CLUMSY LITTLE OAFS! YOU SHOULD BE WORKING INSTEAD OF GETTING IN THE WAY!
AND YOU! CAN'T YOU KEEP YOUR BRATS IN LINE? KNOCKING INTO ME, THE PATRIARCH'S ELDEST--
ELDEST WHAT? WINDBAG?
LUMP OF BEARFAT?
OOOOO! YOU -- YOU --

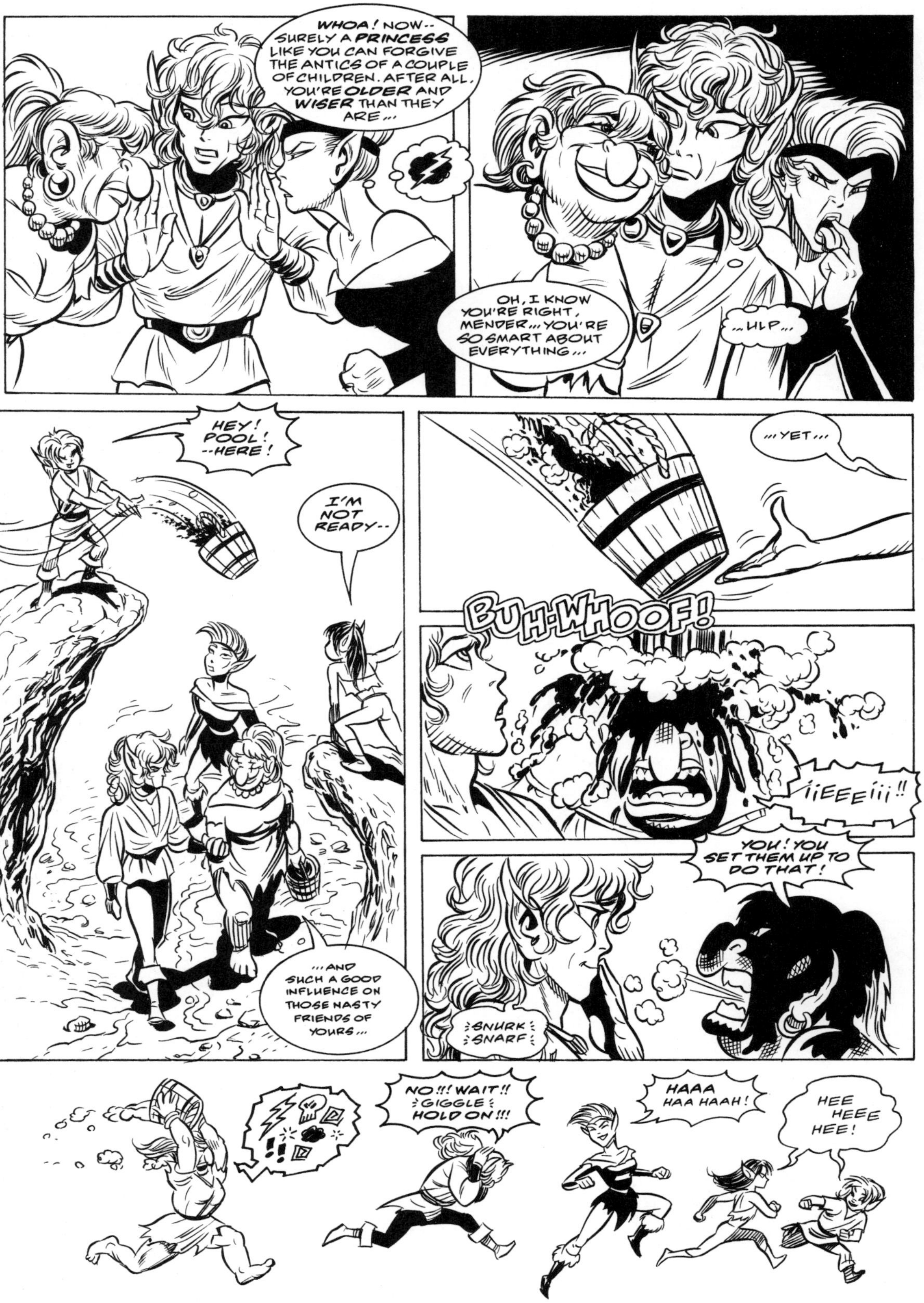

WHOA! NOW-- SURELY A PRINCESS LIKE YOU CAN FORGIVE THE ANTICS OF A COUPLE OF CHILDREN. AFTER ALL, YOU'RE OLDER AND WISER THAN THEY ARE...
OH, I KNOW YOU'RE RIGHT, MENDER... YOU'RE SO SMART ABOUT EVERYTHING...
...ULP...
HEY! POOL! --HERE!
I'M NOT READY--
...AND SUCH A GOOD INFLUENCE ON THOSE NASTY FRIENDS OF YOURS...
...YET...
BUH-WHOOF!
¡¡EEE¡¡¡!!
YOU! YOU SET THEM UP TO DO THAT!
SNURK SNARF
NO!!! WAIT!! GIGGLE HOLD ON!!!
HAAA HAA HAAH!
HEE HEEE HEE!

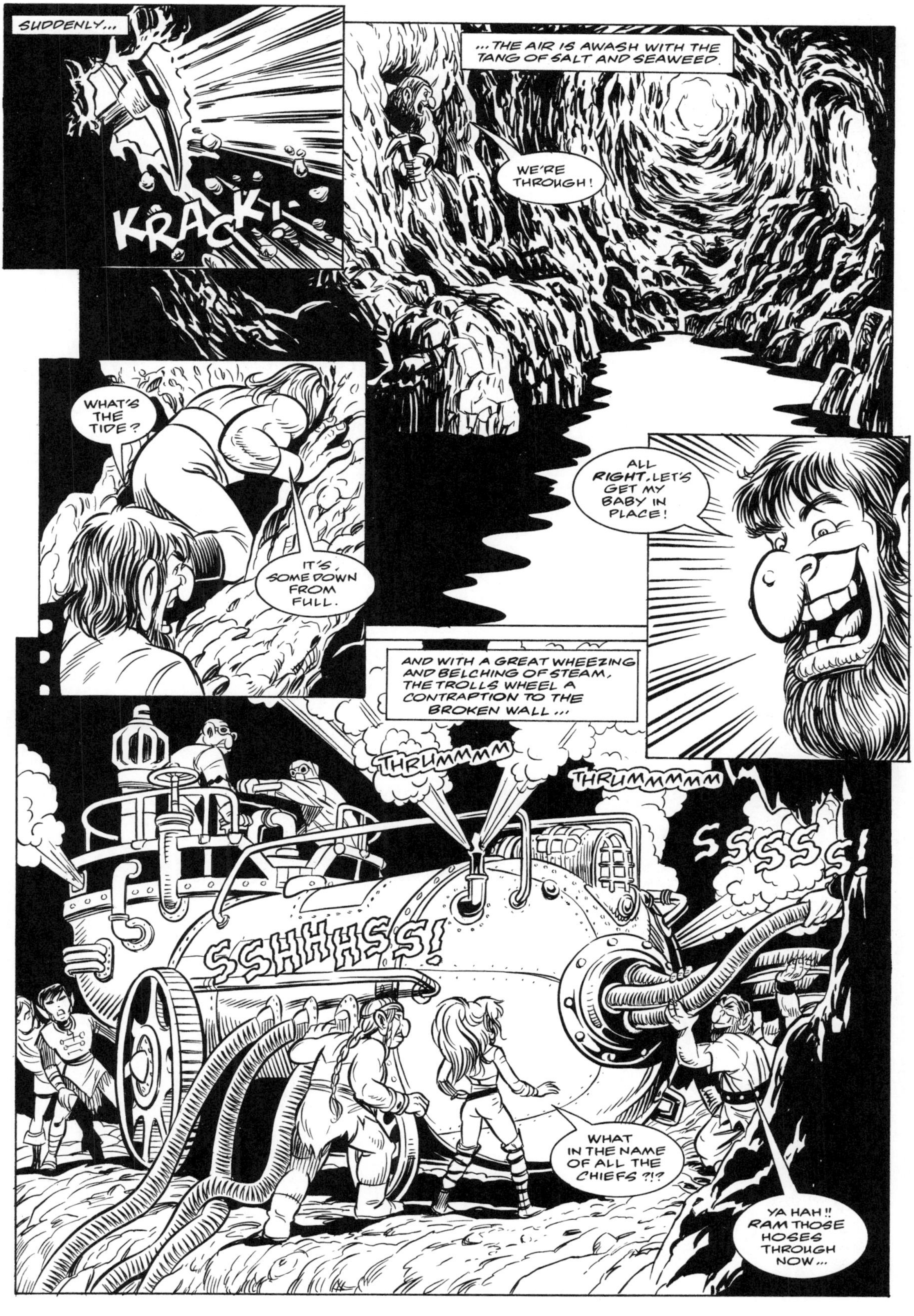

SUDDENLY...
KRACK!
...THE AIR IS AWASH WITH THE TANG OF SALT AND SEAWEED.
WE'RE THROUGH!
WHAT'S THE TIDE?
IT'S SOME DOWN FROM FULL.
ALL RIGHT. LET'S GET MY BABY IN PLACE!
AND WITH A GREAT WHEEZING AND BELCHING OF STEAM, THE TROLLS WHEEL A CONTRAPTION TO THE BROKEN WALL...
THRUMMMM
THRUMMMMM
SSSSS!
SSHHHSSS!
WHAT IN THE NAME OF ALL THE CHIEFS?!?
YA HAH!! RAM THOSE HOSES THROUGH NOW...

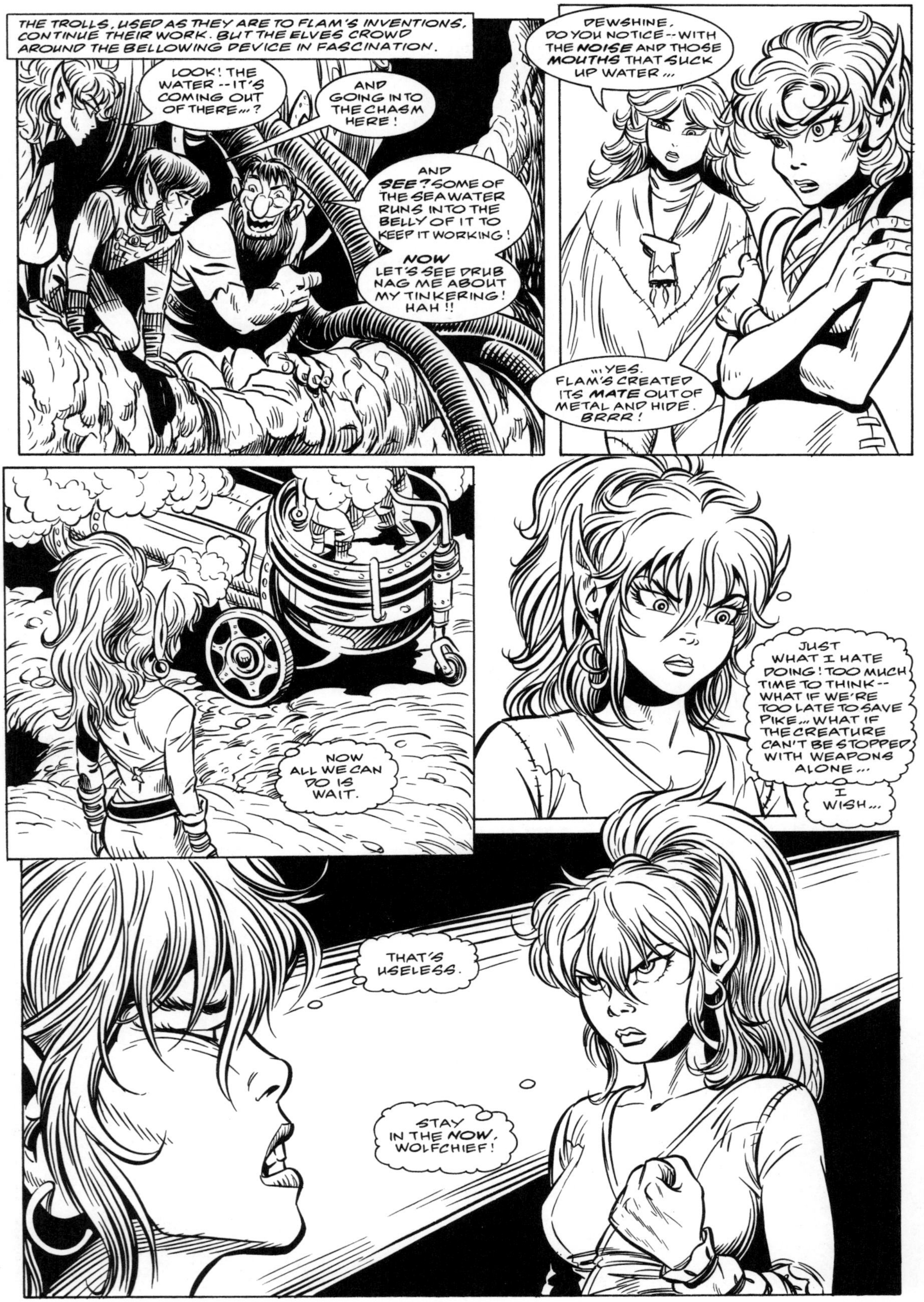
THE TROLLS, USED AS THEY ARE TO FLAM'S INVENTIONS, CONTINUE THEIR WORK. BUT THE ELVES CROWD AROUND THE BELLOWING DEVICE IN FASCINATION.
LOOK! THE WATER --IT'S COMING OUT OF THERE...?
AND GOING INTO THE CHASM HERE!
AND SEE? SOME OF THE SEAWATER RUNS INTO THE BELLY OF IT TO KEEP IT WORKING!
NOW LET'S SEE DRUB NAG ME ABOUT MY TINKERING! HAH!!
DEWSHINE, DO YOU NOTICE-- WITH THE NOISE AND THOSE MOUTHS THAT SUCK UP WATER...
...YES. FLAM'S CREATED ITS MATE OUT OF METAL AND HIDE. BRRR!
NOW ALL WE CAN DO IS WAIT.
JUST WHAT I HATE DOING! TOO MUCH TIME TO THINK-- WHAT IF WE'RE TOO LATE TO SAVE PIKE... WHAT IF THE CREATURE CAN'T BE STOPPED WITH WEAPONS ALONE...
I WISH...
THAT'S USELESS.
STAY IN THE NOW, WOLFCHIEF!

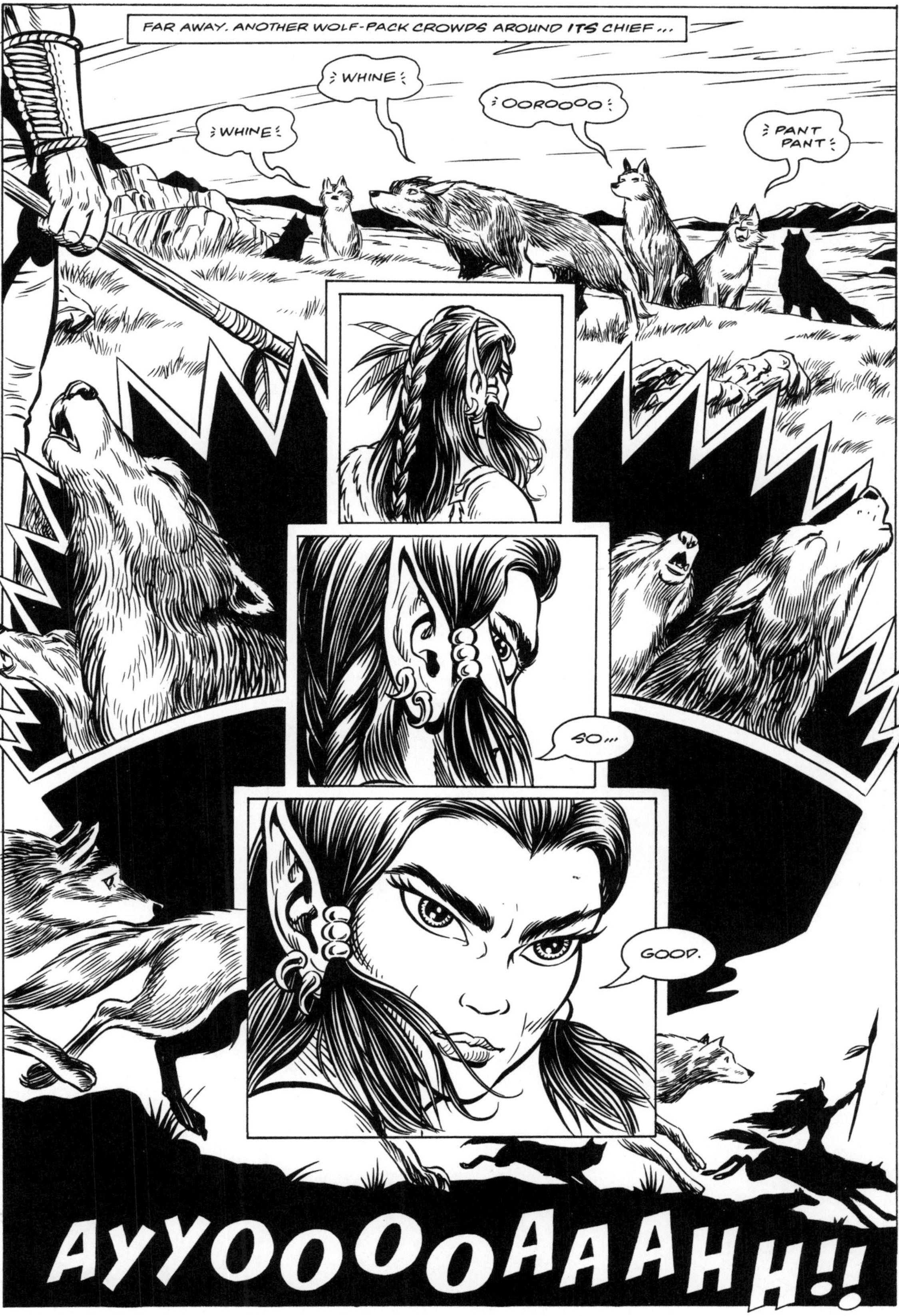
FAR AWAY, ANOTHER WOLF-PACK CROWDS AROUND ITS CHIEF...
WHINE
WHINE
OOROOOO
PANT PANT
SO...
GOOD.
AYYOOOOAAAAHH!!

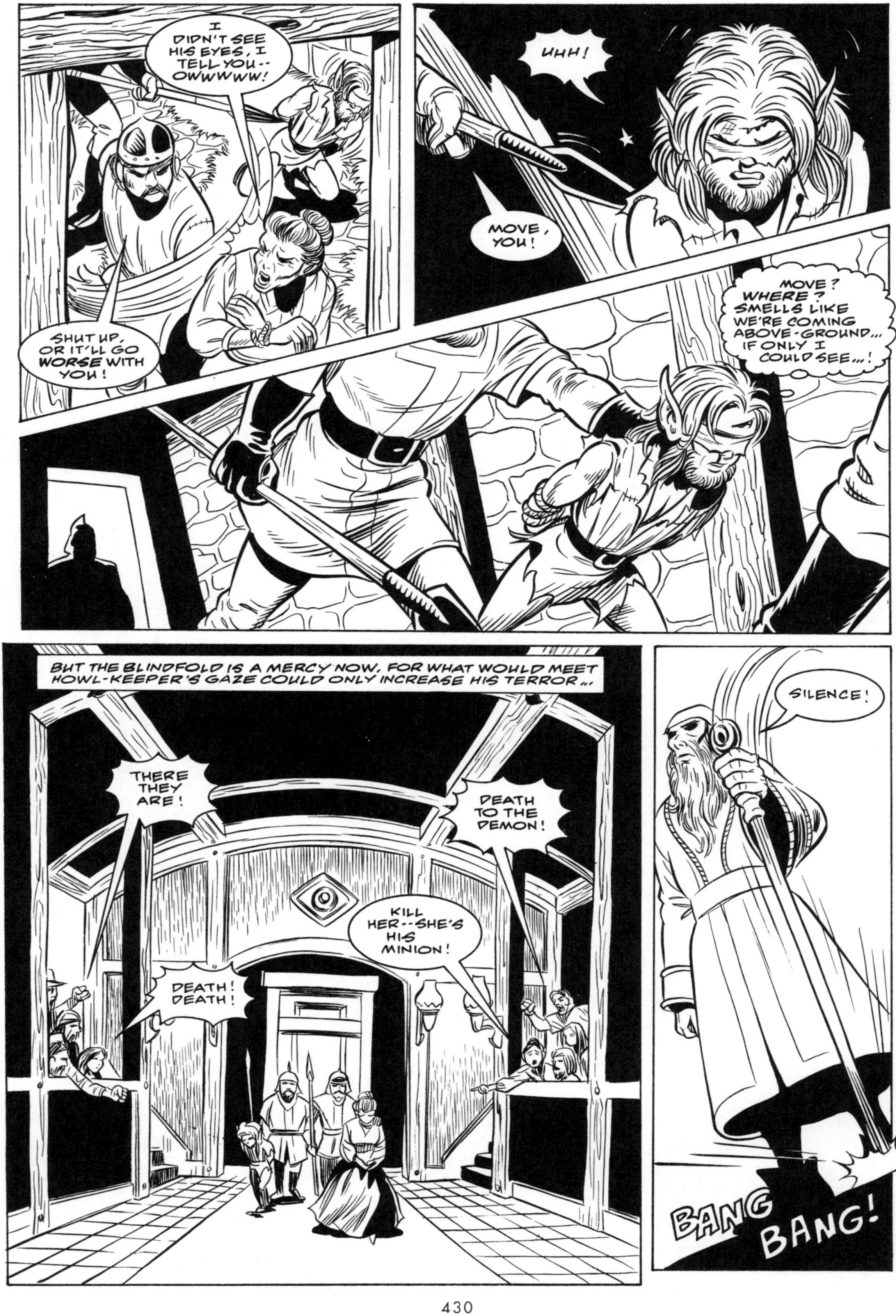

I DIDN'T SEE HIS EYES, I TELL YOU-- OWWWWW!
SHUT UP, OR IT'LL GO WORSE WITH YOU!
UHH!
MOVE, YOU!
MOVE? WHERE? SMELLS LIKE WE'RE COMING ABOVE-GROUND... IF ONLY I COULD SEE...!
BUT THE BLINDFOLD IS A MERCY NOW. FOR WHAT WOULD MEET HOWL-KEEPER'S GAZE COULD ONLY INCREASE HIS TERROR...
THERE THEY ARE!
DEATH TO THE DEMON!
KILL HER--SHE'S HIS MINION!
DEATH! DEATH!
SILENCE!
BANG BANG!

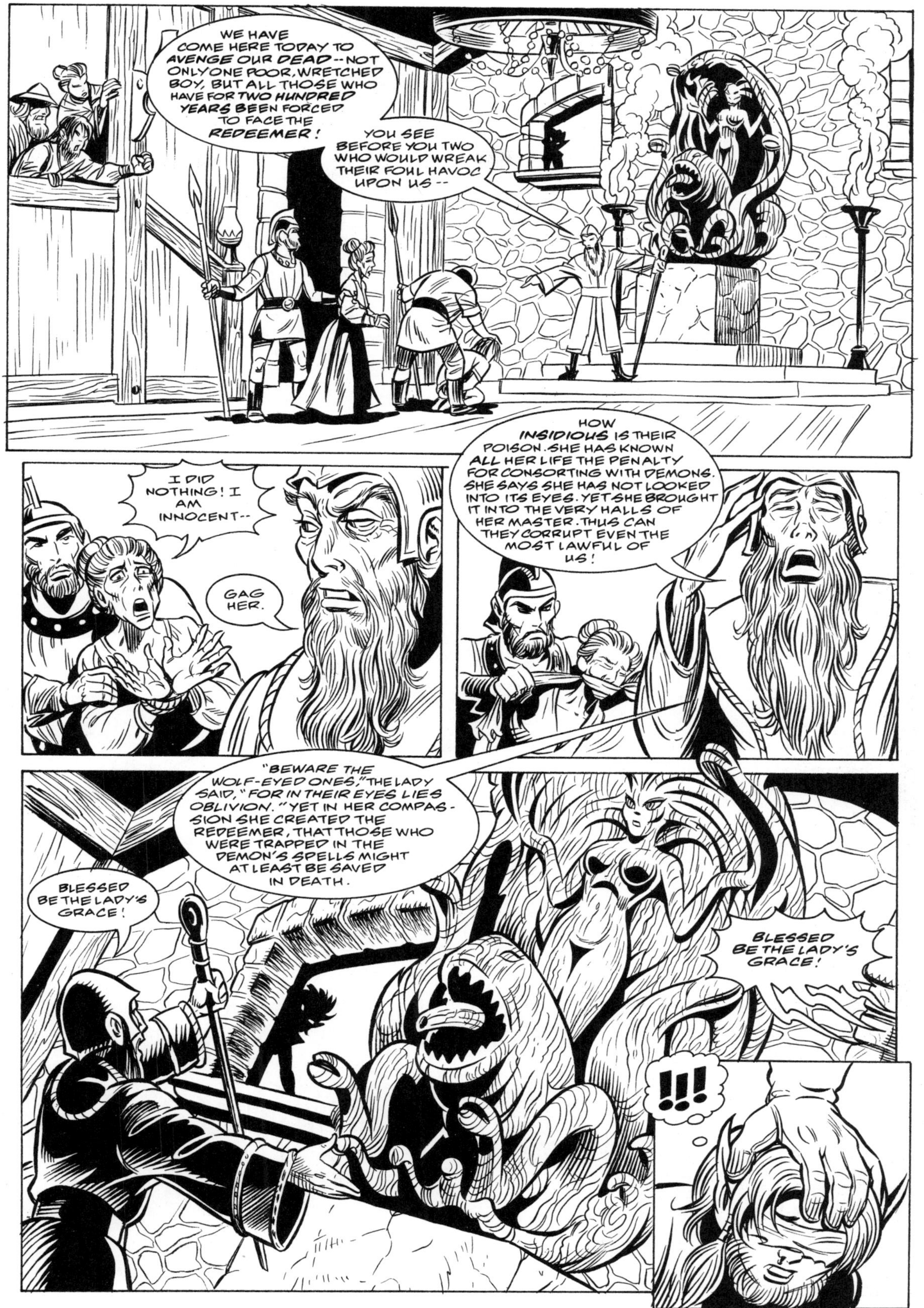

WE HAVE COME HERE TODAY TO AVENGE OUR DEAD--NOT ONLY ONE POOR, WRETCHED BOY, BUT ALL THOSE WHO HAVE FOR TWO HUNDRED YEARS BEEN FORCED TO FACE THE REDEEMER!
YOU SEE BEFORE YOU TWO WHO WOULD WREAK THEIR FOUL HAVOC UPON US--
I DID NOTHING! I AM INNOCENT--
GAG HER.
HOW INSIDIOUS IS THEIR POISON. SHE HAS KNOWN ALL HER LIFE THE PENALTY FOR CONSORTING WITH DEMONS. SHE SAYS SHE HAS NOT LOOKED INTO ITS EYES. YET SHE BROUGHT IT INTO THE VERY HALLS OF HER MASTER. THUS CAN THEY CORRUPT EVEN THE MOST LAWFUL OF US!
"BEWARE THE WOLF-EYED ONES," THE LADY SAID, "FOR IN THEIR EYES LIES OBLIVION." YET IN HER COMPASSION SHE CREATED THE REDEEMER, THAT THOSE WHO WERE TRAPPED IN THE DEMON'S SPELLS MIGHT AT LEAST BE SAVED IN DEATH.
BLESSED BE THE LADY'S GRACE!
BLESSED BE THE LADY'S GRACE!
!!!

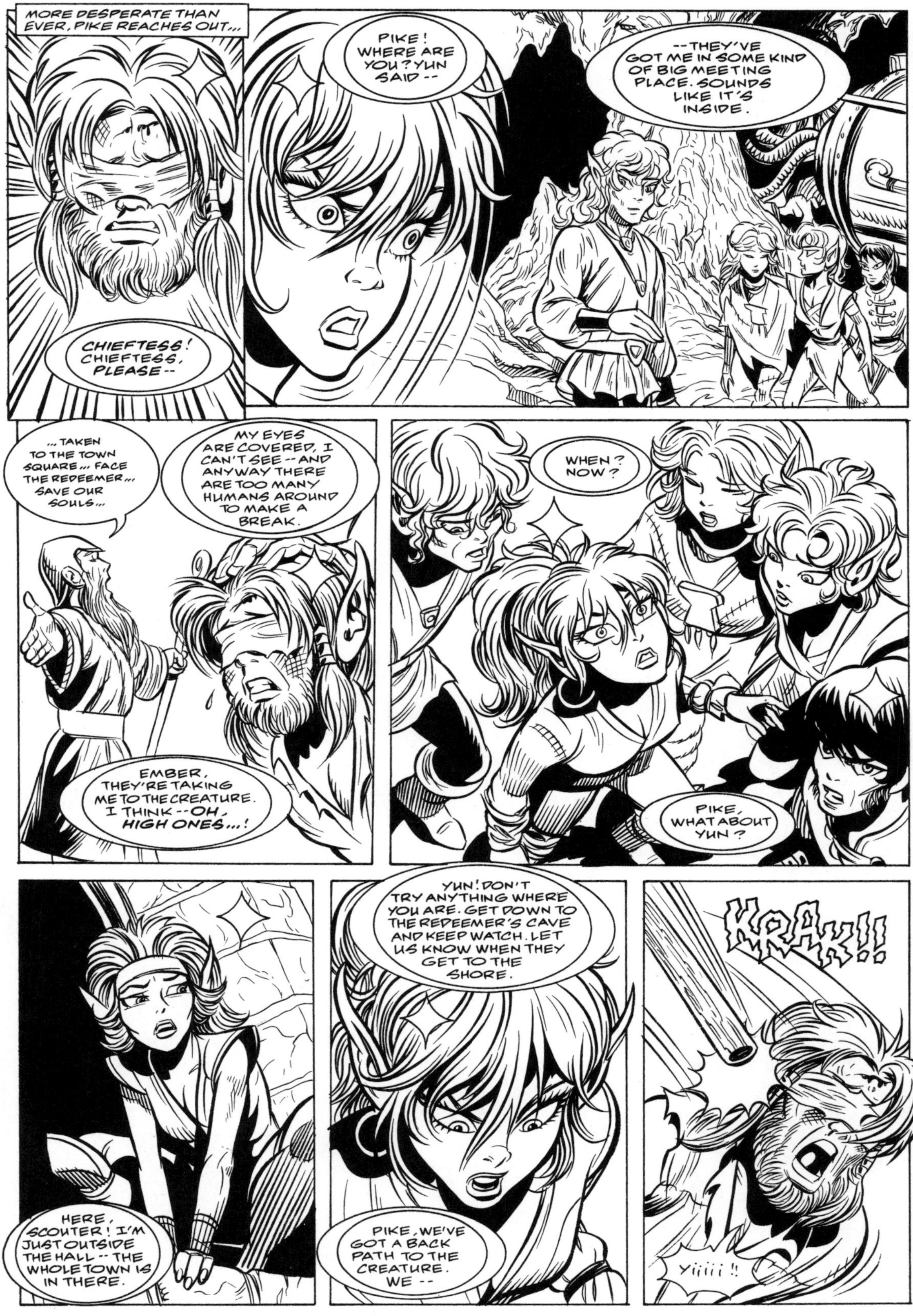
MORE DESPERATE THAN EVER, PIKE REACHES OUT...
CHIEFTESS! CHIEFTESS, PLEASE--
PIKE! WHERE ARE YOU? YUN SAID--
--THEY'VE GOT ME IN SOME KIND OF BIG MEETING PLACE. SOUNDS LIKE IT'S INSIDE.
...TAKEN TO THE TOWN SQUARE... FACE THE REDEEMER... SAVE OUR SOULS...
MY EYES ARE COVERED, I CAN'T SEE--AND ANYWAY THERE ARE TOO MANY HUMANS AROUND TO MAKE A BREAK.
EMBER, THEY'RE TAKING ME TO THE CREATURE. I THINK--OH, HIGH ONES...!
WHEN? NOW?
PIKE, WHAT ABOUT YUN?
HERE, SCOUTER! I'M JUST OUTSIDE THE HALL--THE WHOLE TOWN IS IN THERE.
YUN! DON'T TRY ANYTHING WHERE YOU ARE. GET DOWN TO THE REDEEMER'S CAVE AND KEEP WATCH. LET US KNOW WHEN THEY GET TO THE SHORE.
PIKE, WE'VE GOT A BACK PATH TO THE CREATURE. WE--
KRAK!!
Yiiiii!!

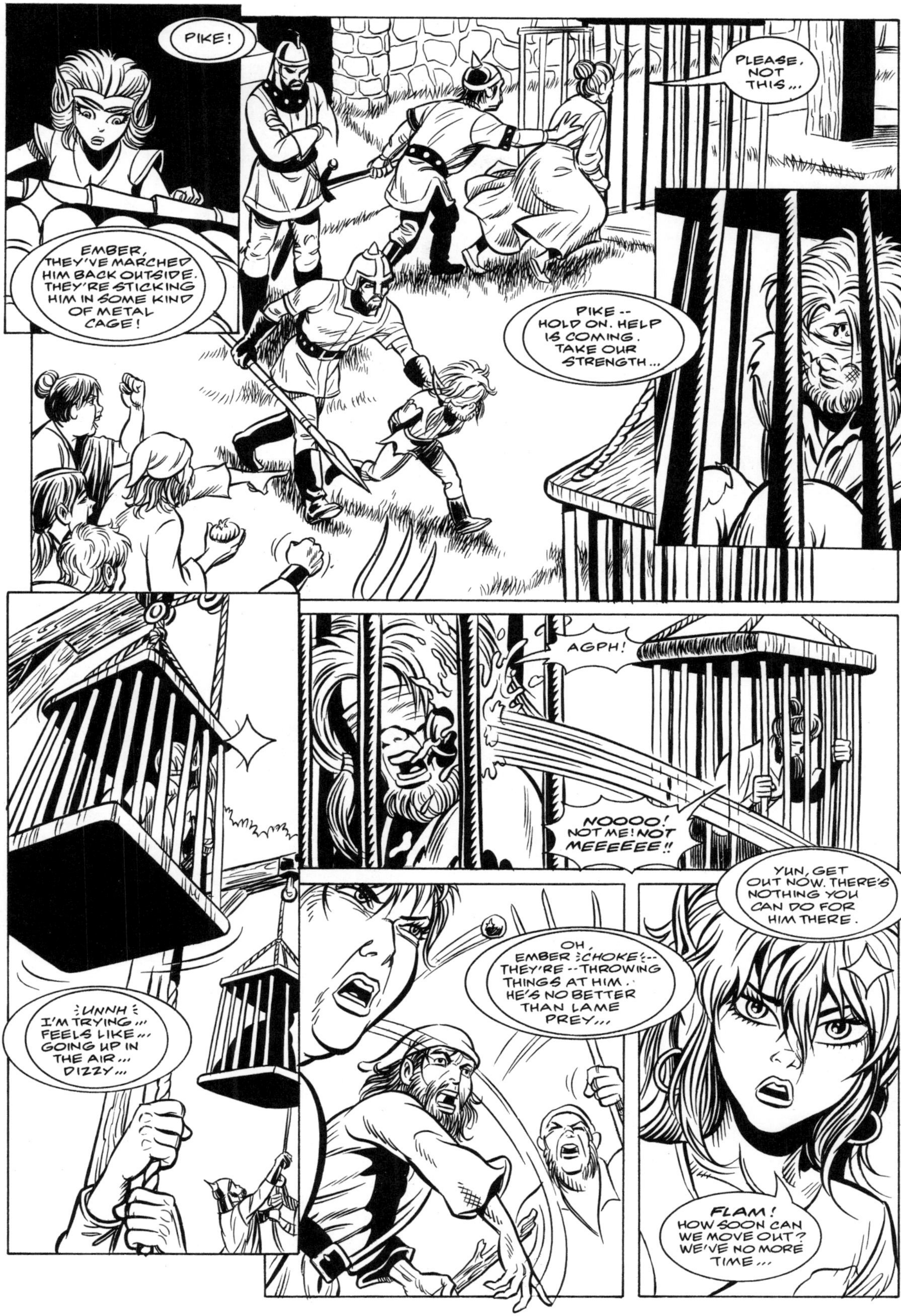
PIKE!
EMBER, THEY'VE MARCHED HIM BACK OUTSIDE. THEY'RE STICKING HIM IN SOME KIND OF METAL CAGE!
PLEASE, NOT THIS...
PIKE -- HOLD ON. HELP IS COMING. TAKE OUR STRENGTH...
UNNH I'M TRYING... FEELS LIKE... GOING UP IN THE AIR... DIZZY...
AGPH!
NOOOO! NOT ME! NOT MEEEEEE!!
OH, EMBER CHOKE -- THEY'RE -- THROWING THINGS AT HIM. HE'S NO BETTER THAN LAME PREY...
YUN, GET OUT NOW. THERE'S NOTHING YOU CAN DO FOR HIM THERE.
FLAM! HOW SOON CAN WE MOVE OUT? WE'VE NO MORE TIME...

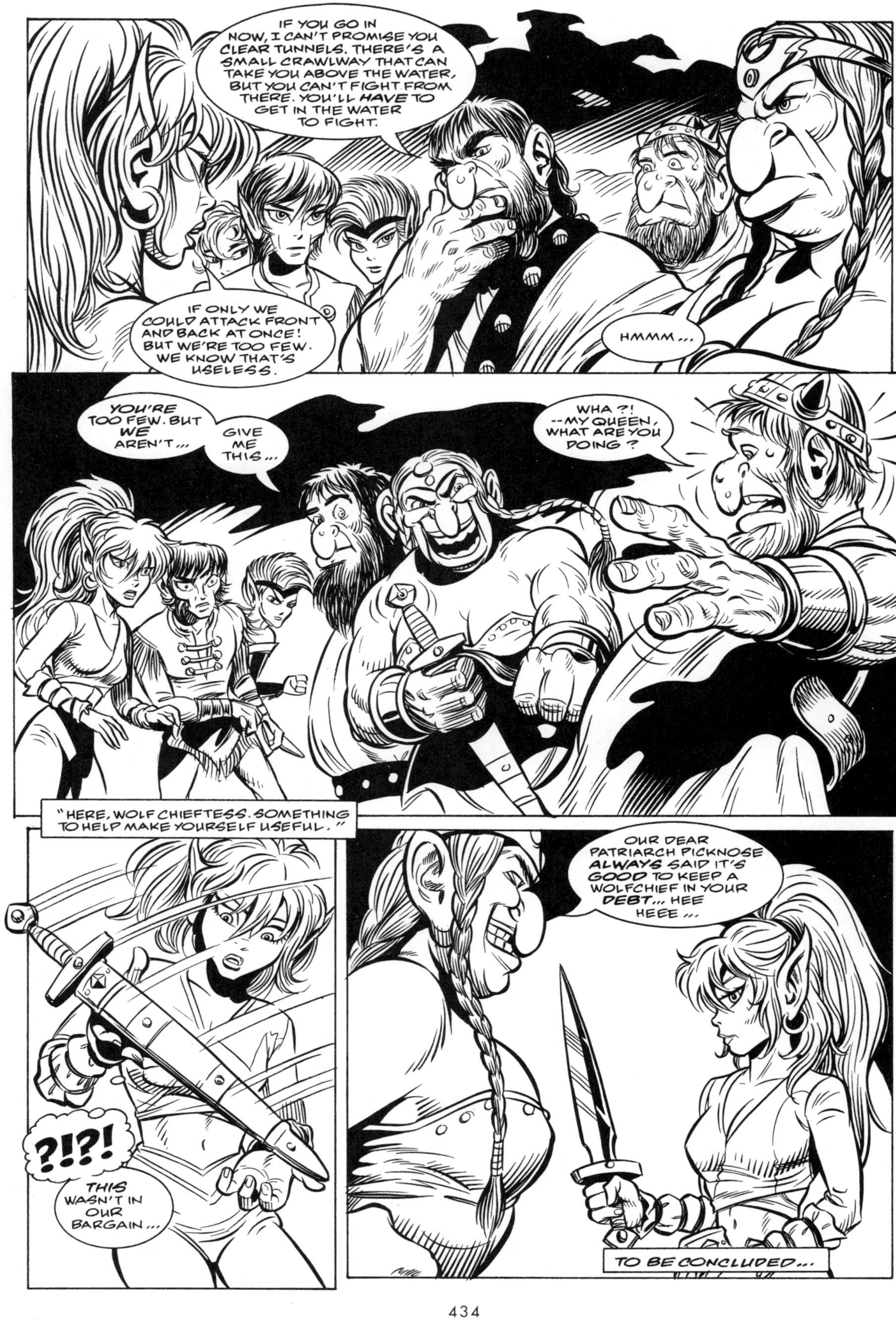
IF YOU GO IN NOW, I CAN'T PROMISE YOU CLEAR TUNNELS. THERE'S A SMALL CRAWLWAY THAT CAN TAKE YOU ABOVE THE WATER, BUT YOU CAN'T FIGHT FROM THERE. YOU'LL HAVE TO GET IN THE WATER TO FIGHT.
IF ONLY WE COULD ATTACK FRONT AND BACK AT ONCE! BUT WE'RE TOO FEW. WE KNOW THAT'S USELESS.
HMMM...
YOU'RE TOO FEW. BUT WE AREN'T...
GIVE ME THIS...
WHA ?! --MY QUEEN, WHAT ARE YOU DOING ?
"HERE, WOLF CHIEFTESS. SOMETHING TO HELP MAKE YOURSELF USEFUL."
?!?!
THIS WASN'T IN OUR BARGAIN...
OUR DEAR PATRIARCH PICKNOSE ALWAYS SAID IT'S GOOD TO KEEP A WOLFCHIEF IN YOUR DEBT... HEE HEEE...
TO BE CONCLUDED...

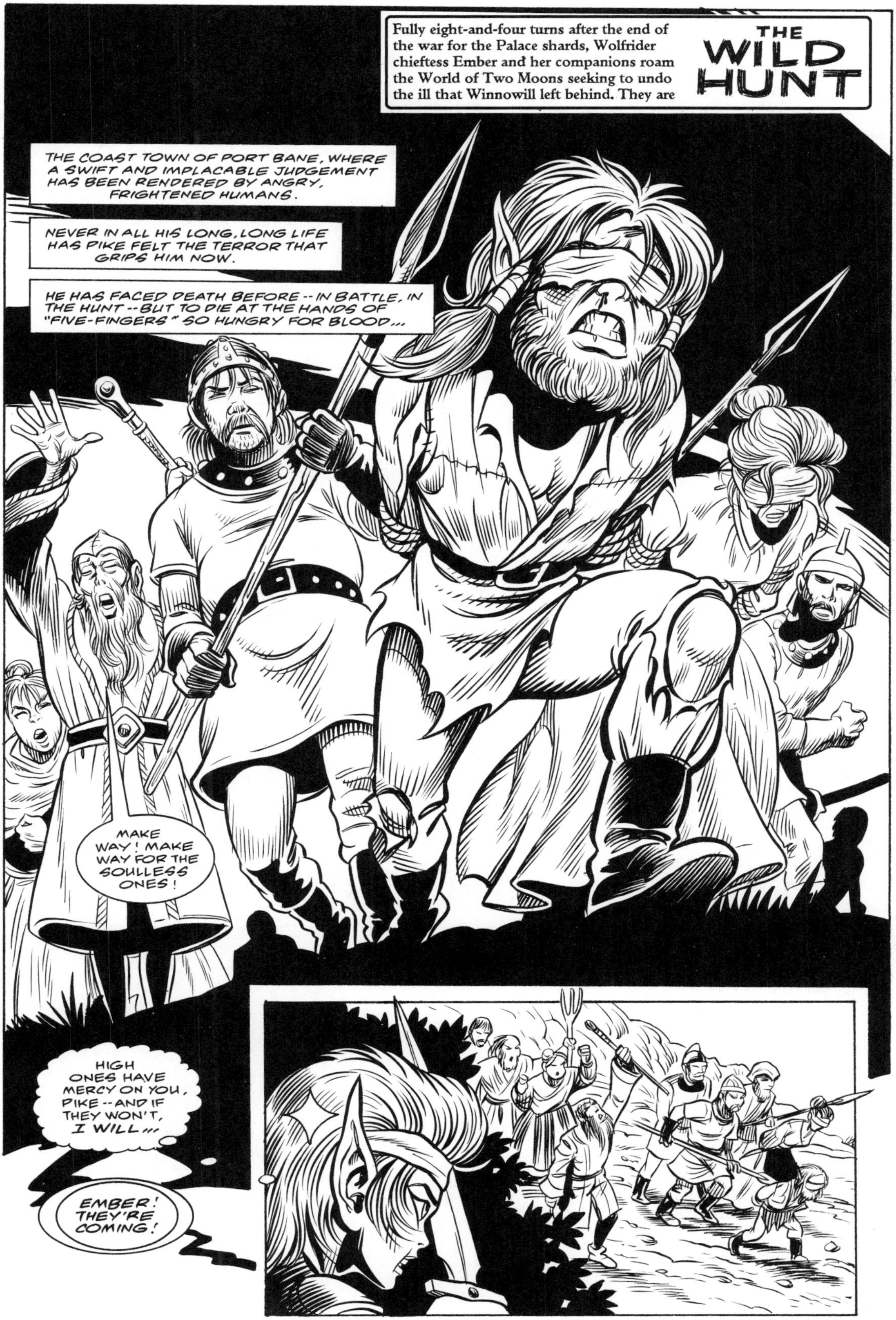

Fully eight-and-four turns after the end of the war for the Palace shards, Wolfrider chieftess Ember and her companions roam the World of Two Moons seeking to undo the ill that Winnowill left behind. They are
THE WILD HUNT
THE COAST TOWN OF PORT BANE, WHERE A SWIFT AND IMPLACABLE JUDGEMENT HAS BEEN RENDERED BY ANGRY, FRIGHTENED HUMANS.
NEVER IN ALL HIS LONG, LONG LIFE HAS PIKE FELT THE TERROR THAT GRIPS HIM NOW.
HE HAS FACED DEATH BEFORE -- IN BATTLE, IN THE HUNT -- BUT TO DIE AT THE HANDS OF "FIVE-FINGERS" SO HUNGRY FOR BLOOD...
MAKE WAY! MAKE WAY FOR THE SOULLESS ONES!
HIGH ONES HAVE MERCY ON YOU, PIKE -- AND IF THEY WON'T, I WILL...
EMBER! THEY'RE COMING!

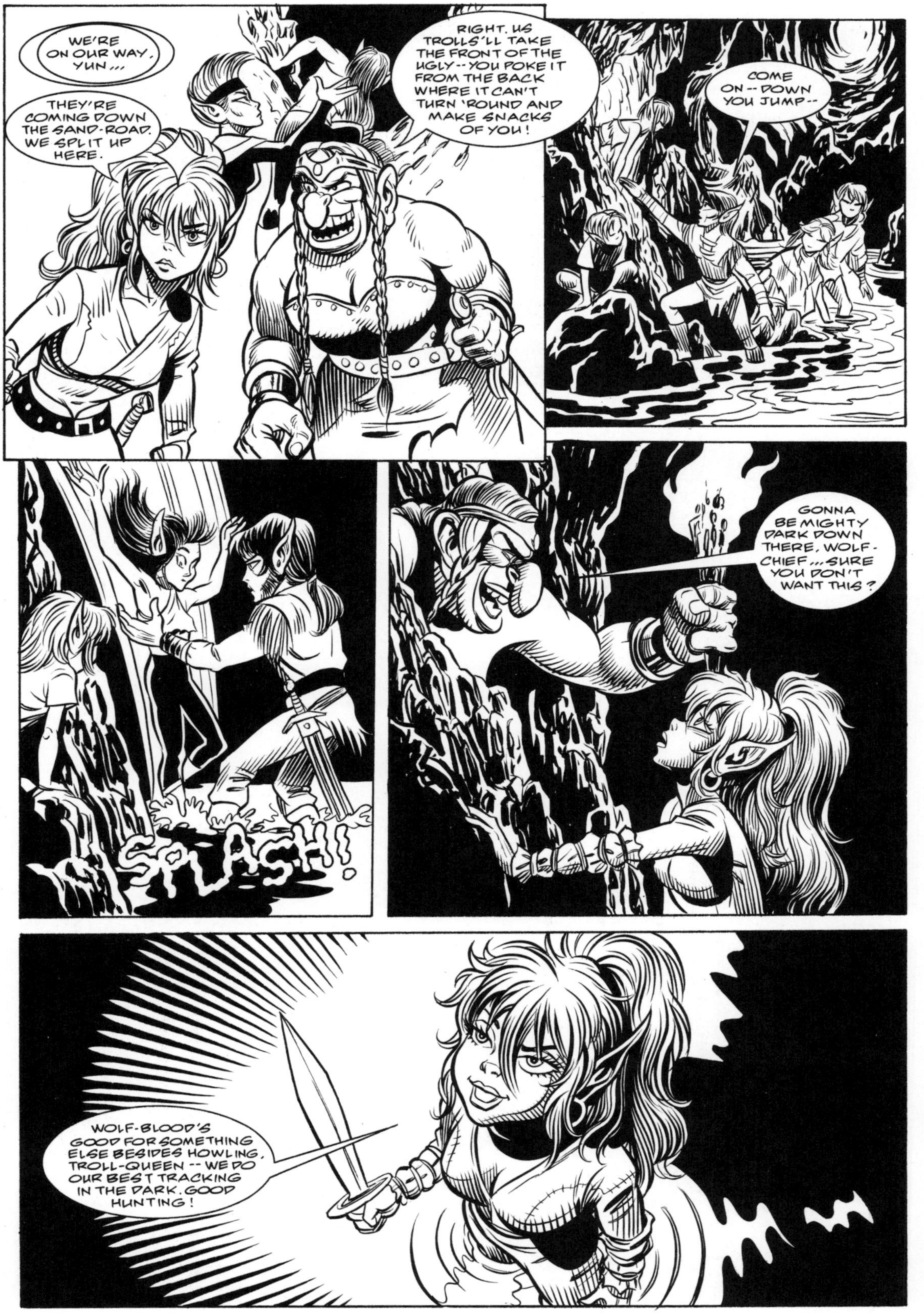
WE'RE ON OUR WAY, YUN ...
THEY'RE COMING DOWN THE SAND-ROAD. WE SPLIT UP HERE.
RIGHT. US TROLLS'LL TAKE THE FRONT OF THE UGLY -- YOU POKE IT FROM THE BACK WHERE IT CAN'T TURN 'ROUND AND MAKE SNACKS OF YOU!
COME ON -- DOWN YOU JUMP --
SPLASH!
GONNA BE MIGHTY DARK DOWN THERE, WOLF-CHIEF ... SURE YOU DON'T WANT THIS?
WOLF-BLOOD'S GOOD FOR SOMETHING ELSE BESIDES HOWLING, TROLL-QUEEN -- WE DO OUR BEST TRACKING IN THE DARK. GOOD HUNTING!

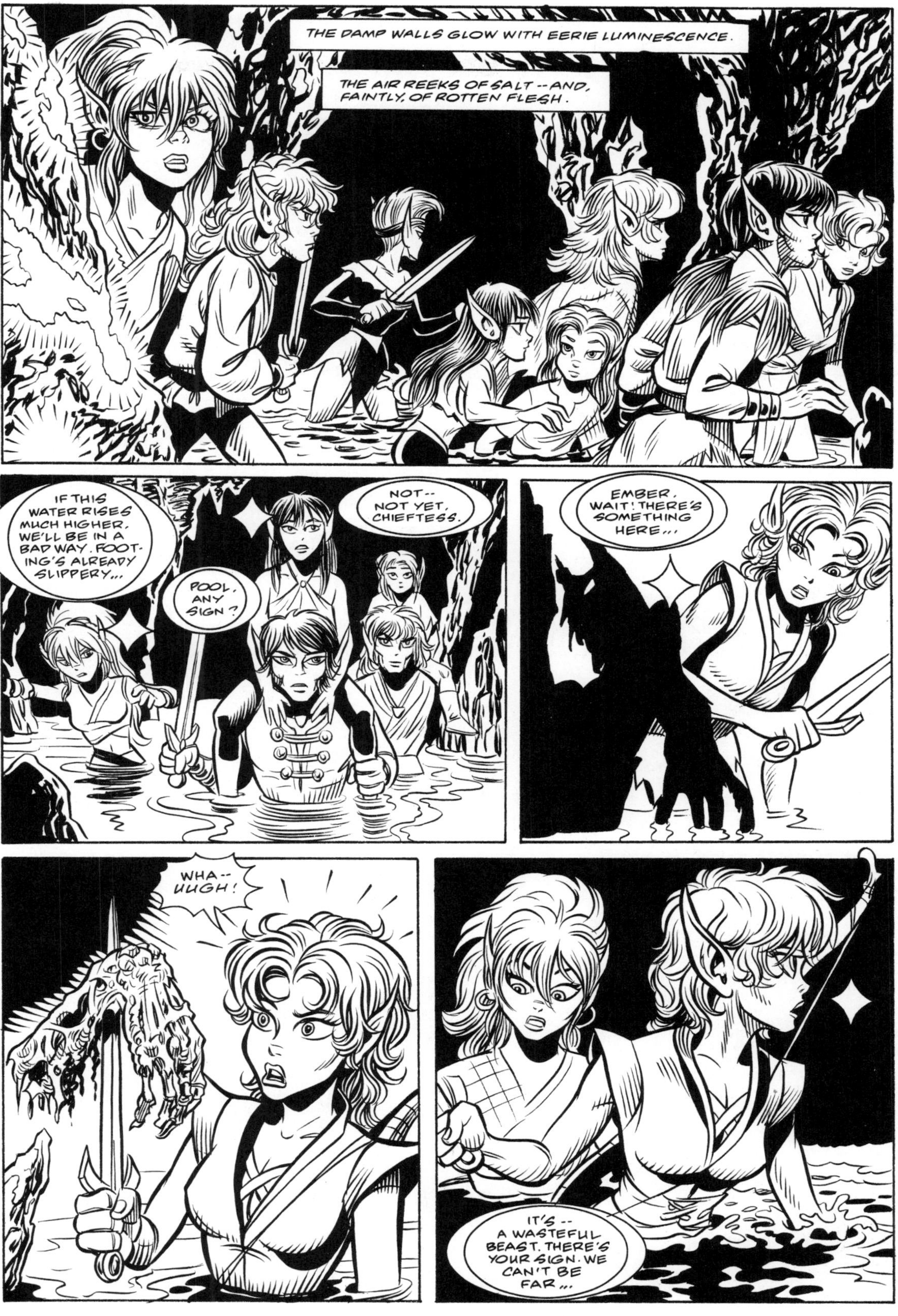
THE DAMP WALLS GLOW WITH EERIE LUMINESCENCE.
THE AIR REEKS OF SALT -- AND, FAINTLY, OF ROTTEN FLESH.
IF THIS WATER RISES MUCH HIGHER, WE'LL BE IN A BAD WAY. FOOTING'S ALREADY SLIPPERY...
NOT -- NOT YET, CHIEFTESS.
POOL, ANY SIGN?
EMBER, WAIT! THERE'S SOMETHING HERE...
WHA -- UUGH!
IT'S -- A WASTEFUL BEAST. THERE'S YOUR SIGN. WE CAN'T BE FAR...

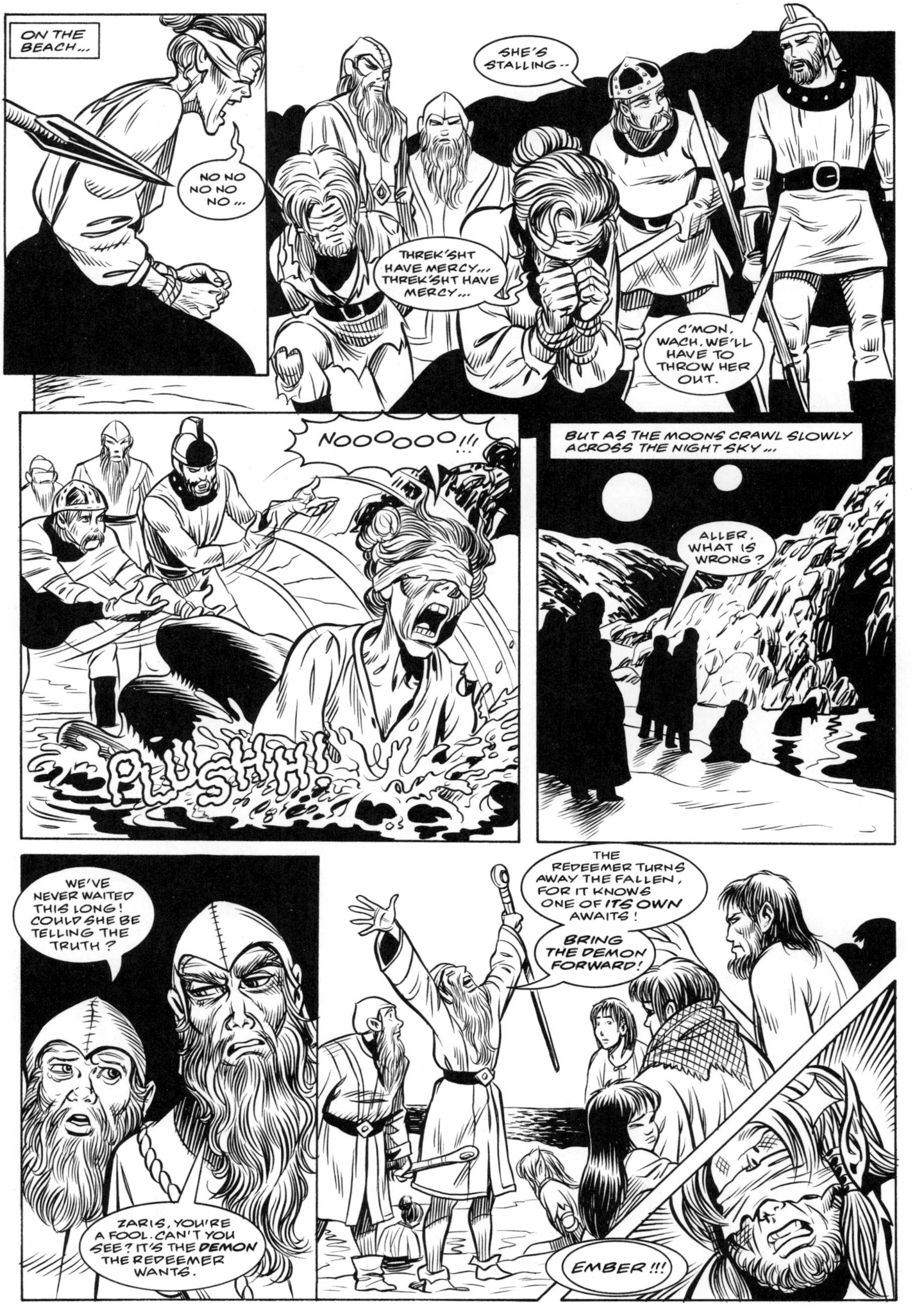

ON THE BEACH...
NO NO NO NO NO...
SHE'S STALLING--
THREK'SHT HAVE MERCY... THREK'SHT HAVE MERCY...
C'MON, WACH. WE'LL HAVE TO THROW HER OUT.
NOOOOOOO!!!
PLUSHH!
BUT AS THE MOONS CRAWL SLOWLY ACROSS THE NIGHT SKY...
ALLER, WHAT IS WRONG?
WE'VE NEVER WAITED THIS LONG! COULD SHE BE TELLING THE TRUTH?
ZARIS, YOU'RE A FOOL. CAN'T YOU SEE? IT'S THE DEMON THE REDEEMER WANTS.
THE REDEEMER TURNS AWAY THE FALLEN, FOR IT KNOWS ONE OF ITS OWN AWAITS!
BRING THE DEMON FORWARD!
EMBER!!!

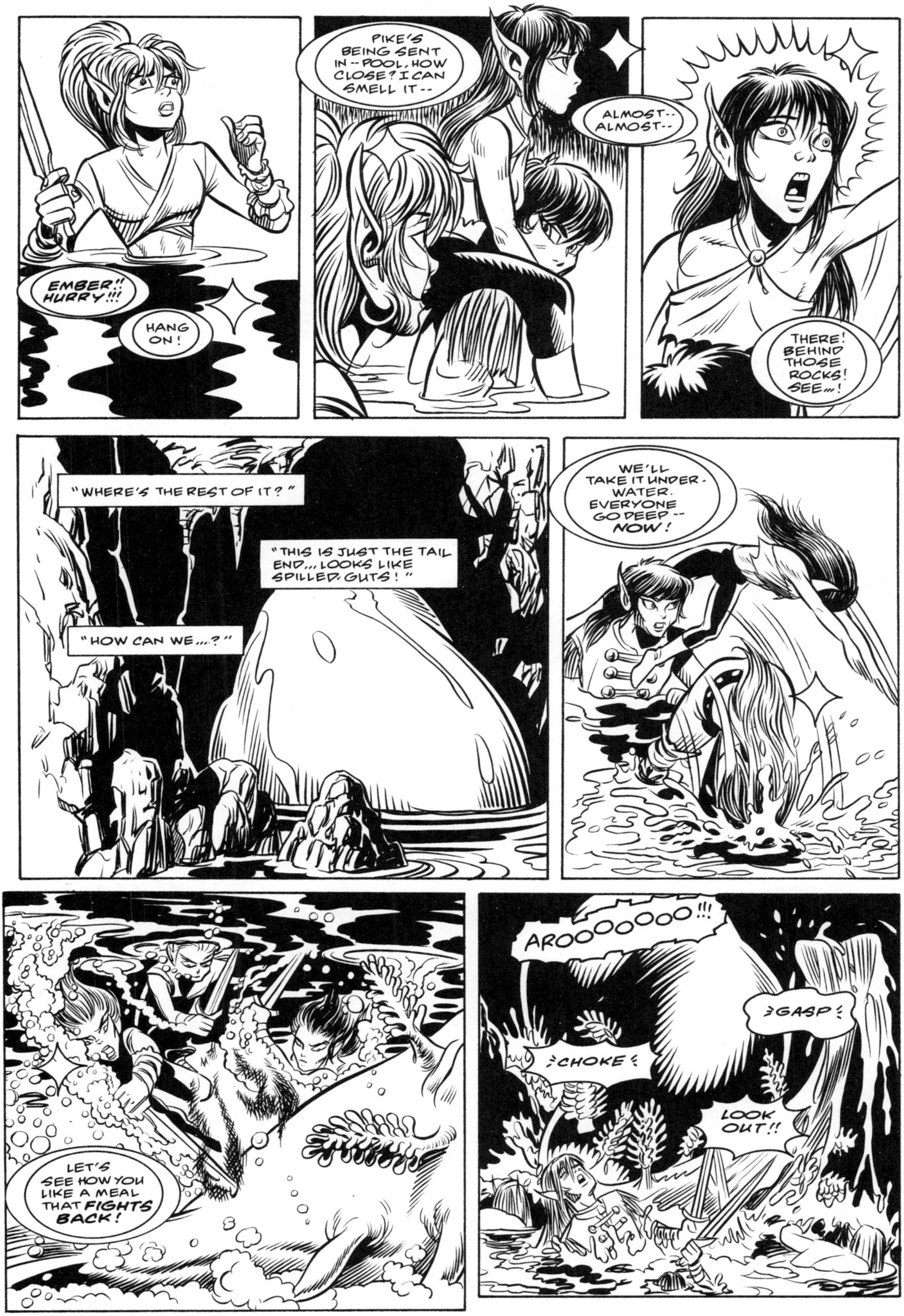
EMBER!! HURRY!!!
HANG ON!
PIKE'S BEING SENT IN -- POOL, HOW CLOSE? I CAN SMELL IT --
ALMOST -- ALMOST --
THERE! BEHIND THOSE ROCKS! SEE...!
"WHERE'S THE REST OF IT?"
"THIS IS JUST THE TAIL END... LOOKS LIKE SPILLED GUTS!"
"HOW CAN WE...?"
WE'LL TAKE IT UNDER-WATER. EVERYONE GO DEEP -- NOW!
LET'S SEE HOW YOU LIKE A MEAL THAT FIGHTS BACK!
AROOOOOOOO!!!
GASP
CHOKE
LOOK OUT!!

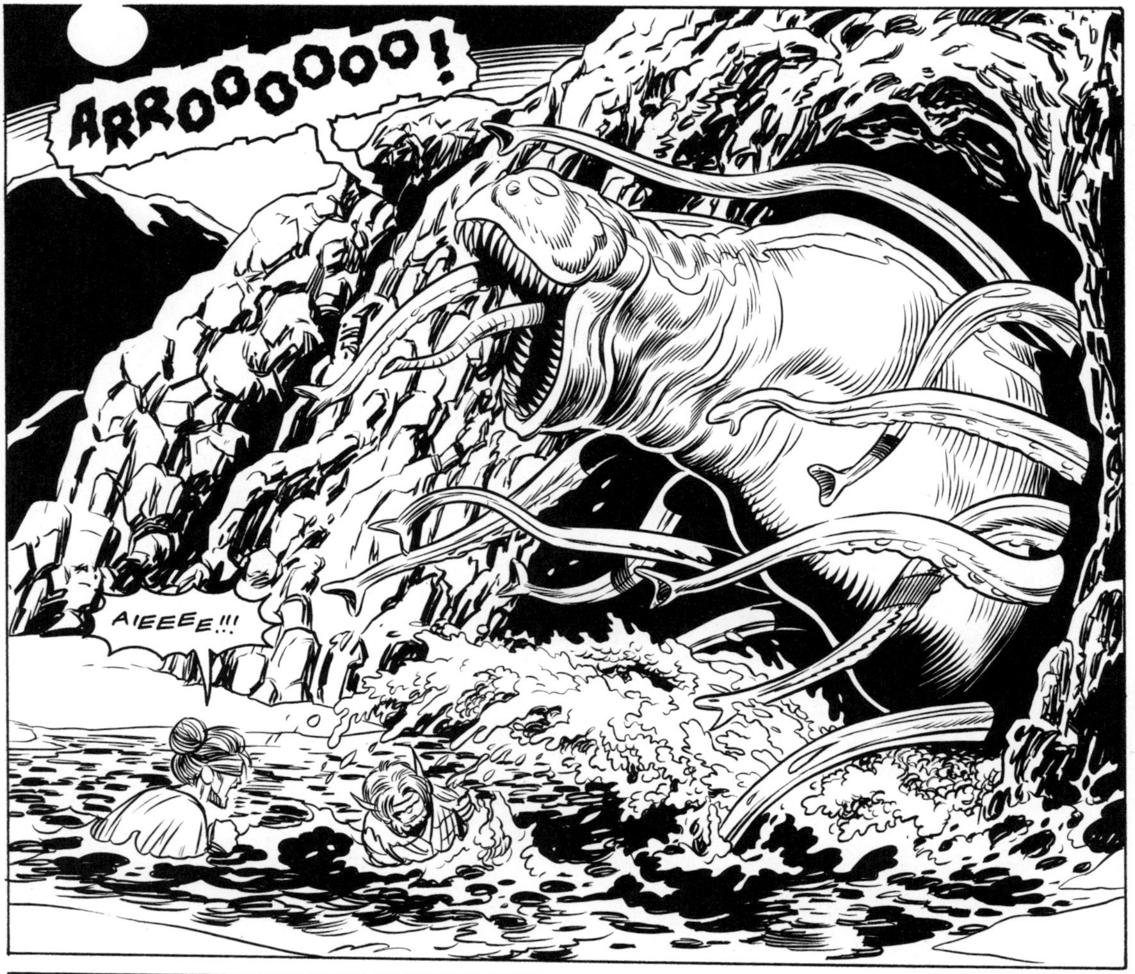
ARROOOOOOO!
AIEEEE!!!
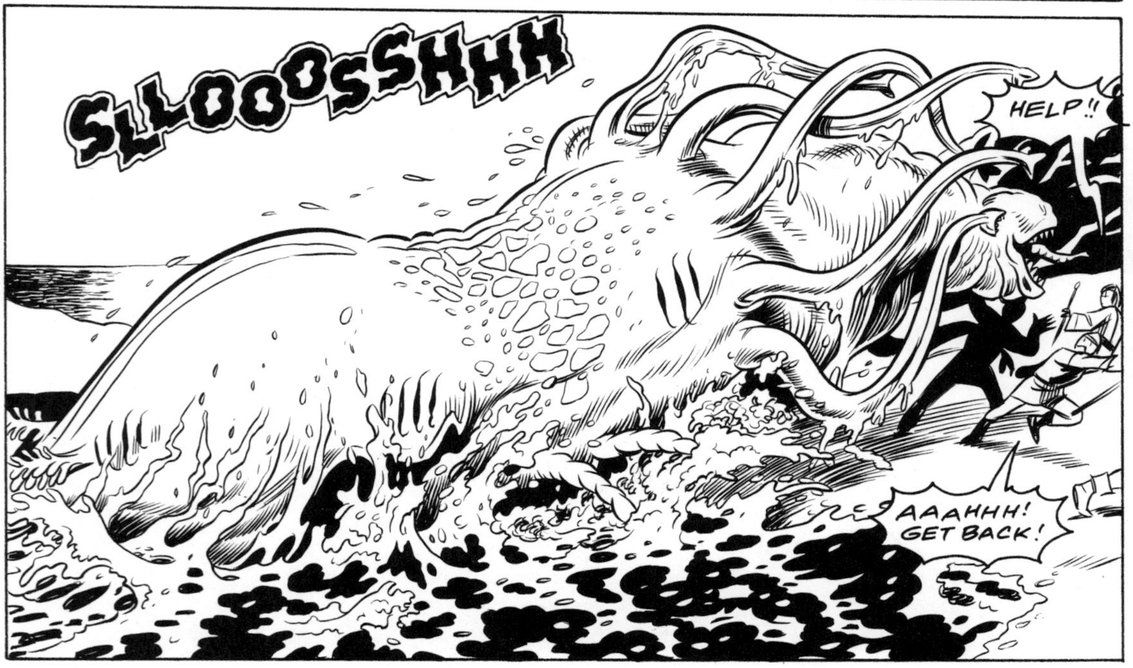
SLLOOOOSSHHH
HELP!!
AAAHHH! GET BACK!

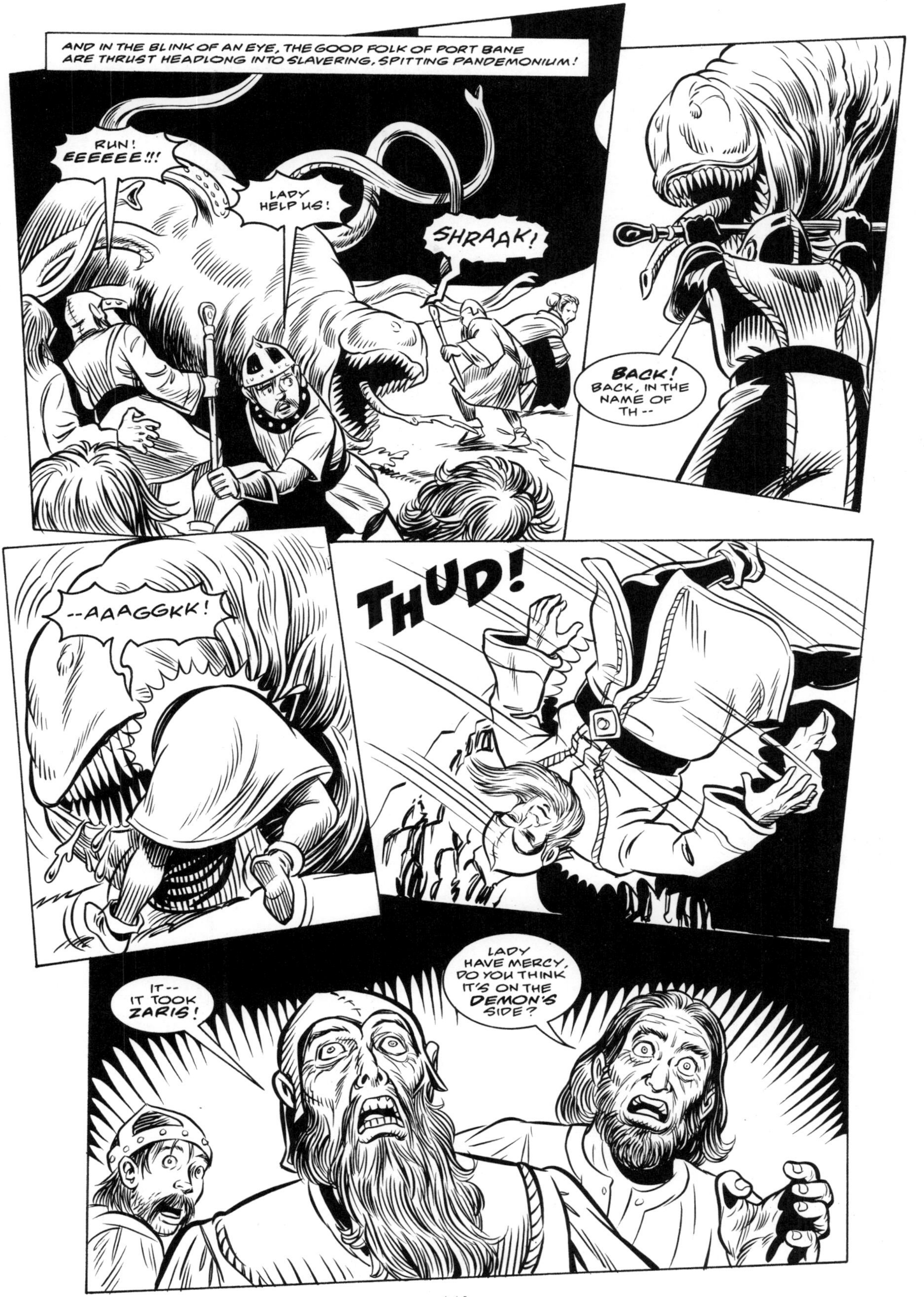
AND IN THE BLINK OF AN EYE, THE GOOD FOLK OF PORT BANE ARE THRUST HEADLONG INTO SLAVERING, SPITTING PANDEMONIUM!
RUN! EEEEEE!!!
LADY HELP US!
SHRAAK!
BACK! BACK, IN THE NAME OF TH--
--AAAGGKK!
THUD!
IT-- IT TOOK ZARIS!
LADY HAVE MERCY, DO YOU THINK IT'S ON THE DEMON'S SIDE?

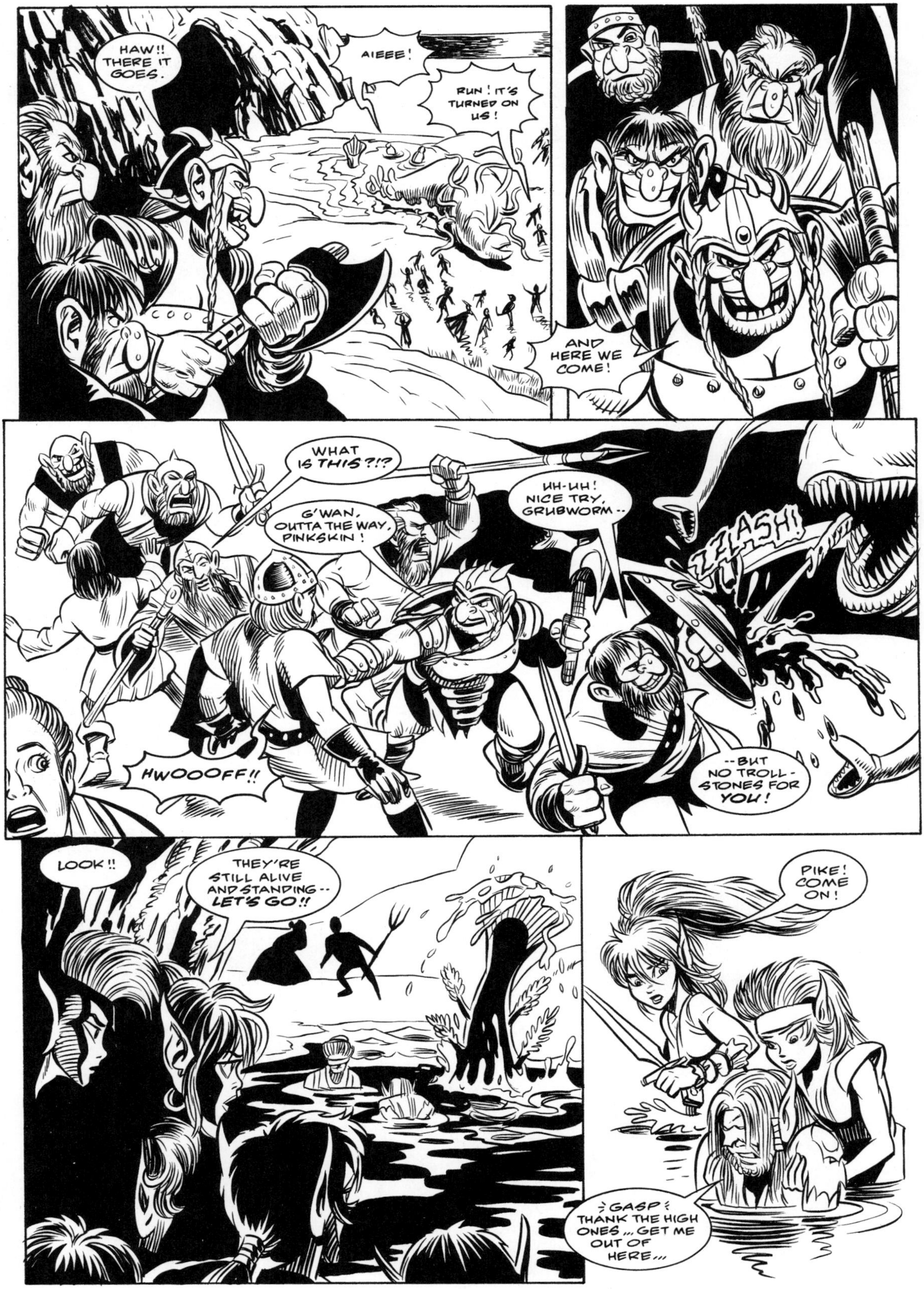
HAW!! THERE IT GOES.
AIEEE!
RUN! IT'S TURNED ON US!
AND HERE WE COME!
WHAT IS THIS?!?
G'WAN, OUTTA THE WAY, PINKSKIN!
UH-UH! NICE TRY, GRUBWORM--
ZZLASH!
HWOOOFF!!
--BUT NO TROLL-STONES FOR YOU!
LOOK!!
THEY'RE STILL ALIVE AND STANDING-- LET'S GO!!
PIKE! COME ON!
GASP THANK THE HIGH ONES ... GET ME OUT OF HERE...

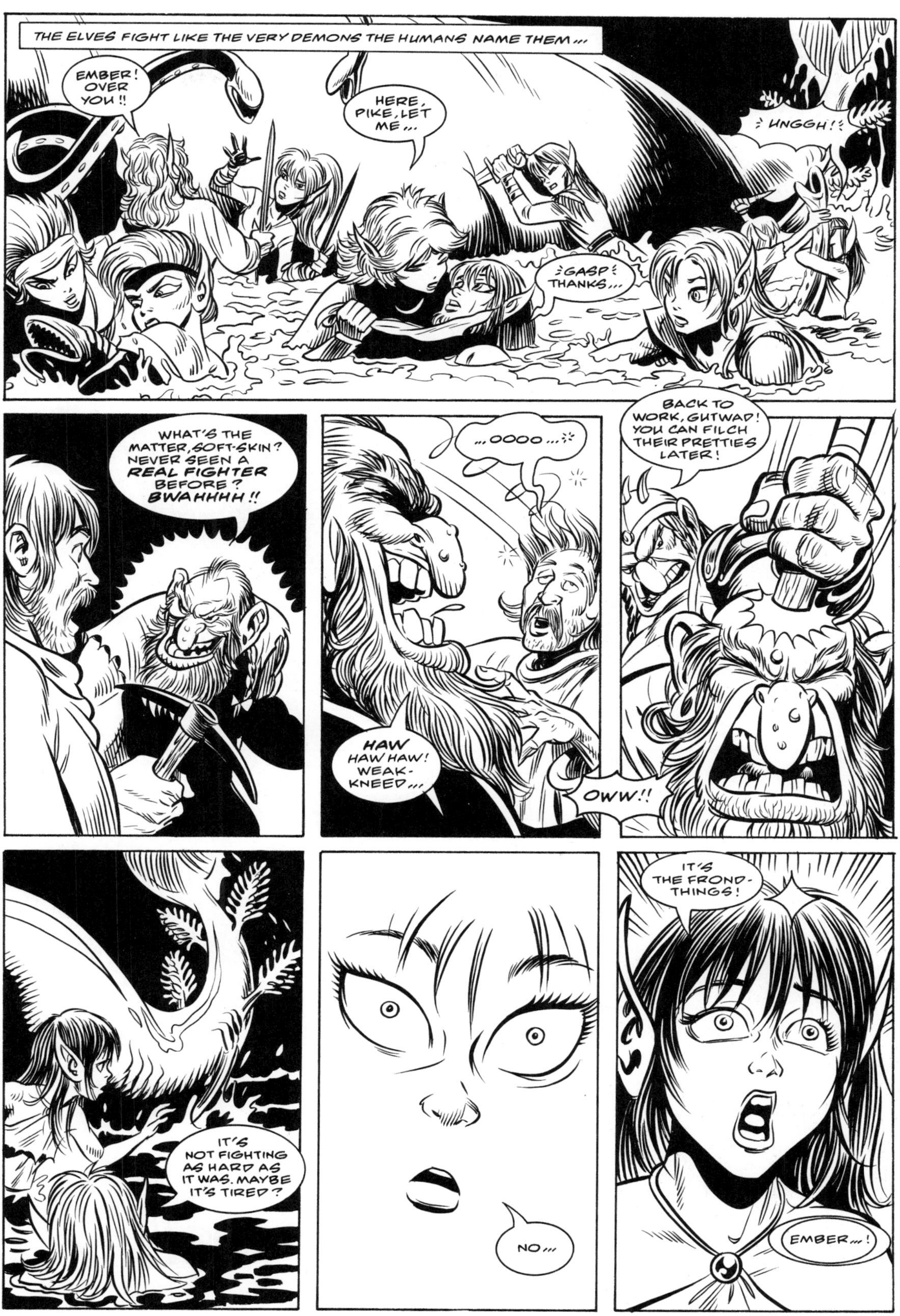
THE ELVES FIGHT LIKE THE VERY DEMONS THE HUMANS NAME THEM...
EMBER! OVER YOU!!
HERE, PIKE, LET ME...
UNGGH!
GASP THANKS...
WHAT'S THE MATTER, SOFT-SKIN? NEVER SEEN A REAL FIGHTER BEFORE? BWAHHHH!!
...OOOO...
HAW HAW HAW! WEAK-KNEED...
BACK TO WORK, GUTWAD! YOU CAN FILCH THEIR PRETTIES LATER!
OWW!!
IT'S NOT FIGHTING AS HARD AS IT WAS. MAYBE IT'S TIRED?
NO...
IT'S THE FROND-THINGS!
EMBER...!

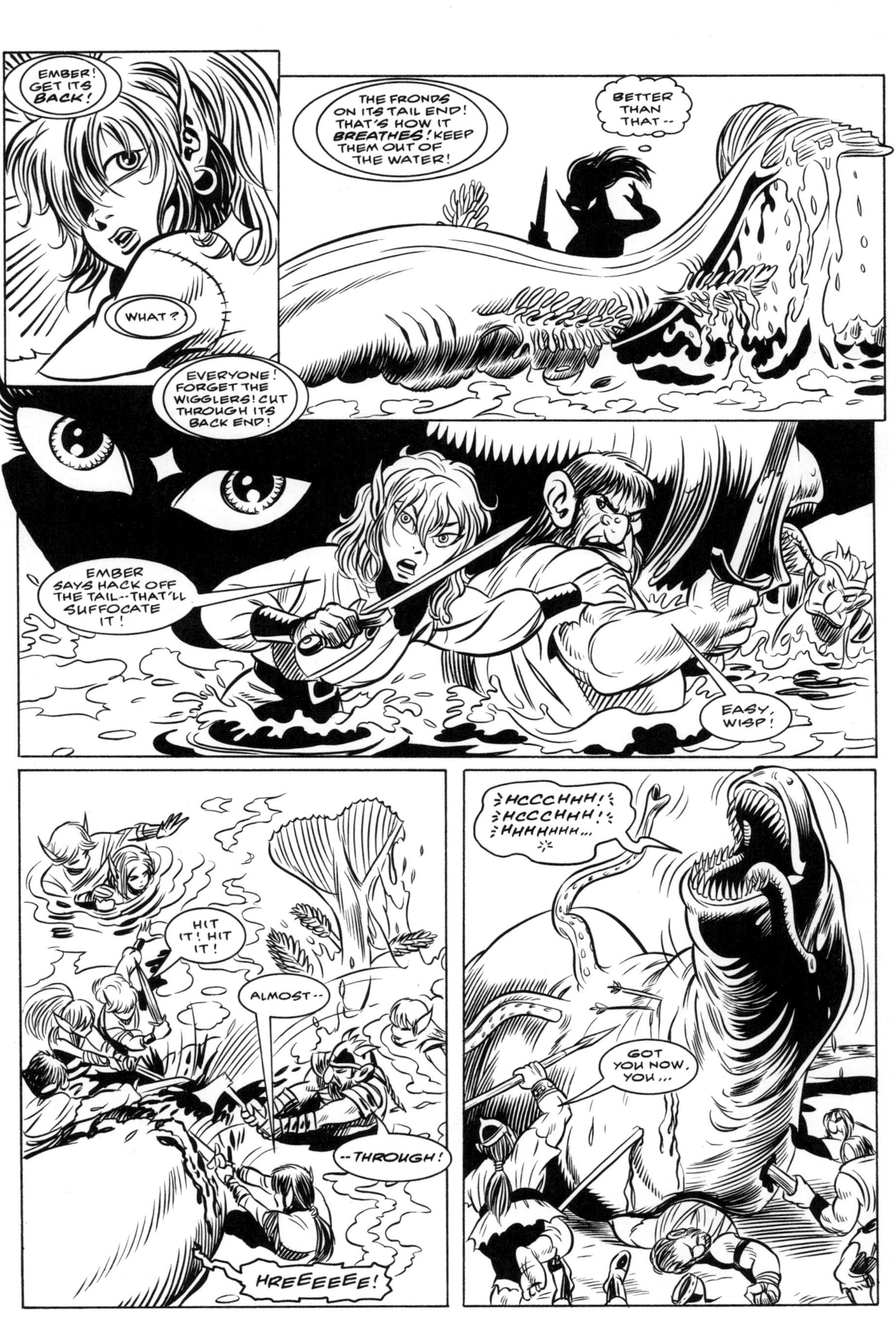
EMBER! GET ITS BACK!
THE FRONDS ON ITS TAIL END! THAT'S HOW IT BREATHES! KEEP THEM OUT OF THE WATER!
BETTER THAN THAT--
WHAT?
EVERYONE! FORGET THE WIGGLERS! CUT THROUGH ITS BACK END!
EMBER SAYS HACK OFF THE TAIL--THAT'LL SUFFOCATE IT!
EASY, WISP!
HIT IT! HIT IT!
ALMOST--
--THROUGH!
HREEEEEE!
HCCCHHH! HCCCHHH! HHHHHHH...
GOT YOU NOW, YOU...

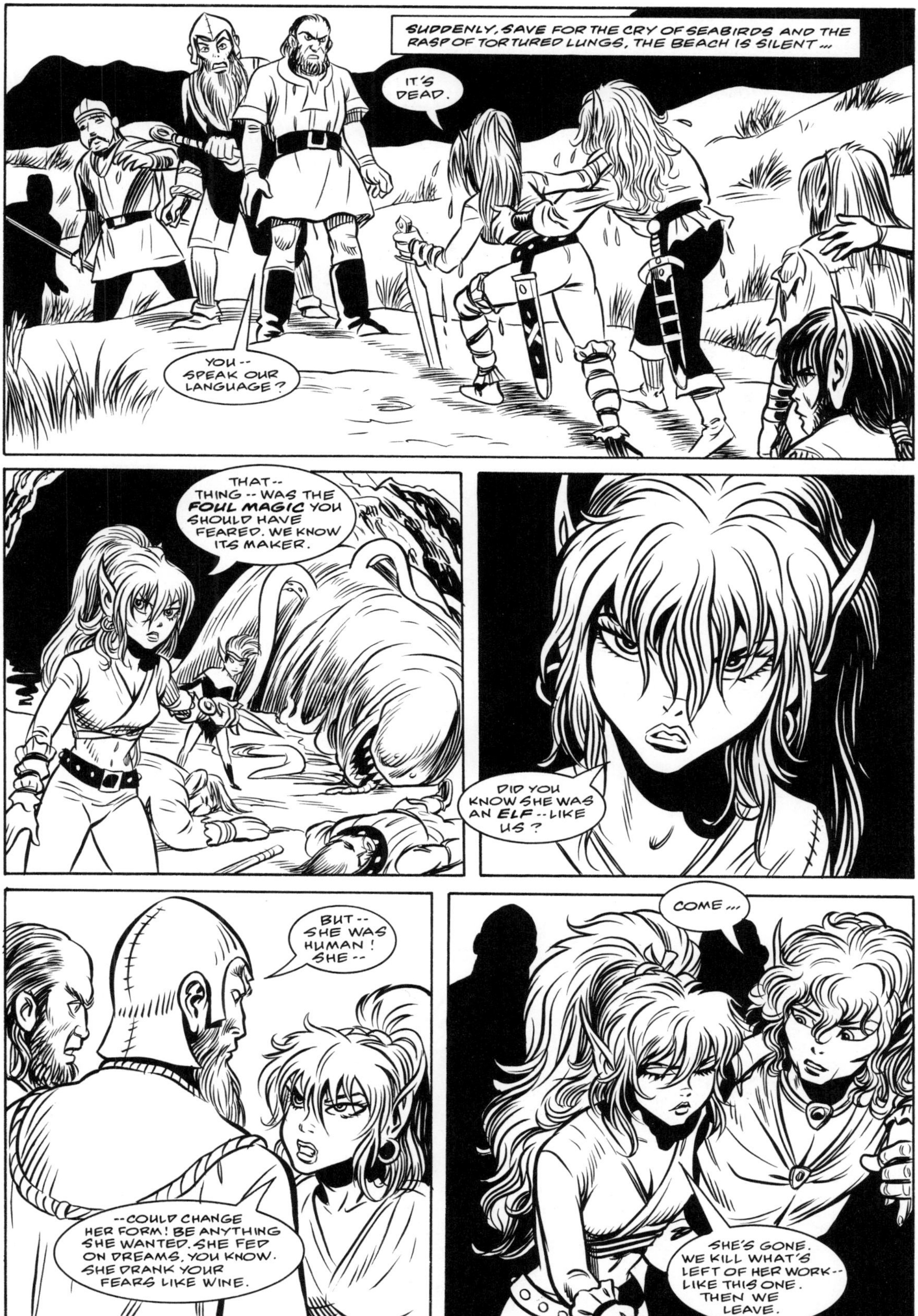
SUDDENLY, SAVE FOR THE CRY OF SEABIRDS AND THE RASP OF TORTURED LUNGS, THE BEACH IS SILENT...
IT'S DEAD.
YOU -- SPEAK OUR LANGUAGE?
THAT -- THING -- WAS THE FOUL MAGIC YOU SHOULD HAVE FEARED. WE KNOW ITS MAKER.
DID YOU KNOW SHE WAS AN ELF -- LIKE US?
BUT -- SHE WAS HUMAN! SHE --
--COULD CHANGE HER FORM! BE ANYTHING SHE WANTED. SHE FED ON DREAMS, YOU KNOW. SHE DRANK YOUR FEARS LIKE WINE.
COME...
SHE'S GONE. WE KILL WHAT'S LEFT OF HER WORK -- LIKE THIS ONE. THEN WE LEAVE.

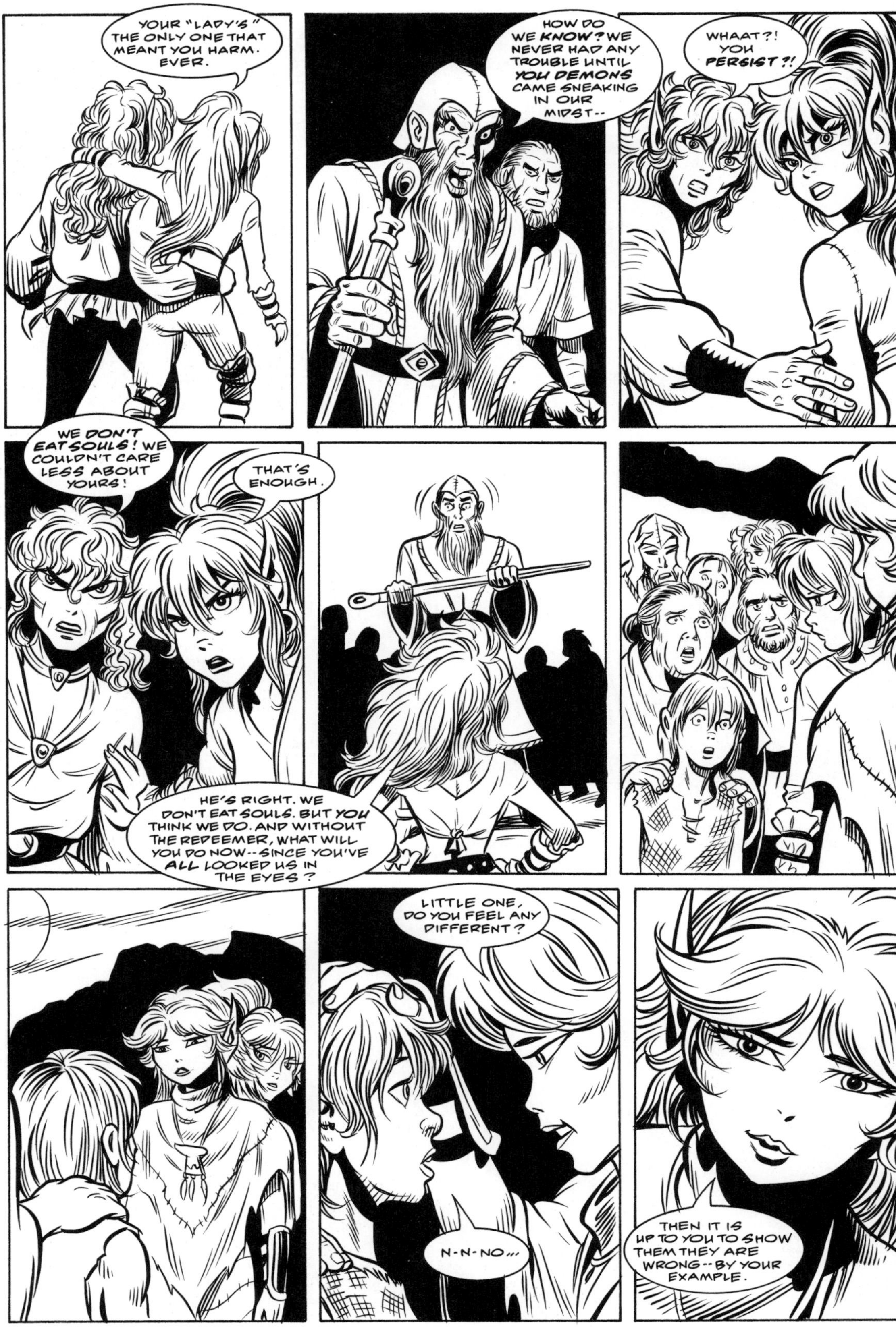
YOUR "LADY'S" THE ONLY ONE THAT MEANT YOU HARM. EVER.
HOW DO WE KNOW? WE NEVER HAD ANY TROUBLE UNTIL YOU DEMONS CAME SNEAKING IN OUR MIDST--
WHAAT?! YOU PERSIST?!
WE DON'T EAT SOULS! WE COULDN'T CARE LESS ABOUT YOURS!
THAT'S ENOUGH.
HE'S RIGHT. WE DON'T EAT SOULS. BUT YOU THINK WE DO. AND WITHOUT THE REDEEMER, WHAT WILL YOU DO NOW--SINCE YOU'VE ALL LOOKED US IN THE EYES?
LITTLE ONE, DO YOU FEEL ANY DIFFERENT?
N-N-NO...
THEN IT IS UP TO YOU TO SHOW THEM THEY ARE WRONG--BY YOUR EXAMPLE.

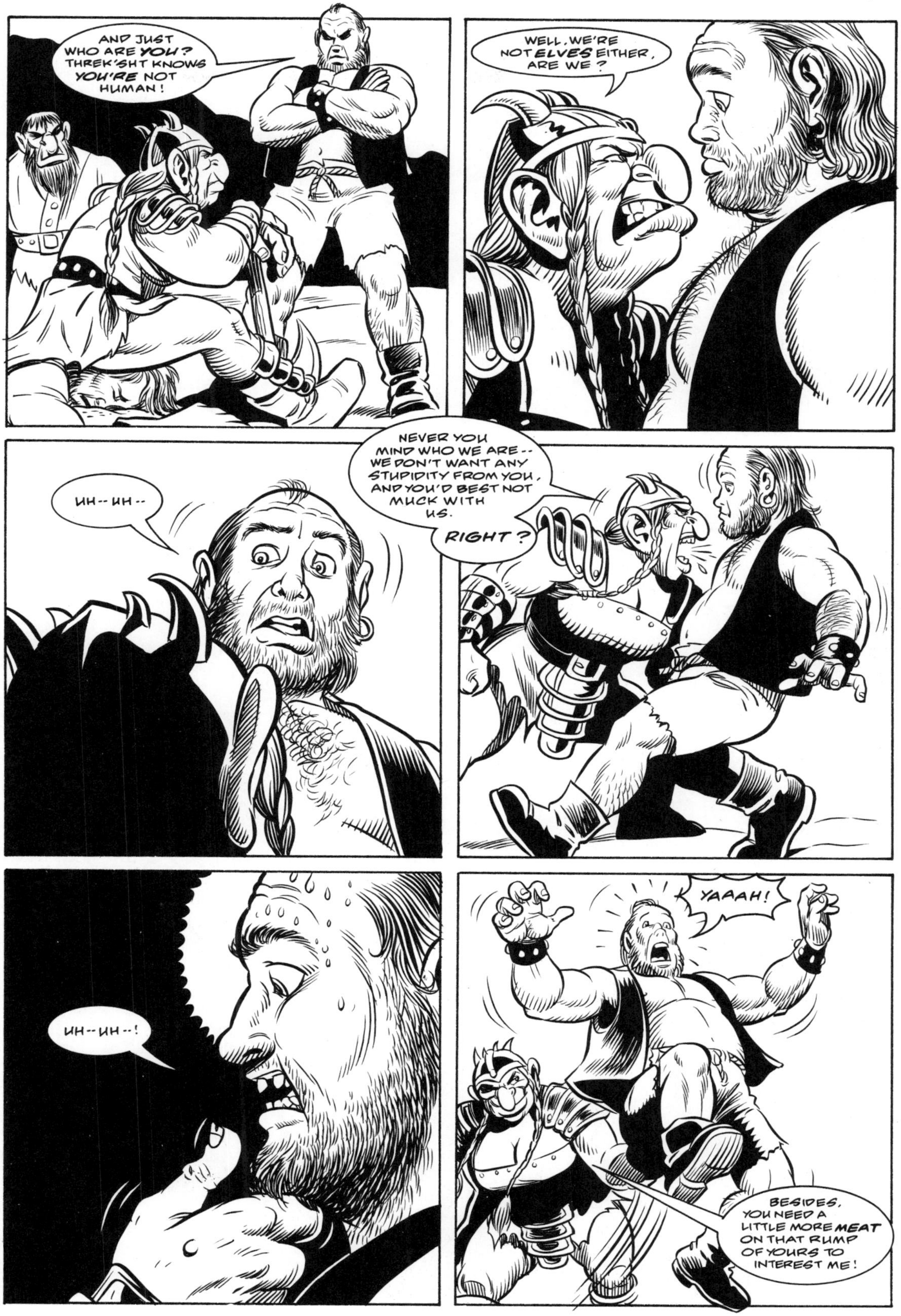
AND JUST WHO ARE YOU? THREK'SHT KNOWS YOU'RE NOT HUMAN!
WELL, WE'RE NOT ELVES EITHER, ARE WE?
UH-- UH--
NEVER YOU MIND WHO WE ARE-- WE DON'T WANT ANY STUPIDITY FROM YOU, AND YOU'D BEST NOT MUCK WITH US.
RIGHT?
UH-- UH--!
YAAAH!
BESIDES, YOU NEED A LITTLE MORE MEAT ON THAT RUMP OF YOURS TO INTEREST ME!

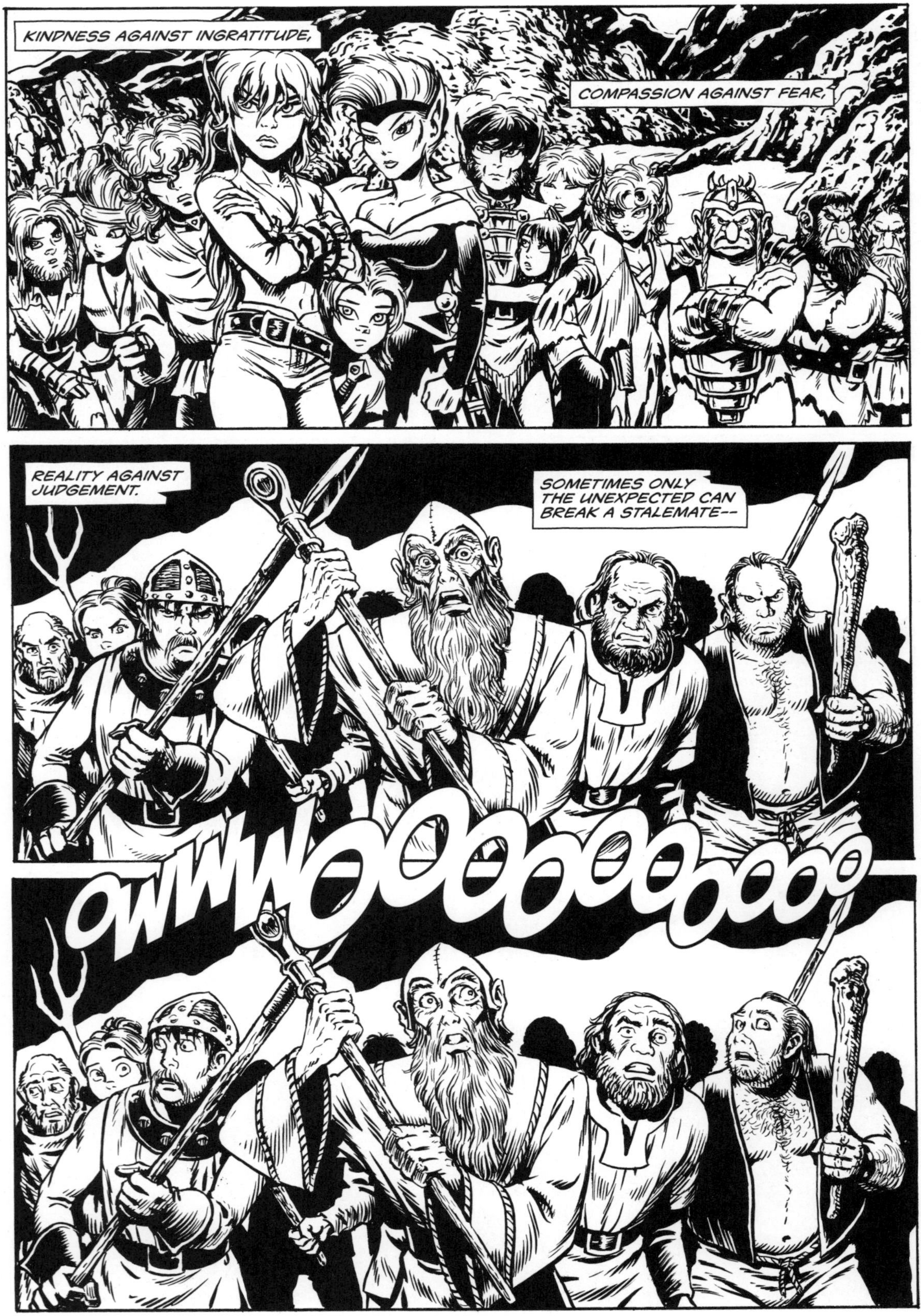
KINDNESS AGAINST INGRATITUDE,
COMPASSION AGAINST FEAR,
REALITY AGAINST JUDGEMENT.
SOMETIMES ONLY THE UNEXPECTED CAN BREAK A STALEMATE--
OWWWOOOOOOOOOOO

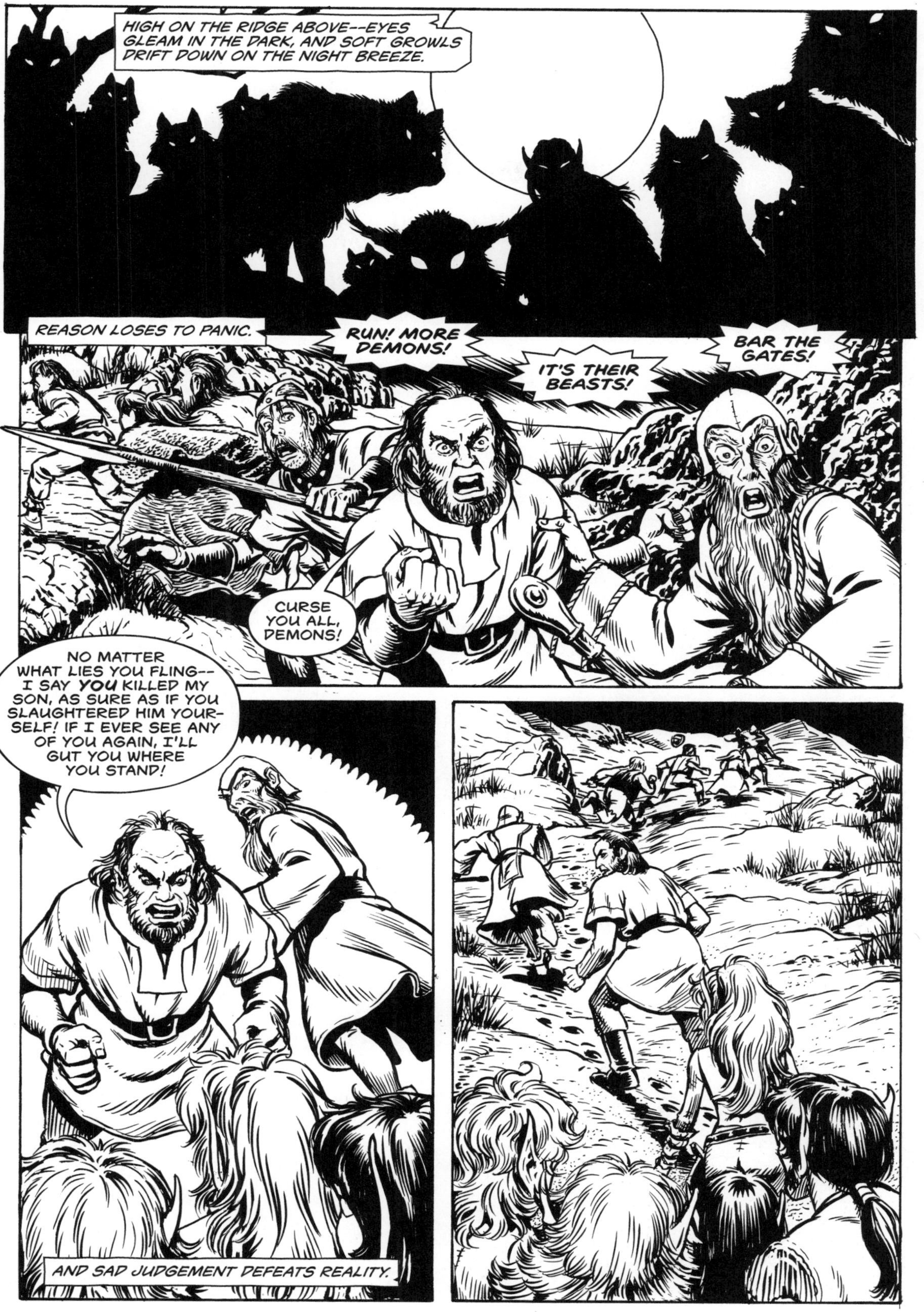
HIGH ON THE RIDGE ABOVE--EYES GLEAM IN THE DARK, AND SOFT GROWLS DRIFT DOWN ON THE NIGHT BREEZE.
REASON LOSES TO PANIC.
RUN! MORE DEMONS!
IT'S THEIR BEASTS!
BAR THE GATES!
CURSE YOU ALL, DEMONS!
NO MATTER WHAT LIES YOU FLING-- I SAY YOU KILLED MY SON, AS SURE AS IF YOU SLAUGHTERED HIM YOURSELF! IF I EVER SEE ANY OF YOU AGAIN, I'LL GUT YOU WHERE YOU STAND!
AND SAD JUDGEMENT DEFEATS REALITY.

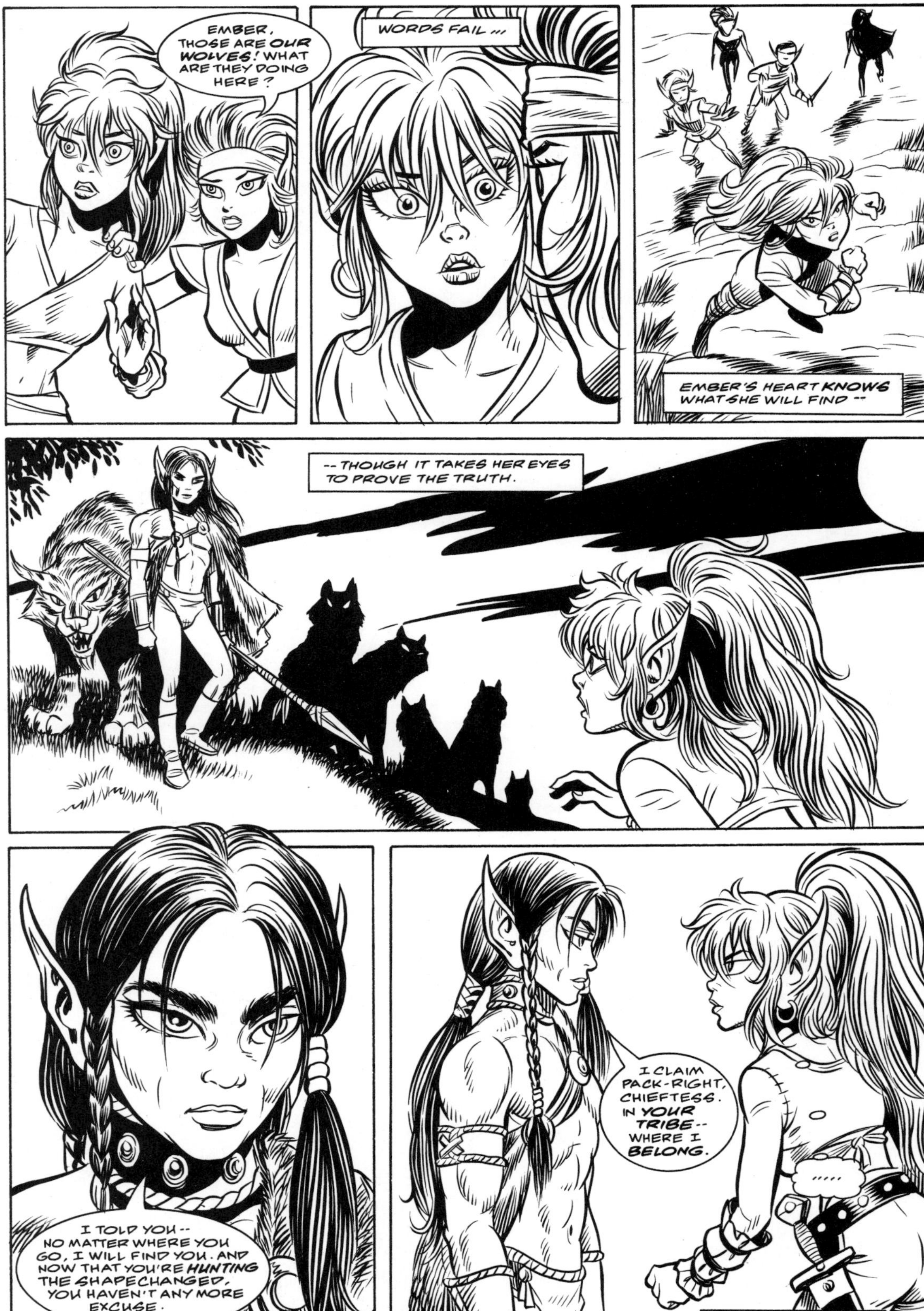
EMBER, THOSE ARE OUR WOLVES! WHAT ARE THEY DOING HERE?
WORDS FAIL...
EMBER'S HEART KNOWS WHAT SHE WILL FIND --
-- THOUGH IT TAKES HER EYES TO PROVE THE TRUTH.
I TOLD YOU -- NO MATTER WHERE YOU GO, I WILL FIND YOU. AND NOW THAT YOU'RE HUNTING THE SHAPECHANGED, YOU HAVEN'T ANY MORE EXCUSE.
I CLAIM PACK-RIGHT, CHIEFTESS. IN YOUR TRIBE -- WHERE I BELONG.
.....
TO BE CONTINUED...

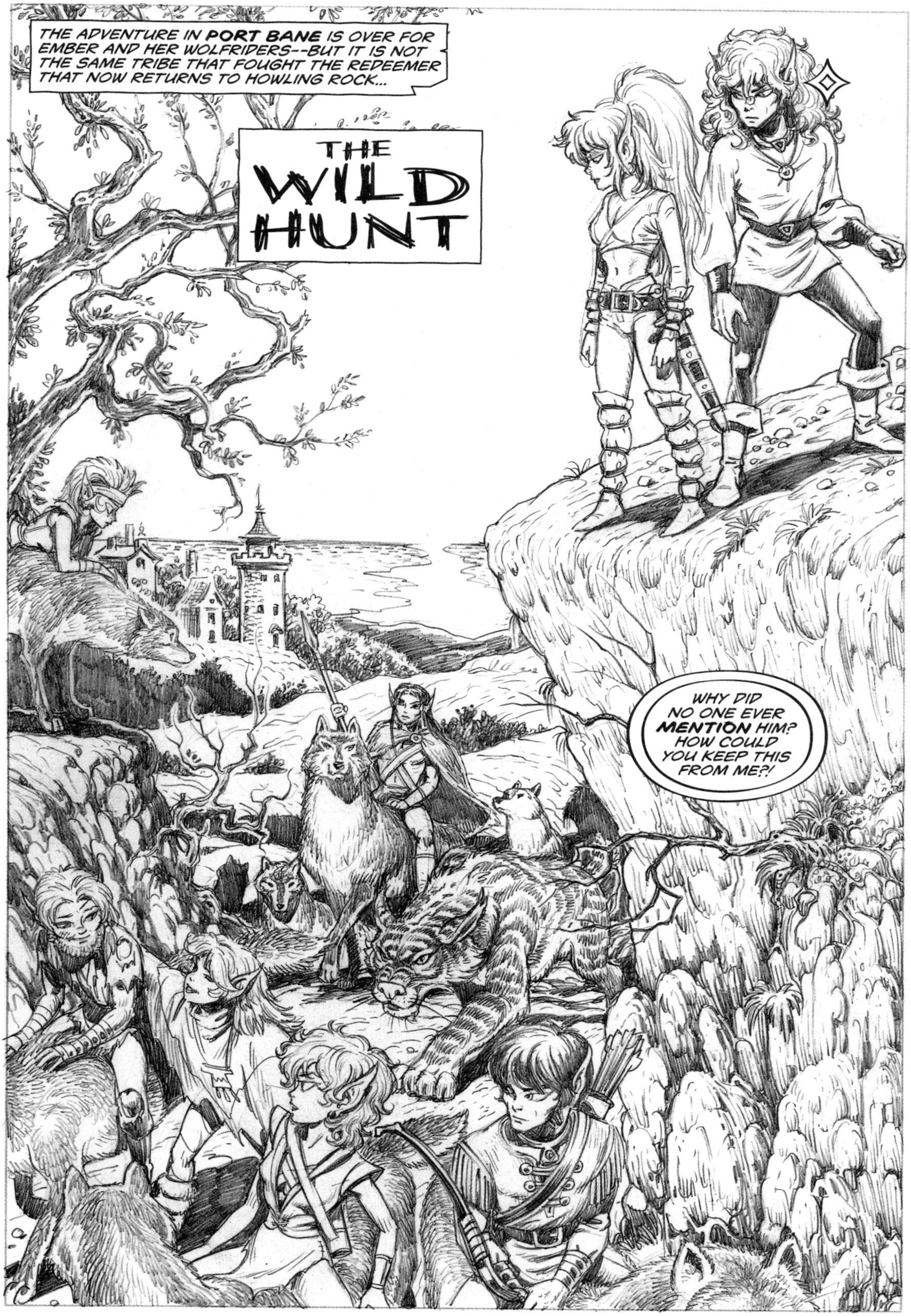
THE ADVENTURE IN PORT BANE IS OVER FOR EMBER AND HER WOLFRIDERS--BUT IT IS NOT THE SAME TRIBE THAT FOUGHT THE REDEEMER THAT NOW RETURNS TO HOWLING ROCK...
THE WILD HUNT
WHY DID NO ONE EVER MENTION HIM? HOW COULD YOU KEEP THIS FROM ME?!

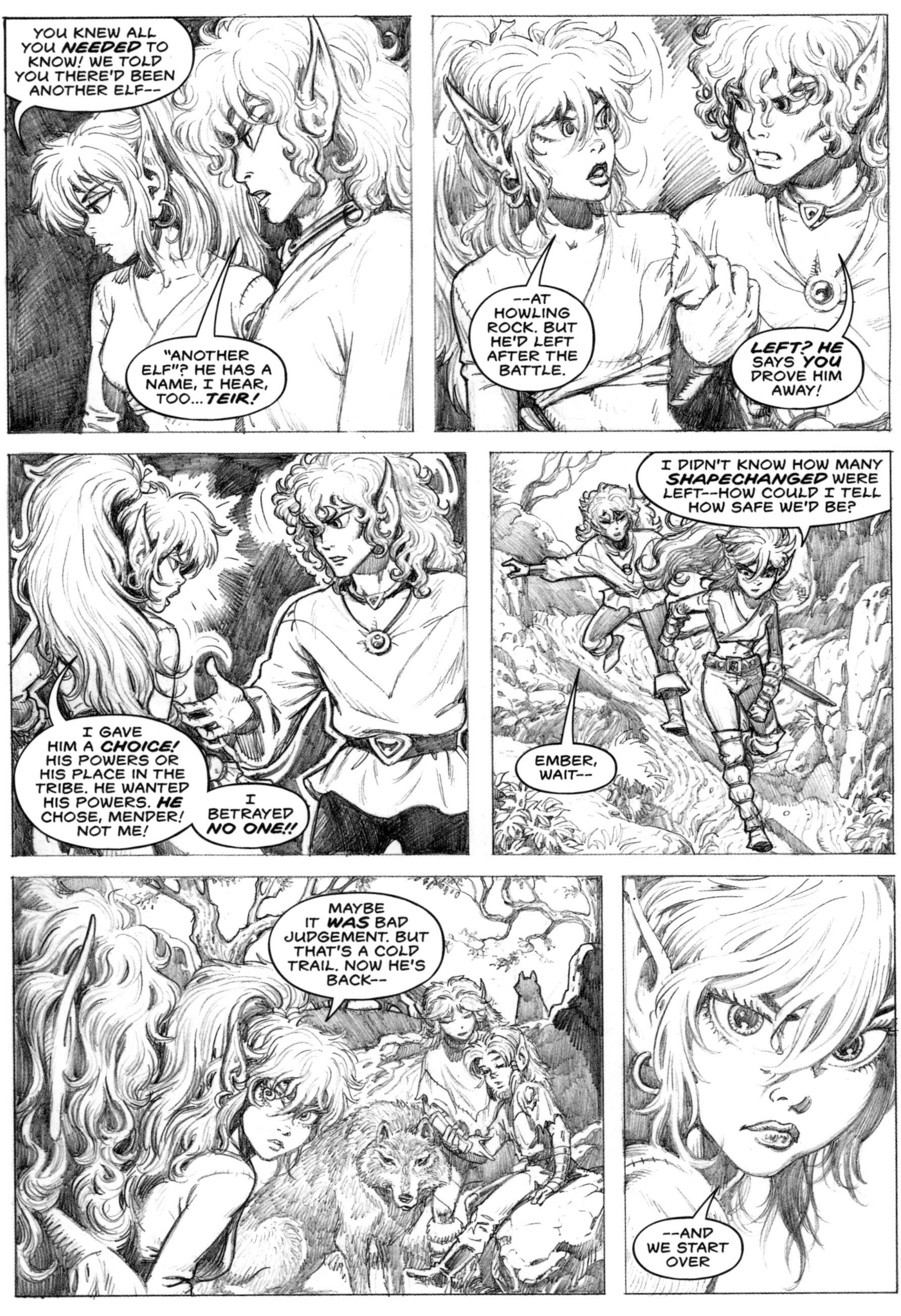

YOU KNEW ALL YOU NEEDED TO KNOW! WE TOLD YOU THERE'D BEEN ANOTHER ELF--
"ANOTHER ELF"? HE HAS A NAME, I HEAR, TOO...TEIR!
--AT HOWLING ROCK. BUT HE'D LEFT AFTER THE BATTLE.
LEFT? HE SAYS YOU DROVE HIM AWAY!
I GAVE HIM A CHOICE! HIS POWERS OR HIS PLACE IN THE TRIBE. HE WANTED HIS POWERS. HE CHOSE, MENDER! NOT ME!
I BETRAYED NO ONE!!
I DIDN'T KNOW HOW MANY SHAPECHANGED WERE LEFT--HOW COULD I TELL HOW SAFE WE'D BE?
EMBER, WAIT--
MAYBE IT WAS BAD JUDGEMENT. BUT THAT'S A COLD TRAIL. NOW HE'S BACK--
--AND WE START OVER

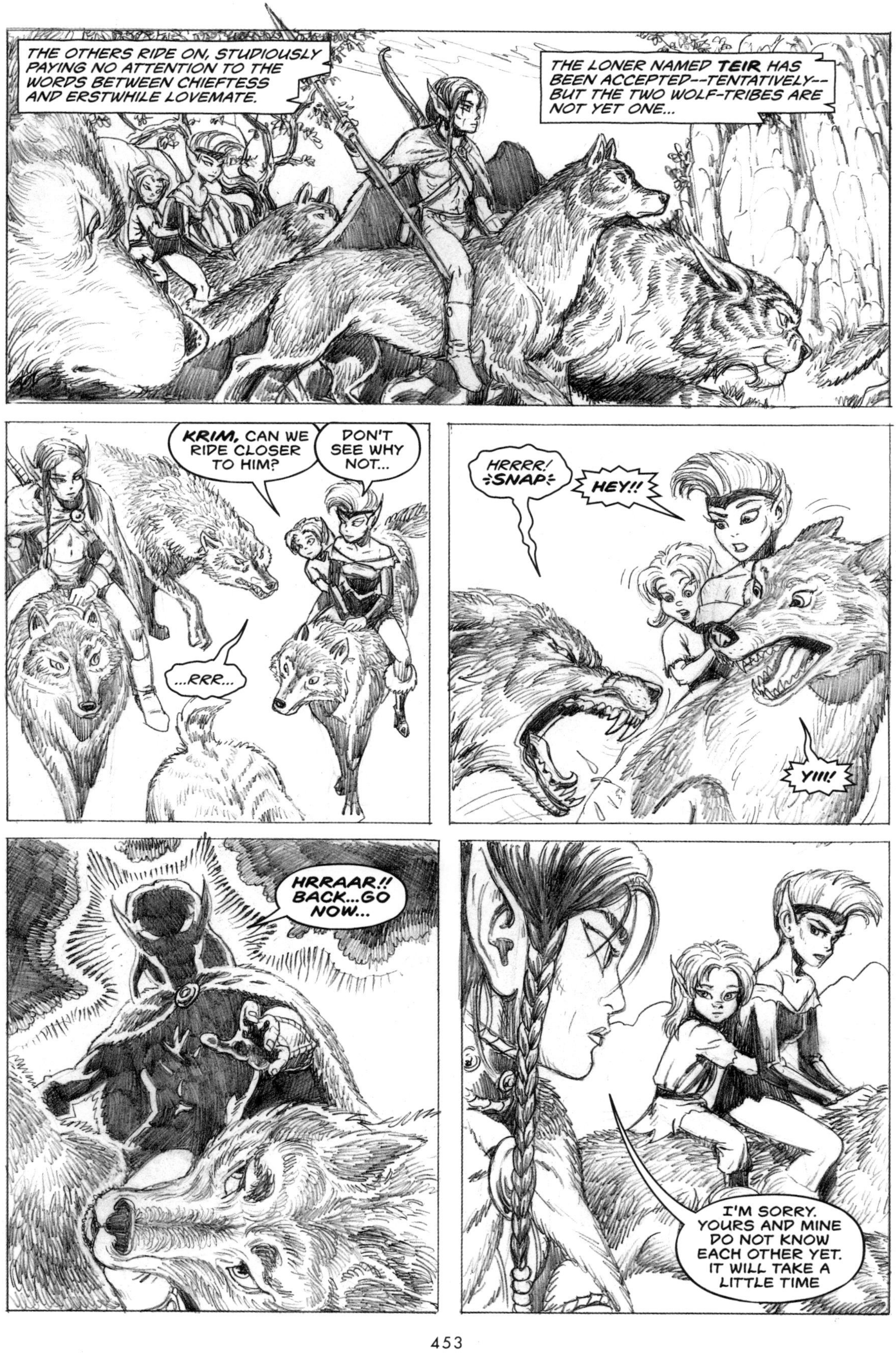

THE OTHERS RIDE ON, STUDIOUSLY PAYING NO ATTENTION TO THE WORDS BETWEEN CHIEFTESS AND ERSTWHILE LOVEMATE.
THE LONER NAMED TEIR HAS BEEN ACCEPTED--TENTATIVELY--BUT THE TWO WOLF-TRIBES ARE NOT YET ONE...
KRIM, CAN WE RIDE CLOSER TO HIM?
DON'T SEE WHY NOT...
...RRR...
HRRRR! SNAP
HEY!!
YIII!
HRRAAR!! BACK...GO NOW...
I'M SORRY. YOURS AND MINE DO NOT KNOW EACH OTHER YET. IT WILL TAKE A LITTLE TIME

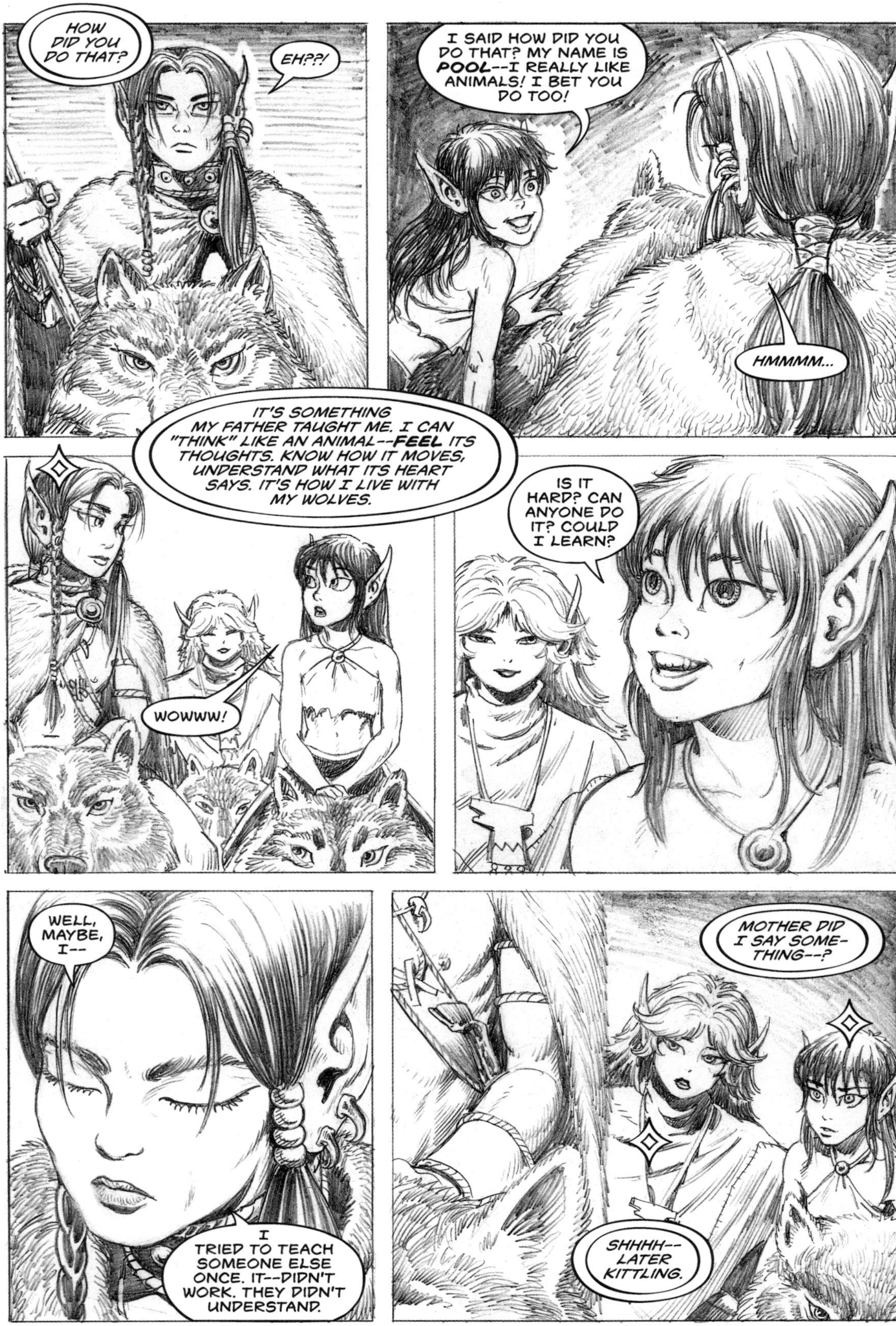
HOW DID YOU DO THAT?
EH??!
I SAID HOW DID YOU DO THAT? MY NAME IS POOL--I REALLY LIKE ANIMALS! I BET YOU DO TOO!
HMMMM...
IT'S SOMETHING MY FATHER TAUGHT ME. I CAN "THINK" LIKE AN ANIMAL--FEEL ITS THOUGHTS. KNOW HOW IT MOVES, UNDERSTAND WHAT ITS HEART SAYS. IT'S HOW I LIVE WITH MY WOLVES.
WOWWW!
IS IT HARD? CAN ANYONE DO IT? COULD I LEARN?
WELL, MAYBE, I--
I TRIED TO TEACH SOMEONE ELSE ONCE. IT--DIDN'T WORK. THEY DIDN'T UNDERSTAND.
MOTHER DID I SAY SOME-THING--?
SHHHH--LATER KITTLING.

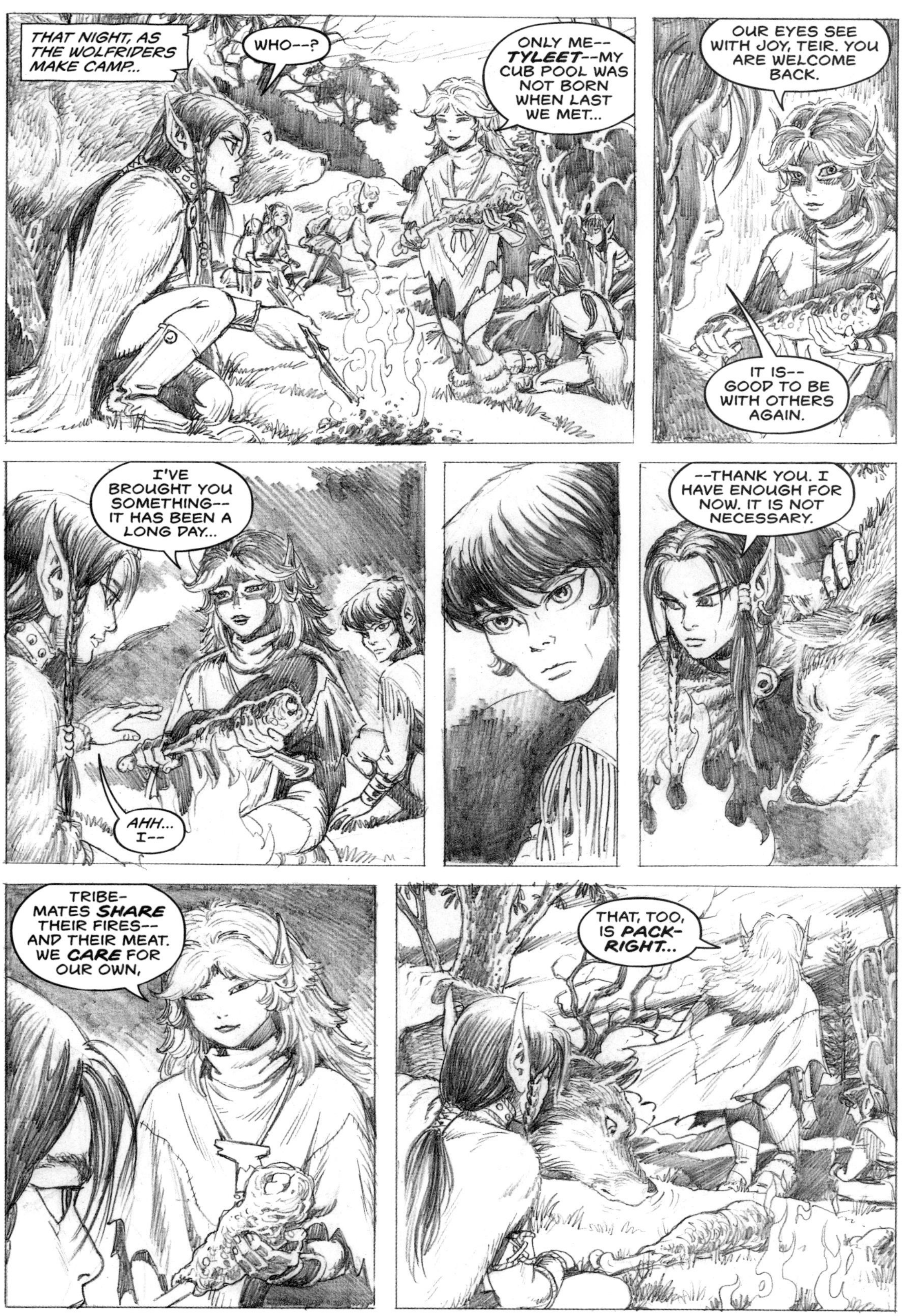

THAT NIGHT, AS THE WOLFRIDERS MAKE CAMP...
WHO--?
ONLY ME-- TYLEET--MY CUB POOL WAS NOT BORN WHEN LAST WE MET...
OUR EYES SEE WITH JOY, TEIR. YOU ARE WELCOME BACK.
IT IS-- GOOD TO BE WITH OTHERS AGAIN.
I'VE BROUGHT YOU SOMETHING-- IT HAS BEEN A LONG DAY...
AHH... I--
--THANK YOU. I HAVE ENOUGH FOR NOW. IT IS NOT NECESSARY.
TRIBE-MATES SHARE THEIR FIRES-- AND THEIR MEAT. WE CARE FOR OUR OWN,
THAT, TOO, IS PACK-RIGHT...

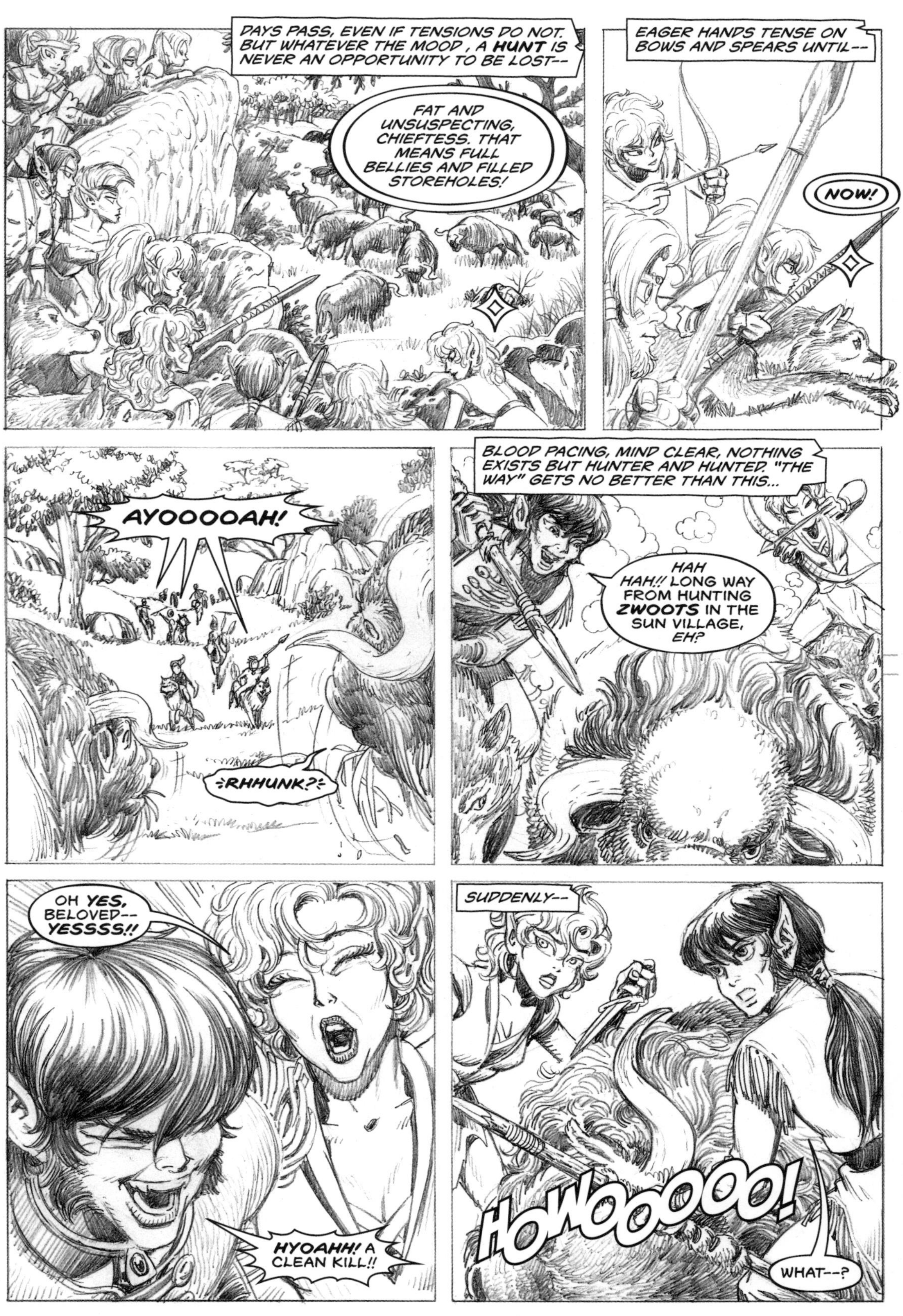
DAYS PASS, EVEN IF TENSIONS DO NOT. BUT WHATEVER THE MOOD, A HUNT IS NEVER AN OPPORTUNITY TO BE LOST--
FAT AND UNSUSPECTING, CHIEFTESS. THAT MEANS FULL BELLIES AND FILLED STOREHOLES!
EAGER HANDS TENSE ON BOWS AND SPEARS UNTIL--
NOW!
AYOOOOAH!
RHHUNK?
BLOOD PACING, MIND CLEAR, NOTHING EXISTS BUT HUNTER AND HUNTED. "THE WAY" GETS NO BETTER THAN THIS...
HAH HAH!! LONG WAY FROM HUNTING ZWOOTS IN THE SUN VILLAGE, EH?
OH YES, BELOVED-- YESSSS!!
HYOAHH! A CLEAN KILL!!
SUDDENLY--
HOWOOOOOO!
WHAT--?

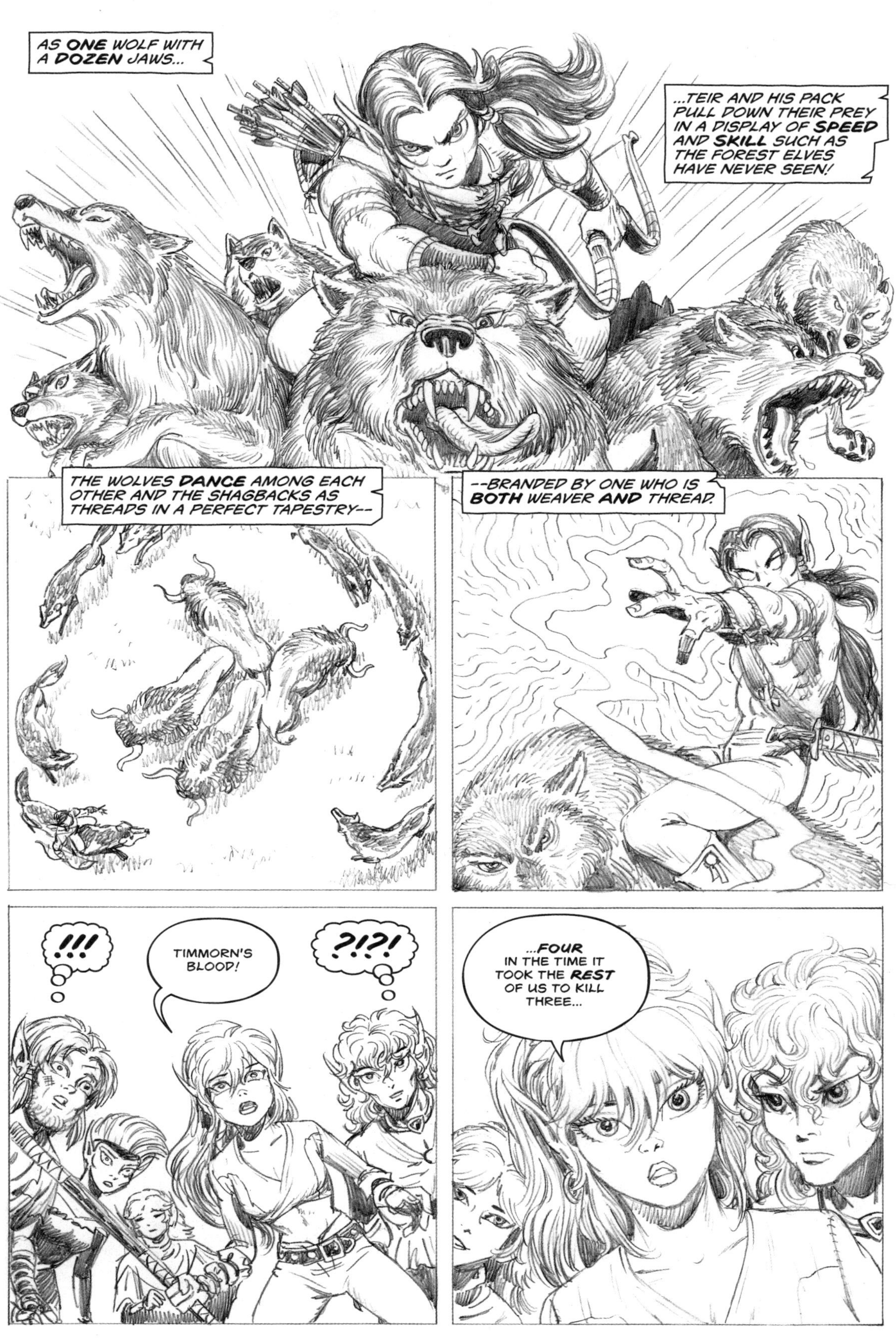
AS ONE WOLF WITH A DOZEN JAWS...
...TEIR AND HIS PACK PULL DOWN THEIR PREY IN A DISPLAY OF SPEED AND SKILL SUCH AS THE FOREST ELVES HAVE NEVER SEEN!
THE WOLVES DANCE AMONG EACH OTHER AND THE SHAGBACKS AS THREADS IN A PERFECT TAPESTRY--
--BRANDED BY ONE WHO IS BOTH WEAVER AND THREAD.
!!!
TIMMORN'S BLOOD!
?!?!
...FOUR IN THE TIME IT TOOK THE REST OF US TO KILL THREE...

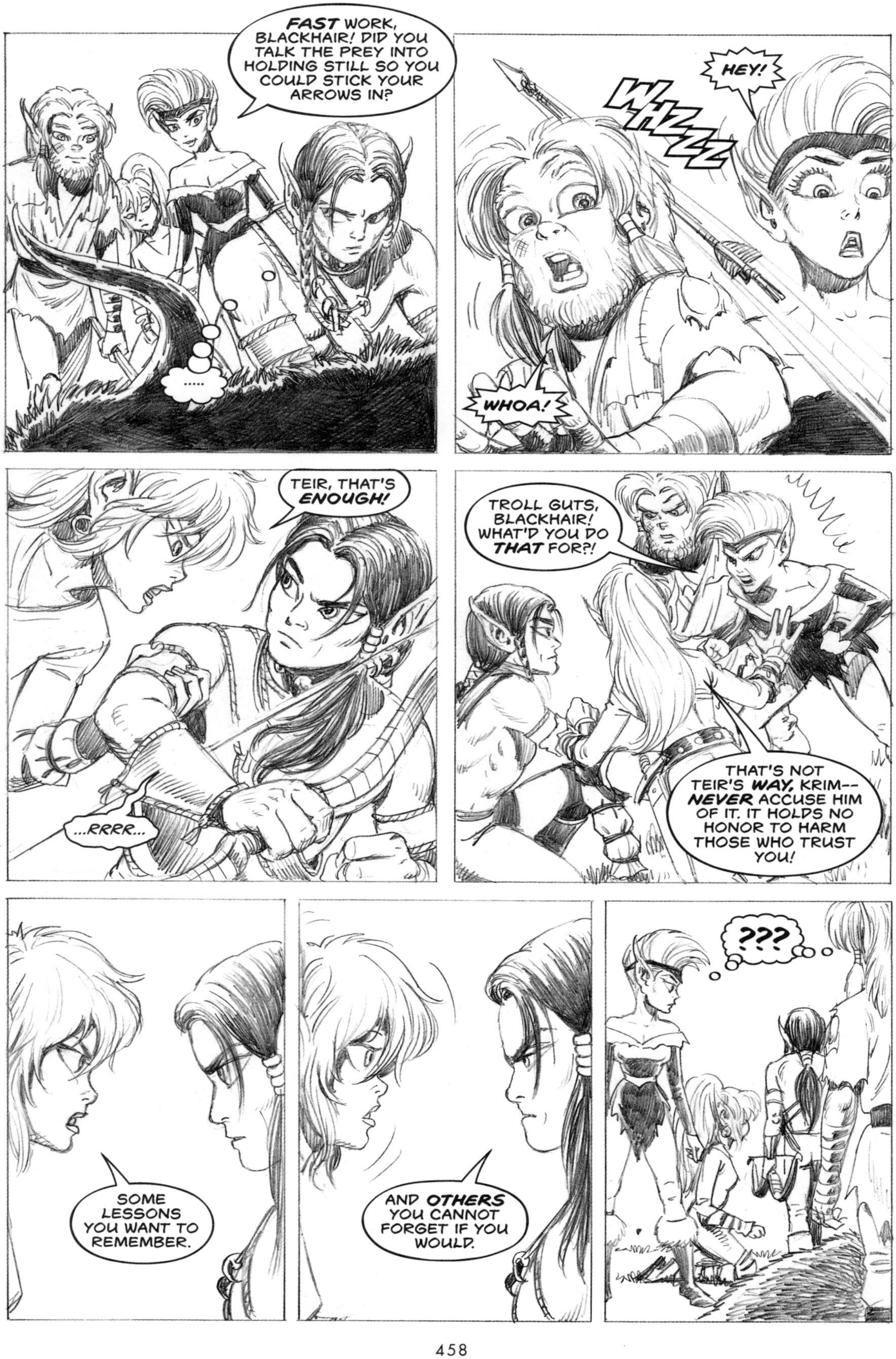

FAST WORK, BLACKHAIR! DID YOU TALK THE PREY INTO HOLDING STILL SO YOU COULD STICK YOUR ARROWS IN?
.....
WHZZZ
HEY!
WHOA!
TEIR, THAT'S ENOUGH!
...RRRR...
TROLL GUTS, BLACKHAIR! WHAT'D YOU DO THAT FOR?!
THAT'S NOT TEIR'S WAY, KRIM--NEVER ACCUSE HIM OF IT. IT HOLDS NO HONOR TO HARM THOSE WHO TRUST YOU!
SOME LESSONS YOU WANT TO REMEMBER.
AND OTHERS YOU CANNOT FORGET IF YOU WOULD.
???

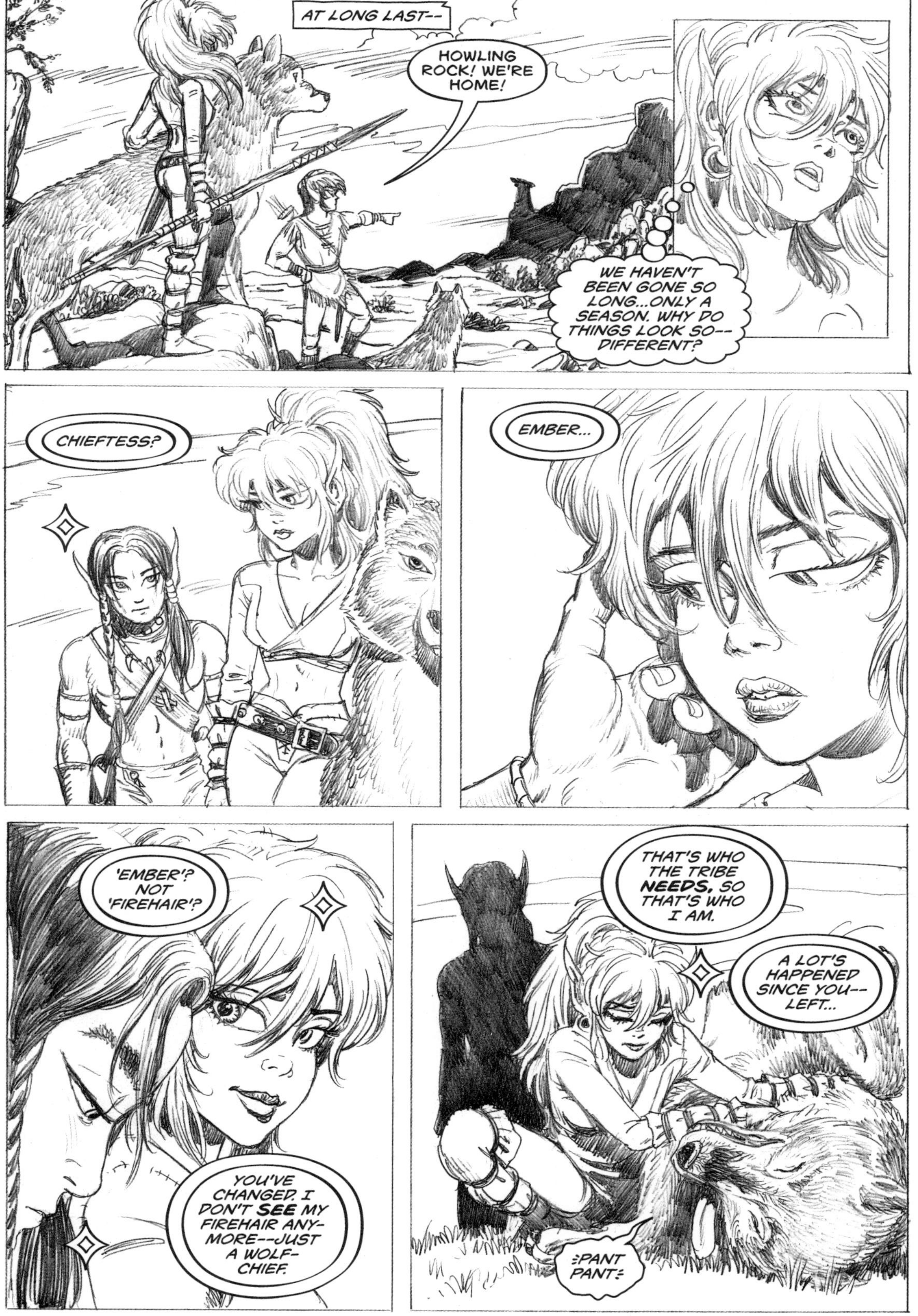
AT LONG LAST--
HOWLING ROCK! WE'RE HOME!
WE HAVEN'T BEEN GONE SO LONG...ONLY A SEASON. WHY DO THINGS LOOK SO-- DIFFERENT?
CHIEFTESS?
EMBER...
'EMBER'? NOT 'FIREHAIR'?
YOU'VE CHANGED. I DON'T SEE MY FIREHAIR ANY-MORE--JUST A WOLF-CHIEF.
THAT'S WHO THE TRIBE NEEDS. SO THAT'S WHO I AM.
A LOT'S HAPPENED SINCE YOU-- LEFT...
PANT PANT

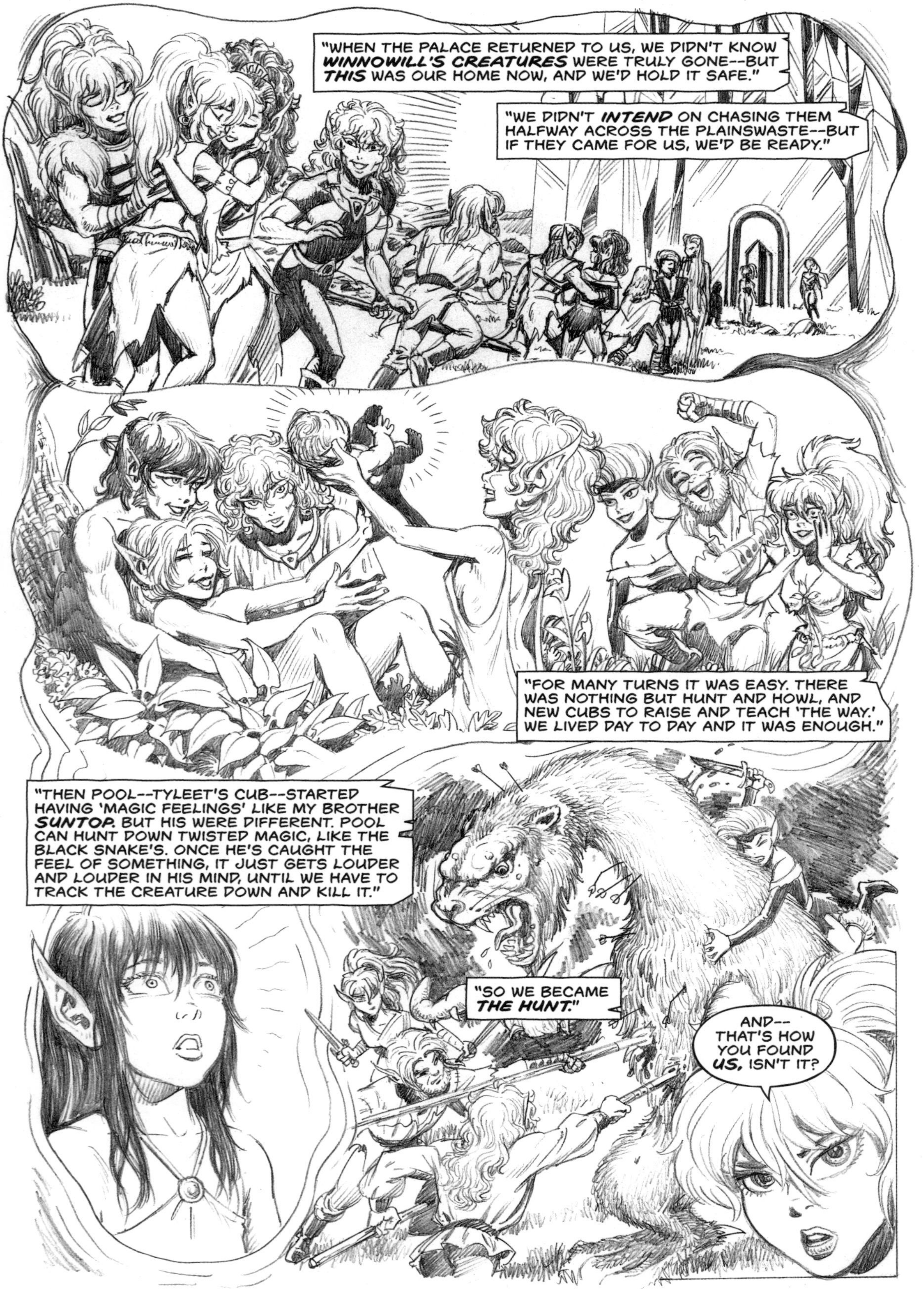
"WHEN THE PALACE RETURNED TO US, WE DIDN'T KNOW **WINNOWILL'S CREATURES** WERE TRULY GONE--BUT **THIS** WAS OUR HOME NOW, AND WE'D HOLD IT SAFE."
"WE DIDN'T **INTEND** ON CHASING THEM HALFWAY ACROSS THE PLAINSWASTE--BUT IF THEY CAME FOR US, WE'D BE READY."
"FOR MANY TURNS IT WAS EASY. THERE WAS NOTHING BUT HUNT AND HOWL, AND NEW CUBS TO RAISE AND TEACH 'THE WAY.' WE LIVED DAY TO DAY AND IT WAS ENOUGH."
"THEN POOL--TYLEET'S CUB--STARTED HAVING 'MAGIC FEELINGS' LIKE MY BROTHER **SUNTOP**. BUT HIS WERE DIFFERENT. POOL CAN HUNT DOWN TWISTED MAGIC, LIKE THE BLACK SNAKE'S. ONCE HE'S CAUGHT THE FEEL OF SOMETHING, IT JUST GETS LOUDER AND LOUDER IN HIS MIND, UNTIL WE HAVE TO TRACK THE CREATURE DOWN AND KILL IT."
"SO WE BECAME **THE HUNT**."
AND-- THAT'S HOW YOU FOUND **US,** ISN'T IT?

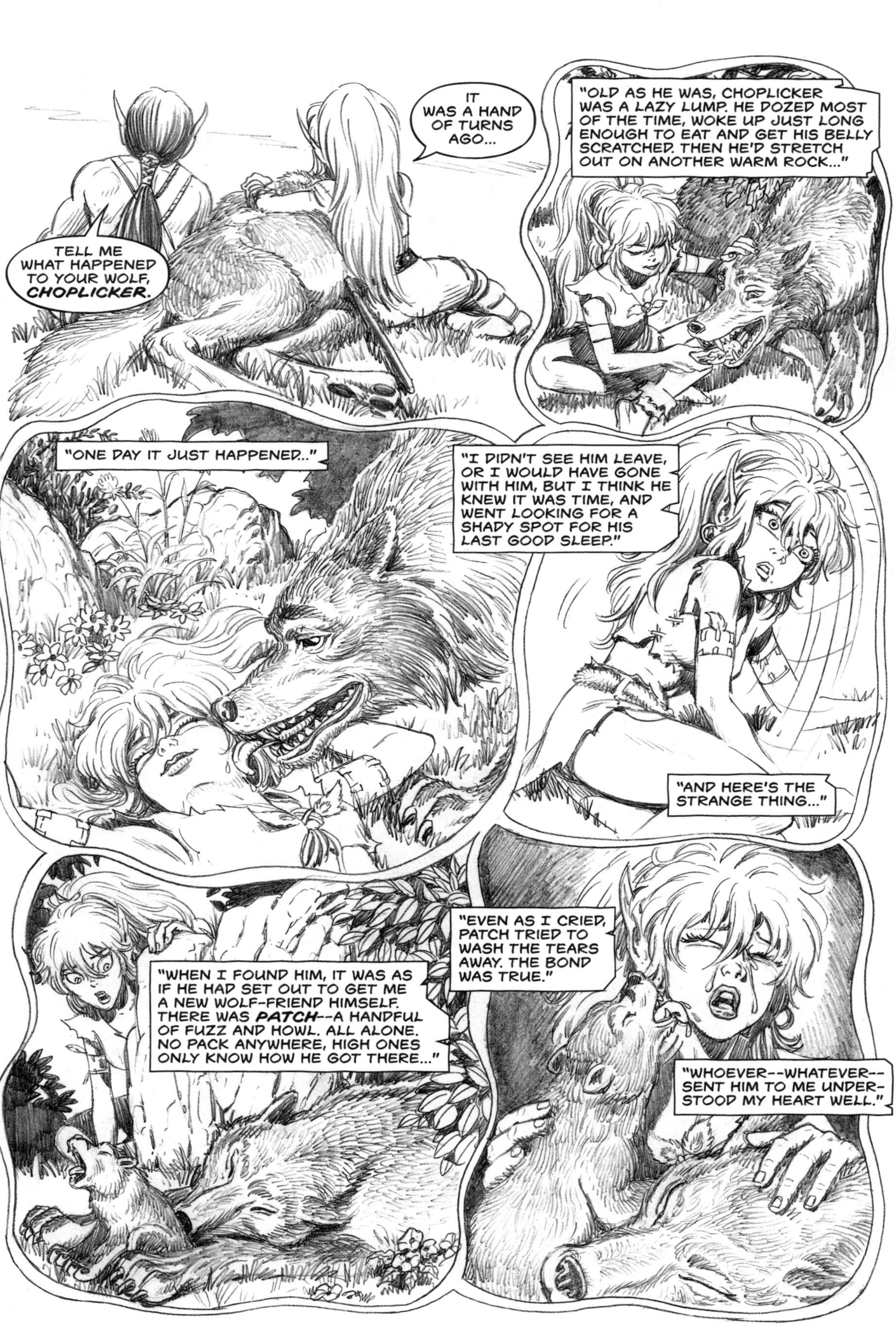

TELL ME WHAT HAPPENED TO YOUR WOLF, CHOPLICKER.
IT WAS A HAND OF TURNS AGO...
"OLD AS HE WAS, CHOPLICKER WAS A LAZY LUMP. HE DOZED MOST OF THE TIME, WOKE UP JUST LONG ENOUGH TO EAT AND GET HIS BELLY SCRATCHED. THEN HE'D STRETCH OUT ON ANOTHER WARM ROCK..."
"ONE DAY IT JUST HAPPENED..."
"I DIDN'T SEE HIM LEAVE, OR I WOULD HAVE GONE WITH HIM, BUT I THINK HE KNEW IT WAS TIME, AND WENT LOOKING FOR A SHADY SPOT FOR HIS LAST GOOD SLEEP."
"AND HERE'S THE STRANGE THING..."
"WHEN I FOUND HIM, IT WAS AS IF HE HAD SET OUT TO GET ME A NEW WOLF-FRIEND HIMSELF. THERE WAS PATCH--A HANDFUL OF FUZZ AND HOWL. ALL ALONE. NO PACK ANYWHERE, HIGH ONES ONLY KNOW HOW HE GOT THERE..."
"EVEN AS I CRIED, PATCH TRIED TO WASH THE TEARS AWAY. THE BOND WAS TRUE."
"WHOEVER--WHATEVER--SENT HIM TO ME UNDERSTOOD MY HEART WELL."

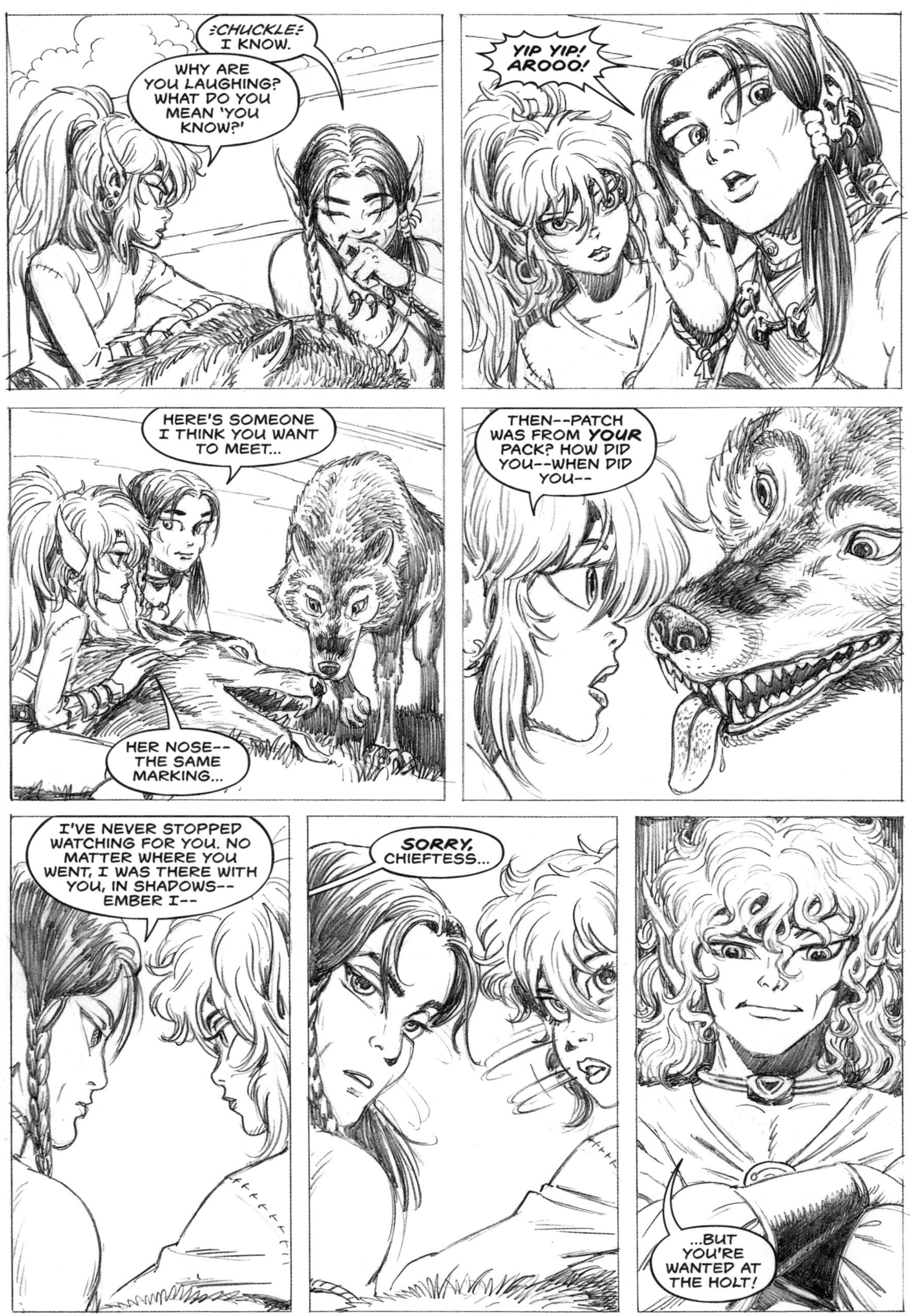

:CHUCKLE: I KNOW.
WHY ARE YOU LAUGHING? WHAT DO YOU MEAN 'YOU KNOW?'
YIP YIP! AROOO!
HERE'S SOMEONE I THINK YOU WANT TO MEET...
HER NOSE-- THE SAME MARKING...
THEN--PATCH WAS FROM *YOUR* PACK? HOW DID YOU--WHEN DID YOU--
I'VE NEVER STOPPED WATCHING FOR YOU. NO MATTER WHERE YOU WENT, I WAS THERE WITH YOU, IN SHADOWS-- EMBER I--
SORRY, CHIEFTESS...
...BUT YOU'RE WANTED AT THE HOLT!

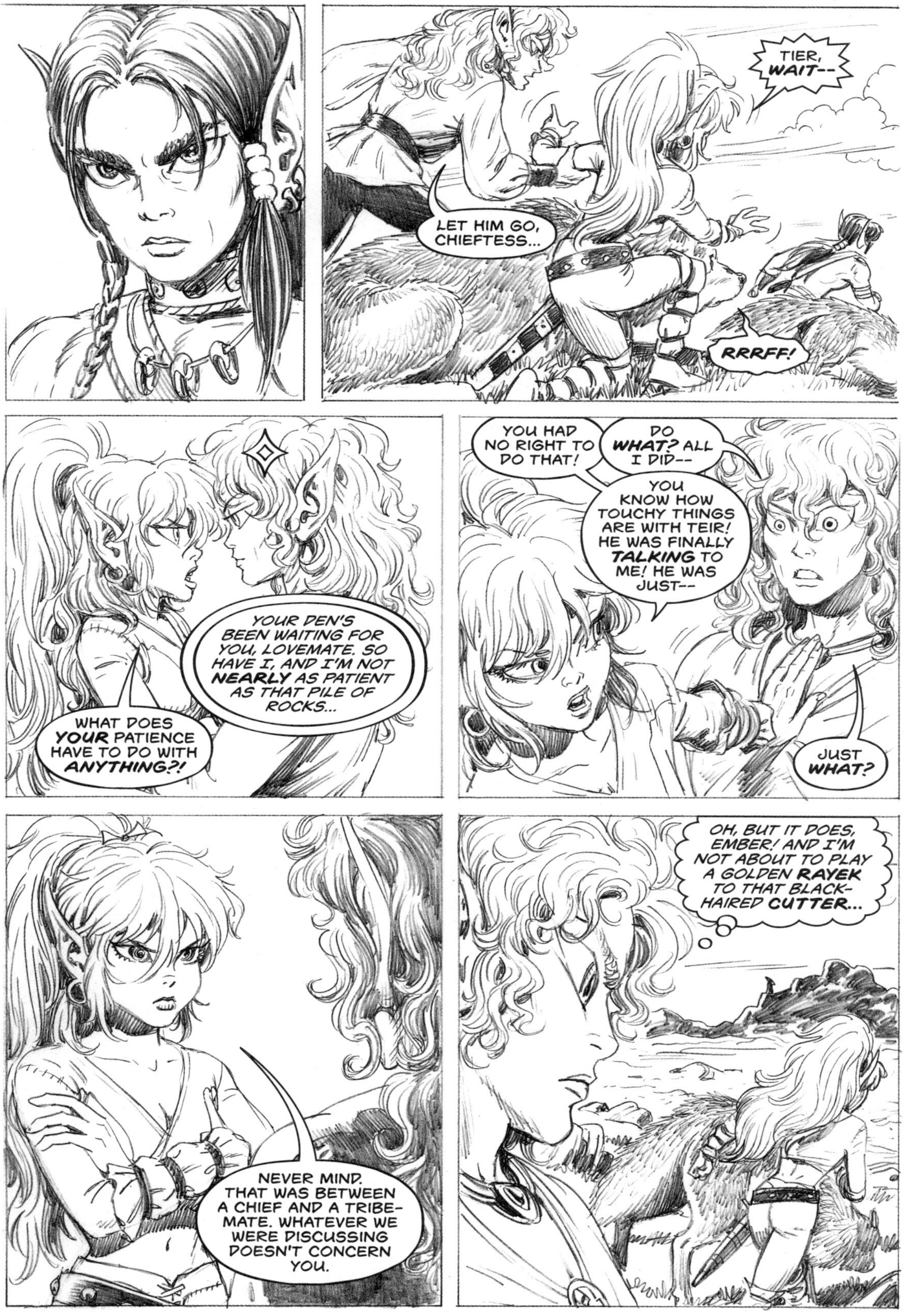
TIER, WAIT--
LET HIM GO, CHIEFTESS...
RRRFF!
YOUR DEN'S BEEN WAITING FOR YOU, LOVEMATE. SO HAVE I, AND I'M NOT NEARLY AS PATIENT AS THAT PILE OF ROCKS...
WHAT DOES YOUR PATIENCE HAVE TO DO WITH ANYTHING?!
YOU HAD NO RIGHT TO DO THAT!
DO WHAT? ALL I DID--
YOU KNOW HOW TOUCHY THINGS ARE WITH TEIR! HE WAS FINALLY TALKING TO ME! HE WAS JUST--
JUST WHAT?
NEVER MIND. THAT WAS BETWEEN A CHIEF AND A TRIBE-MATE. WHATEVER WE WERE DISCUSSING DOESN'T CONCERN YOU.
OH, BUT IT DOES, EMBER! AND I'M NOT ABOUT TO PLAY A GOLDEN RAYEK TO THAT BLACK-HAIRED CUTTER...

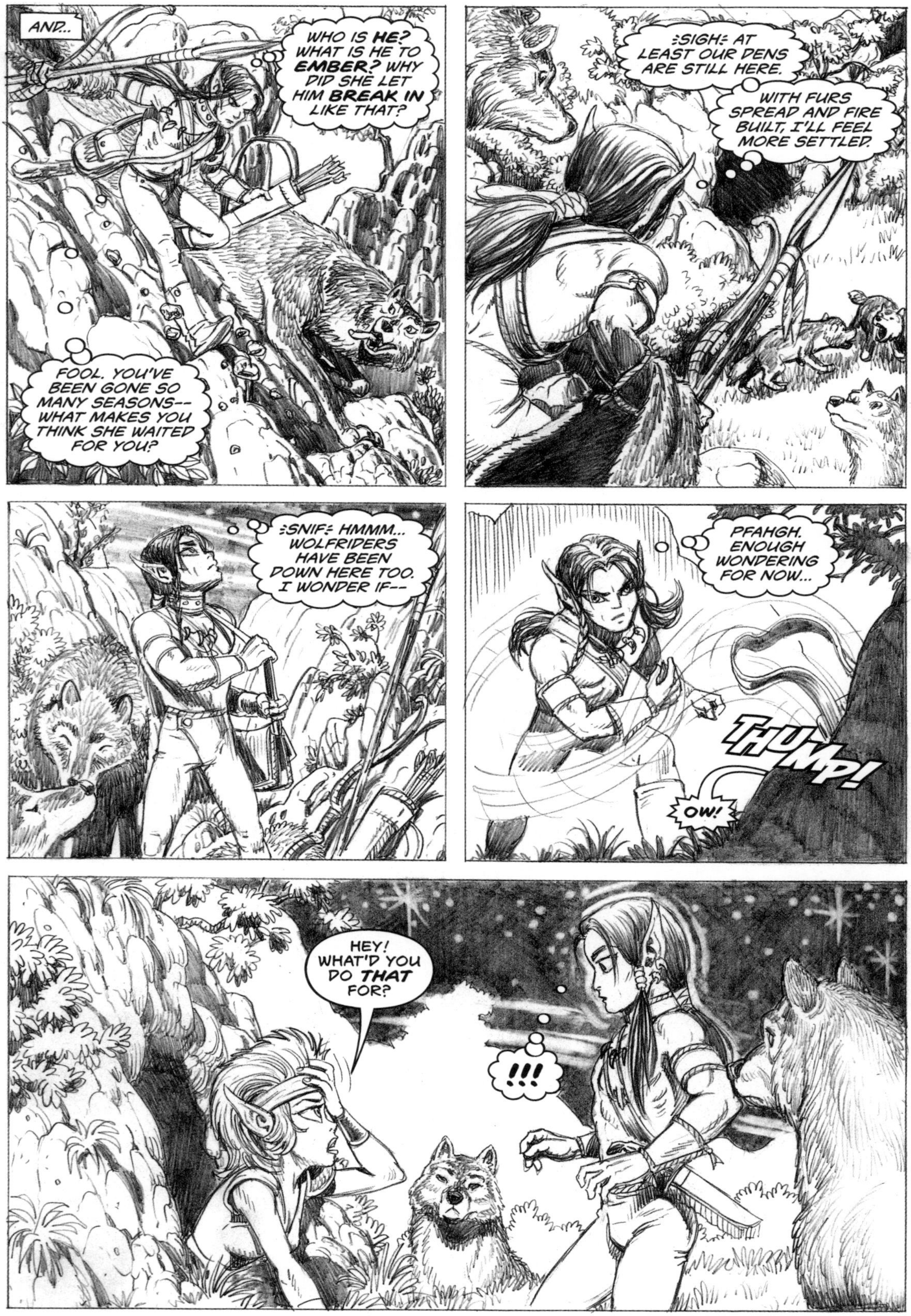
AND...
WHO IS HE? WHAT IS HE TO EMBER? WHY DID SHE LET HIM BREAK IN LIKE THAT?
FOOL. YOU'VE BEEN GONE SO MANY SEASONS--WHAT MAKES YOU THINK SHE WAITED FOR YOU?
:SIGH: AT LEAST OUR DENS ARE STILL HERE.
WITH FURS SPREAD AND FIRE BUILT, I'LL FEEL MORE SETTLED.
:SNIF: HMMM... WOLFRIDERS HAVE BEEN DOWN HERE TOO. I WONDER IF--
PFAHGH. ENOUGH WONDERING FOR NOW...
THUMP!
OW!
HEY! WHAT'D YOU DO THAT FOR?
!!!

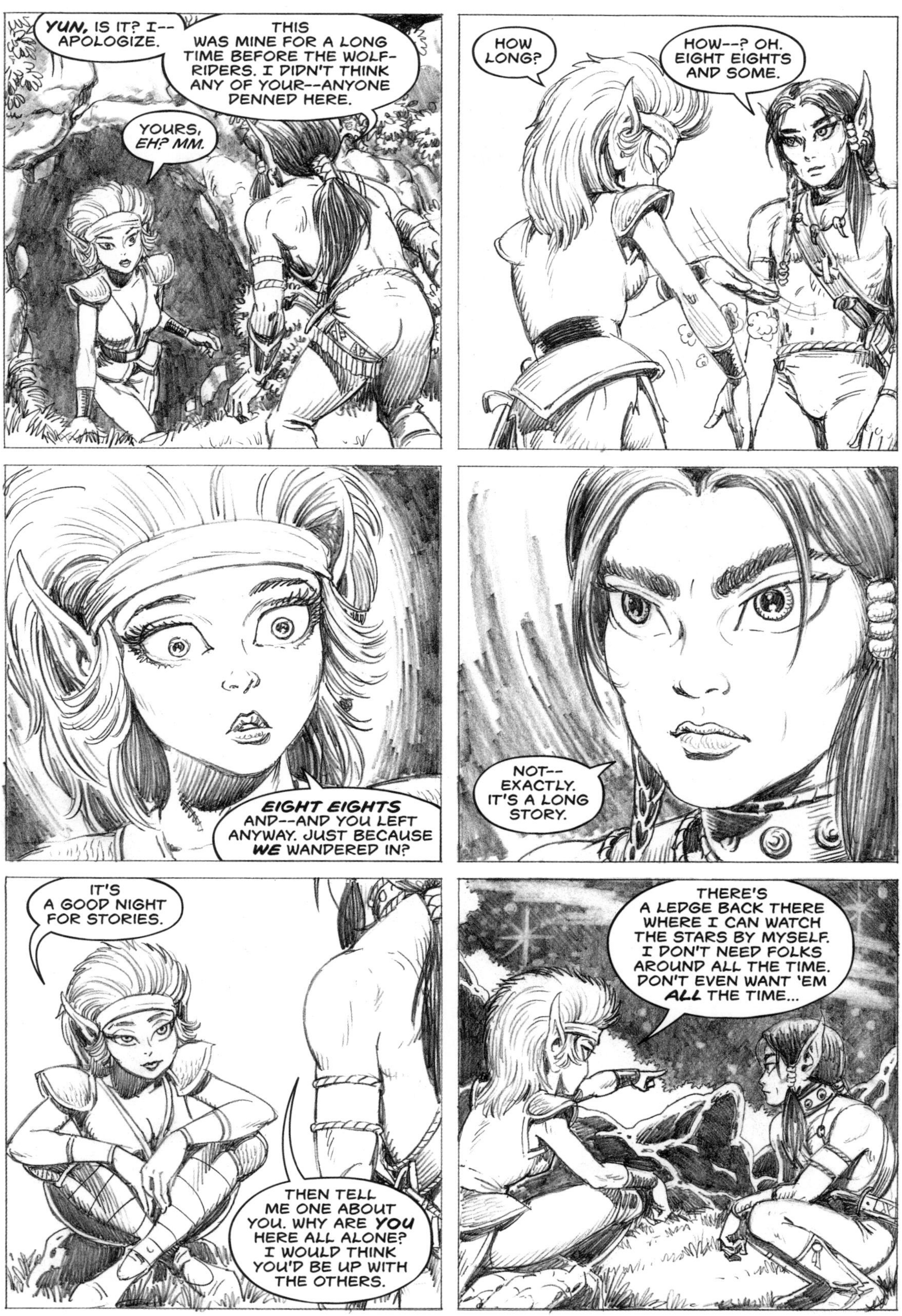
YUN, IS IT? I-- APOLOGIZE.
THIS WAS MINE FOR A LONG TIME BEFORE THE WOLF-RIDERS. I DIDN'T THINK ANY OF YOUR--ANYONE DENNED HERE.
YOURS, EH? MM.
HOW LONG?
HOW--? OH. EIGHT EIGHTS AND SOME.
EIGHT EIGHTS AND--AND YOU LEFT ANYWAY. JUST BECAUSE WE WANDERED IN?
NOT-- EXACTLY. IT'S A LONG STORY.
IT'S A GOOD NIGHT FOR STORIES.
THEN TELL ME ONE ABOUT YOU. WHY ARE YOU HERE ALL ALONE? I WOULD THINK YOU'D BE UP WITH THE OTHERS.
THERE'S A LEDGE BACK THERE WHERE I CAN WATCH THE STARS BY MYSELF. I DON'T NEED FOLKS AROUND ALL THE TIME. DON'T EVEN WANT 'EM ALL THE TIME...

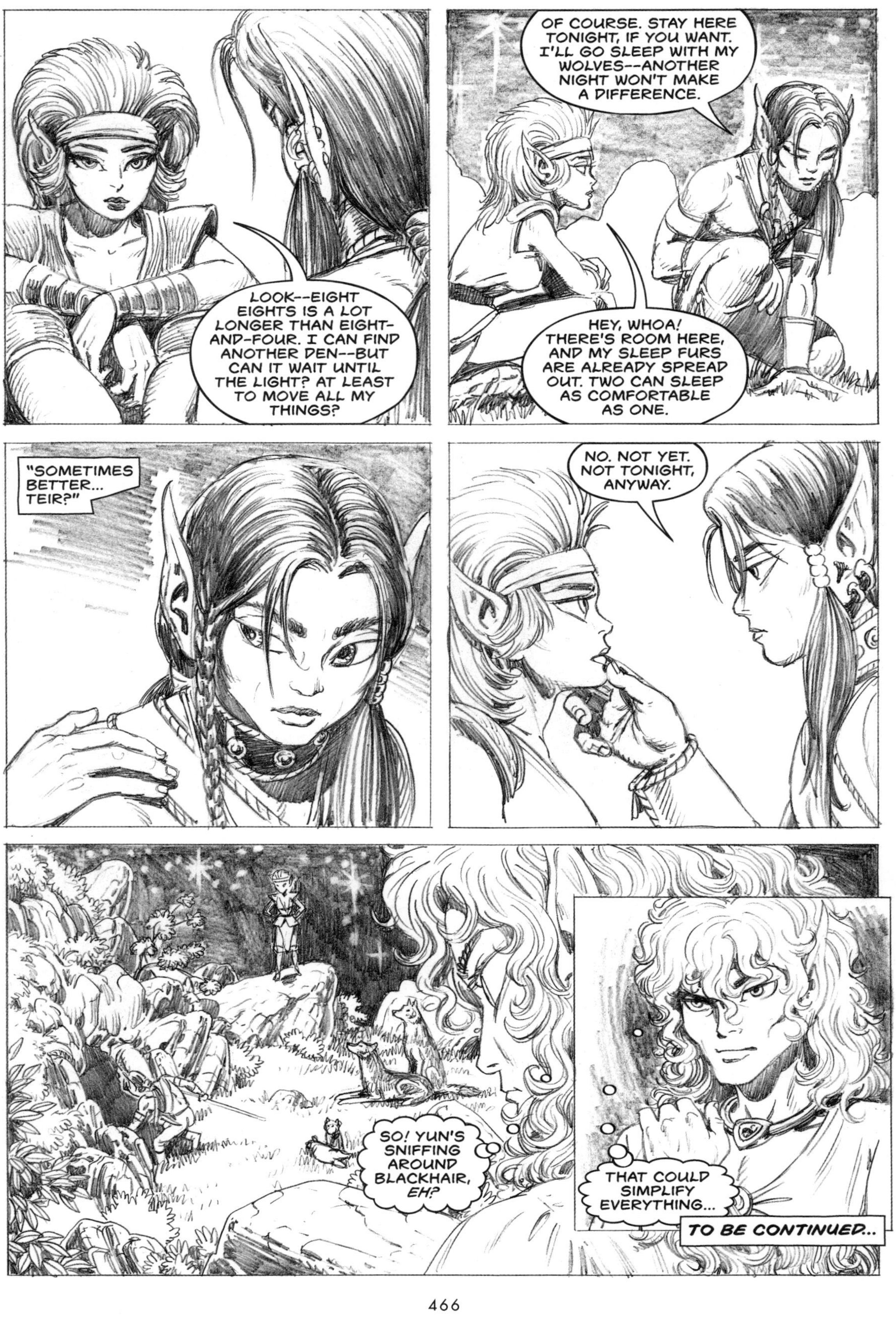
LOOK--EIGHT EIGHTS IS A LOT LONGER THAN EIGHT-AND-FOUR. I CAN FIND ANOTHER DEN--BUT CAN IT WAIT UNTIL THE LIGHT? AT LEAST TO MOVE ALL MY THINGS?
OF COURSE. STAY HERE TONIGHT, IF YOU WANT. I'LL GO SLEEP WITH MY WOLVES--ANOTHER NIGHT WON'T MAKE A DIFFERENCE.
HEY, WHOA! THERE'S ROOM HERE, AND MY SLEEP FURS ARE ALREADY SPREAD OUT. TWO CAN SLEEP AS COMFORTABLE AS ONE.
"SOMETIMES BETTER... TEIR?"
NO. NOT YET. NOT TONIGHT, ANYWAY.
SO! YUN'S SNIFFING AROUND BLACKHAIR, *EH?*
THAT COULD SIMPLIFY EVERYTHING...
TO BE CONTINUED...

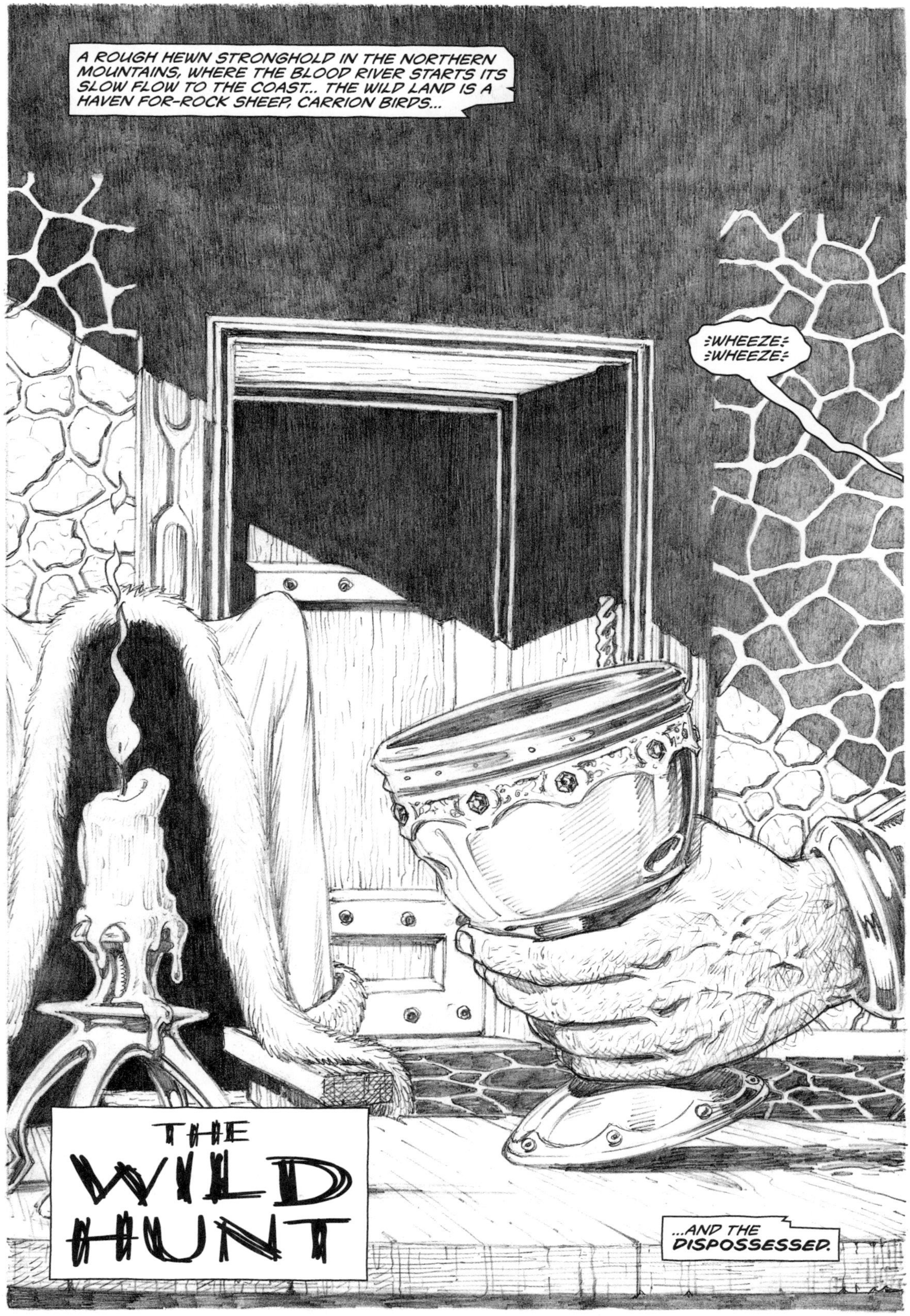
A ROUGH HEWN STRONGHOLD IN THE NORTHERN MOUNTAINS, WHERE THE BLOOD RIVER STARTS ITS SLOW FLOW TO THE COAST... THE WILD LAND IS A HAVEN FOR-ROCK SHEEP, CARRION BIRDS...
WHEEZE WHEEZE
THE WILD HUNT
...AND THE DISPOSSESSED.

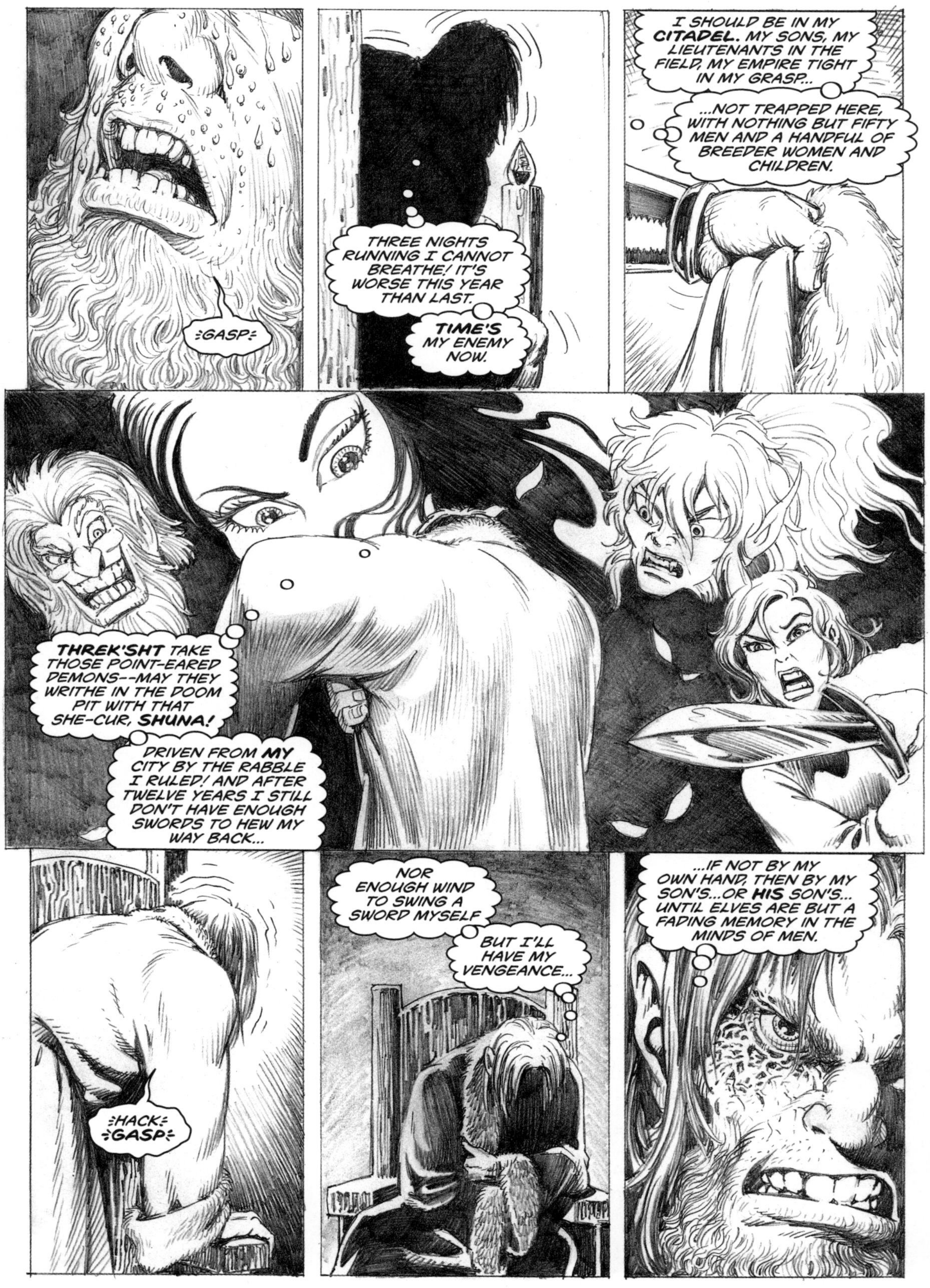
GASP
THREE NIGHTS RUNNING I CANNOT BREATHE! IT'S WORSE THIS YEAR THAN LAST.
TIME'S MY ENEMY NOW.
I SHOULD BE IN MY CITADEL. MY SONS, MY LIEUTENANTS IN THE FIELD, MY EMPIRE TIGHT IN MY GRASP...
...NOT TRAPPED HERE, WITH NOTHING BUT FIFTY MEN AND A HANDFUL OF BREEDER WOMEN AND CHILDREN.
THREK'SHT TAKE THOSE POINT-EARED DEMONS--MAY THEY WRITHE IN THE DOOM PIT WITH THAT SHE-CUR, SHUNA!
DRIVEN FROM MY CITY BY THE RABBLE I RULED! AND AFTER TWELVE YEARS I STILL DON'T HAVE ENOUGH SWORDS TO HEW MY WAY BACK...
HACK GASP
NOR ENOUGH WIND TO SWING A SWORD MYSELF
BUT I'LL HAVE MY VENGEANCE...
...IF NOT BY MY OWN HAND, THEN BY MY SON'S...OR HIS SON'S... UNTIL ELVES ARE BUT A FADING MEMORY IN THE MINDS OF MEN.

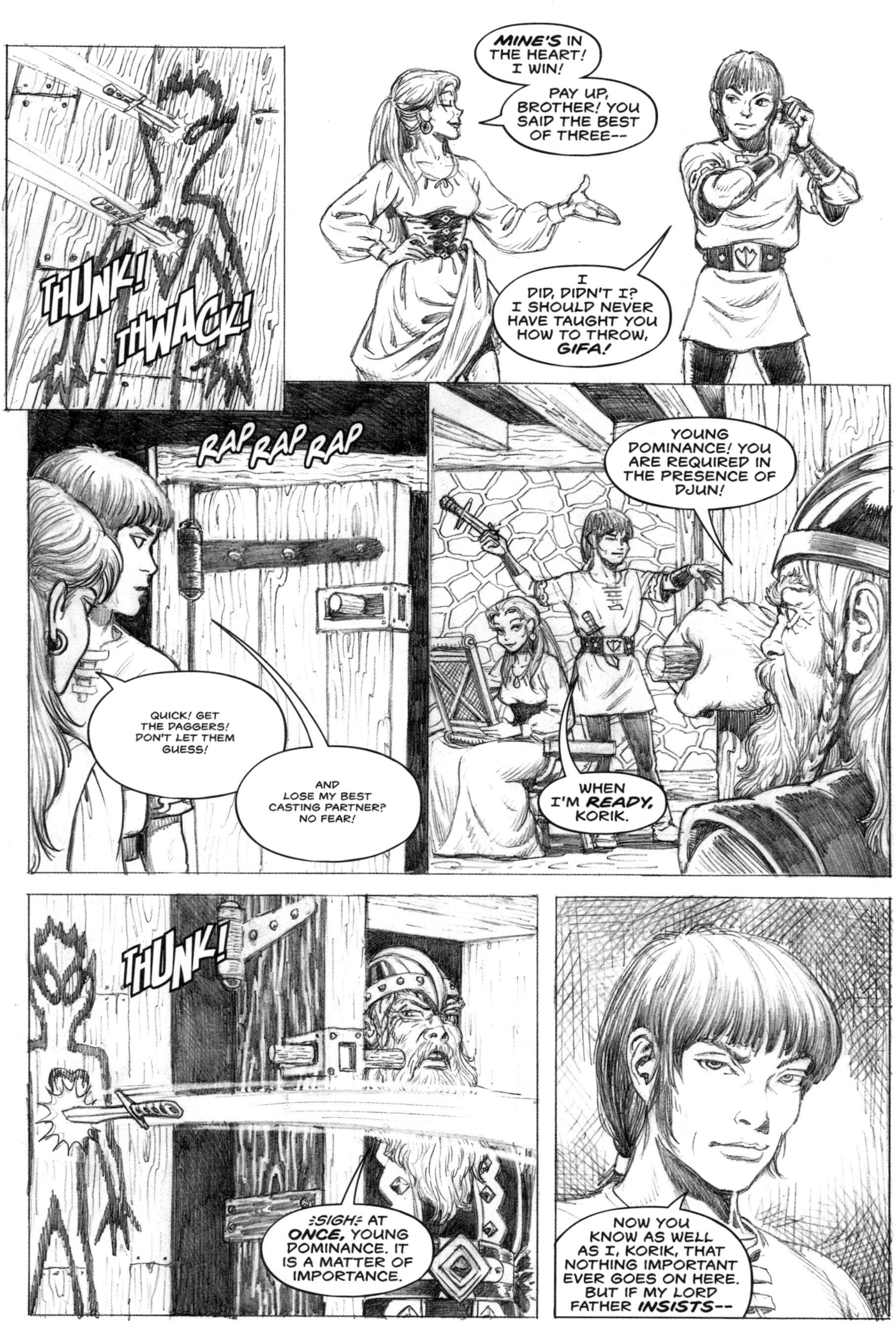
THUNK! THWACK!
MINE'S IN THE HEART! I WIN!
PAY UP, BROTHER! YOU SAID THE BEST OF THREE--
I DID, DIDN'T I? I SHOULD NEVER HAVE TAUGHT YOU HOW TO THROW, GIFA!
RAP RAP RAP
QUICK! GET THE DAGGERS! DON'T LET THEM GUESS!
AND LOSE MY BEST CASTING PARTNER? NO FEAR!
YOUNG DOMINANCE! YOU ARE REQUIRED IN THE PRESENCE OF DJUN!
WHEN I'M READY, KORIK.
THUNK!
:SIGH: AT ONCE, YOUNG DOMINANCE. IT IS A MATTER OF IMPORTANCE.
NOW YOU KNOW AS WELL AS I, KORIK, THAT NOTHING IMPORTANT EVER GOES ON HERE. BUT IF MY LORD FATHER INSISTS--

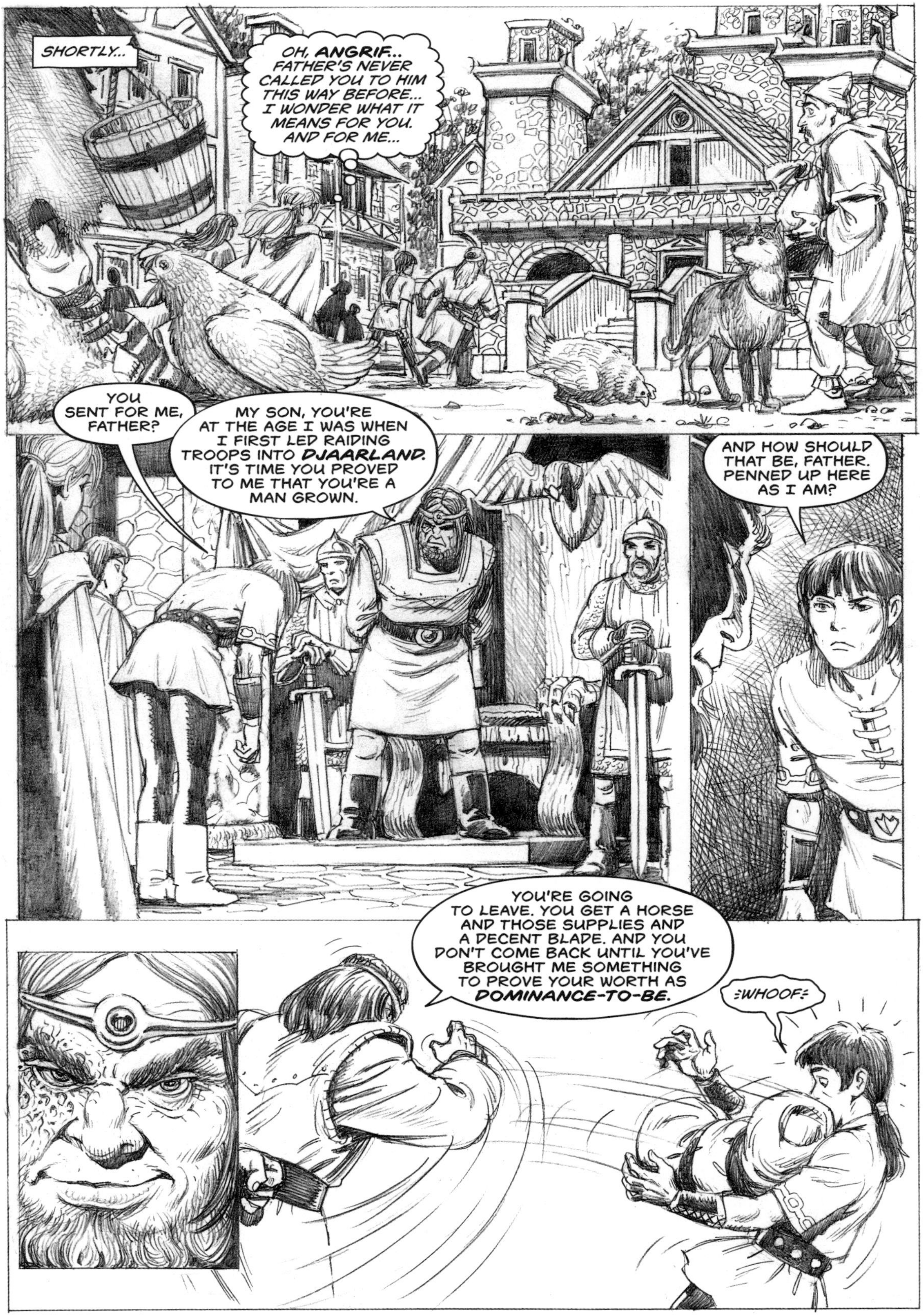

SHORTLY...
OH, ANGRIF... FATHER'S NEVER CALLED YOU TO HIM THIS WAY BEFORE... I WONDER WHAT IT MEANS FOR YOU. AND FOR ME...
YOU SENT FOR ME, FATHER?
MY SON, YOU'RE AT THE AGE I WAS WHEN I FIRST LED RAIDING TROOPS INTO DJAARLAND. IT'S TIME YOU PROVED TO ME THAT YOU'RE A MAN GROWN.
AND HOW SHOULD THAT BE, FATHER. PENNED UP HERE AS I AM?
YOU'RE GOING TO LEAVE. YOU GET A HORSE AND THOSE SUPPLIES AND A DECENT BLADE. AND YOU DON'T COME BACK UNTIL YOU'VE BROUGHT ME SOMETHING TO PROVE YOUR WORTH AS DOMINANCE-TO-BE.
WHOOF

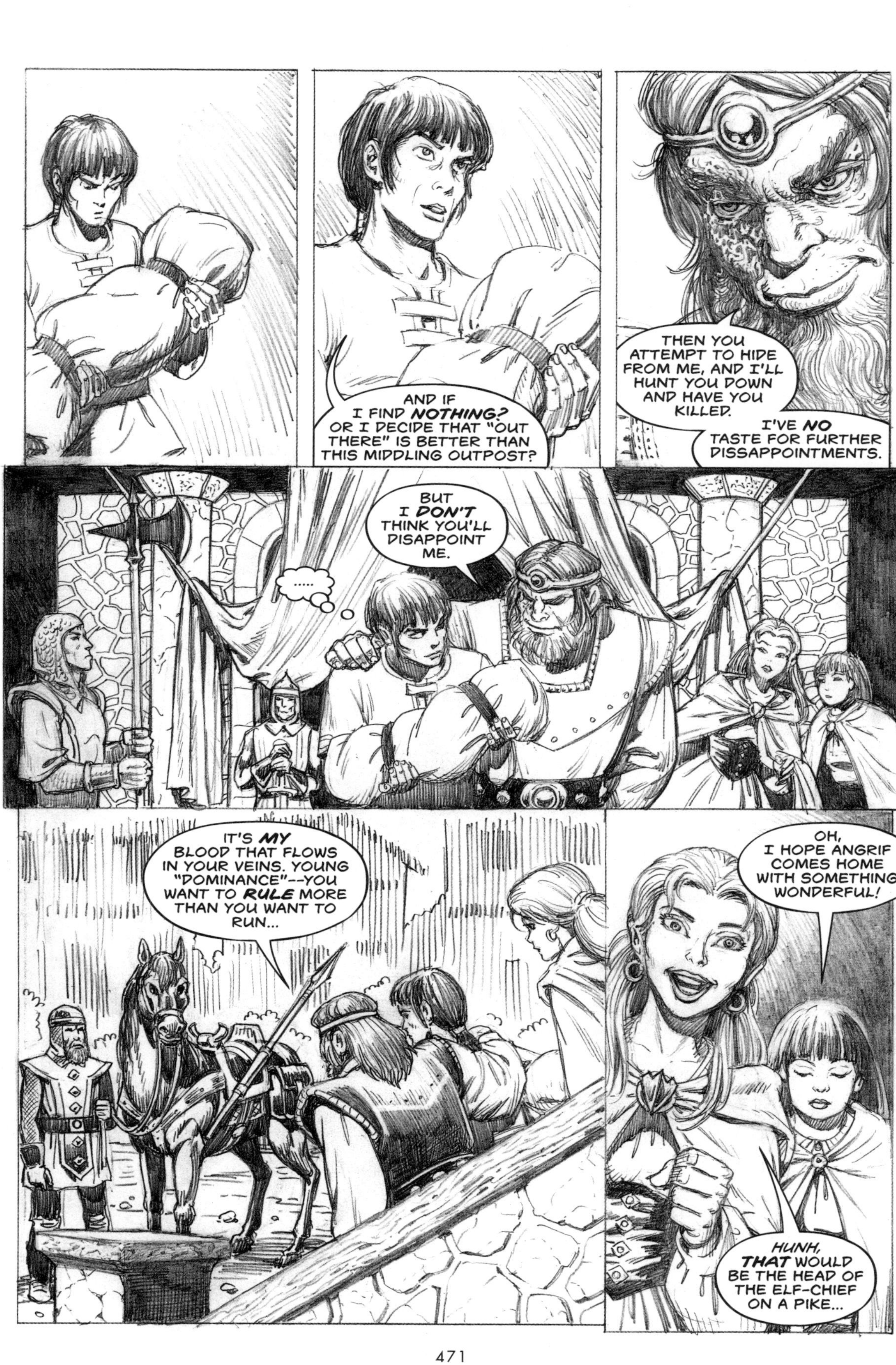
AND IF I FIND NOTHING? OR I DECIDE THAT "OUT THERE" IS BETTER THAN THIS MIDDLING OUTPOST?
THEN YOU ATTEMPT TO HIDE FROM ME, AND I'LL HUNT YOU DOWN AND HAVE YOU KILLED.
I'VE NO TASTE FOR FURTHER DISSAPPOINTMENTS.
BUT I DON'T THINK YOU'LL DISAPPOINT ME.
.....
IT'S MY BLOOD THAT FLOWS IN YOUR VEINS. YOUNG "DOMINANCE"--YOU WANT TO RULE MORE THAN YOU WANT TO RUN...
OH, I HOPE ANGRIF COMES HOME WITH SOMETHING WONDERFUL!
HUNH, THAT WOULD BE THE HEAD OF THE ELF-CHIEF ON A PIKE...

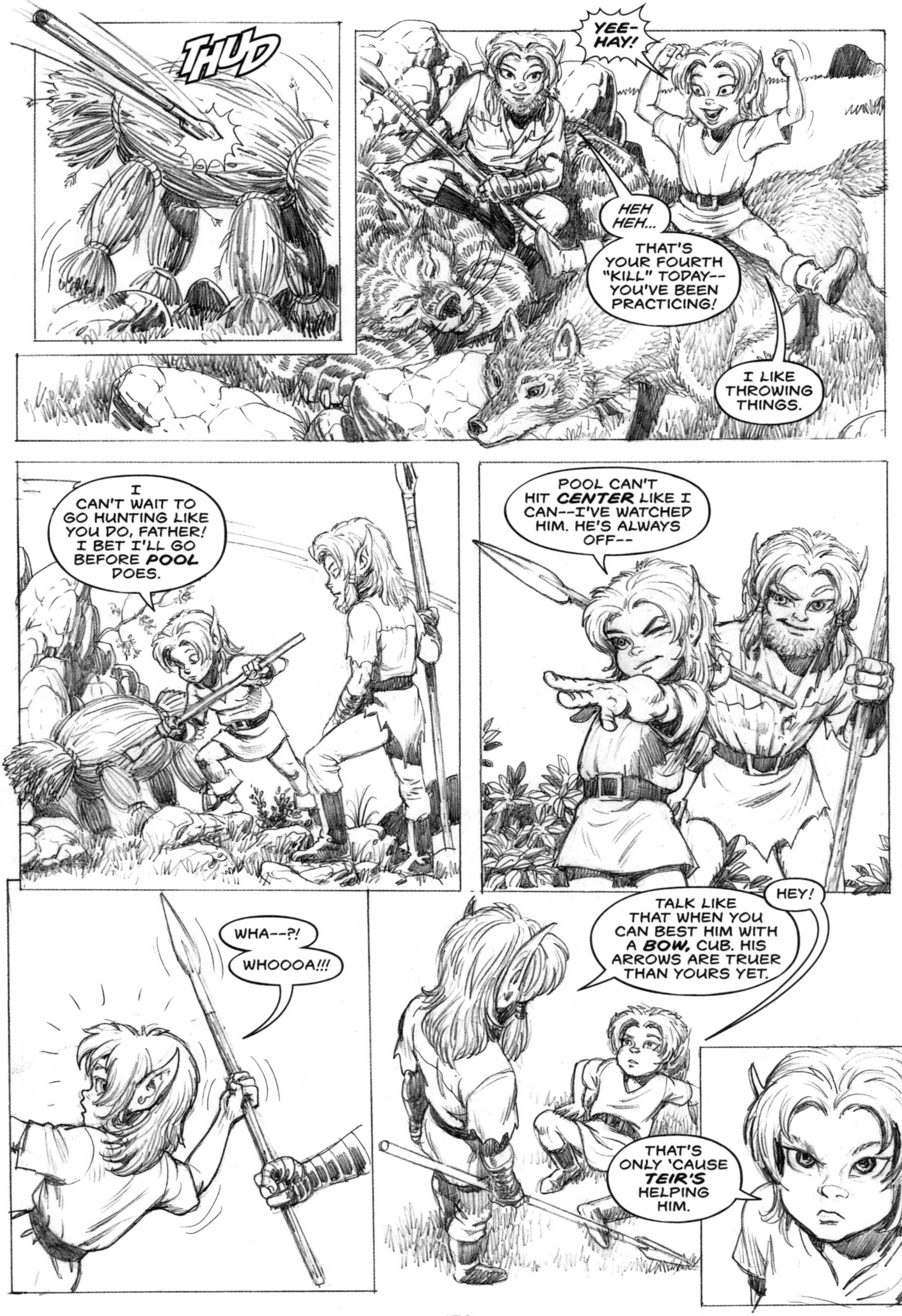
THUD
YEE-HAY!
HEH HEH... THAT'S YOUR FOURTH "KILL" TODAY--YOU'VE BEEN PRACTICING!
I LIKE THROWING THINGS.
I CAN'T WAIT TO GO HUNTING LIKE YOU DO, FATHER! I BET I'LL GO BEFORE POOL DOES.
POOL CAN'T HIT CENTER LIKE I CAN--I'VE WATCHED HIM. HE'S ALWAYS OFF--
WHA--?!
WHOOOA!!!
TALK LIKE THAT WHEN YOU CAN BEST HIM WITH A BOW, CUB. HIS ARROWS ARE TRUER THAN YOURS YET.
HEY!
THAT'S ONLY 'CAUSE TEIR'S HELPING HIM.

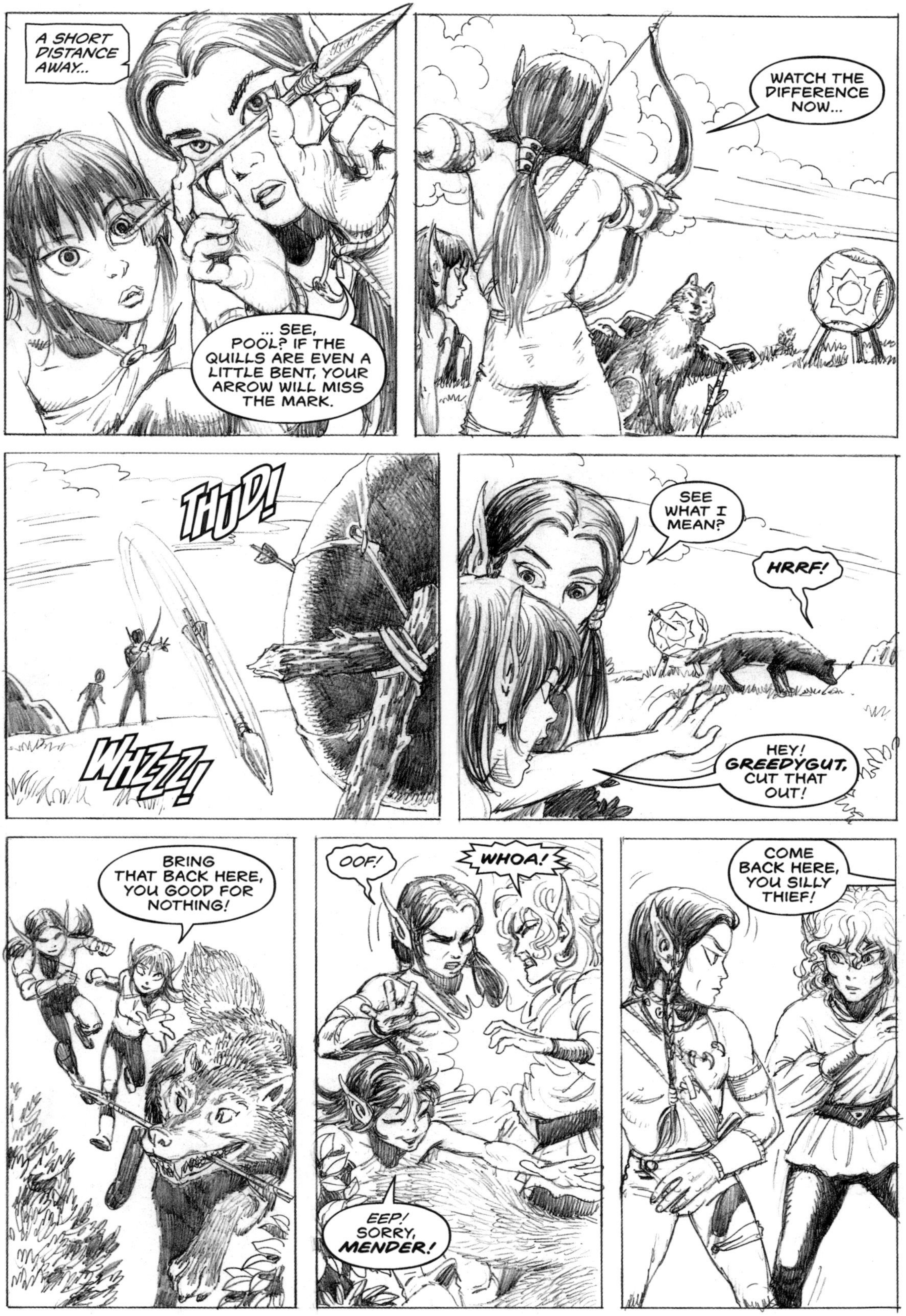
A SHORT DISTANCE AWAY...
... SEE, POOL? IF THE QUILLS ARE EVEN A LITTLE BENT, YOUR ARROW WILL MISS THE MARK.
WATCH THE DIFFERENCE NOW...
THUD!
WHZZZ!
SEE WHAT I MEAN?
HRRF!
HEY! GREEDYGUT, CUT THAT OUT!
BRING THAT BACK HERE, YOU GOOD FOR NOTHING!
OOF!
WHOA!
EEP! SORRY, MENDER!
COME BACK HERE, YOU SILLY THIEF!

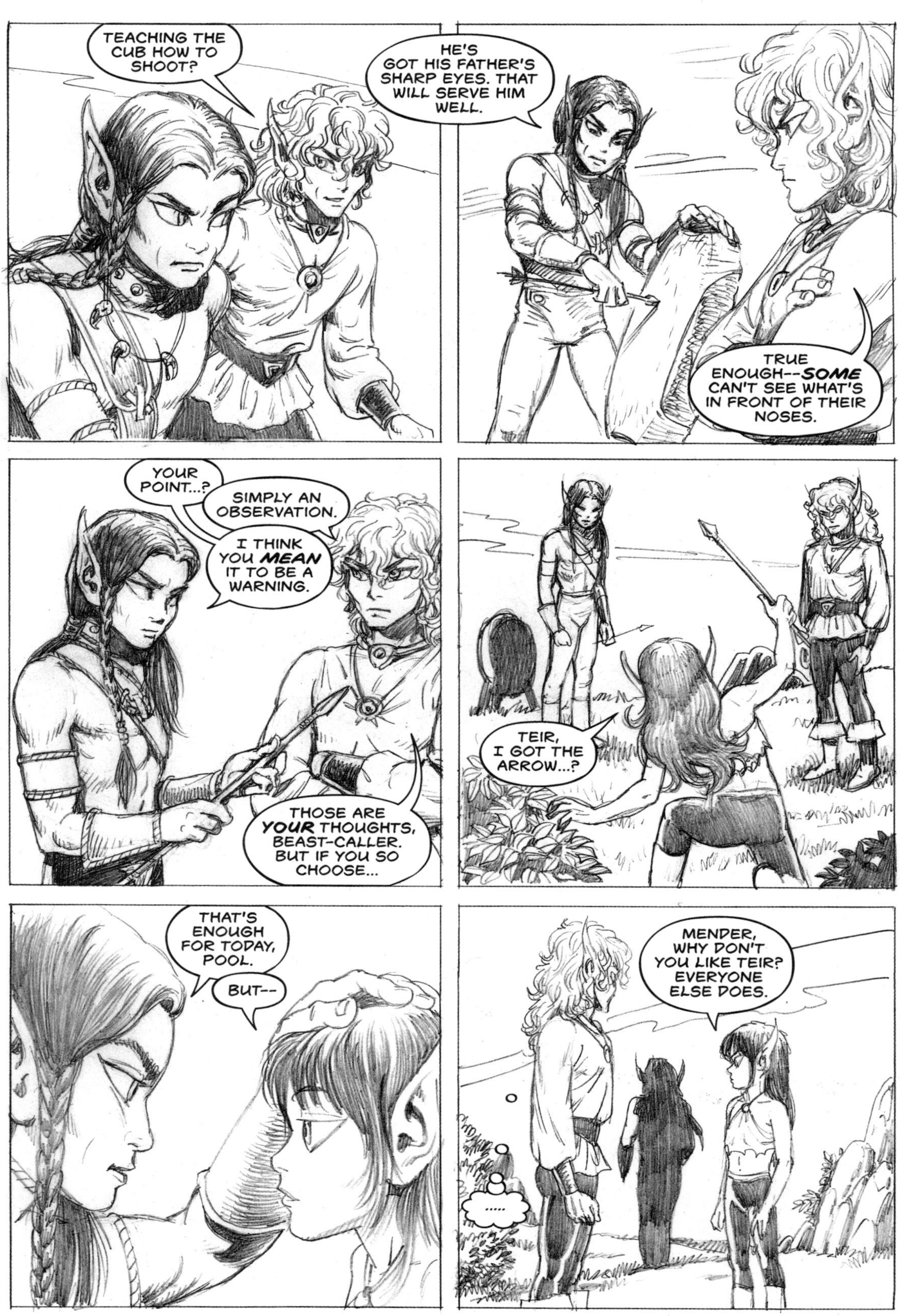
TEACHING THE CUB HOW TO SHOOT?
HE'S GOT HIS FATHER'S SHARP EYES. THAT WILL SERVE HIM WELL.
TRUE ENOUGH--SOME CAN'T SEE WHAT'S IN FRONT OF THEIR NOSES.
YOUR POINT...?
SIMPLY AN OBSERVATION.
I THINK YOU MEAN IT TO BE A WARNING.
THOSE ARE YOUR THOUGHTS, BEAST-CALLER. BUT IF YOU SO CHOOSE...
TEIR, I GOT THE ARROW...?
THAT'S ENOUGH FOR TODAY, POOL.
BUT--
MENDER, WHY DON'T YOU LIKE TEIR? EVERYONE ELSE DOES.
.....

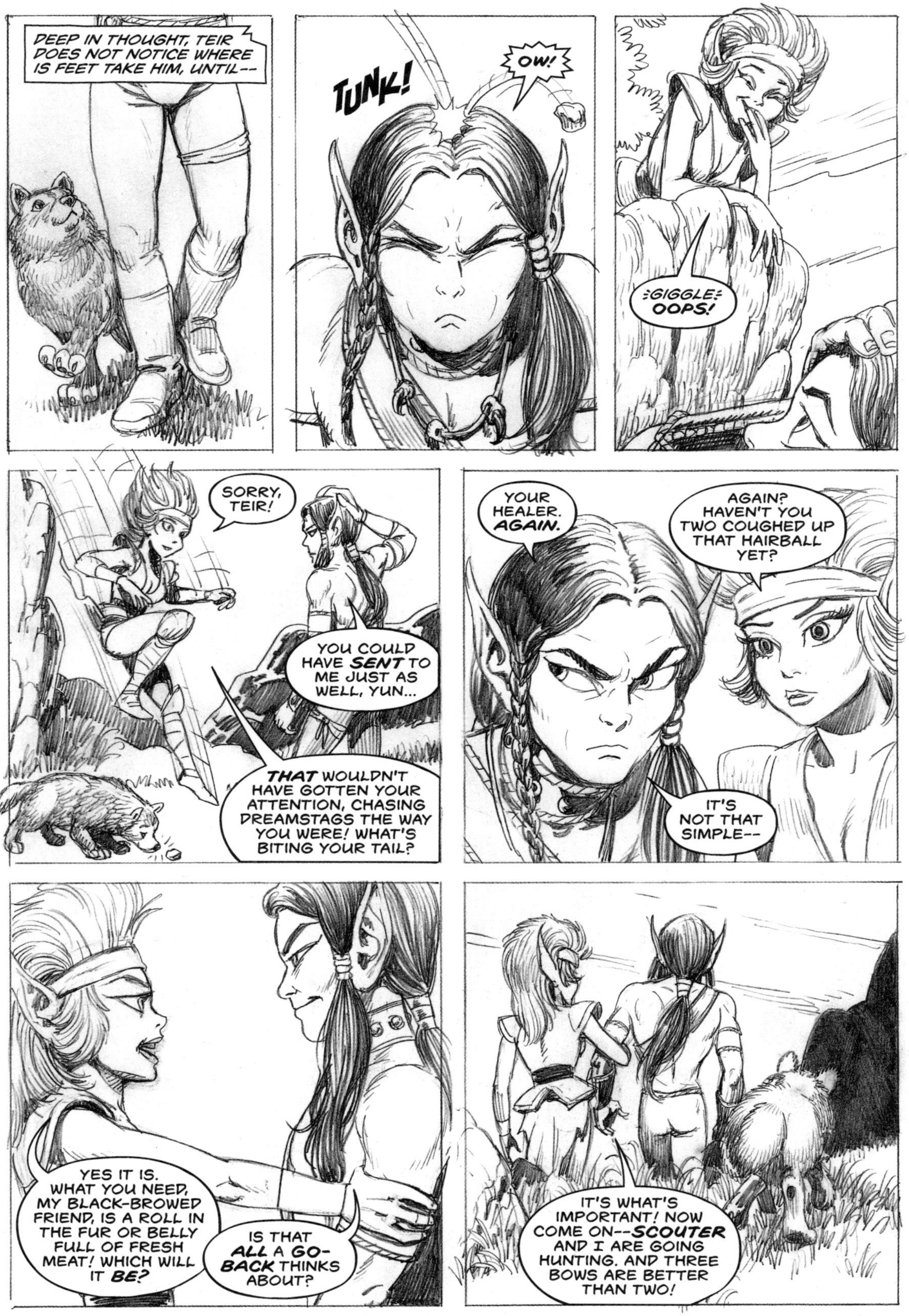
DEEP IN THOUGHT, TEIR DOES NOT NOTICE WHERE IS FEET TAKE HIM, UNTIL--
TUNK!
OW!
GIGGLE OOPS!
SORRY, TEIR!
YOU COULD HAVE SENT TO ME JUST AS WELL, YUN...
THAT WOULDN'T HAVE GOTTEN YOUR ATTENTION, CHASING DREAMSTAGS THE WAY YOU WERE! WHAT'S BITING YOUR TAIL?
YOUR HEALER. AGAIN.
AGAIN? HAVEN'T YOU TWO COUGHED UP THAT HAIRBALL YET?
IT'S NOT THAT SIMPLE--
YES IT IS. WHAT YOU NEED, MY BLACK-BROWED FRIEND, IS A ROLL IN THE FUR OR BELLY FULL OF FRESH MEAT! WHICH WILL IT BE?
IS THAT ALL A GO-BACK THINKS ABOUT?
IT'S WHAT'S IMPORTANT! NOW COME ON--SCOUTER AND I ARE GOING HUNTING. AND THREE BOWS ARE BETTER THAN TWO!

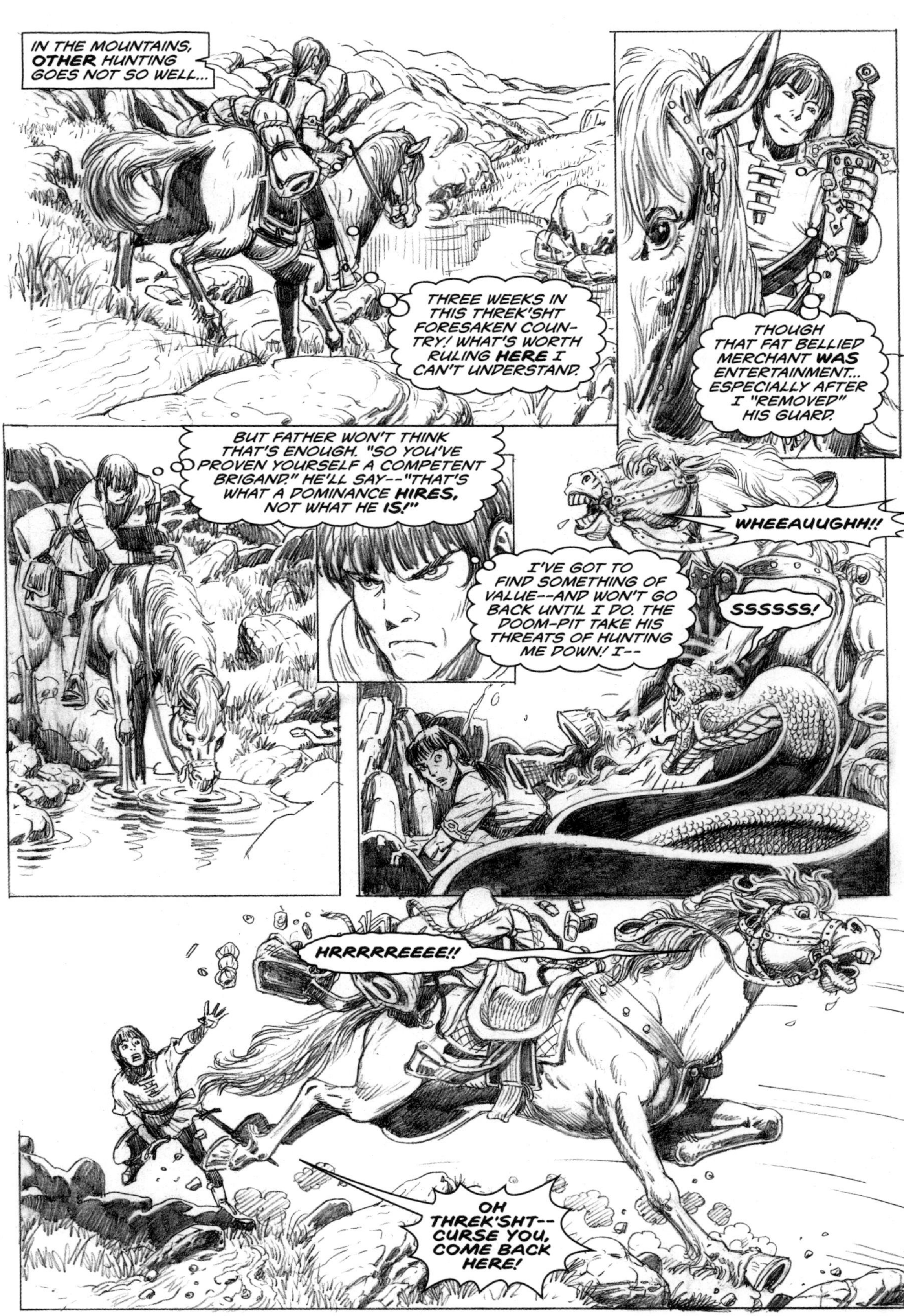
IN THE MOUNTAINS, OTHER HUNTING GOES NOT SO WELL...
THREE WEEKS IN THIS THREK'SHT FORESAKEN COUNTRY! WHAT'S WORTH RULING HERE I CAN'T UNDERSTAND.
THOUGH THAT FAT BELLIED MERCHANT WAS ENTERTAINMENT... ESPECIALLY AFTER I "REMOVED" HIS GUARD.
BUT FATHER WON'T THINK THAT'S ENOUGH. "SO YOU'VE PROVEN YOURSELF A COMPETENT BRIGAND." HE'LL SAY--"THAT'S WHAT A DOMINANCE HIRES, NOT WHAT HE IS!"
I'VE GOT TO FIND SOMETHING OF VALUE--AND WON'T GO BACK UNTIL I DO. THE DOOM-PIT TAKE HIS THREATS OF HUNTING ME DOWN! I--
WHEEAUUGHH!!
SSSSSS!
HRRRRREEEE!!
OH THREK'SHT--CURSE YOU, COME BACK HERE!

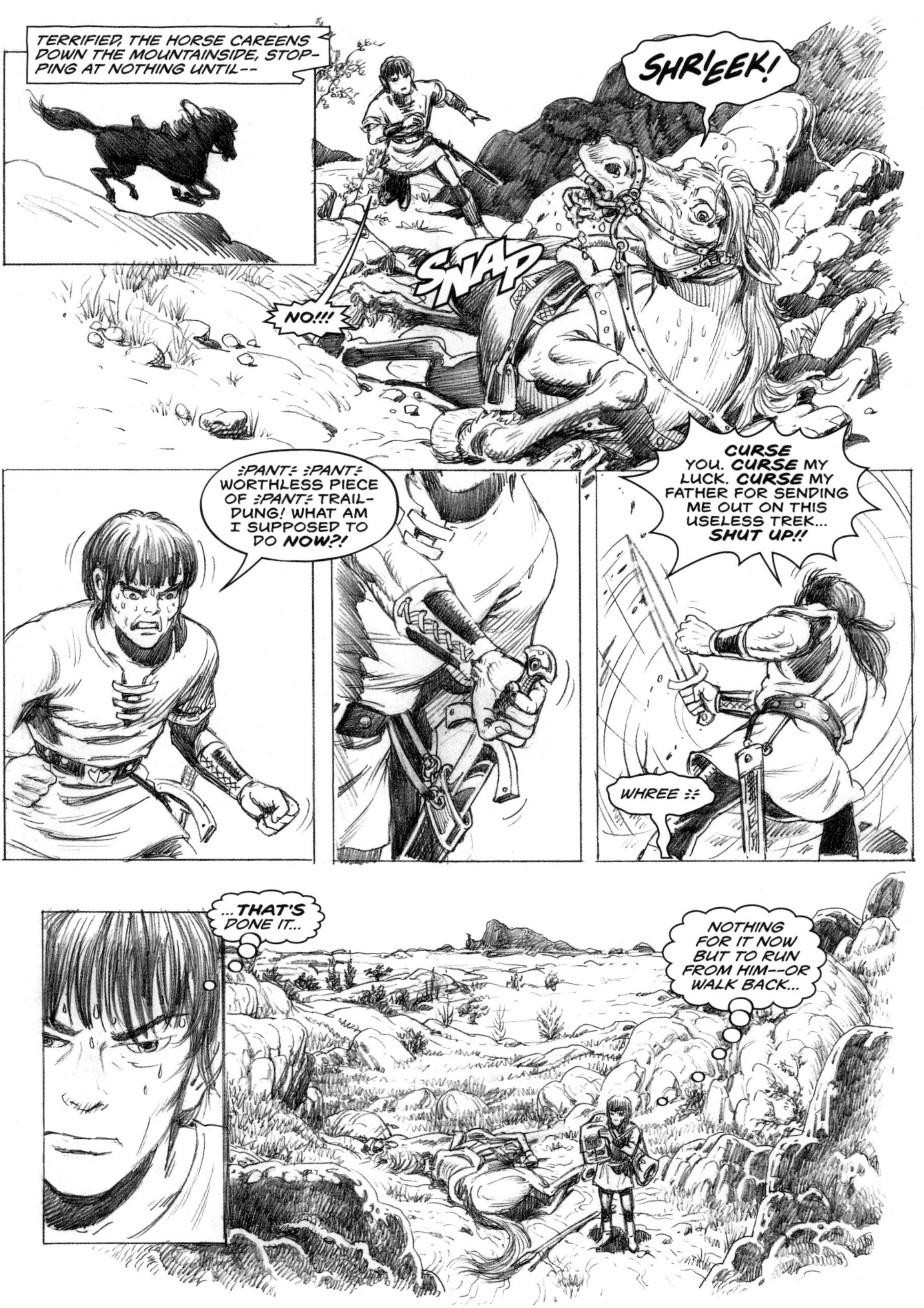
TERRIFIED, THE HORSE CAREENS DOWN THE MOUNTAINSIDE, STOPPING AT NOTHING UNTIL--
SHRIEEK!
SNAP
NO!!!
PANT PANT WORTHLESS PIECE OF PANT TRAIL-DUNG! WHAT AM I SUPPOSED TO DO NOW?!
CURSE YOU. CURSE MY LUCK. CURSE MY FATHER FOR SENDING ME OUT ON THIS USELESS TREK... SHUT UP!!
WHREE
...THAT'S DONE IT...
NOTHING FOR IT NOW BUT TO RUN FROM HIM--OR WALK BACK...

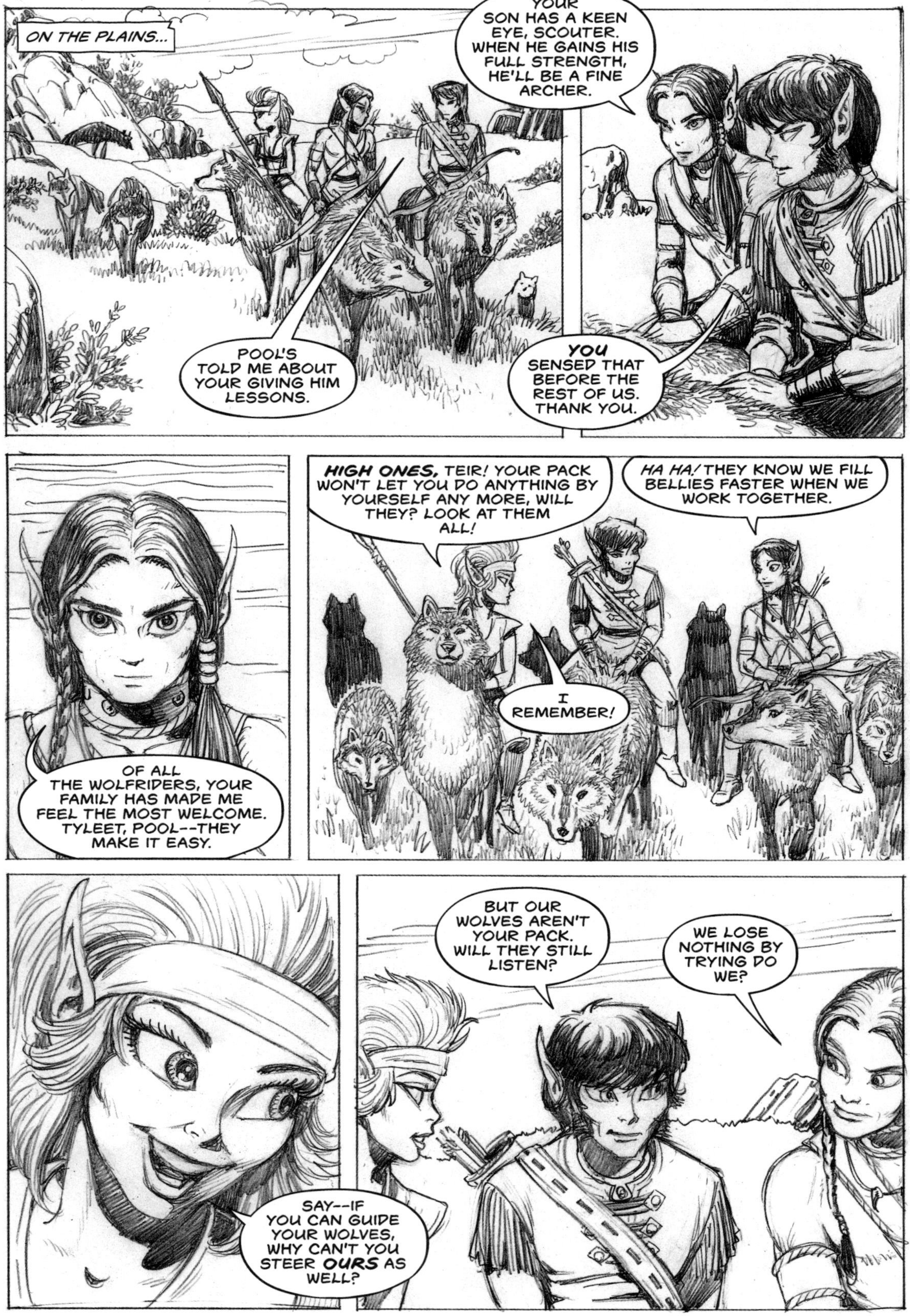

ON THE PLAINS...
POOL'S TOLD ME ABOUT YOUR GIVING HIM LESSONS.
YOUR SON HAS A KEEN EYE, SCOUTER. WHEN HE GAINS HIS FULL STRENGTH, HE'LL BE A FINE ARCHER.
YOU SENSED THAT BEFORE THE REST OF US. THANK YOU.
OF ALL THE WOLFRIDERS, YOUR FAMILY HAS MADE ME FEEL THE MOST WELCOME. TYLEET, POOL--THEY MAKE IT EASY.
HIGH ONES, TEIR! YOUR PACK WON'T LET YOU DO ANYTHING BY YOURSELF ANY MORE, WILL THEY? LOOK AT THEM ALL!
I REMEMBER!
HA HA! THEY KNOW WE FILL BELLIES FASTER WHEN WE WORK TOGETHER.
SAY--IF YOU CAN GUIDE YOUR WOLVES, WHY CAN'T YOU STEER OURS AS WELL?
BUT OUR WOLVES AREN'T YOUR PACK. WILL THEY STILL LISTEN?
WE LOSE NOTHING BY TRYING DO WE?

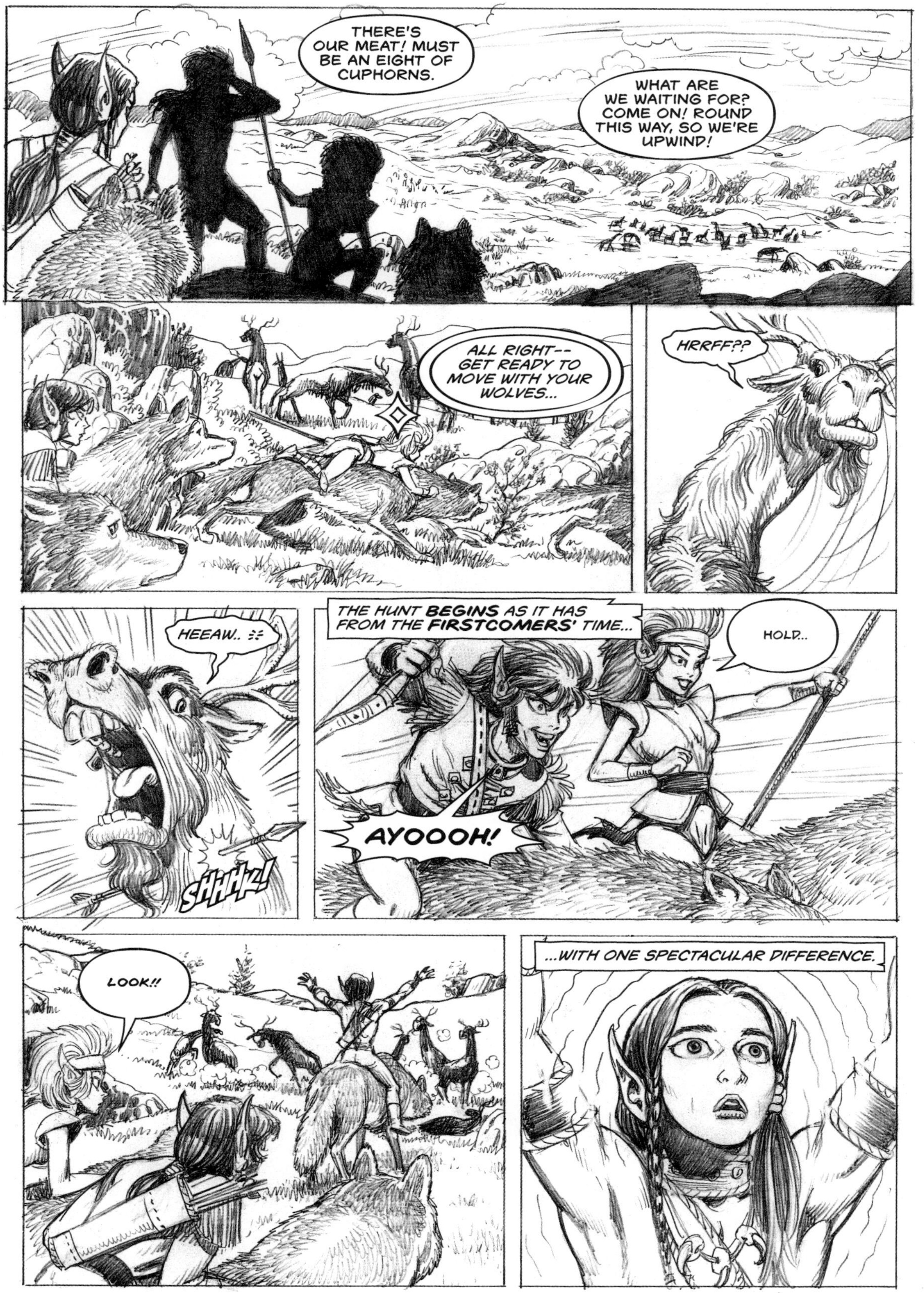
THERE'S OUR MEAT! MUST BE AN EIGHT OF CUPHORNS.
WHAT ARE WE WAITING FOR? COME ON! ROUND THIS WAY, SO WE'RE UPWIND!
ALL RIGHT-- GET READY TO MOVE WITH YOUR WOLVES...
HRRFF??
HEEAW..
SHHHK!
THE HUNT BEGINS AS IT HAS FROM THE FIRSTCOMERS' TIME...
HOLD...
AYOOOH!
LOOK!!
...WITH ONE SPECTACULAR DIFFERENCE.

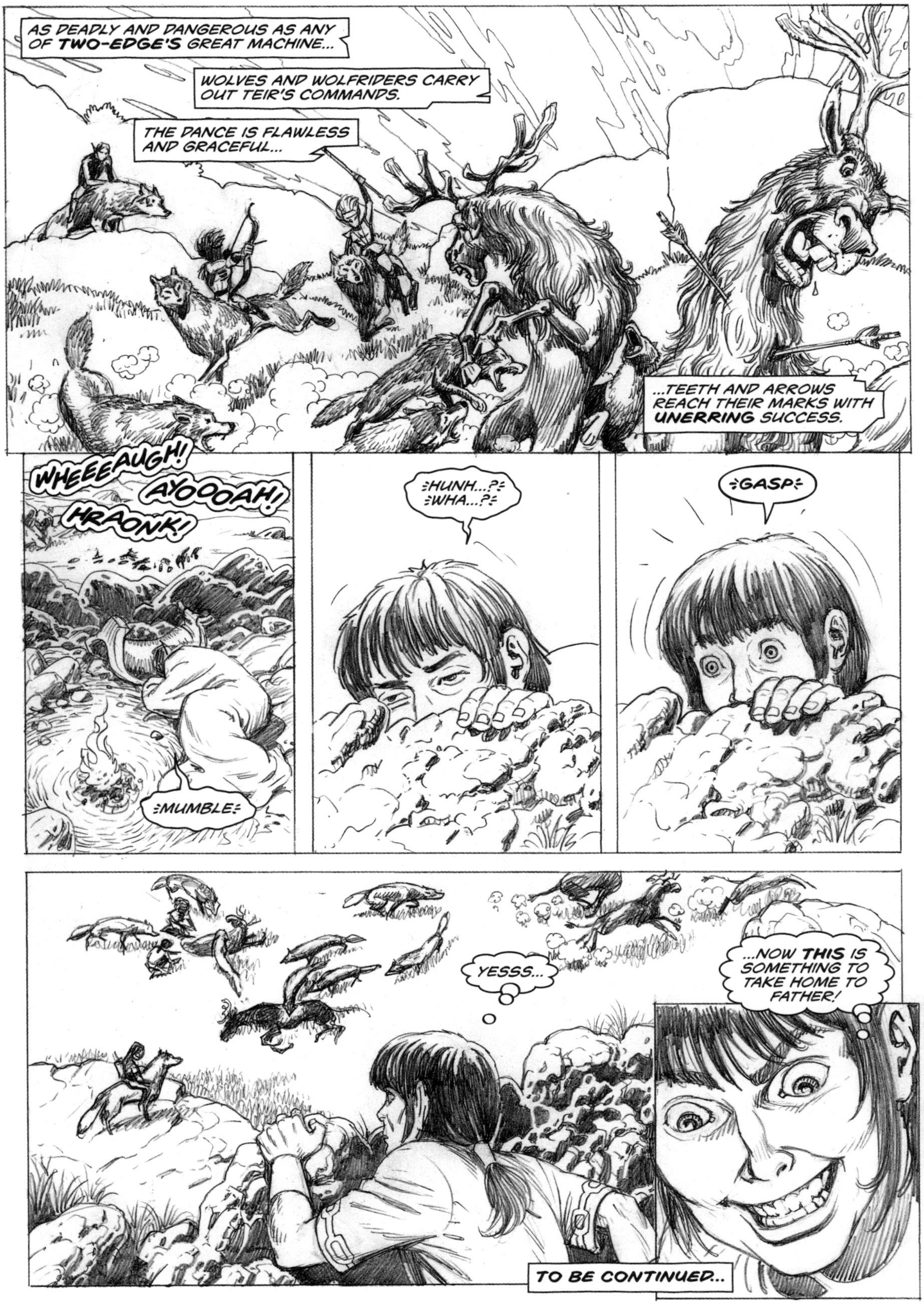
AS DEADLY AND DANGEROUS AS ANY OF TWO-EDGE'S GREAT MACHINE...
WOLVES AND WOLFRIDERS CARRY OUT TEIR'S COMMANDS.
THE DANCE IS FLAWLESS AND GRACEFUL...
...TEETH AND ARROWS REACH THEIR MARKS WITH UNERRING SUCCESS.
WHEEEAUGH!
AYOOOAH!
HRAONK!
MUMBLE
HUNH...? WHA...?
GASP
YESSS...
...NOW THIS IS SOMETHING TO TAKE HOME TO FATHER!
TO BE CONTINUED...

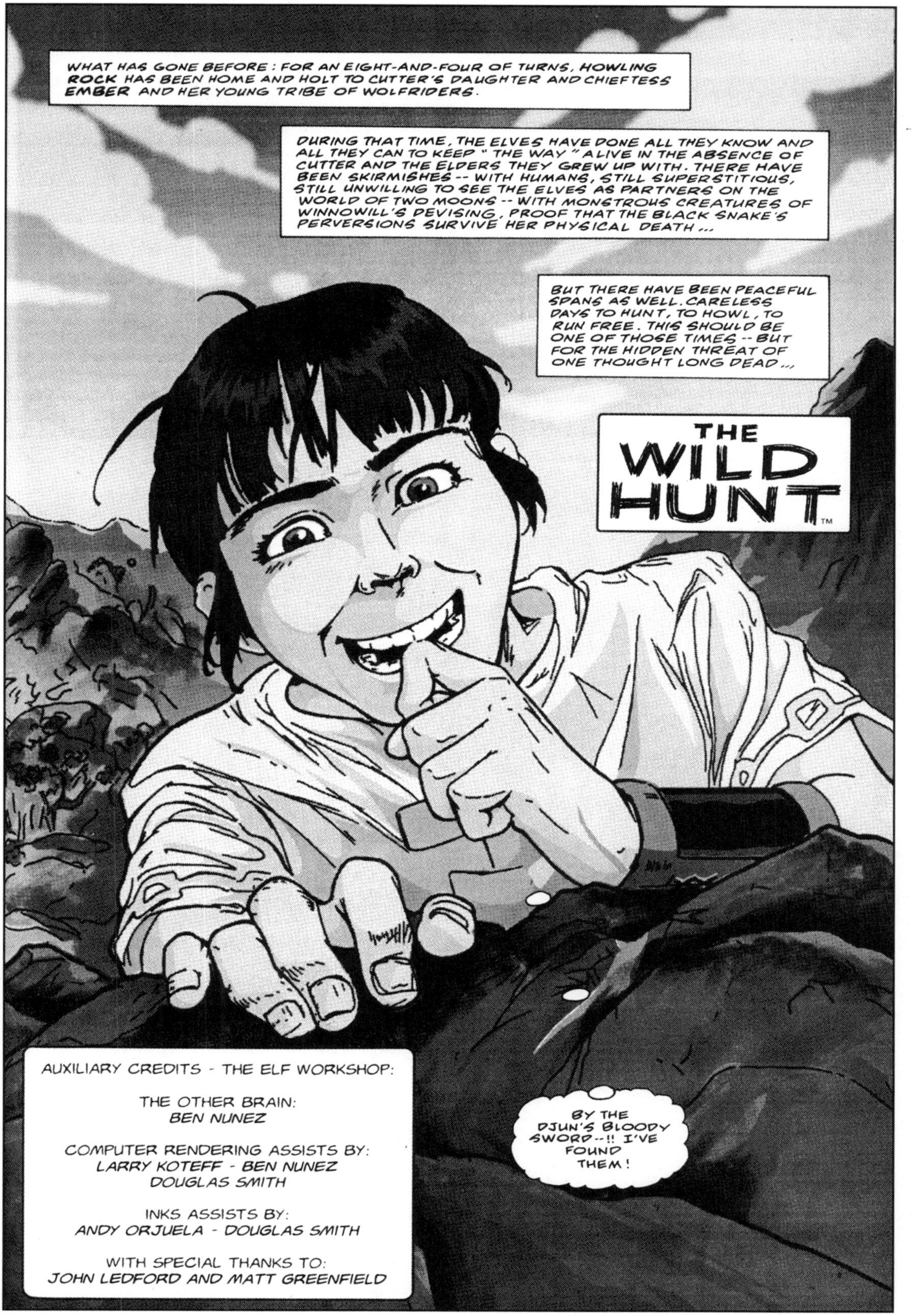
WHAT HAS GONE BEFORE: FOR AN EIGHT-AND-FOUR OF TURNS, HOWLING ROCK HAS BEEN HOME AND HOLT TO CUTTER'S DAUGHTER AND CHIEFTESS EMBER AND HER YOUNG TRIBE OF WOLFRIDERS.
DURING THAT TIME, THE ELVES HAVE DONE ALL THEY KNOW AND ALL THEY CAN TO KEEP "THE WAY" ALIVE IN THE ABSENCE OF CUTTER AND THE ELDERS THEY GREW UP WITH. THERE HAVE BEEN SKIRMISHES -- WITH HUMANS, STILL SUPERSTITIOUS, STILL UNWILLING TO SEE THE ELVES AS PARTNERS ON THE WORLD OF TWO MOONS -- WITH MONSTROUS CREATURES OF WINNOWILL'S DEVISING, PROOF THAT THE BLACK SNAKE'S PERVERSIONS SURVIVE HER PHYSICAL DEATH...
BUT THERE HAVE BEEN PEACEFUL SPANS AS WELL. CARELESS DAYS TO HUNT, TO HOWL, TO RUN FREE. THIS SHOULD BE ONE OF THOSE TIMES -- BUT FOR THE HIDDEN THREAT OF ONE THOUGHT LONG DEAD...
THE WILD HUNT™
AUXILIARY CREDITS - THE ELF WORKSHOP:
THE OTHER BRAIN: BEN NUNEZ
COMPUTER RENDERING ASSISTS BY: LARRY KOTEFF - BEN NUNEZ DOUGLAS SMITH
INKS ASSISTS BY: ANDY ORJUELA - DOUGLAS SMITH
WITH SPECIAL THANKS TO: JOHN LEDFORD AND MATT GREENFIELD
BY THE DJUN'S BLOODY SWORD--!! I'VE FOUND THEM!

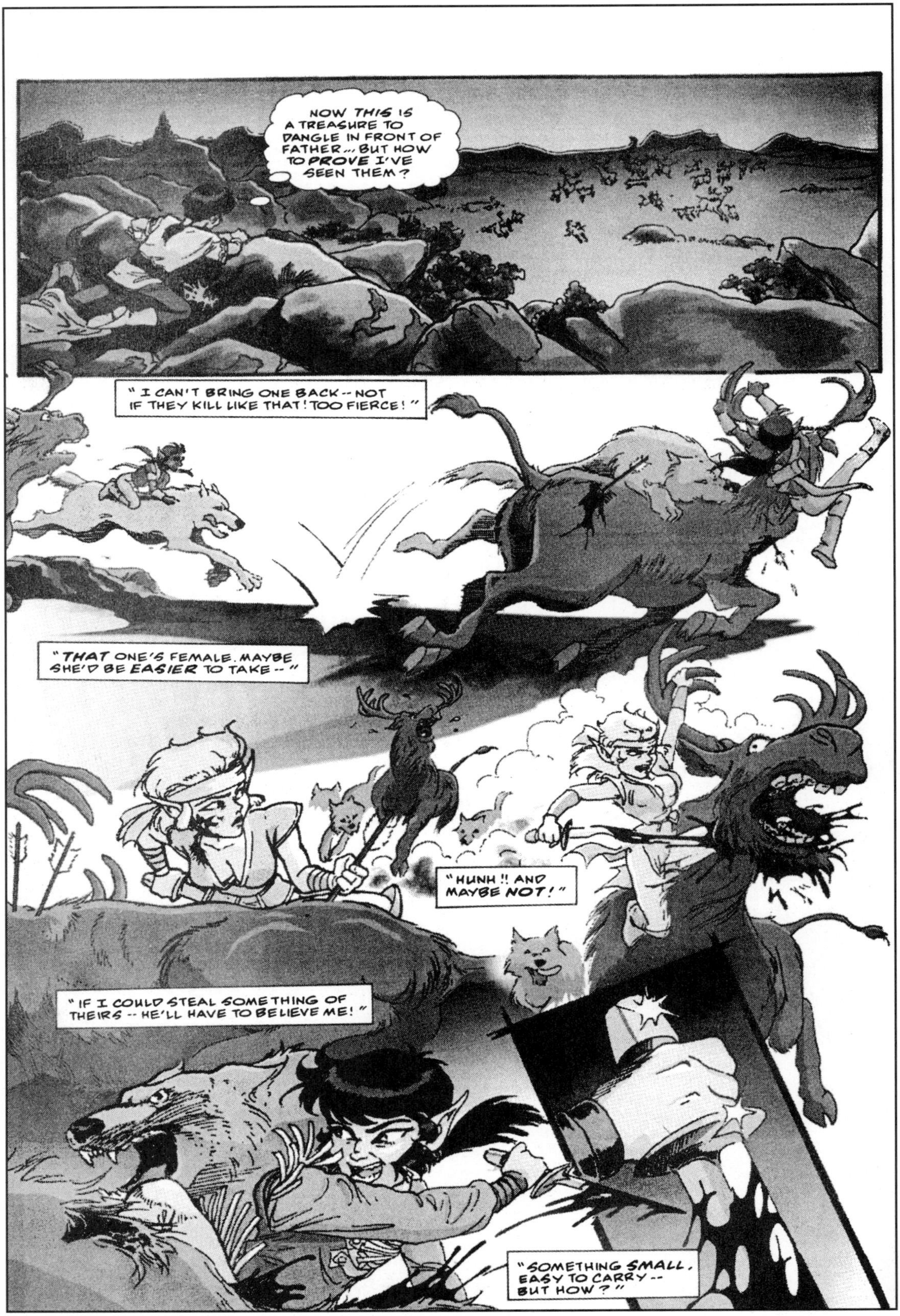

NOW THIS IS A TREASURE TO DANGLE IN FRONT OF FATHER... BUT HOW TO PROVE I'VE SEEN THEM?
"I CAN'T BRING ONE BACK -- NOT IF THEY KILL LIKE THAT! TOO FIERCE!"
"THAT ONE'S FEMALE. MAYBE SHE'D BE EASIER TO TAKE --"
"HUNH!! AND MAYBE NOT!"
"IF I COULD STEAL SOMETHING OF THEIRS -- HE'LL HAVE TO BELIEVE ME!"
"SOMETHING SMALL, EASY TO CARRY -- BUT HOW?"

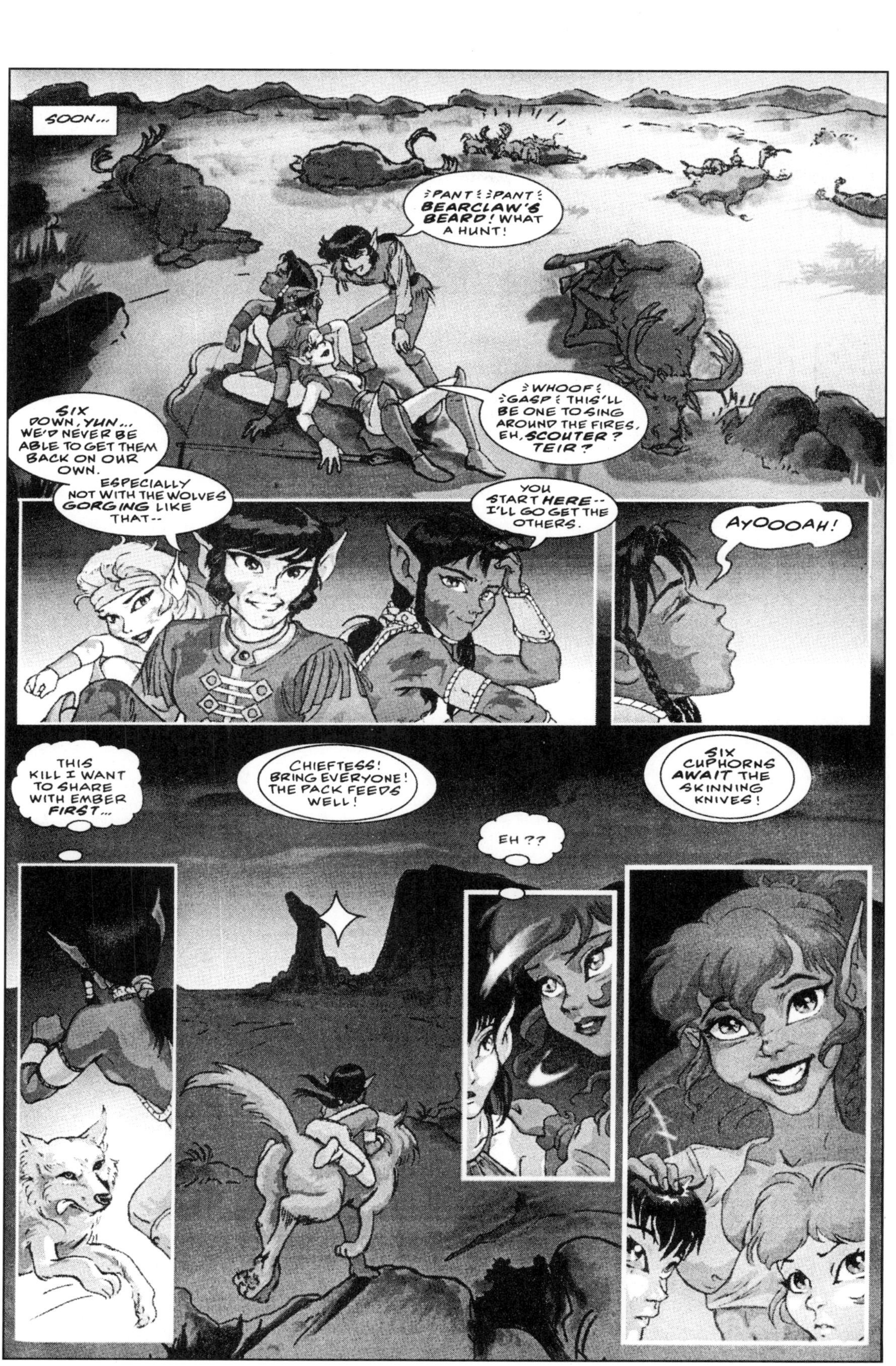
SOON...
PANT PANT BEARCLAW'S BEARD! WHAT A HUNT!
WHOOF GASP THIS'LL BE ONE TO SING AROUND THE FIRES, EH, SCOUTER TEIR?
SIX DOWN, YUN... WE'D NEVER BE ABLE TO GET THEM BACK ON OUR OWN.
ESPECIALLY NOT WITH THE WOLVES GORGING LIKE THAT--
YOU START HERE-- I'LL GO GET THE OTHERS.
AYOOOAH!
THIS KILL I WANT TO SHARE WITH EMBER FIRST...
CHIEFTESS! BRING EVERYONE! THE PACK FEEDS WELL!
EH ??
SIX CUPHORNS AWAIT THE SKINNING KNIVES!

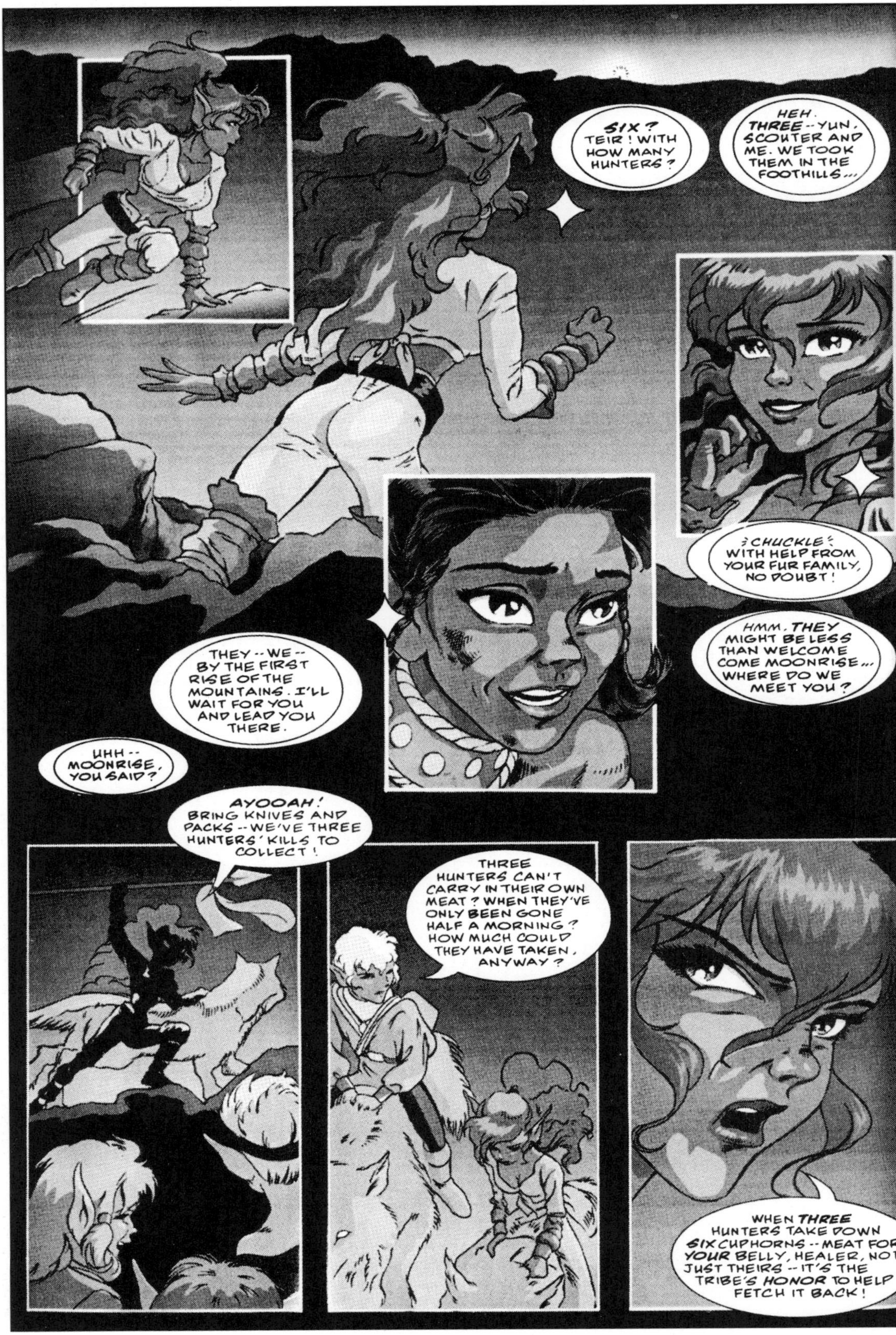
SIX? TEIR! WITH HOW MANY HUNTERS?
HEH. THREE -- YUN, SCOUTER AND ME. WE TOOK THEM IN THE FOOTHILLS...
CHUCKLE WITH HELP FROM YOUR FUR FAMILY, NO DOUBT!
HMM. THEY MIGHT BE LESS THAN WELCOME COME MOONRISE... WHERE DO WE MEET YOU?
THEY -- WE -- BY THE FIRST RISE OF THE MOUNTAINS. I'LL WAIT FOR YOU AND LEAD YOU THERE.
UHH -- MOONRISE, YOU SAID?
AYOOAH! BRING KNIVES AND PACKS -- WE'VE THREE HUNTERS' KILLS TO COLLECT!
THREE HUNTERS CAN'T CARRY IN THEIR OWN MEAT? WHEN THEY'VE ONLY BEEN GONE HALF A MORNING? HOW MUCH COULD THEY HAVE TAKEN, ANYWAY?
WHEN THREE HUNTERS TAKE DOWN SIX CUPHORNS -- MEAT FOR YOUR BELLY, HEALER, NOT JUST THEIRS -- IT'S THE TRIBE'S HONOR TO HELP FETCH IT BACK!

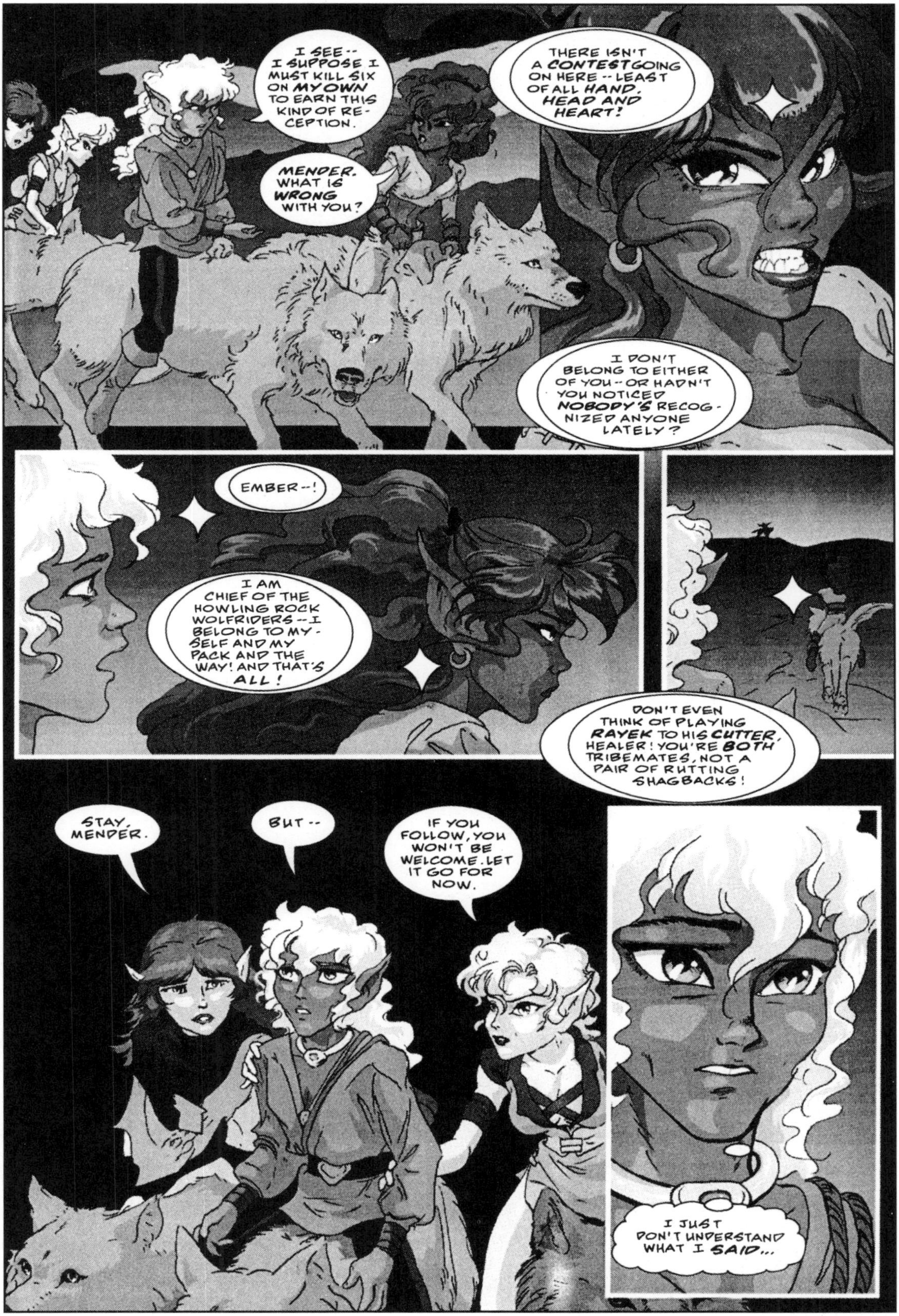
I SEE-- I SUPPOSE I MUST KILL SIX ON MY OWN TO EARN THIS KIND OF RECEPTION.
MENDER. WHAT IS WRONG WITH YOU?
THERE ISN'T A CONTEST GOING ON HERE -- LEAST OF ALL HAND, HEAD AND HEART!
I DON'T BELONG TO EITHER OF YOU -- OR HADN'T YOU NOTICED NOBODY'S RECOGNIZED ANYONE LATELY?
EMBER--!
I AM CHIEF OF THE HOWLING ROCK WOLFRIDERS -- I BELONG TO MYSELF AND MY PACK AND THE WAY! AND THAT'S ALL!
DON'T EVEN THINK OF PLAYING RAYEK TO HIS CUTTER, HEALER! YOU'RE BOTH TRIBEMATES, NOT A PAIR OF RUTTING SHAGBACKS!
STAY, MENDER.
BUT--
IF YOU FOLLOW, YOU WON'T BE WELCOME. LET IT GO FOR NOW.
I JUST DON'T UNDERSTAND WHAT I SAID...

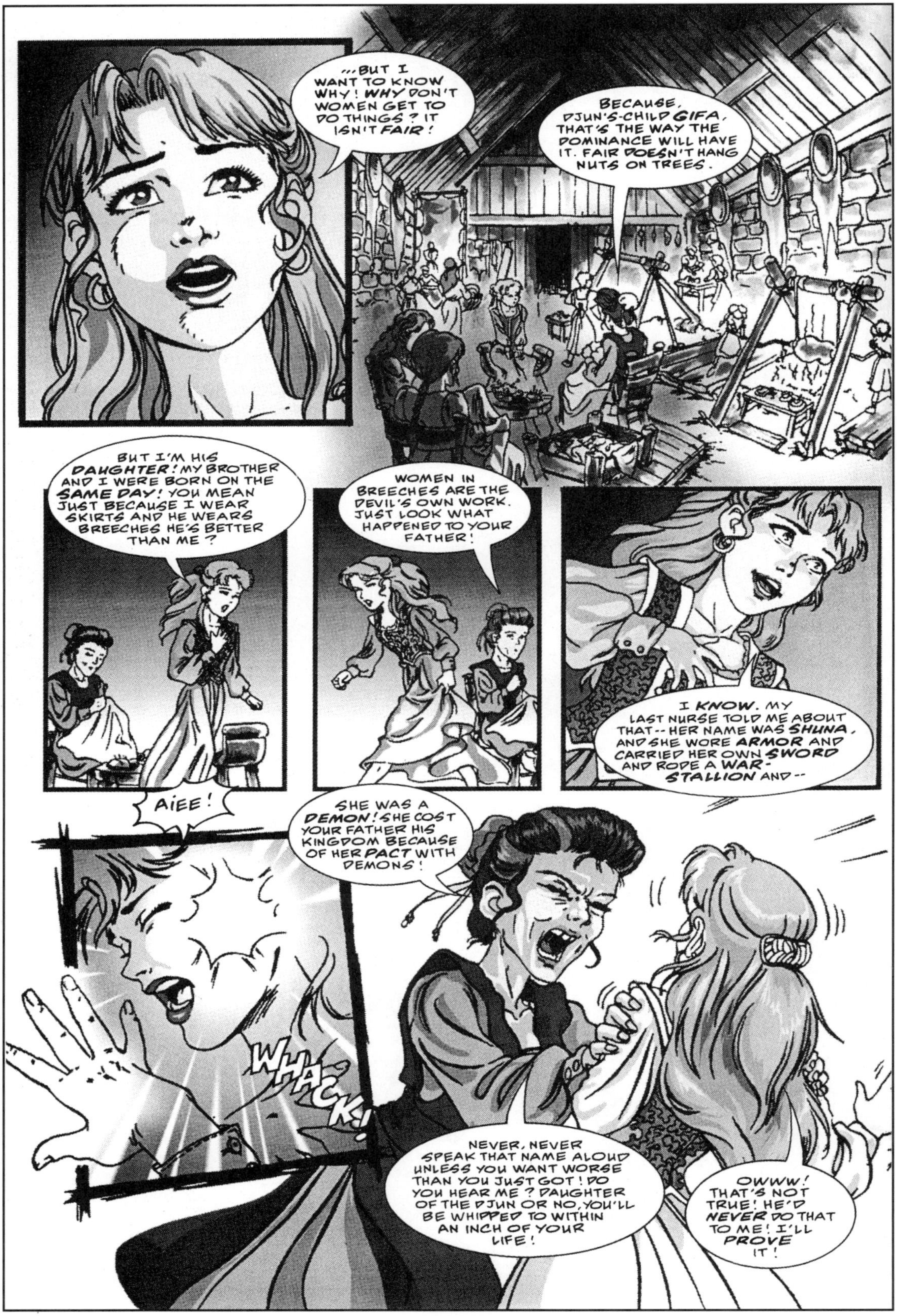
...BUT I WANT TO KNOW WHY! WHY DON'T WOMEN GET TO DO THINGS? IT ISN'T FAIR!
BECAUSE, DJUN'S-CHILD GIFA, THAT'S THE WAY THE DOMINANCE WILL HAVE IT. FAIR DOESN'T HANG NUTS ON TREES.
BUT I'M HIS DAUGHTER! MY BROTHER AND I WERE BORN ON THE SAME DAY! YOU MEAN JUST BECAUSE I WEAR SKIRTS AND HE WEARS BREECHES HE'S BETTER THAN ME?
WOMEN IN BREECHES ARE THE DEVIL'S OWN WORK. JUST LOOK WHAT HAPPENED TO YOUR FATHER!
I KNOW. MY LAST NURSE TOLD ME ABOUT THAT-- HER NAME WAS SHUNA, AND SHE WORE ARMOR AND CARRIED HER OWN SWORD AND RODE A WAR-STALLION AND--
AIEE!
SHE WAS A DEMON! SHE COST YOUR FATHER HIS KINGDOM BECAUSE OF HER PACT WITH DEMONS!
WHACK!
NEVER, NEVER SPEAK THAT NAME ALOUD UNLESS YOU WANT WORSE THAN YOU JUST GOT! DO YOU HEAR ME? DAUGHTER OF THE DJUN OR NO, YOU'LL BE WHIPPED TO WITHIN AN INCH OF YOUR LIFE!
OWWW! THAT'S NOT TRUE! HE'D NEVER DO THAT TO ME! I'LL PROVE IT!

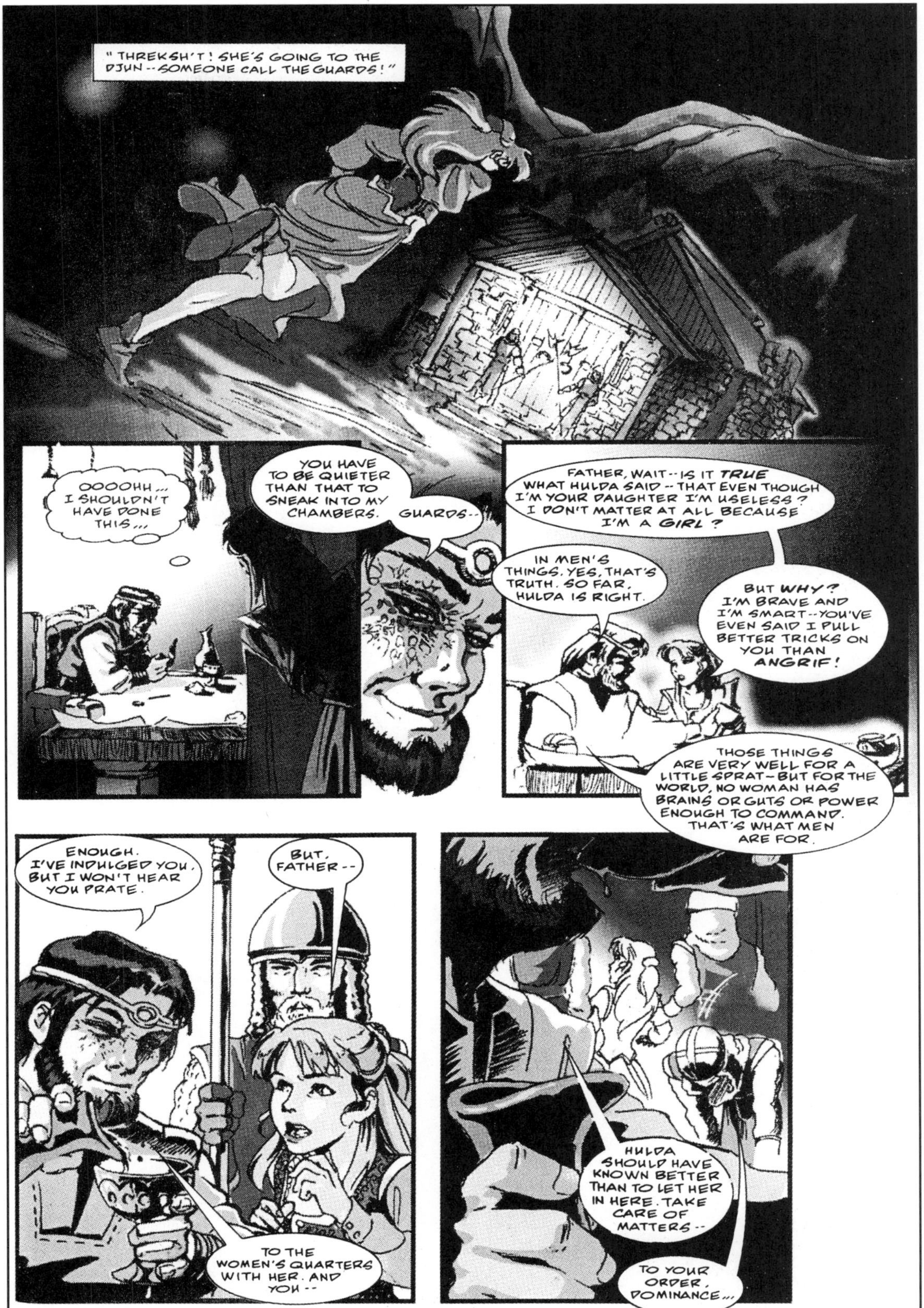
"THREKSH'T! SHE'S GOING TO THE DJUN--SOMEONE CALL THE GUARDS!"
OOOOHH... I SHOULDN'T HAVE DONE THIS...
YOU HAVE TO BE QUIETER THAN THAT TO SNEAK INTO MY CHAMBERS.
GUARDS--
FATHER, WAIT--IS IT TRUE WHAT HULDA SAID--THAT EVEN THOUGH I'M YOUR DAUGHTER I'M USELESS? I DON'T MATTER AT ALL BECAUSE I'M A GIRL?
IN MEN'S THINGS, YES, THAT'S TRUTH. SO FAR, HULDA IS RIGHT.
BUT WHY? I'M BRAVE AND I'M SMART--YOU'VE EVEN SAID I PULL BETTER TRICKS ON YOU THAN ANGRIF!
THOSE THINGS ARE VERY WELL FOR A LITTLE SPRAT--BUT FOR THE WORLD, NO WOMAN HAS BRAINS OR GUTS OR POWER ENOUGH TO COMMAND. THAT'S WHAT MEN ARE FOR.
ENOUGH. I'VE INDULGED YOU, BUT I WON'T HEAR YOU PRATE.
BUT, FATHER--
TO THE WOMEN'S QUARTERS WITH HER. AND YOU--
HULDA SHOULD HAVE KNOWN BETTER THAN TO LET HER IN HERE. TAKE CARE OF MATTERS--
TO YOUR ORDER, DOMINANCE...

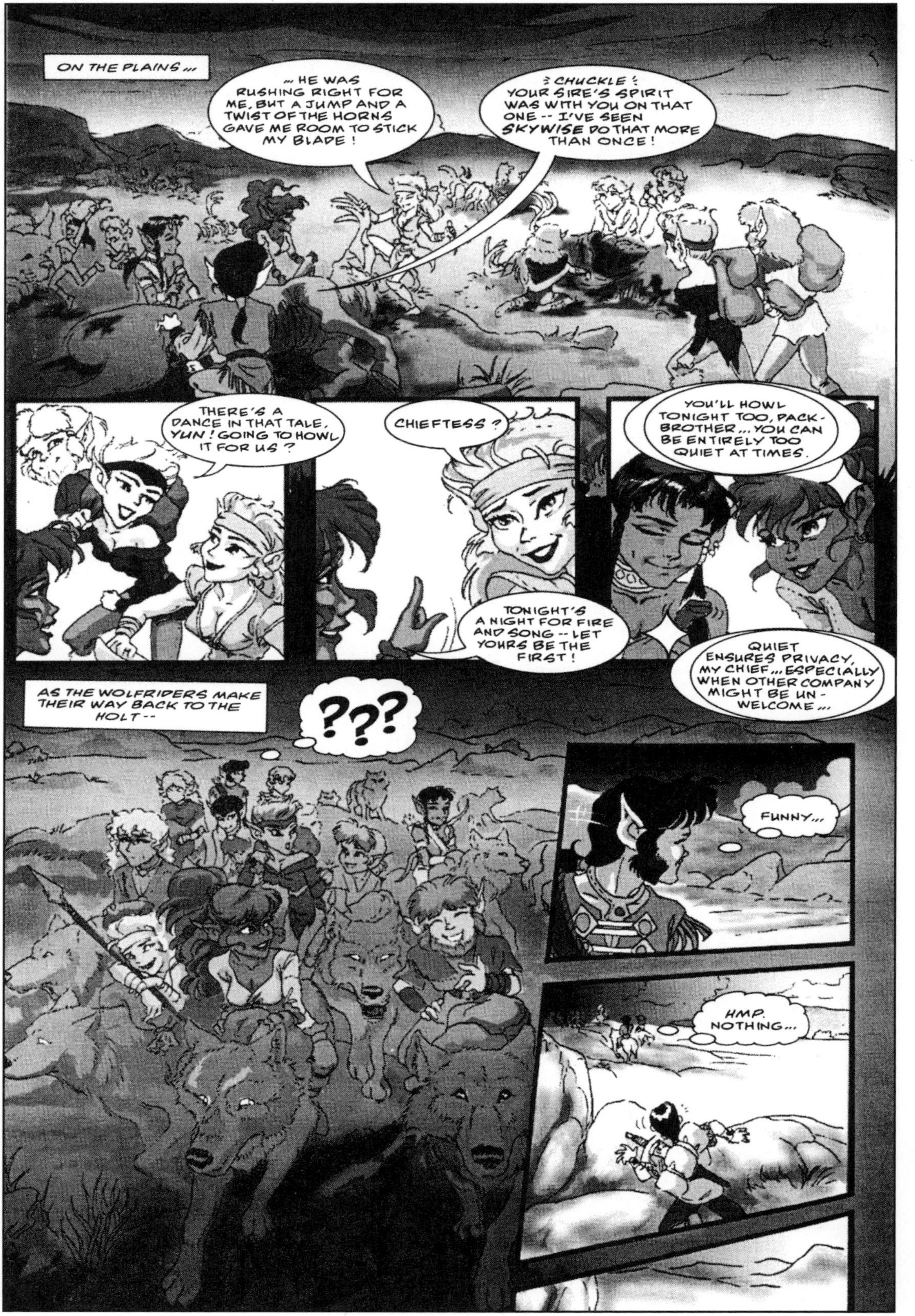
ON THE PLAINS...
...HE WAS RUSHING RIGHT FOR ME, BUT A JUMP AND A TWIST OF THE HORNS GAVE ME ROOM TO STICK MY BLADE!
CHUCKLE
YOUR SIRE'S SPIRIT WAS WITH YOU ON THAT ONE -- I'VE SEEN SKYWISE DO THAT MORE THAN ONCE!
THERE'S A DANCE IN THAT TALE, YUN! GOING TO HOWL IT FOR US?
CHIEFTESS?
TONIGHT'S A NIGHT FOR FIRE AND SONG -- LET YOURS BE THE FIRST!
YOU'LL HOWL TONIGHT TOO, PACK-BROTHER... YOU CAN BE ENTIRELY TOO QUIET AT TIMES.
QUIET ENSURES PRIVACY, MY CHIEF... ESPECIALLY WHEN OTHER COMPANY MIGHT BE UN-WELCOME...
AS THE WOLFRIDERS MAKE THEIR WAY BACK TO THE HOLT--
???
FUNNY...
HMP. NOTHING...

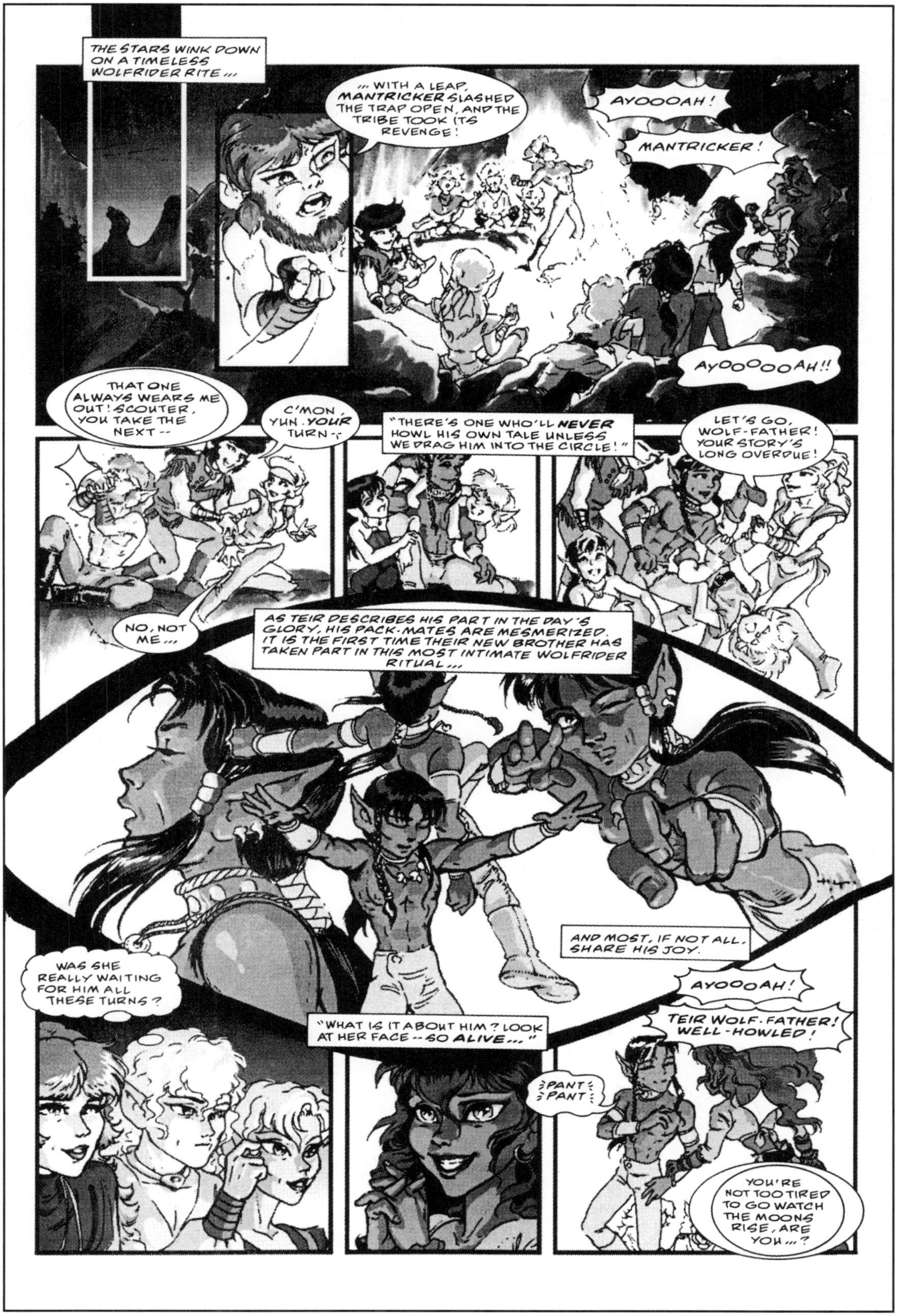
THE STARS WINK DOWN ON A TIMELESS WOLFRIDER RITE...
...WITH A LEAP, MANTRICKER SLASHED THE TRAP OPEN, AND THE TRIBE TOOK ITS REVENGE!
AYOOOAH!
MANTRICKER!
AYOOOOOAH!!
THAT ONE ALWAYS WEARS ME OUT! SCOUTER, YOU TAKE THE NEXT--
C'MON, YUN. YOUR TURN--
NO, NOT ME...
"THERE'S ONE WHO'LL NEVER HOWL HIS OWN TALE UNLESS WE DRAG HIM INTO THE CIRCLE!"
LET'S GO, WOLF-FATHER! YOUR STORY'S LONG OVERDUE!
AS TEIR DESCRIBES HIS PART IN THE DAY'S GLORY, HIS PACK-MATES ARE MESMERIZED. IT IS THE FIRST TIME THEIR NEW BROTHER HAS TAKEN PART IN THIS MOST INTIMATE WOLFRIDER RITUAL...
AND MOST, IF NOT ALL, SHARE HIS JOY.
WAS SHE REALLY WAITING FOR HIM ALL THESE TURNS?
"WHAT IS IT ABOUT HIM? LOOK AT HER FACE -- SO ALIVE..."
AYOOOAH!
TEIR WOLF-FATHER! WELL-HOWLED!
PANT PANT
YOU'RE NOT TOO TIRED TO GO WATCH THE MOONS RISE, ARE YOU...?

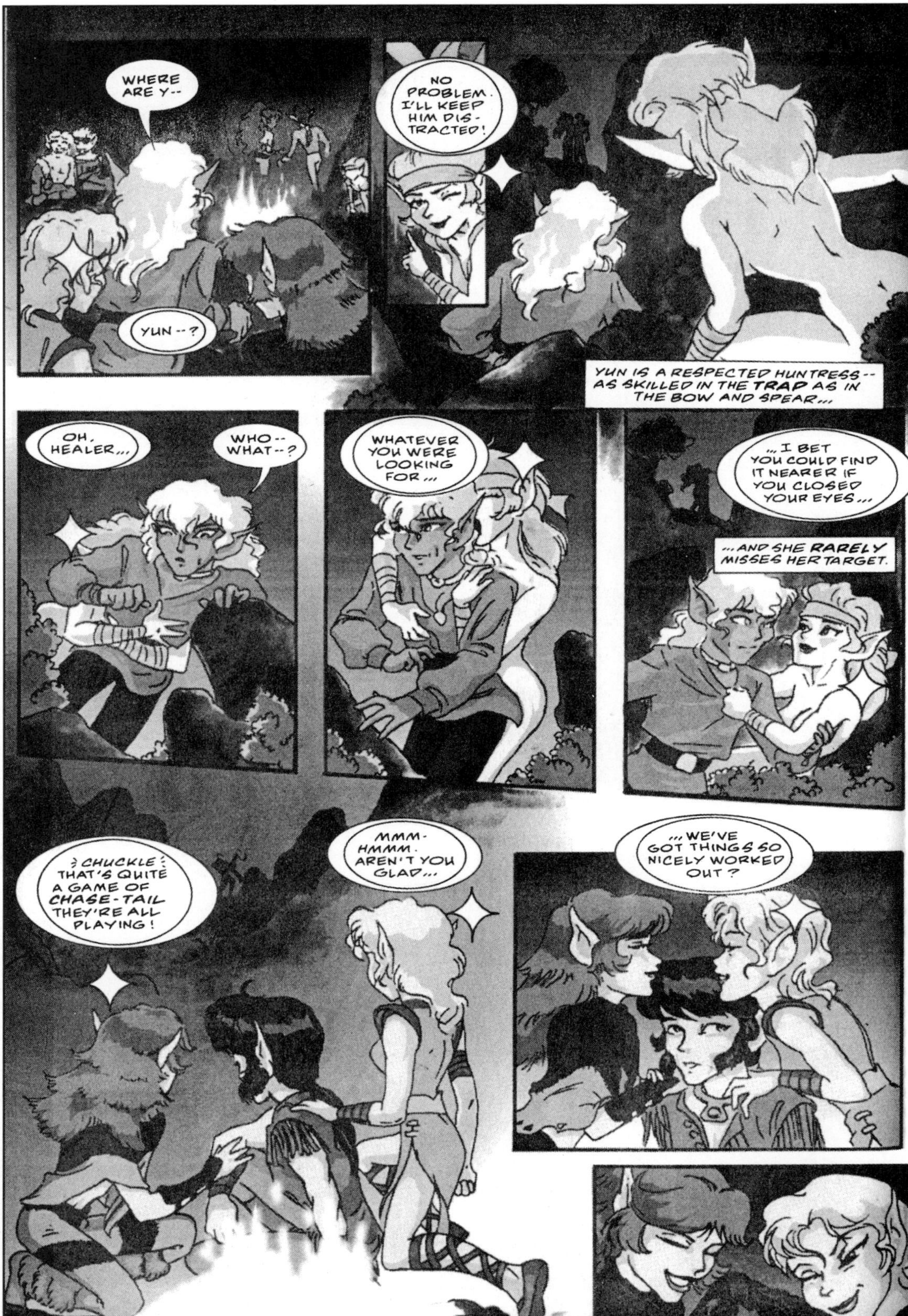

WHERE ARE Y--
YUN--?
NO PROBLEM. I'LL KEEP HIM DISTRACTED!
YUN IS A RESPECTED HUNTRESS-- AS SKILLED IN THE TRAP AS IN THE BOW AND SPEAR...
OH, HEALER...
WHO-- WHAT--?
WHATEVER YOU WERE LOOKING FOR...
...I BET YOU COULD FIND IT NEARER IF YOU CLOSED YOUR EYES...
...AND SHE RARELY MISSES HER TARGET.
:CHUCKLE: THAT'S QUITE A GAME OF CHASE-TAIL THEY'RE ALL PLAYING!
MMM-HMMM. AREN'T YOU GLAD...
...WE'VE GOT THINGS SO NICELY WORKED OUT?

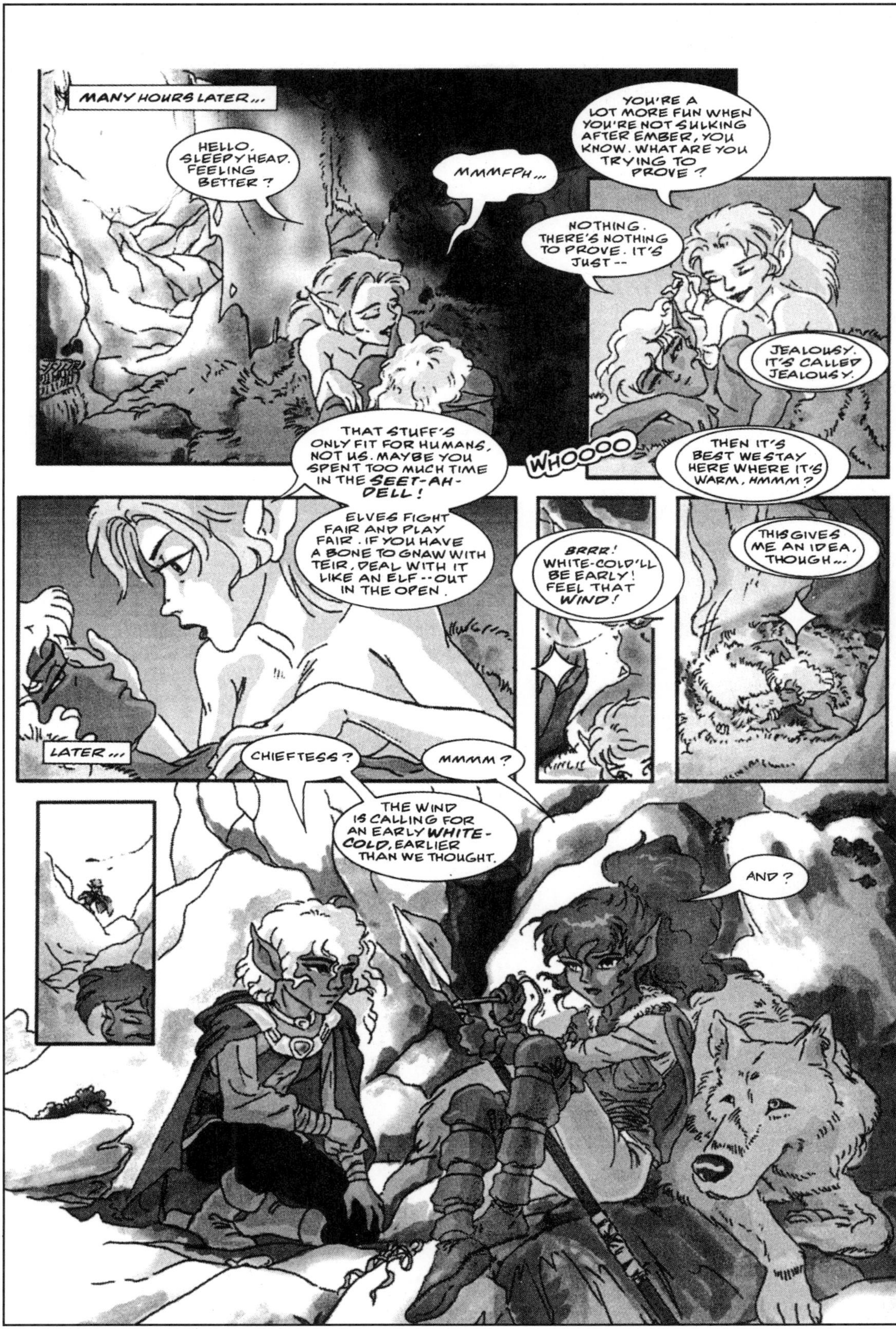

MANY HOURS LATER...
HELLO, SLEEPYHEAD. FEELING BETTER?
MMMFPH...
YOU'RE A LOT MORE FUN WHEN YOU'RE NOT SULKING AFTER EMBER, YOU KNOW. WHAT ARE YOU TRYING TO PROVE?
NOTHING. THERE'S NOTHING TO PROVE. IT'S JUST--
JEALOUSY. IT'S CALLED JEALOUSY.
THAT STUFF'S ONLY FIT FOR HUMANS, NOT US. MAYBE YOU SPENT TOO MUCH TIME IN THE SEET-AH-DELL!
ELVES FIGHT FAIR AND PLAY FAIR. IF YOU HAVE A BONE TO GNAW WITH TEIR, DEAL WITH IT LIKE AN ELF--OUT IN THE OPEN.
WHOOOO
BRRR! WHITE-COLD'LL BE EARLY! FEEL THAT WIND!
THEN IT'S BEST WE STAY HERE WHERE IT'S WARM, HMMM?
THIS GIVES ME AN IDEA, THOUGH...
LATER...
CHIEFTESS?
MMMM?
THE WIND IS CALLING FOR AN EARLY WHITE-COLD, EARLIER THAN WE THOUGHT.
AND?

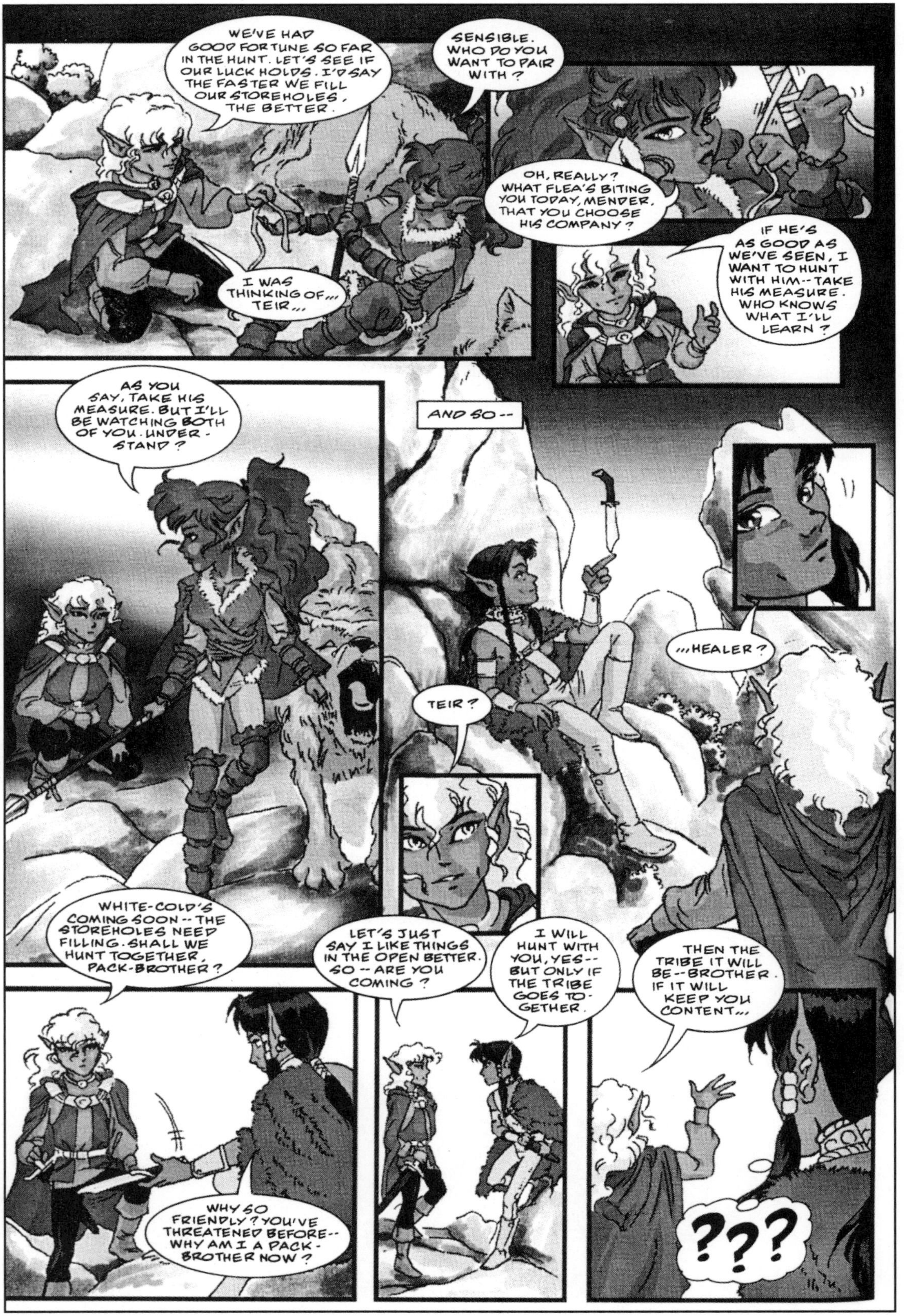
WE'VE HAD GOOD FORTUNE SO FAR IN THE HUNT. LET'S SEE IF OUR LUCK HOLDS. I'D SAY THE FASTER WE FILL OUR STOREHOLES, THE BETTER.
SENSIBLE. WHO DO YOU WANT TO PAIR WITH?
I WAS THINKING OF... TEIR...
OH, REALLY? WHAT FLEA'S BITING YOU TODAY, MENDER, THAT YOU CHOOSE HIS COMPANY?
IF HE'S AS GOOD AS WE'VE SEEN, I WANT TO HUNT WITH HIM--TAKE HIS MEASURE. WHO KNOWS WHAT I'LL LEARN?
AS YOU SAY, TAKE HIS MEASURE. BUT I'LL BE WATCHING BOTH OF YOU. UNDER-STAND?
AND SO--
TEIR?
...HEALER?
WHITE-COLD'S COMING SOON--THE STOREHOLES NEED FILLING. SHALL WE HUNT TOGETHER, PACK-BROTHER?
WHY SO FRIENDLY? YOU'VE THREATENED BEFORE--WHY AM I A PACK-BROTHER NOW?
LET'S JUST SAY I LIKE THINGS IN THE OPEN BETTER. SO--ARE YOU COMING?
I WILL HUNT WITH YOU, YES--BUT ONLY IF THE TRIBE GOES TO-GETHER.
THEN THE TRIBE IT WILL BE--BROTHER. IF IT WILL KEEP YOU CONTENT...
???

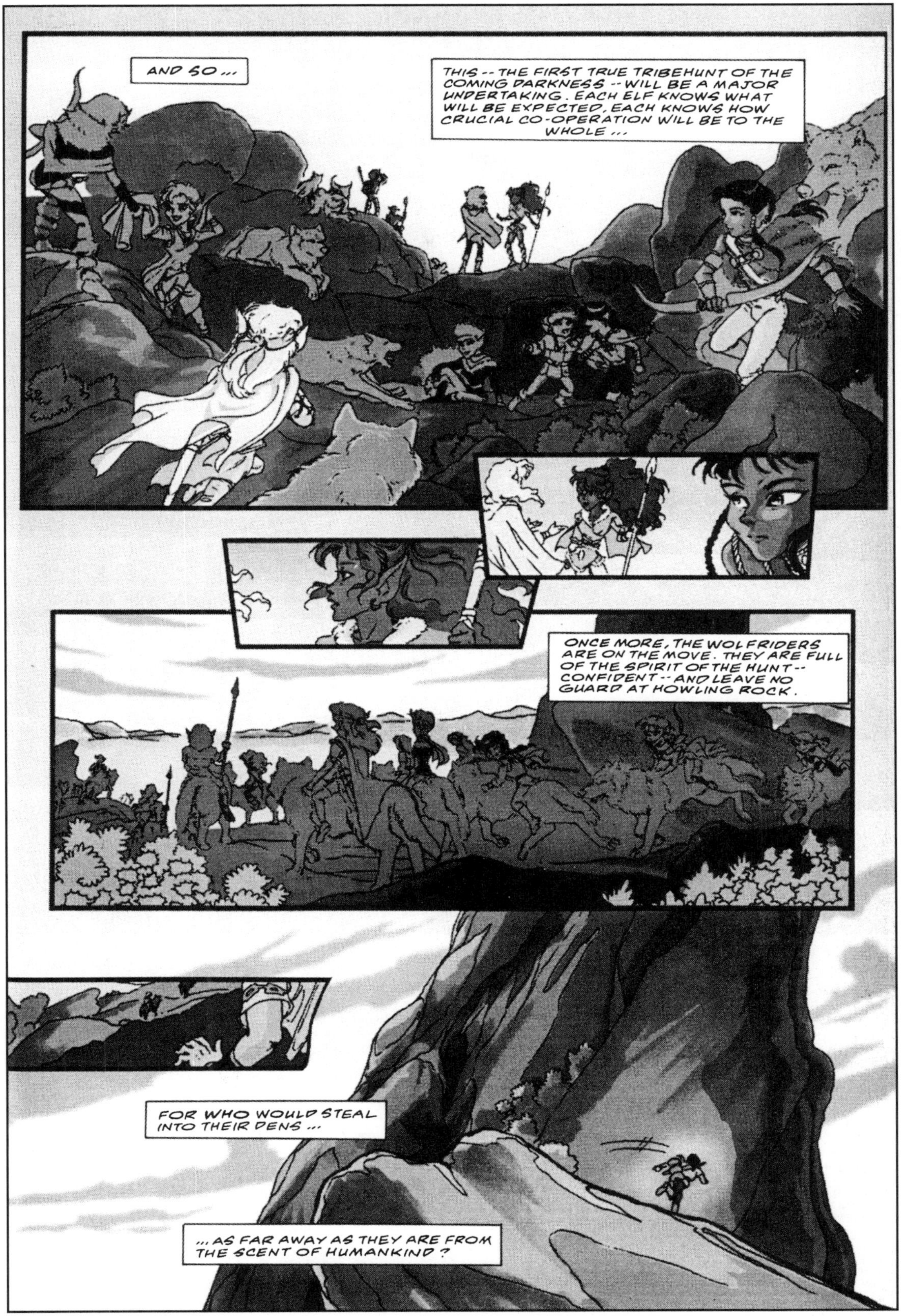
AND SO ...
THIS -- THE FIRST TRUE TRIBEHUNT OF THE COMING DARKNESS -- WILL BE A MAJOR UNDERTAKING. EACH ELF KNOWS WHAT WILL BE EXPECTED, EACH KNOWS HOW CRUCIAL CO-OPERATION WILL BE TO THE WHOLE ...
ONCE MORE, THE WOLFRIDERS ARE ON THE MOVE. THEY ARE FULL OF THE SPIRIT OF THE HUNT -- CONFIDENT -- AND LEAVE NO GUARD AT HOWLING ROCK.
FOR WHO WOULD STEAL INTO THEIR DENS ...
... AS FAR AWAY AS THEY ARE FROM THE SCENT OF HUMANKIND?

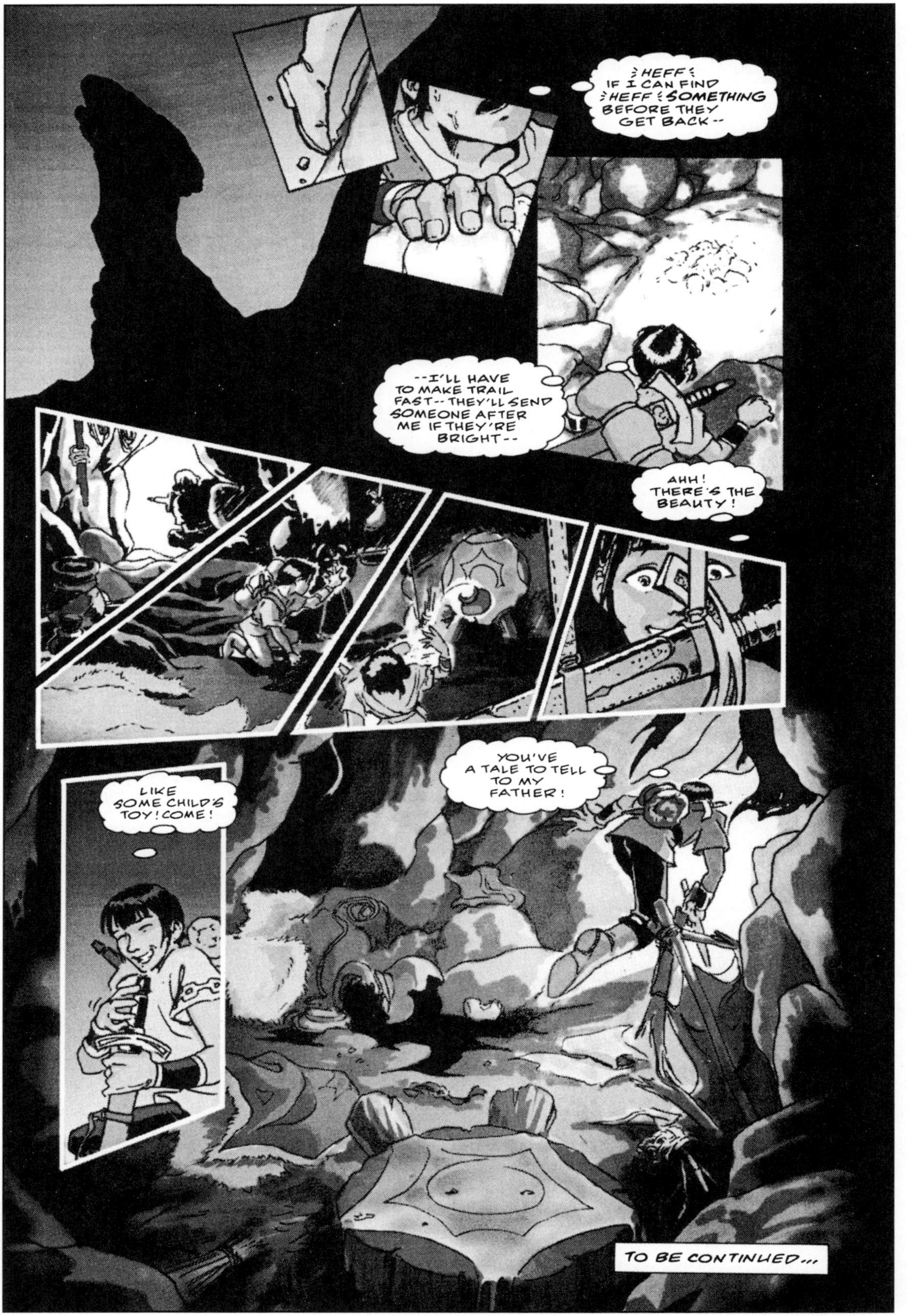
HEFF IF I CAN FIND HEFF SOMETHING BEFORE THEY GET BACK--
--I'LL HAVE TO MAKE TRAIL FAST-- THEY'LL SEND SOMEONE AFTER ME IF THEY'RE BRIGHT--
AHH! THERE'S THE BEAUTY!
LIKE SOME CHILD'S TOY! COME!
YOU'VE A TALE TO TELL TO MY FATHER!
TO BE CONTINUED...

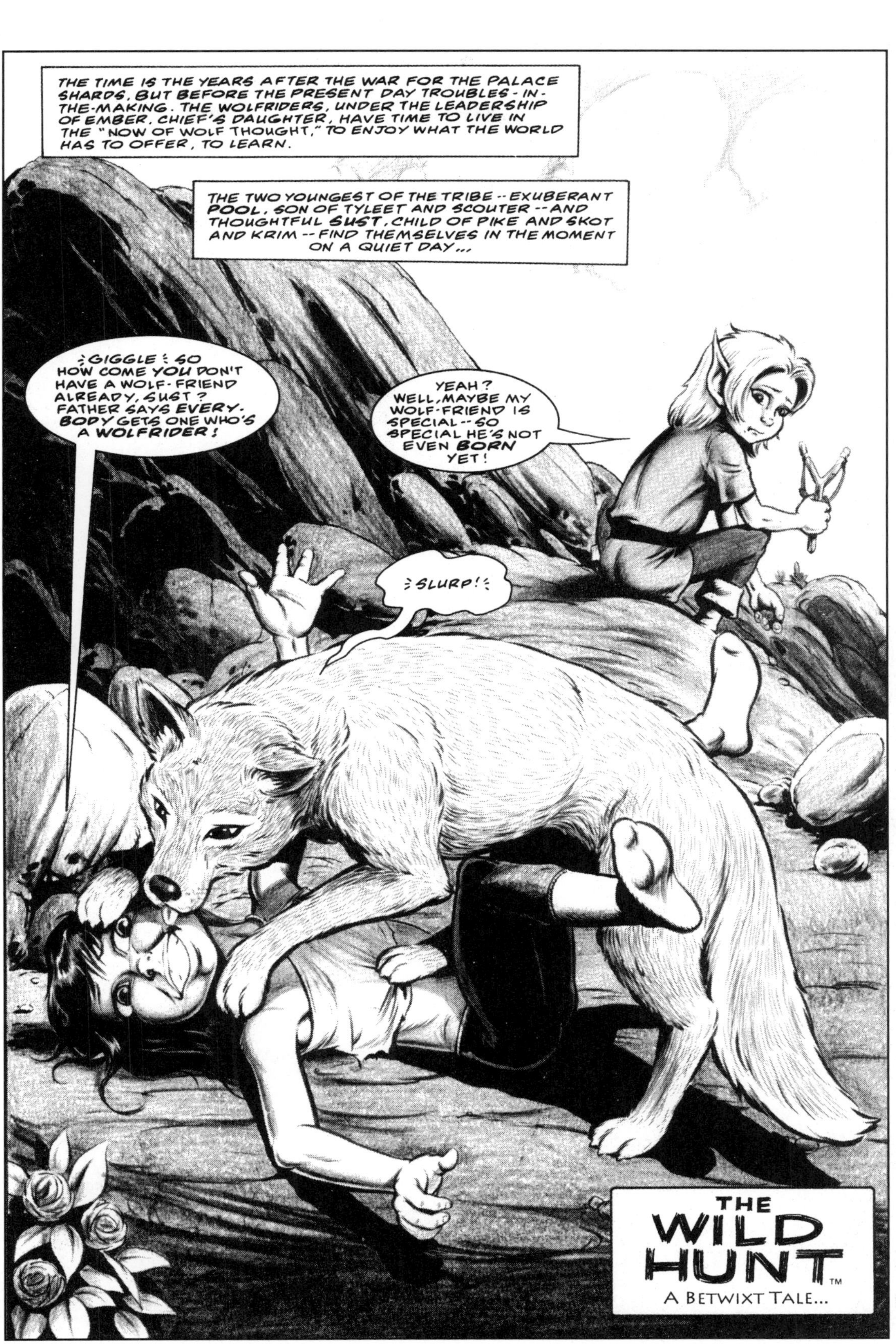
THE TIME IS THE YEARS AFTER THE WAR FOR THE PALACE SHARDS, BUT BEFORE THE PRESENT DAY TROUBLES-IN-THE-MAKING. THE WOLFRIDERS, UNDER THE LEADERSHIP OF EMBER, CHIEF'S DAUGHTER, HAVE TIME TO LIVE IN THE "NOW OF WOLF THOUGHT," TO ENJOY WHAT THE WORLD HAS TO OFFER, TO LEARN.
THE TWO YOUNGEST OF THE TRIBE -- EXUBERANT POOL, SON OF TYLEET AND SCOUTER -- AND THOUGHTFUL SUST, CHILD OF PIKE AND SKOT AND KRIM -- FIND THEMSELVES IN THE MOMENT ON A QUIET DAY...
:GIGGLE: SO HOW COME YOU DON'T HAVE A WOLF-FRIEND ALREADY, SUST? FATHER SAYS EVERYBODY GETS ONE WHO'S A WOLFRIDER!
YEAH? WELL, MAYBE MY WOLF-FRIEND IS SPECIAL -- SO SPECIAL HE'S NOT EVEN BORN YET!
:SLURP!:
THE WILD HUNT™
A BETWIXT TALE...

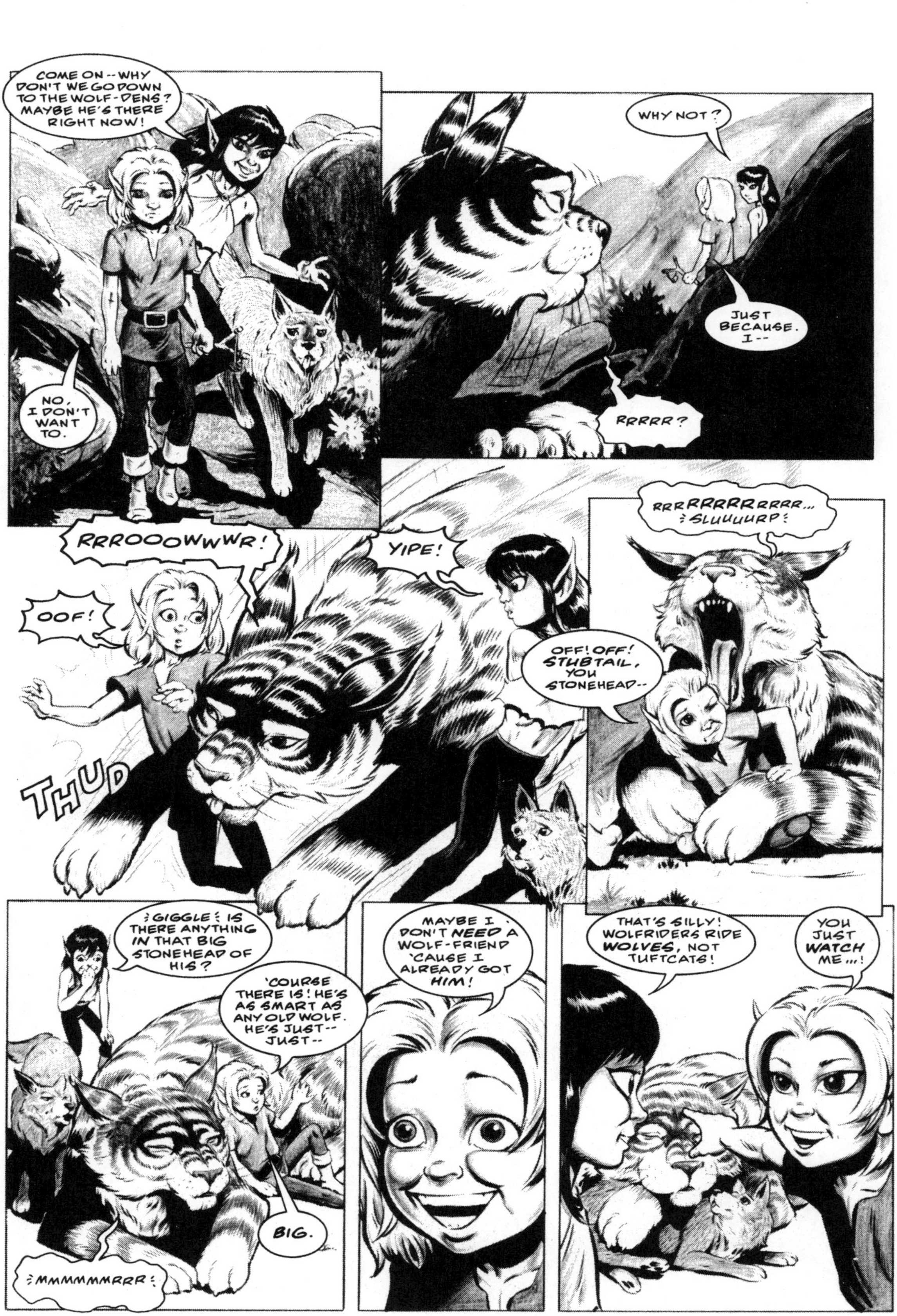
COME ON -- WHY DON'T WE GO DOWN TO THE WOLF-DENS? MAYBE HE'S THERE RIGHT NOW!
NO, I DON'T WANT TO.
WHY NOT?
JUST BECAUSE. I --
RRRRR?
RRROOOOWWWR!
OOF!
YIPE!
THUD
OFF! OFF! STUBTAIL, YOU STONEHEAD--
RRRRRRRRRrrrr... SLUUUURP
GIGGLE IS THERE ANYTHING IN THAT BIG STONEHEAD OF HIS?
'COURSE THERE IS! HE'S AS SMART AS ANY OLD WOLF. HE'S JUST-- JUST--
BIG.
MMMMMMRRR
MAYBE I DON'T NEED A WOLF-FRIEND 'CAUSE I ALREADY GOT HIM!
THAT'S SILLY! WOLFRIDERS RIDE WOLVES, NOT TUFTCATS!
YOU JUST WATCH ME...!

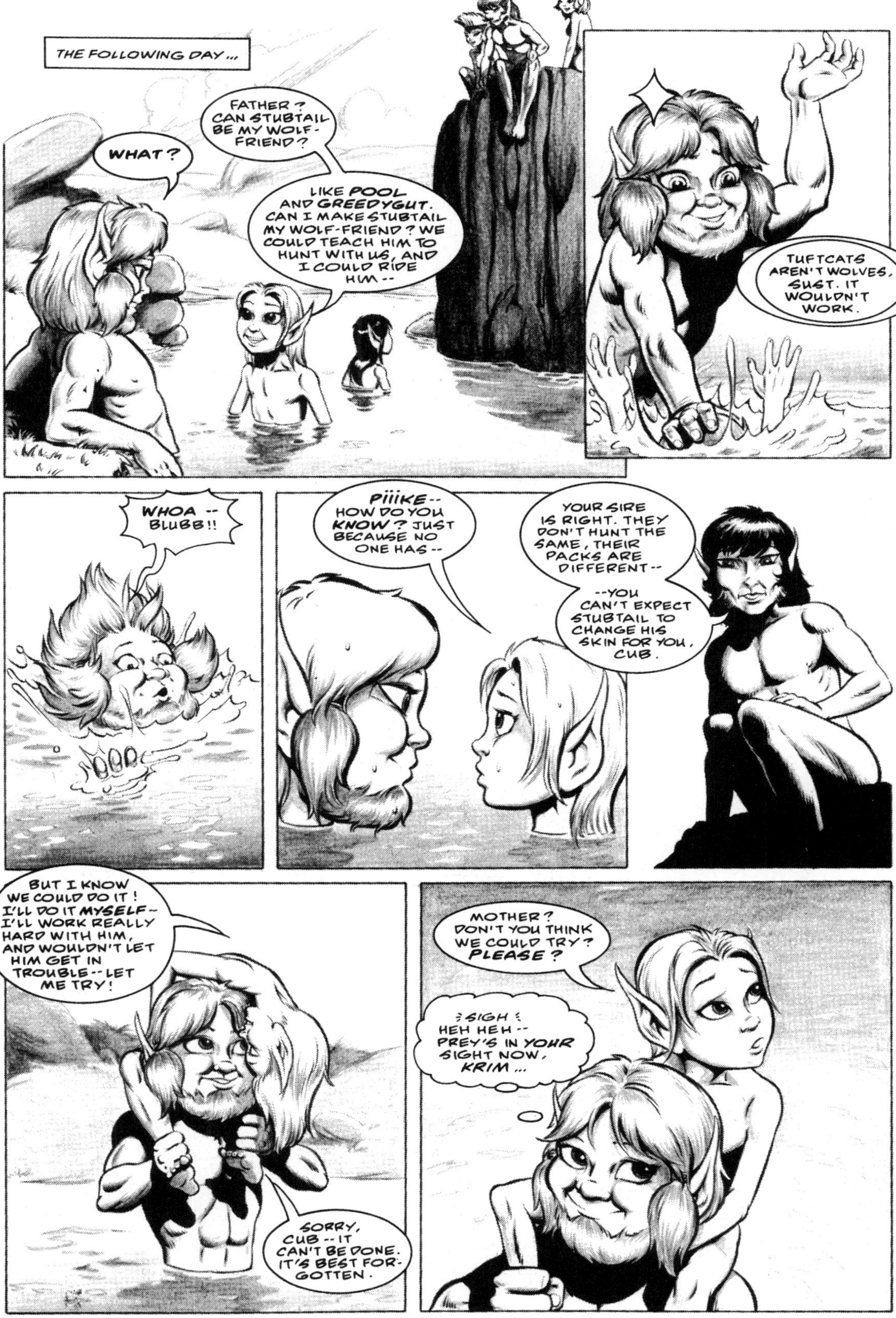
THE FOLLOWING DAY...
FATHER? CAN STUBTAIL BE MY WOLF-FRIEND?
WHAT?
LIKE POOL AND GREEDYGUT. CAN I MAKE STUBTAIL MY WOLF-FRIEND? WE COULD TEACH HIM TO HUNT WITH US, AND I COULD RIDE HIM--
TUFTCATS AREN'T WOLVES, SUST. IT WOULDN'T WORK.
WHOA -- BLUBB!!
PIIIKE-- HOW DO YOU KNOW? JUST BECAUSE NO ONE HAS--
YOUR SIRE IS RIGHT. THEY DON'T HUNT THE SAME, THEIR PACKS ARE DIFFERENT--
--YOU CAN'T EXPECT STUBTAIL TO CHANGE HIS SKIN FOR YOU, CUB.
BUT I KNOW WE COULD DO IT! I'LL DO IT MYSELF-- I'LL WORK REALLY HARD WITH HIM, AND WOULDN'T LET HIM GET IN TROUBLE--LET ME TRY!
SORRY, CUB--IT CAN'T BE DONE. IT'S BEST FOR-GOTTEN.
MOTHER? DON'T YOU THINK WE COULD TRY? PLEASE?
SIGH HEH HEH-- PREY'S IN YOUR SIGHT NOW, KRIM...

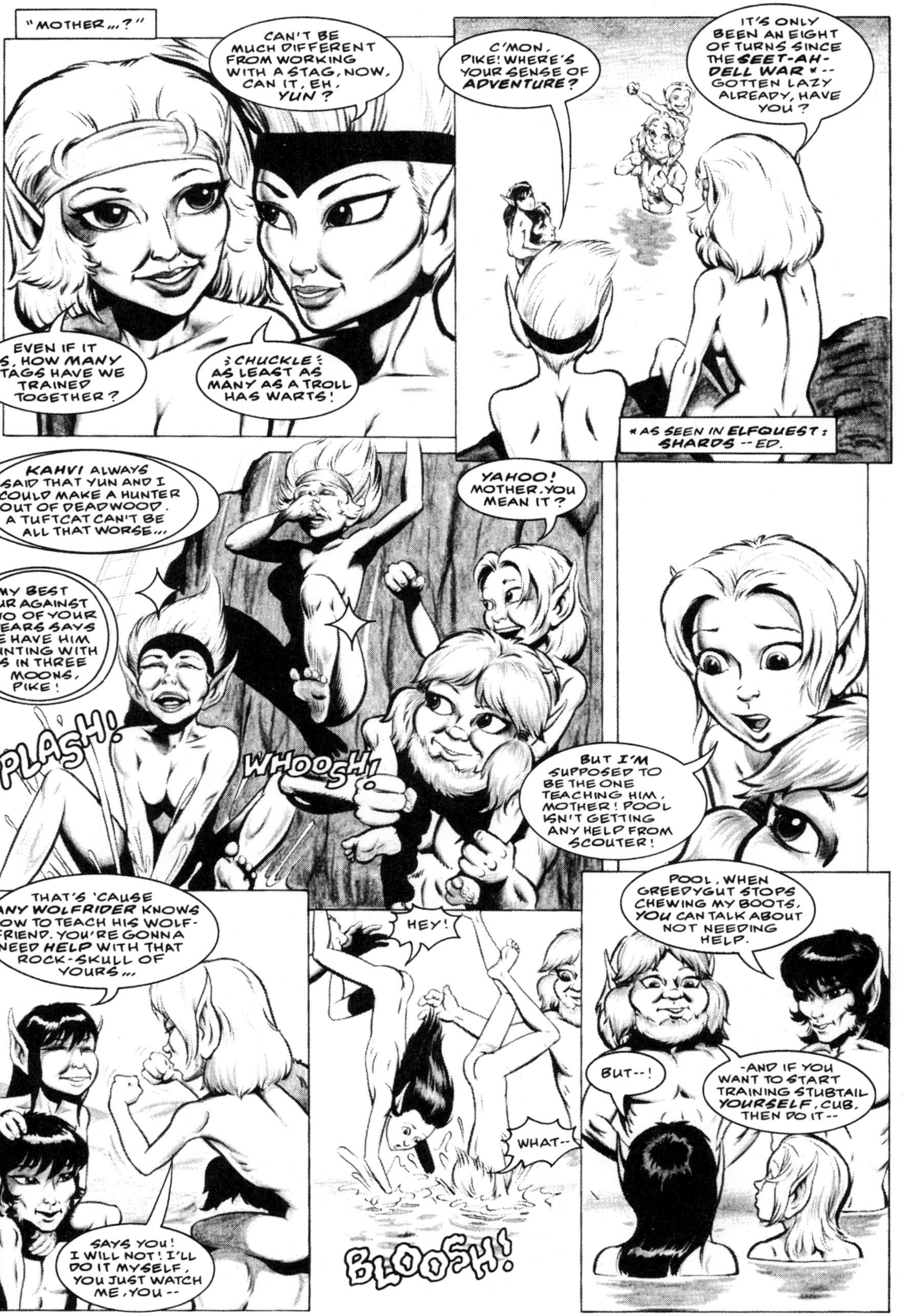
"MOTHER...?"
CAN'T BE MUCH DIFFERENT FROM WORKING WITH A STAG, NOW, CAN IT, EH, YUN?
EVEN IF IT IS, HOW MANY STAGS HAVE WE TRAINED TOGETHER?
CHUCKLE AS LEAST AS MANY AS A TROLL HAS WARTS!
C'MON, PIKE! WHERE'S YOUR SENSE OF ADVENTURE?
IT'S ONLY BEEN AN EIGHT OF TURNS SINCE THE SEET-AH-DELL WAR* -- GOTTEN LAZY ALREADY, HAVE YOU?
*AS SEEN IN ELFQUEST: SHARDS --ED.
KAHVI ALWAYS SAID THAT YUN AND I COULD MAKE A HUNTER OUT OF DEADWOOD. A TUFTCAT CAN'T BE ALL THAT WORSE...
MY BEST FUR AGAINST TWO OF YOUR SPEARS SAYS WE HAVE HIM HUNTING WITH US IN THREE MOONS, PIKE!
YAHOO! MOTHER, YOU MEAN IT?
SPLASH!
WHOOSH!
BUT I'M SUPPOSED TO BE THE ONE TEACHING HIM, MOTHER! POOL ISN'T GETTING ANY HELP FROM SCOUTER!
THAT'S 'CAUSE ANY WOLFRIDER KNOWS HOW TO TEACH HIS WOLF-FRIEND. YOU'RE GONNA NEED HELP WITH THAT ROCK-SKULL OF YOURS...
SAYS YOU! I WILL NOT! I'LL DO IT MYSELF, YOU JUST WATCH ME, YOU --
HEY!
WHAT--
BLOOSH!
POOL, WHEN GREEDYGUT STOPS CHEWING MY BOOTS, YOU CAN TALK ABOUT NOT NEEDING HELP.
BUT--!
-AND IF YOU WANT TO START TRAINING STUBTAIL YOURSELF, CUB, THEN DO IT --

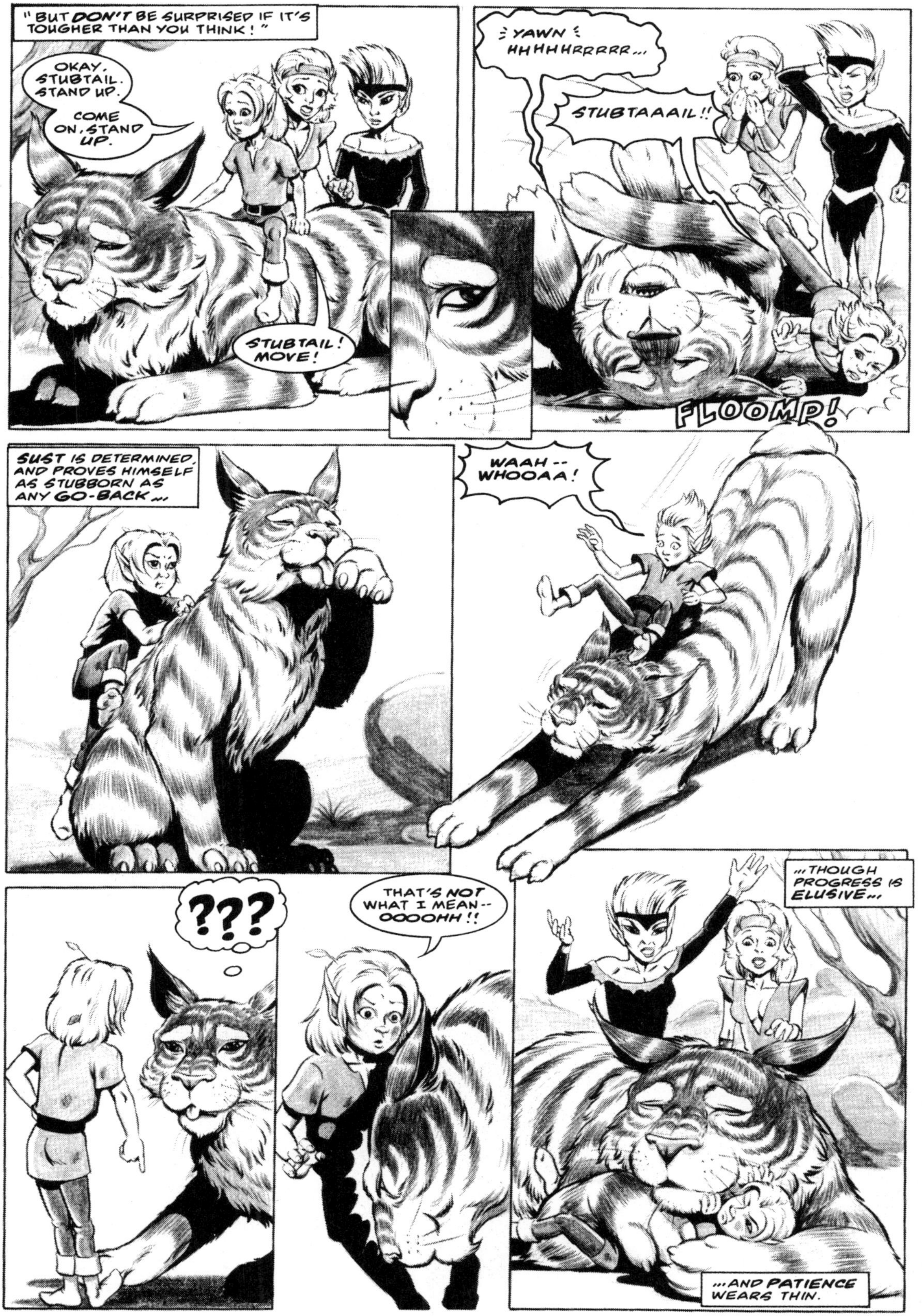
"BUT DON'T BE SURPRISED IF IT'S TOUGHER THAN YOU THINK!"
OKAY, STUBTAIL. STAND UP.
COME ON, STAND UP.
STUBTAIL! MOVE!
YAWN HHHHHRRRRR...
STUBTAAAIL!!
FLOOMP!
SUST IS DETERMINED, AND PROVES HIMSELF AS STUBBORN AS ANY GO-BACK...
WAAH -- WHOOAA!
???
THAT'S NOT WHAT I MEAN -- OOOOHH!!
...THOUGH PROGRESS IS ELUSIVE...
...AND PATIENCE WEARS THIN.

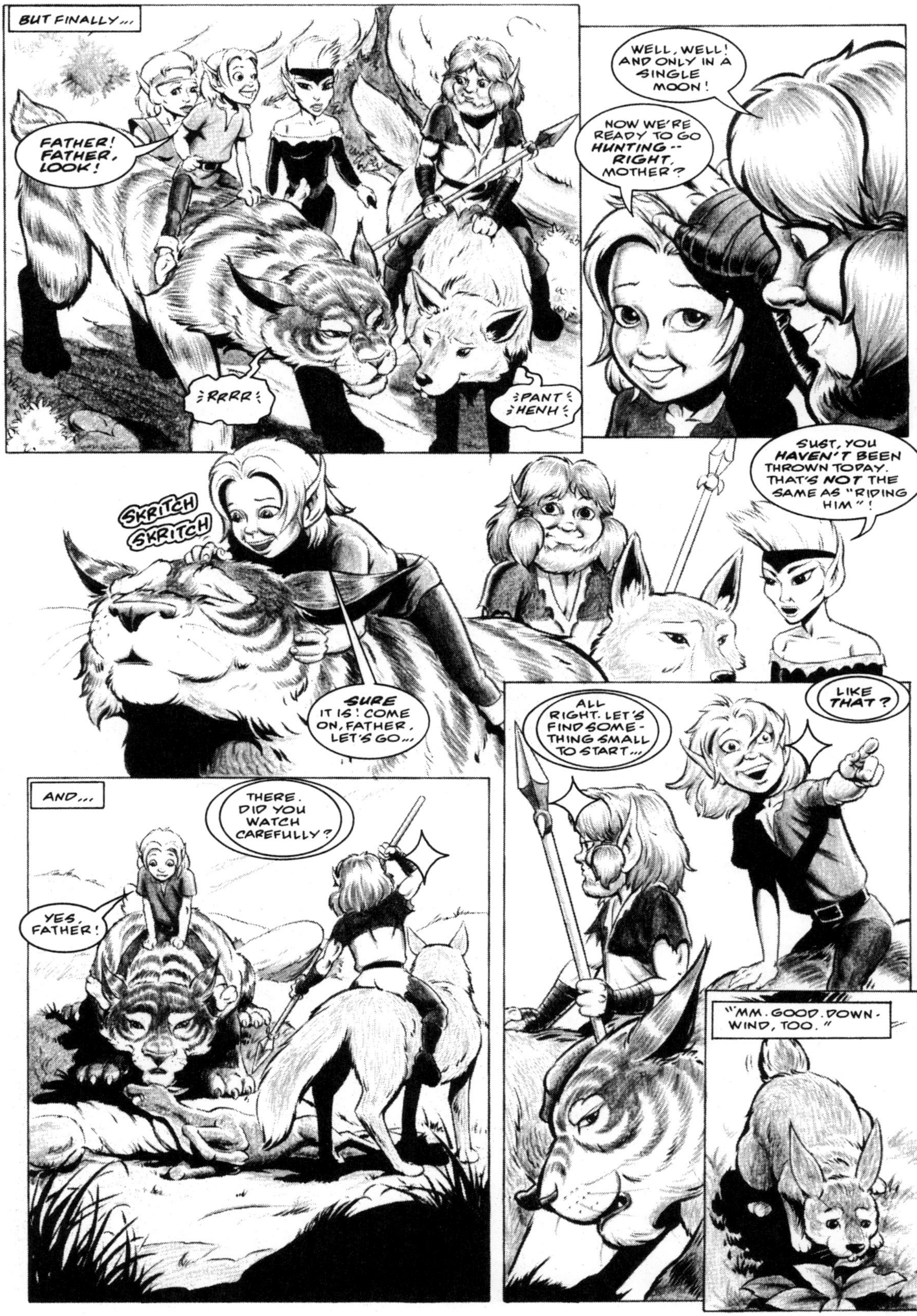

BUT FINALLY...
FATHER! FATHER, LOOK!
RRRR
PANT HENH
WELL, WELL! AND ONLY IN A SINGLE MOON!
NOW WE'RE READY TO GO HUNTING -- RIGHT, MOTHER?
SKRITCH SKRITCH
SUST, YOU HAVEN'T BEEN THROWN TODAY. THAT'S NOT THE SAME AS "RIDING HIM"!
SURE IT IS! COME ON, FATHER, LET'S GO...
ALL RIGHT. LET'S FIND SOME-THING SMALL TO START...
LIKE THAT?
AND...
THERE. DID YOU WATCH CAREFULLY?
YES, FATHER!
"MM. GOOD. DOWN-WIND, TOO."

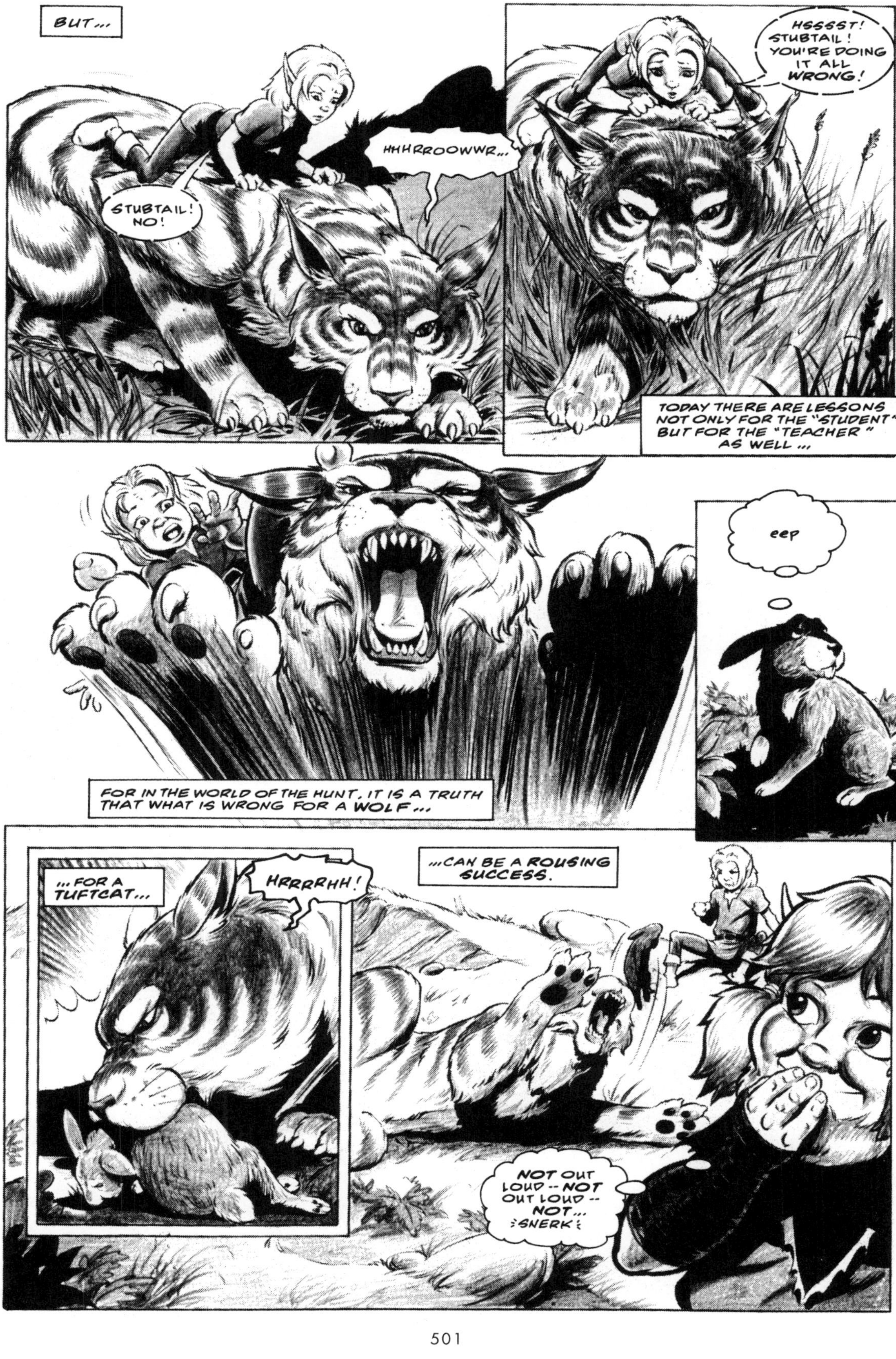

BUT...
STUBTAIL! NO!
HHHRROOWWR...
HSSSST! STUBTAIL! YOU'RE DOING IT ALL WRONG!
TODAY THERE ARE LESSONS NOT ONLY FOR THE "STUDENT" BUT FOR THE "TEACHER" AS WELL...
eep
FOR IN THE WORLD OF THE HUNT, IT IS A TRUTH THAT WHAT IS WRONG FOR A WOLF...
...FOR A TUFTCAT...
HRRRRHH!
...CAN BE A ROUSING SUCCESS.
NOT OUT LOUD -- NOT OUT LOUD -- NOT... SNERK

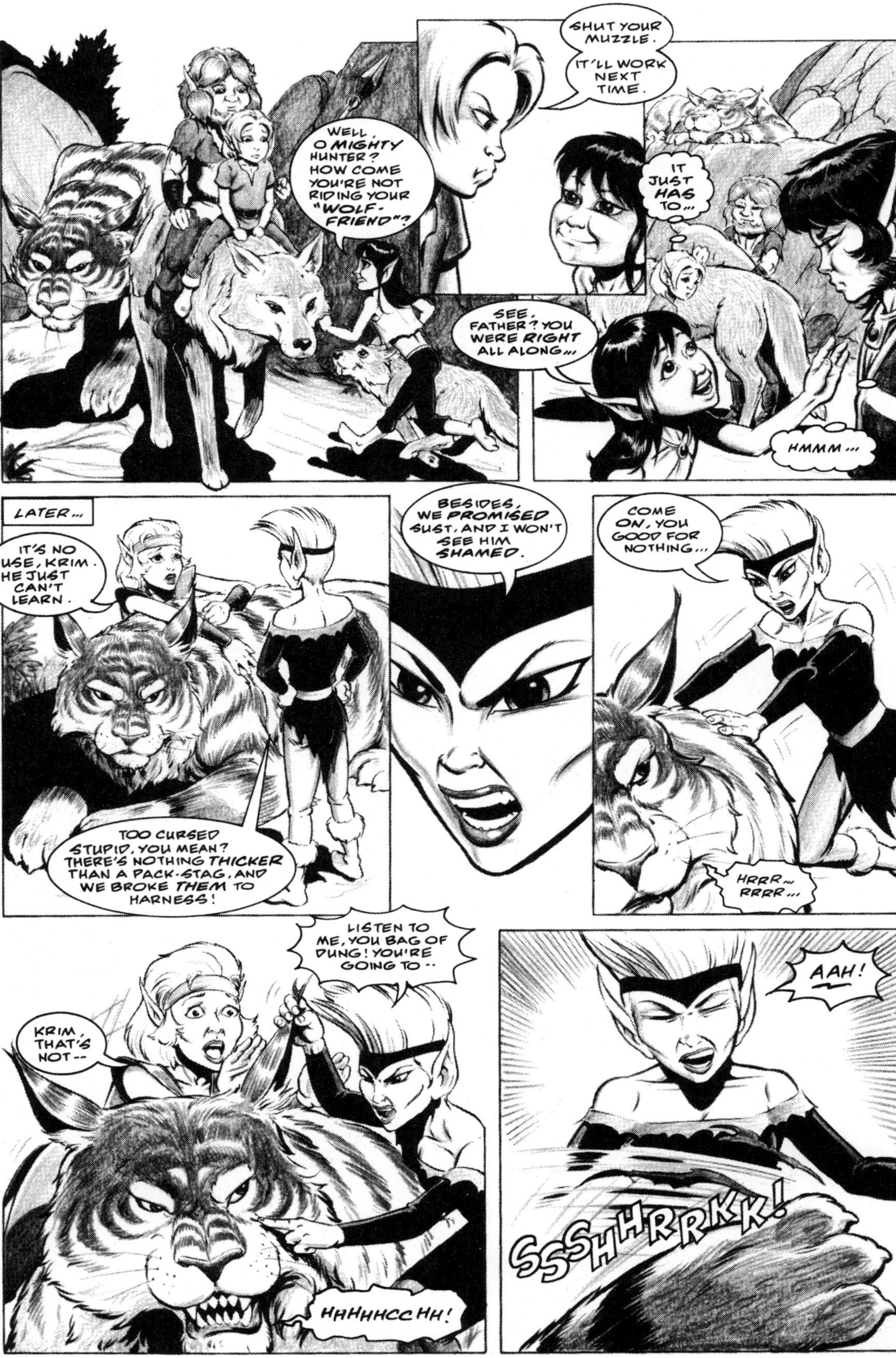
WELL, O MIGHTY HUNTER? HOW COME YOU'RE NOT RIDING YOUR "WOLF-FRIEND"?
SHUT YOUR MUZZLE.
IT'LL WORK NEXT TIME.
IT JUST HAS TO...
SEE, FATHER? YOU WERE RIGHT ALL ALONG...
HMMM...
LATER...
IT'S NO USE, KRIM. HE JUST CAN'T LEARN.
TOO CURSED STUPID, YOU MEAN? THERE'S NOTHING THICKER THAN A PACK-STAG, AND WE BROKE THEM TO HARNESS!
BESIDES, WE PROMISED SUST, AND I WON'T SEE HIM SHAMED.
COME ON, YOU GOOD FOR NOTHING...
HRRR... RRRR...
LISTEN TO ME, YOU BAG OF DUNG! YOU'RE GOING TO --
KRIM, THAT'S NOT --
HHHHCCHH!
AAH!
SSSHHRRKK!

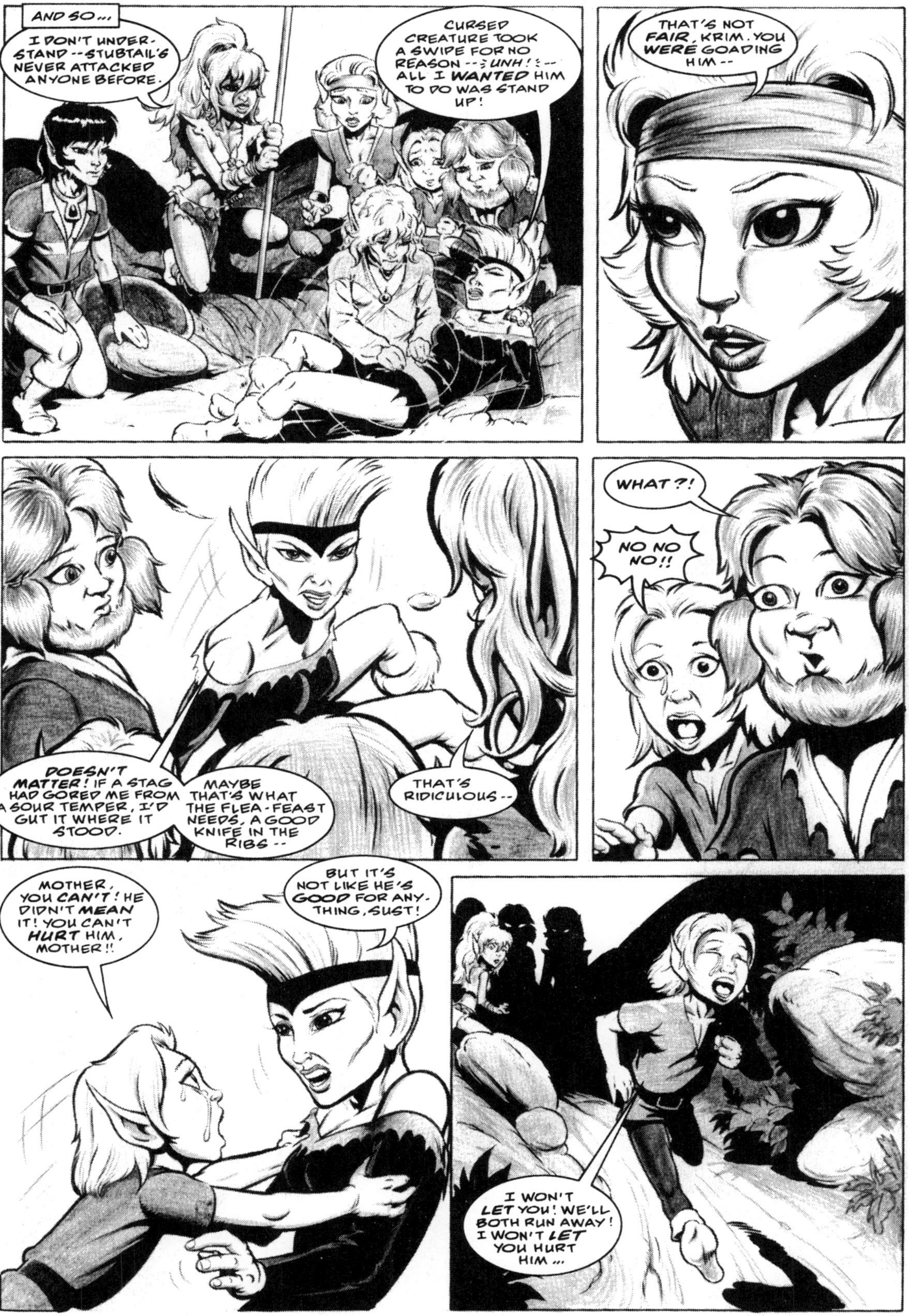
AND SO...
I DON'T UNDER-STAND--STUBTAIL'S NEVER ATTACKED ANYONE BEFORE.
CURSED CREATURE TOOK A SWIPE FOR NO REASON--UNH!--ALL I WANTED HIM TO DO WAS STAND UP!
THAT'S NOT FAIR, KRIM. YOU WERE GOADING HIM--
DOESN'T MATTER! IF A STAG HAD GORED ME FROM A SOUR TEMPER, I'D GUT IT WHERE IT STOOD.
MAYBE THAT'S WHAT THE FLEA-FEAST NEEDS, A GOOD KNIFE IN THE RIBS--
THAT'S RIDICULOUS--
WHAT?!
NO NO NO!!
MOTHER, YOU CAN'T! HE DIDN'T MEAN IT! YOU CAN'T HURT HIM, MOTHER!!
BUT IT'S NOT LIKE HE'S GOOD FOR ANYTHING, SUST!
I WON'T LET YOU! WE'LL BOTH RUN AWAY! I WON'T LET YOU HURT HIM...

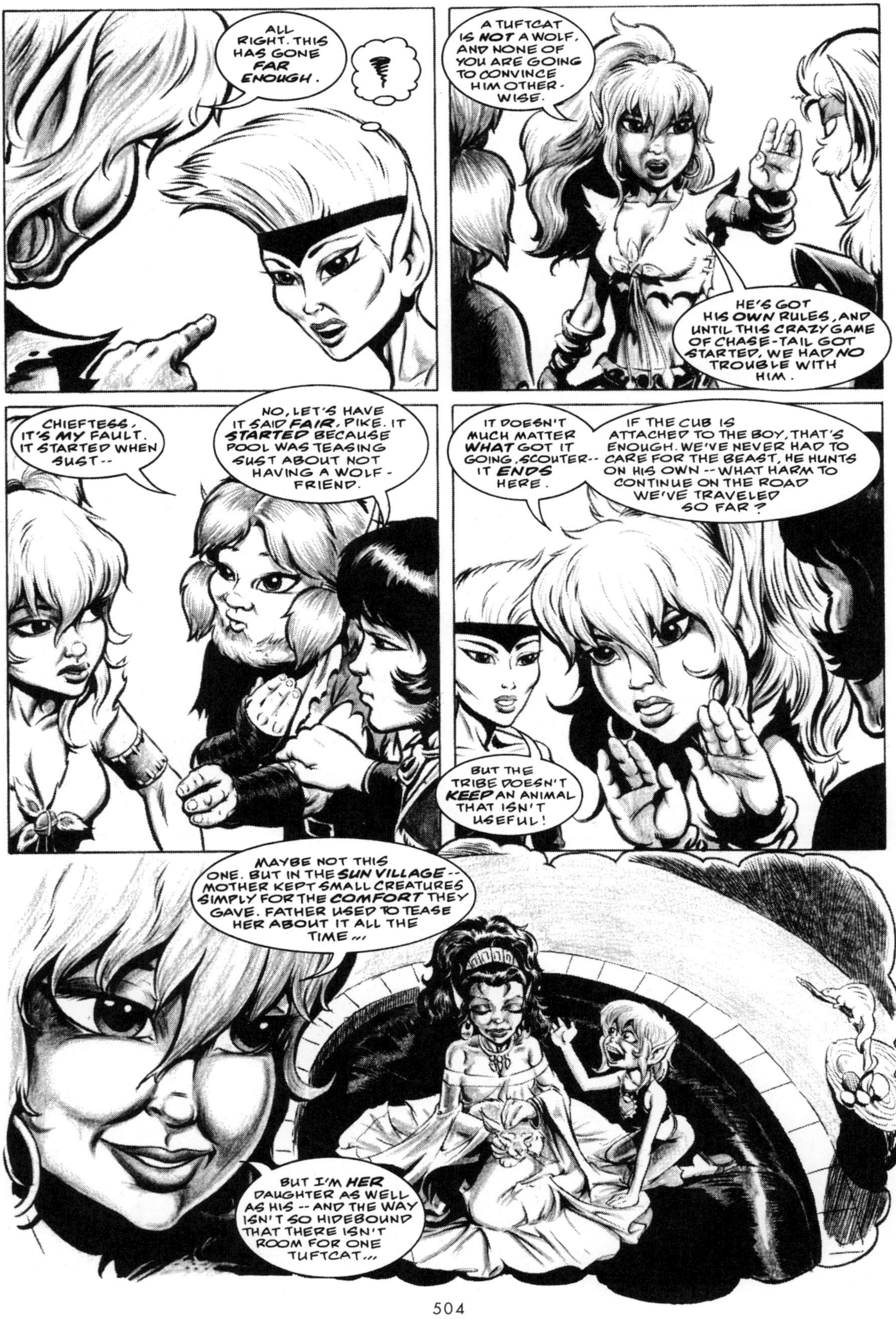
ALL RIGHT. THIS HAS GONE FAR ENOUGH.
A TUFTCAT IS NOT A WOLF, AND NONE OF YOU ARE GOING TO CONVINCE HIM OTHERWISE.
HE'S GOT HIS OWN RULES, AND UNTIL THIS CRAZY GAME OF CHASE-TAIL GOT STARTED, WE HAD NO TROUBLE WITH HIM.
CHIEFTESS, IT'S MY FAULT. IT STARTED WHEN SUST--
NO, LET'S HAVE IT SAID FAIR, PIKE. IT STARTED BECAUSE POOL WAS TEASING SUST ABOUT NOT HAVING A WOLF-FRIEND.
IT DOESN'T MUCH MATTER WHAT GOT IT GOING, SCOUTER-- IT ENDS HERE.
IF THE CUB IS ATTACHED TO THE BOY, THAT'S ENOUGH. WE'VE NEVER HAD TO CARE FOR THE BEAST, HE HUNTS ON HIS OWN -- WHAT HARM TO CONTINUE ON THE ROAD WE'VE TRAVELED SO FAR?
BUT THE TRIBE DOESN'T KEEP AN ANIMAL THAT ISN'T USEFUL!
MAYBE NOT THIS ONE. BUT IN THE SUN VILLAGE-- MOTHER KEPT SMALL CREATURES SIMPLY FOR THE COMFORT THEY GAVE. FATHER USED TO TEASE HER ABOUT IT ALL THE TIME...
BUT I'M HER DAUGHTER AS WELL AS HIS -- AND THE WAY ISN'T SO HIDEBOUND THAT THERE ISN'T ROOM FOR ONE TUFTCAT...

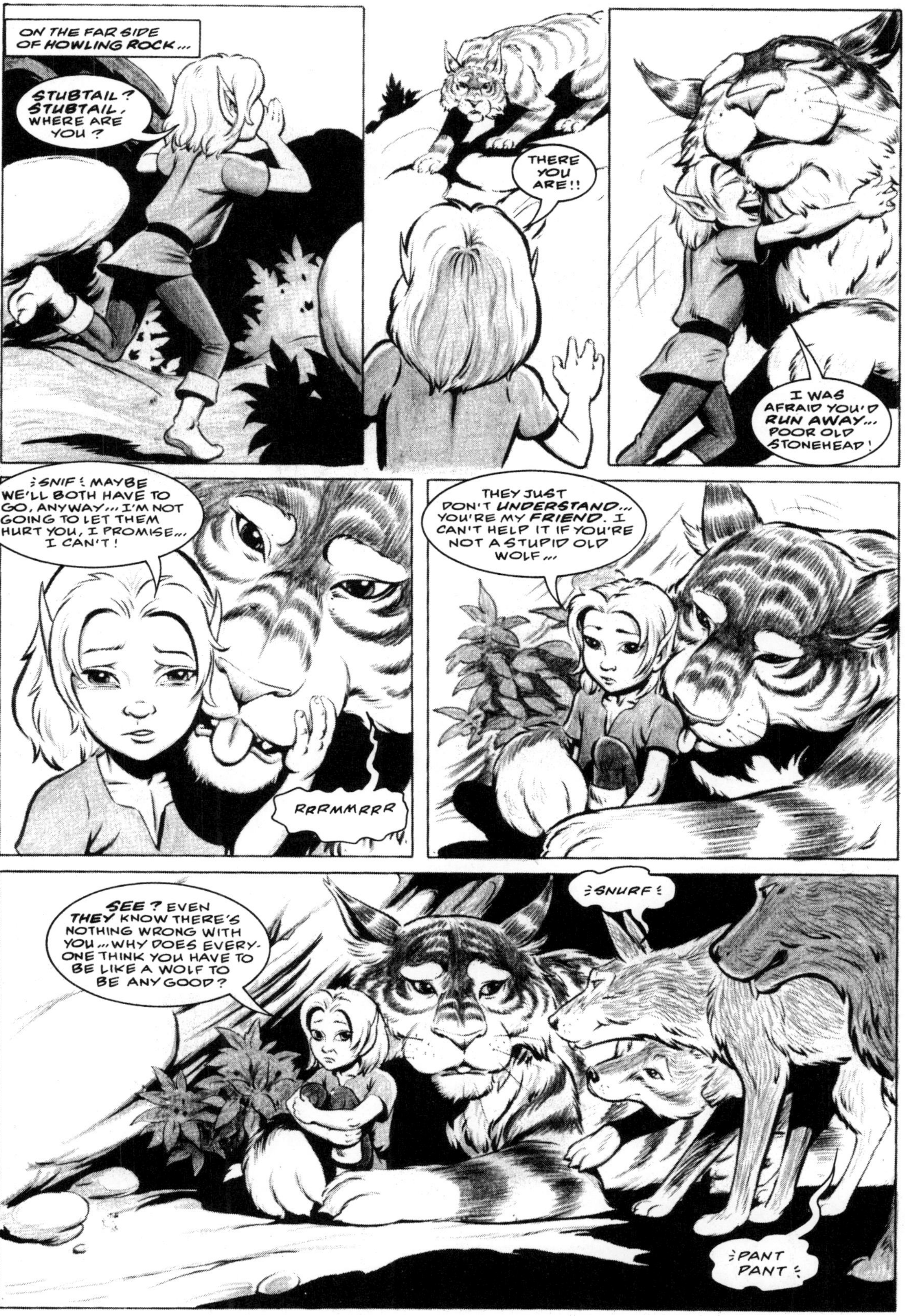

ON THE FAR SIDE OF HOWLING ROCK...
STUBTAIL? STUBTAIL, WHERE ARE YOU?
THERE YOU ARE!!
I WAS AFRAID YOU'D RUN AWAY... POOR OLD STONEHEAD!
SNIF MAYBE WE'LL BOTH HAVE TO GO, ANYWAY... I'M NOT GOING TO LET THEM HURT YOU, I PROMISE... I CAN'T!
RRRMMRRR
THEY JUST DON'T UNDERSTAND... YOU'RE MY FRIEND. I CAN'T HELP IT IF YOU'RE NOT A STUPID OLD WOLF...
SEE? EVEN THEY KNOW THERE'S NOTHING WRONG WITH YOU... WHY DOES EVERYONE THINK YOU HAVE TO BE LIKE A WOLF TO BE ANY GOOD?
SNURF
PANT PANT

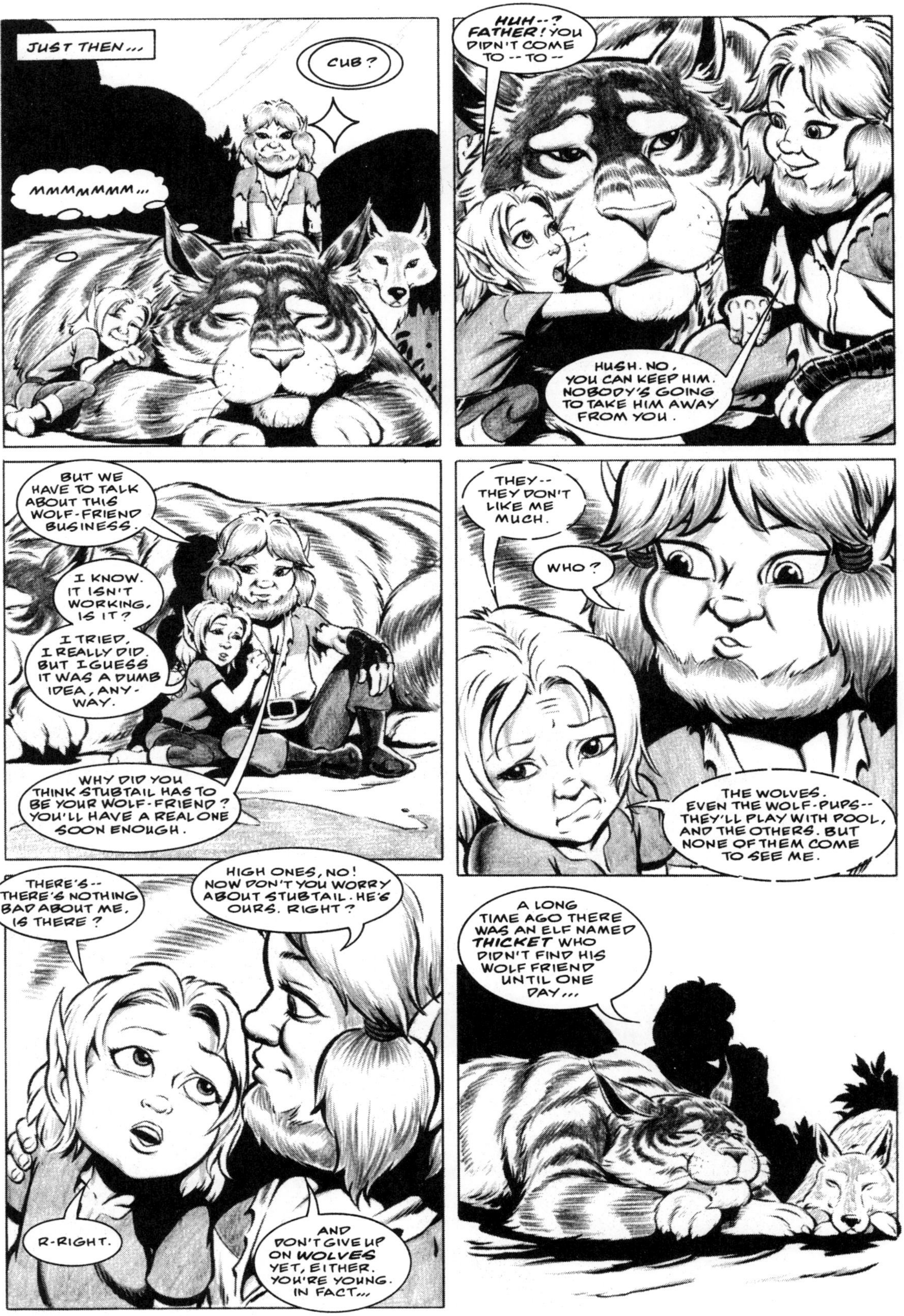
JUST THEN...
CUB?
MMMMMMM...
HUH--? FATHER! YOU DIDN'T COME TO -- TO --
HUSH. NO. YOU CAN KEEP HIM. NOBODY'S GOING TO TAKE HIM AWAY FROM YOU.
BUT WE HAVE TO TALK ABOUT THIS WOLF-FRIEND BUSINESS.
I KNOW. IT ISN'T WORKING, IS IT?
I TRIED, I REALLY DID. BUT I GUESS IT WAS A DUMB IDEA, ANYWAY.
WHY DID YOU THINK STUBTAIL HAS TO BE YOUR WOLF-FRIEND? YOU'LL HAVE A REAL ONE SOON ENOUGH.
THEY-- THEY DON'T LIKE ME MUCH.
WHO?
THE WOLVES. EVEN THE WOLF-PUPS-- THEY'LL PLAY WITH POOL, AND THE OTHERS. BUT NONE OF THEM COME TO SEE ME.
THERE'S-- THERE'S NOTHING BAD ABOUT ME, IS THERE?
HIGH ONES, NO! NOW DON'T YOU WORRY ABOUT STUBTAIL. HE'S OURS. RIGHT?
R-RIGHT.
AND DON'T GIVE UP ON WOLVES YET, EITHER. YOU'RE YOUNG. IN FACT...
A LONG TIME AGO THERE WAS AN ELF NAMED THICKET WHO DIDN'T FIND HIS WOLF FRIEND UNTIL ONE DAY...

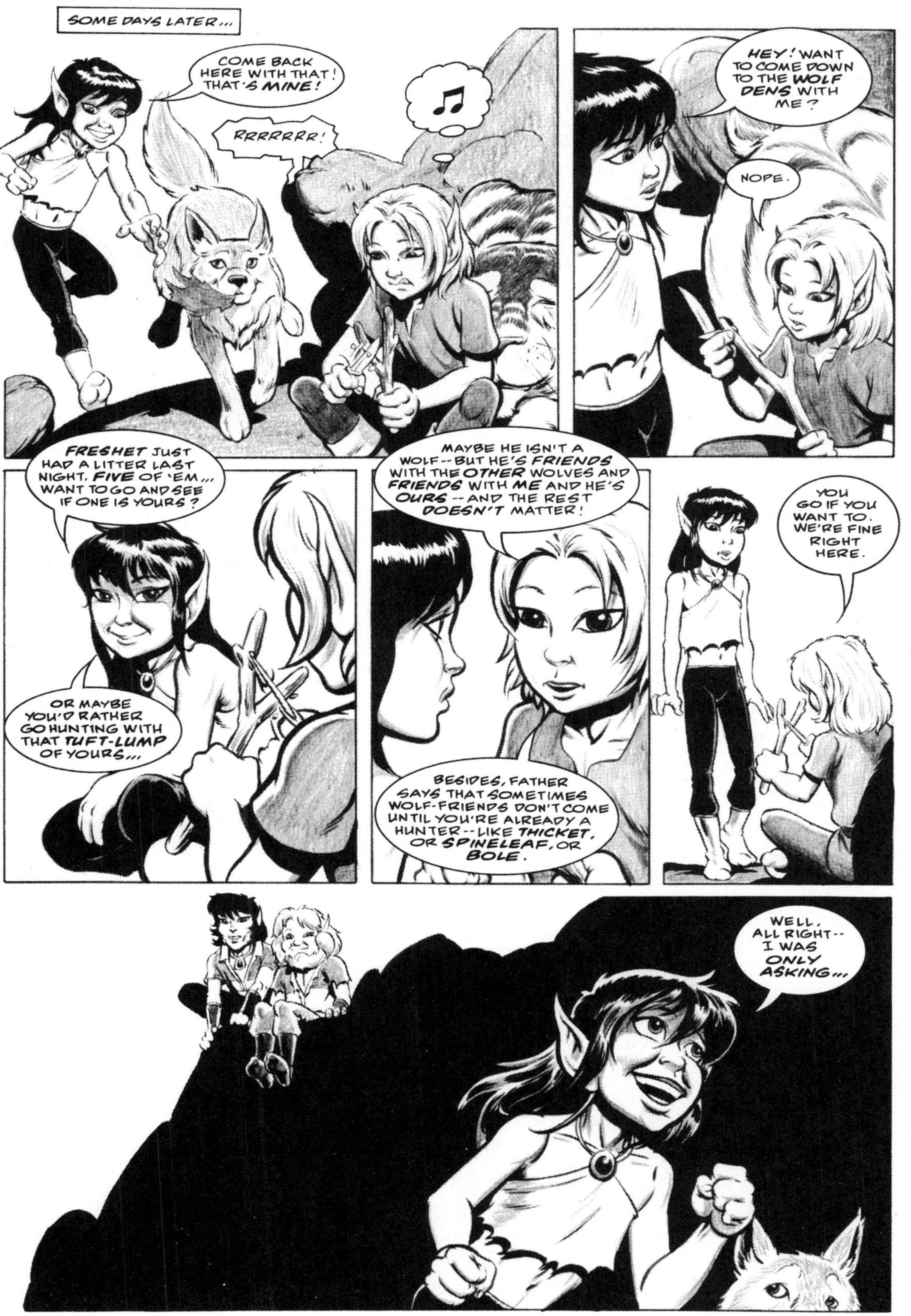
SOME DAYS LATER...
COME BACK HERE WITH THAT! THAT'S MINE!
RRRRRRR!
♫
HEY! WANT TO COME DOWN TO THE WOLF DENS WITH ME?
NOPE.
FRESHET JUST HAD A LITTER LAST NIGHT. FIVE OF 'EM... WANT TO GO AND SEE IF ONE IS YOURS?
OR MAYBE YOU'D RATHER GO HUNTING WITH THAT TUFT-LUMP OF YOURS...
MAYBE HE ISN'T A WOLF--BUT HE'S FRIENDS WITH THE OTHER WOLVES AND FRIENDS WITH ME AND HE'S OURS--AND THE REST DOESN'T MATTER!
BESIDES, FATHER SAYS THAT SOMETIMES WOLF-FRIENDS DON'T COME UNTIL YOU'RE ALREADY A HUNTER--LIKE THICKET, OR SPINELEAF, OR BOLE.
YOU GO IF YOU WANT TO. WE'RE FINE RIGHT HERE.
WELL, ALL RIGHT--I WAS ONLY ASKING...

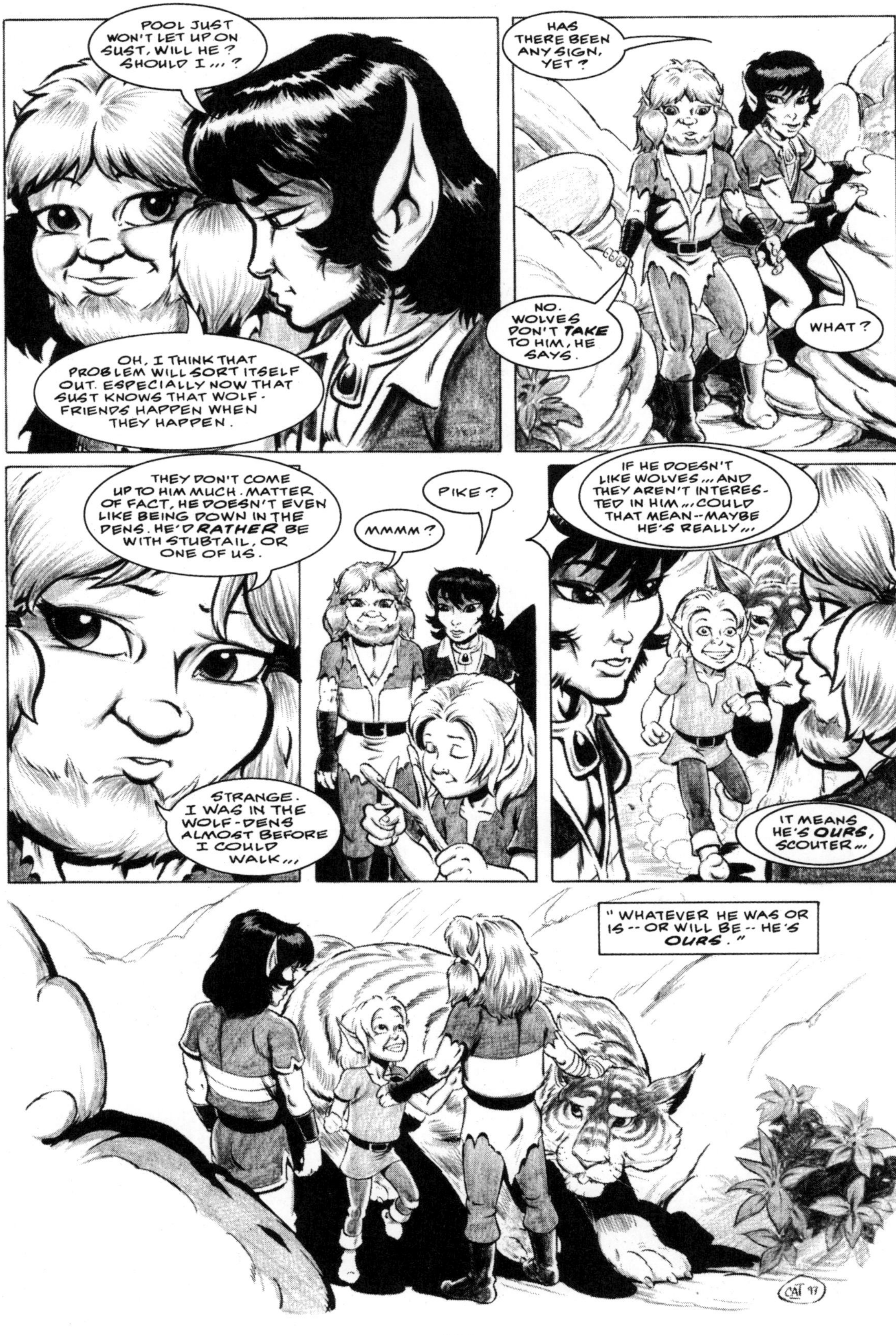
POOL JUST WON'T LET UP ON SUST, WILL HE? SHOULD I...?
OH, I THINK THAT PROBLEM WILL SORT ITSELF OUT. ESPECIALLY NOW THAT SUST KNOWS THAT WOLF-FRIENDS HAPPEN WHEN THEY HAPPEN.
HAS THERE BEEN ANY SIGN, YET?
NO. WOLVES DON'T TAKE TO HIM, HE SAYS.
WHAT?
THEY DON'T COME UP TO HIM MUCH. MATTER OF FACT, HE DOESN'T EVEN LIKE BEING DOWN IN THE DENS. HE'D RATHER BE WITH STUBTAIL, OR ONE OF US.
STRANGE. I WAS IN THE WOLF-DENS ALMOST BEFORE I COULD WALK...
MMMM?
PIKE?
IF HE DOESN'T LIKE WOLVES... AND THEY AREN'T INTERESTED IN HIM... COULD THAT MEAN--MAYBE HE'S REALLY...
IT MEANS HE'S OURS, SCOUTER...
"WHATEVER HE WAS OR IS -- OR WILL BE -- HE'S OURS."
CAT 97

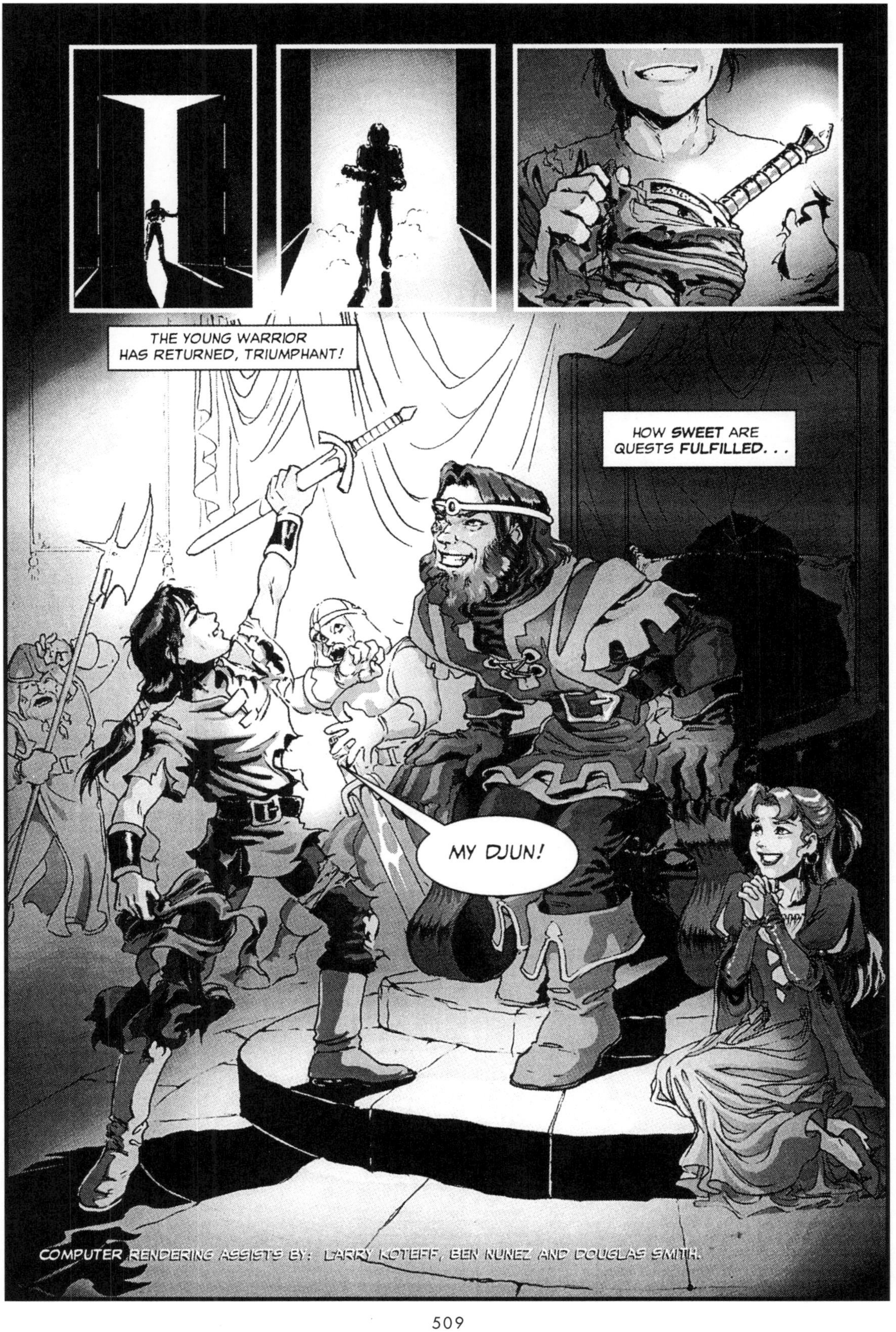
THE YOUNG WARRIOR HAS RETURNED, TRIUMPHANT!
HOW SWEET ARE QUESTS FULFILLED. . .
MY DJUN!
COMPUTER RENDERING ASSISTS BY: LARRY KOTEFF, BEN NUNEZ AND DOUGLAS SMITH.

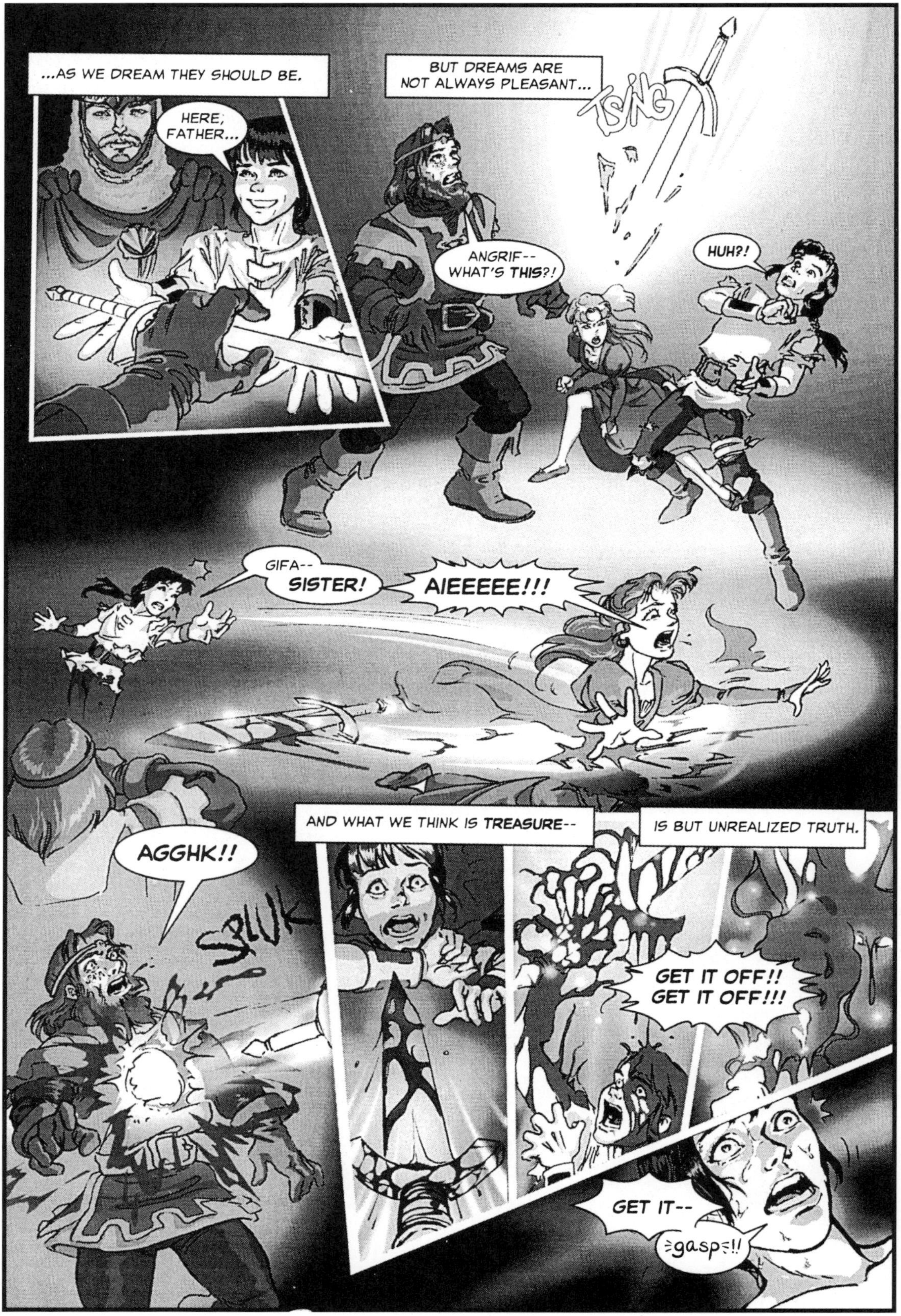
...AS WE DREAM THEY SHOULD BE.
HERE, FATHER...
BUT DREAMS ARE NOT ALWAYS PLEASANT...
TSING
ANGRIF-- WHAT'S THIS?!
HUH?!
GIFA-- SISTER!
AIEEEEE!!!
AGGHK!!
SPLUK
AND WHAT WE THINK IS TREASURE--
IS BUT UNREALIZED TRUTH.
GET IT OFF!! GET IT OFF!!!
GET IT--
gasp!!

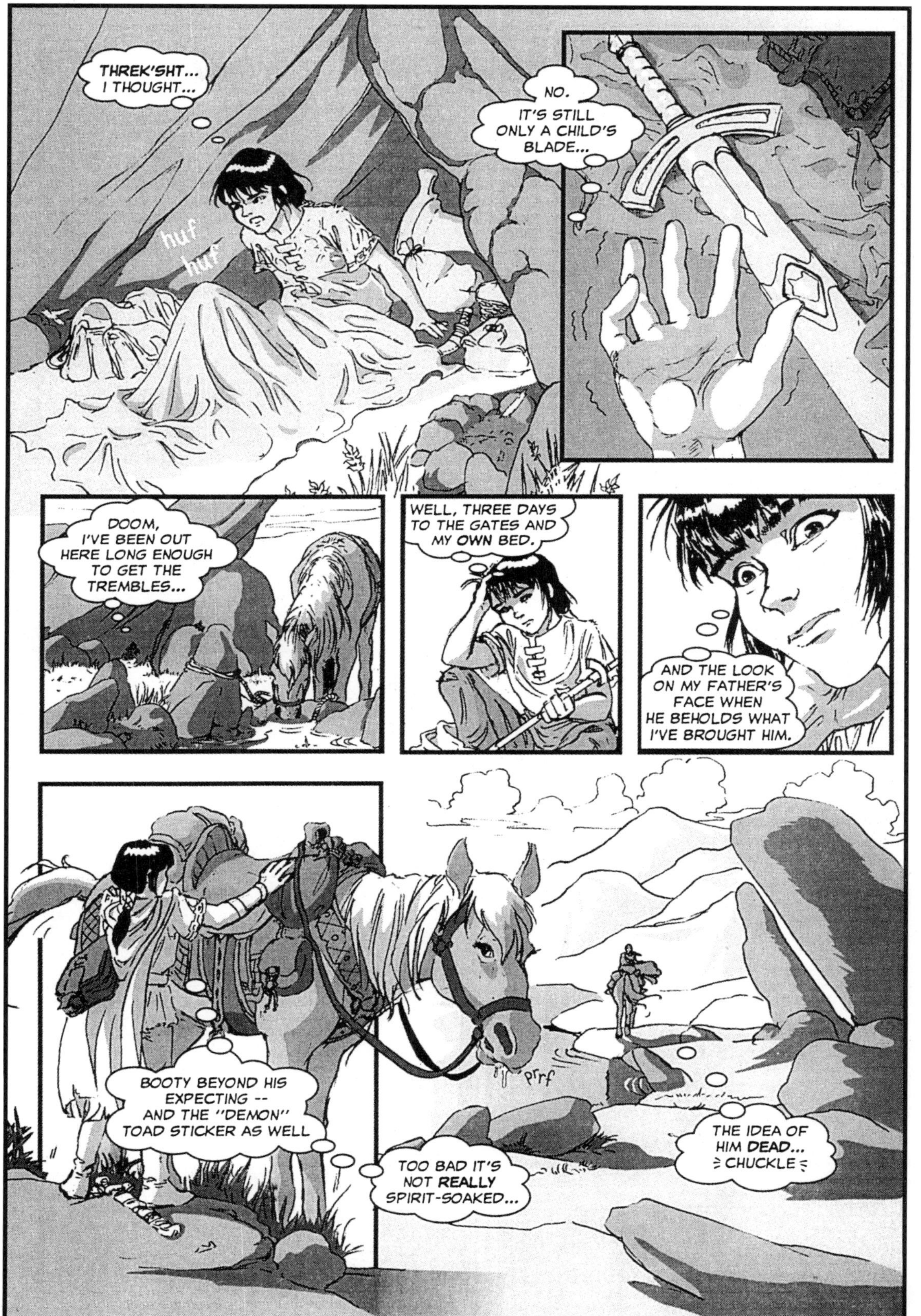
THREK'SHT... I THOUGHT...
huf huf
NO. IT'S STILL ONLY A CHILD'S BLADE...
DOOM, I'VE BEEN OUT HERE LONG ENOUGH TO GET THE TREMBLES...
WELL, THREE DAYS TO THE GATES AND MY OWN BED.
AND THE LOOK ON MY FATHER'S FACE WHEN HE BEHOLDS WHAT I'VE BROUGHT HIM.
BOOTY BEYOND HIS EXPECTING -- AND THE "DEMON" TOAD STICKER AS WELL
prrf
TOO BAD IT'S NOT REALLY SPIRIT-SOAKED...
THE IDEA OF HIM DEAD... CHUCKLE

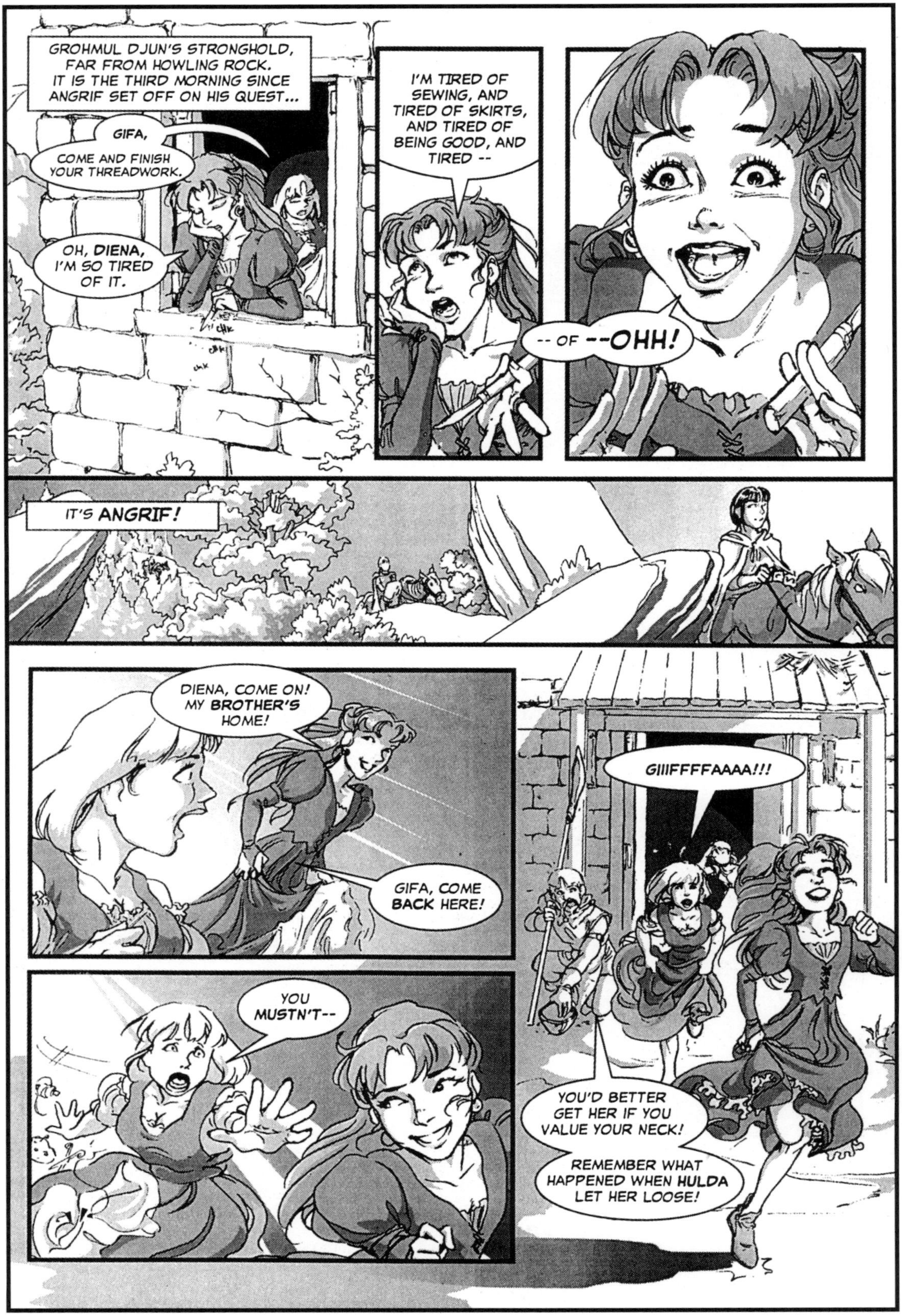
GROHMUL DJUN'S STRONGHOLD, FAR FROM HOWLING ROCK. IT IS THE THIRD MORNING SINCE ANGRIF SET OFF ON HIS QUEST...
GIFA,
COME AND FINISH YOUR THREADWORK.
OH, DIENA, I'M SO TIRED OF IT.
I'M TIRED OF SEWING, AND TIRED OF SKIRTS, AND TIRED OF BEING GOOD, AND TIRED --
-- OF --OHH!
IT'S ANGRIF!
DIENA, COME ON! MY BROTHER'S HOME!
GIFA, COME BACK HERE!
YOU MUSTN'T--
GIIIFFFFAAAA!!!
YOU'D BETTER GET HER IF YOU VALUE YOUR NECK!
REMEMBER WHAT HAPPENED WHEN HULDA LET HER LOOSE!

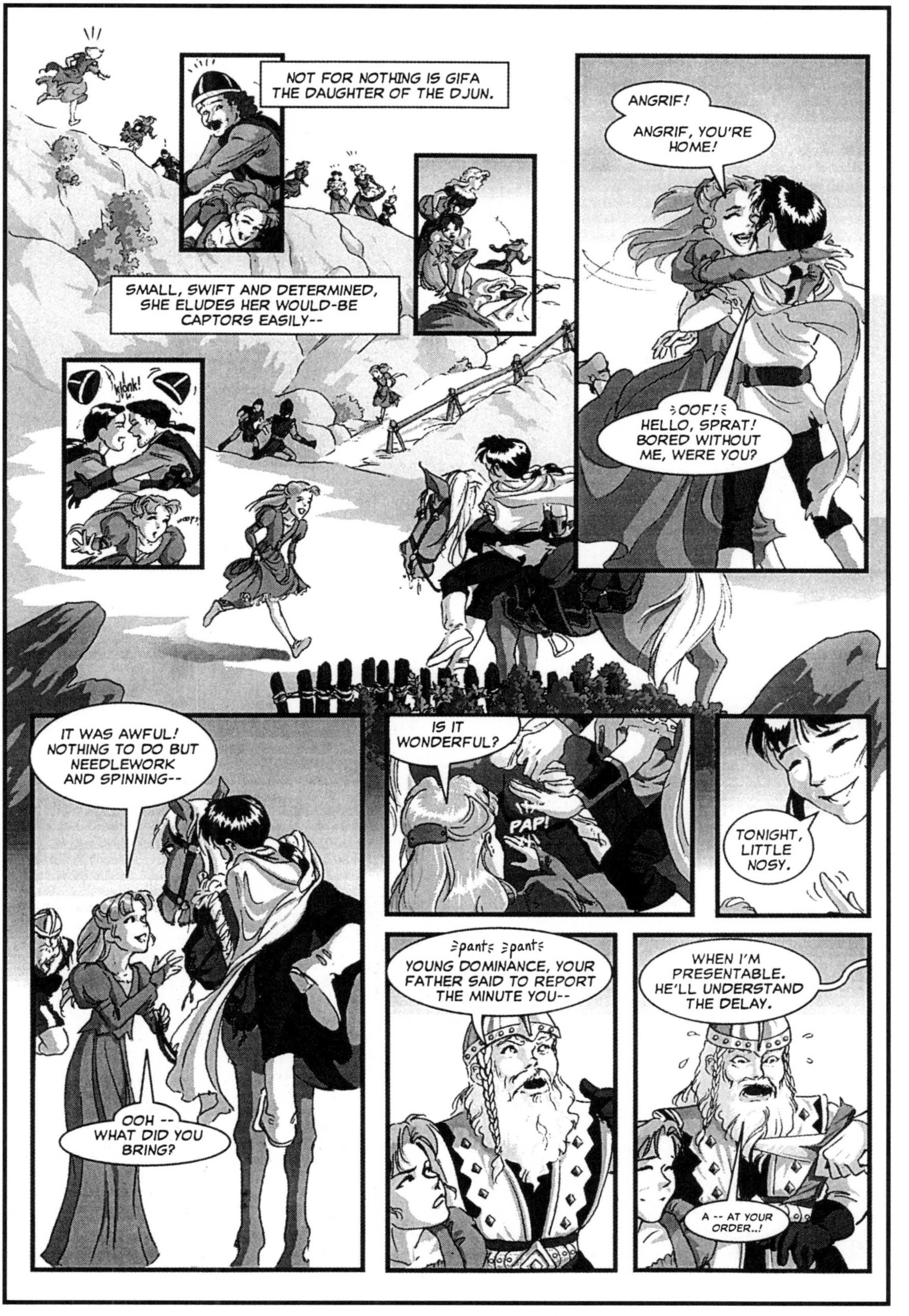
NOT FOR NOTHING IS GIFA THE DAUGHTER OF THE DJUN.
SMALL, SWIFT AND DETERMINED, SHE ELUDES HER WOULD-BE CAPTORS EASILY--
KLONK!
ANGRIF!
ANGRIF, YOU'RE HOME!
OOF!
HELLO, SPRAT! BORED WITHOUT ME, WERE YOU?
IT WAS AWFUL! NOTHING TO DO BUT NEEDLEWORK AND SPINNING--
OOH -- WHAT DID YOU BRING?
IS IT WONDERFUL?
PAP!
TONIGHT, LITTLE NOSY.
PANT PANT
YOUNG DOMINANCE, YOUR FATHER SAID TO REPORT THE MINUTE YOU--
WHEN I'M PRESENTABLE. HE'LL UNDERSTAND THE DELAY.
A -- AT YOUR ORDER..!

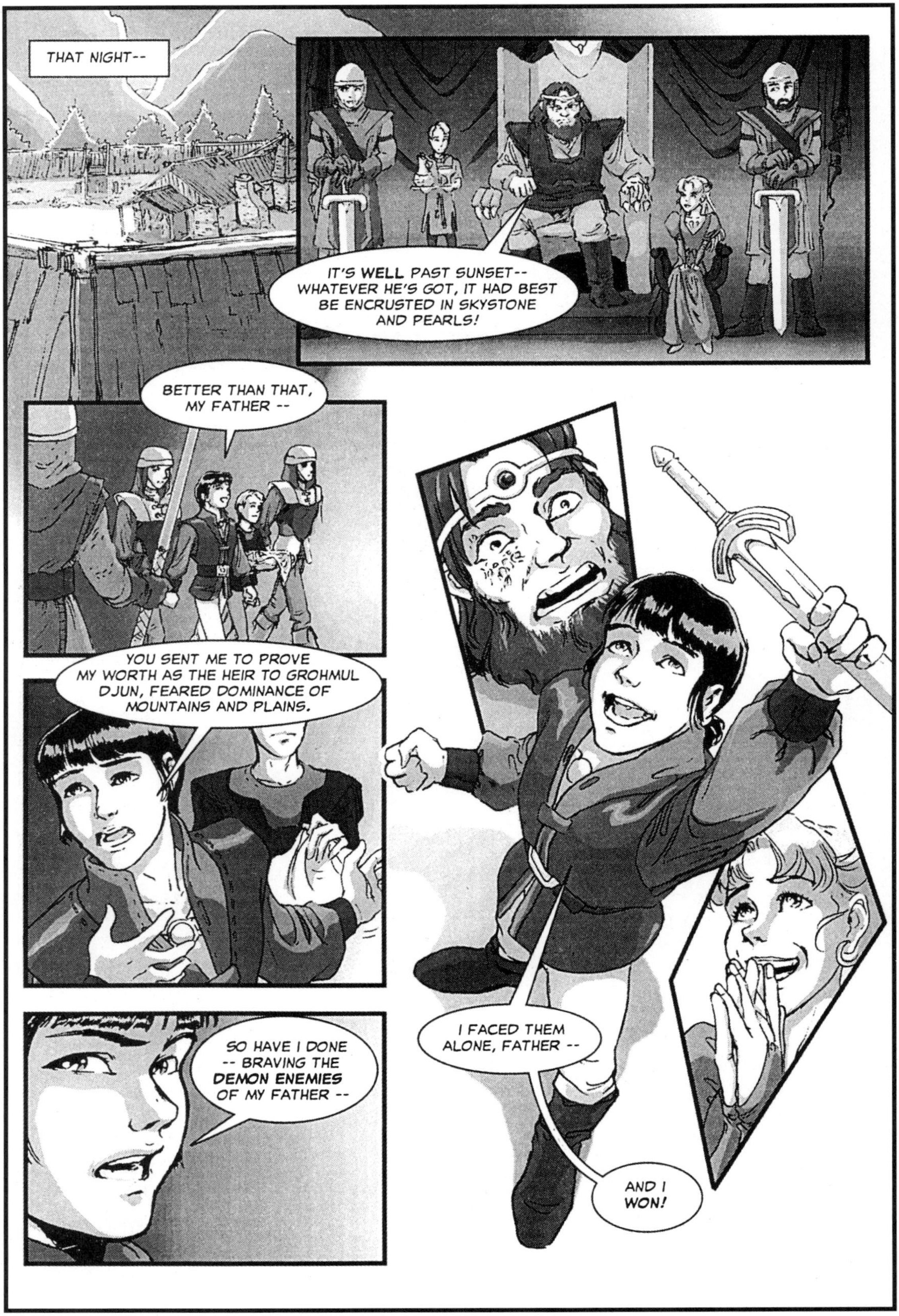
THAT NIGHT--
IT'S WELL PAST SUNSET-- WHATEVER HE'S GOT, IT HAD BEST BE ENCRUSTED IN SKYSTONE AND PEARLS!
BETTER THAN THAT, MY FATHER --
YOU SENT ME TO PROVE MY WORTH AS THE HEIR TO GROHMUL DJUN, FEARED DOMINANCE OF MOUNTAINS AND PLAINS.
SO HAVE I DONE -- BRAVING THE DEMON ENEMIES OF MY FATHER --
I FACED THEM ALONE, FATHER --
AND I WON!

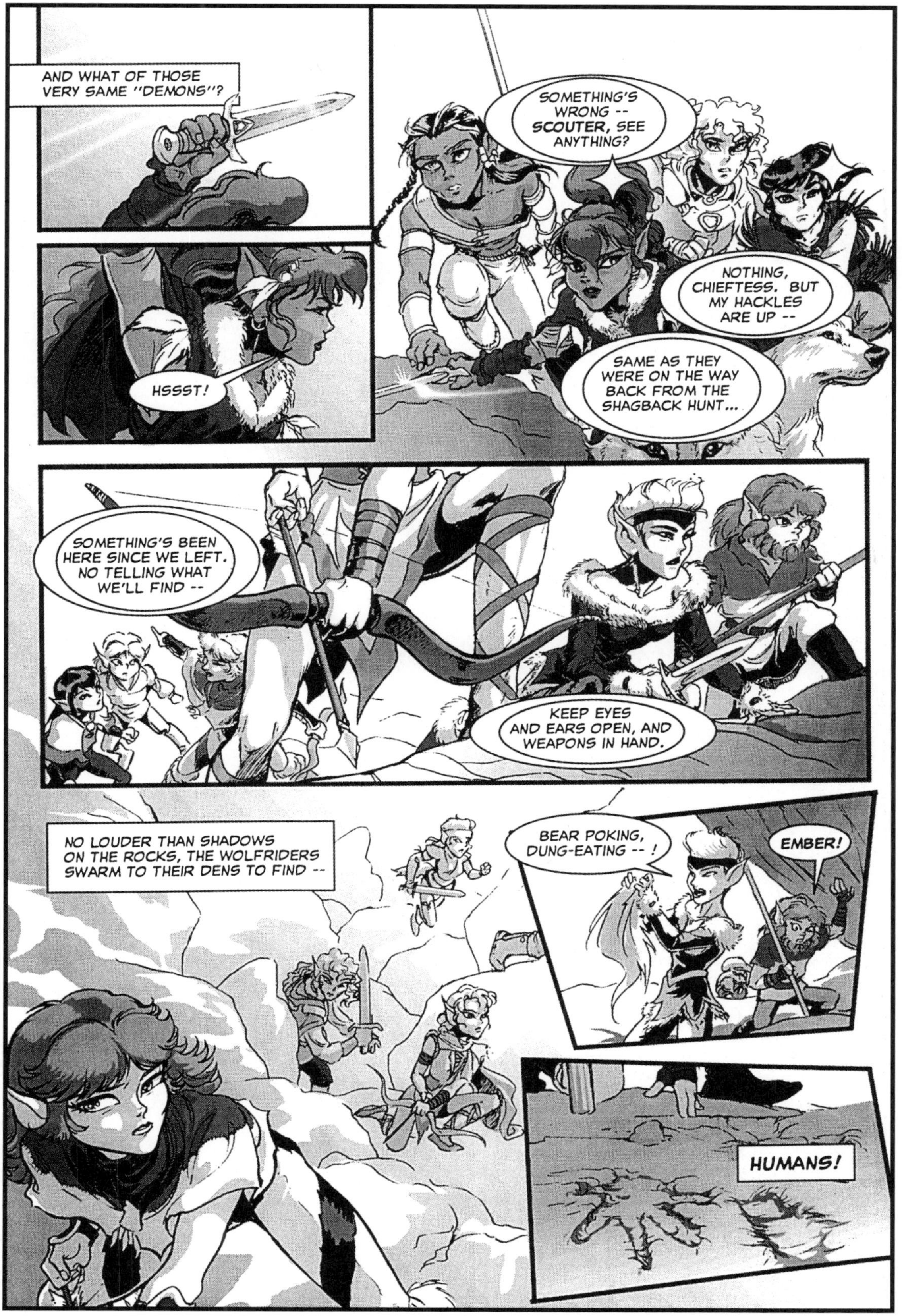
AND WHAT OF THOSE VERY SAME "DEMONS"?
SOMETHING'S WRONG -- SCOUTER, SEE ANYTHING?
HSSST!
NOTHING, CHIEFTESS. BUT MY HACKLES ARE UP --
SAME AS THEY WERE ON THE WAY BACK FROM THE SHAGBACK HUNT...
SOMETHING'S BEEN HERE SINCE WE LEFT. NO TELLING WHAT WE'LL FIND --
KEEP EYES AND EARS OPEN, AND WEAPONS IN HAND.
NO LOUDER THAN SHADOWS ON THE ROCKS, THE WOLFRIDERS SWARM TO THEIR DENS TO FIND --
BEAR POKING, DUNG-EATING -- !
EMBER!
HUMANS!

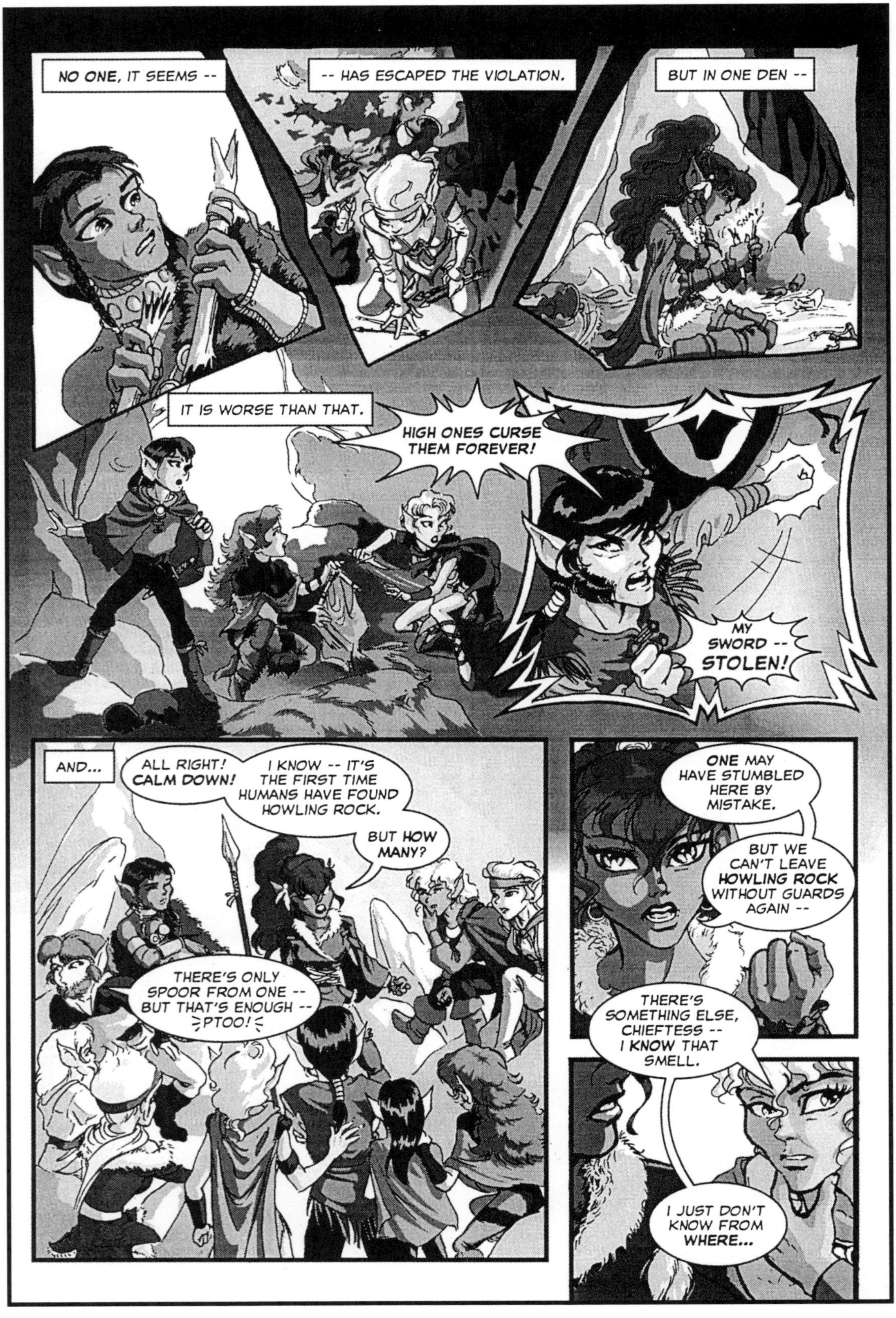

NO ONE, IT SEEMS --
-- HAS ESCAPED THE VIOLATION.
BUT IN ONE DEN --
SNAP!
IT IS WORSE THAN THAT.
HIGH ONES CURSE THEM FOREVER!
MY SWORD -- STOLEN!
AND...
ALL RIGHT! CALM DOWN!
I KNOW -- IT'S THE FIRST TIME HUMANS HAVE FOUND HOWLING ROCK.
BUT HOW MANY?
THERE'S ONLY SPOOR FROM ONE -- BUT THAT'S ENOUGH -- PTOO!
ONE MAY HAVE STUMBLED HERE BY MISTAKE.
BUT WE CAN'T LEAVE HOWLING ROCK WITHOUT GUARDS AGAIN --
THERE'S SOMETHING ELSE, CHIEFTESS -- I KNOW THAT SMELL.
I JUST DON'T KNOW FROM WHERE...

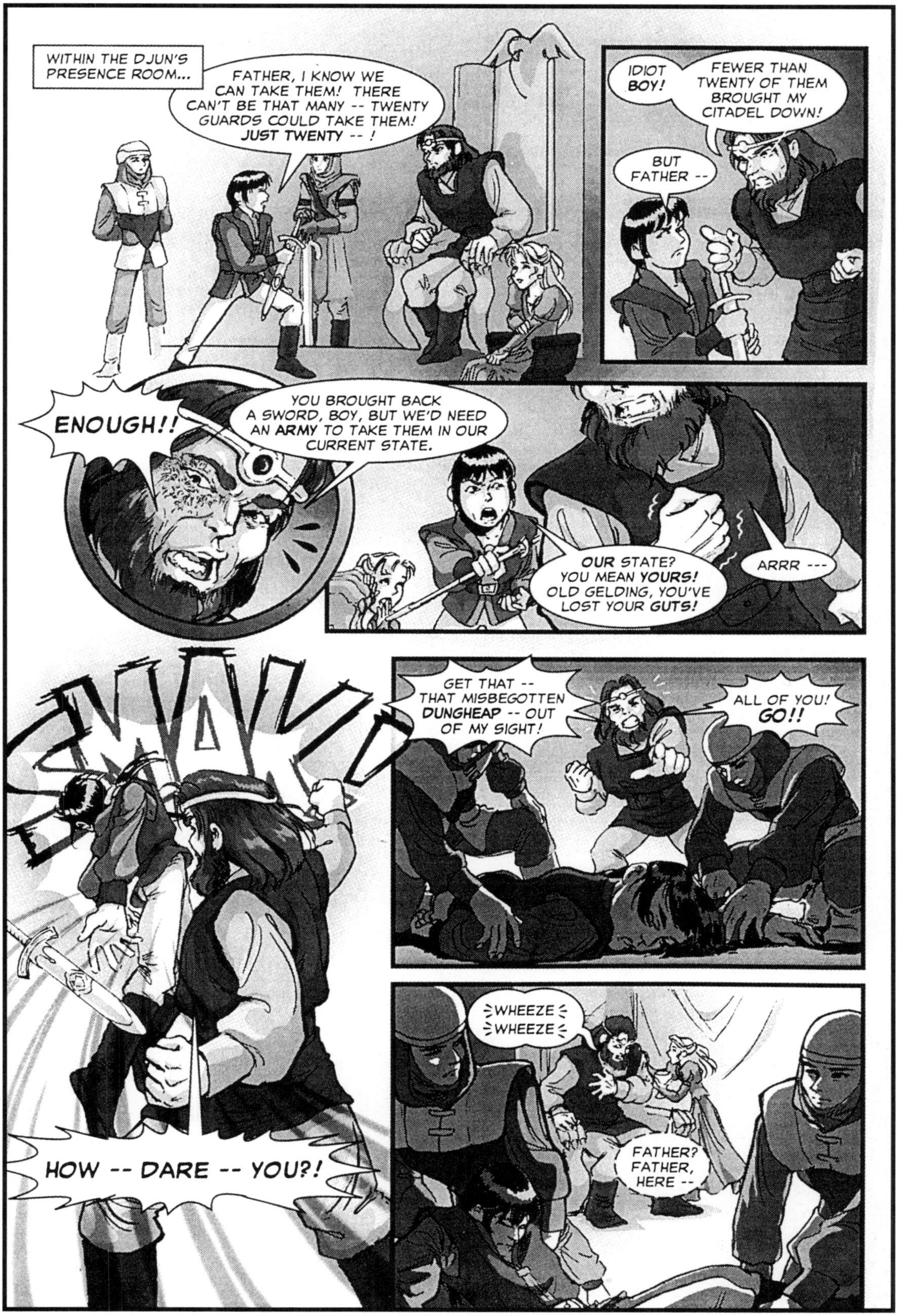
WITHIN THE DJUN'S PRESENCE ROOM...
FATHER, I KNOW WE CAN TAKE THEM! THERE CAN'T BE THAT MANY -- TWENTY GUARDS COULD TAKE THEM! JUST TWENTY -- !
IDIOT BOY!
FEWER THAN TWENTY OF THEM BROUGHT MY CITADEL DOWN!
BUT FATHER --
ENOUGH!!
YOU BROUGHT BACK A SWORD, BOY, BUT WE'D NEED AN ARMY TO TAKE THEM IN OUR CURRENT STATE.
OUR STATE? YOU MEAN YOURS! OLD GELDING, YOU'VE LOST YOUR GUTS!
ARRR ---
HOW -- DARE -- YOU?!
GET THAT -- THAT MISBEGOTTEN DUNGHEAP -- OUT OF MY SIGHT!
ALL OF YOU! GO!!
WHEEZE
WHEEZE
FATHER? FATHER, HERE --

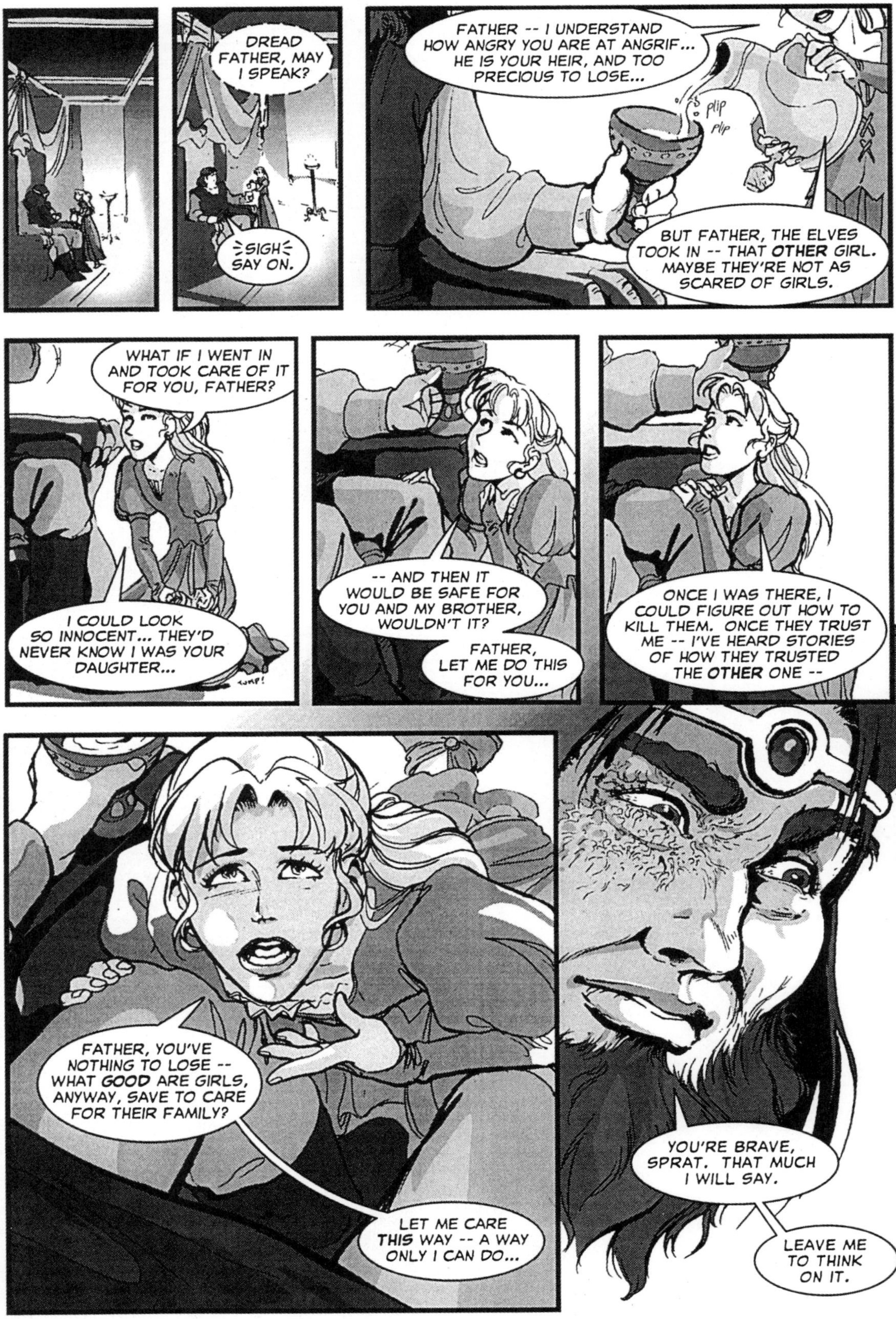
DREAD FATHER, MAY I SPEAK?
SIGH SAY ON.
FATHER -- I UNDERSTAND HOW ANGRY YOU ARE AT ANGRIF... HE IS YOUR HEIR, AND TOO PRECIOUS TO LOSE...
plip
plip
BUT FATHER, THE ELVES TOOK IN -- THAT **OTHER** GIRL. MAYBE THEY'RE NOT AS SCARED OF GIRLS.
WHAT IF I WENT IN AND TOOK CARE OF IT FOR YOU, FATHER?
I COULD LOOK SO INNOCENT... THEY'D NEVER KNOW I WAS YOUR DAUGHTER...
-- AND THEN IT WOULD BE SAFE FOR YOU AND MY BROTHER, WOULDN'T IT?
FATHER, LET ME DO THIS FOR YOU...
ONCE I WAS THERE, I COULD FIGURE OUT HOW TO KILL THEM. ONCE THEY TRUST ME -- I'VE HEARD STORIES OF HOW THEY TRUSTED THE **OTHER** ONE --
FATHER, YOU'VE NOTHING TO LOSE -- WHAT **GOOD** ARE GIRLS, ANYWAY, SAVE TO CARE FOR THEIR FAMILY?
LET ME CARE **THIS** WAY -- A WAY ONLY I CAN DO...
YOU'RE BRAVE, SPRAT. THAT MUCH I WILL SAY.
LEAVE ME TO THINK ON IT.

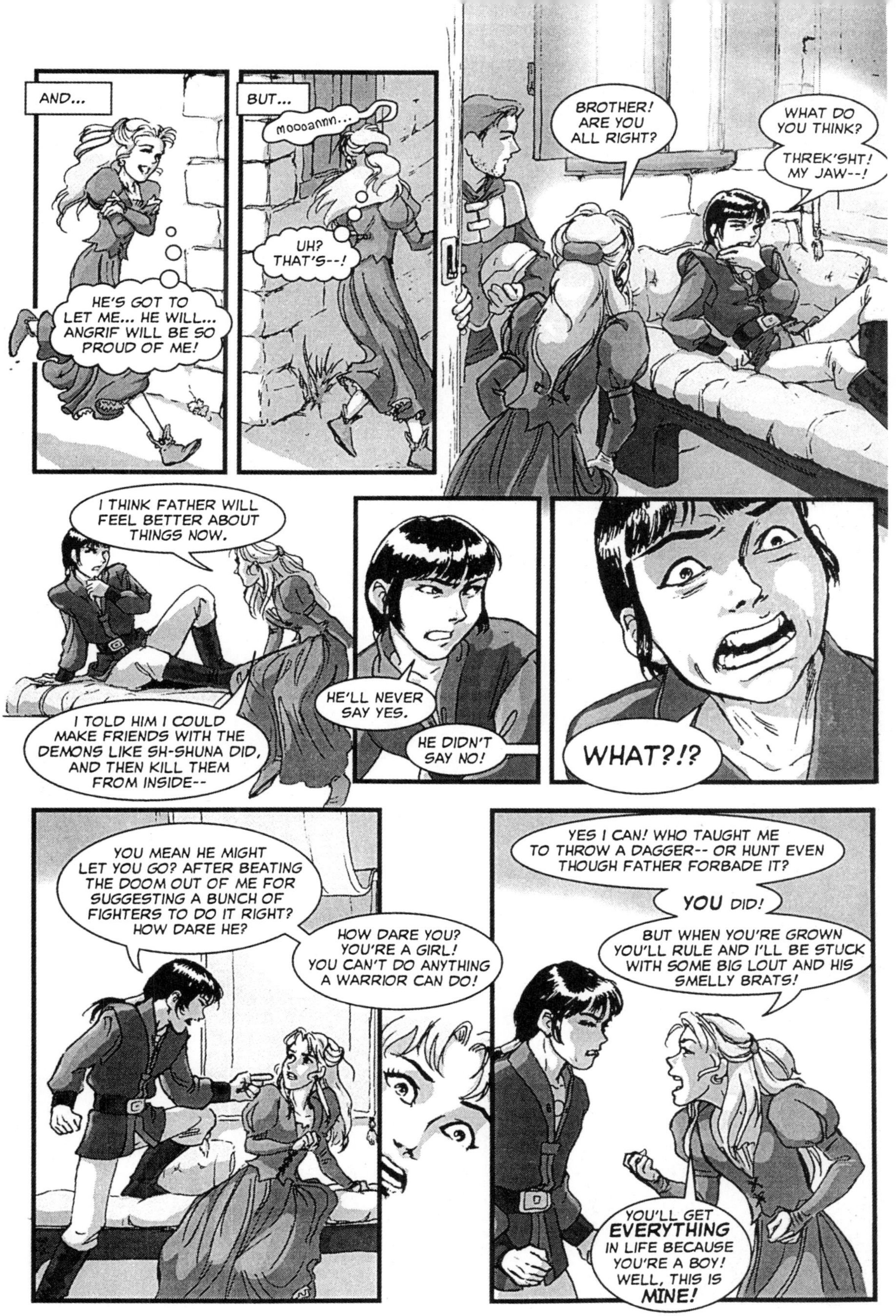
AND...
HE'S GOT TO LET ME... HE WILL... ANGRIF WILL BE SO PROUD OF ME!
BUT...
MOOOANNN...
UH? THAT'S--!
BROTHER! ARE YOU ALL RIGHT?
WHAT DO YOU THINK?
THREK'SHT! MY JAW--!
I THINK FATHER WILL FEEL BETTER ABOUT THINGS NOW.
I TOLD HIM I COULD MAKE FRIENDS WITH THE DEMONS LIKE SH-SHUNA DID, AND THEN KILL THEM FROM INSIDE--
HE'LL NEVER SAY YES.
HE DIDN'T SAY NO!
WHAT?!?
YOU MEAN HE MIGHT LET YOU GO? AFTER BEATING THE DOOM OUT OF ME FOR SUGGESTING A BUNCH OF FIGHTERS TO DO IT RIGHT? HOW DARE HE?
HOW DARE YOU? YOU'RE A GIRL! YOU CAN'T DO ANYTHING A WARRIOR CAN DO!
YES I CAN! WHO TAUGHT ME TO THROW A DAGGER-- OR HUNT EVEN THOUGH FATHER FORBADE IT?
YOU DID!
BUT WHEN YOU'RE GROWN YOU'LL RULE AND I'LL BE STUCK WITH SOME BIG LOUT AND HIS SMELLY BRATS!
YOU'LL GET EVERYTHING IN LIFE BECAUSE YOU'RE A BOY! WELL, THIS IS MINE!

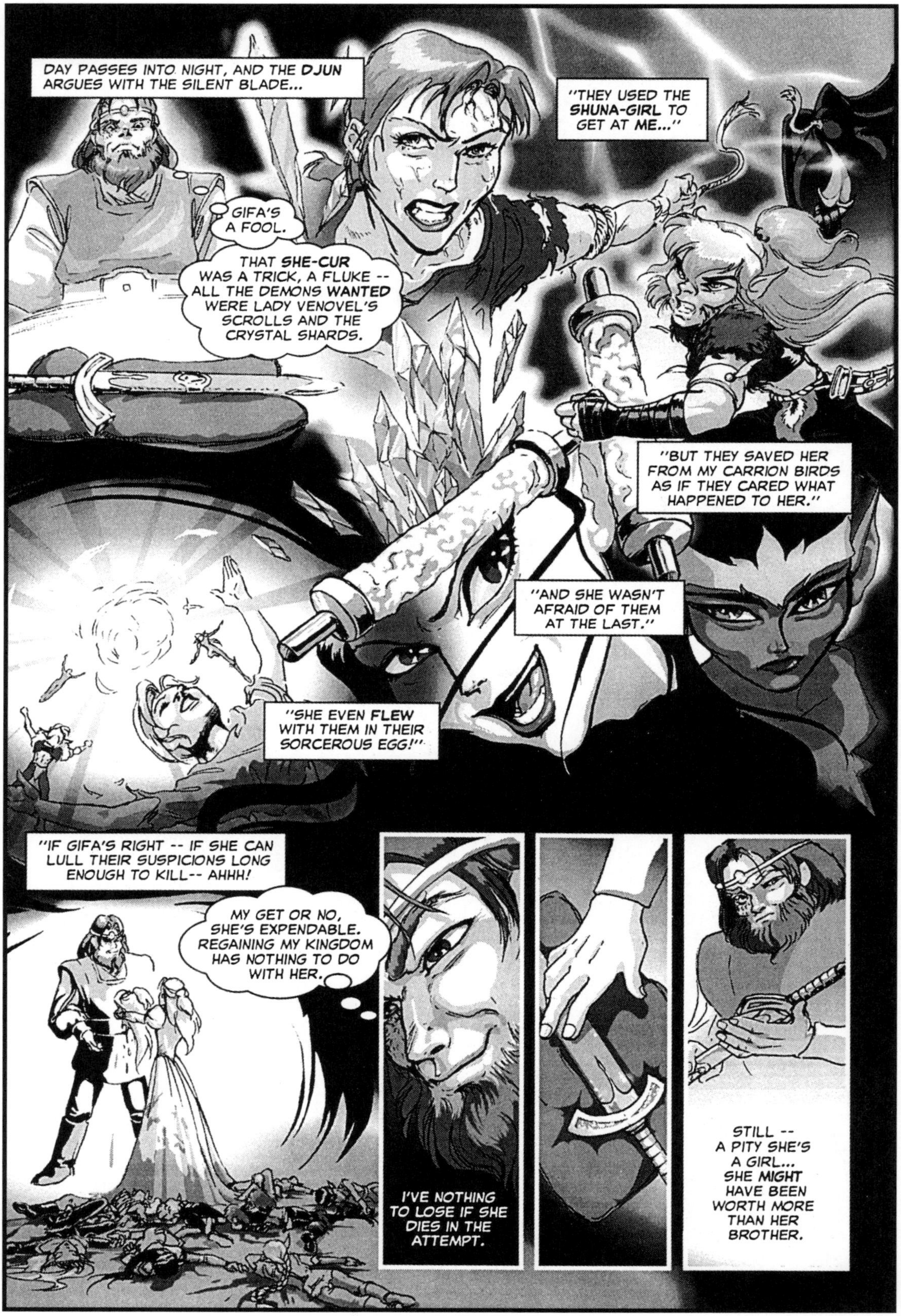
DAY PASSES INTO NIGHT, AND THE DJUN ARGUES WITH THE SILENT BLADE...
"THEY USED THE SHUNA-GIRL TO GET AT ME..."
GIFA'S A FOOL.
THAT SHE-CUR WAS A TRICK, A FLUKE -- ALL THE DEMONS WANTED WERE LADY VENOVEL'S SCROLLS AND THE CRYSTAL SHARDS.
"BUT THEY SAVED HER FROM MY CARRION BIRDS AS IF THEY CARED WHAT HAPPENED TO HER."
"AND SHE WASN'T AFRAID OF THEM AT THE LAST."
"SHE EVEN FLEW WITH THEM IN THEIR SORCEROUS EGG!"
"IF GIFA'S RIGHT -- IF SHE CAN LULL THEIR SUSPICIONS LONG ENOUGH TO KILL-- AHHH!
MY GET OR NO, SHE'S EXPENDABLE. REGAINING MY KINGDOM HAS NOTHING TO DO WITH HER.
I'VE NOTHING TO LOSE IF SHE DIES IN THE ATTEMPT.
STILL -- A PITY SHE'S A GIRL... SHE MIGHT HAVE BEEN WORTH MORE THAN HER BROTHER.

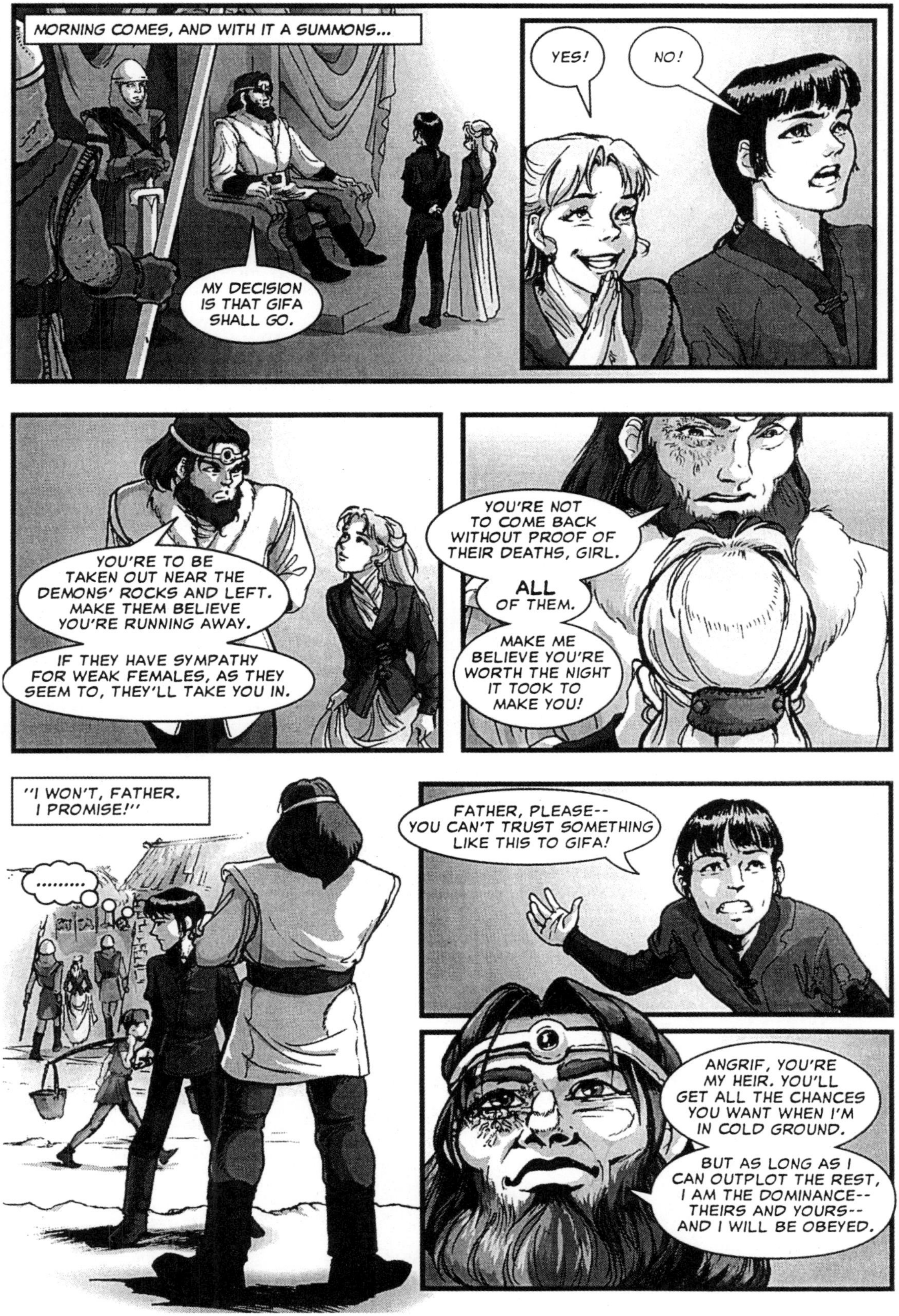
MORNING COMES, AND WITH IT A SUMMONS...
MY DECISION IS THAT GIFA SHALL GO.
YES!
NO!
YOU'RE TO BE TAKEN OUT NEAR THE DEMONS' ROCKS AND LEFT. MAKE THEM BELIEVE YOU'RE RUNNING AWAY.
IF THEY HAVE SYMPATHY FOR WEAK FEMALES, AS THEY SEEM TO, THEY'LL TAKE YOU IN.
YOU'RE NOT TO COME BACK WITHOUT PROOF OF THEIR DEATHS, GIRL.
ALL OF THEM.
MAKE ME BELIEVE YOU'RE WORTH THE NIGHT IT TOOK TO MAKE YOU!
"I WON'T, FATHER. I PROMISE!"
....
FATHER, PLEASE-- YOU CAN'T TRUST SOMETHING LIKE THIS TO GIFA!
ANGRIF, YOU'RE MY HEIR. YOU'LL GET ALL THE CHANCES YOU WANT WHEN I'M IN COLD GROUND.
BUT AS LONG AS I CAN OUTPLOT THE REST, I AM THE DOMINANCE-- THEIRS AND YOURS-- AND I WILL BE OBEYED.

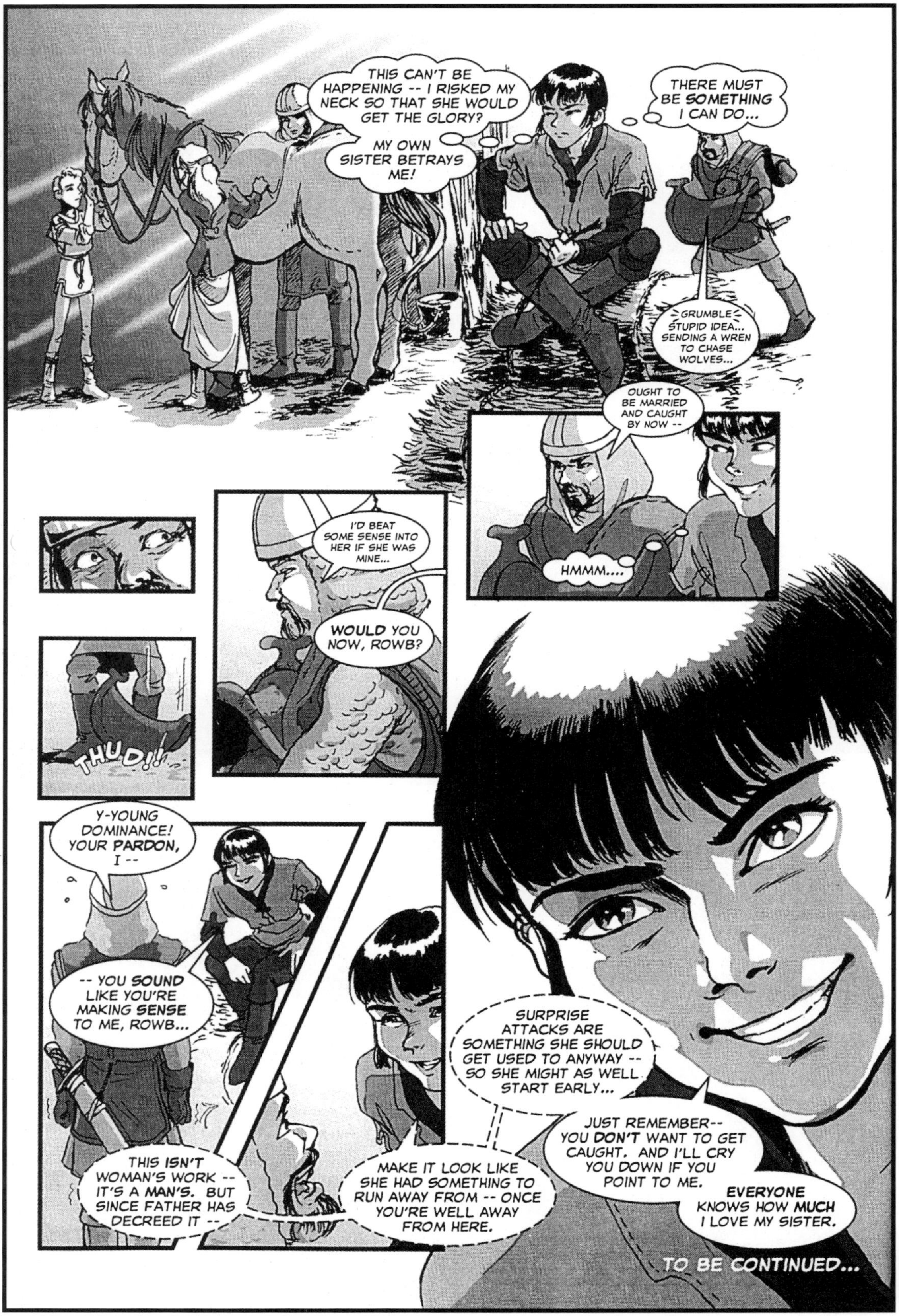
THIS CAN'T BE HAPPENING -- I RISKED MY NECK SO THAT SHE WOULD GET THE GLORY?
MY OWN SISTER BETRAYS ME!
THERE MUST BE SOMETHING I CAN DO...
GRUMBLE STUPID IDEA... SENDING A WREN TO CHASE WOLVES...
OUGHT TO BE MARRIED AND CAUGHT BY NOW --
HMMM....
I'D BEAT SOME SENSE INTO HER IF SHE WAS MINE...
WOULD YOU NOW, ROWB?
THUD!!
Y-YOUNG DOMINANCE! YOUR PARDON, I --
-- YOU SOUND LIKE YOU'RE MAKING SENSE TO ME, ROWB...
SURPRISE ATTACKS ARE SOMETHING SHE SHOULD GET USED TO ANYWAY -- SO SHE MIGHT AS WELL START EARLY...
THIS ISN'T WOMAN'S WORK -- IT'S A MAN'S. BUT SINCE FATHER HAS DECREED IT --
MAKE IT LOOK LIKE SHE HAD SOMETHING TO RUN AWAY FROM -- ONCE YOU'RE WELL AWAY FROM HERE.
JUST REMEMBER-- YOU DON'T WANT TO GET CAUGHT. AND I'LL CRY YOU DOWN IF YOU POINT TO ME.
EVERYONE KNOWS HOW MUCH I LOVE MY SISTER.
TO BE CONTINUED...

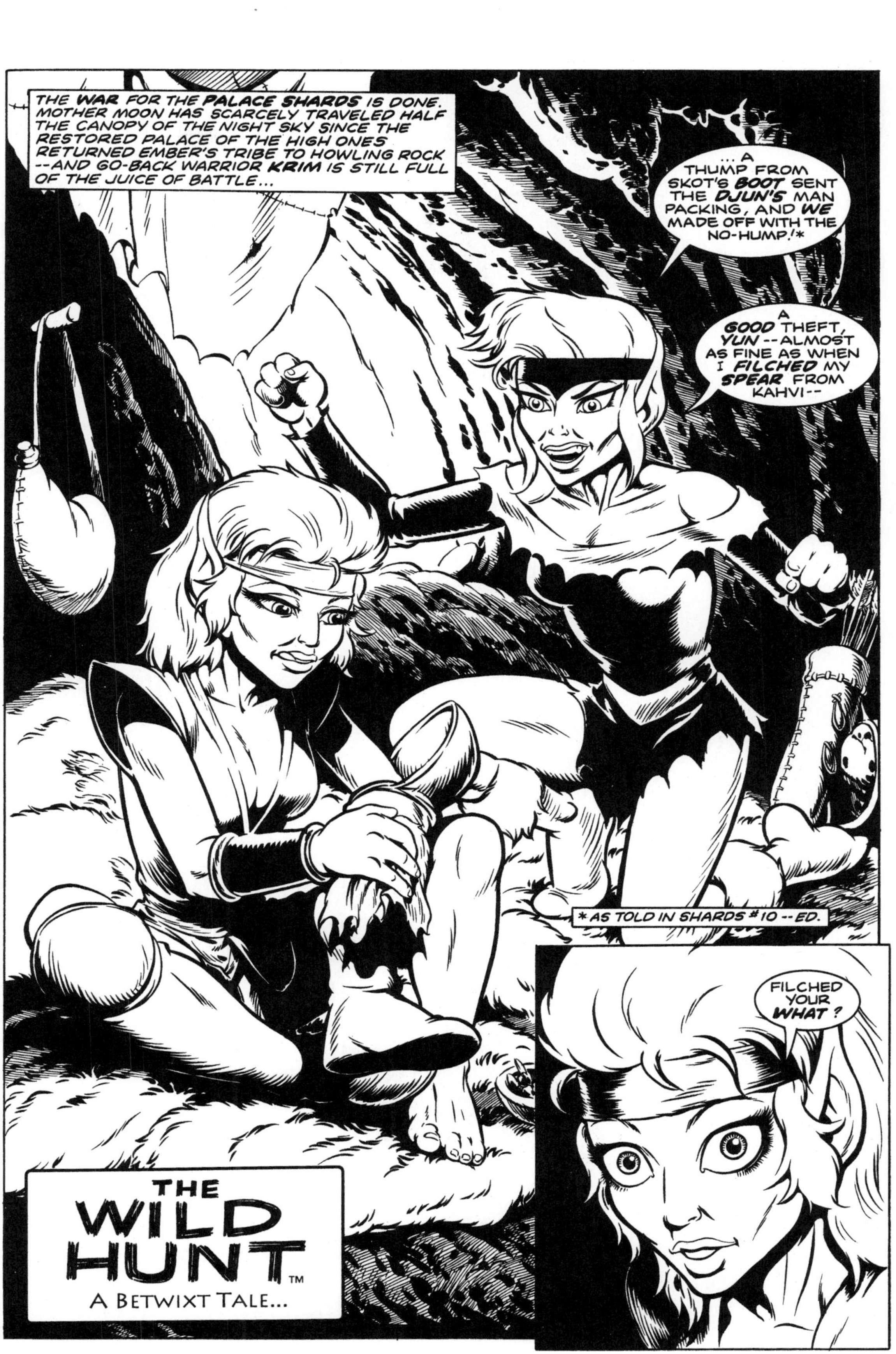
THE WAR FOR THE PALACE SHARDS IS DONE. MOTHER MOON HAS SCARCELY TRAVELED HALF THE CANOPY OF THE NIGHT SKY SINCE THE RESTORED PALACE OF THE HIGH ONES RETURNED EMBER'S TRIBE TO HOWLING ROCK --AND GO-BACK WARRIOR KRIM IS STILL FULL OF THE JUICE OF BATTLE...
... A THUMP FROM SKOT'S BOOT SENT THE DJUN'S MAN PACKING, AND WE MADE OFF WITH THE NO-HUMP!*
A GOOD THEFT, YUN --ALMOST AS FINE AS WHEN I FILCHED MY SPEAR FROM KAHVI--
* AS TOLD IN SHARDS #10 --ED.
THE WILD HUNT™
A BETWIXT TALE...
FILCHED YOUR WHAT?

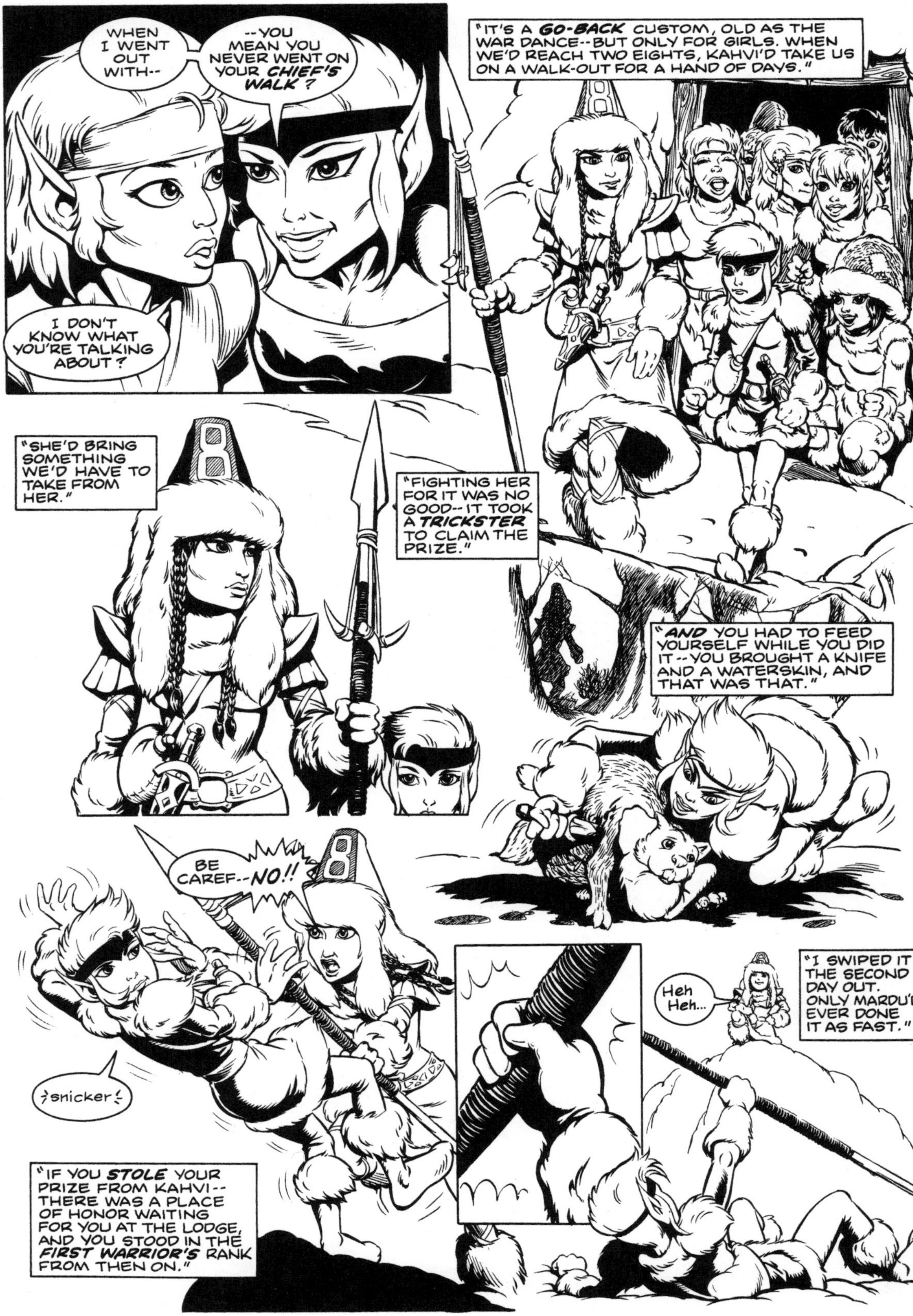
WHEN I WENT OUT WITH--
--YOU MEAN YOU NEVER WENT ON YOUR CHIEF'S WALK?
I DON'T KNOW WHAT YOU'RE TALKING ABOUT?
"IT'S A GO-BACK CUSTOM, OLD AS THE WAR DANCE--BUT ONLY FOR GIRLS. WHEN WE'D REACH TWO EIGHTS, KAHVI'D TAKE US ON A WALK-OUT FOR A HAND OF DAYS."
"SHE'D BRING SOMETHING WE'D HAVE TO TAKE FROM HER."
"FIGHTING HER FOR IT WAS NO GOOD-- IT TOOK A TRICKSTER TO CLAIM THE PRIZE."
"AND YOU HAD TO FEED YOURSELF WHILE YOU DID IT--YOU BROUGHT A KNIFE AND A WATERSKIN, AND THAT WAS THAT."
BE CAREF--NO!!
snicker
"IF YOU STOLE YOUR PRIZE FROM KAHVI-- THERE WAS A PLACE OF HONOR WAITING FOR YOU AT THE LODGE, AND YOU STOOD IN THE FIRST WARRIOR'S RANK FROM THEN ON."
Heh Heh...
"I SWIPED IT THE SECOND DAY OUT. ONLY MARDU'D EVER DONE IT AS FAST."

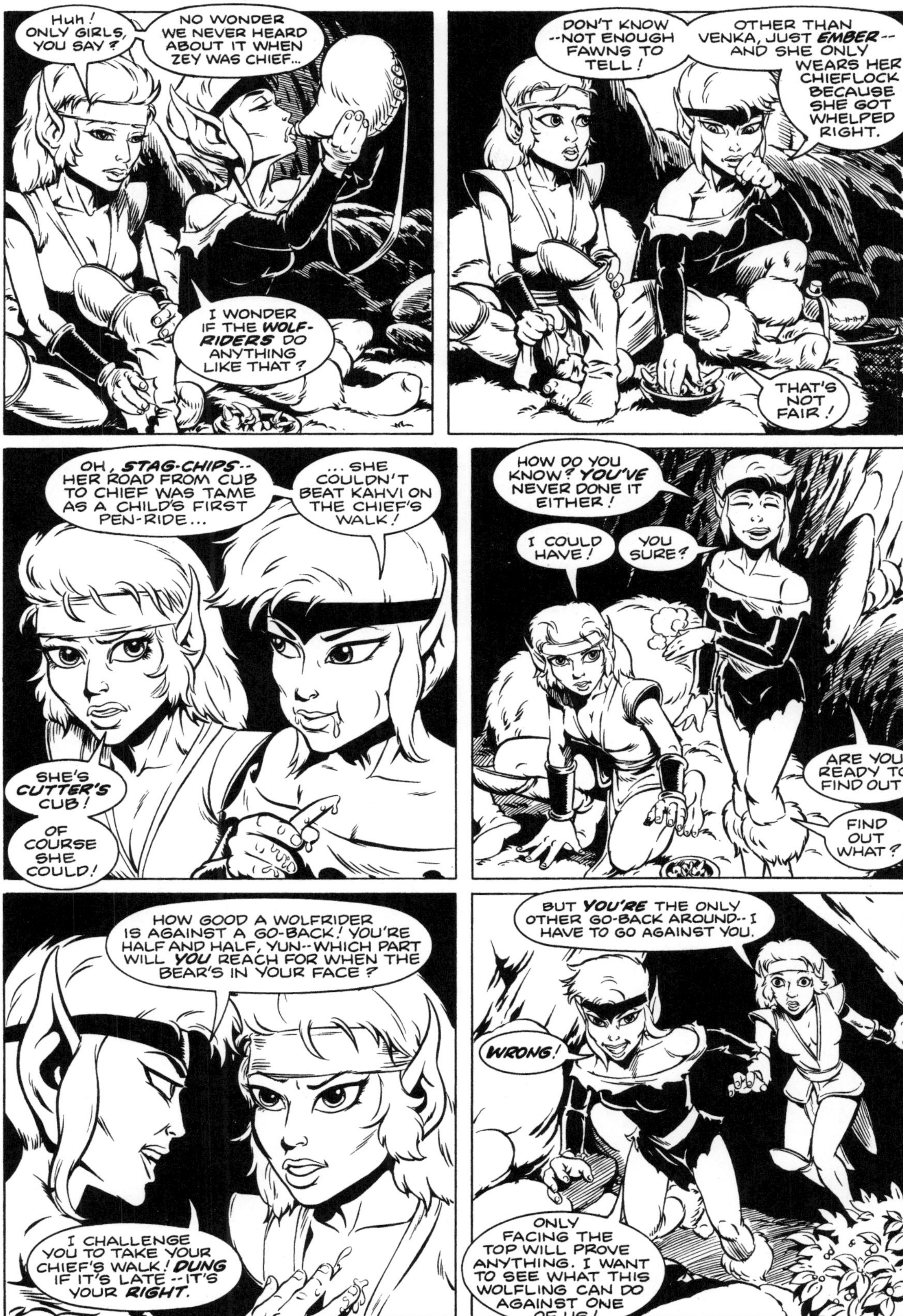

Huh! ONLY GIRLS, YOU SAY?
NO WONDER WE NEVER HEARD ABOUT IT WHEN ZEY WAS CHIEF...
I WONDER IF THE **WOLF-RIDERS** DO ANYTHING LIKE THAT?
DON'T KNOW --NOT ENOUGH FAWNS TO TELL!
OTHER THAN VENKA, JUST **EMBER**-- AND SHE ONLY WEARS HER CHIEFLOCK BECAUSE SHE GOT WHELPED RIGHT.
THAT'S NOT FAIR!
OH, **STAG-CHIPS**-- HER ROAD FROM CUB TO CHIEF WAS TAME AS A CHILD'S FIRST PEN-RIDE...
...SHE COULDN'T BEAT KAHVI ON THE CHIEF'S WALK!
SHE'S **CUTTER'S** CUB!
OF COURSE SHE COULD!
HOW DO YOU KNOW? **YOU'VE** NEVER DONE IT EITHER!
I COULD HAVE!
YOU SURE?
ARE YOU READY TO FIND OUT?
FIND OUT WHAT?
HOW GOOD A WOLFRIDER IS AGAINST A GO-BACK! YOU'RE HALF AND HALF, YUN--WHICH PART WILL **YOU** REACH FOR WHEN THE BEAR'S IN YOUR FACE?
I CHALLENGE YOU TO TAKE YOUR CHIEF'S WALK! **DUNG** IF IT'S LATE --IT'S YOUR **RIGHT**.
BUT **YOU'RE** THE ONLY OTHER GO-BACK AROUND-- I HAVE TO GO AGAINST YOU.
WRONG!
ONLY FACING THE TOP WILL PROVE ANYTHING. I WANT TO SEE WHAT THIS WOLFLING CAN DO AGAINST ONE OF US!

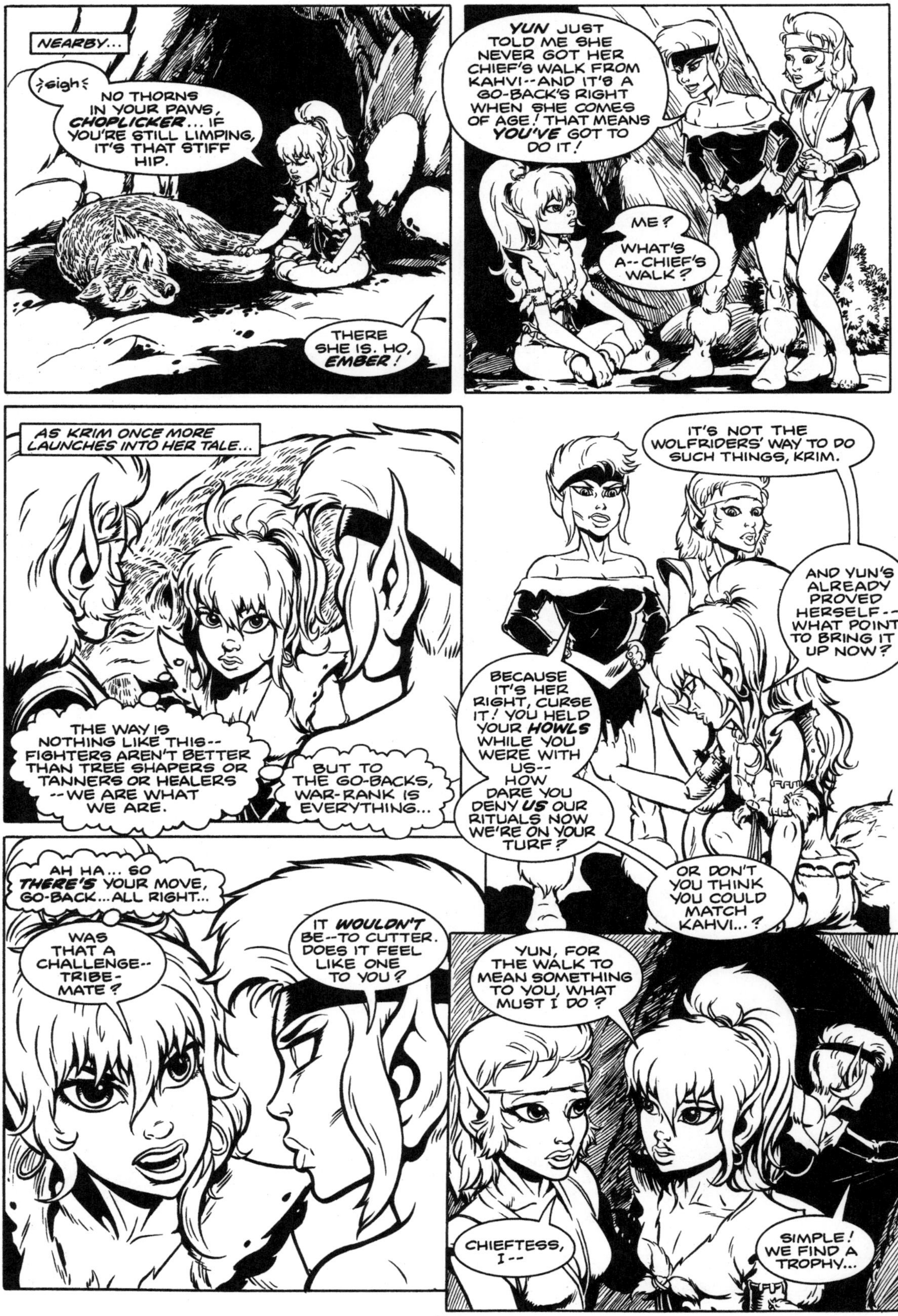
NEARBY...
>sigh< NO THORNS IN YOUR PAWS, CHOPLICKER... IF YOU'RE STILL LIMPING, IT'S THAT STIFF HIP.
THERE SHE IS. HO, EMBER!
YUN JUST TOLD ME SHE NEVER GOT HER CHIEF'S WALK FROM KAHVI--AND IT'S A GO-BACK'S RIGHT WHEN SHE COMES OF AGE! THAT MEANS YOU'VE GOT TO DO IT!
ME? WHAT'S A--CHIEF'S WALK?
AS KRIM ONCE MORE LAUNCHES INTO HER TALE...
THE WAY IS NOTHING LIKE THIS--FIGHTERS AREN'T BETTER THAN TREE SHAPERS OR TANNERS OR HEALERS --WE ARE WHAT WE ARE.
BUT TO THE GO-BACKS, WAR-RANK IS EVERYTHING...
IT'S NOT THE WOLFRIDERS' WAY TO DO SUCH THINGS, KRIM.
AND YUN'S ALREADY PROVED HERSELF--WHAT POINT TO BRING IT UP NOW?
BECAUSE IT'S HER RIGHT, CURSE IT! YOU HELD YOUR HOWLS WHILE YOU WERE WITH US--HOW DARE YOU DENY US OUR RITUALS NOW WE'RE ON YOUR TURF?
OR DON'T YOU THINK YOU COULD MATCH KAHVI...?
AH HA... SO THERE'S YOUR MOVE, GO-BACK...ALL RIGHT...
WAS THAT A CHALLENGE--TRIBE-MATE?
IT WOULDN'T BE--TO CUTTER. DOES IT FEEL LIKE ONE TO YOU?
YUN, FOR THE WALK TO MEAN SOMETHING TO YOU, WHAT MUST I DO?
CHIEFTESS, I--
SIMPLE! WE FIND A TROPHY...

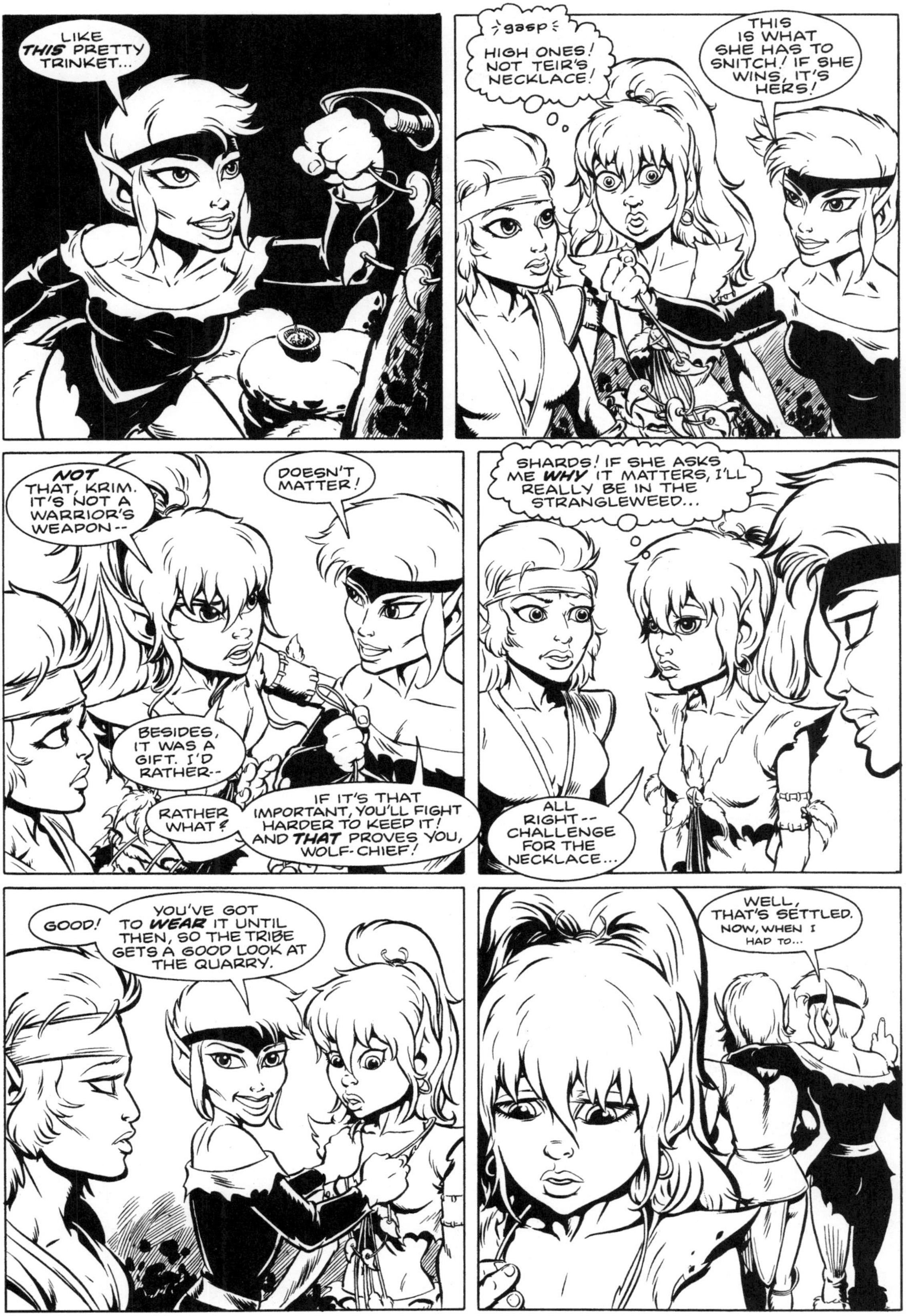
LIKE THIS PRETTY TRINKET...
gasp
HIGH ONES! NOT TEIR'S NECKLACE!
THIS IS WHAT SHE HAS TO SNITCH! IF SHE WINS, IT'S HERS!
NOT THAT, KRIM. IT'S NOT A WARRIOR'S WEAPON--
DOESN'T MATTER!
BESIDES, IT WAS A GIFT. I'D RATHER--
RATHER WHAT?
IF IT'S THAT IMPORTANT, YOU'LL FIGHT HARDER TO KEEP IT! AND THAT PROVES YOU, WOLF-CHIEF!
SHARDS! IF SHE ASKS ME WHY IT MATTERS, I'LL REALLY BE IN THE STRANGLEWEED...
ALL RIGHT-- CHALLENGE FOR THE NECKLACE...
GOOD!
YOU'VE GOT TO WEAR IT UNTIL THEN, SO THE TRIBE GETS A GOOD LOOK AT THE QUARRY.
WELL, THAT'S SETTLED. NOW, WHEN I HAD TO...

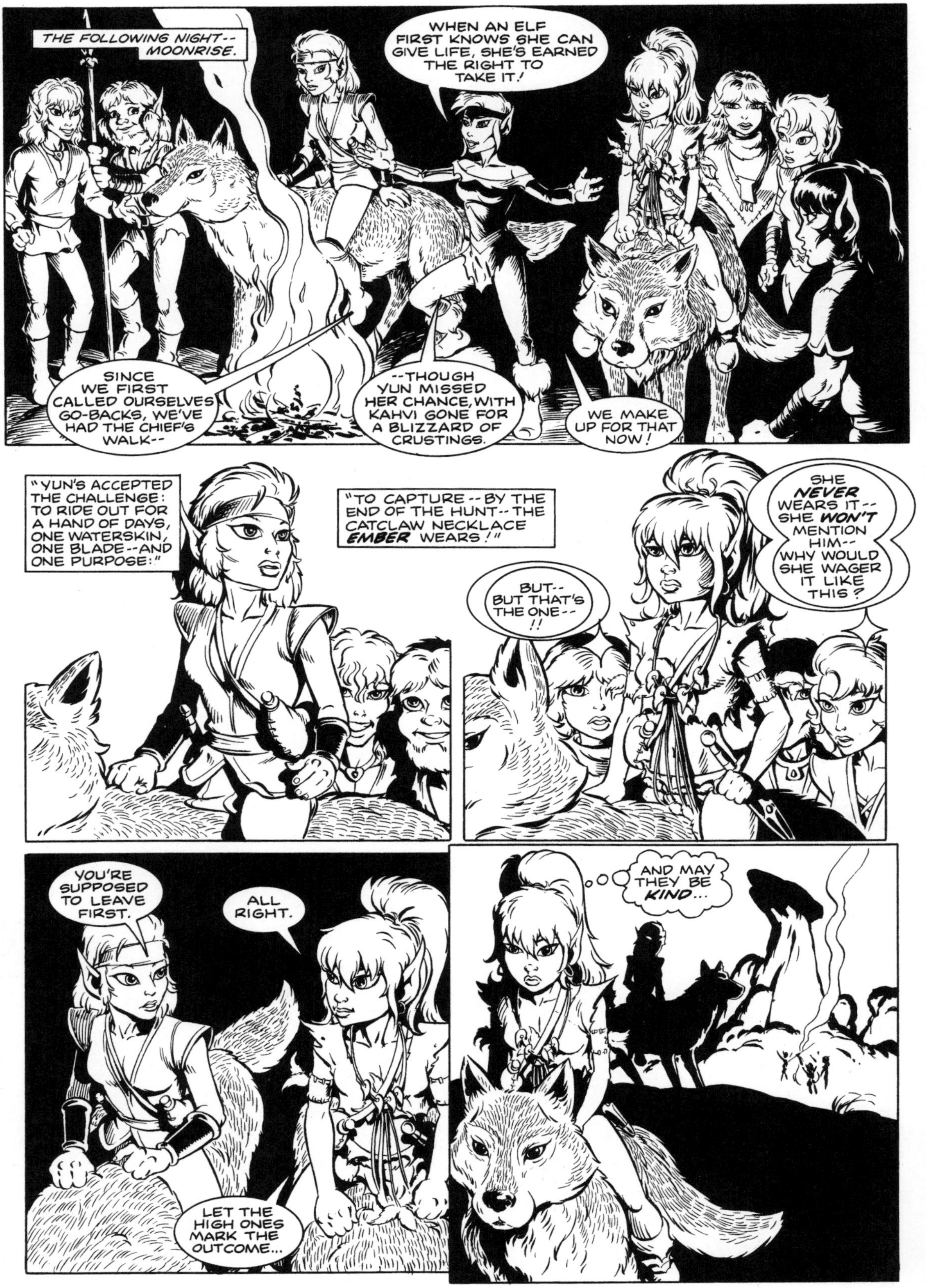
THE FOLLOWING NIGHT-- MOONRISE.
WHEN AN ELF FIRST KNOWS SHE CAN GIVE LIFE, SHE'S EARNED THE RIGHT TO TAKE IT!
SINCE WE FIRST CALLED OURSELVES GO-BACKS, WE'VE HAD THE CHIEF'S WALK--
--THOUGH YUN MISSED HER CHANCE, WITH KAHVI GONE FOR A BLIZZARD OF CRUSTINGS.
WE MAKE UP FOR THAT NOW!
"YUN'S ACCEPTED THE CHALLENGE: TO RIDE OUT FOR A HAND OF DAYS, ONE WATERSKIN, ONE BLADE--AND ONE PURPOSE:"
"TO CAPTURE--BY THE END OF THE HUNT--THE CATCLAW NECKLACE EMBER WEARS!"
BUT-- BUT THAT'S THE ONE-- !!
SHE NEVER WEARS IT-- SHE WON'T MENTION HIM-- WHY WOULD SHE WAGER IT LIKE THIS?
YOU'RE SUPPOSED TO LEAVE FIRST.
ALL RIGHT.
LET THE HIGH ONES MARK THE OUTCOME...
AND MAY THEY BE KIND...

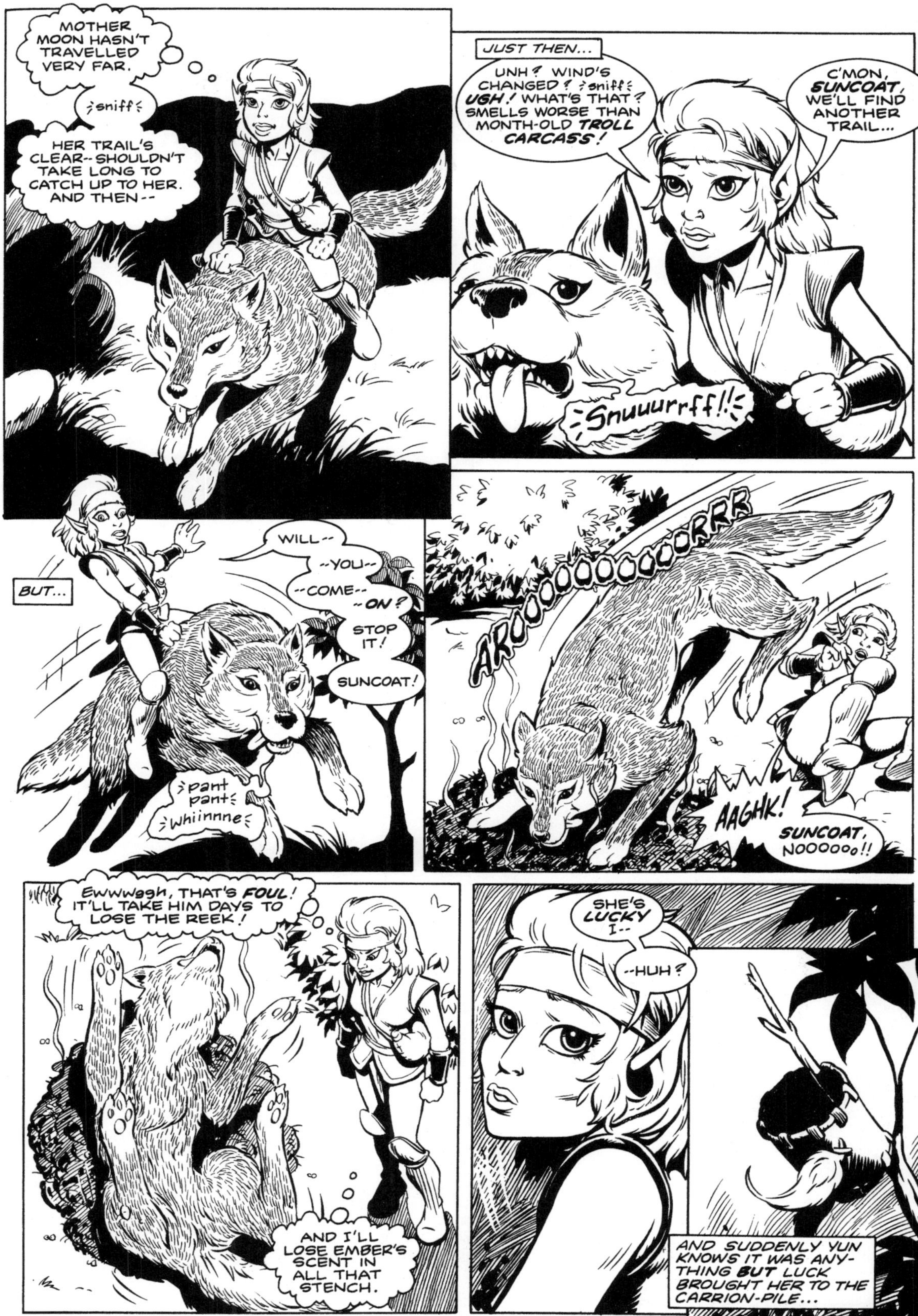
MOTHER MOON HASN'T TRAVELLED VERY FAR.
sniff
HER TRAIL'S CLEAR-- SHOULDN'T TAKE LONG TO CATCH UP TO HER. AND THEN--
JUST THEN...
UNH? WIND'S CHANGED? sniff UGH! WHAT'S THAT? SMELLS WORSE THAN MONTH-OLD TROLL CARCASS!
C'MON, SUNCOAT, WE'LL FIND ANOTHER TRAIL...
Snuuurrff!!
BUT...
WILL--
--YOU--
--COME--
--ON?
STOP IT!
SUNCOAT!
pant pant
whiinnne
AROOOOOOOOOOORRR
AAGHK!
SUNCOAT, NOOOooo!!
Ewwwgh, THAT'S FOUL! IT'LL TAKE HIM DAYS TO LOSE THE REEK!
AND I'LL LOSE EMBER'S SCENT IN ALL THAT STENCH.
SHE'S LUCKY I--
--HUH?
AND SUDDENLY YUN KNOWS IT WAS ANYTHING BUT LUCK BROUGHT HER TO THE CARRION-PILE...

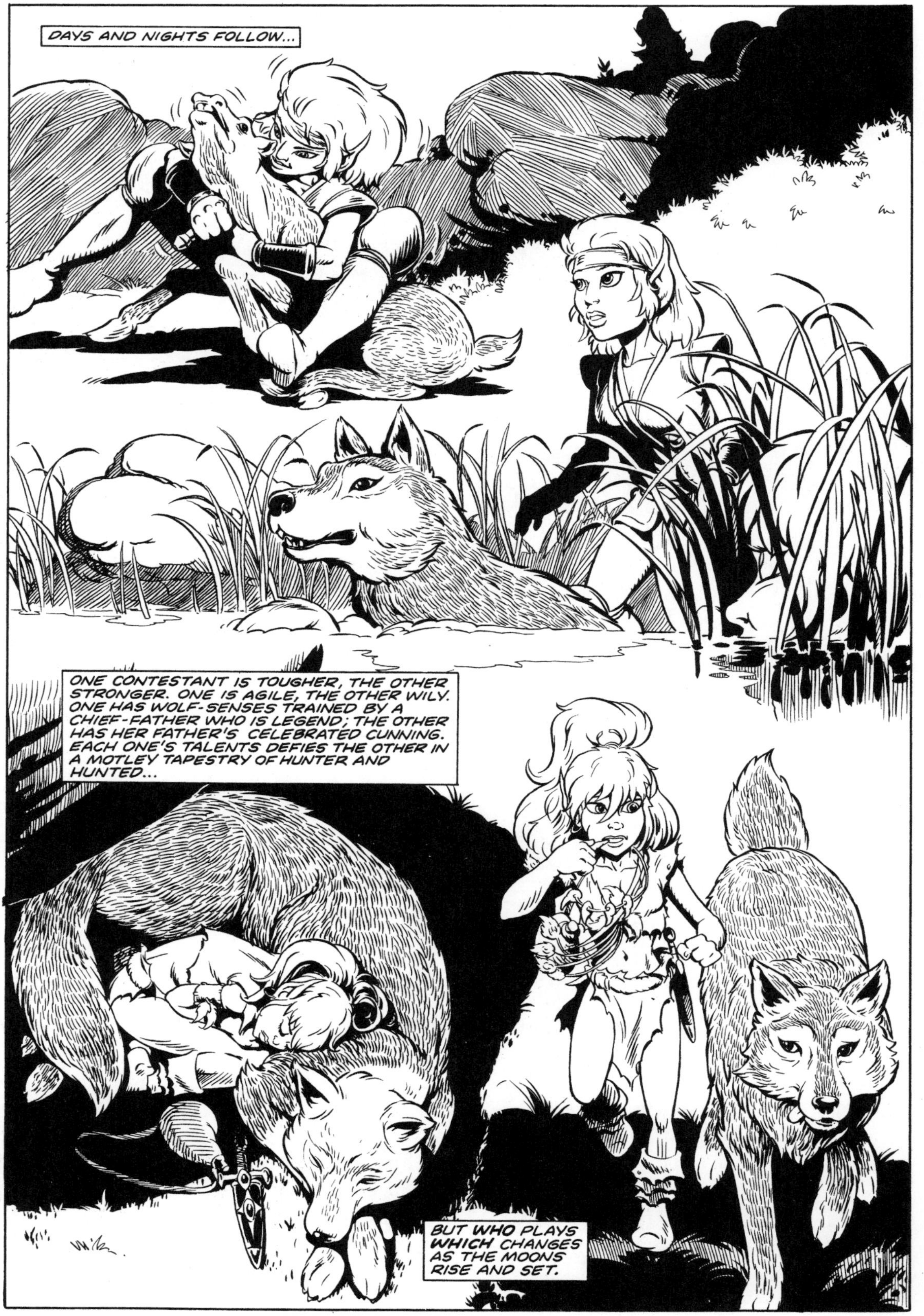
DAYS AND NIGHTS FOLLOW...
ONE CONTESTANT IS TOUGHER, THE OTHER STRONGER. ONE IS AGILE, THE OTHER WILY. ONE HAS WOLF-SENSES TRAINED BY A CHIEF-FATHER WHO IS LEGEND; THE OTHER HAS HER FATHER'S CELEBRATED CUNNING. EACH ONE'S TALENTS DEFIES THE OTHER IN A MOTLEY TAPESTRY OF HUNTER AND HUNTED...
BUT WHO PLAYS WHICH CHANGES AS THE MOONS RISE AND SET.

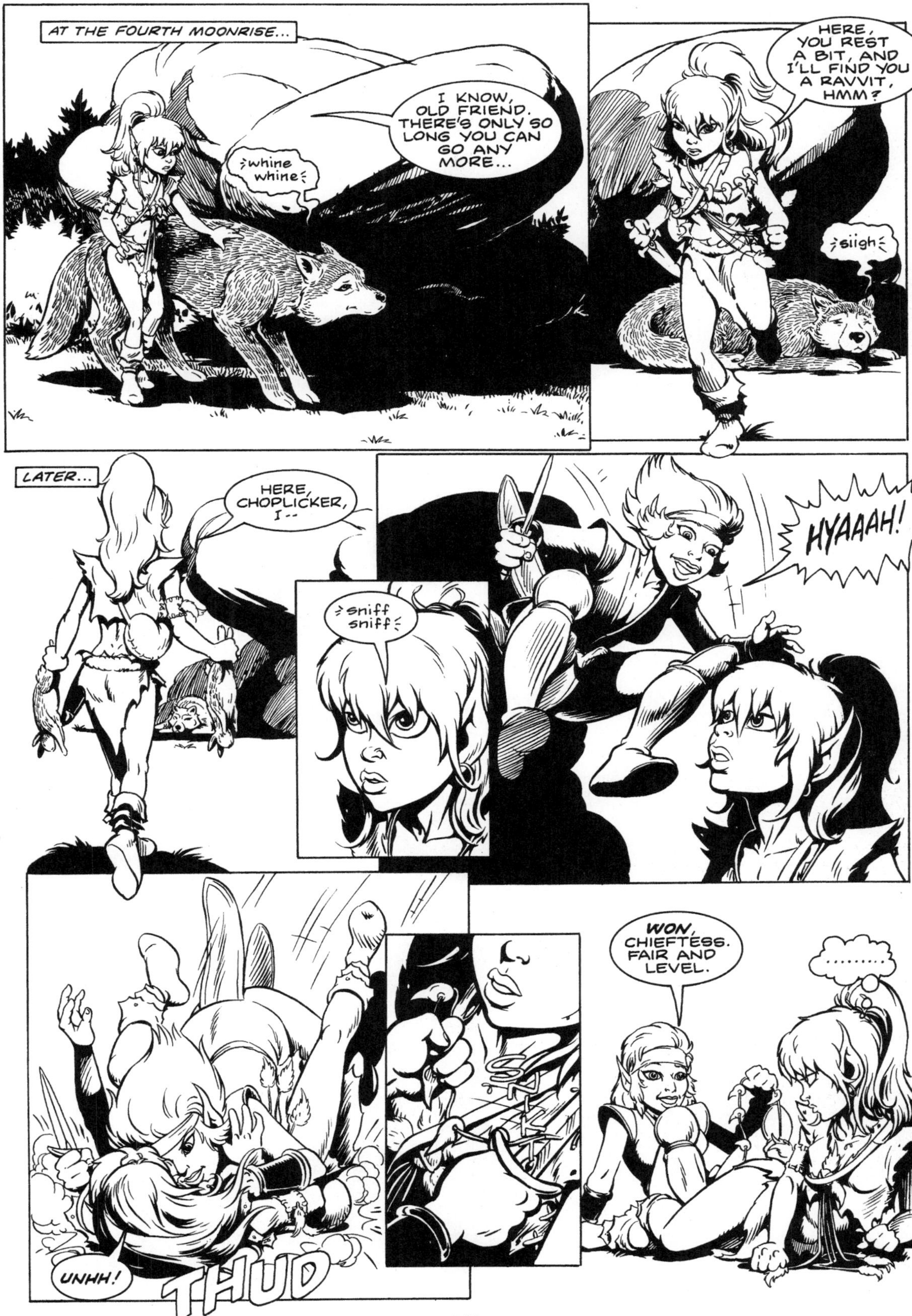

AT THE FOURTH MOONRISE...
whine whine
I KNOW, OLD FRIEND. THERE'S ONLY SO LONG YOU CAN GO ANY MORE...
HERE, YOU REST A BIT, AND I'LL FIND YOU A RAVVIT, HMM?
siigh
LATER...
HERE, CHOPLICKER, I --
HYAAAH!
sniff sniff
UNHH!
THUD
WON, CHIEFTESS. FAIR AND LEVEL.
....

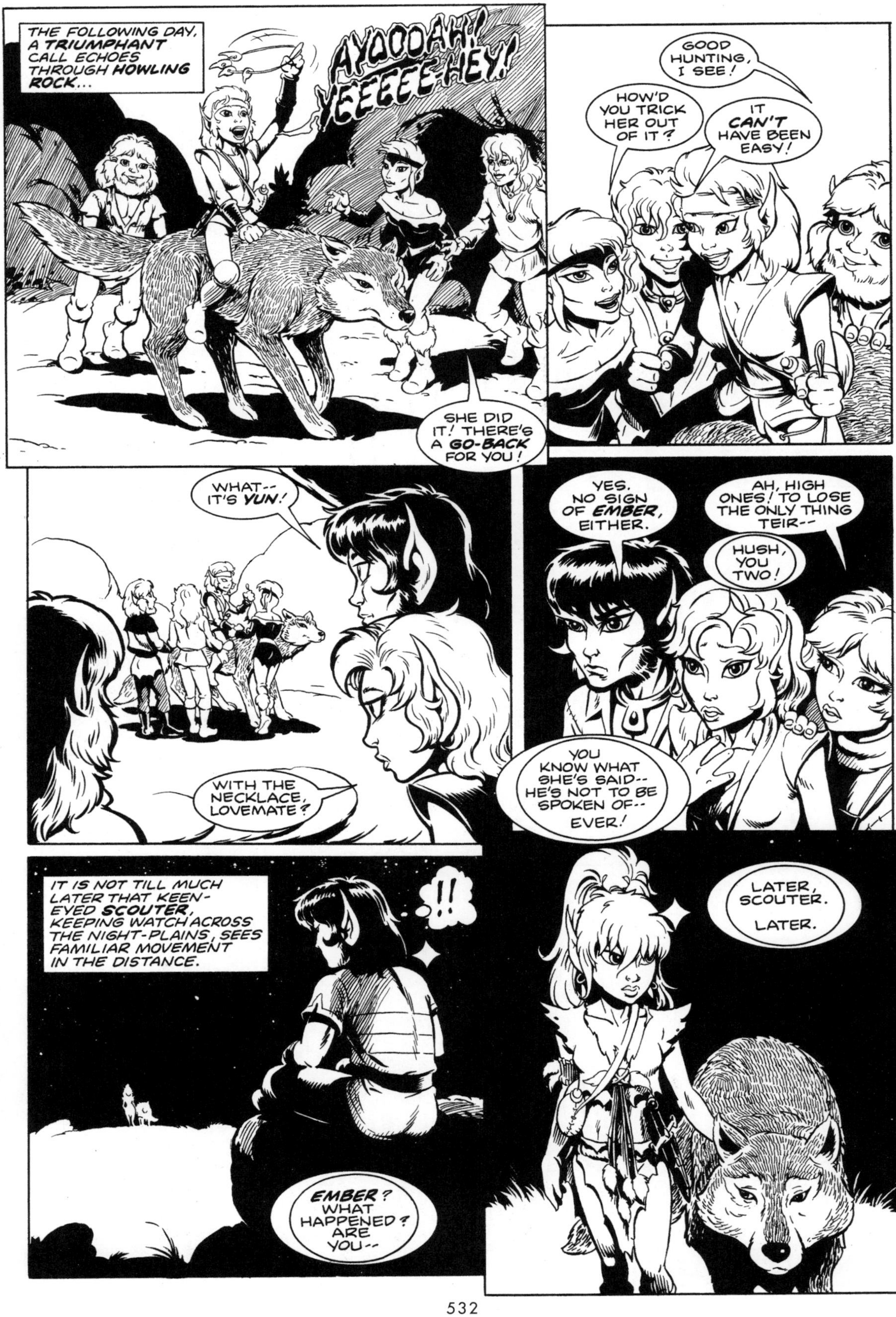
THE FOLLOWING DAY, A TRIUMPHANT CALL ECHOES THROUGH HOWLING ROCK...
AYOOOAH! YEEEEEE-HEY!
SHE DID IT! THERE'S A GO-BACK FOR YOU!
GOOD HUNTING, I SEE!
HOW'D YOU TRICK HER OUT OF IT?
IT CAN'T HAVE BEEN EASY!
WHAT-- IT'S YUN!
WITH THE NECKLACE, LOVEMATE?
YES. NO SIGN OF EMBER, EITHER.
AH, HIGH ONES! TO LOSE THE ONLY THING TEIR--
HUSH, YOU TWO!
YOU KNOW WHAT SHE'S SAID-- HE'S NOT TO BE SPOKEN OF-- EVER!
IT IS NOT TILL MUCH LATER THAT KEEN-EYED SCOUTER, KEEPING WATCH ACROSS THE NIGHT-PLAINS, SEES FAMILIAR MOVEMENT IN THE DISTANCE.
!!
EMBER? WHAT HAPPENED? ARE YOU--
LATER, SCOUTER.
LATER.

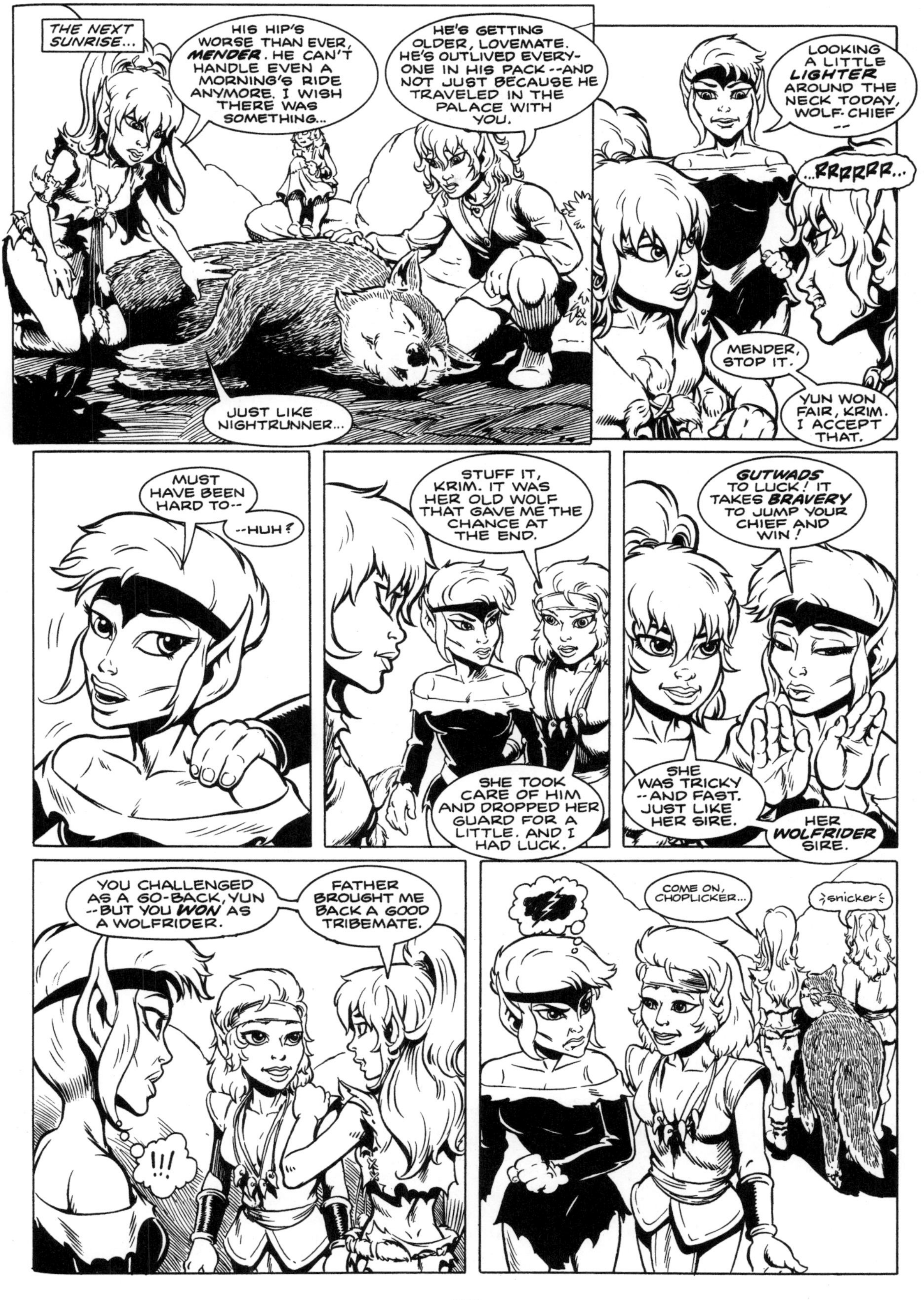

THE NEXT SUNRISE...
HIS HIP'S WORSE THAN EVER, MENDER. HE CAN'T HANDLE EVEN A MORNING'S RIDE ANYMORE. I WISH THERE WAS SOMETHING...
HE'S GETTING OLDER, LOVEMATE. HE'S OUTLIVED EVERYONE IN HIS PACK--AND NOT JUST BECAUSE HE TRAVELED IN THE PALACE WITH YOU.
JUST LIKE NIGHTRUNNER...
LOOKING A LITTLE LIGHTER AROUND THE NECK TODAY, WOLF-CHIEF--
...RRRRRR...
MENDER, STOP IT.
YUN WON FAIR, KRIM. I ACCEPT THAT.
MUST HAVE BEEN HARD TO--
--HUH?
STUFF IT, KRIM. IT WAS HER OLD WOLF THAT GAVE ME THE CHANCE AT THE END.
SHE TOOK CARE OF HIM AND DROPPED HER GUARD FOR A LITTLE. AND I HAD LUCK.
GUTWADS TO LUCK! IT TAKES BRAVERY TO JUMP YOUR CHIEF AND WIN!
SHE WAS TRICKY --AND FAST. JUST LIKE HER SIRE.
HER WOLFRIDER SIRE.
YOU CHALLENGED AS A GO-BACK, YUN --BUT YOU WON AS A WOLFRIDER.
FATHER BROUGHT ME BACK A GOOD TRIBEMATE.
!!!
COME ON, CHOPLICKER...
snicker

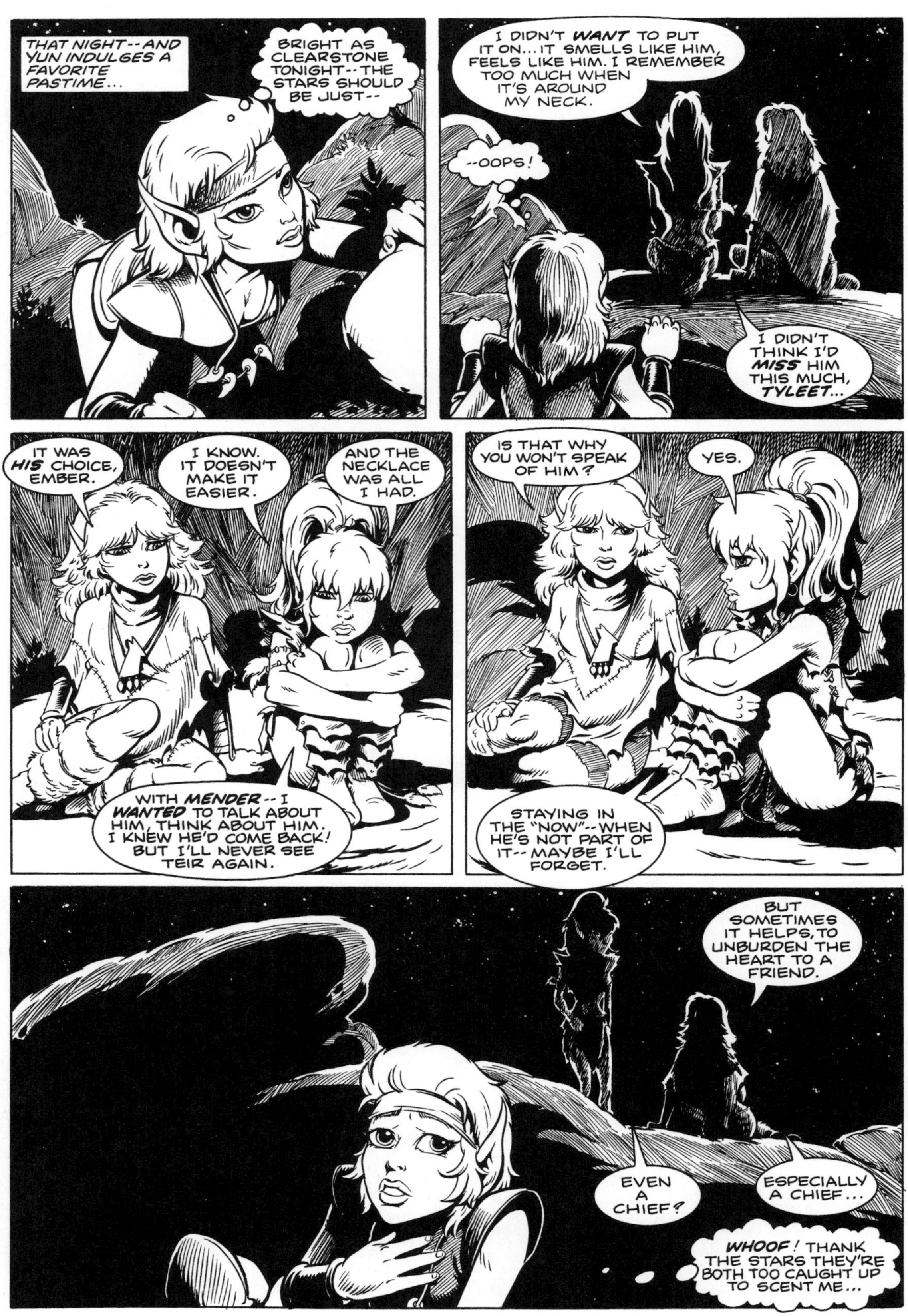
THAT NIGHT--AND YUN INDULGES A FAVORITE PASTIME...
BRIGHT AS CLEARSTONE TONIGHT--THE STARS SHOULD BE JUST--
I DIDN'T WANT TO PUT IT ON... IT SMELLS LIKE HIM, FEELS LIKE HIM. I REMEMBER TOO MUCH WHEN IT'S AROUND MY NECK.
--OOPS!
I DIDN'T THINK I'D MISS HIM THIS MUCH, TYLEET...
IT WAS HIS CHOICE, EMBER.
I KNOW. IT DOESN'T MAKE IT EASIER.
AND THE NECKLACE WAS ALL I HAD.
WITH MENDER--I WANTED TO TALK ABOUT HIM, THINK ABOUT HIM. I KNEW HE'D COME BACK! BUT I'LL NEVER SEE TEIR AGAIN.
IS THAT WHY YOU WON'T SPEAK OF HIM?
YES.
STAYING IN THE "NOW"--WHEN HE'S NOT PART OF IT--MAYBE I'LL FORGET.
BUT SOMETIMES IT HELPS, TO UNBURDEN THE HEART TO A FRIEND.
EVEN A CHIEF?
ESPECIALLY A CHIEF...
WHOOF! THANK THE STARS THEY'RE BOTH TOO CAUGHT UP TO SCENT ME...

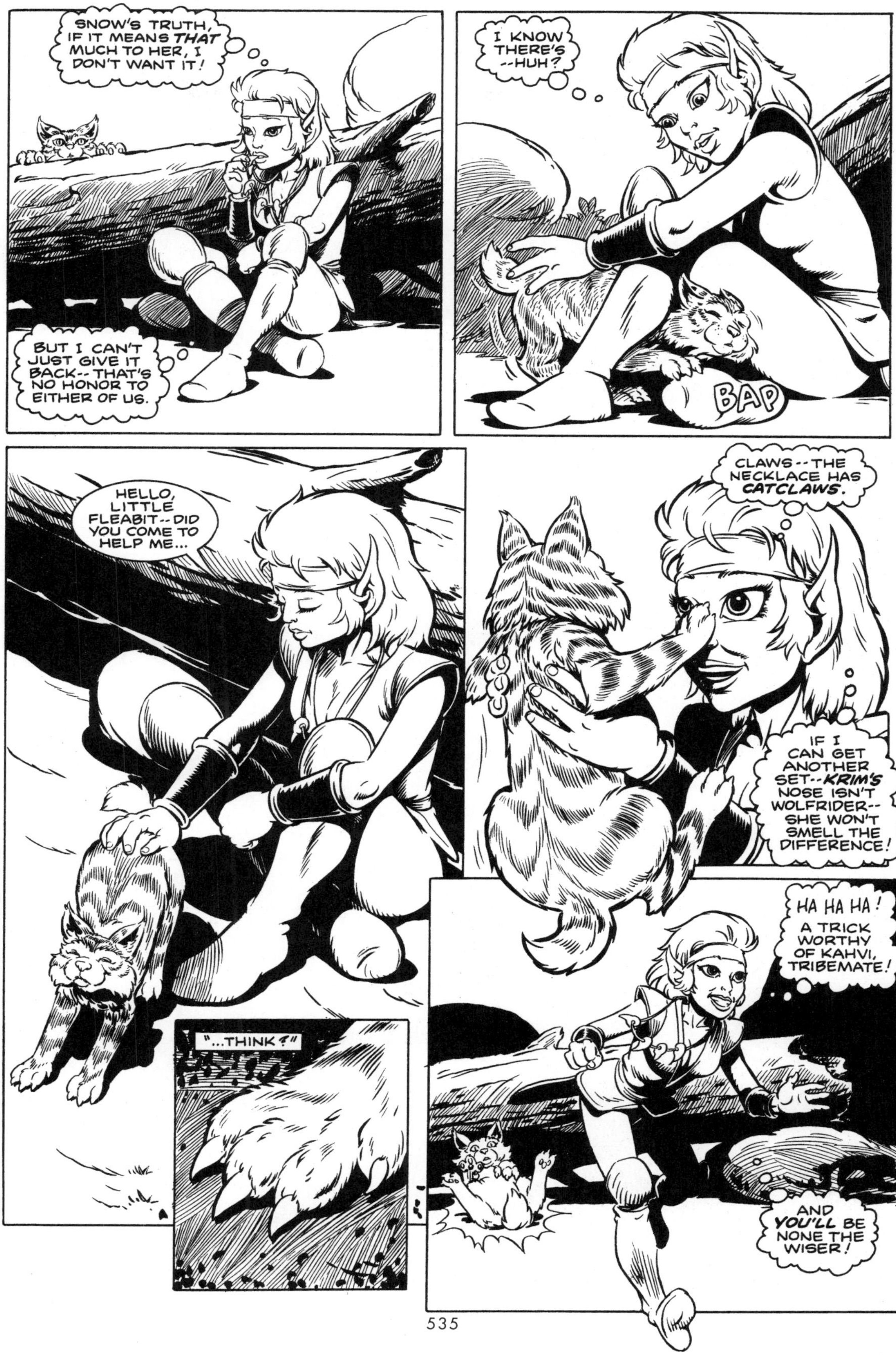

SNOW'S TRUTH, IF IT MEANS **THAT** MUCH TO HER, I DON'T WANT IT!
BUT I CAN'T JUST GIVE IT BACK-- THAT'S NO HONOR TO EITHER OF US.
I KNOW THERE'S --HUH?
BAP
HELLO, LITTLE FLEABIT-- DID YOU COME TO HELP ME...
"...THINK?"
CLAWS--THE NECKLACE HAS **CATCLAWS**.
IF I CAN GET ANOTHER SET--**KRIM'S** NOSE ISN'T WOLFRIDER-- SHE WON'T SMELL THE DIFFERENCE!
HA HA HA! A TRICK WORTHY OF KAHVI, TRIBEMATE!
AND **YOU'LL** BE NONE THE WISER!

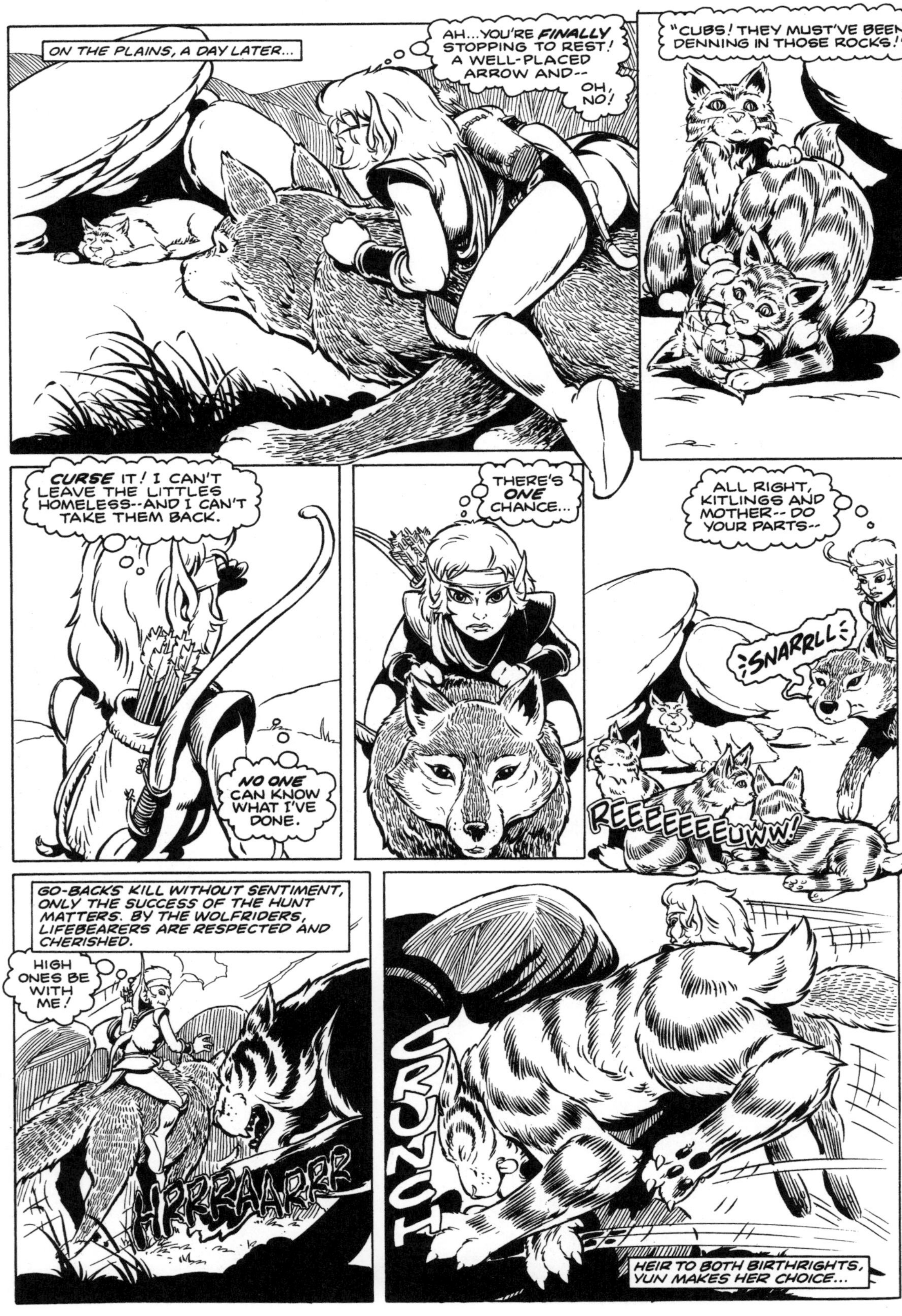
ON THE PLAINS, A DAY LATER...
AH... YOU'RE FINALLY STOPPING TO REST! A WELL-PLACED ARROW AND--
OH, NO!
"CUBS! THEY MUST'VE BEEN DENNING IN THOSE ROCKS!"
CURSE IT! I CAN'T LEAVE THE LITTLES HOMELESS--AND I CAN'T TAKE THEM BACK.
NO ONE CAN KNOW WHAT I'VE DONE.
THERE'S ONE CHANCE...
ALL RIGHT, KITLINGS AND MOTHER-- DO YOUR PARTS--
SNARRLL
REEEEEEEEEUWW!
GO-BACKS KILL WITHOUT SENTIMENT, ONLY THE SUCCESS OF THE HUNT MATTERS. BY THE WOLFRIDERS, LIFEBEARERS ARE RESPECTED AND CHERISHED.
HIGH ONES BE WITH ME!
HRRRAARRR
CRUNCH
HEIR TO BOTH BIRTHRIGHTS, YUN MAKES HER CHOICE...

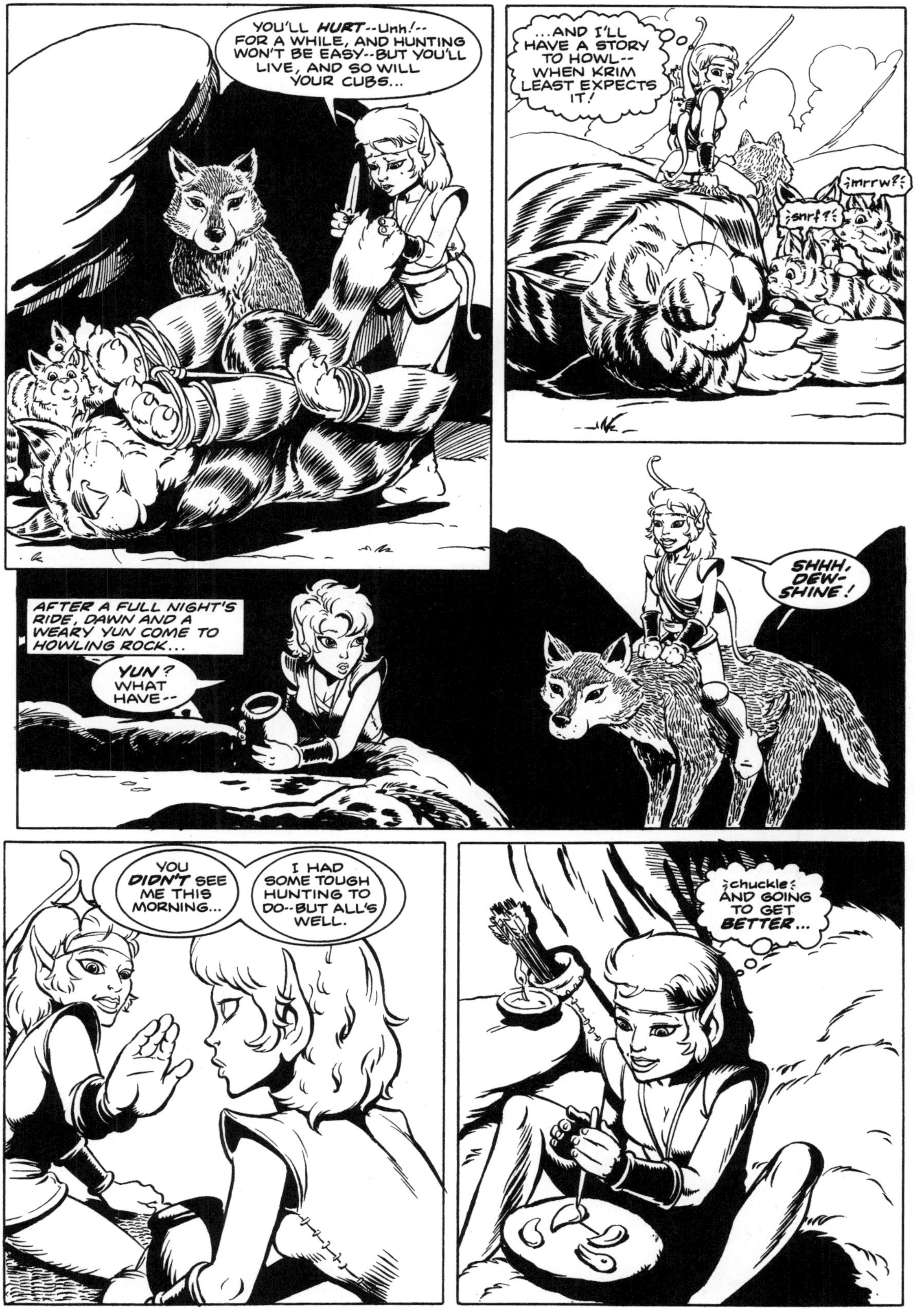
YOU'LL HURT--Unh!--FOR A WHILE, AND HUNTING WON'T BE EASY--BUT YOU'LL LIVE, AND SO WILL YOUR CUBS...
...AND I'LL HAVE A STORY TO HOWL--WHEN KRIM LEAST EXPECTS IT!
snrf?
mrrw?
AFTER A FULL NIGHT'S RIDE, DAWN AND A WEARY YUN COME TO HOWLING ROCK...
YUN? WHAT HAVE--
SHHH, DEW-SHINE!
YOU DIDN'T SEE ME THIS MORNING...
I HAD SOME TOUGH HUNTING TO DO--BUT ALL'S WELL.
chuckle AND GOING TO GET BETTER...

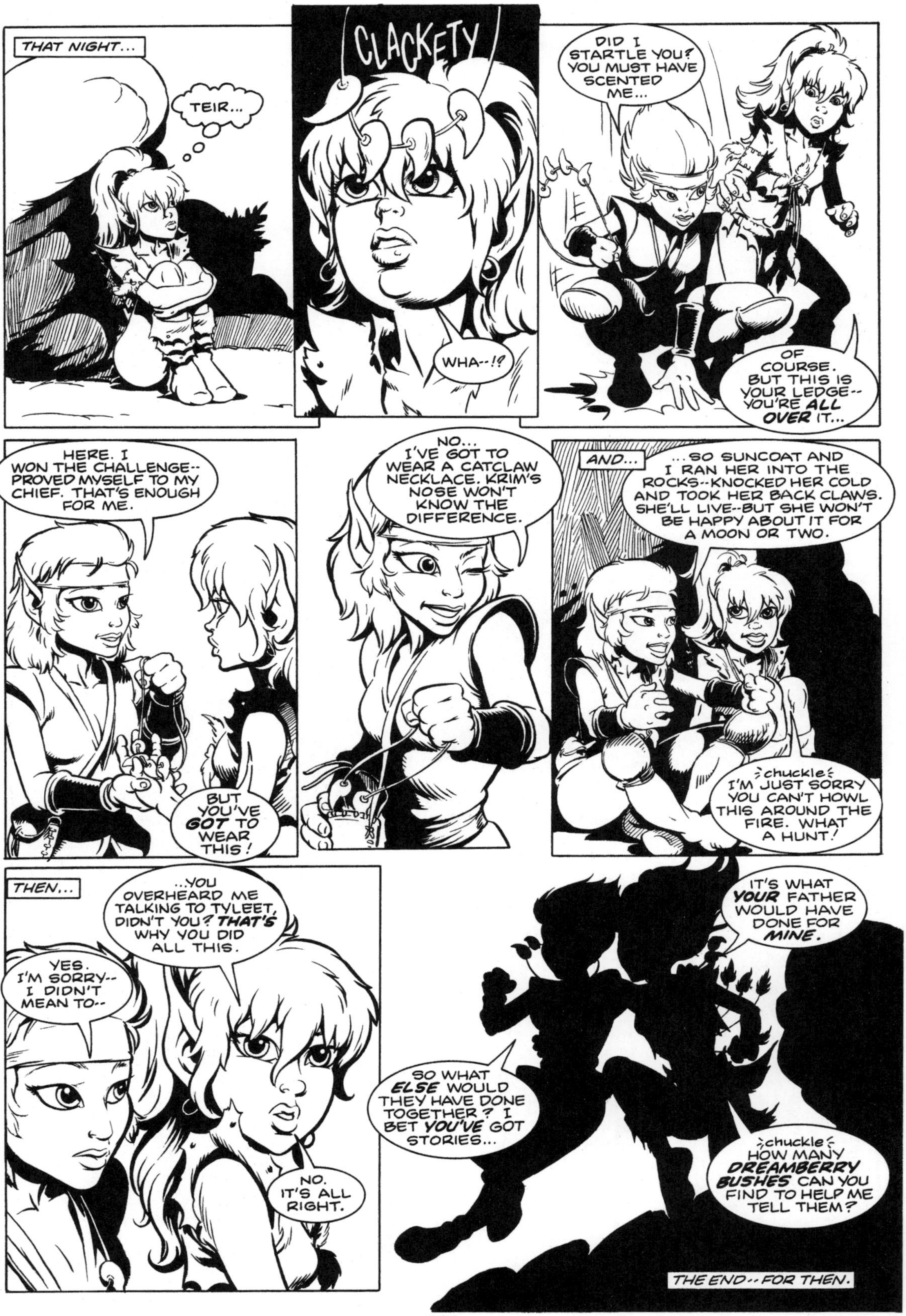
THAT NIGHT...
TEIR...
CLACKETY
WHA--!?
DID I STARTLE YOU? YOU MUST HAVE SCENTED ME...
OF COURSE. BUT THIS IS YOUR LEDGE-- YOU'RE ALL OVER IT...
HERE. I WON THE CHALLENGE-- PROVED MYSELF TO MY CHIEF. THAT'S ENOUGH FOR ME.
BUT YOU'VE GOT TO WEAR THIS!
NO... I'VE GOT TO WEAR A CATCLAW NECKLACE. KRIM'S NOSE WON'T KNOW THE DIFFERENCE.
AND...
...SO SUNCOAT AND I RAN HER INTO THE ROCKS--KNOCKED HER COLD AND TOOK HER BACK CLAWS. SHE'LL LIVE--BUT SHE WON'T BE HAPPY ABOUT IT FOR A MOON OR TWO.
chuckle I'M JUST SORRY YOU CAN'T HOWL THIS AROUND THE FIRE. WHAT A HUNT!
THEN...
...YOU OVERHEARD ME TALKING TO TYLEET, DIDN'T YOU? THAT'S WHY YOU DID ALL THIS.
YES. I'M SORRY-- I DIDN'T MEAN TO--
NO. IT'S ALL RIGHT.
IT'S WHAT YOUR FATHER WOULD HAVE DONE FOR MINE.
SO WHAT ELSE WOULD THEY HAVE DONE TOGETHER? I BET YOU'VE GOT STORIES...
chuckle HOW MANY DREAMBERRY BUSHES CAN YOU FIND TO HELP ME TELL THEM?
THE END--FOR THEN.

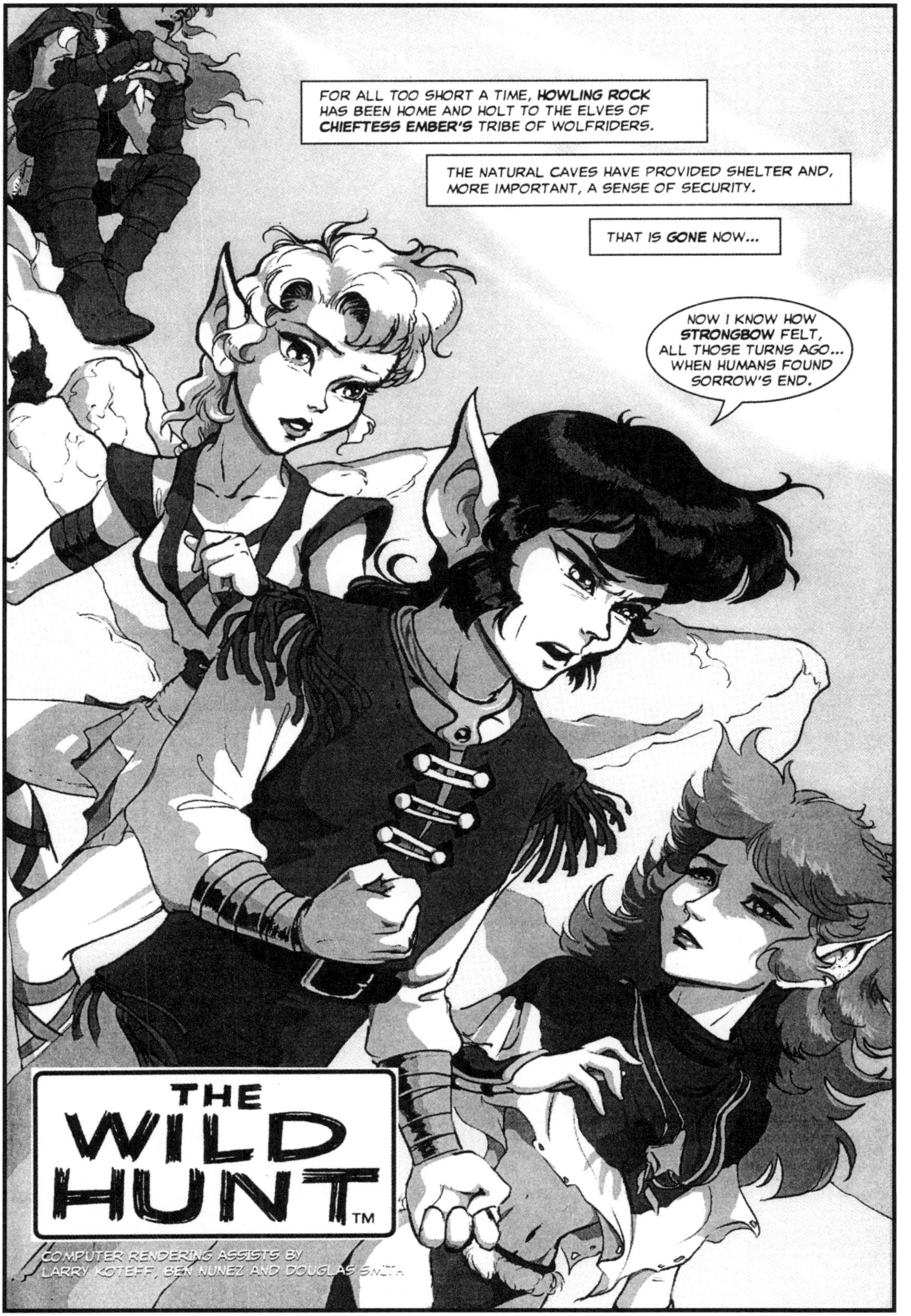
FOR ALL TOO SHORT A TIME, HOWLING ROCK HAS BEEN HOME AND HOLT TO THE ELVES OF CHIEFTESS EMBER'S TRIBE OF WOLFRIDERS.
THE NATURAL CAVES HAVE PROVIDED SHELTER AND, MORE IMPORTANT, A SENSE OF SECURITY.
THAT IS GONE NOW...
NOW I KNOW HOW STRONGBOW FELT, ALL THOSE TURNS AGO... WHEN HUMANS FOUND SORROW'S END.
THE WILD HUNT™
COMPUTER RENDERING ASSISTS BY LARRY KOTEFF, BEN NUNEZ AND DOUGLAS SMITH

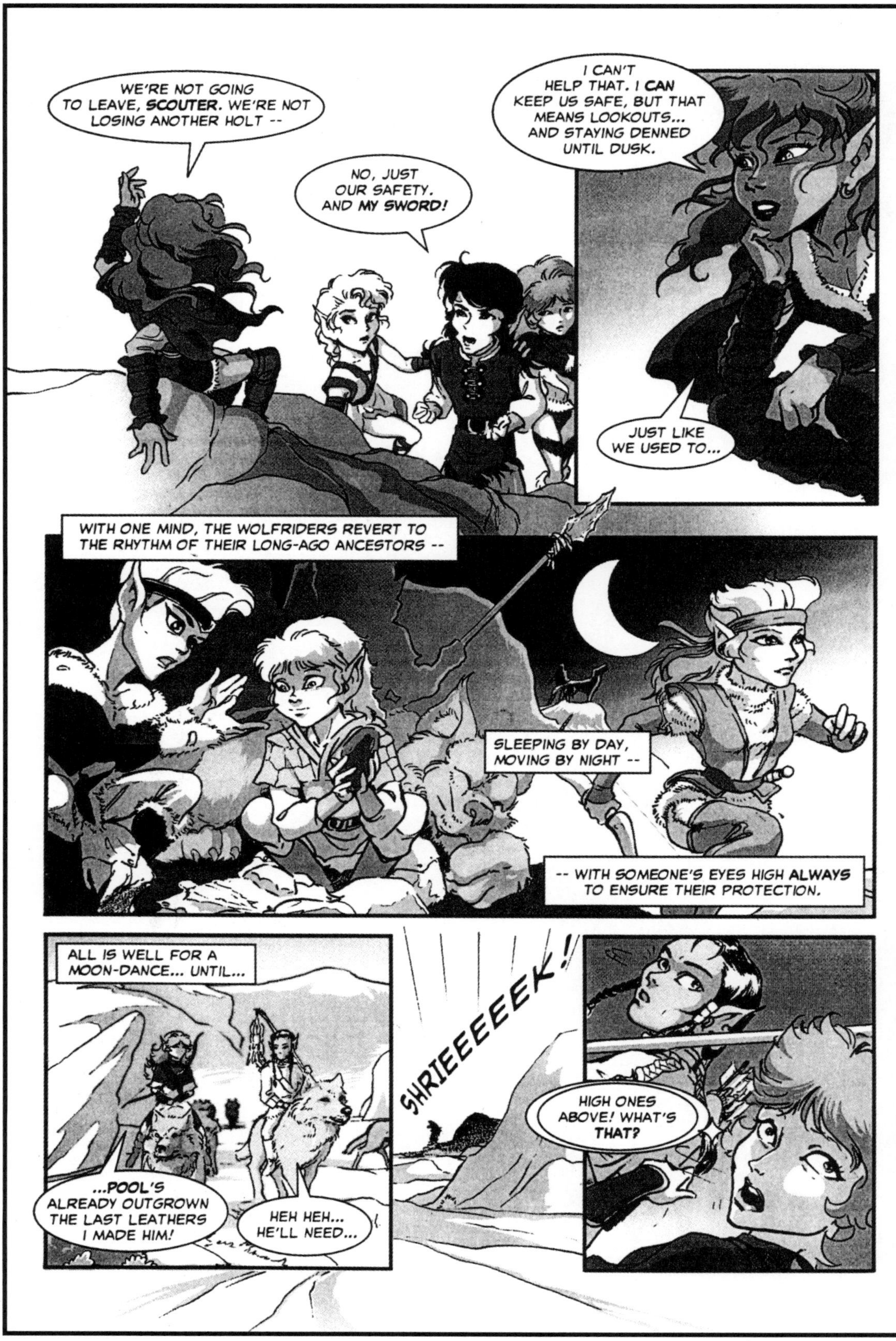
WE'RE NOT GOING TO LEAVE, SCOUTER. WE'RE NOT LOSING ANOTHER HOLT --
NO, JUST OUR SAFETY. AND MY SWORD!
I CAN'T HELP THAT. I CAN KEEP US SAFE, BUT THAT MEANS LOOKOUTS... AND STAYING DENNED UNTIL DUSK.
JUST LIKE WE USED TO...
WITH ONE MIND, THE WOLFRIDERS REVERT TO THE RHYTHM OF THEIR LONG-AGO ANCESTORS --
SLEEPING BY DAY, MOVING BY NIGHT --
-- WITH SOMEONE'S EYES HIGH ALWAYS TO ENSURE THEIR PROTECTION.
ALL IS WELL FOR A MOON-DANCE... UNTIL...
...POOL'S ALREADY OUTGROWN THE LAST LEATHERS I MADE HIM!
HEH HEH... HE'LL NEED...
SHRIEEEEEK!
HIGH ONES ABOVE! WHAT'S THAT?

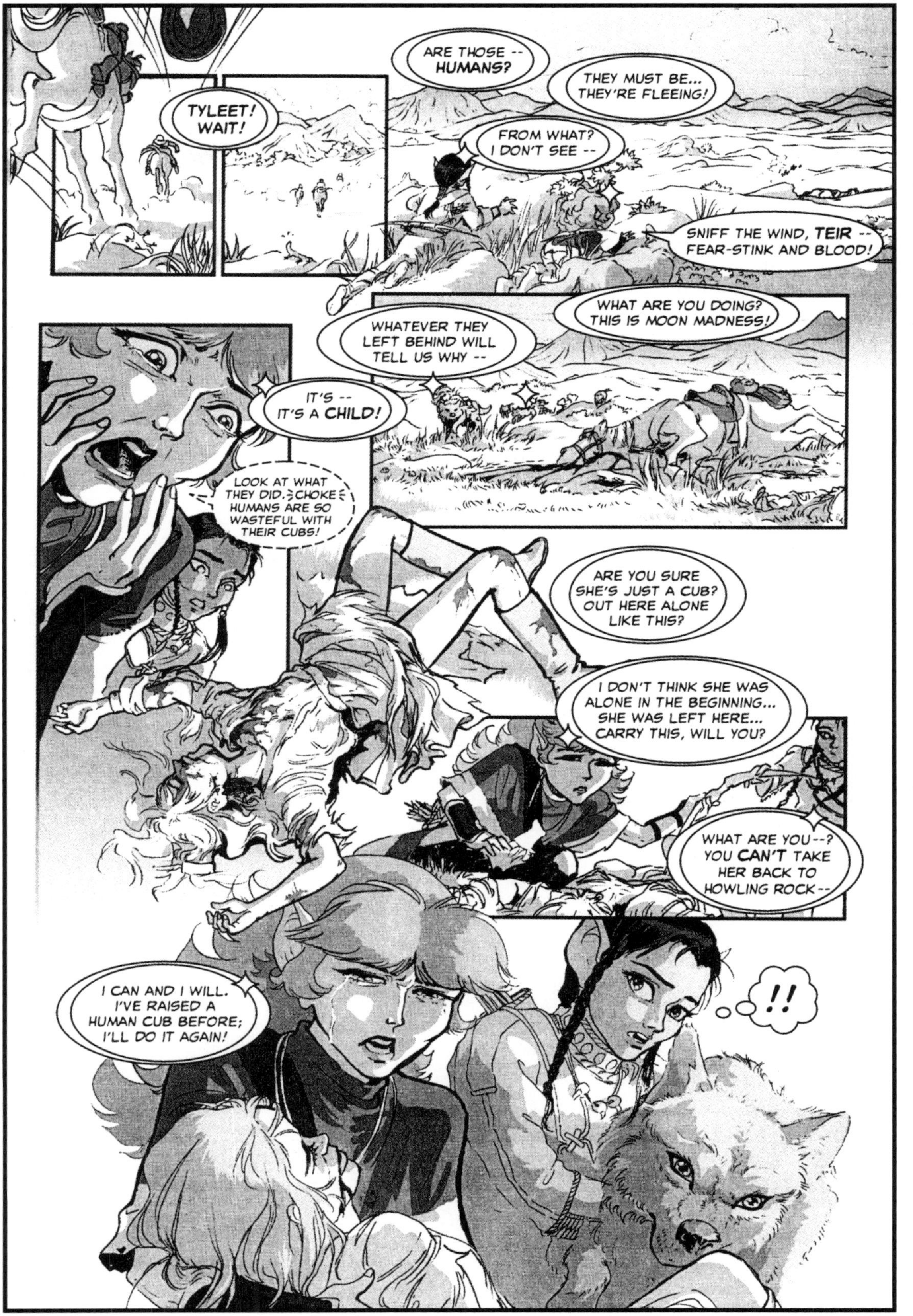
TYLEET! WAIT!
ARE THOSE -- HUMANS?
THEY MUST BE... THEY'RE FLEEING!
FROM WHAT? I DON'T SEE --
SNIFF THE WIND, TEIR -- FEAR-STINK AND BLOOD!
WHAT ARE YOU DOING? THIS IS MOON MADNESS!
WHATEVER THEY LEFT BEHIND WILL TELL US WHY --
IT'S -- IT'S A CHILD!
LOOK AT WHAT THEY DID. CHOKE HUMANS ARE SO WASTEFUL WITH THEIR CUBS!
ARE YOU SURE SHE'S JUST A CUB? OUT HERE ALONE LIKE THIS?
I DON'T THINK SHE WAS ALONE IN THE BEGINNING... SHE WAS LEFT HERE... CARRY THIS, WILL YOU?
WHAT ARE YOU--? YOU CAN'T TAKE HER BACK TO HOWLING ROCK--
I CAN AND I WILL. I'VE RAISED A HUMAN CUB BEFORE; I'LL DO IT AGAIN!
!!

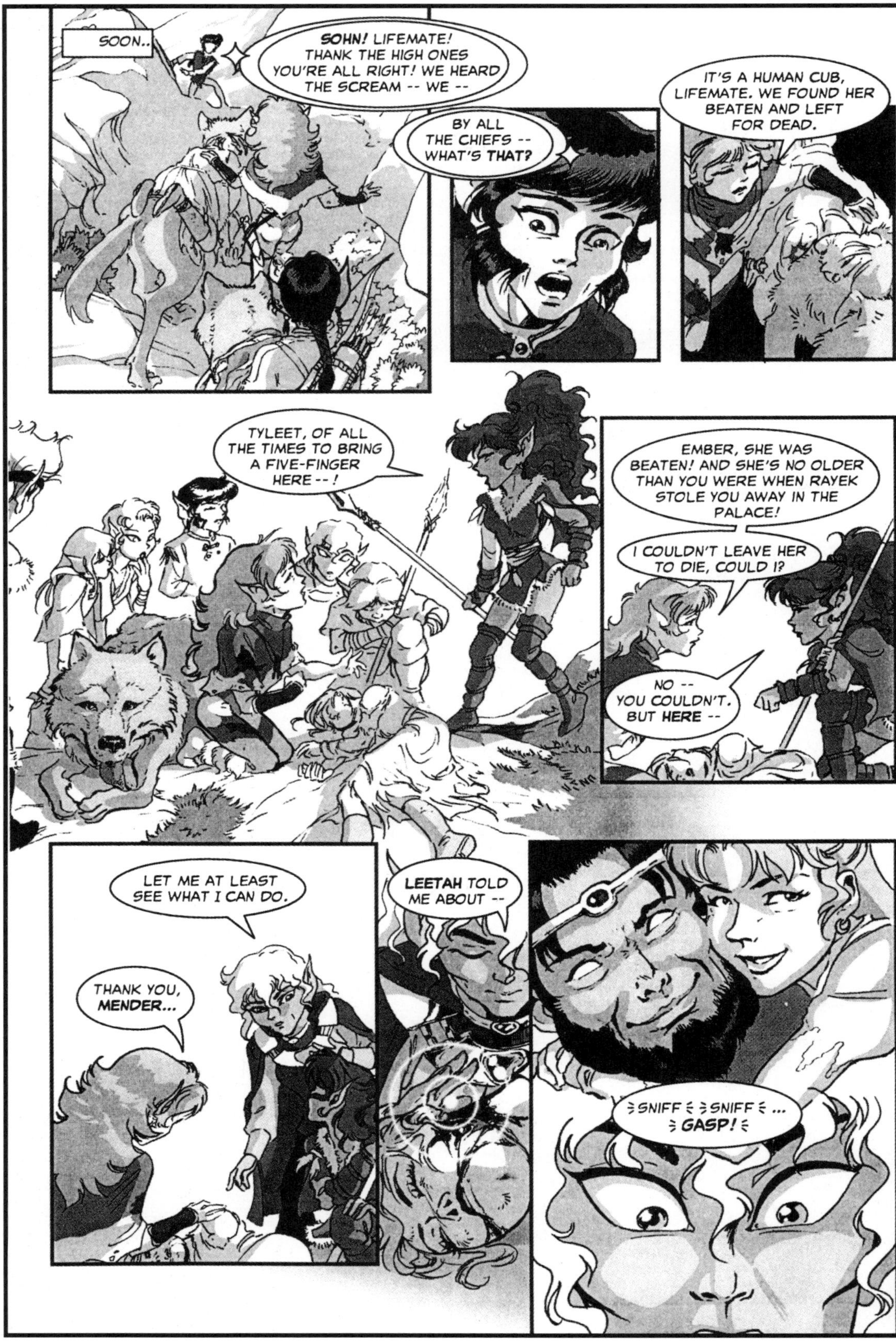
SOON..
SOHN! LIFEMATE! THANK THE HIGH ONES YOU'RE ALL RIGHT! WE HEARD THE SCREAM -- WE --
BY ALL THE CHIEFS -- WHAT'S THAT?
IT'S A HUMAN CUB, LIFEMATE. WE FOUND HER BEATEN AND LEFT FOR DEAD.
TYLEET, OF ALL THE TIMES TO BRING A FIVE-FINGER HERE -- !
EMBER, SHE WAS BEATEN! AND SHE'S NO OLDER THAN YOU WERE WHEN RAYEK STOLE YOU AWAY IN THE PALACE!
I COULDN'T LEAVE HER TO DIE, COULD I?
NO -- YOU COULDN'T. BUT HERE --
LET ME AT LEAST SEE WHAT I CAN DO.
THANK YOU, MENDER...
LEETAH TOLD ME ABOUT --
SNIFF SNIFF ... GASP!

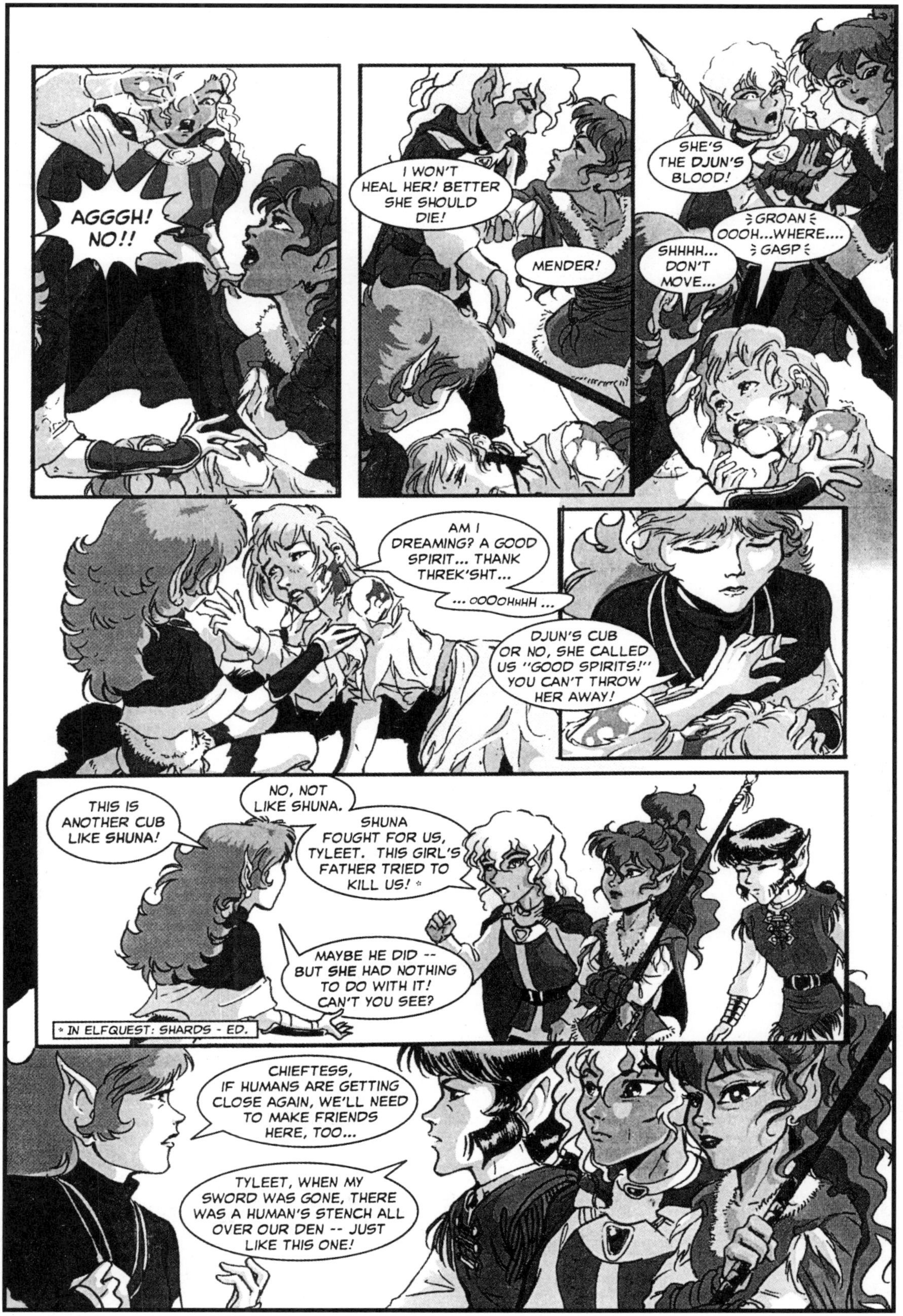

AGGGH! NO!!
I WON'T HEAL HER! BETTER SHE SHOULD DIE!
MENDER!
SHE'S THE DJUN'S BLOOD!
GROAN OOOH...WHERE.... GASP
SHHHH... DON'T MOVE...
AM I DREAMING? A GOOD SPIRIT... THANK THREK'SHT...
... OOOOHHHH ...
DJUN'S CUB OR NO, SHE CALLED US "GOOD SPIRITS!" YOU CAN'T THROW HER AWAY!
THIS IS ANOTHER CUB LIKE SHUNA!
NO, NOT LIKE SHUNA.
SHUNA FOUGHT FOR US, TYLEET. THIS GIRL'S FATHER TRIED TO KILL US! *
MAYBE HE DID -- BUT SHE HAD NOTHING TO DO WITH IT! CAN'T YOU SEE?
* IN ELFQUEST: SHARDS - ED.
CHIEFTESS, IF HUMANS ARE GETTING CLOSE AGAIN, WE'LL NEED TO MAKE FRIENDS HERE, TOO...
TYLEET, WHEN MY SWORD WAS GONE, THERE WAS A HUMAN'S STENCH ALL OVER OUR DEN -- JUST LIKE THIS ONE!

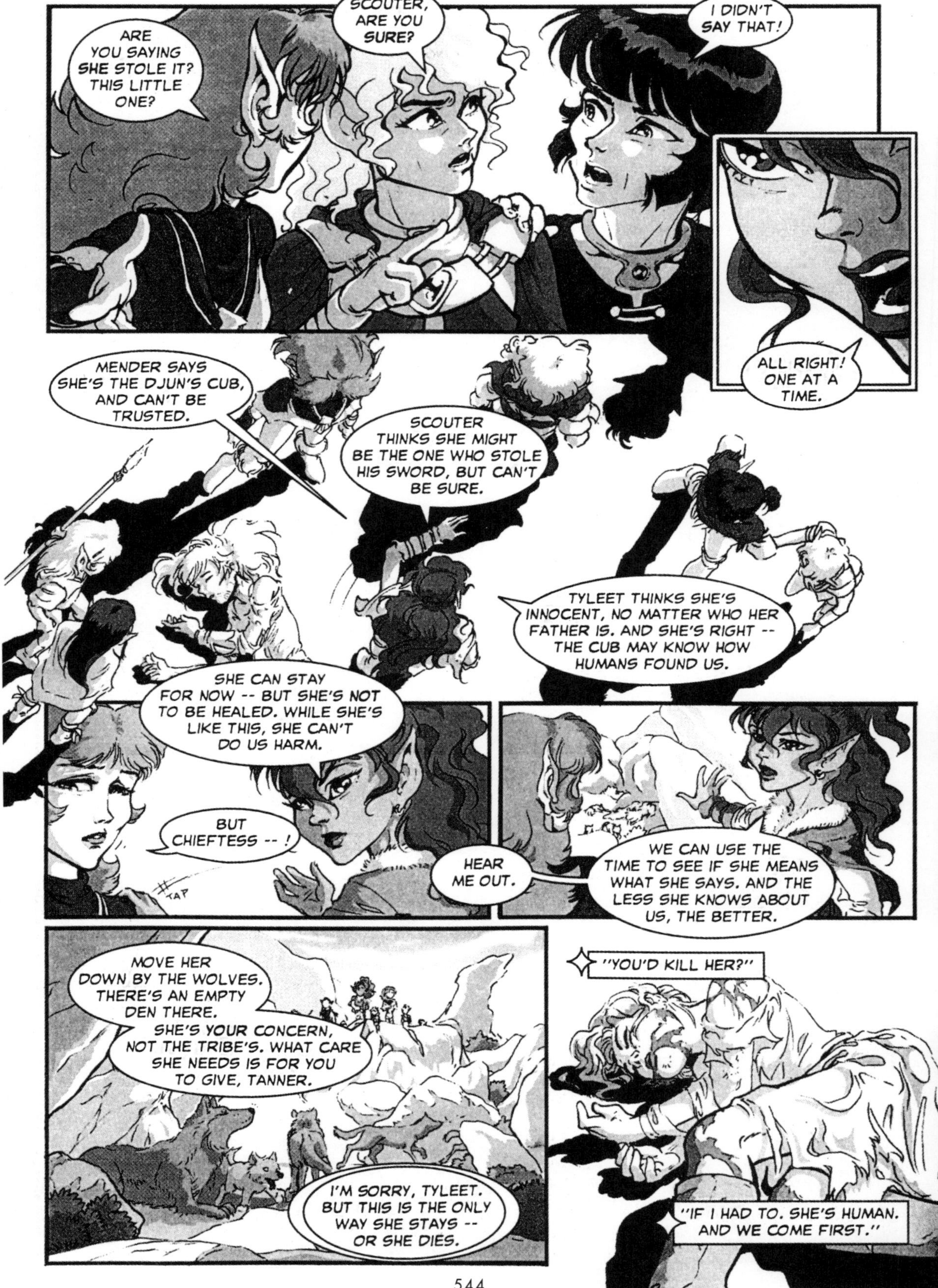

ARE YOU SAYING SHE STOLE IT? THIS LITTLE ONE?
SCOUTER, ARE YOU SURE?
I DIDN'T SAY THAT!
ALL RIGHT! ONE AT A TIME.
MENDER SAYS SHE'S THE DJUN'S CUB, AND CAN'T BE TRUSTED.
SCOUTER THINKS SHE MIGHT BE THE ONE WHO STOLE HIS SWORD, BUT CAN'T BE SURE.
TYLEET THINKS SHE'S INNOCENT, NO MATTER WHO HER FATHER IS. AND SHE'S RIGHT -- THE CUB MAY KNOW HOW HUMANS FOUND US.
SHE CAN STAY FOR NOW -- BUT SHE'S NOT TO BE HEALED. WHILE SHE'S LIKE THIS, SHE CAN'T DO US HARM.
BUT CHIEFTESS -- !
TAP
HEAR ME OUT.
WE CAN USE THE TIME TO SEE IF SHE MEANS WHAT SHE SAYS. AND THE LESS SHE KNOWS ABOUT US, THE BETTER.
MOVE HER DOWN BY THE WOLVES. THERE'S AN EMPTY DEN THERE.
SHE'S YOUR CONCERN, NOT THE TRIBE'S. WHAT CARE SHE NEEDS IS FOR YOU TO GIVE, TANNER.
I'M SORRY, TYLEET. BUT THIS IS THE ONLY WAY SHE STAYS -- OR SHE DIES.
"YOU'D KILL HER?"
"IF I HAD TO. SHE'S HUMAN. AND WE COME FIRST."

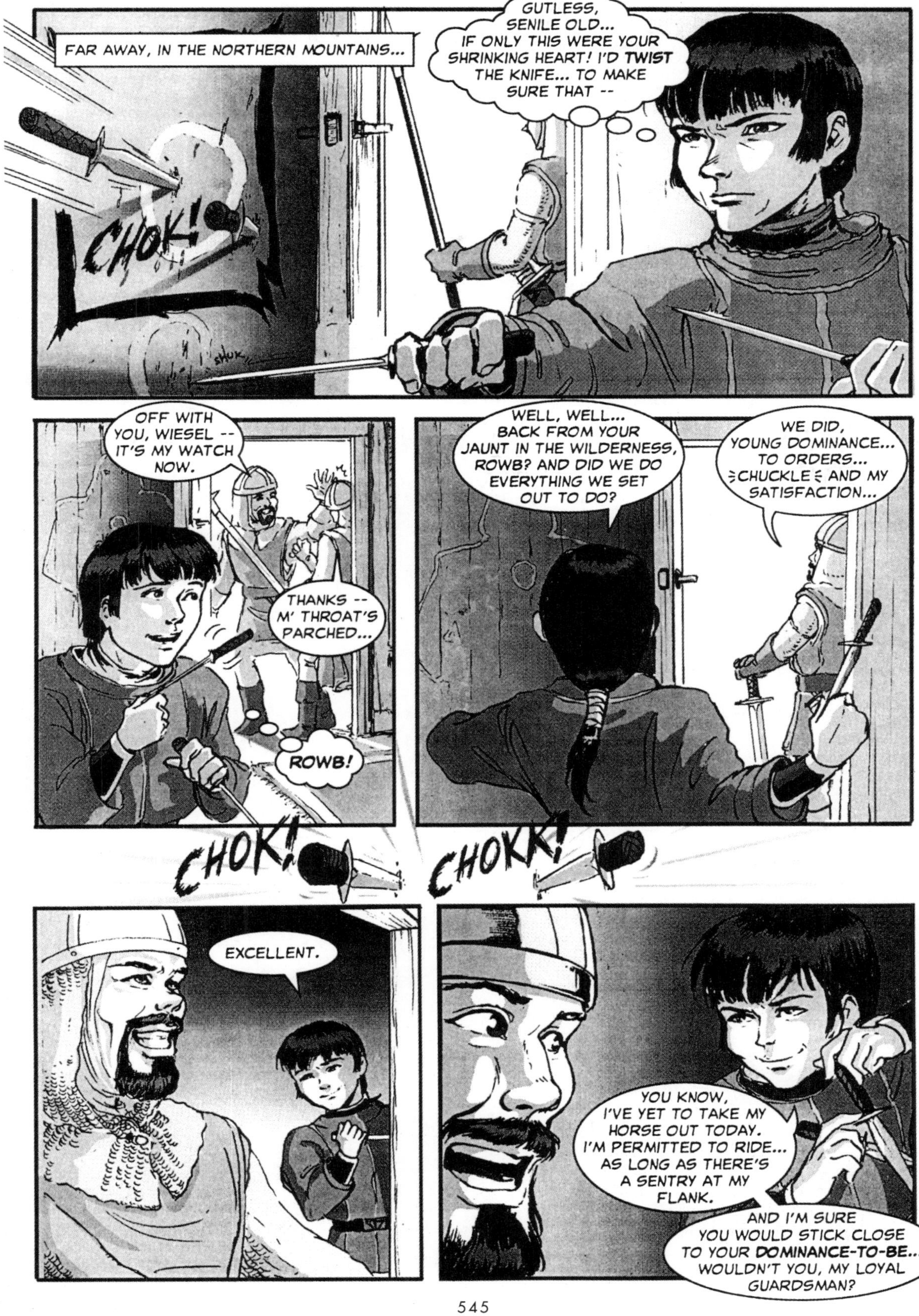
FAR AWAY, IN THE NORTHERN MOUNTAINS...
GUTLESS, SENILE OLD... IF ONLY THIS WERE YOUR SHRINKING HEART! I'D TWIST THE KNIFE... TO MAKE SURE THAT --
CHOK!
SHUK
OFF WITH YOU, WIESEL -- IT'S MY WATCH NOW.
THANKS -- M' THROAT'S PARCHED...
ROWB!
WELL, WELL... BACK FROM YOUR JAUNT IN THE WILDERNESS, ROWB? AND DID WE DO EVERYTHING WE SET OUT TO DO?
WE DID, YOUNG DOMINANCE... TO ORDERS... CHUCKLE AND MY SATISFACTION...
CHOK!
CHOKK!
EXCELLENT.
YOU KNOW, I'VE YET TO TAKE MY HORSE OUT TODAY. I'M PERMITTED TO RIDE... AS LONG AS THERE'S A SENTRY AT MY FLANK.
AND I'M SURE YOU WOULD STICK CLOSE TO YOUR DOMINANCE-TO-BE... WOULDN'T YOU, MY LOYAL GUARDSMAN?

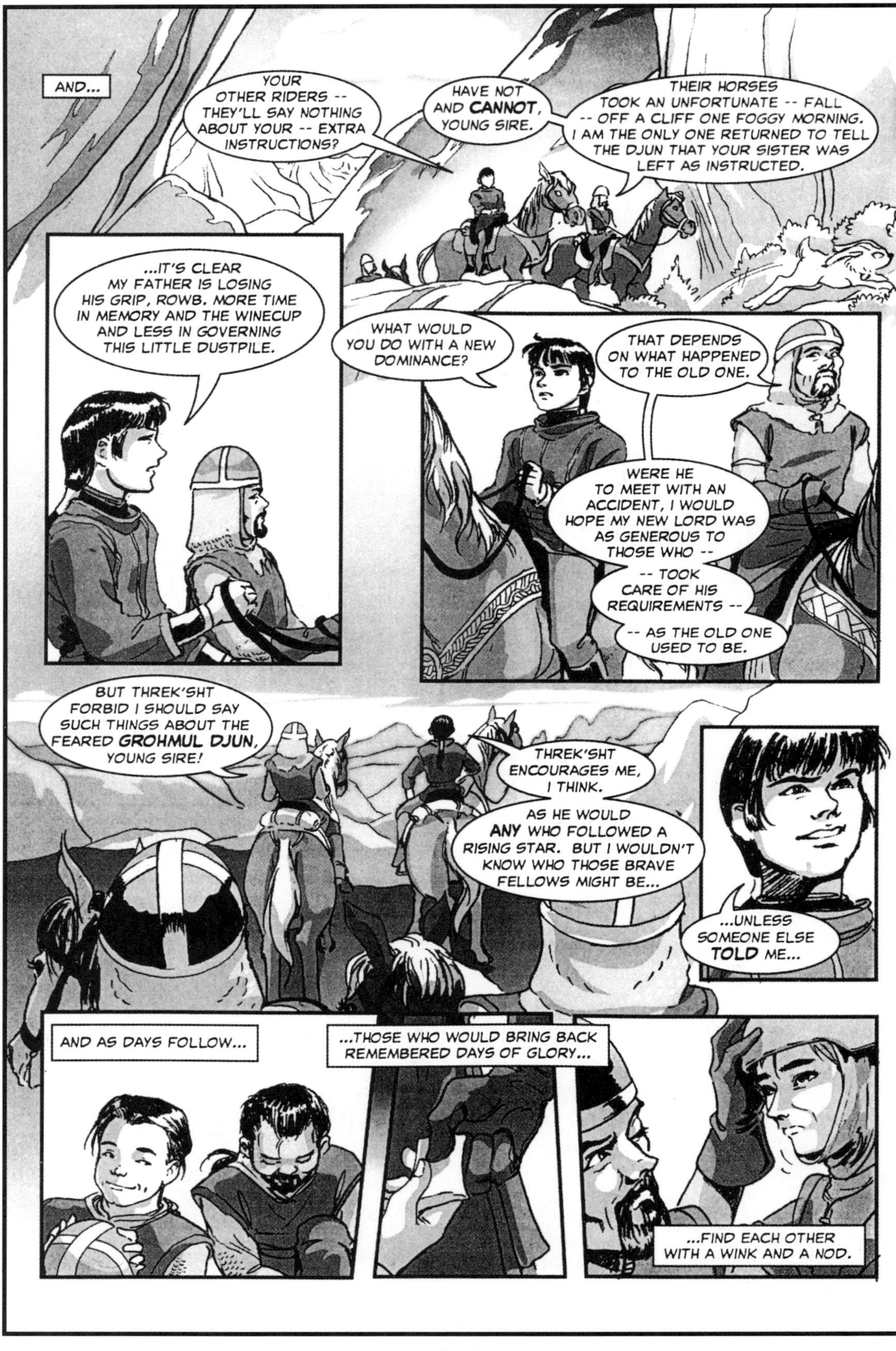
AND...
YOUR OTHER RIDERS -- THEY'LL SAY NOTHING ABOUT YOUR -- EXTRA INSTRUCTIONS?
HAVE NOT AND CANNOT, YOUNG SIRE.
THEIR HORSES TOOK AN UNFORTUNATE -- FALL -- OFF A CLIFF ONE FOGGY MORNING. I AM THE ONLY ONE RETURNED TO TELL THE DJUN THAT YOUR SISTER WAS LEFT AS INSTRUCTED.
...IT'S CLEAR MY FATHER IS LOSING HIS GRIP, ROWB. MORE TIME IN MEMORY AND THE WINECUP AND LESS IN GOVERNING THIS LITTLE DUSTPILE.
WHAT WOULD YOU DO WITH A NEW DOMINANCE?
THAT DEPENDS ON WHAT HAPPENED TO THE OLD ONE.
WERE HE TO MEET WITH AN ACCIDENT, I WOULD HOPE MY NEW LORD WAS AS GENEROUS TO THOSE WHO --
-- TOOK CARE OF HIS REQUIREMENTS --
-- AS THE OLD ONE USED TO BE.
BUT THREK'SHT FORBID I SHOULD SAY SUCH THINGS ABOUT THE FEARED GROHMUL DJUN, YOUNG SIRE!
THREK'SHT ENCOURAGES ME, I THINK.
AS HE WOULD ANY WHO FOLLOWED A RISING STAR. BUT I WOULDN'T KNOW WHO THOSE BRAVE FELLOWS MIGHT BE...
...UNLESS SOMEONE ELSE TOLD ME...
AND AS DAYS FOLLOW...
...THOSE WHO WOULD BRING BACK REMEMBERED DAYS OF GLORY...
...FIND EACH OTHER WITH A WINK AND A NOD.

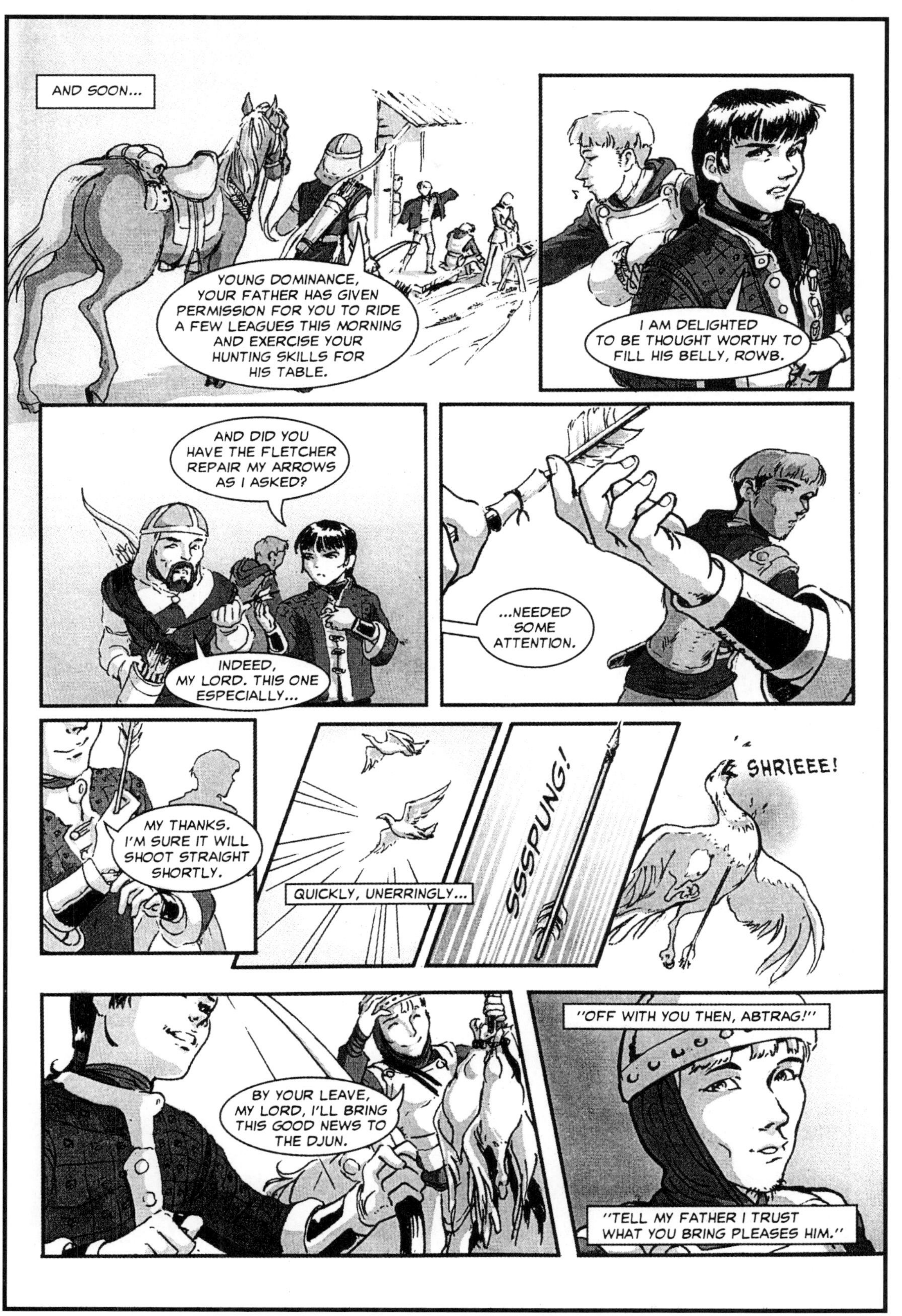

AND SOON...
YOUNG DOMINANCE, YOUR FATHER HAS GIVEN PERMISSION FOR YOU TO RIDE A FEW LEAGUES THIS MORNING AND EXERCISE YOUR HUNTING SKILLS FOR HIS TABLE.
I AM DELIGHTED TO BE THOUGHT WORTHY TO FILL HIS BELLY, ROWB.
AND DID YOU HAVE THE FLETCHER REPAIR MY ARROWS AS I ASKED?
INDEED, MY LORD. THIS ONE ESPECIALLY...
...NEEDED SOME ATTENTION.
MY THANKS. I'M SURE IT WILL SHOOT STRAIGHT SHORTLY.
QUICKLY, UNERRINGLY...
SSSPUNG!
SHRIEEE!
BY YOUR LEAVE, MY LORD, I'LL BRING THIS GOOD NEWS TO THE DJUN.
"OFF WITH YOU THEN, ABTRAG!"
"TELL MY FATHER I TRUST WHAT YOU BRING PLEASES HIM."

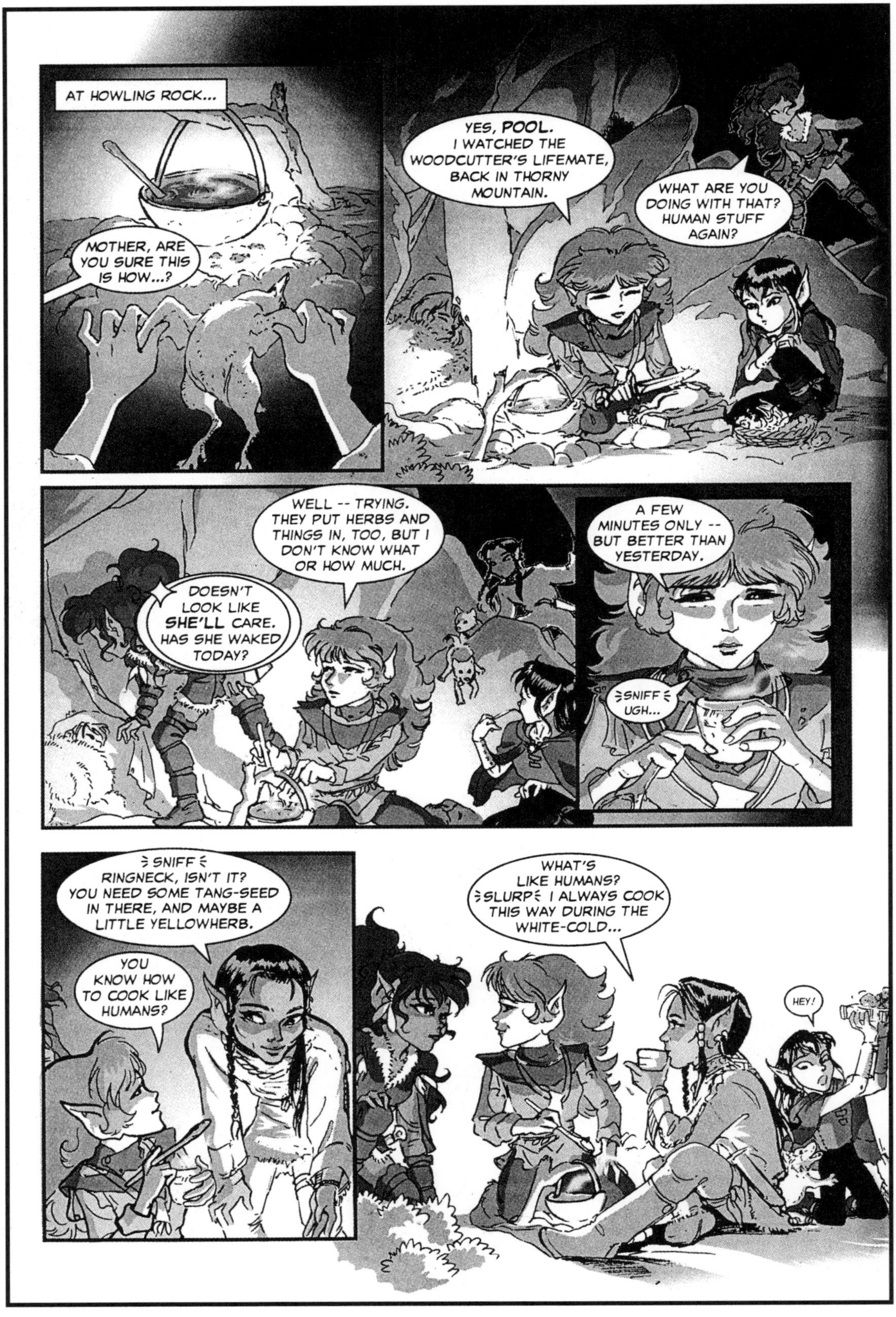

AT HOWLING ROCK...
MOTHER, ARE YOU SURE THIS IS HOW...?
YES, POOL. I WATCHED THE WOODCUTTER'S LIFEMATE, BACK IN THORNY MOUNTAIN.
WHAT ARE YOU DOING WITH THAT? HUMAN STUFF AGAIN?
WELL -- TRYING. THEY PUT HERBS AND THINGS IN, TOO, BUT I DON'T KNOW WHAT OR HOW MUCH.
DOESN'T LOOK LIKE SHE'LL CARE. HAS SHE WAKED TODAY?
A FEW MINUTES ONLY -- BUT BETTER THAN YESTERDAY.
SNIFF UGH...
SNIFF RINGNECK, ISN'T IT? YOU NEED SOME TANG-SEED IN THERE, AND MAYBE A LITTLE YELLOWHERB.
YOU KNOW HOW TO COOK LIKE HUMANS?
WHAT'S LIKE HUMANS? SLURP I ALWAYS COOK THIS WAY DURING THE WHITE-COLD...
HEY!

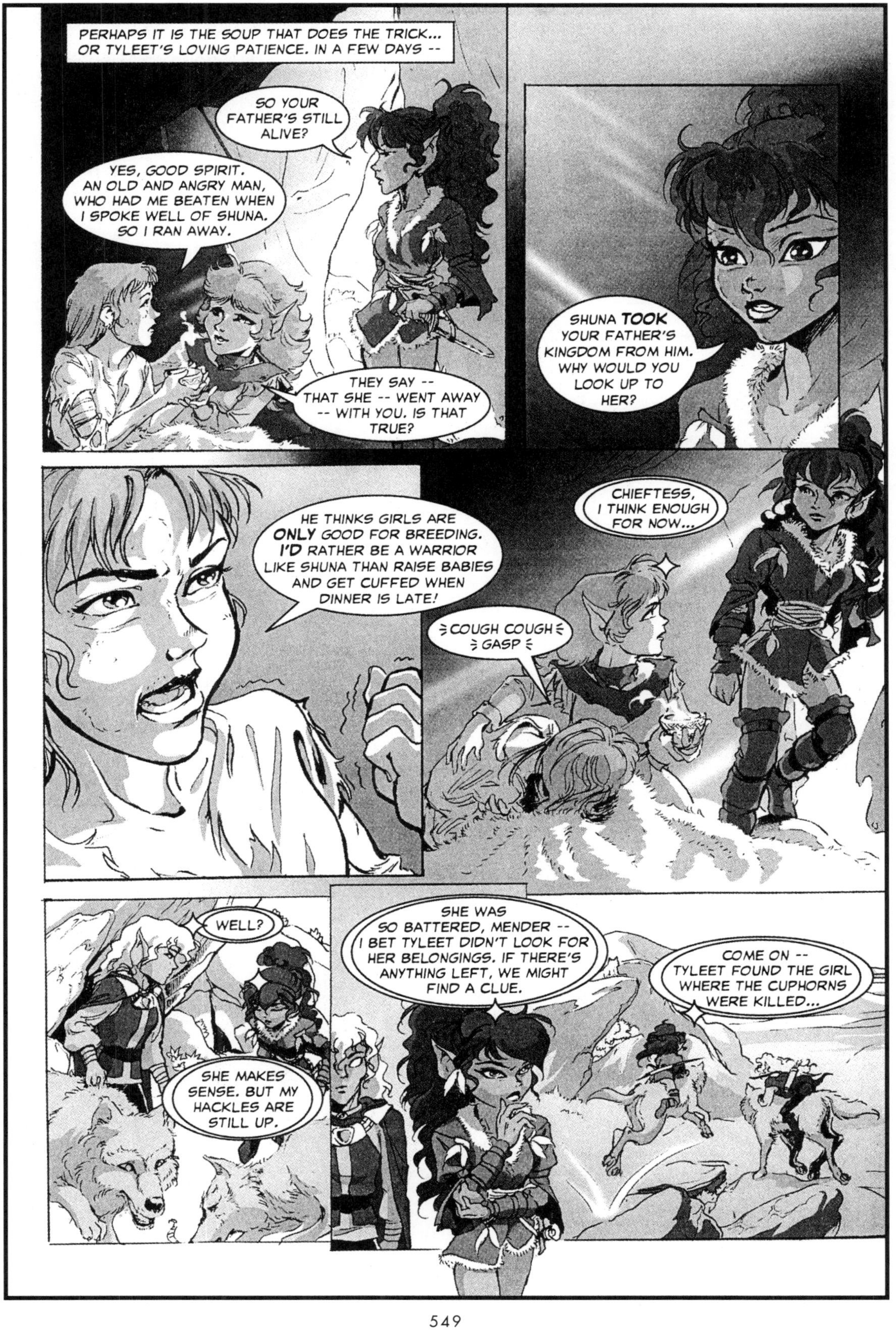

PERHAPS IT IS THE SOUP THAT DOES THE TRICK... OR TYLEET'S LOVING PATIENCE. IN A FEW DAYS --
SO YOUR FATHER'S STILL ALIVE?
YES, GOOD SPIRIT. AN OLD AND ANGRY MAN, WHO HAD ME BEATEN WHEN I SPOKE WELL OF SHUNA. SO I RAN AWAY.
THEY SAY -- THAT SHE -- WENT AWAY -- WITH YOU. IS THAT TRUE?
SHUNA **TOOK** YOUR FATHER'S KINGDOM FROM HIM. WHY WOULD YOU LOOK UP TO HER?
HE THINKS GIRLS ARE **ONLY** GOOD FOR BREEDING. **I'D** RATHER BE A WARRIOR LIKE SHUNA THAN RAISE BABIES AND GET CUFFED WHEN DINNER IS LATE!
CHIEFTESS, I THINK ENOUGH FOR NOW...
COUGH COUGH GASP
WELL?
SHE MAKES SENSE. BUT MY HACKLES ARE STILL UP.
SHE WAS SO BATTERED, MENDER -- I BET TYLEET DIDN'T LOOK FOR HER BELONGINGS. IF THERE'S ANYTHING LEFT, WE MIGHT FIND A CLUE.
COME ON -- TYLEET FOUND THE GIRL WHERE THE CUPHORNS WERE KILLED...

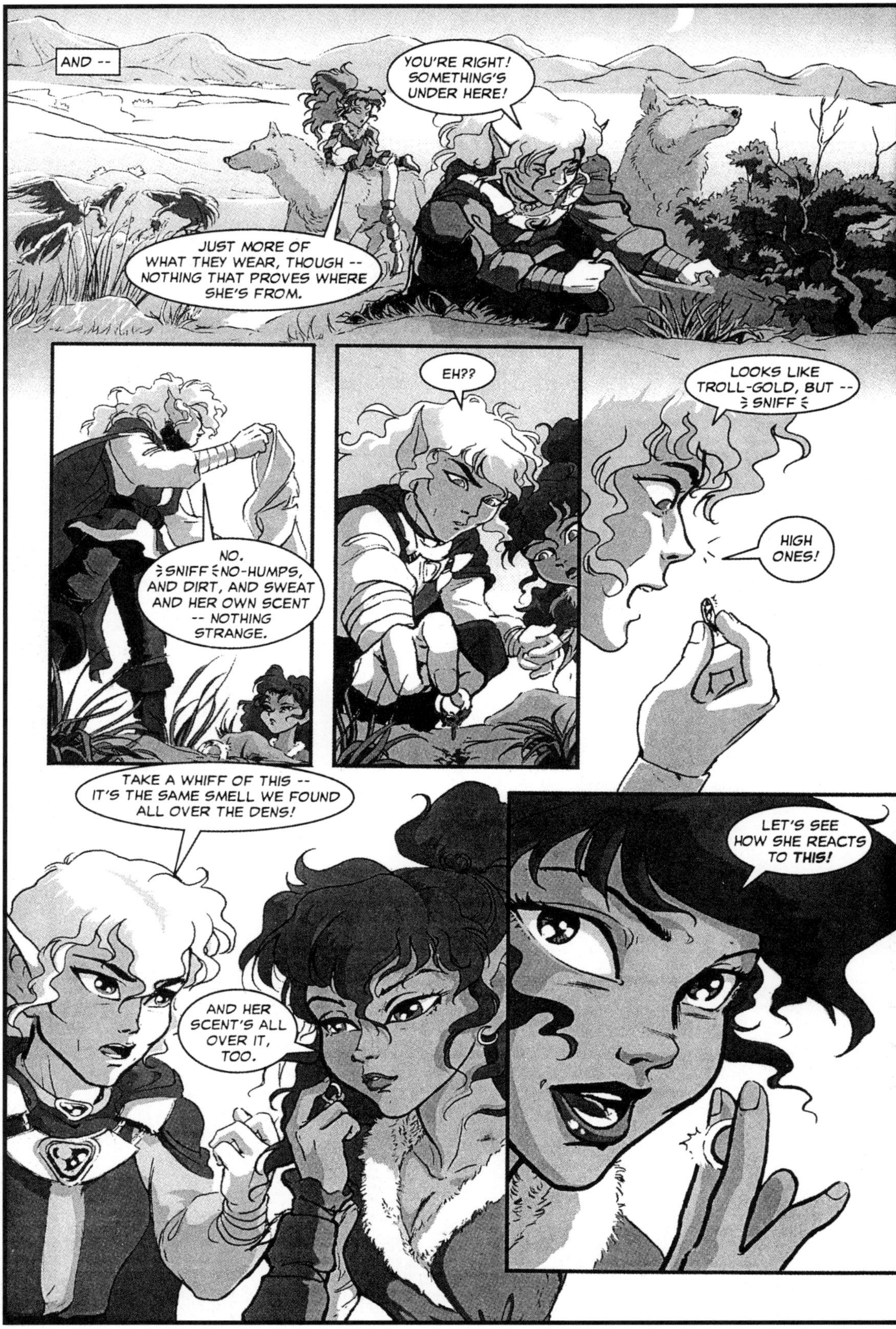
AND --
YOU'RE RIGHT! SOMETHING'S UNDER HERE!
JUST MORE OF WHAT THEY WEAR, THOUGH -- NOTHING THAT PROVES WHERE SHE'S FROM.
NO. ≷SNIFF≶ NO-HUMPS, AND DIRT, AND SWEAT AND HER OWN SCENT -- NOTHING STRANGE.
EH??
LOOKS LIKE TROLL-GOLD, BUT -- ≷SNIFF≶
HIGH ONES!
TAKE A WHIFF OF THIS -- IT'S THE SAME SMELL WE FOUND ALL OVER THE DENS!
AND HER SCENT'S ALL OVER IT, TOO.
LET'S SEE HOW SHE REACTS TO THIS!

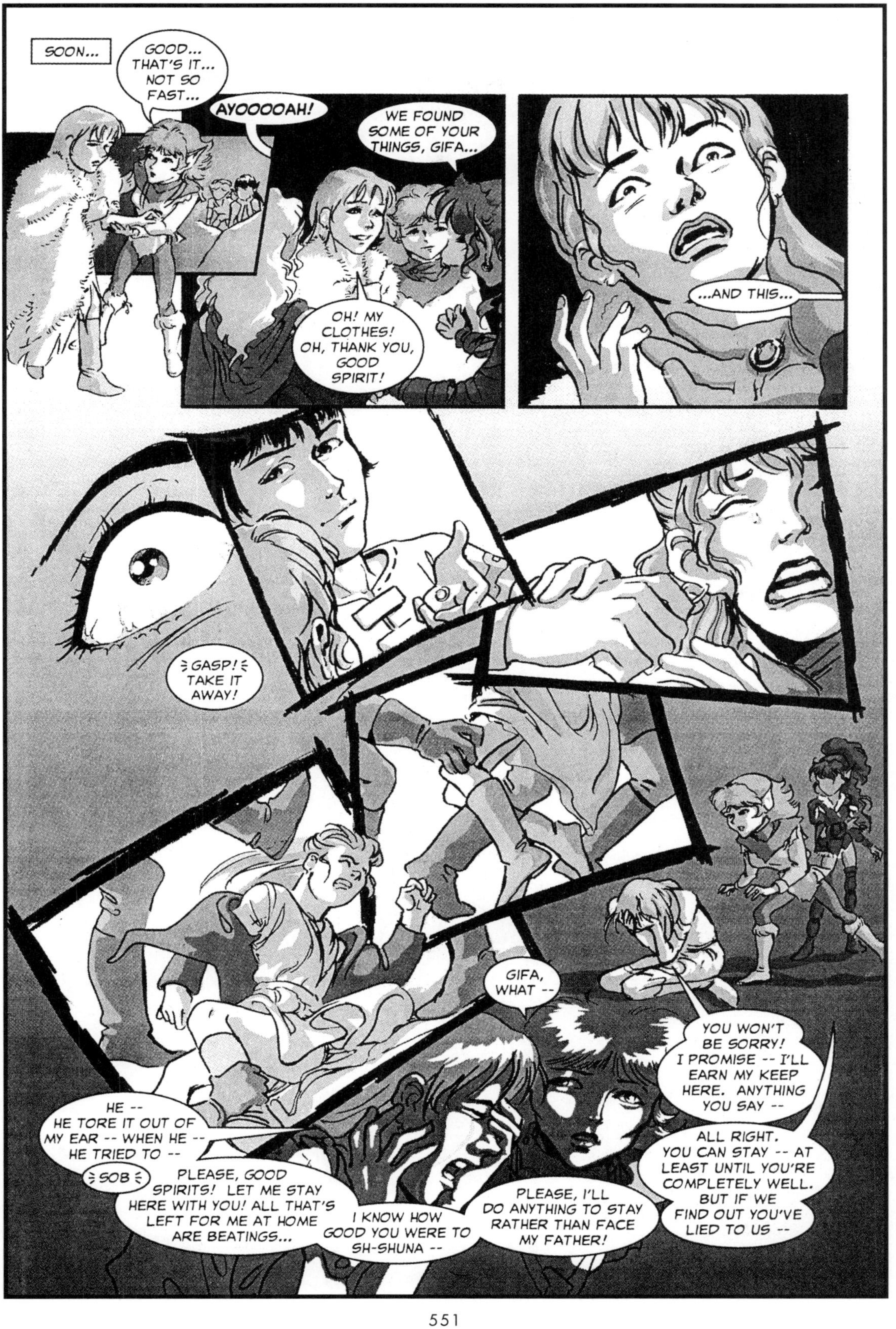

SOON...
GOOD... THAT'S IT... NOT SO FAST...
AYOOOOAH!
WE FOUND SOME OF YOUR THINGS, GIFA...
OH! MY CLOTHES! OH, THANK YOU, GOOD SPIRIT!
...AND THIS...
GASP! TAKE IT AWAY!
GIFA, WHAT --
YOU WON'T BE SORRY! I PROMISE -- I'LL EARN MY KEEP HERE. ANYTHING YOU SAY --
HE -- HE TORE IT OUT OF MY EAR -- WHEN HE -- HE TRIED TO --
SOB
PLEASE, GOOD SPIRITS! LET ME STAY HERE WITH YOU! ALL THAT'S LEFT FOR ME AT HOME ARE BEATINGS...
I KNOW HOW GOOD YOU WERE TO SH-SHUNA --
PLEASE, I'LL DO ANYTHING TO STAY RATHER THAN FACE MY FATHER!
ALL RIGHT. YOU CAN STAY -- AT LEAST UNTIL YOU'RE COMPLETELY WELL. BUT IF WE FIND OUT YOU'VE LIED TO US --

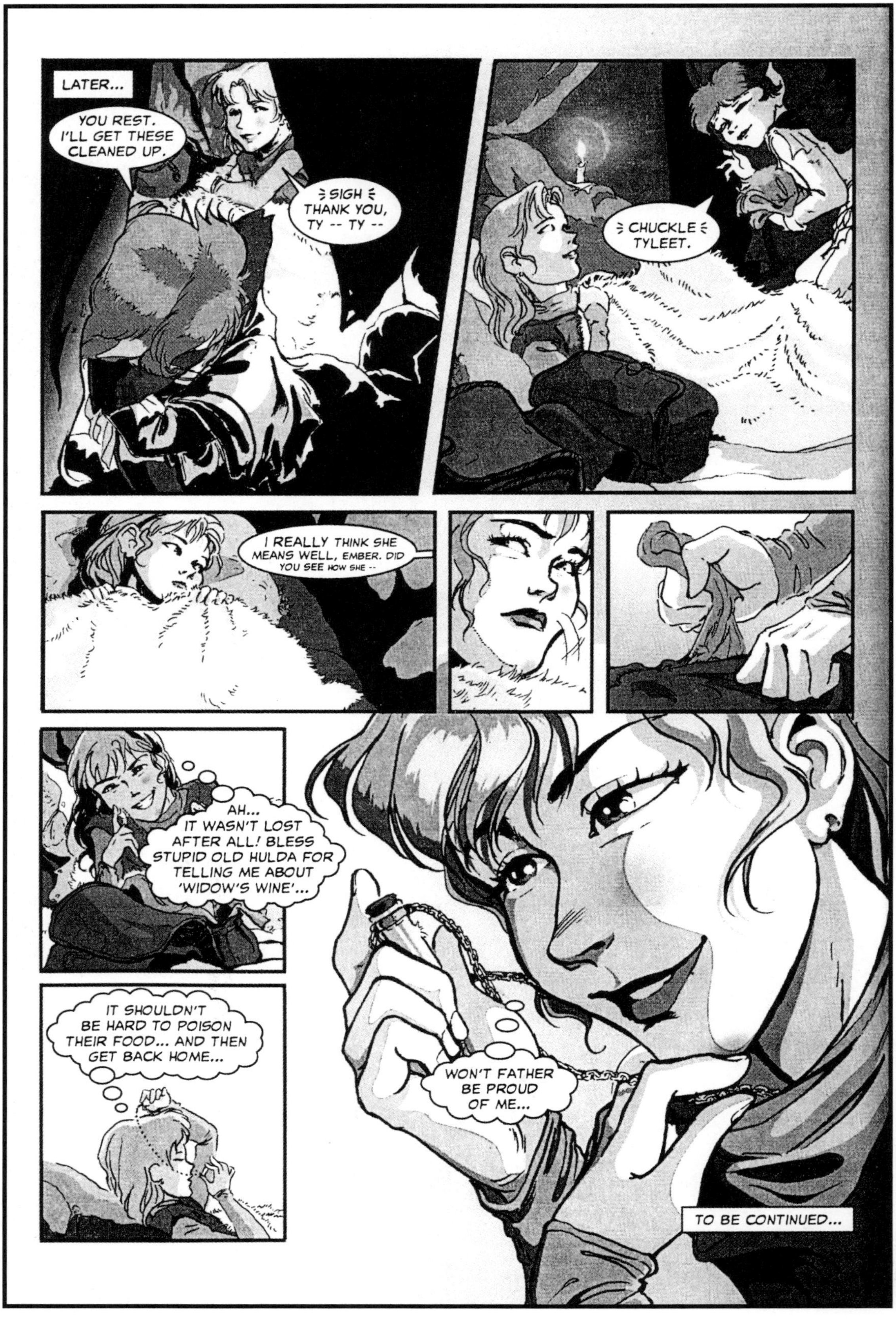

LATER...
YOU REST. I'LL GET THESE CLEANED UP.
SIGH THANK YOU, TY -- TY --
CHUCKLE TYLEET.
I REALLY THINK SHE MEANS WELL, EMBER. DID YOU SEE HOW SHE --
AH... IT WASN'T LOST AFTER ALL! BLESS STUPID OLD HULDA FOR TELLING ME ABOUT 'WIDOW'S WINE'...
IT SHOULDN'T BE HARD TO POISON THEIR FOOD... AND THEN GET BACK HOME...
WON'T FATHER BE PROUD OF ME...
TO BE CONTINUED...

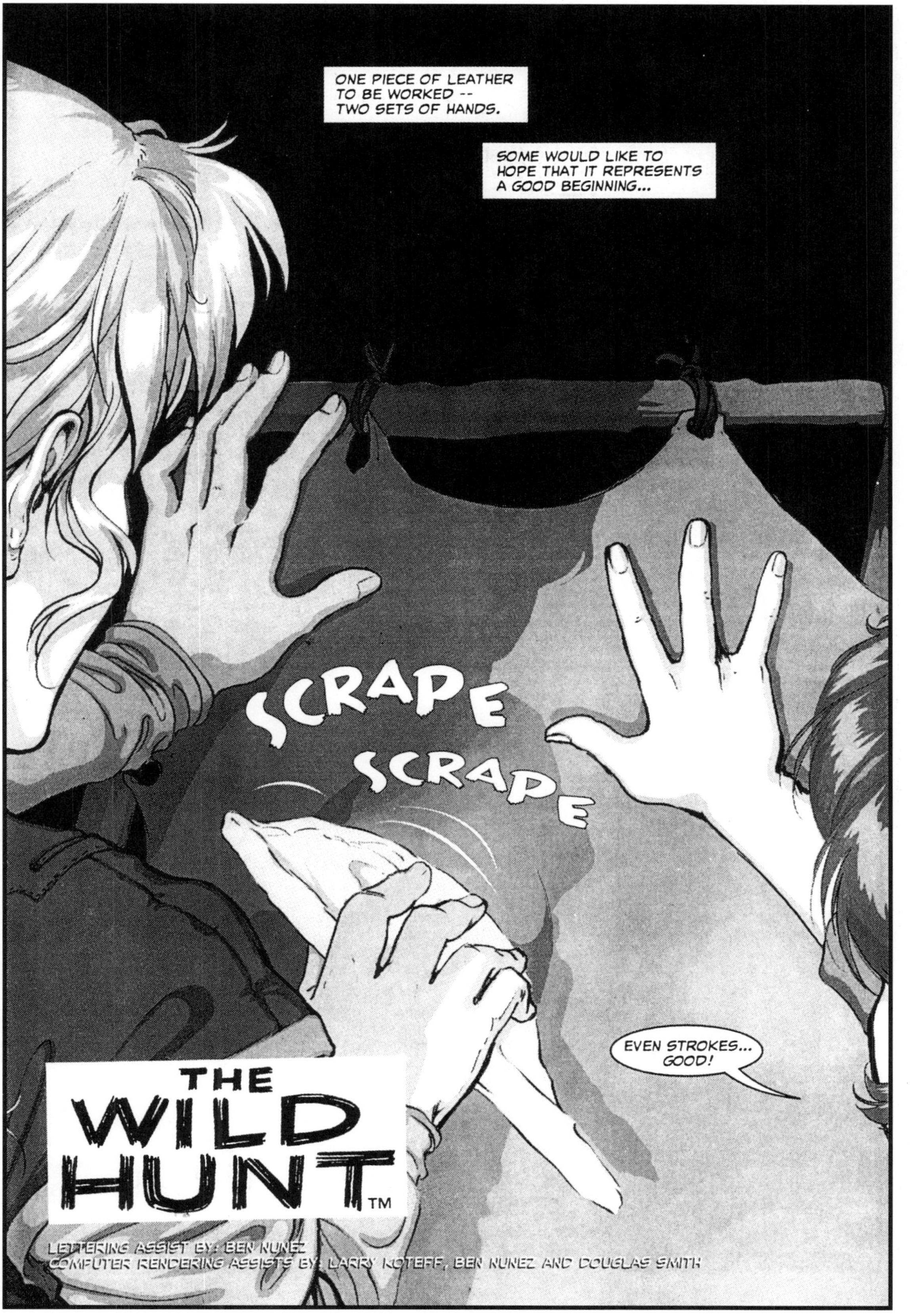
ONE PIECE OF LEATHER TO BE WORKED -- TWO SETS OF HANDS.
SOME WOULD LIKE TO HOPE THAT IT REPRESENTS A GOOD BEGINNING...
SCRAPE
SCRAPE
EVEN STROKES... GOOD!
THE WILD HUNT™
LETTERING ASSIST BY: BEN NUNEZ
COMPUTER RENDERING ASSISTS BY: LARRY KOTEFF, BEN NUNEZ AND DOUGLAS SMITH

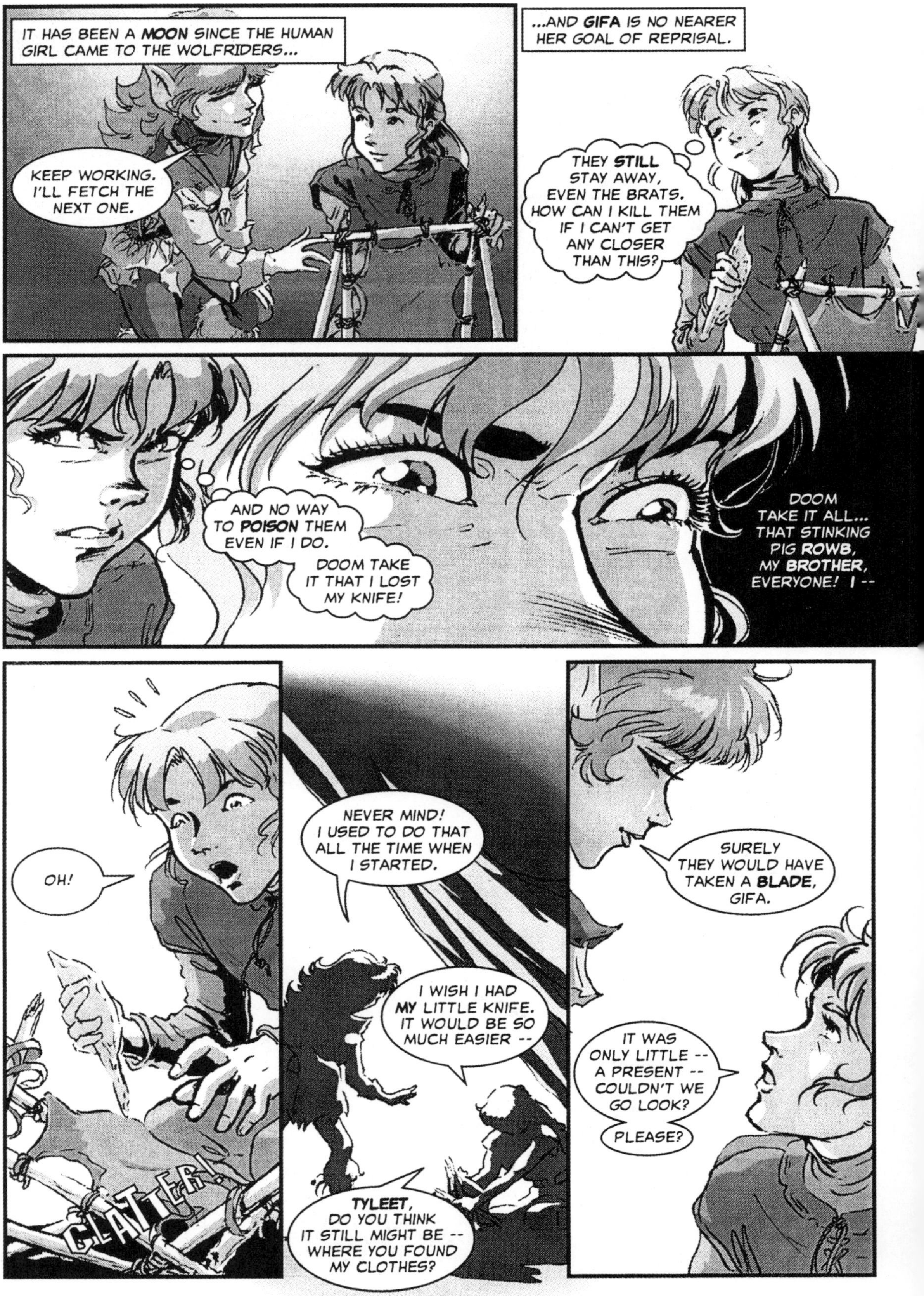
IT HAS BEEN A MOON SINCE THE HUMAN GIRL CAME TO THE WOLFRIDERS...
KEEP WORKING. I'LL FETCH THE NEXT ONE.
...AND GIFA IS NO NEARER HER GOAL OF REPRISAL.
THEY STILL STAY AWAY, EVEN THE BRATS. HOW CAN I KILL THEM IF I CAN'T GET ANY CLOSER THAN THIS?
AND NO WAY TO POISON THEM EVEN IF I DO.
DOOM TAKE IT THAT I LOST MY KNIFE!
DOOM TAKE IT ALL... THAT STINKING PIG ROWB, MY BROTHER, EVERYONE! I --
OH!
CLATTER!
NEVER MIND! I USED TO DO THAT ALL THE TIME WHEN I STARTED.
I WISH I HAD MY LITTLE KNIFE. IT WOULD BE SO MUCH EASIER --
TYLEET, DO YOU THINK IT STILL MIGHT BE -- WHERE YOU FOUND MY CLOTHES?
SURELY THEY WOULD HAVE TAKEN A BLADE, GIFA.
IT WAS ONLY LITTLE -- A PRESENT -- COULDN'T WE GO LOOK?
PLEASE?

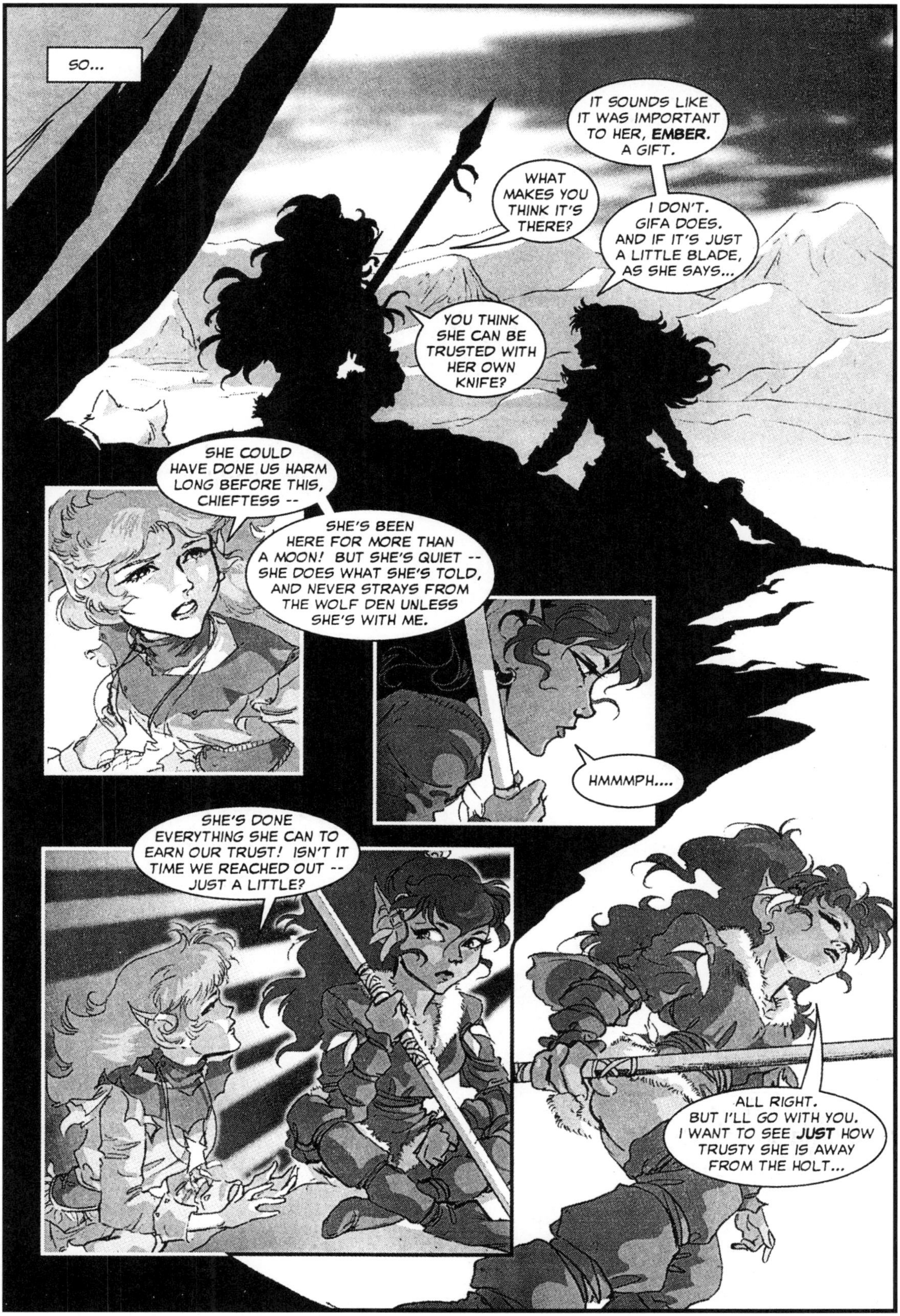
SO...
IT SOUNDS LIKE IT WAS IMPORTANT TO HER, EMBER. A GIFT.
WHAT MAKES YOU THINK IT'S THERE?
I DON'T. GIFA DOES. AND IF IT'S JUST A LITTLE BLADE, AS SHE SAYS...
YOU THINK SHE CAN BE TRUSTED WITH HER OWN KNIFE?
SHE COULD HAVE DONE US HARM LONG BEFORE THIS, CHIEFTESS --
SHE'S BEEN HERE FOR MORE THAN A MOON! BUT SHE'S QUIET -- SHE DOES WHAT SHE'S TOLD, AND NEVER STRAYS FROM THE WOLF DEN UNLESS SHE'S WITH ME.
HMMMPH....
SHE'S DONE EVERYTHING SHE CAN TO EARN OUR TRUST! ISN'T IT TIME WE REACHED OUT -- JUST A LITTLE?
ALL RIGHT. BUT I'LL GO WITH YOU. I WANT TO SEE JUST HOW TRUSTY SHE IS AWAY FROM THE HOLT...

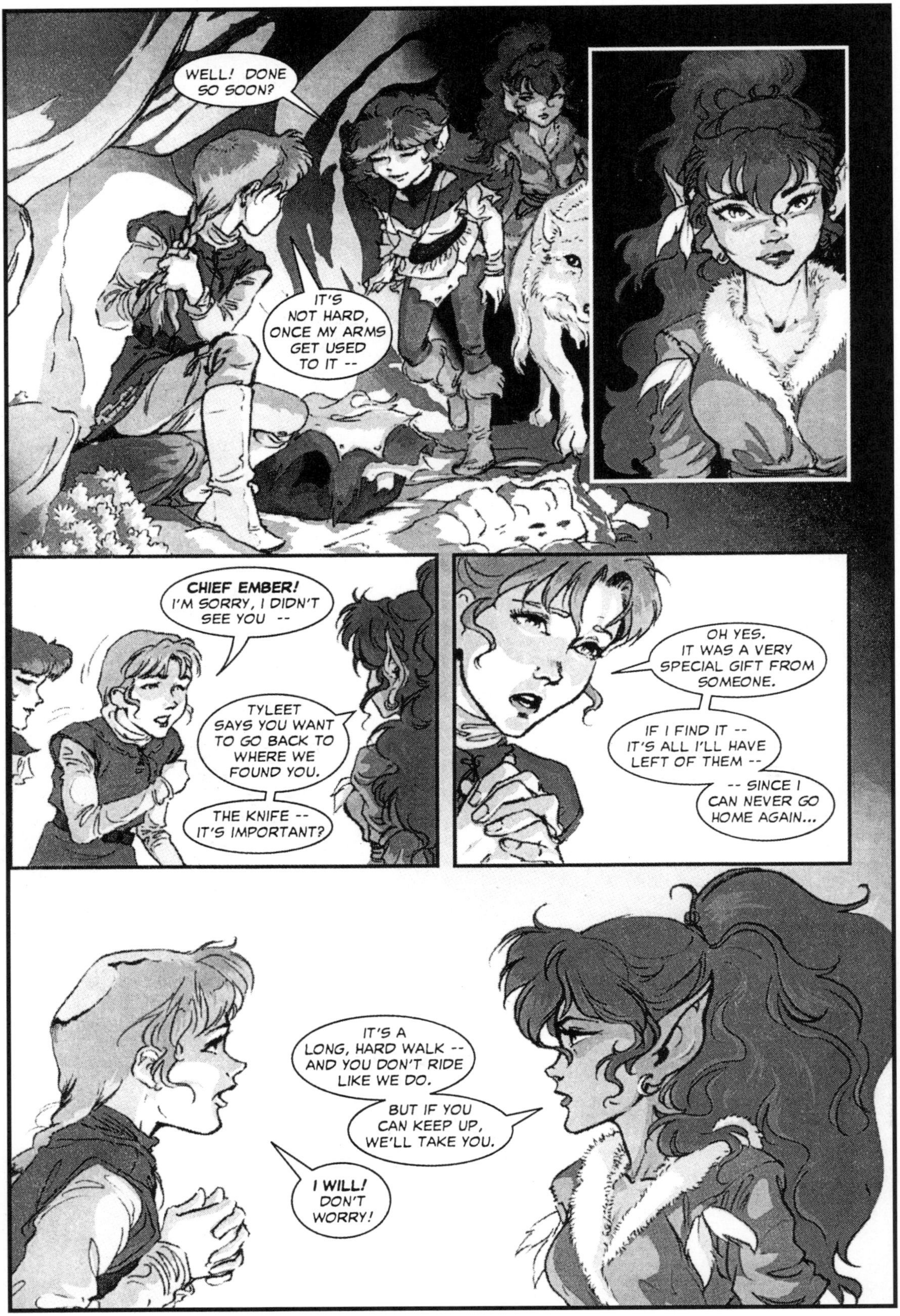

WELL! DONE SO SOON?
IT'S NOT HARD, ONCE MY ARMS GET USED TO IT --
CHIEF EMBER! I'M SORRY, I DIDN'T SEE YOU --
TYLEET SAYS YOU WANT TO GO BACK TO WHERE WE FOUND YOU.
THE KNIFE -- IT'S IMPORTANT?
OH YES. IT WAS A VERY SPECIAL GIFT FROM SOMEONE.
IF I FIND IT -- IT'S ALL I'LL HAVE LEFT OF THEM --
-- SINCE I CAN NEVER GO HOME AGAIN...
IT'S A LONG, HARD WALK -- AND YOU DON'T RIDE LIKE WE DO.
BUT IF YOU CAN KEEP UP, WE'LL TAKE YOU.
I WILL! DON'T WORRY!

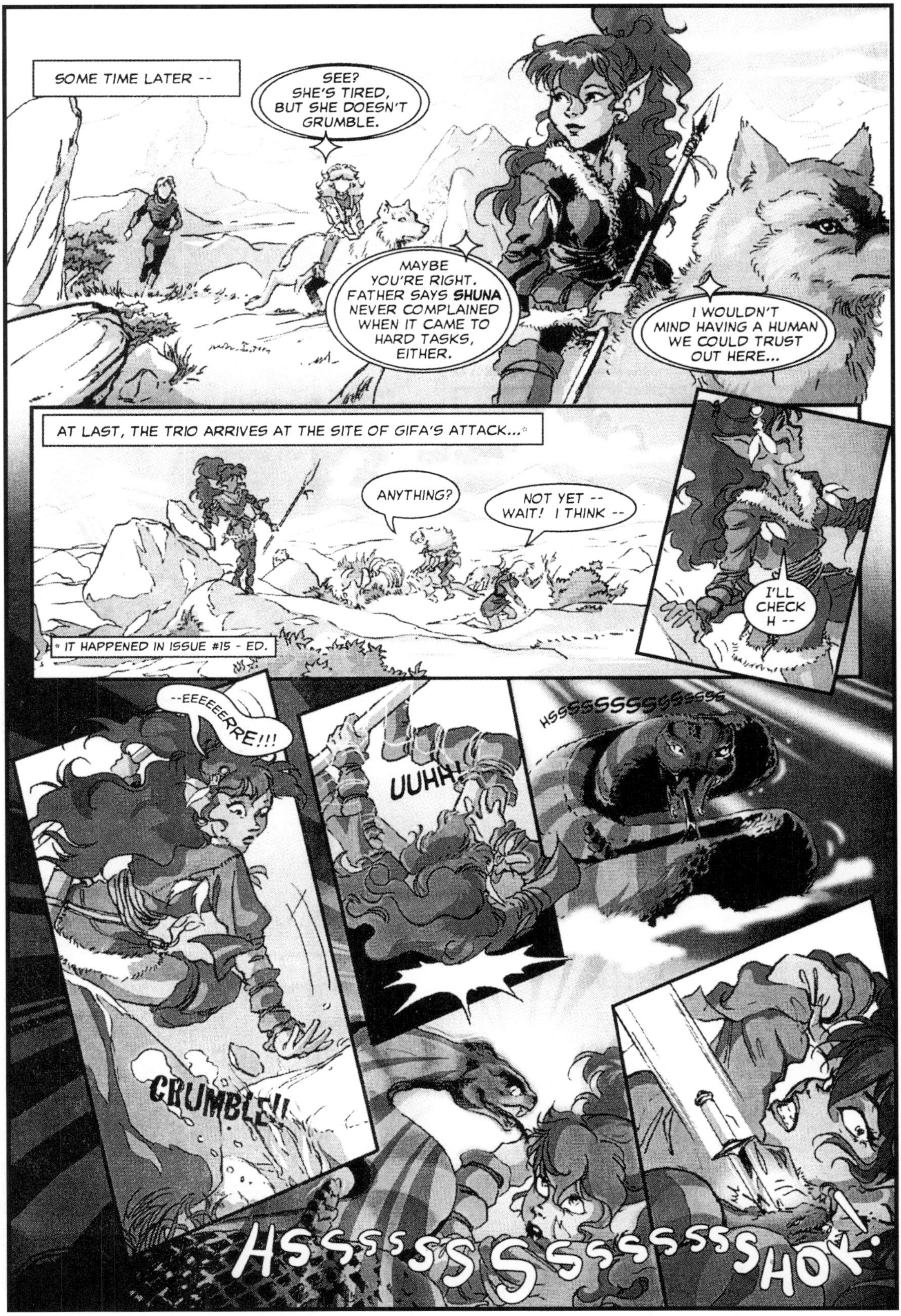

SOME TIME LATER --
SEE? SHE'S TIRED, BUT SHE DOESN'T GRUMBLE.
MAYBE YOU'RE RIGHT. FATHER SAYS SHUNA NEVER COMPLAINED WHEN IT CAME TO HARD TASKS, EITHER.
I WOULDN'T MIND HAVING A HUMAN WE COULD TRUST OUT HERE...
AT LAST, THE TRIO ARRIVES AT THE SITE OF GIFA'S ATTACK...*
ANYTHING?
NOT YET -- WAIT! I THINK --
* IT HAPPENED IN ISSUE #15 - ED.
I'LL CHECK H --
--EEEEEERRE!!!
UUHH!
HSSSSSSSSSSSSSS
CRUMBLE!!
HSSSSSSSSSSSSSSHOK!

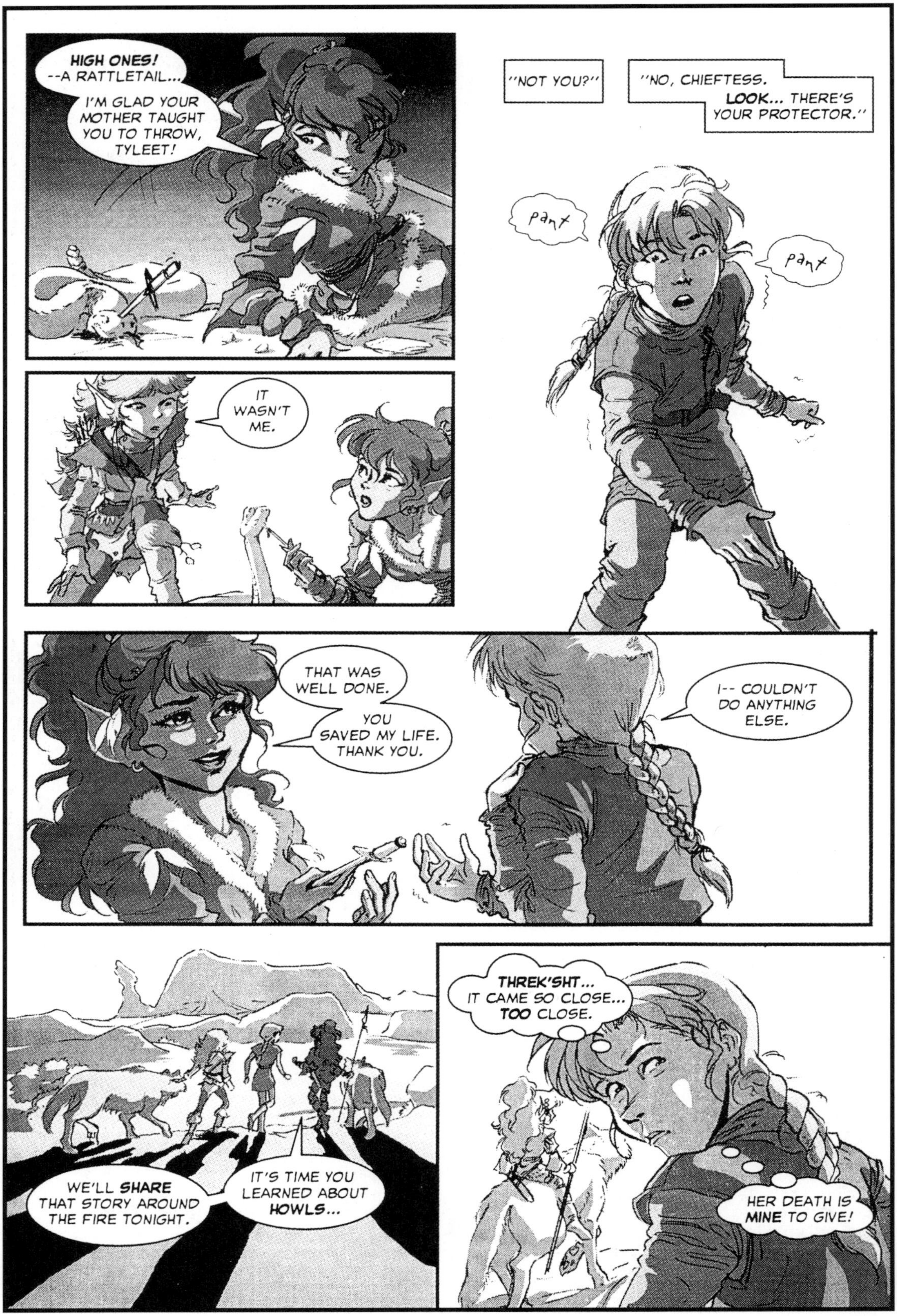
HIGH ONES!
--A RATTLETAIL...
I'M GLAD YOUR MOTHER TAUGHT YOU TO THROW, TYLEET!
IT WASN'T ME.
"NOT YOU?"
"NO, CHIEFTESS. LOOK... THERE'S YOUR PROTECTOR."
pant
pant
THAT WAS WELL DONE.
YOU SAVED MY LIFE. THANK YOU.
I-- COULDN'T DO ANYTHING ELSE.
WE'LL SHARE THAT STORY AROUND THE FIRE TONIGHT.
IT'S TIME YOU LEARNED ABOUT HOWLS...
THREK'SHT... IT CAME SO CLOSE... TOO CLOSE.
HER DEATH IS MINE TO GIVE!

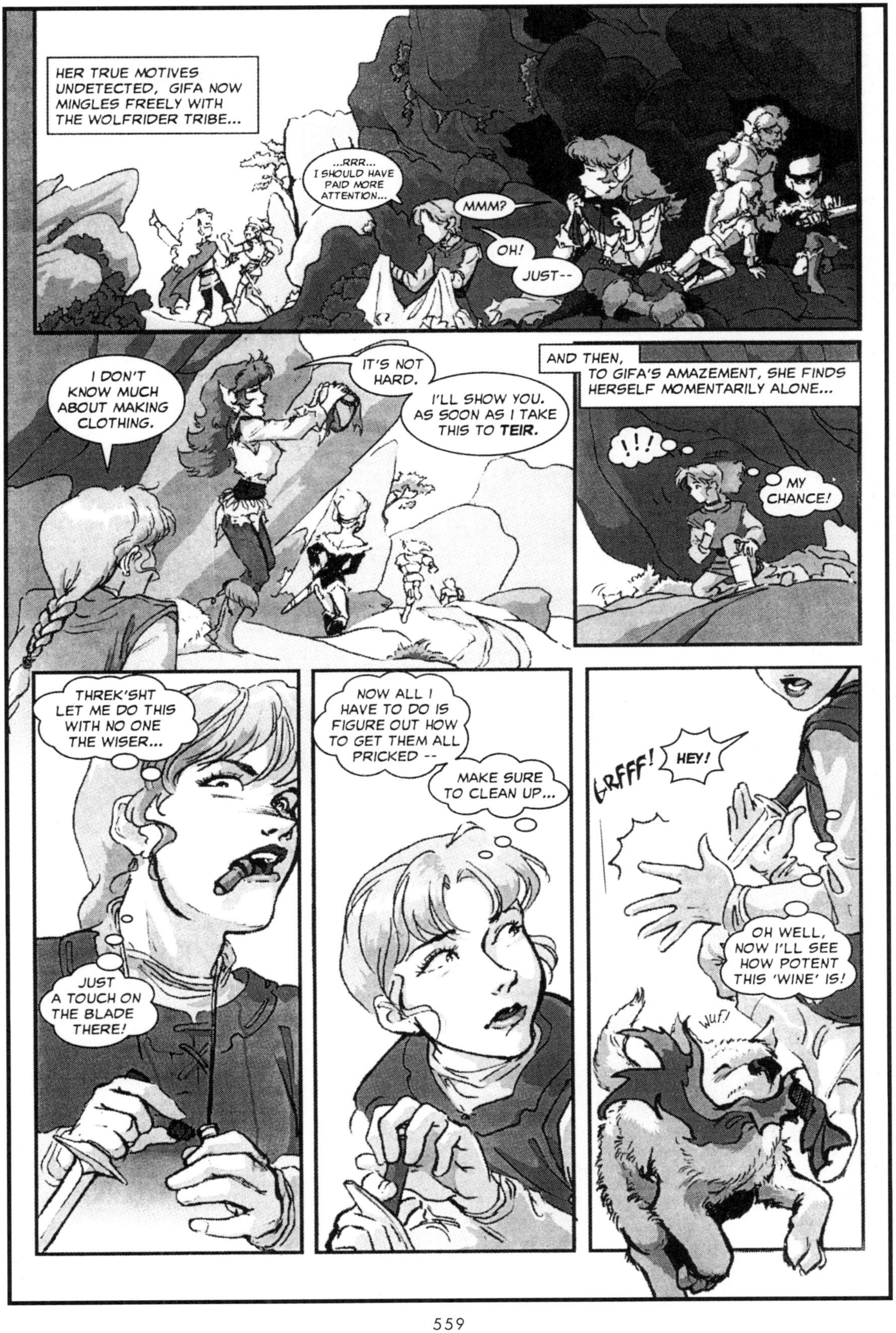
HER TRUE MOTIVES UNDETECTED, GIFA NOW MINGLES FREELY WITH THE WOLFRIDER TRIBE...
...RRR... I SHOULD HAVE PAID MORE ATTENTION...
MMM?
OH!
JUST--
I DON'T KNOW MUCH ABOUT MAKING CLOTHING.
IT'S NOT HARD.
I'LL SHOW YOU. AS SOON AS I TAKE THIS TO TEIR.
AND THEN, TO GIFA'S AMAZEMENT, SHE FINDS HERSELF MOMENTARILY ALONE...
!!!
MY CHANCE!
THREK'SHT LET ME DO THIS WITH NO ONE THE WISER...
JUST A TOUCH ON THE BLADE THERE!
NOW ALL I HAVE TO DO IS FIGURE OUT HOW TO GET THEM ALL PRICKED --
MAKE SURE TO CLEAN UP...
GRFFF!
HEY!
OH WELL, NOW I'LL SEE HOW POTENT THIS 'WINE' IS!
WUF!

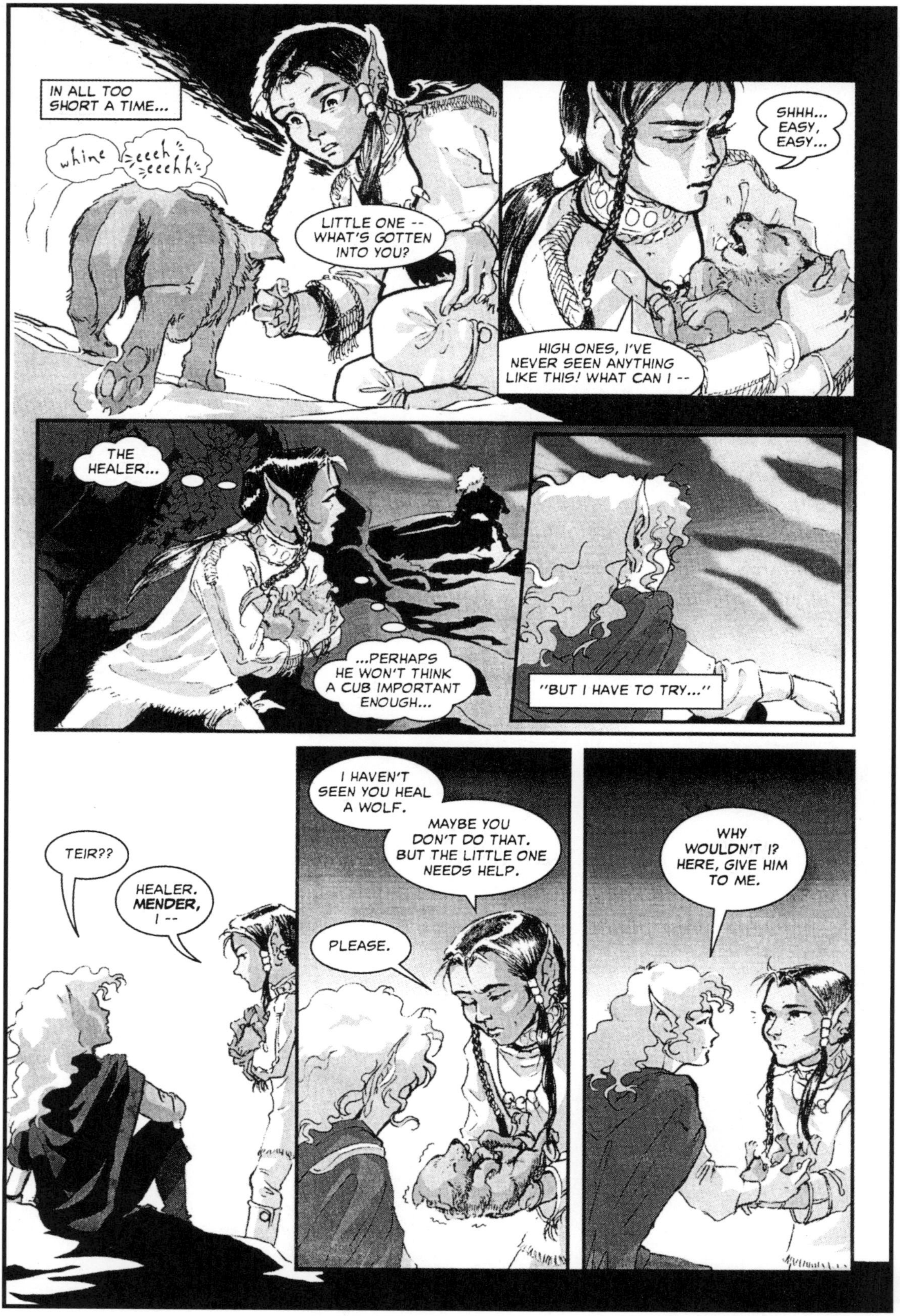
IN ALL TOO SHORT A TIME...
whine
eeeh eeehh
LITTLE ONE -- WHAT'S GOTTEN INTO YOU?
SHHH... EASY, EASY...
HIGH ONES, I'VE NEVER SEEN ANYTHING LIKE THIS! WHAT CAN I --
THE HEALER...
...PERHAPS HE WON'T THINK A CUB IMPORTANT ENOUGH...
"BUT I HAVE TO TRY..."
TEIR??
HEALER. **MENDER,** I --
I HAVEN'T SEEN YOU HEAL A WOLF.
MAYBE YOU DON'T DO THAT. BUT THE LITTLE ONE NEEDS HELP.
PLEASE.
WHY WOULDN'T I? HERE, GIVE HIM TO ME.

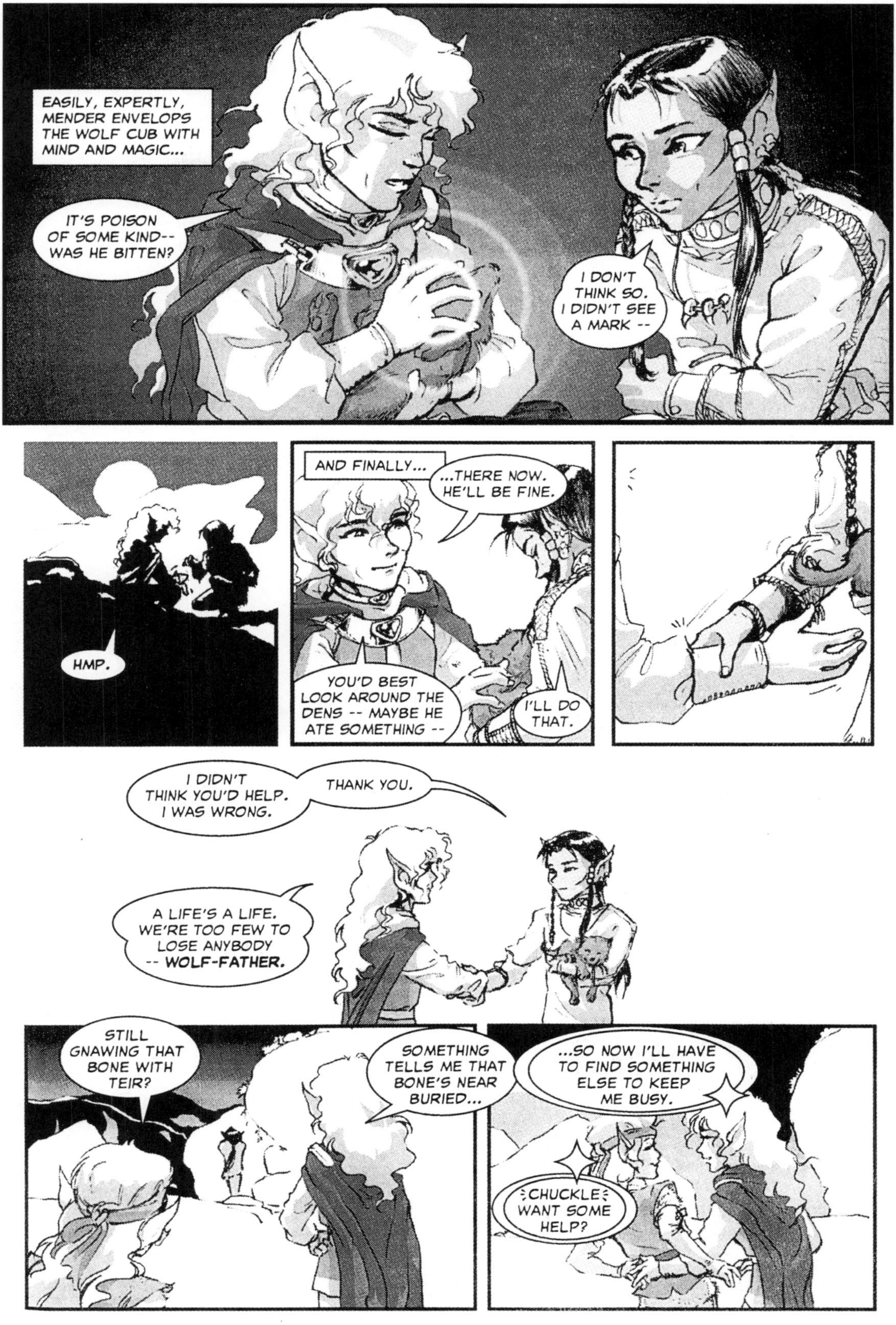
EASILY, EXPERTLY, MENDER ENVELOPS THE WOLF CUB WITH MIND AND MAGIC...
IT'S POISON OF SOME KIND-- WAS HE BITTEN?
I DON'T THINK SO. I DIDN'T SEE A MARK --
HMP.
AND FINALLY...
...THERE NOW. HE'LL BE FINE.
YOU'D BEST LOOK AROUND THE DENS -- MAYBE HE ATE SOMETHING --
I'LL DO THAT.
I DIDN'T THINK YOU'D HELP. I WAS WRONG.
THANK YOU.
A LIFE'S A LIFE. WE'RE TOO FEW TO LOSE ANYBODY -- **WOLF-FATHER.**
STILL GNAWING THAT BONE WITH TEIR?
SOMETHING TELLS ME THAT BONE'S NEAR BURIED...
...SO NOW I'LL HAVE TO FIND SOMETHING ELSE TO KEEP ME BUSY.
CHUCKLE WANT SOME HELP?

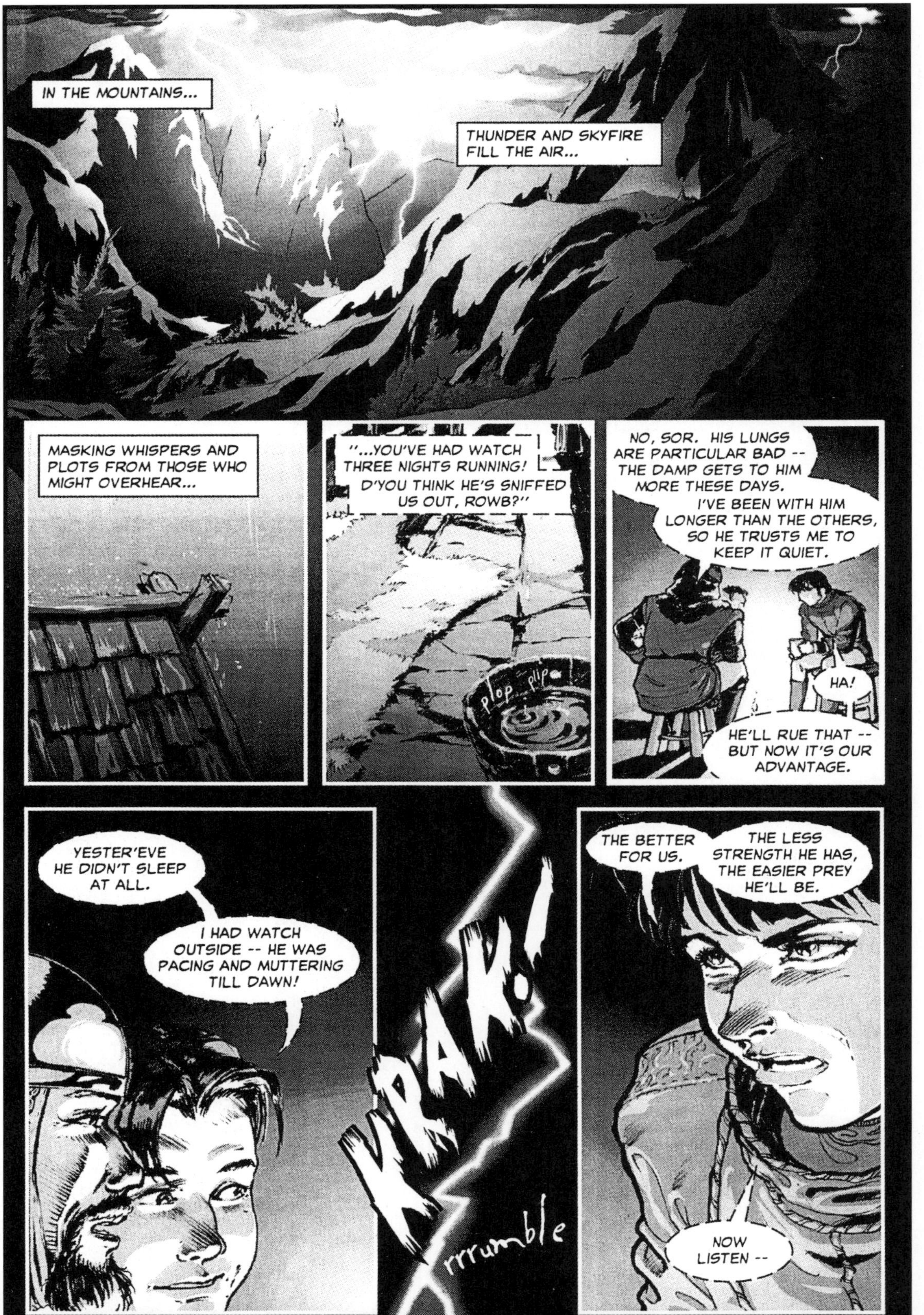

IN THE MOUNTAINS...
THUNDER AND SKYFIRE FILL THE AIR...
MASKING WHISPERS AND PLOTS FROM THOSE WHO MIGHT OVERHEAR...
"...YOU'VE HAD WATCH THREE NIGHTS RUNNING! D'YOU THINK HE'S SNIFFED US OUT, ROWB?"
plop plip
NO, SOR. HIS LUNGS ARE PARTICULAR BAD -- THE DAMP GETS TO HIM MORE THESE DAYS.
I'VE BEEN WITH HIM LONGER THAN THE OTHERS, SO HE TRUSTS ME TO KEEP IT QUIET.
HA!
HE'LL RUE THAT -- BUT NOW IT'S OUR ADVANTAGE.
YESTER'EVE HE DIDN'T SLEEP AT ALL.
I HAD WATCH OUTSIDE -- HE WAS PACING AND MUTTERING TILL DAWN!
KRAK!
rrrumble
THE BETTER FOR US.
THE LESS STRENGTH HE HAS, THE EASIER PREY HE'LL BE.
NOW LISTEN --

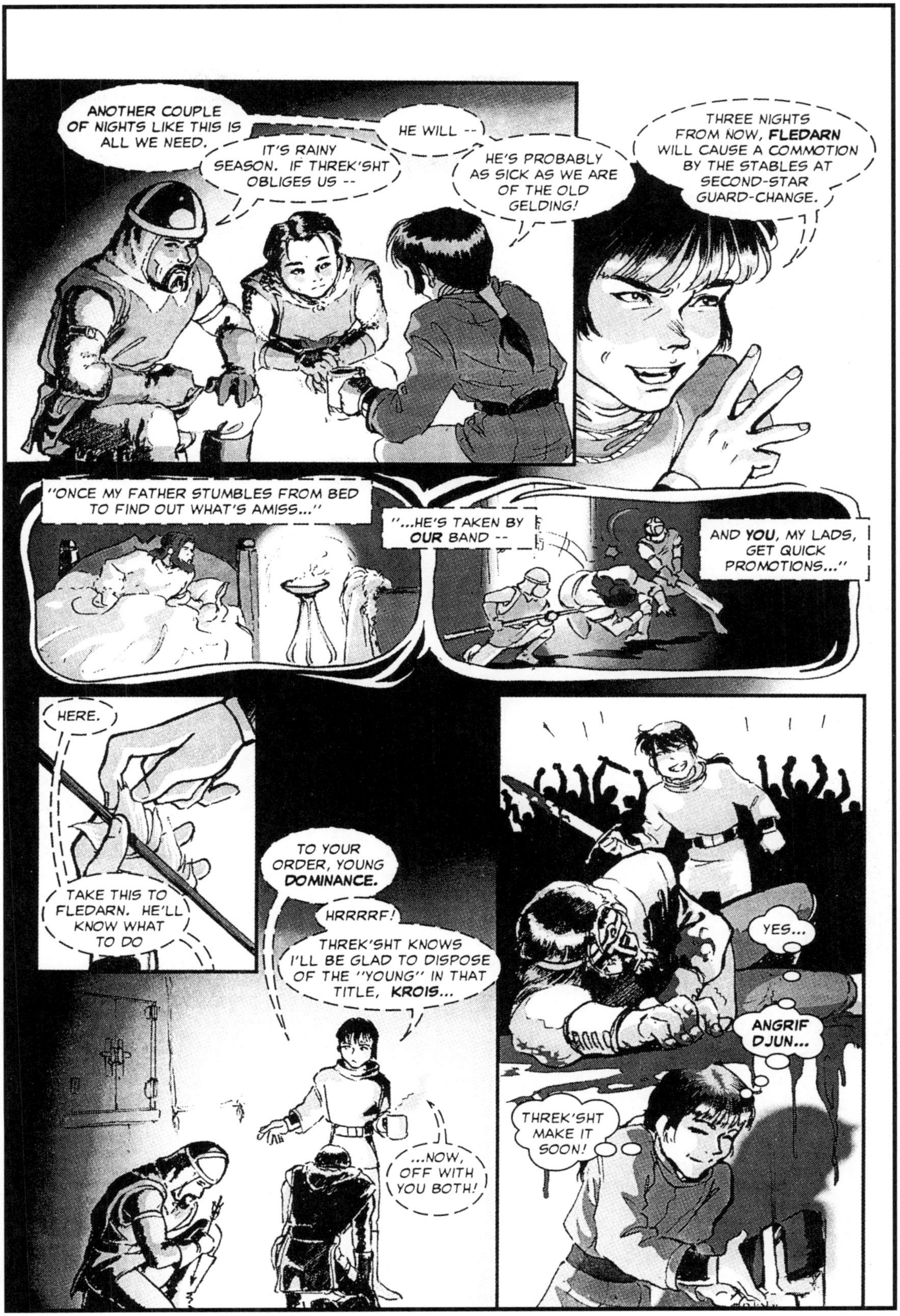
ANOTHER COUPLE OF NIGHTS LIKE THIS IS ALL WE NEED.
IT'S RAINY SEASON. IF THREK'SHT OBLIGES US --
HE WILL --
HE'S PROBABLY AS SICK AS WE ARE OF THE OLD GELDING!
THREE NIGHTS FROM NOW, FLEDARN WILL CAUSE A COMMOTION BY THE STABLES AT SECOND-STAR GUARD-CHANGE.
"ONCE MY FATHER STUMBLES FROM BED TO FIND OUT WHAT'S AMISS..."
"...HE'S TAKEN BY OUR BAND --
AND YOU, MY LADS, GET QUICK PROMOTIONS..."
HERE.
TAKE THIS TO FLEDARN. HE'LL KNOW WHAT TO DO
TO YOUR ORDER, YOUNG DOMINANCE.
HRRRRF!
THREK'SHT KNOWS I'LL BE GLAD TO DISPOSE OF THE "YOUNG" IN THAT TITLE, KROIS...
...NOW, OFF WITH YOU BOTH!
YES...
ANGRIF DJUN...
THREK'SHT MAKE IT SOON!

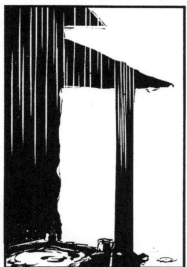

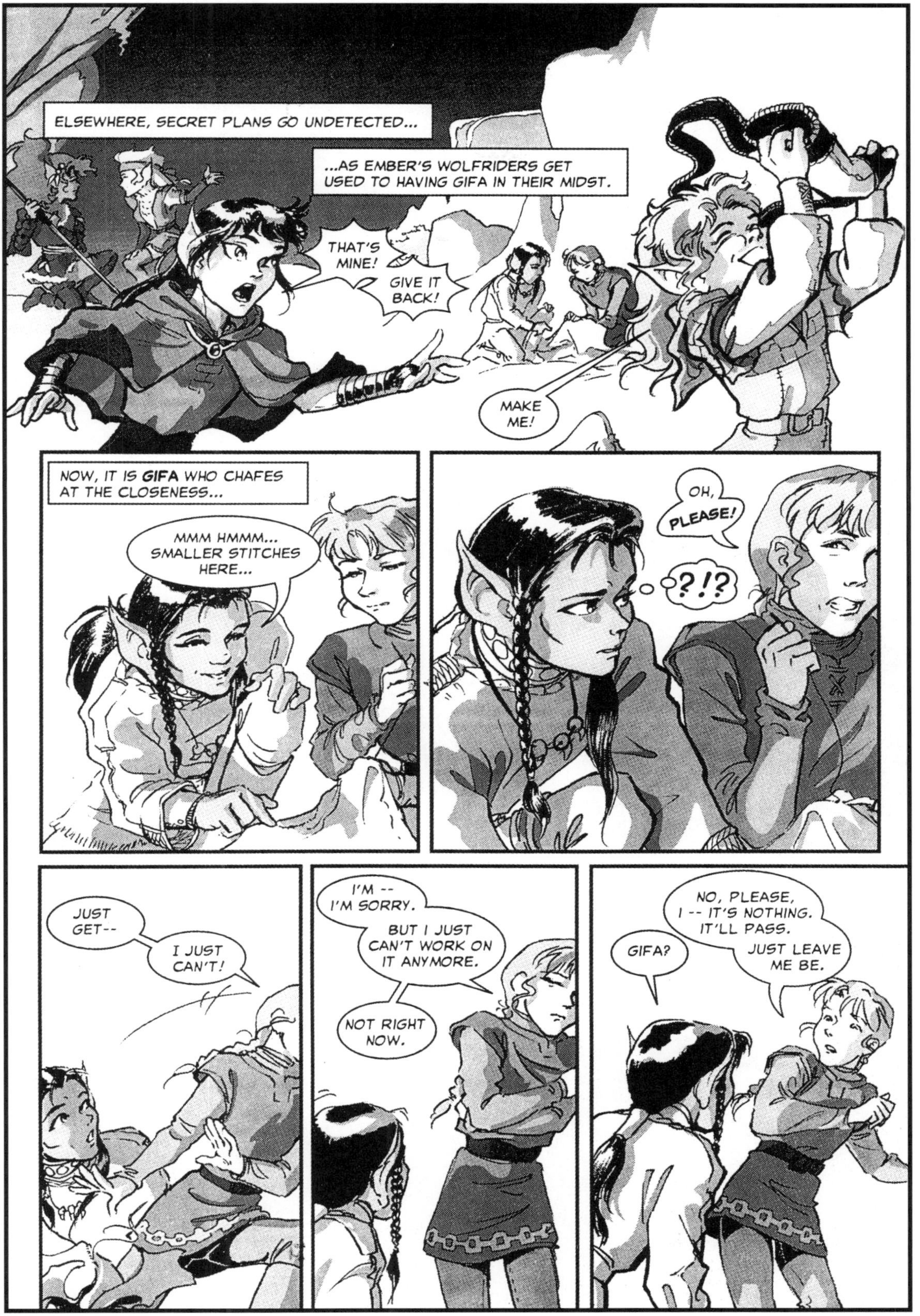
ELSEWHERE, SECRET PLANS GO UNDETECTED...
...AS EMBER'S WOLFRIDERS GET USED TO HAVING GIFA IN THEIR MIDST.
THAT'S MINE!
GIVE IT BACK!
MAKE ME!
NOW, IT IS **GIFA** WHO CHAFES AT THE CLOSENESS...
MMM HMMM... SMALLER STITCHES HERE...
OH, **PLEASE!**
?!?
JUST GET--
I JUST CAN'T!
I'M -- I'M SORRY.
BUT I JUST CAN'T WORK ON IT ANYMORE.
NOT RIGHT NOW.
GIFA?
NO, PLEASE, I -- IT'S NOTHING. IT'LL PASS.
JUST LEAVE ME BE.

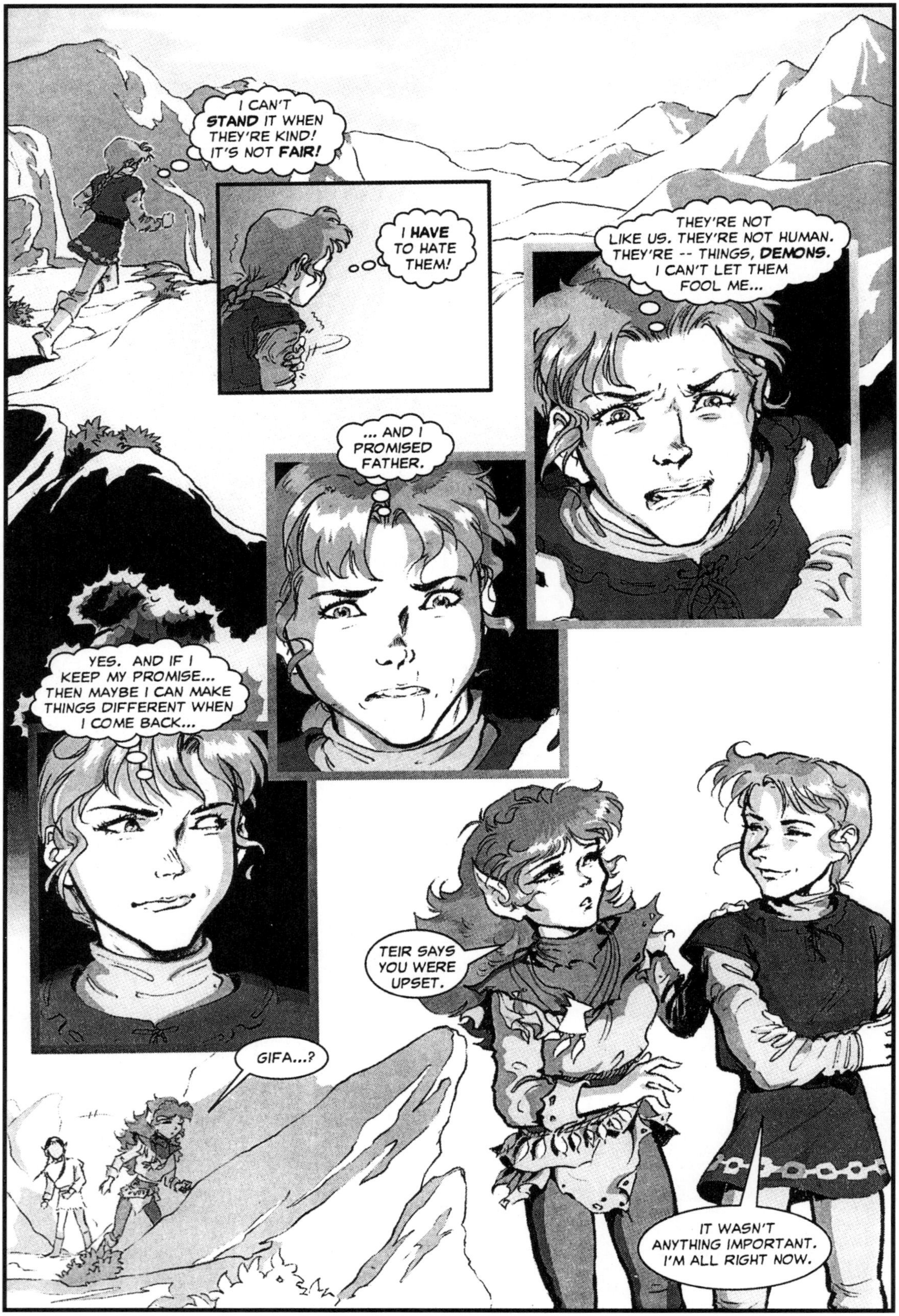
I CAN'T STAND IT WHEN THEY'RE KIND! IT'S NOT FAIR!
I HAVE TO HATE THEM!
THEY'RE NOT LIKE US. THEY'RE NOT HUMAN. THEY'RE -- THINGS, DEMONS. I CAN'T LET THEM FOOL ME...
... AND I PROMISED FATHER.
YES. AND IF I KEEP MY PROMISE... THEN MAYBE I CAN MAKE THINGS DIFFERENT WHEN I COME BACK...
GIFA...?
TEIR SAYS YOU WERE UPSET.
IT WASN'T ANYTHING IMPORTANT. I'M ALL RIGHT NOW.

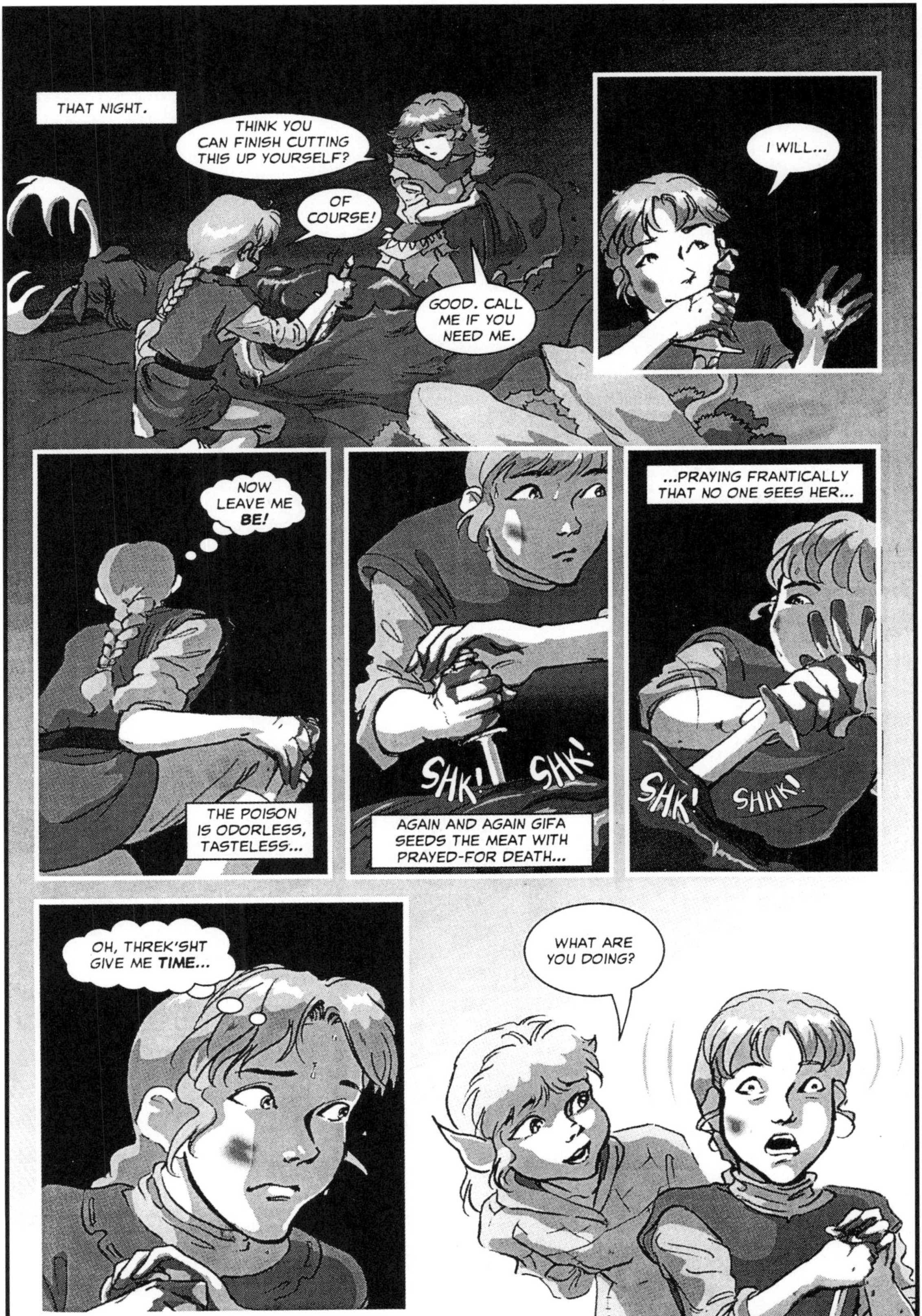
THAT NIGHT.
THINK YOU CAN FINISH CUTTING THIS UP YOURSELF?
OF COURSE!
GOOD. CALL ME IF YOU NEED ME.
I WILL...
NOW LEAVE ME BE!
THE POISON IS ODORLESS, TASTELESS...
SHK! SHK!
AGAIN AND AGAIN GIFA SEEDS THE MEAT WITH PRAYED-FOR DEATH...
...PRAYING FRANTICALLY THAT NO ONE SEES HER...
SHK! SHHK!
OH, THREK'SHT GIVE ME TIME...
WHAT ARE YOU DOING?

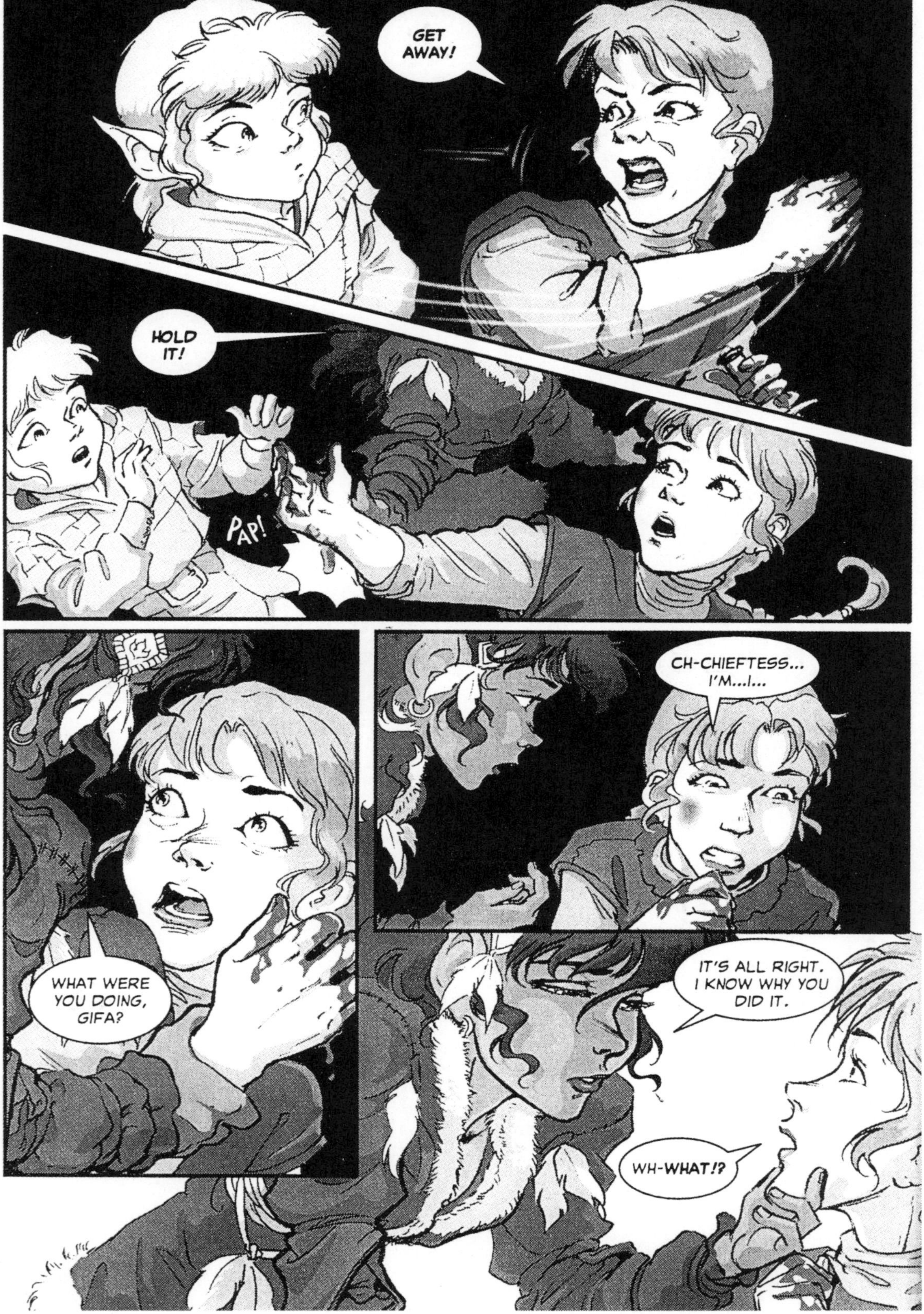
GET AWAY!
HOLD IT!
PAP!
WHAT WERE YOU DOING, GIFA?
CH-CHIEFTESS... I'M...I...
IT'S ALL RIGHT. I KNOW WHY YOU DID IT.
WH-WHAT!?

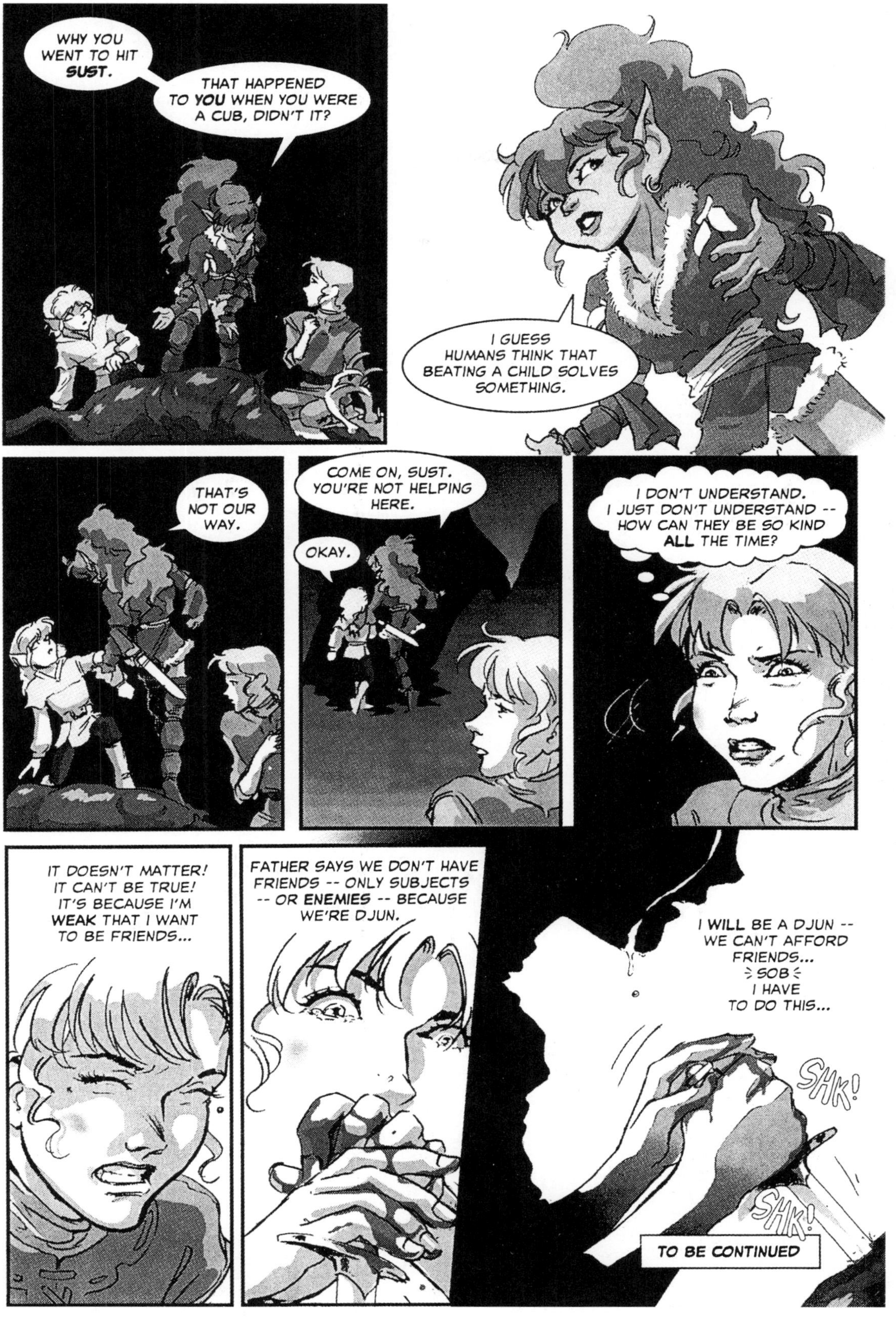

WHY YOU WENT TO HIT SUST.
THAT HAPPENED TO YOU WHEN YOU WERE A CUB, DIDN'T IT?
I GUESS HUMANS THINK THAT BEATING A CHILD SOLVES SOMETHING.
THAT'S NOT OUR WAY.
COME ON, SUST. YOU'RE NOT HELPING HERE.
OKAY.
I DON'T UNDERSTAND. I JUST DON'T UNDERSTAND -- HOW CAN THEY BE SO KIND ALL THE TIME?
IT DOESN'T MATTER! IT CAN'T BE TRUE! IT'S BECAUSE I'M WEAK THAT I WANT TO BE FRIENDS...
FATHER SAYS WE DON'T HAVE FRIENDS -- ONLY SUBJECTS -- OR ENEMIES -- BECAUSE WE'RE DJUN.
I WILL BE A DJUN -- WE CAN'T AFFORD FRIENDS... SOB I HAVE TO DO THIS...
SHK!
SHK!
TO BE CONTINUED

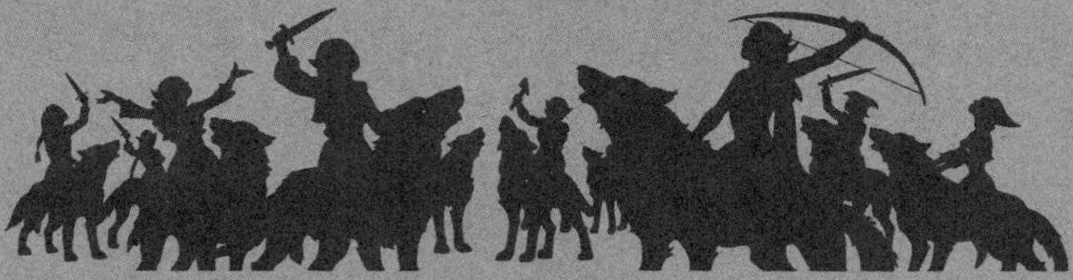

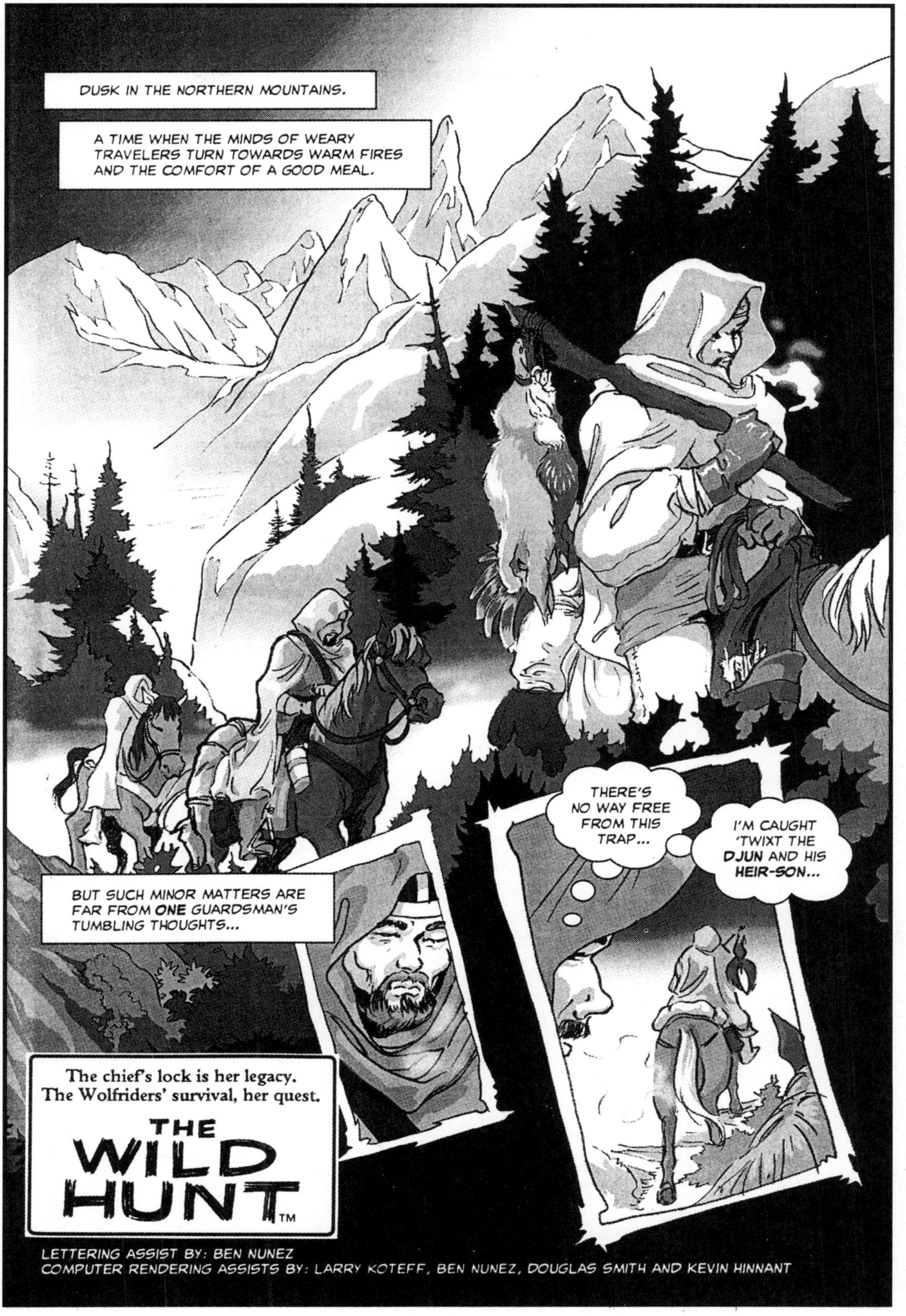

DUSK IN THE NORTHERN MOUNTAINS.
A TIME WHEN THE MINDS OF WEARY TRAVELERS TURN TOWARDS WARM FIRES AND THE COMFORT OF A GOOD MEAL.
BUT SUCH MINOR MATTERS ARE FAR FROM ONE GUARDSMAN'S TUMBLING THOUGHTS...
THERE'S NO WAY FREE FROM THIS TRAP...
I'M CAUGHT 'TWIXT THE DJUN AND HIS HEIR-SON...
The chief's lock is her legacy. The Wolfriders' survival, her quest.
THE WILD HUNT™
LETTERING ASSIST BY: BEN NUNEZ
COMPUTER RENDERING ASSISTS BY: LARRY KOTEFF, BEN NUNEZ, DOUGLAS SMITH AND KEVIN HINNANT

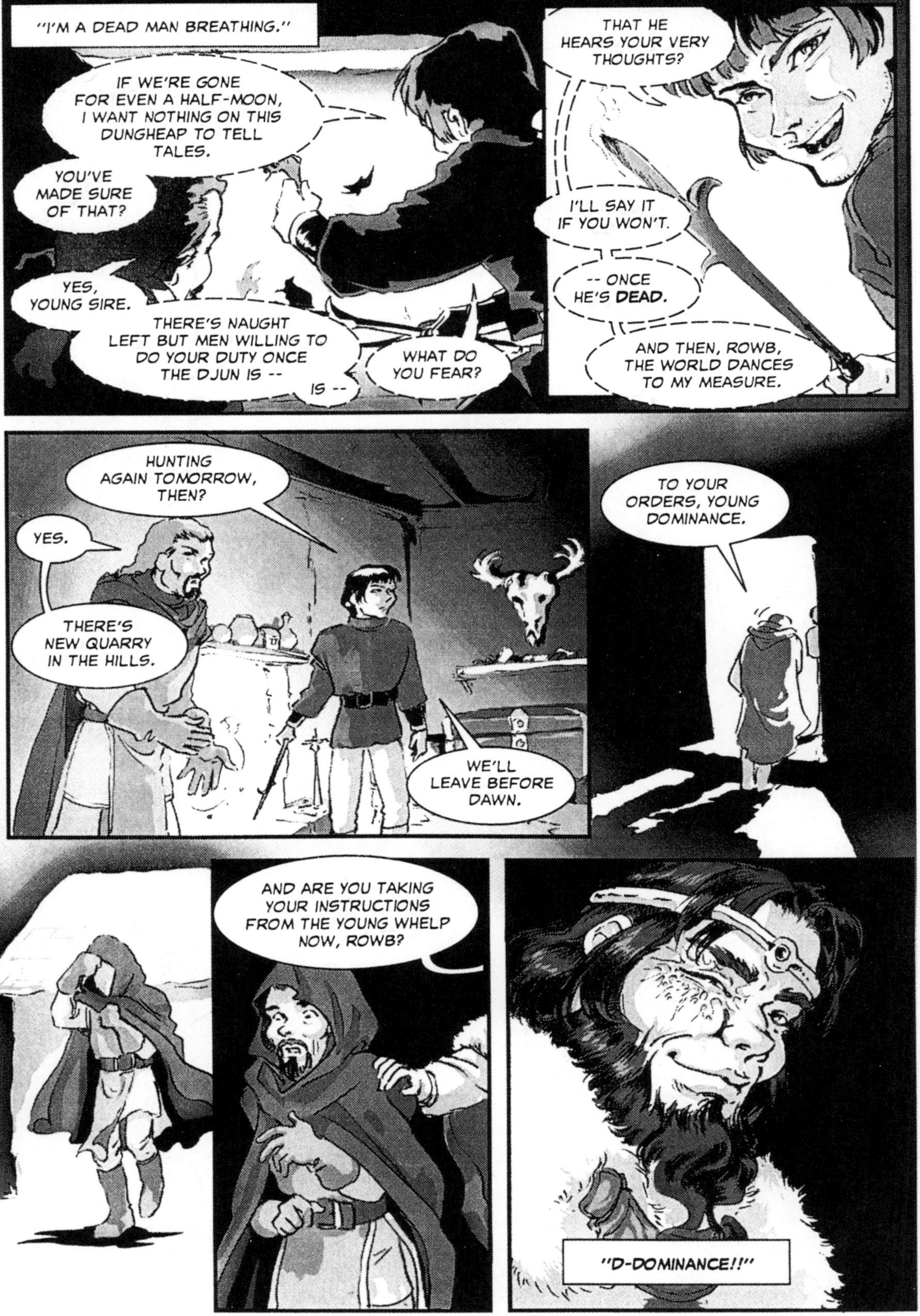
"I'M A DEAD MAN BREATHING."
IF WE'RE GONE FOR EVEN A HALF-MOON, I WANT NOTHING ON THIS DUNGHEAP TO TELL TALES.
YOU'VE MADE SURE OF THAT?
YES, YOUNG SIRE.
THERE'S NAUGHT LEFT BUT MEN WILLING TO DO YOUR DUTY ONCE THE DJUN IS --
IS --
WHAT DO YOU FEAR?
THAT HE HEARS YOUR VERY THOUGHTS?
I'LL SAY IT IF YOU WON'T.
-- ONCE HE'S **DEAD.**
AND THEN, ROWB, THE WORLD DANCES TO MY MEASURE.
HUNTING AGAIN TOMORROW, THEN?
YES.
THERE'S NEW QUARRY IN THE HILLS.
WE'LL LEAVE BEFORE DAWN.
TO YOUR ORDERS, YOUNG DOMINANCE.
AND ARE YOU TAKING YOUR INSTRUCTIONS FROM THE YOUNG WHELP NOW, ROWB?
"D-DOMINANCE!!"

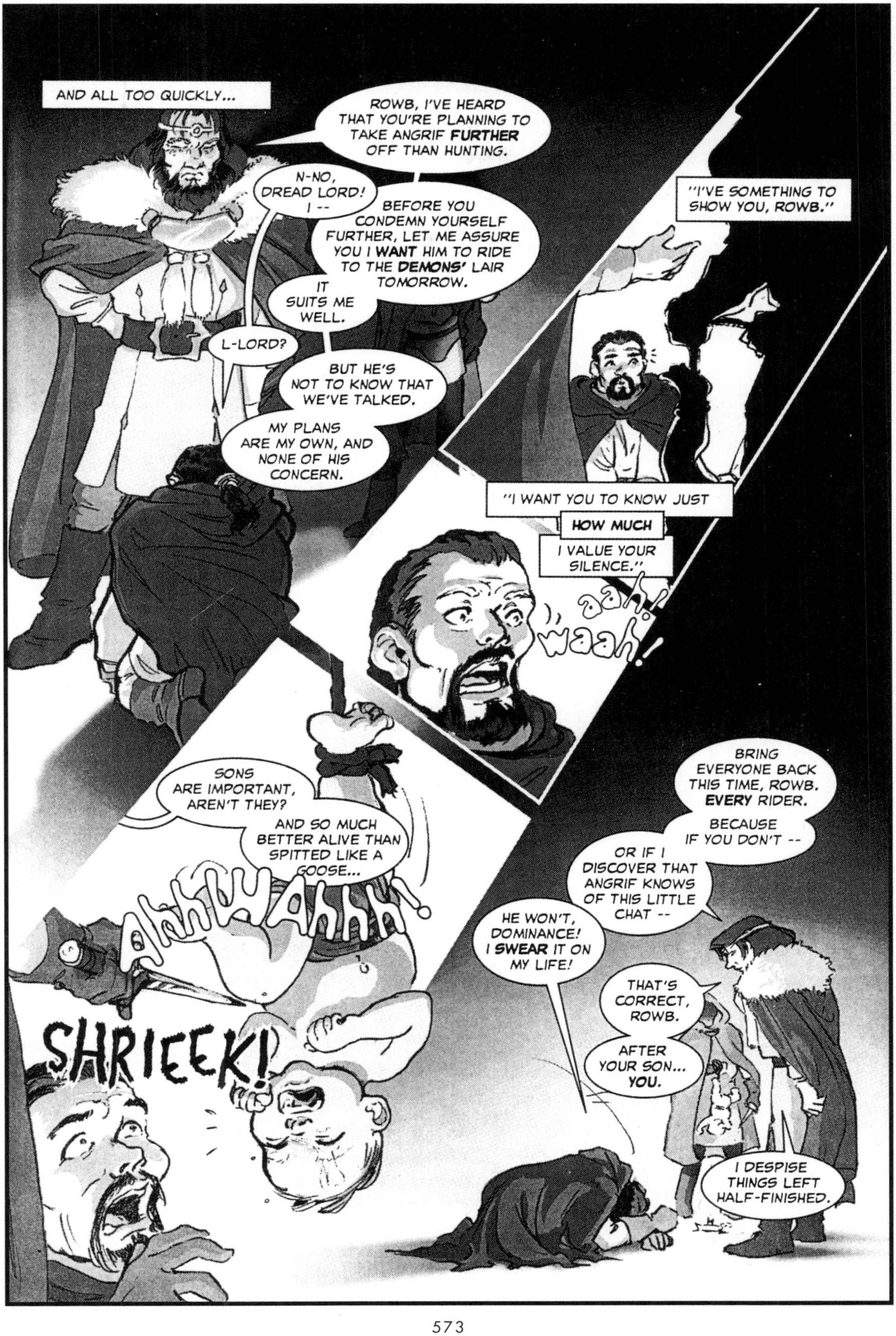
AND ALL TOO QUICKLY...
ROWB, I'VE HEARD THAT YOU'RE PLANNING TO TAKE ANGRIF FURTHER OFF THAN HUNTING.
N-NO, DREAD LORD! I --
BEFORE YOU CONDEMN YOURSELF FURTHER, LET ME ASSURE YOU I WANT HIM TO RIDE TO THE DEMONS' LAIR TOMORROW.
IT SUITS ME WELL.
L-LORD?
BUT HE'S NOT TO KNOW THAT WE'VE TALKED.
MY PLANS ARE MY OWN, AND NONE OF HIS CONCERN.
"I'VE SOMETHING TO SHOW YOU, ROWB."
"I WANT YOU TO KNOW JUST
HOW MUCH
I VALUE YOUR SILENCE."
WAAH! WAAH!
SONS ARE IMPORTANT, AREN'T THEY?
AND SO MUCH BETTER ALIVE THAN SPITTED LIKE A GOOSE...
AHHWAHHH!
SHRIEEK!
BRING EVERYONE BACK THIS TIME, ROWB. EVERY RIDER.
BECAUSE IF YOU DON'T --
OR IF I DISCOVER THAT ANGRIF KNOWS OF THIS LITTLE CHAT --
HE WON'T, DOMINANCE! I SWEAR IT ON MY LIFE!
THAT'S CORRECT, ROWB.
AFTER YOUR SON... YOU.
I DESPISE THINGS LEFT HALF-FINISHED.

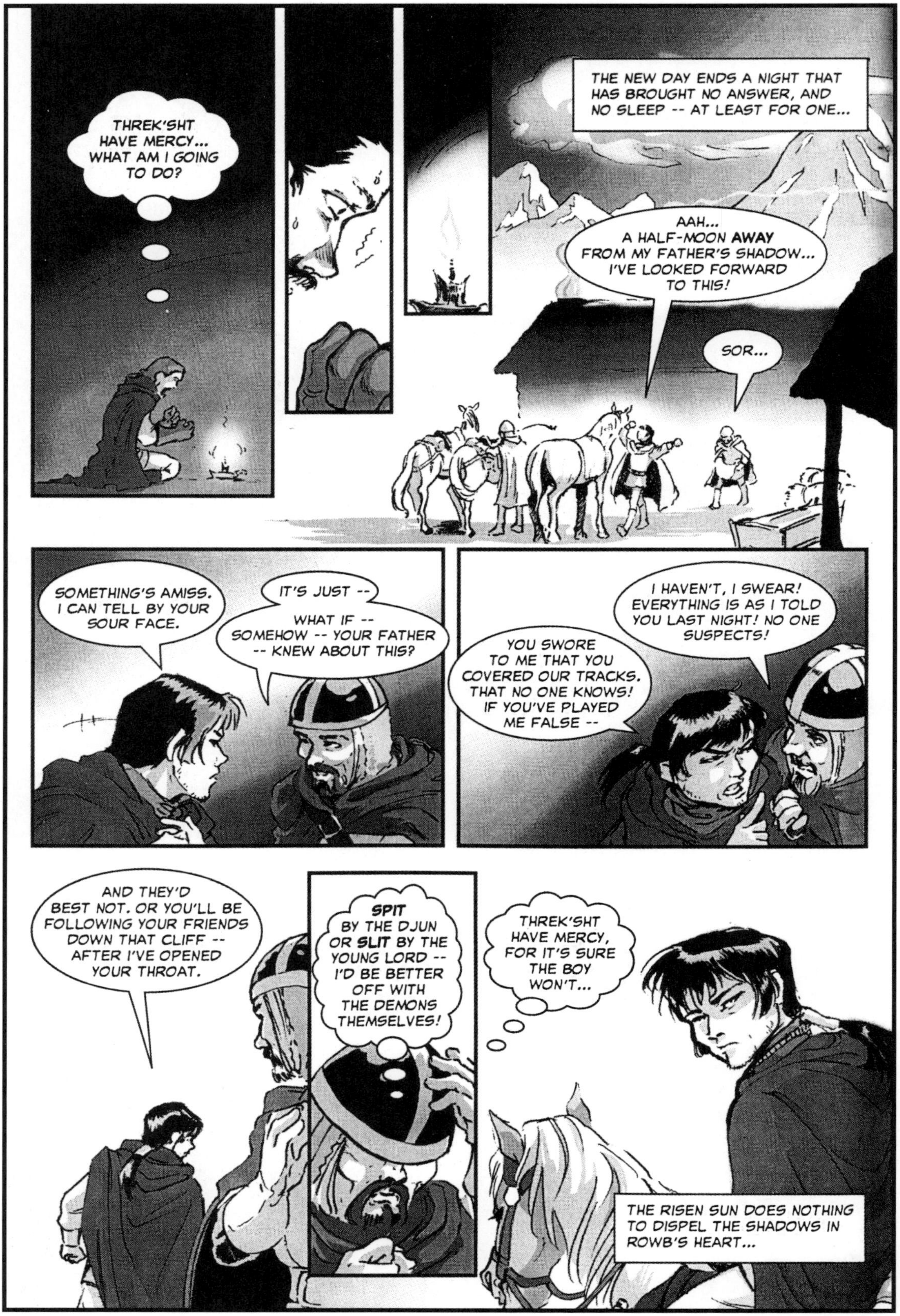

THREK'SHT HAVE MERCY... WHAT AM I GOING TO DO?
THE NEW DAY ENDS A NIGHT THAT HAS BROUGHT NO ANSWER, AND NO SLEEP -- AT LEAST FOR ONE...
AAH... A HALF-MOON AWAY FROM MY FATHER'S SHADOW... I'VE LOOKED FORWARD TO THIS!
SOR...
SOMETHING'S AMISS. I CAN TELL BY YOUR SOUR FACE.
IT'S JUST --
WHAT IF -- SOMEHOW -- YOUR FATHER -- KNEW ABOUT THIS?
YOU SWORE TO ME THAT YOU COVERED OUR TRACKS. THAT NO ONE KNOWS! IF YOU'VE PLAYED ME FALSE --
I HAVEN'T, I SWEAR! EVERYTHING IS AS I TOLD YOU LAST NIGHT! NO ONE SUSPECTS!
AND THEY'D BEST NOT. OR YOU'LL BE FOLLOWING YOUR FRIENDS DOWN THAT CLIFF -- AFTER I'VE OPENED YOUR THROAT.
SPIT BY THE DJUN OR SLIT BY THE YOUNG LORD -- I'D BE BETTER OFF WITH THE DEMONS THEMSELVES!
THREK'SHT HAVE MERCY, FOR IT'S SURE THE BOY WON'T...
THE RISEN SUN DOES NOTHING TO DISPEL THE SHADOWS IN ROWB'S HEART...

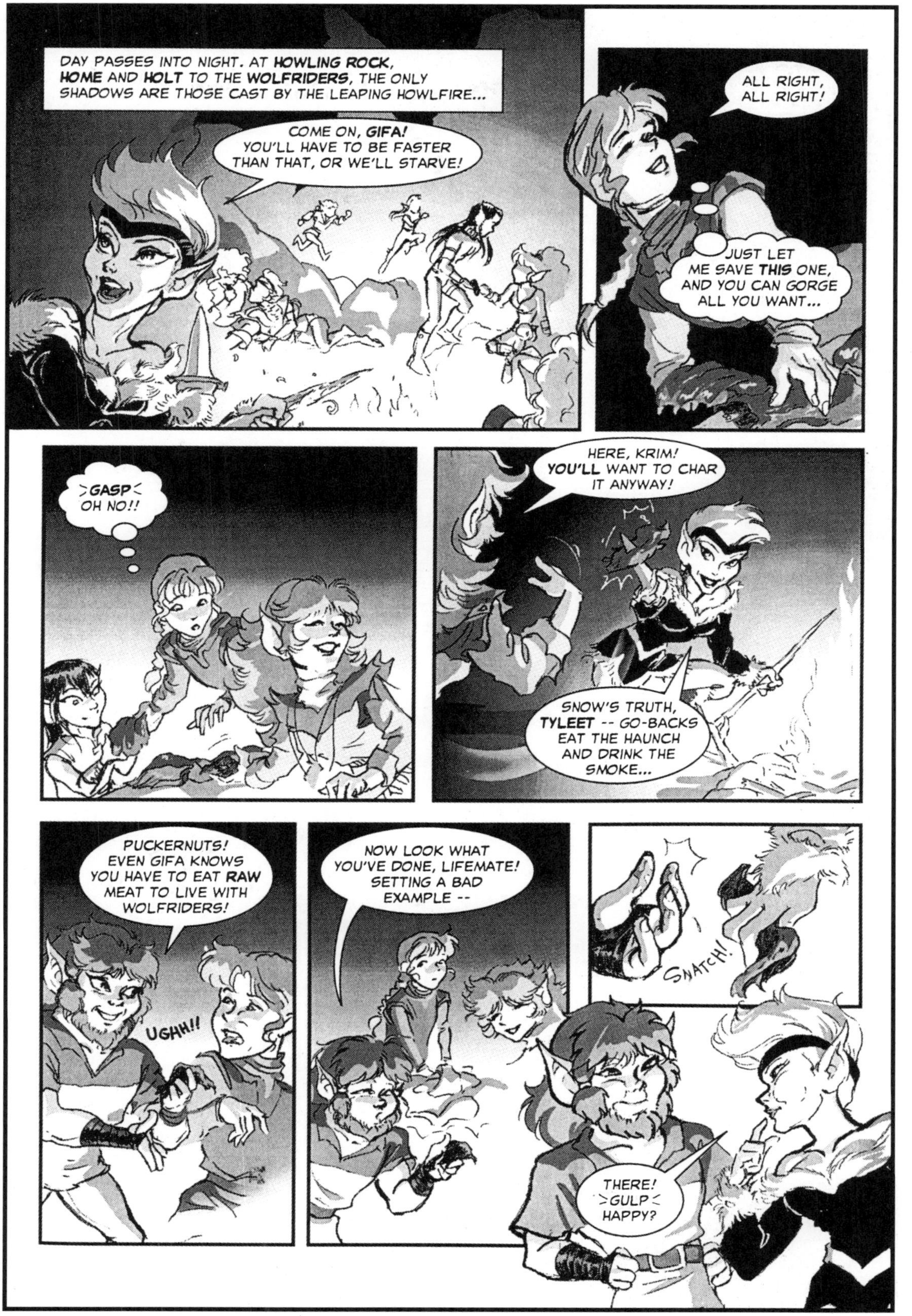
DAY PASSES INTO NIGHT. AT **HOWLING ROCK**, **HOME** AND **HOLT** TO THE **WOLFRIDERS**, THE ONLY SHADOWS ARE THOSE CAST BY THE LEAPING HOWLFIRE...
COME ON, **GIFA!** YOU'LL HAVE TO BE FASTER THAN THAT, OR WE'LL STARVE!
ALL RIGHT, ALL RIGHT!
JUST LET ME SAVE **THIS** ONE, AND YOU CAN GORGE ALL YOU WANT...
>GASP< OH NO!!
HERE, KRIM! **YOU'LL** WANT TO CHAR IT ANYWAY!
SNOW'S TRUTH, **TYLEET** -- GO-BACKS EAT THE HAUNCH AND DRINK THE SMOKE...
PUCKERNUTS! EVEN GIFA KNOWS YOU HAVE TO EAT **RAW** MEAT TO LIVE WITH WOLFRIDERS!
UGHH!!
NOW LOOK WHAT YOU'VE DONE, LIFEMATE! SETTING A BAD EXAMPLE --
SNATCH!
THERE! >GULP< HAPPY?

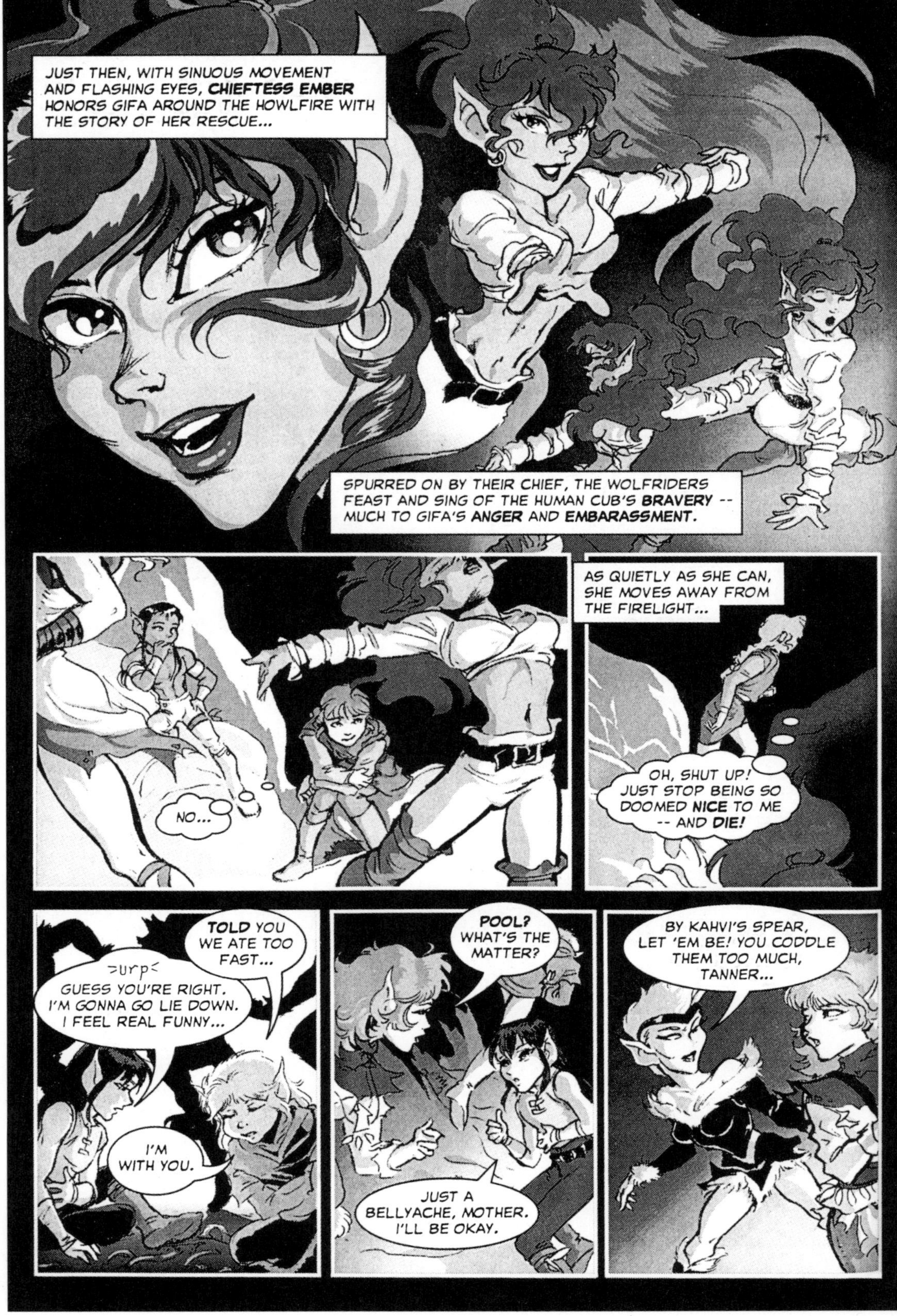

JUST THEN, WITH SINUOUS MOVEMENT AND FLASHING EYES, **CHIEFTESS EMBER** HONORS GIFA AROUND THE HOWLFIRE WITH THE STORY OF HER RESCUE...
SPURRED ON BY THEIR CHIEF, THE WOLFRIDERS FEAST AND SING OF THE HUMAN CUB'S **BRAVERY** -- MUCH TO GIFA'S **ANGER** AND **EMBARASSMENT.**
NO...
AS QUIETLY AS SHE CAN, SHE MOVES AWAY FROM THE FIRELIGHT...
OH, SHUT UP! JUST STOP BEING SO DOOMED **NICE** TO ME -- AND **DIE!**
TOLD YOU WE ATE TOO FAST...
>URP< GUESS YOU'RE RIGHT. I'M GONNA GO LIE DOWN. I FEEL REAL FUNNY...
I'M WITH YOU.
POOL? WHAT'S THE MATTER?
JUST A BELLYACHE, MOTHER. I'LL BE OKAY.
BY KAHVI'S SPEAR, LET 'EM BE! YOU CODDLE THEM TOO MUCH, TANNER...

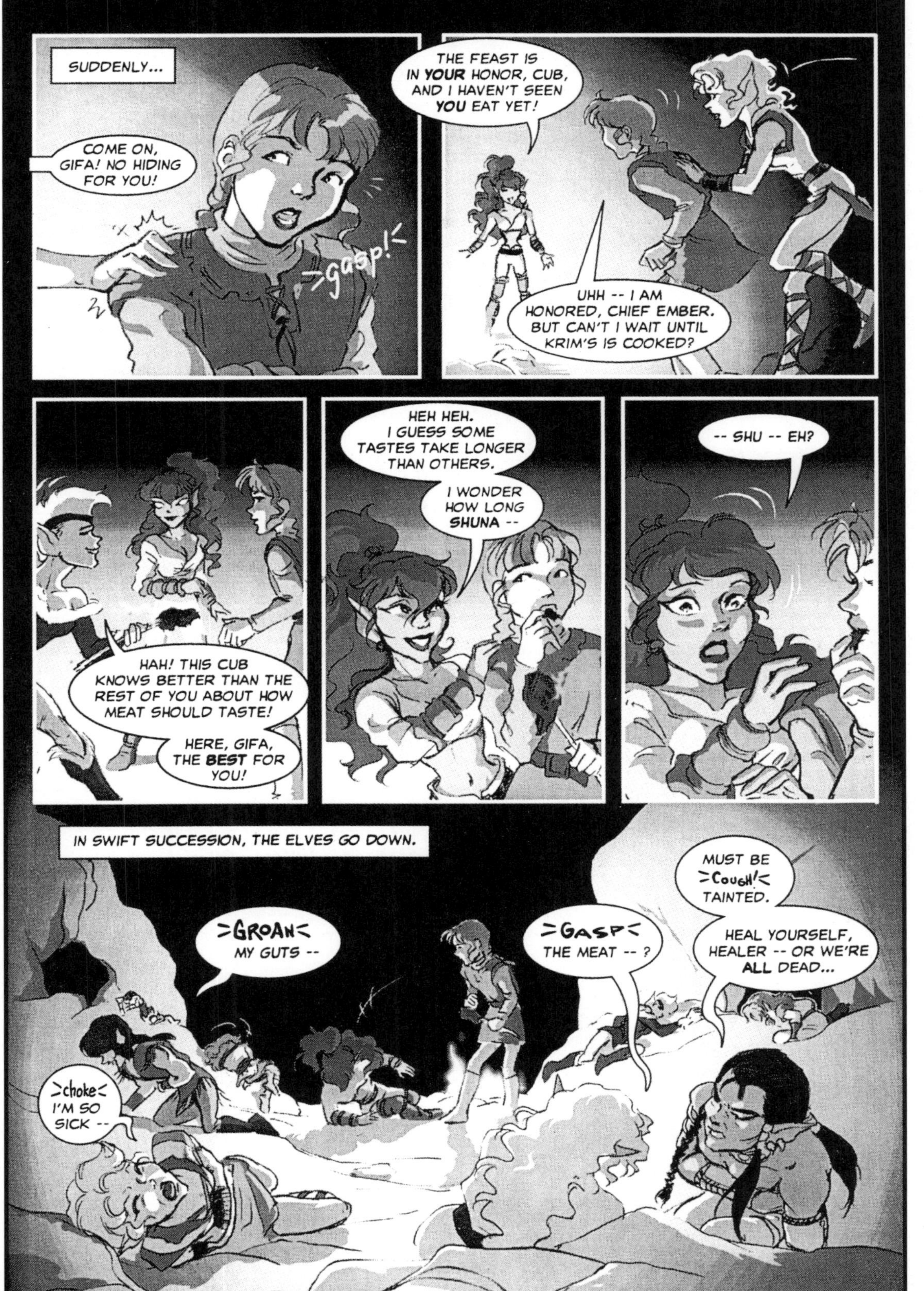
SUDDENLY...
COME ON, GIFA! NO HIDING FOR YOU!
>gasp!<
THE FEAST IS IN YOUR HONOR, CUB, AND I HAVEN'T SEEN YOU EAT YET!
UHH -- I AM HONORED, CHIEF EMBER. BUT CAN'T I WAIT UNTIL KRIM'S IS COOKED?
HAH! THIS CUB KNOWS BETTER THAN THE REST OF YOU ABOUT HOW MEAT SHOULD TASTE!
HERE, GIFA, THE BEST FOR YOU!
HEH HEH. I GUESS SOME TASTES TAKE LONGER THAN OTHERS.
I WONDER HOW LONG SHUNA --
-- SHU -- EH?
IN SWIFT SUCCESSION, THE ELVES GO DOWN.
>GROAN< MY GUTS --
>GASP< THE MEAT -- ?
MUST BE >COUGH!< TAINTED.
HEAL YOURSELF, HEALER -- OR WE'RE ALL DEAD...
>choke< I'M SO SICK --

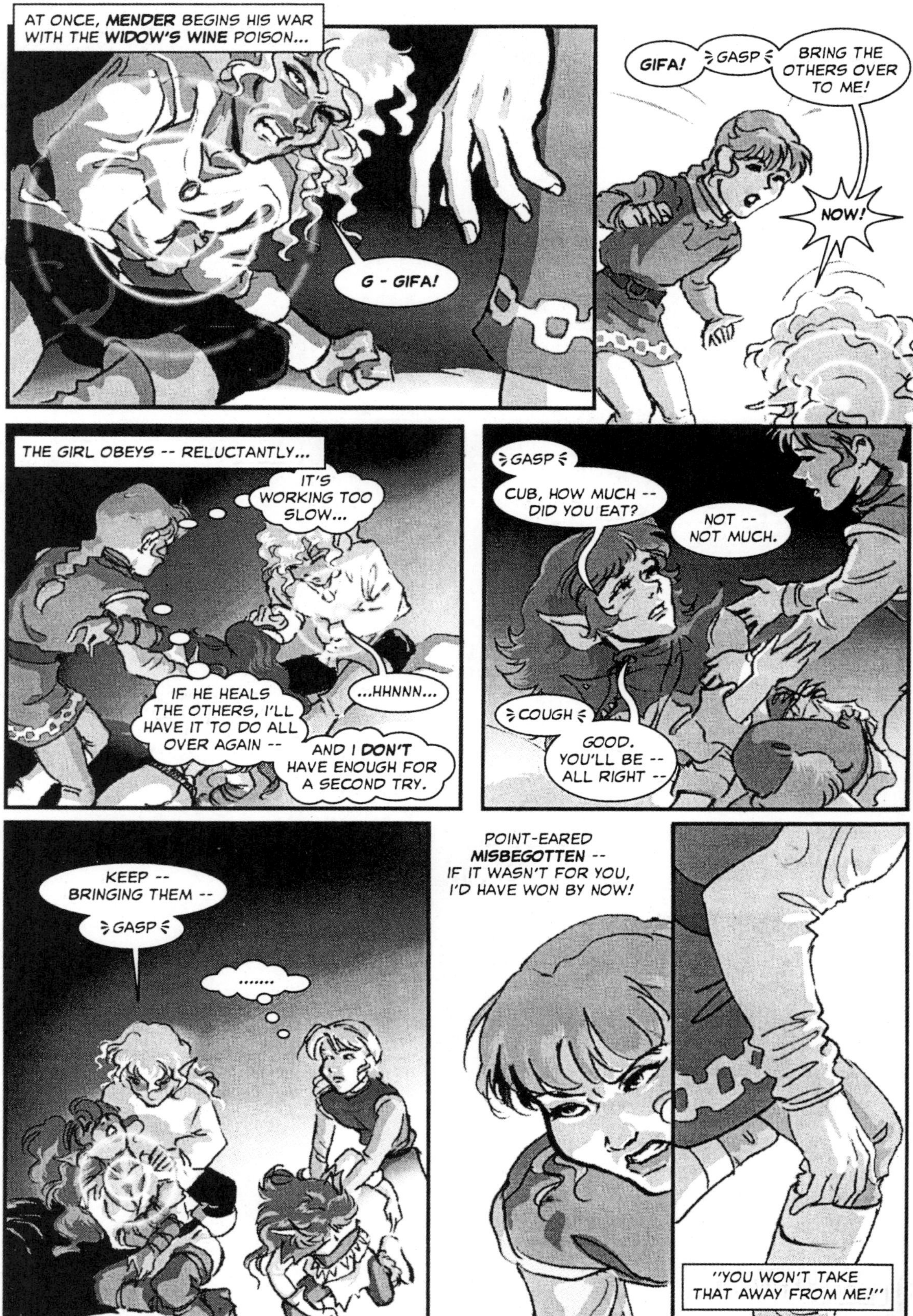
AT ONCE, MENDER BEGINS HIS WAR WITH THE WIDOW'S WINE POISON...
G - GIFA!
GIFA!
GASP
BRING THE OTHERS OVER TO ME!
NOW!
THE GIRL OBEYS -- RELUCTANTLY...
IT'S WORKING TOO SLOW...
IF HE HEALS THE OTHERS, I'LL HAVE IT TO DO ALL OVER AGAIN --
...HHNNN...
AND I DON'T HAVE ENOUGH FOR A SECOND TRY.
GASP
CUB, HOW MUCH -- DID YOU EAT?
NOT -- NOT MUCH.
COUGH
GOOD. YOU'LL BE -- ALL RIGHT --
KEEP -- BRINGING THEM --
GASP
....
POINT-EARED MISBEGOTTEN -- IF IT WASN'T FOR YOU, I'D HAVE WON BY NOW!
"YOU WON'T TAKE THAT AWAY FROM ME!"

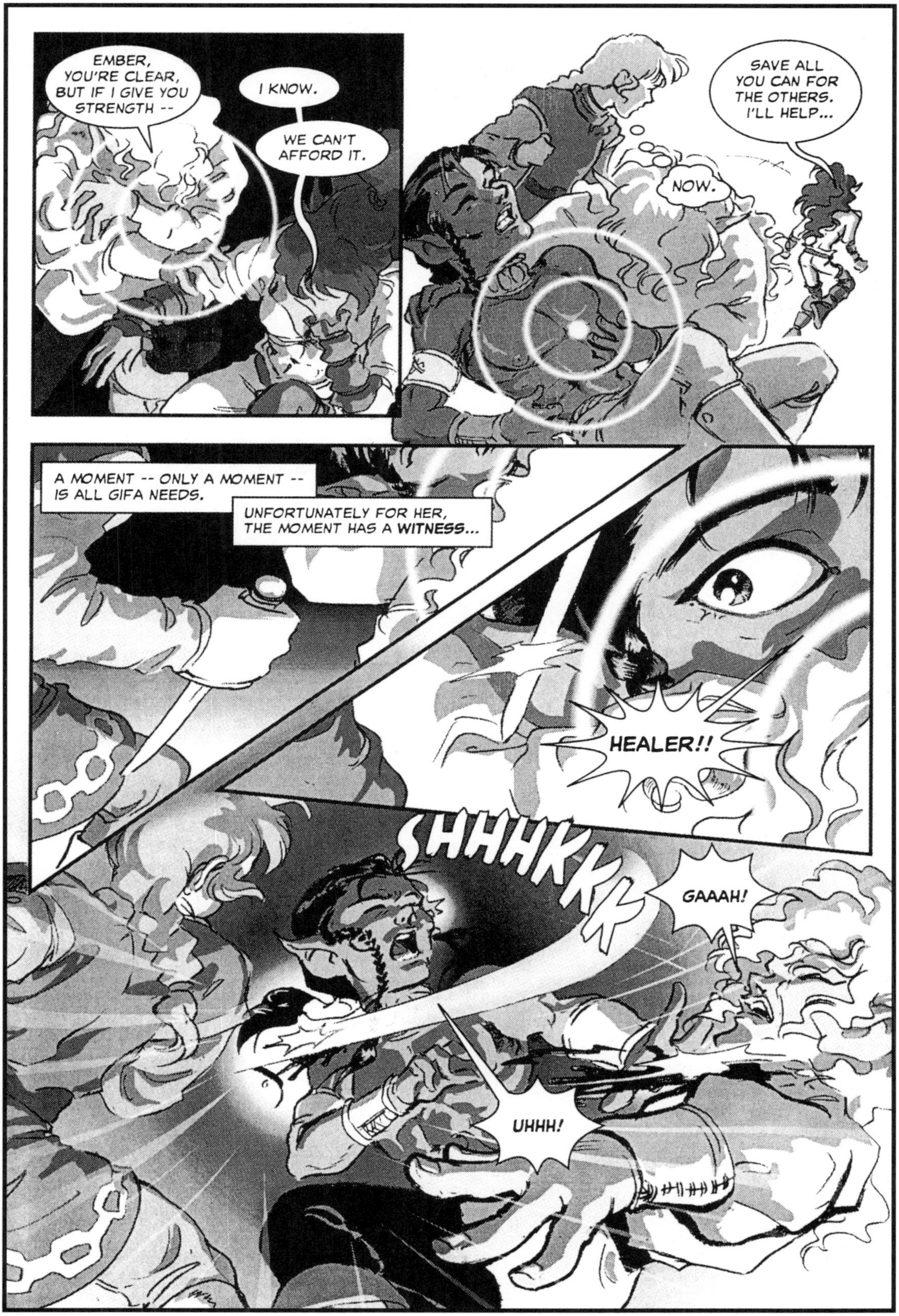

EMBER, YOU'RE CLEAR, BUT IF I GIVE YOU STRENGTH --
I KNOW.
WE CAN'T AFFORD IT.
NOW.
SAVE ALL YOU CAN FOR THE OTHERS. I'LL HELP...
A MOMENT -- ONLY A MOMENT -- IS ALL GIFA NEEDS.
UNFORTUNATELY FOR HER, THE MOMENT HAS A WITNESS...
HEALER!!
SHHHKKK
GAAAH!
UHHH!

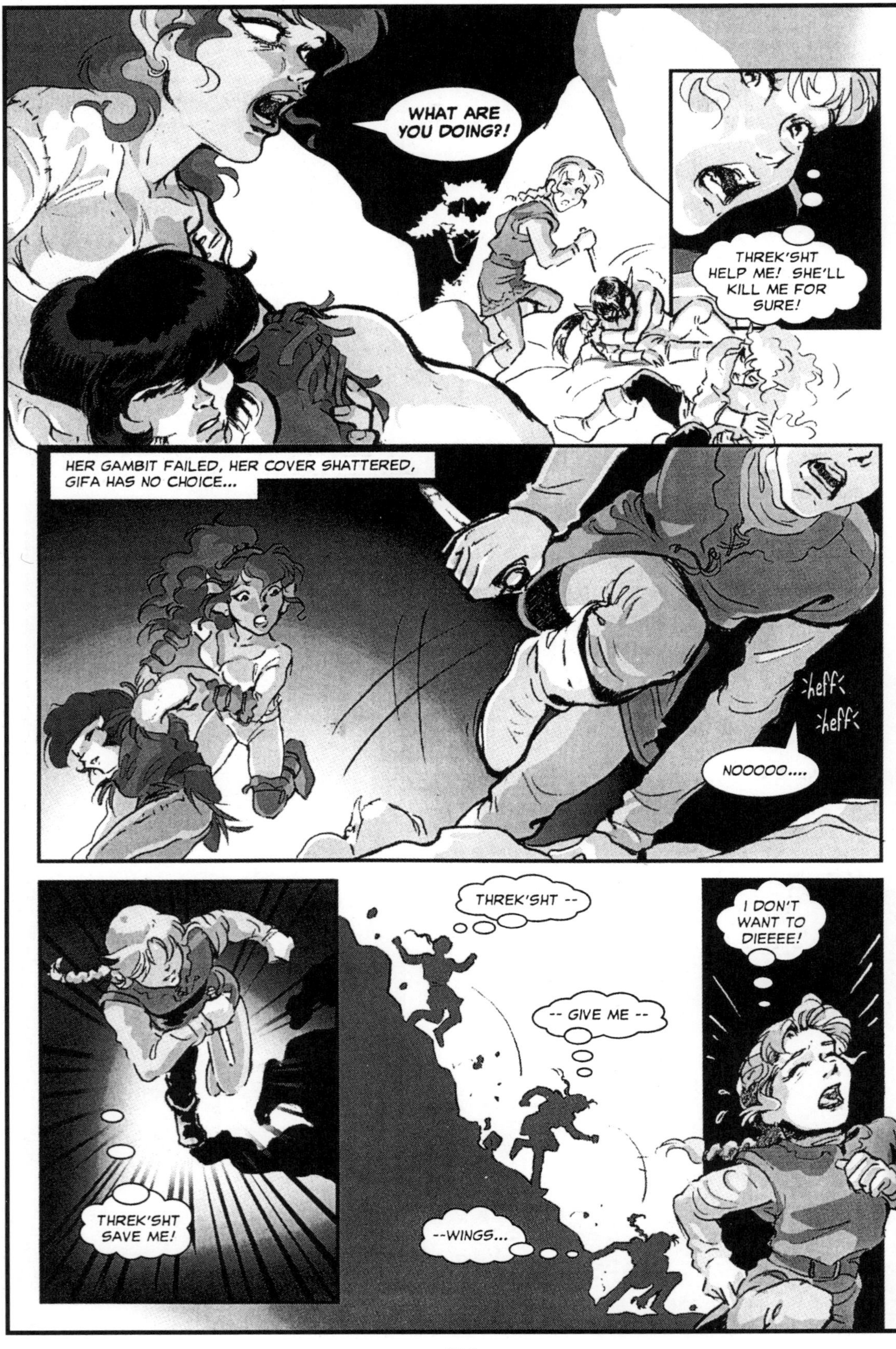
WHAT ARE YOU DOING?!
THREK'SHT HELP ME! SHE'LL KILL ME FOR SURE!
HER GAMBIT FAILED, HER COVER SHATTERED, GIFA HAS NO CHOICE...
heff
heff
NOOOOO....
THREK'SHT SAVE ME!
THREK'SHT --
-- GIVE ME --
--WINGS...
I DON'T WANT TO DIEEEE!

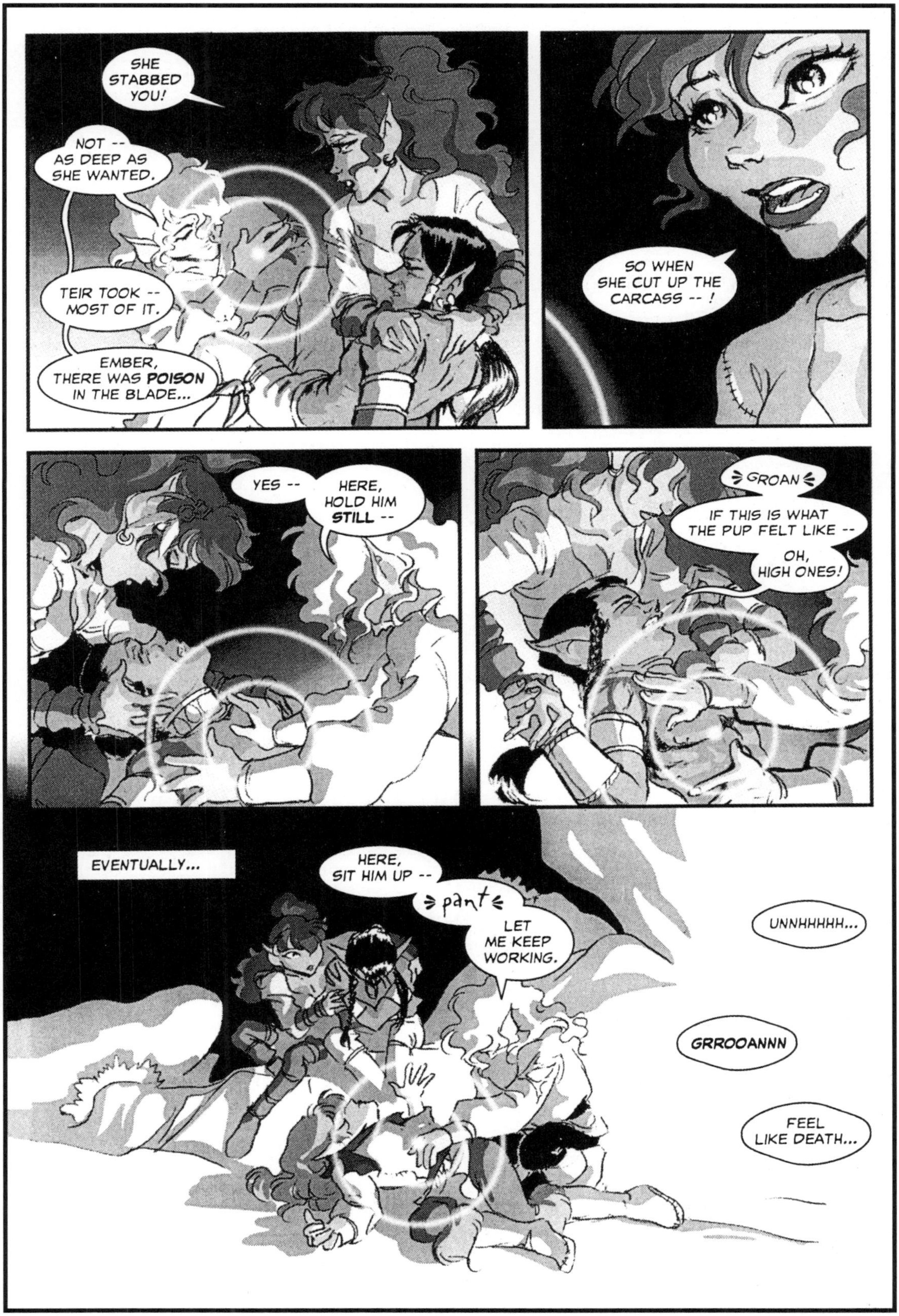
SHE STABBED YOU!
NOT -- AS DEEP AS SHE WANTED.
TEIR TOOK -- MOST OF IT.
EMBER, THERE WAS POISON IN THE BLADE...
SO WHEN SHE CUT UP THE CARCASS -- !
YES --
HERE, HOLD HIM STILL --
GROAN
IF THIS IS WHAT THE PUP FELT LIKE --
OH, HIGH ONES!
EVENTUALLY...
HERE, SIT HIM UP --
pant
LET ME KEEP WORKING.
UNNHHHHH...
GRROOANNN
FEEL LIKE DEATH...

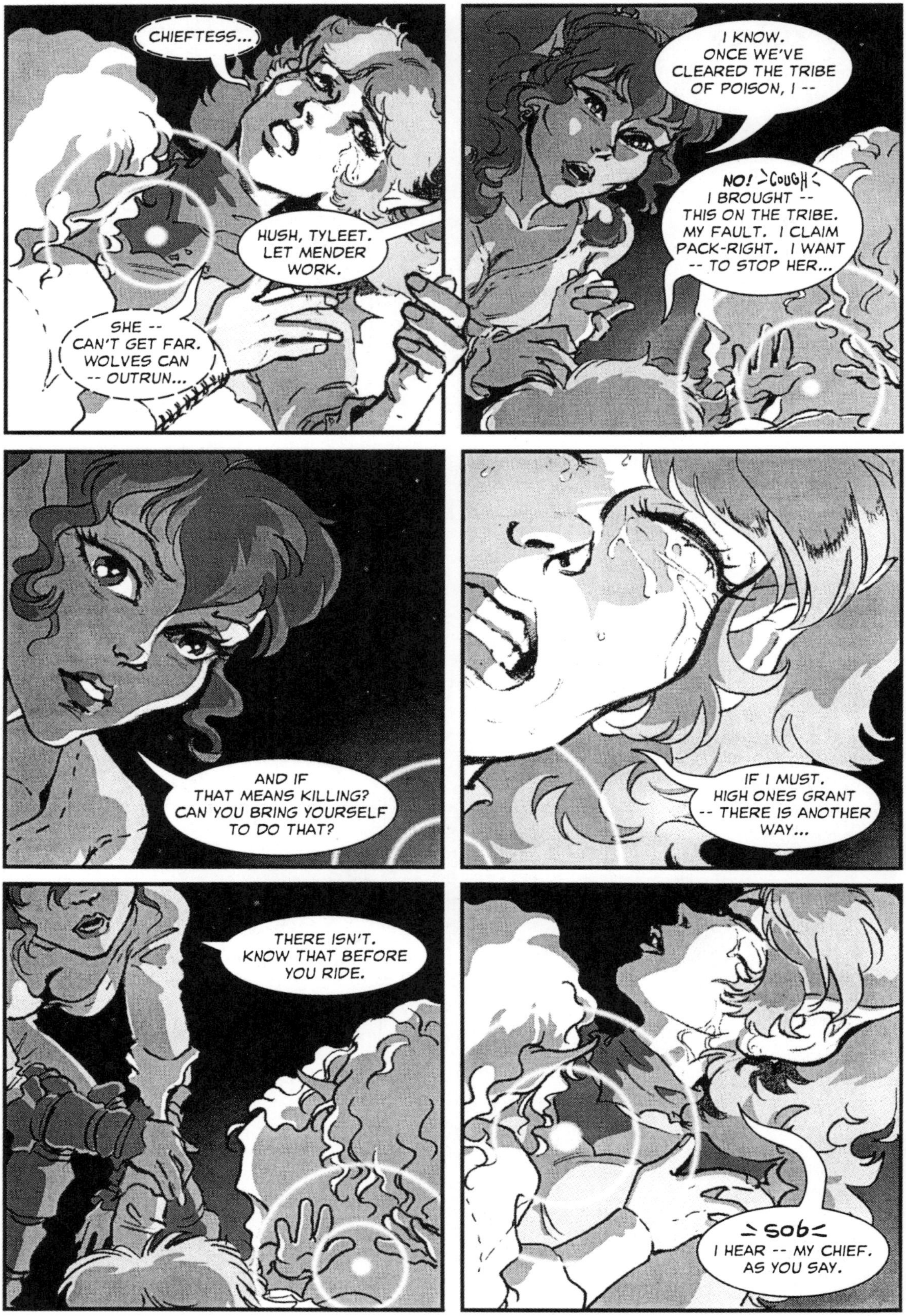
CHIEFTESS...
HUSH, TYLEET. LET MENDER WORK.
SHE -- CAN'T GET FAR. WOLVES CAN -- OUTRUN...
I KNOW. ONCE WE'VE CLEARED THE TRIBE OF POISON, I --
NO! COUGH I BROUGHT -- THIS ON THE TRIBE. MY FAULT. I CLAIM PACK-RIGHT. I WANT -- TO STOP HER...
AND IF THAT MEANS KILLING? CAN YOU BRING YOURSELF TO DO THAT?
IF I MUST. HIGH ONES GRANT -- THERE IS ANOTHER WAY...
THERE ISN'T. KNOW THAT BEFORE YOU RIDE.
SOB I HEAR -- MY CHIEF. AS YOU SAY.

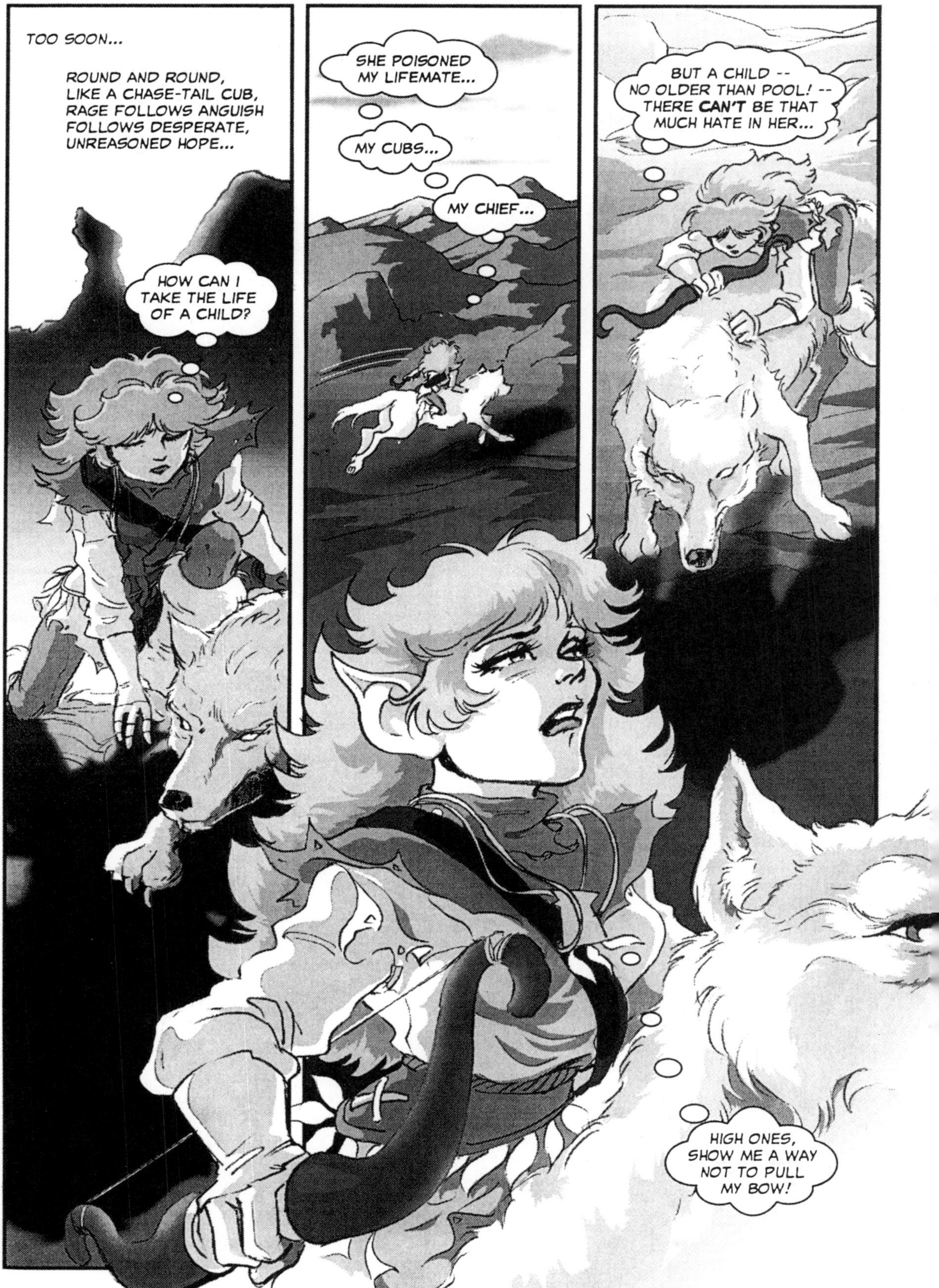
TOO SOON...
ROUND AND ROUND, LIKE A CHASE-TAIL CUB, RAGE FOLLOWS ANGUISH FOLLOWS DESPERATE, UNREASONED HOPE...
HOW CAN I TAKE THE LIFE OF A CHILD?
SHE POISONED MY LIFEMATE...
MY CUBS...
MY CHIEF...
BUT A CHILD -- NO OLDER THAN POOL! -- THERE **CAN'T** BE THAT MUCH HATE IN HER...
HIGH ONES, SHOW ME A WAY NOT TO PULL MY BOW!

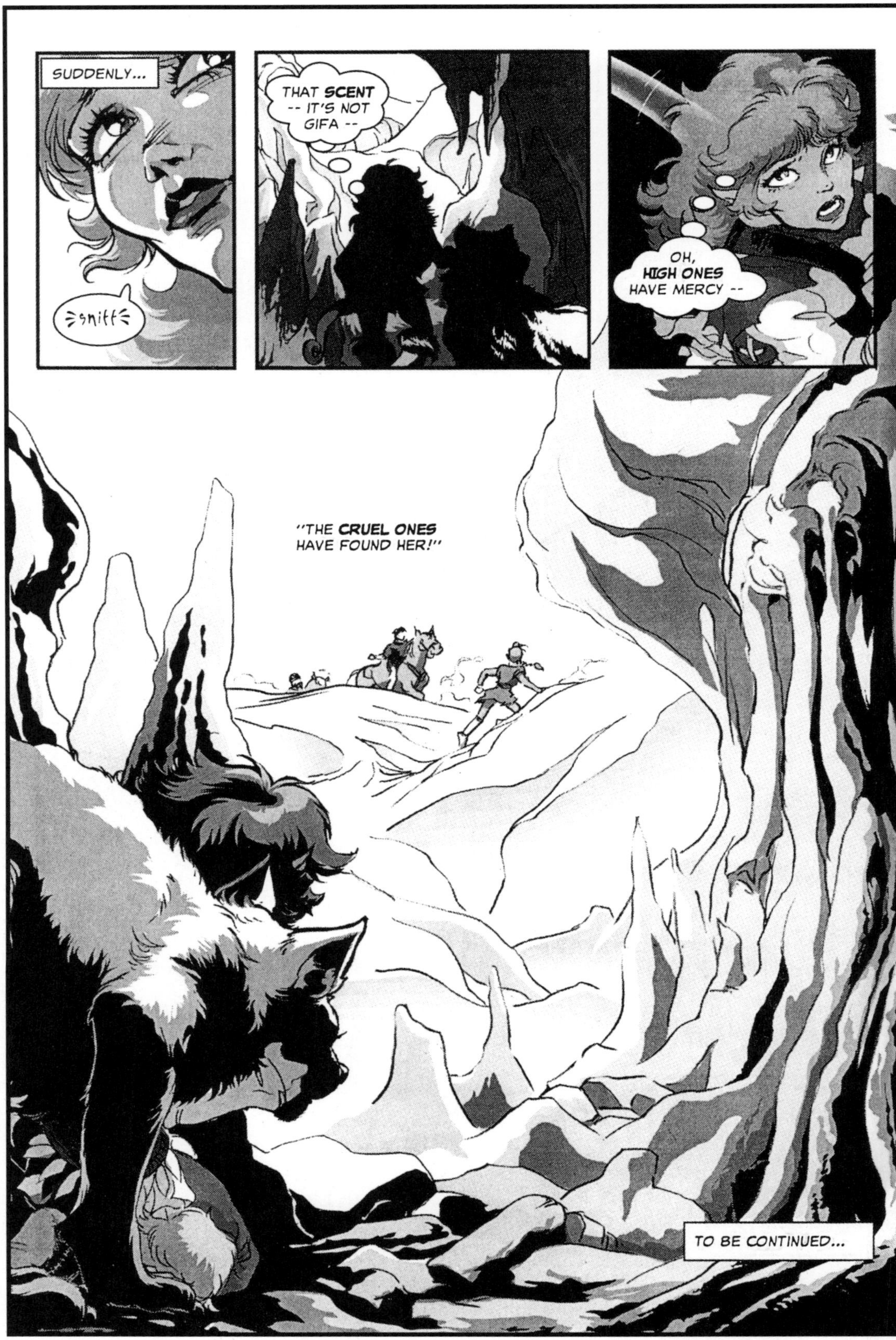
SUDDENLY...
snitt
THAT SCENT -- IT'S NOT GIFA --
OH, HIGH ONES HAVE MERCY --
"THE CRUEL ONES HAVE FOUND HER!"
TO BE CONTINUED...

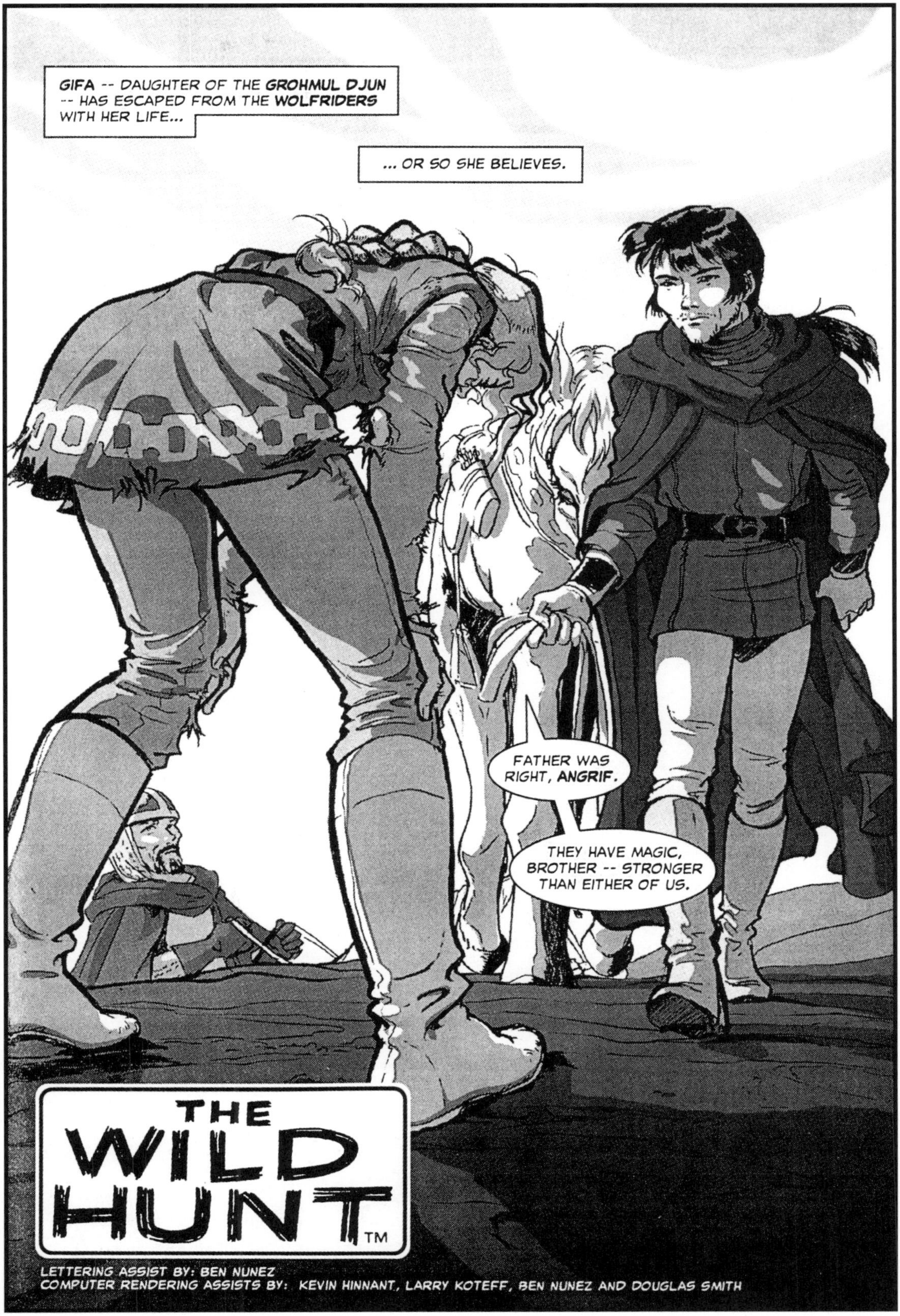
GIFA -- DAUGHTER OF THE GROHMUL DJUN -- HAS ESCAPED FROM THE WOLFRIDERS WITH HER LIFE...
... OR SO SHE BELIEVES.
FATHER WAS RIGHT, ANGRIF.
THEY HAVE MAGIC, BROTHER -- STRONGER THAN EITHER OF US.
THE WILD HUNT™
LETTERING ASSIST BY: BEN NUNEZ
COMPUTER RENDERING ASSISTS BY: KEVIN HINNANT, LARRY KOTEFF, BEN NUNEZ AND DOUGLAS SMITH

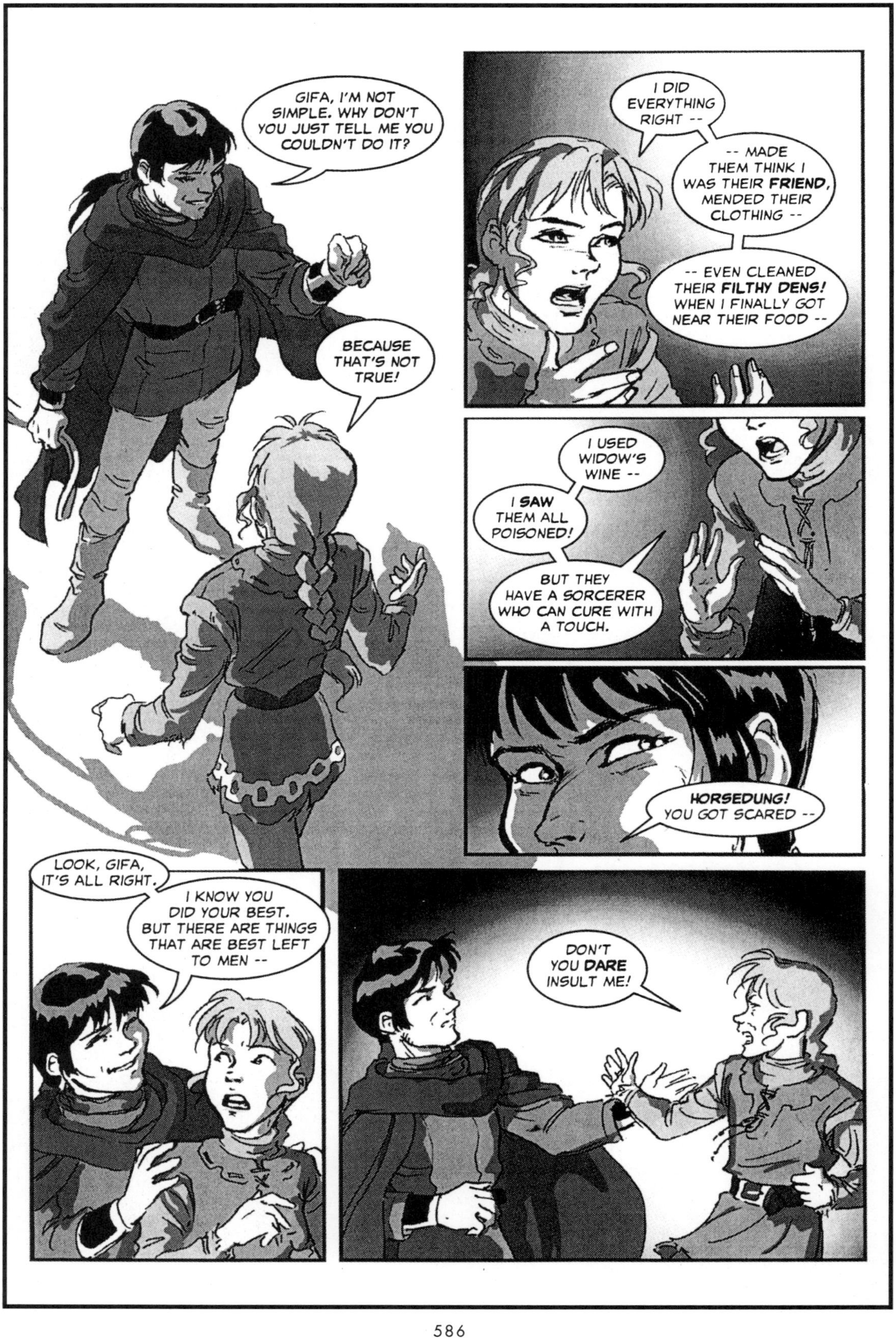
GIFA, I'M NOT SIMPLE. WHY DON'T YOU JUST TELL ME YOU COULDN'T DO IT?
BECAUSE THAT'S NOT TRUE!
I DID EVERYTHING RIGHT --
-- MADE THEM THINK I WAS THEIR FRIEND, MENDED THEIR CLOTHING --
-- EVEN CLEANED THEIR FILTHY DENS! WHEN I FINALLY GOT NEAR THEIR FOOD --
I USED WIDOW'S WINE --
I SAW THEM ALL POISONED!
BUT THEY HAVE A SORCERER WHO CAN CURE WITH A TOUCH.
HORSEDUNG! YOU GOT SCARED --
LOOK, GIFA, IT'S ALL RIGHT.
I KNOW YOU DID YOUR BEST. BUT THERE ARE THINGS THAT ARE BEST LEFT TO MEN --
DON'T YOU DARE INSULT ME!

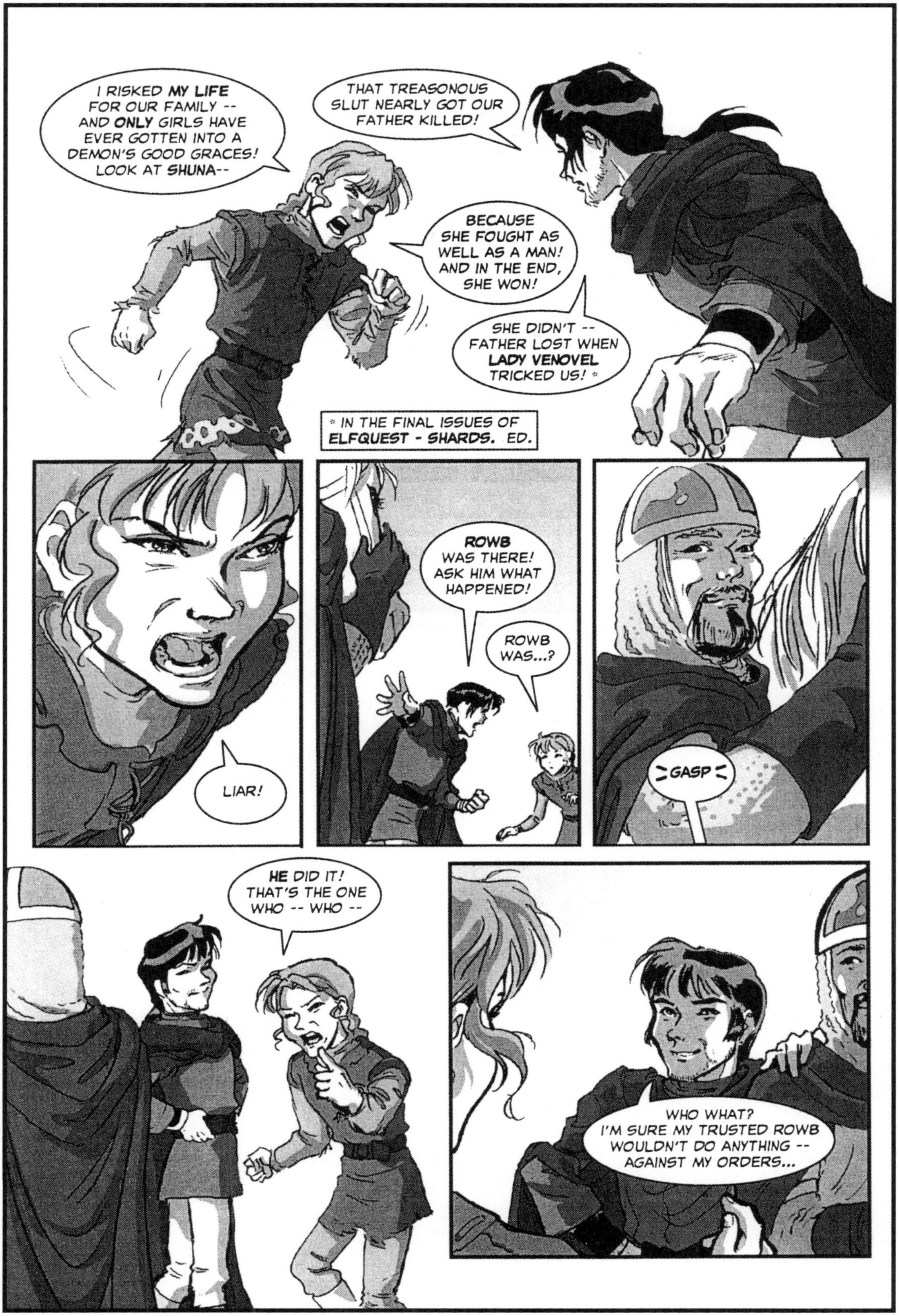
I RISKED MY LIFE FOR OUR FAMILY -- AND ONLY GIRLS HAVE EVER GOTTEN INTO A DEMON'S GOOD GRACES! LOOK AT SHUNA--
THAT TREASONOUS SLUT NEARLY GOT OUR FATHER KILLED!
BECAUSE SHE FOUGHT AS WELL AS A MAN! AND IN THE END, SHE WON!
SHE DIDN'T -- FATHER LOST WHEN LADY VENOVEL TRICKED US! *
* IN THE FINAL ISSUES OF ELFQUEST - SHARDS. ED.
LIAR!
ROWB WAS THERE! ASK HIM WHAT HAPPENED!
ROWB WAS...?
GASP
HE DID IT! THAT'S THE ONE WHO -- WHO --
WHO WHAT? I'M SURE MY TRUSTED ROWB WOULDN'T DO ANYTHING -- AGAINST MY ORDERS...

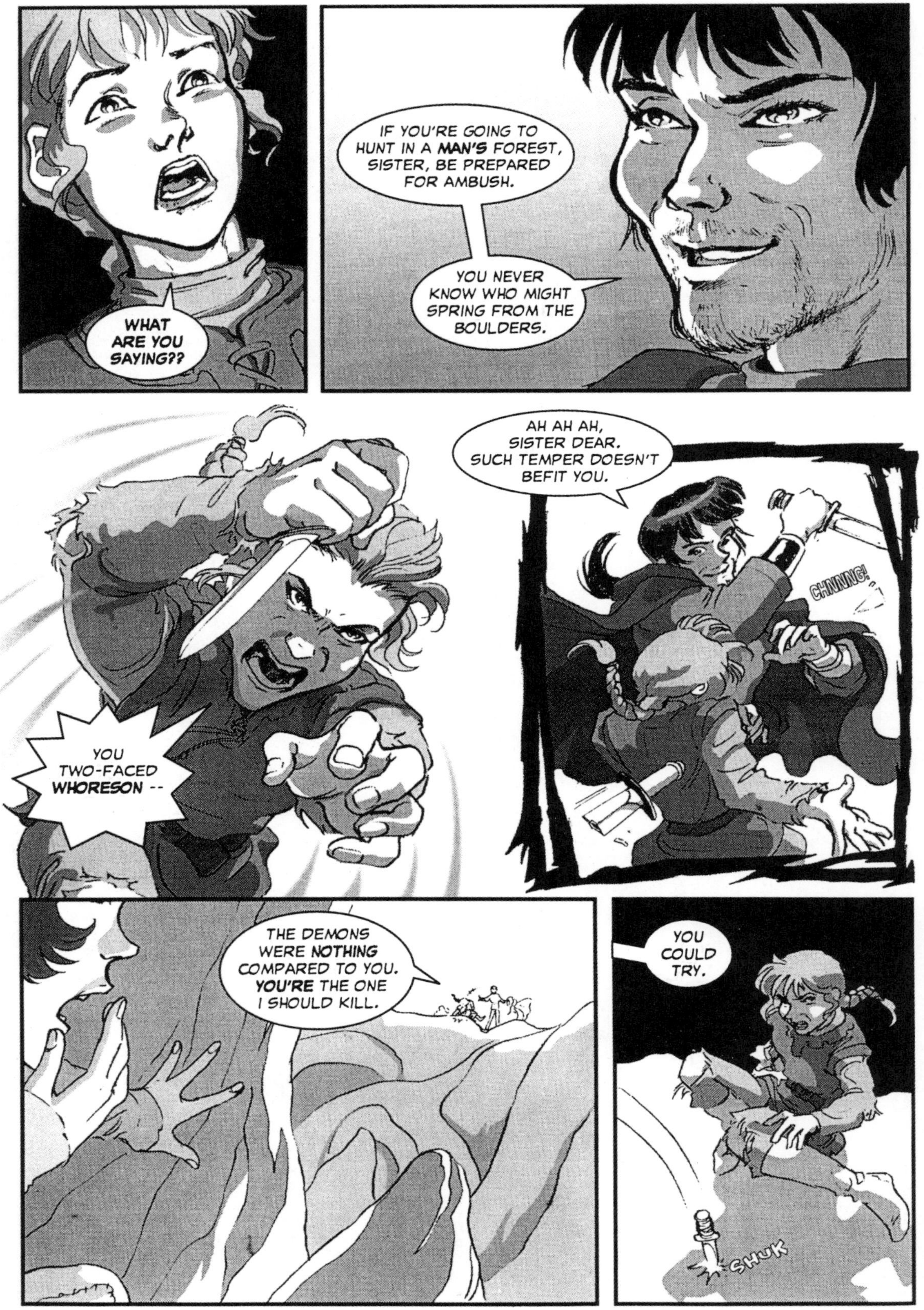
WHAT ARE YOU SAYING??
IF YOU'RE GOING TO HUNT IN A MAN'S FOREST, SISTER, BE PREPARED FOR AMBUSH.
YOU NEVER KNOW WHO MIGHT SPRING FROM THE BOULDERS.
YOU TWO-FACED WHORESON --
AH AH AH, SISTER DEAR. SUCH TEMPER DOESN'T BEFIT YOU.
CHNNNG!
THE DEMONS WERE NOTHING COMPARED TO YOU. YOU'RE THE ONE I SHOULD KILL.
YOU COULD TRY.
SHUK

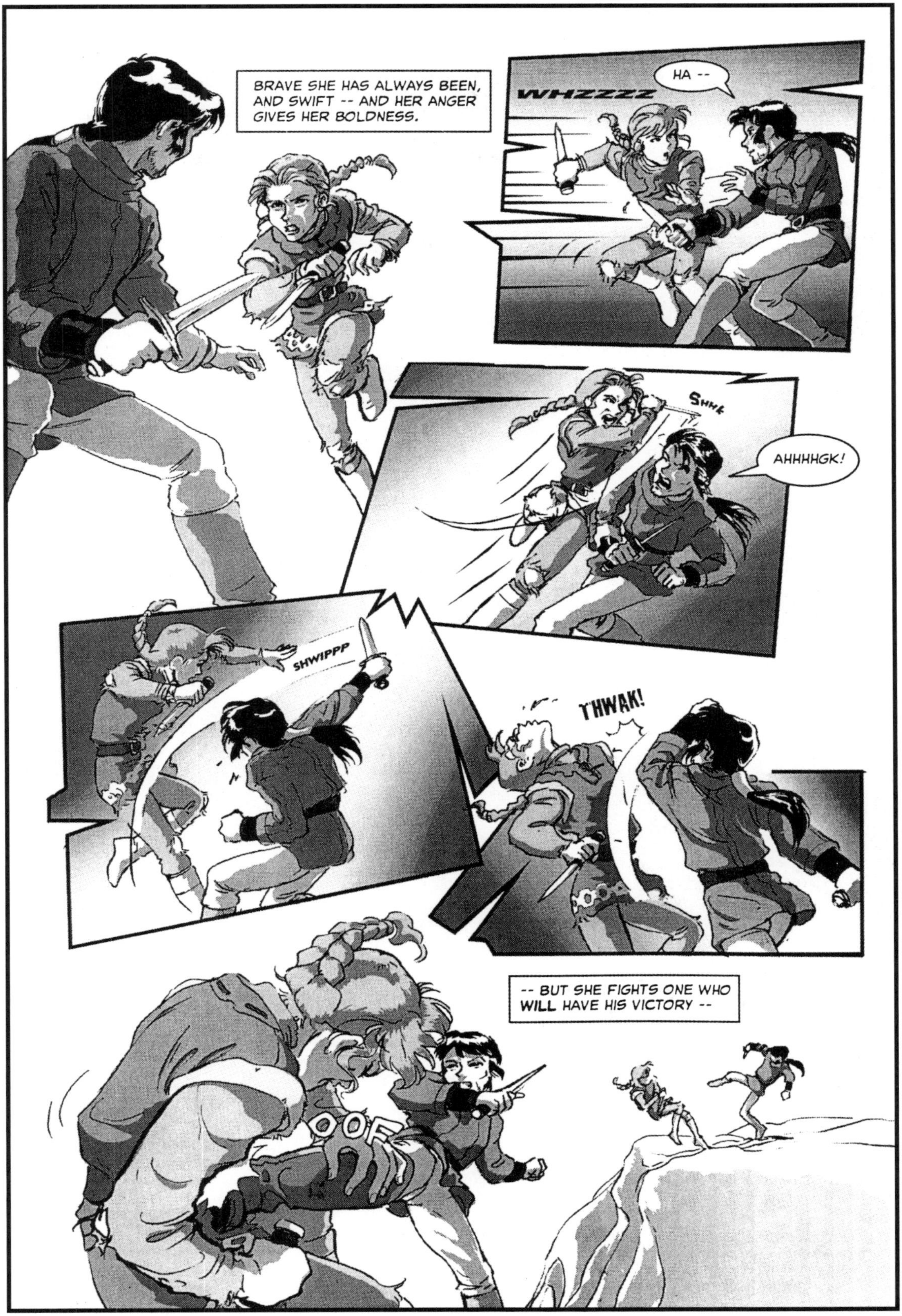
BRAVE SHE HAS ALWAYS BEEN, AND SWIFT -- AND HER ANGER GIVES HER BOLDNESS.
WHZZZZ
HA --
SHHK
AHHHHGK!
SHWIPPP
THWAK!
-- BUT SHE FIGHTS ONE WHO WILL HAVE HIS VICTORY --
OOF

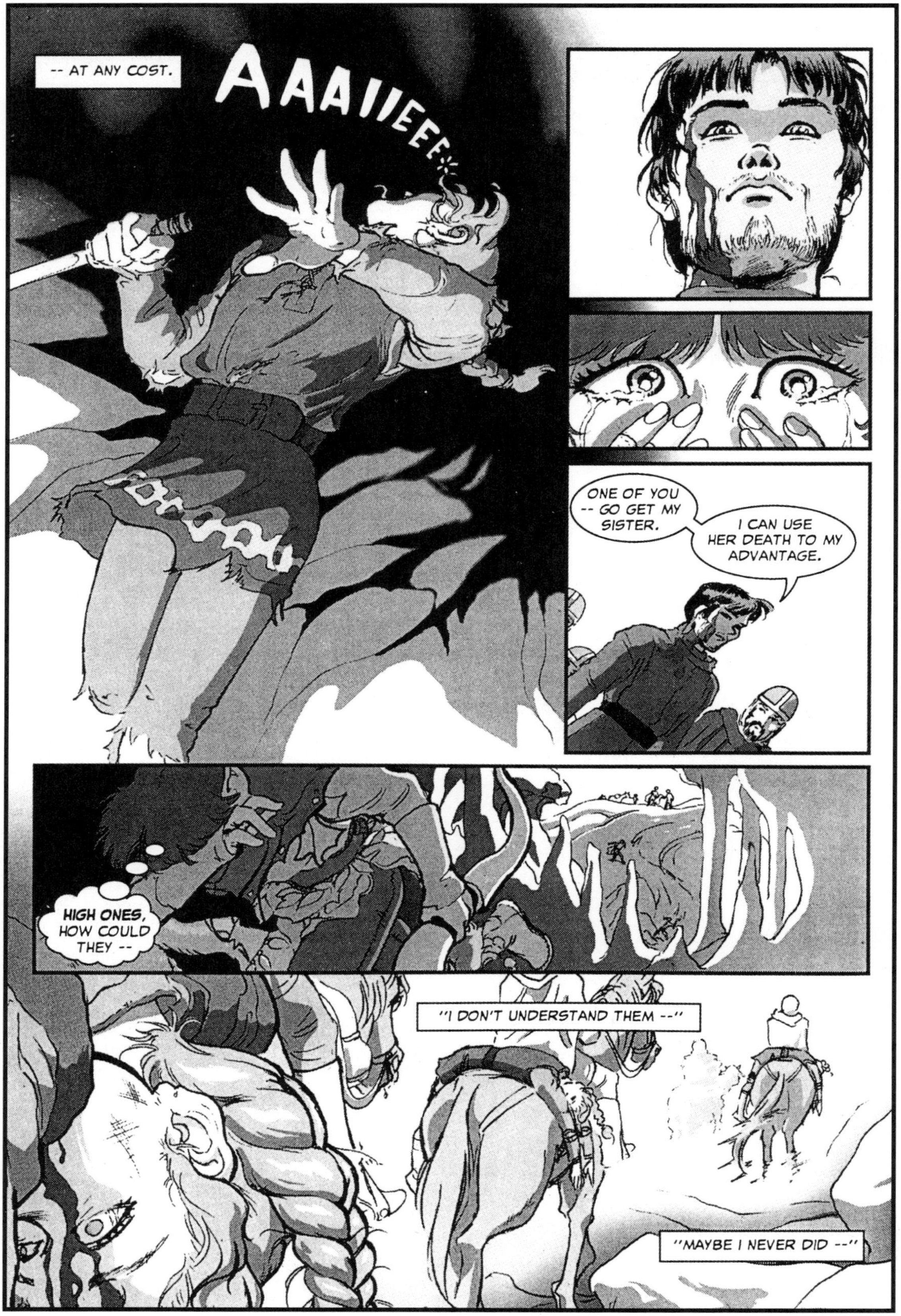
-- AT ANY COST.
AAAIIEEE
ONE OF YOU -- GO GET MY SISTER.
I CAN USE HER DEATH TO MY ADVANTAGE.
HIGH ONES, HOW COULD THEY --
"I DON'T UNDERSTAND THEM --"
"MAYBE I NEVER DID --"

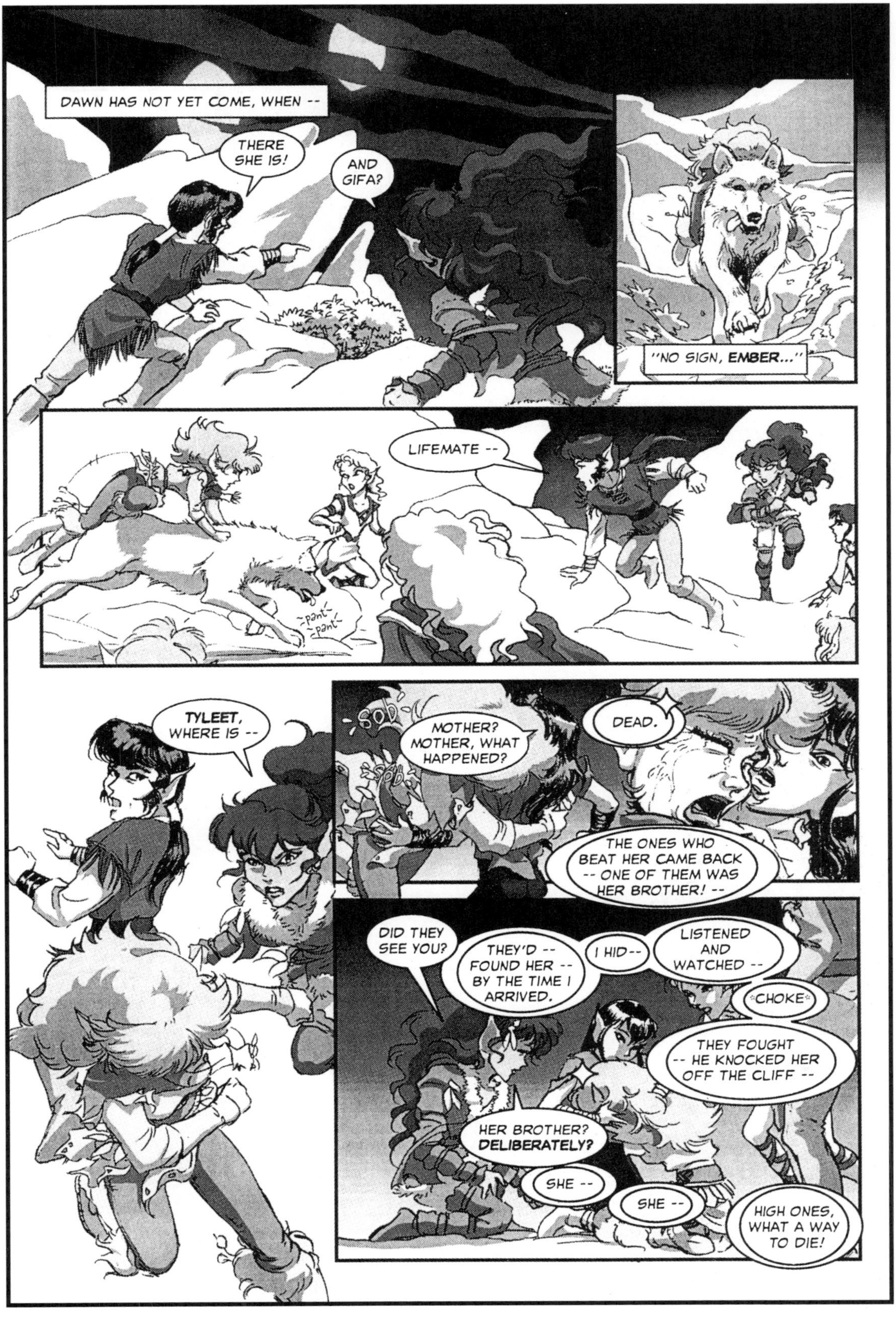
DAWN HAS NOT YET COME, WHEN --
THERE SHE IS!
AND GIFA?
"NO SIGN, EMBER..."
LIFEMATE --
pant pant
TYLEET, WHERE IS --
MOTHER? MOTHER, WHAT HAPPENED?
DEAD.
THE ONES WHO BEAT HER CAME BACK -- ONE OF THEM WAS HER BROTHER! --
DID THEY SEE YOU?
THEY'D -- FOUND HER -- BY THE TIME I ARRIVED.
I HID--
LISTENED AND WATCHED --
CHOKE
THEY FOUGHT -- HE KNOCKED HER OFF THE CLIFF --
HER BROTHER? DELIBERATELY?
SHE --
SHE --
HIGH ONES, WHAT A WAY TO DIE!

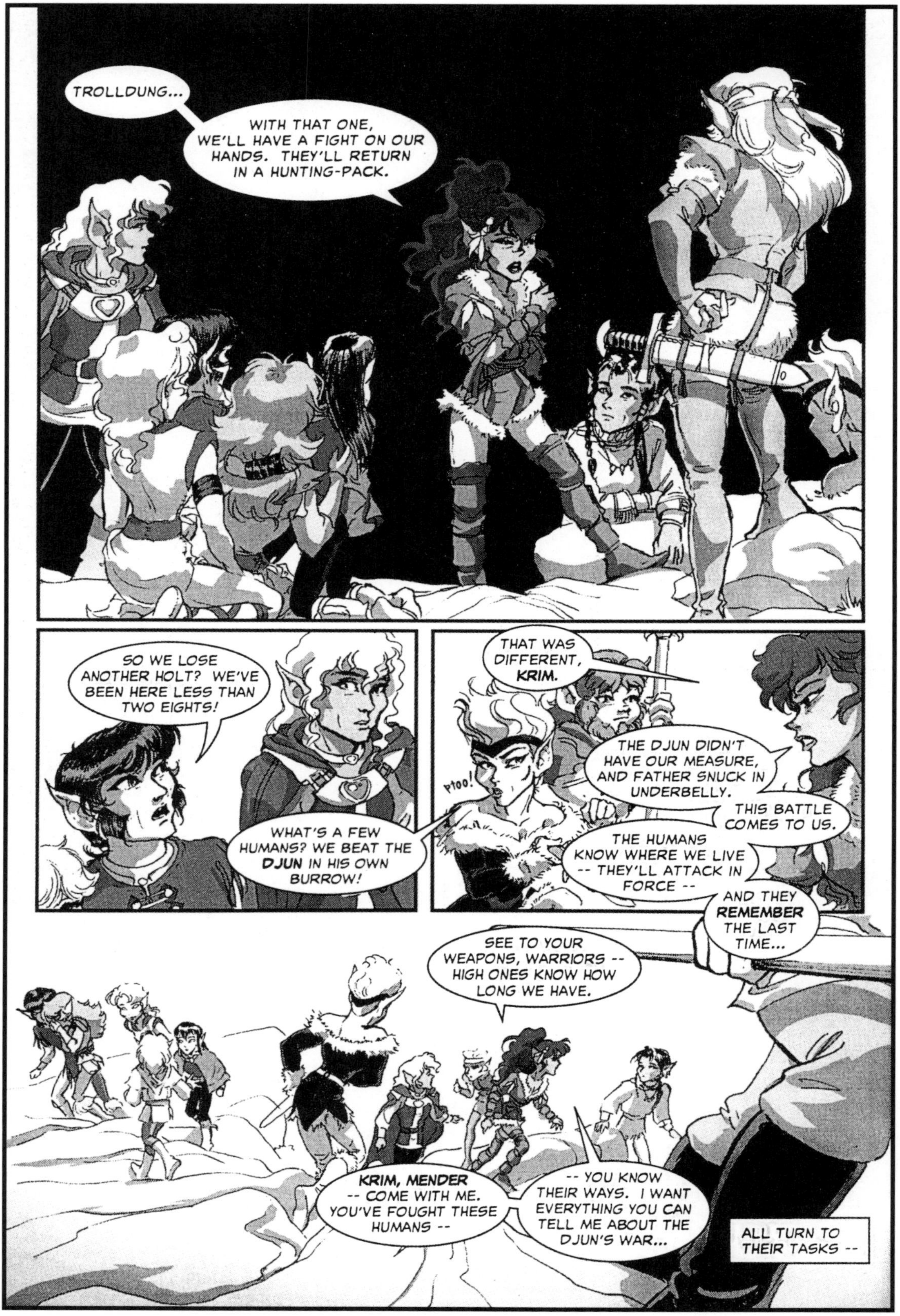
TROLLDUNG...
WITH THAT ONE, WE'LL HAVE A FIGHT ON OUR HANDS. THEY'LL RETURN IN A HUNTING-PACK.
SO WE LOSE ANOTHER HOLT? WE'VE BEEN HERE LESS THAN TWO EIGHTS!
WHAT'S A FEW HUMANS? WE BEAT THE **DJUN** IN HIS OWN BURROW!
PTOO!
THAT WAS DIFFERENT, **KRIM.**
THE DJUN DIDN'T HAVE OUR MEASURE, AND FATHER SNUCK IN UNDERBELLY.
THIS BATTLE COMES TO US.
THE HUMANS KNOW WHERE WE LIVE -- THEY'LL ATTACK IN FORCE --
AND THEY **REMEMBER** THE LAST TIME...
SEE TO YOUR WEAPONS, WARRIORS -- HIGH ONES KNOW HOW LONG WE HAVE.
KRIM, MENDER -- COME WITH ME. YOU'VE FOUGHT THESE HUMANS --
-- YOU KNOW THEIR WAYS. I WANT EVERYTHING YOU **CAN** TELL ME ABOUT THE DJUN'S WAR...
ALL TURN TO THEIR TASKS --

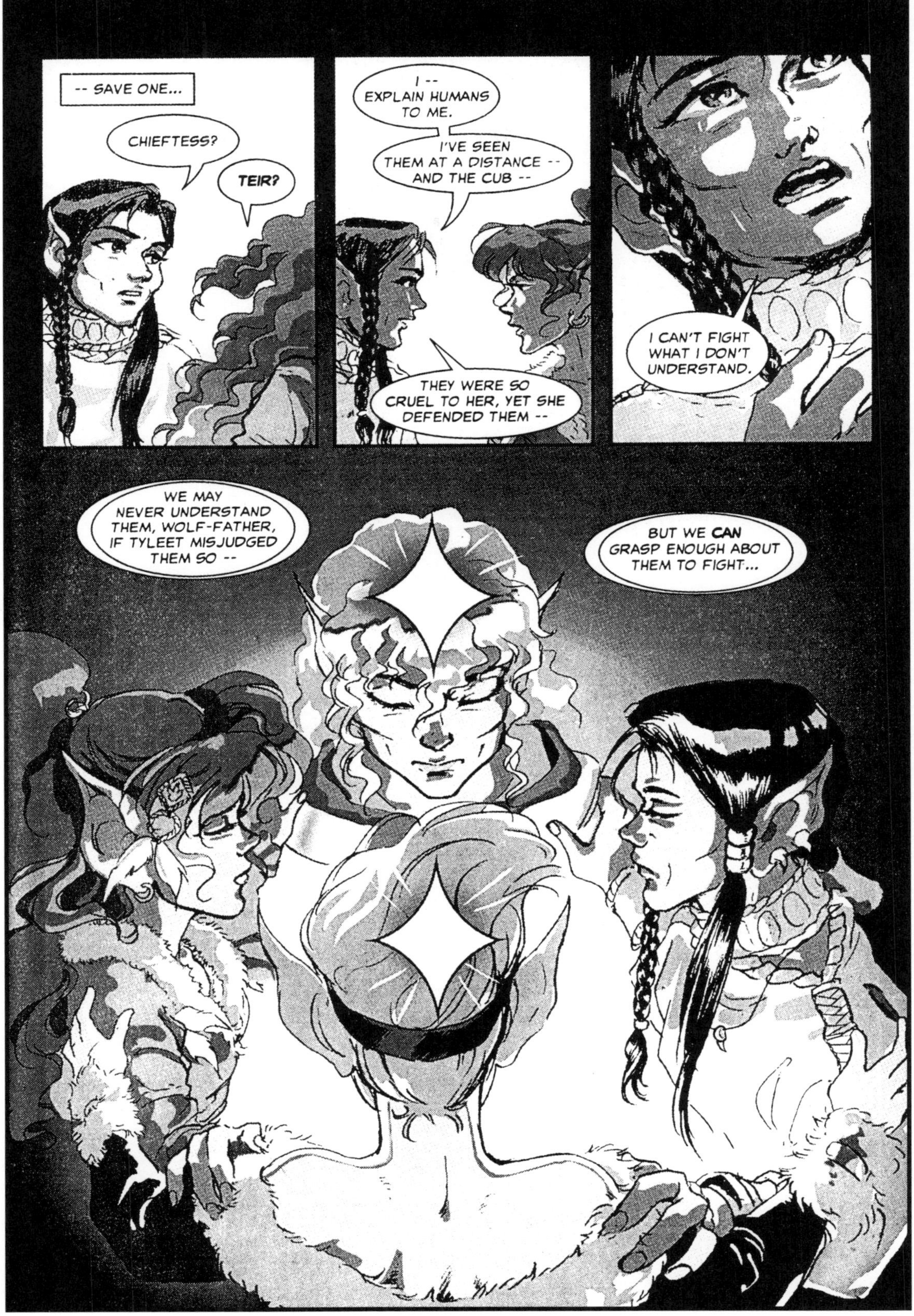
-- SAVE ONE...
CHIEFTESS?
TEIR?
I -- EXPLAIN HUMANS TO ME.
I'VE SEEN THEM AT A DISTANCE -- AND THE CUB --
THEY WERE SO CRUEL TO HER, YET SHE DEFENDED THEM --
I CAN'T FIGHT WHAT I DON'T UNDERSTAND.
WE MAY NEVER UNDERSTAND THEM, WOLF-FATHER, IF TYLEET MISJUDGED THEM SO --
BUT WE CAN GRASP ENOUGH ABOUT THEM TO FIGHT...

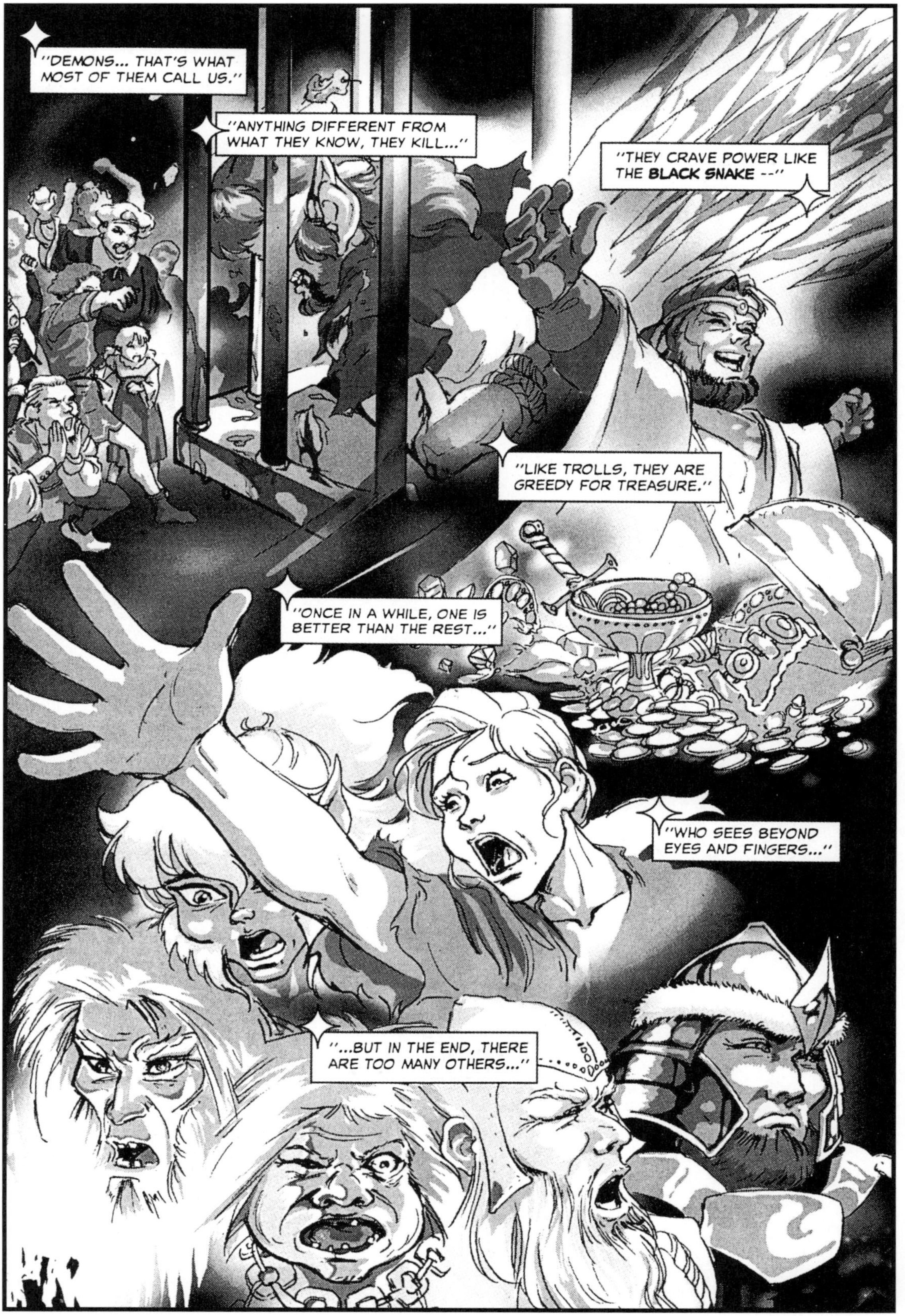
''DEMONS... THAT'S WHAT MOST OF THEM CALL US.''
''ANYTHING DIFFERENT FROM WHAT THEY KNOW, THEY KILL...''
''THEY CRAVE POWER LIKE THE **BLACK SNAKE** --''
''LIKE TROLLS, THEY ARE GREEDY FOR TREASURE.''
''ONCE IN A WHILE, ONE IS BETTER THAN THE REST...''
''WHO SEES BEYOND EYES AND FINGERS...''
''...BUT IN THE END, THERE ARE TOO MANY OTHERS...''

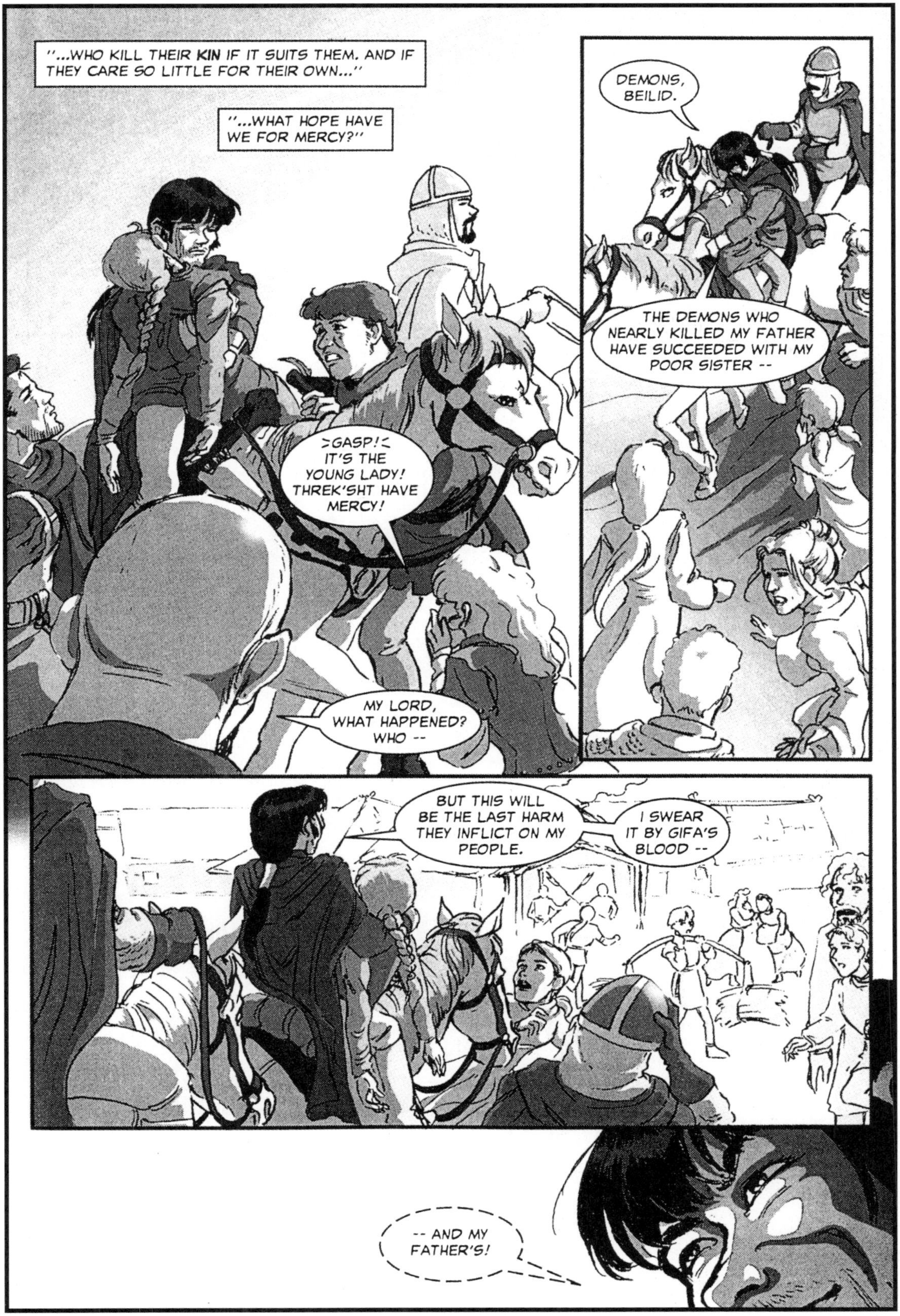
"...WHO KILL THEIR KIN IF IT SUITS THEM. AND IF THEY CARE SO LITTLE FOR THEIR OWN..."
"...WHAT HOPE HAVE WE FOR MERCY?"
>GASP!< IT'S THE YOUNG LADY! THREK'SHT HAVE MERCY!
MY LORD, WHAT HAPPENED? WHO --
DEMONS, BEILID.
THE DEMONS WHO NEARLY KILLED MY FATHER HAVE SUCCEEDED WITH MY POOR SISTER --
BUT THIS WILL BE THE LAST HARM THEY INFLICT ON MY PEOPLE.
I SWEAR IT BY GIFA'S BLOOD --
-- AND MY FATHER'S!

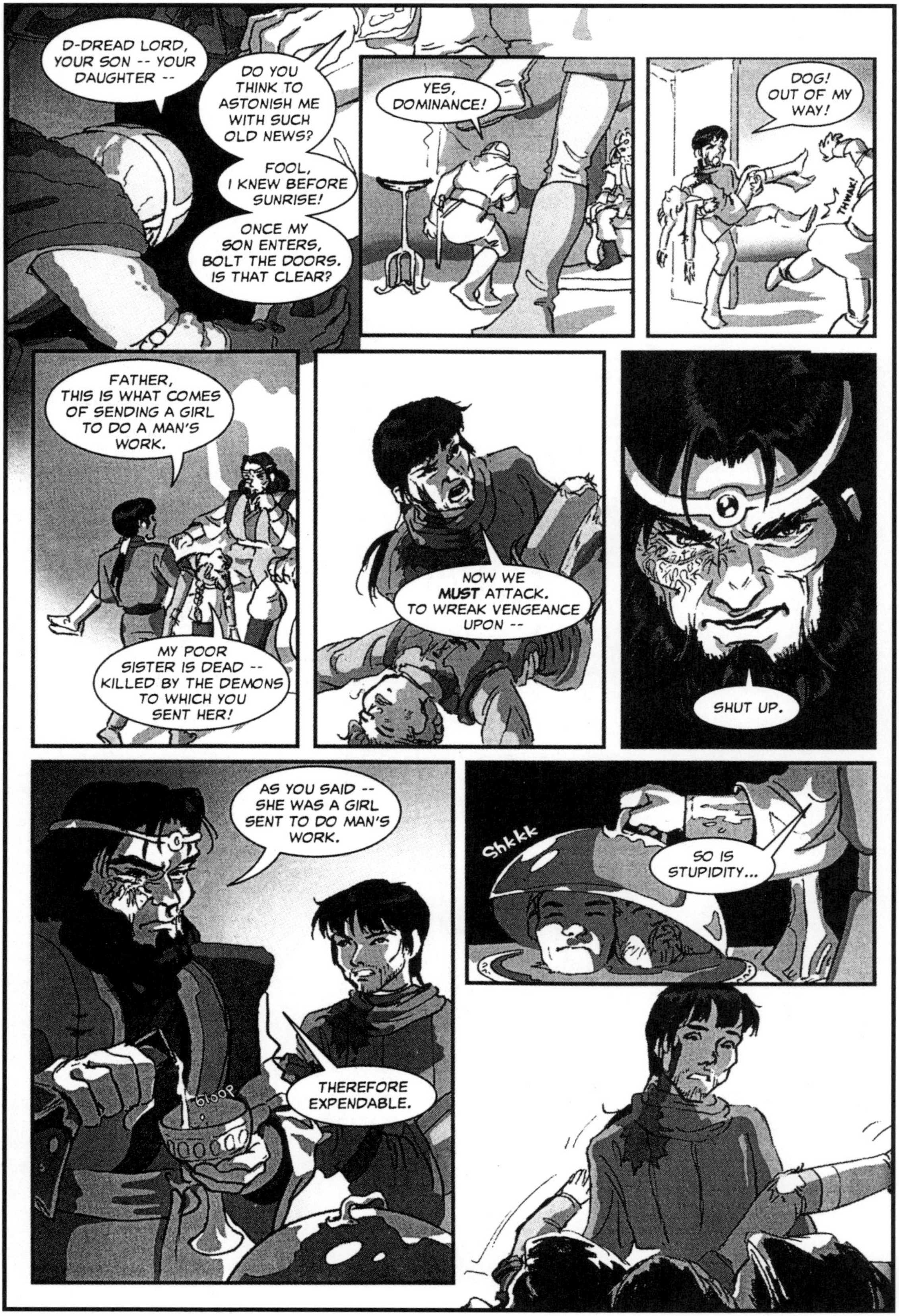
D-DREAD LORD, YOUR SON -- YOUR DAUGHTER --
DO YOU THINK TO ASTONISH ME WITH SUCH OLD NEWS?
FOOL, I KNEW BEFORE SUNRISE!
ONCE MY SON ENTERS, BOLT THE DOORS. IS THAT CLEAR?
YES, DOMINANCE!
DOG! OUT OF MY WAY!
THWAK!
FATHER, THIS IS WHAT COMES OF SENDING A GIRL TO DO A MAN'S WORK.
MY POOR SISTER IS DEAD -- KILLED BY THE DEMONS TO WHICH YOU SENT HER!
NOW WE MUST ATTACK. TO WREAK VENGEANCE UPON --
SHUT UP.
AS YOU SAID -- SHE WAS A GIRL SENT TO DO MAN'S WORK.
THEREFORE EXPENDABLE.
Gloop
Shkkk
SO IS STUPIDITY...

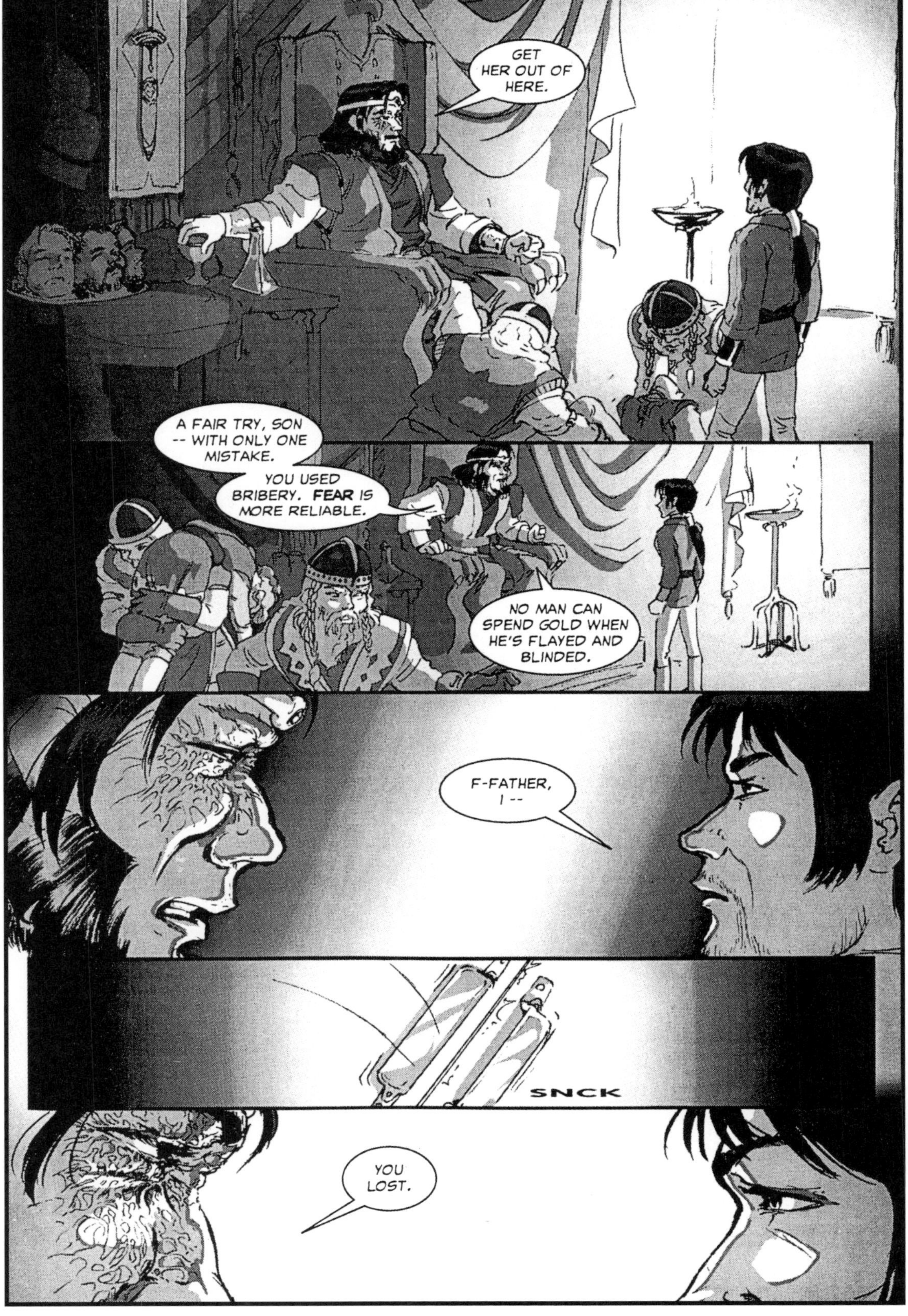

GET HER OUT OF HERE.
A FAIR TRY, SON -- WITH ONLY ONE MISTAKE.
YOU USED BRIBERY. FEAR IS MORE RELIABLE.
NO MAN CAN SPEND GOLD WHEN HE'S FLAYED AND BLINDED.
F-FATHER, I --
SNCK
YOU LOST.

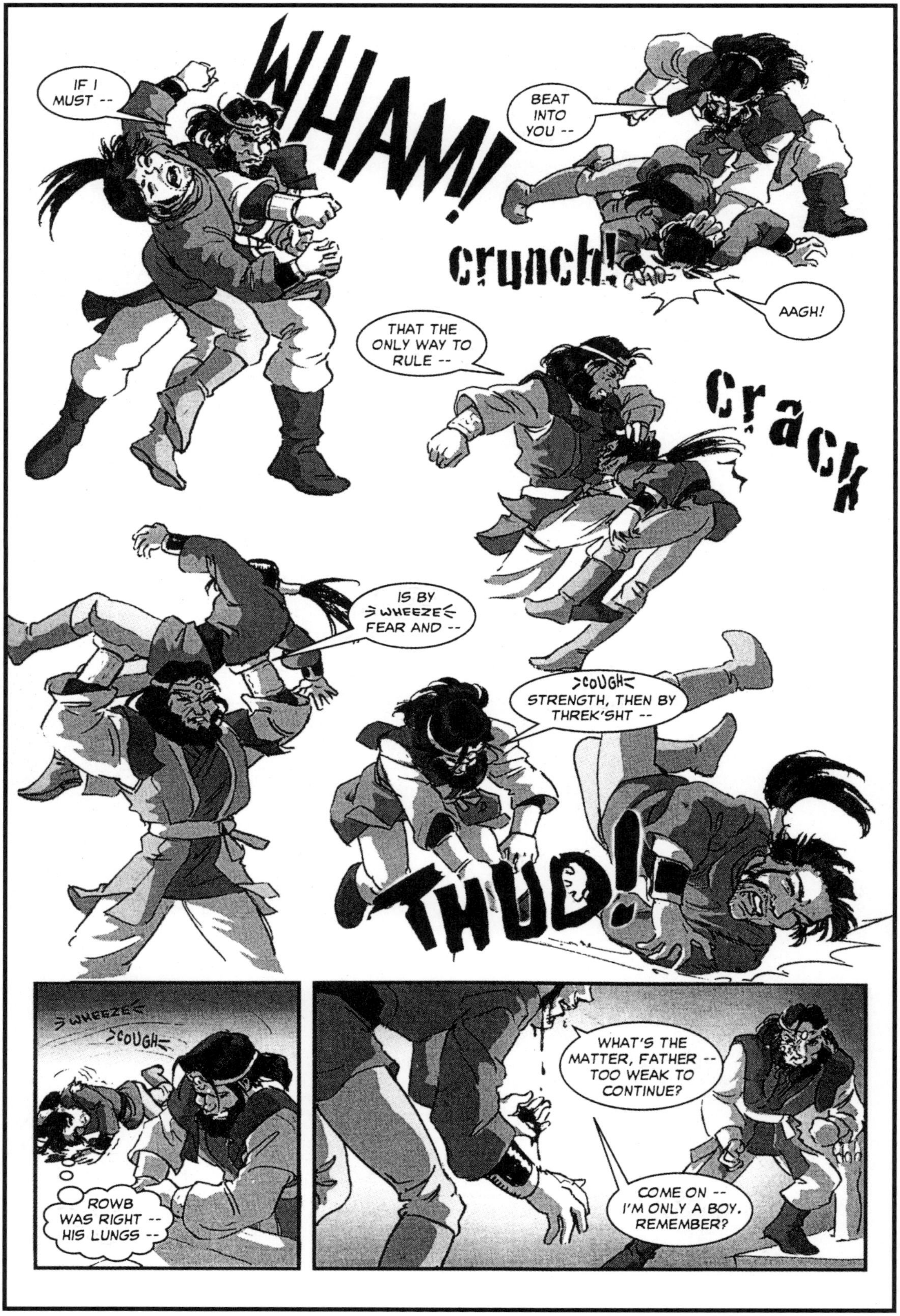
IF I MUST --
WHAM!
BEAT INTO YOU --
crunch!
AAGH!
THAT THE ONLY WAY TO RULE --
Crack
IS BY >WHEEZE< FEAR AND --
>COUGH< STRENGTH, THEN BY THREK'SHT --
THUD!!
>WHEEZE<
>COUGH<
ROWB WAS RIGHT -- HIS LUNGS --
WHAT'S THE MATTER, FATHER -- TOO WEAK TO CONTINUE?
COME ON -- I'M ONLY A BOY. REMEMBER?

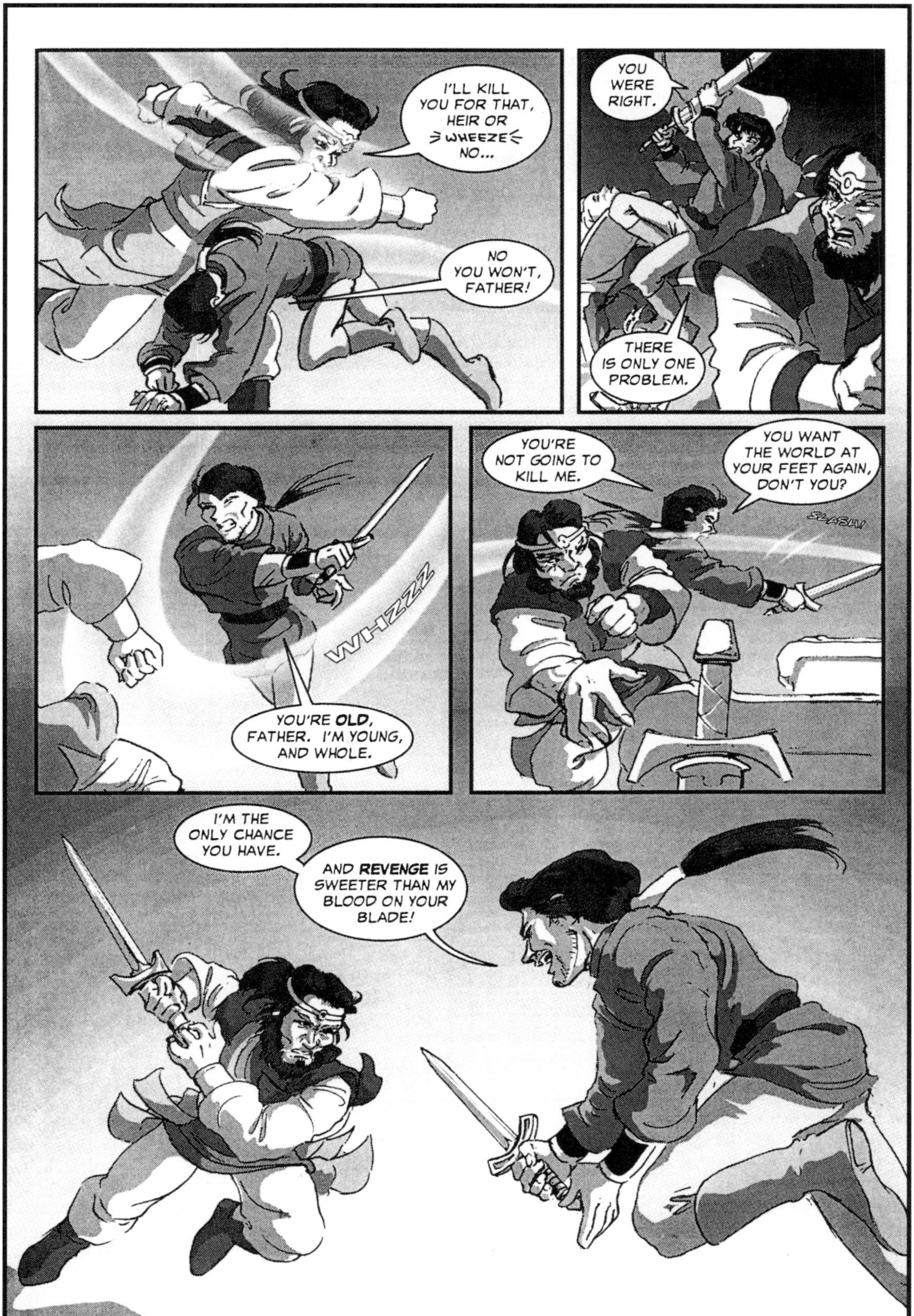

I'LL KILL YOU FOR THAT, HEIR OR ≷WHEEZE≶ NO...
NO YOU WON'T, FATHER!
YOU WERE RIGHT.
THERE IS ONLY ONE PROBLEM.
WHZZZ
YOU'RE OLD, FATHER. I'M YOUNG, AND WHOLE.
YOU'RE NOT GOING TO KILL ME.
YOU WANT THE WORLD AT YOUR FEET AGAIN, DON'T YOU?
SLASH!
I'M THE ONLY CHANCE YOU HAVE.
AND REVENGE IS SWEETER THAN MY BLOOD ON YOUR BLADE!

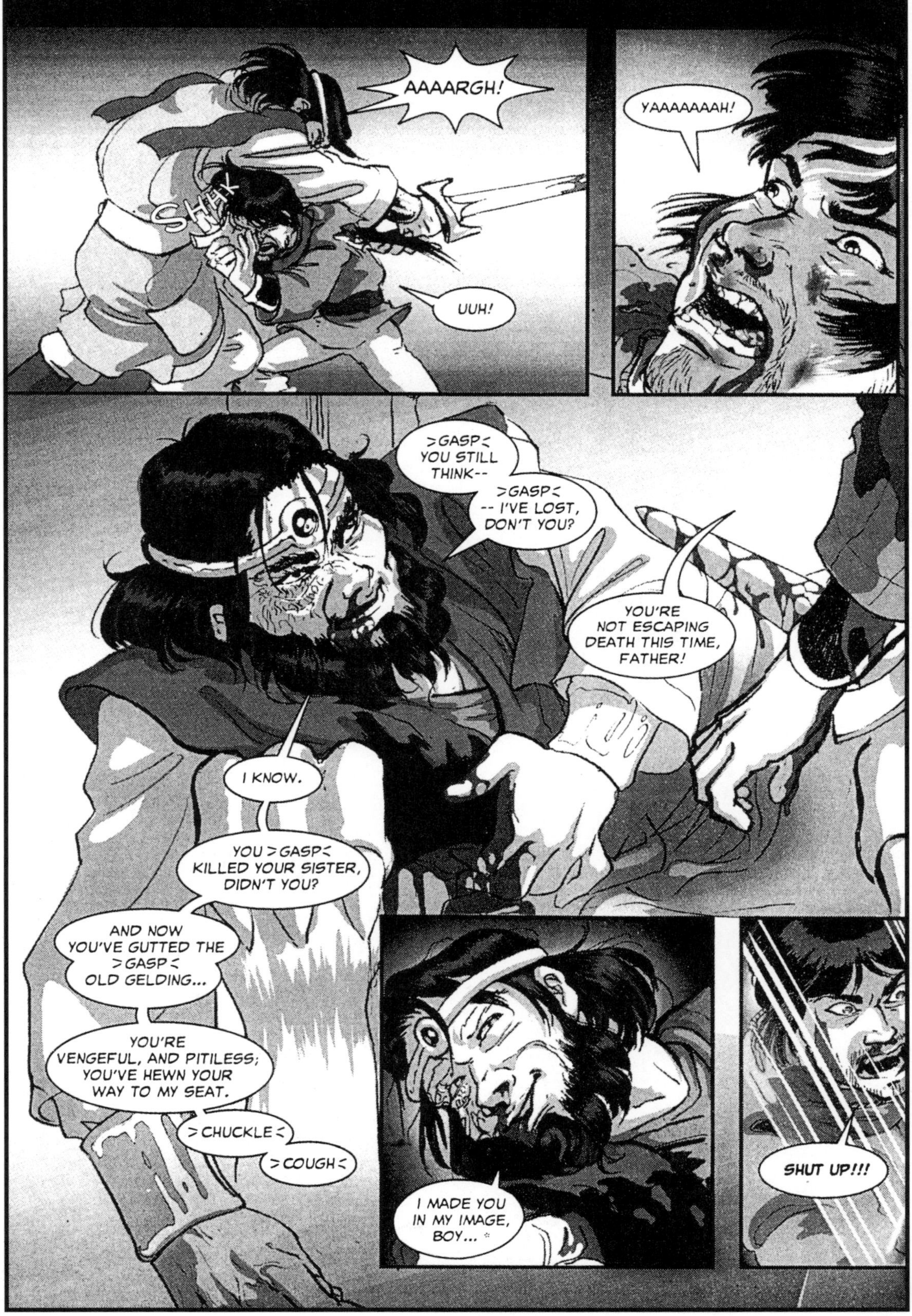
AAAARGH!
SHHK
UUH!
YAAAAAAAH!
>GASP< YOU STILL THINK--
>GASP< -- I'VE LOST, DON'T YOU?
YOU'RE NOT ESCAPING DEATH THIS TIME, FATHER!
I KNOW.
YOU >GASP< KILLED YOUR SISTER, DIDN'T YOU?
AND NOW YOU'VE GUTTED THE >GASP< OLD GELDING...
YOU'RE VENGEFUL, AND PITILESS; YOU'VE HEWN YOUR WAY TO MY SEAT.
>CHUCKLE<
>COUGH<
I MADE YOU IN MY IMAGE, BOY... *
SHUT UP!!!

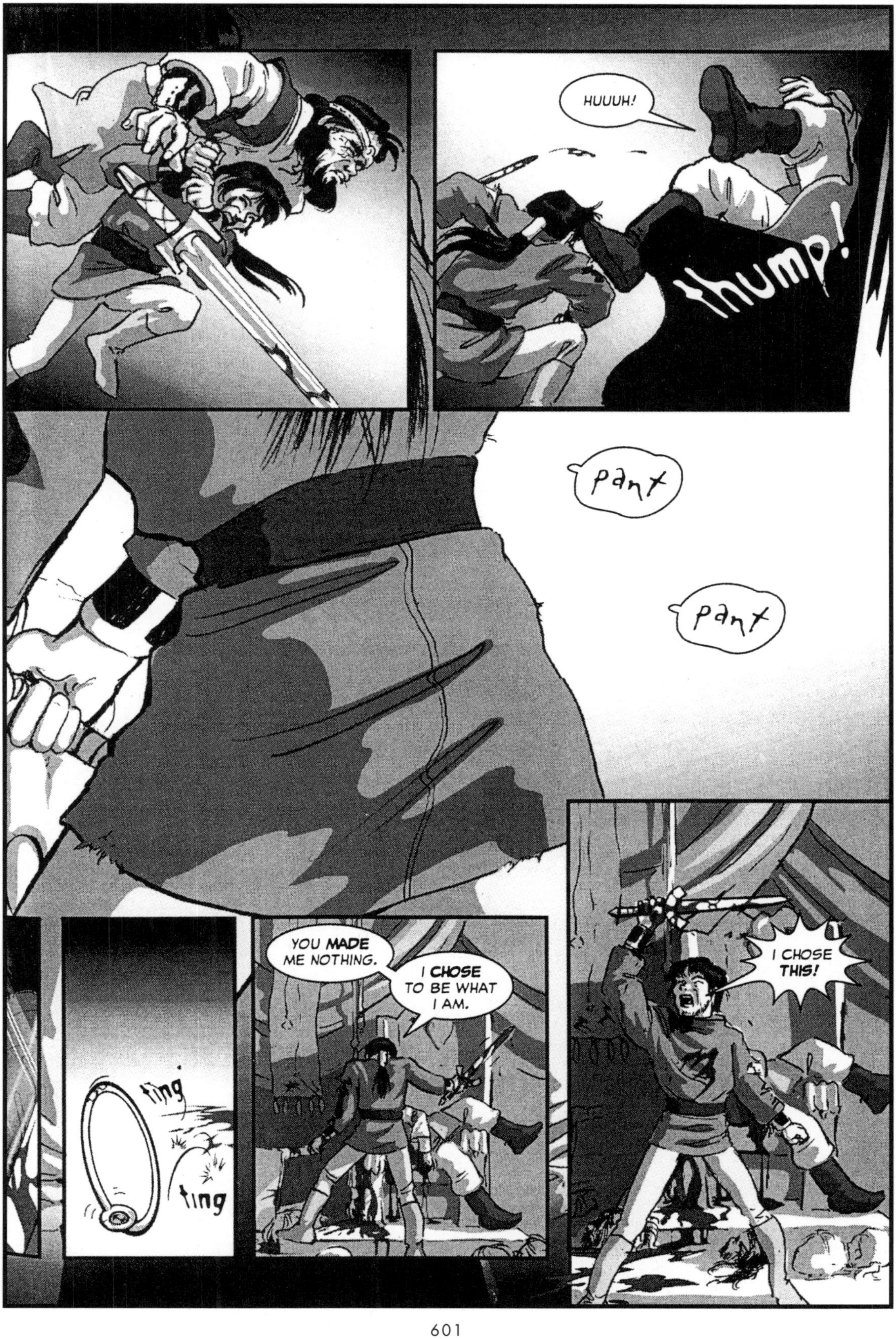
HUUUH!
thump!
pant
pant
ting
ting
YOU MADE ME NOTHING.
I CHOSE TO BE WHAT I AM.
I CHOSE THIS!

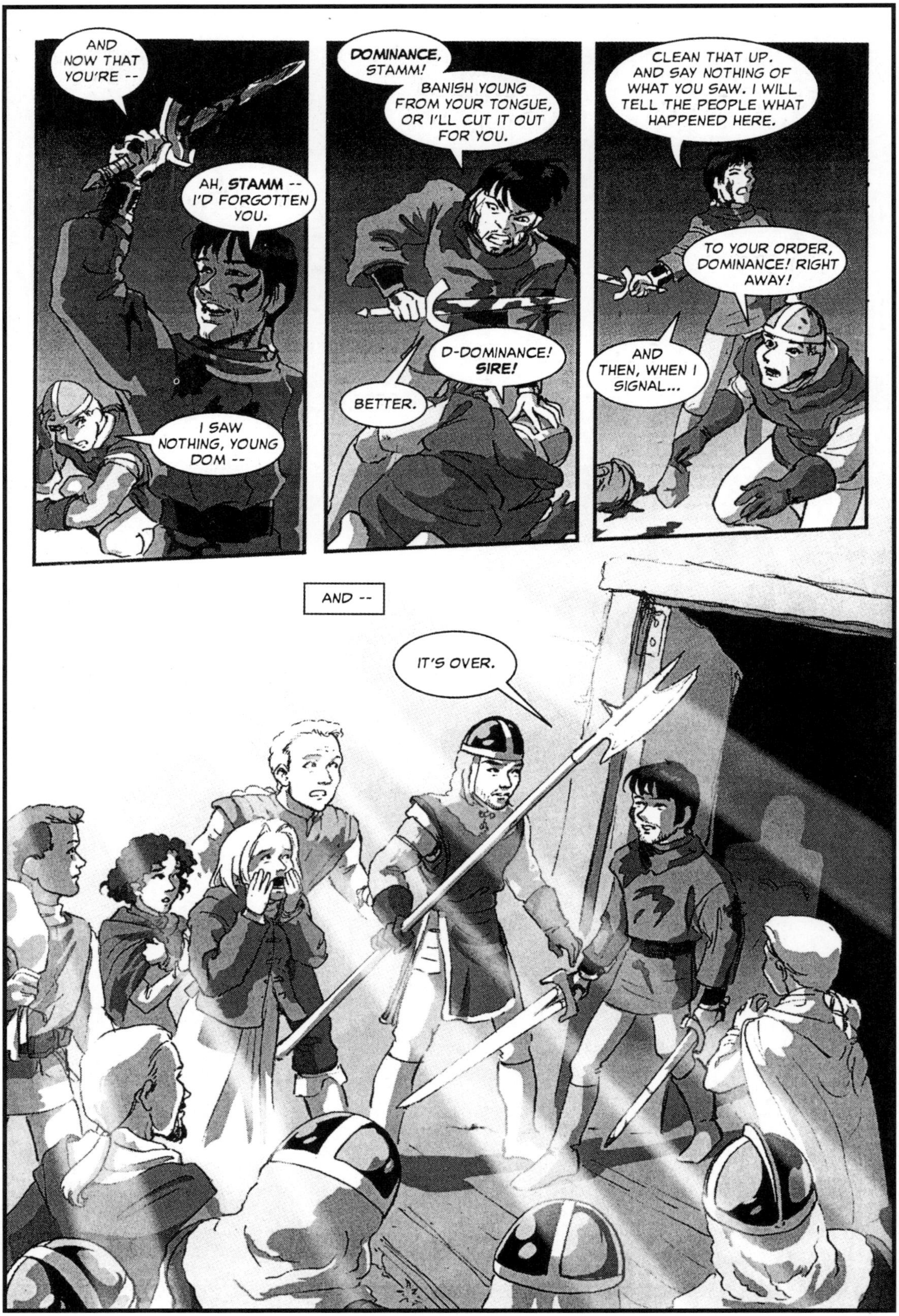
AND NOW THAT YOU'RE --
AH, STAMM -- I'D FORGOTTEN YOU.
I SAW NOTHING, YOUNG DOM --
DOMINANCE, STAMM!
BANISH YOUNG FROM YOUR TONGUE, OR I'LL CUT IT OUT FOR YOU.
D-DOMINANCE! SIRE!
BETTER.
CLEAN THAT UP. AND SAY NOTHING OF WHAT YOU SAW. I WILL TELL THE PEOPLE WHAT HAPPENED HERE.
TO YOUR ORDER, DOMINANCE! RIGHT AWAY!
AND THEN, WHEN I SIGNAL...
AND --
IT'S OVER.

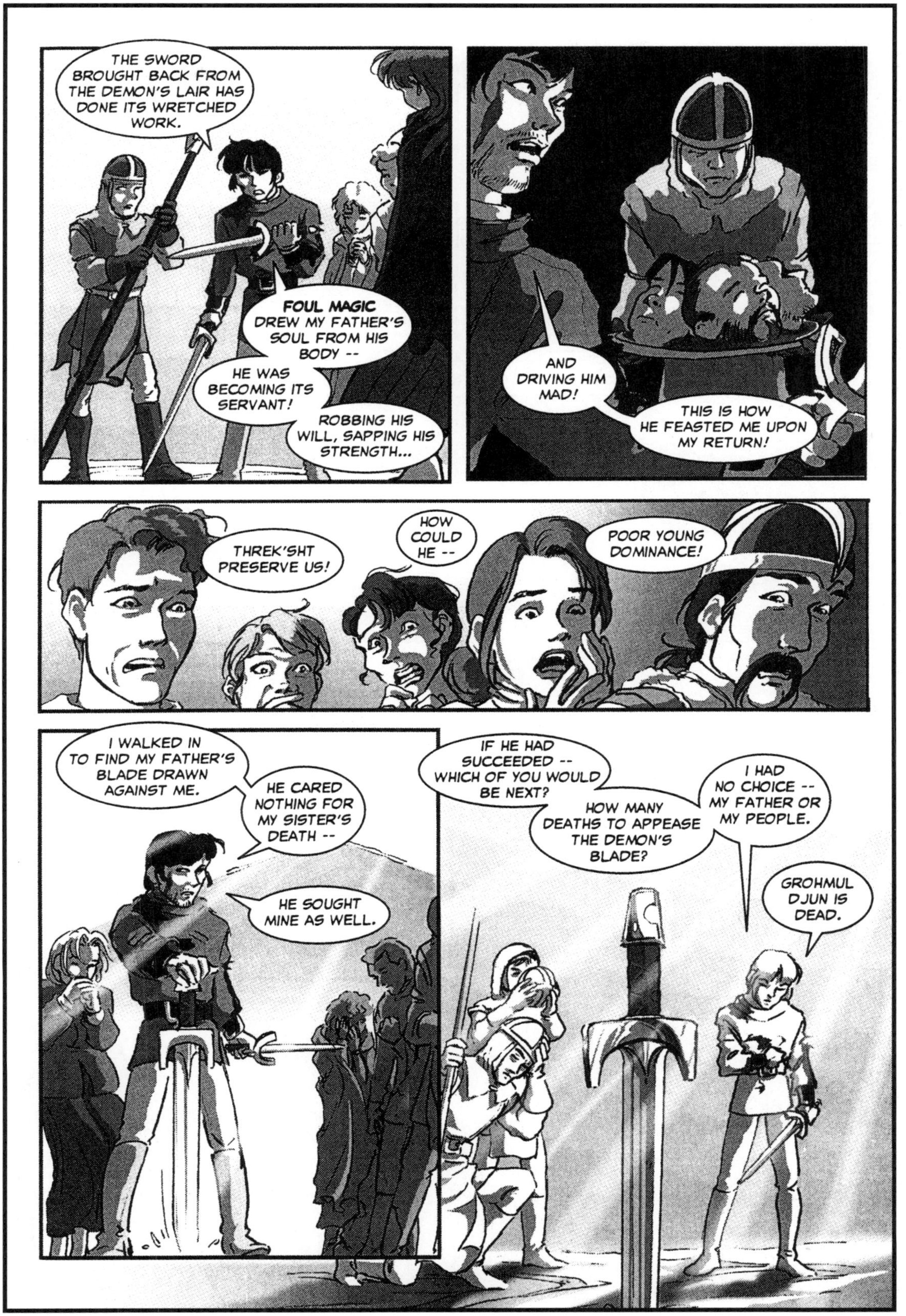
THE SWORD BROUGHT BACK FROM THE DEMON'S LAIR HAS DONE ITS WRETCHED WORK.
FOUL MAGIC DREW MY FATHER'S SOUL FROM HIS BODY --
HE WAS BECOMING ITS SERVANT!
ROBBING HIS WILL, SAPPING HIS STRENGTH...
AND DRIVING HIM MAD!
THIS IS HOW HE FEASTED ME UPON MY RETURN!
THREK'SHT PRESERVE US!
HOW COULD HE --
POOR YOUNG DOMINANCE!
I WALKED IN TO FIND MY FATHER'S BLADE DRAWN AGAINST ME.
HE CARED NOTHING FOR MY SISTER'S DEATH --
HE SOUGHT MINE AS WELL.
IF HE HAD SUCCEEDED -- WHICH OF YOU WOULD BE NEXT?
HOW MANY DEATHS TO APPEASE THE DEMON'S BLADE?
I HAD NO CHOICE -- MY FATHER OR MY PEOPLE.
GROHMUL DJUN IS DEAD.

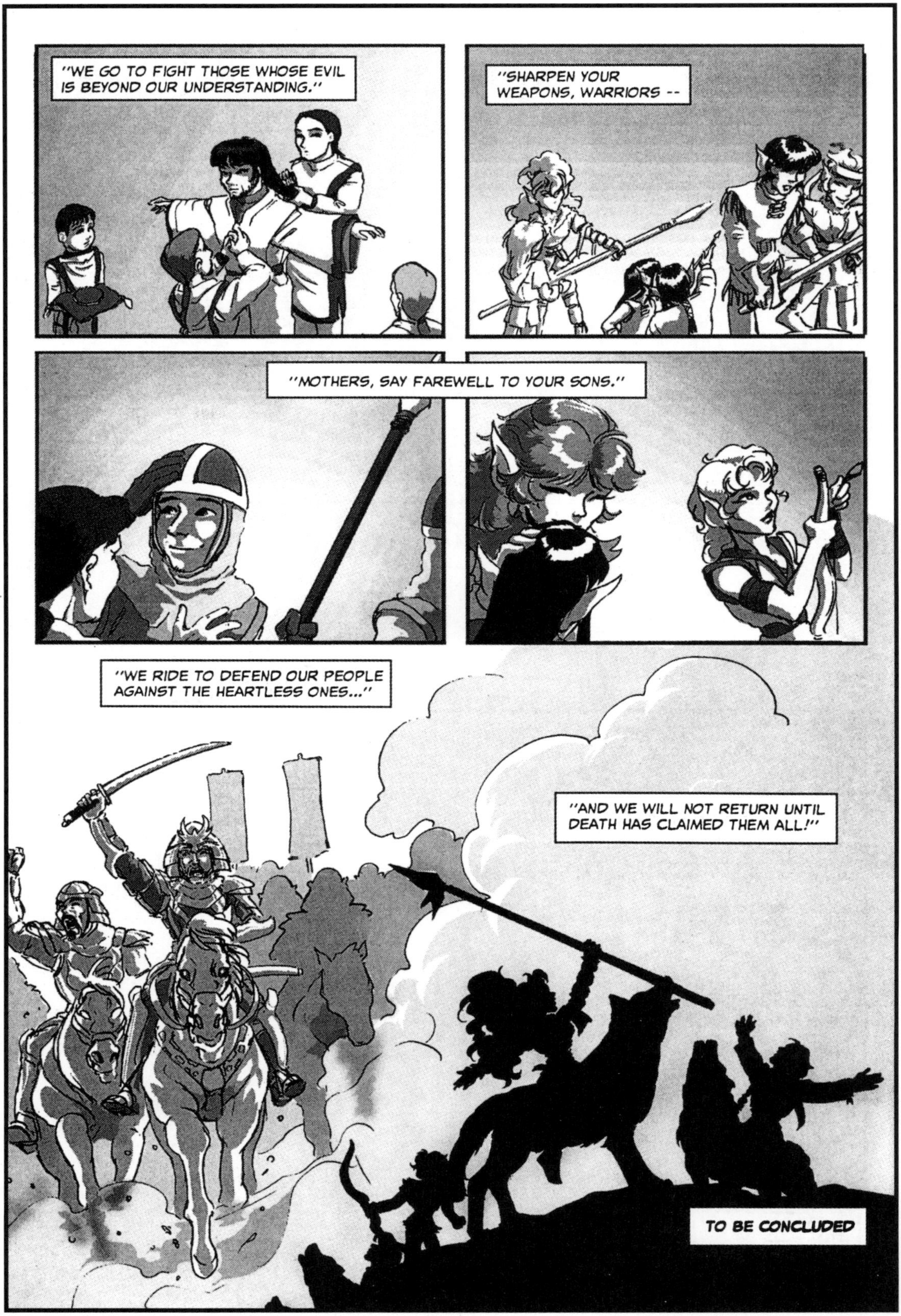
"WE GO TO FIGHT THOSE WHOSE EVIL IS BEYOND OUR UNDERSTANDING."
"SHARPEN YOUR WEAPONS, WARRIORS --
"MOTHERS, SAY FAREWELL TO YOUR SONS."
"WE RIDE TO DEFEND OUR PEOPLE AGAINST THE HEARTLESS ONES..."
"AND WE WILL NOT RETURN UNTIL DEATH HAS CLAIMED THEM ALL!"
TO BE CONCLUDED

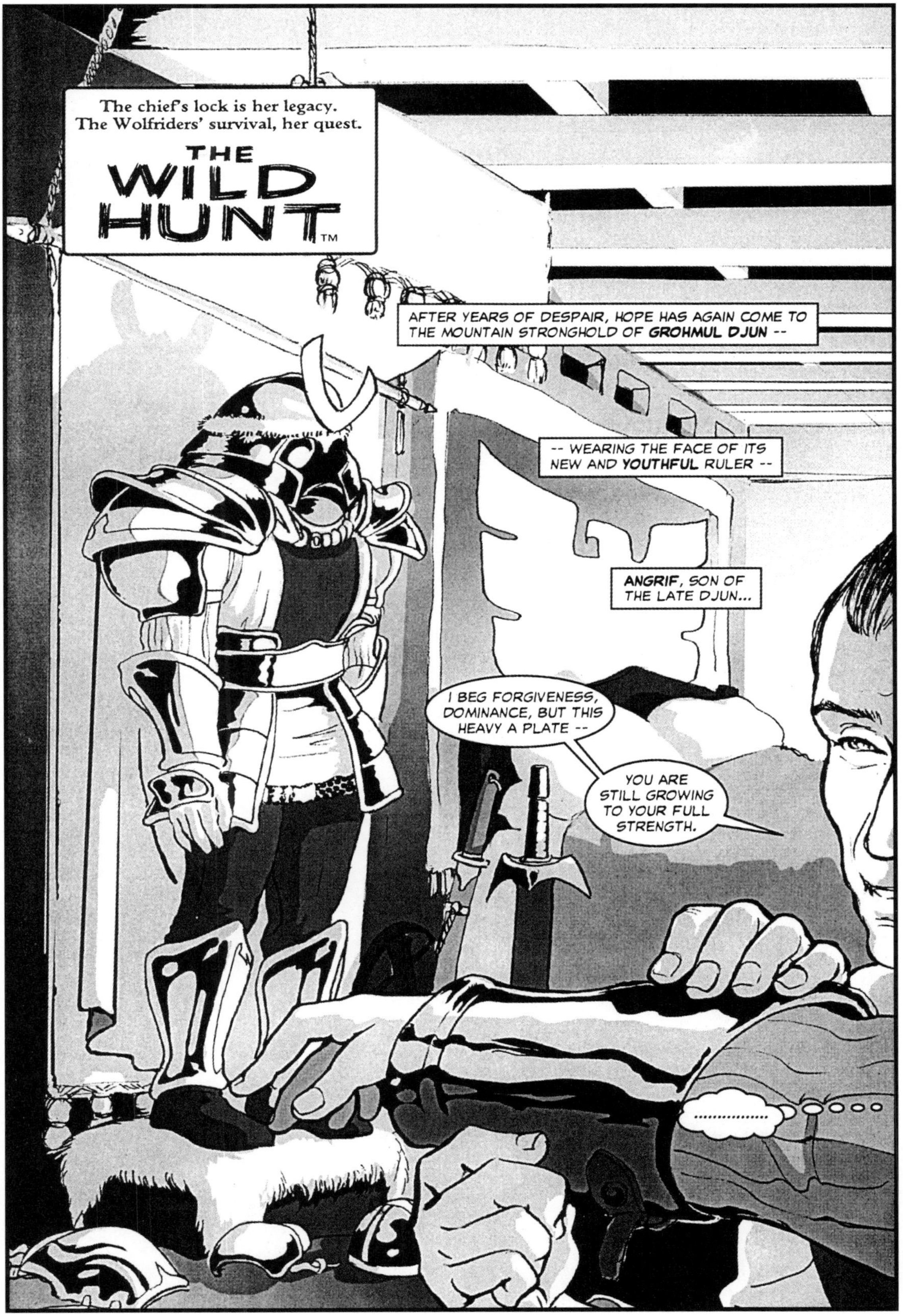
The chief's lock is her legacy.
The Wolfriders' survival, her quest.
THE WILD HUNT™
AFTER YEARS OF DESPAIR, HOPE HAS AGAIN COME TO THE MOUNTAIN STRONGHOLD OF GROHMUL DJUN --
-- WEARING THE FACE OF ITS NEW AND YOUTHFUL RULER --
ANGRIF, SON OF THE LATE DJUN...
I BEG FORGIVENESS, DOMINANCE, BUT THIS HEAVY A PLATE --
YOU ARE STILL GROWING TO YOUR FULL STRENGTH.
....

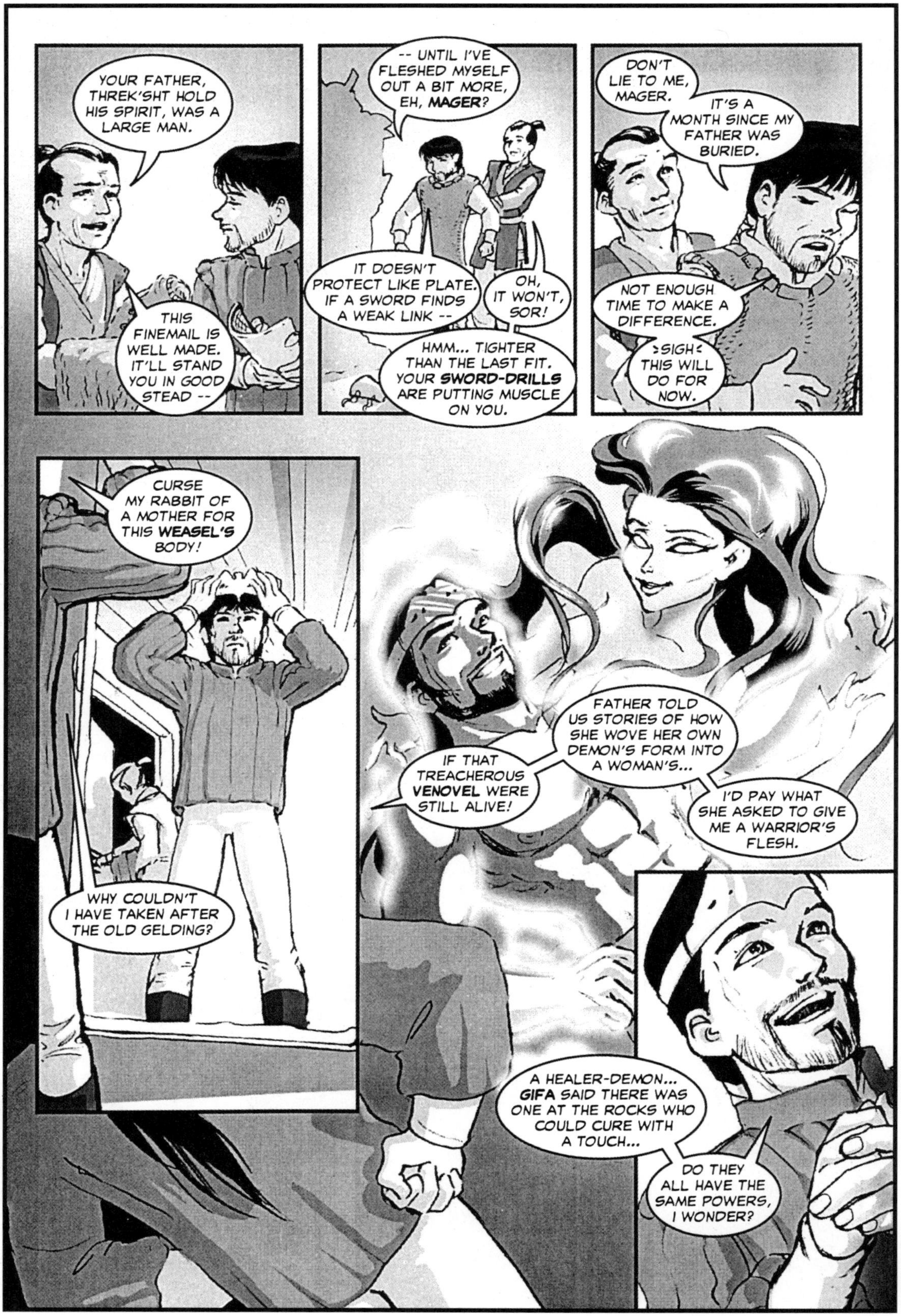
YOUR FATHER, THREK'SHT HOLD HIS SPIRIT, WAS A LARGE MAN.
THIS FINEMAIL IS WELL MADE. IT'LL STAND YOU IN GOOD STEAD --
-- UNTIL I'VE FLESHED MYSELF OUT A BIT MORE, EH, MAGER?
IT DOESN'T PROTECT LIKE PLATE. IF A SWORD FINDS A WEAK LINK --
OH, IT WON'T, SOR!
HMM... TIGHTER THAN THE LAST FIT. YOUR SWORD-DRILLS ARE PUTTING MUSCLE ON YOU.
DON'T LIE TO ME, MAGER.
IT'S A MONTH SINCE MY FATHER WAS BURIED.
NOT ENOUGH TIME TO MAKE A DIFFERENCE.
>SIGH< THIS WILL DO FOR NOW.
CURSE MY RABBIT OF A MOTHER FOR THIS WEASEL'S BODY!
WHY COULDN'T I HAVE TAKEN AFTER THE OLD GELDING?
IF THAT TREACHEROUS VENOVEL WERE STILL ALIVE!
FATHER TOLD US STORIES OF HOW SHE WOVE HER OWN DEMON'S FORM INTO A WOMAN'S...
I'D PAY WHAT SHE ASKED TO GIVE ME A WARRIOR'S FLESH.
A HEALER-DEMON... GIFA SAID THERE WAS ONE AT THE ROCKS WHO COULD CURE WITH A TOUCH...
DO THEY ALL HAVE THE SAME POWERS, I WONDER?

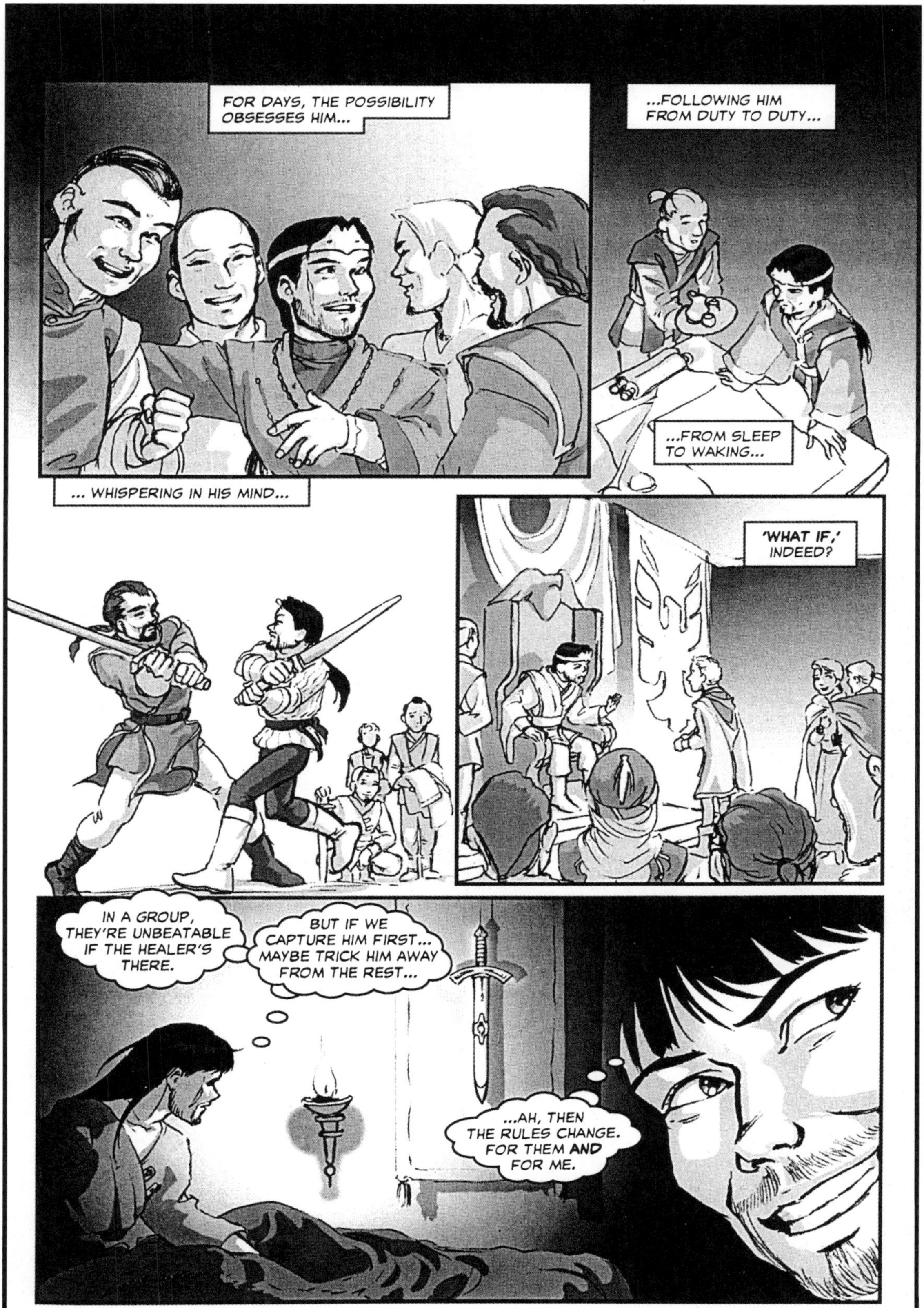

FOR DAYS, THE POSSIBILITY OBSESSES HIM...
...FOLLOWING HIM FROM DUTY TO DUTY...
...FROM SLEEP TO WAKING...
... WHISPERING IN HIS MIND...
'WHAT IF,' INDEED?
IN A GROUP, THEY'RE UNBEATABLE IF THE HEALER'S THERE.
BUT IF WE CAPTURE HIM FIRST... MAYBE TRICK HIM AWAY FROM THE REST...
...AH, THEN THE RULES CHANGE. FOR THEM AND FOR ME.

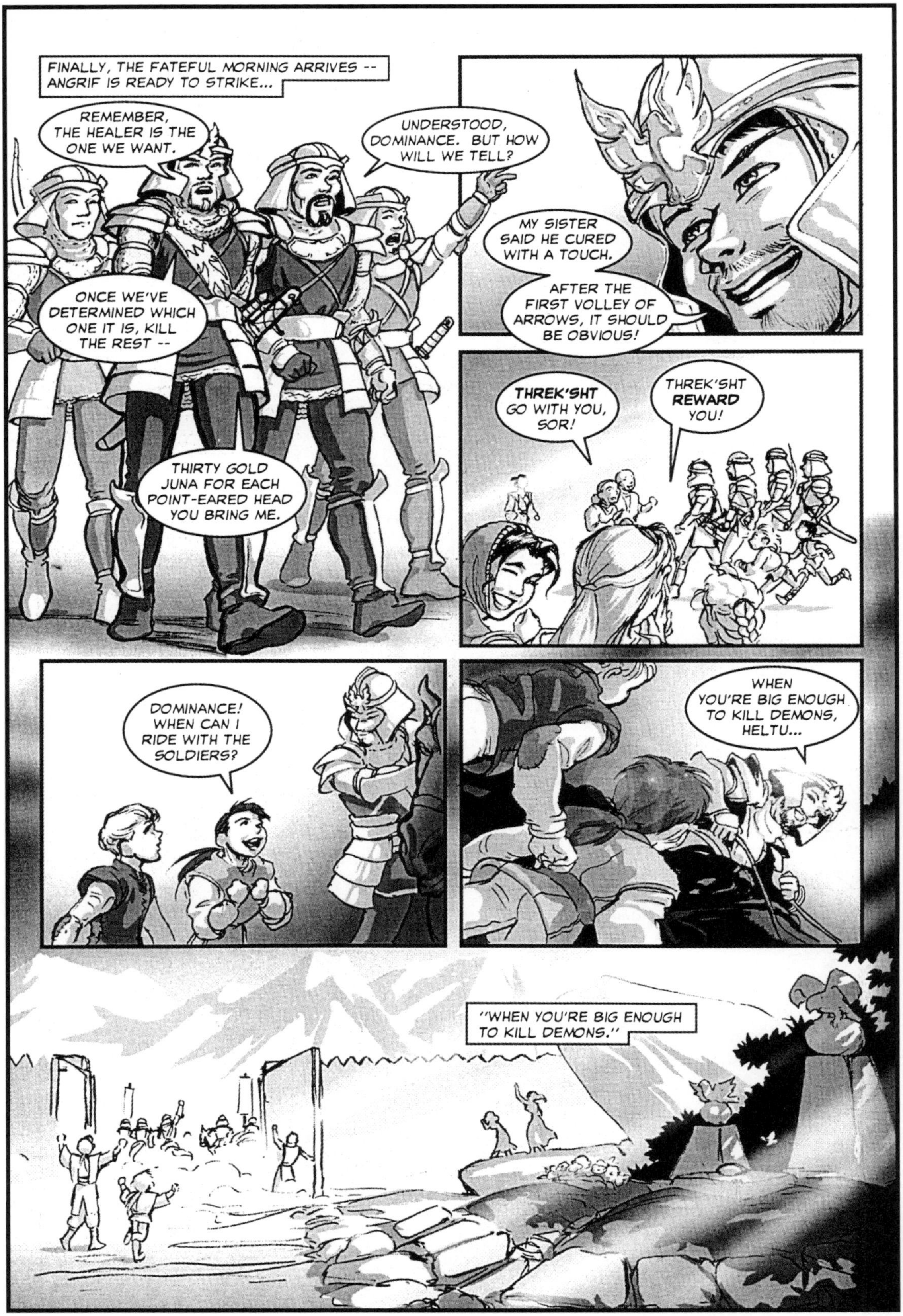
FINALLY, THE FATEFUL MORNING ARRIVES -- ANGRIF IS READY TO STRIKE...
REMEMBER, THE HEALER IS THE ONE WE WANT.
UNDERSTOOD, DOMINANCE. BUT HOW WILL WE TELL?
ONCE WE'VE DETERMINED WHICH ONE IT IS, KILL THE REST --
THIRTY GOLD JUNA FOR EACH POINT-EARED HEAD YOU BRING ME.
MY SISTER SAID HE CURED WITH A TOUCH.
AFTER THE FIRST VOLLEY OF ARROWS, IT SHOULD BE OBVIOUS!
THREK'SHT GO WITH YOU, SOR!
THREK'SHT REWARD YOU!
DOMINANCE! WHEN CAN I RIDE WITH THE SOLDIERS?
WHEN YOU'RE BIG ENOUGH TO KILL DEMONS, HELTU...
"WHEN YOU'RE BIG ENOUGH TO KILL DEMONS."

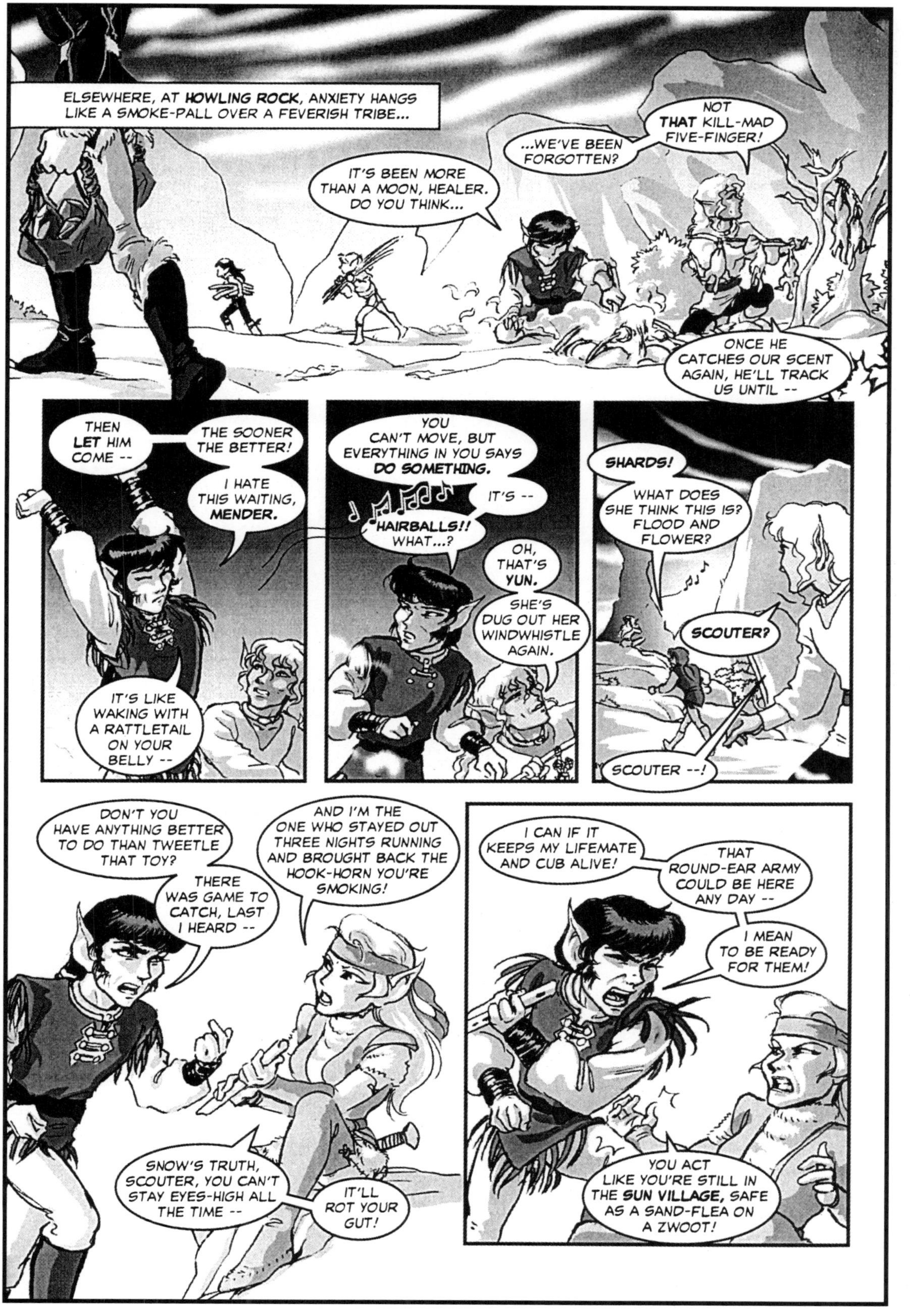

ELSEWHERE, AT HOWLING ROCK, ANXIETY HANGS LIKE A SMOKE-PALL OVER A FEVERISH TRIBE...
IT'S BEEN MORE THAN A MOON, HEALER. DO YOU THINK...
...WE'VE BEEN FORGOTTEN?
NOT THAT KILL-MAD FIVE-FINGER!
ONCE HE CATCHES OUR SCENT AGAIN, HE'LL TRACK US UNTIL --
THEN LET HIM COME --
THE SOONER THE BETTER!
I HATE THIS WAITING, MENDER.
IT'S LIKE WAKING WITH A RATTLETAIL ON YOUR BELLY --
YOU CAN'T MOVE, BUT EVERYTHING IN YOU SAYS DO SOMETHING.
IT'S --
HAIRBALLS!! WHAT...?
OH, THAT'S YUN.
SHE'S DUG OUT HER WINDWHISTLE AGAIN.
SHARDS!
WHAT DOES SHE THINK THIS IS? FLOOD AND FLOWER?
SCOUTER?
SCOUTER --!
DON'T YOU HAVE ANYTHING BETTER TO DO THAN TWEETLE THAT TOY?
THERE WAS GAME TO CATCH, LAST I HEARD --
AND I'M THE ONE WHO STAYED OUT THREE NIGHTS RUNNING AND BROUGHT BACK THE HOOK-HORN YOU'RE SMOKING!
SNOW'S TRUTH, SCOUTER, YOU CAN'T STAY EYES-HIGH ALL THE TIME --
IT'LL ROT YOUR GUT!
I CAN IF IT KEEPS MY LIFEMATE AND CUB ALIVE!
THAT ROUND-EAR ARMY COULD BE HERE ANY DAY --
I MEAN TO BE READY FOR THEM!
YOU ACT LIKE YOU'RE STILL IN THE SUN VILLAGE, SAFE AS A SAND-FLEA ON A ZWOOT!

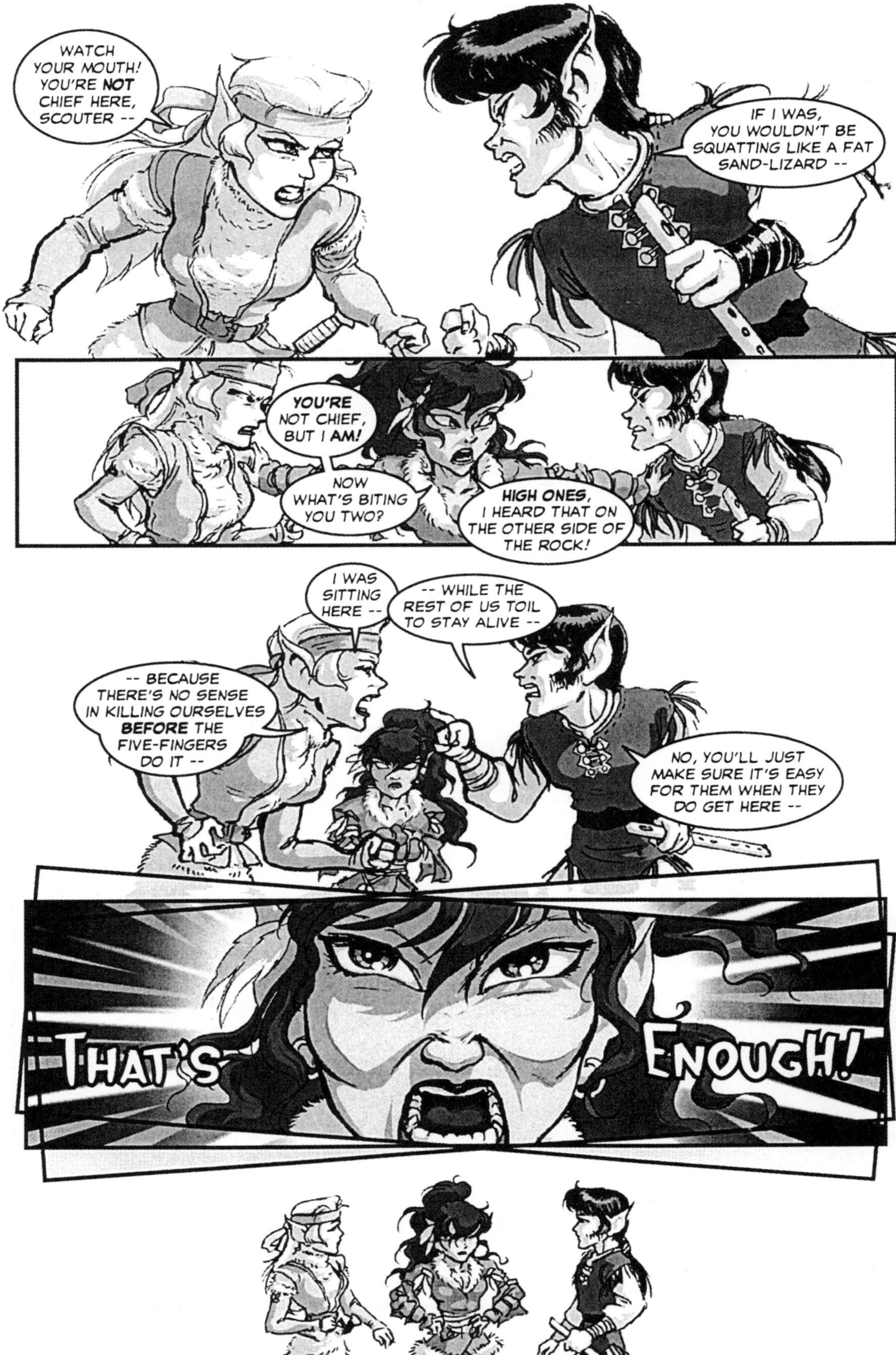
WATCH YOUR MOUTH! YOU'RE **NOT** CHIEF HERE, SCOUTER --
IF I WAS, YOU WOULDN'T BE SQUATTING LIKE A FAT SAND-LIZARD --
YOU'RE NOT CHIEF, BUT I **AM!**
NOW WHAT'S BITING YOU TWO?
HIGH ONES, I HEARD THAT ON THE OTHER SIDE OF THE ROCK!
I WAS SITTING HERE --
-- WHILE THE REST OF US TOIL TO STAY ALIVE --
-- BECAUSE THERE'S NO SENSE IN KILLING OURSELVES **BEFORE** THE FIVE-FINGERS DO IT --
NO, YOU'LL JUST MAKE SURE IT'S EASY FOR THEM WHEN THEY DO GET HERE --
THAT'S ENOUGH!

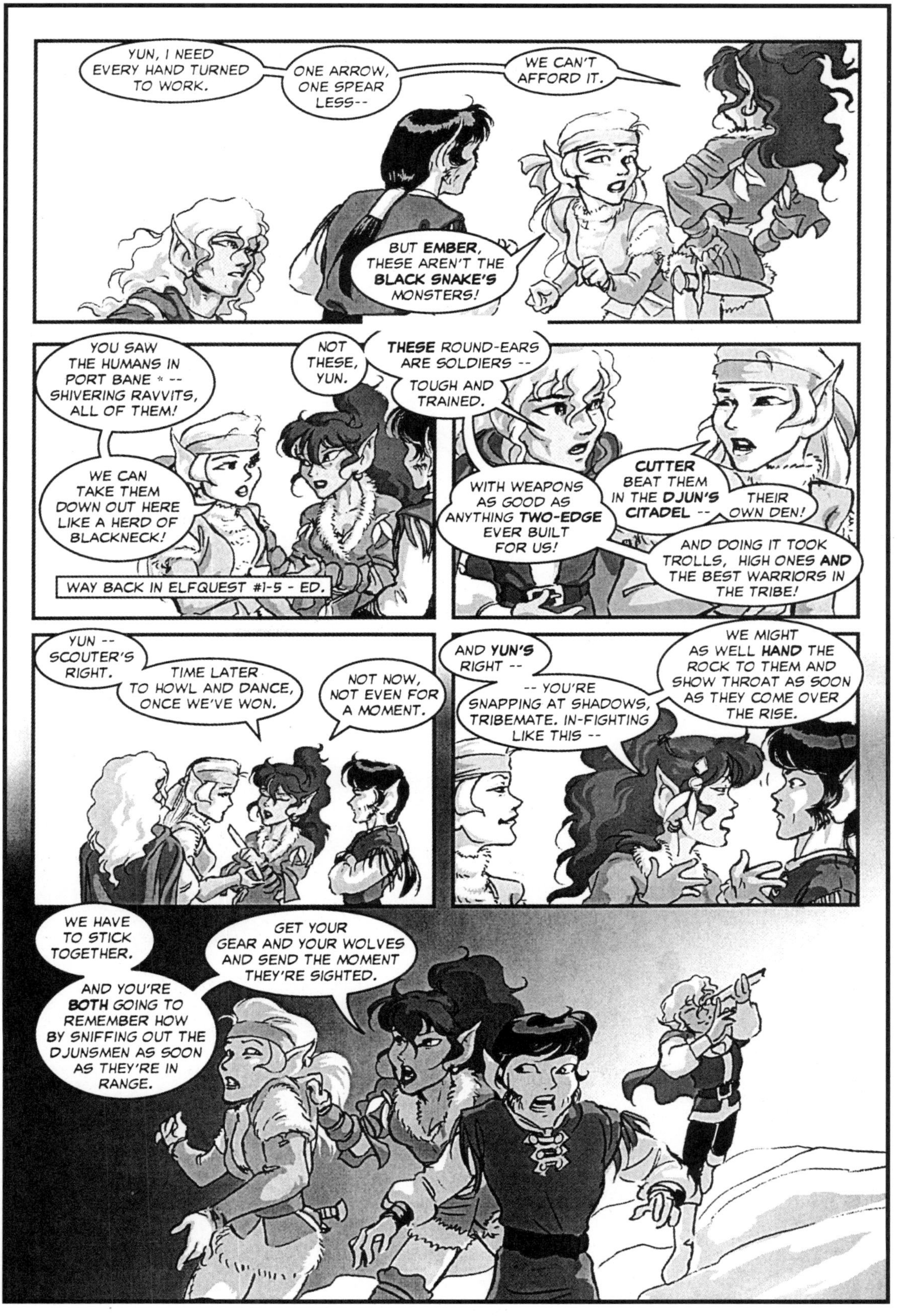
YUN, I NEED EVERY HAND TURNED TO WORK.
ONE ARROW, ONE SPEAR LESS--
WE CAN'T AFFORD IT.
BUT EMBER, THESE AREN'T THE BLACK SNAKE'S MONSTERS!
YOU SAW THE HUMANS IN PORT BANE * -- SHIVERING RAVVITS, ALL OF THEM!
WE CAN TAKE THEM DOWN OUT HERE LIKE A HERD OF BLACKNECK!
WAY BACK IN ELFQUEST #1-5 - ED.
NOT THESE, YUN.
THESE ROUND-EARS ARE SOLDIERS --
TOUGH AND TRAINED.
WITH WEAPONS AS GOOD AS ANYTHING TWO-EDGE EVER BUILT FOR US!
CUTTER BEAT THEM IN THE DJUN'S CITADEL --
THEIR OWN DEN!
AND DOING IT TOOK TROLLS, HIGH ONES AND THE BEST WARRIORS IN THE TRIBE!
YUN -- SCOUTER'S RIGHT.
TIME LATER TO HOWL AND DANCE, ONCE WE'VE WON.
NOT NOW, NOT EVEN FOR A MOMENT.
AND YUN'S RIGHT --
-- YOU'RE SNAPPING AT SHADOWS, TRIBEMATE. IN-FIGHTING LIKE THIS --
WE MIGHT AS WELL HAND THE ROCK TO THEM AND SHOW THROAT AS SOON AS THEY COME OVER THE RISE.
WE HAVE TO STICK TOGETHER.
AND YOU'RE BOTH GOING TO REMEMBER HOW BY SNIFFING OUT THE DJUNSMEN AS SOON AS THEY'RE IN RANGE.
GET YOUR GEAR AND YOUR WOLVES AND SEND THE MOMENT THEY'RE SIGHTED.

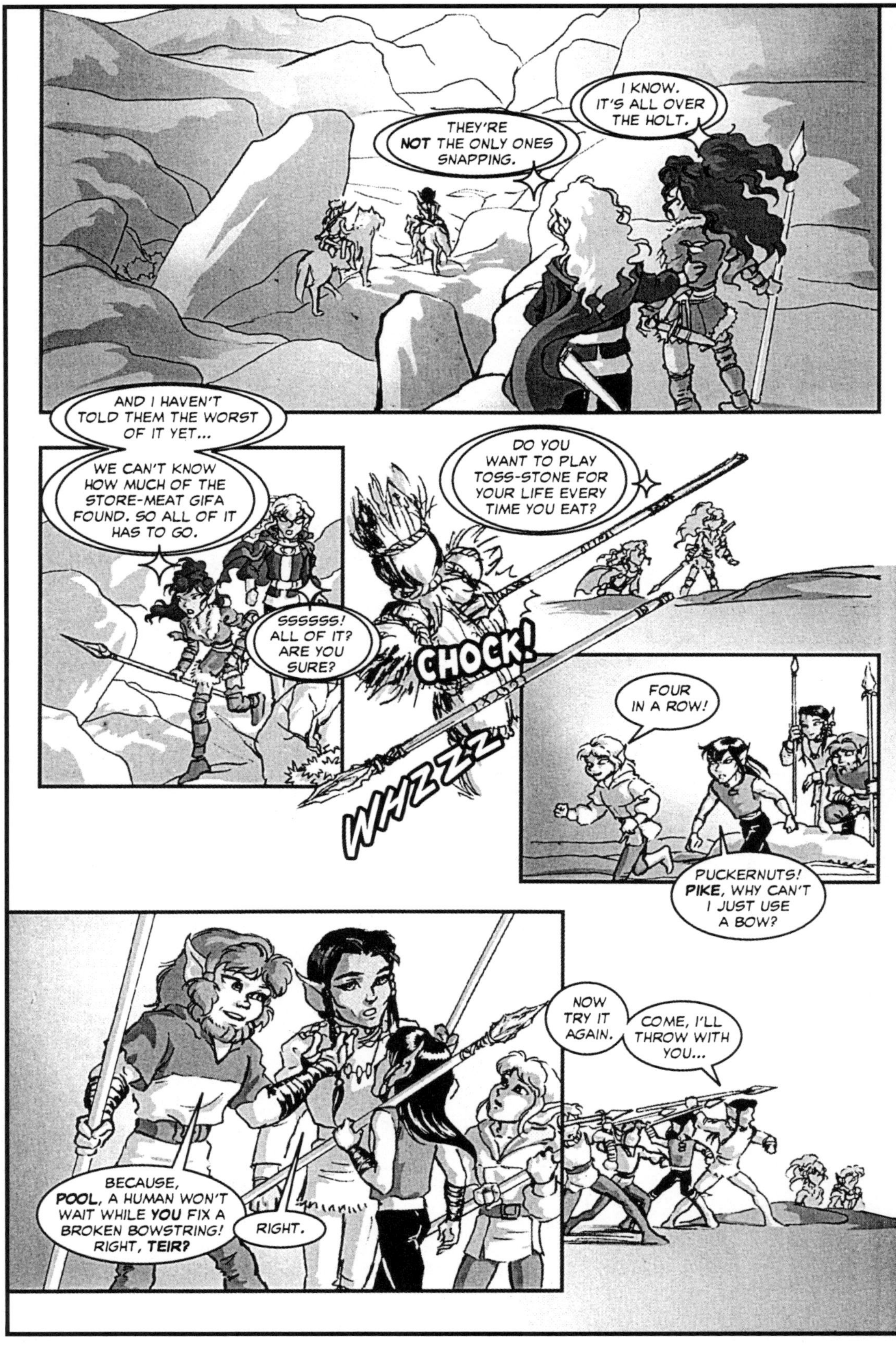
THEY'RE NOT THE ONLY ONES SNAPPING.
I KNOW. IT'S ALL OVER THE HOLT.
AND I HAVEN'T TOLD THEM THE WORST OF IT YET...
WE CAN'T KNOW HOW MUCH OF THE STORE-MEAT GIFA FOUND. SO ALL OF IT HAS TO GO.
SSSSSS! ALL OF IT? ARE YOU SURE?
DO YOU WANT TO PLAY TOSS-STONE FOR YOUR LIFE EVERY TIME YOU EAT?
CHOCK!
WHZZZ
FOUR IN A ROW!
PUCKERNUTS! PIKE, WHY CAN'T I JUST USE A BOW?
BECAUSE, POOL, A HUMAN WON'T WAIT WHILE YOU FIX A BROKEN BOWSTRING! RIGHT, TEIR?
RIGHT.
NOW TRY IT AGAIN.
COME, I'LL THROW WITH YOU...

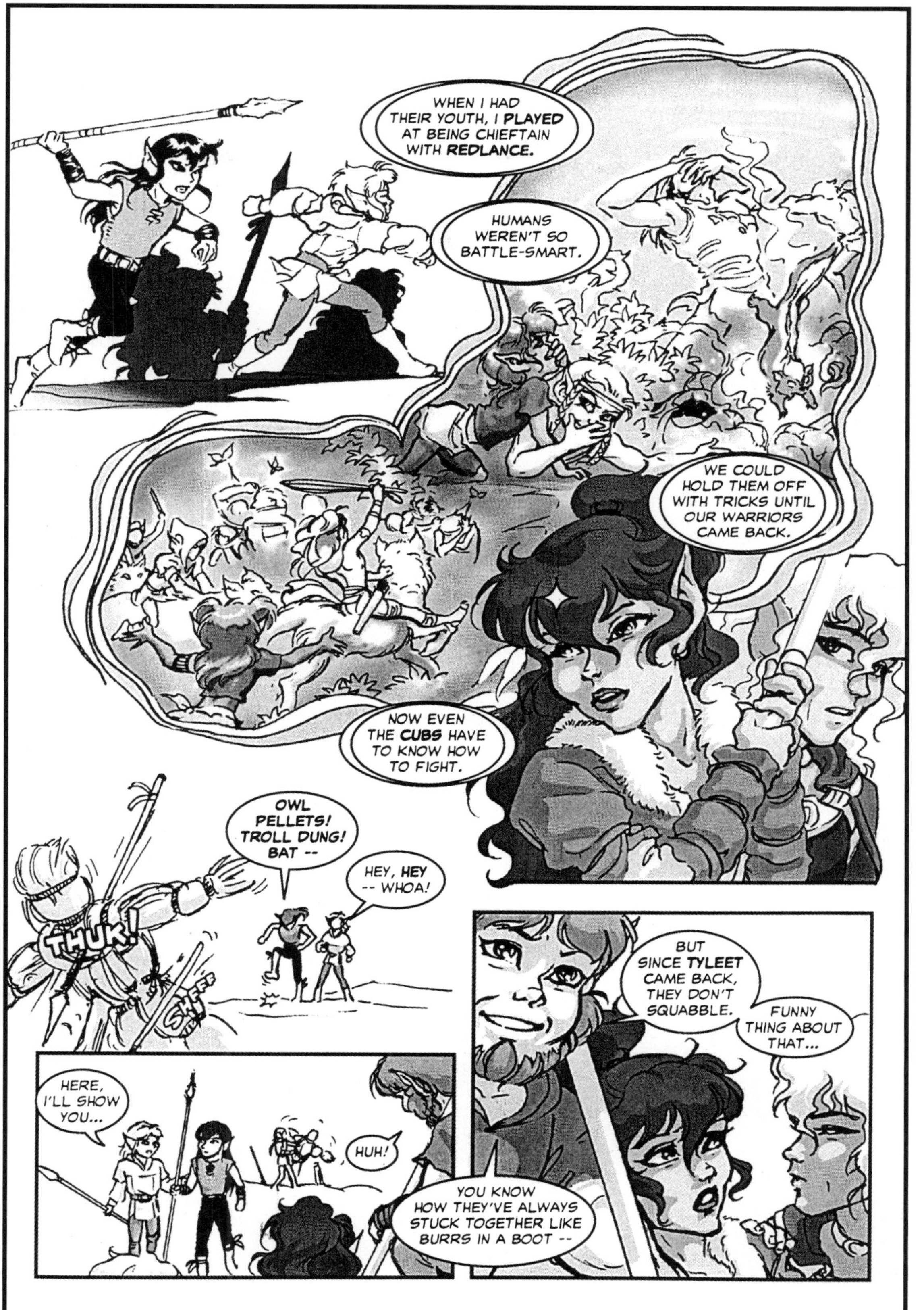
WHEN I HAD THEIR YOUTH, I PLAYED AT BEING CHIEFTAIN WITH REDLANCE.
HUMANS WEREN'T SO BATTLE-SMART.
WE COULD HOLD THEM OFF WITH TRICKS UNTIL OUR WARRIORS CAME BACK.
NOW EVEN THE CUBS HAVE TO KNOW HOW TO FIGHT.
OWL PELLETS! TROLL DUNG! BAT --
HEY, HEY -- WHOA!
THUK!
SHFF
BUT SINCE TYLEET CAME BACK, THEY DON'T SQUABBLE.
FUNNY THING ABOUT THAT...
HERE, I'LL SHOW YOU...
HUH!
YOU KNOW HOW THEY'VE ALWAYS STUCK TOGETHER LIKE BURRS IN A BOOT --

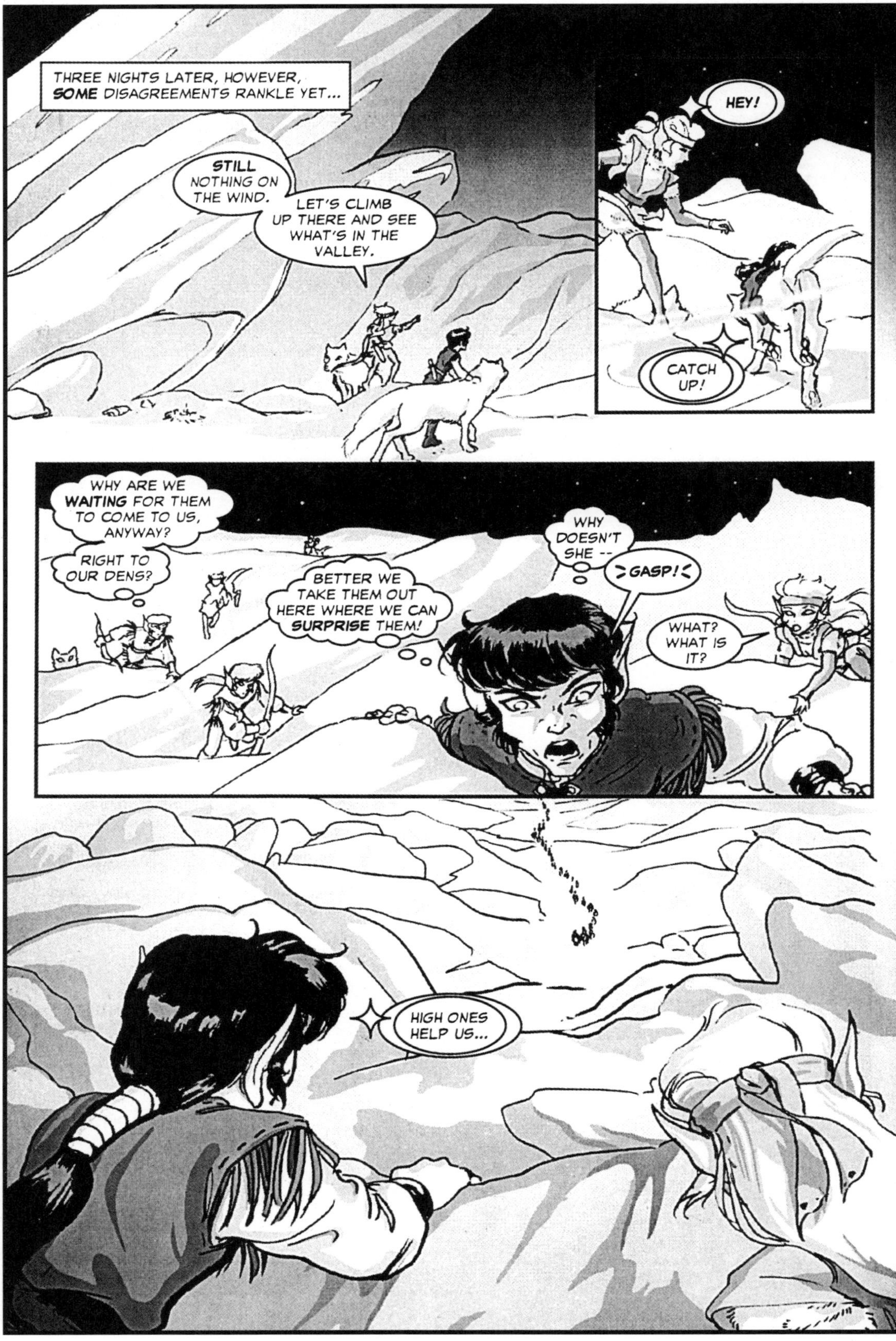

THREE NIGHTS LATER, HOWEVER, SOME DISAGREEMENTS RANKLE YET...
STILL NOTHING ON THE WIND.
LET'S CLIMB UP THERE AND SEE WHAT'S IN THE VALLEY.
HEY!
CATCH UP!
WHY ARE WE WAITING FOR THEM TO COME TO US, ANYWAY?
RIGHT TO OUR DENS?
BETTER WE TAKE THEM OUT HERE WHERE WE CAN SURPRISE THEM!
WHY DOESN'T SHE --
GASP!
WHAT? WHAT IS IT?
HIGH ONES HELP US...

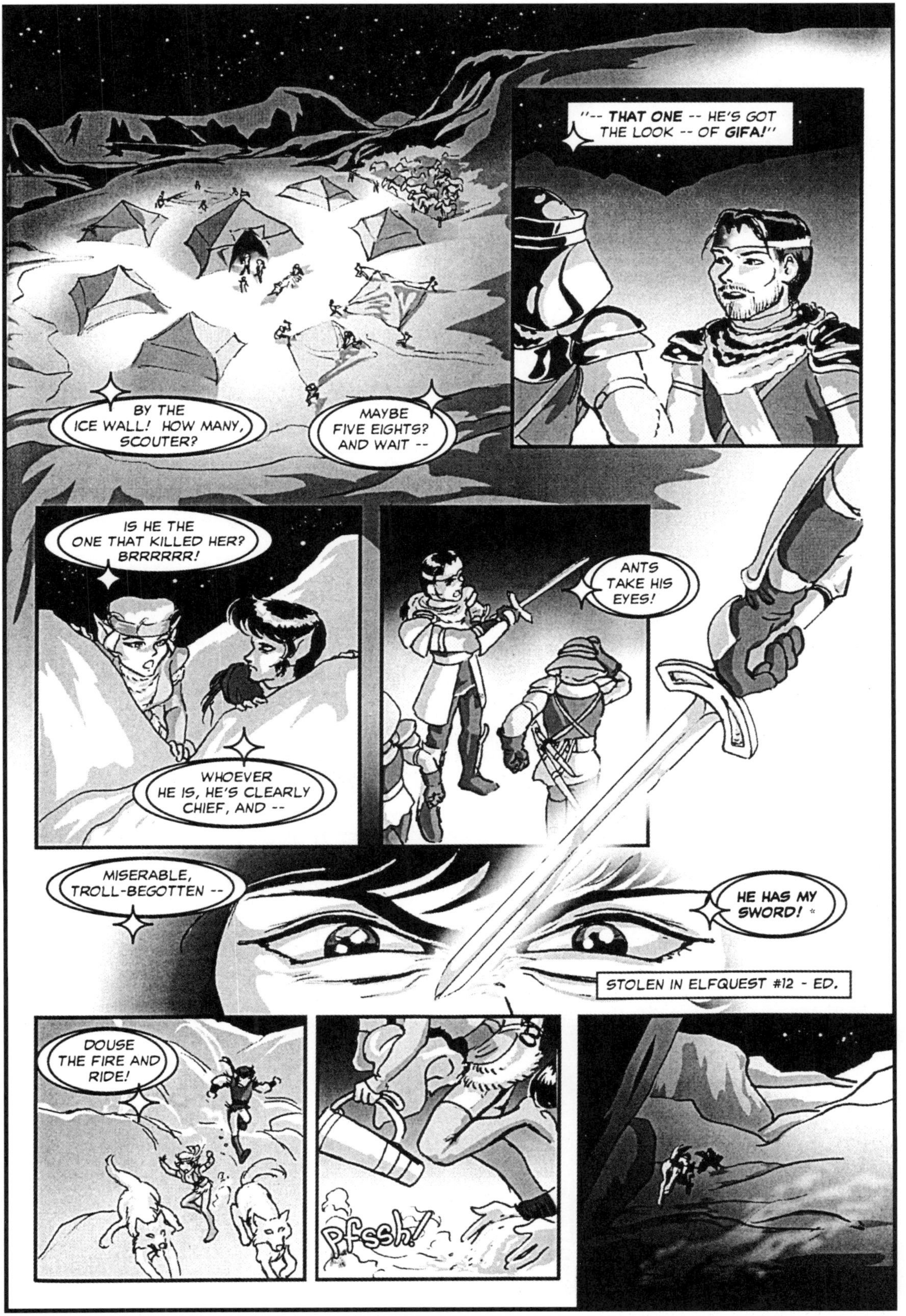

BY THE ICE WALL! HOW MANY, SCOUTER?
MAYBE FIVE EIGHTS? AND WAIT --
"-- THAT ONE -- HE'S GOT THE LOOK -- OF GIFA!"
IS HE THE ONE THAT KILLED HER? BRRRRRR!
WHOEVER HE IS, HE'S CLEARLY CHIEF, AND --
ANTS TAKE HIS EYES!
MISERABLE, TROLL-BEGOTTEN --
HE HAS MY SWORD! *
* STOLEN IN ELFQUEST #12 - ED.
DOUSE THE FIRE AND RIDE!
PFSSH!

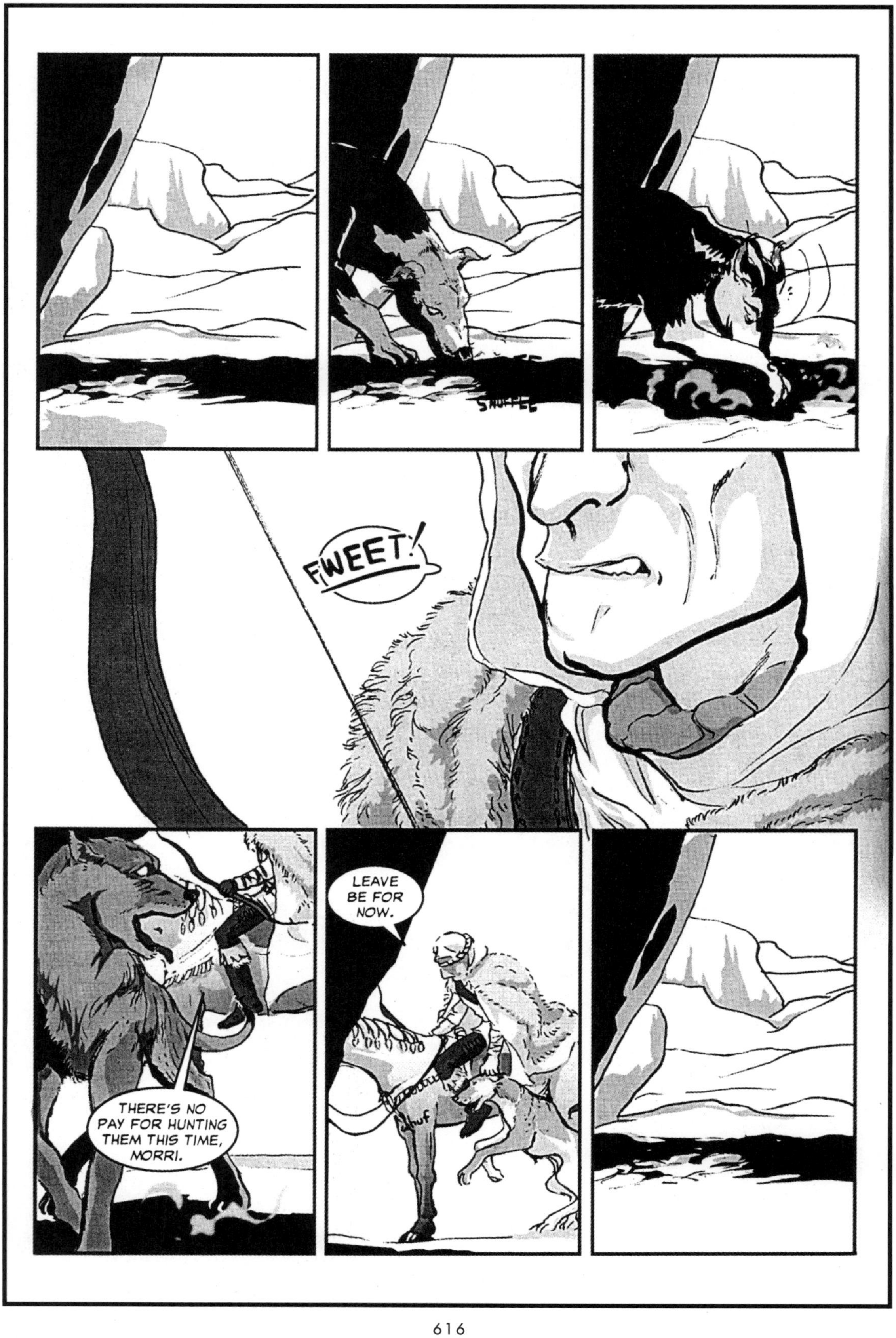

SNUFFLE
FWEET!
THERE'S NO PAY FOR HUNTING THEM THIS TIME, MORRI.
LEAVE BE FOR NOW.

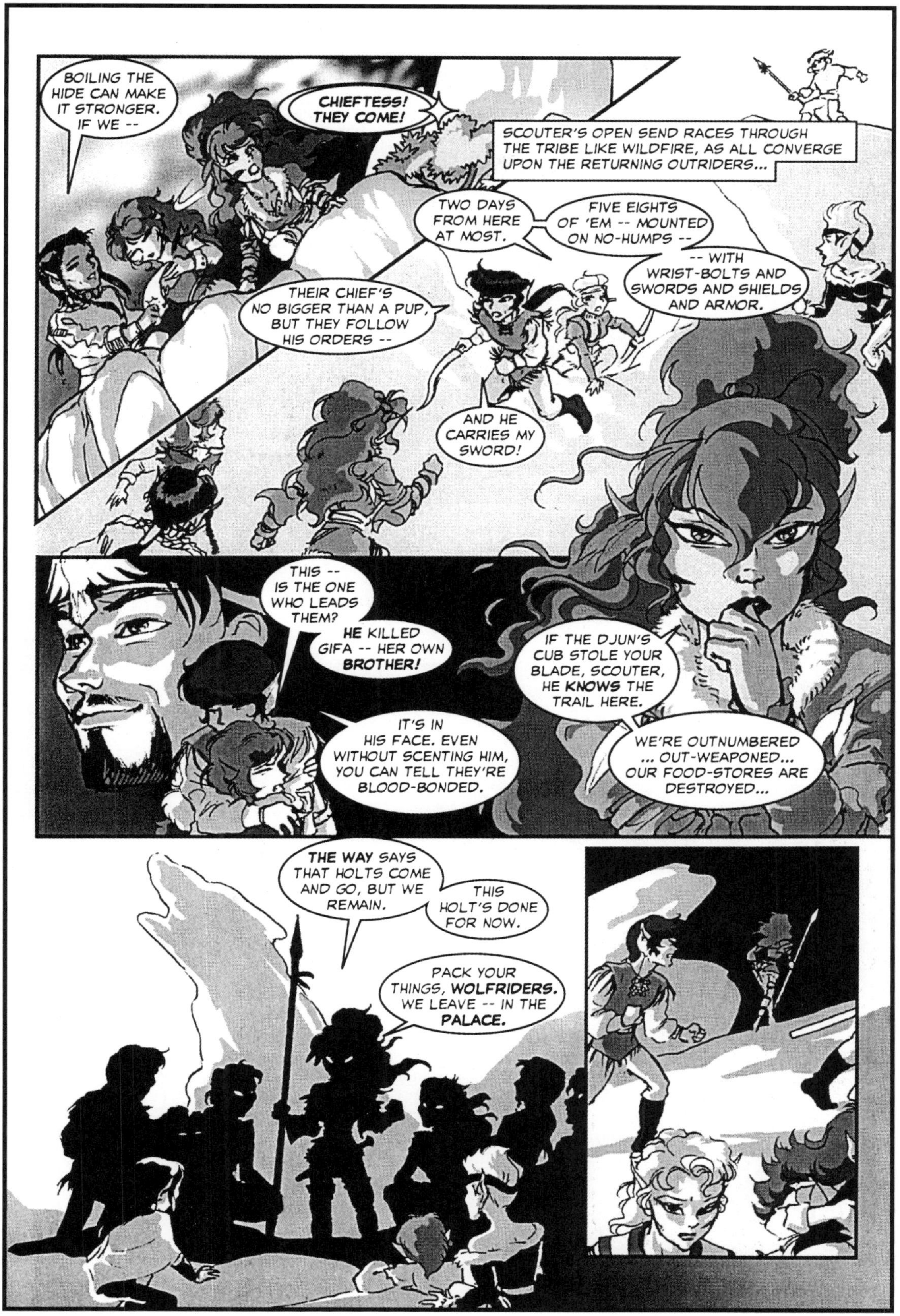
BOILING THE HIDE CAN MAKE IT STRONGER. IF WE --
CHIEFTESS! THEY COME!
SCOUTER'S OPEN SEND RACES THROUGH THE TRIBE LIKE WILDFIRE, AS ALL CONVERGE UPON THE RETURNING OUTRIDERS...
TWO DAYS FROM HERE AT MOST.
FIVE EIGHTS OF 'EM -- MOUNTED ON NO-HUMPS --
-- WITH WRIST-BOLTS AND SWORDS AND SHIELDS AND ARMOR.
THEIR CHIEF'S NO BIGGER THAN A PUP, BUT THEY FOLLOW HIS ORDERS --
AND HE CARRIES MY SWORD!
THIS -- IS THE ONE WHO LEADS THEM?
HE KILLED GIFA -- HER OWN BROTHER!
IT'S IN HIS FACE. EVEN WITHOUT SCENTING HIM, YOU CAN TELL THEY'RE BLOOD-BONDED.
IF THE DJUN'S CUB STOLE YOUR BLADE, SCOUTER, HE KNOWS THE TRAIL HERE.
WE'RE OUTNUMBERED ... OUT-WEAPONED... OUR FOOD-STORES ARE DESTROYED...
THE WAY SAYS THAT HOLTS COME AND GO, BUT WE REMAIN.
THIS HOLT'S DONE FOR NOW.
PACK YOUR THINGS, WOLFRIDERS. WE LEAVE -- IN THE PALACE.

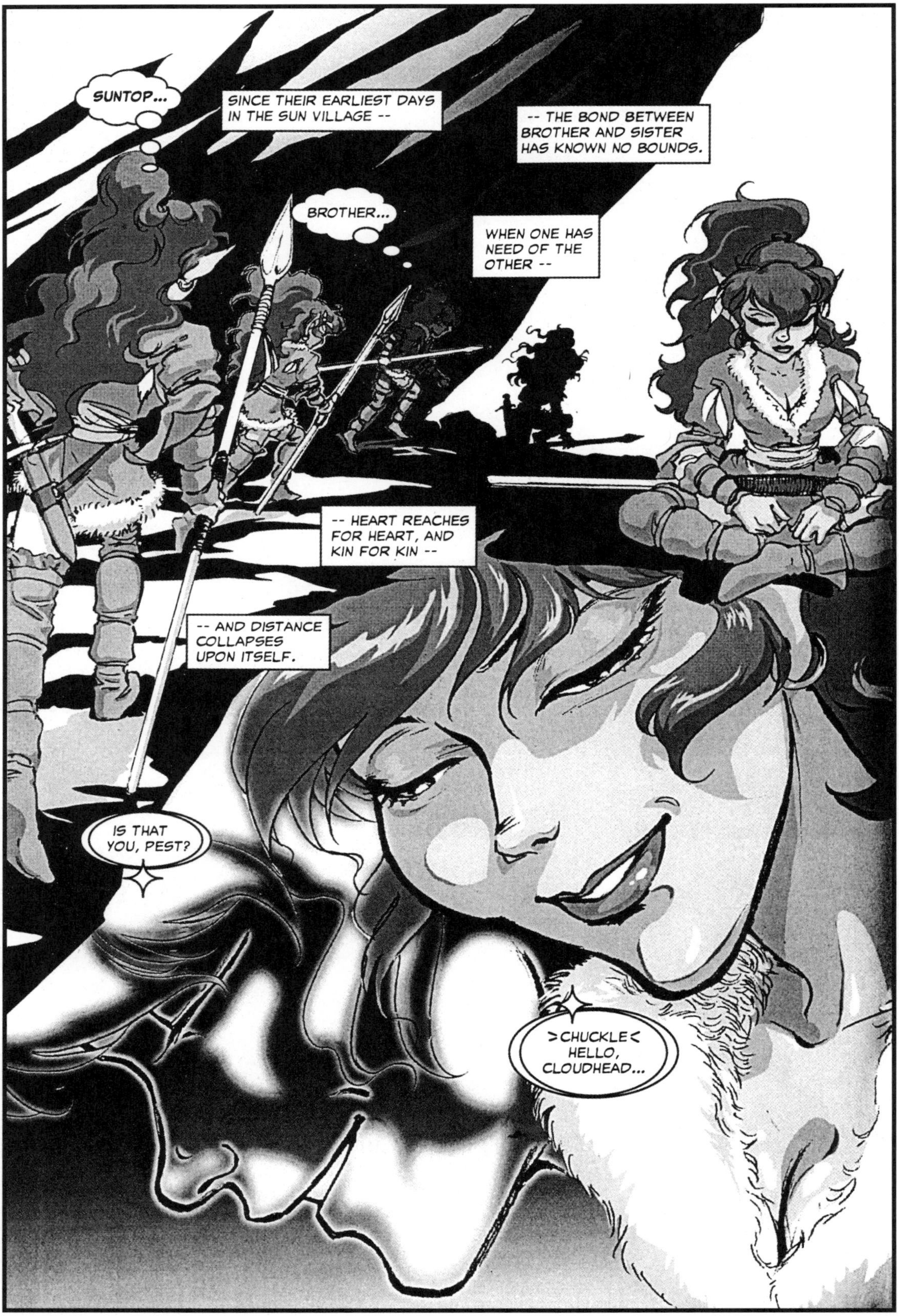
SUNTOP...
SINCE THEIR EARLIEST DAYS IN THE SUN VILLAGE --
-- THE BOND BETWEEN BROTHER AND SISTER HAS KNOWN NO BOUNDS.
BROTHER...
WHEN ONE HAS NEED OF THE OTHER --
-- HEART REACHES FOR HEART, AND KIN FOR KIN --
-- AND DISTANCE COLLAPSES UPON ITSELF.
IS THAT YOU, PEST?
>CHUCKLE< HELLO, CLOUDHEAD...

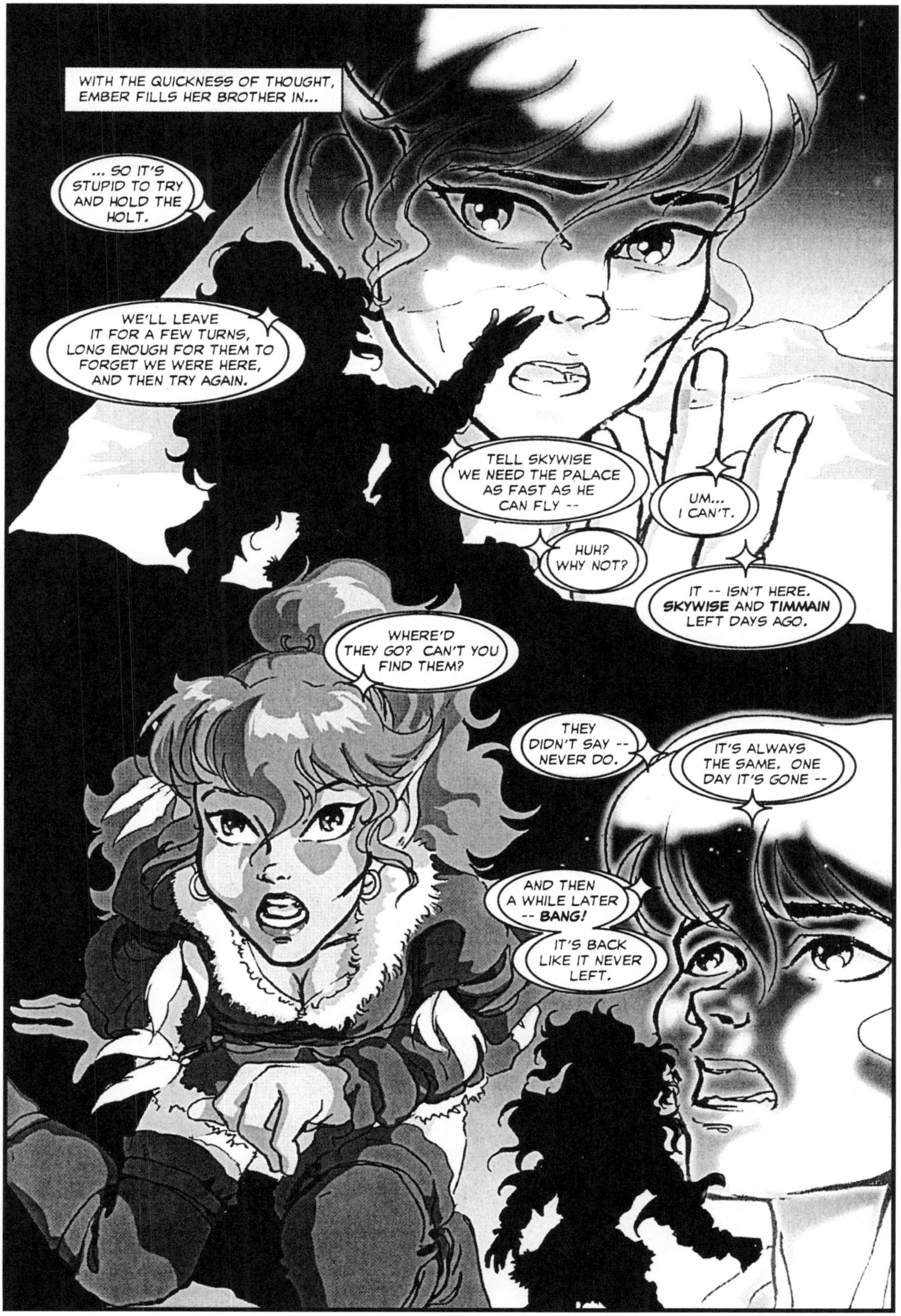
WITH THE QUICKNESS OF THOUGHT, EMBER FILLS HER BROTHER IN...
... SO IT'S STUPID TO TRY AND HOLD THE HOLT.
WE'LL LEAVE IT FOR A FEW TURNS, LONG ENOUGH FOR THEM TO FORGET WE WERE HERE, AND THEN TRY AGAIN.
TELL SKYWISE WE NEED THE PALACE AS FAST AS HE CAN FLY --
UM... I CAN'T.
HUH? WHY NOT?
IT -- ISN'T HERE. **SKYWISE** AND **TIMMAIN** LEFT DAYS AGO.
WHERE'D THEY GO? CAN'T YOU FIND THEM?
THEY DIDN'T SAY -- NEVER DO.
IT'S ALWAYS THE SAME. ONE DAY IT'S GONE --
AND THEN A WHILE LATER -- **BANG!**
IT'S BACK LIKE IT NEVER LEFT.

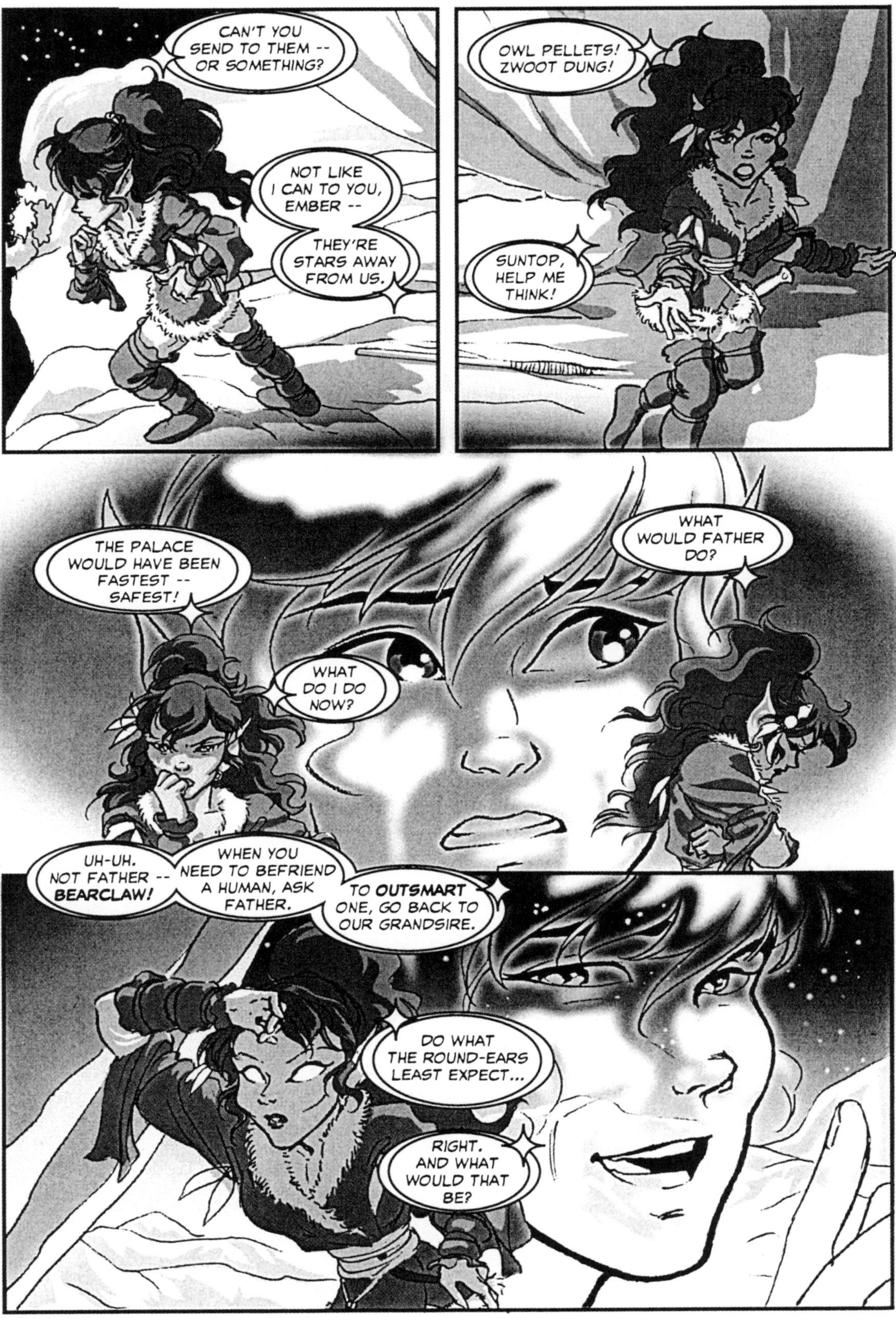
CAN'T YOU SEND TO THEM -- OR SOMETHING?
NOT LIKE I CAN TO YOU, EMBER --
THEY'RE STARS AWAY FROM US.
OWL PELLETS! ZWOOT DUNG!
SUNTOP, HELP ME THINK!
THE PALACE WOULD HAVE BEEN FASTEST -- SAFEST!
WHAT DO I DO NOW?
WHAT WOULD FATHER DO?
UH-UH. NOT FATHER -- **BEARCLAW!**
WHEN YOU NEED TO BEFRIEND A HUMAN, ASK FATHER.
TO **OUTSMART** ONE, GO BACK TO OUR GRANDSIRE.
DO WHAT THE ROUND-EARS LEAST EXPECT...
RIGHT. AND WHAT WOULD THAT BE?

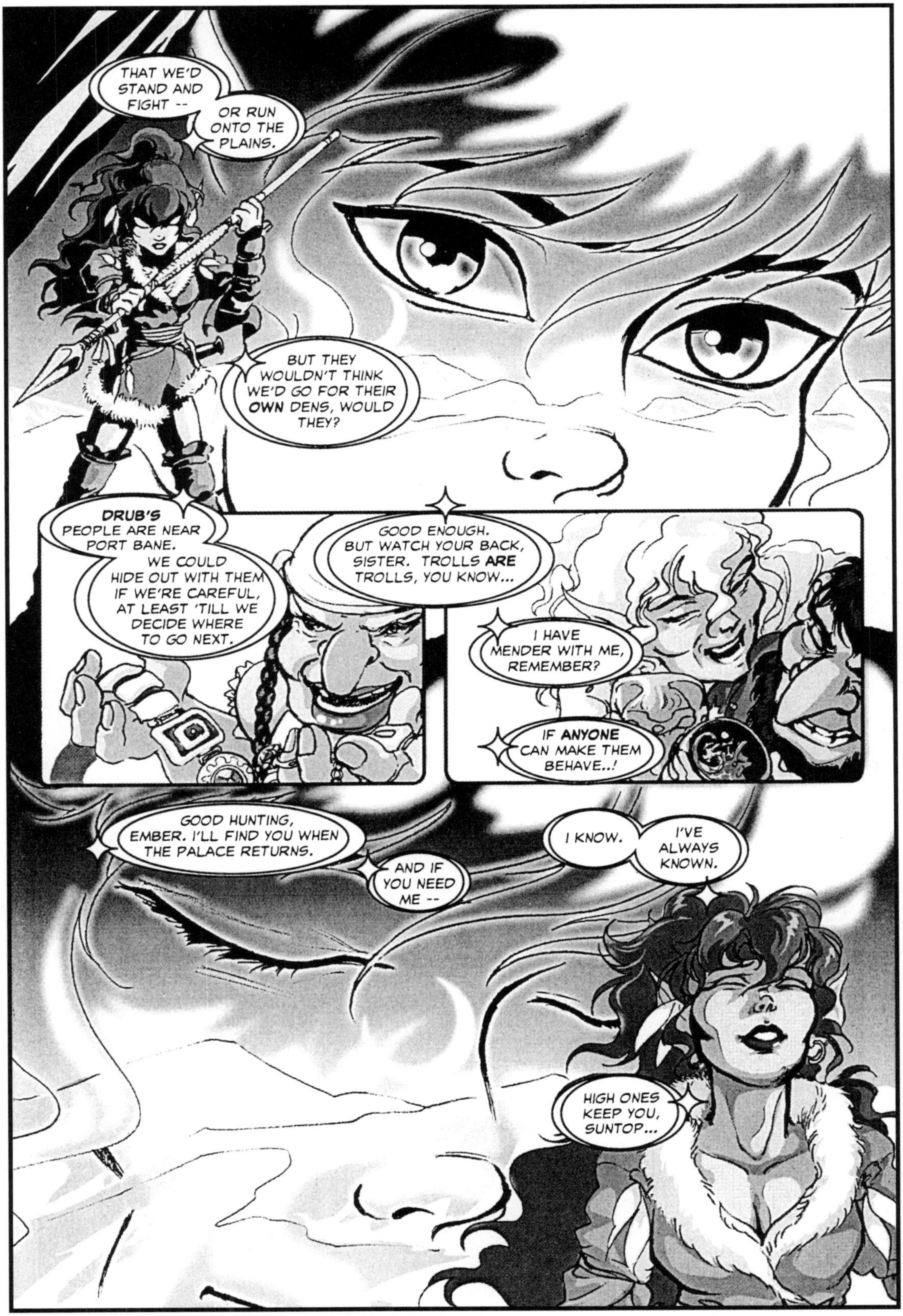
THAT WE'D STAND AND FIGHT --
OR RUN ONTO THE PLAINS.
BUT THEY WOULDN'T THINK WE'D GO FOR THEIR OWN DENS, WOULD THEY?
DRUB'S PEOPLE ARE NEAR PORT BANE.
WE COULD HIDE OUT WITH THEM IF WE'RE CAREFUL, AT LEAST 'TILL WE DECIDE WHERE TO GO NEXT.
GOOD ENOUGH. BUT WATCH YOUR BACK, SISTER. TROLLS ARE TROLLS, YOU KNOW...
I HAVE MENDER WITH ME, REMEMBER?
IF ANYONE CAN MAKE THEM BEHAVE..!
GOOD HUNTING, EMBER. I'LL FIND YOU WHEN THE PALACE RETURNS.
AND IF YOU NEED ME --
I KNOW.
I'VE ALWAYS KNOWN.
HIGH ONES KEEP YOU, SUNTOP...

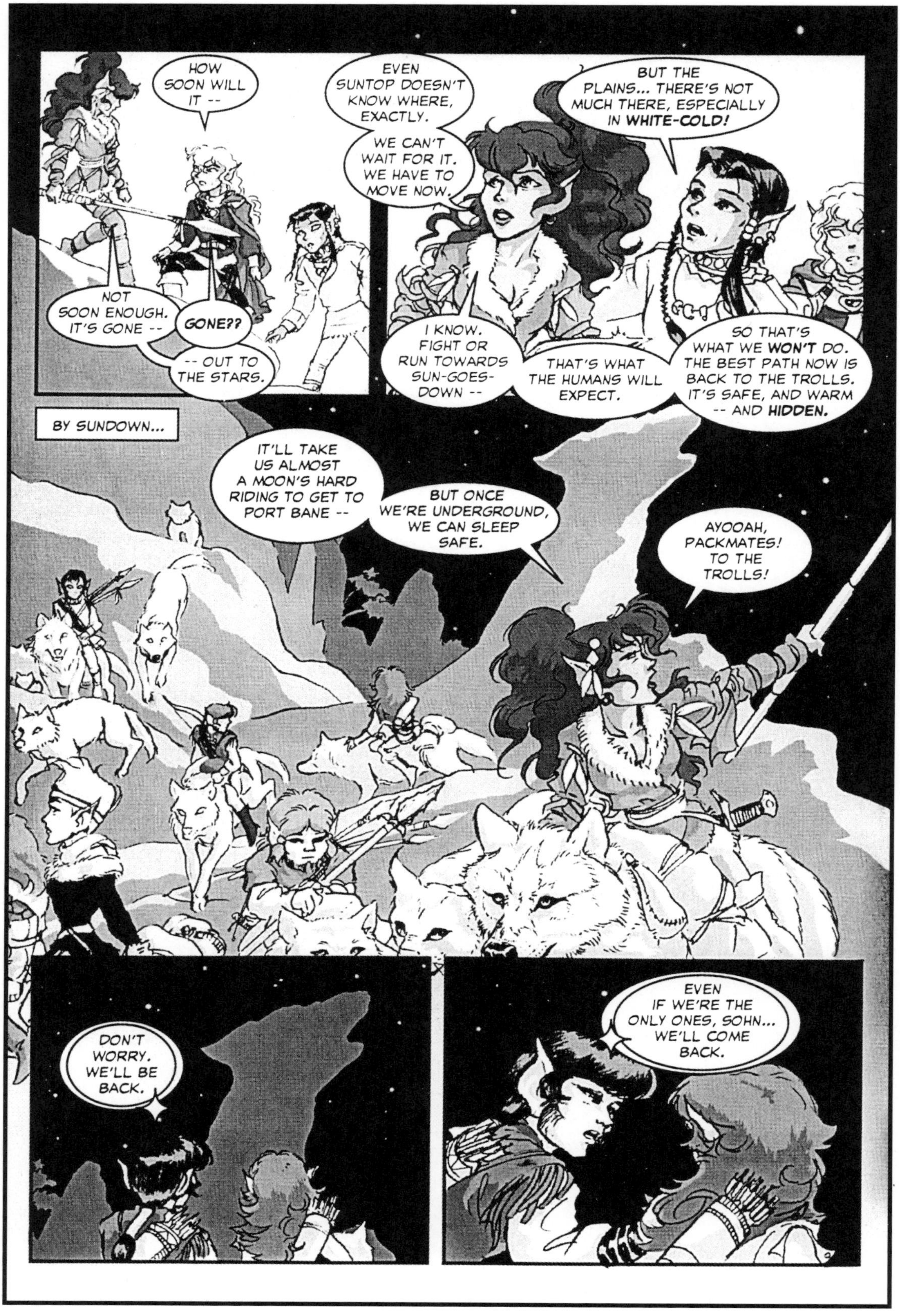
HOW SOON WILL IT --
NOT SOON ENOUGH. IT'S GONE --
GONE??
-- OUT TO THE STARS.
EVEN SUNTOP DOESN'T KNOW WHERE, EXACTLY.
WE CAN'T WAIT FOR IT. WE HAVE TO MOVE NOW.
BUT THE PLAINS... THERE'S NOT MUCH THERE, ESPECIALLY IN WHITE-COLD!
I KNOW. FIGHT OR RUN TOWARDS SUN-GOES-DOWN --
THAT'S WHAT THE HUMANS WILL EXPECT.
SO THAT'S WHAT WE WON'T DO. THE BEST PATH NOW IS BACK TO THE TROLLS. IT'S SAFE, AND WARM -- AND HIDDEN.
BY SUNDOWN...
IT'LL TAKE US ALMOST A MOON'S HARD RIDING TO GET TO PORT BANE --
BUT ONCE WE'RE UNDERGROUND, WE CAN SLEEP SAFE.
AYOOAH, PACKMATES! TO THE TROLLS!
DON'T WORRY. WE'LL BE BACK.
EVEN IF WE'RE THE ONLY ONES, SOHN... WE'LL COME BACK.

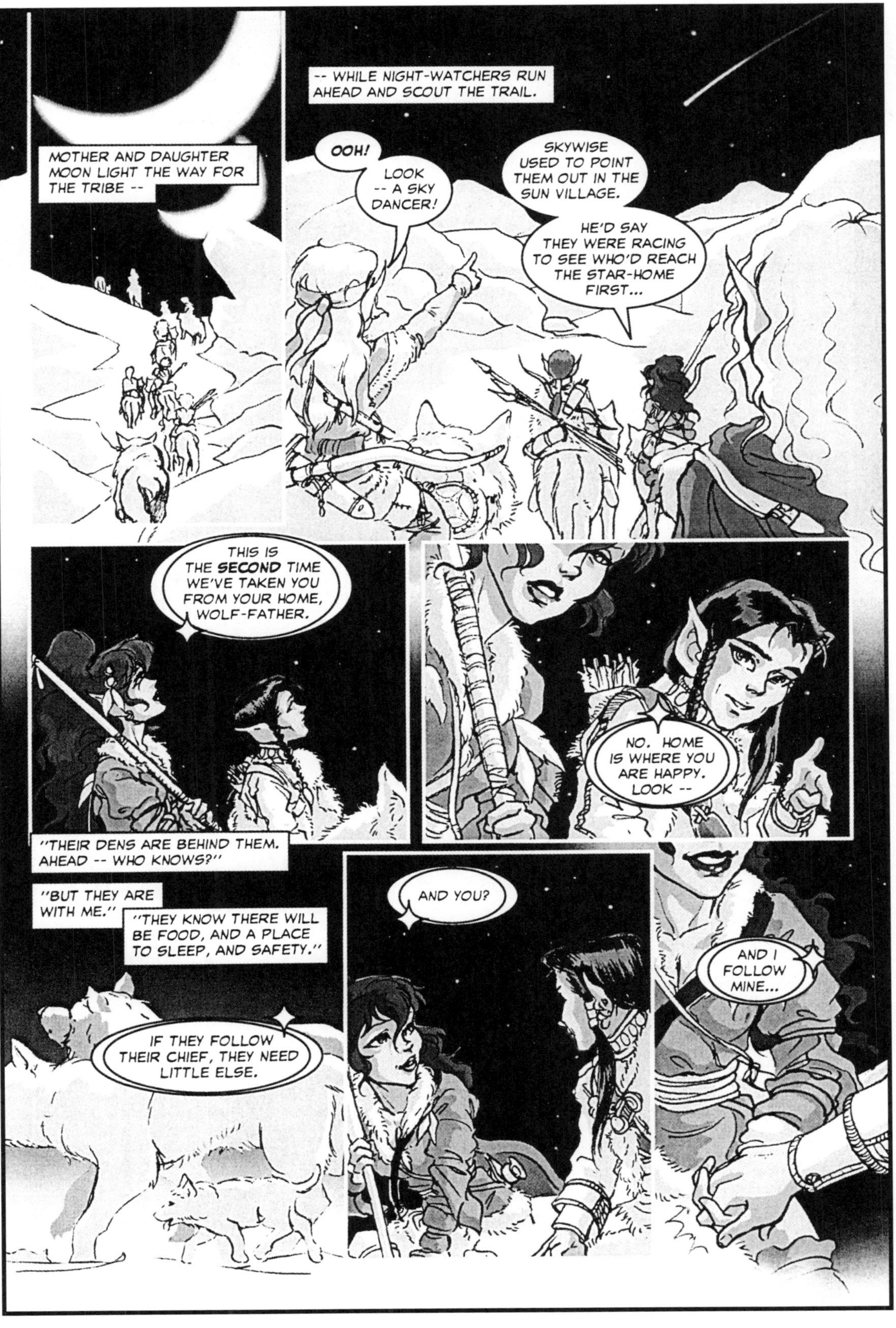
MOTHER AND DAUGHTER MOON LIGHT THE WAY FOR THE TRIBE --
-- WHILE NIGHT-WATCHERS RUN AHEAD AND SCOUT THE TRAIL.
OOH!
LOOK -- A SKY DANCER!
SKYWISE USED TO POINT THEM OUT IN THE SUN VILLAGE.
HE'D SAY THEY WERE RACING TO SEE WHO'D REACH THE STAR-HOME FIRST...
THIS IS THE SECOND TIME WE'VE TAKEN YOU FROM YOUR HOME, WOLF-FATHER.
NO. HOME IS WHERE YOU ARE HAPPY. LOOK --
"THEIR DENS ARE BEHIND THEM. AHEAD -- WHO KNOWS?"
"BUT THEY ARE WITH ME."
"THEY KNOW THERE WILL BE FOOD, AND A PLACE TO SLEEP, AND SAFETY."
IF THEY FOLLOW THEIR CHIEF, THEY NEED LITTLE ELSE.
AND YOU?
AND I FOLLOW MINE...

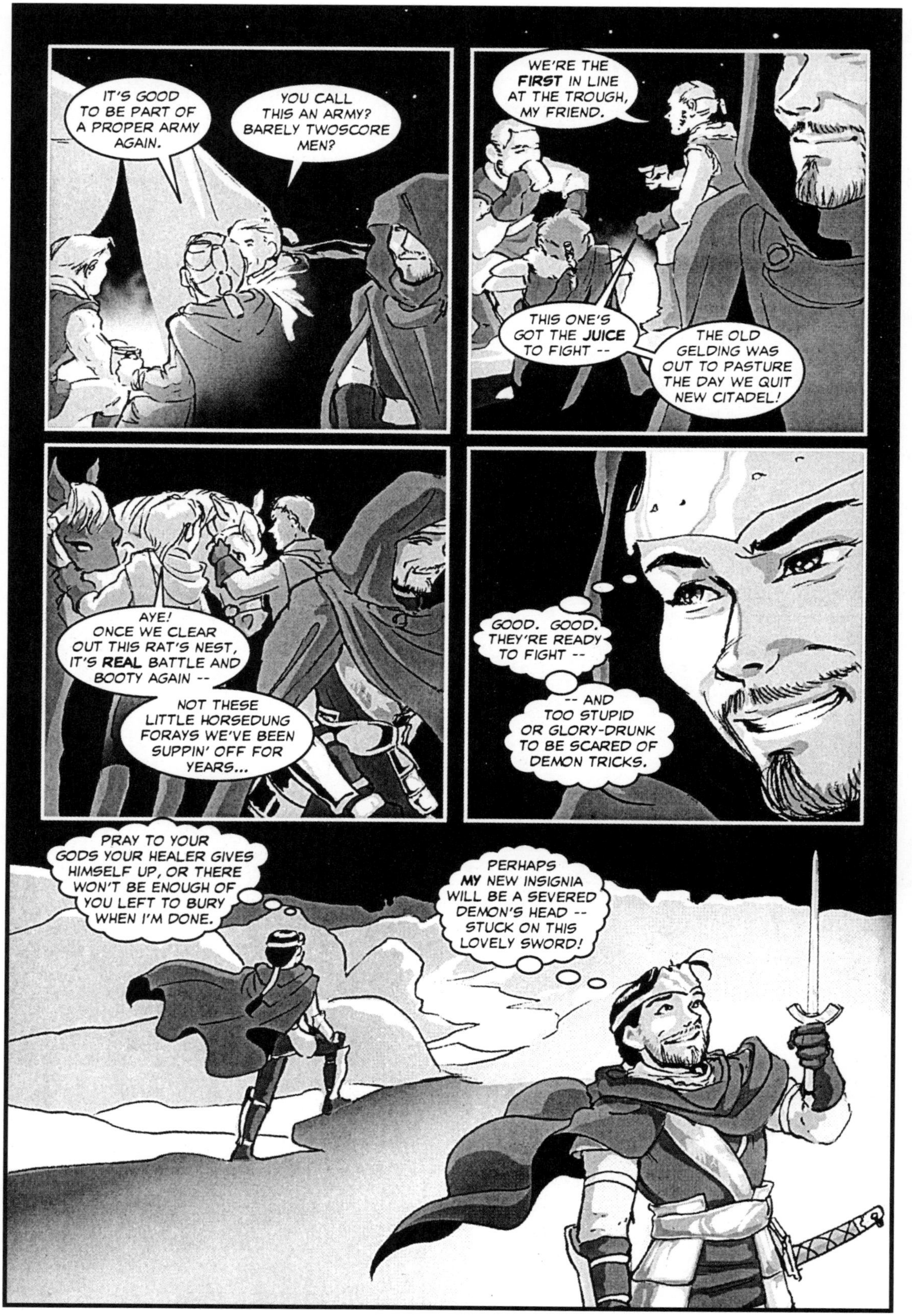

IT'S GOOD TO BE PART OF A PROPER ARMY AGAIN.
YOU CALL THIS AN ARMY? BARELY TWOSCORE MEN?
WE'RE THE **FIRST** IN LINE AT THE TROUGH, MY FRIEND.
THIS ONE'S GOT THE **JUICE** TO FIGHT --
THE OLD GELDING WAS OUT TO PASTURE THE DAY WE QUIT NEW CITADEL!
AYE! ONCE WE CLEAR OUT THIS RAT'S NEST, IT'S **REAL** BATTLE AND BOOTY AGAIN --
NOT THESE LITTLE HORSEDUNG FORAYS WE'VE BEEN SUPPIN' OFF FOR YEARS...
GOOD. GOOD. THEY'RE READY TO FIGHT --
-- AND TOO STUPID OR GLORY-DRUNK TO BE SCARED OF DEMON TRICKS.
PRAY TO YOUR GODS YOUR HEALER GIVES HIMSELF UP, OR THERE WON'T BE ENOUGH OF YOU LEFT TO BURY WHEN I'M DONE.
PERHAPS **MY** NEW INSIGNIA WILL BE A SEVERED DEMON'S HEAD -- STUCK ON THIS LOVELY SWORD!

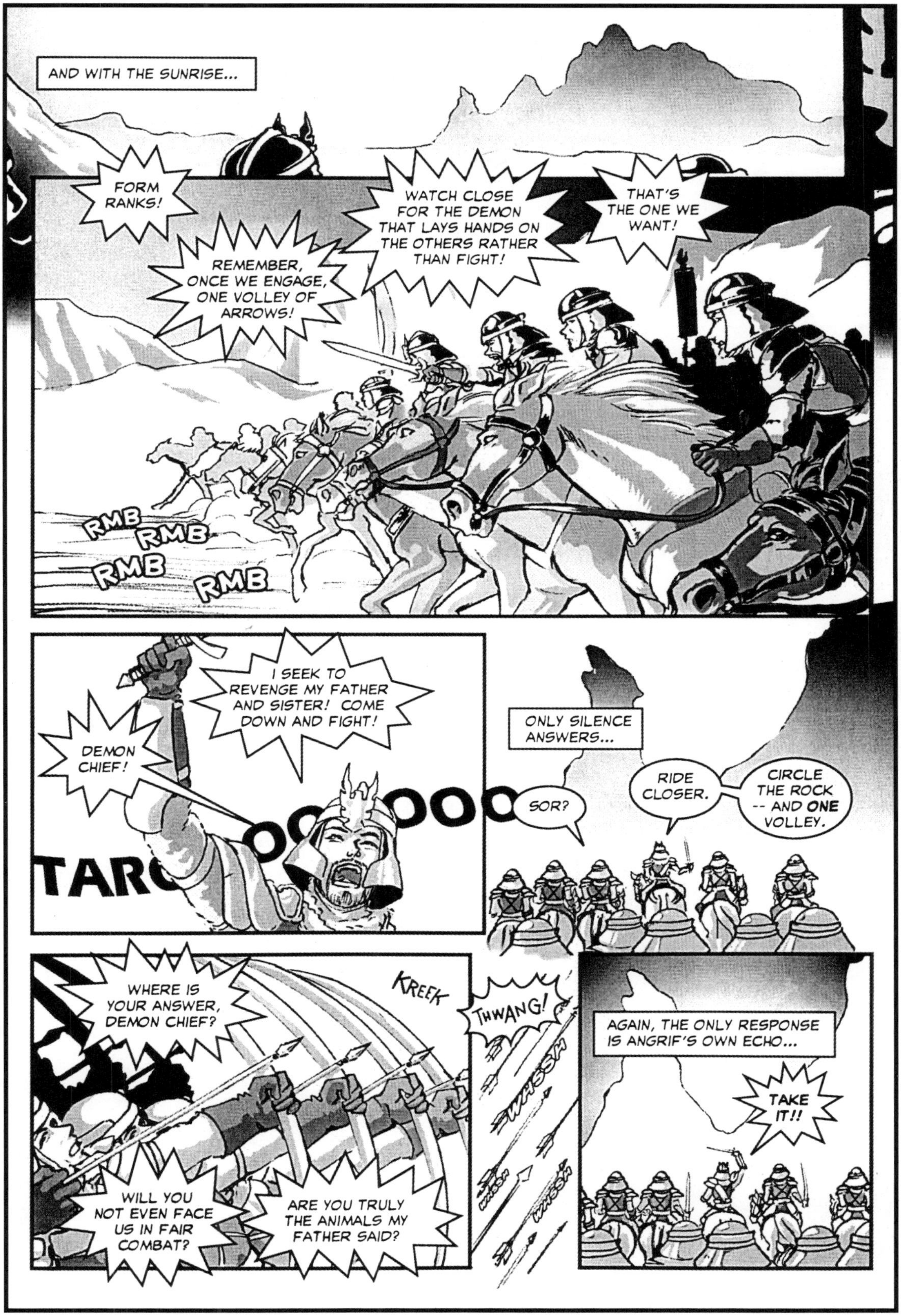
AND WITH THE SUNRISE...
FORM RANKS!
REMEMBER, ONCE WE ENGAGE, ONE VOLLEY OF ARROWS!
WATCH CLOSE FOR THE DEMON THAT LAYS HANDS ON THE OTHERS RATHER THAN FIGHT!
THAT'S THE ONE WE WANT!
RMB RMB RMB RMB
DEMON CHIEF!
I SEEK TO REVENGE MY FATHER AND SISTER! COME DOWN AND FIGHT!
TAROOOOOOO
ONLY SILENCE ANSWERS...
SOR?
RIDE CLOSER.
CIRCLE THE ROCK -- AND ONE VOLLEY.
WHERE IS YOUR ANSWER, DEMON CHIEF?
KREEK
THWANG!
WILL YOU NOT EVEN FACE US IN FAIR COMBAT?
ARE YOU TRULY THE ANIMALS MY FATHER SAID?
WHSSH
AGAIN, THE ONLY RESPONSE IS ANGRIF'S OWN ECHO...
TAKE IT!!

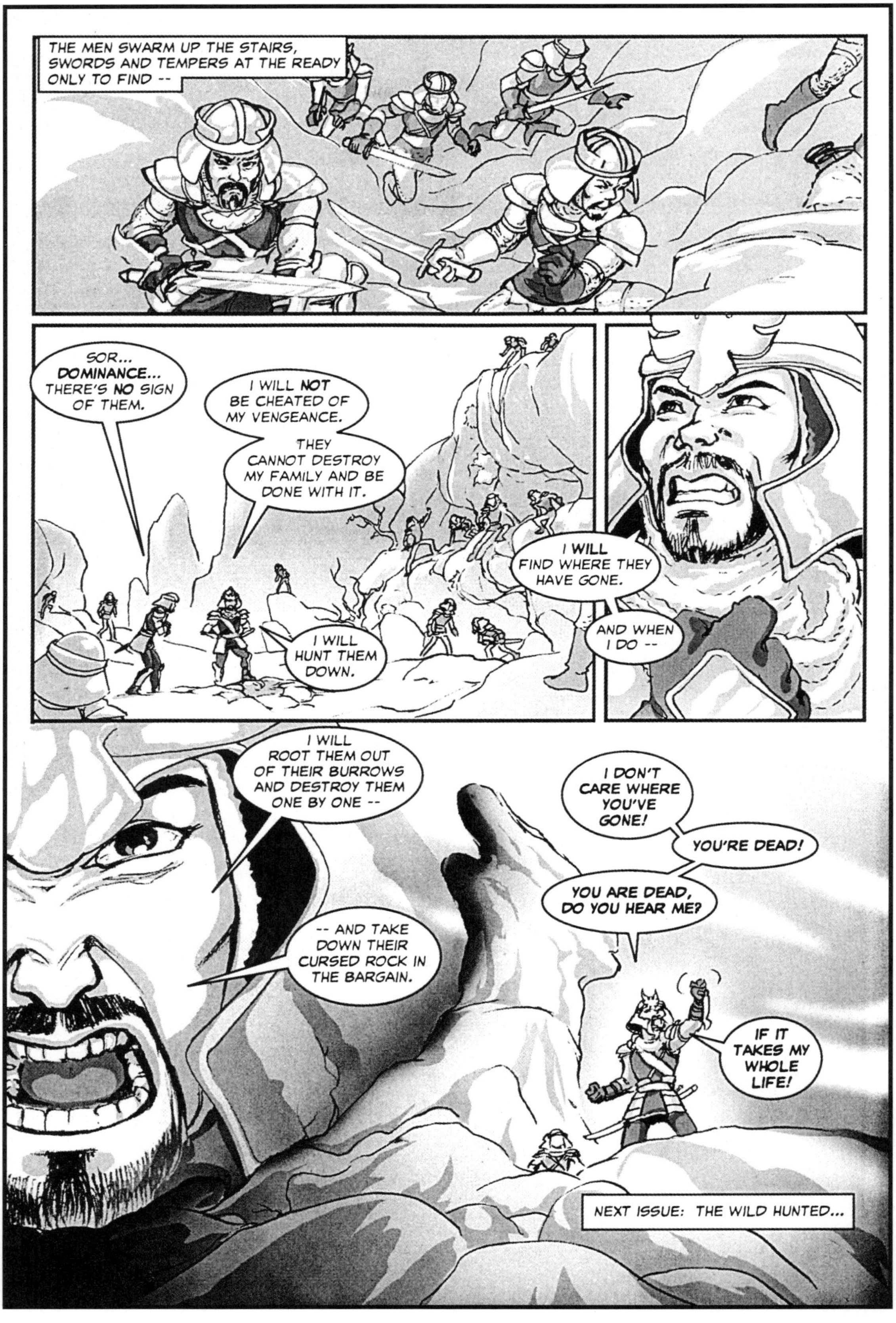
THE MEN SWARM UP THE STAIRS, SWORDS AND TEMPERS AT THE READY ONLY TO FIND --
SOR... DOMINANCE... THERE'S NO SIGN OF THEM.
I WILL NOT BE CHEATED OF MY VENGEANCE.
THEY CANNOT DESTROY MY FAMILY AND BE DONE WITH IT.
I WILL HUNT THEM DOWN.
I WILL FIND WHERE THEY HAVE GONE.
AND WHEN I DO --
I WILL ROOT THEM OUT OF THEIR BURROWS AND DESTROY THEM ONE BY ONE --
-- AND TAKE DOWN THEIR CURSED ROCK IN THE BARGAIN.
I DON'T CARE WHERE YOU'VE GONE!
YOU'RE DEAD!
YOU ARE DEAD, DO YOU HEAR ME?
IF IT TAKES MY WHOLE LIFE!
NEXT ISSUE: THE WILD HUNTED...

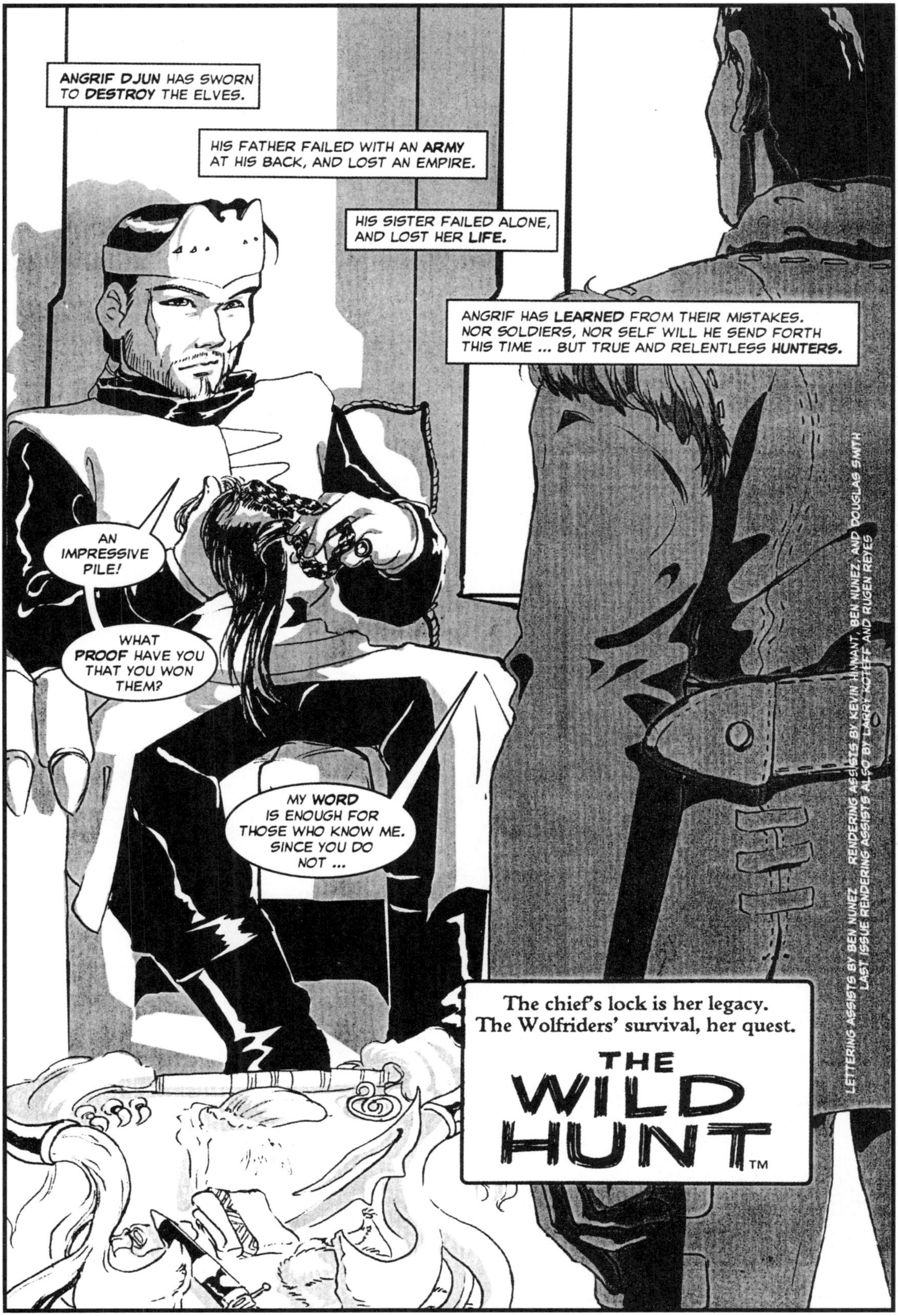

ANGRIF DJUN HAS SWORN TO DESTROY THE ELVES.
HIS FATHER FAILED WITH AN ARMY AT HIS BACK, AND LOST AN EMPIRE.
HIS SISTER FAILED ALONE, AND LOST HER LIFE.
ANGRIF HAS LEARNED FROM THEIR MISTAKES. NOR SOLDIERS, NOR SELF WILL HE SEND FORTH THIS TIME ... BUT TRUE AND RELENTLESS HUNTERS.
AN IMPRESSIVE PILE!
WHAT PROOF HAVE YOU THAT YOU WON THEM?
MY WORD IS ENOUGH FOR THOSE WHO KNOW ME. SINCE YOU DO NOT ...
The chief's lock is her legacy.
The Wolfriders' survival, her quest.
THE WILD HUNT™
LETTERING ASSISTS BY BEN NUNEZ RENDERING ASSISTS BY KEVIN HINNANT, BEN NUNEZ, AND DOUGLAS SMITH
LAST ISSUE RENDERING ASSISTS ALSO BY LARRY KOTEFF AND RUGEN REYES

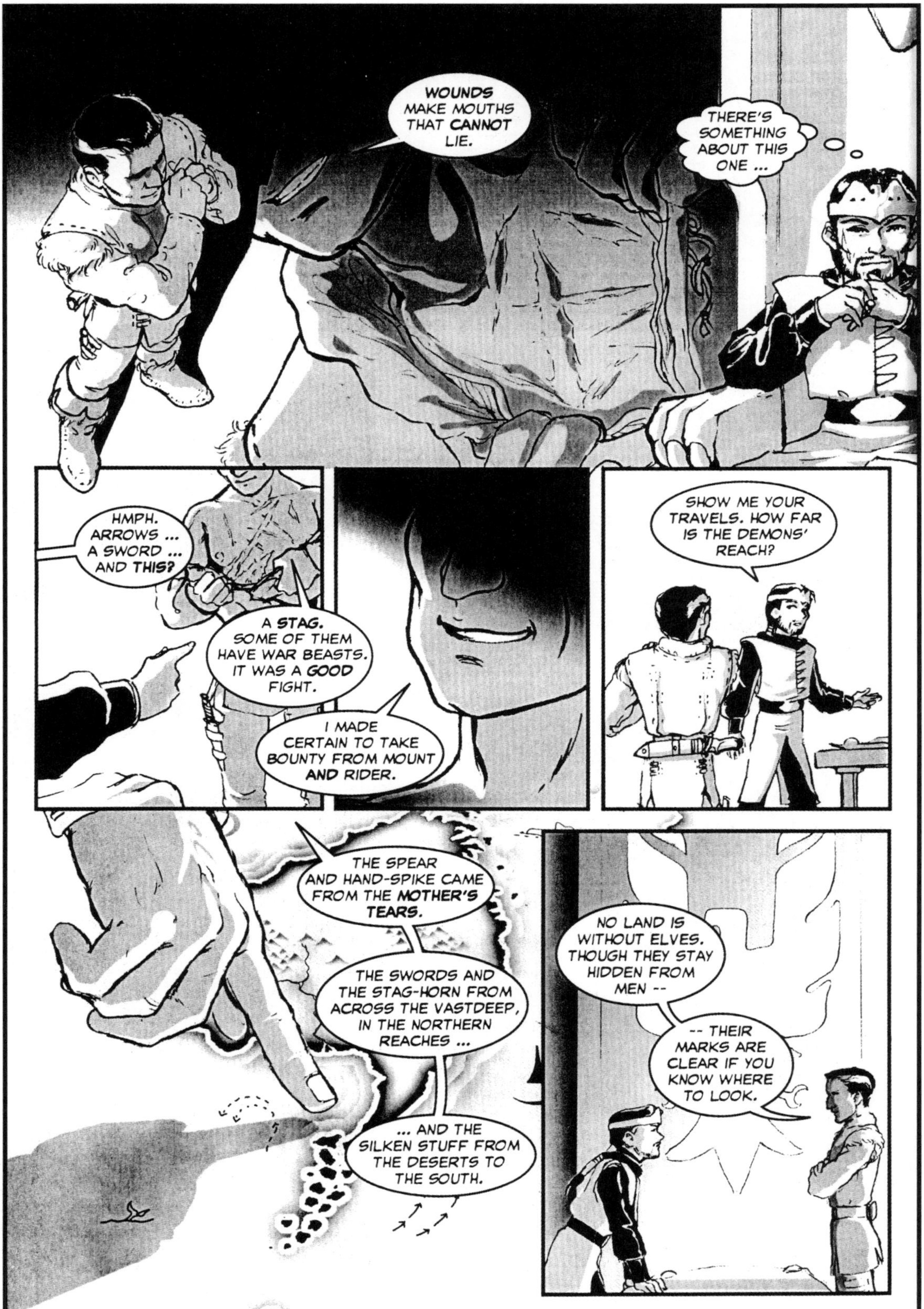
WOUNDS MAKE MOUTHS THAT CANNOT LIE.
THERE'S SOMETHING ABOUT THIS ONE ...
HMPH. ARROWS ... A SWORD ... AND THIS?
A STAG. SOME OF THEM HAVE WAR BEASTS. IT WAS A GOOD FIGHT.
I MADE CERTAIN TO TAKE BOUNTY FROM MOUNT AND RIDER.
SHOW ME YOUR TRAVELS. HOW FAR IS THE DEMONS' REACH?
THE SPEAR AND HAND-SPIKE CAME FROM THE MOTHER'S TEARS.
THE SWORDS AND THE STAG-HORN FROM ACROSS THE VASTDEEP, IN THE NORTHERN REACHES ...
... AND THE SILKEN STUFF FROM THE DESERTS TO THE SOUTH.
NO LAND IS WITHOUT ELVES. THOUGH THEY STAY HIDDEN FROM MEN --
-- THEIR MARKS ARE CLEAR IF YOU KNOW WHERE TO LOOK.

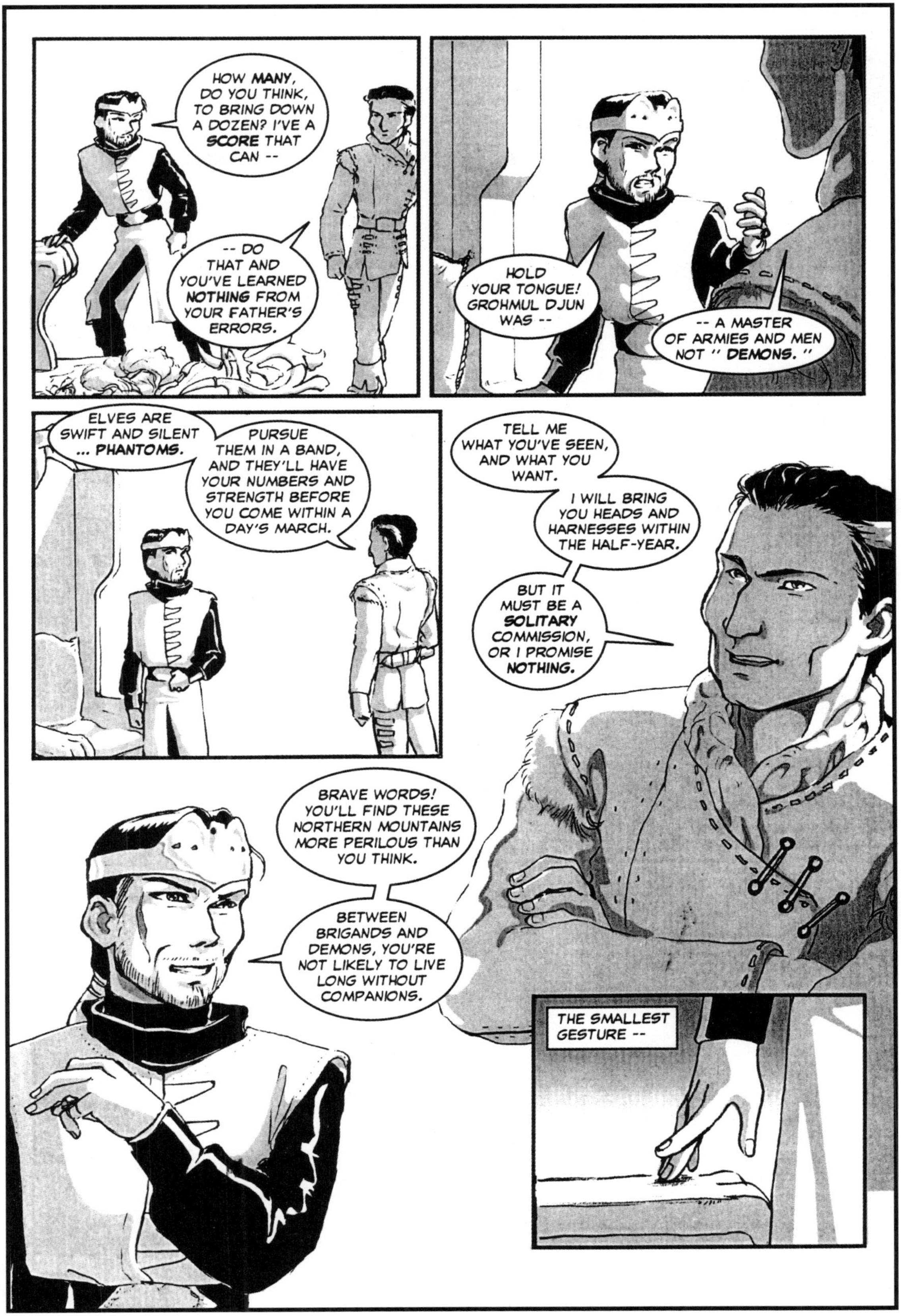

HOW MANY, DO YOU THINK, TO BRING DOWN A DOZEN? I'VE A SCORE THAT CAN --
-- DO THAT AND YOU'VE LEARNED NOTHING FROM YOUR FATHER'S ERRORS.
HOLD YOUR TONGUE! GROHMUL DJUN WAS --
-- A MASTER OF ARMIES AND MEN NOT " DEMONS. "
ELVES ARE SWIFT AND SILENT ... PHANTOMS.
PURSUE THEM IN A BAND, AND THEY'LL HAVE YOUR NUMBERS AND STRENGTH BEFORE YOU COME WITHIN A DAY'S MARCH.
TELL ME WHAT YOU'VE SEEN, AND WHAT YOU WANT.
I WILL BRING YOU HEADS AND HARNESSES WITHIN THE HALF-YEAR.
BUT IT MUST BE A SOLITARY COMMISSION, OR I PROMISE NOTHING.
BRAVE WORDS! YOU'LL FIND THESE NORTHERN MOUNTAINS MORE PERILOUS THAN YOU THINK.
BETWEEN BRIGANDS AND DEMONS, YOU'RE NOT LIKELY TO LIVE LONG WITHOUT COMPANIONS.
THE SMALLEST GESTURE --

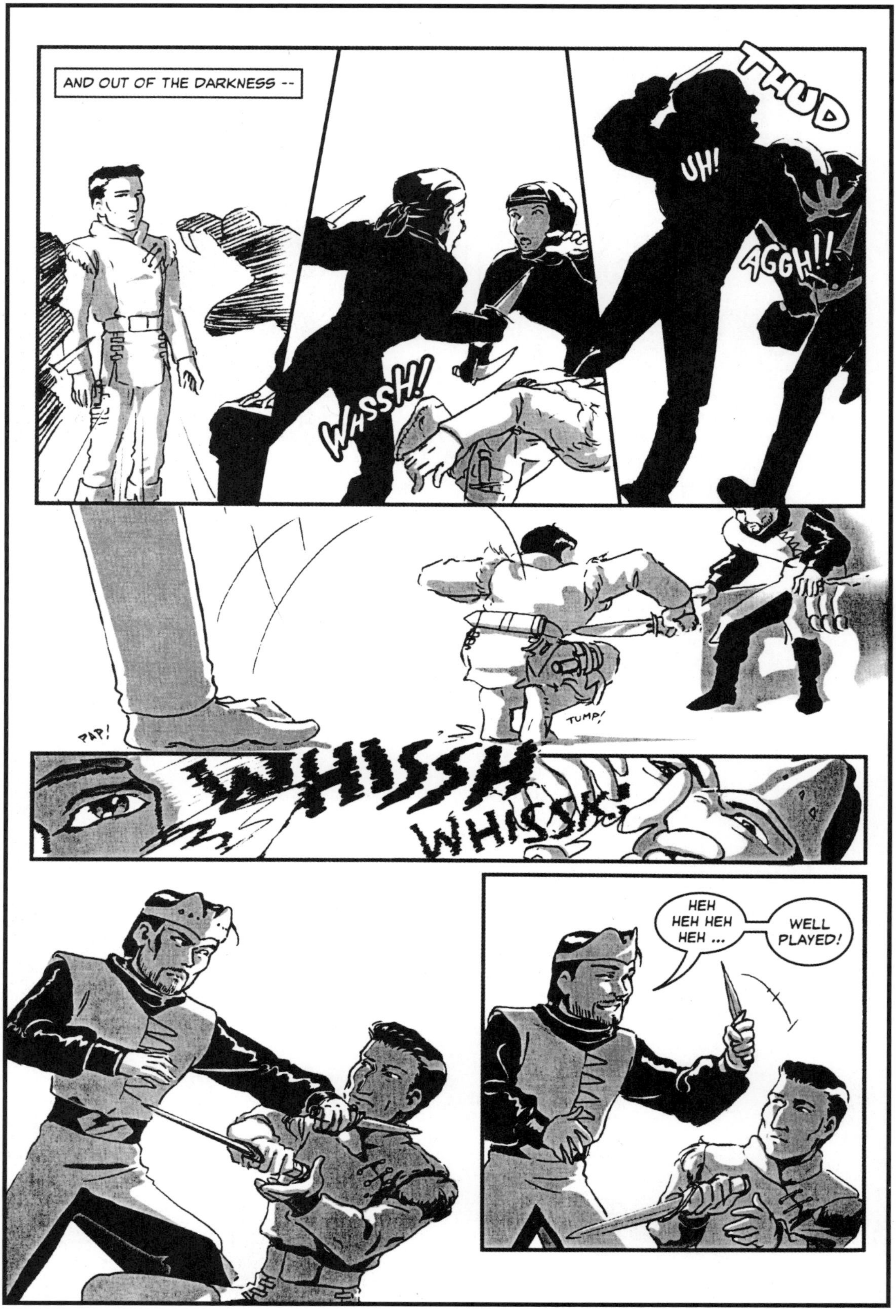
AND OUT OF THE DARKNESS --
WHSSH!
THUD
UH!
AGGH!!
PAP!
TUMP!
WHISSH
WHISSK!
HEH HEH HEH HEH ...
WELL PLAYED!

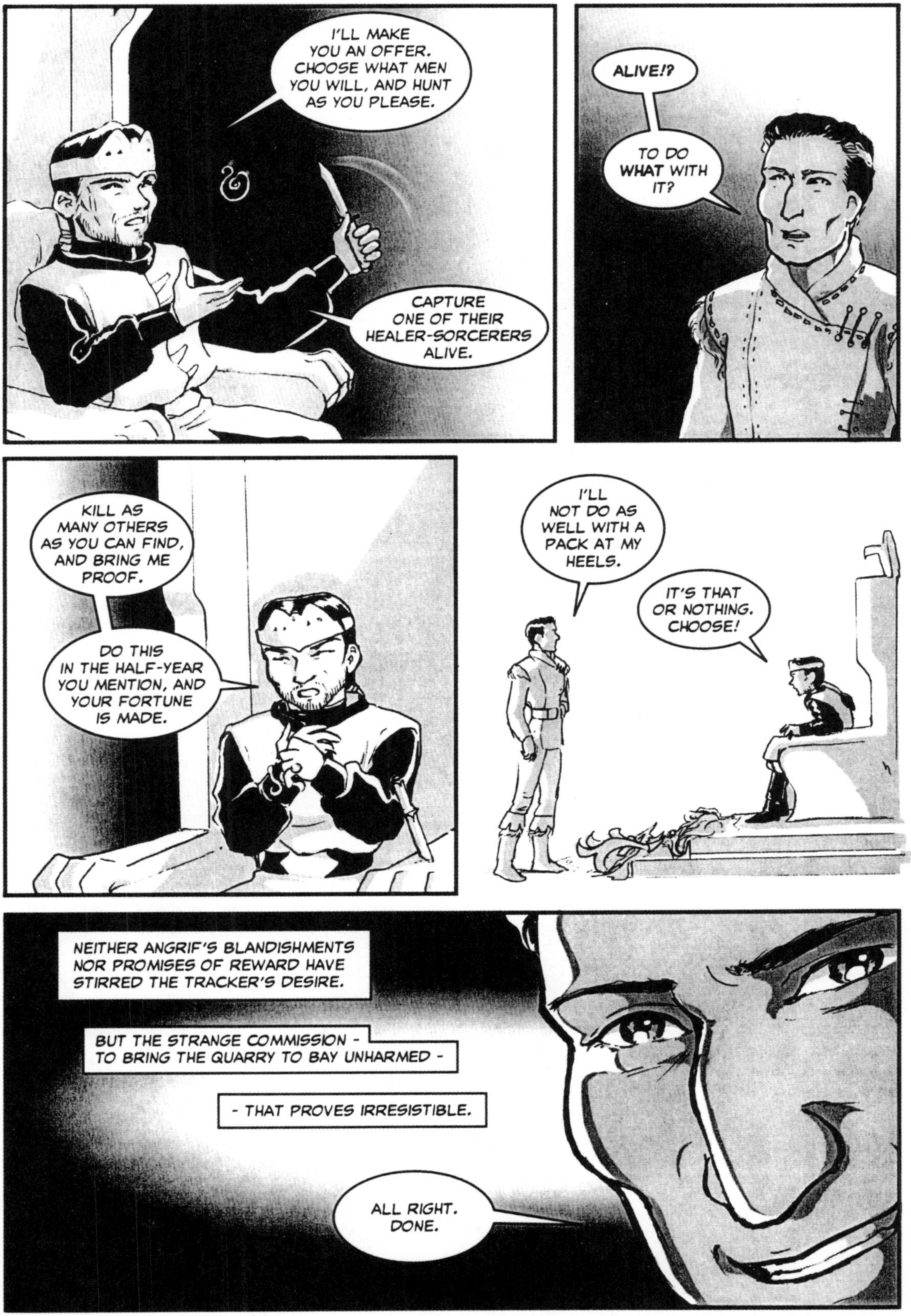
I'LL MAKE YOU AN OFFER. CHOOSE WHAT MEN YOU WILL, AND HUNT AS YOU PLEASE.
CAPTURE ONE OF THEIR HEALER-SORCERERS ALIVE.
ALIVE!?
TO DO WHAT WITH IT?
KILL AS MANY OTHERS AS YOU CAN FIND, AND BRING ME PROOF.
DO THIS IN THE HALF-YEAR YOU MENTION, AND YOUR FORTUNE IS MADE.
I'LL NOT DO AS WELL WITH A PACK AT MY HEELS.
IT'S THAT OR NOTHING. CHOOSE!
NEITHER ANGRIF'S BLANDISHMENTS NOR PROMISES OF REWARD HAVE STIRRED THE TRACKER'S DESIRE.
BUT THE STRANGE COMMISSION - TO BRING THE QUARRY TO BAY UNHARMED -
- THAT PROVES IRRESISTIBLE.
ALL RIGHT. DONE.

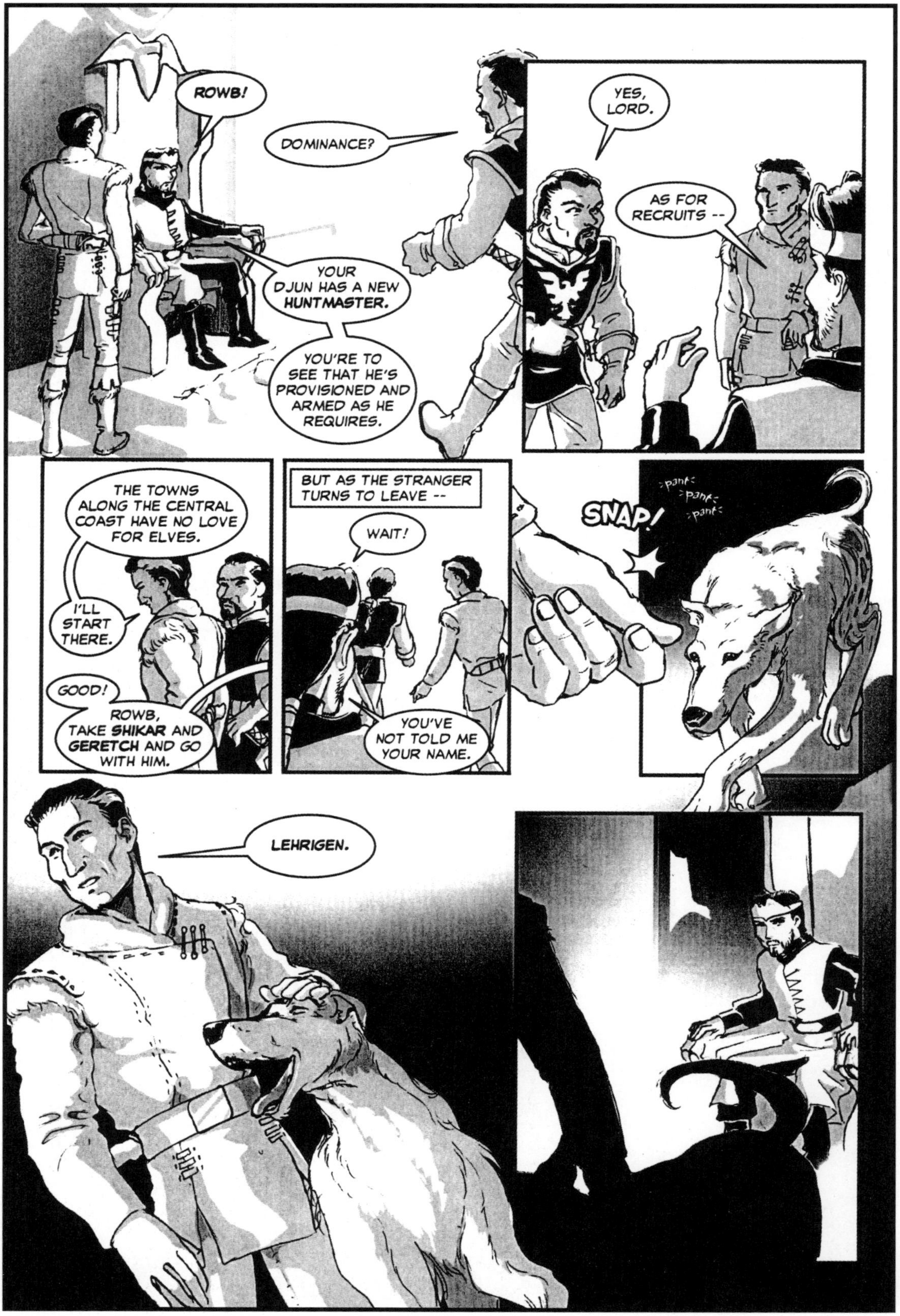
ROWB!
DOMINANCE?
YOUR DJUN HAS A NEW HUNTMASTER.
YOU'RE TO SEE THAT HE'S PROVISIONED AND ARMED AS HE REQUIRES.
YES, LORD.
AS FOR RECRUITS --
THE TOWNS ALONG THE CENTRAL COAST HAVE NO LOVE FOR ELVES.
I'LL START THERE.
GOOD!
ROWB, TAKE SHIKAR AND GERETCH AND GO WITH HIM.
BUT AS THE STRANGER TURNS TO LEAVE --
WAIT!
YOU'VE NOT TOLD ME YOUR NAME.
SNAP!
pant pant pant
LEHRIGEN.

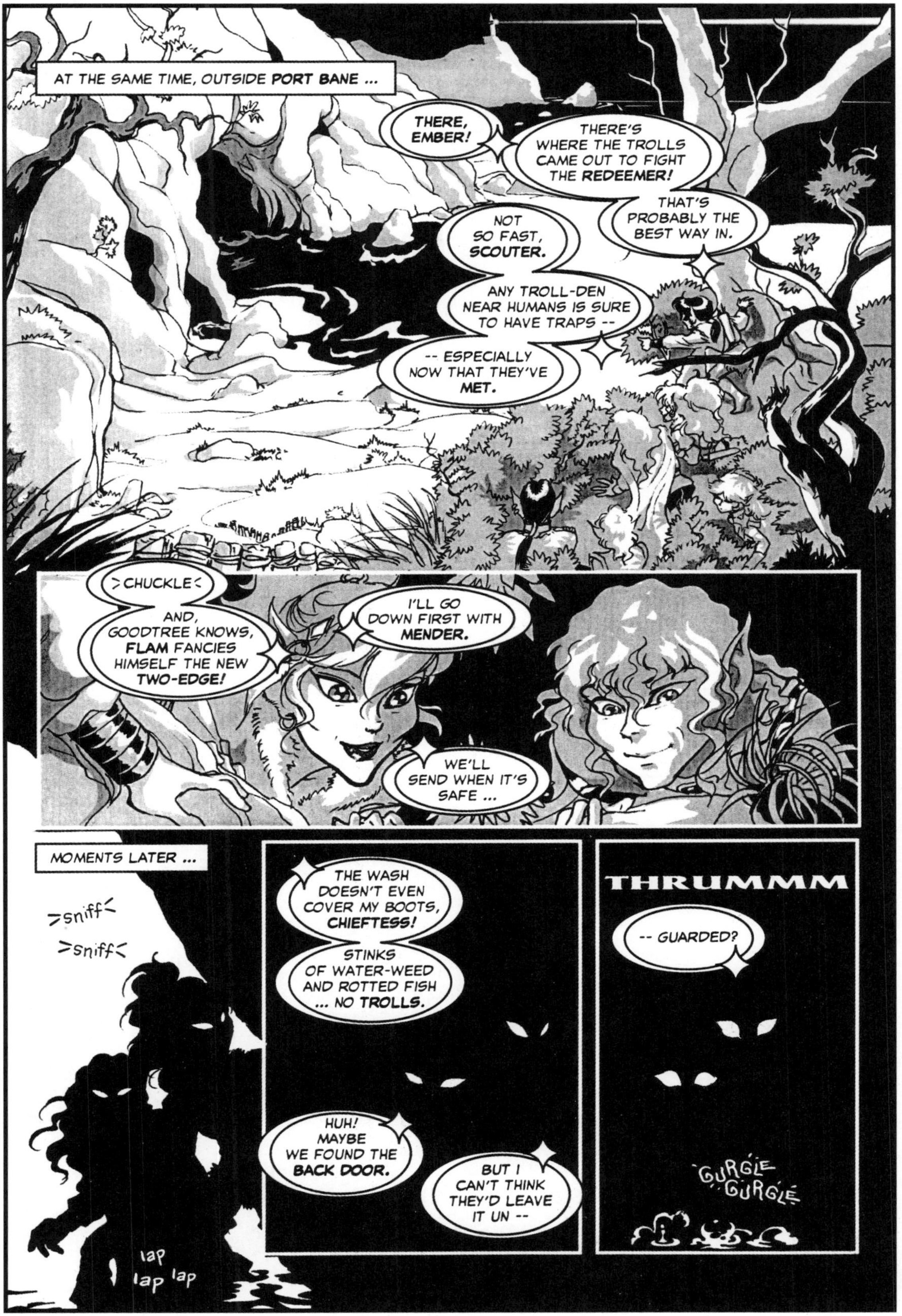
AT THE SAME TIME, OUTSIDE PORT BANE ...
THERE, EMBER!
THERE'S WHERE THE TROLLS CAME OUT TO FIGHT THE REDEEMER!
THAT'S PROBABLY THE BEST WAY IN.
NOT SO FAST, SCOUTER.
ANY TROLL-DEN NEAR HUMANS IS SURE TO HAVE TRAPS --
-- ESPECIALLY NOW THAT THEY'VE MET.
>CHUCKLE<
AND, GOODTREE KNOWS, FLAM FANCIES HIMSELF THE NEW TWO-EDGE!
I'LL GO DOWN FIRST WITH MENDER.
WE'LL SEND WHEN IT'S SAFE ...
MOMENTS LATER ...
>sniff<
>sniff<
lap lap lap
THE WASH DOESN'T EVEN COVER MY BOOTS, CHIEFTESS!
STINKS OF WATER-WEED AND ROTTED FISH ... NO TROLLS.
HUH! MAYBE WE FOUND THE BACK DOOR.
BUT I CAN'T THINK THEY'D LEAVE IT UN --
THRUMMM
-- GUARDED?
GURGLE GURGLE

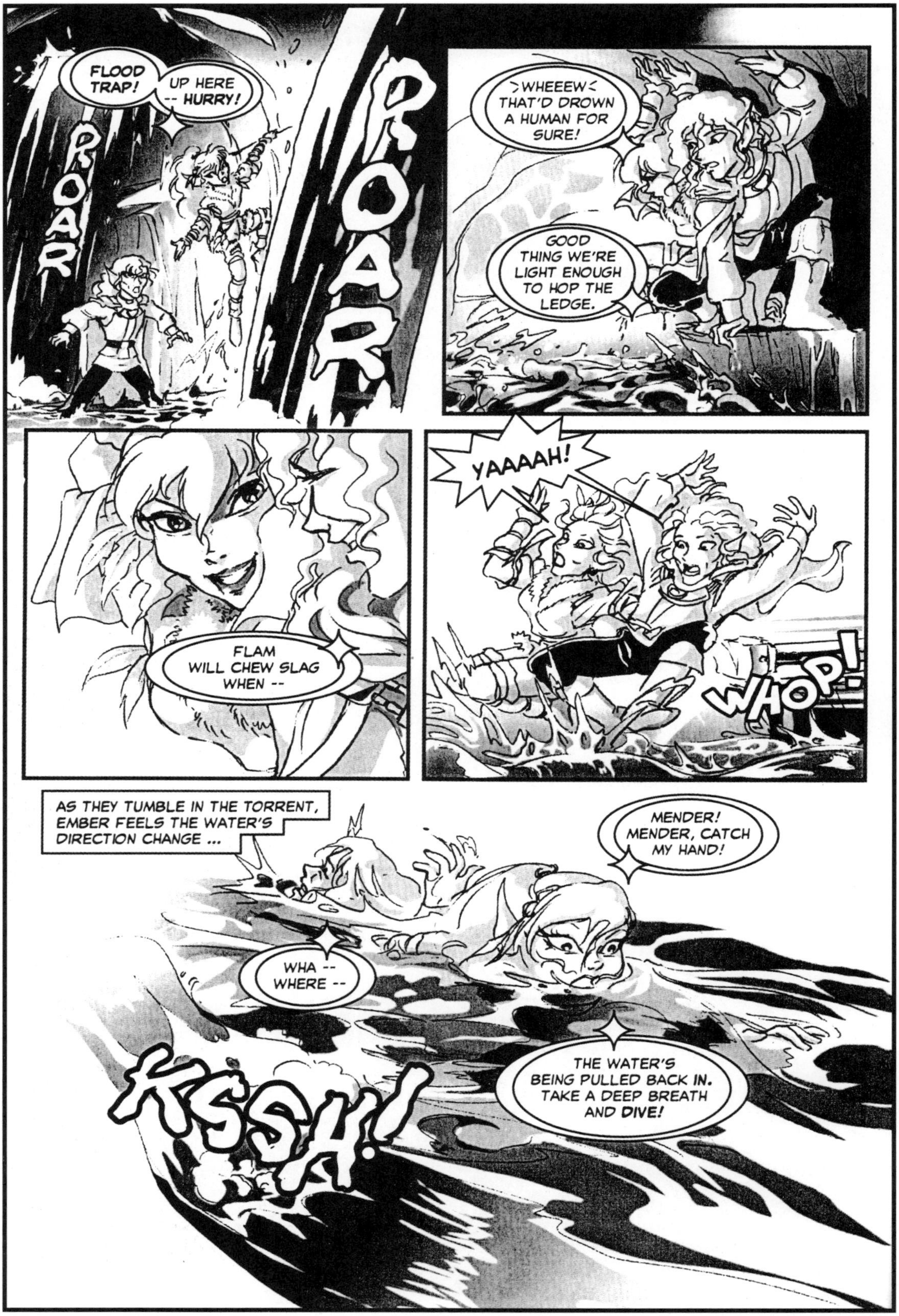

FLOOD TRAP!
UP HERE -- HURRY!
ROAR
ROAR
>WHEEEW< THAT'D DROWN A HUMAN FOR SURE!
GOOD THING WE'RE LIGHT ENOUGH TO HOP THE LEDGE.
FLAM WILL CHEW SLAG WHEN --
YAAAAH!
WHOP!
AS THEY TUMBLE IN THE TORRENT, EMBER FEELS THE WATER'S DIRECTION CHANGE ...
MENDER! MENDER, CATCH MY HAND!
WHA -- WHERE --
THE WATER'S BEING PULLED BACK IN. TAKE A DEEP BREATH AND DIVE!
KSSH!

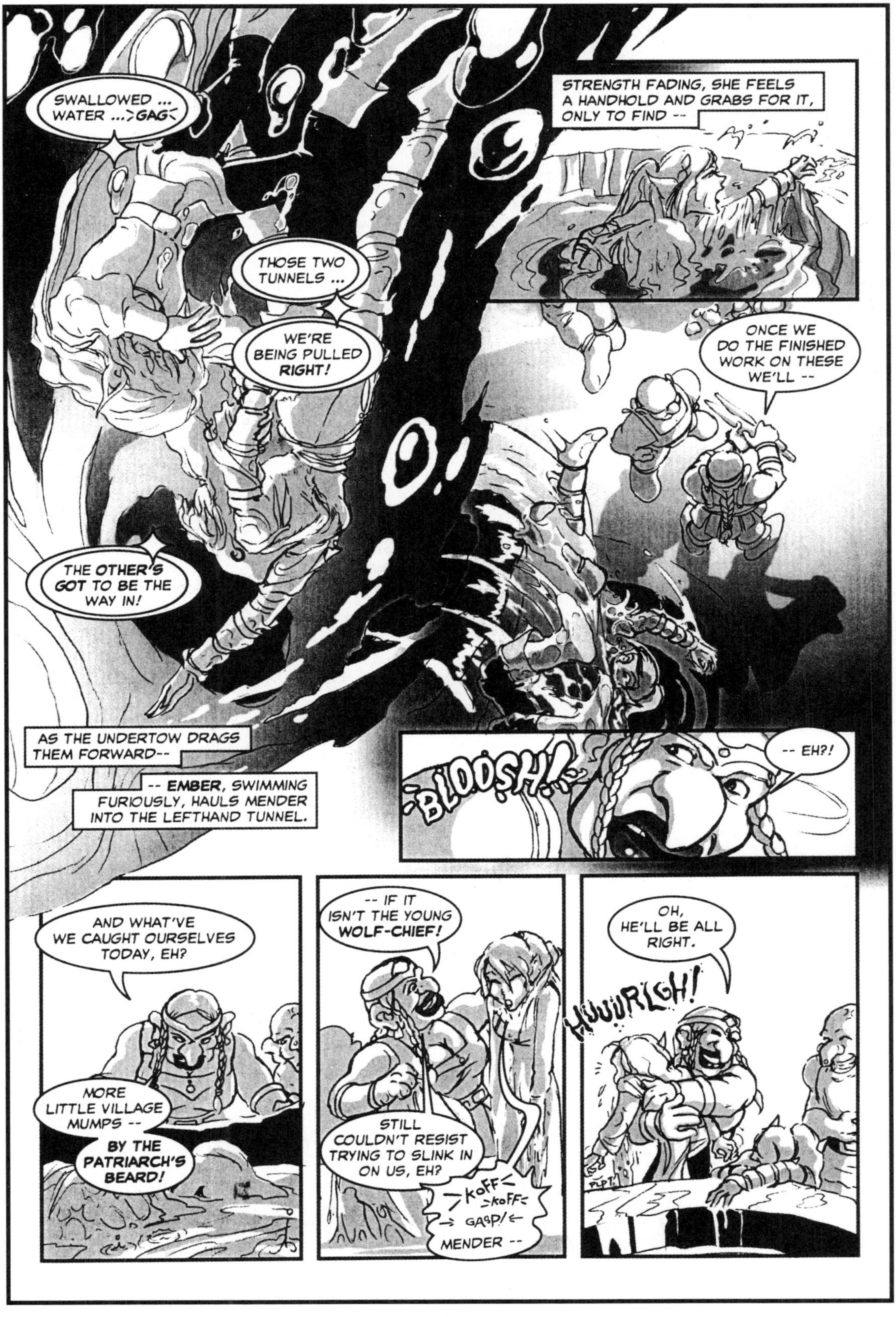

SWALLOWED ... WATER ... >GAG<
STRENGTH FADING, SHE FEELS A HANDHOLD AND GRABS FOR IT, ONLY TO FIND --
THOSE TWO TUNNELS ...
WE'RE BEING PULLED RIGHT!
THE OTHER'S GOT TO BE THE WAY IN!
ONCE WE DO THE FINISHED WORK ON THESE WE'LL --
AS THE UNDERTOW DRAGS THEM FORWARD--
-- EMBER, SWIMMING FURIOUSLY, HAULS MENDER INTO THE LEFTHAND TUNNEL.
BLOOSH!
-- EH?!
AND WHAT'VE WE CAUGHT OURSELVES TODAY, EH?
MORE LITTLE VILLAGE MUMPS --
BY THE PATRIARCH'S BEARD!
-- IF IT ISN'T THE YOUNG WOLF-CHIEF!
STILL COULDN'T RESIST TRYING TO SLINK IN ON US, EH?
>KOFF< >KOFF< GASP! MENDER --
OH, HE'LL BE ALL RIGHT.
HUUURLGH!

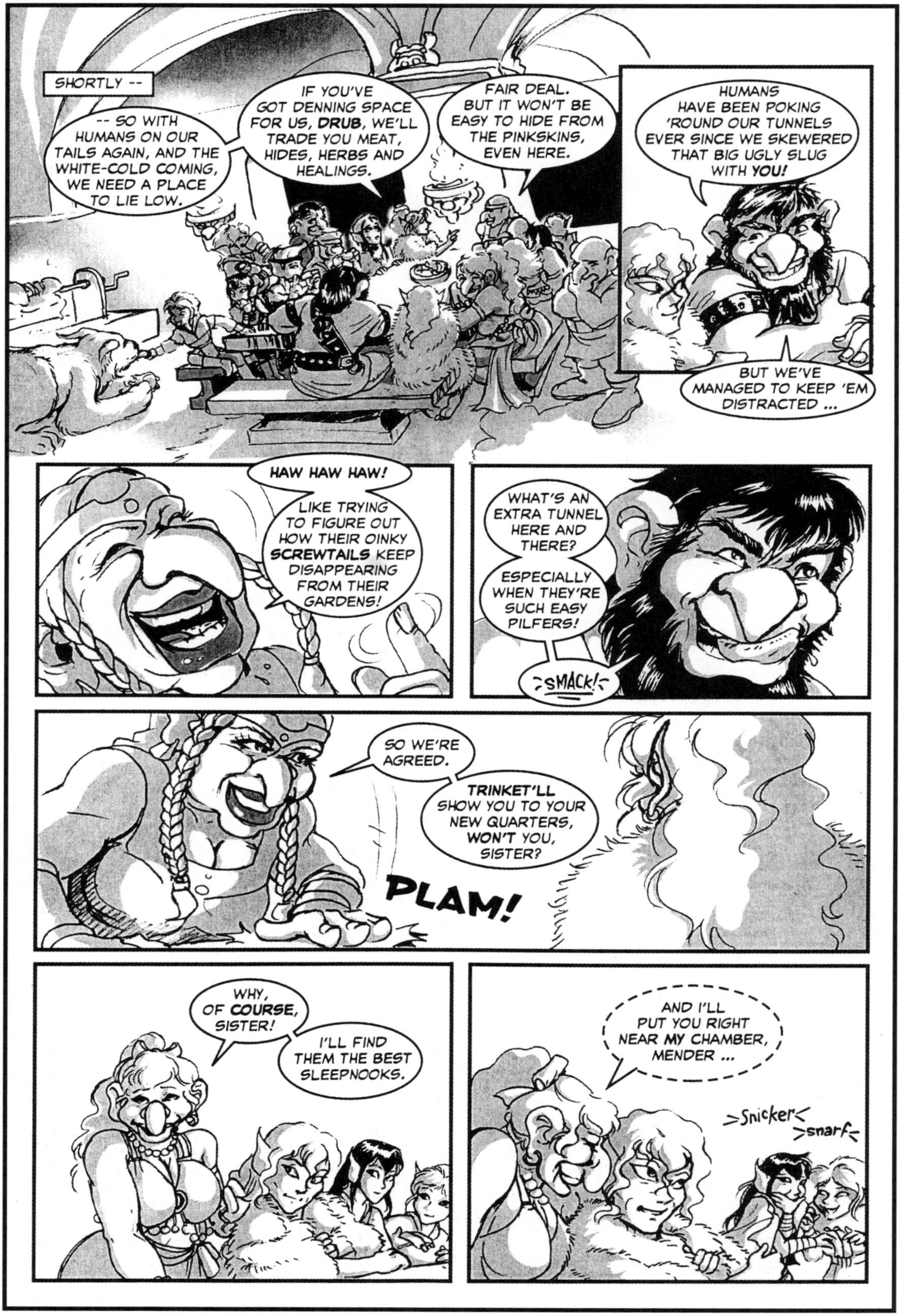
SHORTLY --
-- SO WITH HUMANS ON OUR TAILS AGAIN, AND THE WHITE-COLD COMING, WE NEED A PLACE TO LIE LOW.
IF YOU'VE GOT DENNING SPACE FOR US, DRUB, WE'LL TRADE YOU MEAT, HIDES, HERBS AND HEALINGS.
FAIR DEAL. BUT IT WON'T BE EASY TO HIDE FROM THE PINKSKINS, EVEN HERE.
HUMANS HAVE BEEN POKING 'ROUND OUR TUNNELS EVER SINCE WE SKEWERED THAT BIG UGLY SLUG WITH YOU!
BUT WE'VE MANAGED TO KEEP 'EM DISTRACTED ...
HAW HAW HAW!
LIKE TRYING TO FIGURE OUT HOW THEIR OINKY SCREWTAILS KEEP DISAPPEARING FROM THEIR GARDENS!
WHAT'S AN EXTRA TUNNEL HERE AND THERE?
ESPECIALLY WHEN THEY'RE SUCH EASY PILFERS!
SMACK!
SO WE'RE AGREED.
TRINKET'LL SHOW YOU TO YOUR NEW QUARTERS, WON'T YOU, SISTER?
PLAM!
WHY, OF COURSE, SISTER!
I'LL FIND THEM THE BEST SLEEPNOOKS.
AND I'LL PUT YOU RIGHT NEAR MY CHAMBER, MENDER ...
Snicker
snarf

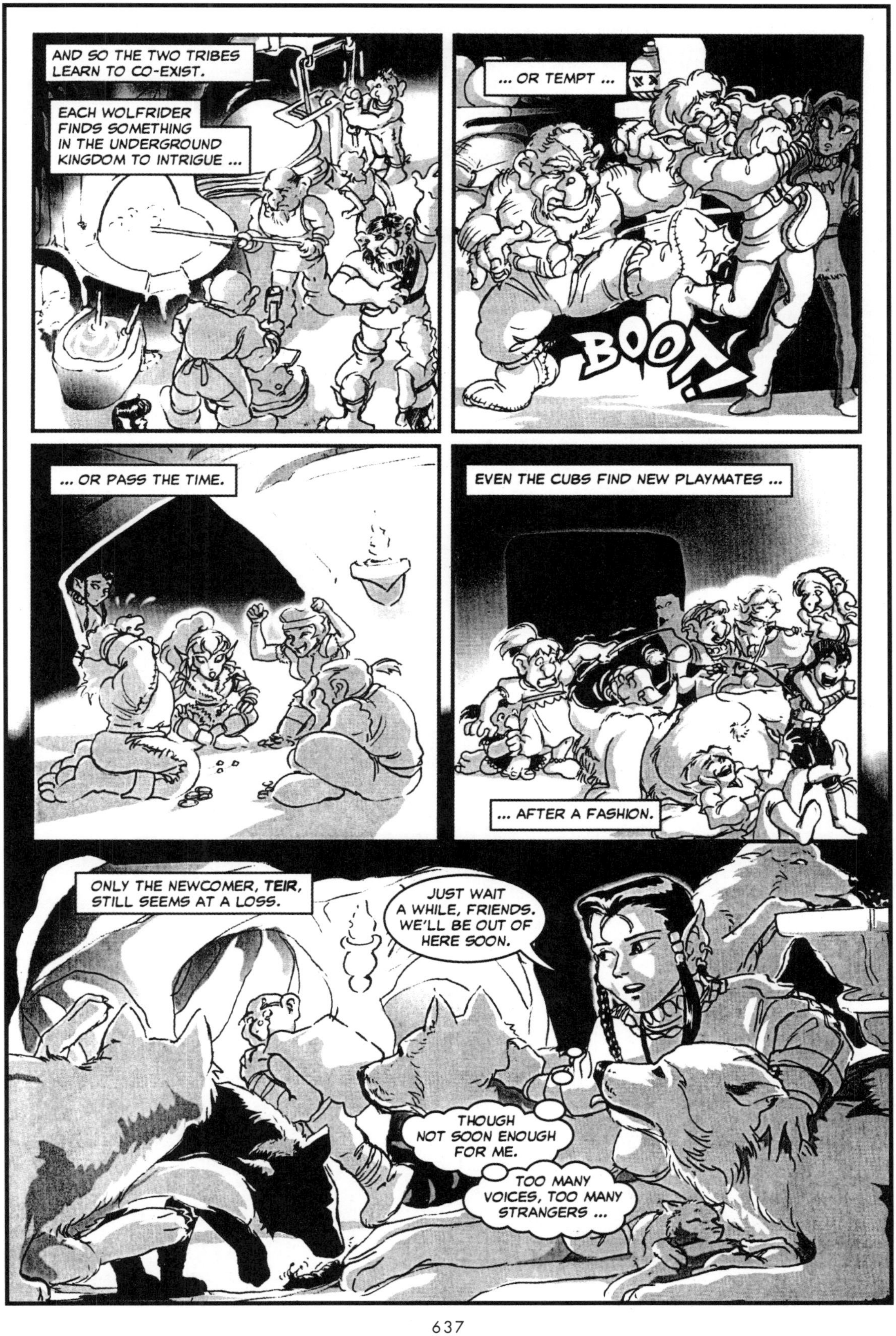
AND SO THE TWO TRIBES LEARN TO CO-EXIST.
EACH WOLFRIDER FINDS SOMETHING IN THE UNDERGROUND KINGDOM TO INTRIGUE ...
... OR TEMPT ...
BOOT!
... OR PASS THE TIME.
EVEN THE CUBS FIND NEW PLAYMATES ...
... AFTER A FASHION.
ONLY THE NEWCOMER, TEIR, STILL SEEMS AT A LOSS.
JUST WAIT A WHILE, FRIENDS. WE'LL BE OUT OF HERE SOON.
THOUGH NOT SOON ENOUGH FOR ME.
TOO MANY VOICES, TOO MANY STRANGERS ...

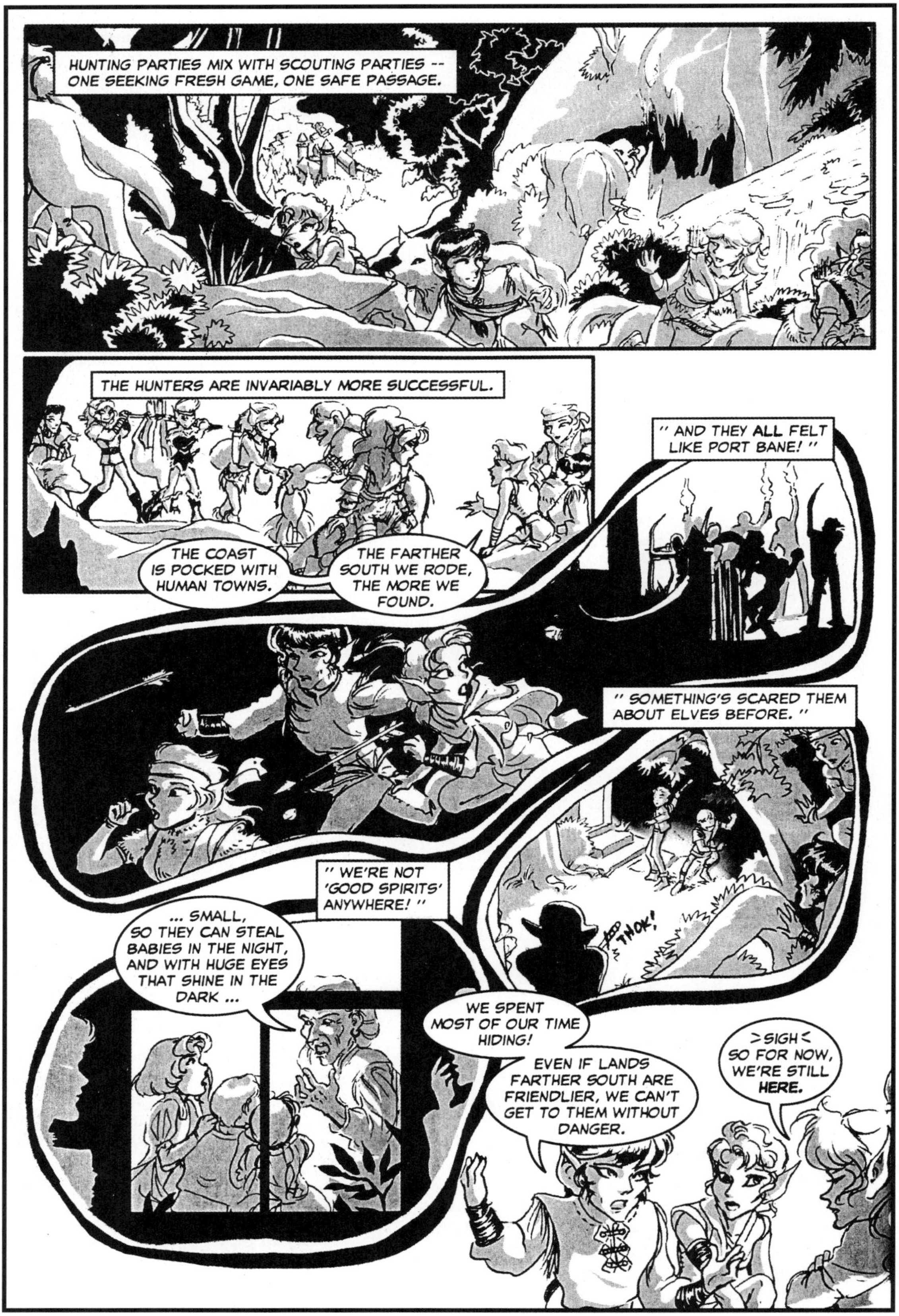
HUNTING PARTIES MIX WITH SCOUTING PARTIES -- ONE SEEKING FRESH GAME, ONE SAFE PASSAGE.
THE HUNTERS ARE INVARIABLY MORE SUCCESSFUL.
THE COAST IS POCKED WITH HUMAN TOWNS.
THE FARTHER SOUTH WE RODE, THE MORE WE FOUND.
" AND THEY ALL FELT LIKE PORT BANE! "
" SOMETHING'S SCARED THEM ABOUT ELVES BEFORE. "
THOK!
" WE'RE NOT 'GOOD SPIRITS' ANYWHERE! "
... SMALL, SO THEY CAN STEAL BABIES IN THE NIGHT, AND WITH HUGE EYES THAT SHINE IN THE DARK ...
WE SPENT MOST OF OUR TIME HIDING!
EVEN IF LANDS FARTHER SOUTH ARE FRIENDLIER, WE CAN'T GET TO THEM WITHOUT DANGER.
>SIGH< SO FOR NOW, WE'RE STILL HERE.

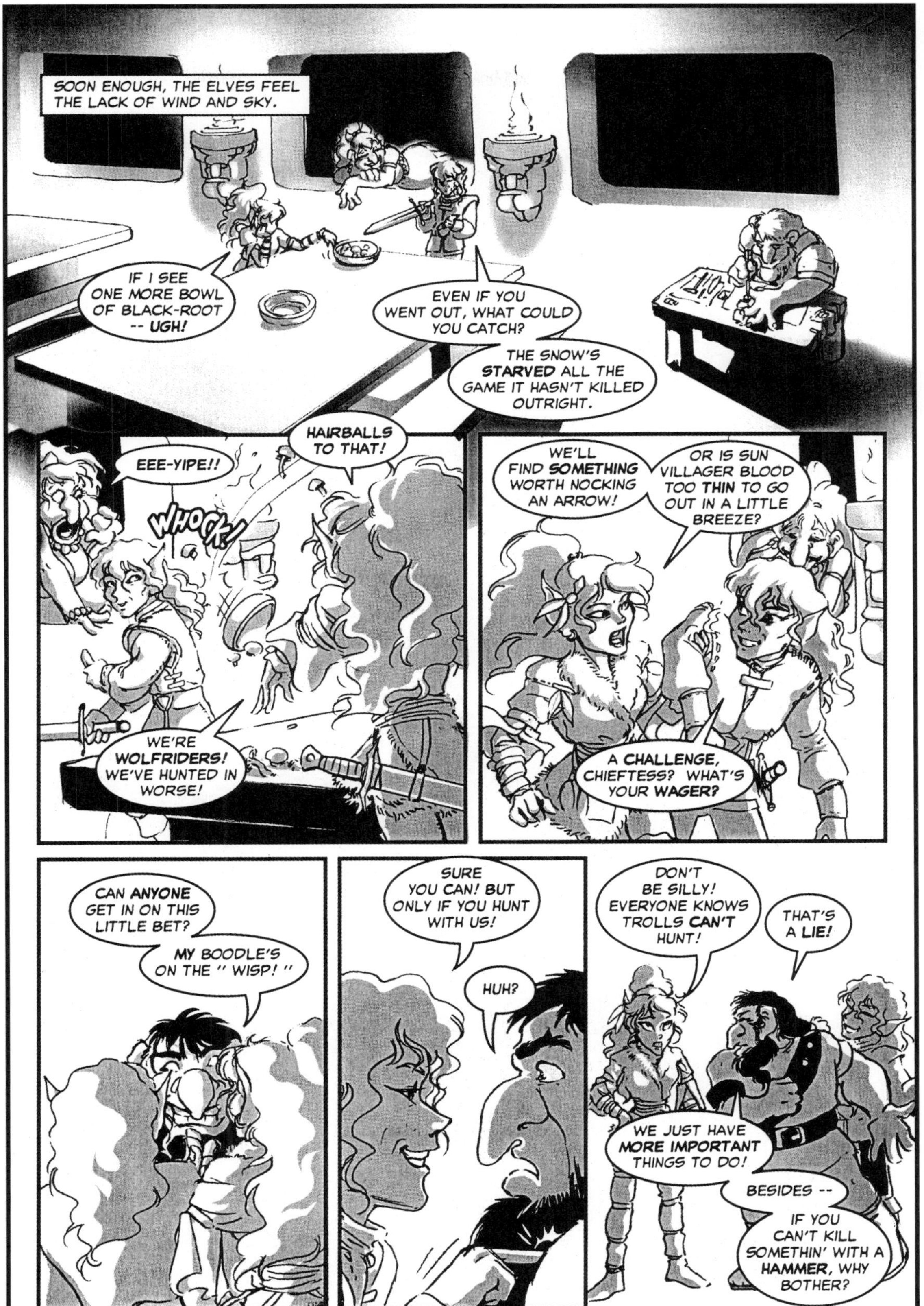
SOON ENOUGH, THE ELVES FEEL THE LACK OF WIND AND SKY.
IF I SEE ONE MORE BOWL OF BLACK-ROOT -- UGH!
EVEN IF YOU WENT OUT, WHAT COULD YOU CATCH?
THE SNOW'S STARVED ALL THE GAME IT HASN'T KILLED OUTRIGHT.
EEE-YIPE!!
HAIRBALLS TO THAT!
WHOCK!
WE'RE WOLFRIDERS! WE'VE HUNTED IN WORSE!
WE'LL FIND SOMETHING WORTH NOCKING AN ARROW!
OR IS SUN VILLAGER BLOOD TOO THIN TO GO OUT IN A LITTLE BREEZE?
A CHALLENGE, CHIEFTESS? WHAT'S YOUR WAGER?
CAN ANYONE GET IN ON THIS LITTLE BET?
MY BOODLE'S ON THE " WISP! "
SURE YOU CAN! BUT ONLY IF YOU HUNT WITH US!
HUH?
DON'T BE SILLY! EVERYONE KNOWS TROLLS CAN'T HUNT!
THAT'S A LIE!
WE JUST HAVE MORE IMPORTANT THINGS TO DO!
BESIDES --
IF YOU CAN'T KILL SOMETHIN' WITH A HAMMER, WHY BOTHER?

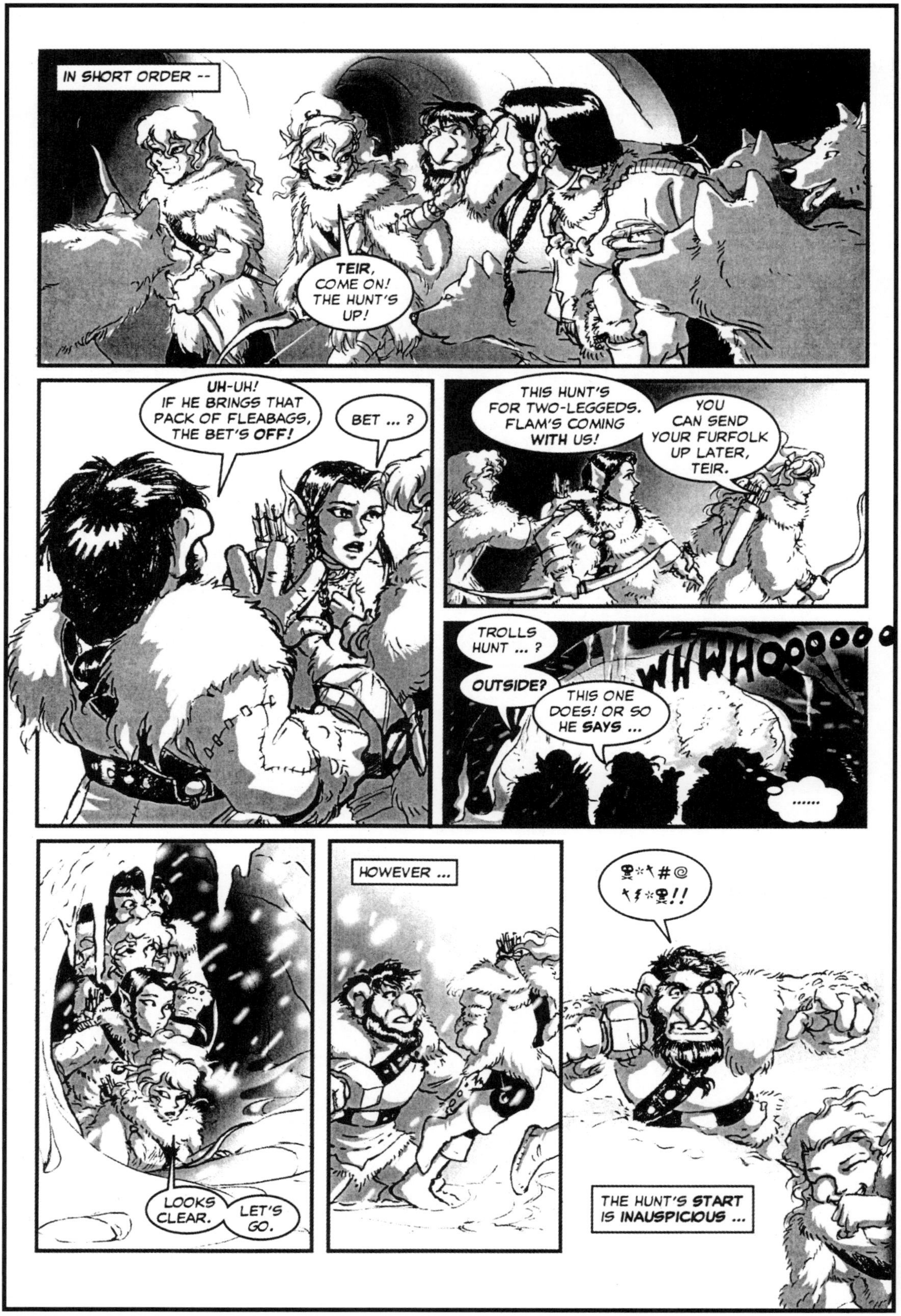
IN SHORT ORDER --
TEIR, COME ON! THE HUNT'S UP!
UH-UH! IF HE BRINGS THAT PACK OF FLEABAGS, THE BET'S OFF!
BET ... ?
THIS HUNT'S FOR TWO-LEGGEDS. FLAM'S COMING WITH US!
YOU CAN SEND YOUR FURFOLK UP LATER, TEIR.
TROLLS HUNT ... ?
OUTSIDE?
THIS ONE DOES! OR SO HE SAYS ...
WHWHOOOOOOO
......
LOOKS CLEAR.
LET'S GO.
HOWEVER ...
THE HUNT'S START IS INAUSPICIOUS ...

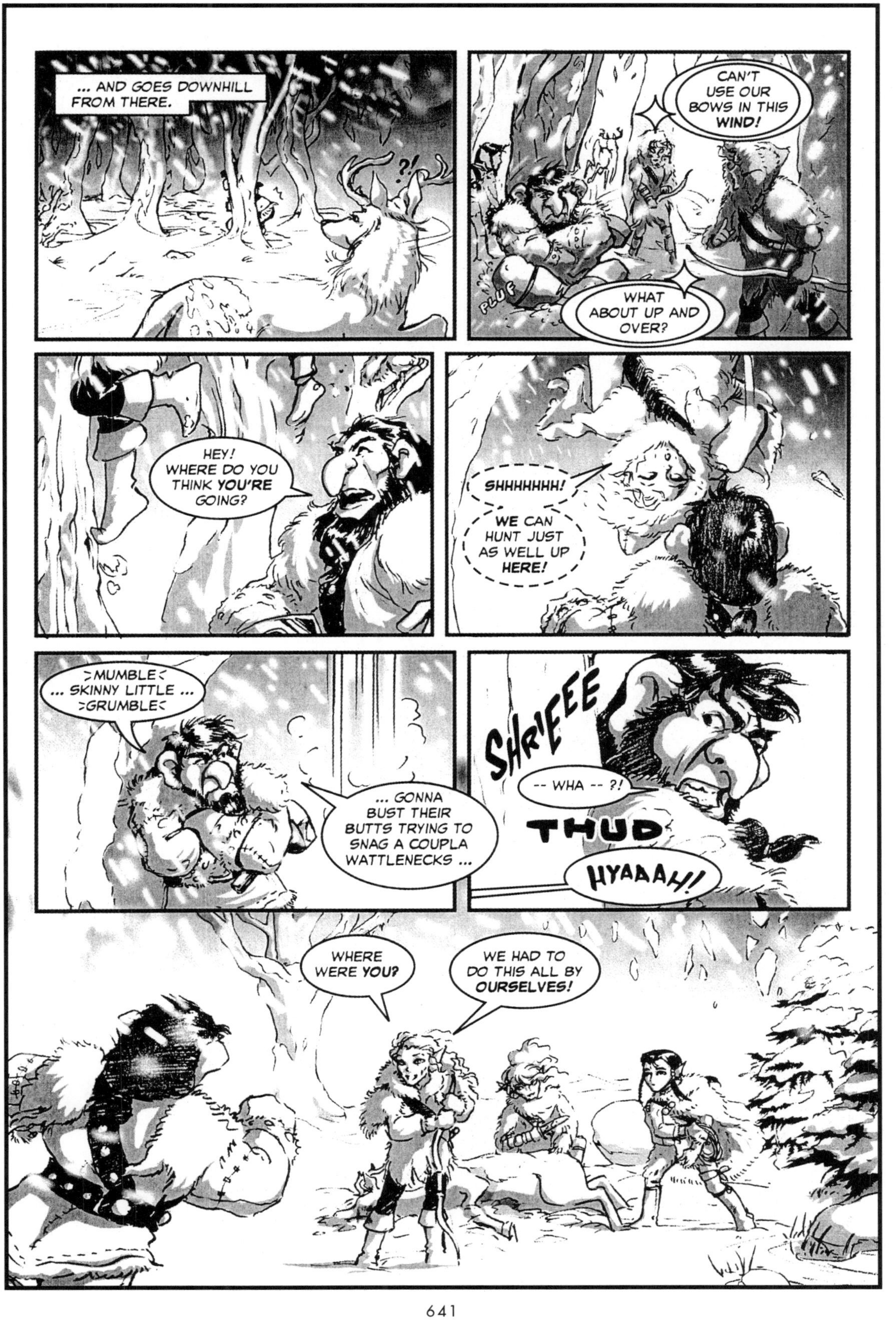
... AND GOES DOWNHILL FROM THERE.
?!
CAN'T USE OUR BOWS IN THIS WIND!
PLUF
WHAT ABOUT UP AND OVER?
HEY! WHERE DO YOU THINK YOU'RE GOING?
SHHHHHHH!
WE CAN HUNT JUST AS WELL UP HERE!
>MUMBLE< ... SKINNY LITTLE ... >GRUMBLE<
... GONNA BUST THEIR BUTTS TRYING TO SNAG A COUPLA WATTLENECKS ...
SHRIEEE
-- WHA -- ?!
THUD
HYAAAH!
WHERE WERE YOU?
WE HAD TO DO THIS ALL BY OURSELVES!

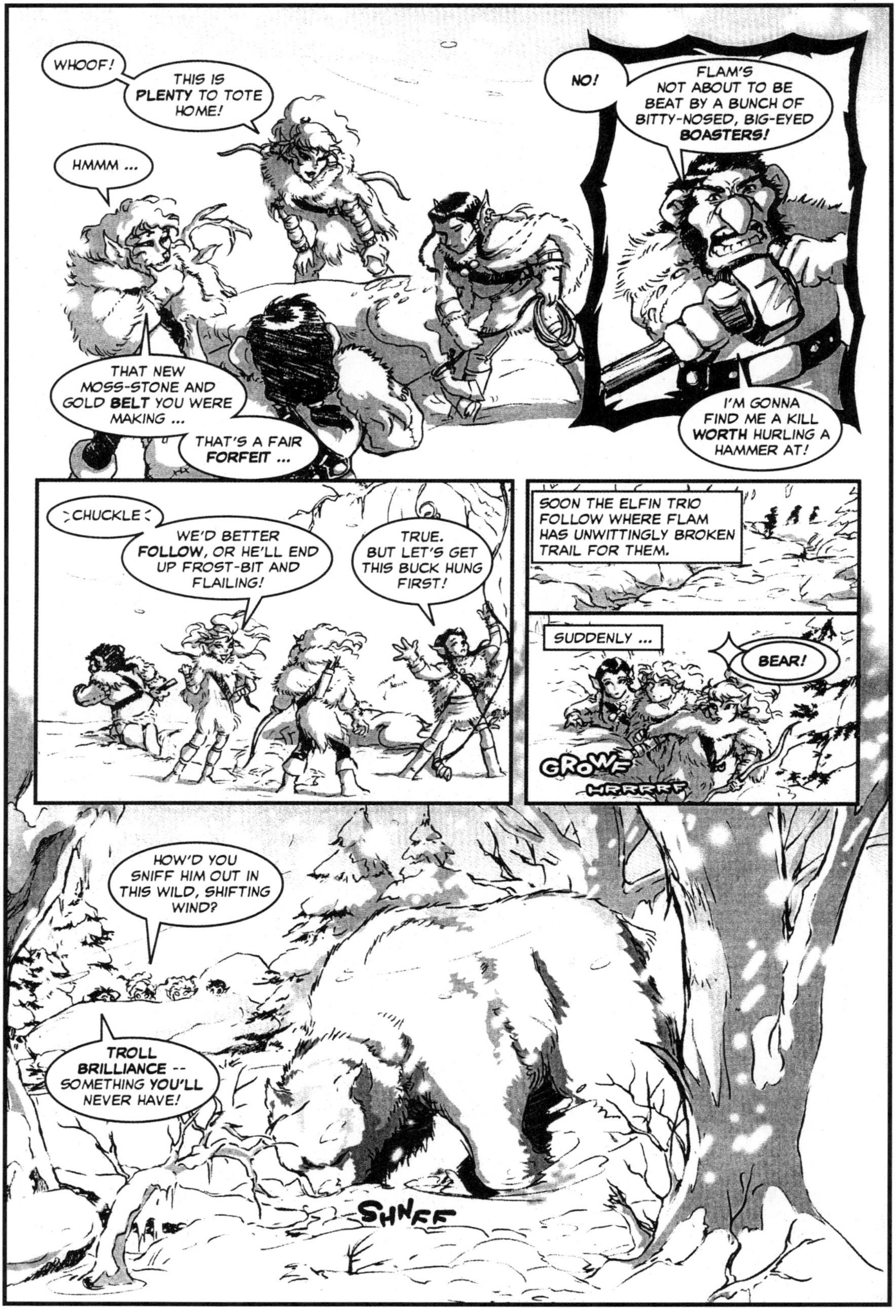
WHOOF!
THIS IS PLENTY TO TOTE HOME!
HMMM ...
THAT NEW MOSS-STONE AND GOLD BELT YOU WERE MAKING ...
THAT'S A FAIR FORFEIT ...
NO!
FLAM'S NOT ABOUT TO BE BEAT BY A BUNCH OF BITTY-NOSED, BIG-EYED BOASTERS!
I'M GONNA FIND ME A KILL WORTH HURLING A HAMMER AT!
CHUCKLE
WE'D BETTER FOLLOW, OR HE'LL END UP FROST-BIT AND FLAILING!
TRUE. BUT LET'S GET THIS BUCK HUNG FIRST!
SOON THE ELFIN TRIO FOLLOW WHERE FLAM HAS UNWITTINGLY BROKEN TRAIL FOR THEM.
SUDDENLY ...
BEAR!
GROWF
HRRRRF
HOW'D YOU SNIFF HIM OUT IN THIS WILD, SHIFTING WIND?
TROLL BRILLIANCE -- SOMETHING YOU'LL NEVER HAVE!
SHNFF

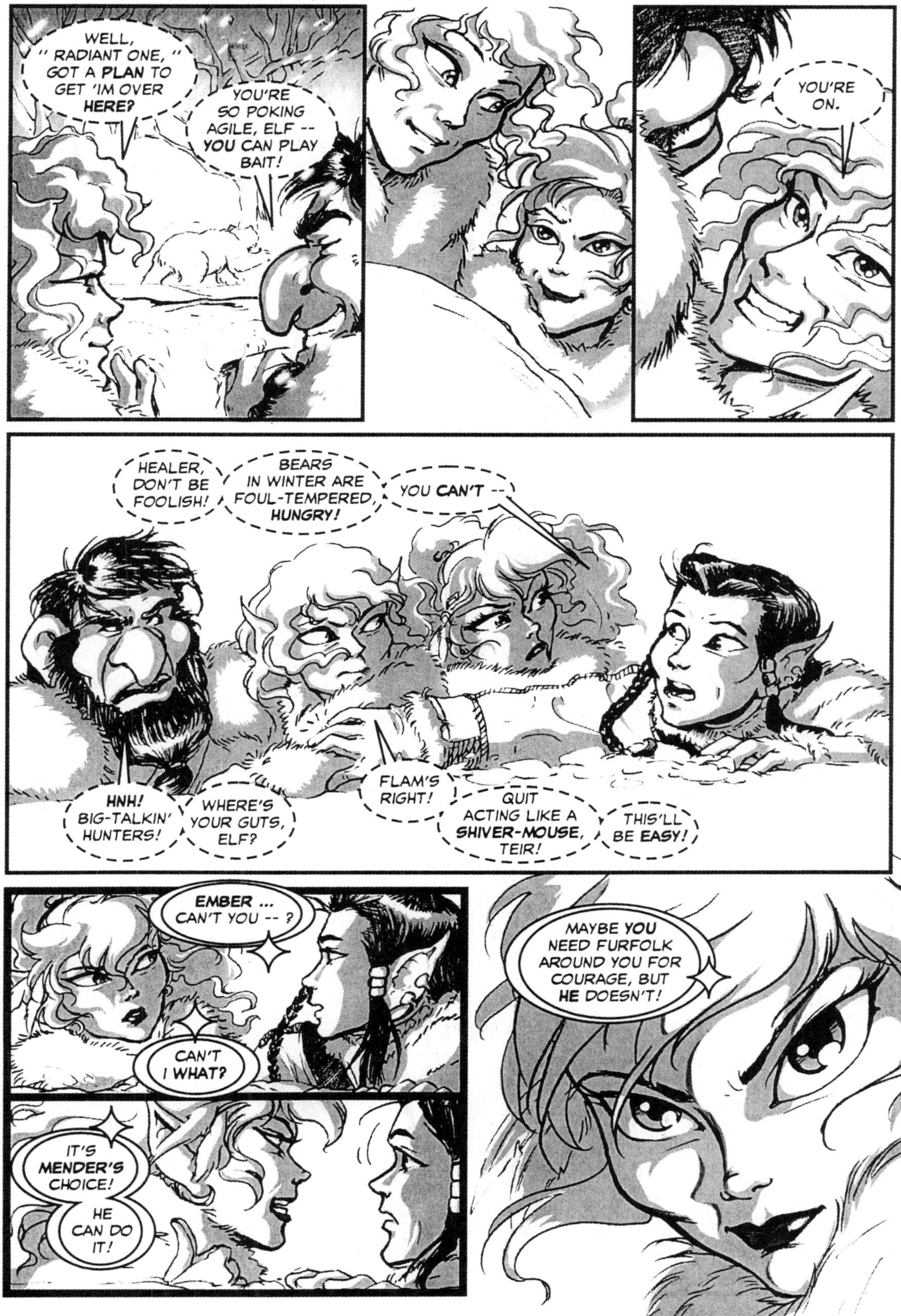
WELL, '' RADIANT ONE, '' GOT A **PLAN** TO GET 'IM OVER **HERE?**
YOU'RE SO POKING AGILE, ELF -- **YOU** CAN PLAY BAIT!
YOU'RE ON.
HEALER, DON'T BE FOOLISH!
BEARS IN WINTER ARE FOUL-TEMPERED, **HUNGRY!**
YOU **CAN'T** --
HNH! BIG-TALKIN' HUNTERS!
WHERE'S YOUR GUTS, ELF?
FLAM'S RIGHT!
QUIT ACTING LIKE A **SHIVER-MOUSE**, TEIR!
THIS'LL BE **EASY!**
EMBER ... CAN'T YOU -- ?
CAN'T I **WHAT?**
IT'S **MENDER'S** CHOICE!
HE CAN DO IT!
MAYBE **YOU** NEED FURFOLK AROUND YOU FOR COURAGE, BUT **HE** DOESN'T!

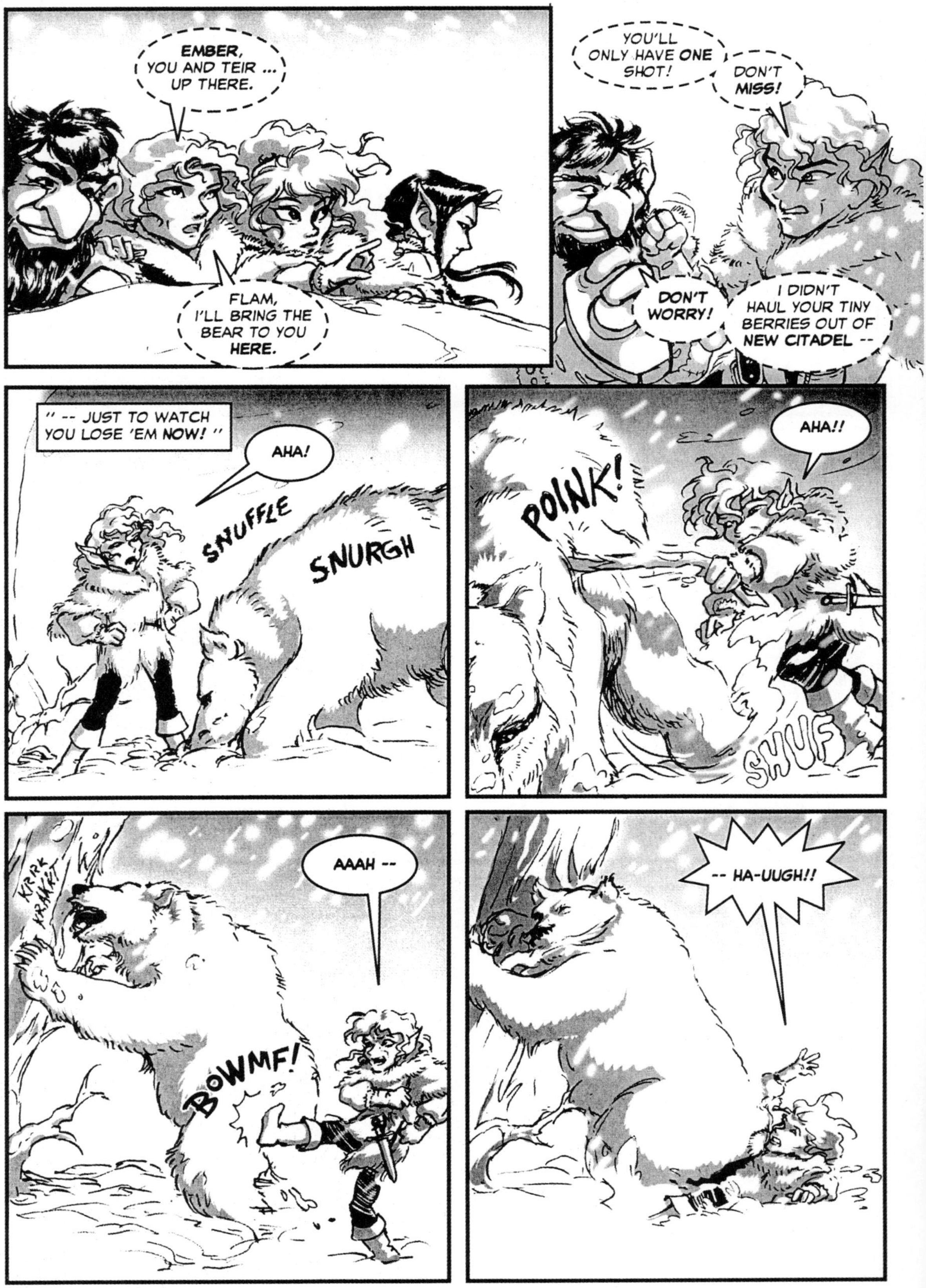
EMBER, YOU AND TEIR ... UP THERE.
FLAM, I'LL BRING THE BEAR TO YOU HERE.
YOU'LL ONLY HAVE ONE SHOT!
DON'T MISS!
DON'T WORRY!
I DIDN'T HAUL YOUR TINY BERRIES OUT OF NEW CITADEL --
" -- JUST TO WATCH YOU LOSE 'EM NOW! "
AHA!
SNUFFLE
SNURGH
AHA!!
POINK!
SHUF
AAAH --
BOWMF!
-- HA-UUGH!!

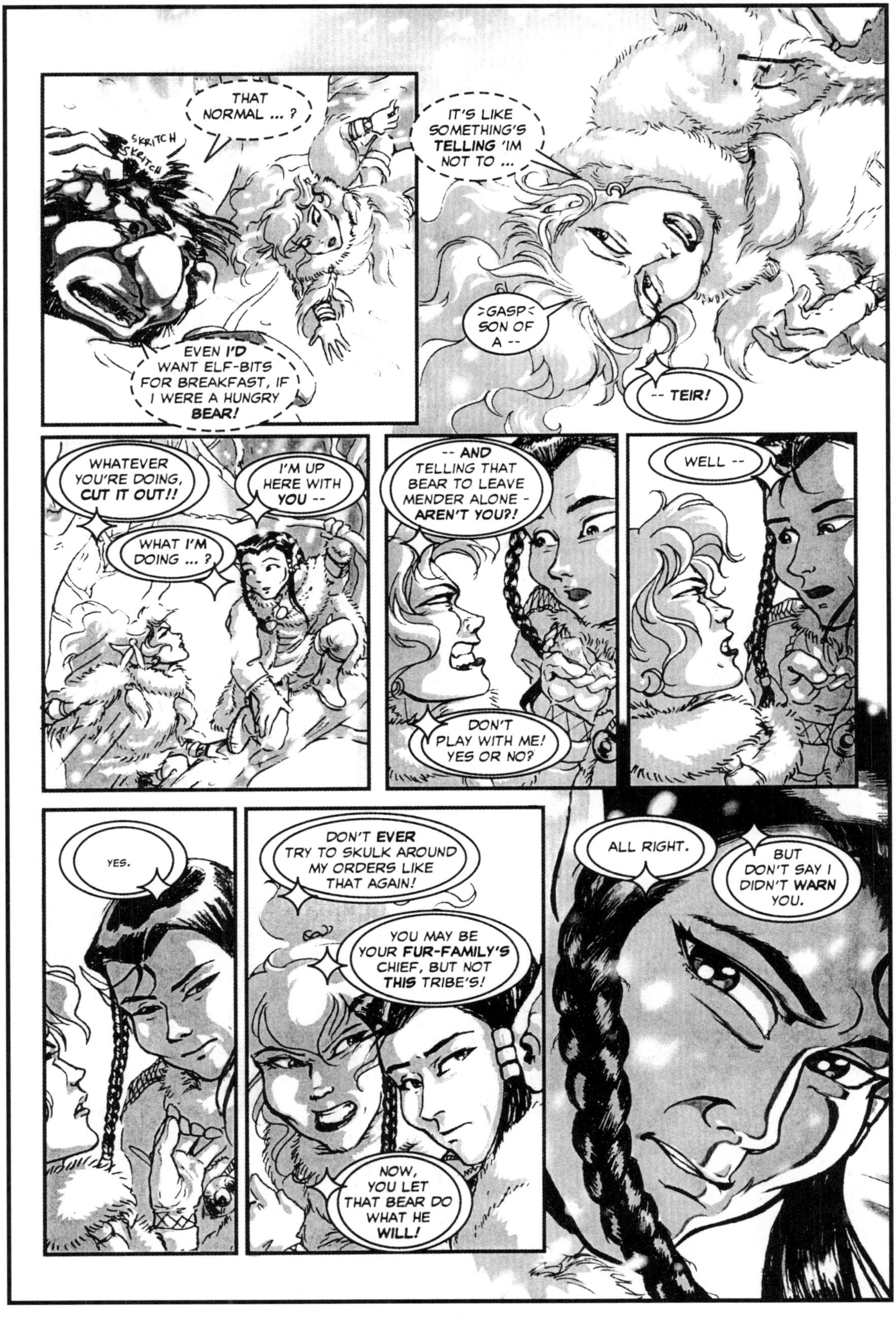
SKRITCH
SKRITCH
THAT NORMAL ... ?
EVEN I'D WANT ELF-BITS FOR BREAKFAST, IF I WERE A HUNGRY BEAR!
IT'S LIKE SOMETHING'S TELLING 'IM NOT TO ...
GASP SON OF A --
-- TEIR!
WHATEVER YOU'RE DOING, CUT IT OUT!!
I'M UP HERE WITH YOU --
WHAT I'M DOING ... ?
-- AND TELLING THAT BEAR TO LEAVE MENDER ALONE - AREN'T YOU?!
DON'T PLAY WITH ME! YES OR NO?
WELL --
YES.
DON'T EVER TRY TO SKULK AROUND MY ORDERS LIKE THAT AGAIN!
YOU MAY BE YOUR FUR-FAMILY'S CHIEF, BUT NOT THIS TRIBE'S!
NOW, YOU LET THAT BEAR DO WHAT HE WILL!
ALL RIGHT.
BUT DON'T SAY I DIDN'T WARN YOU.

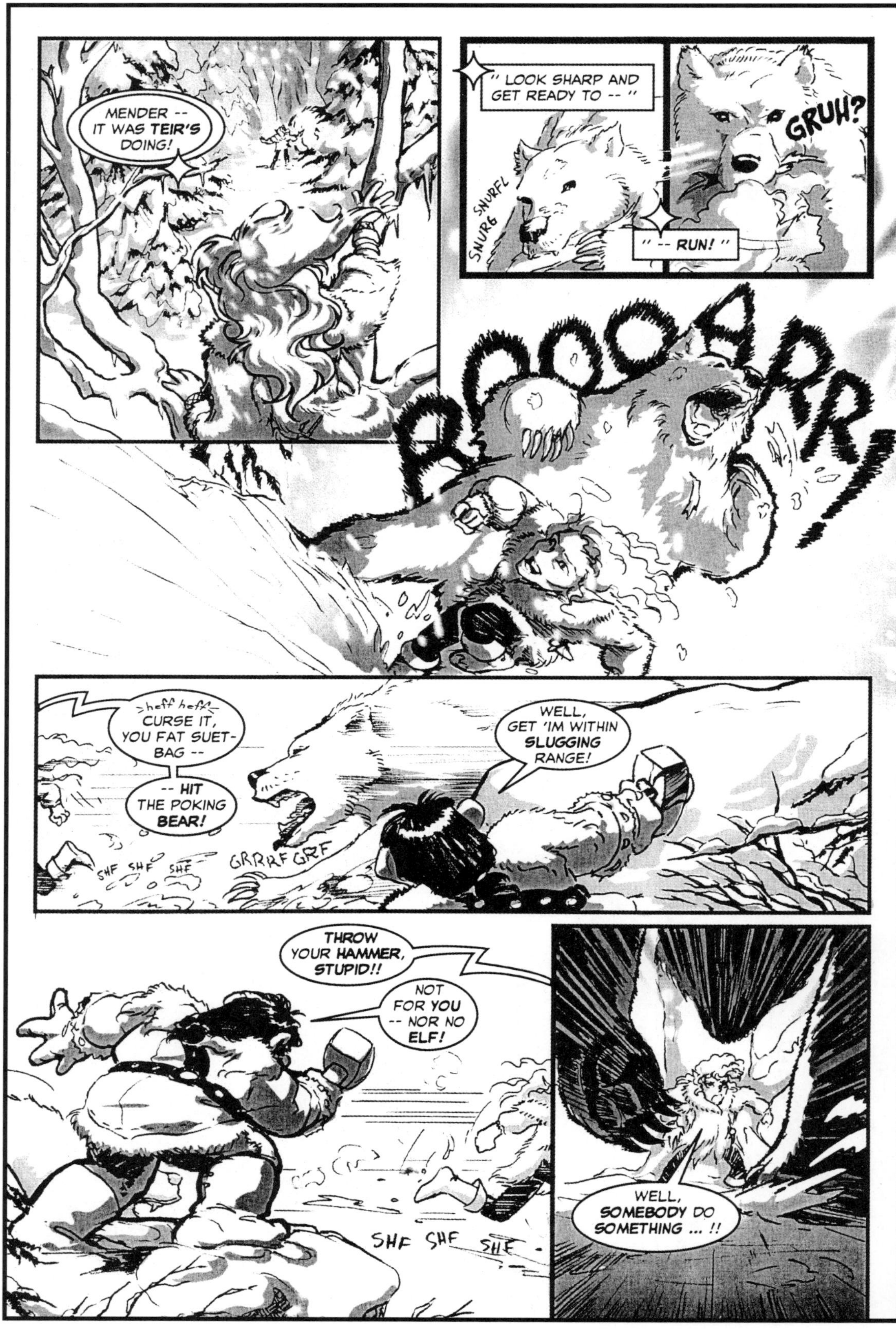
MENDER -- IT WAS TEIR'S DOING!
" LOOK SHARP AND GET READY TO -- "
SNURFL SNURG SNURG
GRUH?
" -- RUN! "
BROOOARR!
heff heff CURSE IT, YOU FAT SUET-BAG --
-- HIT THE POKING BEAR!
WELL, GET 'IM WITHIN SLUGGING RANGE!
SHF SHF SHF
GRRRF GRF
THROW YOUR HAMMER, STUPID!!
NOT FOR YOU -- NOR NO ELF!
SHF SHF SHF
WELL, SOMEBODY DO SOMETHING ... !!

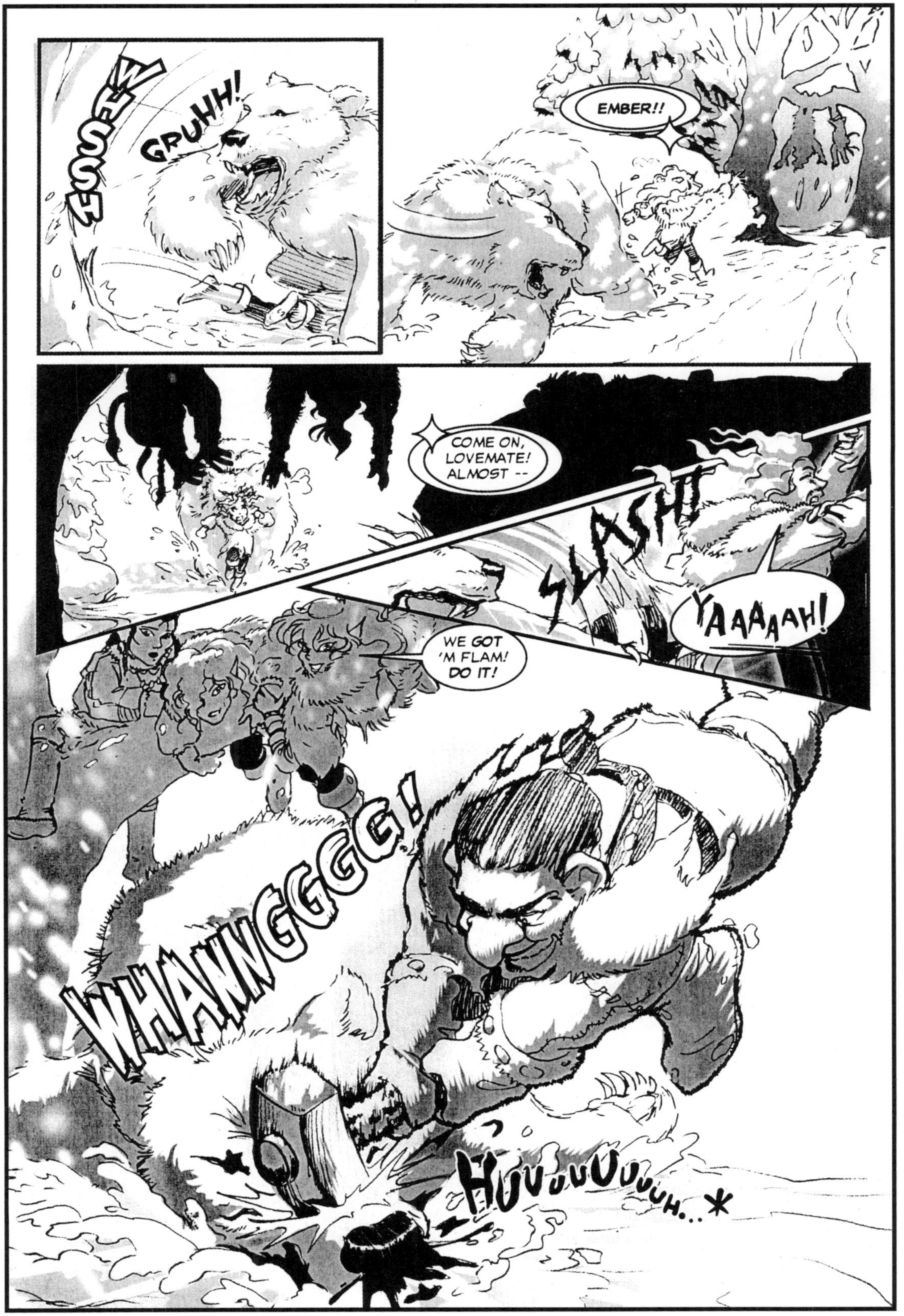
WHSSST
GRUHH!
EMBER!!
COME ON, LOVEMATE! ALMOST --
SLASH!
YAAAAAH!
WE GOT 'M FLAM! DO IT!
WHANNGGGG!
HUUUUUUUUH...*

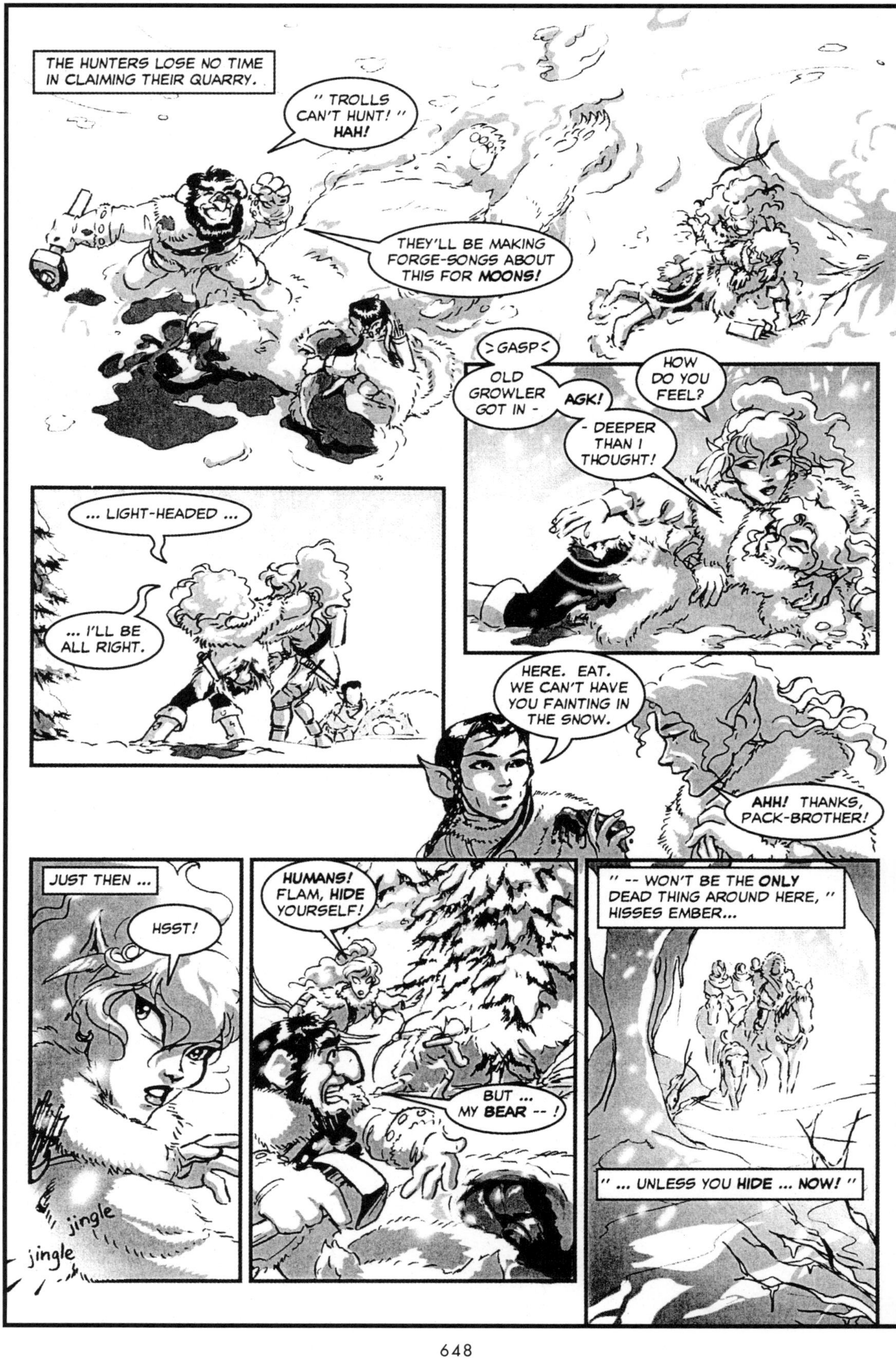
THE HUNTERS LOSE NO TIME IN CLAIMING THEIR QUARRY.
" TROLLS CAN'T HUNT! " HAH!
THEY'LL BE MAKING FORGE-SONGS ABOUT THIS FOR MOONS!
>GASP<
OLD GROWLER GOT IN -
AGK!
- DEEPER THAN I THOUGHT!
HOW DO YOU FEEL?
... LIGHT-HEADED ...
... I'LL BE ALL RIGHT.
HERE. EAT. WE CAN'T HAVE YOU FAINTING IN THE SNOW.
AHH! THANKS, PACK-BROTHER!
JUST THEN ...
HSST!
jingle
jingle
HUMANS! FLAM, HIDE YOURSELF!
BUT ... MY BEAR -- !
" -- WON'T BE THE ONLY DEAD THING AROUND HERE, " HISSES EMBER...
" ... UNLESS YOU HIDE ... NOW! "

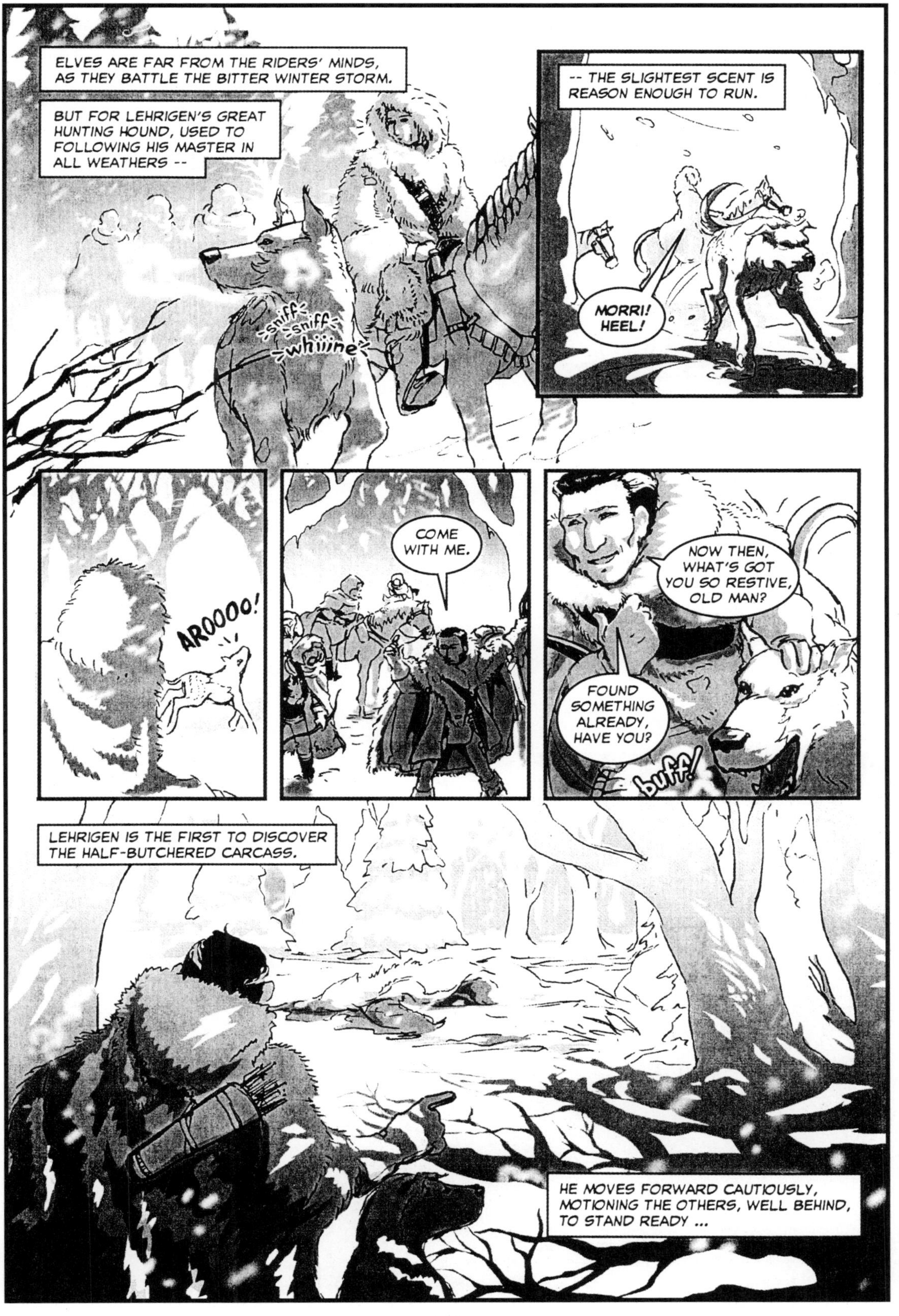
ELVES ARE FAR FROM THE RIDERS' MINDS, AS THEY BATTLE THE BITTER WINTER STORM.
BUT FOR LEHRIGEN'S GREAT HUNTING HOUND, USED TO FOLLOWING HIS MASTER IN ALL WEATHERS --
sniff
sniff
whiiine
-- THE SLIGHTEST SCENT IS REASON ENOUGH TO RUN.
MORRI! HEEL!
AROOOO!
COME WITH ME.
NOW THEN, WHAT'S GOT YOU SO RESTIVE, OLD MAN?
FOUND SOMETHING ALREADY, HAVE YOU?
buff!
LEHRIGEN IS THE FIRST TO DISCOVER THE HALF-BUTCHERED CARCASS.
HE MOVES FORWARD CAUTIOUSLY, MOTIONING THE OTHERS, WELL BEHIND, TO STAND READY ...

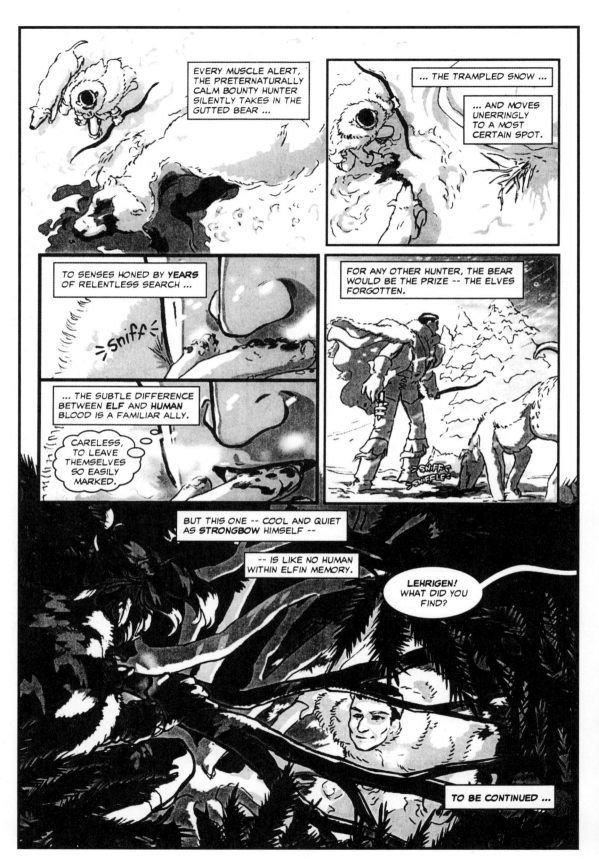

EVERY MUSCLE ALERT, THE PRETERNATURALLY CALM BOUNTY HUNTER SILENTLY TAKES IN THE GUTTED BEAR ...

... THE TRAMPLED SNOW ...

... AND MOVES UNERRINGLY TO A MOST CERTAIN SPOT.

TO SENSES HONED BY **YEARS** OF RELENTLESS SEARCH ...

Sniff

... THE SUBTLE DIFFERENCE BETWEEN **ELF** AND **HUMAN** BLOOD IS A FAMILIAR ALLY.

CARELESS, TO LEAVE THEMSELVES SO EASILY MARKED.

FOR ANY OTHER HUNTER, THE BEAR WOULD BE THE PRIZE -- THE ELVES FORGOTTEN.

SNIFF SNIFFLES

BUT THIS ONE -- COOL AND QUIET AS **STRONGBOW** HIMSELF --

-- IS LIKE NO HUMAN WITHIN ELFIN MEMORY.

LEHRIGEN! WHAT DID YOU FIND?

TO BE CONTINUED ...

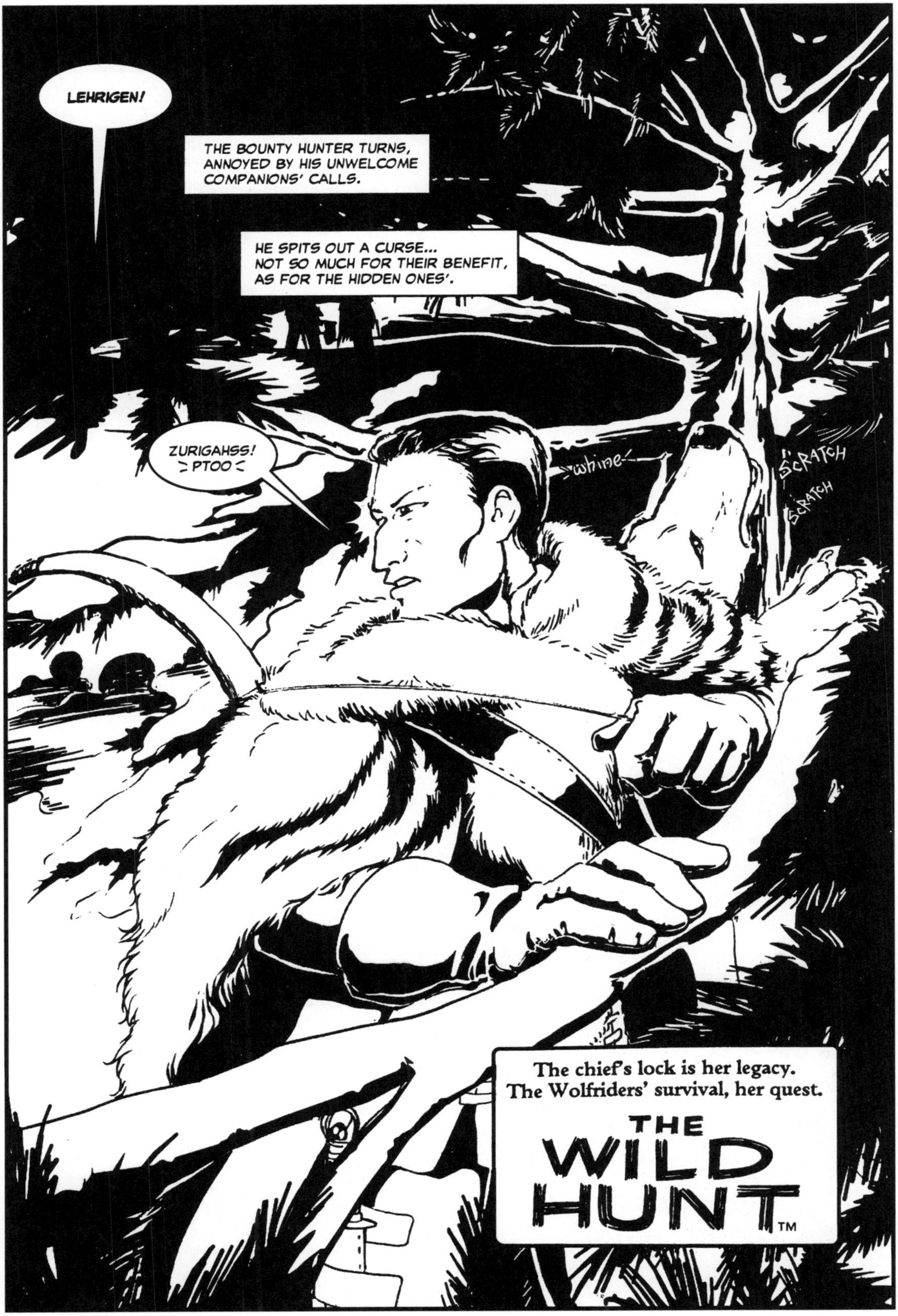
LEHRIGEN!
THE BOUNTY HUNTER TURNS, ANNOYED BY HIS UNWELCOME COMPANIONS' CALLS.
HE SPITS OUT A CURSE... NOT SO MUCH FOR THEIR BENEFIT, AS FOR THE HIDDEN ONES'.
ZURIGAHSS! PTOO
whine
SCRATCH
SCRATCH
The chief's lock is her legacy.
The Wolfriders' survival, her quest.
THE WILD HUNT™

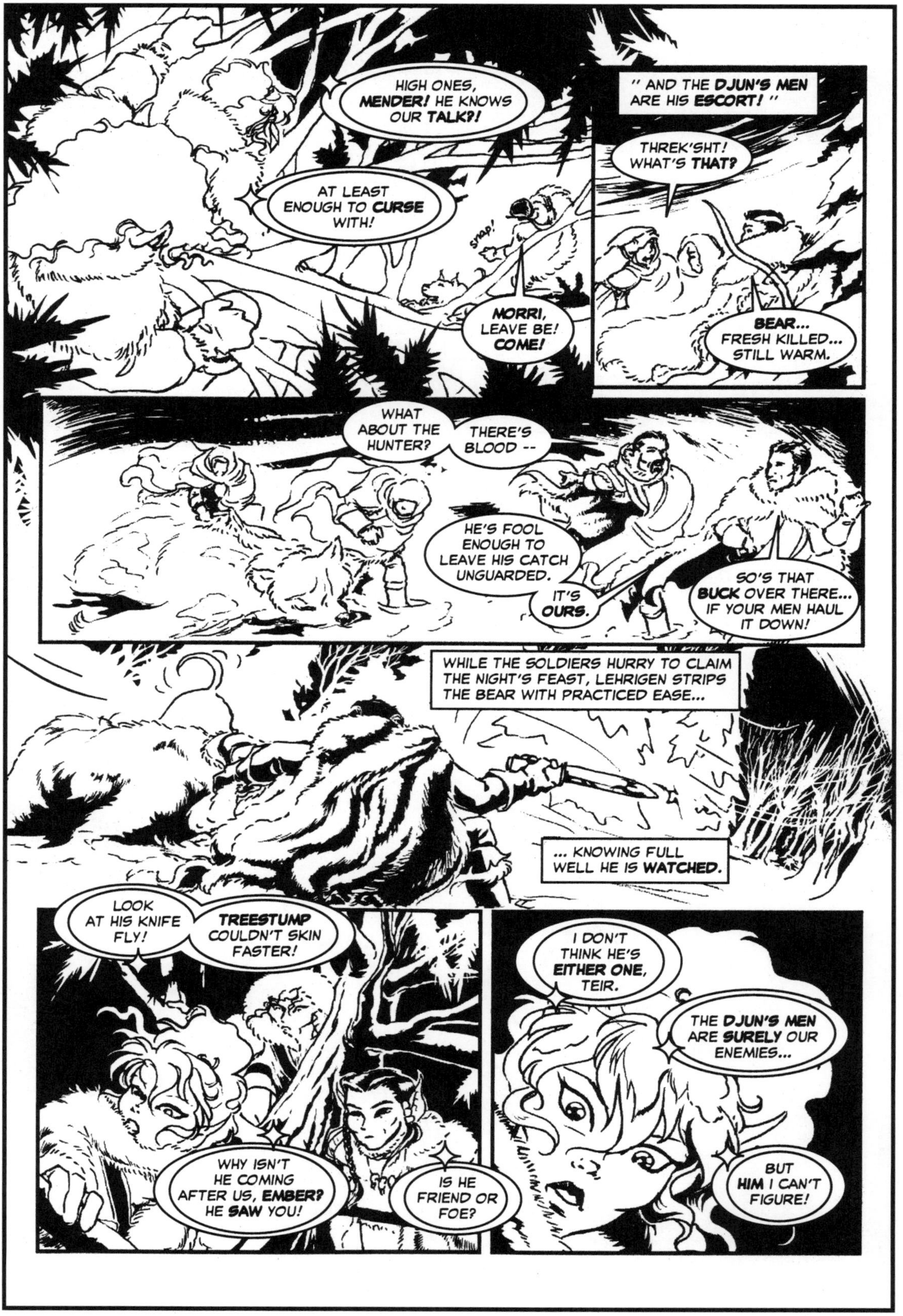
HIGH ONES, MENDER! HE KNOWS OUR TALK?!
AT LEAST ENOUGH TO CURSE WITH!
snap!
MORRI, LEAVE BE! COME!
" AND THE DJUN'S MEN ARE HIS ESCORT! "
THREK'SHT! WHAT'S THAT?
BEAR... FRESH KILLED... STILL WARM.
WHAT ABOUT THE HUNTER?
THERE'S BLOOD --
HE'S FOOL ENOUGH TO LEAVE HIS CATCH UNGUARDED.
IT'S OURS.
SO'S THAT BUCK OVER THERE... IF YOUR MEN HAUL IT DOWN!
WHILE THE SOLDIERS HURRY TO CLAIM THE NIGHT'S FEAST, LEHRIGEN STRIPS THE BEAR WITH PRACTICED EASE...
... KNOWING FULL WELL HE IS WATCHED.
LOOK AT HIS KNIFE FLY!
TREESTUMP COULDN'T SKIN FASTER!
WHY ISN'T HE COMING AFTER US, EMBER? HE SAW YOU!
IS HE FRIEND OR FOE?
I DON'T THINK HE'S EITHER ONE, TEIR.
THE DJUN'S MEN ARE SURELY OUR ENEMIES...
BUT HIM I CAN'T FIGURE!

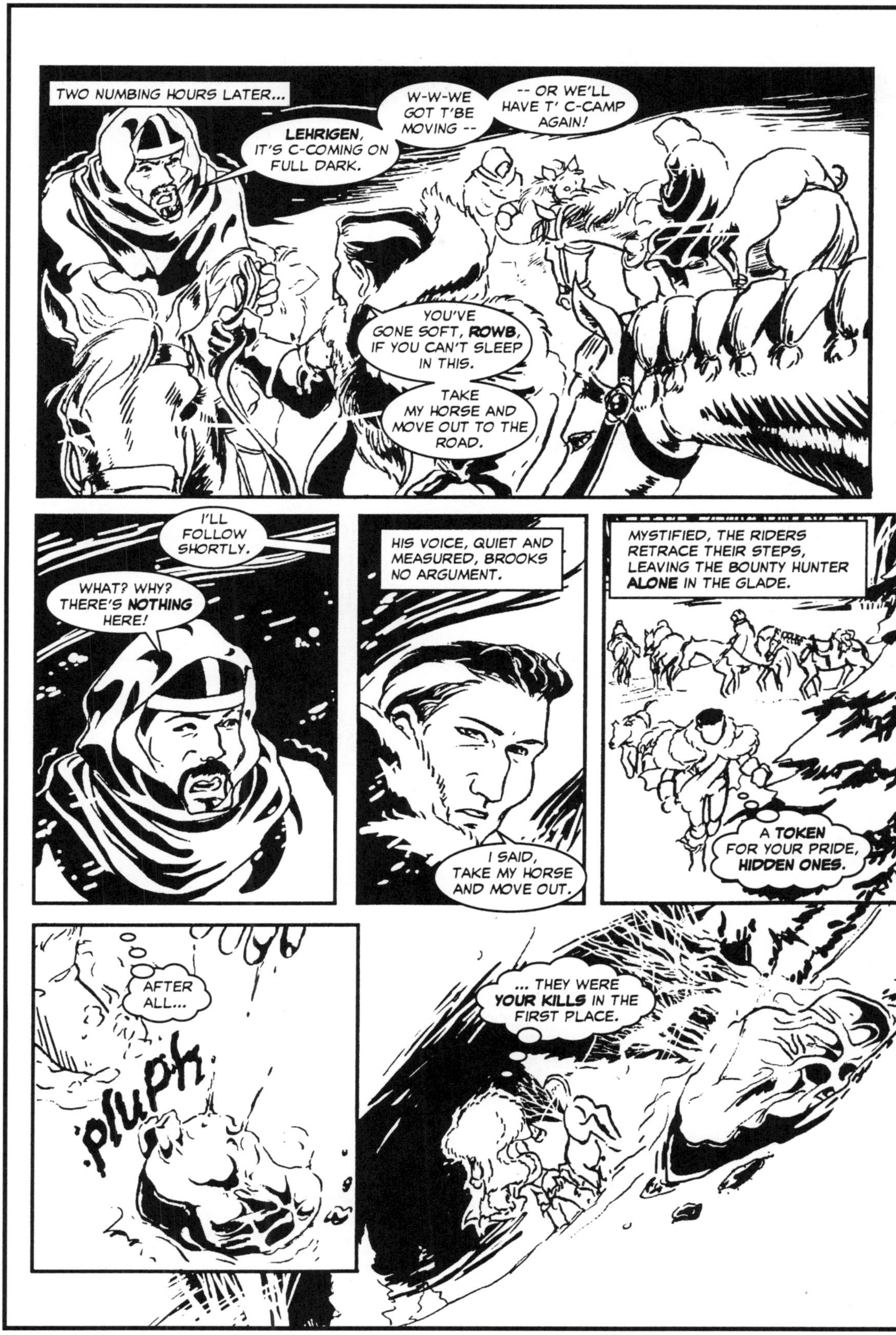

TWO NUMBING HOURS LATER...
LEHRIGEN, IT'S C-COMING ON FULL DARK.
W-W-WE GOT T'BE MOVING --
-- OR WE'LL HAVE T' C-CAMP AGAIN!
YOU'VE GONE SOFT, ROWB, IF YOU CAN'T SLEEP IN THIS.
TAKE MY HORSE AND MOVE OUT TO THE ROAD.
I'LL FOLLOW SHORTLY.
WHAT? WHY? THERE'S NOTHING HERE!
HIS VOICE, QUIET AND MEASURED, BROOKS NO ARGUMENT.
I SAID, TAKE MY HORSE AND MOVE OUT.
MYSTIFIED, THE RIDERS RETRACE THEIR STEPS, LEAVING THE BOUNTY HUNTER ALONE IN THE GLADE.
A TOKEN FOR YOUR PRIDE, HIDDEN ONES.
AFTER ALL...
plph
... THEY WERE YOUR KILLS IN THE FIRST PLACE.

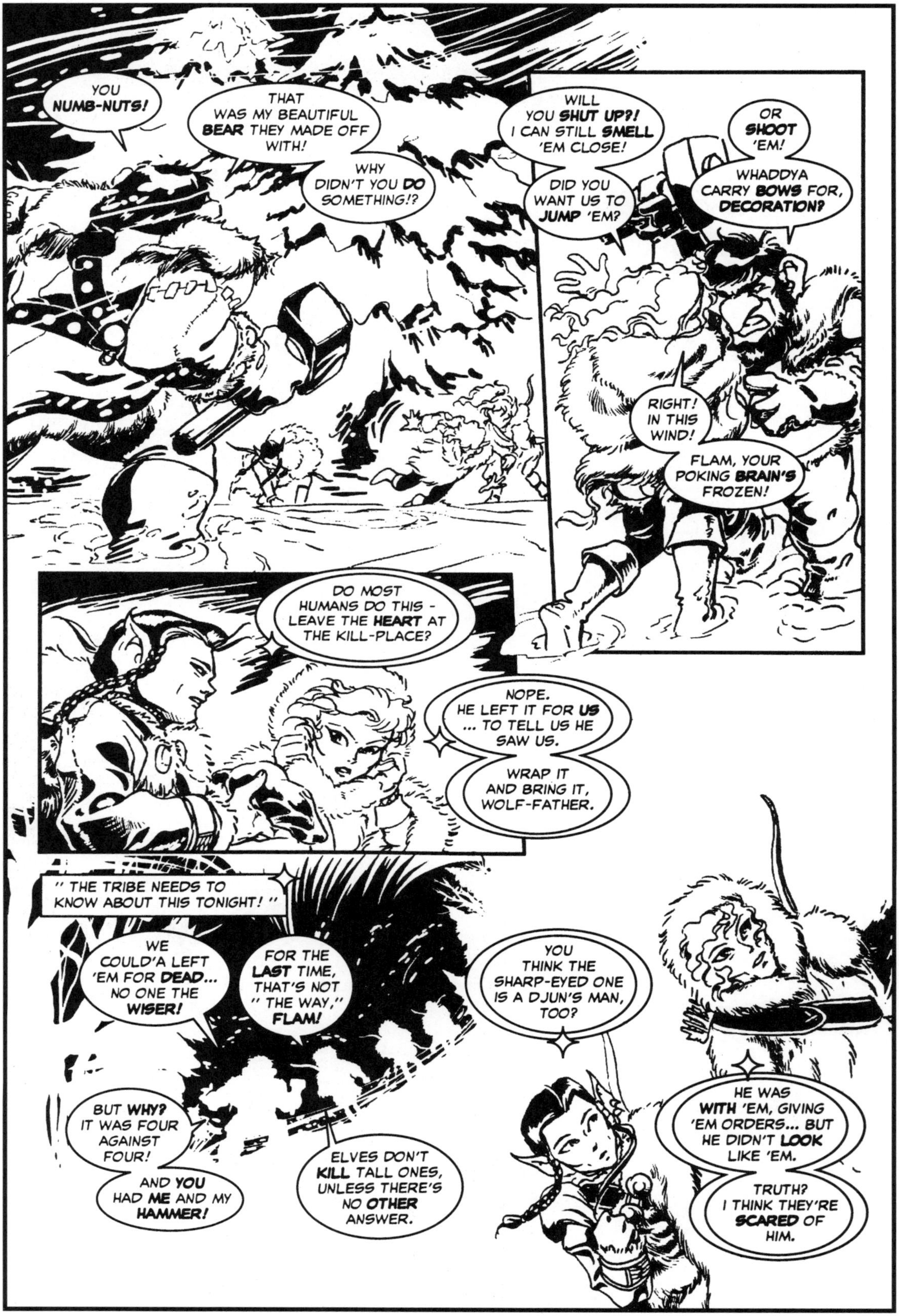
YOU NUMB-NUTS!
THAT WAS MY BEAUTIFUL BEAR THEY MADE OFF WITH!
WHY DIDN'T YOU DO SOMETHING!?
WILL YOU SHUT UP?! I CAN STILL SMELL 'EM CLOSE!
DID YOU WANT US TO JUMP 'EM?
OR SHOOT 'EM!
WHADDYA CARRY BOWS FOR, DECORATION?
RIGHT! IN THIS WIND!
FLAM, YOUR POKING BRAIN'S FROZEN!
DO MOST HUMANS DO THIS - LEAVE THE HEART AT THE KILL-PLACE?
NOPE. HE LEFT IT FOR US ... TO TELL US HE SAW US.
WRAP IT AND BRING IT, WOLF-FATHER.
" THE TRIBE NEEDS TO KNOW ABOUT THIS TONIGHT! "
WE COULD'A LEFT 'EM FOR DEAD... NO ONE THE WISER!
FOR THE LAST TIME, THAT'S NOT " THE WAY," FLAM!
BUT WHY? IT WAS FOUR AGAINST FOUR!
AND YOU HAD ME AND MY HAMMER!
ELVES DON'T KILL TALL ONES, UNLESS THERE'S NO OTHER ANSWER.
YOU THINK THE SHARP-EYED ONE IS A DJUN'S MAN, TOO?
HE WAS WITH 'EM, GIVING 'EM ORDERS... BUT HE DIDN'T LOOK LIKE 'EM.
TRUTH? I THINK THEY'RE SCARED OF HIM.

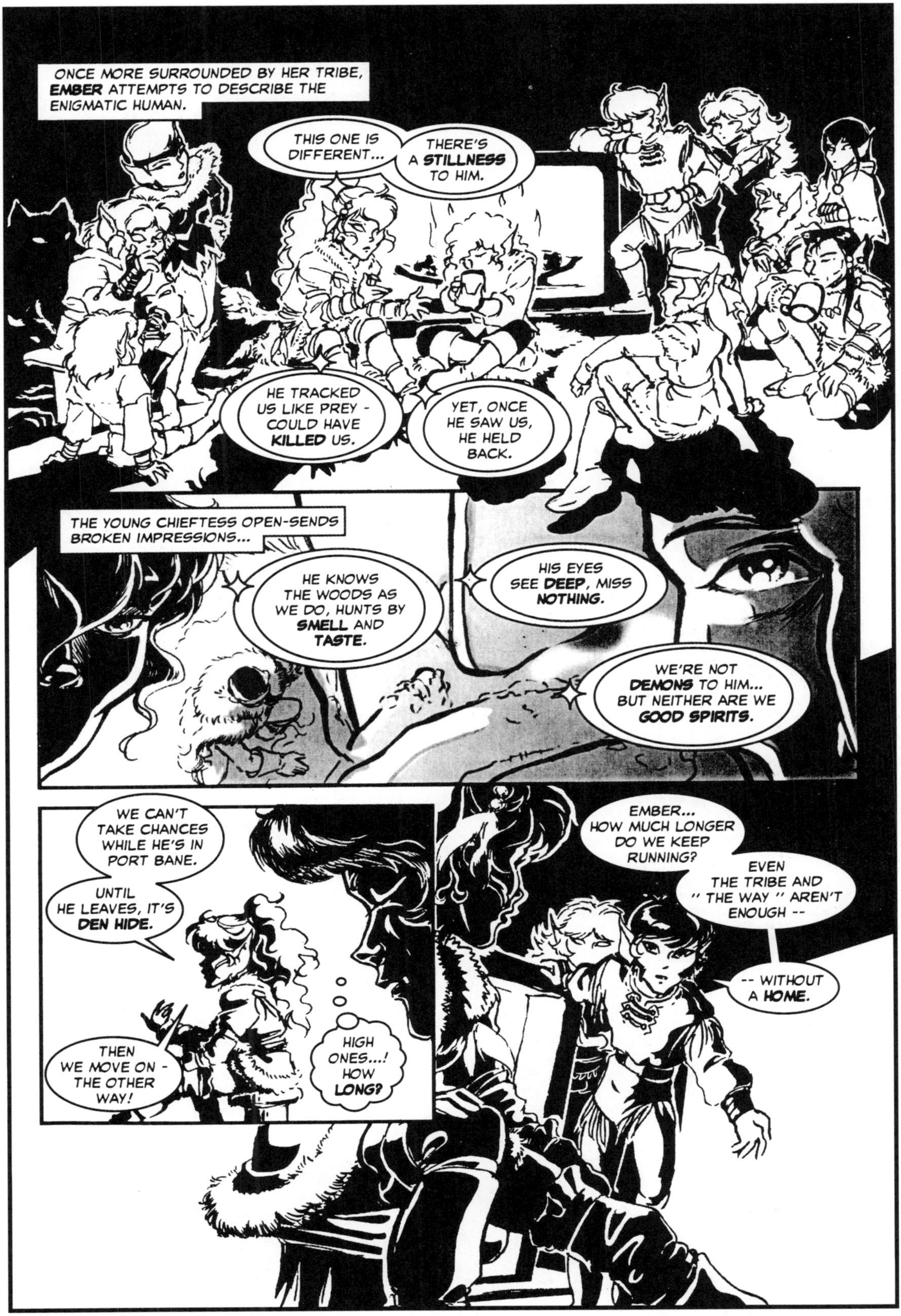
ONCE MORE SURROUNDED BY HER TRIBE, EMBER ATTEMPTS TO DESCRIBE THE ENIGMATIC HUMAN.
THIS ONE IS DIFFERENT...
THERE'S A STILLNESS TO HIM.
HE TRACKED US LIKE PREY - COULD HAVE KILLED US.
YET, ONCE HE SAW US, HE HELD BACK.
THE YOUNG CHIEFTESS OPEN-SENDS BROKEN IMPRESSIONS...
HE KNOWS THE WOODS AS WE DO, HUNTS BY SMELL AND TASTE.
HIS EYES SEE DEEP, MISS NOTHING.
WE'RE NOT DEMONS TO HIM... BUT NEITHER ARE WE GOOD SPIRITS.
WE CAN'T TAKE CHANCES WHILE HE'S IN PORT BANE.
UNTIL HE LEAVES, IT'S DEN HIDE.
THEN WE MOVE ON - THE OTHER WAY!
HIGH ONES...! HOW LONG?
EMBER... HOW MUCH LONGER DO WE KEEP RUNNING?
EVEN THE TRIBE AND " THE WAY " AREN'T ENOUGH --
-- WITHOUT A HOME.

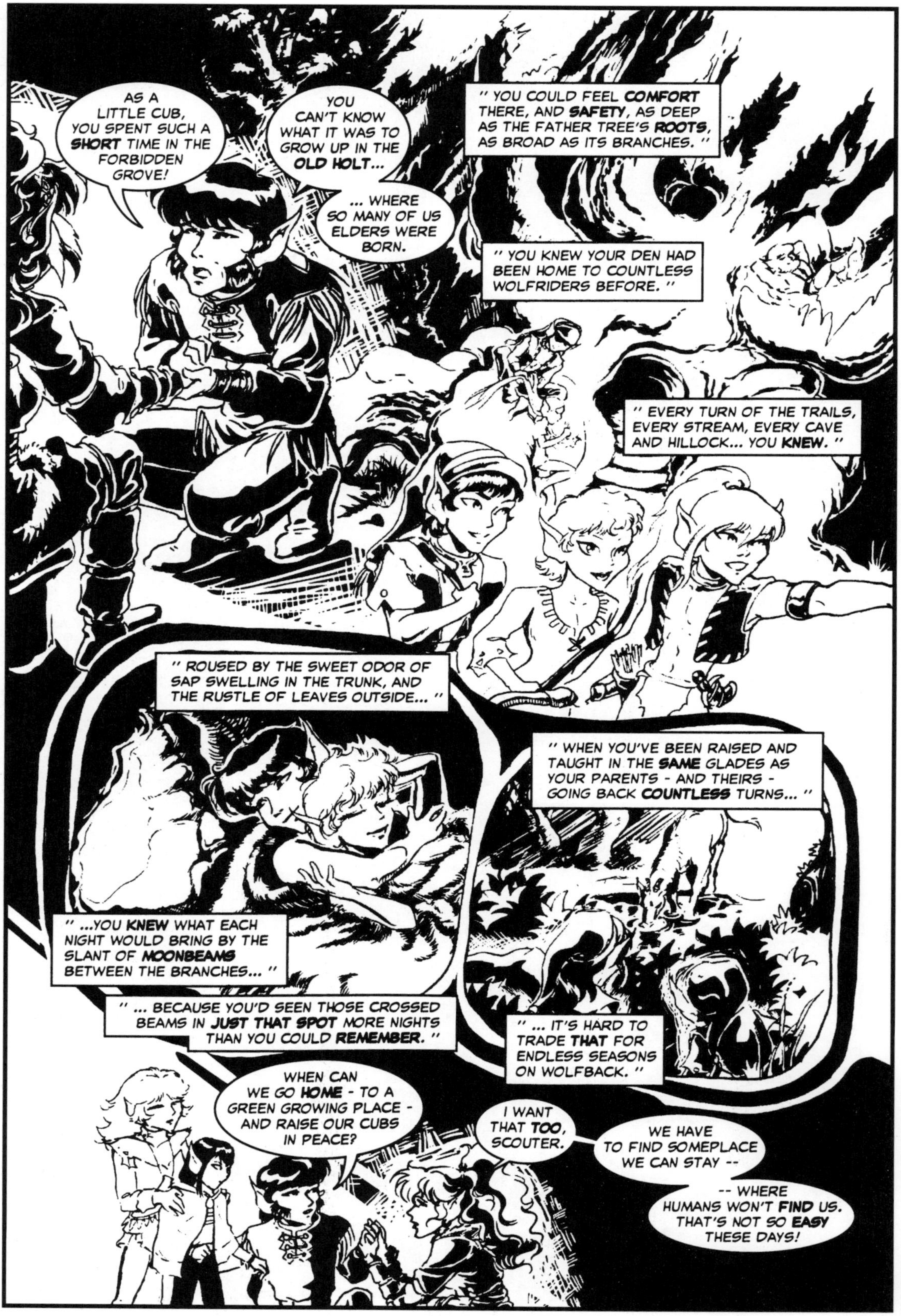
AS A LITTLE CUB, YOU SPENT SUCH A SHORT TIME IN THE FORBIDDEN GROVE!
YOU CAN'T KNOW WHAT IT WAS TO GROW UP IN THE OLD HOLT...
... WHERE SO MANY OF US ELDERS WERE BORN.
" YOU COULD FEEL COMFORT THERE, AND SAFETY, AS DEEP AS THE FATHER TREE'S ROOTS, AS BROAD AS ITS BRANCHES. "
" YOU KNEW YOUR DEN HAD BEEN HOME TO COUNTLESS WOLFRIDERS BEFORE. "
" EVERY TURN OF THE TRAILS, EVERY STREAM, EVERY CAVE AND HILLOCK... YOU KNEW. "
" ROUSED BY THE SWEET ODOR OF SAP SWELLING IN THE TRUNK, AND THE RUSTLE OF LEAVES OUTSIDE... "
" ...YOU KNEW WHAT EACH NIGHT WOULD BRING BY THE SLANT OF MOONBEAMS BETWEEN THE BRANCHES... "
" ... BECAUSE YOU'D SEEN THOSE CROSSED BEAMS IN JUST THAT SPOT MORE NIGHTS THAN YOU COULD REMEMBER. "
" WHEN YOU'VE BEEN RAISED AND TAUGHT IN THE SAME GLADES AS YOUR PARENTS - AND THEIRS - GOING BACK COUNTLESS TURNS... "
" ... IT'S HARD TO TRADE THAT FOR ENDLESS SEASONS ON WOLFBACK. "
WHEN CAN WE GO HOME - TO A GREEN GROWING PLACE - AND RAISE OUR CUBS IN PEACE?
I WANT THAT TOO, SCOUTER.
WE HAVE TO FIND SOMEPLACE WE CAN STAY --
-- WHERE HUMANS WON'T FIND US. THAT'S NOT SO EASY THESE DAYS!

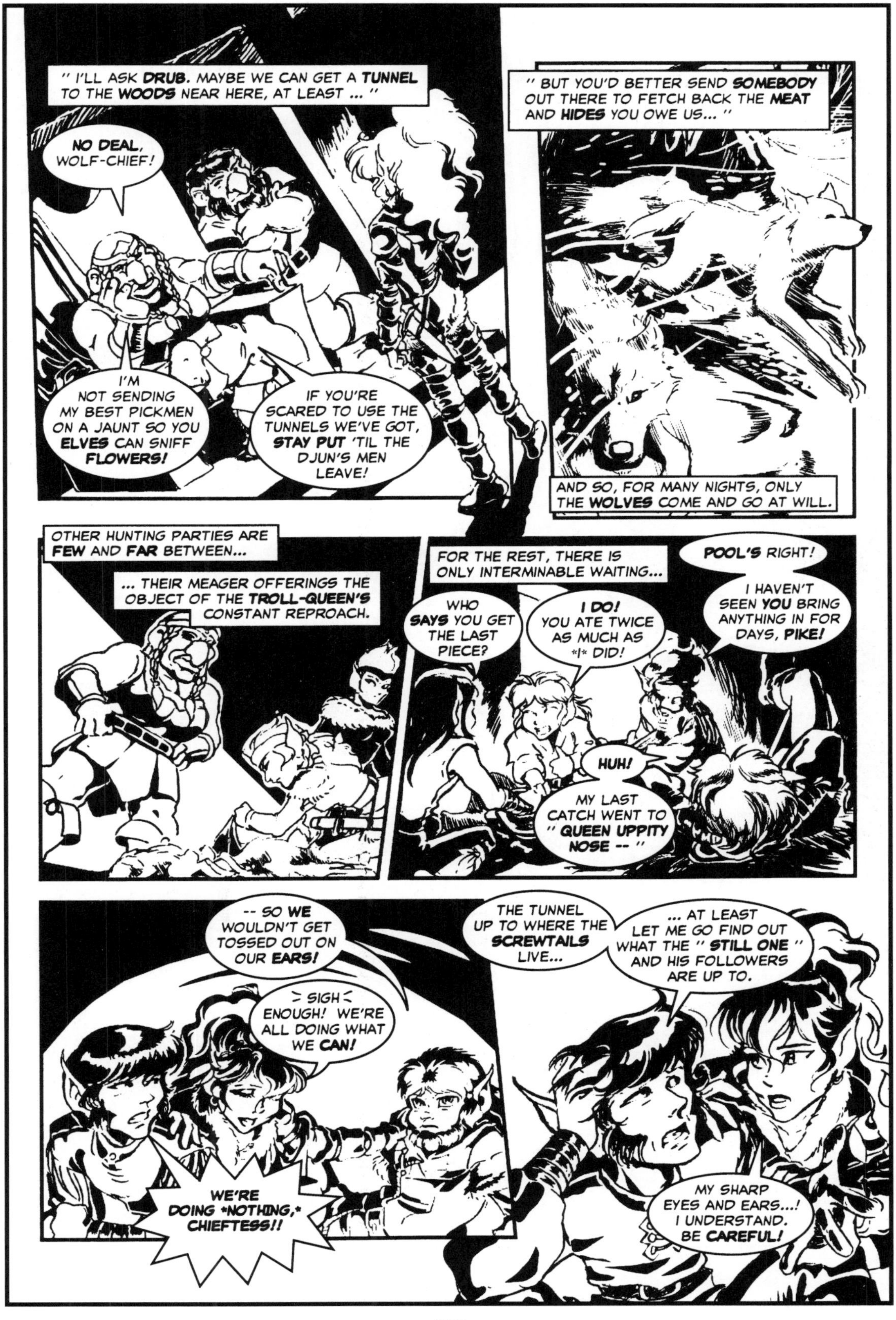
" I'LL ASK DRUB. MAYBE WE CAN GET A TUNNEL TO THE WOODS NEAR HERE, AT LEAST ... "
NO DEAL, WOLF-CHIEF!
I'M NOT SENDING MY BEST PICKMEN ON A JAUNT SO YOU ELVES CAN SNIFF FLOWERS!
IF YOU'RE SCARED TO USE THE TUNNELS WE'VE GOT, STAY PUT 'TIL THE DJUN'S MEN LEAVE!
" BUT YOU'D BETTER SEND SOMEBODY OUT THERE TO FETCH BACK THE MEAT AND HIDES YOU OWE US... "
AND SO, FOR MANY NIGHTS, ONLY THE WOLVES COME AND GO AT WILL.
OTHER HUNTING PARTIES ARE FEW AND FAR BETWEEN...
... THEIR MEAGER OFFERINGS THE OBJECT OF THE TROLL-QUEEN'S CONSTANT REPROACH.
FOR THE REST, THERE IS ONLY INTERMINABLE WAITING...
WHO SAYS YOU GET THE LAST PIECE?
I DO! YOU ATE TWICE AS MUCH AS *I* DID!
POOL'S RIGHT!
I HAVEN'T SEEN YOU BRING ANYTHING IN FOR DAYS, PIKE!
HUH!
MY LAST CATCH WENT TO " QUEEN UPPITY NOSE -- "
-- SO WE WOULDN'T GET TOSSED OUT ON OUR EARS!
> SIGH < ENOUGH! WE'RE ALL DOING WHAT WE CAN!
WE'RE DOING *NOTHING,* CHIEFTESS!!
THE TUNNEL UP TO WHERE THE SCREWTAILS LIVE...
... AT LEAST LET ME GO FIND OUT WHAT THE " STILL ONE " AND HIS FOLLOWERS ARE UP TO.
MY SHARP EYES AND EARS...! I UNDERSTAND. BE CAREFUL!

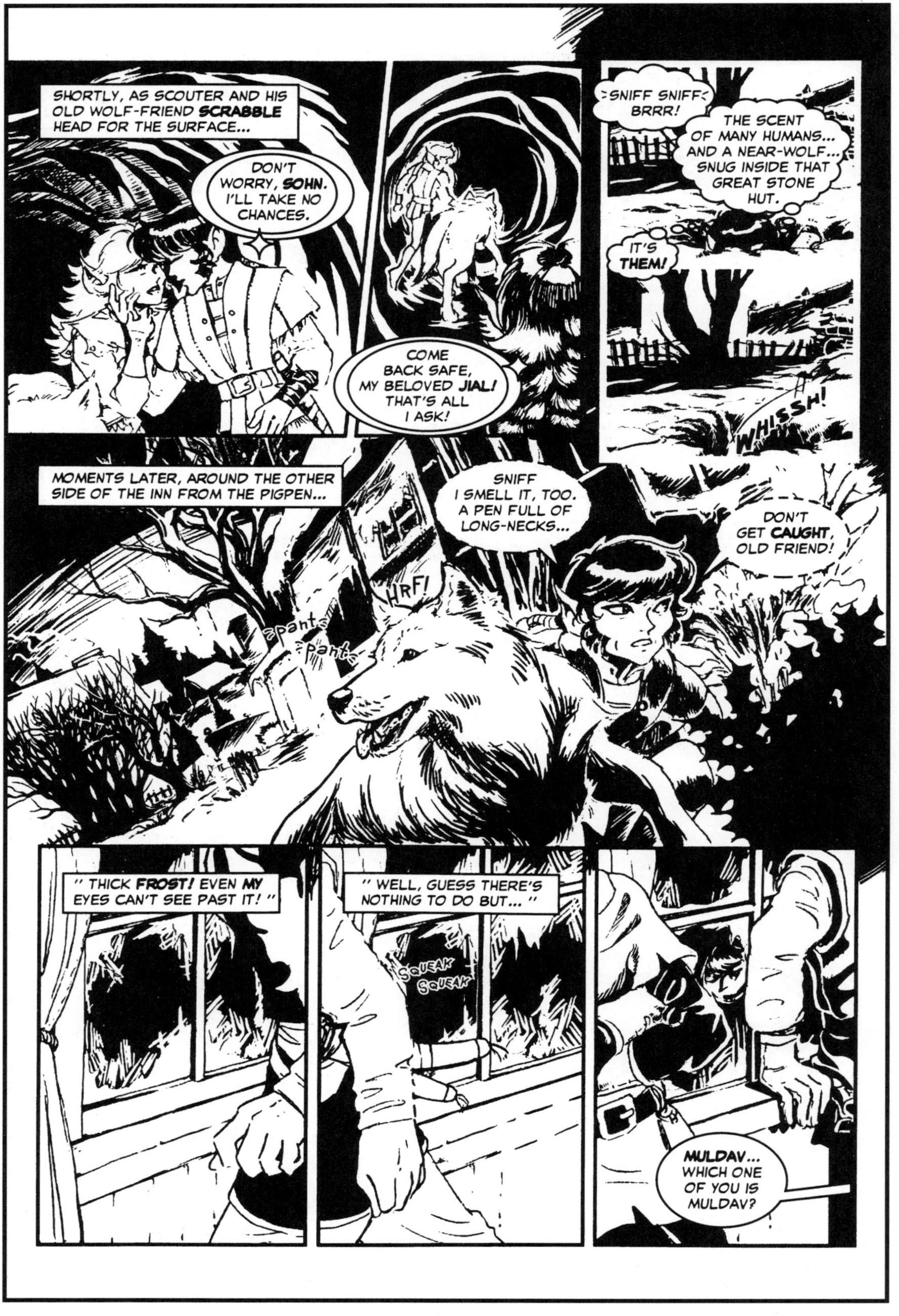
SHORTLY, AS SCOUTER AND HIS OLD WOLF-FRIEND SCRABBLE HEAD FOR THE SURFACE...
DON'T WORRY, SOHN. I'LL TAKE NO CHANCES.
COME BACK SAFE, MY BELOVED JIAL! THAT'S ALL I ASK!
SNIFF SNIFF BRRR!
THE SCENT OF MANY HUMANS... AND A NEAR-WOLF... SNUG INSIDE THAT GREAT STONE HUT.
IT'S THEM!
WHISSSH!
MOMENTS LATER, AROUND THE OTHER SIDE OF THE INN FROM THE PIGPEN...
SNIFF I SMELL IT, TOO. A PEN FULL OF LONG-NECKS...
DON'T GET CAUGHT, OLD FRIEND!
HRF!
pant pant
" THICK FROST! EVEN MY EYES CAN'T SEE PAST IT! "
" WELL, GUESS THERE'S NOTHING TO DO BUT... "
SQUEAK SQUEAK
MULDAV... WHICH ONE OF YOU IS MULDAV?

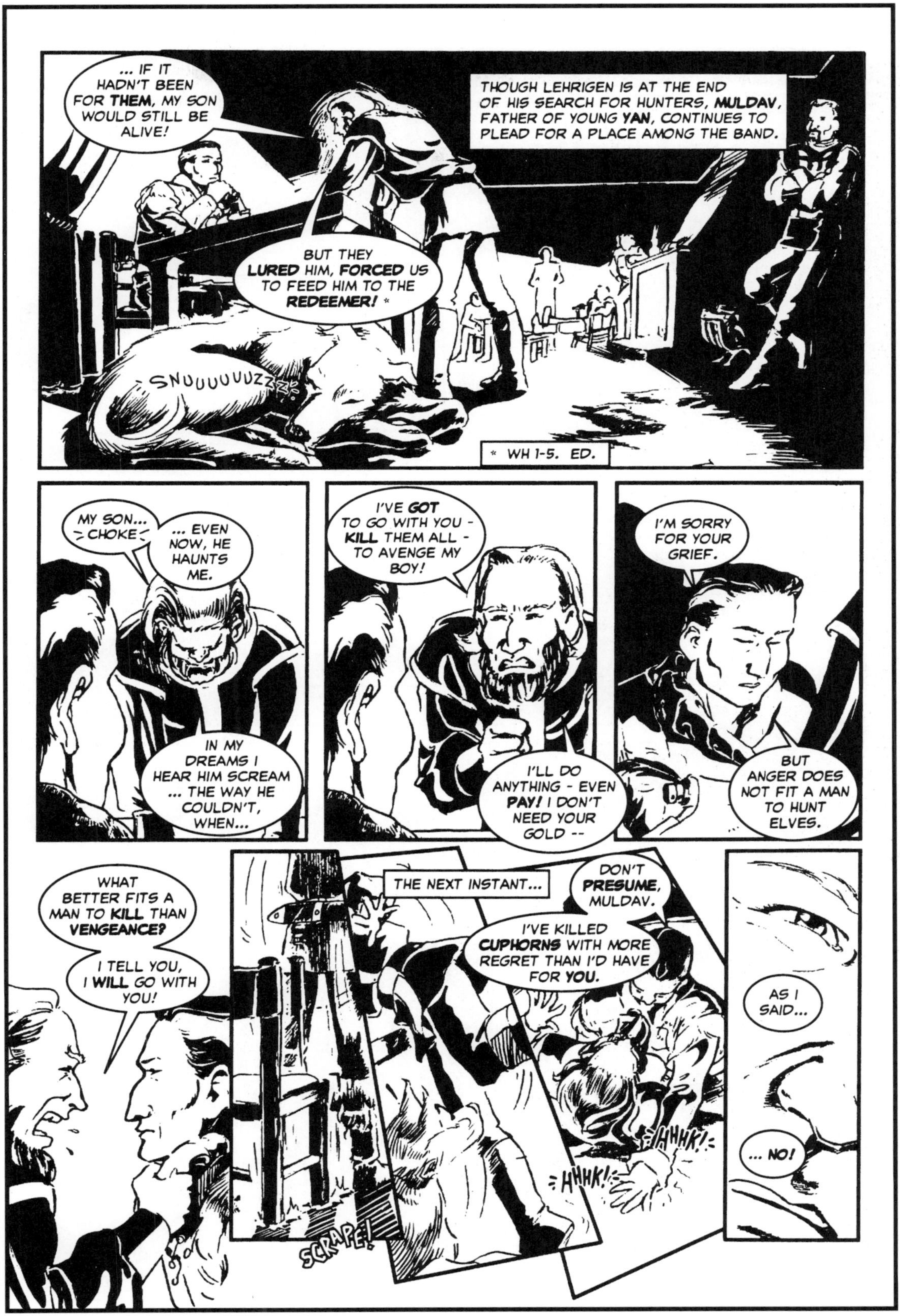
... IF IT HADN'T BEEN FOR THEM, MY SON WOULD STILL BE ALIVE!
THOUGH LEHRIGEN IS AT THE END OF HIS SEARCH FOR HUNTERS, MULDAV, FATHER OF YOUNG YAN, CONTINUES TO PLEAD FOR A PLACE AMONG THE BAND.
BUT THEY LURED HIM, FORCED US TO FEED HIM TO THE REDEEMER! *
SNUUUUUUZZZ
* WH 1-5. ED.
MY SON... CHOKE
... EVEN NOW, HE HAUNTS ME.
IN MY DREAMS I HEAR HIM SCREAM ... THE WAY HE COULDN'T, WHEN...
I'VE GOT TO GO WITH YOU - KILL THEM ALL - TO AVENGE MY BOY!
I'LL DO ANYTHING - EVEN PAY! I DON'T NEED YOUR GOLD --
I'M SORRY FOR YOUR GRIEF.
BUT ANGER DOES NOT FIT A MAN TO HUNT ELVES.
WHAT BETTER FITS A MAN TO KILL THAN VENGEANCE?
I TELL YOU, I WILL GO WITH YOU!
THE NEXT INSTANT...
DON'T PRESUME, MULDAV.
I'VE KILLED CUPHORNS WITH MORE REGRET THAN I'D HAVE FOR YOU.
HHHK!
HHHK!
SCRAPE!
AS I SAID...
... NO!

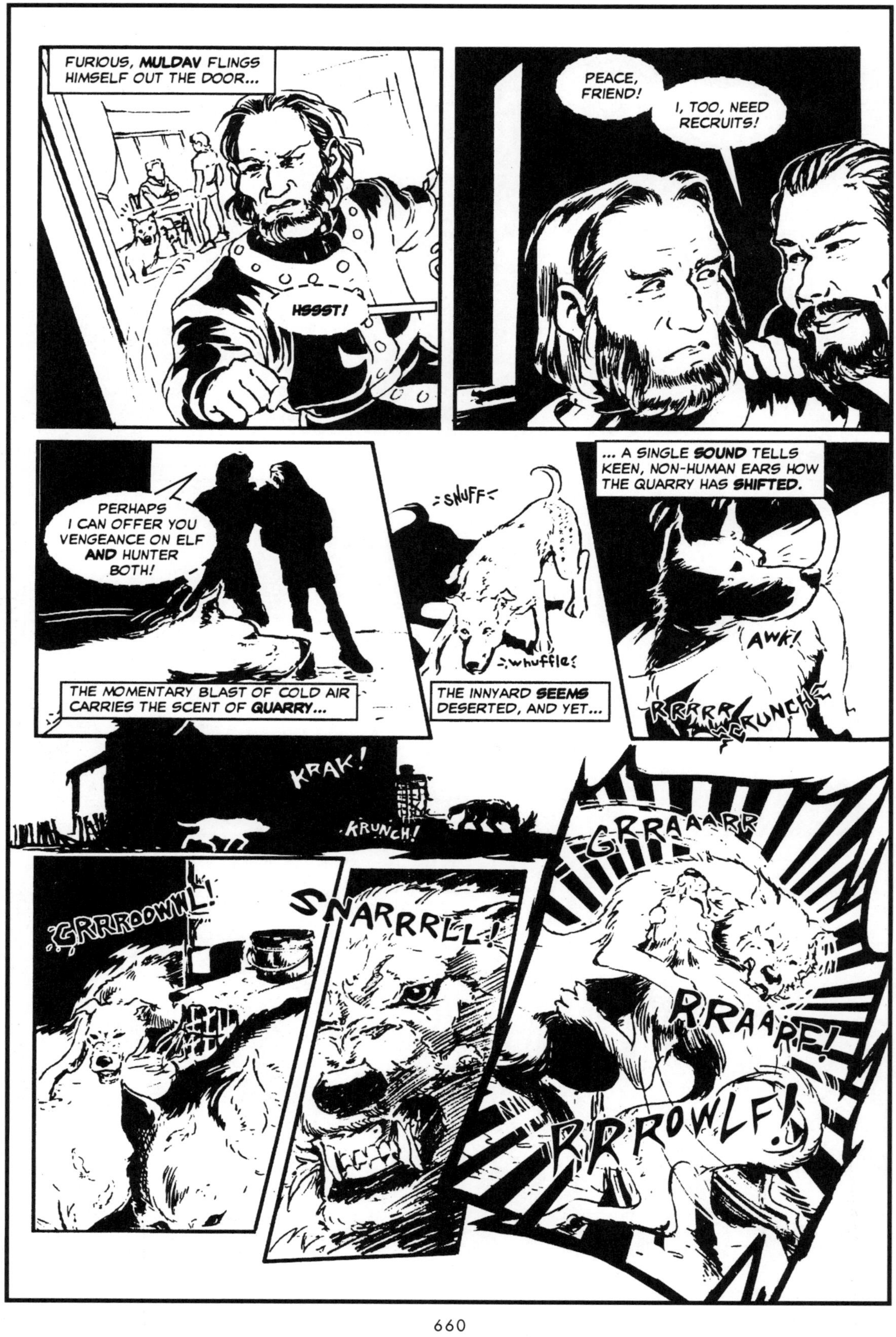
FURIOUS, MULDAV FLINGS HIMSELF OUT THE DOOR...
HSSST!
PEACE, FRIEND!
I, TOO, NEED RECRUITS!
PERHAPS I CAN OFFER YOU VENGEANCE ON ELF AND HUNTER BOTH!
THE MOMENTARY BLAST OF COLD AIR CARRIES THE SCENT OF QUARRY...
SNUFF
WHUFFLE
THE INNYARD SEEMS DESERTED, AND YET...
... A SINGLE SOUND TELLS KEEN, NON-HUMAN EARS HOW THE QUARRY HAS SHIFTED.
AWK!
RRRRR
CRUNCH
KRAK!
KRUNCH!
GRRROOWWL!
SNARRRLL!
GRRAAARR
RRAARF!
RRROWLF!

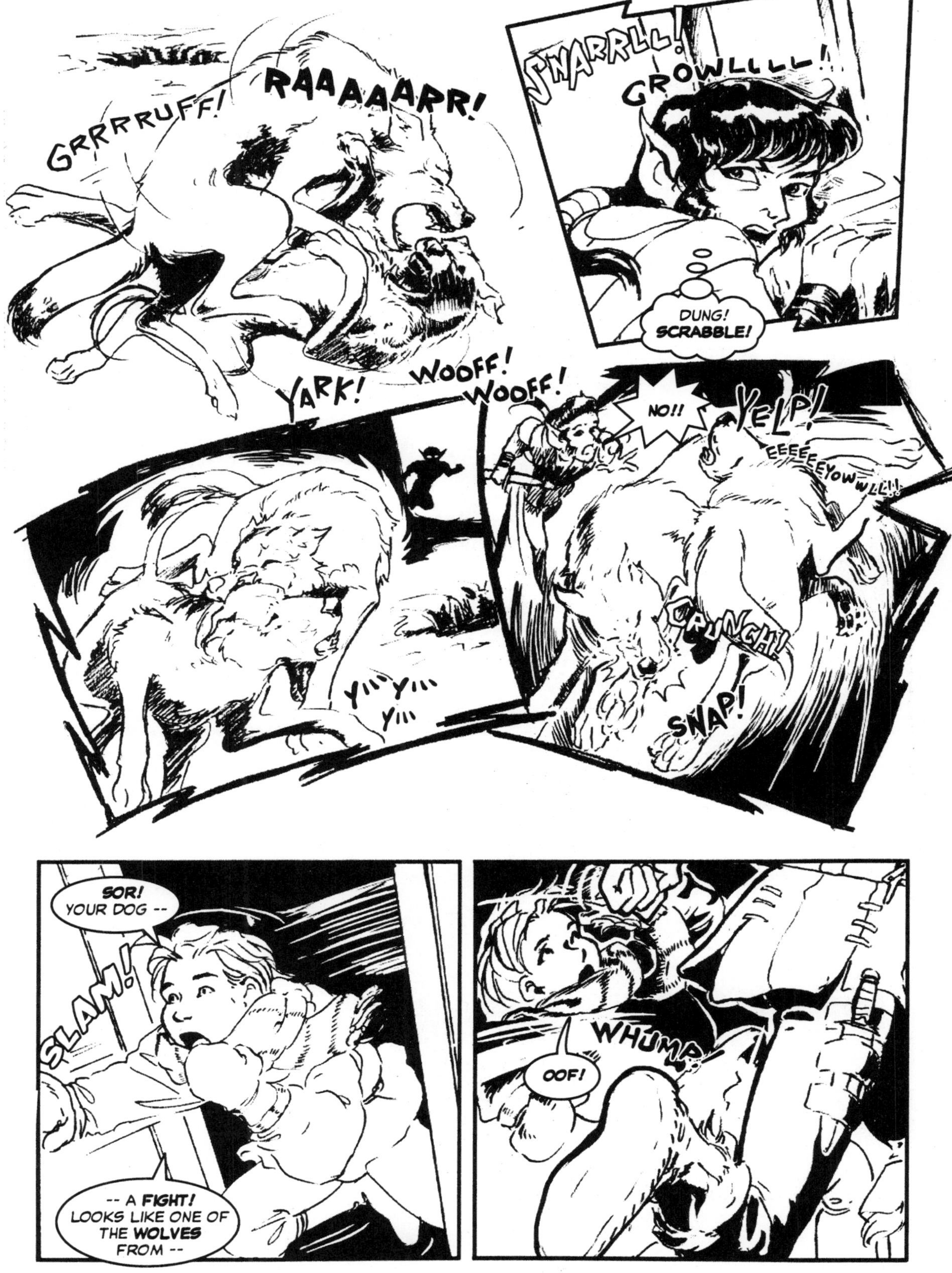
GRRRRUFF!
RAAAAAARR!
SNARRLLL!
GROWLLLLL!
DUNG! SCRABBLE!
YARK!
WOOFF!
WOOFF!
NO!!
YELP!
EEEEEEYOWLL!!
CRUNCH!
SNAP!
SOR! YOUR DOG --
SLAM!
-- A FIGHT! LOOKS LIKE ONE OF THE WOLVES FROM --
WHUMP
OOF!

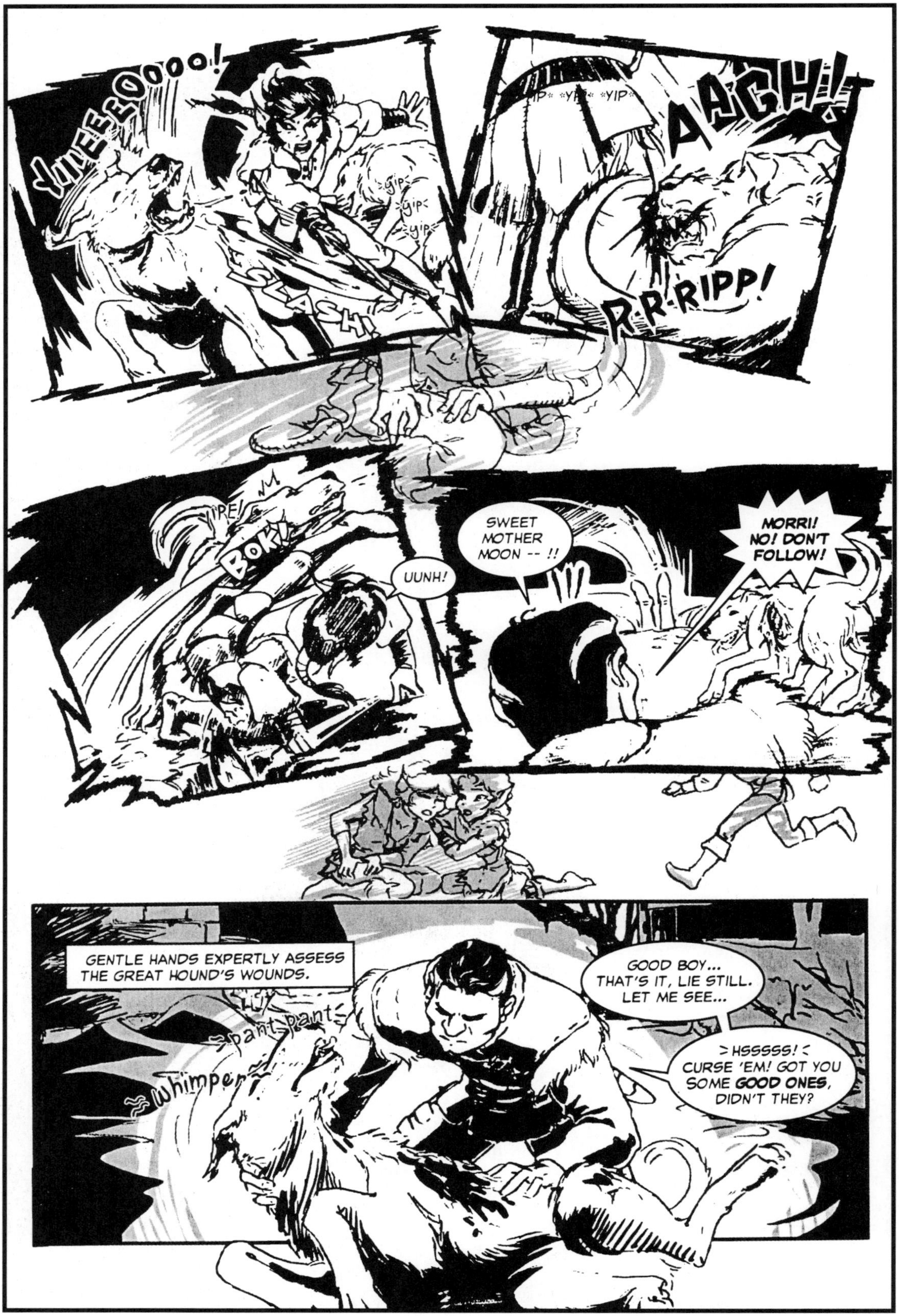
YIEEEOOOO!
yip
yip
yip
SLASH!
YIP YIP YIP
AAGH!!
RRRIPP!
YIPE!
BOK!
UUNH!
SWEET MOTHER MOON -- !!
MORRI! NO! DON'T FOLLOW!
GENTLE HANDS EXPERTLY ASSESS THE GREAT HOUND'S WOUNDS.
GOOD BOY... THAT'S IT, LIE STILL. LET ME SEE...
pant pant
whimper
HSSSSS! CURSE 'EM! GOT YOU SOME GOOD ONES, DIDN'T THEY?

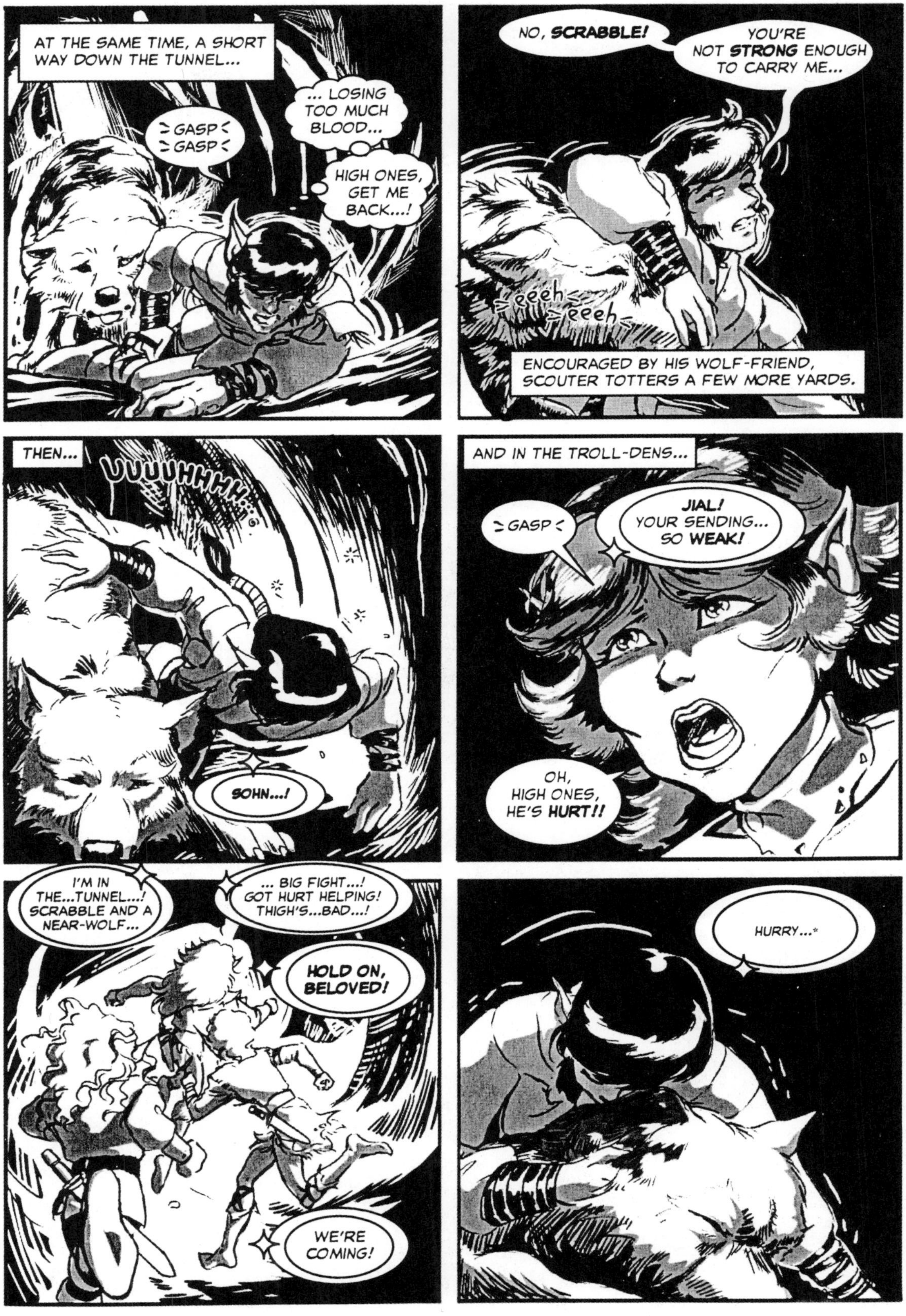

AT THE SAME TIME, A SHORT WAY DOWN THE TUNNEL...
GASP GASP
... LOSING TOO MUCH BLOOD...
HIGH ONES, GET ME BACK...!
NO, SCRABBLE!
YOU'RE NOT STRONG ENOUGH TO CARRY ME...
eeeh eeeh
ENCOURAGED BY HIS WOLF-FRIEND, SCOUTER TOTTERS A FEW MORE YARDS.
THEN...
UUUUHHHH...
SOHN...!
AND IN THE TROLL-DENS...
GASP
JIAL! YOUR SENDING... SO WEAK!
OH, HIGH ONES, HE'S HURT!!
I'M IN THE...TUNNEL...! SCRABBLE AND A NEAR-WOLF...
... BIG FIGHT...! GOT HURT HELPING! THIGH'S...BAD...!
HOLD ON, BELOVED!
WE'RE COMING!
HURRY...*

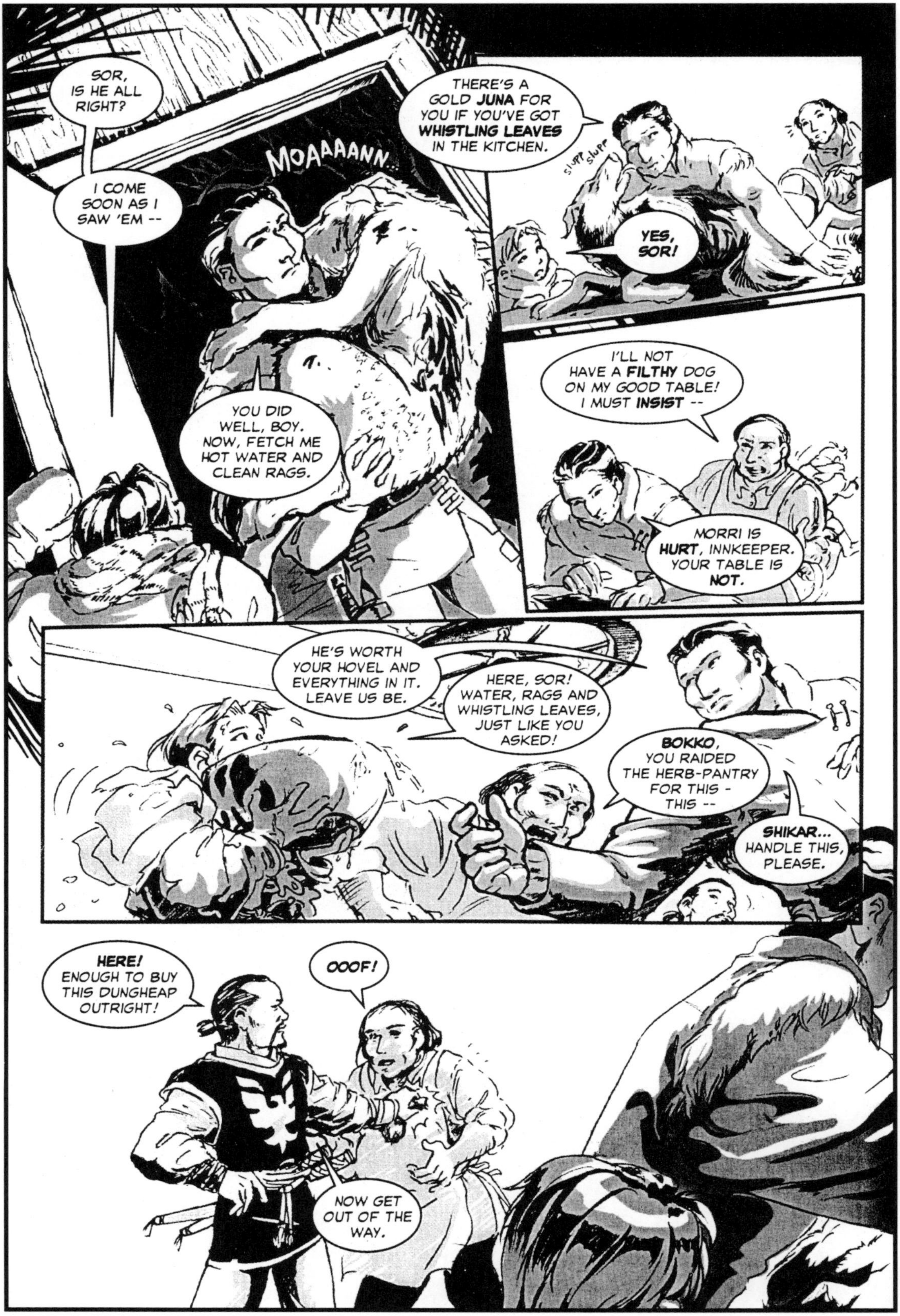
SOR, IS HE ALL RIGHT?
I COME SOON AS I SAW 'EM --
MOAAAANN...
YOU DID WELL, BOY. NOW, FETCH ME HOT WATER AND CLEAN RAGS.
THERE'S A GOLD JUNA FOR YOU IF YOU'VE GOT WHISTLING LEAVES IN THE KITCHEN.
SLUPP SLUPP
YES, SOR!
I'LL NOT HAVE A FILTHY DOG ON MY GOOD TABLE! I MUST INSIST --
MORRI IS HURT, INNKEEPER. YOUR TABLE IS NOT.
HE'S WORTH YOUR HOVEL AND EVERYTHING IN IT. LEAVE US BE.
HERE, SOR! WATER, RAGS AND WHISTLING LEAVES, JUST LIKE YOU ASKED!
BOKKO, YOU RAIDED THE HERB-PANTRY FOR THIS - THIS --
SHIKAR... HANDLE THIS, PLEASE.
HERE! ENOUGH TO BUY THIS DUNGHEAP OUTRIGHT!
OOOF!
NOW GET OUT OF THE WAY.

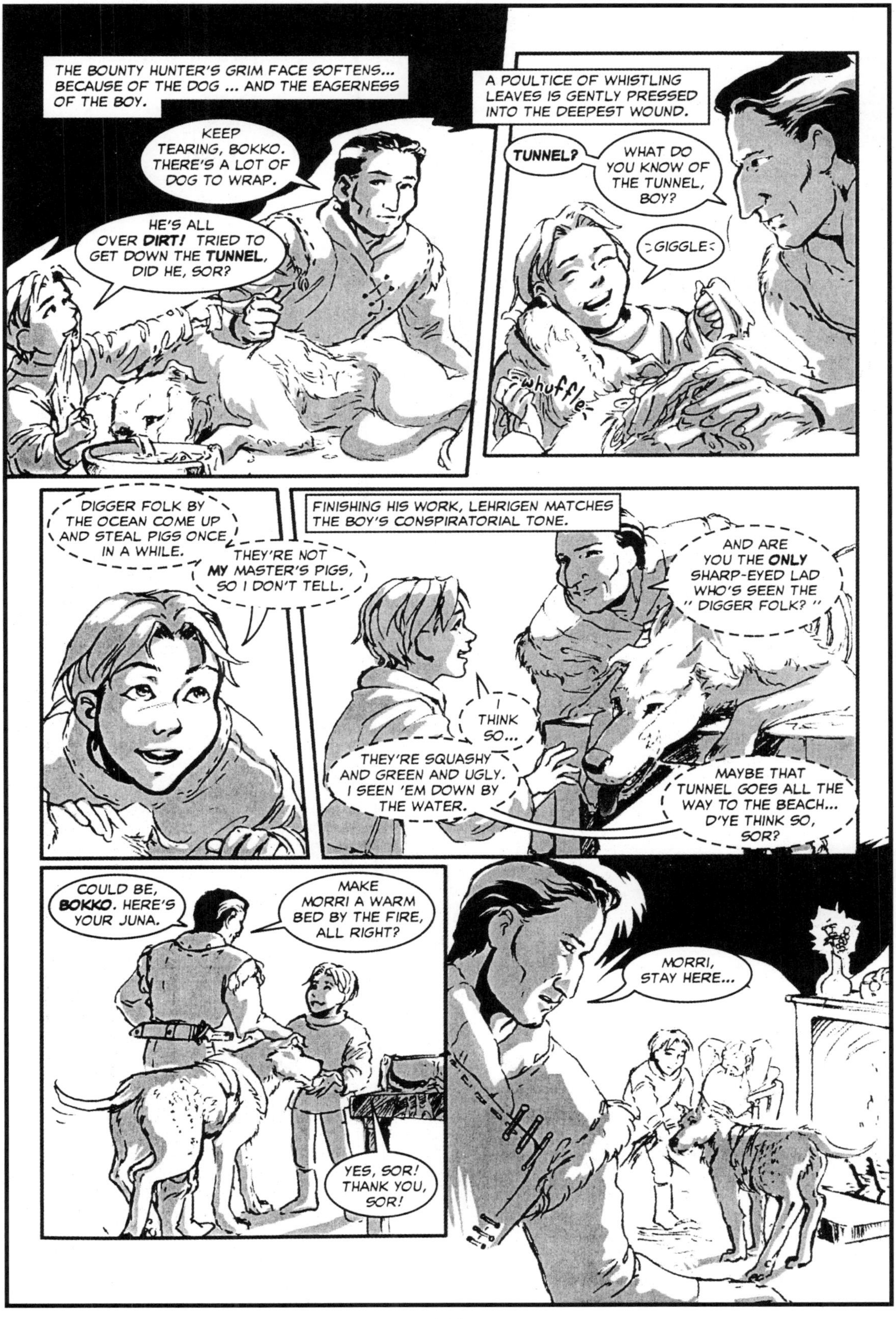
THE BOUNTY HUNTER'S GRIM FACE SOFTENS... BECAUSE OF THE DOG ... AND THE EAGERNESS OF THE BOY.
KEEP TEARING, BOKKO. THERE'S A LOT OF DOG TO WRAP.
HE'S ALL OVER DIRT! TRIED TO GET DOWN THE TUNNEL, DID HE, SOR?
A POULTICE OF WHISTLING LEAVES IS GENTLY PRESSED INTO THE DEEPEST WOUND.
TUNNEL?
WHAT DO YOU KNOW OF THE TUNNEL, BOY?
GIGGLE
whuffle
DIGGER FOLK BY THE OCEAN COME UP AND STEAL PIGS ONCE IN A WHILE.
THEY'RE NOT MY MASTER'S PIGS, SO I DON'T TELL.
FINISHING HIS WORK, LEHRIGEN MATCHES THE BOY'S CONSPIRATORIAL TONE.
AND ARE YOU THE ONLY SHARP-EYED LAD WHO'S SEEN THE "DIGGER FOLK?"
I THINK SO...
THEY'RE SQUASHY AND GREEN AND UGLY. I SEEN 'EM DOWN BY THE WATER.
MAYBE THAT TUNNEL GOES ALL THE WAY TO THE BEACH... D'YE THINK SO, SOR?
COULD BE, BOKKO. HERE'S YOUR JUNA.
MAKE MORRI A WARM BED BY THE FIRE, ALL RIGHT?
YES, SOR! THANK YOU, SOR!
MORRI, STAY HERE...

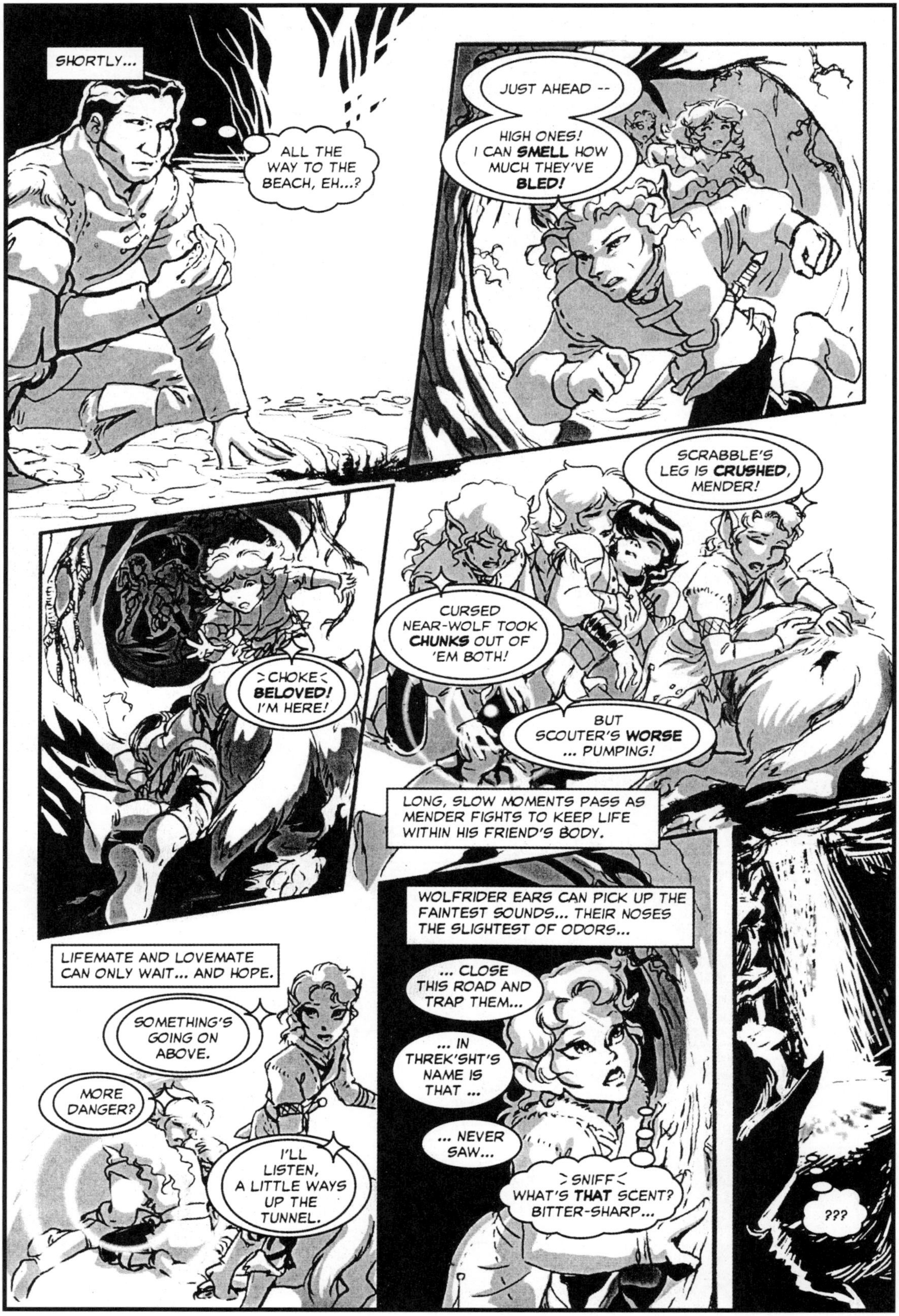

SHORTLY...
ALL THE WAY TO THE BEACH, EH...?
JUST AHEAD --
HIGH ONES! I CAN SMELL HOW MUCH THEY'VE BLED!
>CHOKE< BELOVED! I'M HERE!
SCRABBLE'S LEG IS CRUSHED, MENDER!
CURSED NEAR-WOLF TOOK CHUNKS OUT OF 'EM BOTH!
BUT SCOUTER'S WORSE ... PUMPING!
LONG, SLOW MOMENTS PASS AS MENDER FIGHTS TO KEEP LIFE WITHIN HIS FRIEND'S BODY.
LIFEMATE AND LOVEMATE CAN ONLY WAIT... AND HOPE.
SOMETHING'S GOING ON ABOVE.
MORE DANGER?
I'LL LISTEN, A LITTLE WAYS UP THE TUNNEL.
WOLFRIDER EARS CAN PICK UP THE FAINTEST SOUNDS... THEIR NOSES THE SLIGHTEST OF ODORS...
... CLOSE THIS ROAD AND TRAP THEM...
... IN THREK'SHT'S NAME IS THAT ...
... NEVER SAW...
>SNIFF< WHAT'S THAT SCENT? BITTER-SHARP...
???

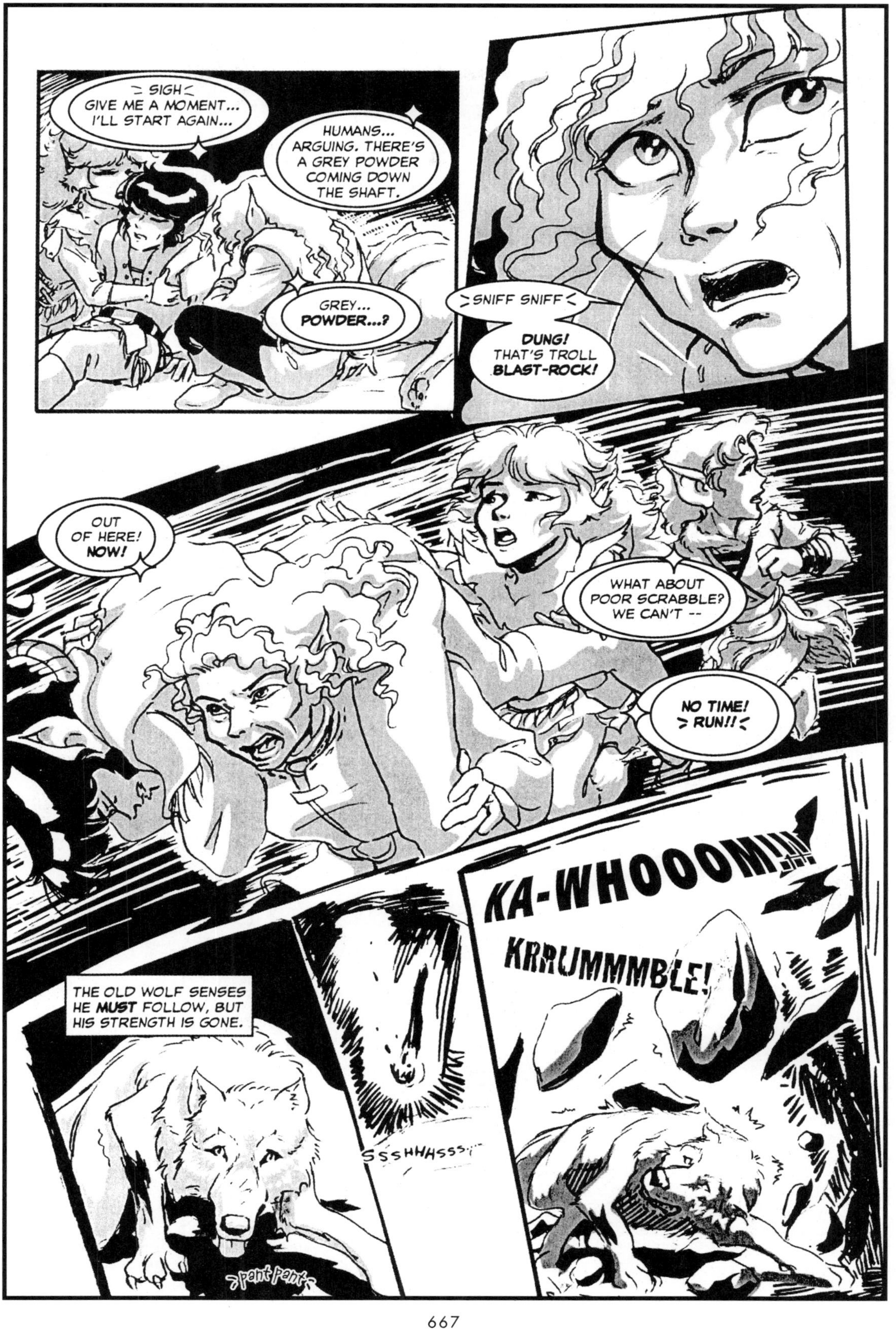

SIGH
GIVE ME A MOMENT... I'LL START AGAIN...
HUMANS... ARGUING. THERE'S A GREY POWDER COMING DOWN THE SHAFT.
GREY... POWDER...?
SNIFF SNIFF
DUNG! THAT'S TROLL BLAST-ROCK!
OUT OF HERE! NOW!
WHAT ABOUT POOR SCRABBLE? WE CAN'T --
NO TIME! RUN!!
KA-WHOOOM!!!
KRRUMMMBLE!
THE OLD WOLF SENSES HE MUST FOLLOW, BUT HIS STRENGTH IS GONE.
SSSHHHSSS
pant pant

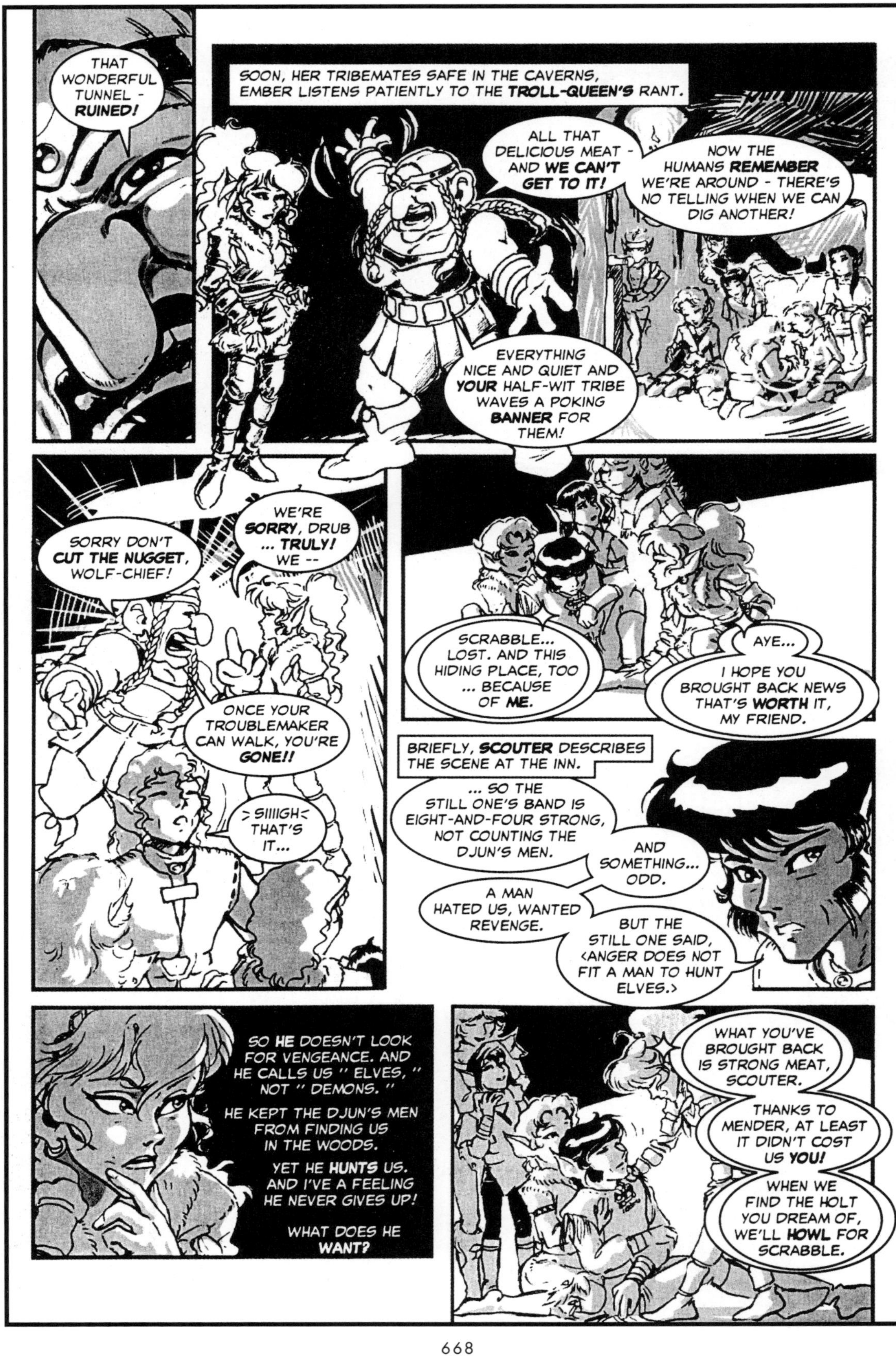
THAT WONDERFUL TUNNEL - RUINED!
SOON, HER TRIBEMATES SAFE IN THE CAVERNS, EMBER LISTENS PATIENTLY TO THE TROLL-QUEEN'S RANT.
ALL THAT DELICIOUS MEAT - AND WE CAN'T GET TO IT!
NOW THE HUMANS REMEMBER WE'RE AROUND - THERE'S NO TELLING WHEN WE CAN DIG ANOTHER!
EVERYTHING NICE AND QUIET AND YOUR HALF-WIT TRIBE WAVES A POKING BANNER FOR THEM!
SORRY DON'T CUT THE NUGGET, WOLF-CHIEF!
WE'RE SORRY, DRUB ... TRULY! WE --
ONCE YOUR TROUBLEMAKER CAN WALK, YOU'RE GONE!!
>SIIIIGH< THAT'S IT...
SCRABBLE... LOST. AND THIS HIDING PLACE, TOO ... BECAUSE OF ME.
AYE...
I HOPE YOU BROUGHT BACK NEWS THAT'S WORTH IT, MY FRIEND.
BRIEFLY, SCOUTER DESCRIBES THE SCENE AT THE INN.
... SO THE STILL ONE'S BAND IS EIGHT-AND-FOUR STRONG, NOT COUNTING THE DJUN'S MEN.
AND SOMETHING... ODD.
A MAN HATED US, WANTED REVENGE.
BUT THE STILL ONE SAID, <ANGER DOES NOT FIT A MAN TO HUNT ELVES.>
SO HE DOESN'T LOOK FOR VENGEANCE. AND HE CALLS US " ELVES, " NOT " DEMONS. "
HE KEPT THE DJUN'S MEN FROM FINDING US IN THE WOODS.
YET HE HUNTS US. AND I'VE A FEELING HE NEVER GIVES UP!
WHAT DOES HE WANT?
WHAT YOU'VE BROUGHT BACK IS STRONG MEAT, SCOUTER.
THANKS TO MENDER, AT LEAST IT DIDN'T COST US YOU!
WHEN WE FIND THE HOLT YOU DREAM OF, WE'LL HOWL FOR SCRABBLE.

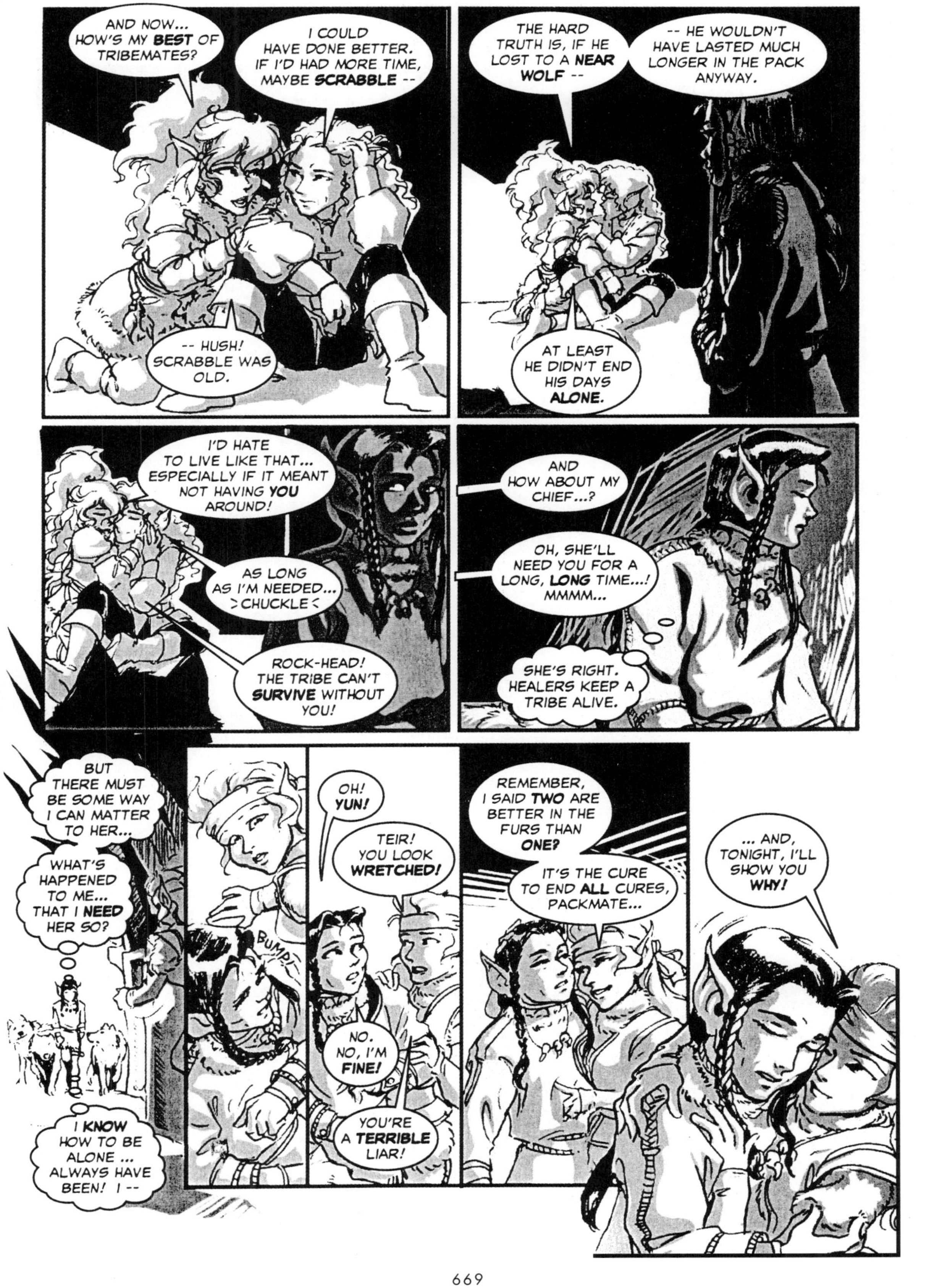
AND NOW... HOW'S MY BEST OF TRIBEMATES?
I COULD HAVE DONE BETTER. IF I'D HAD MORE TIME, MAYBE SCRABBLE --
-- HUSH! SCRABBLE WAS OLD.
THE HARD TRUTH IS, IF HE LOST TO A NEAR WOLF --
-- HE WOULDN'T HAVE LASTED MUCH LONGER IN THE PACK ANYWAY.
AT LEAST HE DIDN'T END HIS DAYS ALONE.
I'D HATE TO LIVE LIKE THAT... ESPECIALLY IF IT MEANT NOT HAVING YOU AROUND!
AS LONG AS I'M NEEDED... >CHUCKLE<
ROCK-HEAD! THE TRIBE CAN'T SURVIVE WITHOUT YOU!
AND HOW ABOUT MY CHIEF...?
OH, SHE'LL NEED YOU FOR A LONG, LONG TIME...! MMMM...
SHE'S RIGHT. HEALERS KEEP A TRIBE ALIVE.
BUT THERE MUST BE SOME WAY I CAN MATTER TO HER...
WHAT'S HAPPENED TO ME... THAT I NEED HER SO?
I KNOW HOW TO BE ALONE ... ALWAYS HAVE BEEN! I --
BUMP!
OH! YUN!
TEIR! YOU LOOK WRETCHED!
NO. NO, I'M FINE!
YOU'RE A TERRIBLE LIAR!
REMEMBER, I SAID TWO ARE BETTER IN THE FURS THAN ONE?
IT'S THE CURE TO END ALL CURES, PACKMATE...
... AND, TONIGHT, I'LL SHOW YOU WHY!

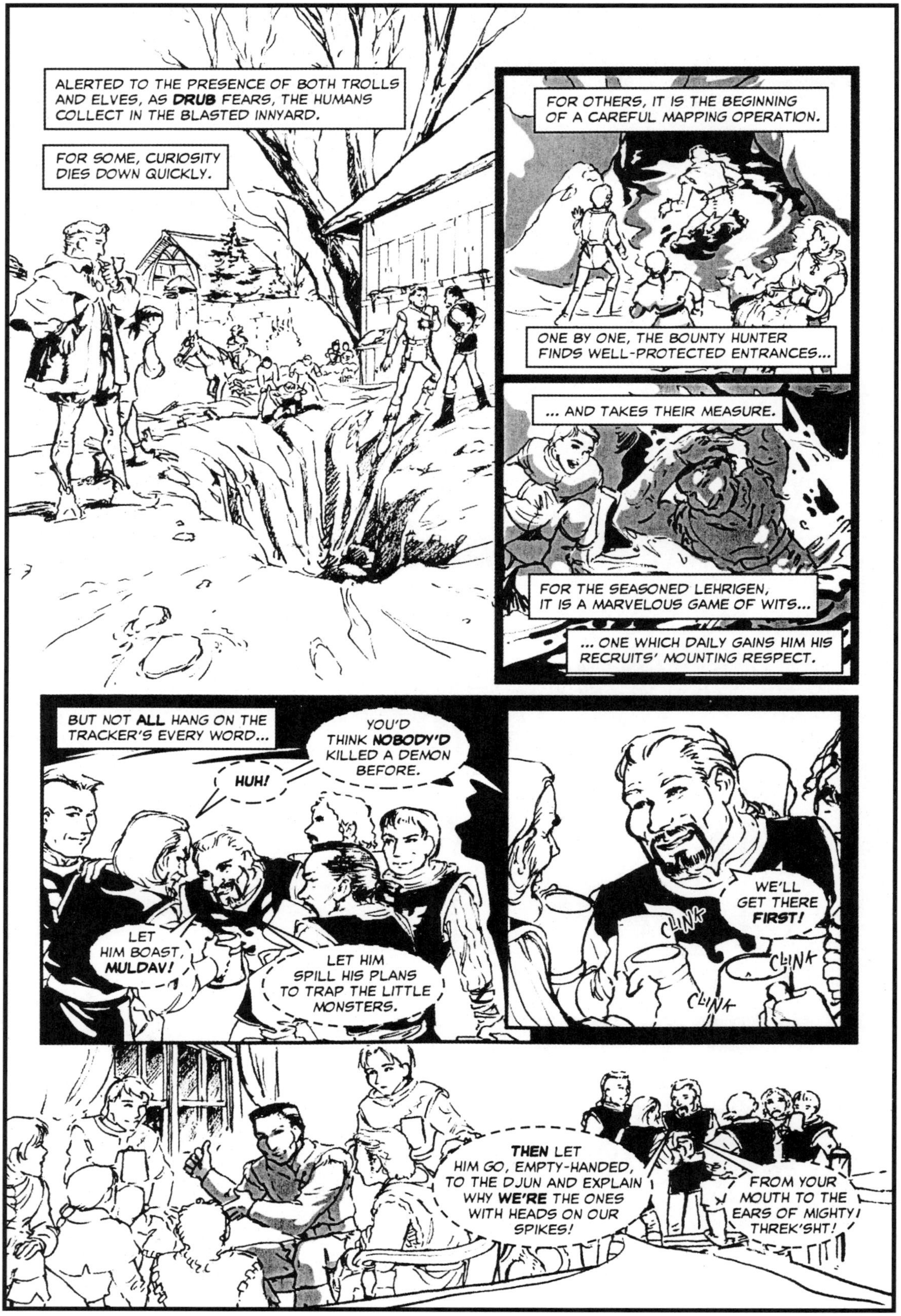

ALERTED TO THE PRESENCE OF BOTH TROLLS AND ELVES, AS DRUB FEARS, THE HUMANS COLLECT IN THE BLASTED INNYARD.
FOR SOME, CURIOSITY DIES DOWN QUICKLY.
FOR OTHERS, IT IS THE BEGINNING OF A CAREFUL MAPPING OPERATION.
ONE BY ONE, THE BOUNTY HUNTER FINDS WELL-PROTECTED ENTRANCES...
... AND TAKES THEIR MEASURE.
FOR THE SEASONED LEHRIGEN, IT IS A MARVELOUS GAME OF WITS...
... ONE WHICH DAILY GAINS HIM HIS RECRUITS' MOUNTING RESPECT.
BUT NOT ALL HANG ON THE TRACKER'S EVERY WORD...
YOU'D THINK NOBODY'D KILLED A DEMON BEFORE.
HUH!
LET HIM BOAST, MULDAV!
LET HIM SPILL HIS PLANS TO TRAP THE LITTLE MONSTERS.
WE'LL GET THERE FIRST!
CLINK
CLINK
CLINK
THEN LET HIM GO, EMPTY-HANDED, TO THE DJUN AND EXPLAIN WHY WE'RE THE ONES WITH HEADS ON OUR SPIKES!
FROM YOUR MOUTH TO THE EARS OF MIGHTY THREK'SHT!

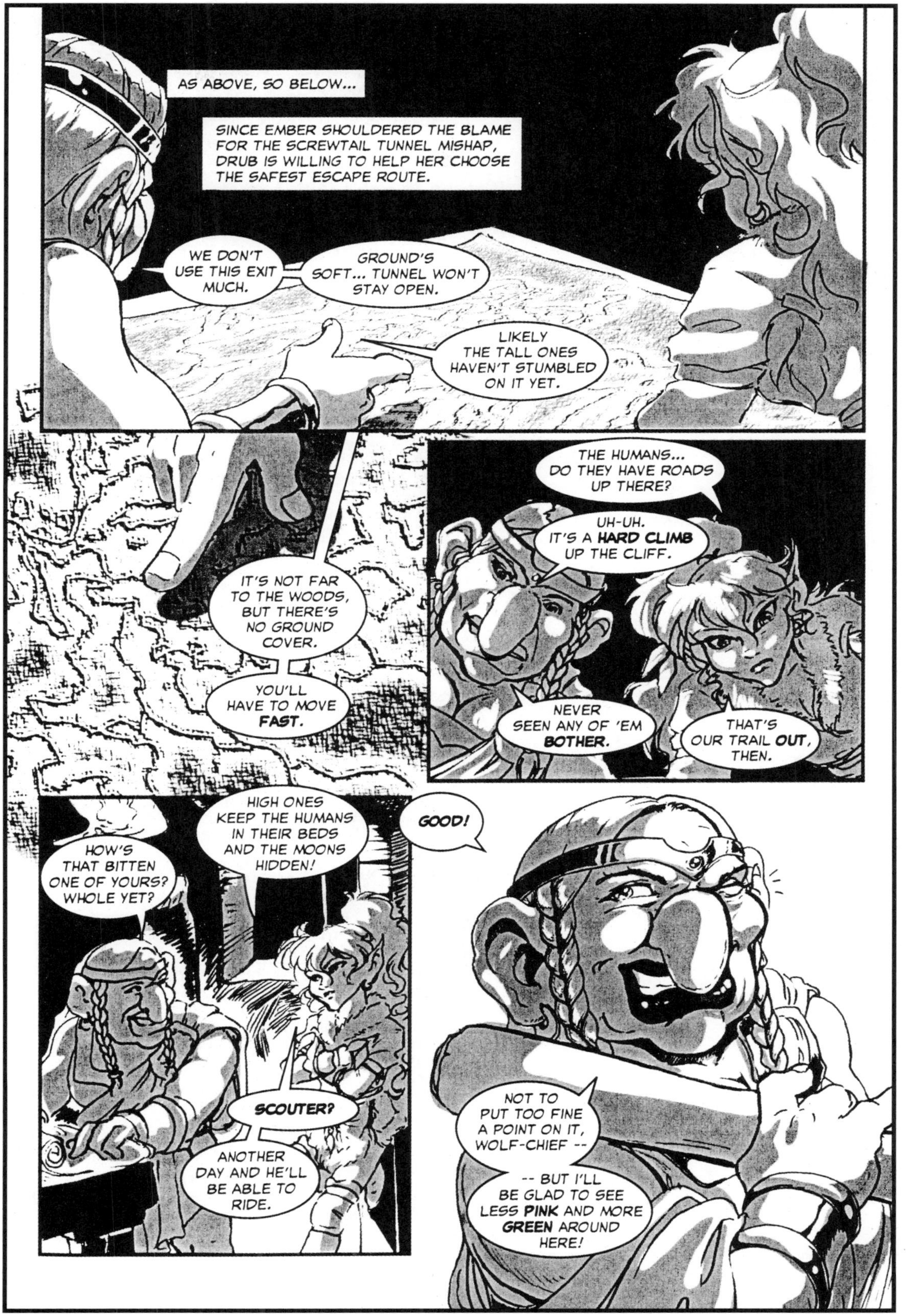
AS ABOVE, SO BELOW...
SINCE EMBER SHOULDERED THE BLAME FOR THE SCREWTAIL TUNNEL MISHAP, DRUB IS WILLING TO HELP HER CHOOSE THE SAFEST ESCAPE ROUTE.
WE DON'T USE THIS EXIT MUCH.
GROUND'S SOFT... TUNNEL WON'T STAY OPEN.
LIKELY THE TALL ONES HAVEN'T STUMBLED ON IT YET.
IT'S NOT FAR TO THE WOODS, BUT THERE'S NO GROUND COVER.
YOU'LL HAVE TO MOVE FAST.
THE HUMANS... DO THEY HAVE ROADS UP THERE?
UH-UH. IT'S A HARD CLIMB UP THE CLIFF.
NEVER SEEN ANY OF 'EM BOTHER.
THAT'S OUR TRAIL OUT, THEN.
HOW'S THAT BITTEN ONE OF YOURS? WHOLE YET?
SCOUTER?
ANOTHER DAY AND HE'LL BE ABLE TO RIDE.
HIGH ONES KEEP THE HUMANS IN THEIR BEDS AND THE MOONS HIDDEN!
GOOD!
NOT TO PUT TOO FINE A POINT ON IT, WOLF-CHIEF --
-- BUT I'LL BE GLAD TO SEE LESS PINK AND MORE GREEN AROUND HERE!

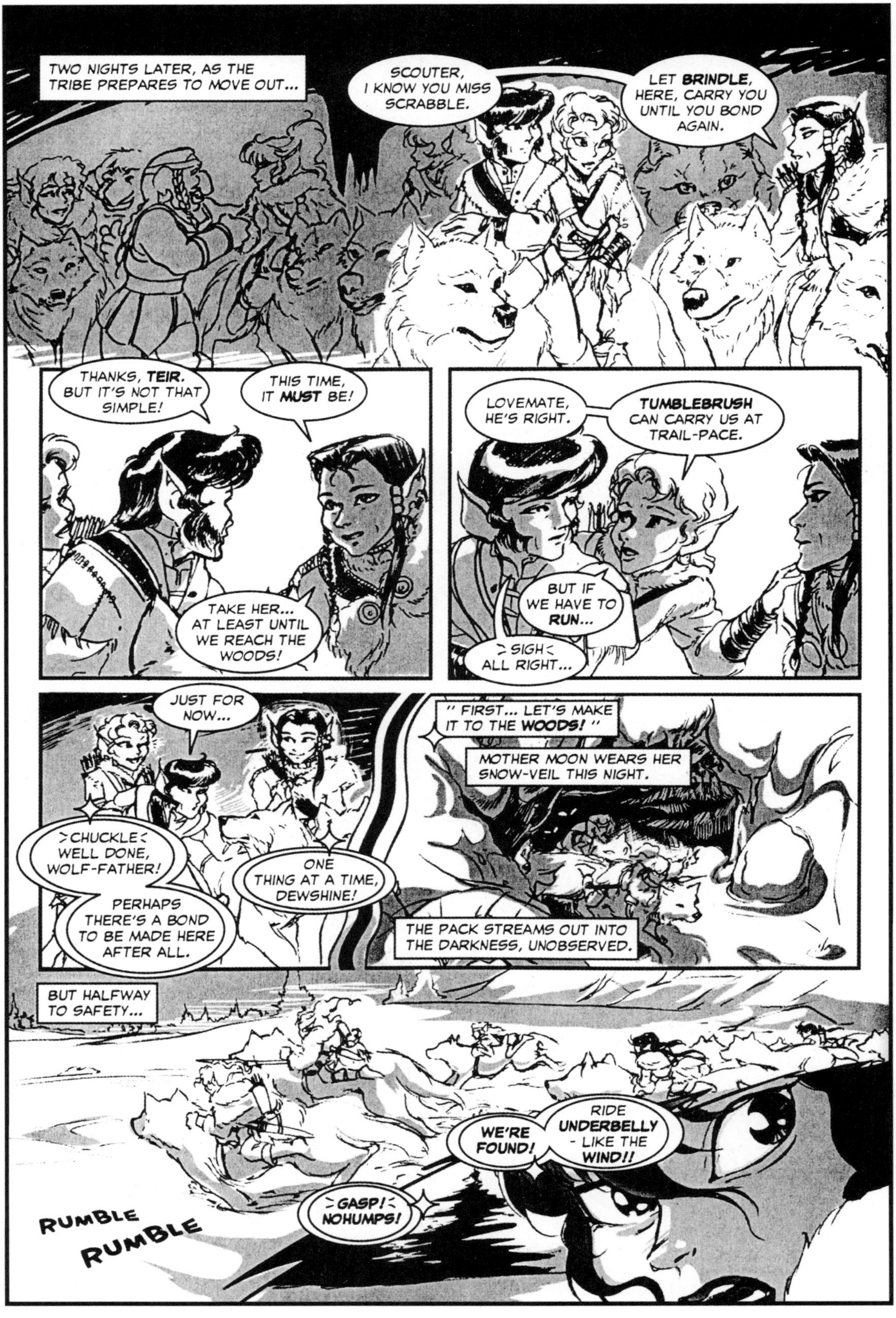
TWO NIGHTS LATER, AS THE TRIBE PREPARES TO MOVE OUT...
SCOUTER, I KNOW YOU MISS SCRABBLE.
LET **BRINDLE**, HERE, CARRY YOU UNTIL YOU BOND AGAIN.
THANKS, **TEIR**. BUT IT'S NOT THAT SIMPLE!
THIS TIME, IT **MUST** BE!
TAKE HER... AT LEAST UNTIL WE REACH THE WOODS!
LOVEMATE, HE'S RIGHT.
TUMBLEBRUSH CAN CARRY US AT TRAIL-PACE.
BUT IF WE HAVE TO **RUN**...
>SIGH< ALL RIGHT...
JUST FOR NOW...
>CHUCKLE< WELL DONE, WOLF-FATHER!
PERHAPS THERE'S A BOND TO BE MADE HERE AFTER ALL.
ONE THING AT A TIME, DEWSHINE!
" FIRST... LET'S MAKE IT TO THE **WOODS!** "
MOTHER MOON WEARS HER SNOW-VEIL THIS NIGHT.
THE PACK STREAMS OUT INTO THE DARKNESS, UNOBSERVED.
BUT HALFWAY TO SAFETY...
WE'RE FOUND!
RIDE **UNDERBELLY** - LIKE THE **WIND!!**
>GASP!< NOHUMPS!
RUMBLE RUMBLE

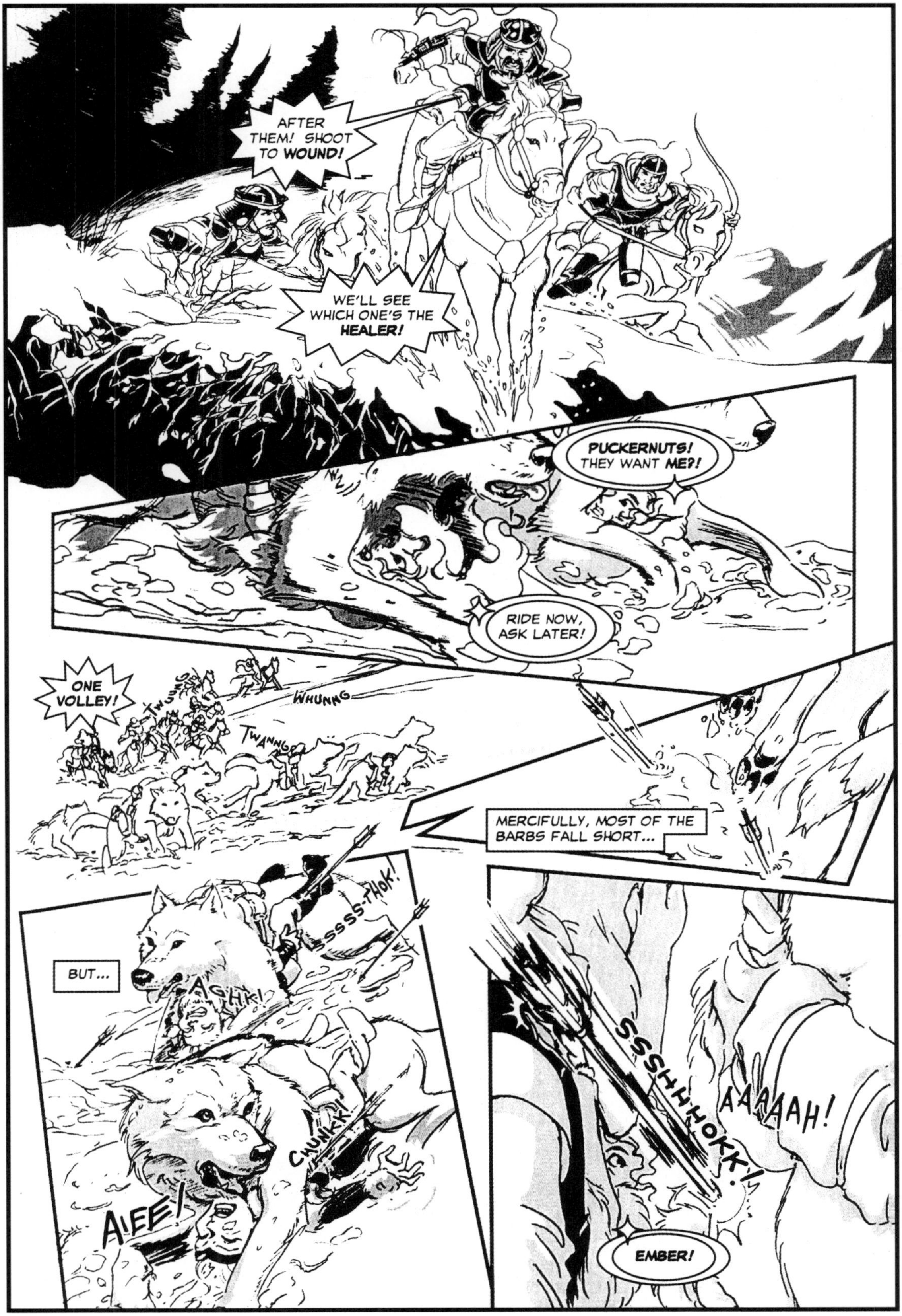
AFTER THEM! SHOOT TO WOUND!
WE'LL SEE WHICH ONE'S THE HEALER!
PUCKERNUTS! THEY WANT ME?!
RIDE NOW, ASK LATER!
ONE VOLLEY!
TWUNG
WHUNNG
TWANNG
MERCIFULLY, MOST OF THE BARBS FALL SHORT...
BUT...
SSSSS-THOK!
AGHK!
CHUNKK!
AIEE!
SSSHHHOKK!
AAAAAH!
EMBER!

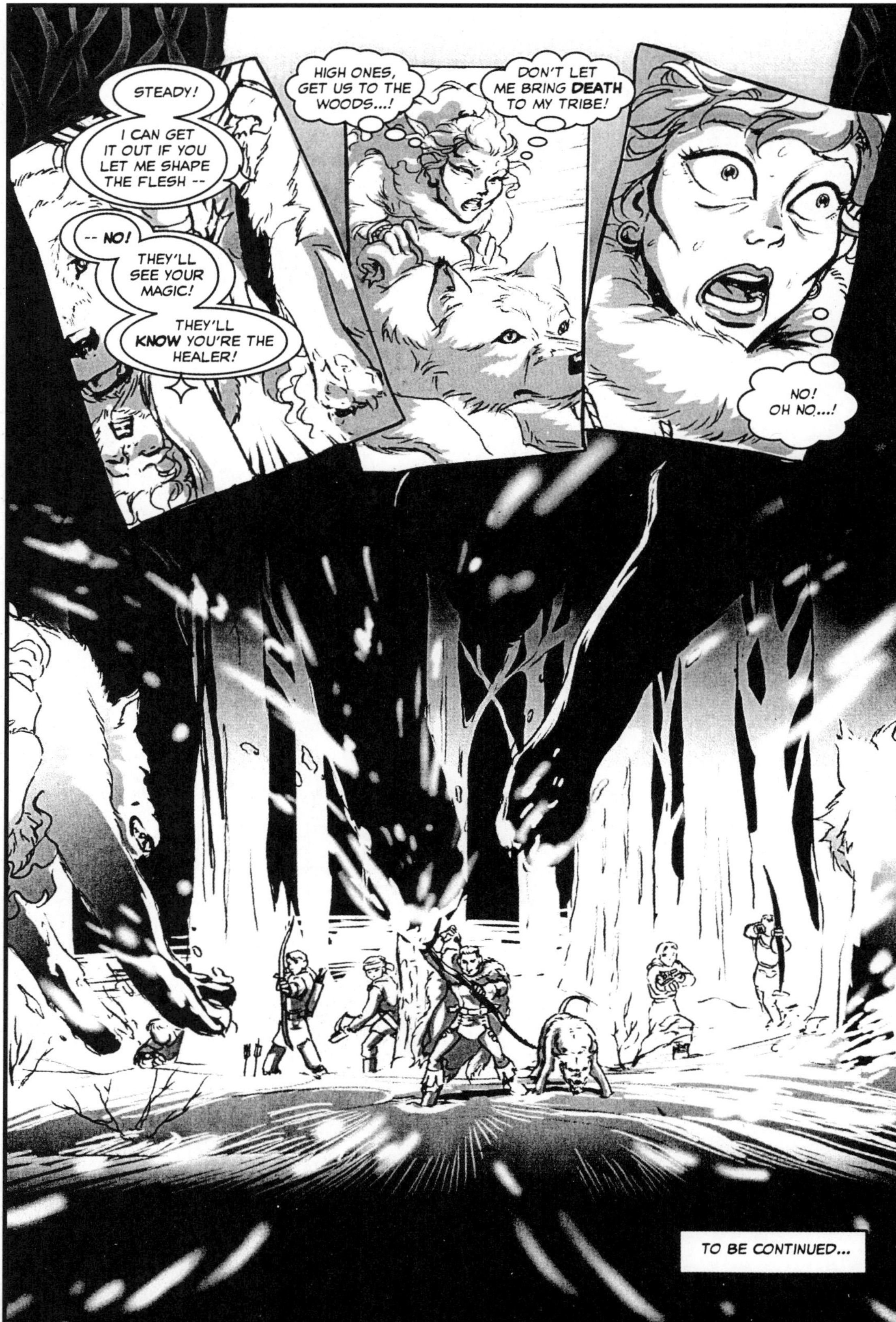

STEADY!
I CAN GET IT OUT IF YOU LET ME SHAPE THE FLESH --
-- NO!
THEY'LL SEE YOUR MAGIC!
THEY'LL KNOW YOU'RE THE HEALER!
HIGH ONES, GET US TO THE WOODS...!
DON'T LET ME BRING DEATH TO MY TRIBE!
NO! OH NO...!
TO BE CONTINUED...

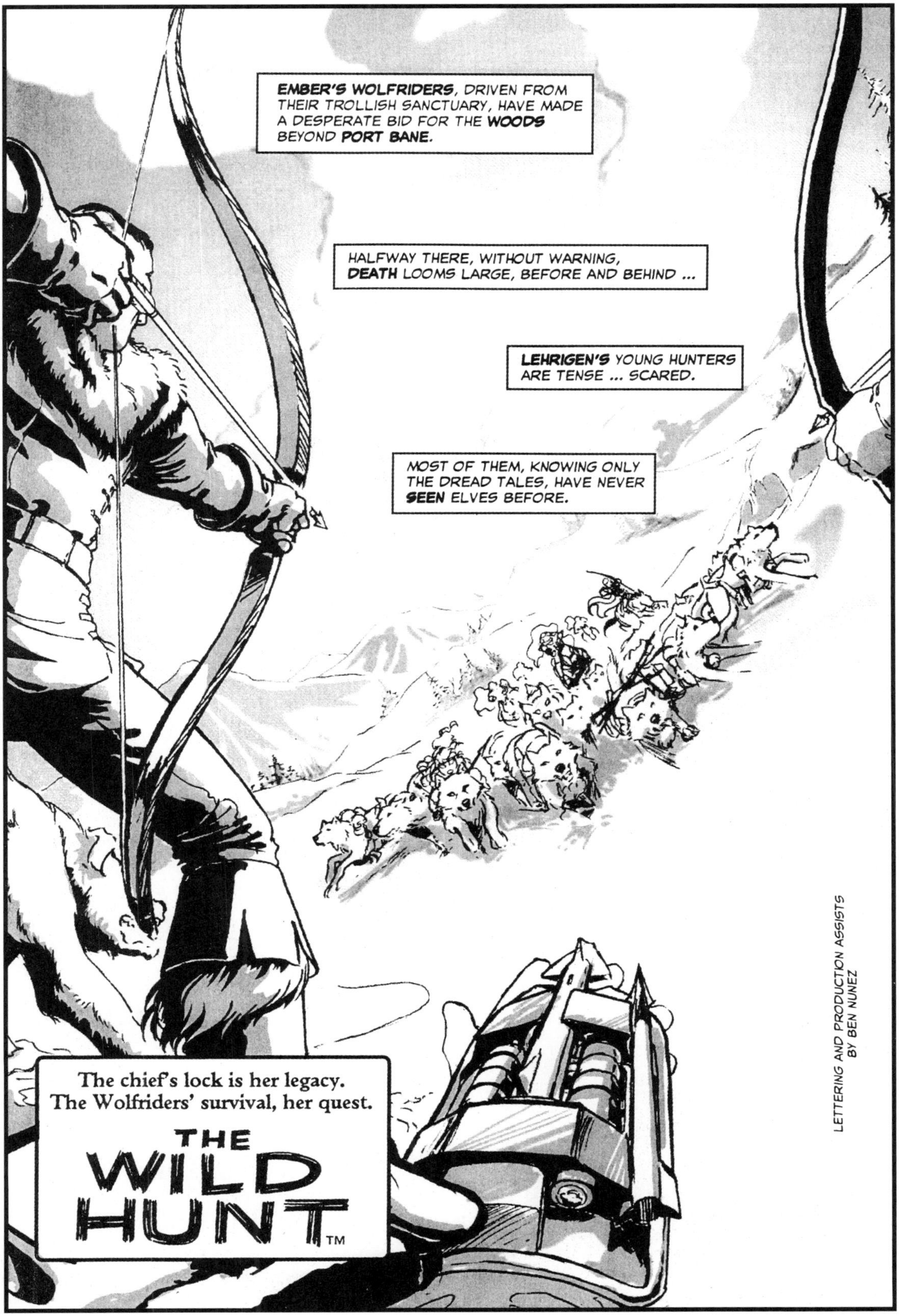
EMBER'S WOLFRIDERS, DRIVEN FROM THEIR TROLLISH SANCTUARY, HAVE MADE A DESPERATE BID FOR THE WOODS BEYOND PORT BANE.
HALFWAY THERE, WITHOUT WARNING, DEATH LOOMS LARGE, BEFORE AND BEHIND ...
LEHRIGEN'S YOUNG HUNTERS ARE TENSE ... SCARED.
MOST OF THEM, KNOWING ONLY THE DREAD TALES, HAVE NEVER SEEN ELVES BEFORE.
The chief's lock is her legacy.
The Wolfriders' survival, her quest.
THE WILD HUNT™
LETTERING AND PRODUCTION ASSISTS BY BEN NUNEZ

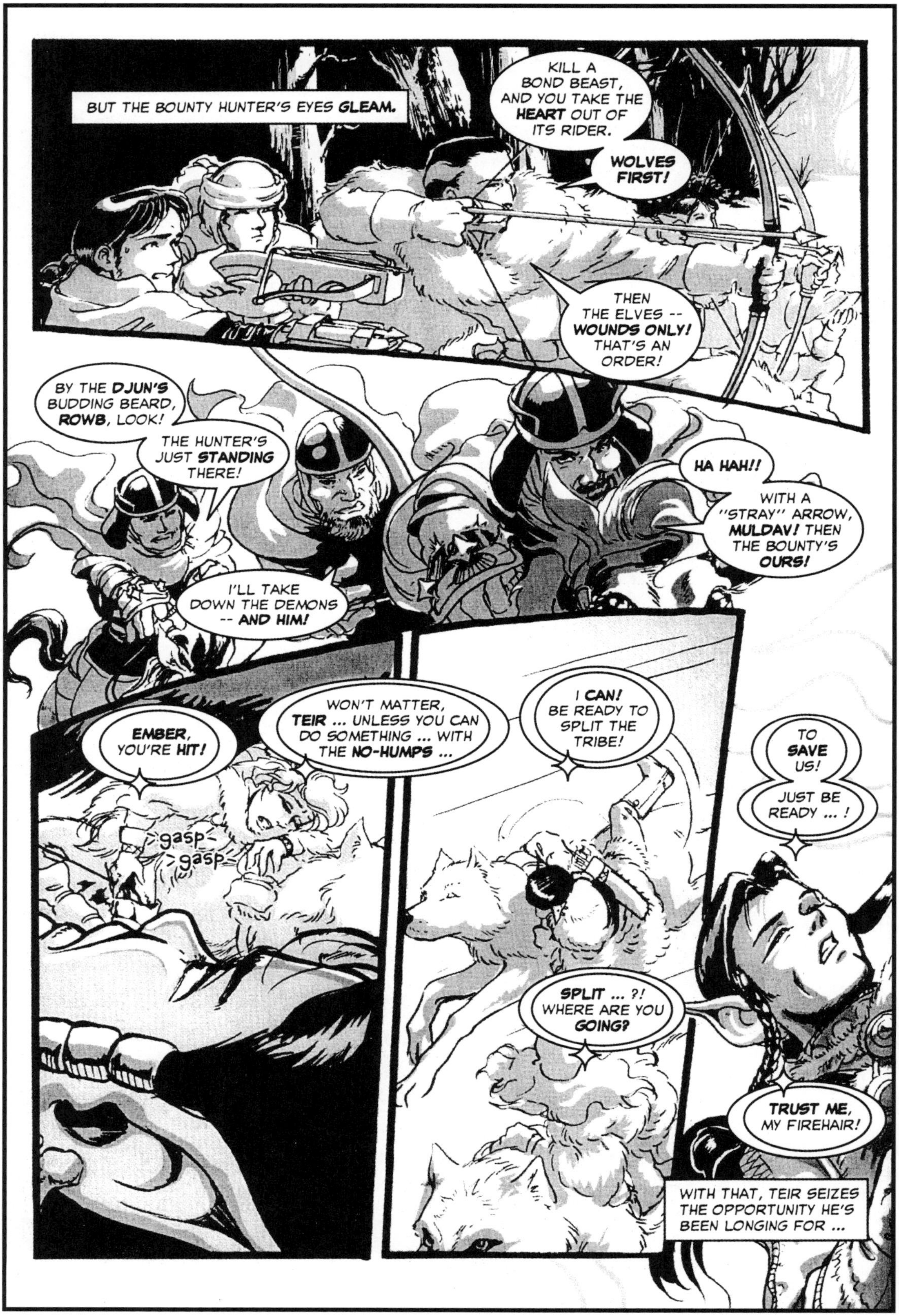
BUT THE BOUNTY HUNTER'S EYES GLEAM.
KILL A BOND BEAST, AND YOU TAKE THE HEART OUT OF ITS RIDER.
WOLVES FIRST!
THEN THE ELVES -- WOUNDS ONLY! THAT'S AN ORDER!
BY THE DJUN'S BUDDING BEARD, ROWB, LOOK!
THE HUNTER'S JUST STANDING THERE!
I'LL TAKE DOWN THE DEMONS -- AND HIM!
HA HAH!!
WITH A "STRAY" ARROW, MULDAV! THEN THE BOUNTY'S OURS!
EMBER, YOU'RE HIT!
>gasp<
>gasp<
WON'T MATTER, TEIR ... UNLESS YOU CAN DO SOMETHING ... WITH THE NO-HUMPS ...
I CAN! BE READY TO SPLIT THE TRIBE!
TO SAVE US!
JUST BE READY ... !
SPLIT ... ?! WHERE ARE YOU GOING?
TRUST ME, MY FIREHAIR!
WITH THAT, TEIR SEIZES THE OPPORTUNITY HE'S BEEN LONGING FOR ...

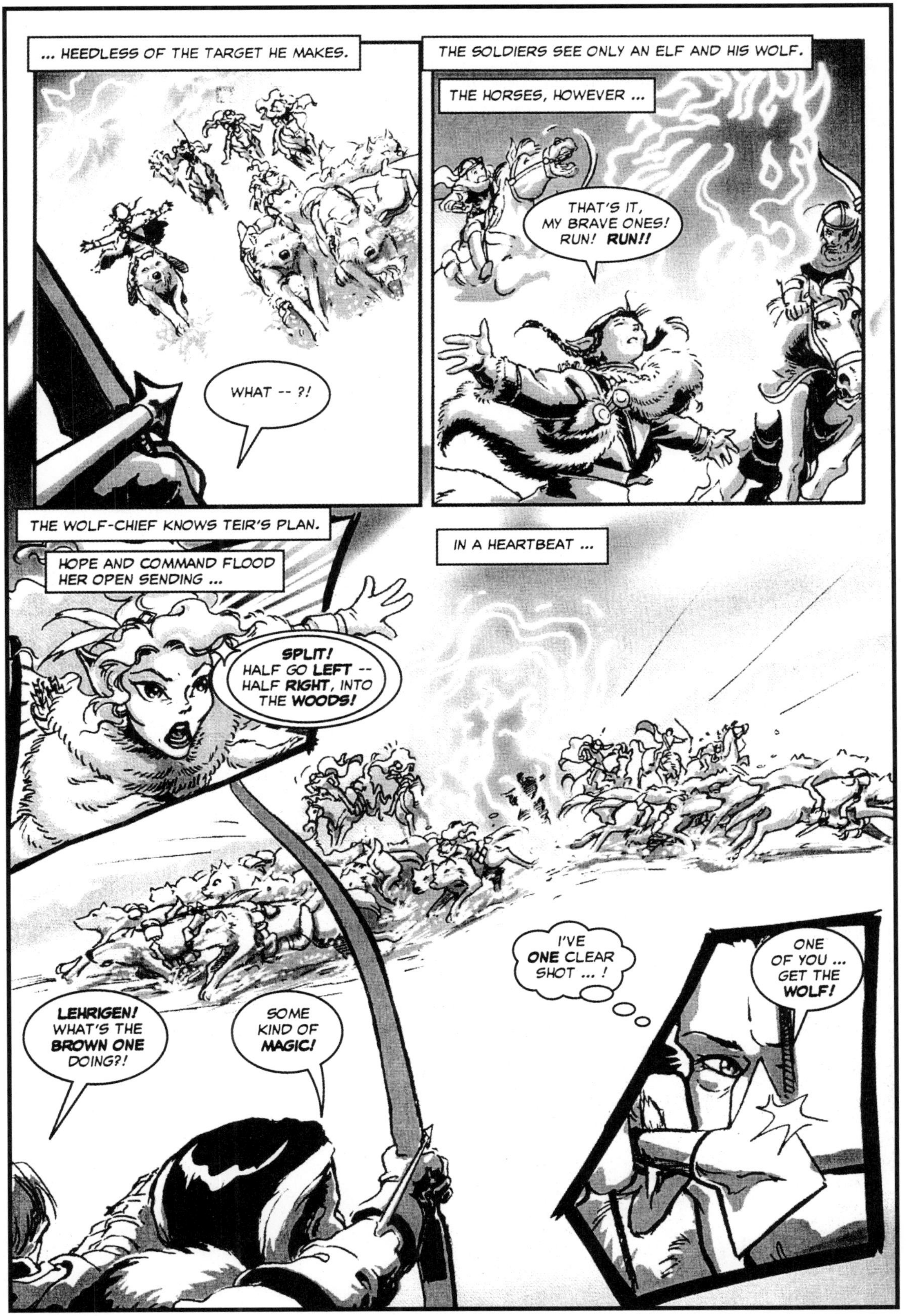
... HEEDLESS OF THE TARGET HE MAKES.
WHAT -- ?!
THE SOLDIERS SEE ONLY AN ELF AND HIS WOLF.
THE HORSES, HOWEVER ...
THAT'S IT, MY BRAVE ONES! RUN! RUN!!
THE WOLF-CHIEF KNOWS TEIR'S PLAN.
HOPE AND COMMAND FLOOD HER OPEN SENDING ...
SPLIT! HALF GO LEFT -- HALF RIGHT, INTO THE WOODS!
IN A HEARTBEAT ...
I'VE ONE CLEAR SHOT ... !
ONE OF YOU ... GET THE WOLF!
LEHRIGEN! WHAT'S THE BROWN ONE DOING?!
SOME KIND OF MAGIC!

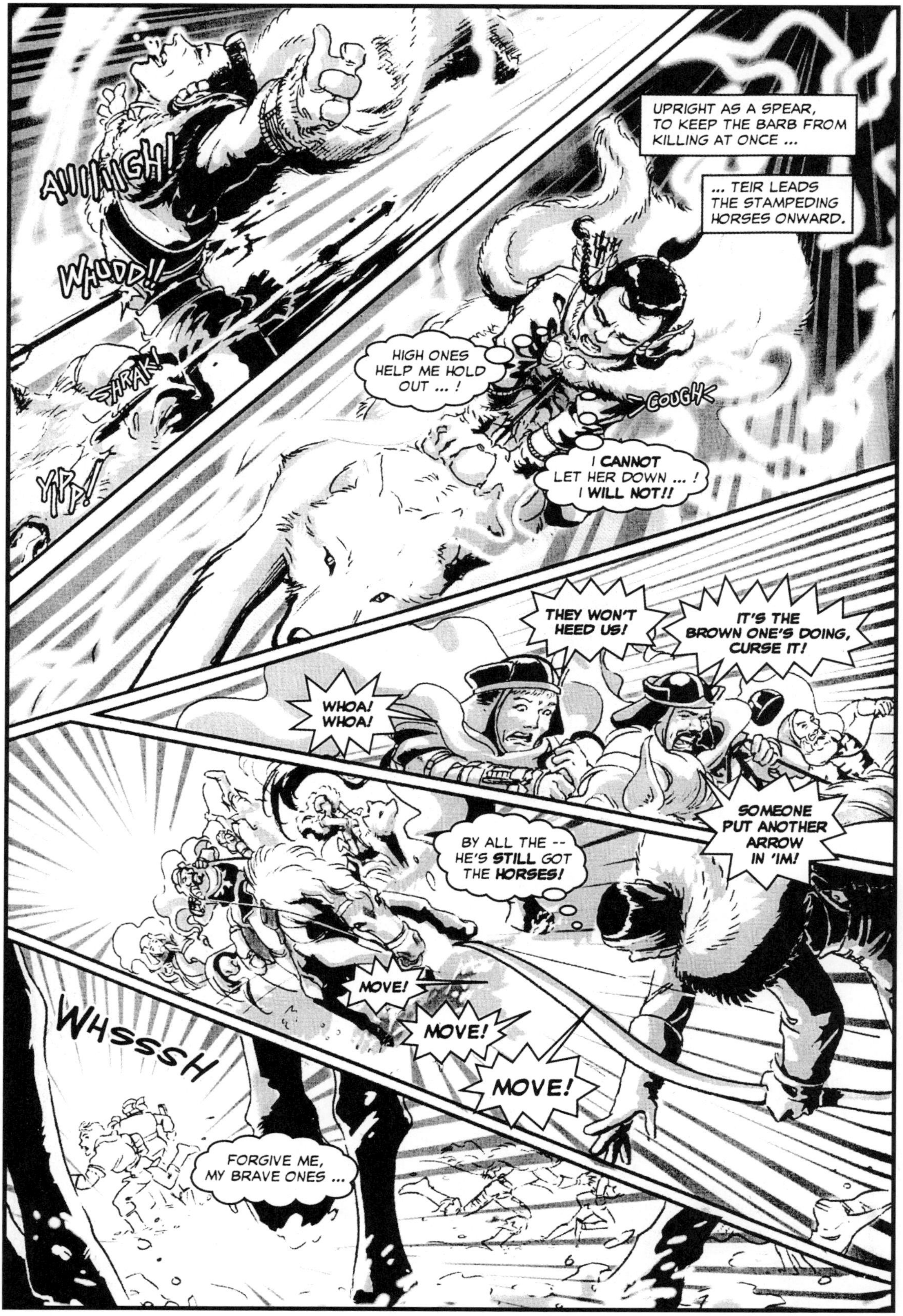
UPRIGHT AS A SPEAR, TO KEEP THE BARB FROM KILLING AT ONCE ...
... TEIR LEADS THE STAMPEDING HORSES ONWARD.
AIIIIIIGH!
WHUDD!!
SHRAK!
YIPP!
HIGH ONES HELP ME HOLD OUT ... !
COUGH
I CANNOT LET HER DOWN ... ! I WILL NOT!!
THEY WON'T HEED US!
IT'S THE BROWN ONE'S DOING, CURSE IT!
WHOA! WHOA!
SOMEONE PUT ANOTHER ARROW IN 'IM!
BY ALL THE -- HE'S STILL GOT THE HORSES!
MOVE!
MOVE!
MOVE!
WHSSSSH
FORGIVE ME, MY BRAVE ONES ...

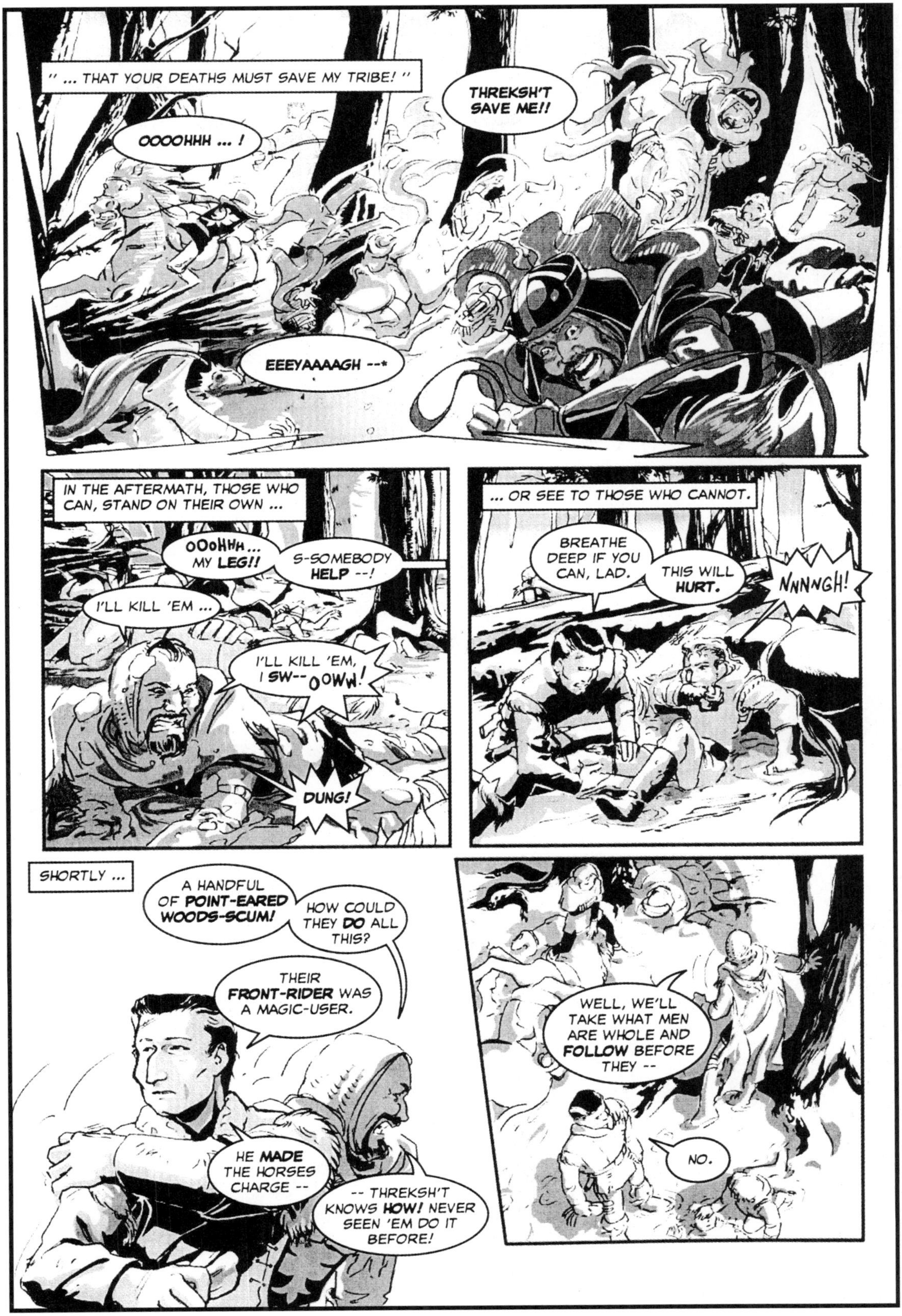

" ... THAT YOUR DEATHS MUST SAVE MY TRIBE! "
THREKSH'T SAVE ME!!
OOOOHHH ... !
EEEYAAAAGH --*
IN THE AFTERMATH, THOSE WHO CAN, STAND ON THEIR OWN ...
OOOHHH... MY LEG!!
S-SOMEBODY HELP --!
I'LL KILL 'EM ...
I'LL KILL 'EM, I SW-- OOWW!
DUNG!
... OR SEE TO THOSE WHO CANNOT.
BREATHE DEEP IF YOU CAN, LAD.
THIS WILL HURT.
NNNNGH!
SHORTLY ...
A HANDFUL OF POINT-EARED WOODS-SCUM!
HOW COULD THEY DO ALL THIS?
THEIR FRONT-RIDER WAS A MAGIC-USER.
HE MADE THE HORSES CHARGE --
-- THREKSH'T KNOWS HOW! NEVER SEEN 'EM DO IT BEFORE!
WELL, WE'LL TAKE WHAT MEN ARE WHOLE AND FOLLOW BEFORE THEY --
NO.

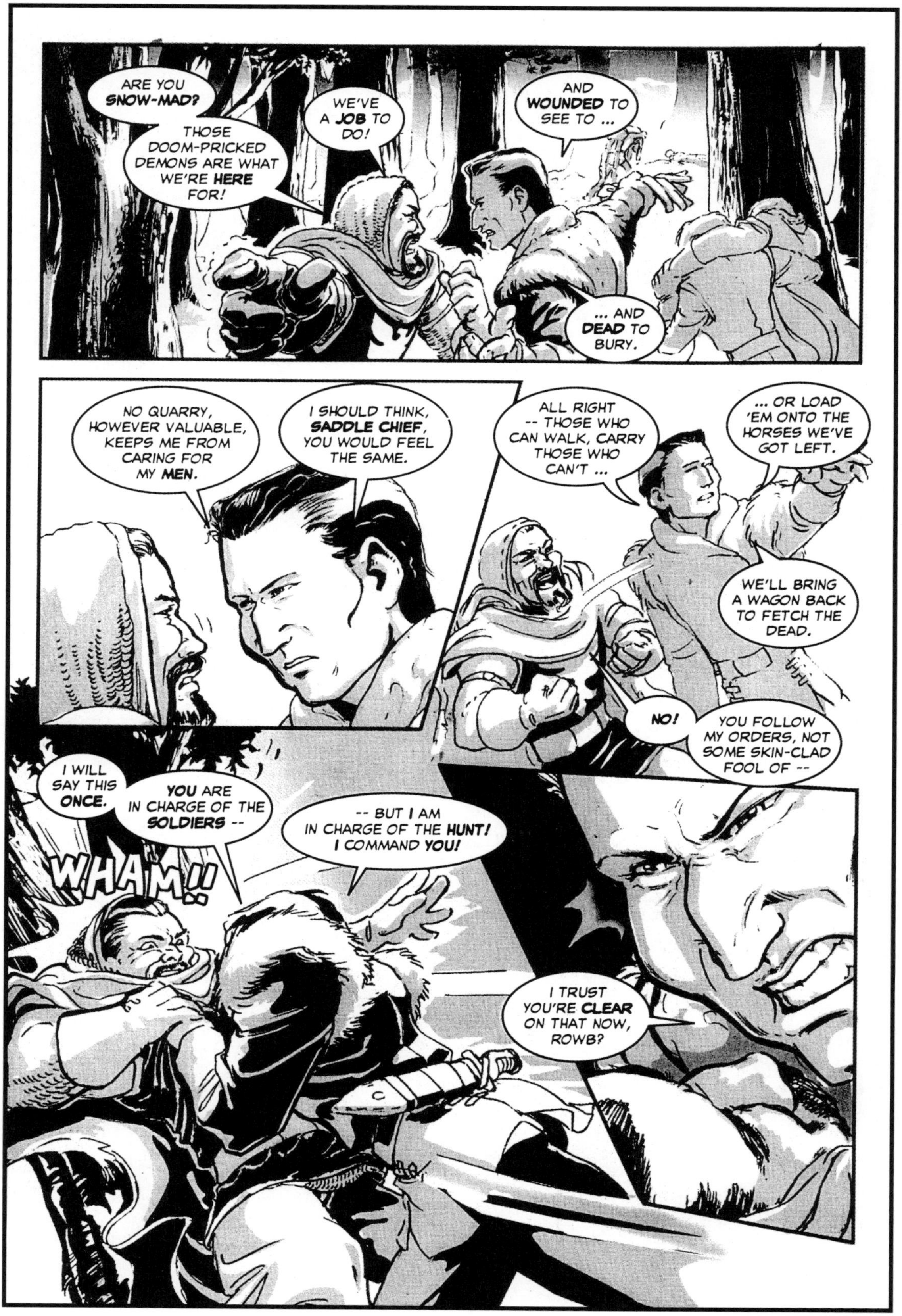

ARE YOU SNOW-MAD?
THOSE DOOM-PRICKED DEMONS ARE WHAT WE'RE HERE FOR!
WE'VE A JOB TO DO!
AND WOUNDED TO SEE TO ...
... AND DEAD TO BURY.
NO QUARRY, HOWEVER VALUABLE, KEEPS ME FROM CARING FOR MY MEN.
I SHOULD THINK, SADDLE CHIEF, YOU WOULD FEEL THE SAME.
ALL RIGHT -- THOSE WHO CAN WALK, CARRY THOSE WHO CAN'T ...
... OR LOAD 'EM ONTO THE HORSES WE'VE GOT LEFT.
WE'LL BRING A WAGON BACK TO FETCH THE DEAD.
NO!
YOU FOLLOW MY ORDERS, NOT SOME SKIN-CLAD FOOL OF --
I WILL SAY THIS ONCE.
YOU ARE IN CHARGE OF THE SOLDIERS --
-- BUT I AM IN CHARGE OF THE HUNT! I COMMAND YOU!
WHAM!!
I TRUST YOU'RE CLEAR ON THAT NOW, ROWB?

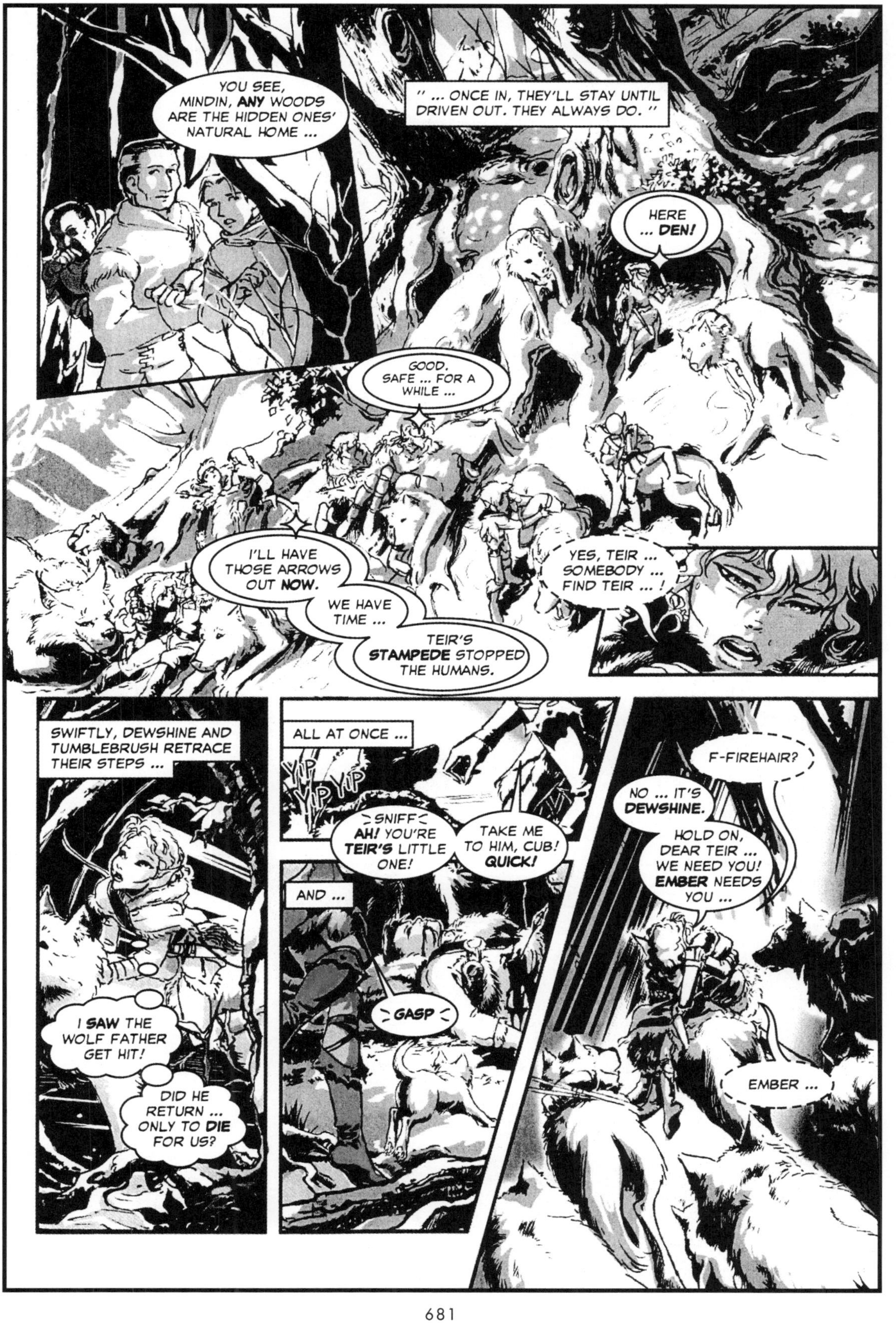
YOU SEE, MINDIN, ANY WOODS ARE THE HIDDEN ONES' NATURAL HOME ...
" ... ONCE IN, THEY'LL STAY UNTIL DRIVEN OUT. THEY ALWAYS DO. "
HERE ... DEN!
GOOD. SAFE ... FOR A WHILE ...
I'LL HAVE THOSE ARROWS OUT NOW.
WE HAVE TIME ...
TEIR'S STAMPEDE STOPPED THE HUMANS.
YES, TEIR ... SOMEBODY ... FIND TEIR ... !
SWIFTLY, DEWSHINE AND TUMBLEBRUSH RETRACE THEIR STEPS ...
I SAW THE WOLF FATHER GET HIT!
DID HE RETURN ... ONLY TO DIE FOR US?
ALL AT ONCE ...
YIP YIP YIP
SNIFF AH! YOU'RE TEIR'S LITTLE ONE!
TAKE ME TO HIM, CUB! QUICK!
AND ...
GASP
F-FIREHAIR?
NO ... IT'S DEWSHINE.
HOLD ON, DEAR TEIR ... WE NEED YOU! EMBER NEEDS YOU ...
EMBER ...

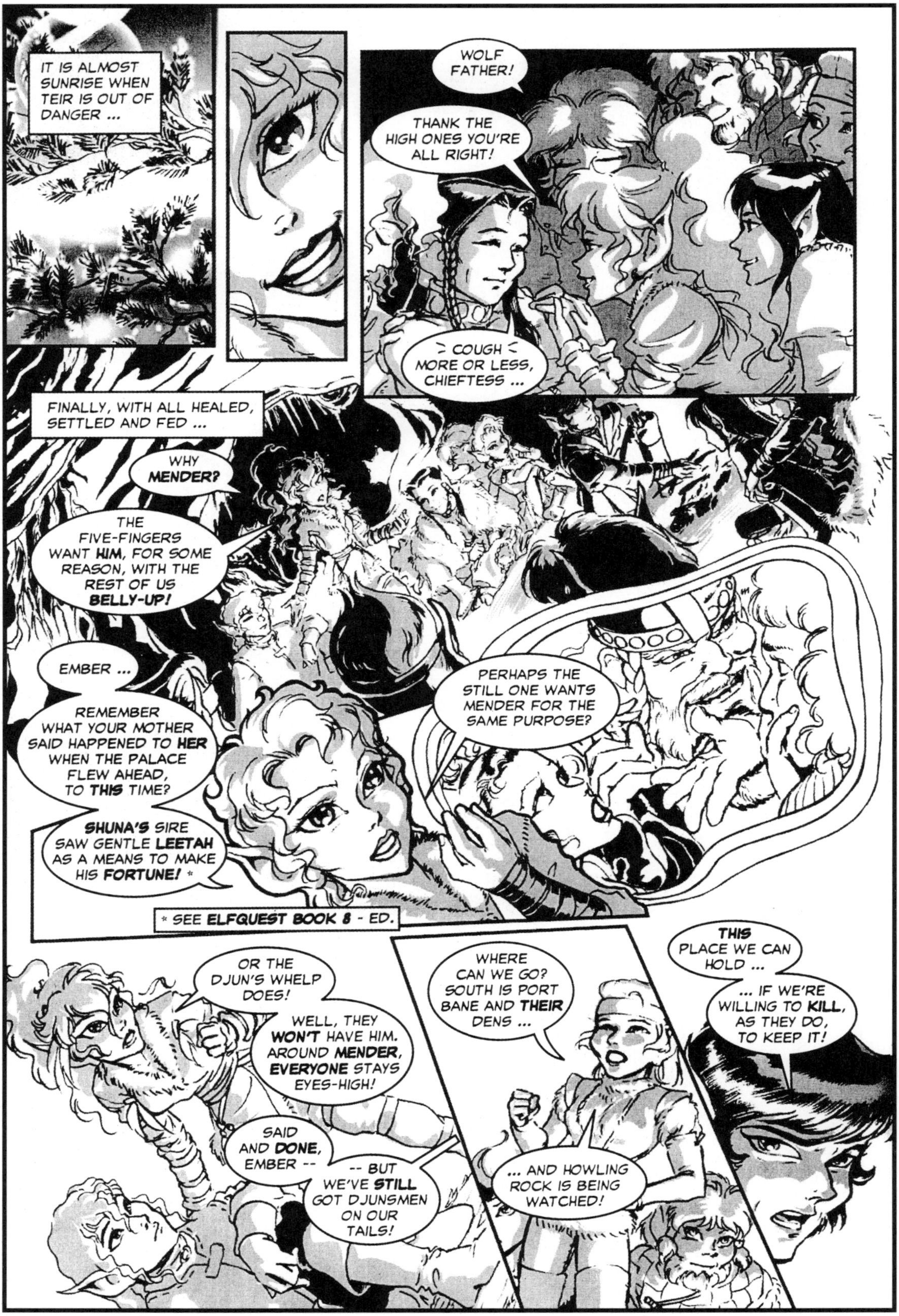

IT IS ALMOST SUNRISE WHEN TEIR IS OUT OF DANGER ...
WOLF FATHER!
THANK THE HIGH ONES YOU'RE ALL RIGHT!
> COUGH < MORE OR LESS, CHIEFTESS ...
FINALLY, WITH ALL HEALED, SETTLED AND FED ...
WHY MENDER?
THE FIVE-FINGERS WANT HIM, FOR SOME REASON, WITH THE REST OF US BELLY-UP!
EMBER ...
REMEMBER WHAT YOUR MOTHER SAID HAPPENED TO HER WHEN THE PALACE FLEW AHEAD, TO THIS TIME?
SHUNA'S SIRE SAW GENTLE LEETAH AS A MEANS TO MAKE HIS FORTUNE! *
PERHAPS THE STILL ONE WANTS MENDER FOR THE SAME PURPOSE?
* SEE ELFQUEST BOOK 8 - ED.
OR THE DJUN'S WHELP DOES!
WELL, THEY WON'T HAVE HIM. AROUND MENDER, EVERYONE STAYS EYES-HIGH!
SAID AND DONE, EMBER --
-- BUT WE'VE STILL GOT DJUNSMEN ON OUR TAILS!
WHERE CAN WE GO? SOUTH IS PORT BANE AND THEIR DENS ...
... AND HOWLING ROCK IS BEING WATCHED!
THIS PLACE WE CAN HOLD ...
... IF WE'RE WILLING TO KILL, AS THEY DO, TO KEEP IT!

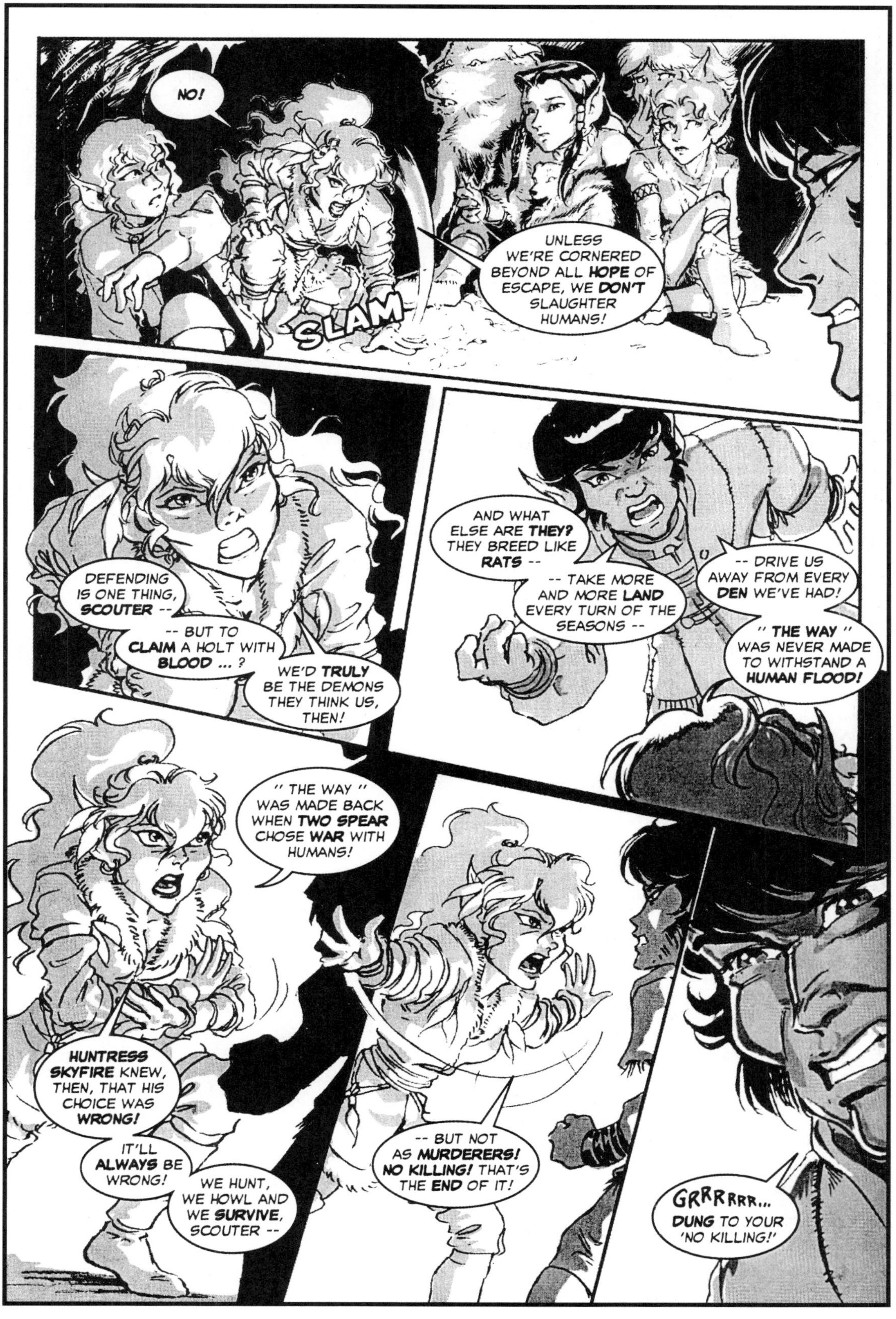

NO!
UNLESS WE'RE CORNERED BEYOND ALL HOPE OF ESCAPE, WE DON'T SLAUGHTER HUMANS!
SLAM
DEFENDING IS ONE THING, SCOUTER --
-- BUT TO CLAIM A HOLT WITH BLOOD ... ?
WE'D TRULY BE THE DEMONS THEY THINK US, THEN!
AND WHAT ELSE ARE THEY? THEY BREED LIKE RATS --
-- TAKE MORE AND MORE LAND EVERY TURN OF THE SEASONS --
-- DRIVE US AWAY FROM EVERY DEN WE'VE HAD!
" THE WAY " WAS NEVER MADE TO WITHSTAND A HUMAN FLOOD!
" THE WAY " WAS MADE BACK WHEN TWO SPEAR CHOSE WAR WITH HUMANS!
HUNTRESS SKYFIRE KNEW, THEN, THAT HIS CHOICE WAS WRONG!
IT'LL ALWAYS BE WRONG!
WE HUNT, WE HOWL AND WE SURVIVE, SCOUTER --
-- BUT NOT AS MURDERERS! NO KILLING! THAT'S THE END OF IT!
GRRRRRR... DUNG TO YOUR 'NO KILLING!'

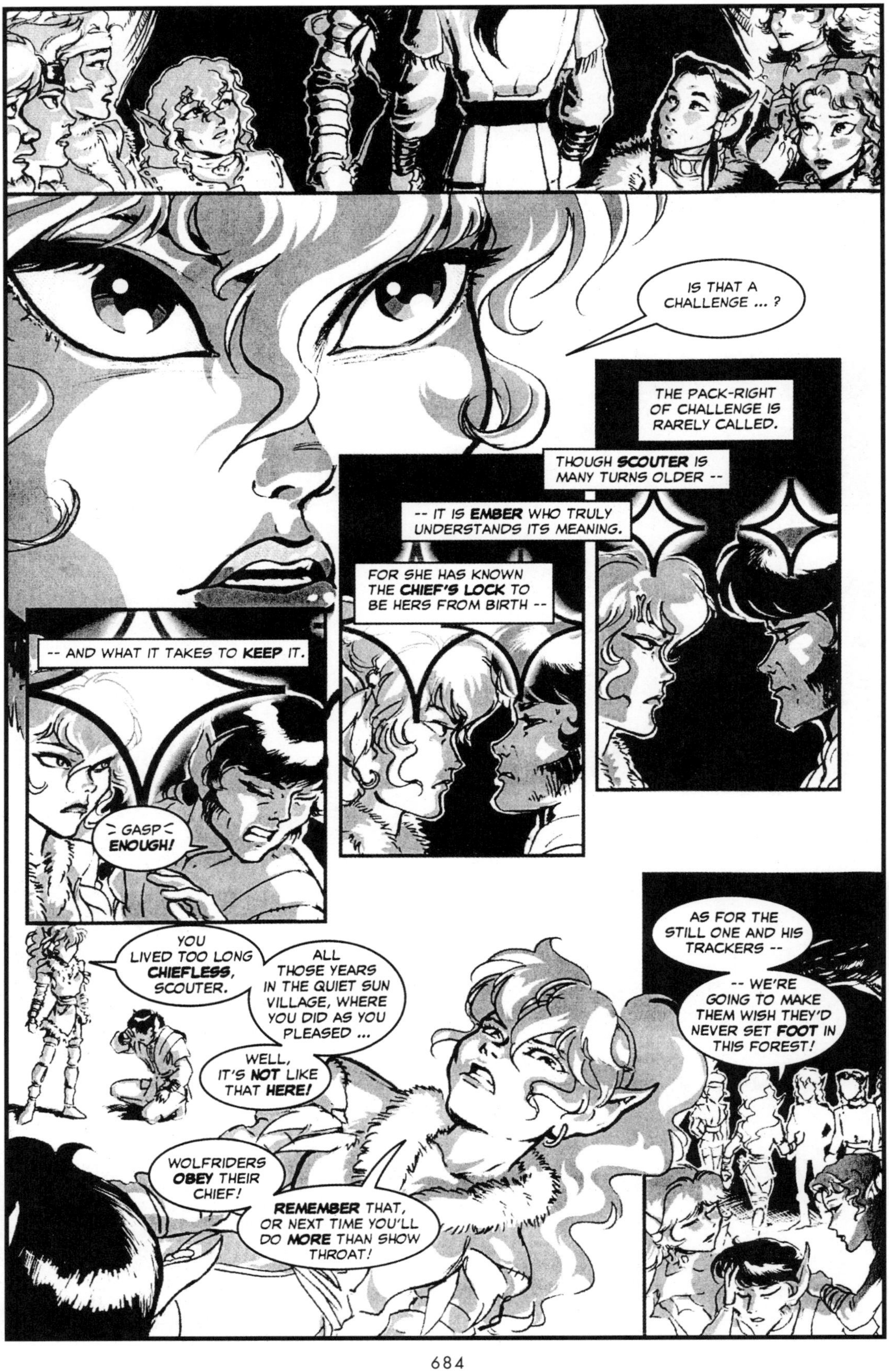

IS THAT A CHALLENGE ... ?
THE PACK-RIGHT OF CHALLENGE IS RARELY CALLED.
THOUGH SCOUTER IS MANY TURNS OLDER --
-- IT IS EMBER WHO TRULY UNDERSTANDS ITS MEANING.
FOR SHE HAS KNOWN THE CHIEF'S LOCK TO BE HERS FROM BIRTH --
-- AND WHAT IT TAKES TO KEEP IT.
GASP ENOUGH!
YOU LIVED TOO LONG CHIEFLESS, SCOUTER.
ALL THOSE YEARS IN THE QUIET SUN VILLAGE, WHERE YOU DID AS YOU PLEASED ...
WELL, IT'S NOT LIKE THAT HERE!
WOLFRIDERS OBEY THEIR CHIEF!
REMEMBER THAT, OR NEXT TIME YOU'LL DO MORE THAN SHOW THROAT!
AS FOR THE STILL ONE AND HIS TRACKERS --
-- WE'RE GOING TO MAKE THEM WISH THEY'D NEVER SET FOOT IN THIS FOREST!

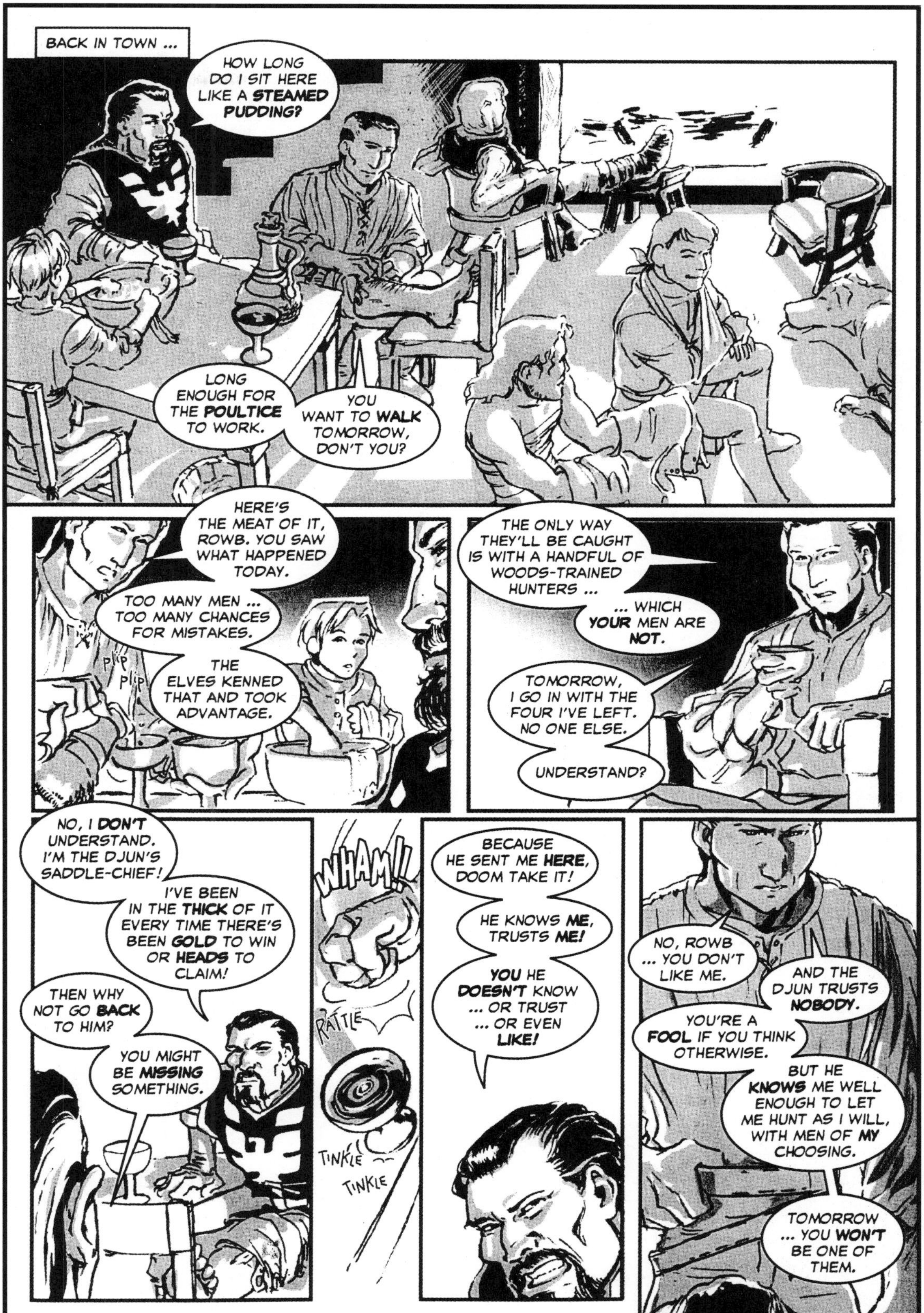
BACK IN TOWN ...
HOW LONG DO I SIT HERE LIKE A **STEAMED PUDDING?**
LONG ENOUGH FOR THE **POULTICE** TO WORK.
YOU WANT TO **WALK** TOMORROW, DON'T YOU?
HERE'S THE MEAT OF IT, ROWB. YOU SAW WHAT HAPPENED TODAY.
TOO MANY MEN ... TOO MANY CHANCES FOR MISTAKES.
THE ELVES KENNED THAT AND TOOK ADVANTAGE.
PLIP PLIP
THE ONLY WAY THEY'LL BE CAUGHT IS WITH A HANDFUL OF WOODS-TRAINED HUNTERS ...
... WHICH **YOUR** MEN ARE **NOT**.
TOMORROW, I GO IN WITH THE FOUR I'VE LEFT. NO ONE ELSE.
UNDERSTAND?
NO, I **DON'T** UNDERSTAND. I'M THE DJUN'S SADDLE-CHIEF!
I'VE BEEN IN THE **THICK** OF IT EVERY TIME THERE'S BEEN **GOLD** TO WIN OR **HEADS** TO CLAIM!
THEN WHY NOT GO **BACK** TO HIM?
YOU MIGHT BE **MISSING** SOMETHING.
WHAM!!
RATTLE
TINKLE
TINKLE
BECAUSE HE SENT ME **HERE**, DOOM TAKE IT!
HE KNOWS **ME**, TRUSTS **ME!**
YOU HE **DOESN'T** KNOW ... OR TRUST ... OR EVEN **LIKE!**
NO, ROWB ... YOU DON'T LIKE ME.
AND THE DJUN TRUSTS **NOBODY**.
YOU'RE A **FOOL** IF YOU THINK OTHERWISE.
BUT HE **KNOWS** ME WELL ENOUGH TO LET ME HUNT AS I WILL, WITH MEN OF **MY** CHOOSING.
TOMORROW ... YOU **WON'T** BE ONE OF THEM.

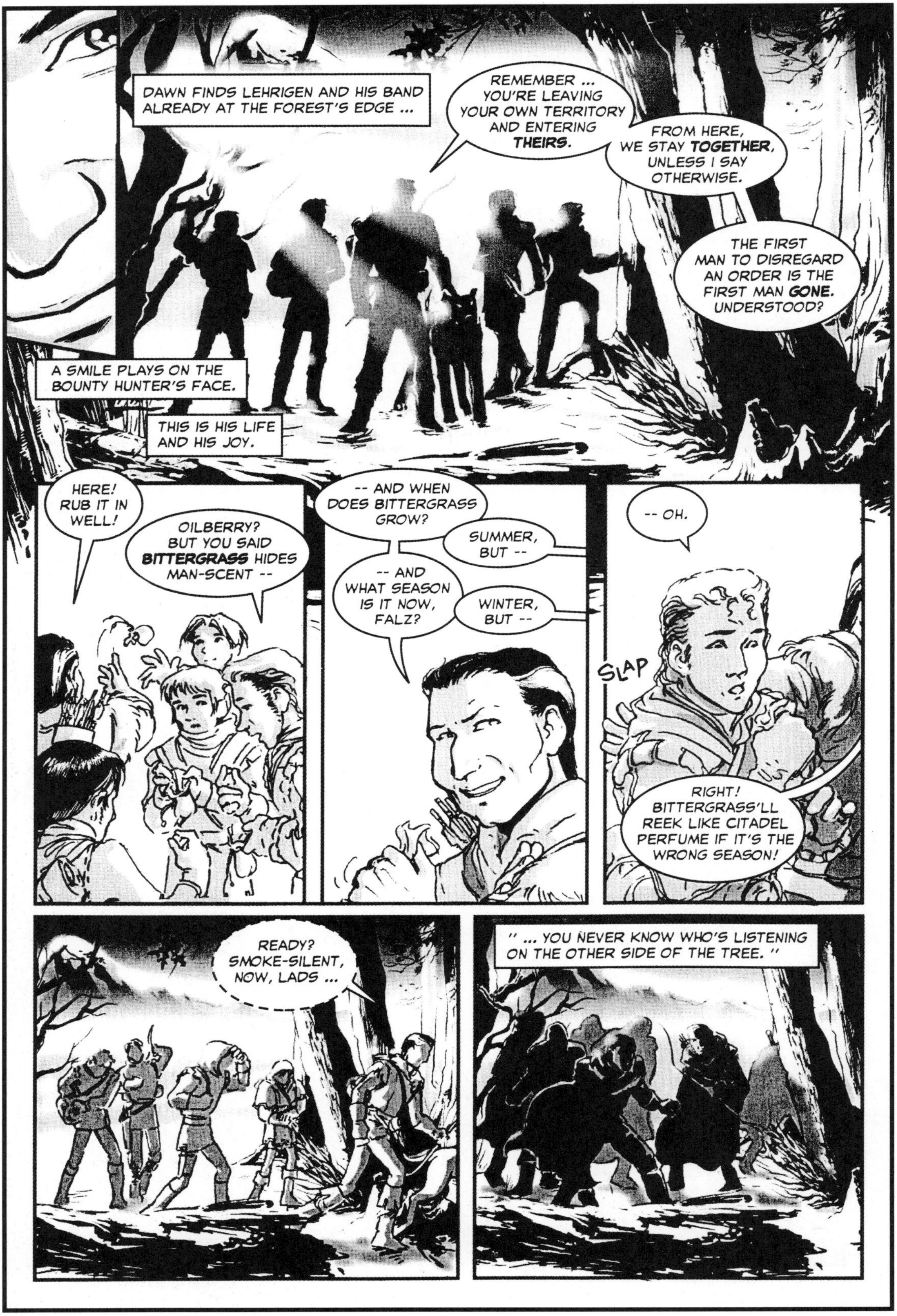
DAWN FINDS LEHRIGEN AND HIS BAND ALREADY AT THE FOREST'S EDGE ...
REMEMBER ... YOU'RE LEAVING YOUR OWN TERRITORY AND ENTERING **THEIRS**.
FROM HERE, WE STAY **TOGETHER**, UNLESS I SAY OTHERWISE.
THE FIRST MAN TO DISREGARD AN ORDER IS THE FIRST MAN **GONE**. UNDERSTOOD?
A SMILE PLAYS ON THE BOUNTY HUNTER'S FACE.
THIS IS HIS LIFE AND HIS JOY.
HERE! RUB IT IN WELL!
OILBERRY? BUT YOU SAID **BITTERGRASS** HIDES MAN-SCENT --
-- AND WHEN DOES BITTERGRASS GROW?
SUMMER, BUT --
-- AND WHAT SEASON IS IT NOW, FALZ?
WINTER, BUT --
-- OH.
SLAP
RIGHT! BITTERGRASS'LL REEK LIKE CITADEL PERFUME IF IT'S THE WRONG SEASON!
READY? SMOKE-SILENT, NOW, LADS ...
" ... YOU NEVER KNOW WHO'S LISTENING ON THE OTHER SIDE OF THE TREE. "

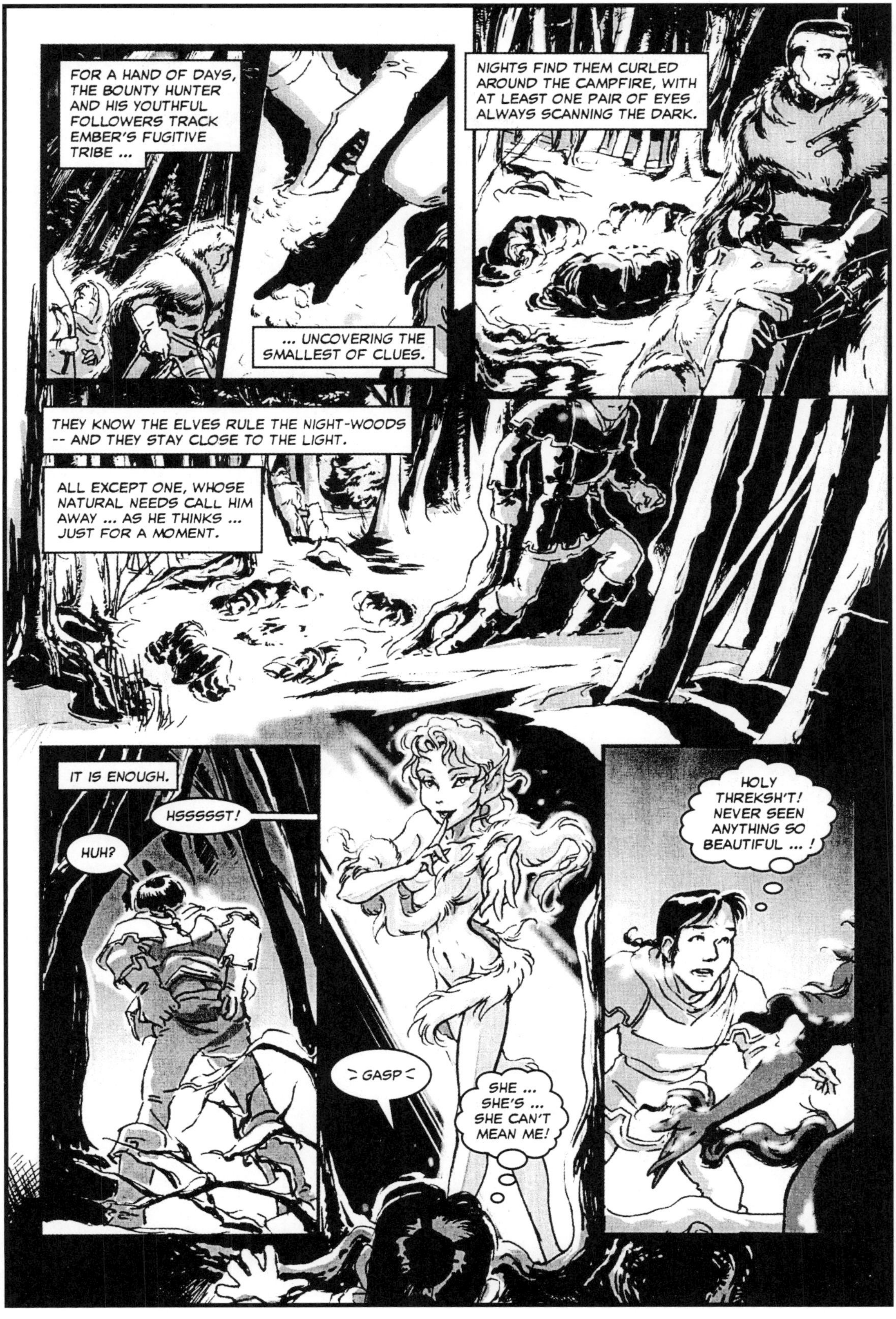
FOR A HAND OF DAYS, THE BOUNTY HUNTER AND HIS YOUTHFUL FOLLOWERS TRACK EMBER'S FUGITIVE TRIBE ...
... UNCOVERING THE SMALLEST OF CLUES.
NIGHTS FIND THEM CURLED AROUND THE CAMPFIRE, WITH AT LEAST ONE PAIR OF EYES ALWAYS SCANNING THE DARK.
THEY KNOW THE ELVES RULE THE NIGHT-WOODS -- AND THEY STAY CLOSE TO THE LIGHT.
ALL EXCEPT ONE, WHOSE NATURAL NEEDS CALL HIM AWAY ... AS HE THINKS ... JUST FOR A MOMENT.
IT IS ENOUGH.
HSSSSST!
HUH?
HOLY THREKSH'T! NEVER SEEN ANYTHING SO BEAUTIFUL ... !
GASP
SHE ... SHE'S ... SHE CAN'T MEAN ME!

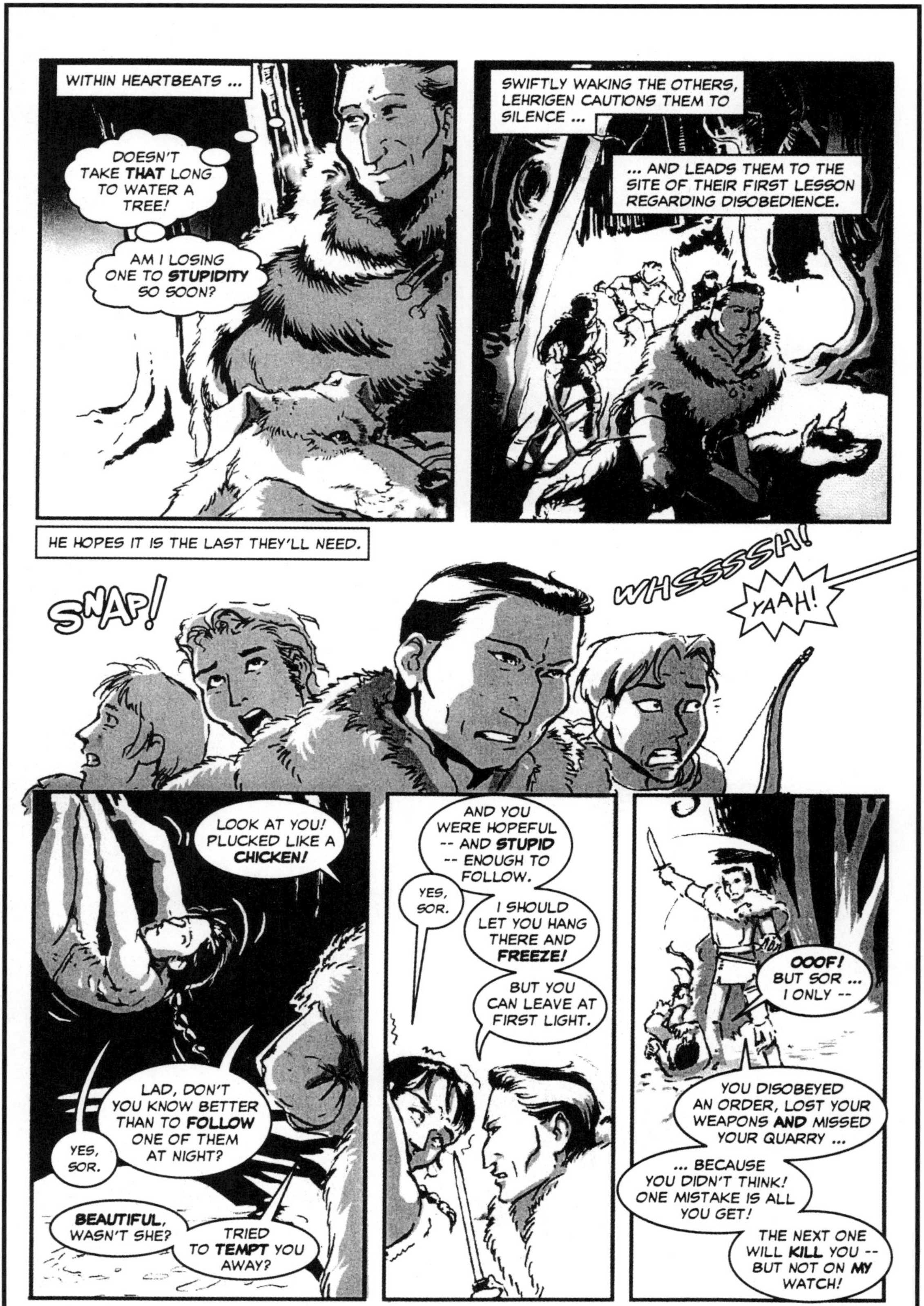

WITHIN HEARTBEATS ...
DOESN'T TAKE THAT LONG TO WATER A TREE!
AM I LOSING ONE TO STUPIDITY SO SOON?
SWIFTLY WAKING THE OTHERS, LEHRIGEN CAUTIONS THEM TO SILENCE ...
... AND LEADS THEM TO THE SITE OF THEIR FIRST LESSON REGARDING DISOBEDIENCE.
HE HOPES IT IS THE LAST THEY'LL NEED.
SNAP!
WHSSSSSH!
YAAH!
LOOK AT YOU! PLUCKED LIKE A CHICKEN!
LAD, DON'T YOU KNOW BETTER THAN TO FOLLOW ONE OF THEM AT NIGHT?
YES, SOR.
BEAUTIFUL, WASN'T SHE?
TRIED TO TEMPT YOU AWAY?
AND YOU WERE HOPEFUL -- AND STUPID -- ENOUGH TO FOLLOW.
YES, SOR.
I SHOULD LET YOU HANG THERE AND FREEZE!
BUT YOU CAN LEAVE AT FIRST LIGHT.
OOOF! BUT SOR ... I ONLY --
YOU DISOBEYED AN ORDER, LOST YOUR WEAPONS AND MISSED YOUR QUARRY ...
... BECAUSE YOU DIDN'T THINK! ONE MISTAKE IS ALL YOU GET!
THE NEXT ONE WILL KILL YOU -- BUT NOT ON MY WATCH!

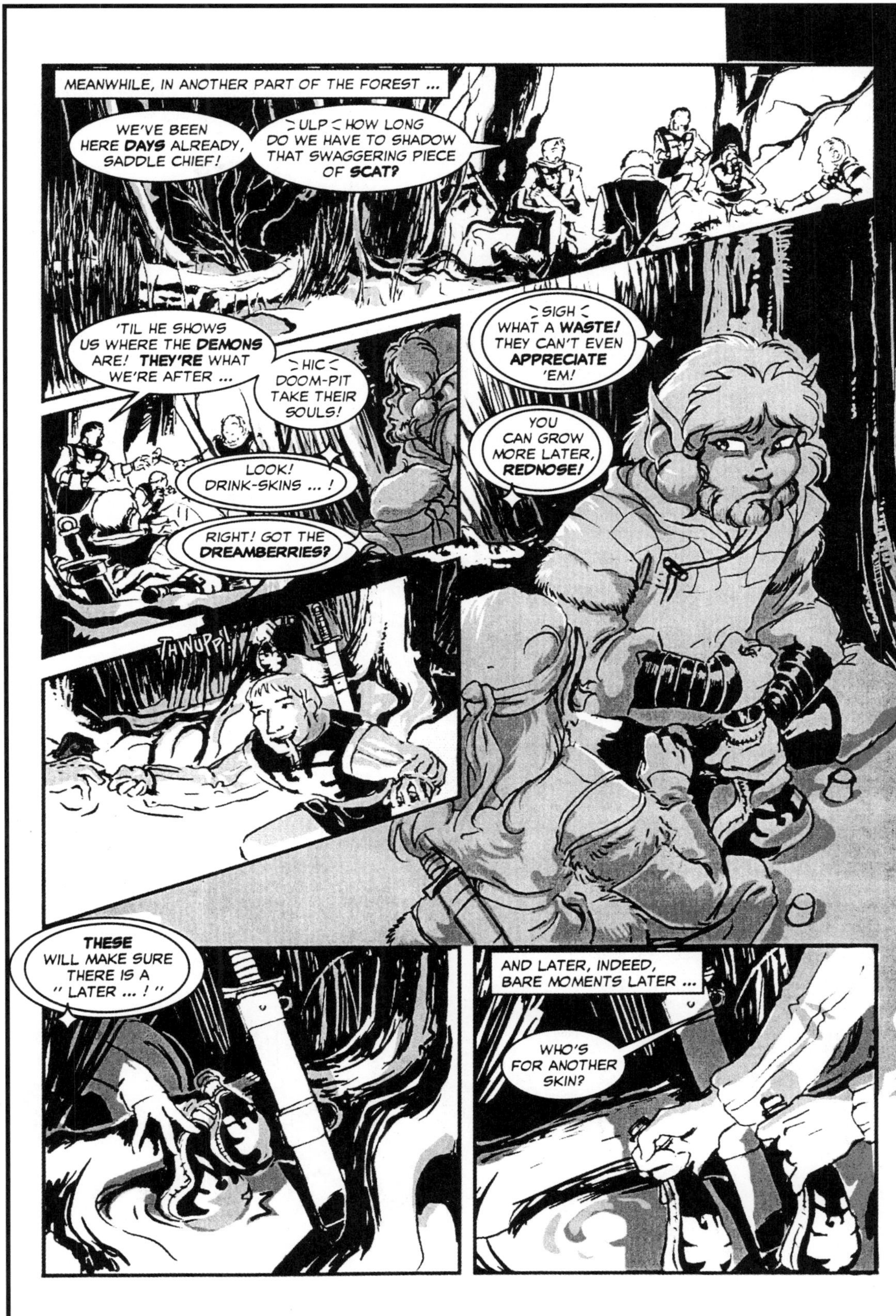

MEANWHILE, IN ANOTHER PART OF THE FOREST ...
WE'VE BEEN HERE DAYS ALREADY, SADDLE CHIEF!
>ULP< HOW LONG DO WE HAVE TO SHADOW THAT SWAGGERING PIECE OF SCAT?
'TIL HE SHOWS US WHERE THE DEMONS ARE! THEY'RE WHAT WE'RE AFTER ...
>HIC< DOOM-PIT TAKE THEIR SOULS!
>SIGH< WHAT A WASTE! THEY CAN'T EVEN APPRECIATE 'EM!
YOU CAN GROW MORE LATER, REDNOSE!
LOOK! DRINK-SKINS ... !
RIGHT! GOT THE DREAMBERRIES?
THWUPP!
THESE WILL MAKE SURE THERE IS A " LATER ... ! "
AND LATER, INDEED, BARE MOMENTS LATER ...
WHO'S FOR ANOTHER SKIN?

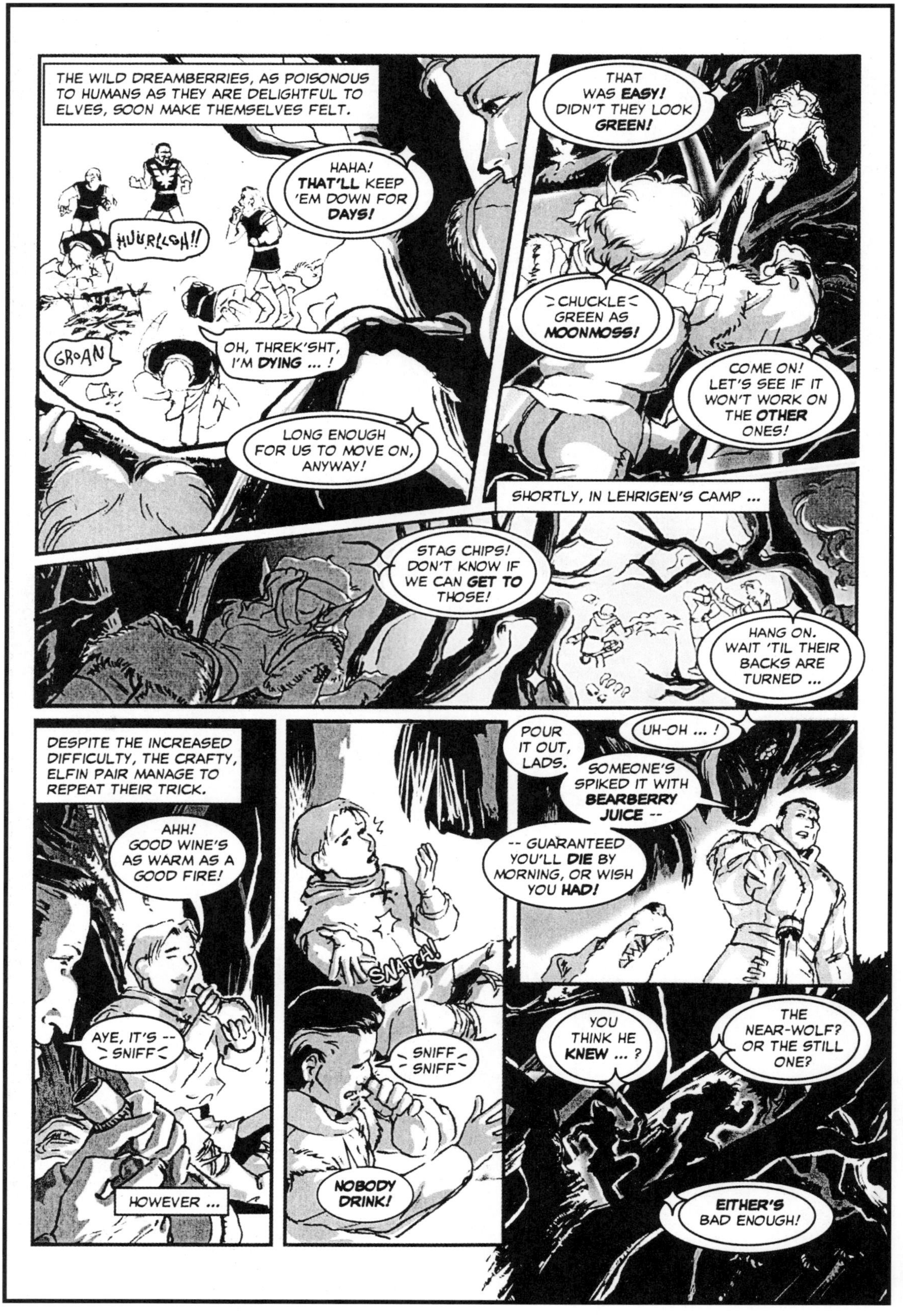
THE WILD DREAMBERRIES, AS POISONOUS TO HUMANS AS THEY ARE DELIGHTFUL TO ELVES, SOON MAKE THEMSELVES FELT.
HAHA! THAT'LL KEEP 'EM DOWN FOR DAYS!
HUURLLGH!!
GROAN
OH, THREK'SHT, I'M DYING ... !
LONG ENOUGH FOR US TO MOVE ON, ANYWAY!
THAT WAS EASY! DIDN'T THEY LOOK GREEN!
CHUCKLE GREEN AS MOONMOSS!
COME ON! LET'S SEE IF IT WON'T WORK ON THE OTHER ONES!
SHORTLY, IN LEHRIGEN'S CAMP ...
STAG CHIPS! DON'T KNOW IF WE CAN GET TO THOSE!
HANG ON. WAIT 'TIL THEIR BACKS ARE TURNED ...
DESPITE THE INCREASED DIFFICULTY, THE CRAFTY, ELFIN PAIR MANAGE TO REPEAT THEIR TRICK.
AHH! GOOD WINE'S AS WARM AS A GOOD FIRE!
AYE, IT'S -- SNIFF
HOWEVER ...
SNATCH!
SNIFF SNIFF
NOBODY DRINK!
UH-OH ... !
POUR IT OUT, LADS.
SOMEONE'S SPIKED IT WITH BEARBERRY JUICE --
-- GUARANTEED YOU'LL DIE BY MORNING, OR WISH YOU HAD!
YOU THINK HE KNEW ... ?
THE NEAR-WOLF? OR THE STILL ONE?
EITHER'S BAD ENOUGH!

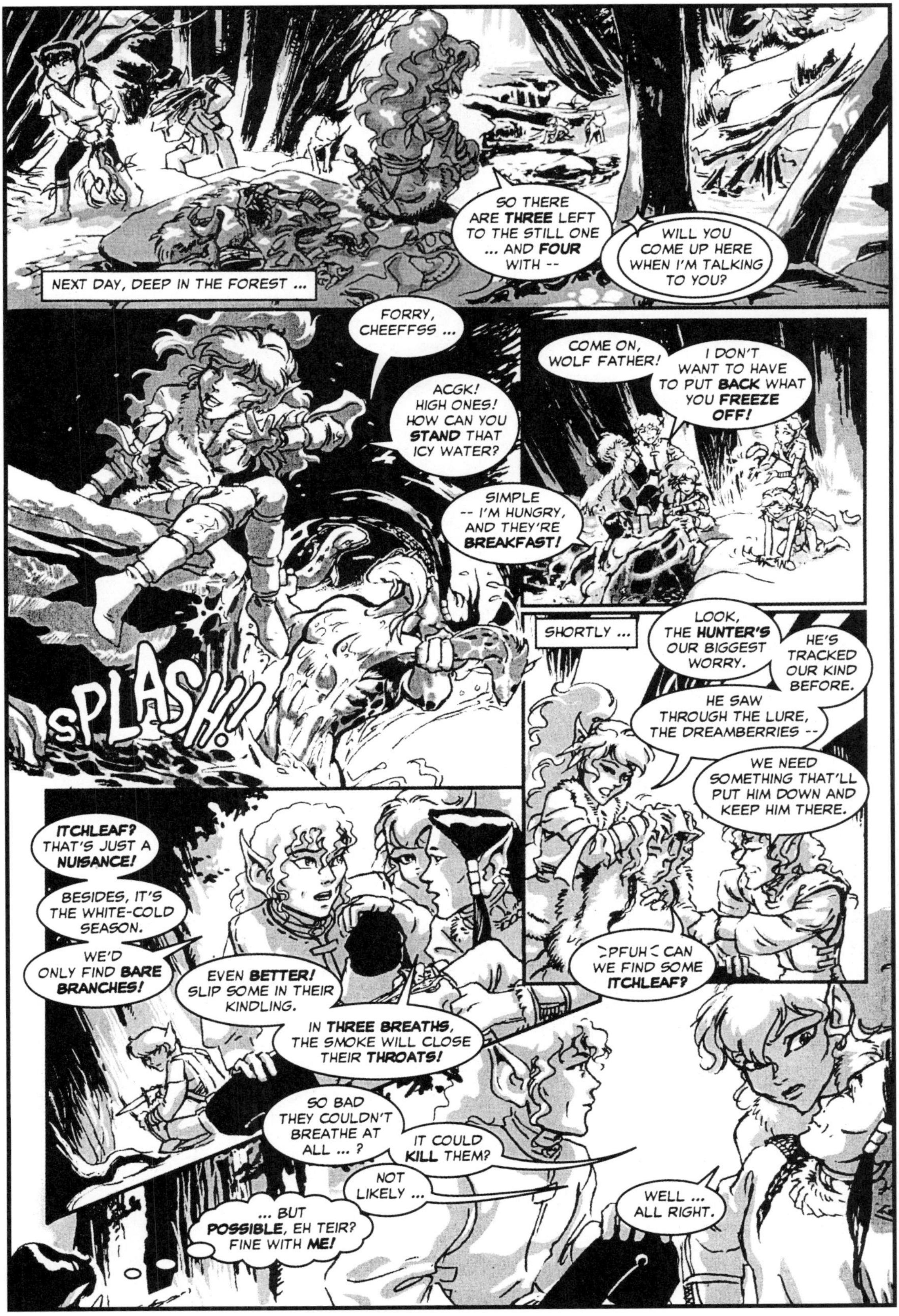
NEXT DAY, DEEP IN THE FOREST ...
SO THERE ARE THREE LEFT TO THE STILL ONE ... AND FOUR WITH --
WILL YOU COME UP HERE WHEN I'M TALKING TO YOU?
FORRY, CHEEFFSS ...
ACGK! HIGH ONES! HOW CAN YOU STAND THAT ICY WATER?
SIMPLE -- I'M HUNGRY, AND THEY'RE BREAKFAST!
SPLASH!!
COME ON, WOLF FATHER!
I DON'T WANT TO HAVE TO PUT BACK WHAT YOU FREEZE OFF!
SHORTLY ...
LOOK, THE HUNTER'S OUR BIGGEST WORRY.
HE'S TRACKED OUR KIND BEFORE.
HE SAW THROUGH THE LURE, THE DREAMBERRIES --
WE NEED SOMETHING THAT'LL PUT HIM DOWN AND KEEP HIM THERE.
PFUH CAN WE FIND SOME ITCHLEAF?
ITCHLEAF? THAT'S JUST A NUISANCE!
BESIDES, IT'S THE WHITE-COLD SEASON.
WE'D ONLY FIND BARE BRANCHES!
EVEN BETTER! SLIP SOME IN THEIR KINDLING.
IN THREE BREATHS, THE SMOKE WILL CLOSE THEIR THROATS!
SO BAD THEY COULDN'T BREATHE AT ALL ... ?
IT COULD KILL THEM?
NOT LIKELY ...
... BUT POSSIBLE, EH TEIR? FINE WITH ME!
WELL ... ALL RIGHT.

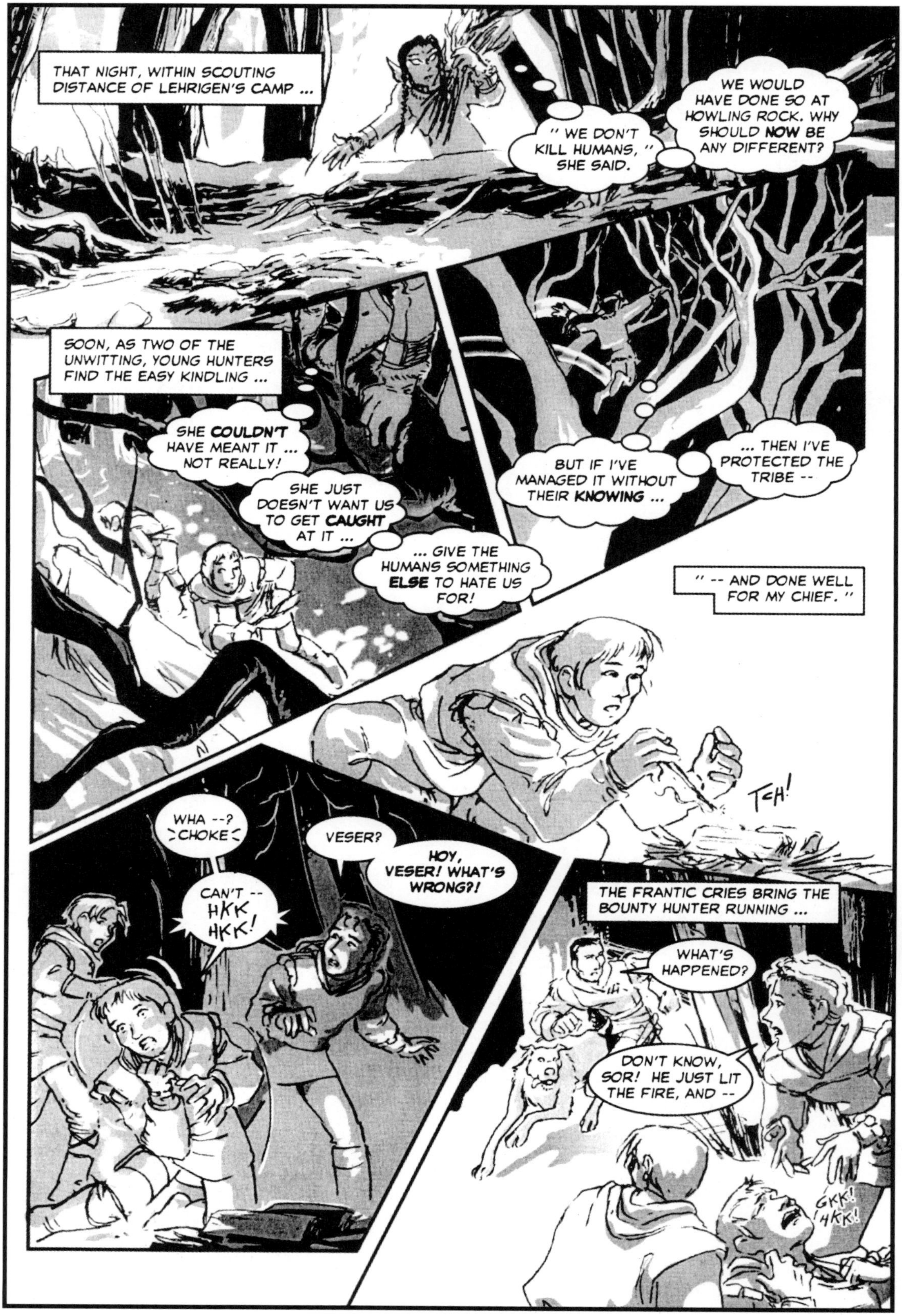

THAT NIGHT, WITHIN SCOUTING DISTANCE OF LEHRIGEN'S CAMP ...
" WE DON'T KILL HUMANS, " SHE SAID.
WE WOULD HAVE DONE SO AT HOWLING ROCK. WHY SHOULD NOW BE ANY DIFFERENT?
SOON, AS TWO OF THE UNWITTING, YOUNG HUNTERS FIND THE EASY KINDLING ...
SHE COULDN'T HAVE MEANT IT ... NOT REALLY!
SHE JUST DOESN'T WANT US TO GET CAUGHT AT IT ...
... GIVE THE HUMANS SOMETHING ELSE TO HATE US FOR!
BUT IF I'VE MANAGED IT WITHOUT THEIR KNOWING ...
... THEN I'VE PROTECTED THE TRIBE --
" -- AND DONE WELL FOR MY CHIEF. "
TCH!
WHA --? CHOKE
CAN'T -- HKK HKK!
VESER?
HOY, VESER! WHAT'S WRONG?!
THE FRANTIC CRIES BRING THE BOUNTY HUNTER RUNNING ...
WHAT'S HAPPENED?
DON'T KNOW, SOR! HE JUST LIT THE FIRE, AND --
GKK! HKK!

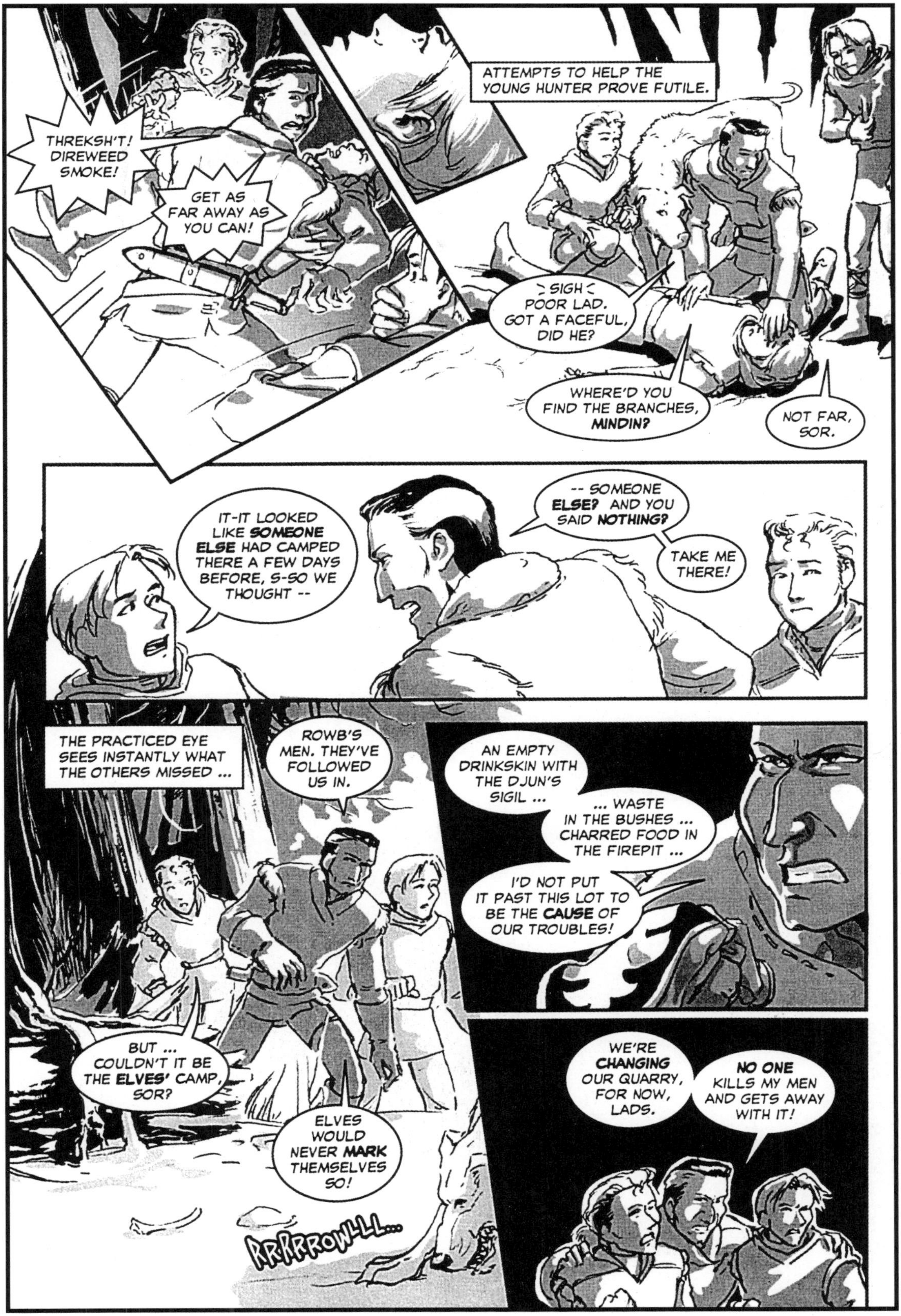
THREKSH'T! DIREWEED SMOKE!
GET AS FAR AWAY AS YOU CAN!
ATTEMPTS TO HELP THE YOUNG HUNTER PROVE FUTILE.
SIGH
POOR LAD. GOT A FACEFUL, DID HE?
WHERE'D YOU FIND THE BRANCHES, MINDIN?
NOT FAR, SOR.
IT-IT LOOKED LIKE SOMEONE ELSE HAD CAMPED THERE A FEW DAYS BEFORE, S-SO WE THOUGHT --
-- SOMEONE ELSE? AND YOU SAID NOTHING?
TAKE ME THERE!
THE PRACTICED EYE SEES INSTANTLY WHAT THE OTHERS MISSED ...
ROWB'S MEN. THEY'VE FOLLOWED US IN.
BUT ... COULDN'T IT BE THE ELVES' CAMP, SOR?
ELVES WOULD NEVER MARK THEMSELVES SO!
RRRRROWLLL...
AN EMPTY DRINKSKIN WITH THE DJUN'S SIGIL ...
... WASTE IN THE BUSHES ... CHARRED FOOD IN THE FIREPIT ...
I'D NOT PUT IT PAST THIS LOT TO BE THE CAUSE OF OUR TROUBLES!
WE'RE CHANGING OUR QUARRY, FOR NOW, LADS.
NO ONE KILLS MY MEN AND GETS AWAY WITH IT!

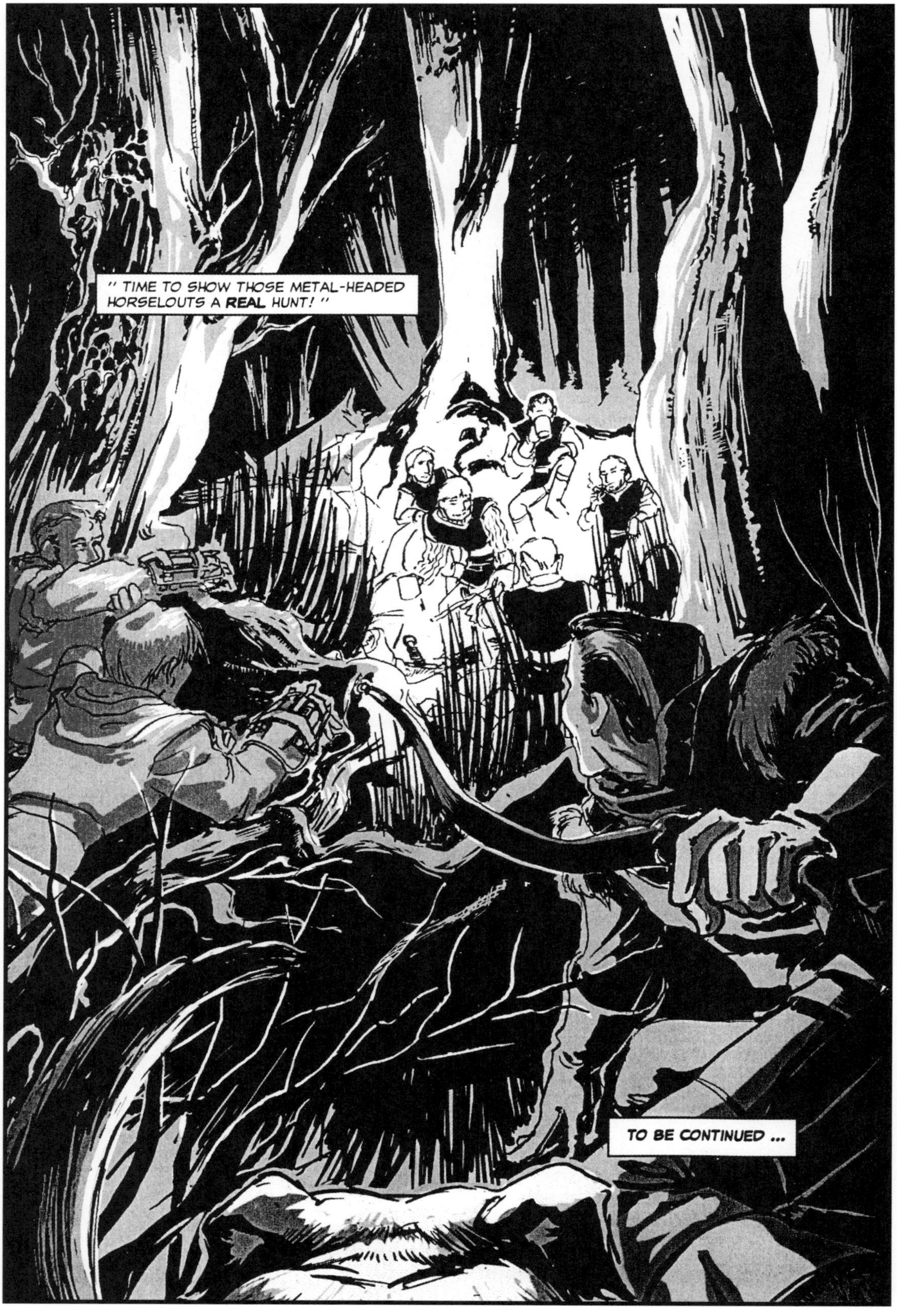
" TIME TO SHOW THOSE METAL-HEADED HORSELOUTS A **REAL** HUNT! "
TO BE CONTINUED ...

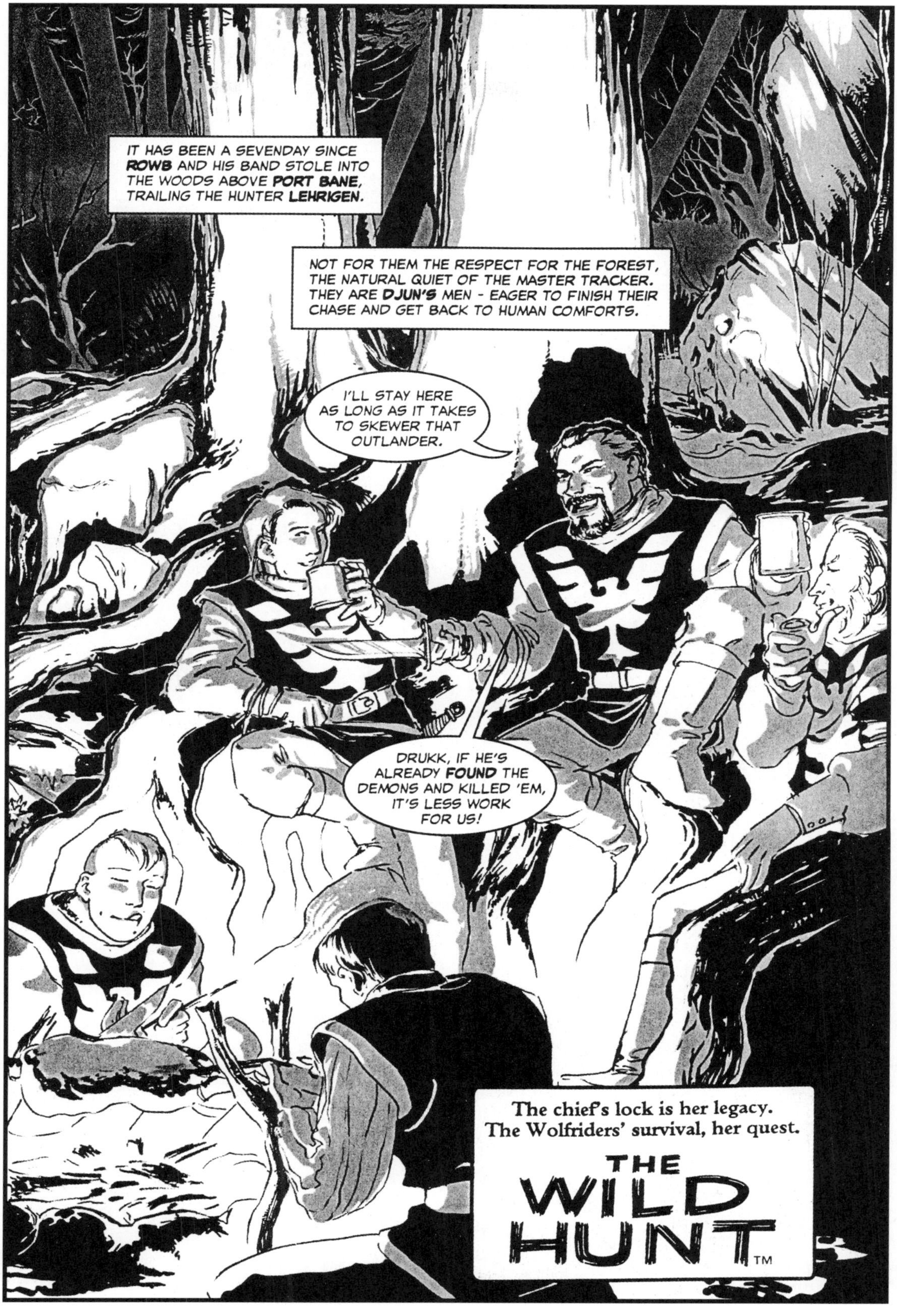
IT HAS BEEN A SEVENDAY SINCE ROWB AND HIS BAND STOLE INTO THE WOODS ABOVE PORT BANE, TRAILING THE HUNTER LEHRIGEN.
NOT FOR THEM THE RESPECT FOR THE FOREST, THE NATURAL QUIET OF THE MASTER TRACKER. THEY ARE DJUN'S MEN - EAGER TO FINISH THEIR CHASE AND GET BACK TO HUMAN COMFORTS.
I'LL STAY HERE AS LONG AS IT TAKES TO SKEWER THAT OUTLANDER.
DRUKK, IF HE'S ALREADY FOUND THE DEMONS AND KILLED 'EM, IT'S LESS WORK FOR US!
The chief's lock is her legacy. The Wolfriders' survival, her quest.
THE WILD HUNT™

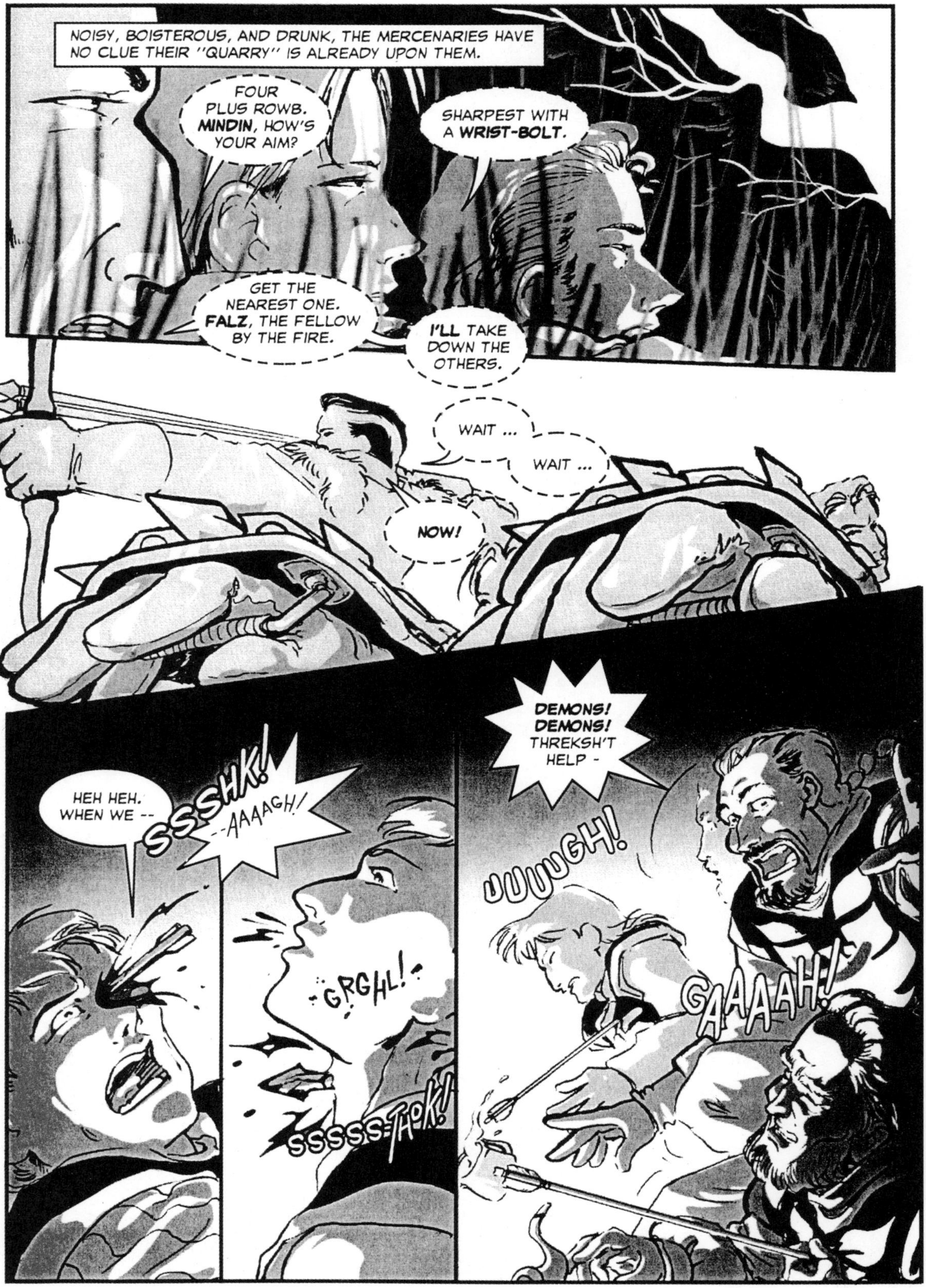

NOISY, BOISTEROUS, AND DRUNK, THE MERCENARIES HAVE NO CLUE THEIR "QUARRY" IS ALREADY UPON THEM.
FOUR PLUS ROWB. MINDIN, HOW'S YOUR AIM?
SHARPEST WITH A WRIST-BOLT.
GET THE NEAREST ONE. FALZ, THE FELLOW BY THE FIRE.
I'LL TAKE DOWN THE OTHERS.
WAIT ...
WAIT ...
NOW!
HEH HEH. WHEN WE --
SSSHK!
--AAAAGH!
GRGHL!
SSSSSTHOK!
DEMONS! DEMONS! THREKSH'T HELP -
UUUUGH!
GAAAAH!

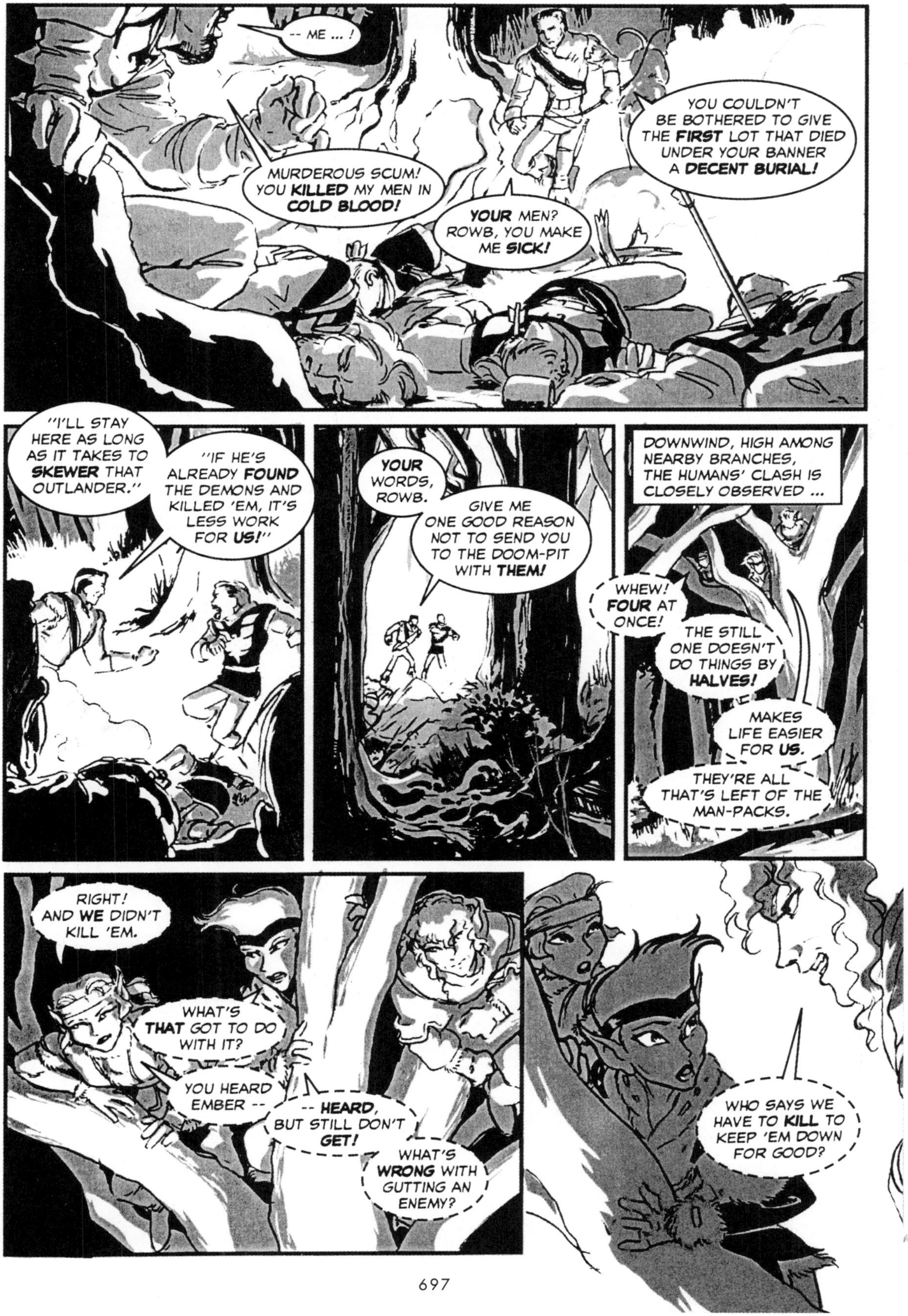
-- ME ... !
MURDEROUS SCUM! YOU KILLED MY MEN IN COLD BLOOD!
YOUR MEN? ROWB, YOU MAKE ME SICK!
YOU COULDN'T BE BOTHERED TO GIVE THE FIRST LOT THAT DIED UNDER YOUR BANNER A DECENT BURIAL!
"I'LL STAY HERE AS LONG AS IT TAKES TO SKEWER THAT OUTLANDER."
"IF HE'S ALREADY FOUND THE DEMONS AND KILLED 'EM, IT'S LESS WORK FOR US!"
YOUR WORDS, ROWB.
GIVE ME ONE GOOD REASON NOT TO SEND YOU TO THE DOOM-PIT WITH THEM!
DOWNWIND, HIGH AMONG NEARBY BRANCHES, THE HUMANS' CLASH IS CLOSELY OBSERVED ...
WHEW! FOUR AT ONCE!
THE STILL ONE DOESN'T DO THINGS BY HALVES!
MAKES LIFE EASIER FOR US.
THEY'RE ALL THAT'S LEFT OF THE MAN-PACKS.
RIGHT! AND WE DIDN'T KILL 'EM.
WHAT'S THAT GOT TO DO WITH IT?
YOU HEARD EMBER --
-- HEARD, BUT STILL DON'T GET!
WHAT'S WRONG WITH GUTTING AN ENEMY?
WHO SAYS WE HAVE TO KILL TO KEEP 'EM DOWN FOR GOOD?

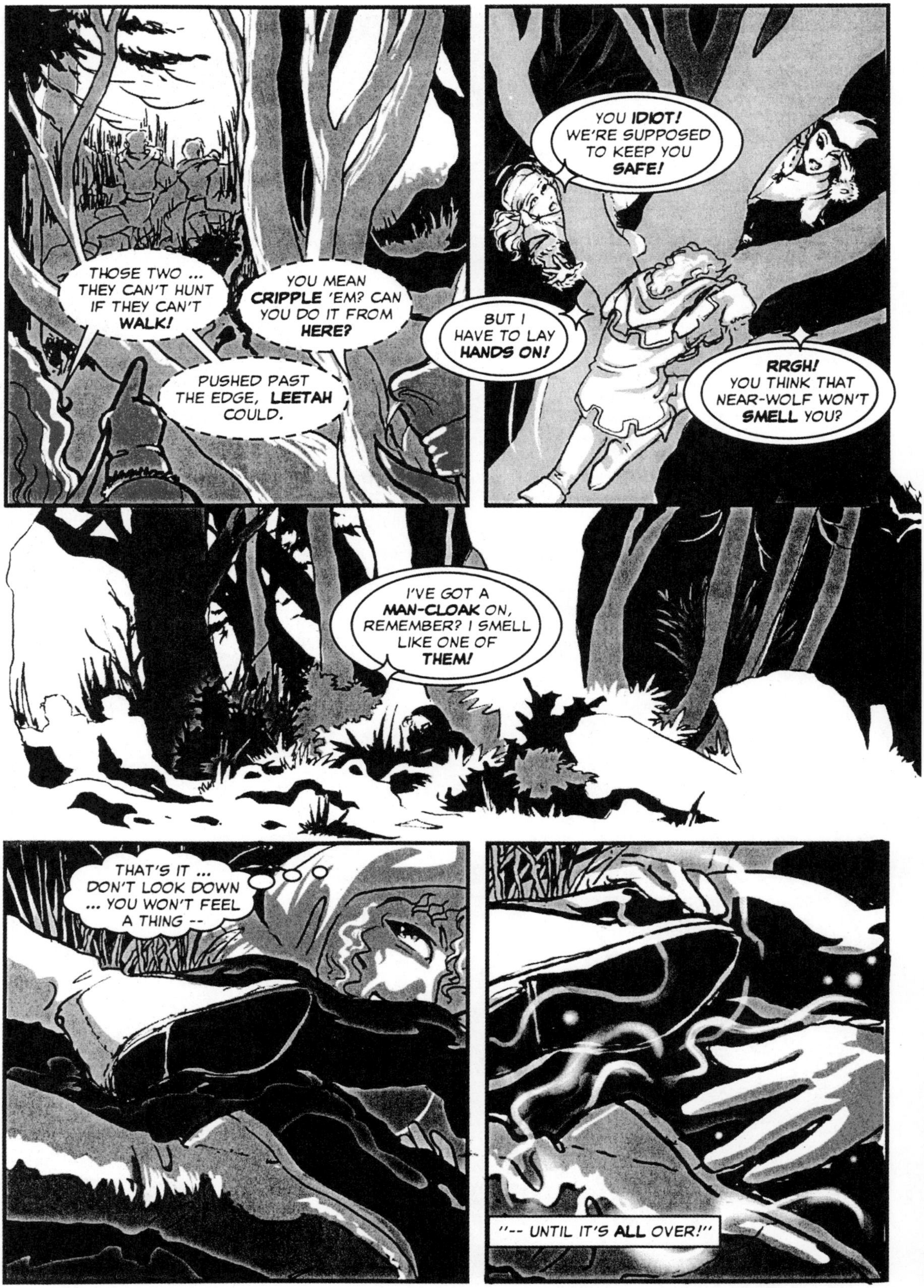
THOSE TWO ... THEY CAN'T HUNT IF THEY CAN'T WALK!
YOU MEAN CRIPPLE 'EM? CAN YOU DO IT FROM HERE?
PUSHED PAST THE EDGE, LEETAH COULD.
YOU IDIOT! WE'RE SUPPOSED TO KEEP YOU SAFE!
BUT I HAVE TO LAY HANDS ON!
RRGH! YOU THINK THAT NEAR-WOLF WON'T SMELL YOU?
I'VE GOT A MAN-CLOAK ON, REMEMBER? I SMELL LIKE ONE OF THEM!
THAT'S IT ... DON'T LOOK DOWN ... YOU WON'T FEEL A THING --
"-- UNTIL IT'S ALL OVER!"

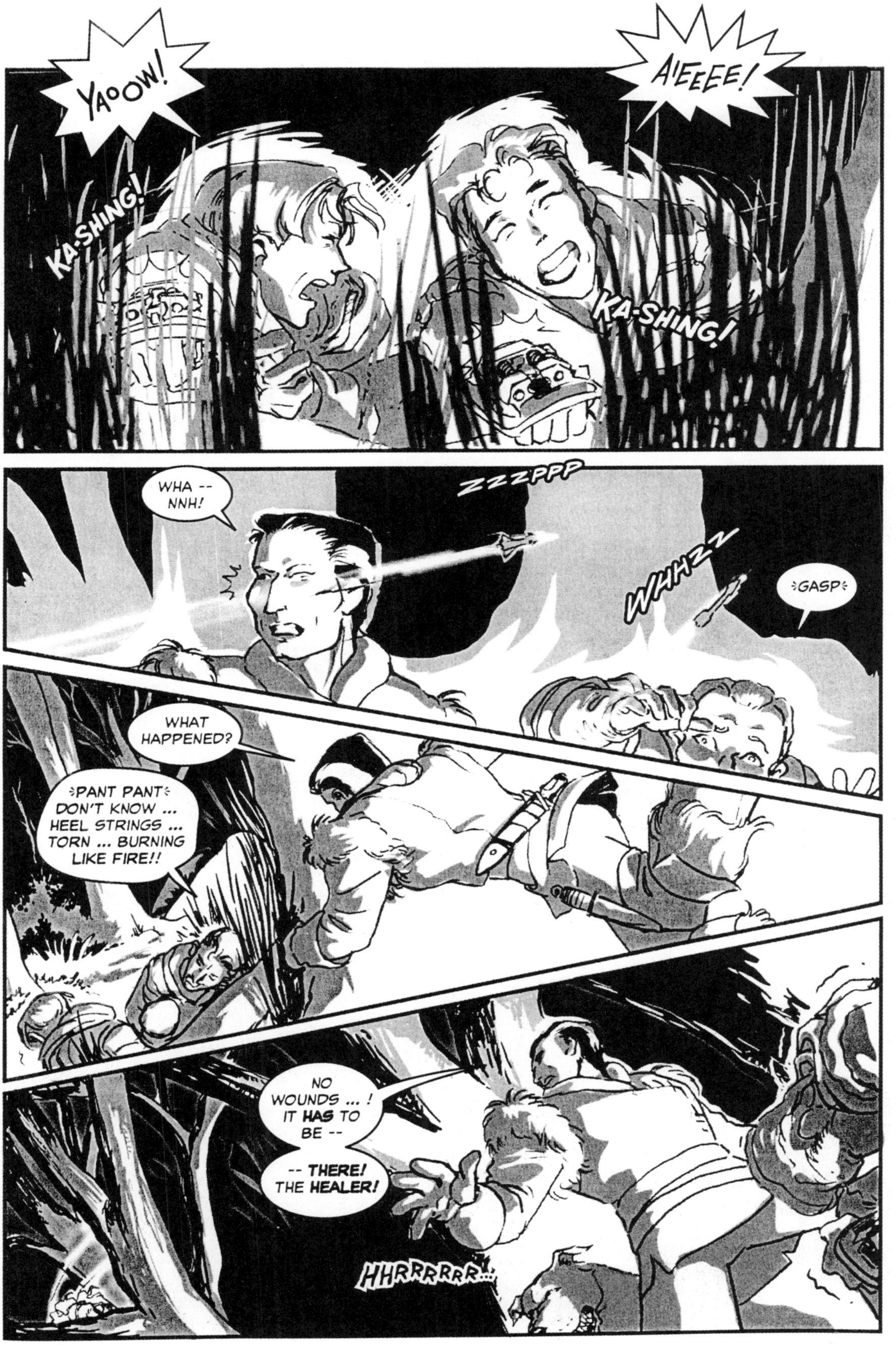
YAOOW!
A'EEEEE!
KA-SHING!
KA-SHING!
WHA -- NNH!
ZZZPPP
WHHZZ
GASP
WHAT HAPPENED?
PANT PANT
DON'T KNOW ... HEEL STRINGS ... TORN ... BURNING LIKE FIRE!!
NO WOUNDS ... ! IT **HAS** TO BE --
-- **THERE!** THE **HEALER!**
HHRRRRRR...!

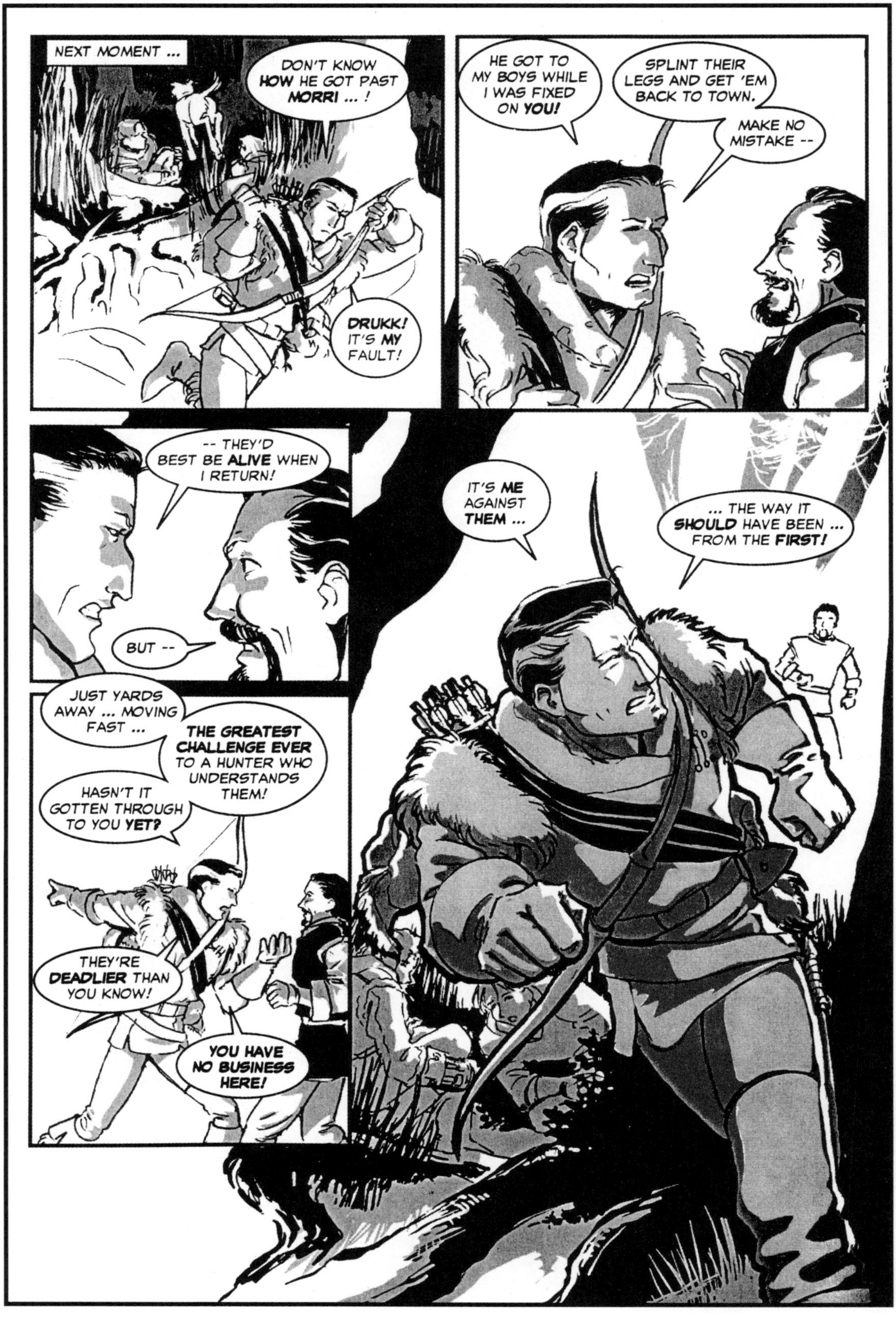
NEXT MOMENT ...
DON'T KNOW HOW HE GOT PAST MORRI ... !
DRUKK! IT'S MY FAULT!
HE GOT TO MY BOYS WHILE I WAS FIXED ON YOU!
SPLINT THEIR LEGS AND GET 'EM BACK TO TOWN.
MAKE NO MISTAKE --
-- THEY'D BEST BE ALIVE WHEN I RETURN!
BUT --
JUST YARDS AWAY ... MOVING FAST ...
THE GREATEST CHALLENGE EVER TO A HUNTER WHO UNDERSTANDS THEM!
HASN'T IT GOTTEN THROUGH TO YOU YET?
THEY'RE DEADLIER THAN YOU KNOW!
YOU HAVE NO BUSINESS HERE!
IT'S ME AGAINST THEM ...
... THE WAY IT SHOULD HAVE BEEN ... FROM THE FIRST!

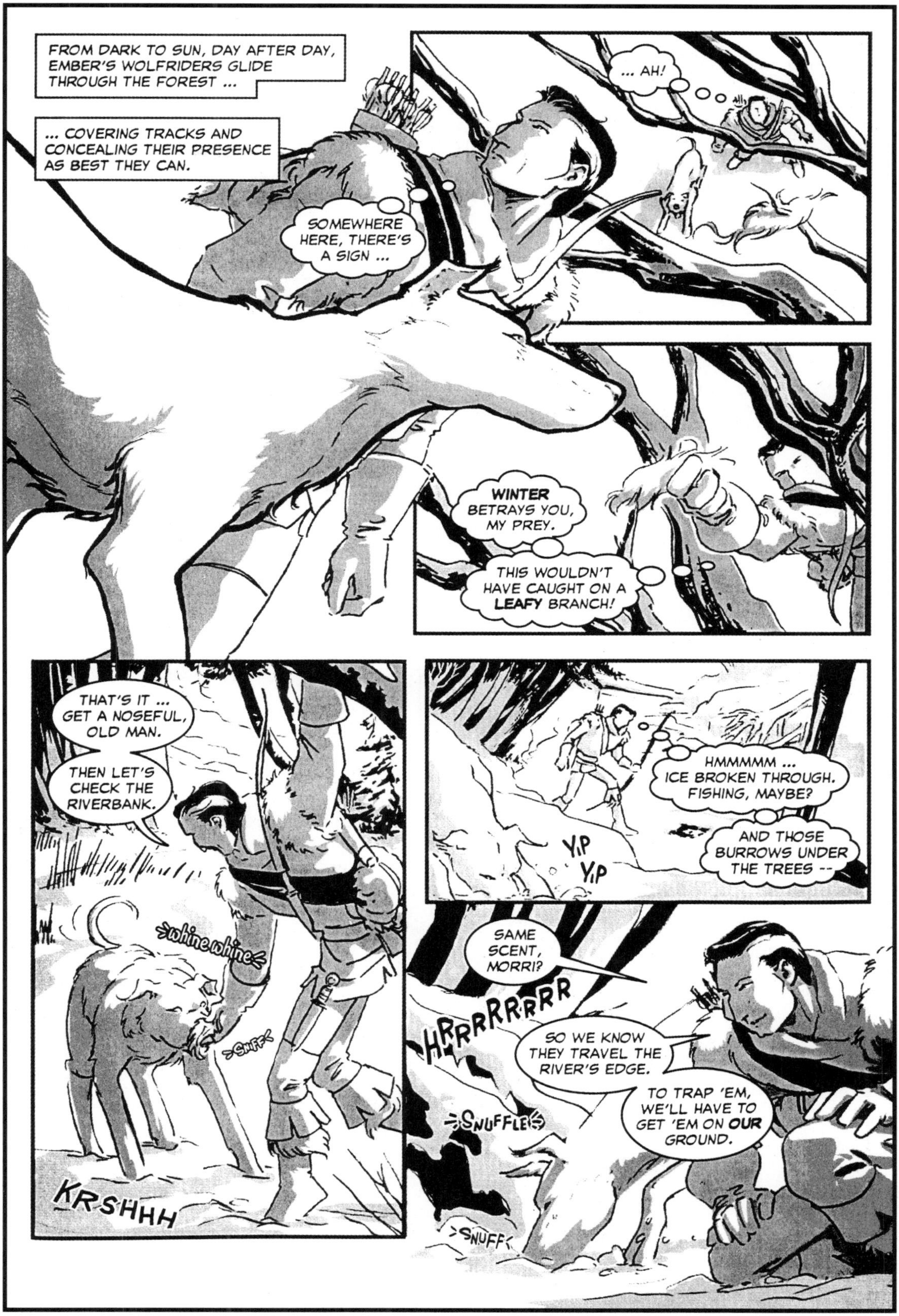

FROM DARK TO SUN, DAY AFTER DAY, EMBER'S WOLFRIDERS GLIDE THROUGH THE FOREST ...
... COVERING TRACKS AND CONCEALING THEIR PRESENCE AS BEST THEY CAN.
... AH!
SOMEWHERE HERE, THERE'S A SIGN ...
WINTER BETRAYS YOU, MY PREY.
THIS WOULDN'T HAVE CAUGHT ON A **LEAFY** BRANCH!
THAT'S IT ... GET A NOSEFUL, OLD MAN.
THEN LET'S CHECK THE RIVERBANK.
whine whine
SNIFF
KRSHHH
HMMMMM ... ICE BROKEN THROUGH. FISHING, MAYBE?
AND THOSE BURROWS UNDER THE TREES --
YIP
YIP
SAME SCENT, MORRI?
HRRRRRRRR
SO WE KNOW THEY TRAVEL THE RIVER'S EDGE.
TO TRAP 'EM, WE'LL HAVE TO GET 'EM ON **OUR** GROUND.
SNUFFLE
SNUFF

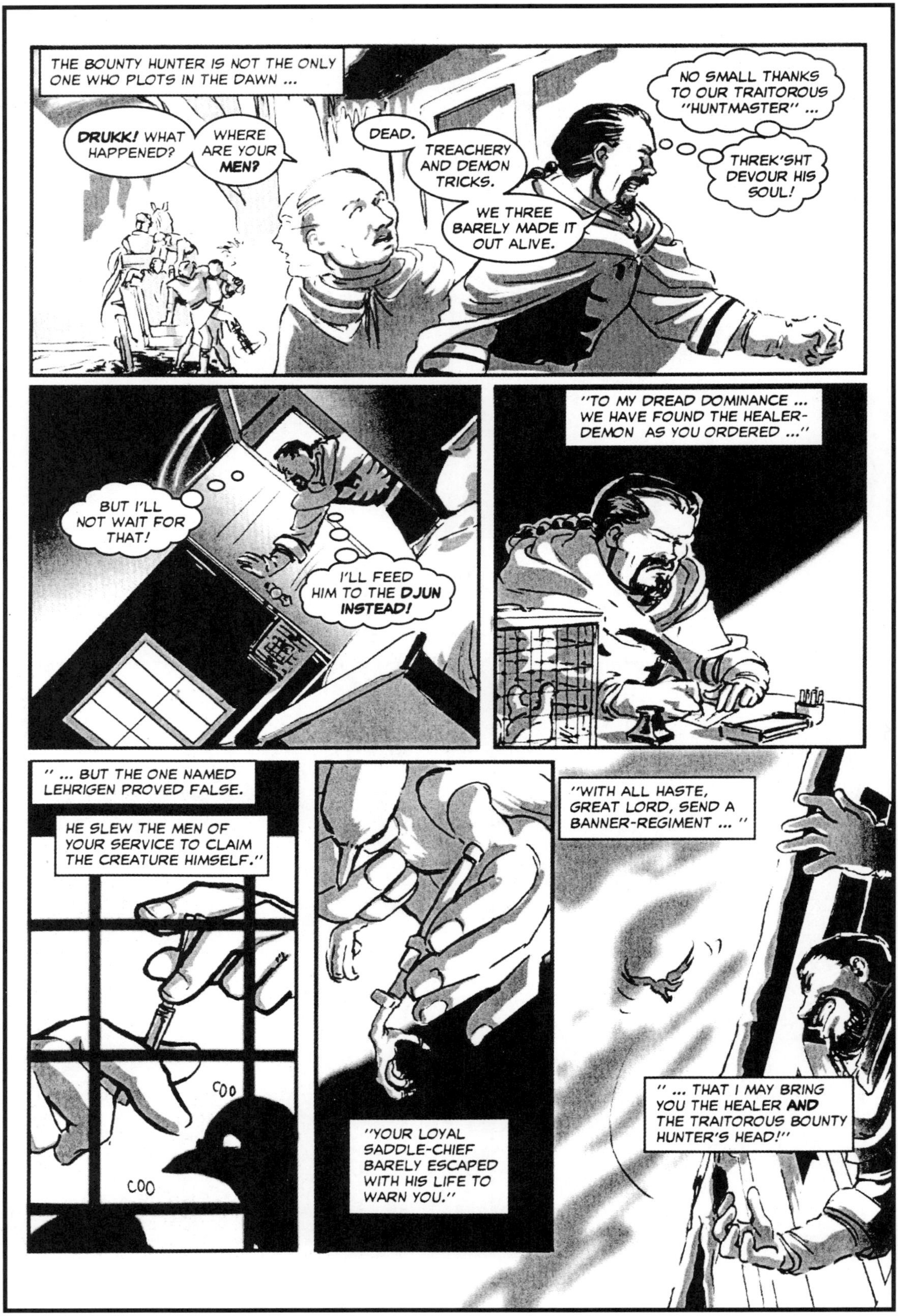
THE BOUNTY HUNTER IS NOT THE ONLY ONE WHO PLOTS IN THE DAWN ...
DRUKK! WHAT HAPPENED?
WHERE ARE YOUR **MEN?**
DEAD.
TREACHERY AND DEMON TRICKS.
WE THREE BARELY MADE IT OUT ALIVE.
NO SMALL THANKS TO OUR TRAITOROUS "HUNTMASTER" ...
THREK'SHT DEVOUR HIS SOUL!
BUT I'LL NOT WAIT FOR THAT!
I'LL FEED HIM TO THE **DJUN** **INSTEAD!**
"TO MY DREAD DOMINANCE ... WE HAVE FOUND THE HEALER-DEMON AS YOU ORDERED ..."
" ... BUT THE ONE NAMED LEHRIGEN PROVED FALSE.
HE SLEW THE MEN OF YOUR SERVICE TO CLAIM THE CREATURE HIMSELF."
COO
COO
"YOUR LOYAL SADDLE-CHIEF BARELY ESCAPED WITH HIS LIFE TO WARN YOU."
"WITH ALL HASTE, GREAT LORD, SEND A BANNER-REGIMENT ... "
" ... THAT I MAY BRING YOU THE HEALER **AND** THE TRAITOROUS BOUNTY HUNTER'S HEAD!"

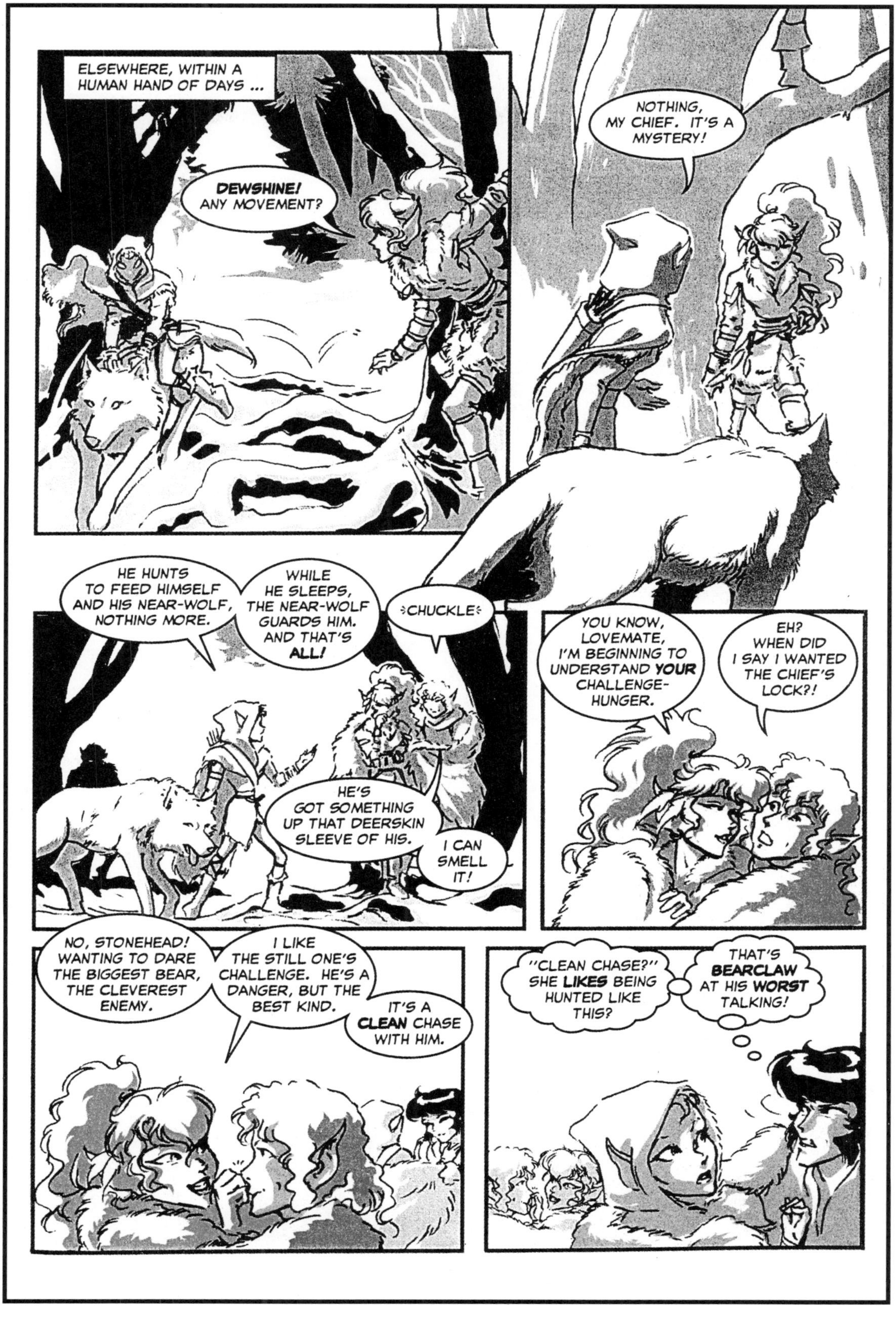
ELSEWHERE, WITHIN A HUMAN HAND OF DAYS ...
DEWSHINE! ANY MOVEMENT?
NOTHING, MY CHIEF. IT'S A MYSTERY!
HE HUNTS TO FEED HIMSELF AND HIS NEAR-WOLF, NOTHING MORE.
WHILE HE SLEEPS, THE NEAR-WOLF GUARDS HIM. AND THAT'S ALL!
CHUCKLE
HE'S GOT SOMETHING UP THAT DEERSKIN SLEEVE OF HIS.
I CAN SMELL IT!
YOU KNOW, LOVEMATE, I'M BEGINNING TO UNDERSTAND YOUR CHALLENGE-HUNGER.
EH? WHEN DID I SAY I WANTED THE CHIEF'S LOCK?!
NO, STONEHEAD! WANTING TO DARE THE BIGGEST BEAR, THE CLEVEREST ENEMY.
I LIKE THE STILL ONE'S CHALLENGE. HE'S A DANGER, BUT THE BEST KIND.
IT'S A CLEAN CHASE WITH HIM.
"CLEAN CHASE?" SHE LIKES BEING HUNTED LIKE THIS?
THAT'S BEARCLAW AT HIS WORST TALKING!

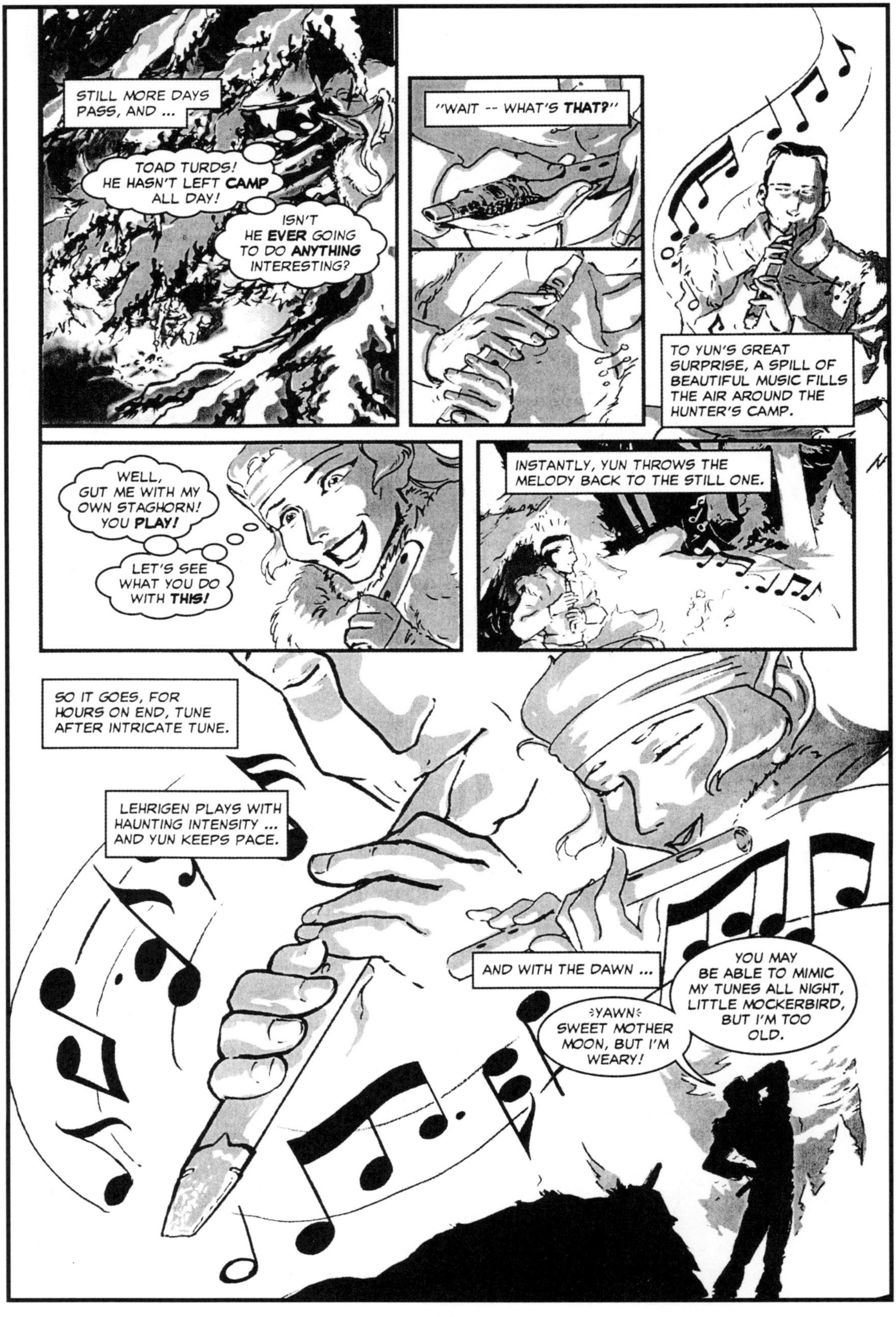
STILL MORE DAYS PASS, AND ...
TOAD TURDS! HE HASN'T LEFT **CAMP** ALL DAY!
ISN'T HE **EVER** GOING TO DO **ANYTHING** INTERESTING?
"WAIT -- WHAT'S **THAT?**"
TO YUN'S GREAT SURPRISE, A SPILL OF BEAUTIFUL MUSIC FILLS THE AIR AROUND THE HUNTER'S CAMP.
WELL, GUT ME WITH MY OWN STAGHORN! YOU **PLAY!**
LET'S SEE WHAT YOU DO WITH **THIS!**
INSTANTLY, YUN THROWS THE MELODY BACK TO THE STILL ONE.
SO IT GOES, FOR HOURS ON END, TUNE AFTER INTRICATE TUNE.
LEHRIGEN PLAYS WITH HAUNTING INTENSITY ... AND YUN KEEPS PACE.
AND WITH THE DAWN ...
YOU MAY BE ABLE TO MIMIC MY TUNES ALL NIGHT, LITTLE MOCKERBIRD, BUT I'M TOO OLD.
YAWN SWEET MOTHER MOON, BUT I'M WEARY!

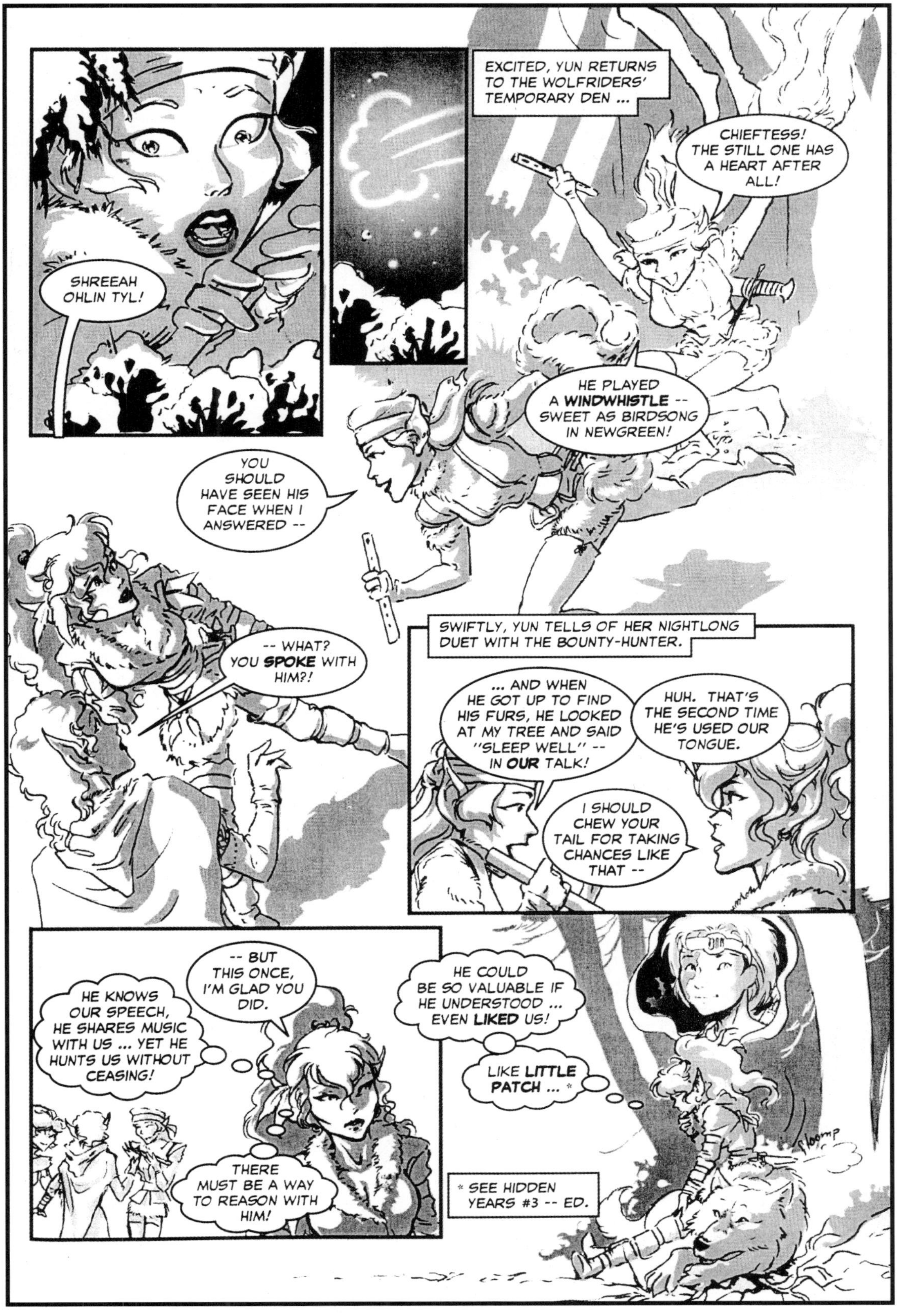
SHREEAH OHLIN TYL!
EXCITED, YUN RETURNS TO THE WOLFRIDERS' TEMPORARY DEN ...
CHIEFTESS! THE STILL ONE HAS A HEART AFTER ALL!
HE PLAYED A WINDWHISTLE -- SWEET AS BIRDSONG IN NEWGREEN!
YOU SHOULD HAVE SEEN HIS FACE WHEN I ANSWERED --
-- WHAT? YOU SPOKE WITH HIM?!
SWIFTLY, YUN TELLS OF HER NIGHTLONG DUET WITH THE BOUNTY-HUNTER.
... AND WHEN HE GOT UP TO FIND HIS FURS, HE LOOKED AT MY TREE AND SAID "SLEEP WELL" -- IN OUR TALK!
HUH. THAT'S THE SECOND TIME HE'S USED OUR TONGUE.
I SHOULD CHEW YOUR TAIL FOR TAKING CHANCES LIKE THAT --
-- BUT THIS ONCE, I'M GLAD YOU DID.
HE KNOWS OUR SPEECH, HE SHARES MUSIC WITH US ... YET HE HUNTS US WITHOUT CEASING!
THERE MUST BE A WAY TO REASON WITH HIM!
HE COULD BE SO VALUABLE IF HE UNDERSTOOD ... EVEN LIKED US!
LIKE LITTLE PATCH ... *
FLOOMP
* SEE HIDDEN YEARS #3 -- ED.

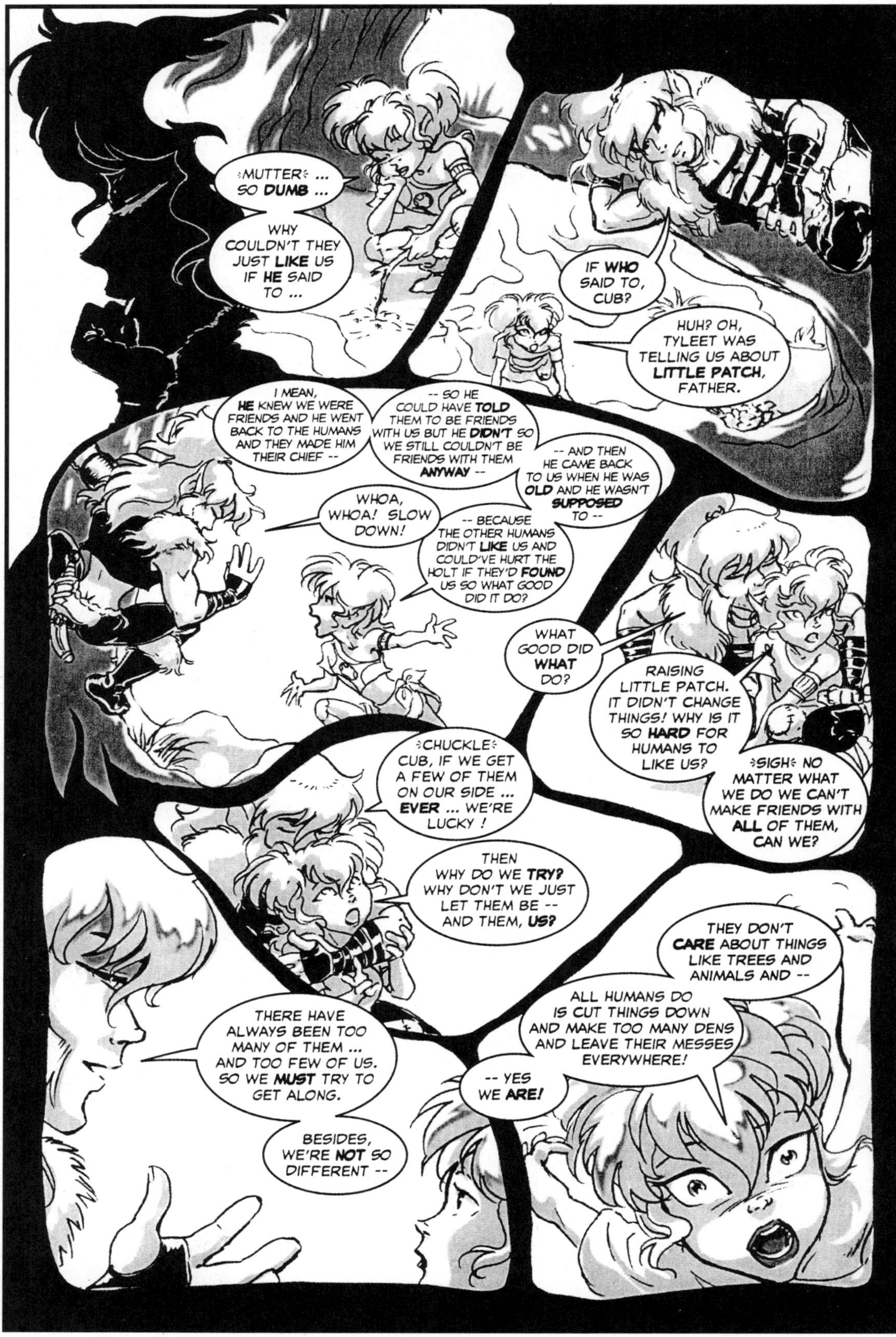

∻MUTTER∻ ... SO DUMB ...
WHY COULDN'T THEY JUST LIKE US IF HE SAID TO ...
IF WHO SAID TO, CUB?
HUH? OH, TYLEET WAS TELLING US ABOUT LITTLE PATCH, FATHER.
I MEAN, HE KNEW WE WERE FRIENDS AND HE WENT BACK TO THE HUMANS AND THEY MADE HIM THEIR CHIEF --
-- SO HE COULD HAVE TOLD THEM TO BE FRIENDS WITH US BUT HE DIDN'T SO WE STILL COULDN'T BE FRIENDS WITH THEM ANYWAY --
-- AND THEN HE CAME BACK TO US WHEN HE WAS OLD AND HE WASN'T SUPPOSED TO --
WHOA, WHOA! SLOW DOWN!
-- BECAUSE THE OTHER HUMANS DIDN'T LIKE US AND COULD'VE HURT THE HOLT IF THEY'D FOUND US SO WHAT GOOD DID IT DO?
WHAT GOOD DID WHAT DO?
RAISING LITTLE PATCH. IT DIDN'T CHANGE THINGS! WHY IS IT SO HARD FOR HUMANS TO LIKE US?
∻SIGH∻ NO MATTER WHAT WE DO WE CAN'T MAKE FRIENDS WITH ALL OF THEM, CAN WE?
∻CHUCKLE∻ CUB, IF WE GET A FEW OF THEM ON OUR SIDE ... EVER ... WE'RE LUCKY !
THEN WHY DO WE TRY? WHY DON'T WE JUST LET THEM BE -- AND THEM, US?
THERE HAVE ALWAYS BEEN TOO MANY OF THEM ... AND TOO FEW OF US. SO WE MUST TRY TO GET ALONG.
BESIDES, WE'RE NOT SO DIFFERENT --
THEY DON'T CARE ABOUT THINGS LIKE TREES AND ANIMALS AND --
ALL HUMANS DO IS CUT THINGS DOWN AND MAKE TOO MANY DENS AND LEAVE THEIR MESSES EVERYWHERE!
-- YES WE ARE!

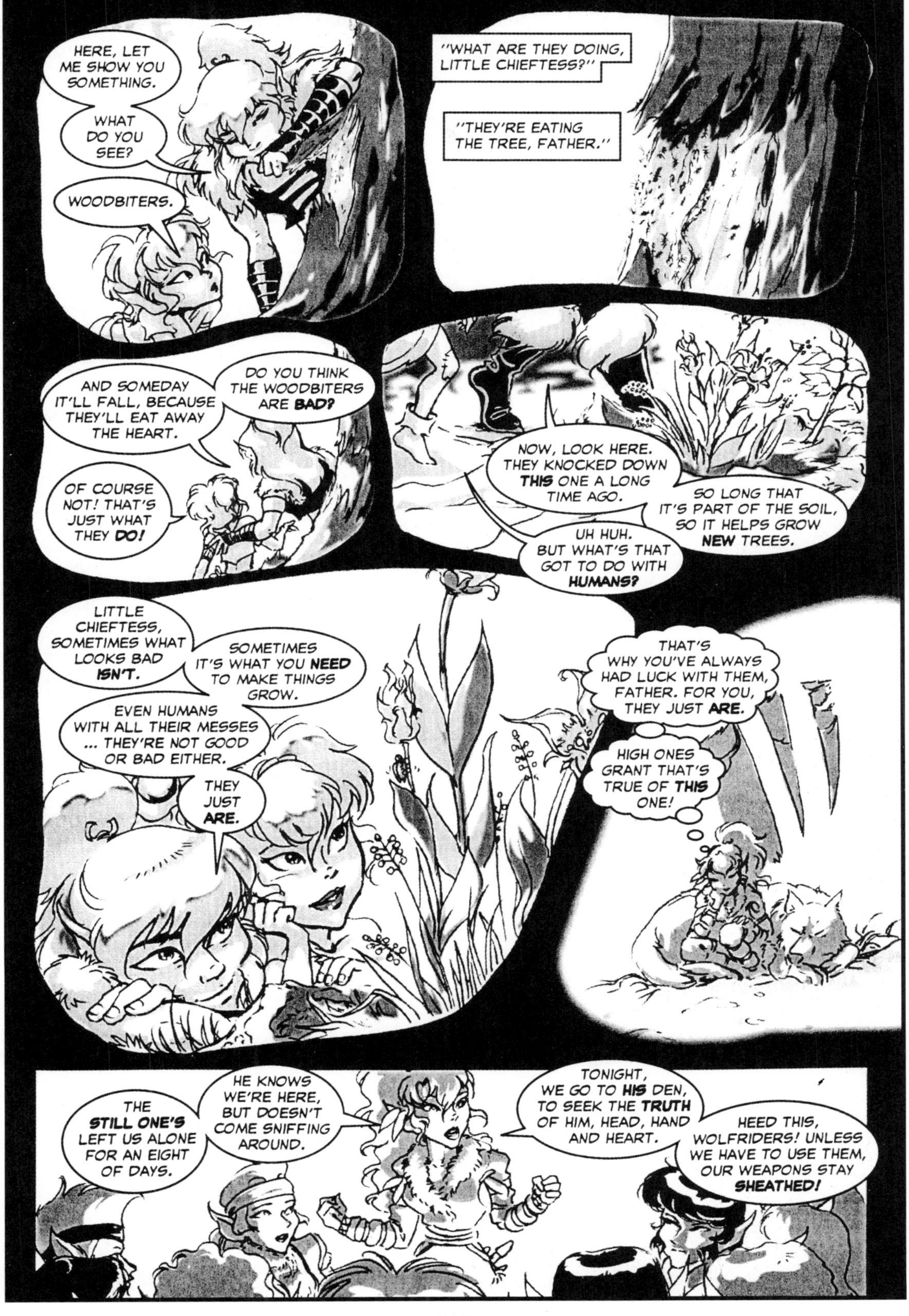
HERE, LET ME SHOW YOU SOMETHING.
WHAT DO YOU SEE?
WOODBITERS.
"WHAT ARE THEY DOING, LITTLE CHIEFTESS?"
"THEY'RE EATING THE TREE, FATHER."
AND SOMEDAY IT'LL FALL, BECAUSE THEY'LL EAT AWAY THE HEART.
DO YOU THINK THE WOODBITERS ARE BAD?
OF COURSE NOT! THAT'S JUST WHAT THEY DO!
NOW, LOOK HERE. THEY KNOCKED DOWN THIS ONE A LONG TIME AGO.
SO LONG THAT IT'S PART OF THE SOIL, SO IT HELPS GROW NEW TREES.
UH HUH. BUT WHAT'S THAT GOT TO DO WITH HUMANS?
LITTLE CHIEFTESS, SOMETIMES WHAT LOOKS BAD ISN'T.
SOMETIMES IT'S WHAT YOU NEED TO MAKE THINGS GROW.
EVEN HUMANS WITH ALL THEIR MESSES ... THEY'RE NOT GOOD OR BAD EITHER.
THEY JUST ARE.
THAT'S WHY YOU'VE ALWAYS HAD LUCK WITH THEM, FATHER. FOR YOU, THEY JUST ARE.
HIGH ONES GRANT THAT'S TRUE OF THIS ONE!
THE STILL ONE'S LEFT US ALONE FOR AN EIGHT OF DAYS.
HE KNOWS WE'RE HERE, BUT DOESN'T COME SNIFFING AROUND.
TONIGHT, WE GO TO HIS DEN, TO SEEK THE TRUTH OF HIM, HEAD, HAND AND HEART.
HEED THIS, WOLFRIDERS! UNLESS WE HAVE TO USE THEM, OUR WEAPONS STAY SHEATHED!

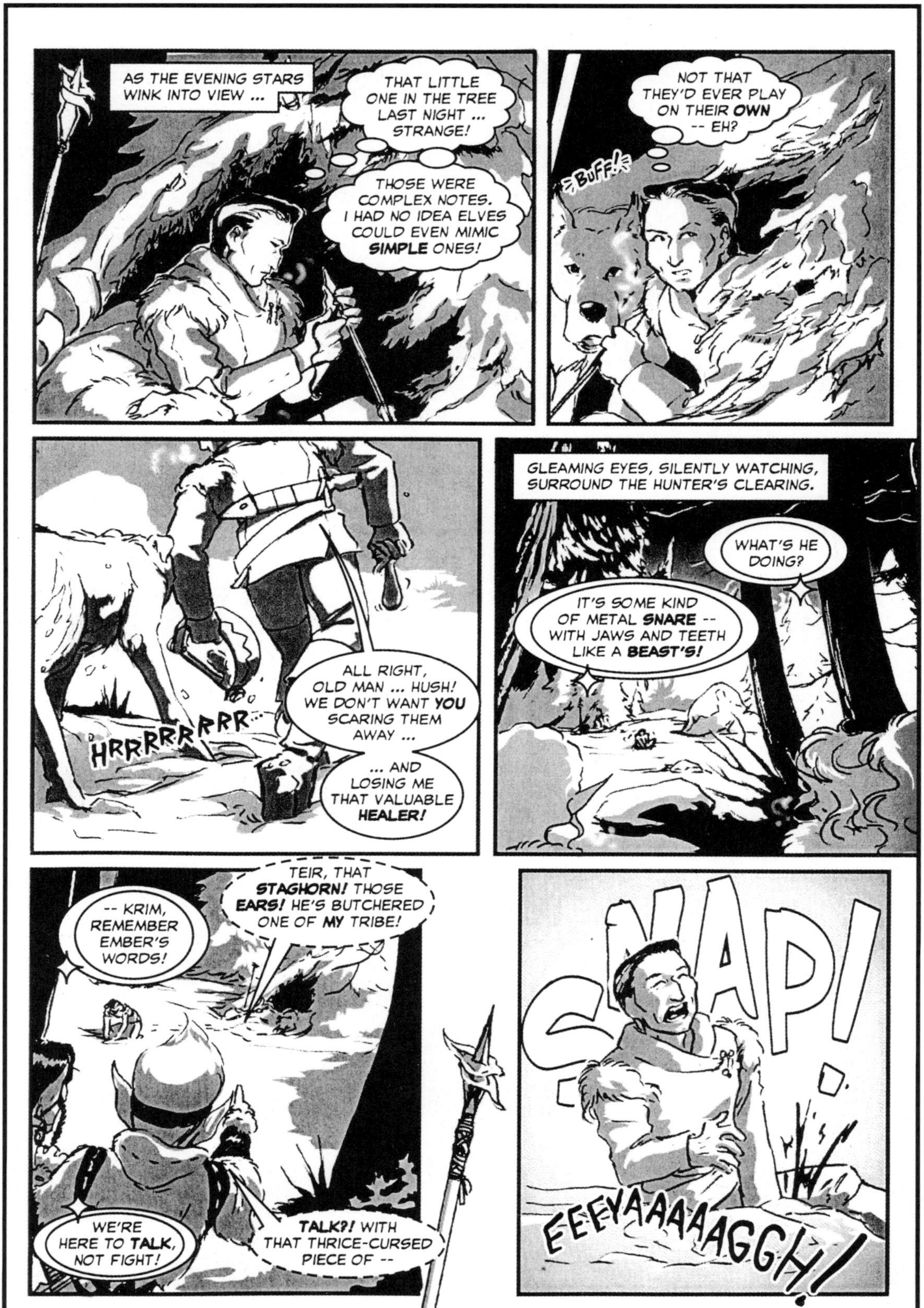

AS THE EVENING STARS WINK INTO VIEW ...
THAT LITTLE ONE IN THE TREE LAST NIGHT ... STRANGE!
THOSE WERE COMPLEX NOTES. I HAD NO IDEA ELVES COULD EVEN MIMIC **SIMPLE** ONES!
NOT THAT THEY'D EVER PLAY ON THEIR **OWN** -- EH?
BUFF!
HRRRRRRRR...
ALL RIGHT, OLD MAN ... HUSH! WE DON'T WANT **YOU** SCARING THEM AWAY ...
... AND LOSING ME THAT VALUABLE **HEALER!**
GLEAMING EYES, SILENTLY WATCHING, SURROUND THE HUNTER'S CLEARING.
WHAT'S HE DOING?
IT'S SOME KIND OF METAL **SNARE** -- WITH JAWS AND TEETH LIKE A **BEAST'S!**
-- KRIM, REMEMBER EMBER'S WORDS!
TEIR, THAT **STAGHORN!** THOSE **EARS!** HE'S BUTCHERED ONE OF **MY** TRIBE!
WE'RE HERE TO **TALK**, NOT FIGHT!
TALK?! WITH THAT THRICE-CURSED PIECE OF --
SNAP!
EEEYAAAAAGGH!

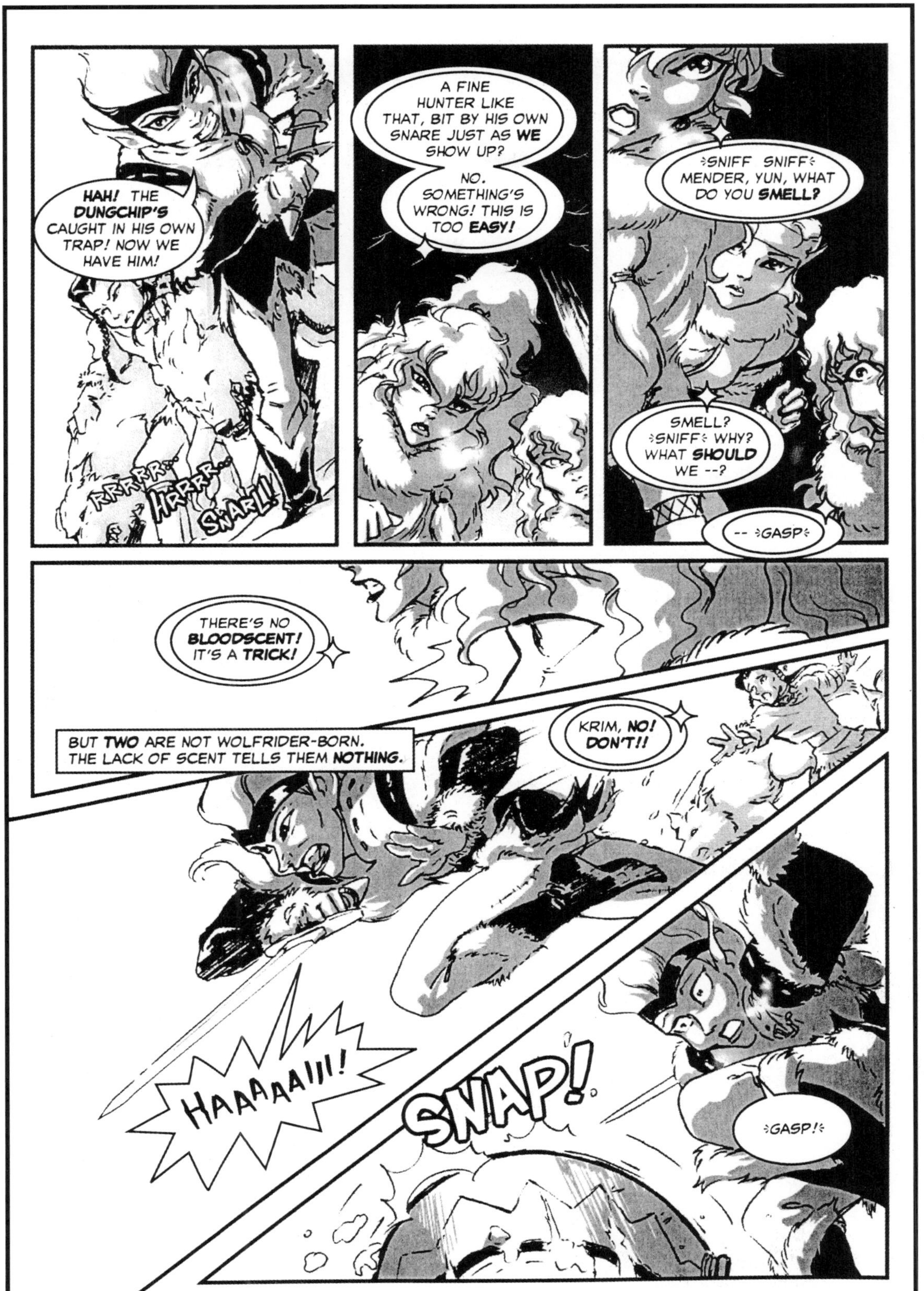
HAH! THE DUNGCHIP'S CAUGHT IN HIS OWN TRAP! NOW WE HAVE HIM!
RRRRR.. HRRRR... SNARL!
A FINE HUNTER LIKE THAT, BIT BY HIS OWN SNARE JUST AS WE SHOW UP?
NO. SOMETHING'S WRONG! THIS IS TOO EASY!
SNIFF SNIFF MENDER, YUN, WHAT DO YOU SMELL?
SMELL? SNIFF WHY? WHAT SHOULD WE --?
-- GASP
THERE'S NO BLOODSCENT! IT'S A TRICK!
BUT TWO ARE NOT WOLFRIDER-BORN. THE LACK OF SCENT TELLS THEM NOTHING.
KRIM, NO! DON'T!!
HAAAAIII!
SNAP!
GASP!

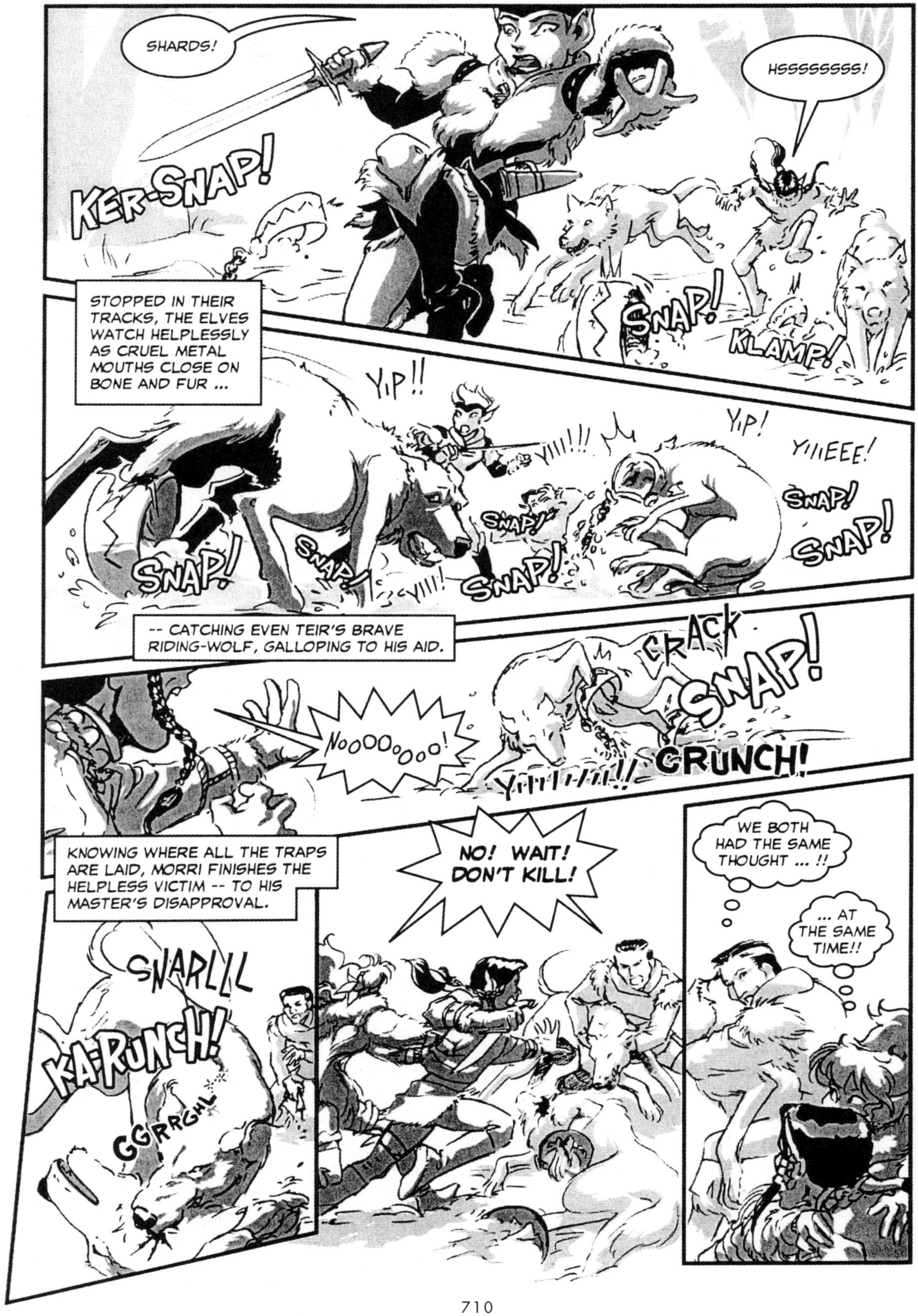
SHARDS!
HSSSSSSSS!
KER-SNAP!
SNAP!
KLAMP!
STOPPED IN THEIR TRACKS, THE ELVES WATCH HELPLESSLY AS CRUEL METAL MOUTHS CLOSE ON BONE AND FUR ...
YIP!!
YIP!
YIIIEEE!
SNAP!
SNAP!
SNAP!
SNAP!
SNAP!
SNAP!
SNAP!
-- CATCHING EVEN TEIR'S BRAVE RIDING-WOLF, GALLOPING TO HIS AID.
CRACK
SNAP!
NOOOOOOOO!
CRUNCH!
KNOWING WHERE ALL THE TRAPS ARE LAID, MORRI FINISHES THE HELPLESS VICTIM -- TO HIS MASTER'S DISAPPROVAL.
NO! WAIT! DON'T KILL!
WE BOTH HAD THE SAME THOUGHT ... !!
... AT THE SAME TIME!!
SNARLLL
KA-RUNCH!
GGRRRGHL

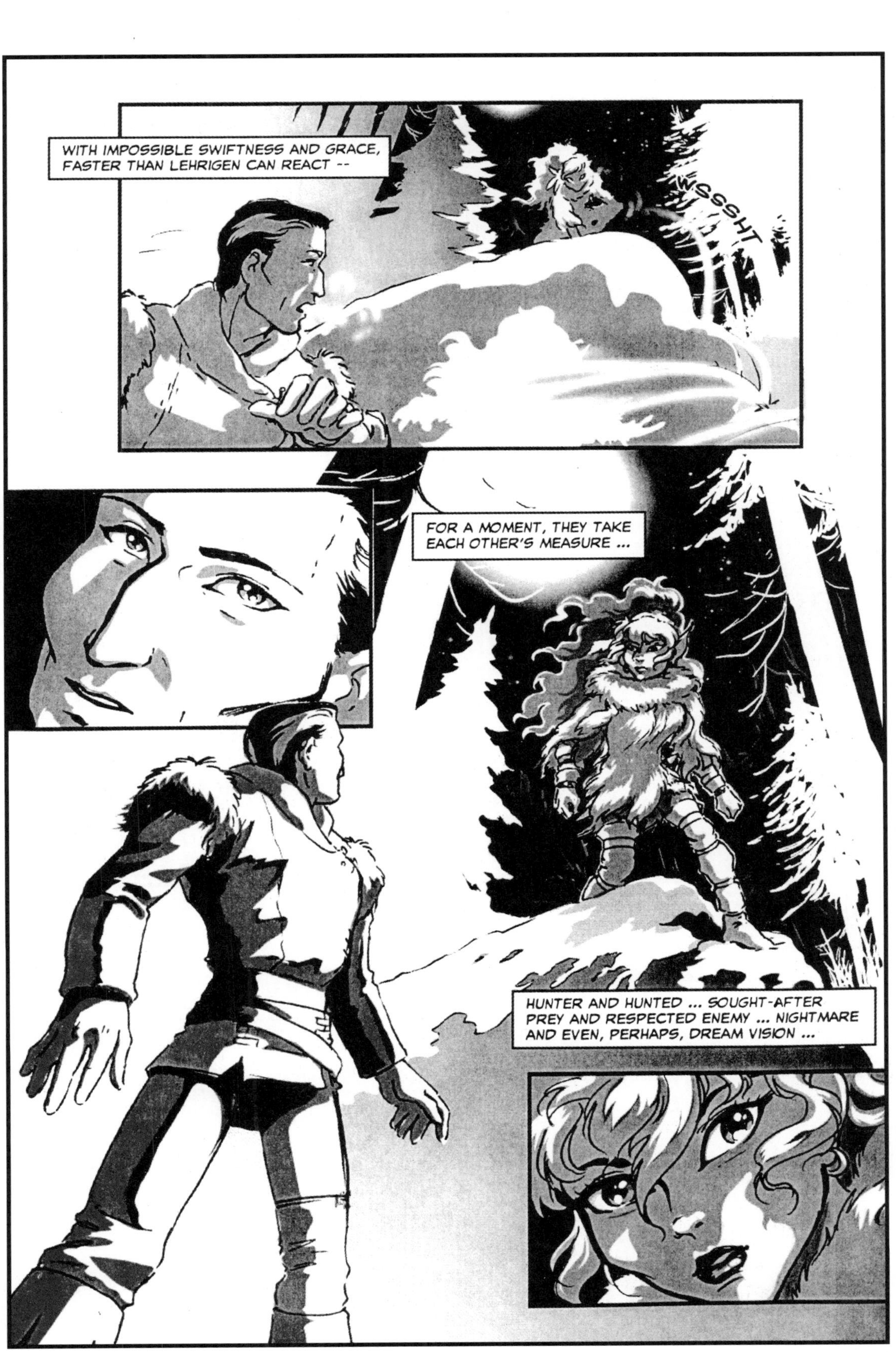
WITH IMPOSSIBLE SWIFTNESS AND GRACE, FASTER THAN LEHRIGEN CAN REACT --
WSSSHT
FOR A MOMENT, THEY TAKE EACH OTHER'S MEASURE ...
HUNTER AND HUNTED ... SOUGHT-AFTER PREY AND RESPECTED ENEMY ... NIGHTMARE AND EVEN, PERHAPS, DREAM VISION ...

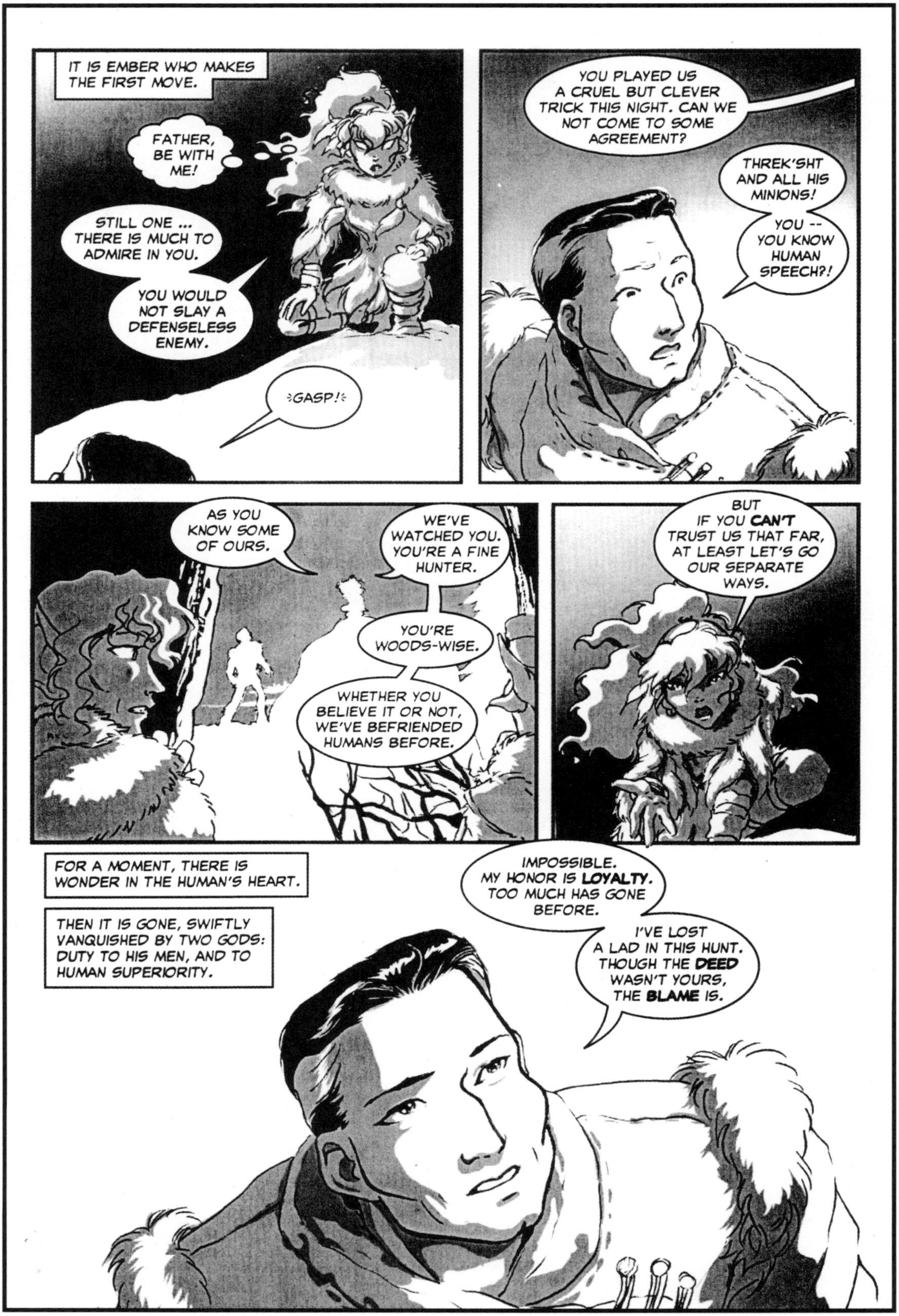
IT IS EMBER WHO MAKES THE FIRST MOVE.
FATHER, BE WITH ME!
STILL ONE ... THERE IS MUCH TO ADMIRE IN YOU.
YOU WOULD NOT SLAY A DEFENSELESS ENEMY.
GASP!
YOU PLAYED US A CRUEL BUT CLEVER TRICK THIS NIGHT. CAN WE NOT COME TO SOME AGREEMENT?
THREK'SHT AND ALL HIS MINIONS!
YOU -- YOU KNOW HUMAN SPEECH?!
AS YOU KNOW SOME OF OURS.
WE'VE WATCHED YOU. YOU'RE A FINE HUNTER.
YOU'RE WOODS-WISE.
WHETHER YOU BELIEVE IT OR NOT, WE'VE BEFRIENDED HUMANS BEFORE.
BUT IF YOU CAN'T TRUST US THAT FAR, AT LEAST LET'S GO OUR SEPARATE WAYS.
FOR A MOMENT, THERE IS WONDER IN THE HUMAN'S HEART.
THEN IT IS GONE, SWIFTLY VANQUISHED BY TWO GODS: DUTY TO HIS MEN, AND TO HUMAN SUPERIORITY.
IMPOSSIBLE. MY HONOR IS LOYALTY. TOO MUCH HAS GONE BEFORE.
I'VE LOST A LAD IN THIS HUNT. THOUGH THE DEED WASN'T YOURS, THE BLAME IS.

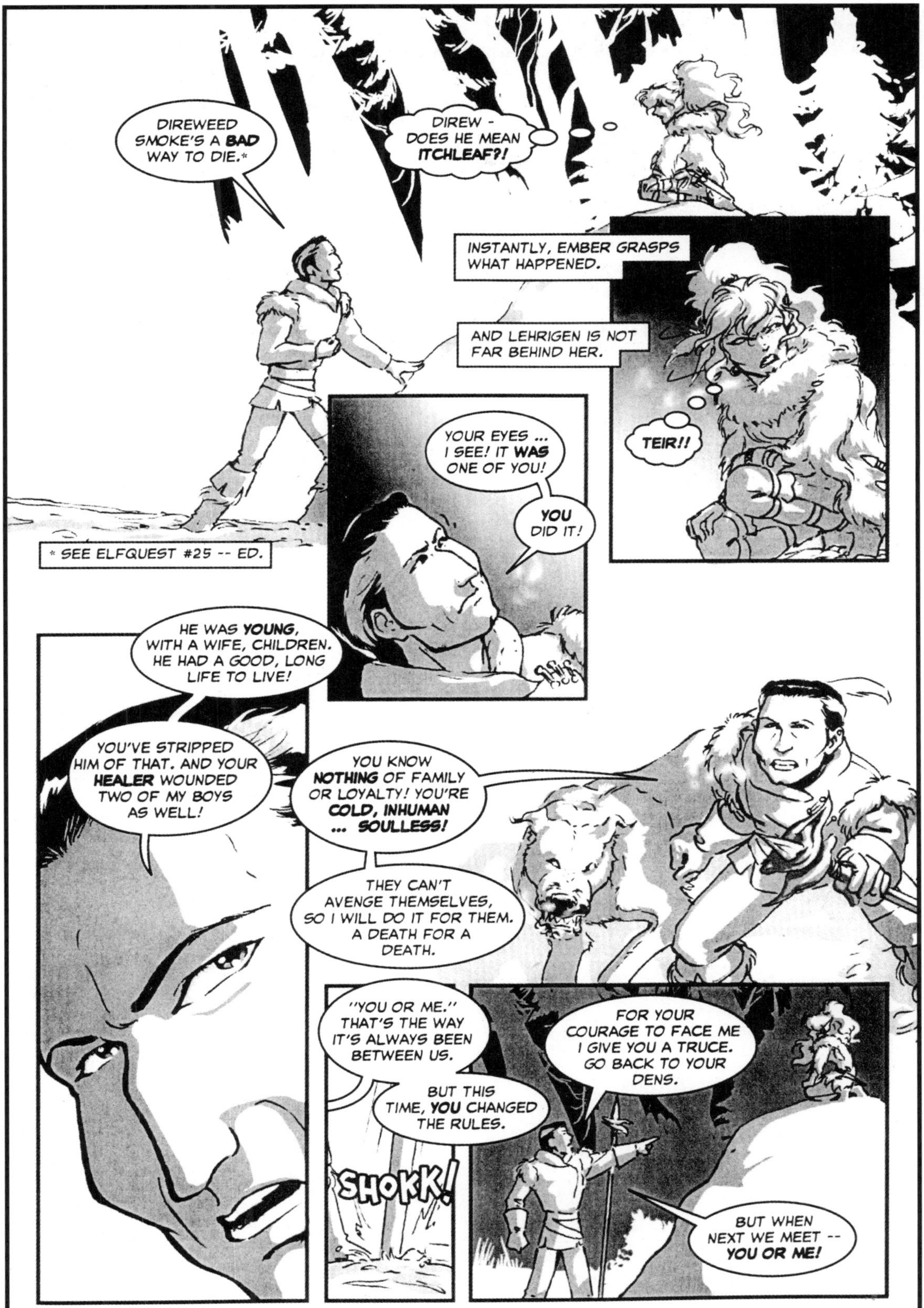
DIREWEED SMOKE'S A BAD WAY TO DIE.*
DIREW - DOES HE MEAN ITCHLEAF?!
INSTANTLY, EMBER GRASPS WHAT HAPPENED.
AND LEHRIGEN IS NOT FAR BEHIND HER.
TEIR!!
YOUR EYES ... I SEE! IT WAS ONE OF YOU!
YOU DID IT!
* SEE ELFQUEST #25 -- ED.
HE WAS YOUNG, WITH A WIFE, CHILDREN. HE HAD A GOOD, LONG LIFE TO LIVE!
YOU'VE STRIPPED HIM OF THAT. AND YOUR HEALER WOUNDED TWO OF MY BOYS AS WELL!
YOU KNOW NOTHING OF FAMILY OR LOYALTY! YOU'RE COLD, INHUMAN ... SOULLESS!
THEY CAN'T AVENGE THEMSELVES, SO I WILL DO IT FOR THEM. A DEATH FOR A DEATH.
"YOU OR ME." THAT'S THE WAY IT'S ALWAYS BEEN BETWEEN US.
BUT THIS TIME, YOU CHANGED THE RULES.
SHOKK!
FOR YOUR COURAGE TO FACE ME I GIVE YOU A TRUCE. GO BACK TO YOUR DENS.
BUT WHEN NEXT WE MEET -- YOU OR ME!

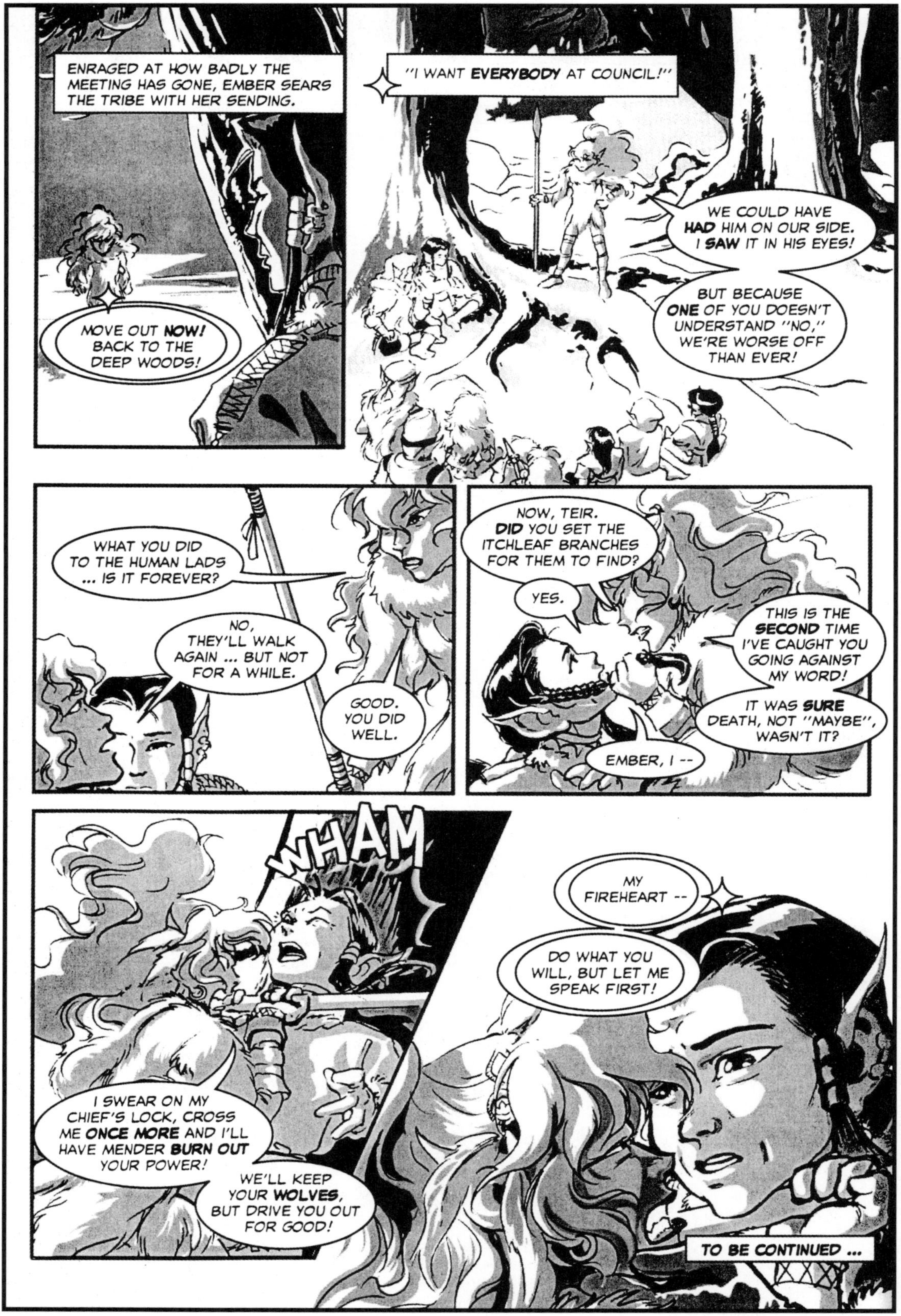
ENRAGED AT HOW BADLY THE MEETING HAS GONE, EMBER SEARS THE TRIBE WITH HER SENDING.
MOVE OUT **NOW!** BACK TO THE DEEP WOODS!
"I WANT **EVERYBODY** AT COUNCIL!"
WE COULD HAVE **HAD** HIM ON OUR SIDE. I **SAW** IT IN HIS EYES!
BUT BECAUSE **ONE** OF YOU DOESN'T UNDERSTAND "NO," WE'RE WORSE OFF THAN EVER!
WHAT YOU DID TO THE HUMAN LADS ... IS IT FOREVER?
NO, THEY'LL WALK AGAIN ... BUT NOT FOR A WHILE.
GOOD. YOU DID WELL.
NOW, TEIR. **DID** YOU SET THE ITCHLEAF BRANCHES FOR THEM TO FIND?
YES.
THIS IS THE **SECOND** TIME I'VE CAUGHT YOU GOING AGAINST MY WORD!
IT WAS **SURE** DEATH, NOT "MAYBE", WASN'T IT?
EMBER, I --
WHAM
I SWEAR ON MY CHIEF'S LOCK, CROSS ME **ONCE MORE** AND I'LL HAVE MENDER **BURN OUT** YOUR POWER!
WE'LL KEEP YOUR **WOLVES**, BUT DRIVE YOU OUT FOR GOOD!
MY FIREHEART --
DO WHAT YOU WILL, BUT LET ME SPEAK FIRST!
TO BE CONTINUED ...

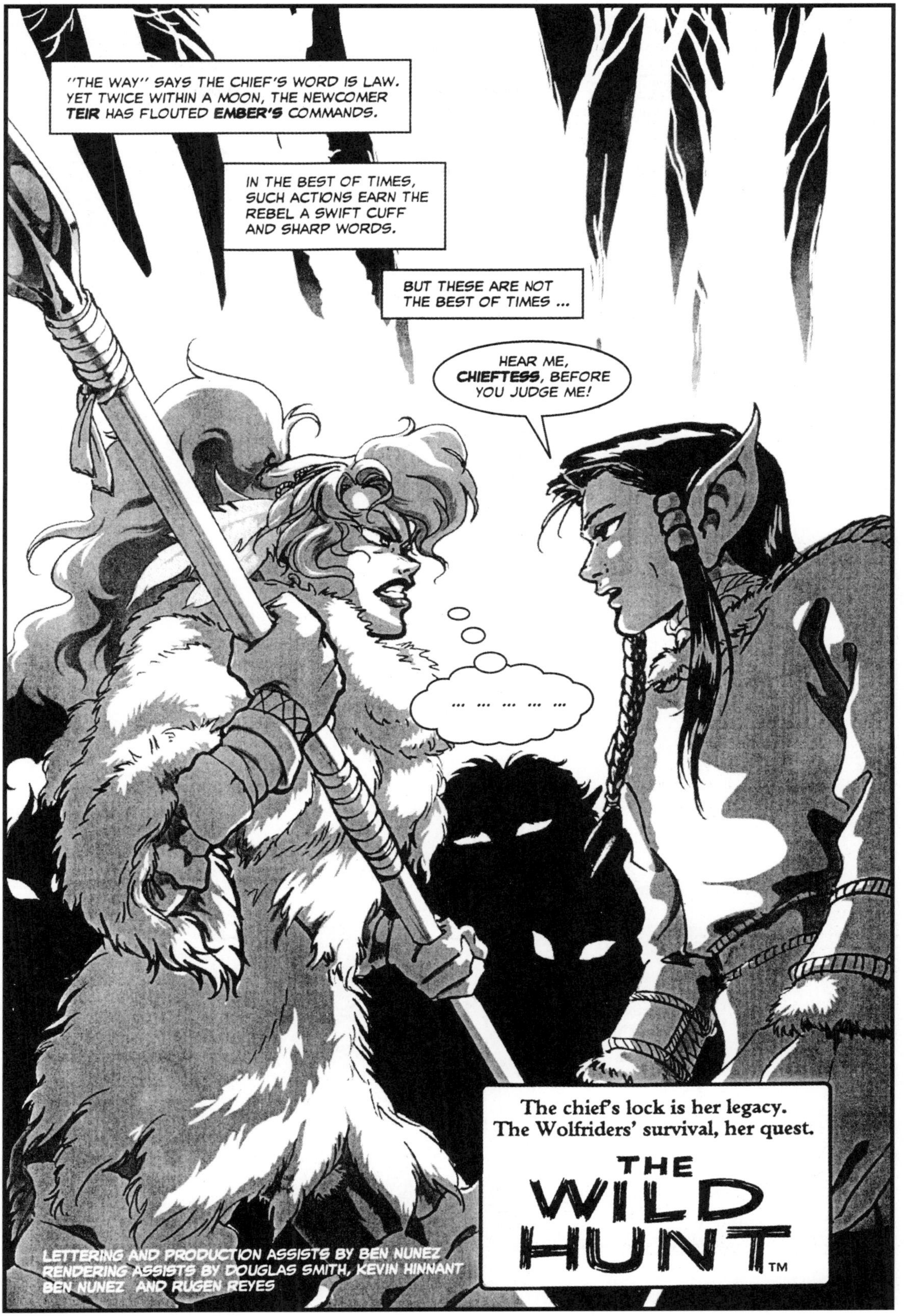
"THE WAY" SAYS THE CHIEF'S WORD IS LAW. YET TWICE WITHIN A MOON, THE NEWCOMER TEIR HAS FLOUTED EMBER'S COMMANDS.
IN THE BEST OF TIMES, SUCH ACTIONS EARN THE REBEL A SWIFT CUFF AND SHARP WORDS.
BUT THESE ARE NOT THE BEST OF TIMES ...
HEAR ME, CHIEFTESS, BEFORE YOU JUDGE ME!
... ...
The chief's lock is her legacy. The Wolfriders' survival, her quest.
THE WILD HUNT™
LETTERING AND PRODUCTION ASSISTS BY BEN NUNEZ
RENDERING ASSISTS BY DOUGLAS SMITH, KEVIN HINNANT BEN NUNEZ AND RUGEN REYES

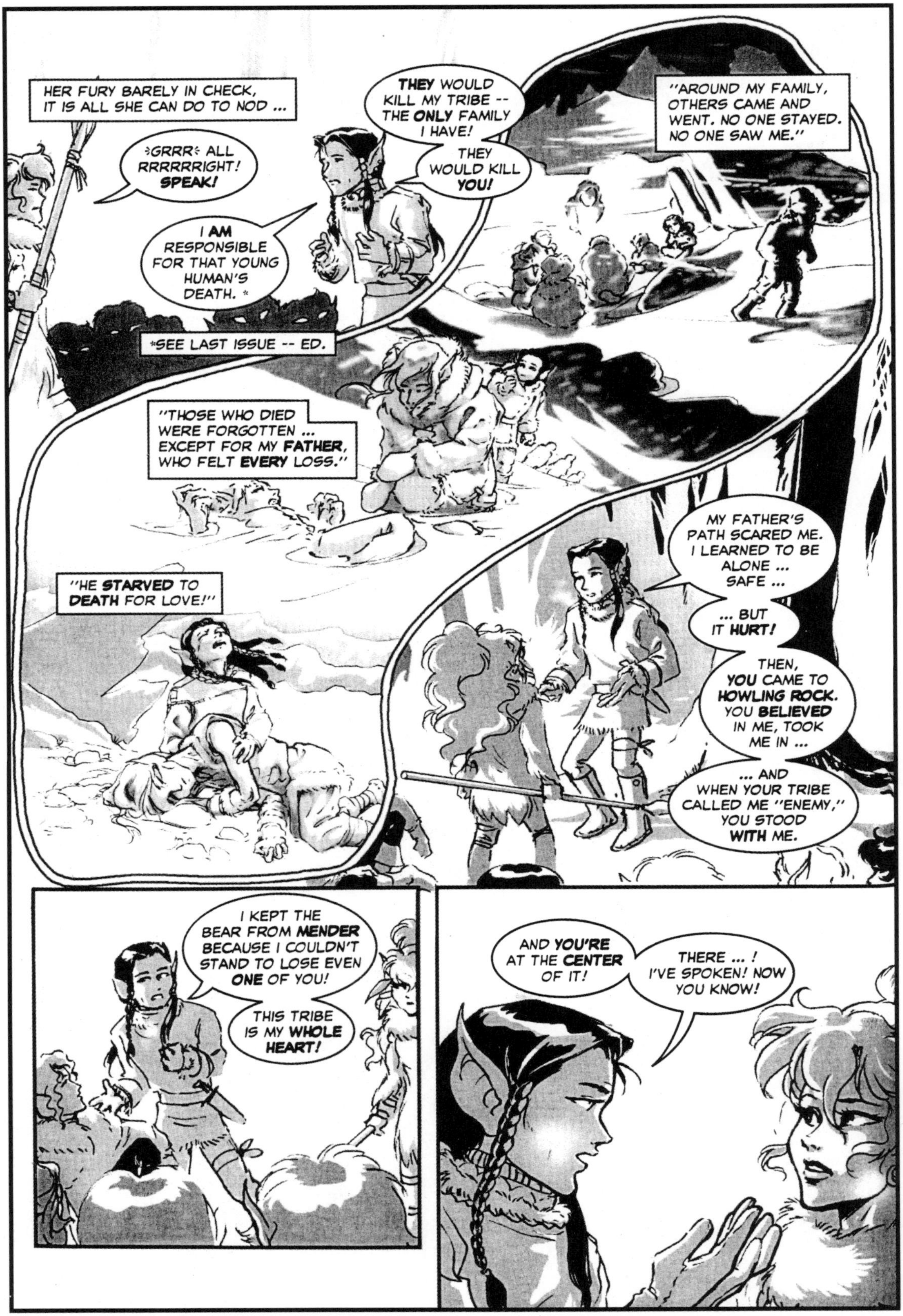

HER FURY BARELY IN CHECK, IT IS ALL SHE CAN DO TO NOD ...
⊰GRRR⊱ ALL RRRRRRIGHT! SPEAK!
I AM RESPONSIBLE FOR THAT YOUNG HUMAN'S DEATH. *
*SEE LAST ISSUE -- ED.
THEY WOULD KILL MY TRIBE -- THE ONLY FAMILY I HAVE!
THEY WOULD KILL YOU!
"AROUND MY FAMILY, OTHERS CAME AND WENT. NO ONE STAYED. NO ONE SAW ME."
"THOSE WHO DIED WERE FORGOTTEN ... EXCEPT FOR MY FATHER, WHO FELT EVERY LOSS."
"HE STARVED TO DEATH FOR LOVE!"
MY FATHER'S PATH SCARED ME. I LEARNED TO BE ALONE ... SAFE ...
... BUT IT HURT!
THEN, YOU CAME TO HOWLING ROCK. YOU BELIEVED IN ME, TOOK ME IN ...
... AND WHEN YOUR TRIBE CALLED ME "ENEMY," YOU STOOD WITH ME.
I KEPT THE BEAR FROM MENDER BECAUSE I COULDN'T STAND TO LOSE EVEN ONE OF YOU!
THIS TRIBE IS MY WHOLE HEART!
AND YOU'RE AT THE CENTER OF IT!
THERE ... ! I'VE SPOKEN! NOW YOU KNOW!

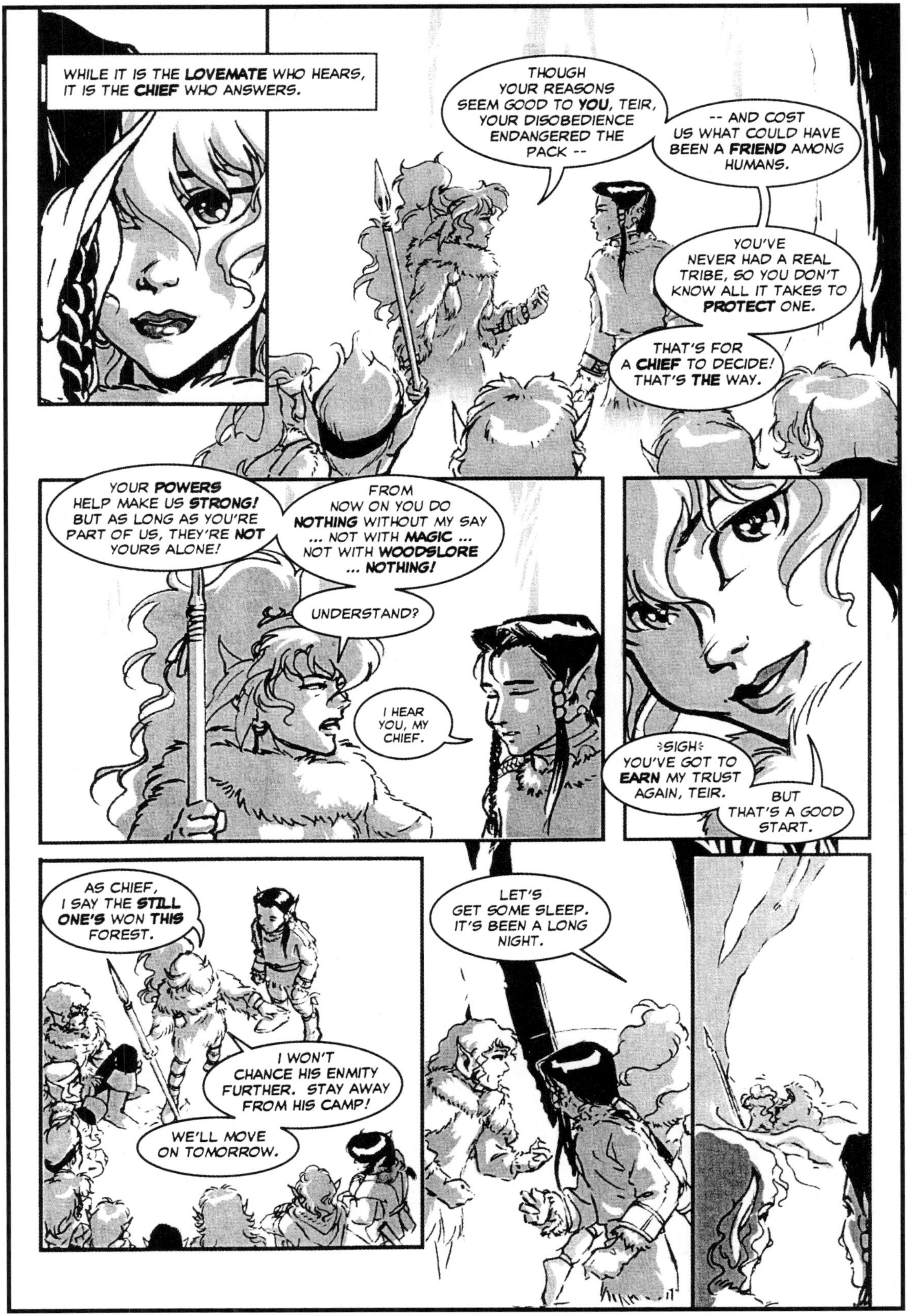
WHILE IT IS THE LOVEMATE WHO HEARS, IT IS THE CHIEF WHO ANSWERS.
THOUGH YOUR REASONS SEEM GOOD TO YOU, TEIR, YOUR DISOBEDIENCE ENDANGERED THE PACK --
-- AND COST US WHAT COULD HAVE BEEN A FRIEND AMONG HUMANS.
YOU'VE NEVER HAD A REAL TRIBE, SO YOU DON'T KNOW ALL IT TAKES TO PROTECT ONE.
THAT'S FOR A CHIEF TO DECIDE! THAT'S THE WAY.
YOUR POWERS HELP MAKE US STRONG! BUT AS LONG AS YOU'RE PART OF US, THEY'RE NOT YOURS ALONE!
FROM NOW ON YOU DO NOTHING WITHOUT MY SAY ... NOT WITH MAGIC ... NOT WITH WOODSLORE ... NOTHING!
UNDERSTAND?
I HEAR YOU, MY CHIEF.
SIGH
YOU'VE GOT TO EARN MY TRUST AGAIN, TEIR.
BUT THAT'S A GOOD START.
AS CHIEF, I SAY THE STILL ONE'S WON THIS FOREST.
I WON'T CHANCE HIS ENMITY FURTHER. STAY AWAY FROM HIS CAMP!
WE'LL MOVE ON TOMORROW.
LET'S GET SOME SLEEP. IT'S BEEN A LONG NIGHT.

AS THE WOLFRIDERS BED DOWN FOR THE DAY, POOL TENTATIVELY DRAWS NEAR THE BOWMASTER HE HERO-WORSHIPS.

I'M ALL RIGHT! HERE, SETTLE DOWN, NOW ...

¿schlup shlurp

¿mmmb mmmb¿

TEIR?

WHAT IF -- WHAT IF I WENT WITH YOU TO KILL THE NEAR-WOLF? WE'D GET REVENGE AND --

I'M-I'M **SORRY** ABOUT YOUR WOLF-FRIEND.*

CAN I DO ... ANYTHING?

TEIR SHAKES HIS HEAD, WORDS FAILING.

*AGAIN, LAST ISSUE -- ED.

-- **WHAT?!** NO! DON'T EVEN **THINK** IT! WE CAN'T!

BUT HE WAS YOUR **WOLF FRIEND!**

AREN'T YOU GOING TO DO **ANYTHING?!!**

POOL, I WON'T GO AGAINST EMBER AGAIN. I CAN'T. NOT AFTER ...

¿SIGH¿ SOMETIMES YOU **MUST** ACCEPT THERE'S NOTHING YOU CAN DO.

NO! IF THAT NEAR-WOLF GOT MY GREEDYGUT, I'D ...

... WELL, I'D MAKE **SURE** HE **PAID!**

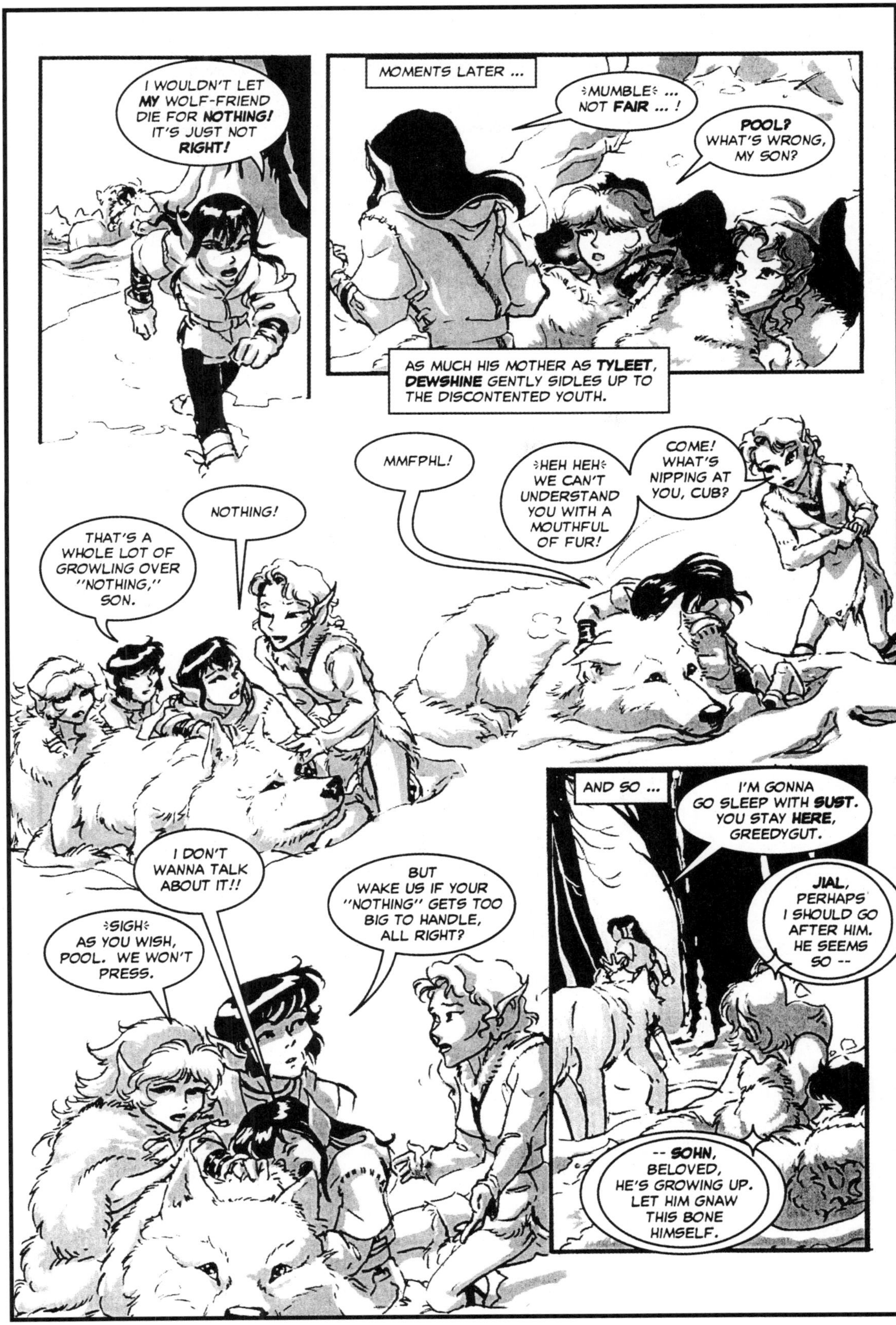

I WOULDN'T LET MY WOLF-FRIEND DIE FOR NOTHING! IT'S JUST NOT RIGHT!
MOMENTS LATER ...
MUMBLE ... NOT FAIR ... !
POOL? WHAT'S WRONG, MY SON?
AS MUCH HIS MOTHER AS TYLEET, DEWSHINE GENTLY SIDLES UP TO THE DISCONTENTED YOUTH.
COME! WHAT'S NIPPING AT YOU, CUB?
MMFPHL!
HEH HEH WE CAN'T UNDERSTAND YOU WITH A MOUTHFUL OF FUR!
NOTHING!
THAT'S A WHOLE LOT OF GROWLING OVER "NOTHING," SON.
I DON'T WANNA TALK ABOUT IT!!
SIGH AS YOU WISH, POOL. WE WON'T PRESS.
BUT WAKE US IF YOUR "NOTHING" GETS TOO BIG TO HANDLE, ALL RIGHT?
AND SO ...
I'M GONNA GO SLEEP WITH SUST. YOU STAY HERE, GREEDYGUT.
JIAL, PERHAPS I SHOULD GO AFTER HIM. HE SEEMS SO --
-- SOHN, BELOVED, HE'S GROWING UP. LET HIM GNAW THIS BONE HIMSELF.

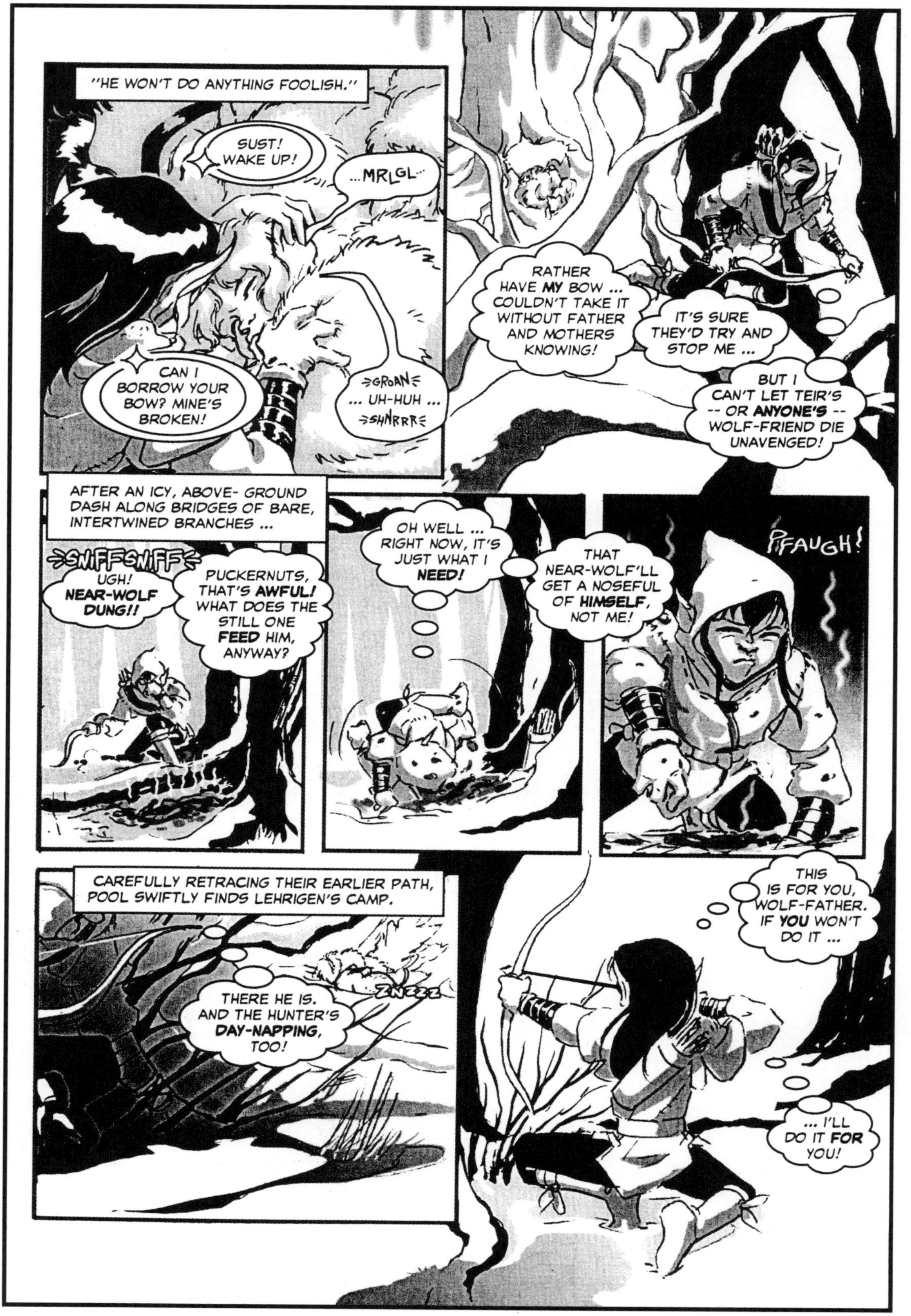
"HE WON'T DO ANYTHING FOOLISH."
SUST! WAKE UP!
...MRLGL...
CAN I BORROW YOUR BOW? MINE'S BROKEN!
GROAN ... UH-HUH ... SHNRRR
RATHER HAVE **MY** BOW ... COULDN'T TAKE IT WITHOUT FATHER AND MOTHERS KNOWING!
IT'S SURE THEY'D TRY AND STOP ME ...
BUT I CAN'T LET TEIR'S -- OR **ANYONE'S** -- WOLF-FRIEND DIE UNAVENGED!
AFTER AN ICY, ABOVE- GROUND DASH ALONG BRIDGES OF BARE, INTERTWINED BRANCHES ...
SNIFFSNIFF
UGH! **NEAR-WOLF DUNG!!**
PUCKERNUTS, THAT'S **AWFUL!** WHAT DOES THE STILL ONE **FEED** HIM, ANYWAY?
OH WELL ... RIGHT NOW, IT'S JUST WHAT I **NEED!**
THAT NEAR-WOLF'LL GET A NOSEFUL OF **HIMSELF**, NOT ME!
PFAUGH!
CAREFULLY RETRACING THEIR EARLIER PATH, POOL SWIFTLY FINDS LEHRIGEN'S CAMP.
THERE HE IS. AND THE HUNTER'S **DAY-NAPPING**, TOO!
ZNZZZ
THIS IS FOR YOU, WOLF-FATHER. IF **YOU** WON'T DO IT ...
... I'LL DO IT **FOR** YOU!

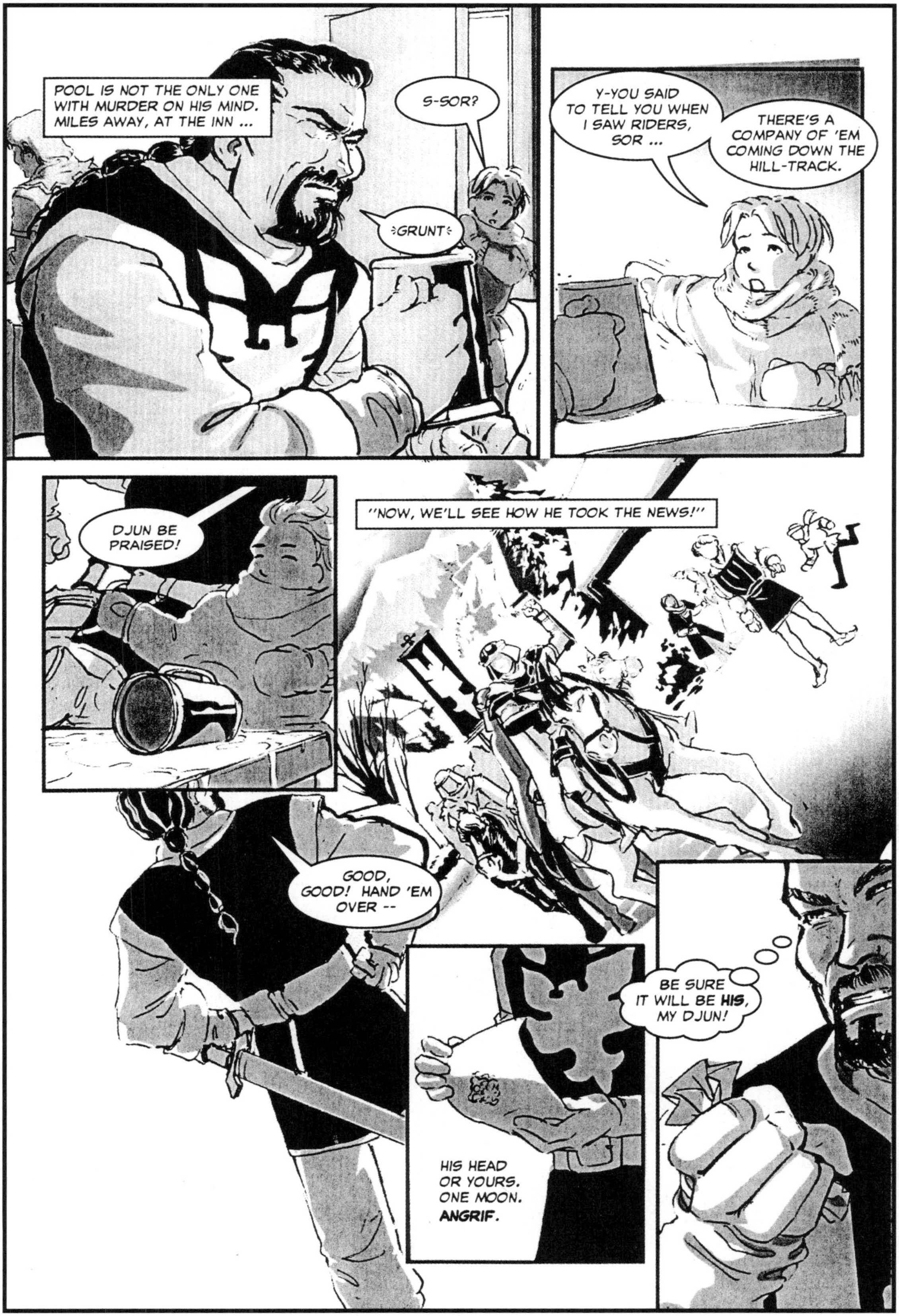
POOL IS NOT THE ONLY ONE WITH MURDER ON HIS MIND. MILES AWAY, AT THE INN ...
S-SOR?
GRUNT
Y-YOU SAID TO TELL YOU WHEN I SAW RIDERS, SOR ...
THERE'S A COMPANY OF 'EM COMING DOWN THE HILL-TRACK.
DJUN BE PRAISED!
"NOW, WE'LL SEE HOW HE TOOK THE NEWS!"
GOOD, GOOD! HAND 'EM OVER --
BE SURE IT WILL BE **HIS**, MY DJUN!
HIS HEAD OR YOURS. ONE MOON. **ANGRIF**.

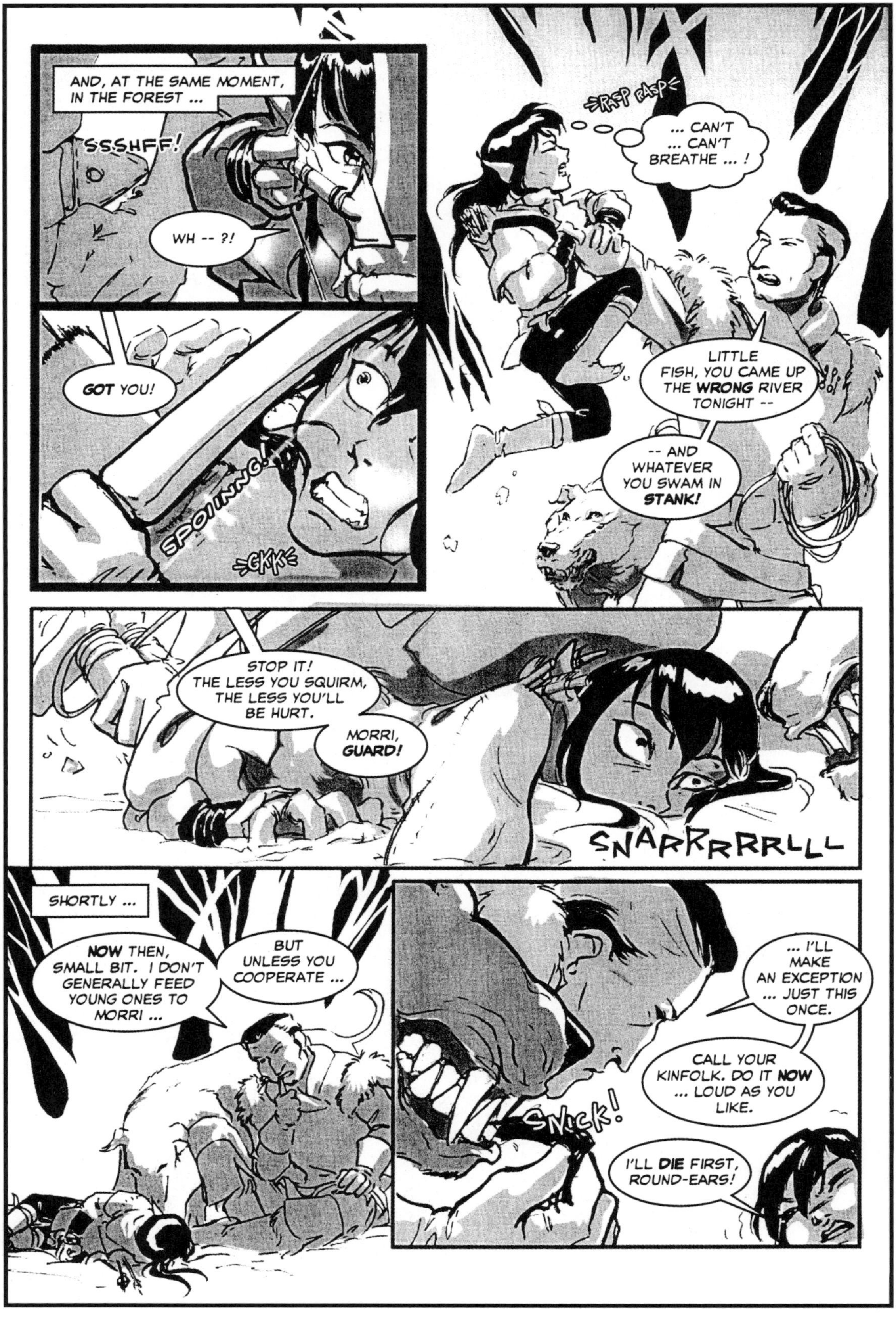
AND, AT THE SAME MOMENT, IN THE FOREST ...
SSSHFF!
WH -- ?!
GOT YOU!
SPOIINNG!
GKK
RASP RASP
... CAN'T ... CAN'T BREATHE ... !
LITTLE FISH, YOU CAME UP THE WRONG RIVER TONIGHT --
-- AND WHATEVER YOU SWAM IN STANK!
STOP IT! THE LESS YOU SQUIRM, THE LESS YOU'LL BE HURT.
MORRI, GUARD!
SNARRRRRLLL
SHORTLY ...
NOW THEN, SMALL BIT. I DON'T GENERALLY FEED YOUNG ONES TO MORRI ...
BUT UNLESS YOU COOPERATE ...
... I'LL MAKE AN EXCEPTION ... JUST THIS ONCE.
CALL YOUR KINFOLK. DO IT NOW ... LOUD AS YOU LIKE.
SNICK!
I'LL DIE FIRST, ROUND-EARS!

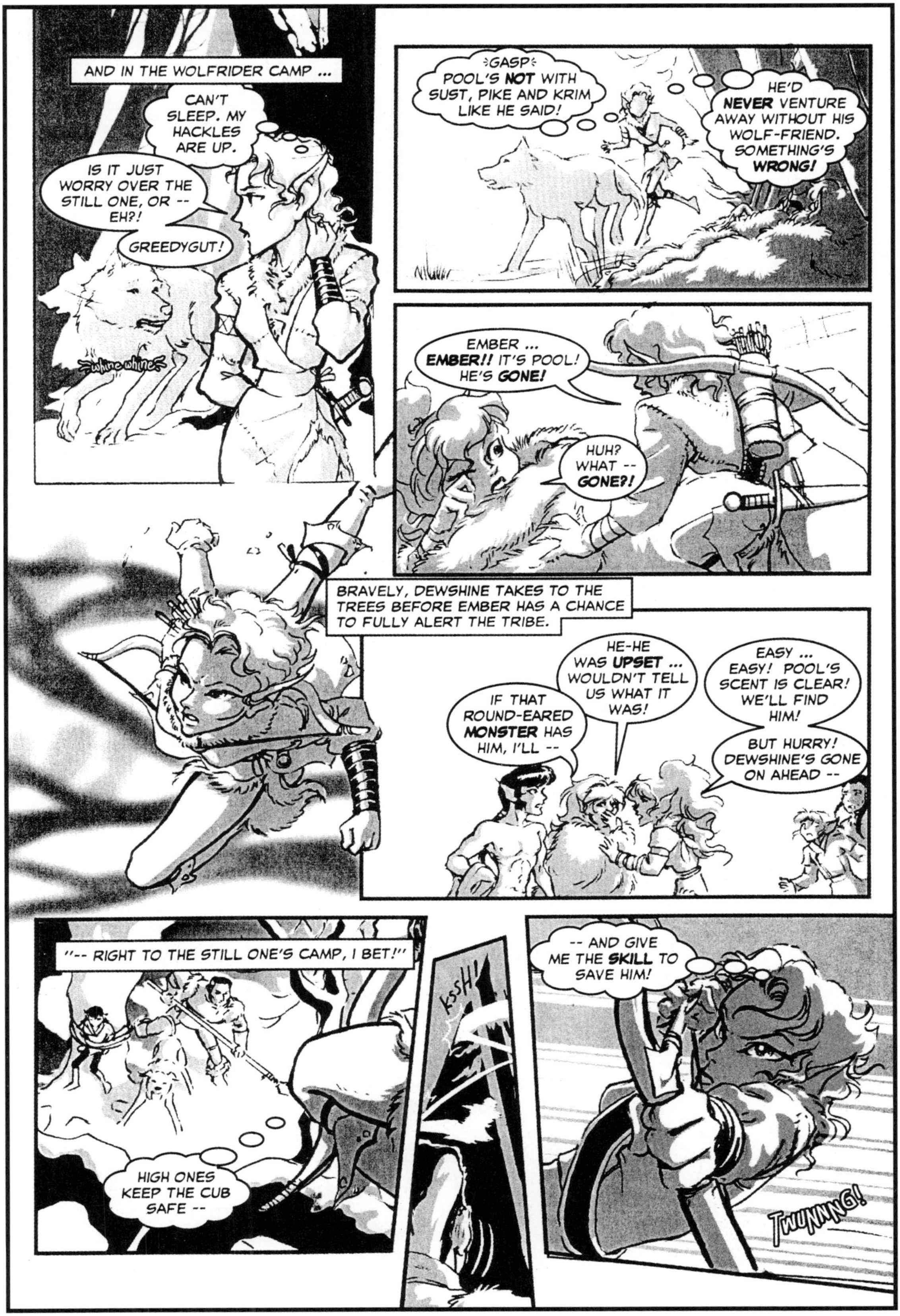
AND IN THE WOLFRIDER CAMP ...
CAN'T SLEEP. MY HACKLES ARE UP.
IS IT JUST WORRY OVER THE STILL ONE, OR -- EH?!
GREEDYGUT!
whine whine
GASP
POOL'S NOT WITH SUST, PIKE AND KRIM LIKE HE SAID!
HE'D NEVER VENTURE AWAY WITHOUT HIS WOLF-FRIEND. SOMETHING'S WRONG!
EMBER ... EMBER!! IT'S POOL! HE'S GONE!
HUH? WHAT -- GONE?!
BRAVELY, DEWSHINE TAKES TO THE TREES BEFORE EMBER HAS A CHANCE TO FULLY ALERT THE TRIBE.
IF THAT ROUND-EARED MONSTER HAS HIM, I'LL --
HE-HE WAS UPSET ... WOULDN'T TELL US WHAT IT WAS!
EASY ... EASY! POOL'S SCENT IS CLEAR! WE'LL FIND HIM!
BUT HURRY! DEWSHINE'S GONE ON AHEAD --
"-- RIGHT TO THE STILL ONE'S CAMP, I BET!"
HIGH ONES KEEP THE CUB SAFE --
KSSH!
-- AND GIVE ME THE SKILL TO SAVE HIM!
TWUNNNG!

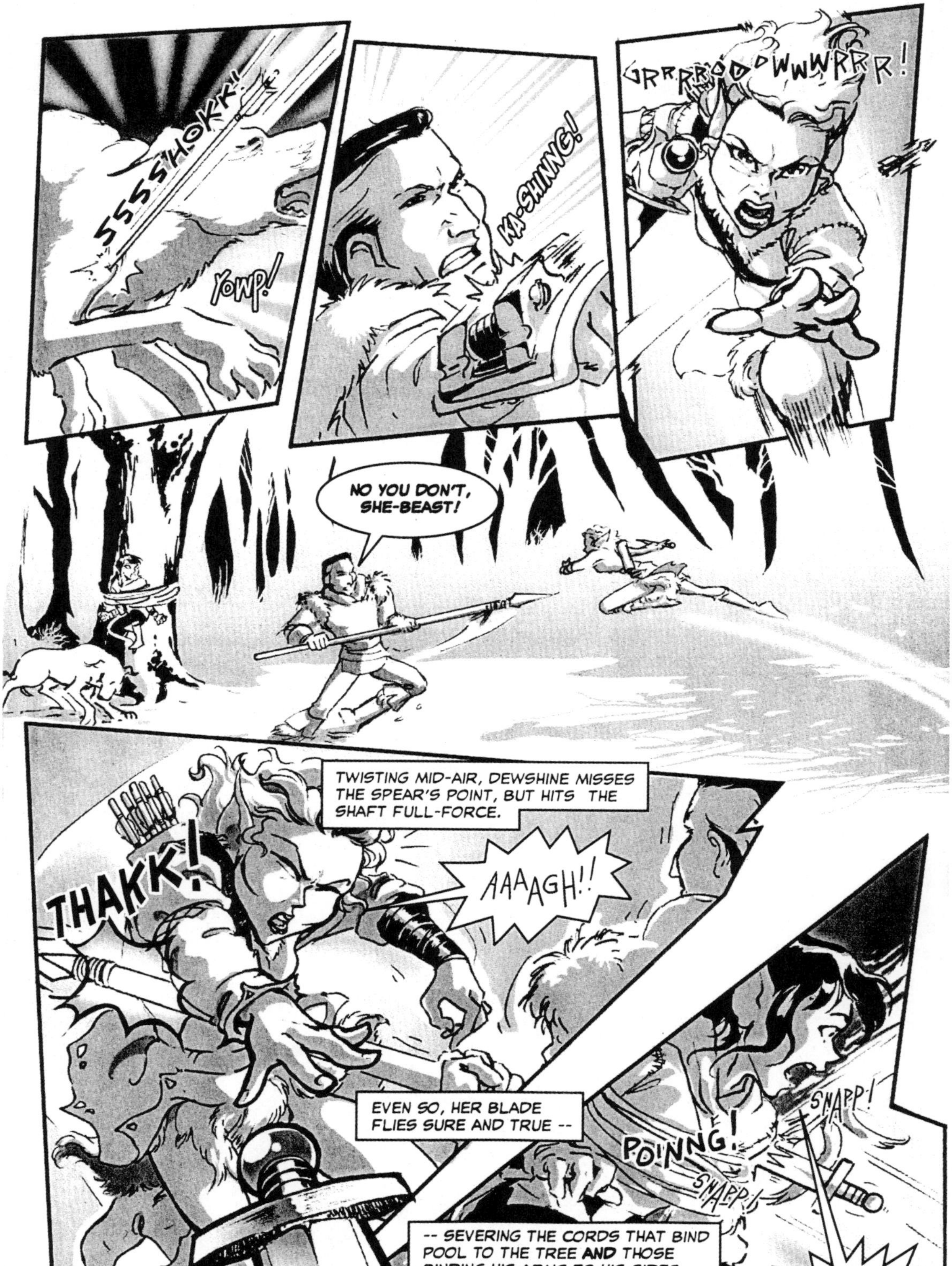
SSSSHOKK!
YOWP!
KA-SHINNG!
GRRRROOOWWWRRR!
NO YOU DON'T, SHE-BEAST!
TWISTING MID-AIR, DEWSHINE MISSES THE SPEAR'S POINT, BUT HITS THE SHAFT FULL-FORCE.
THAKK!
AAAAGH!!
EVEN SO, HER BLADE FLIES SURE AND TRUE --
SNAPP!
POINNG!
SNAPP!
-- SEVERING THE CORDS THAT BIND POOL TO THE TREE AND THOSE BINDING HIS ARMS TO HIS SIDES.
DEWSHINE! NOOOO!!

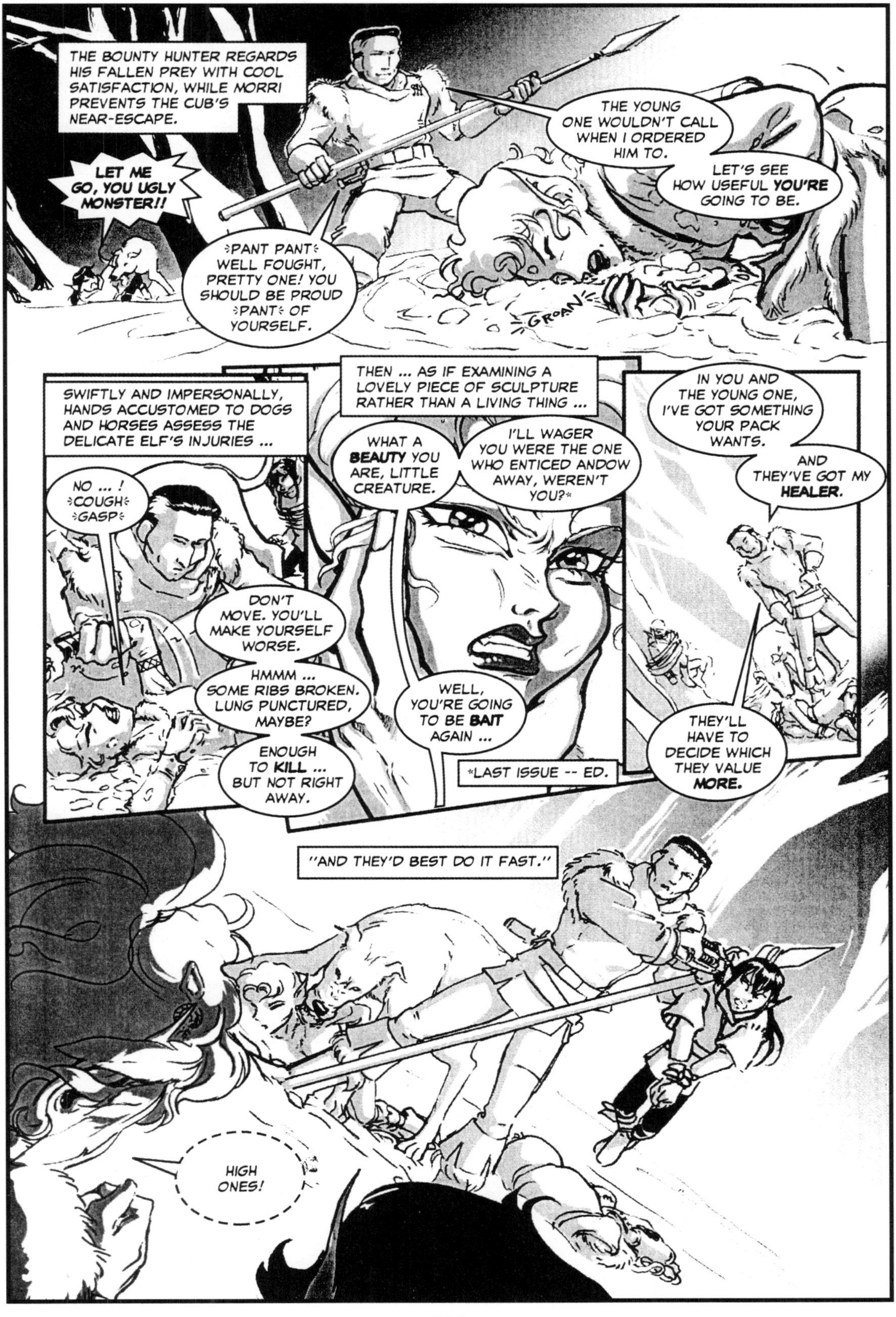
THE BOUNTY HUNTER REGARDS HIS FALLEN PREY WITH COOL SATISFACTION, WHILE MORRI PREVENTS THE CUB'S NEAR-ESCAPE.
LET ME GO, YOU UGLY MONSTER!!
THE YOUNG ONE WOULDN'T CALL WHEN I ORDERED HIM TO.
LET'S SEE HOW USEFUL YOU'RE GOING TO BE.
PANT PANT WELL FOUGHT, PRETTY ONE! YOU SHOULD BE PROUD *PANT* OF YOURSELF.
GROAN
SWIFTLY AND IMPERSONALLY, HANDS ACCUSTOMED TO DOGS AND HORSES ASSESS THE DELICATE ELF'S INJURIES ...
NO ... ! *COUGH* *GASP*
DON'T MOVE. YOU'LL MAKE YOURSELF WORSE.
HMMM ... SOME RIBS BROKEN. LUNG PUNCTURED, MAYBE?
ENOUGH TO KILL ... BUT NOT RIGHT AWAY.
THEN ... AS IF EXAMINING A LOVELY PIECE OF SCULPTURE RATHER THAN A LIVING THING ...
WHAT A BEAUTY YOU ARE, LITTLE CREATURE.
I'LL WAGER YOU WERE THE ONE WHO ENTICED ANDOW AWAY, WEREN'T YOU?*
WELL, YOU'RE GOING TO BE BAIT AGAIN ...
*LAST ISSUE -- ED.
IN YOU AND THE YOUNG ONE, I'VE GOT SOMETHING YOUR PACK WANTS.
AND THEY'VE GOT MY HEALER.
THEY'LL HAVE TO DECIDE WHICH THEY VALUE MORE.
"AND THEY'D BEST DO IT FAST."
HIGH ONES!

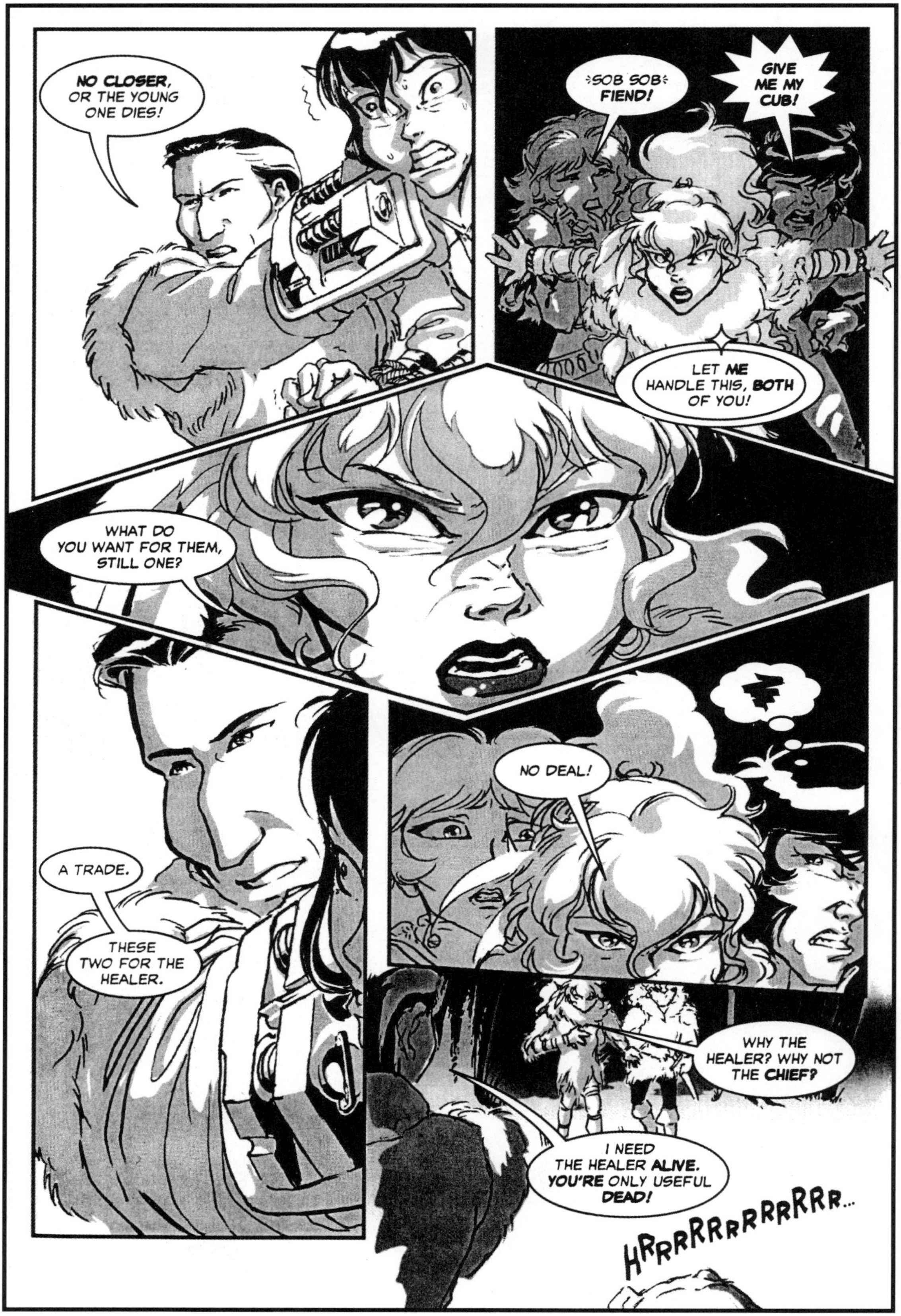
NO CLOSER, OR THE YOUNG ONE DIES!
SOB SOB FIEND!
GIVE ME MY CUB!
LET ME HANDLE THIS, BOTH OF YOU!
WHAT DO YOU WANT FOR THEM, STILL ONE?
A TRADE.
THESE TWO FOR THE HEALER.
NO DEAL!
WHY THE HEALER? WHY NOT THE CHIEF?
I NEED THE HEALER ALIVE. YOU'RE ONLY USEFUL DEAD!
HRRRRRRRRRRRRR...

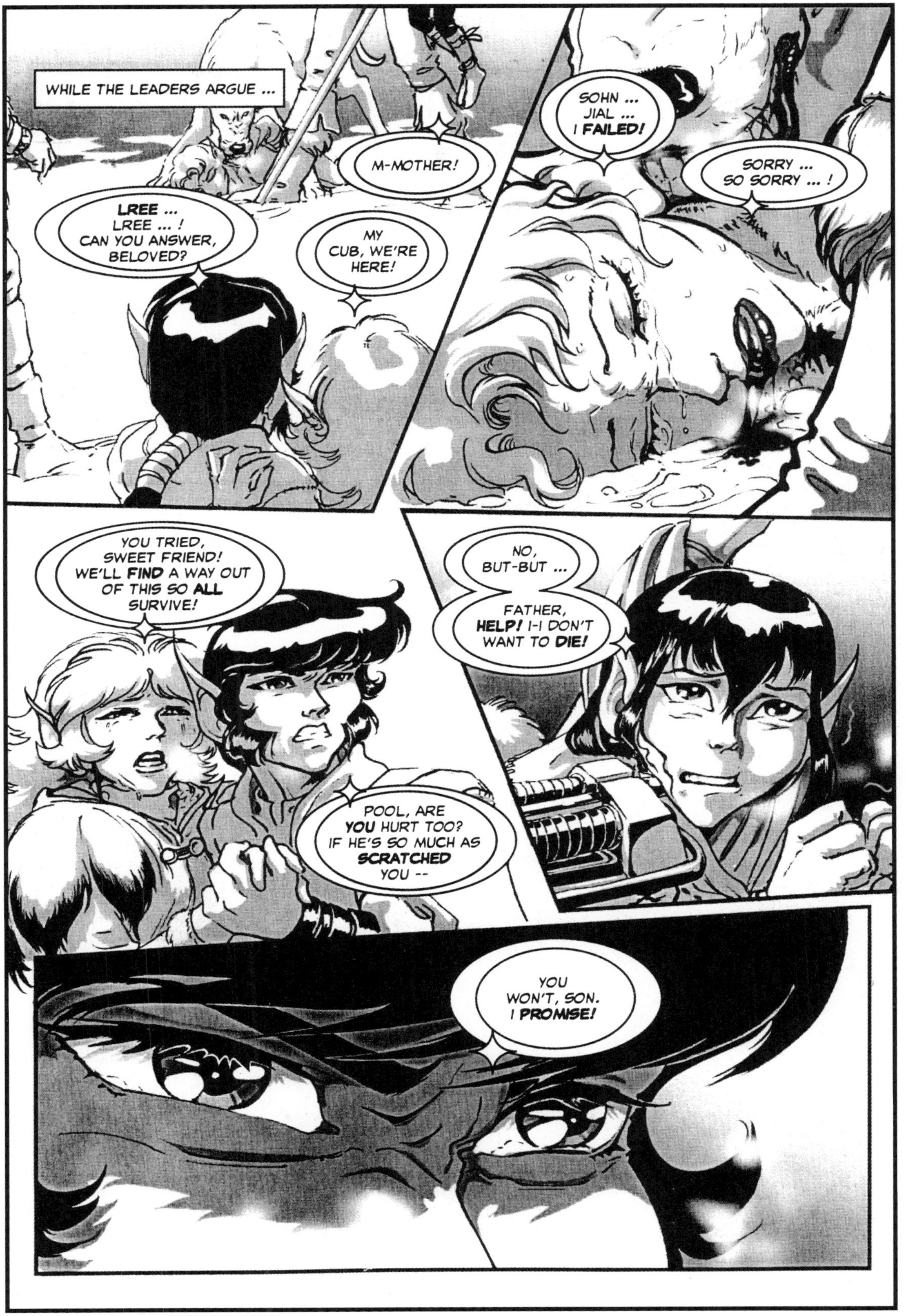
WHILE THE LEADERS ARGUE ...
M-MOTHER!
LREE ... LREE ... ! CAN YOU ANSWER, BELOVED?
MY CUB, WE'RE HERE!
SOHN ... JIAL ... I FAILED!
SORRY ... SO SORRY ... !
YOU TRIED, SWEET FRIEND! WE'LL FIND A WAY OUT OF THIS SO ALL SURVIVE!
POOL, ARE YOU HURT TOO? IF HE'S SO MUCH AS SCRATCHED YOU --
NO, BUT-BUT ...
FATHER, HELP! I-I DON'T WANT TO DIE!
YOU WON'T, SON. I PROMISE!

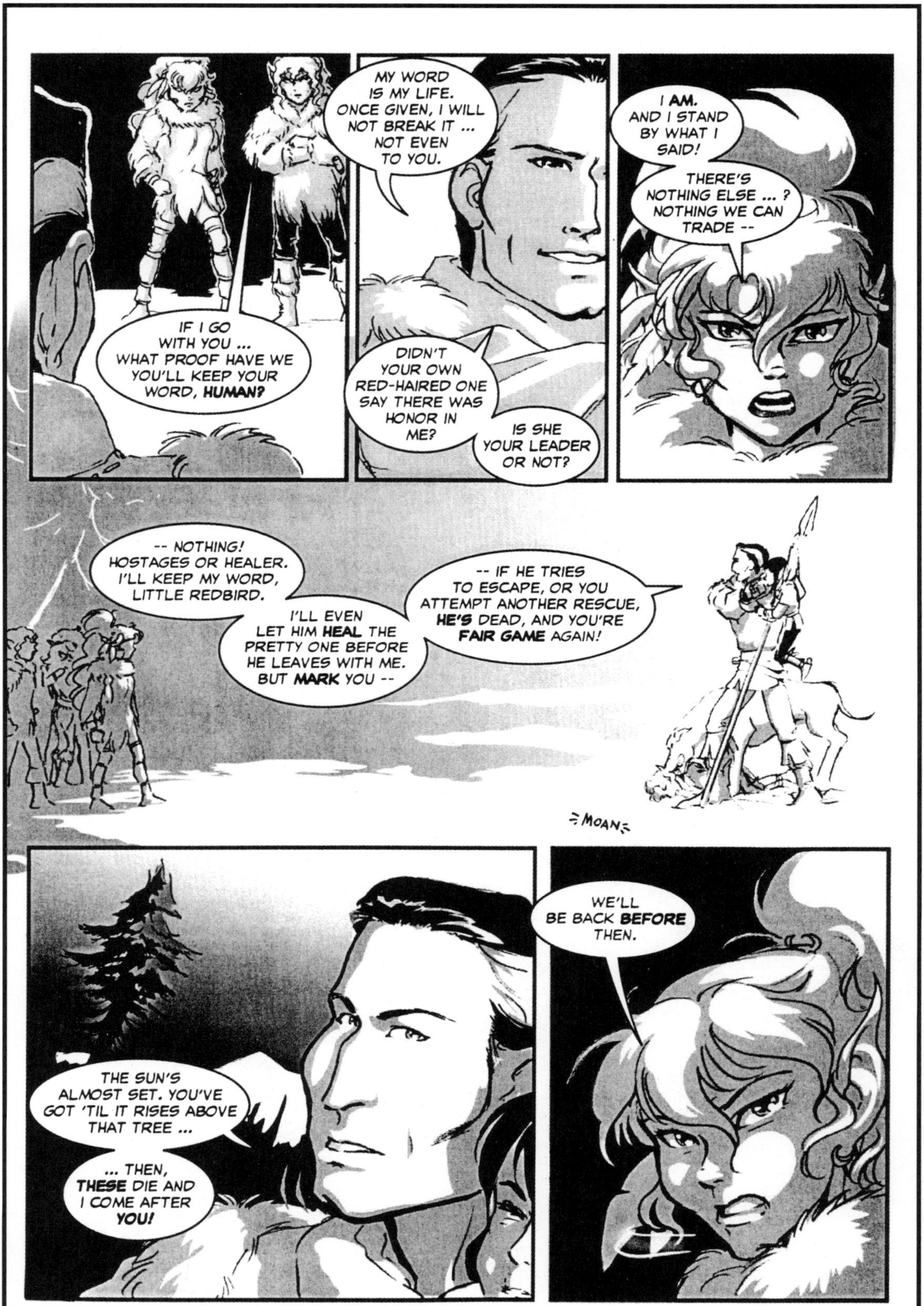
IF I GO WITH YOU ... WHAT PROOF HAVE WE YOU'LL KEEP YOUR WORD, HUMAN?
MY WORD IS MY LIFE. ONCE GIVEN, I WILL NOT BREAK IT ... NOT EVEN TO YOU.
DIDN'T YOUR OWN RED-HAIRED ONE SAY THERE WAS HONOR IN ME?
IS SHE YOUR LEADER OR NOT?
I AM. AND I STAND BY WHAT I SAID!
THERE'S NOTHING ELSE ... ? NOTHING WE CAN TRADE --
-- NOTHING! HOSTAGES OR HEALER. I'LL KEEP MY WORD, LITTLE REDBIRD.
I'LL EVEN LET HIM HEAL THE PRETTY ONE BEFORE HE LEAVES WITH ME. BUT MARK YOU --
-- IF HE TRIES TO ESCAPE, OR YOU ATTEMPT ANOTHER RESCUE, HE'S DEAD, AND YOU'RE FAIR GAME AGAIN!
MOAN
THE SUN'S ALMOST SET. YOU'VE GOT 'TIL IT RISES ABOVE THAT TREE ...
... THEN, THESE DIE AND I COME AFTER YOU!
WE'LL BE BACK BEFORE THEN.

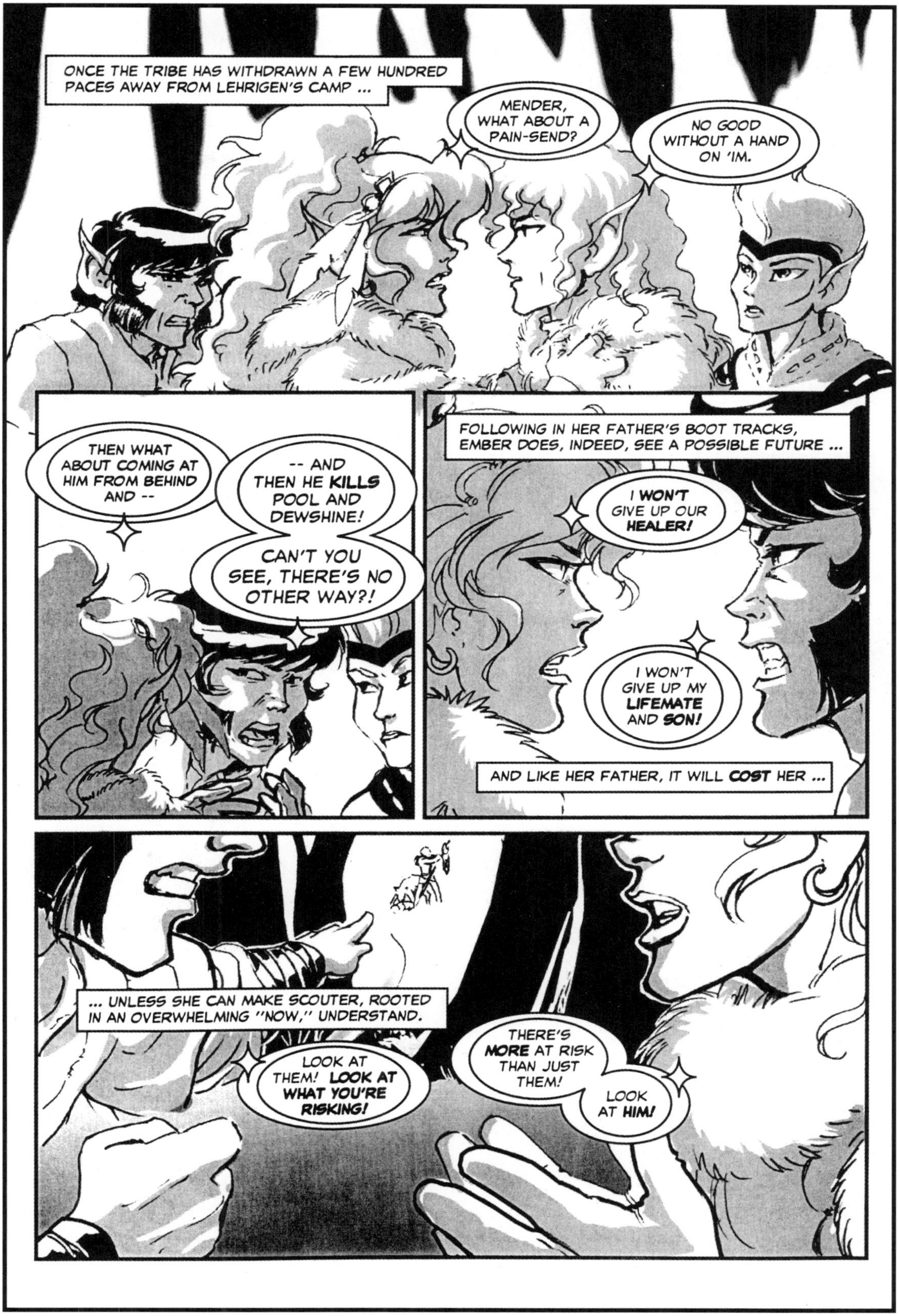
ONCE THE TRIBE HAS WITHDRAWN A FEW HUNDRED PACES AWAY FROM LEHRIGEN'S CAMP ...
MENDER, WHAT ABOUT A PAIN-SEND?
NO GOOD WITHOUT A HAND ON 'IM.
THEN WHAT ABOUT COMING AT HIM FROM BEHIND AND --
-- AND THEN HE KILLS POOL AND DEWSHINE!
CAN'T YOU SEE, THERE'S NO OTHER WAY?!
FOLLOWING IN HER FATHER'S BOOT TRACKS, EMBER DOES, INDEED, SEE A POSSIBLE FUTURE ...
I WON'T GIVE UP OUR HEALER!
I WON'T GIVE UP MY LIFEMATE AND SON!
AND LIKE HER FATHER, IT WILL COST HER ...
... UNLESS SHE CAN MAKE SCOUTER, ROOTED IN AN OVERWHELMING "NOW," UNDERSTAND.
LOOK AT THEM! LOOK AT WHAT YOU'RE RISKING!
THERE'S MORE AT RISK THAN JUST THEM!
LOOK AT HIM!

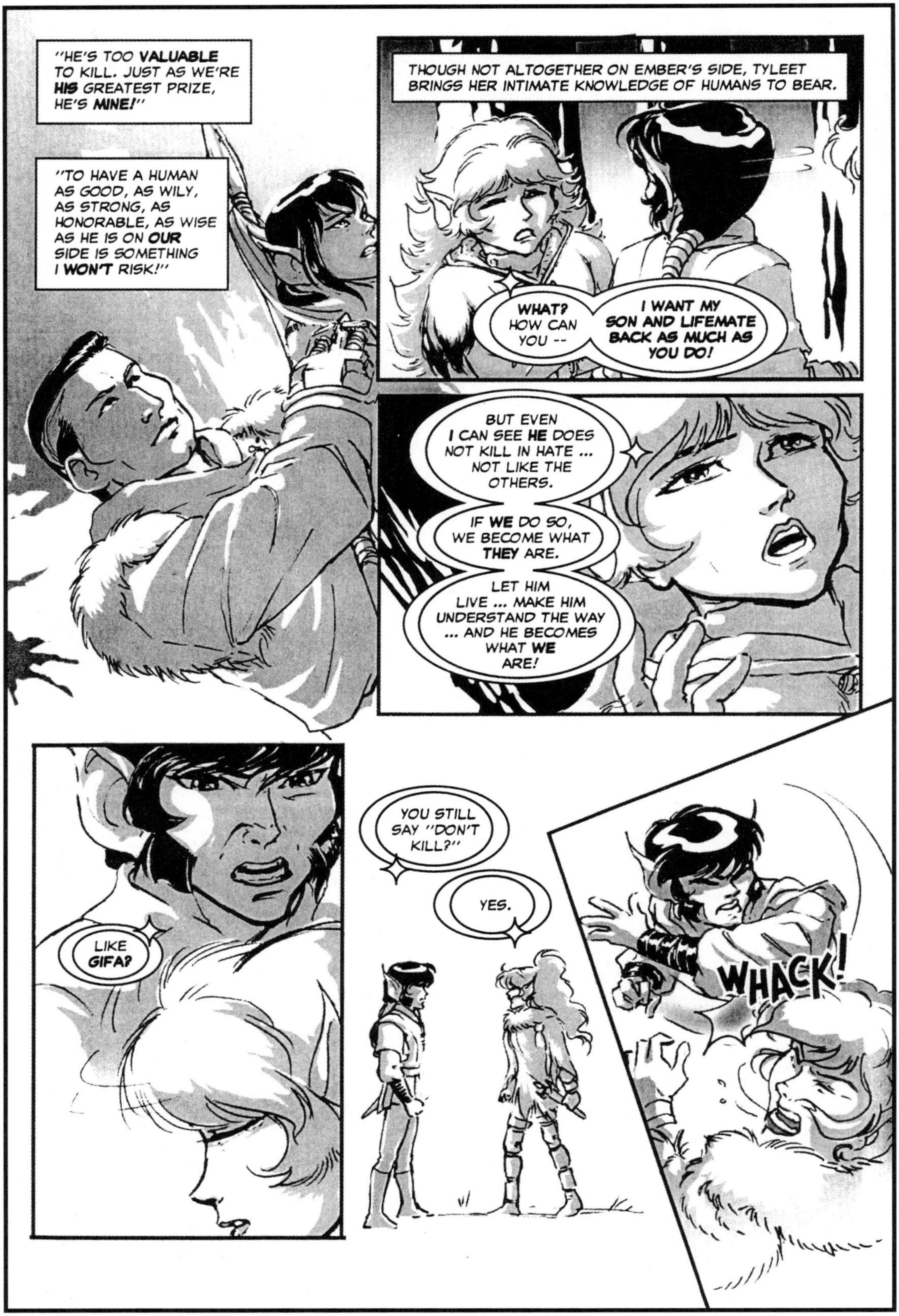
"HE'S TOO VALUABLE TO KILL. JUST AS WE'RE HIS GREATEST PRIZE, HE'S MINE!"
"TO HAVE A HUMAN AS GOOD, AS WILY, AS STRONG, AS HONORABLE, AS WISE AS HE IS ON OUR SIDE IS SOMETHING I WON'T RISK!"
THOUGH NOT ALTOGETHER ON EMBER'S SIDE, TYLEET BRINGS HER INTIMATE KNOWLEDGE OF HUMANS TO BEAR.
WHAT? HOW CAN YOU --
I WANT MY SON AND LIFEMATE BACK AS MUCH AS YOU DO!
BUT EVEN I CAN SEE HE DOES NOT KILL IN HATE ... NOT LIKE THE OTHERS.
IF WE DO SO, WE BECOME WHAT THEY ARE.
LET HIM LIVE ... MAKE HIM UNDERSTAND THE WAY ... AND HE BECOMES WHAT WE ARE!
LIKE GIFA?
YOU STILL SAY "DON'T KILL?"
YES.
WHACK!

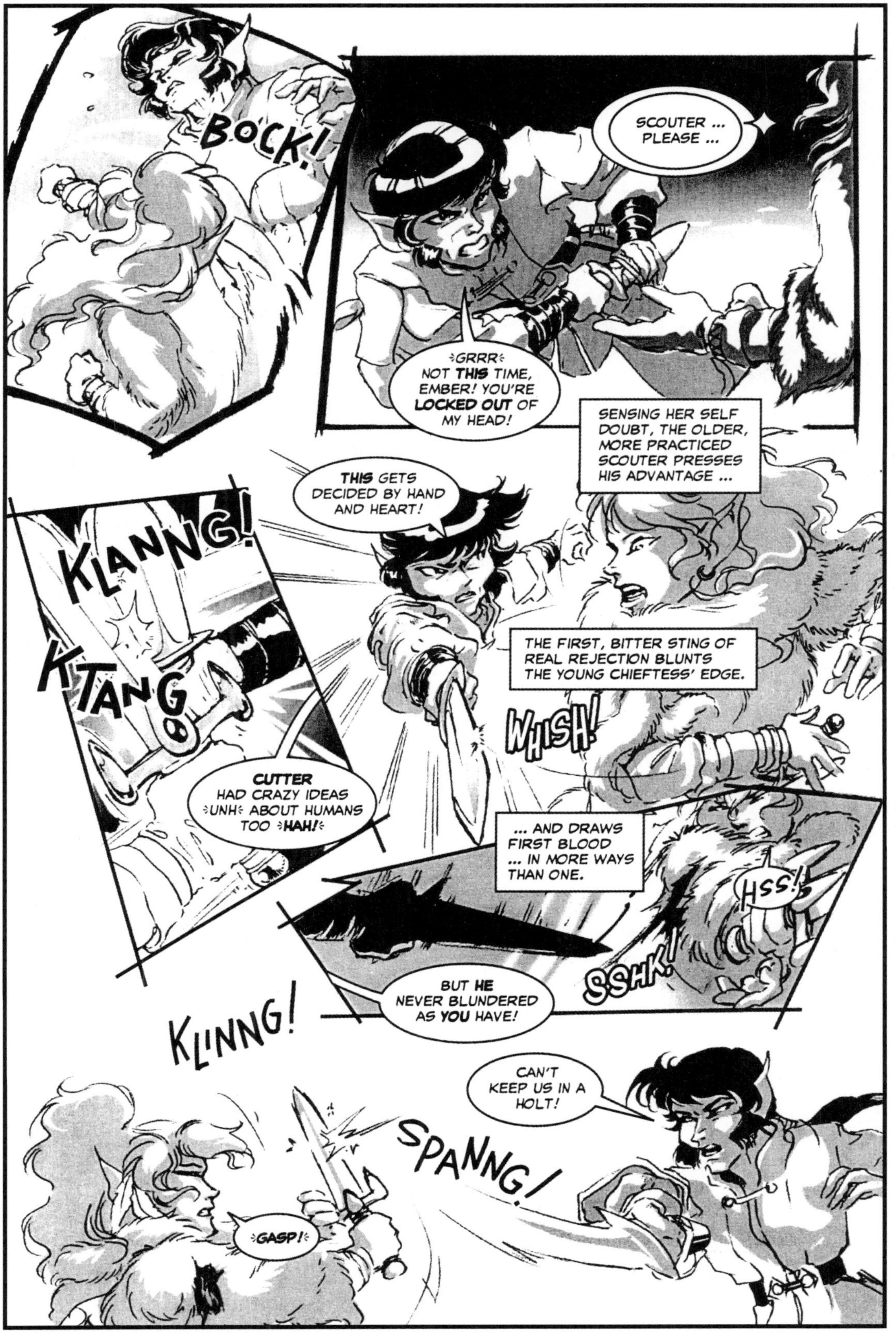

BOCK!
SCOUTER ... PLEASE ...
GRRR NOT THIS TIME, EMBER! YOU'RE LOCKED OUT OF MY HEAD!
SENSING HER SELF DOUBT, THE OLDER, MORE PRACTICED SCOUTER PRESSES HIS ADVANTAGE ...
THIS GETS DECIDED BY HAND AND HEART!
KLANNG!
KTANG
THE FIRST, BITTER STING OF REAL REJECTION BLUNTS THE YOUNG CHIEFTESS' EDGE.
WHISH!
CUTTER HAD CRAZY IDEAS UNH ABOUT HUMANS TOO HAH!
... AND DRAWS FIRST BLOOD ... IN MORE WAYS THAN ONE.
HSS!
SSHK!
BUT HE NEVER BLUNDERED AS YOU HAVE!
KLINNG!
CAN'T KEEP US IN A HOLT!
SPANNG!
GASP!

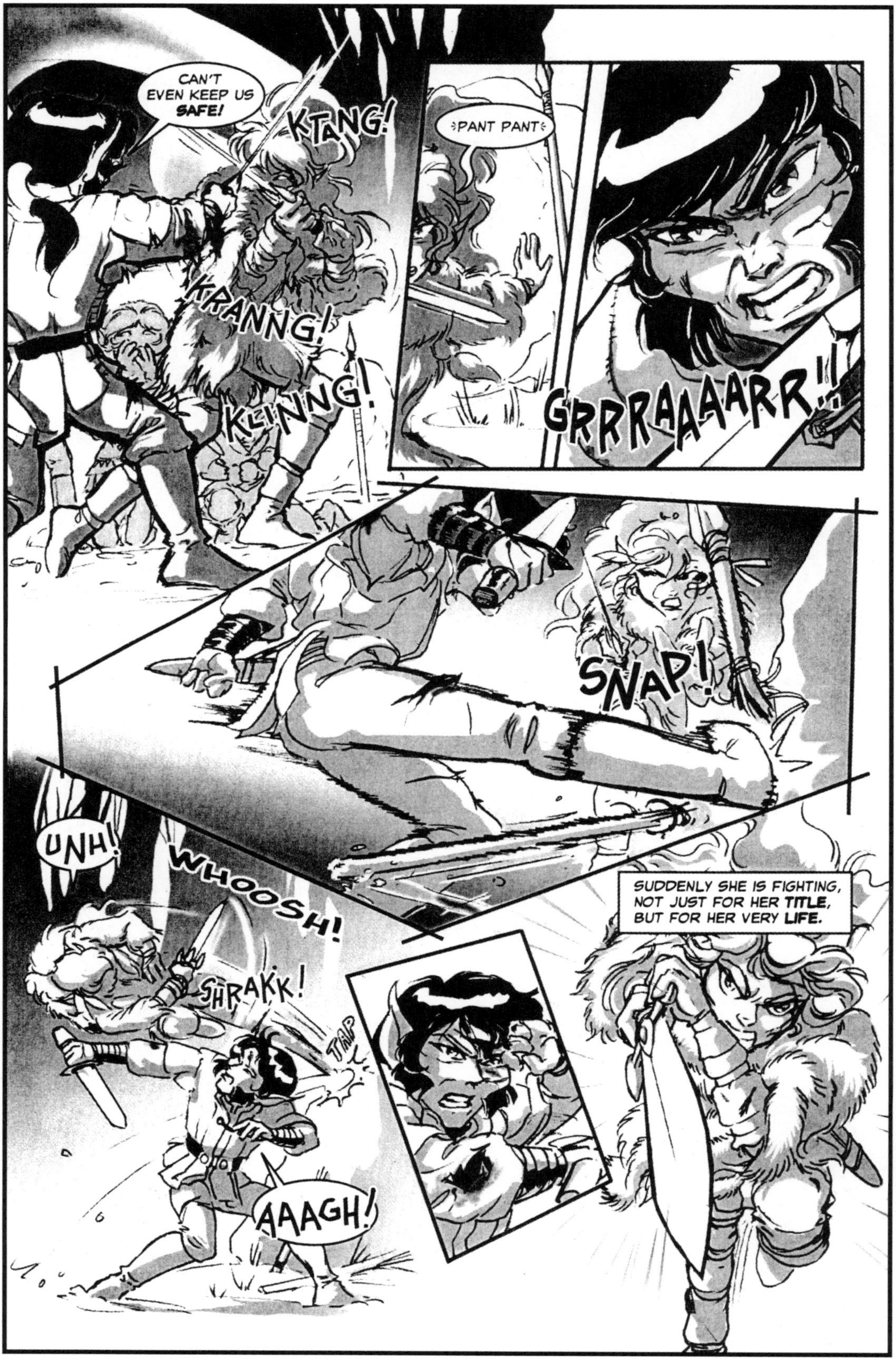
CAN'T EVEN KEEP US SAFE!
KTANG!
KRANNG!
KLINNG!
PANT PANT
GRRRAAAARR!!
SNAP!
UNH!
WHOOSH!
SUDDENLY SHE IS FIGHTING, NOT JUST FOR HER TITLE, BUT FOR HER VERY LIFE.
SHRAKK!
TAP
AAAGH!

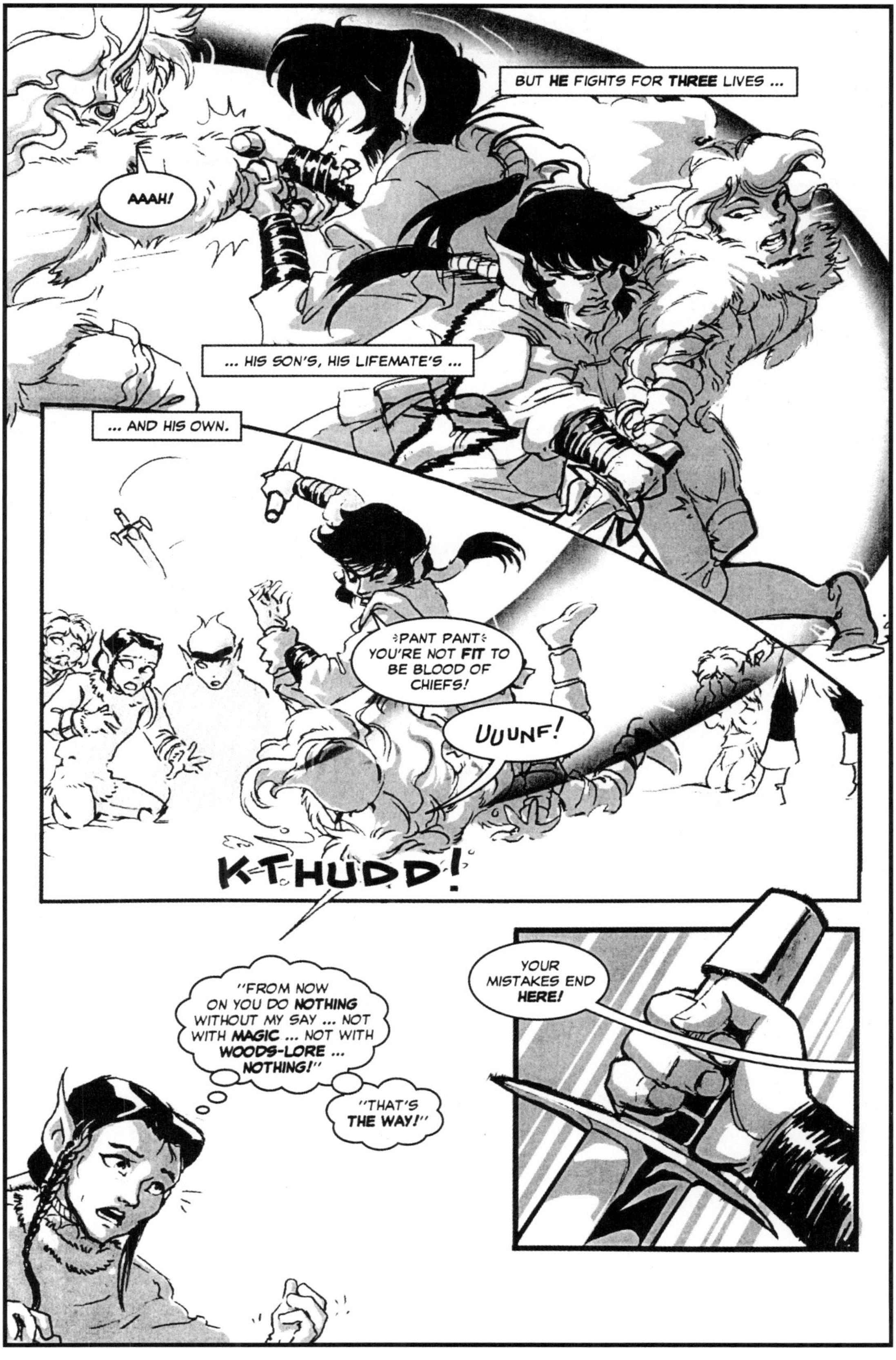
BUT HE FIGHTS FOR THREE LIVES ...
AAAH!
... HIS SON'S, HIS LIFEMATE'S ...
... AND HIS OWN.
PANT PANT YOU'RE NOT FIT TO BE BLOOD OF CHIEFS!
UUUNF!
K-THUDD!
"FROM NOW ON YOU DO NOTHING WITHOUT MY SAY ... NOT WITH MAGIC ... NOT WITH WOODS-LORE ... NOTHING!"
"THAT'S THE WAY!"
YOUR MISTAKES END HERE!

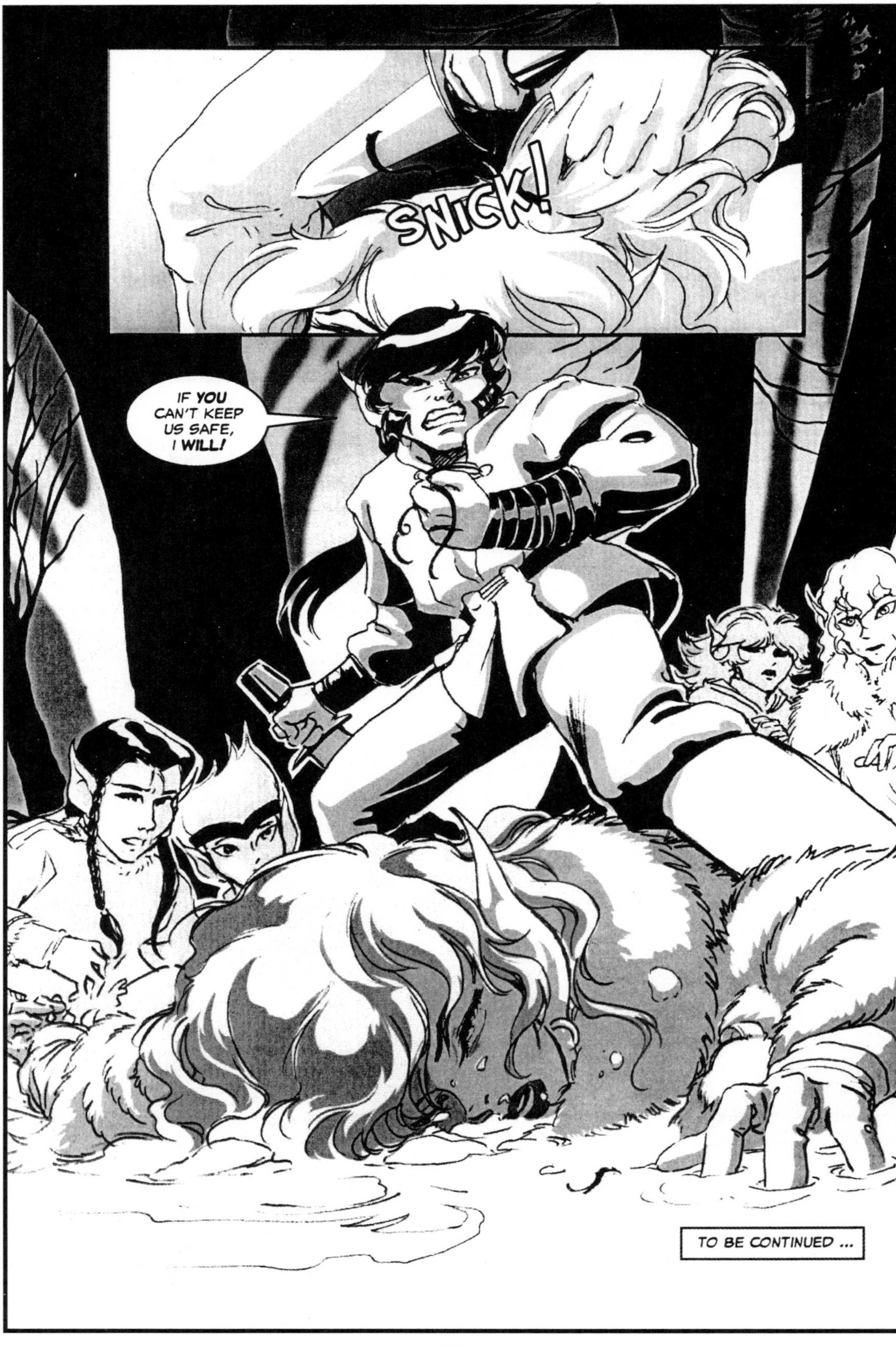
SNICK!
IF YOU CAN'T KEEP US SAFE, I WILL!
TO BE CONTINUED ...

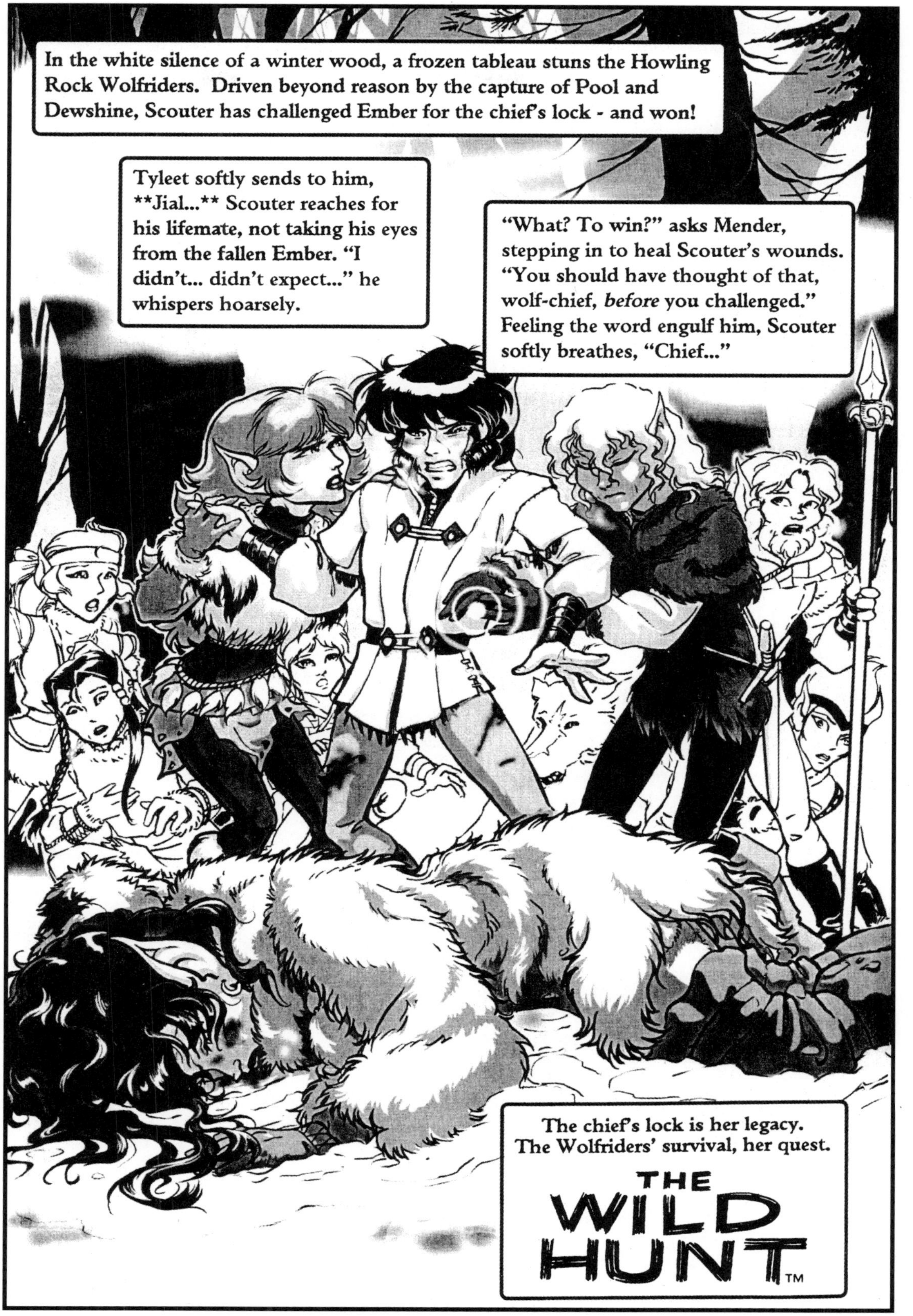

In the white silence of a winter wood, a frozen tableau stuns the Howling Rock Wolfriders. Driven beyond reason by the capture of Pool and Dewshine, Scouter has challenged Ember for the chief's lock - and won!
Tyleet softly sends to him, **Jial...** Scouter reaches for his lifemate, not taking his eyes from the fallen Ember. "I didn't... didn't expect..." he whispers hoarsely.
"What? To win?" asks Mender, stepping in to heal Scouter's wounds. "You should have thought of that, wolf-chief, *before* you challenged." Feeling the word engulf him, Scouter softly breathes, "Chief..."
The chief's lock is her legacy. The Wolfriders' survival, her quest.
THE WILD HUNT™

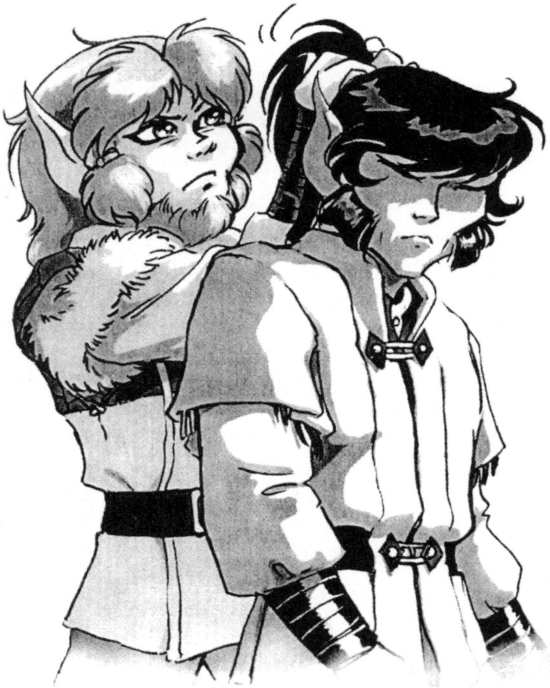

"That's right. Now we're YOUR litter to lead." Pike, the eldest, gathers Scouter's hair back into a lock and binds it with a leather thong. "Hold still! You'd best get used to wearing this."

Marked with the emblem of all Wolfrider leaders since Timmorn Yellow-Eyes, Scouter feels all eyes upon him. "This isn't what I wanted," he says. "But I've dug my den and must live in it."

Turning to Mender, Scouter explains, "There's no other way, packmate. We've got to trade you to the Still One so you can heal Dewshine...make him give her and my son back." Knowing this may mean his death, Mender gravely nods. But Scouter's next order astonishes him.

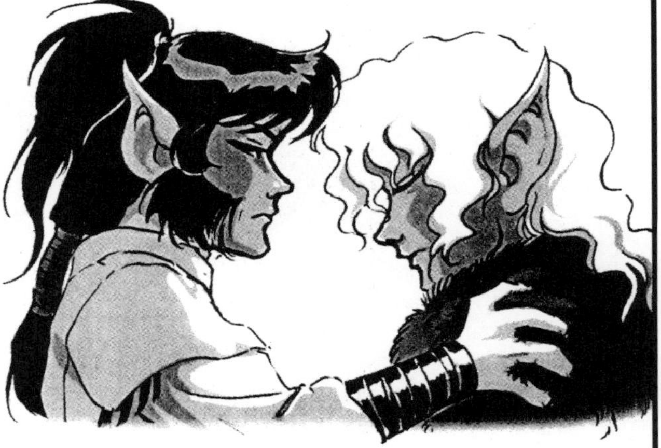

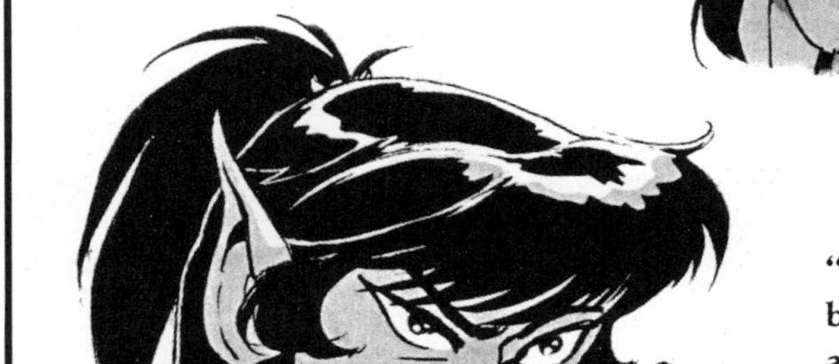

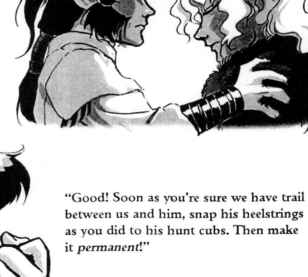

"Good! Soon as you're sure we have trail between us and him, snap his heelstrings as you did to his hunt cubs. Then make it *permanent*!"

Tyleet's lock-send bursts into Scouter's mind. **But we *promised*! Cutter, in his worst trials, never broke faith with humans like this! Where's my good Jial... already strangled by the chief's lock?**

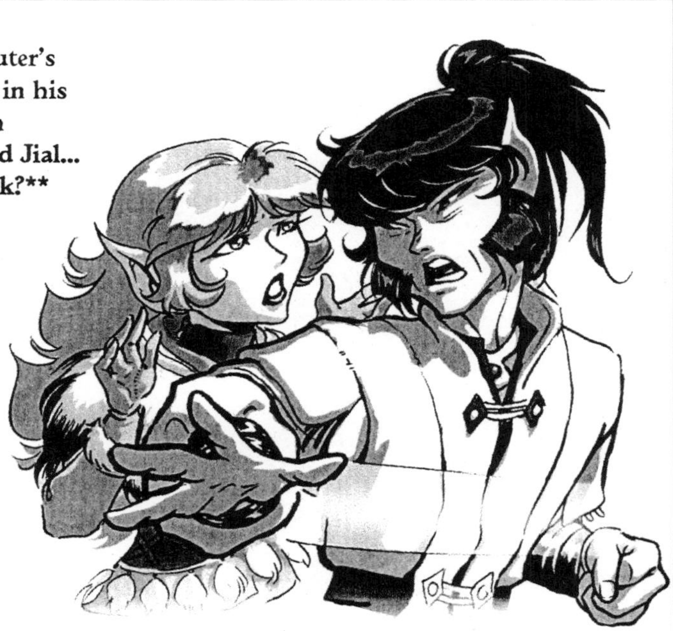

Scouter whirls on her fiercely, shouting so all can hear, "He's *human*! A human who's *tricked* us and makes it clear he wants us dead!
The Way is the Way. When a new chief fairly wins his place, you obey without question!"

With that, Scouter strides back to the clearing where Lehrigen awaits. Silently, the elves fall in behind their new, inwardly terrified chief, leaving the conquered Ember abandoned in the snow...

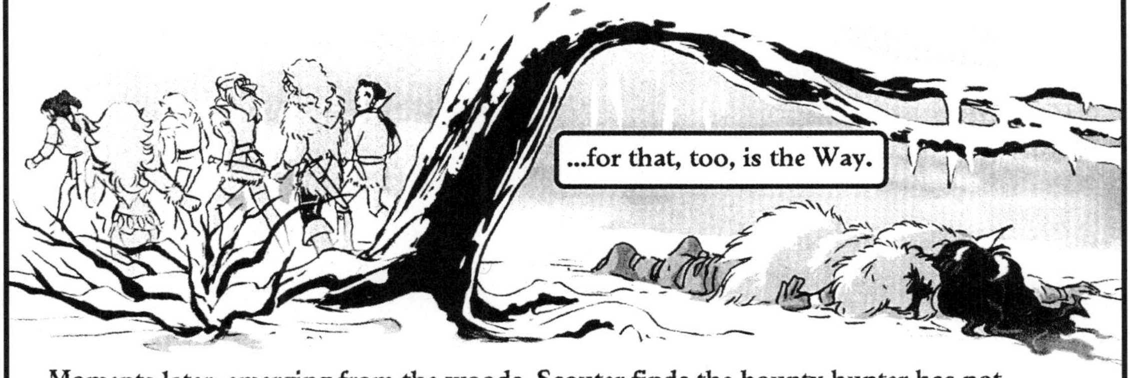
...for that, too, is the Way.

Moments later, emerging from the woods, Scouter finds the bounty hunter has not moved. Lehrigen's deadly wristbolt still rests under young Pool's jaw. Dewshine lies, pale and immobile, between Morri's massive paws. Surprised, Lehrigen asks,
"Where's the little redbird?"

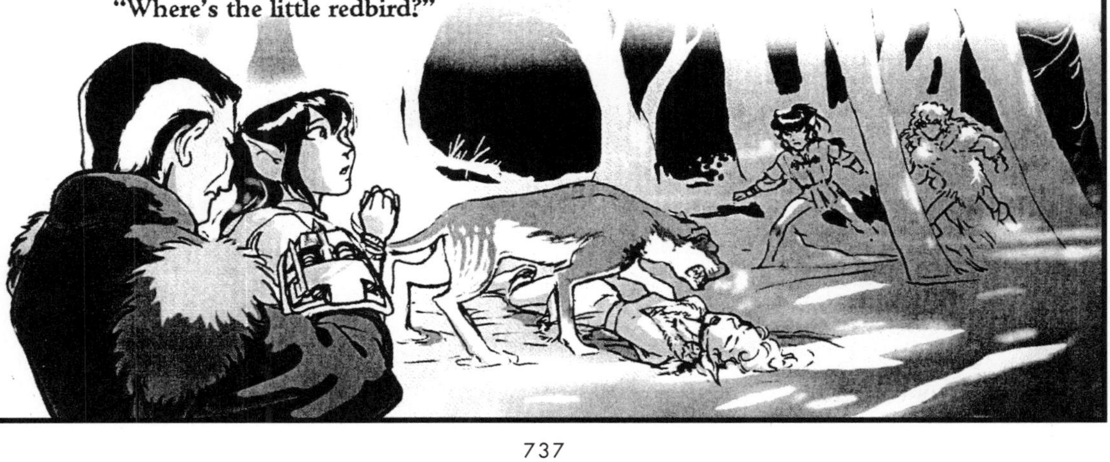

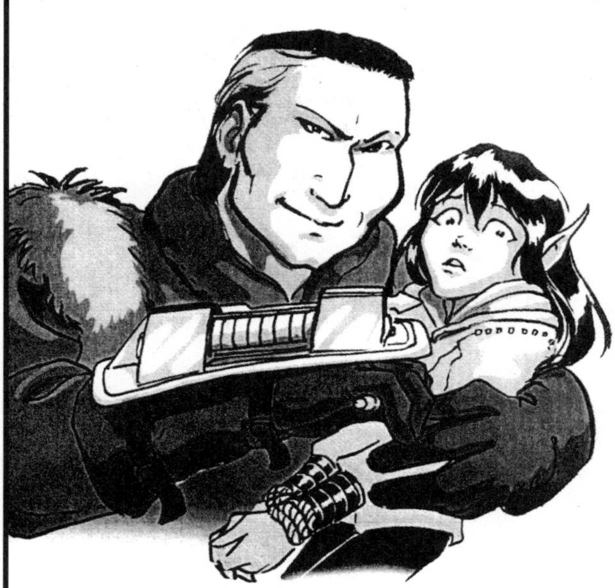

"Gone!" Scouter retorts, "I'm chief now. Do you trade, or do we fight?" At that, Lehrigen smiles thinly. *These* elves he understands - fierce, angry animals out to protect their territory at all costs.

"Trade," he coolly replies. "Healer for hostages."

Mender sprints to Dewshine's aid, reaching to hold her close. "Hang on, dear packsister," he whispers, as the warmth and gentleness of his restorative powers encompass her. Soon, his work done, the tired healer slumps.

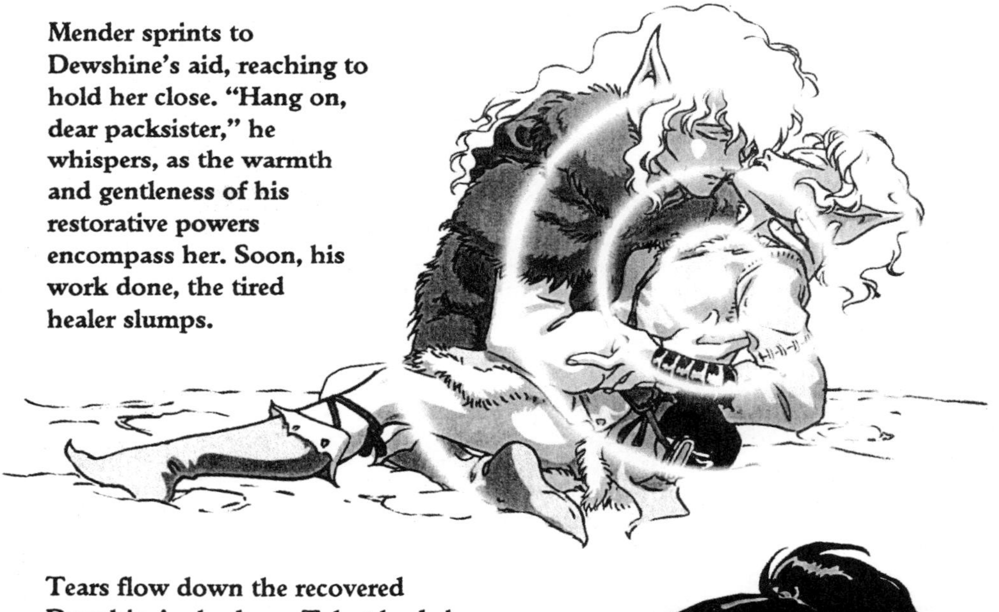

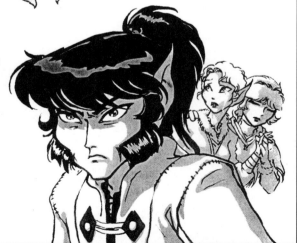

Tears flow down the recovered Dewshine's cheeks as Tyleet leads her back to the tribe. "Mender... his sacrifice is for *all* of us!" she whispers.

Meanwhile, Scouter has not taken his eyes from the tall human. "And now my..." he pauses, thinking better of it, "...and now the *other.*" True to his word, Lehrigen lowers his wristbolt and undoes the elfin boy's bonds. "Go on, little fish," he says, not unkindly, "Swim home."

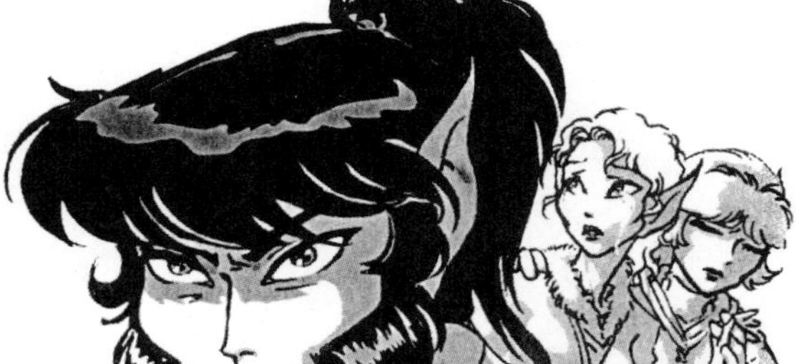

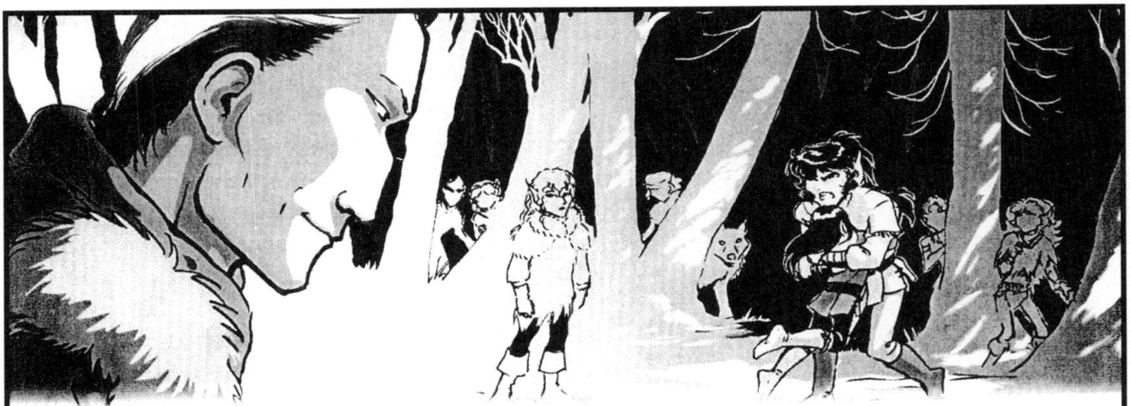

Pool bolts for Scouter, who enfolds him in a ferocious embrace. "Ah, so that's it!" the bounty hunter chuckles, "You're his *sire*, are you?" Scouter answers with a glare of pure loathing. "You needn't fear for your life, elf," Lehrigen acknowledges Mender's courage as the healer surrenders, letting himself be bound. "But I WON'T let you catch me unawares with those wicked hands of yours!"

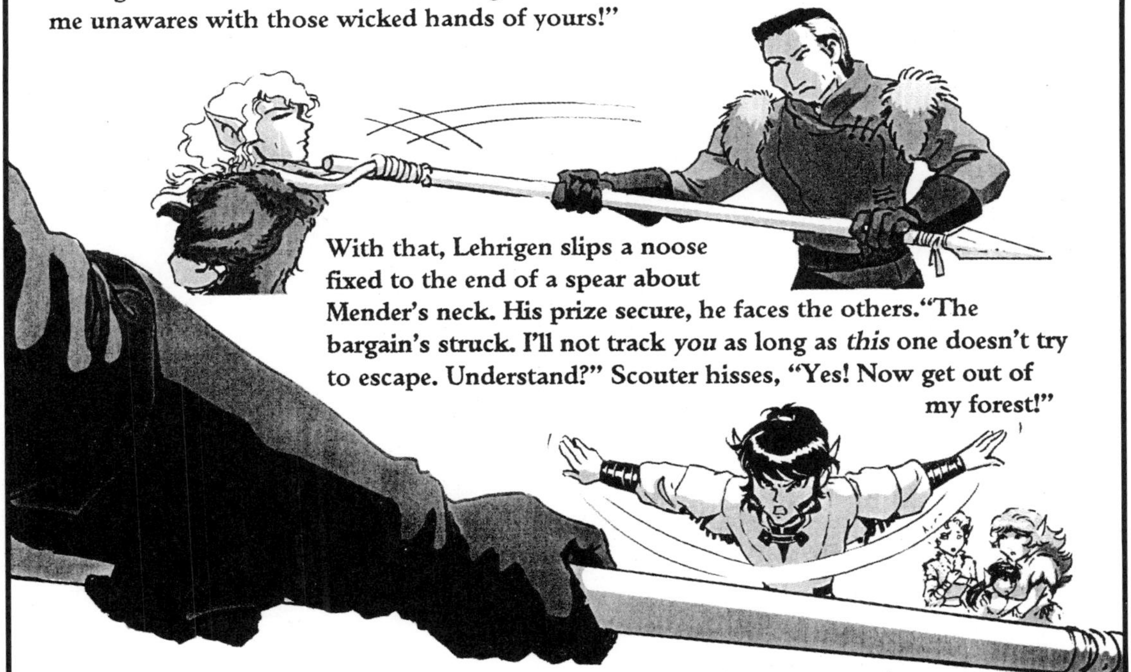

With that, Lehrigen slips a noose fixed to the end of a spear about Mender's neck. His prize secure, he faces the others."The bargain's struck. I'll not track *you* as long as *this* one doesn't try to escape. Understand?" Scouter hisses, "Yes! Now get out of my forest!"

With not a word more, the bounty hunter wheels and strides away, tugging Mender after him at a trot. The gallant healer twists, sending back to his tribe, **Don't worry. This isn't over... not by a bowshot!**

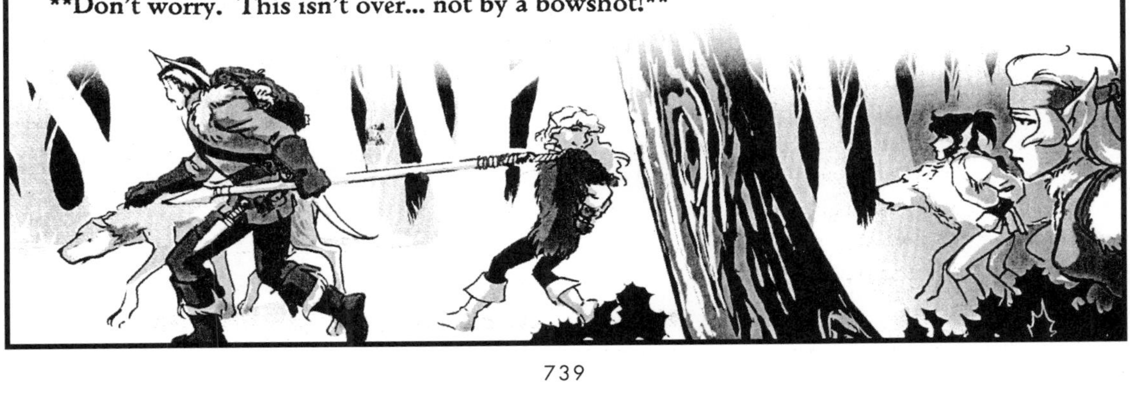

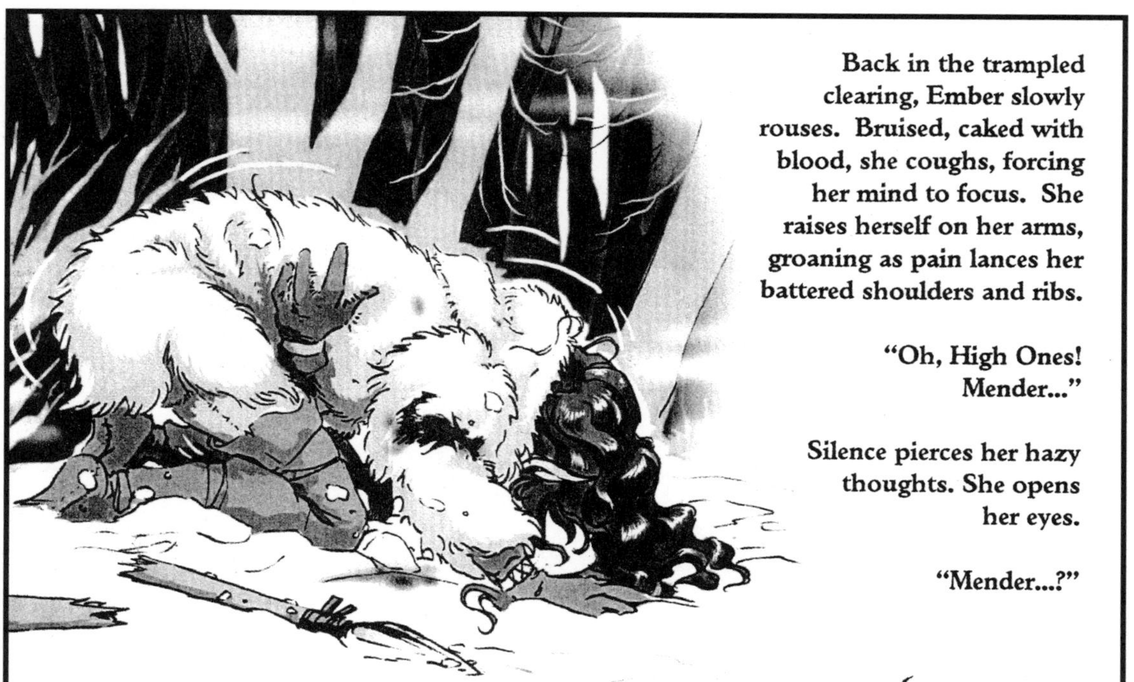

Back in the trampled clearing, Ember slowly rouses. Bruised, caked with blood, she coughs, forcing her mind to focus. She raises herself on her arms, groaning as pain lances her battered shoulders and ribs.

"Oh, High Ones! Mender..."

Silence pierces her hazy thoughts. She opens her eyes.

"Mender...?"

Gingerly exploring a tender knot on her scalp, she puts a hand to the back of her head. Her eyes go wide with realization.

"My chief's lock!"

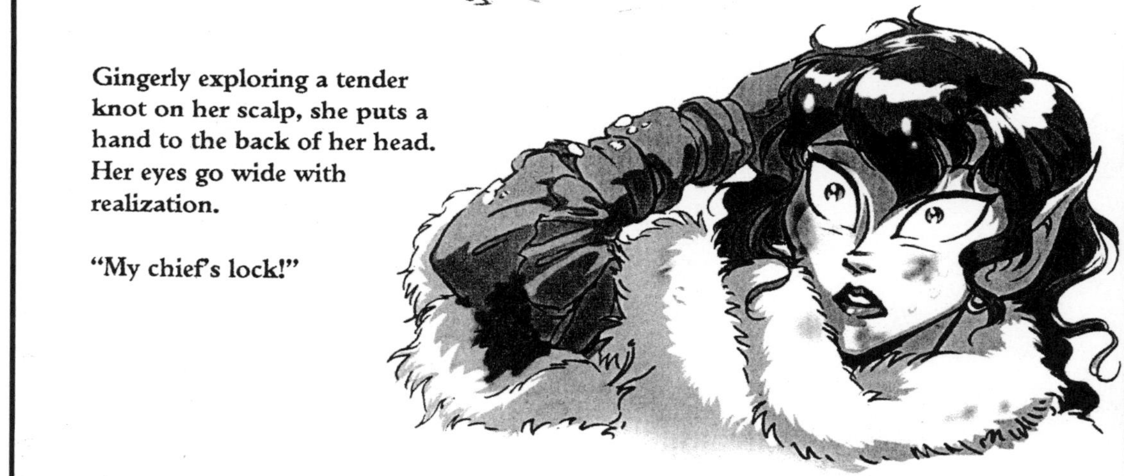

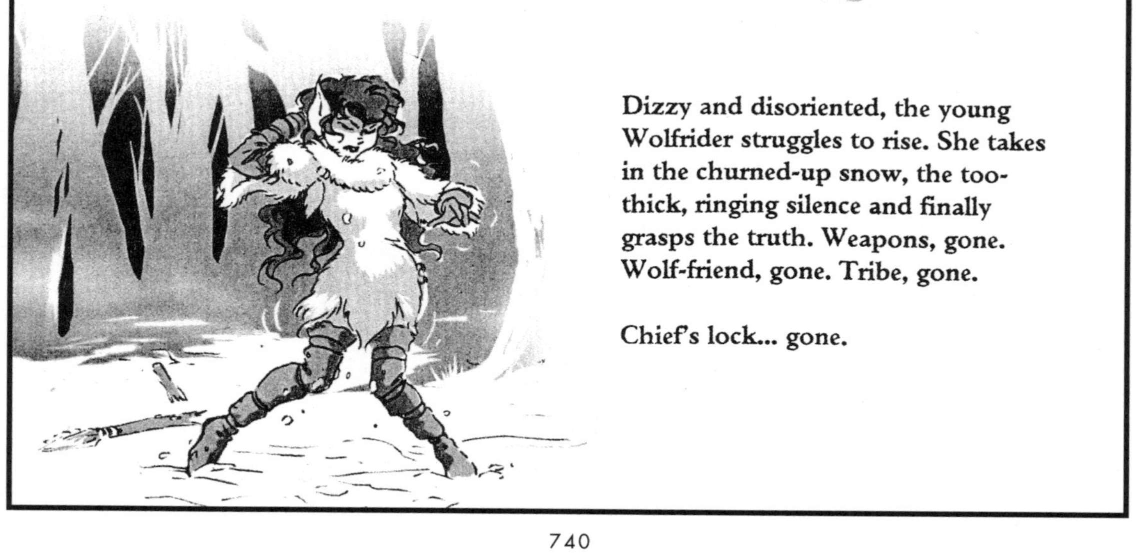

Dizzy and disoriented, the young Wolfrider struggles to rise. She takes in the churned-up snow, the too-thick, ringing silence and finally grasps the truth. Weapons, gone. Wolf-friend, gone. Tribe, gone.

Chief's lock... gone.

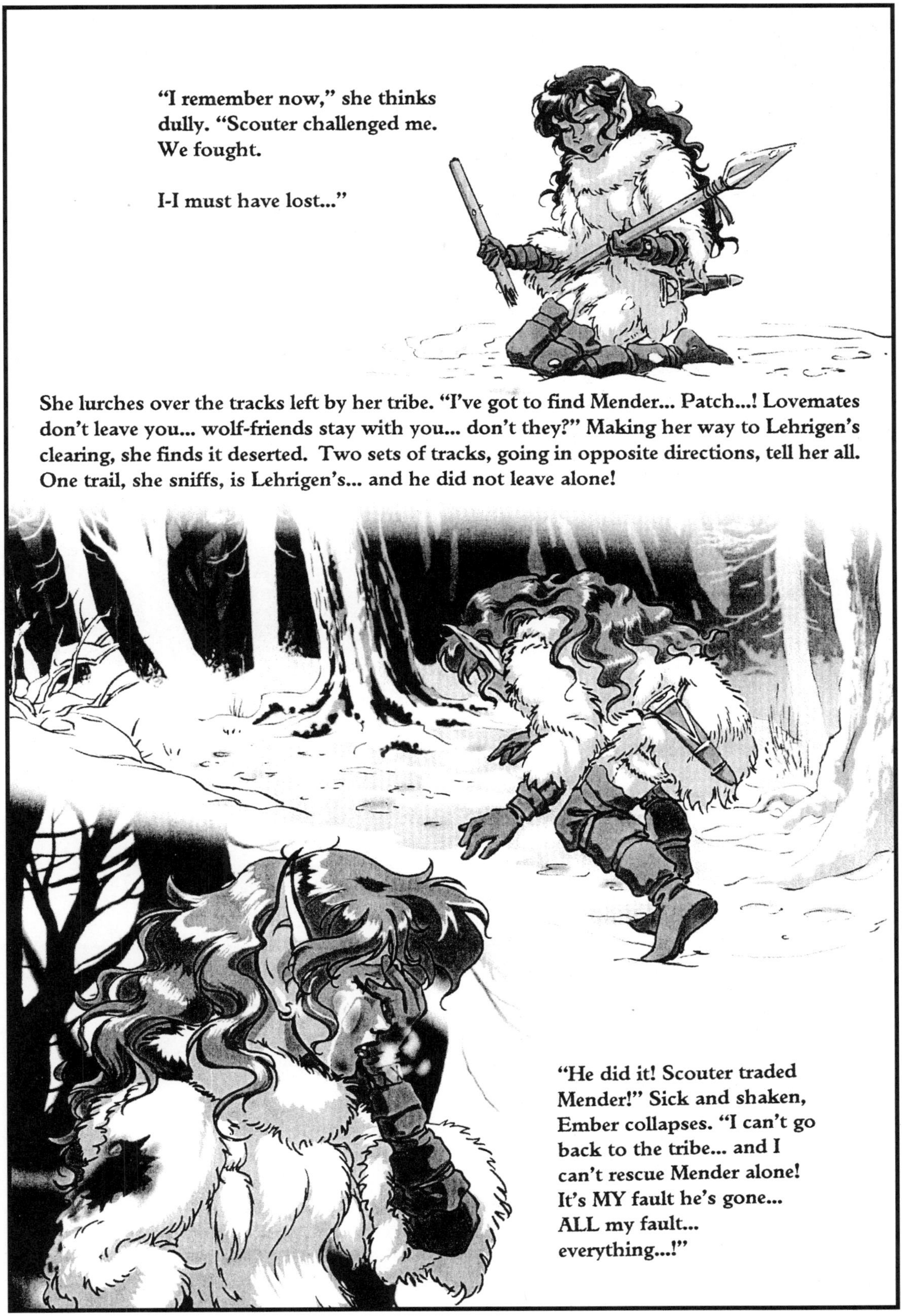
"I remember now," she thinks dully. "Scouter challenged me. We fought.
I-I must have lost..."
She lurches over the tracks left by her tribe. "I've got to find Mender... Patch...! Lovemates don't leave you... wolf-friends stay with you... don't they?" Making her way to Lehrigen's clearing, she finds it deserted. Two sets of tracks, going in opposite directions, tell her all. One trail, she sniffs, is Lehrigen's... and he did not leave alone!
"He did it! Scouter traded Mender!" Sick and shaken, Ember collapses. "I can't go back to the tribe... and I can't rescue Mender alone! It's MY fault he's gone... ALL my fault... everything...!"

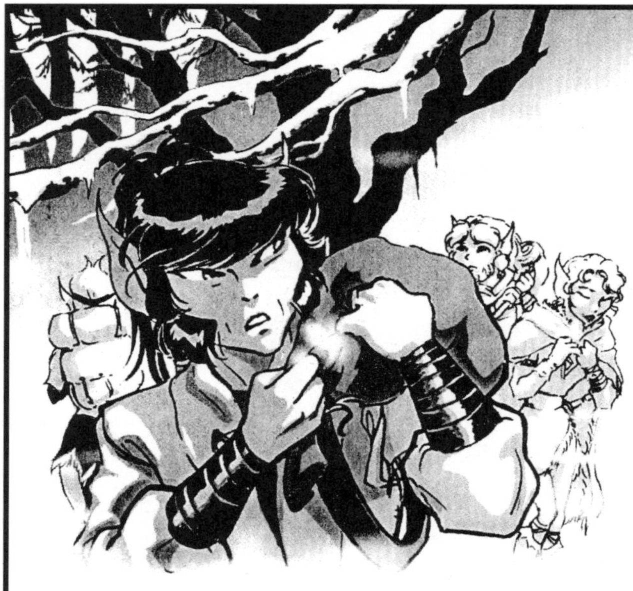

Elsewhere, deeper in the forest, uneasy chief Scouter's tribe is packed and ready to move. His family safe, his thoughts are all on the bounty hunter.

"Best thing now is to side-trail the Still One... find out where he's taking Mender."

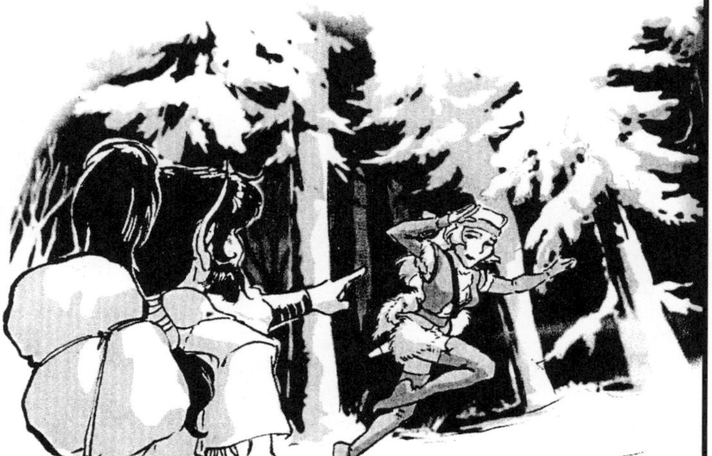

"Yun, tree-scout 'em and stay eyes high," orders Scouter, passing on the role that, once, he proudly called his. "Send their movements back to us. We'll be right behind you."

With a nod and a bound, the Go-Back is away.

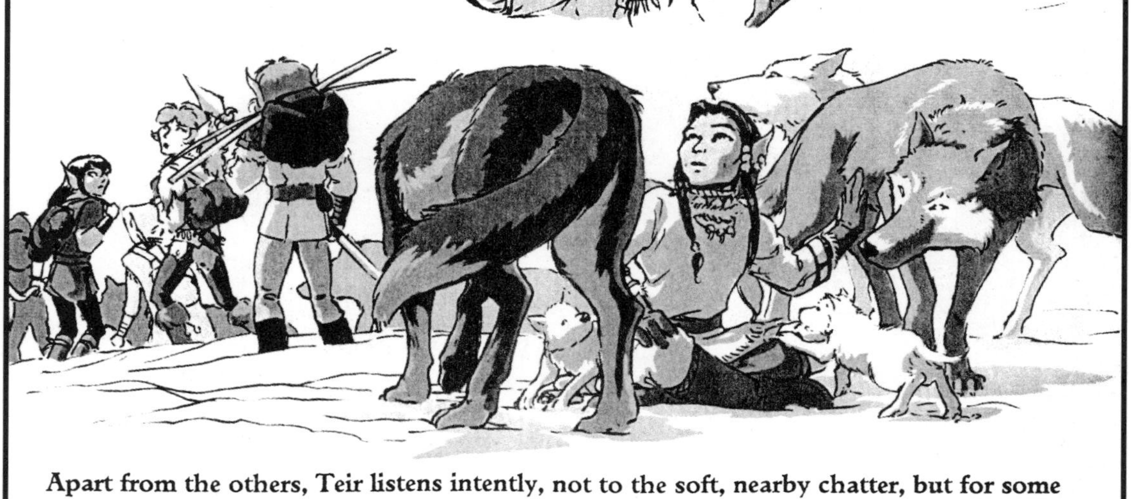

Apart from the others, Teir listens intently, not to the soft, nearby chatter, but for some hint of Ember's thoughts. "Nothing..." he sighs. As the tribe moves out, the Wolf-Father gestures to his lupine companions. "Not yet, friends. I'll tell you when..."

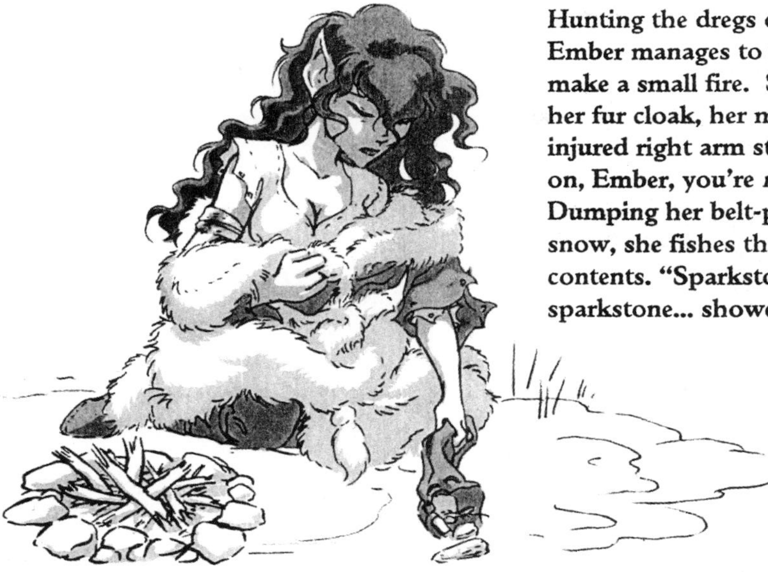

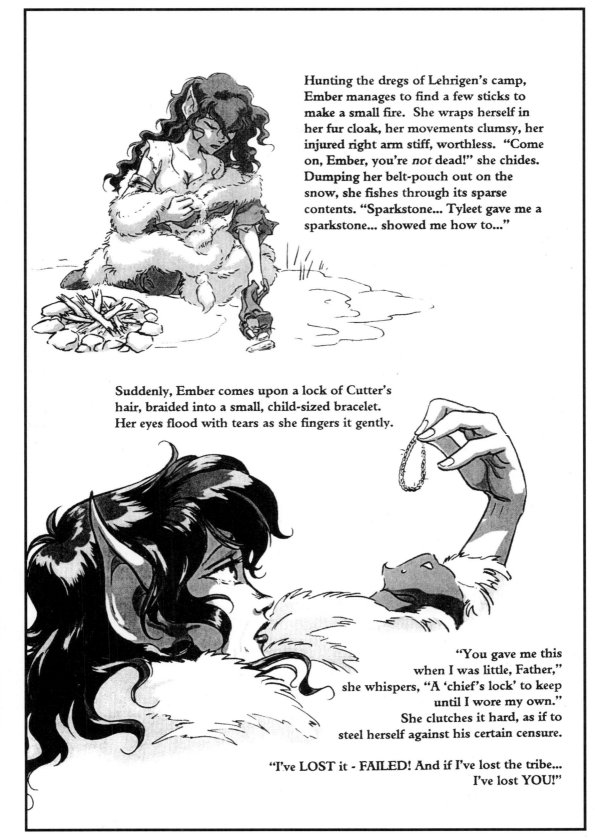

Hunting the dregs of Lehrigen's camp, Ember manages to find a few sticks to make a small fire. She wraps herself in her fur cloak, her movements clumsy, her injured right arm stiff, worthless. "Come on, Ember, you're *not* dead!" she chides. Dumping her belt-pouch out on the snow, she fishes through its sparse contents. "Sparkstone... Tyleet gave me a sparkstone... showed me how to..."

Suddenly, Ember comes upon a lock of Cutter's hair, braided into a small, child-sized bracelet. Her eyes flood with tears as she fingers it gently.

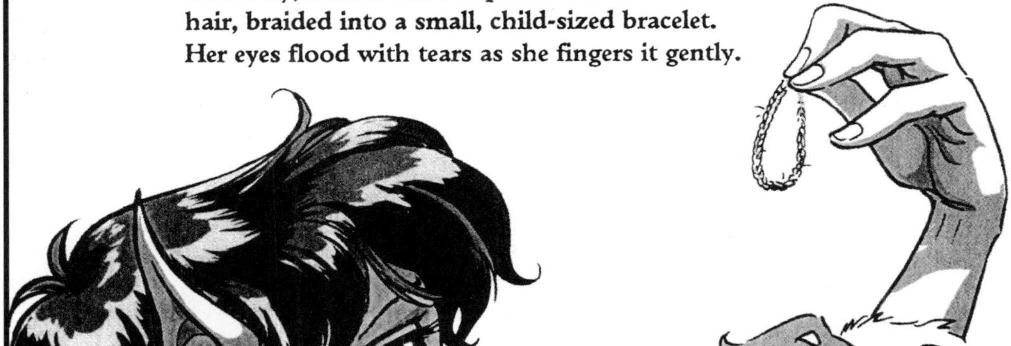

"You gave me this when I was little, Father," she whispers, "A 'chief's lock' to keep until I wore my own." She clutches it hard, as if to steel herself against his certain censure.

"I've LOST it - FAILED! And if I've lost the tribe... I've lost YOU!"

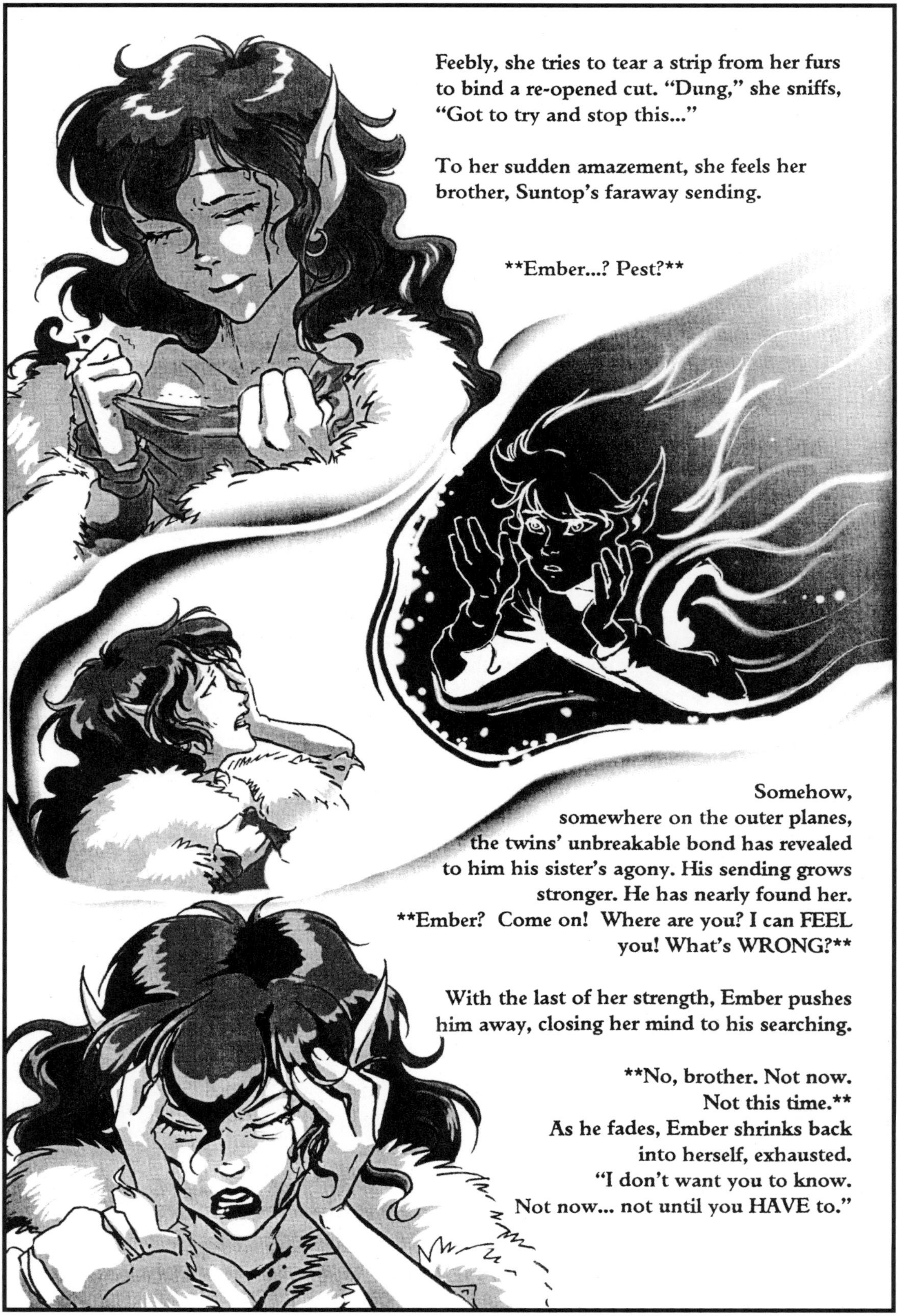
Feebly, she tries to tear a strip from her furs to bind a re-opened cut. "Dung," she sniffs, "Got to try and stop this..."
To her sudden amazement, she feels her brother, Suntop's faraway sending.
Ember...? Pest?
Somehow, somewhere on the outer planes, the twins' unbreakable bond has revealed to him his sister's agony. His sending grows stronger. He has nearly found her.
Ember? Come on! Where are you? I can FEEL you! What's WRONG?
With the last of her strength, Ember pushes him away, closing her mind to his searching.
No, brother. Not now. Not this time.
As he fades, Ember shrinks back into herself, exhausted.
"I don't want you to know. Not now... not until you HAVE to."

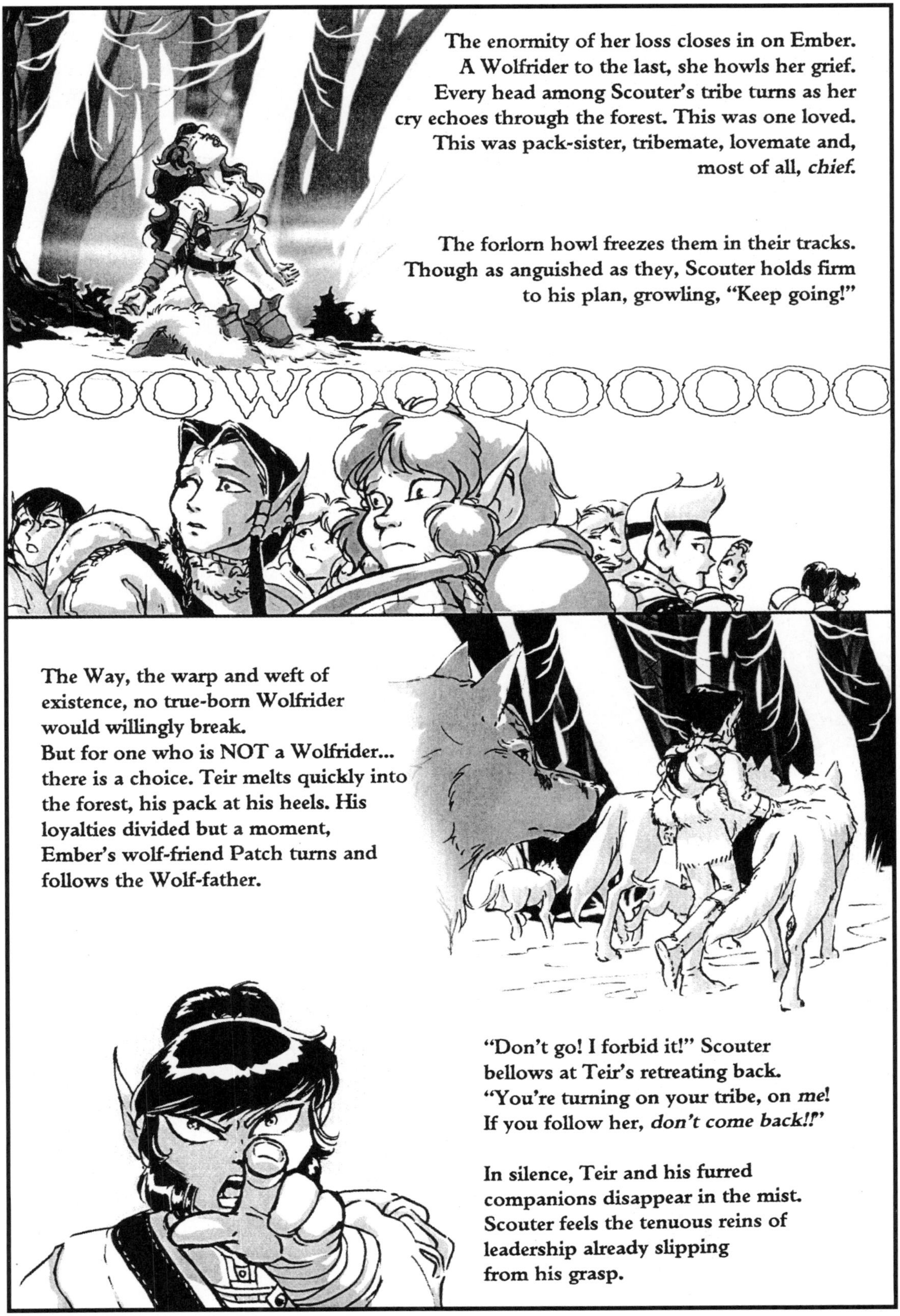
The enormity of her loss closes in on Ember. A Wolfrider to the last, she howls her grief. Every head among Scouter's tribe turns as her cry echoes through the forest. This was one loved. This was pack-sister, tribemate, lovemate and, most of all, *chief.*
The forlorn howl freezes them in their tracks. Though as anguished as they, Scouter holds firm to his plan, growling, "Keep going!"
OOOWOOOOOOOOOO
The Way, the warp and weft of existence, no true-born Wolfrider would willingly break.
But for one who is NOT a Wolfrider... there is a choice. Teir melts quickly into the forest, his pack at his heels. His loyalties divided but a moment, Ember's wolf-friend Patch turns and follows the Wolf-father.
"Don't go! I forbid it!" Scouter bellows at Teir's retreating back. "You're turning on your tribe, on *me*! If you follow her, *don't come back!!*"
In silence, Teir and his furred companions disappear in the mist. Scouter feels the tenuous reins of leadership already slipping from his grasp.

After several days' trudge through snowdrifts, and several closely guarded nights tightly tethered to trees, Mender notes his captor has offered him no greater cruelty. As he has done every night since the trade, Mender watches Lehrigen tend the knife wound that Dewshine gave to Morri.

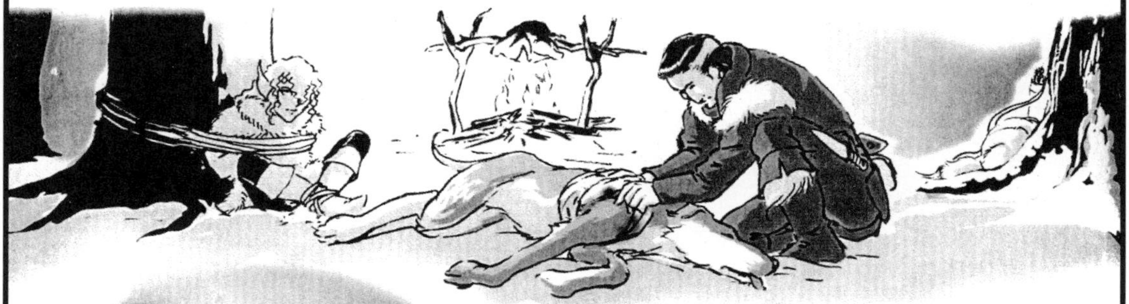

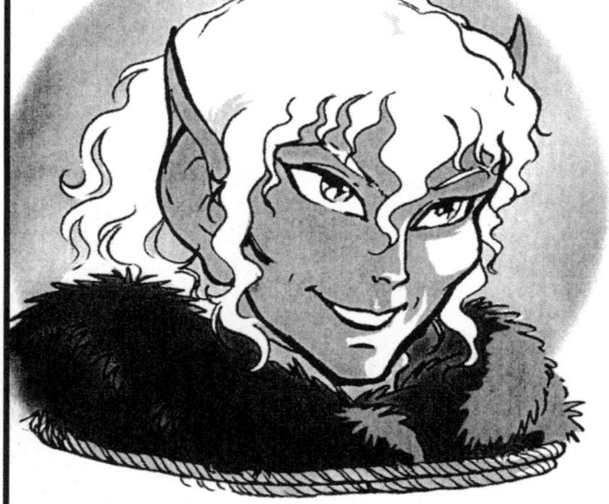

"He's every bit what Ember saw in him," thinks the healer. "Cares for that how-und like a wolf-friend... doesn't talk much... has a nose for a trail like Redlance. What a waste as an enemy!"

Suddenly, a daring thought blossoms. "Still One...?" Mender calls, "I can heal that wound for you. Come, why not? Unless you think *he'd* mind."

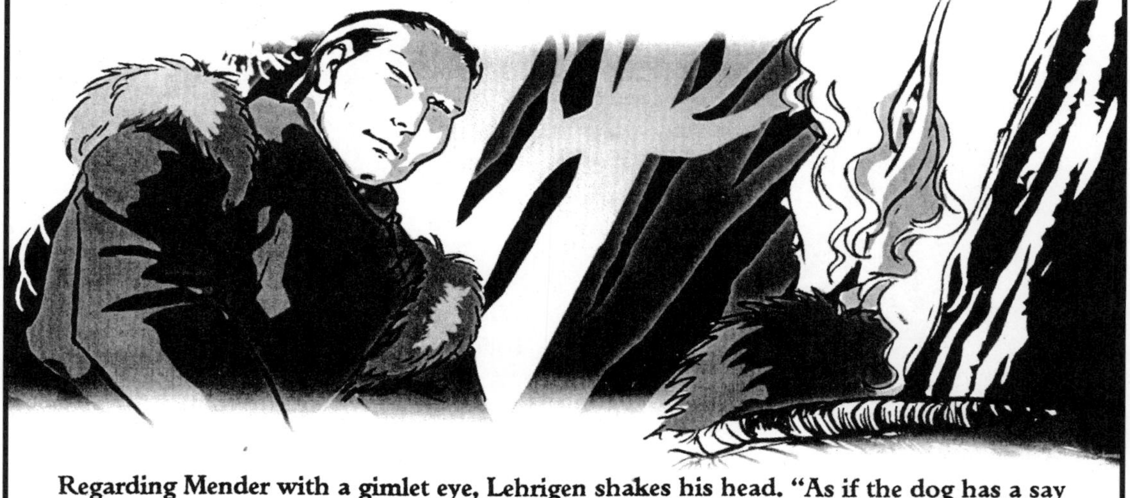

Regarding Mender with a gimlet eye, Lehrigen shakes his head. "As if the dog has a say in it! No, I can't chance your giving him WORSE." But the elf challenges, "What if I gave you *my* word? I'll heal him. Nothing else." Lehrigen's eyes narrow even more. "Morri is your enemy... your guard. It makes no sense."

Mender sighs with exasperation. "For all you've hunted us, Still One, you *still* don't understand how we work. All... *all* life is sacred to elves!"

Lehrigen studies his prisoner. "I'll snap your neck if you cry me false!"

Mender chuckles, "All the more reason for me to deal straight, then!"

The bounty hunter holds Morri's muzzle safely shut. The great dog flinches as the tingling magic emanates from the freed elf's four-fingered hands. Unwinding the bandage, Mender nods at Lehrigen. "Hmmm...you've done well. Know about whistling leaves, do you?" Sinking into a healing trance, Mender closes the gash and stops the seepage.

In a few moments, Mender opens his eyes, examining his handiwork. "There... that's not so bad, now."

Searching Morri for a trace of the wound, the astonished bounty hunter breathes, "Sweet mother moon! Can you do this to humans too? Grow...flesh?"

Mender replies matter-of-factly, "It's harder, but yes, I can."

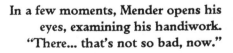

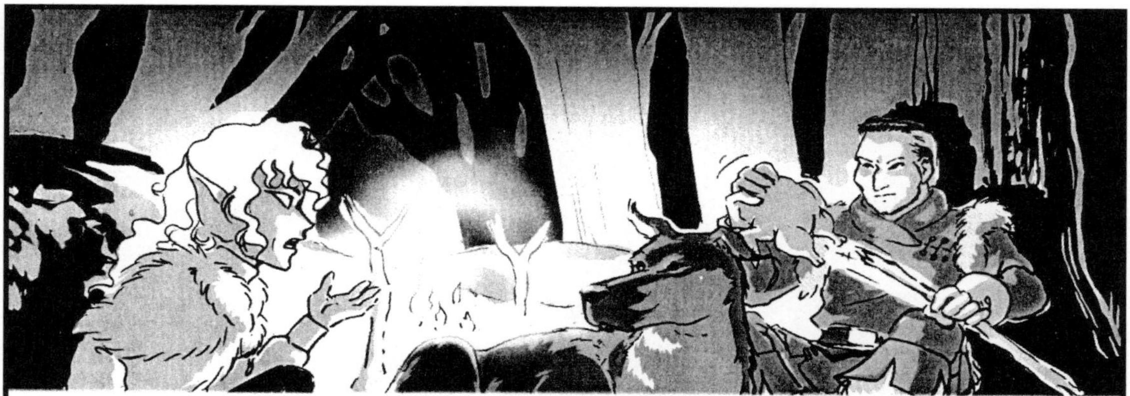

"Well, that explains the Djun," says Lehrigen, pulling a succulent bird from its roasting spit and settling back. "He wants a healer. Alive. That's you."

Mender's hackles rise. "You're one of *his*...?!"

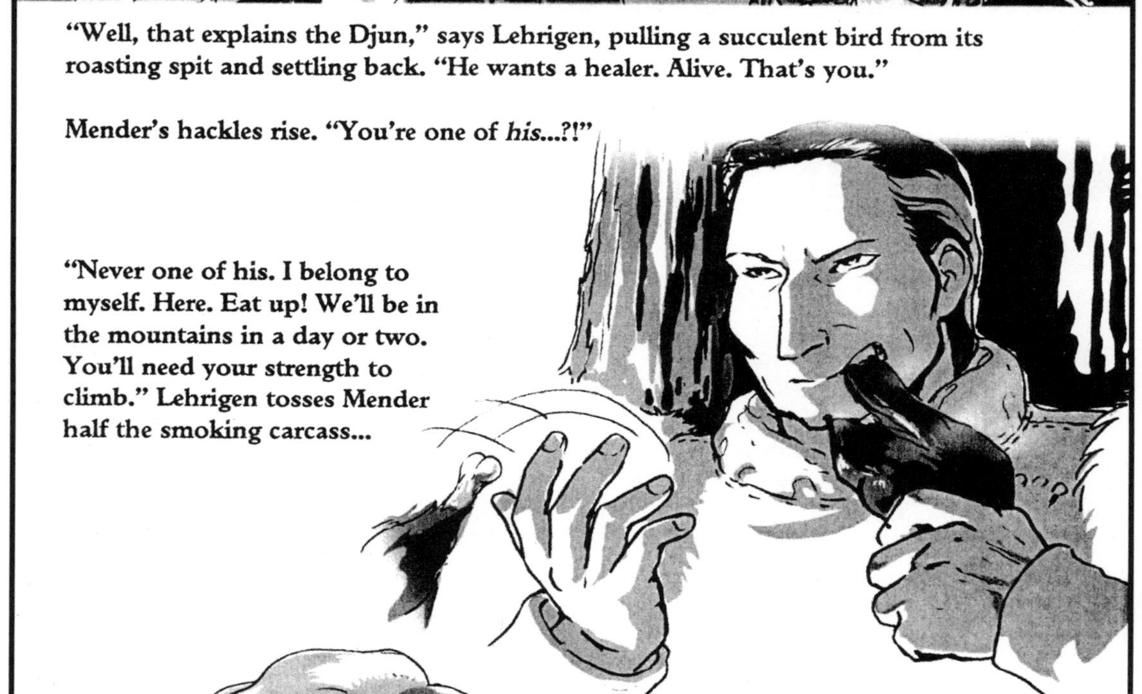

"Never one of his. I belong to myself. Here. Eat up! We'll be in the mountains in a day or two. You'll need your strength to climb." Lehrigen tosses Mender half the smoking carcass...

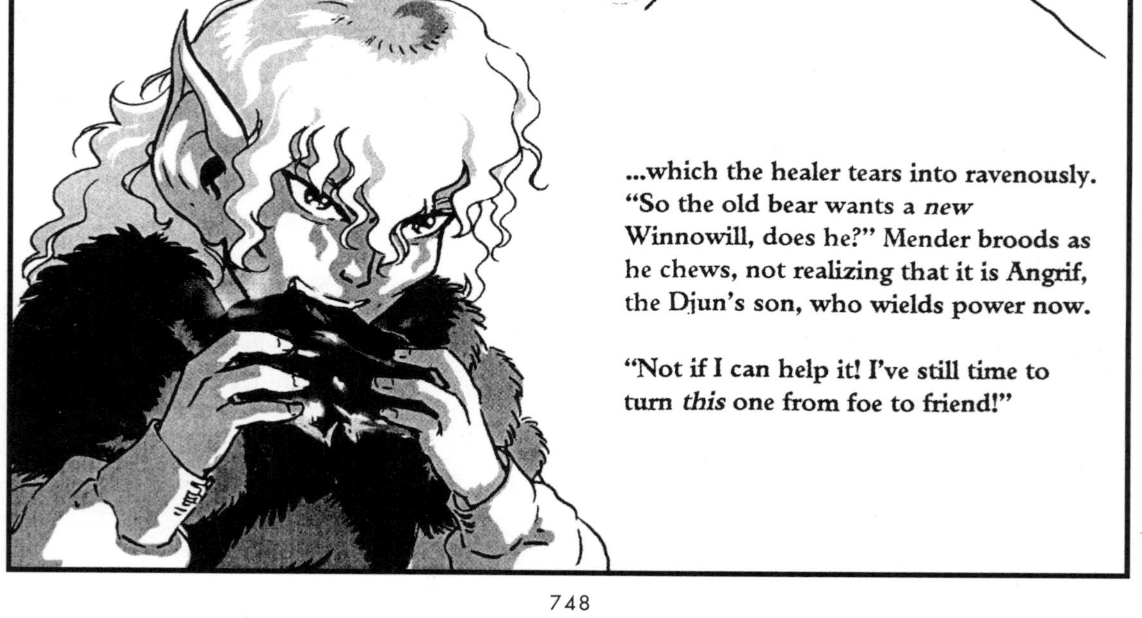

...which the healer tears into ravenously. "So the old bear wants a *new* Winnowill, does he?" Mender broods as he chews, not realizing that it is Angrif, the Djun's son, who wields power now.

"Not if I can help it! I've still time to turn *this* one from foe to friend!"

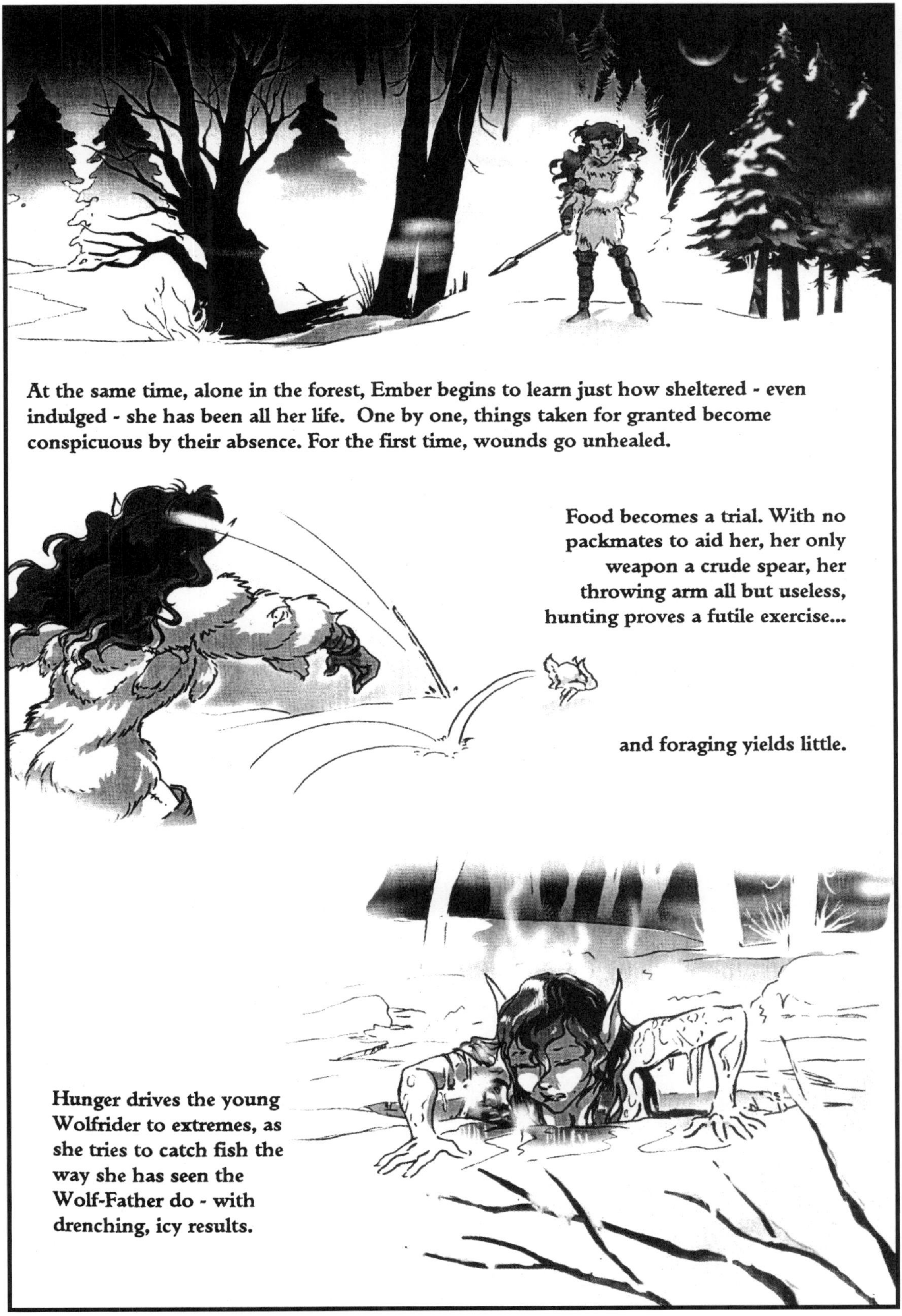
At the same time, alone in the forest, Ember begins to learn just how sheltered - even indulged - she has been all her life. One by one, things taken for granted become conspicuous by their absence. For the first time, wounds go unhealed.
Food becomes a trial. With no packmates to aid her, her only weapon a crude spear, her throwing arm all but useless, hunting proves a futile exercise...
and foraging yields little.
Hunger drives the young Wolfrider to extremes, as she tries to catch fish the way she has seen the Wolf-Father do - with drenching, icy results.

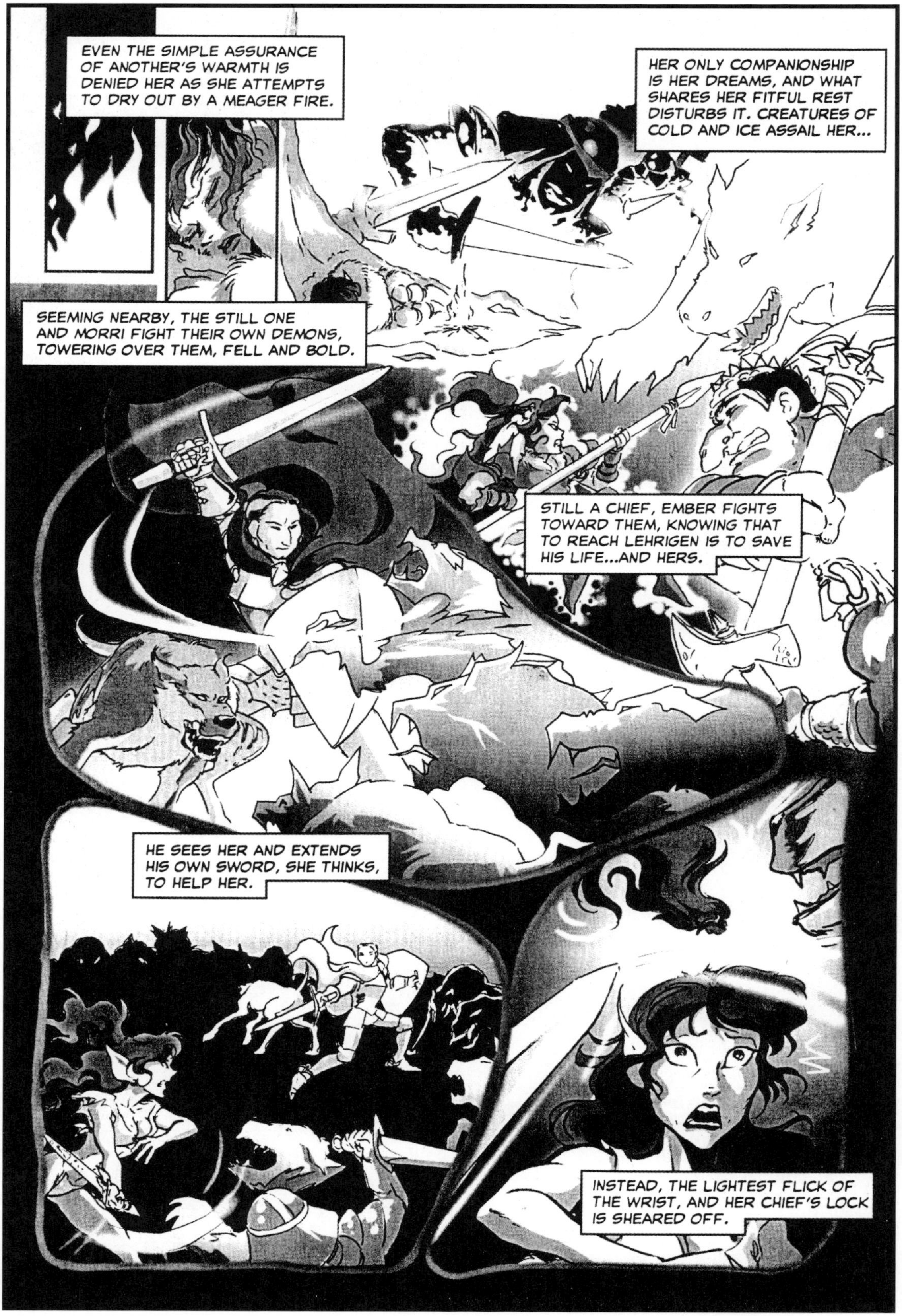
EVEN THE SIMPLE ASSURANCE OF ANOTHER'S WARMTH IS DENIED HER AS SHE ATTEMPTS TO DRY OUT BY A MEAGER FIRE.
HER ONLY COMPANIONSHIP IS HER DREAMS, AND WHAT SHARES HER FITFUL REST DISTURBS IT. CREATURES OF COLD AND ICE ASSAIL HER...
SEEMING NEARBY, THE STILL ONE AND MORRI FIGHT THEIR OWN DEMONS, TOWERING OVER THEM, FELL AND BOLD.
STILL A CHIEF, EMBER FIGHTS TOWARD THEM, KNOWING THAT TO REACH LEHRIGEN IS TO SAVE HIS LIFE...AND HERS.
HE SEES HER AND EXTENDS HIS OWN SWORD, SHE THINKS, TO HELP HER.
INSTEAD, THE LIGHTEST FLICK OF THE WRIST, AND HER CHIEF'S LOCK IS SHEARED OFF.

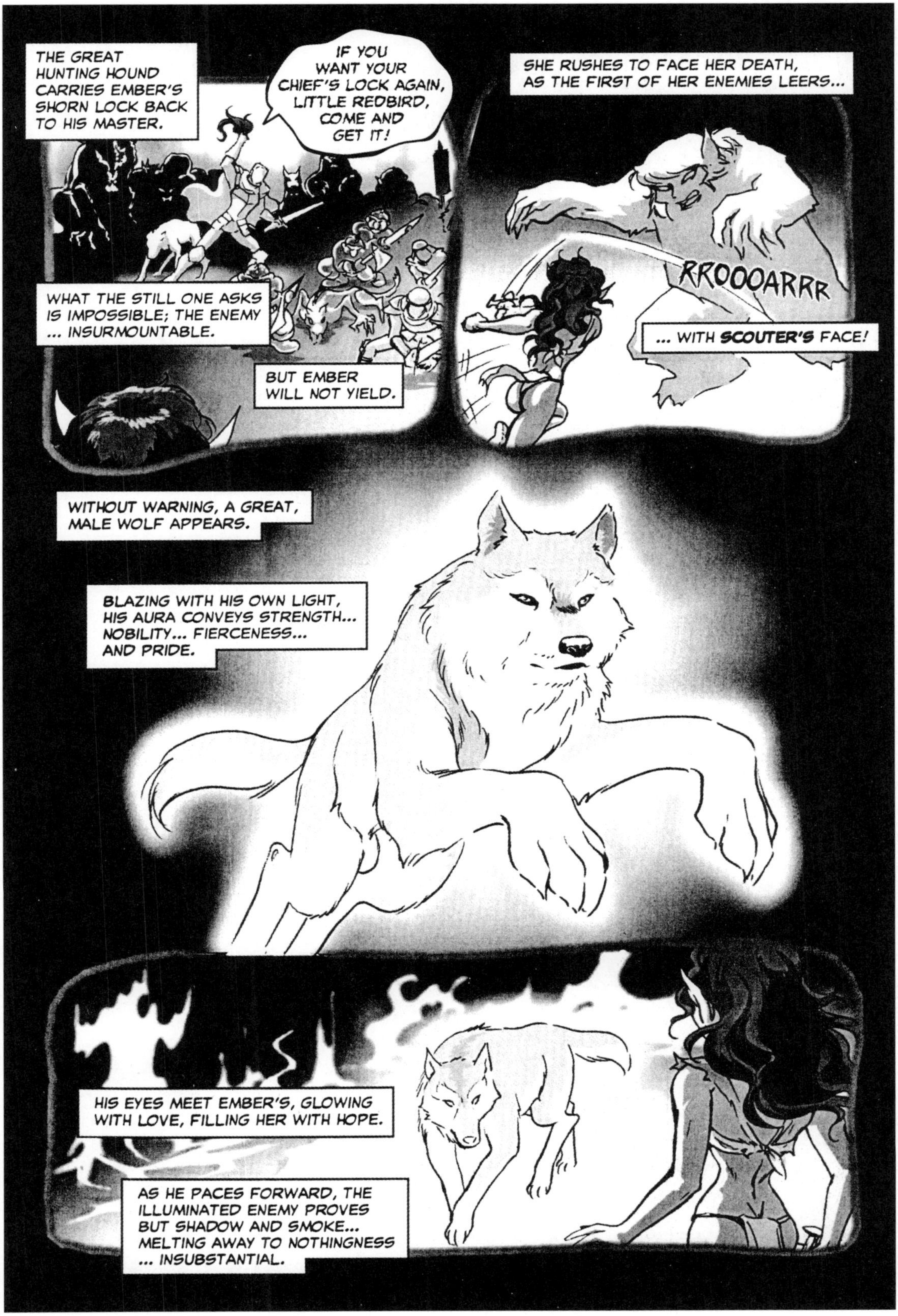
THE GREAT HUNTING HOUND CARRIES EMBER'S SHORN LOCK BACK TO HIS MASTER.
IF YOU WANT YOUR CHIEF'S LOCK AGAIN, LITTLE REDBIRD, COME AND GET IT!
WHAT THE STILL ONE ASKS IS IMPOSSIBLE; THE ENEMY ... INSURMOUNTABLE.
BUT EMBER WILL NOT YIELD.
SHE RUSHES TO FACE HER DEATH, AS THE FIRST OF HER ENEMIES LEERS...
RROOOARRR
... WITH SCOUTER'S FACE!
WITHOUT WARNING, A GREAT, MALE WOLF APPEARS.
BLAZING WITH HIS OWN LIGHT, HIS AURA CONVEYS STRENGTH... NOBILITY... FIERCENESS... AND PRIDE.
HIS EYES MEET EMBER'S, GLOWING WITH LOVE, FILLING HER WITH HOPE.
AS HE PACES FORWARD, THE ILLUMINATED ENEMY PROVES BUT SHADOW AND SMOKE... MELTING AWAY TO NOTHINGNESS ... INSUBSTANTIAL.

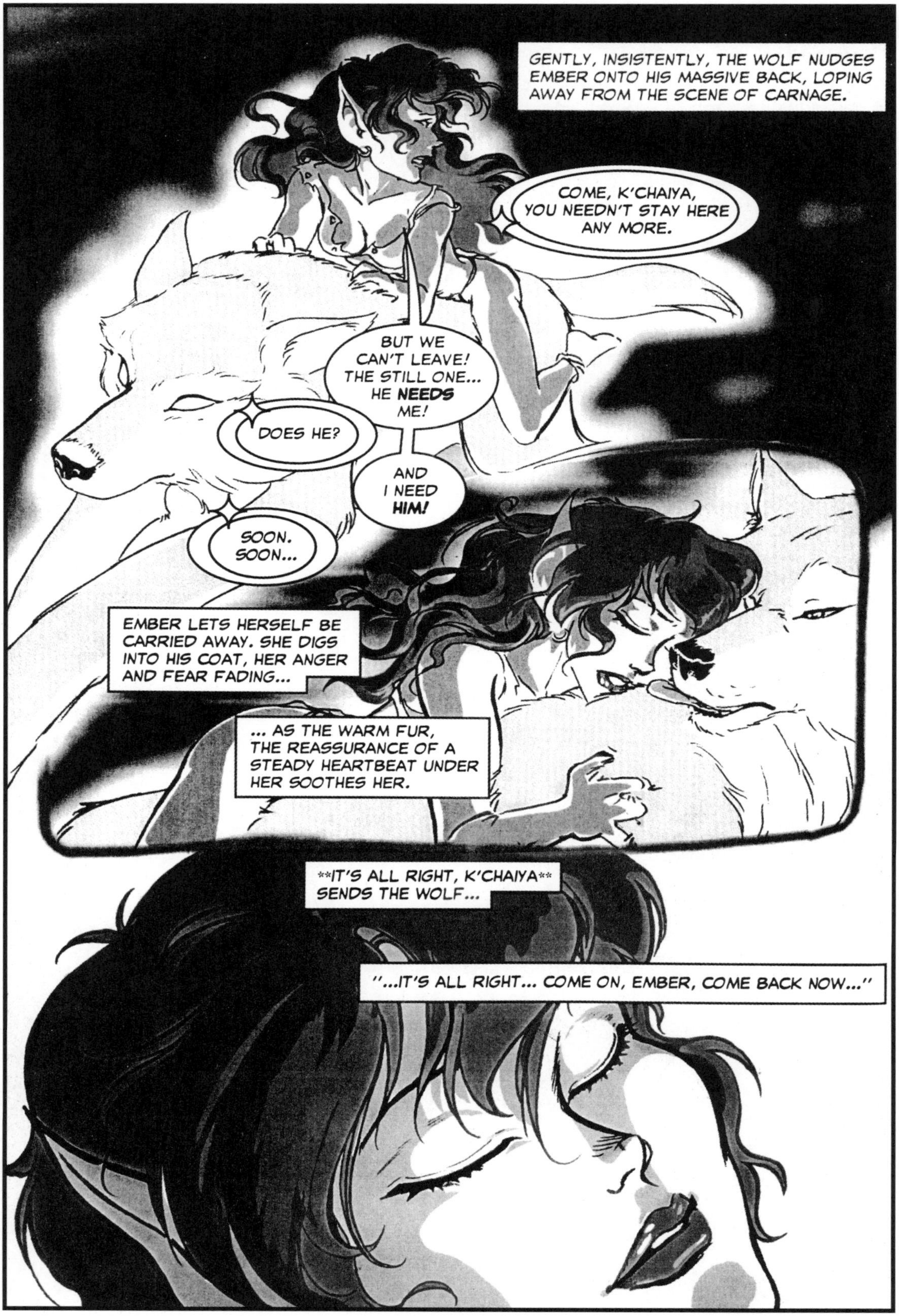
GENTLY, INSISTENTLY, THE WOLF NUDGES EMBER ONTO HIS MASSIVE BACK, LOPING AWAY FROM THE SCENE OF CARNAGE.
COME, K'CHAIYA, YOU NEEDN'T STAY HERE ANY MORE.
BUT WE CAN'T LEAVE! THE STILL ONE... HE **NEEDS** ME!
DOES HE?
AND I NEED **HIM!**
SOON. SOON...
EMBER LETS HERSELF BE CARRIED AWAY. SHE DIGS INTO HIS COAT, HER ANGER AND FEAR FADING...
... AS THE WARM FUR, THE REASSURANCE OF A STEADY HEARTBEAT UNDER HER SOOTHES HER.
IT'S ALL RIGHT, K'CHAIYA SENDS THE WOLF...
"...IT'S ALL RIGHT... COME ON, EMBER, COME BACK NOW..."

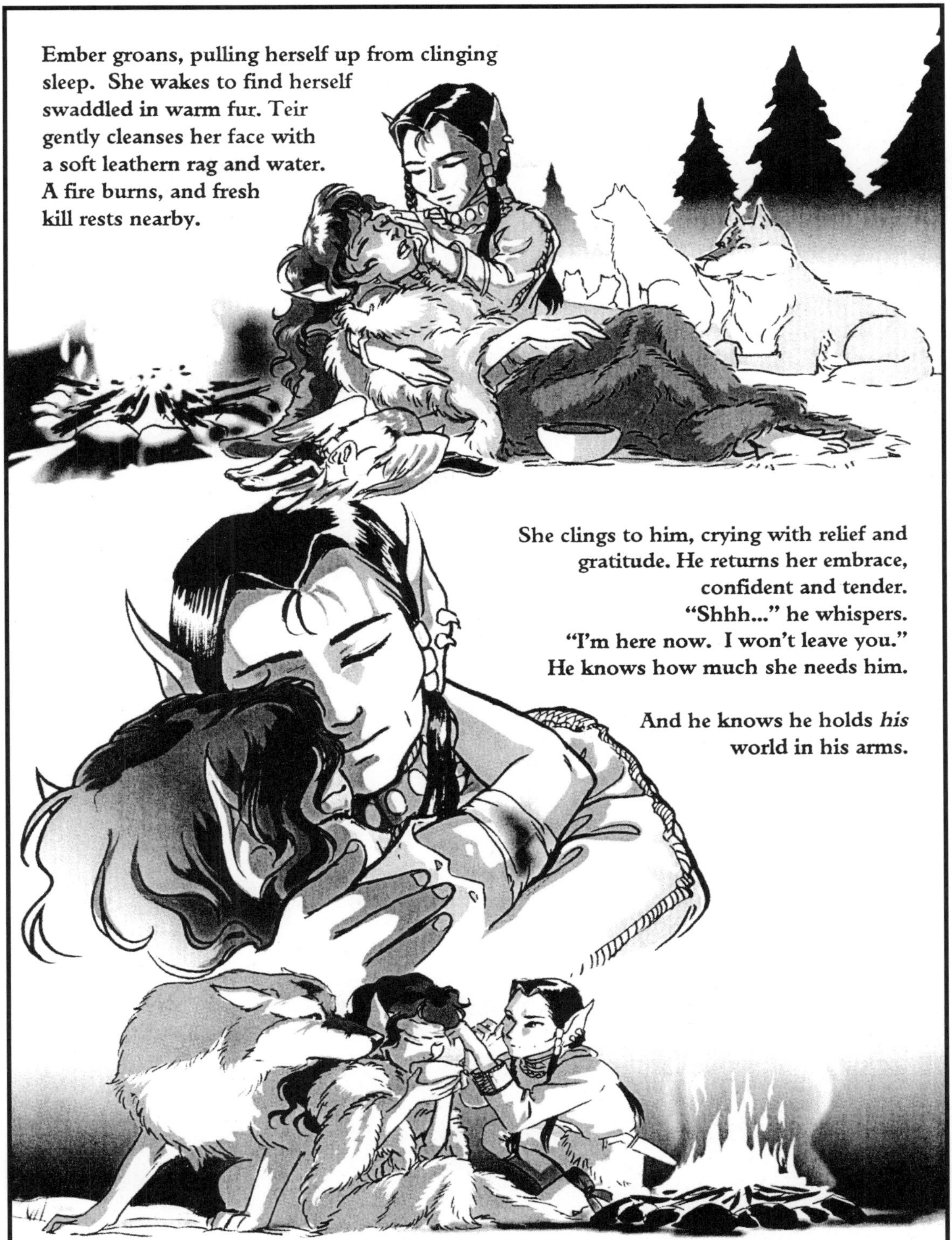
Ember groans, pulling herself up from clinging sleep. She wakes to find herself swaddled in warm fur. Teir gently cleanses her face with a soft leathern rag and water. A fire burns, and fresh kill rests nearby.
She clings to him, crying with relief and gratitude. He returns her embrace, confident and tender. "Shhh..." he whispers. "I'm here now. I won't leave you." He knows how much she needs him.
And he knows he holds *his* world in his arms.
As she drinks hot broth, Ember drinks in inexpressible comfort. Teir skillfully dresses her wounds while the wolves mill about. Happy to be with his elf-friend once more, Patch whines eagerly. "I followed you for days..." Teir explains. "...wanted you to find your own strength. But when I saw you about to give up... I couldn't LET you!"

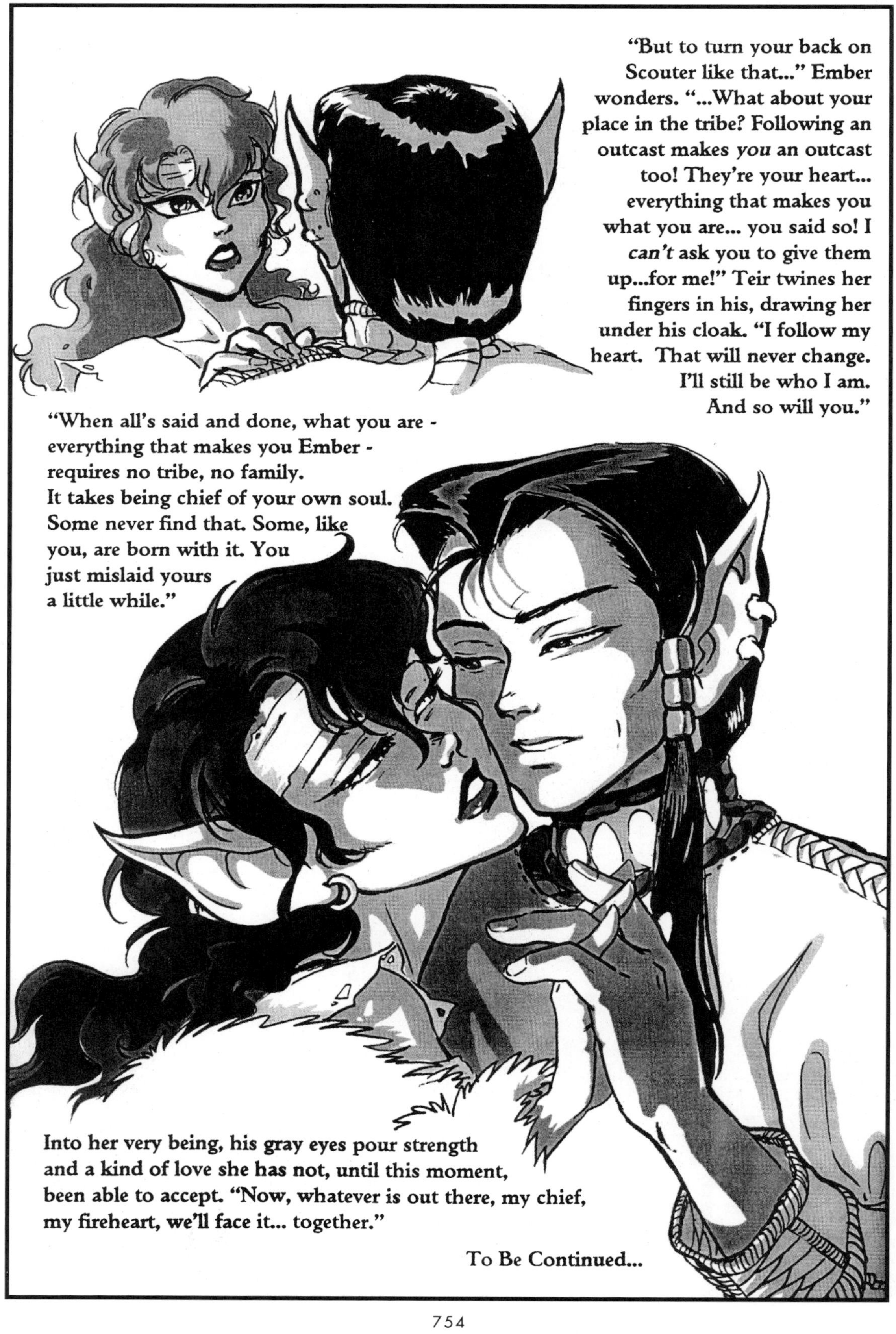
"But to turn your back on Scouter like that..." Ember wonders. "...What about your place in the tribe? Following an outcast makes *you* an outcast too! They're your heart... everything that makes you what you are... you said so! I *can't* ask you to give them up...for me!" Teir twines her fingers in his, drawing her under his cloak. "I follow my heart. That will never change. I'll still be who I am. And so will you."
"When all's said and done, what you are - everything that makes you Ember - requires no tribe, no family. It takes being chief of your own soul. Some never find that. Some, like you, are born with it. You just mislaid yours a little while."
Into her very being, his gray eyes pour strength and a kind of love she has not, until this moment, been able to accept. "Now, whatever is out there, my chief, my fireheart, we'll face it... together."
To Be Continued...

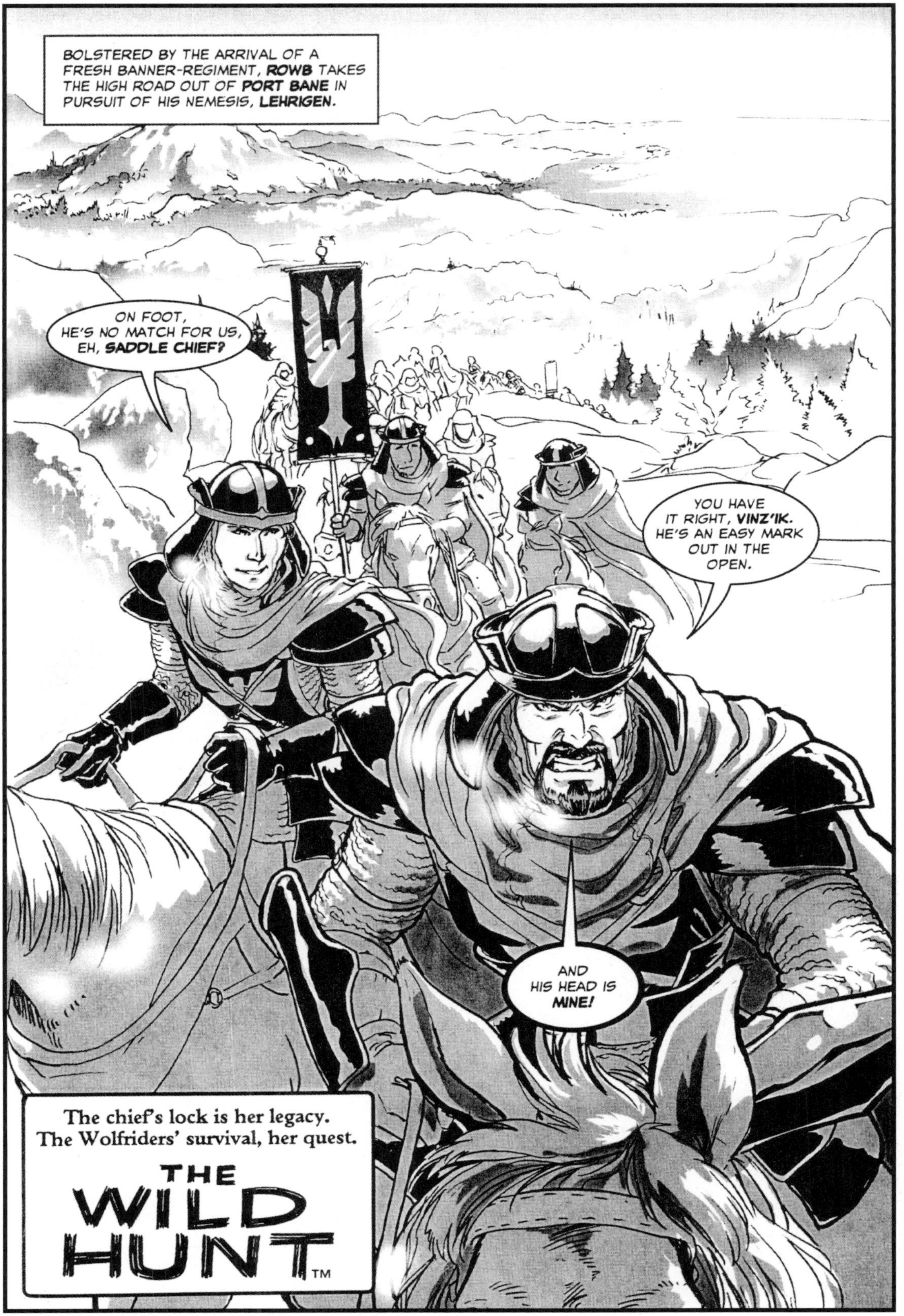

BOLSTERED BY THE ARRIVAL OF A FRESH BANNER-REGIMENT, ROWB TAKES THE HIGH ROAD OUT OF PORT BANE IN PURSUIT OF HIS NEMESIS, LEHRIGEN.
ON FOOT, HE'S NO MATCH FOR US, EH, SADDLE CHIEF?
YOU HAVE IT RIGHT, VINZ'IK. HE'S AN EASY MARK OUT IN THE OPEN.
AND HIS HEAD IS MINE!
The chief's lock is her legacy.
The Wolfriders' survival, her quest.
THE WILD HUNT™

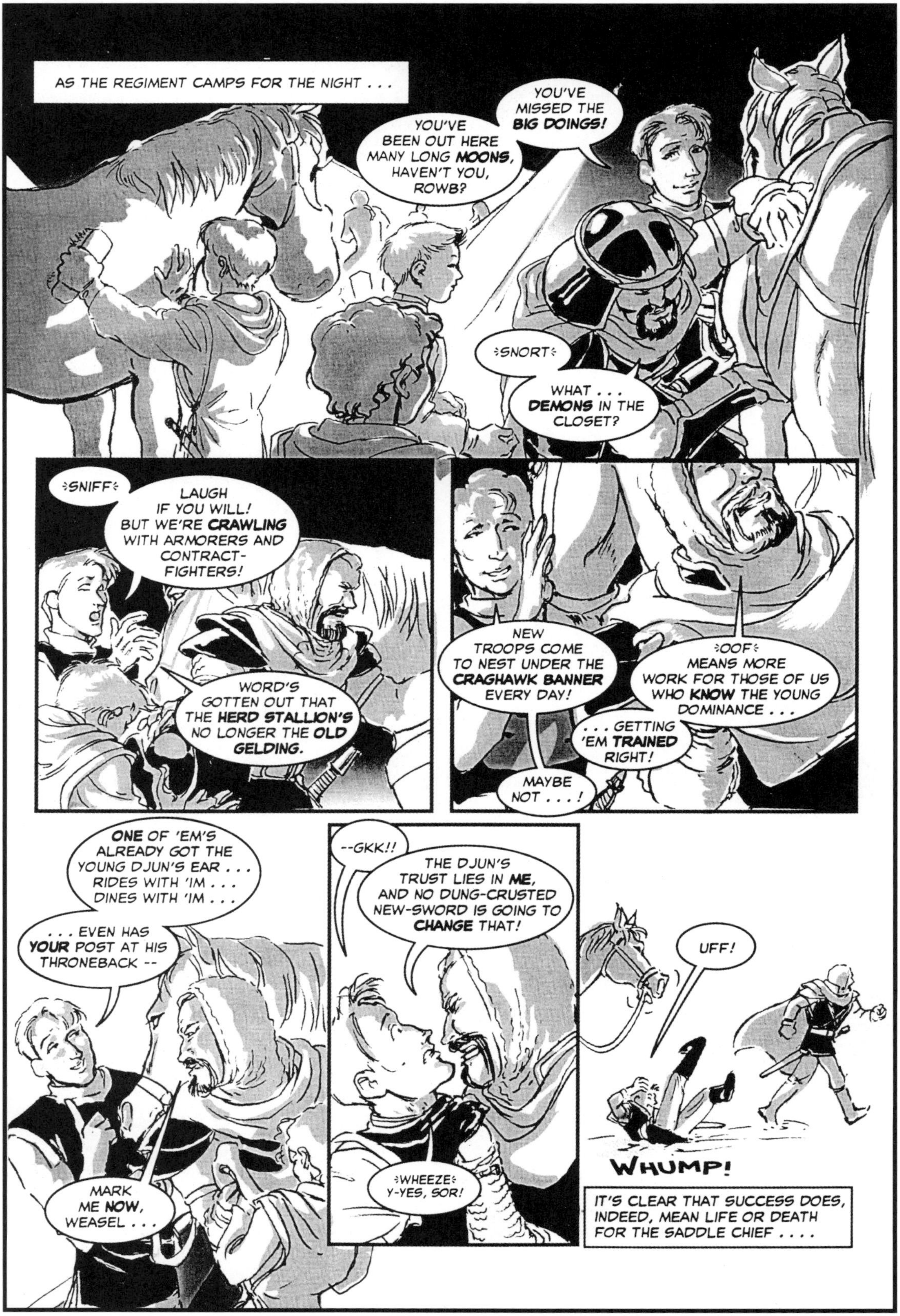
AS THE REGIMENT CAMPS FOR THE NIGHT . . .
YOU'VE BEEN OUT HERE MANY LONG MOONS, HAVEN'T YOU, ROWB?
YOU'VE MISSED THE BIG DOINGS!
SNORT
WHAT . . . DEMONS IN THE CLOSET?
SNIFF
LAUGH IF YOU WILL! BUT WE'RE CRAWLING WITH ARMORERS AND CONTRACT-FIGHTERS!
WORD'S GOTTEN OUT THAT THE HERD STALLION'S NO LONGER THE OLD GELDING.
NEW TROOPS COME TO NEST UNDER THE CRAGHAWK BANNER EVERY DAY!
OOF
MEANS MORE WORK FOR THOSE OF US WHO KNOW THE YOUNG DOMINANCE . . .
. . . GETTING 'EM TRAINED RIGHT!
MAYBE NOT . . . !
ONE OF 'EM'S ALREADY GOT THE YOUNG DJUN'S EAR . . . RIDES WITH 'IM . . . DINES WITH 'IM . . .
. . . EVEN HAS YOUR POST AT HIS THRONEBACK --
MARK ME NOW, WEASEL . . .
--GKK!!
THE DJUN'S TRUST LIES IN ME, AND NO DUNG-CRUSTED NEW-SWORD IS GOING TO CHANGE THAT!
WHEEZE
Y-YES, SOR!
UFF!
WHUMP!
IT'S CLEAR THAT SUCCESS DOES, INDEED, MEAN LIFE OR DEATH FOR THE SADDLE CHIEF . . . .

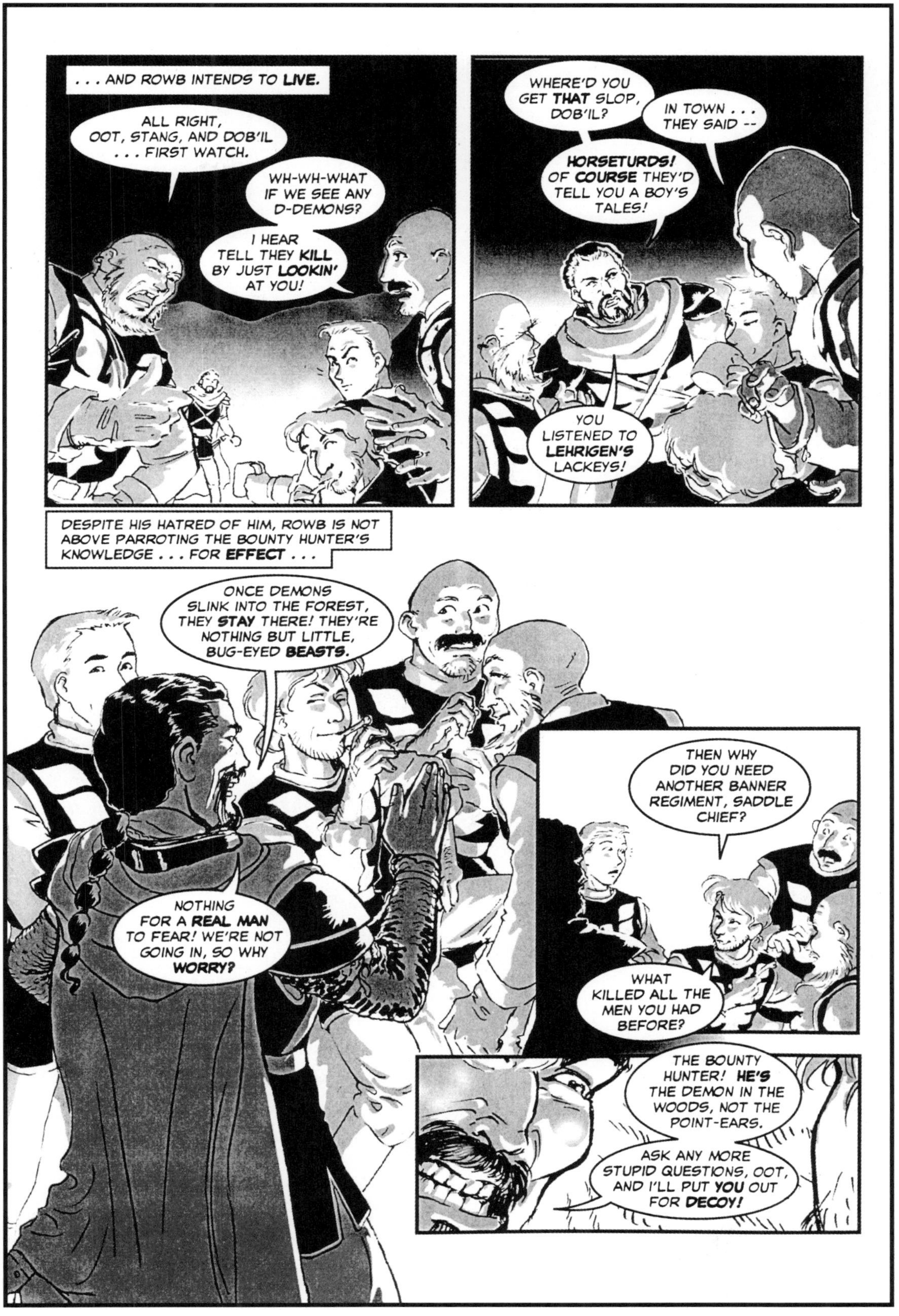
. . . AND ROWB INTENDS TO LIVE.
ALL RIGHT, OOT, STANG, AND DOB'IL . . . FIRST WATCH.
WH-WH-WHAT IF WE SEE ANY D-DEMONS?
I HEAR TELL THEY KILL BY JUST LOOKIN' AT YOU!
WHERE'D YOU GET THAT SLOP, DOB'IL?
IN TOWN . . . THEY SAID --
HORSETURDS! OF COURSE THEY'D TELL YOU A BOY'S TALES!
YOU LISTENED TO LEHRIGEN'S LACKEYS!
DESPITE HIS HATRED OF HIM, ROWB IS NOT ABOVE PARROTING THE BOUNTY HUNTER'S KNOWLEDGE . . . FOR EFFECT . . .
ONCE DEMONS SLINK INTO THE FOREST, THEY STAY THERE! THEY'RE NOTHING BUT LITTLE, BUG-EYED BEASTS.
NOTHING FOR A REAL MAN TO FEAR! WE'RE NOT GOING IN, SO WHY WORRY?
THEN WHY DID YOU NEED ANOTHER BANNER REGIMENT, SADDLE CHIEF?
WHAT KILLED ALL THE MEN YOU HAD BEFORE?
THE BOUNTY HUNTER! HE'S THE DEMON IN THE WOODS, NOT THE POINT-EARS.
ASK ANY MORE STUPID QUESTIONS, OOT, AND I'LL PUT YOU OUT FOR DECOY!

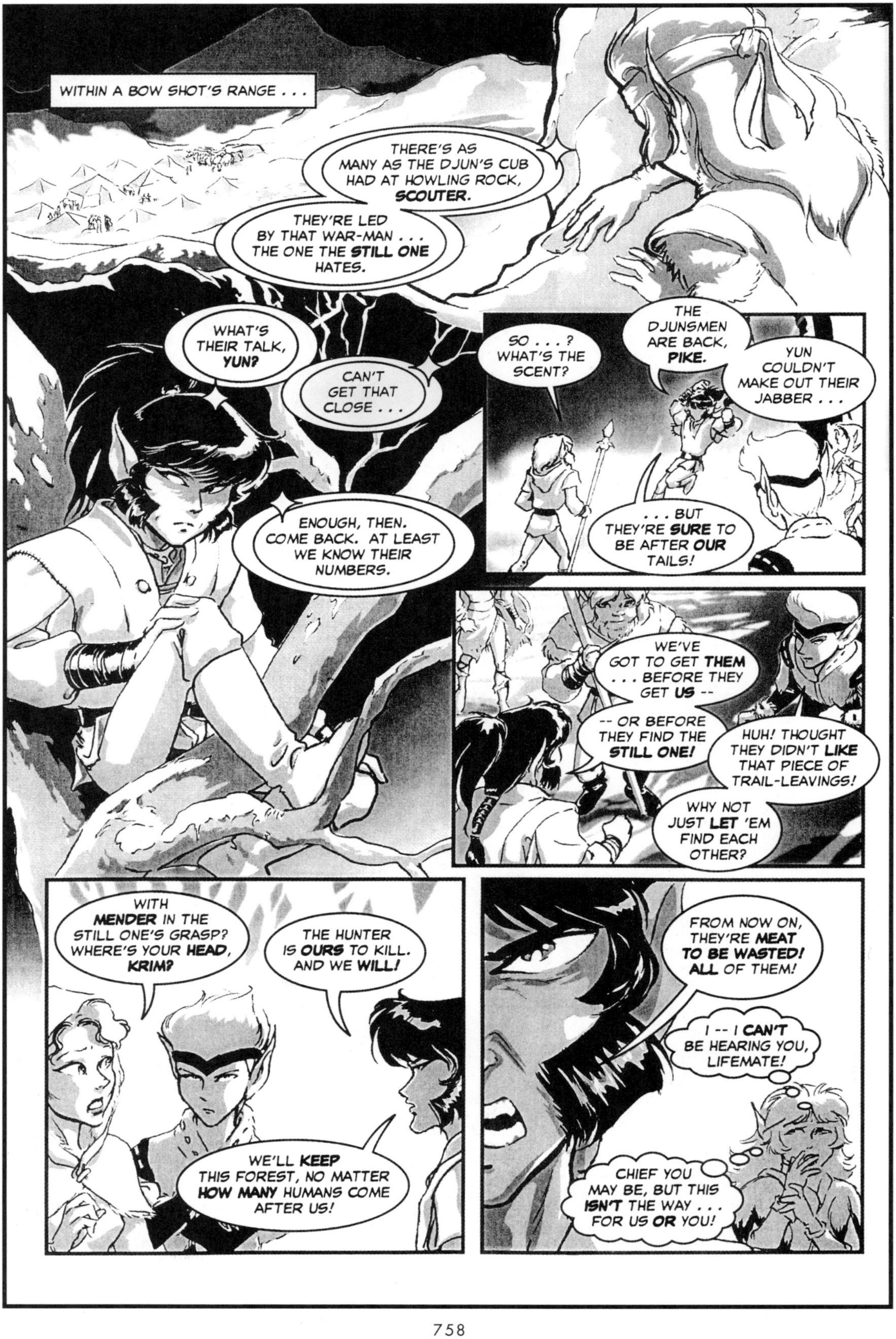
WITHIN A BOW SHOT'S RANGE . . .
THERE'S AS MANY AS THE DJUN'S CUB HAD AT HOWLING ROCK, SCOUTER.
THEY'RE LED BY THAT WAR-MAN . . . THE ONE THE STILL ONE HATES.
WHAT'S THEIR TALK, YUN?
CAN'T GET THAT CLOSE . . .
ENOUGH, THEN. COME BACK. AT LEAST WE KNOW THEIR NUMBERS.
SO . . .? WHAT'S THE SCENT?
THE DJUNSMEN ARE BACK, PIKE.
YUN COULDN'T MAKE OUT THEIR JABBER . . .
. . . BUT THEY'RE SURE TO BE AFTER OUR TAILS!
WE'VE GOT TO GET THEM . . . BEFORE THEY GET US --
-- OR BEFORE THEY FIND THE STILL ONE!
HUH! THOUGHT THEY DIDN'T LIKE THAT PIECE OF TRAIL-LEAVINGS!
WHY NOT JUST LET 'EM FIND EACH OTHER?
WITH MENDER IN THE STILL ONE'S GRASP? WHERE'S YOUR HEAD, KRIM?
THE HUNTER IS OURS TO KILL. AND WE WILL!
WE'LL KEEP THIS FOREST, NO MATTER HOW MANY HUMANS COME AFTER US!
FROM NOW ON, THEY'RE MEAT TO BE WASTED! ALL OF THEM!
I -- I CAN'T BE HEARING YOU, LIFEMATE!
CHIEF YOU MAY BE, BUT THIS ISN'T THE WAY . . . FOR US OR YOU!

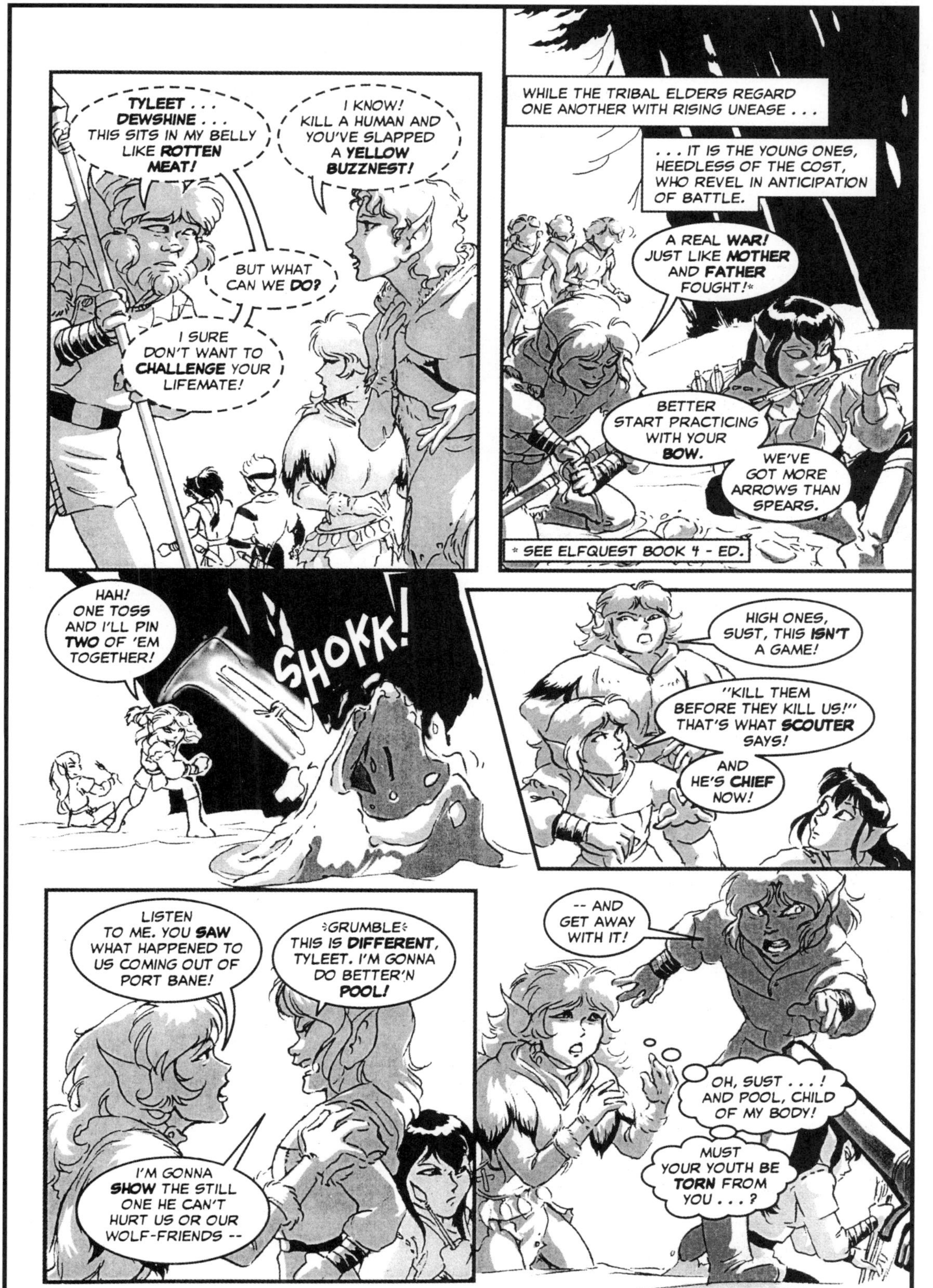
TYLEET . . . DEWSHINE . . . THIS SITS IN MY BELLY LIKE ROTTEN MEAT!
I KNOW! KILL A HUMAN AND YOU'VE SLAPPED A YELLOW BUZZNEST!
BUT WHAT CAN WE DO?
I SURE DON'T WANT TO CHALLENGE YOUR LIFEMATE!
WHILE THE TRIBAL ELDERS REGARD ONE ANOTHER WITH RISING UNEASE . . .
. . . IT IS THE YOUNG ONES, HEEDLESS OF THE COST, WHO REVEL IN ANTICIPATION OF BATTLE.
A REAL WAR! JUST LIKE MOTHER AND FATHER FOUGHT!*
BETTER START PRACTICING WITH YOUR BOW.
WE'VE GOT MORE ARROWS THAN SPEARS.
* SEE ELFQUEST BOOK 4 - ED.
HAH! ONE TOSS AND I'LL PIN TWO OF 'EM TOGETHER!
SHOKK!
HIGH ONES, SUST, THIS ISN'T A GAME!
"KILL THEM BEFORE THEY KILL US!" THAT'S WHAT SCOUTER SAYS!
AND HE'S CHIEF NOW!
LISTEN TO ME. YOU SAW WHAT HAPPENED TO US COMING OUT OF PORT BANE!
GRUMBLE THIS IS DIFFERENT, TYLEET. I'M GONNA DO BETTER'N POOL!
I'M GONNA SHOW THE STILL ONE HE CAN'T HURT US OR OUR WOLF-FRIENDS --
-- AND GET AWAY WITH IT!
OH, SUST . . . ! AND POOL, CHILD OF MY BODY!
MUST YOUR YOUTH BE TORN FROM YOU . . . ?

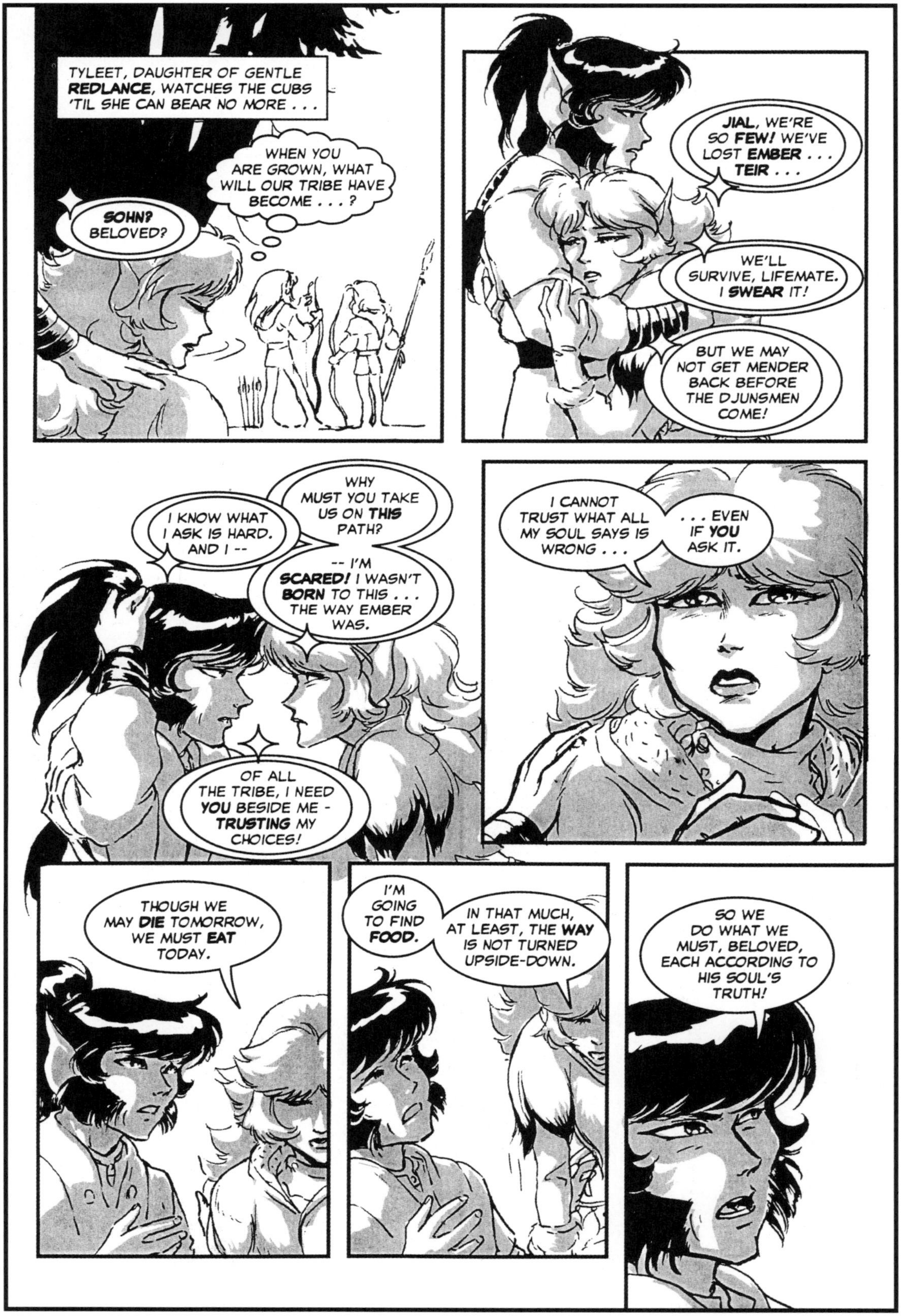
TYLEET, DAUGHTER OF GENTLE REDLANCE, WATCHES THE CUBS 'TIL SHE CAN BEAR NO MORE . . .
WHEN YOU ARE GROWN, WHAT WILL OUR TRIBE HAVE BECOME . . . ?
SOHN? BELOVED?
JIAL, WE'RE SO FEW! WE'VE LOST EMBER . . . TEIR . . .
WE'LL SURVIVE, LIFEMATE. I SWEAR IT!
BUT WE MAY NOT GET MENDER BACK BEFORE THE DJUNSMEN COME!
I KNOW WHAT I ASK IS HARD. AND I --
WHY MUST YOU TAKE US ON THIS PATH?
-- I'M SCARED! I WASN'T BORN TO THIS . . . THE WAY EMBER WAS.
OF ALL THE TRIBE, I NEED YOU BESIDE ME - TRUSTING MY CHOICES!
I CANNOT TRUST WHAT ALL MY SOUL SAYS IS WRONG . . .
. . . EVEN IF YOU ASK IT.
THOUGH WE MAY DIE TOMORROW, WE MUST EAT TODAY.
I'M GOING TO FIND FOOD.
IN THAT MUCH, AT LEAST, THE WAY IS NOT TURNED UPSIDE-DOWN.
SO WE DO WHAT WE MUST, BELOVED, EACH ACCORDING TO HIS SOUL'S TRUTH!

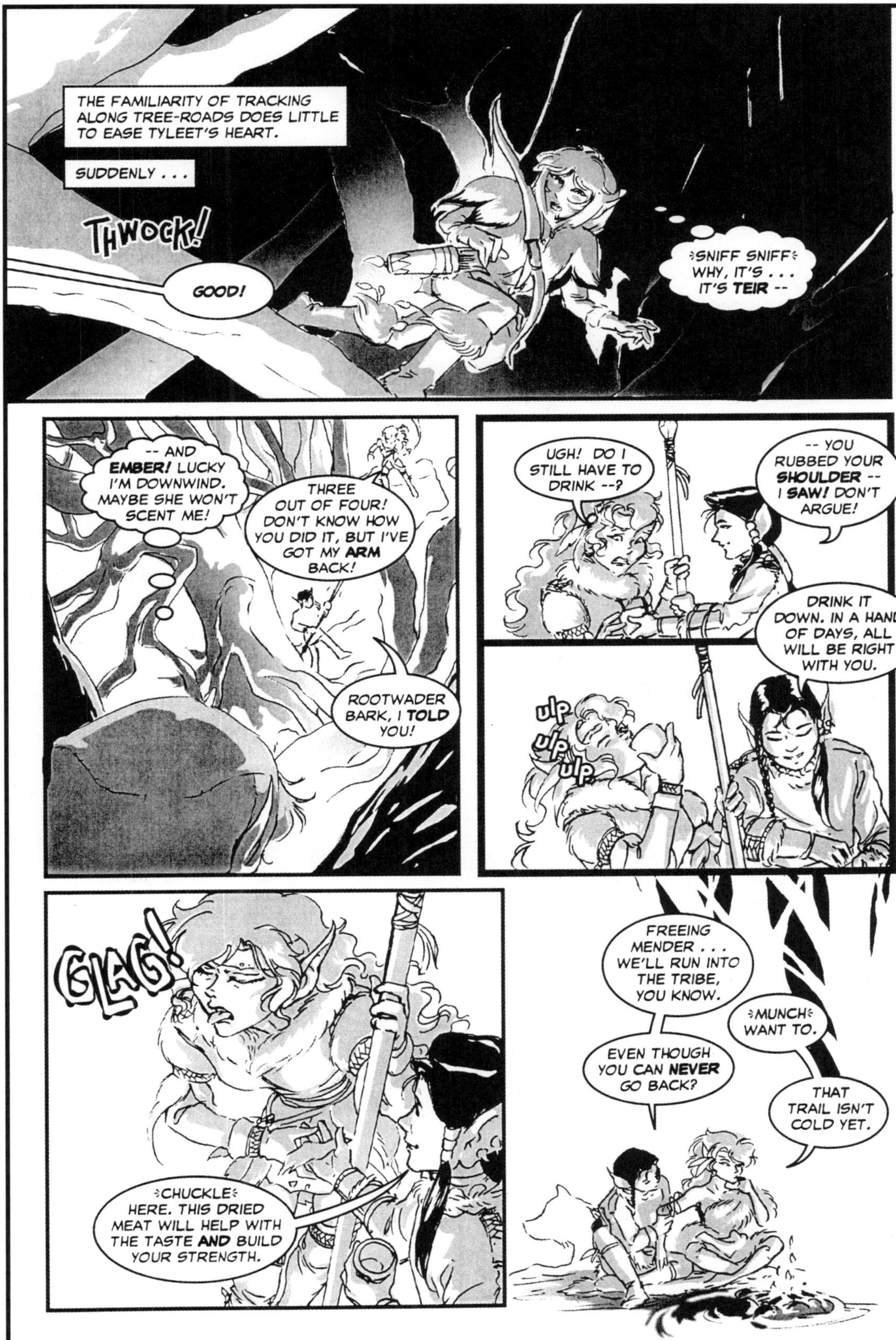
THE FAMILIARITY OF TRACKING ALONG TREE-ROADS DOES LITTLE TO EASE TYLEET'S HEART.
SUDDENLY . . .
THWOCK!
GOOD!
SNIFF SNIFF WHY, IT'S . . . IT'S TEIR --
-- AND EMBER! LUCKY I'M DOWNWIND. MAYBE SHE WON'T SCENT ME!
THREE OUT OF FOUR! DON'T KNOW HOW YOU DID IT, BUT I'VE GOT MY ARM BACK!
ROOTWADER BARK, I TOLD YOU!
UGH! DO I STILL HAVE TO DRINK --?
-- YOU RUBBED YOUR SHOULDER -- I SAW! DON'T ARGUE!
DRINK IT DOWN. IN A HAND OF DAYS, ALL WILL BE RIGHT WITH YOU.
ulp ulp ulp
GLAG!
CHUCKLE HERE. THIS DRIED MEAT WILL HELP WITH THE TASTE AND BUILD YOUR STRENGTH.
FREEING MENDER . . . WE'LL RUN INTO THE TRIBE, YOU KNOW.
EVEN THOUGH YOU CAN NEVER GO BACK?
MUNCH WANT TO.
THAT TRAIL ISN'T COLD YET.

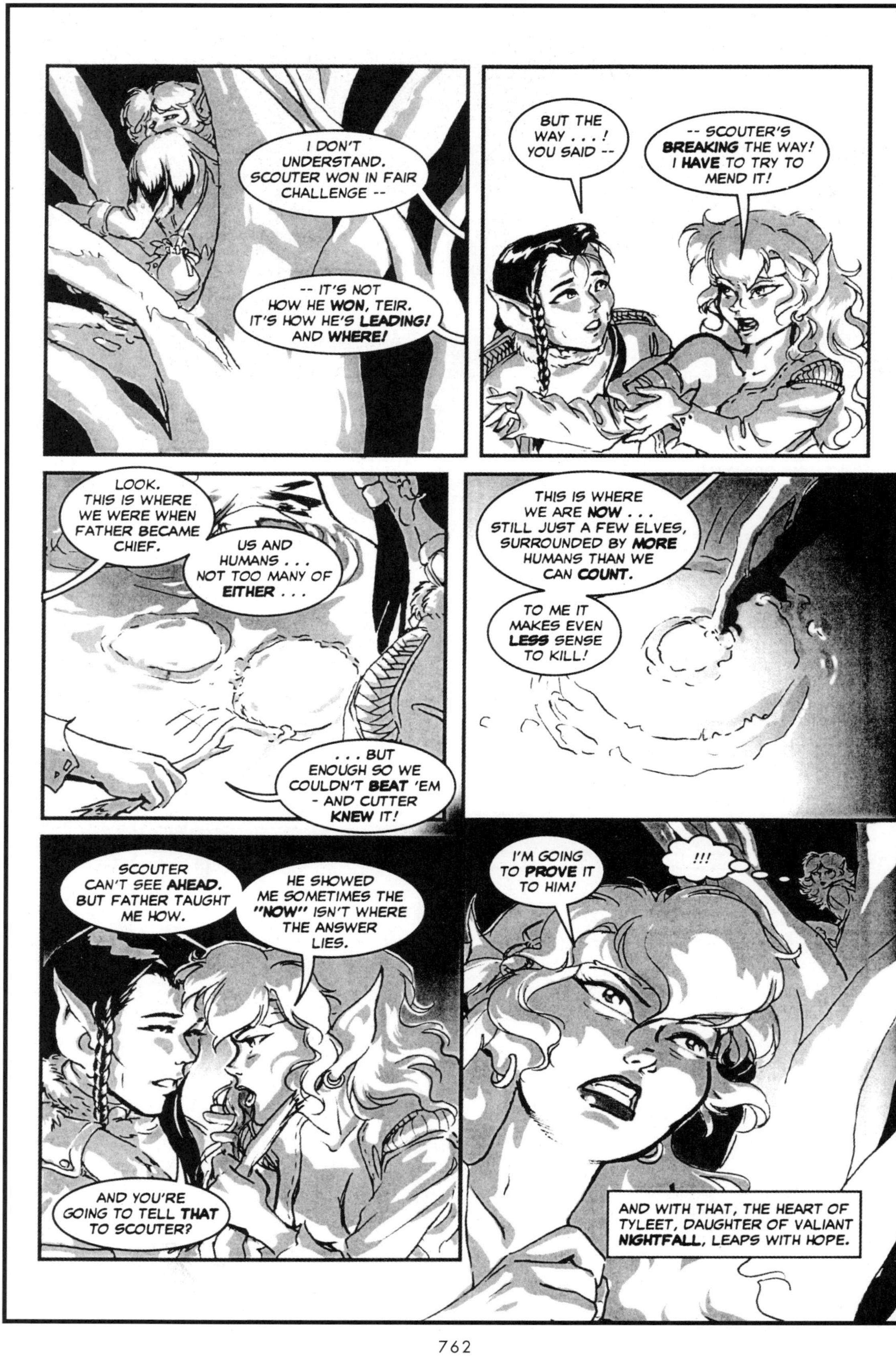
I DON'T UNDERSTAND. SCOUTER WON IN FAIR CHALLENGE --
-- IT'S NOT HOW HE WON, TEIR. IT'S HOW HE'S LEADING! AND WHERE!
BUT THE WAY . . . ! YOU SAID --
-- SCOUTER'S BREAKING THE WAY! I HAVE TO TRY TO MEND IT!
LOOK. THIS IS WHERE WE WERE WHEN FATHER BECAME CHIEF.
US AND HUMANS . . . NOT TOO MANY OF EITHER . . .
. . . BUT ENOUGH SO WE COULDN'T BEAT 'EM - AND CUTTER KNEW IT!
THIS IS WHERE WE ARE NOW . . . STILL JUST A FEW ELVES, SURROUNDED BY MORE HUMANS THAN WE CAN COUNT.
TO ME IT MAKES EVEN LESS SENSE TO KILL!
SCOUTER CAN'T SEE AHEAD. BUT FATHER TAUGHT ME HOW.
HE SHOWED ME SOMETIMES THE "NOW" ISN'T WHERE THE ANSWER LIES.
AND YOU'RE GOING TO TELL THAT TO SCOUTER?
I'M GOING TO PROVE IT TO HIM!
!!!
AND WITH THAT, THE HEART OF TYLEET, DAUGHTER OF VALIANT NIGHTFALL, LEAPS WITH HOPE.

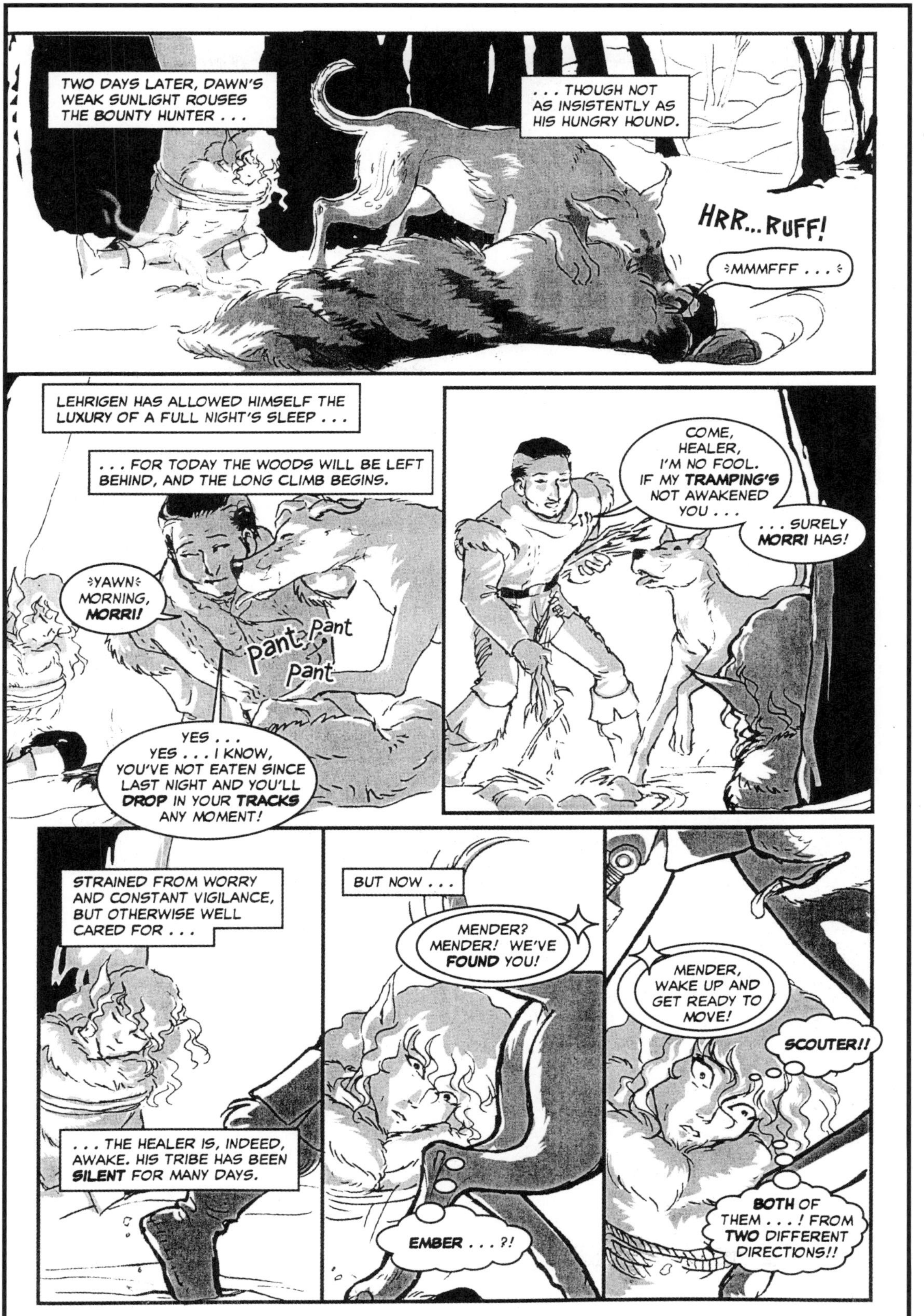
TWO DAYS LATER, DAWN'S WEAK SUNLIGHT ROUSES THE BOUNTY HUNTER . . .
. . . THOUGH NOT AS INSISTENTLY AS HIS HUNGRY HOUND.
HRR... RUFF!
MMMFFF . . .
LEHRIGEN HAS ALLOWED HIMSELF THE LUXURY OF A FULL NIGHT'S SLEEP . . .
. . . FOR TODAY THE WOODS WILL BE LEFT BEHIND, AND THE LONG CLIMB BEGINS.
YAWN MORNING, MORRI!
pant pant pant
YES . . . YES . . . I KNOW, YOU'VE NOT EATEN SINCE LAST NIGHT AND YOU'LL DROP IN YOUR TRACKS ANY MOMENT!
COME, HEALER, I'M NO FOOL. IF MY TRAMPING'S NOT AWAKENED YOU . . .
. . . SURELY MORRI HAS!
STRAINED FROM WORRY AND CONSTANT VIGILANCE, BUT OTHERWISE WELL CARED FOR . . .
. . . THE HEALER IS, INDEED, AWAKE. HIS TRIBE HAS BEEN SILENT FOR MANY DAYS.
BUT NOW . . .
MENDER? MENDER! WE'VE FOUND YOU!
EMBER . . . ?!
MENDER, WAKE UP AND GET READY TO MOVE!
SCOUTER!!
BOTH OF THEM . . . ! FROM TWO DIFFERENT DIRECTIONS!!

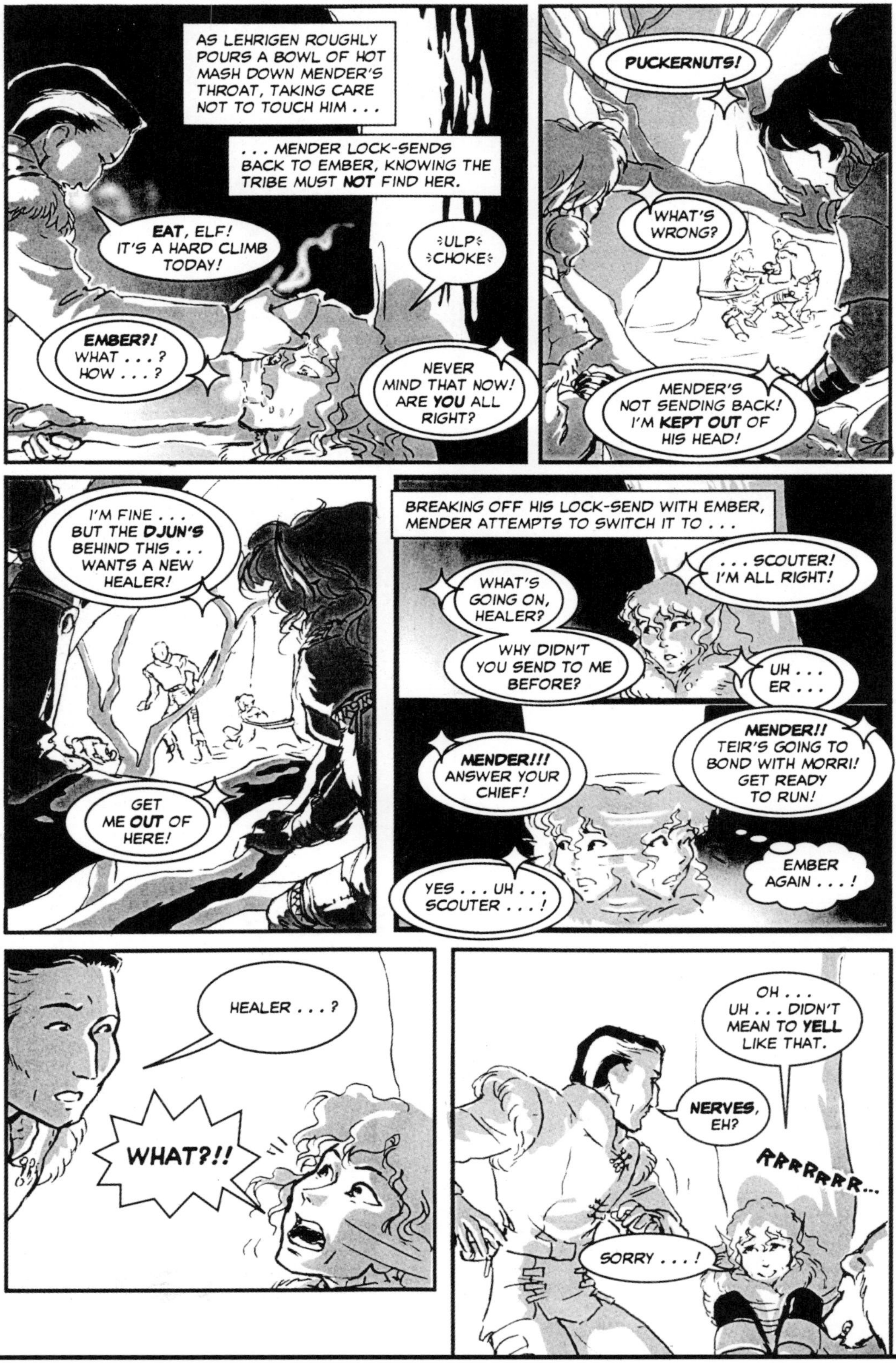
AS LEHRIGEN ROUGHLY POURS A BOWL OF HOT MASH DOWN MENDER'S THROAT, TAKING CARE NOT TO TOUCH HIM . . .
. . . MENDER LOCK-SENDS BACK TO EMBER, KNOWING THE TRIBE MUST NOT FIND HER.
EAT, ELF! IT'S A HARD CLIMB TODAY!
ULP CHOKE
EMBER?! WHAT . . . ? HOW . . . ?
NEVER MIND THAT NOW! ARE YOU ALL RIGHT?
PUCKERNUTS!
WHAT'S WRONG?
MENDER'S NOT SENDING BACK! I'M KEPT OUT OF HIS HEAD!
I'M FINE . . . BUT THE DJUN'S BEHIND THIS . . . WANTS A NEW HEALER!
GET ME OUT OF HERE!
BREAKING OFF HIS LOCK-SEND WITH EMBER, MENDER ATTEMPTS TO SWITCH IT TO . . .
. . . SCOUTER! I'M ALL RIGHT!
WHAT'S GOING ON, HEALER?
WHY DIDN'T YOU SEND TO ME BEFORE?
UH . . . ER . . .
MENDER!!! ANSWER YOUR CHIEF!
MENDER!! TEIR'S GOING TO BOND WITH MORRI! GET READY TO RUN!
YES . . . UH . . . SCOUTER . . . !
EMBER AGAIN . . . !
HEALER . . . ?
WHAT?!!
OH . . . UH . . . DIDN'T MEAN TO YELL LIKE THAT.
NERVES, EH?
RRRRRRR...
SORRY . . . !

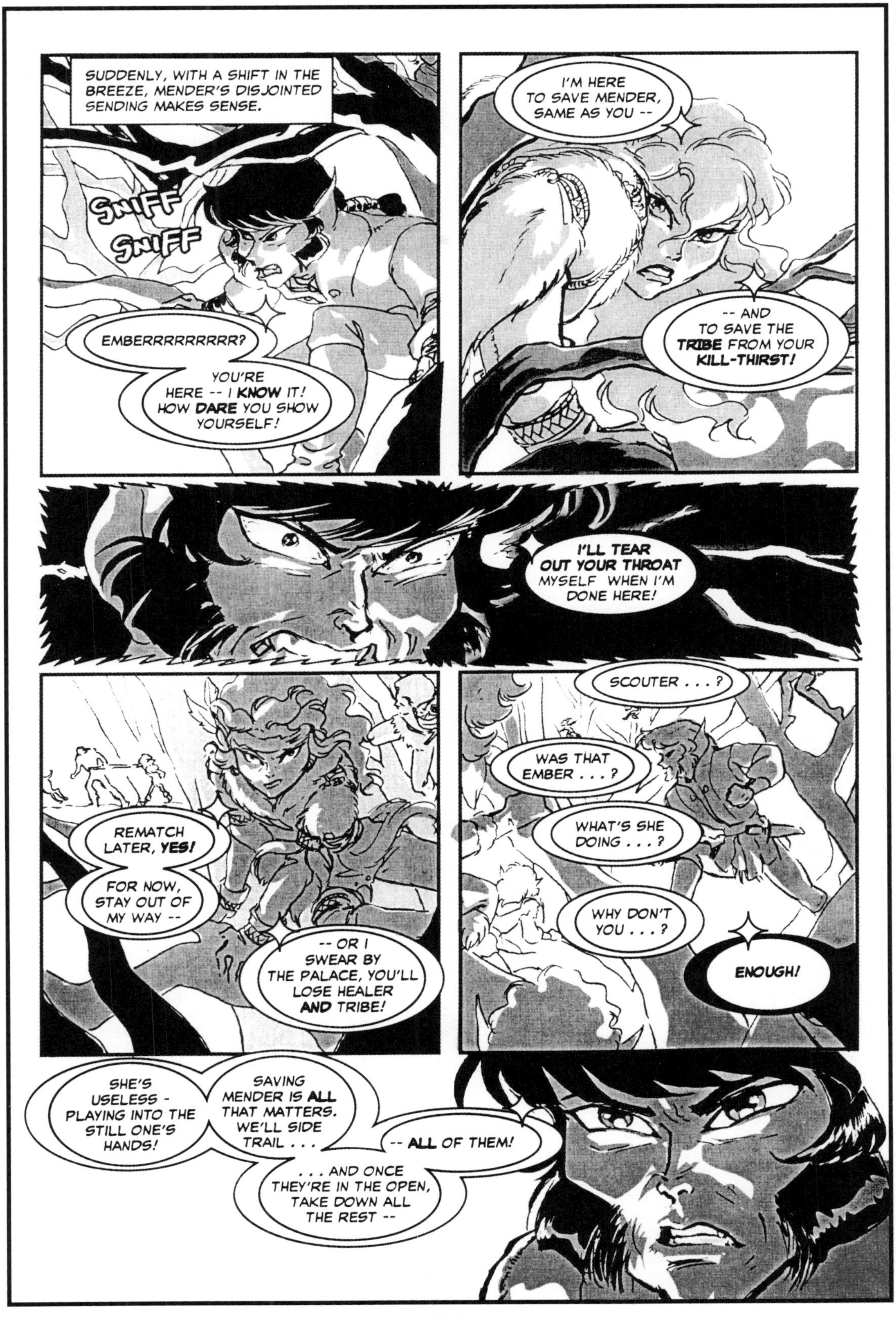
SUDDENLY, WITH A SHIFT IN THE BREEZE, MENDER'S DISJOINTED SENDING MAKES SENSE.
SNIFF
SNIFF
EMBERRRRRRRRR?
YOU'RE HERE -- I KNOW IT! HOW DARE YOU SHOW YOURSELF!
I'M HERE TO SAVE MENDER, SAME AS YOU --
-- AND TO SAVE THE TRIBE FROM YOUR KILL-THIRST!
I'LL TEAR OUT YOUR THROAT MYSELF WHEN I'M DONE HERE!
REMATCH LATER, YES!
FOR NOW, STAY OUT OF MY WAY --
-- OR I SWEAR BY THE PALACE, YOU'LL LOSE HEALER AND TRIBE!
SCOUTER . . . ?
WAS THAT EMBER . . . ?
WHAT'S SHE DOING . . . ?
WHY DON'T YOU . . . ?
ENOUGH!
SHE'S USELESS - PLAYING INTO THE STILL ONE'S HANDS!
SAVING MENDER IS ALL THAT MATTERS. WE'LL SIDE TRAIL . . .
. . . AND ONCE THEY'RE IN THE OPEN, TAKE DOWN ALL THE REST --
-- ALL OF THEM!

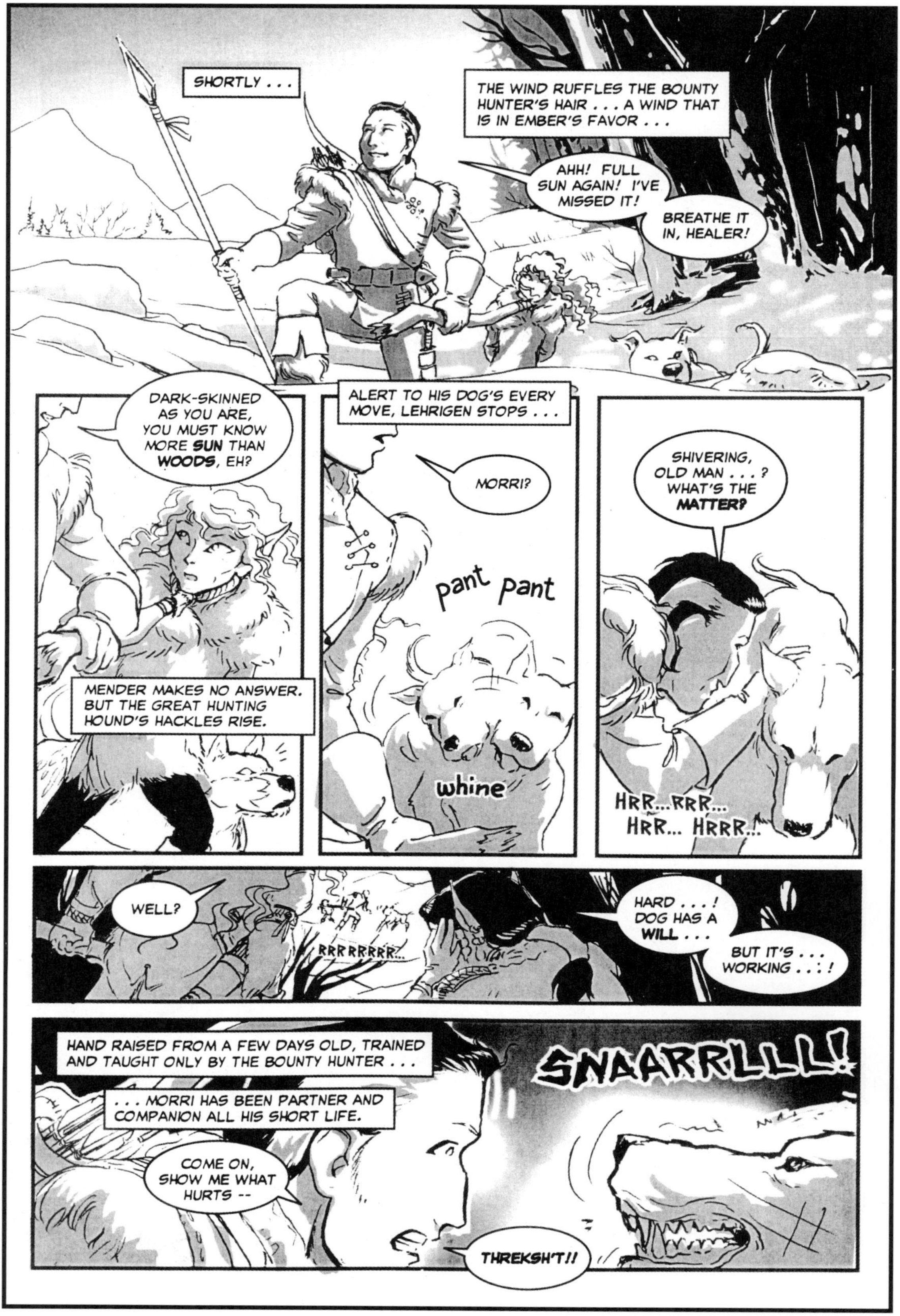
SHORTLY . . .
THE WIND RUFFLES THE BOUNTY HUNTER'S HAIR . . . A WIND THAT IS IN EMBER'S FAVOR . . .
AHH! FULL SUN AGAIN! I'VE MISSED IT!
BREATHE IT IN, HEALER!
DARK-SKINNED AS YOU ARE, YOU MUST KNOW MORE SUN THAN WOODS, EH?
MENDER MAKES NO ANSWER. BUT THE GREAT HUNTING HOUND'S HACKLES RISE.
ALERT TO HIS DOG'S EVERY MOVE, LEHRIGEN STOPS . . .
MORRI?
pant pant
whine
SHIVERING, OLD MAN . . . ? WHAT'S THE MATTER?
HRR... RRR... HRR... HRRR...
WELL?
RRRRRRRR...
HARD . . . ! DOG HAS A WILL . . .
BUT IT'S . . . WORKING . . . !
HAND RAISED FROM A FEW DAYS OLD, TRAINED AND TAUGHT ONLY BY THE BOUNTY HUNTER . . .
. . . MORRI HAS BEEN PARTNER AND COMPANION ALL HIS SHORT LIFE.
SNAARRLLL!
COME ON, SHOW ME WHAT HURTS --
THREKSH'T!!

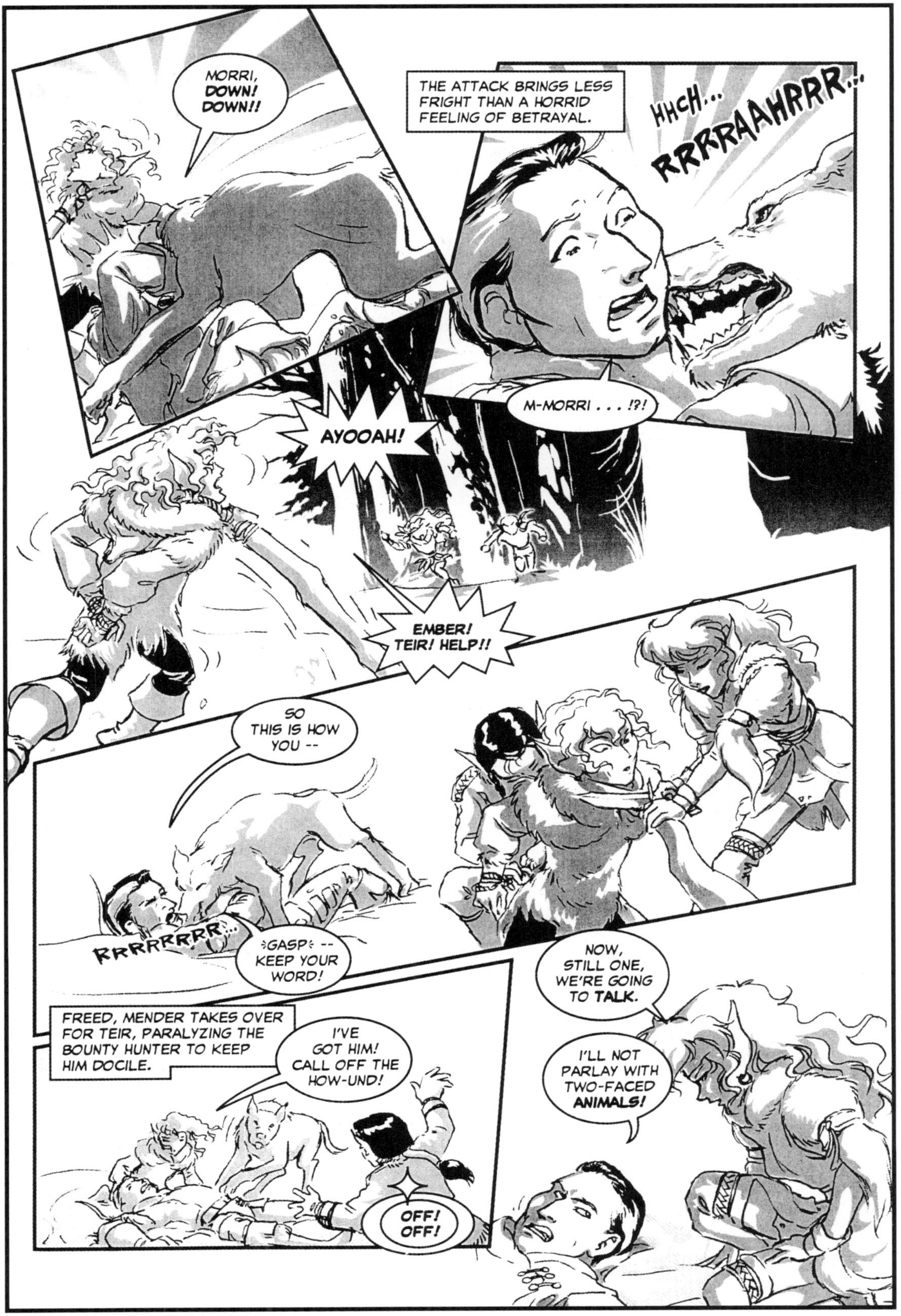
MORRI, DOWN! DOWN!!
THE ATTACK BRINGS LESS FRIGHT THAN A HORRID FEELING OF BETRAYAL.
HHCH... RRRRAAHRRR...
M-MORRI . . . !?!
AYOOAH!
EMBER! TEIR! HELP!!
SO THIS IS HOW YOU --
RRRRRRRR...
GASP -- KEEP YOUR WORD!
NOW, STILL ONE, WE'RE GOING TO TALK.
I'LL NOT PARLAY WITH TWO-FACED ANIMALS!
FREED, MENDER TAKES OVER FOR TEIR, PARALYZING THE BOUNTY HUNTER TO KEEP HIM DOCILE.
I'VE GOT HIM! CALL OFF THE HOW-UND!
OFF! OFF!

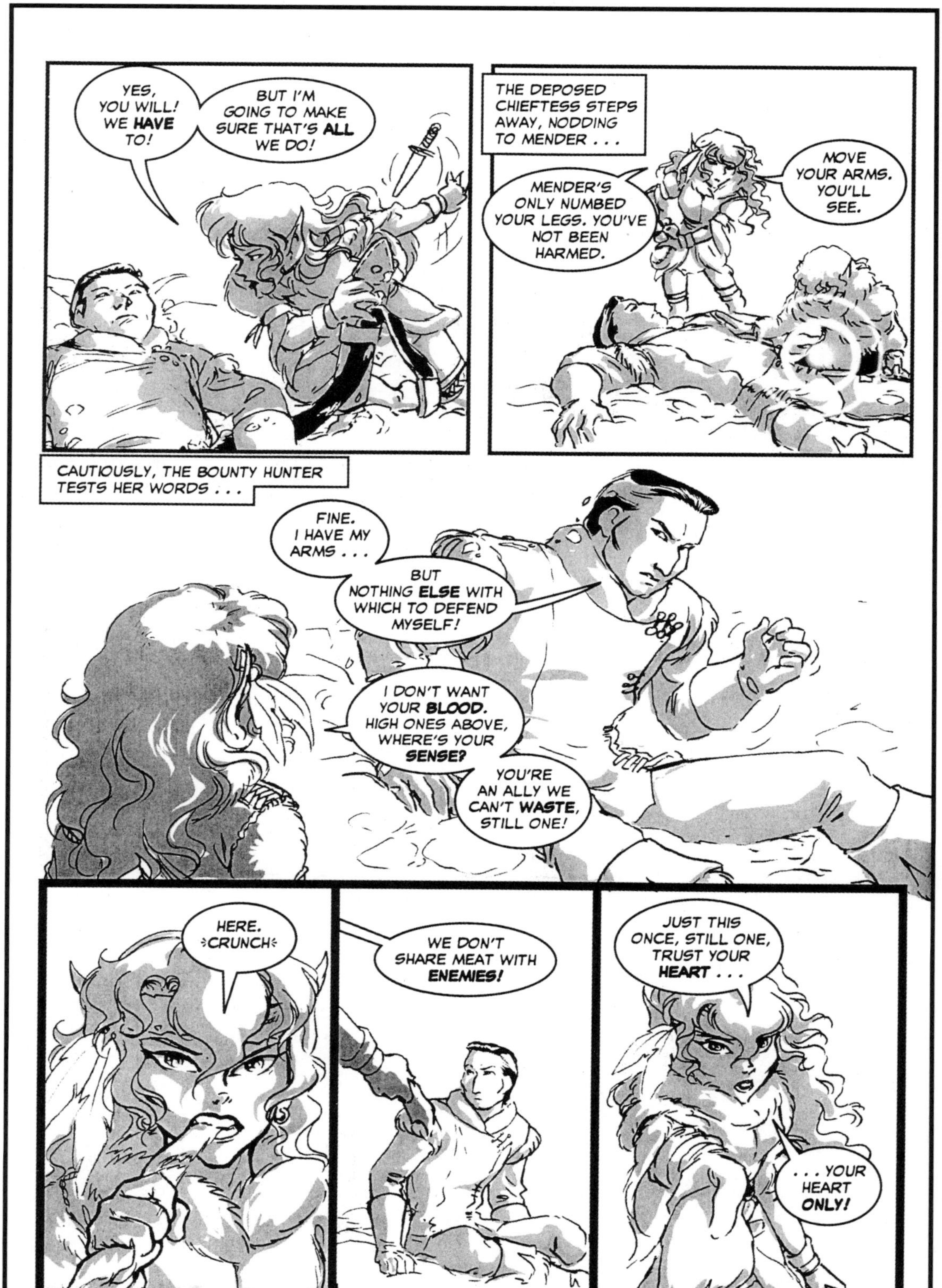
YES, YOU WILL! WE HAVE TO!
BUT I'M GOING TO MAKE SURE THAT'S ALL WE DO!
THE DEPOSED CHIEFTESS STEPS AWAY, NODDING TO MENDER . . .
MENDER'S ONLY NUMBED YOUR LEGS. YOU'VE NOT BEEN HARMED.
MOVE YOUR ARMS. YOU'LL SEE.
CAUTIOUSLY, THE BOUNTY HUNTER TESTS HER WORDS . . .
FINE. I HAVE MY ARMS . . .
BUT NOTHING ELSE WITH WHICH TO DEFEND MYSELF!
I DON'T WANT YOUR BLOOD. HIGH ONES ABOVE, WHERE'S YOUR SENSE?
YOU'RE AN ALLY WE CAN'T WASTE, STILL ONE!
HERE. CRUNCH
WE DON'T SHARE MEAT WITH ENEMIES!
JUST THIS ONCE, STILL ONE, TRUST YOUR HEART . . .
. . . YOUR HEART ONLY!

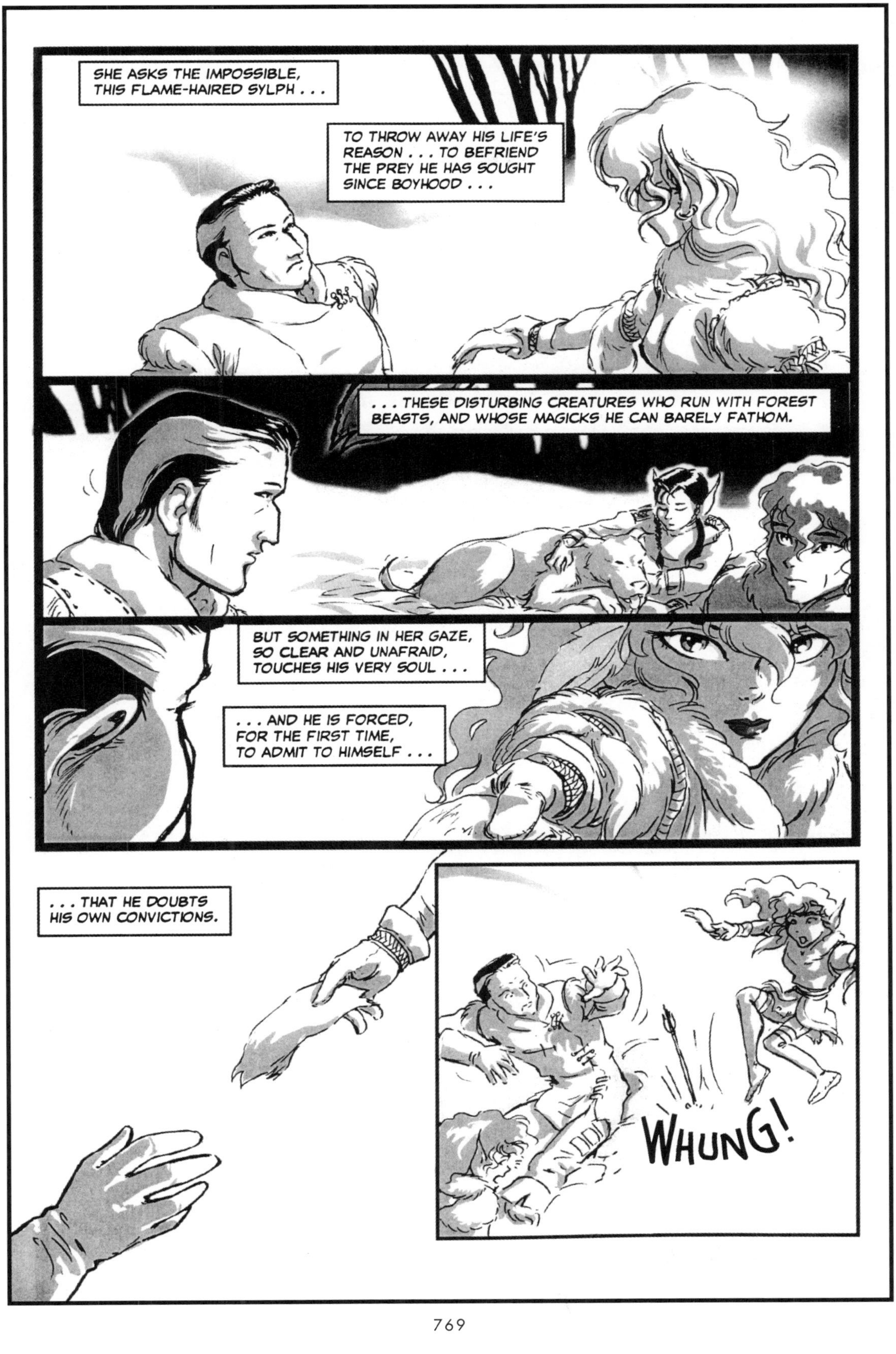
SHE ASKS THE IMPOSSIBLE, THIS FLAME-HAIRED SYLPH . . .
TO THROW AWAY HIS LIFE'S REASON . . . TO BEFRIEND THE PREY HE HAS SOUGHT SINCE BOYHOOD . . .
. . . THESE DISTURBING CREATURES WHO RUN WITH FOREST BEASTS, AND WHOSE MAGICKS HE CAN BARELY FATHOM.
BUT SOMETHING IN HER GAZE, SO CLEAR AND UNAFRAID, TOUCHES HIS VERY SOUL . . .
. . . AND HE IS FORCED, FOR THE FIRST TIME, TO ADMIT TO HIMSELF . . .
. . . THAT HE DOUBTS HIS OWN CONVICTIONS.
WHUNG!

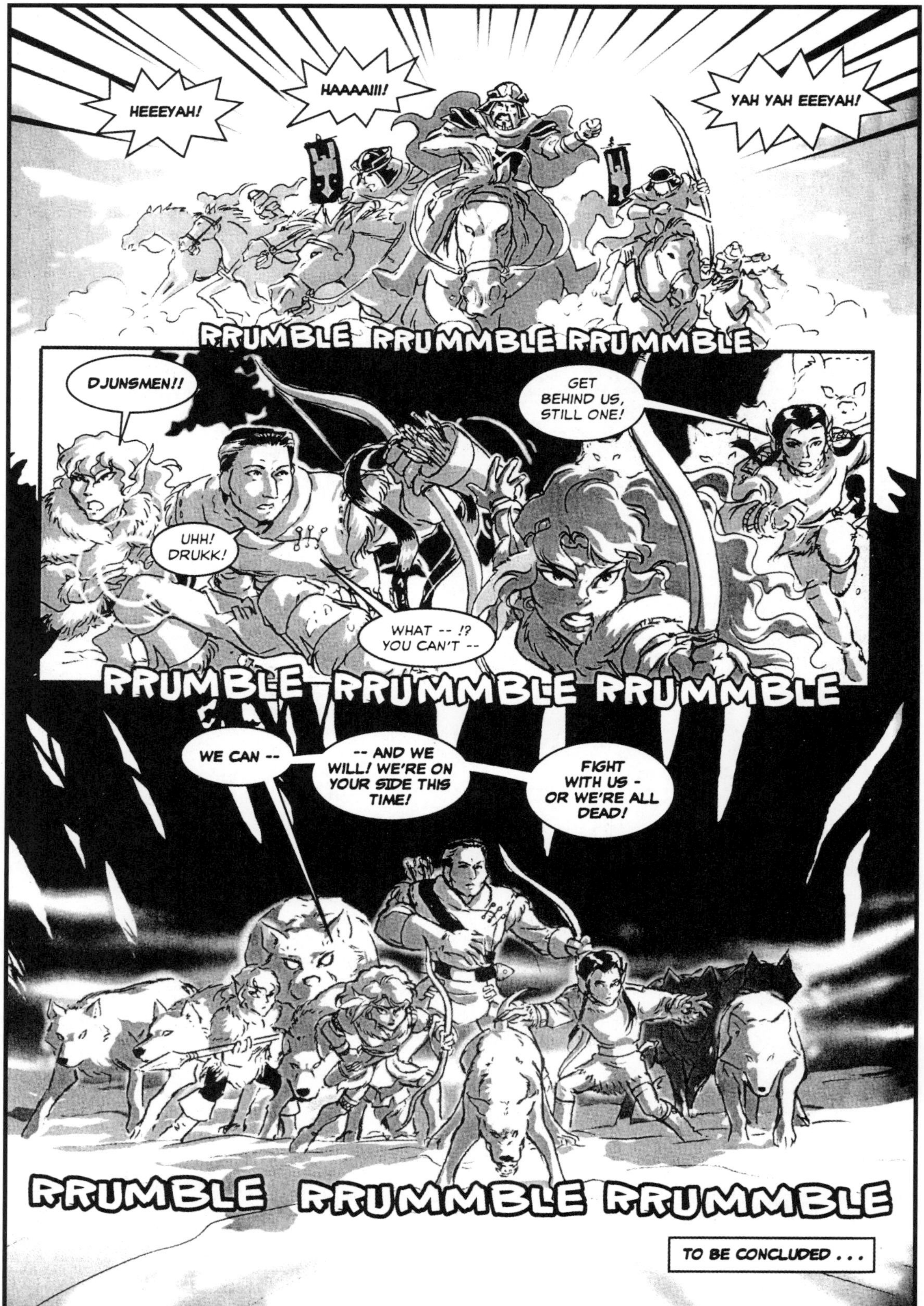
HEEEYAH!
HAAAAIII!
YAH YAH EEEYAH!
RRUMBLE RRUMMBLE RRUMMBLE
DJUNSMEN!!
GET BEHIND US, STILL ONE!
UHH! DRUKK!
WHAT -- !? YOU CAN'T --
RRUMBLE RRUMMBLE RRUMMBLE
WE CAN --
-- AND WE WILL! WE'RE ON YOUR SIDE THIS TIME!
FIGHT WITH US - OR WE'RE ALL DEAD!
RRUMBLE RRUMMBLE RRUMMBLE
TO BE CONCLUDED . . .

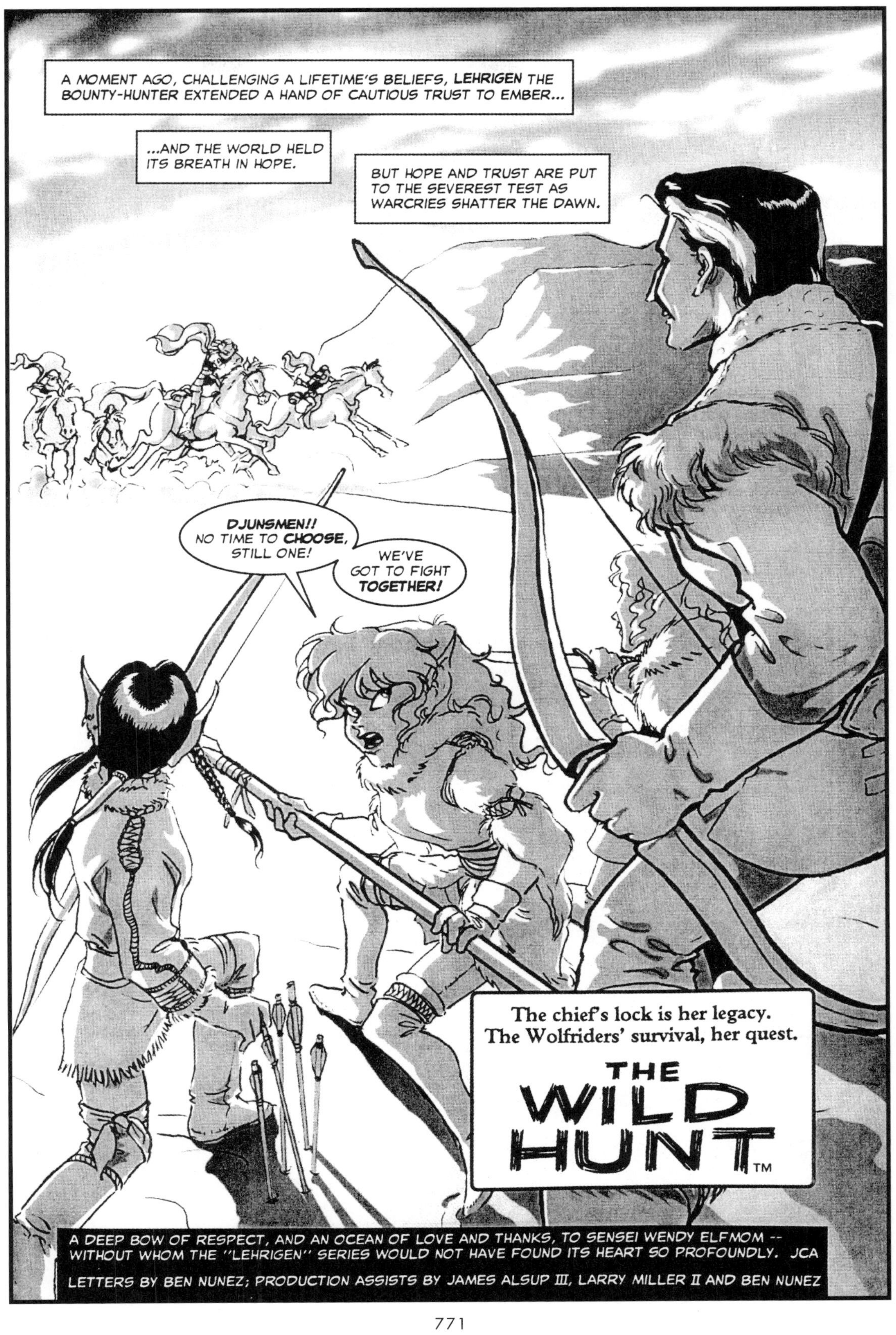

A MOMENT AGO, CHALLENGING A LIFETIME'S BELIEFS, LEHRIGEN THE BOUNTY-HUNTER EXTENDED A HAND OF CAUTIOUS TRUST TO EMBER...
...AND THE WORLD HELD ITS BREATH IN HOPE.
BUT HOPE AND TRUST ARE PUT TO THE SEVEREST TEST AS WARCRIES SHATTER THE DAWN.
DJUNSMEN!! NO TIME TO CHOOSE, STILL ONE!
WE'VE GOT TO FIGHT TOGETHER!
The chief's lock is her legacy.
The Wolfriders' survival, her quest.
THE WILD HUNT ™
A DEEP BOW OF RESPECT, AND AN OCEAN OF LOVE AND THANKS, TO SENSEI WENDY ELFMOM -- WITHOUT WHOM THE "LEHRIGEN" SERIES WOULD NOT HAVE FOUND ITS HEART SO PROFOUNDLY. JCA
LETTERS BY BEN NUNEZ; PRODUCTION ASSISTS BY JAMES ALSUP III, LARRY MILLER II AND BEN NUNEZ

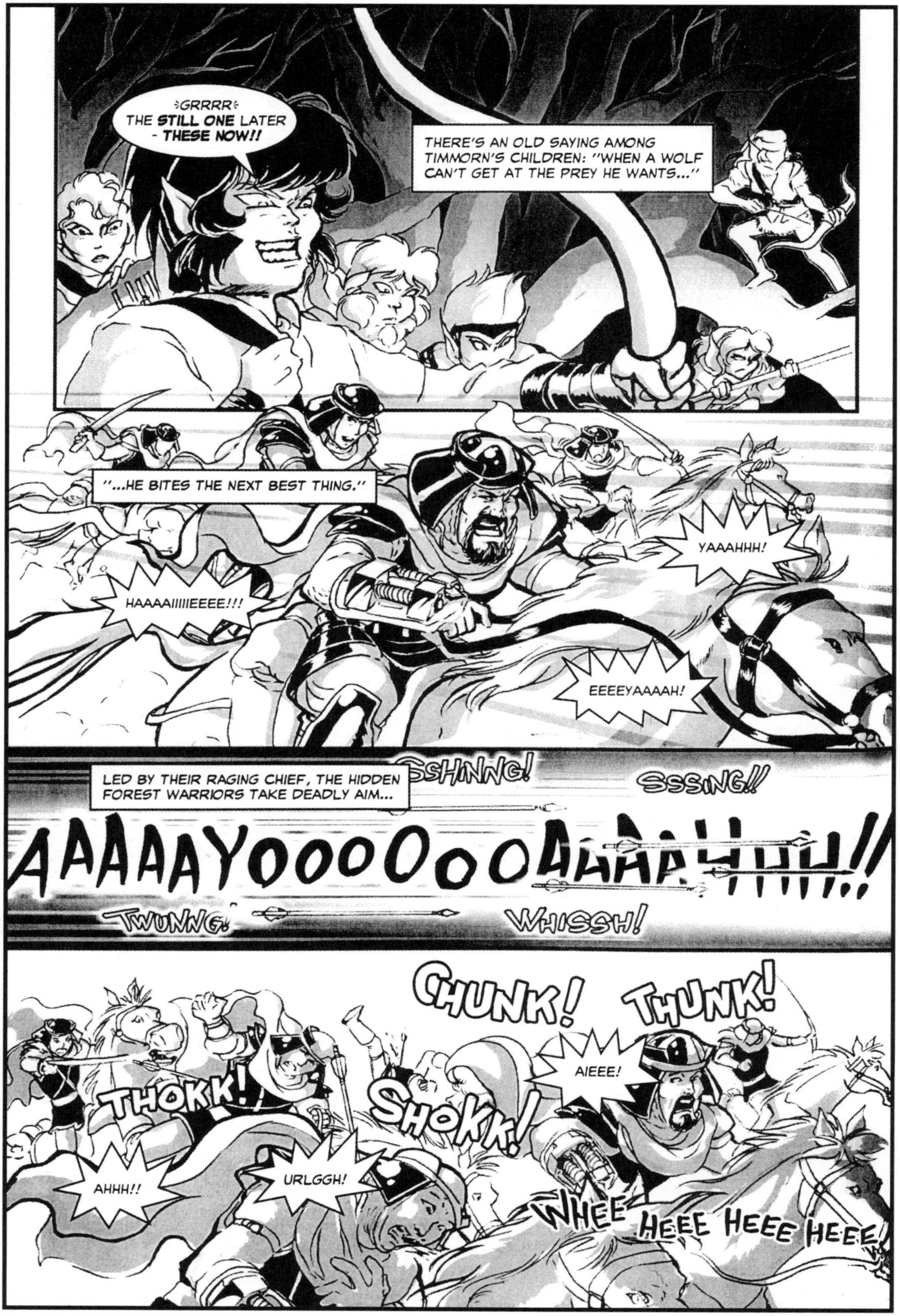
GRRRR
THE STILL ONE LATER - THESE NOW!!
THERE'S AN OLD SAYING AMONG TIMMORN'S CHILDREN: "WHEN A WOLF CAN'T GET AT THE PREY HE WANTS..."
"...HE BITES THE NEXT BEST THING."
YAAAHHH!
HAAAAIIIIIEEEE!!!
EEEEYAAAAH!
LED BY THEIR RAGING CHIEF, THE HIDDEN FOREST WARRIORS TAKE DEADLY AIM...
SSHINNG!
SSSING!!
AAAAAYOOOOOOOAAAAHHHH!!
TWUNNG!
WHISSH!
CHUNK!
THUNK!
AIEEE!
THOKK!
SHOKK!
AHHH!!
URLGGH!
WHEE HEEE HEEE HEEE

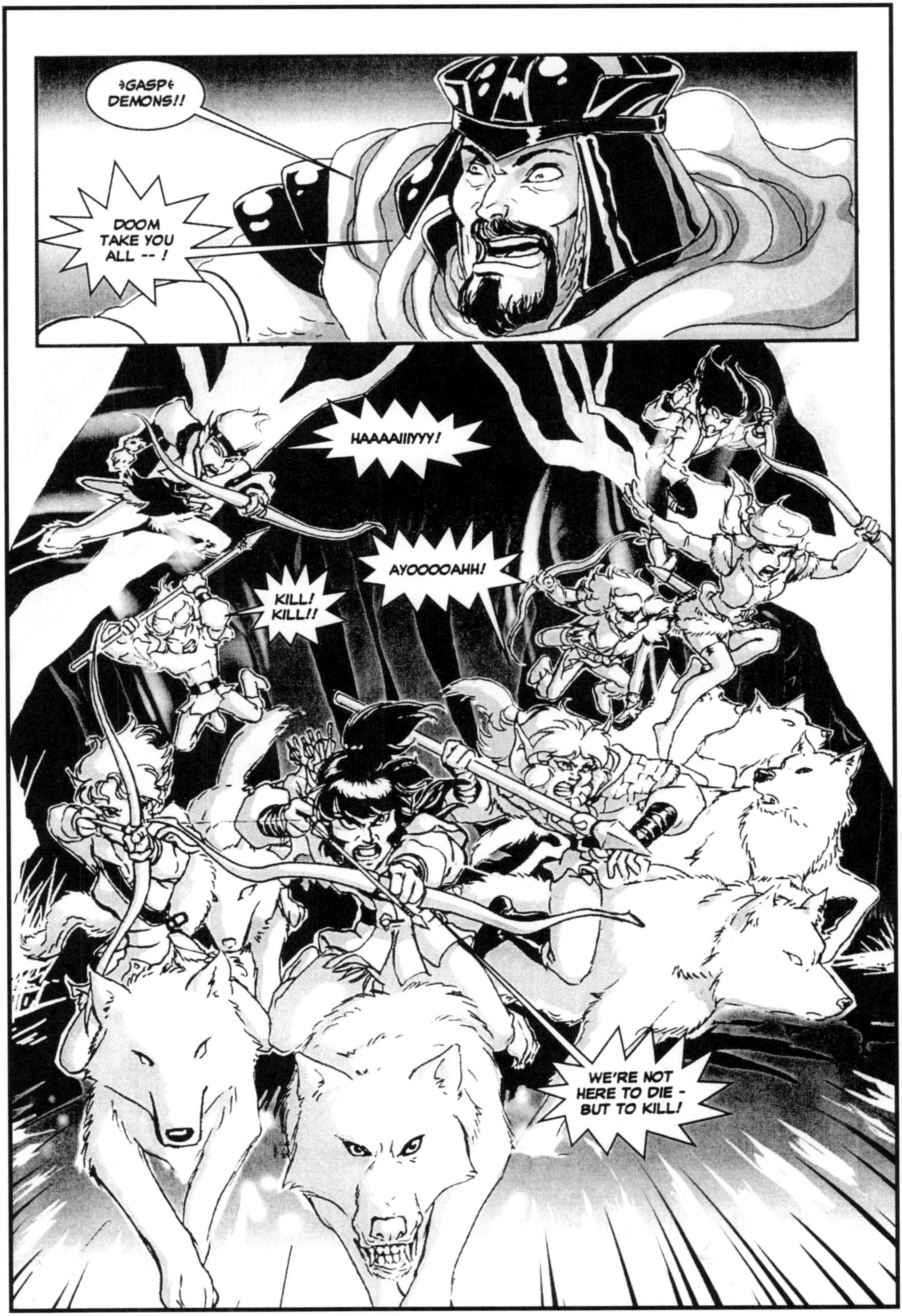

GASP DEMONS!!
DOOM TAKE YOU ALL -- !
HAAAAIIIYYY!
AYOOOOAHH!
KILL! KILL!!
WE'RE NOT HERE TO DIE - BUT TO KILL!

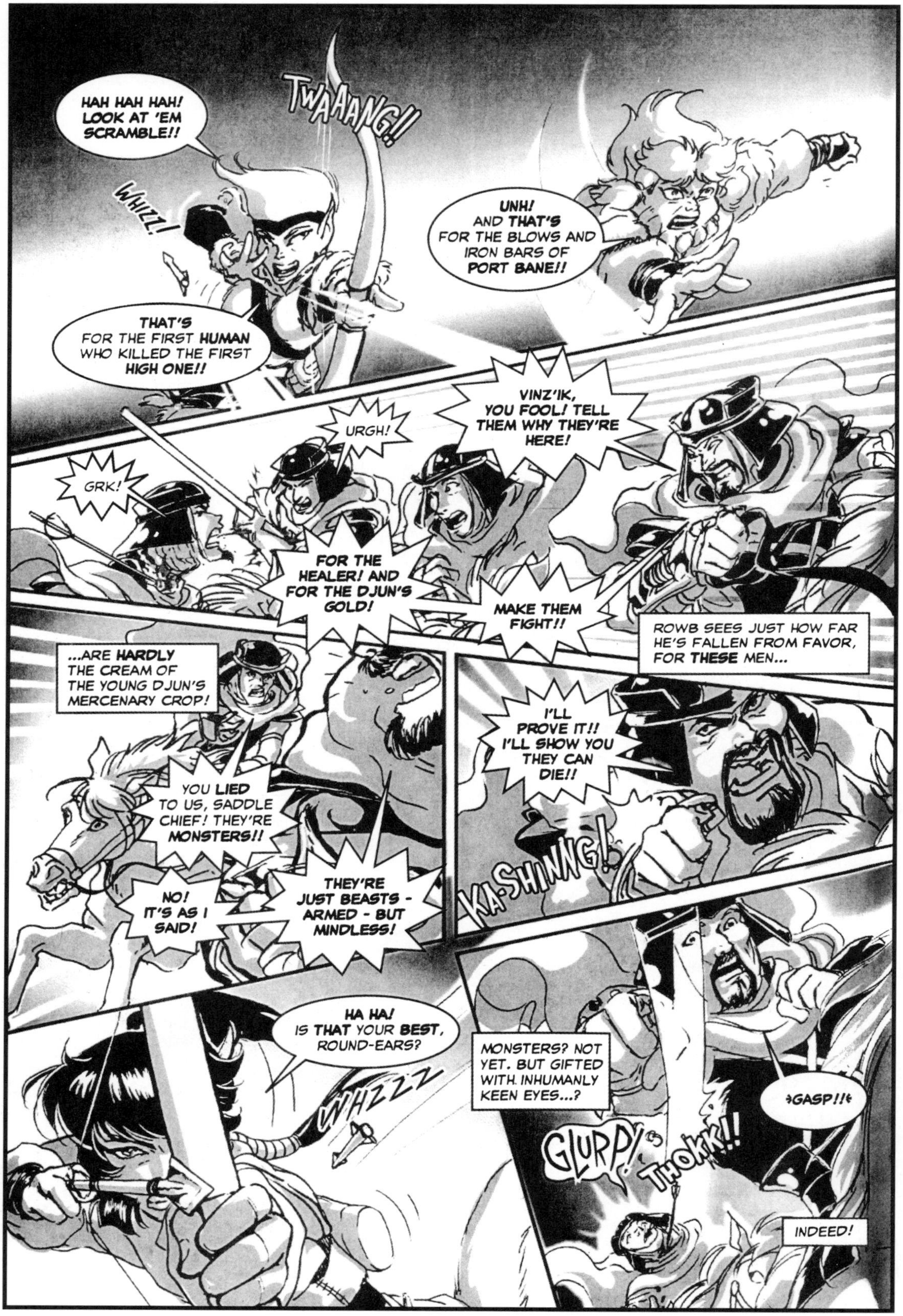
HAH HAH HAH! LOOK AT 'EM SCRAMBLE!!
TWAAANG!!
WHIZZ!
UNH! AND THAT'S FOR THE BLOWS AND IRON BARS OF PORT BANE!!
THAT'S FOR THE FIRST HUMAN WHO KILLED THE FIRST HIGH ONE!!
GRK!
URGH!
VINZ'IK, YOU FOOL! TELL THEM WHY THEY'RE HERE!
FOR THE HEALER! AND FOR THE DJUN'S GOLD!
MAKE THEM FIGHT!!
ROWB SEES JUST HOW FAR HE'S FALLEN FROM FAVOR, FOR THESE MEN...
...ARE HARDLY THE CREAM OF THE YOUNG DJUN'S MERCENARY CROP!
YOU LIED TO US, SADDLE CHIEF! THEY'RE MONSTERS!!
NO! IT'S AS I SAID!
THEY'RE JUST BEASTS - ARMED - BUT MINDLESS!
I'LL PROVE IT!! I'LL SHOW YOU THEY CAN DIE!!
KA-SHINNG!
HA HA! IS THAT YOUR BEST, ROUND-EARS?
WHZZZ
MONSTERS? NOT YET. BUT GIFTED WITH INHUMANLY KEEN EYES...?
GASP!!
GLURP!
THOKK!!
INDEED!

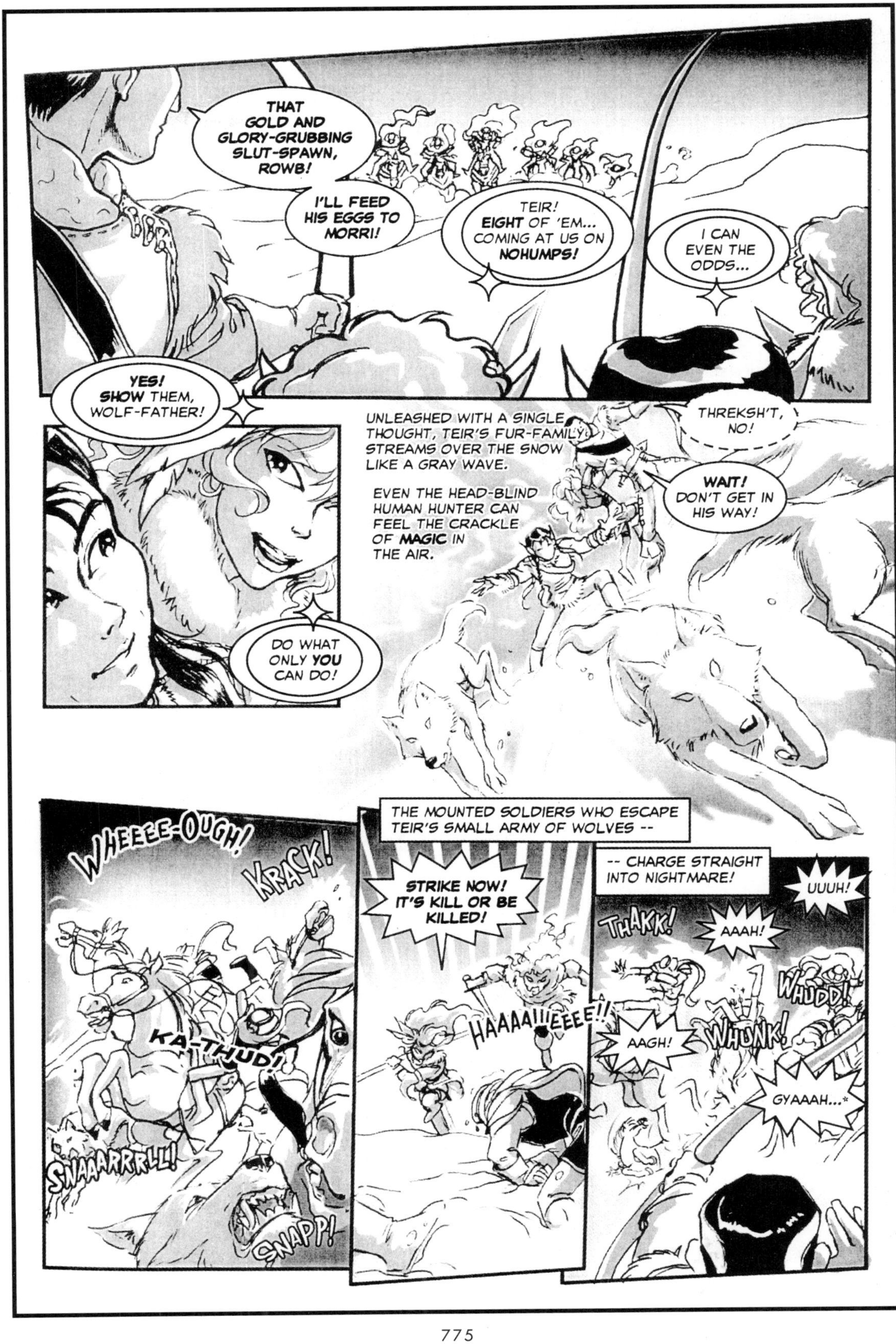
THAT GOLD AND GLORY-GRUBBING SLUT-SPAWN, ROWB!
I'LL FEED HIS EGGS TO MORRI!
TEIR! EIGHT OF 'EM... COMING AT US ON NOHUMPS!
I CAN EVEN THE ODDS...
YES! SHOW THEM, WOLF-FATHER!
DO WHAT ONLY YOU CAN DO!
UNLEASHED WITH A SINGLE THOUGHT, TEIR'S FUR-FAMILY STREAMS OVER THE SNOW LIKE A GRAY WAVE.
EVEN THE HEAD-BLIND HUMAN HUNTER CAN FEEL THE CRACKLE OF MAGIC IN THE AIR.
THREKSH'T, NO!
WAIT! DON'T GET IN HIS WAY!
WHEEEE-OUGH!
KRACK!
KA-THUD!
SNAAARRRLLL!
SNAPP!
THE MOUNTED SOLDIERS WHO ESCAPE TEIR'S SMALL ARMY OF WOLVES --
STRIKE NOW! IT'S KILL OR BE KILLED!
HAAAA!!!EEEE!!
-- CHARGE STRAIGHT INTO NIGHTMARE!
UUUH!
THAKK!
AAAH!
WHUDD!
AAGH!
WHUNK!
GYAAAH...*

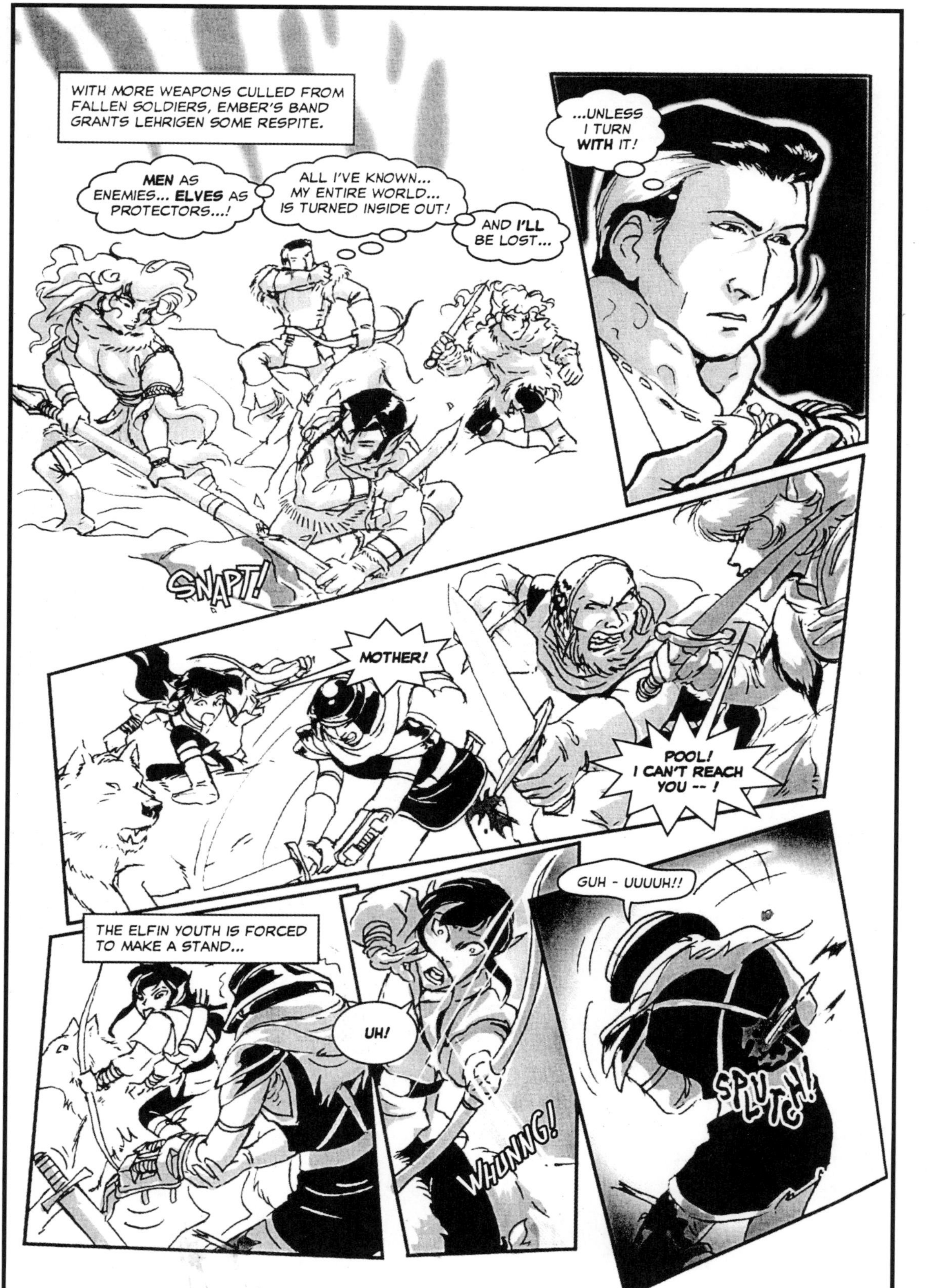
WITH MORE WEAPONS CULLED FROM FALLEN SOLDIERS, EMBER'S BAND GRANTS LEHRIGEN SOME RESPITE.
MEN AS ENEMIES... ELVES AS PROTECTORS...!
ALL I'VE KNOWN... MY ENTIRE WORLD... IS TURNED INSIDE OUT!
AND I'LL BE LOST...
...UNLESS I TURN WITH IT!
SNAPT!
MOTHER!
POOL! I CAN'T REACH YOU -- !
THE ELFIN YOUTH IS FORCED TO MAKE A STAND...
UH!
WHUNNG!
GUH - UUUUH!!
SPLUTCH!

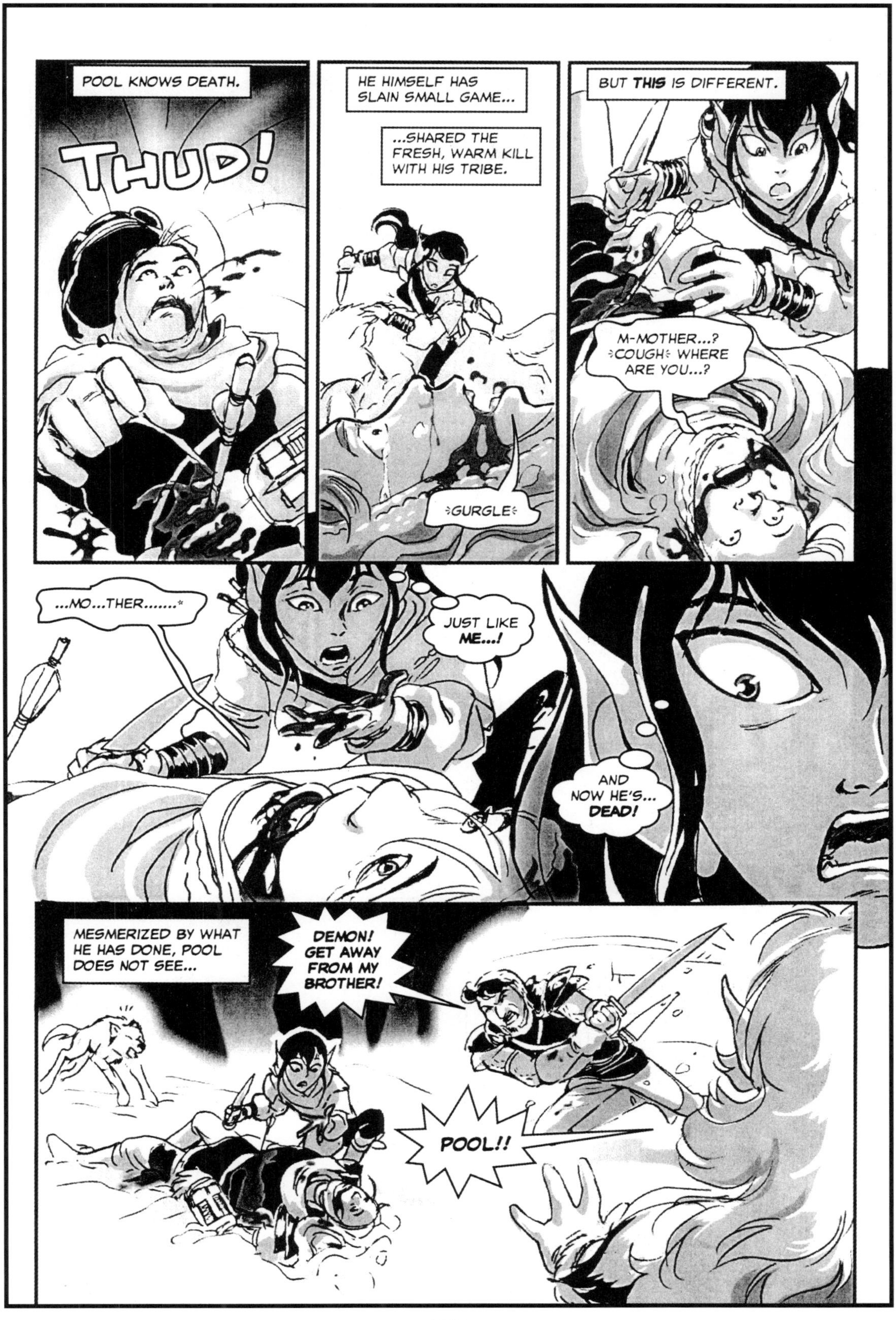
POOL KNOWS DEATH.
THUD!
HE HIMSELF HAS SLAIN SMALL GAME...
...SHARED THE FRESH, WARM KILL WITH HIS TRIBE.
GURGLE
BUT THIS IS DIFFERENT.
M-MOTHER...? COUGH WHERE ARE YOU...?
...MO...THER.......*
JUST LIKE ME...!
AND NOW HE'S... DEAD!
MESMERIZED BY WHAT HE HAS DONE, POOL DOES NOT SEE...
DEMON! GET AWAY FROM MY BROTHER!
POOL!!

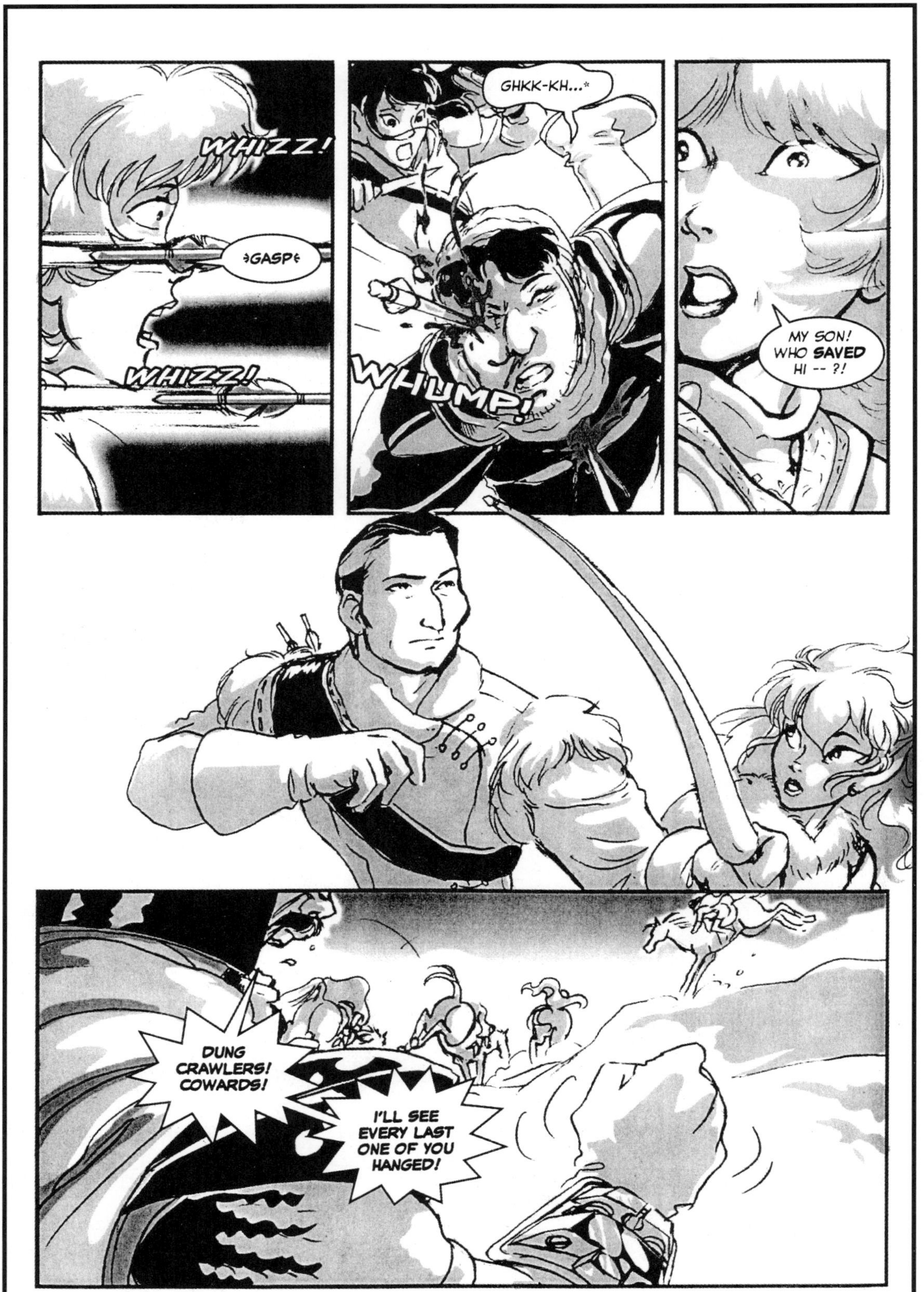
WHIZZ!
GASP
WHIZZ!
GHKK-KH...*
WHUMP!
MY SON! WHO SAVED HI -- ?!
DUNG CRAWLERS! COWARDS!
I'LL SEE EVERY LAST ONE OF YOU HANGED!

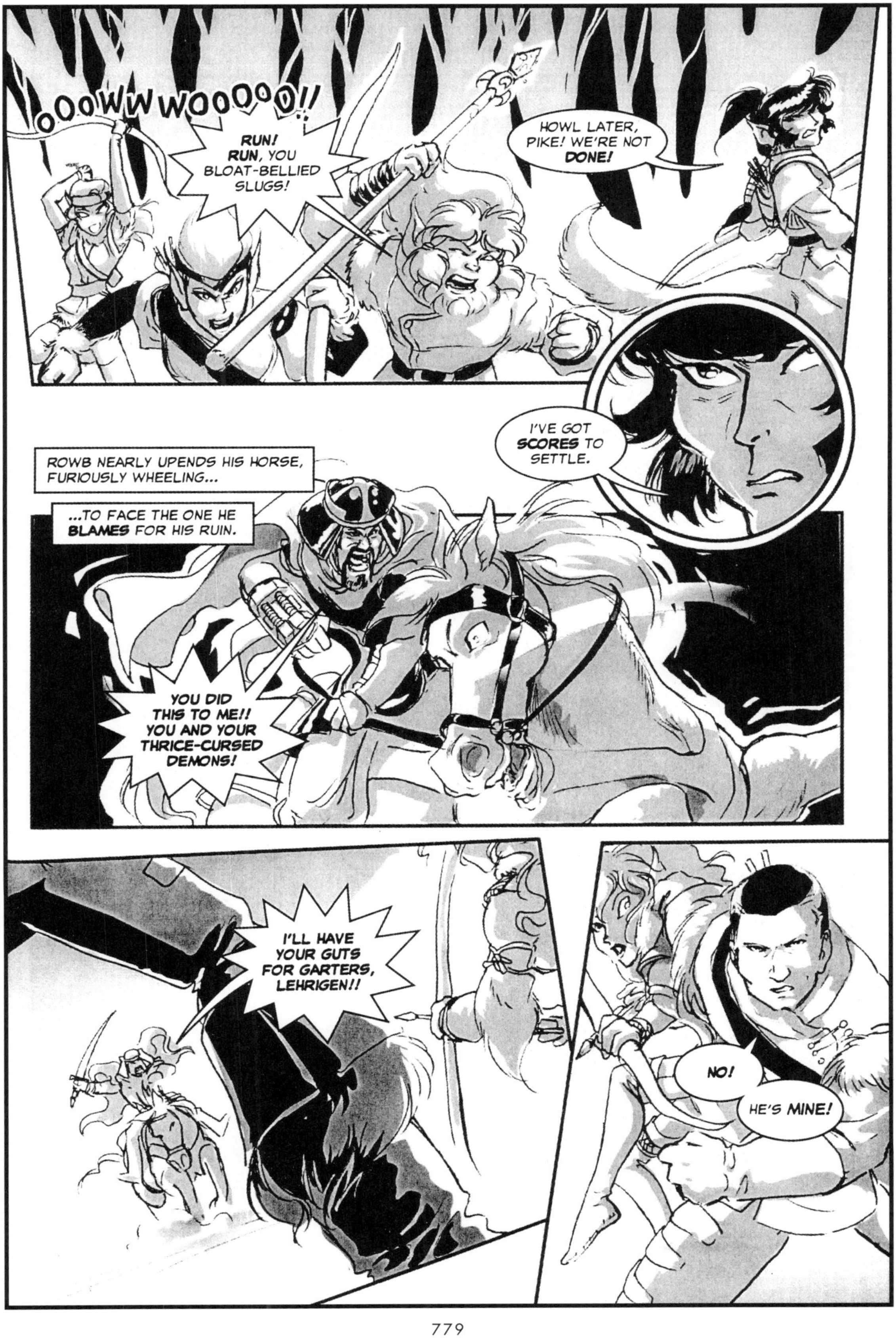
OOOWWWOOOOD!!
RUN! RUN, YOU BLOAT-BELLIED SLUGS!
HOWL LATER, PIKE! WE'RE NOT DONE!
I'VE GOT SCORES TO SETTLE.
ROWB NEARLY UPENDS HIS HORSE, FURIOUSLY WHEELING...
...TO FACE THE ONE HE BLAMES FOR HIS RUIN.
YOU DID THIS TO ME!! YOU AND YOUR THRICE-CURSED DEMONS!
I'LL HAVE YOUR GUTS FOR GARTERS, LEHRIGEN!!
NO!
HE'S MINE!

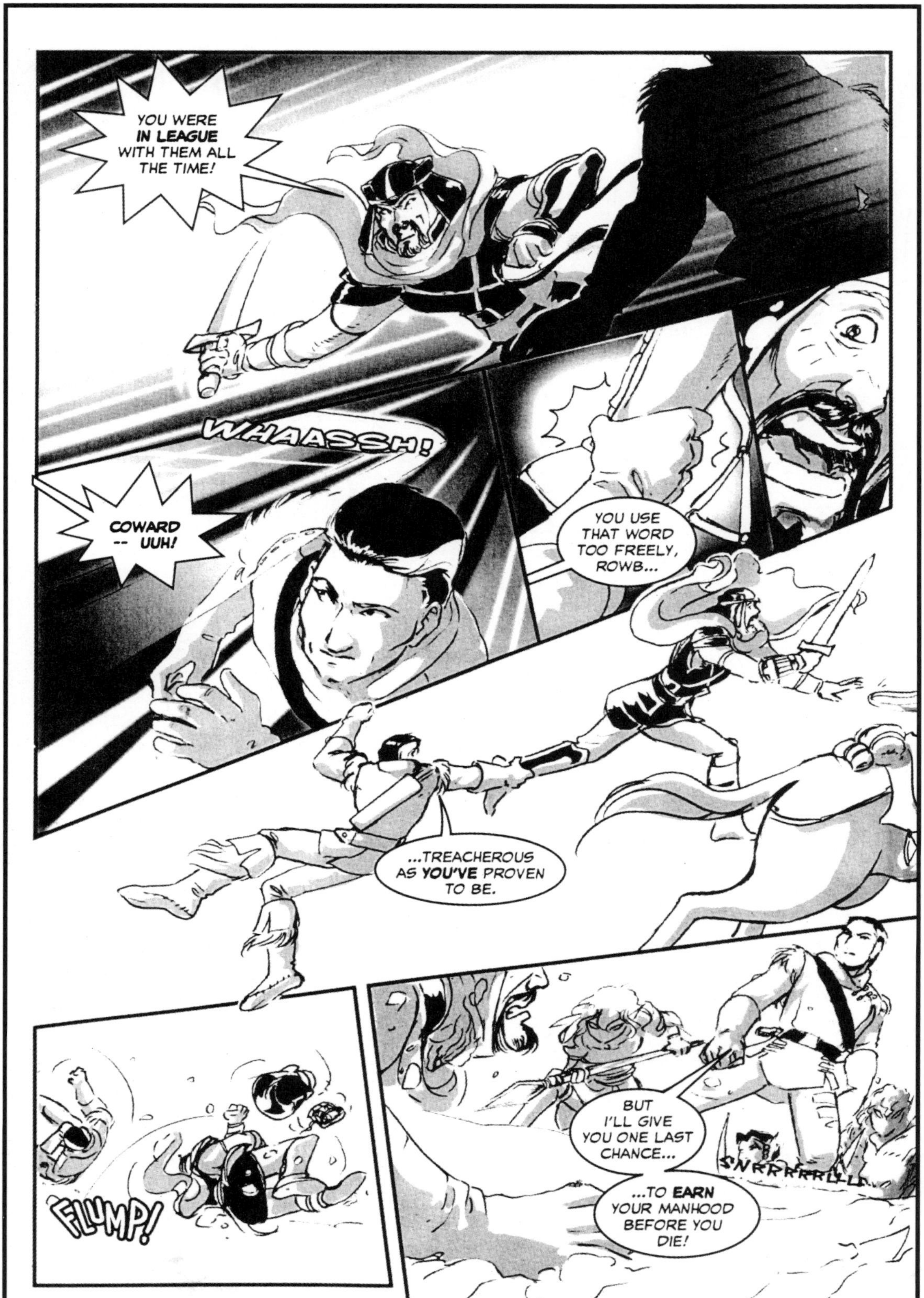
YOU WERE IN LEAGUE WITH THEM ALL THE TIME!
WHAASSH!
COWARD -- UUH!
YOU USE THAT WORD TOO FREELY, ROWB...
...TREACHEROUS AS YOU'VE PROVEN TO BE.
FLUMP!
BUT I'LL GIVE YOU ONE LAST CHANCE...
...TO EARN YOUR MANHOOD BEFORE YOU DIE!
SNRRRRRLLL

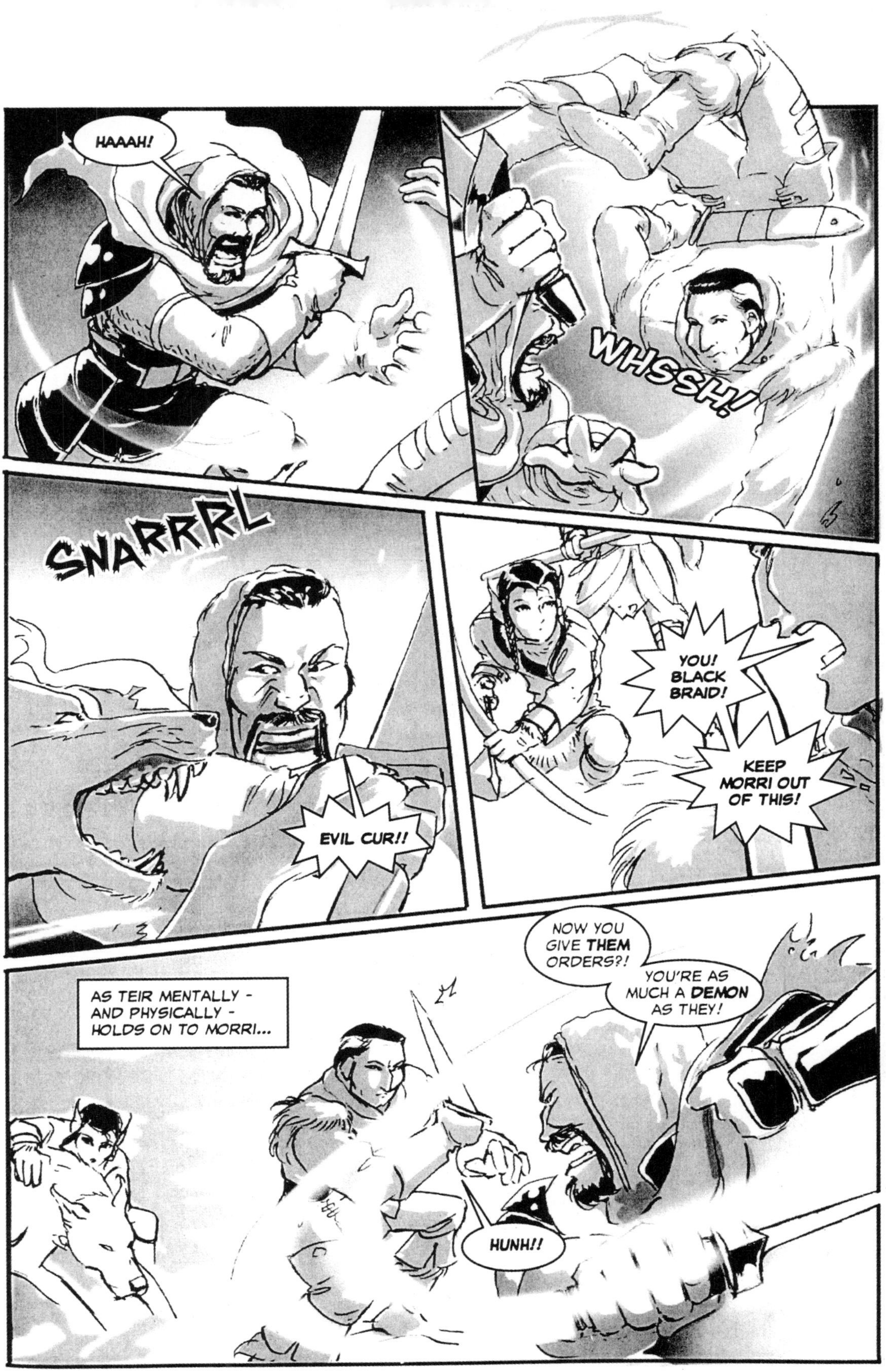
HAAAH!
WHSSH!
SNARRRL
EVIL CUR!!
YOU! BLACK BRAID!
KEEP MORRI OUT OF THIS!
AS TEIR MENTALLY - AND PHYSICALLY - HOLDS ON TO MORRI...
NOW YOU GIVE THEM ORDERS?!
YOU'RE AS MUCH A DEMON AS THEY!
HUNH!!

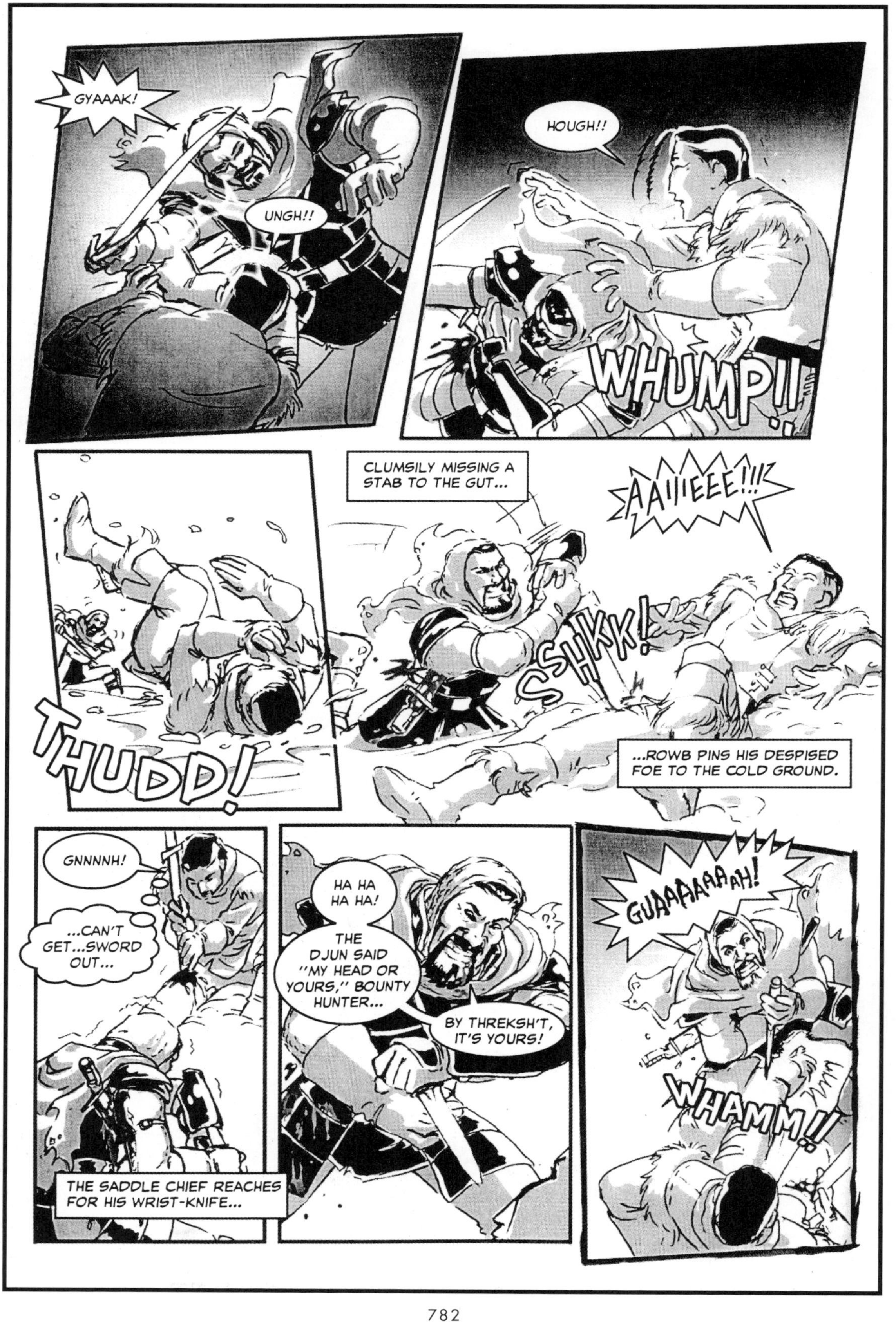
GYAAAK!
UNGH!!
HOUGH!!
WHUMP!!
CLUMSILY MISSING A STAB TO THE GUT...
AAIIEEE!!!
THUDD!
SSHKK!
...ROWB PINS HIS DESPISED FOE TO THE COLD GROUND.
GNNNNH!
...CAN'T GET...SWORD OUT...
THE SADDLE CHIEF REACHES FOR HIS WRIST-KNIFE...
HA HA HA HA!
THE DJUN SAID "MY HEAD OR YOURS," BOUNTY HUNTER...
BY THREKSH'T, IT'S YOURS!
GUAAAAAAAH!
WHAMM!!

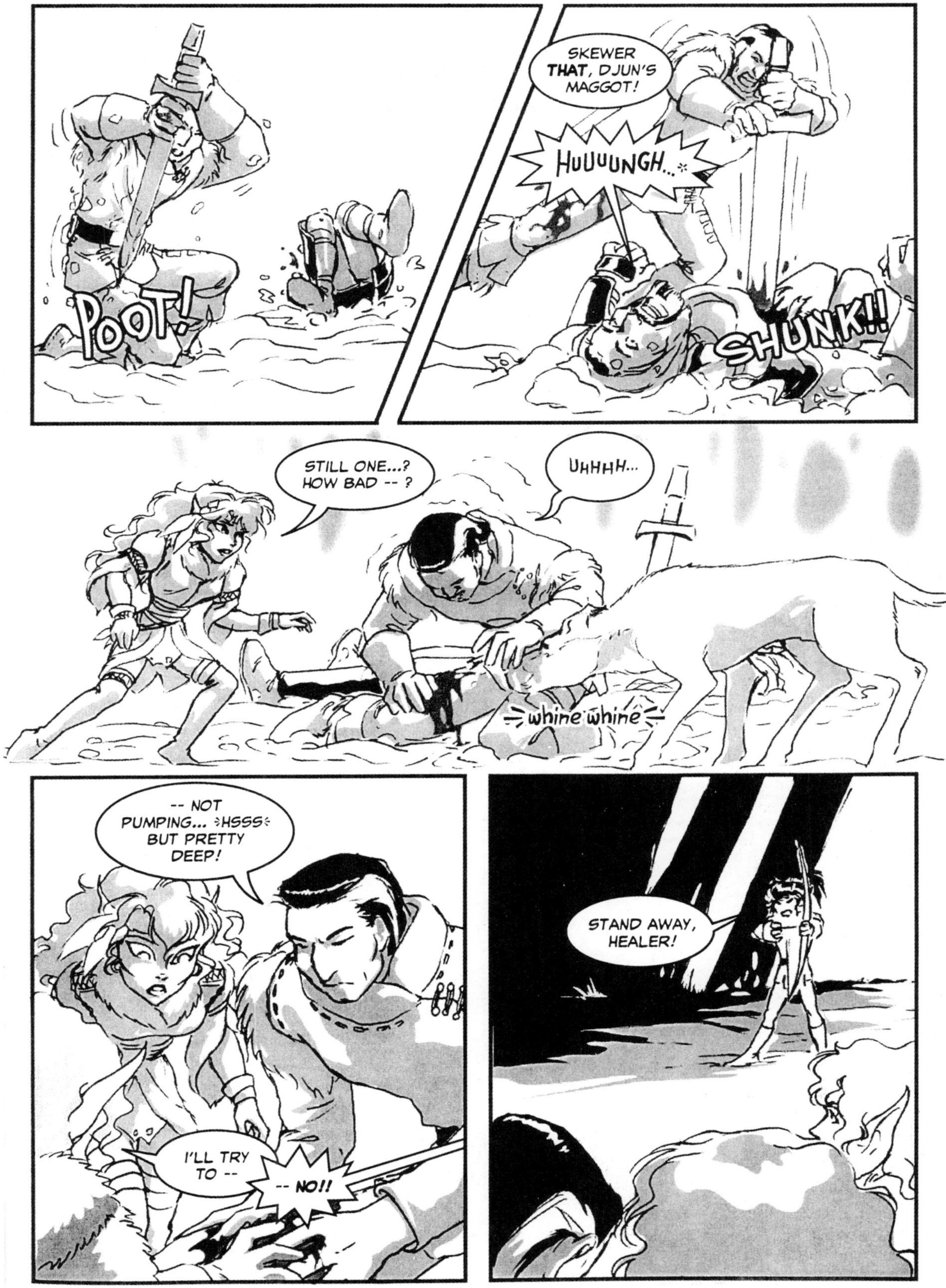
POOT!
SKEWER THAT, DJUN'S MAGGOT!
HUUUUNGH...
SHUNK!!
STILL ONE...? HOW BAD -- ?
UHHHH...
whine whine
-- NOT PUMPING... HSSS BUT PRETTY DEEP!
I'LL TRY TO --
-- NO!!
STAND AWAY, HEALER!

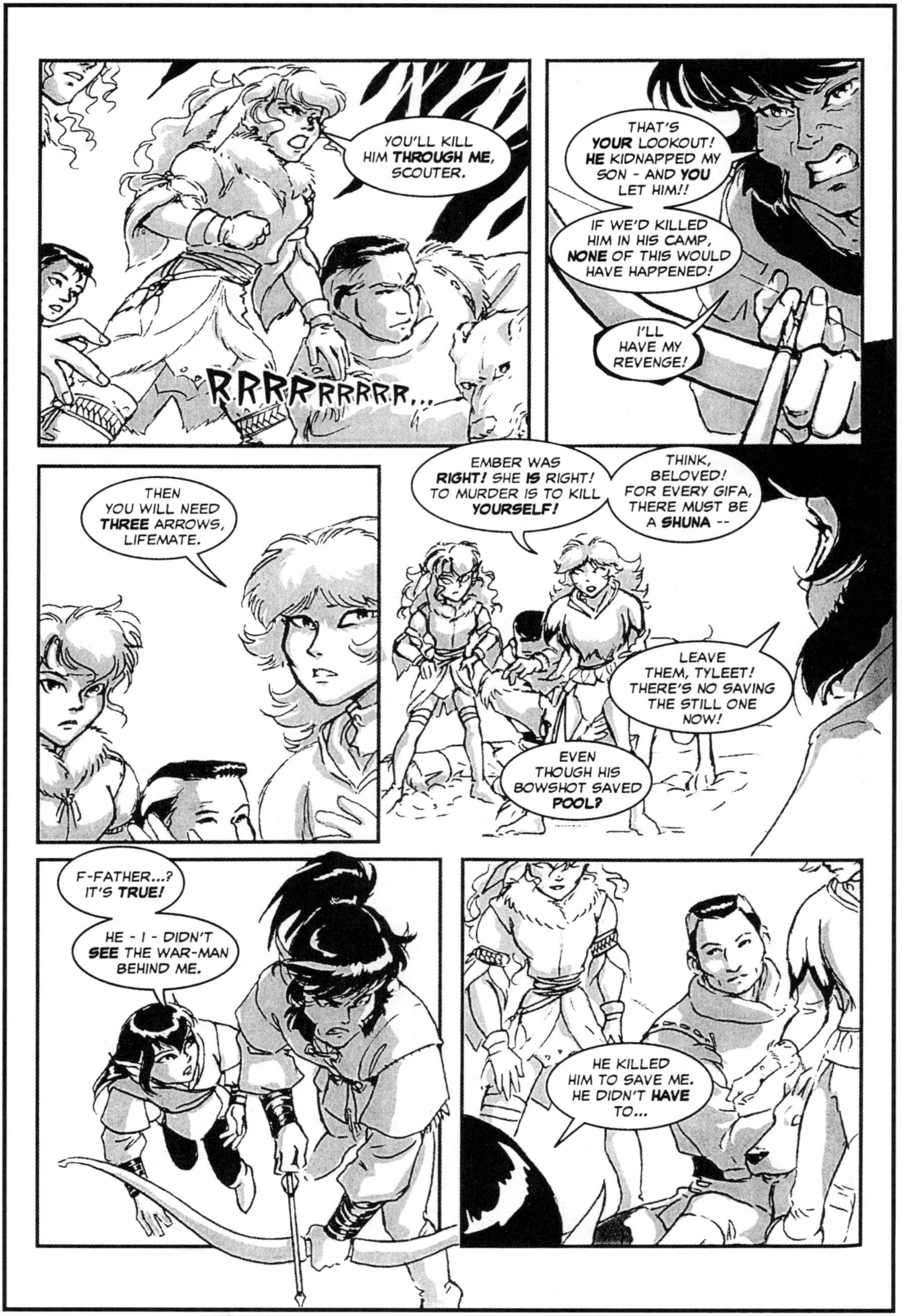
YOU'LL KILL HIM THROUGH ME, SCOUTER.
RRRRRRRRR...
THAT'S YOUR LOOKOUT! HE KIDNAPPED MY SON - AND YOU LET HIM!!
IF WE'D KILLED HIM IN HIS CAMP, NONE OF THIS WOULD HAVE HAPPENED!
I'LL HAVE MY REVENGE!
THEN YOU WILL NEED THREE ARROWS, LIFEMATE.
EMBER WAS RIGHT! SHE IS RIGHT! TO MURDER IS TO KILL YOURSELF!
THINK, BELOVED! FOR EVERY GIFA, THERE MUST BE A SHUNA --
LEAVE THEM, TYLEET! THERE'S NO SAVING THE STILL ONE NOW!
EVEN THOUGH HIS BOWSHOT SAVED POOL?
F-FATHER...? IT'S TRUE!
HE - I - DIDN'T SEE THE WAR-MAN BEHIND ME.
HE KILLED HIM TO SAVE ME. HE DIDN'T HAVE TO...

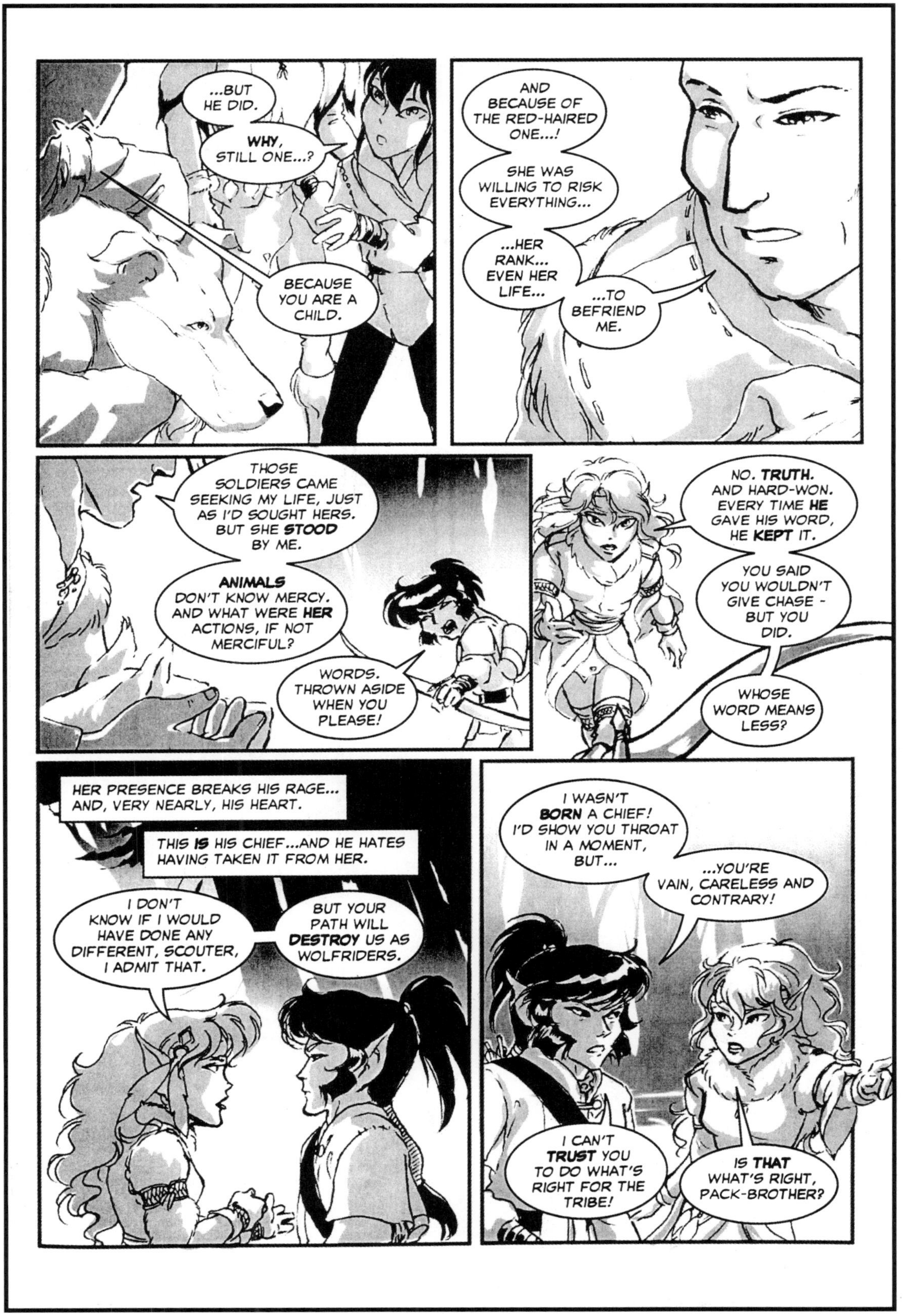

...BUT HE DID.
WHY, STILL ONE...?
BECAUSE YOU ARE A CHILD.
AND BECAUSE OF THE RED-HAIRED ONE...!
SHE WAS WILLING TO RISK EVERYTHING...
...HER RANK... EVEN HER LIFE...
...TO BEFRIEND ME.
THOSE SOLDIERS CAME SEEKING MY LIFE, JUST AS I'D SOUGHT HERS. BUT SHE STOOD BY ME.
ANIMALS DON'T KNOW MERCY. AND WHAT WERE HER ACTIONS, IF NOT MERCIFUL?
WORDS. THROWN ASIDE WHEN YOU PLEASE!
NO. TRUTH. AND HARD-WON. EVERY TIME HE GAVE HIS WORD, HE KEPT IT.
YOU SAID YOU WOULDN'T GIVE CHASE - BUT YOU DID.
WHOSE WORD MEANS LESS?
HER PRESENCE BREAKS HIS RAGE... AND, VERY NEARLY, HIS HEART.
THIS IS HIS CHIEF...AND HE HATES HAVING TAKEN IT FROM HER.
I DON'T KNOW IF I WOULD HAVE DONE ANY DIFFERENT, SCOUTER, I ADMIT THAT.
BUT YOUR PATH WILL DESTROY US AS WOLFRIDERS.
I WASN'T BORN A CHIEF! I'D SHOW YOU THROAT IN A MOMENT, BUT...
...YOU'RE VAIN, CARELESS AND CONTRARY!
I CAN'T TRUST YOU TO DO WHAT'S RIGHT FOR THE TRIBE!
IS THAT WHAT'S RIGHT, PACK-BROTHER?

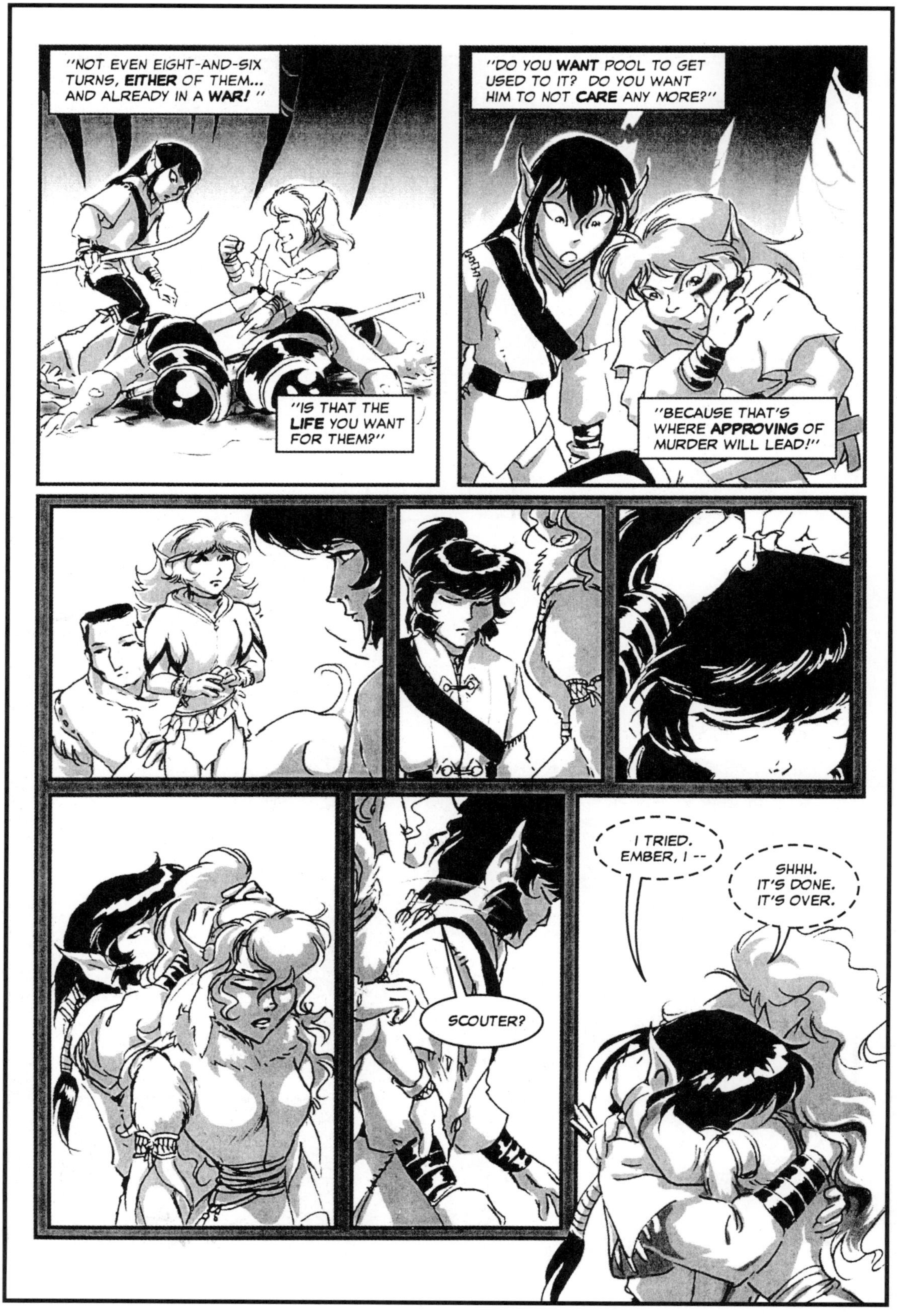
"NOT EVEN EIGHT-AND-SIX TURNS, EITHER OF THEM... AND ALREADY IN A WAR!"
"IS THAT THE LIFE YOU WANT FOR THEM?"
"DO YOU WANT POOL TO GET USED TO IT? DO YOU WANT HIM TO NOT CARE ANY MORE?"
"BECAUSE THAT'S WHERE APPROVING OF MURDER WILL LEAD!"
SCOUTER?
I TRIED. EMBER, I --
SHHH. IT'S DONE. IT'S OVER.

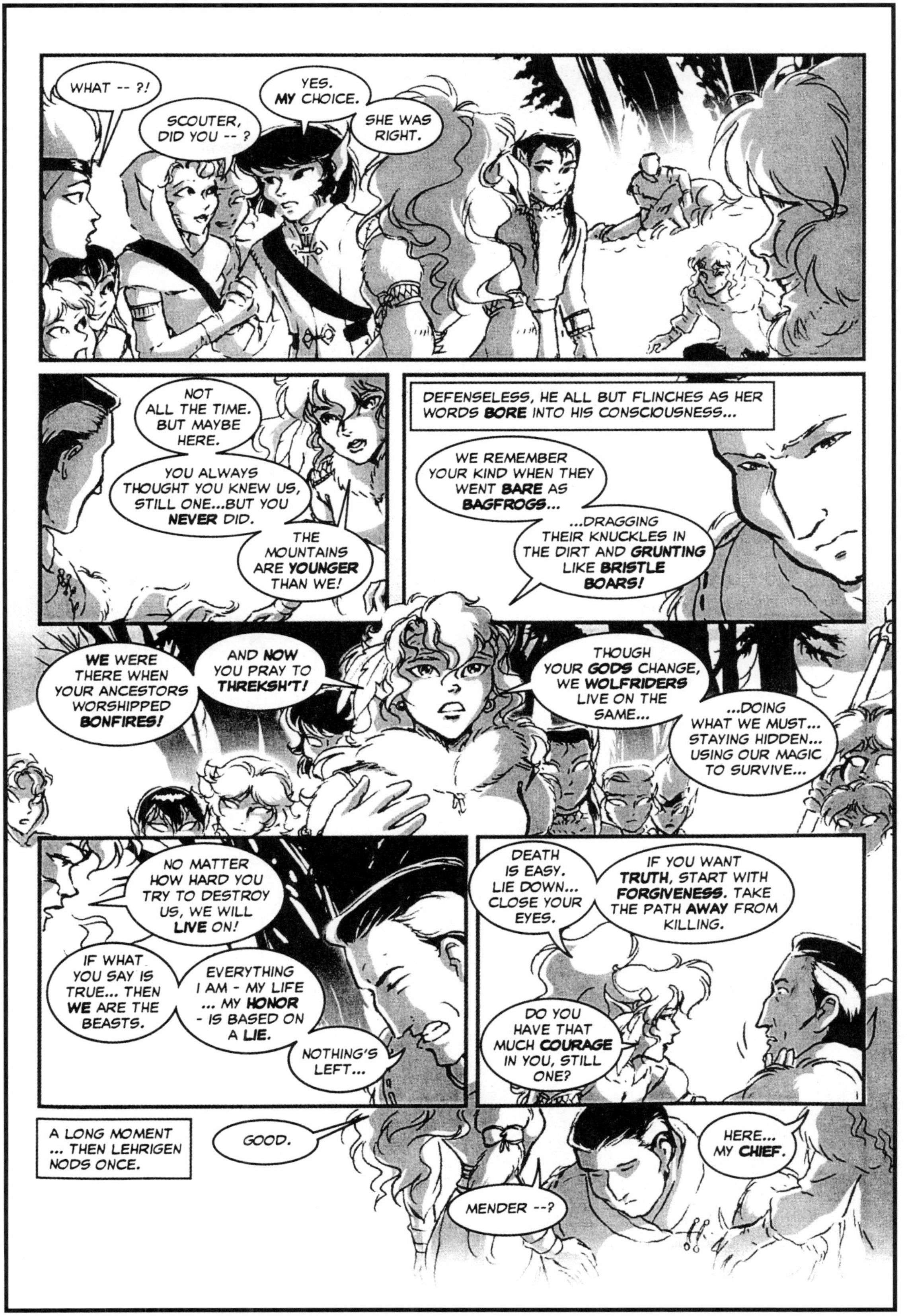

WHAT -- ?!
SCOUTER, DID YOU -- ?
YES. MY CHOICE.
SHE WAS RIGHT.
NOT ALL THE TIME. BUT MAYBE HERE.
YOU ALWAYS THOUGHT YOU KNEW US, STILL ONE...BUT YOU NEVER DID.
THE MOUNTAINS ARE YOUNGER THAN WE!
DEFENSELESS, HE ALL BUT FLINCHES AS HER WORDS BORE INTO HIS CONSCIOUSNESS...
WE REMEMBER YOUR KIND WHEN THEY WENT BARE AS BAGFROGS...
...DRAGGING THEIR KNUCKLES IN THE DIRT AND GRUNTING LIKE BRISTLE BOARS!
WE WERE THERE WHEN YOUR ANCESTORS WORSHIPPED BONFIRES!
AND NOW YOU PRAY TO THREKSH'T!
THOUGH YOUR GODS CHANGE, WE WOLFRIDERS LIVE ON THE SAME...
...DOING WHAT WE MUST... STAYING HIDDEN... USING OUR MAGIC TO SURVIVE...
NO MATTER HOW HARD YOU TRY TO DESTROY US, WE WILL LIVE ON!
IF WHAT YOU SAY IS TRUE... THEN WE ARE THE BEASTS.
EVERYTHING I AM - MY LIFE ... MY HONOR - IS BASED ON A LIE.
NOTHING'S LEFT...
DEATH IS EASY. LIE DOWN... CLOSE YOUR EYES.
IF YOU WANT TRUTH, START WITH FORGIVENESS. TAKE THE PATH AWAY FROM KILLING.
DO YOU HAVE THAT MUCH COURAGE IN YOU, STILL ONE?
A LONG MOMENT ... THEN LEHRIGEN NODS ONCE.
GOOD.
MENDER --?
HERE... MY CHIEF.

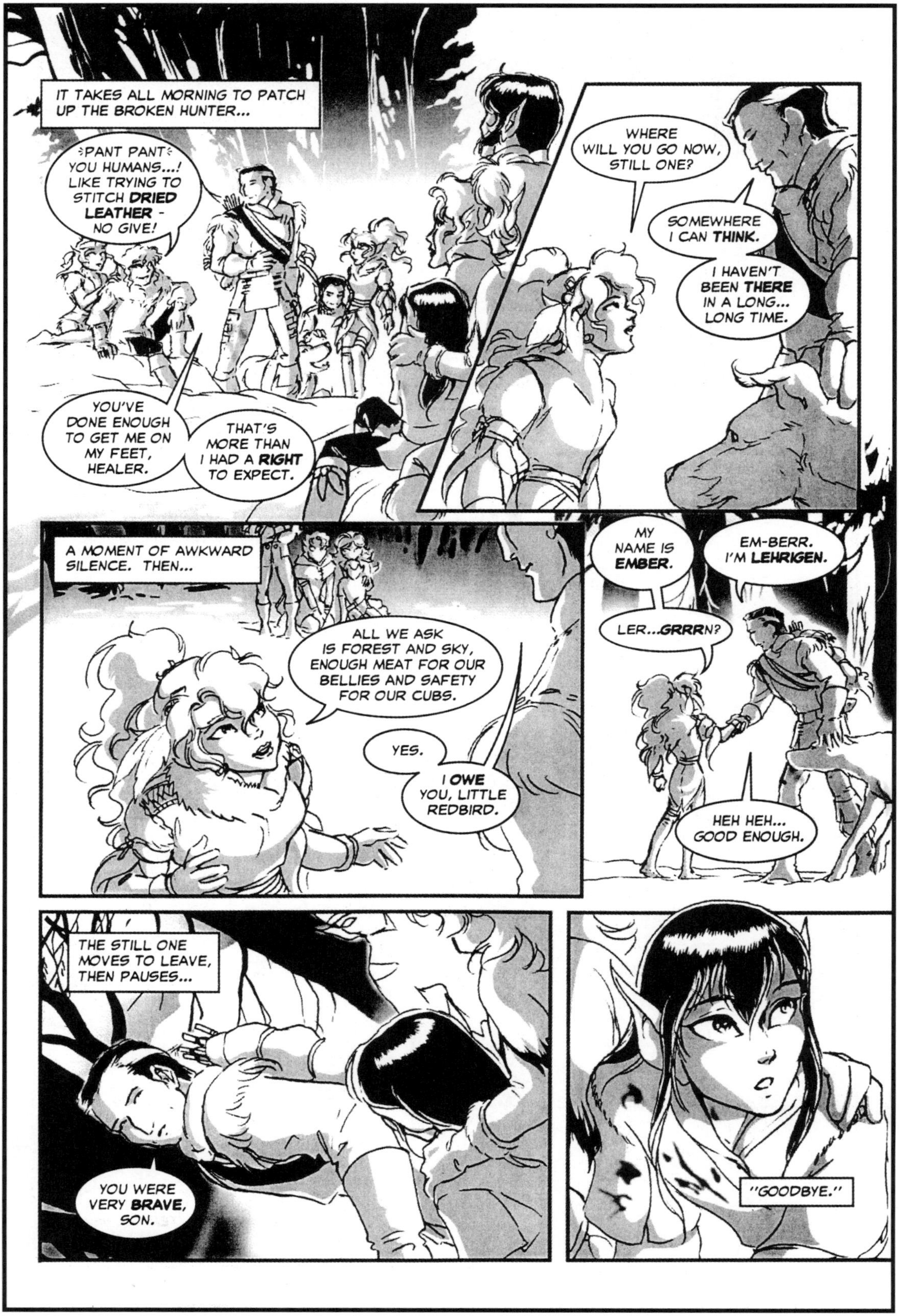
IT TAKES ALL MORNING TO PATCH UP THE BROKEN HUNTER...
PANT PANT YOU HUMANS...! LIKE TRYING TO STITCH DRIED LEATHER - NO GIVE!
YOU'VE DONE ENOUGH TO GET ME ON MY FEET, HEALER.
THAT'S MORE THAN I HAD A RIGHT TO EXPECT.
WHERE WILL YOU GO NOW, STILL ONE?
SOMEWHERE I CAN THINK.
I HAVEN'T BEEN THERE IN A LONG... LONG TIME.
A MOMENT OF AWKWARD SILENCE. THEN...
ALL WE ASK IS FOREST AND SKY, ENOUGH MEAT FOR OUR BELLIES AND SAFETY FOR OUR CUBS.
YES.
I OWE YOU, LITTLE REDBIRD.
MY NAME IS EMBER.
EM-BERR. I'M LEHRIGEN.
LER...GRRRN?
HEH HEH... GOOD ENOUGH.
THE STILL ONE MOVES TO LEAVE, THEN PAUSES...
YOU WERE VERY BRAVE, SON.
"GOODBYE."

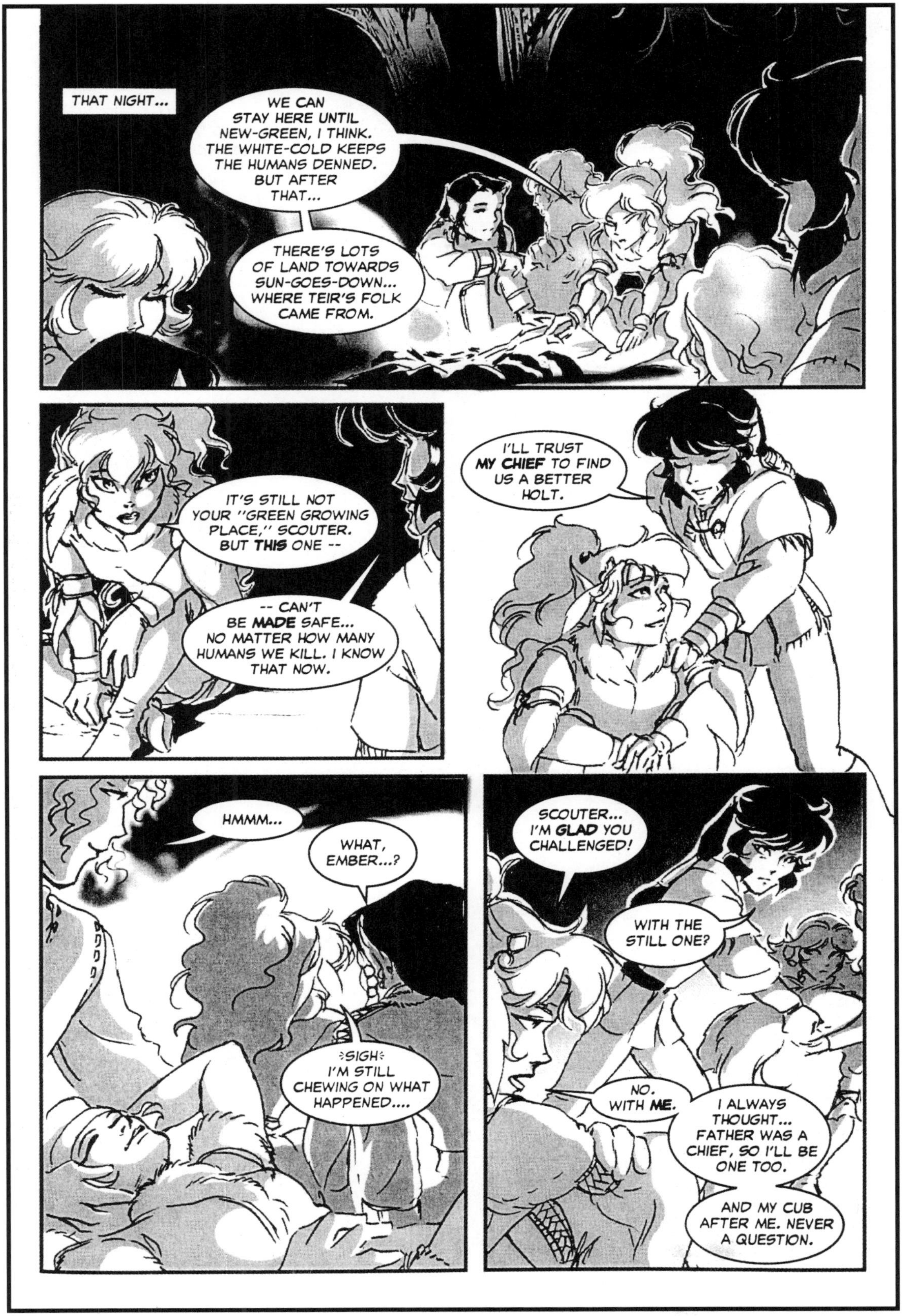
THAT NIGHT...
WE CAN STAY HERE UNTIL NEW-GREEN, I THINK. THE WHITE-COLD KEEPS THE HUMANS DENNED. BUT AFTER THAT...
THERE'S LOTS OF LAND TOWARDS SUN-GOES-DOWN... WHERE TEIR'S FOLK CAME FROM.
IT'S STILL NOT YOUR "GREEN GROWING PLACE," SCOUTER. BUT **THIS** ONE --
-- CAN'T BE **MADE** SAFE... NO MATTER HOW MANY HUMANS WE KILL. I KNOW THAT NOW.
I'LL TRUST **MY CHIEF** TO FIND US A BETTER HOLT.
HMMM...
WHAT, EMBER...?
SIGH I'M STILL CHEWING ON WHAT HAPPENED....
SCOUTER... I'M **GLAD** YOU CHALLENGED!
WITH THE STILL ONE?
NO. WITH **ME.**
I ALWAYS THOUGHT... FATHER WAS A CHIEF, SO I'LL BE ONE TOO.
AND MY CUB AFTER ME. NEVER A QUESTION.

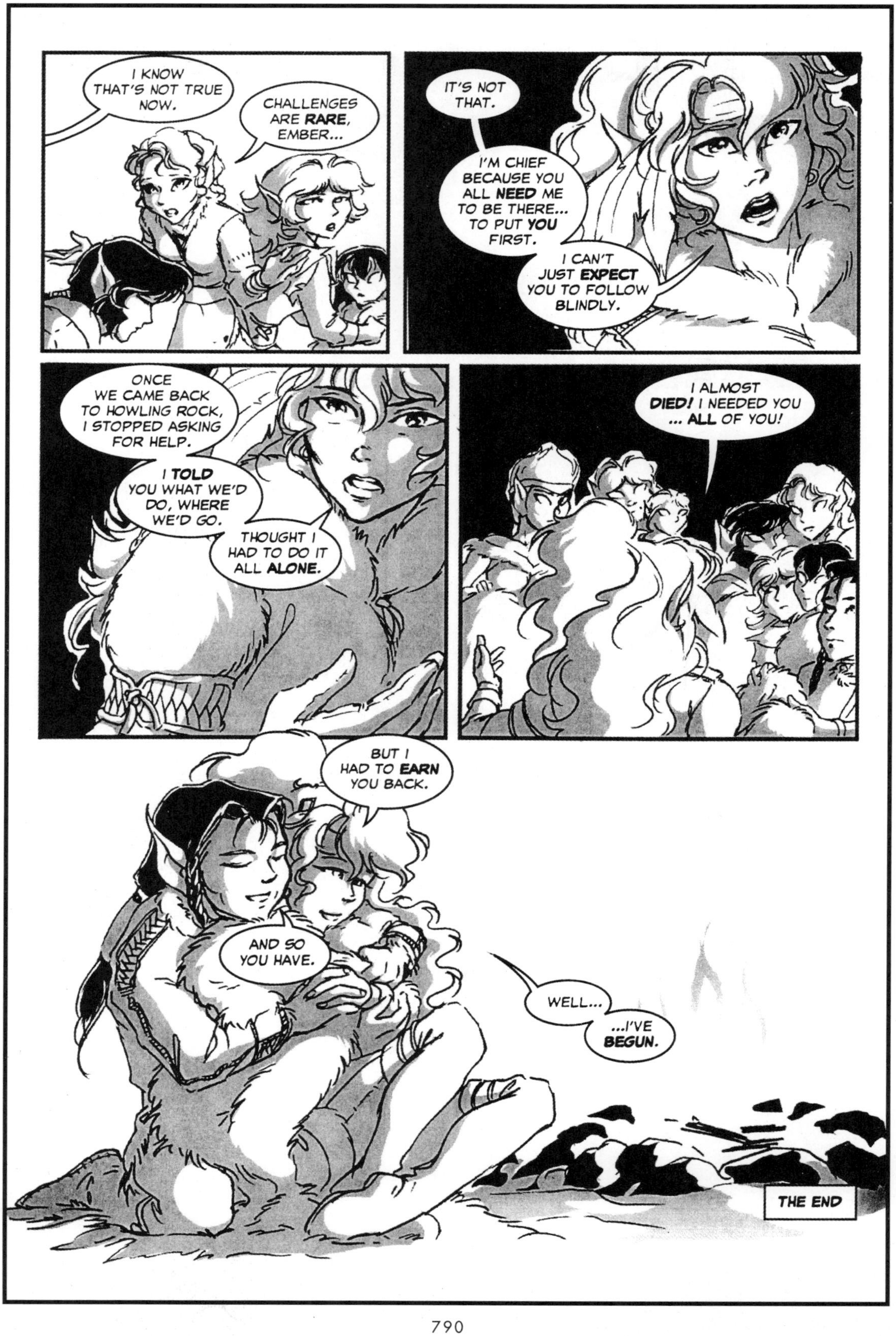
I KNOW THAT'S NOT TRUE NOW.
CHALLENGES ARE RARE, EMBER...
IT'S NOT THAT.
I'M CHIEF BECAUSE YOU ALL NEED ME TO BE THERE... TO PUT YOU FIRST.
I CAN'T JUST EXPECT YOU TO FOLLOW BLINDLY.
ONCE WE CAME BACK TO HOWLING ROCK, I STOPPED ASKING FOR HELP.
I TOLD YOU WHAT WE'D DO, WHERE WE'D GO.
THOUGHT I HAD TO DO IT ALL ALONE.
I ALMOST DIED! I NEEDED YOU ... ALL OF YOU!
BUT I HAD TO EARN YOU BACK.
AND SO YOU HAVE.
WELL...
...I'VE BEGUN.
THE END

ELFQUEST®

DISCOVER THE LEGEND OF *ELFQUEST*! ALLIANCES ARE FORGED, ENEMIES DISCOVERED, AND SAVAGE BATTLES FOUGHT IN THIS EPIC FANTASY ADVENTURE, HANDSOMELY PRESENTED BY DARK HORSE BOOKS!

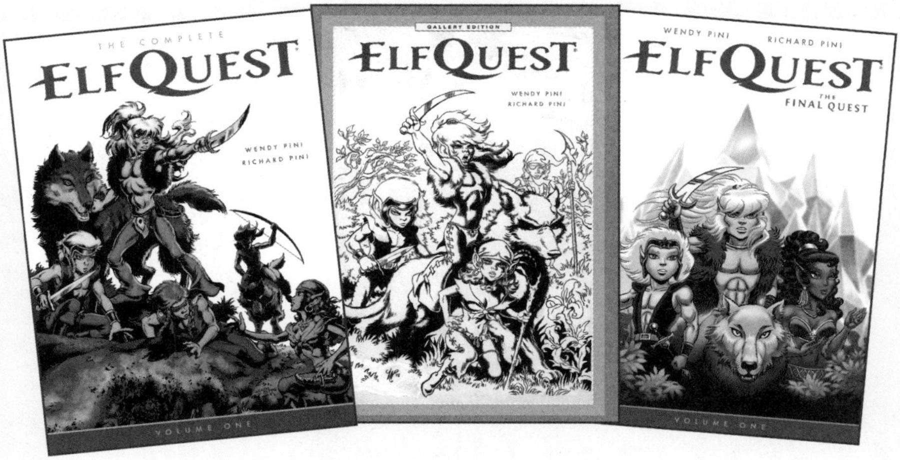
THE COMPLETE
ELFQUEST
WENDY PINI
RICHARD PINI
VOLUME ONE
GALLERY EDITION
ELFQUEST
WENDY PINI
RICHARD PINI
WENDY PINI
RICHARD PINI
ELFQUEST
THE FINAL QUEST
VOLUME ONE

THE COMPLETE ELFQUEST
Volume 1: The Original Quest
978-1-61655-407-1 | $24.99

Volume 2
978-1-61655-408-8 | $24.99

Volume 3
978-1-50670-080-9 | $24.99

Volume 4
978-1-50670-158-5 | $24.99

Volume 5
978-1-50670-606-1 | $24.99

ELFQUEST: THE ORIGINAL QUEST GALLERY EDITION
978-1-61655-411-8 | $125.00

ELFQUEST: THE FINAL QUEST
Volume 1
978-1-61655-409-5 | $17.99

Volume 2
978-1-61655-410-1 | $17.99

Volume 3
978-1-50670-138-7 | $17.99

Volume 4
978-1-50670-492-0 | $17.99

DARK HORSE BOOKS

AVAILABLE AT YOUR LOCAL COMICS SHOP OR BOOKSTORE
To find a comics shop in your area, visit comicshoplocator.com. For more information or to order direct visit DarkHorse.com or call 1-800-862-0052.